CW00840983

Birds in Cheshire and Wirral

A breeding and wintering atlas

Birds in Cheshire and Wirral

A breeding and wintering atlas

David Norman

on behalf of CAWOS

First published 2008 by
Liverpool University Press
4 Cambridge Street
Liverpool L69 7ZU

Copyright © 2008 David Norman on behalf of Cheshire and Wirral Ornithological Society

The author's rights have been asserted in accordance with
the Copyright, Designs and Patents Act, 1988.

All rights reserved. No part of this book may be reproduced, stored in a retrieval system, or transmitted, in any form or by any means, electronic, mechanical, photocopying, recording, or otherwise, without the prior written permission of the publisher.

British Library Cataloguing-in-Publication data
A British Library CIP record is available

ISBN 978-1-84631-152-9

Edited, designed and typeset by BBR (bbr-online.com)

Cartography by Steve Ramsey, David Norman and BBR

Cover illustrations by David Quinn

Printed and bound by Gutenberg Press, Malta

The paper used for this book is FSC-certified and totally chlorine-free. FSC (the Forest Stewardship Council) is an international network to promote responsible management of the world's forests.

Contents

Foreword

Many people enjoy the fun and excitement of Atlas work. It has also given some observers their rewarding first taste of systematic bird recording. The collective efforts of large numbers of observers, each working to a consistent methodology in a different area, gives Atlas projects their special value. After the fieldwork is done, and the results are analysed, they provide an accurate snapshot of bird distributions at the time, and provide a firm basis for assessing future distributional changes. Not surprisingly, Atlas results now play a vital role in setting national conservation policy. For example, they feed invaluably into Biodiversity Action Plans (BAPs) and into the Red and Amber listing system for species of conservation concern. For all these reasons, it is a pleasure to welcome this new Atlas, which maps the distributions of bird species across Cheshire and Wirral in the period 2004–06 (and early 2007 for wintering birds).

This is not the first Atlas to be produced for this region. Its predecessor covered the period 1978–84, but dealt only with summer breeding birds. This new Atlas updates the findings for breeding birds, showing the main distributional changes that have occurred in the intervening twenty years, and also provides information at the same scale for wintering birds. In addition, for the recording of breeding status, three categories are used (confirmed, probable or possible, with supporting details), rather than the two categories (breeding and seen) widely adopted in previous Atlases.

The publication of this new county Atlas coincides with the start of a new national Atlas project, run by the British Trust for Ornithology (BTO), which is scheduled to cover the period 2007–11. Like previous national Atlases, it will map bird distributions in 10 km squares. Set against these national projects, local Atlases generally operate at finer scales. This new Atlas for Cheshire and Wirral shows birds in every tetrad (2 × 2 km square) rather than in every 10 × 10 km square, giving 25 times more resolution. This extra detail can give early warning of distributional changes not visible at a national level. For instance, widespread species such as Skylark and Linnet have shown large population declines over the past twenty years, but their distributions have not noticeably contracted at the scale of the 10 km square. In Cheshire and Wirral, both species still breed in every 10 km square but, since the previous Atlas, the Skylark has gone from 150 tetrads (almost one-quarter of the county's 670) and the Linnet from 161. Such fine-scale information helps to alert us to ongoing distributional declines not yet obvious at the larger scale, and helps to set the context for Local BAPs and county-level conservation targets.

Two other novel aspects of this new Cheshire and Wirral Atlas warrant comment, as they could also be employed in other counties. In collaboration with the BTO, the county's population of more than sixty breeding species was estimated from the Breeding Bird Survey transects and, for many species, maps show relative abundance across the county. The difference between distribution and abundance can sometimes be striking: the House Sparrow, for instance, is no longer amongst the top ten most widespread species in Cheshire and Wirral, but remains the most numerous.

The other new feature of this Atlas is the recording of habitat alongside every bird record. Using an easy but effective coding system, already familiar to participants in BTO surveys, the habitat data provide insights into the factors underlying species' distributions. They have additional value when linked with land-use statistics from the Centre for Ecology and Hydrology at Monks Wood, Cambridgeshire. Simply recording the size and type of waterbody, for instance, confirms that several species of waterfowl, including Canada Goose, Greylag Goose and Coot, now readily breed on ponds and small waters, but in winter almost all move to lakes and reservoirs, especially Cheshire's meres.

The organizers of this Atlas were intent on completing the work in as short a period as possible to avoid the distorting effect of population changes during the survey period: the county's *First Atlas* took seven years of fieldwork (1978–84), during which the populations of several farmland species halved as agricultural changes took effect. On the other hand, the benefits of shortening the survey period had to be balanced against the numbers of dedicated fieldworkers available, and the desire to record as high a level of proof of breeding as possible. A three-year project was an acceptable compromise, and the organizers have followed this up with rapid progress towards publication.

As the years pass, some may remember this Atlas project for particular events, such as the discovery of a wintering Pallas's Warbler, the first breeding in the county of Mediterranean Gull, the largest recorded winter numbers of Leach's Petrels, or the unprecedented invasion of Waxwings in the winter of 2004–05. However, the major value of the Atlas is in quantifying recent distributional changes, as shown, for example, in the welcome spread of some raptors. During 1978–84 the Buzzard was present in just 10 tetrads and was proved to breed in only two, yet in 2004–06 it was found in no less than 560 tetrads, breeding throughout the county except for treeless areas and conurbations. Twenty years ago, no Hobbies were found breeding in the county but, during the current Atlas period, around 50 pairs were found. Peregrines and Ravens showed similarly impressive range expansions. It was also good to learn of the ample distribution and high population of breeding Swallows; and that Grey Herons may be more numerous here than in any other part of England, benefiting from what gave Cheshire its reputation as the pond capital of Britain. On the other hand, this book documents the rapid demise of the Turtle Dove, present in more than one-fifth of the county twenty years ago, but now apparently no longer breeding here. Likewise, the Yellow Wagtail, for which Cheshire was once renowned, was found in 385 tetrads in 1978–84, shrinking to 126 tetrads in 2004–06. Similar statistics are given for some other declining species.

Turning to wintering birds, Cheshire and Wirral cover one of the most important regions in Britain for water-birds, as confirmed by recent Wetland Bird Surveys. This is not surprising, for in addition to abundant fresh waters, the area contains two internationally important estuaries, the Dee and the Mersey, which still support large numbers of wintering wildfowl and waders. Some other wintering species have become more numerous over the past twenty years, probably benefiting from the warming climate. In the recent survey, wintering Blackcaps were present in almost one-quarter of the county, and wintering Stonechats were also more numerous than ever before. Some other resident species show intriguing differences between their distributions at the two seasons. For example, the maps show a winter withdrawal of Dippers from high to low ground within the county, not previously quantified.

Wherever one dips into this publication, there are gems to be found, and many of the findings provoke suggestions for further work. This Atlas results from more than 50,000 hours of fieldwork from hundreds of 'citizen scientists'. It gives unprecedented understanding of the region's birds. I congratulate Cheshire and Wirral Ornithological Society and their members and other fieldworkers in delivering this Atlas, all operating under the inspirational leadership of David Norman. Whether you live locally or further afield, you will find much of interest in the pages of this volume.

Ian Newton OBE FRS FRSE
Chairman, RSPB

Acknowledgements

Although David Norman has taken primary responsibility for this whole project, including for any errors and omissions that remain, it needed a collaborative effort from hundreds of people to make it work.

The prime acknowledgments must be to the fieldworkers who surveyed the entire county for this Atlas, who are listed in full below; and to all the landowners who allowed access for survey work and in many instances provided extra information themselves.

The bird atlasing community, within Britain and elsewhere, is a friendly bunch of people, open and helpful and happy to pass on their knowledge and advice. Thanks are especially due to Mike Hodgson (Northumbria), for advice and copies of their instructions and recording forms, and discussions on offshore tetrads; to colleagues in Cumbria and in Lancashire and North Merseyside, especially for information on funding; to Dan Brauning, Bob Mulvihill and Mike Lanzone (Pennsylvania) for ideas about methods and organization; and to Ian Francis (North-East Scotland) and Iain Main (North Cotswolds) for fruitful discussions on publication and presentation of results.

Several of the staff of the British Trust for Ornithology (BTO) made invaluable contributions at various stages, including Rob Fuller, Simon Gillings and especially Stuart Newson who calculated the abundance figures and maps.

We acknowledge the Centre for Ecology and Hydrology, Monks Wood, for provision of a licence to use their 'landcover 2000' data for the county.

The electronic receipt and processing of data was vital for the rapid progress of the project, and we are indebted to Geoff Blamire for his expertise in database management, designing an offshoot of the database used by CAWOS for the records collected annually by the society, and rapidly providing numerous extracts of the data.

All the dot maps were produced using the DMAP software, and Alan Morton, its author, gave helpful advice on various aspects of its use.

Ted Lock, Noreen Yaqoob and Gill Barber compiled the annual county bird reports on a species-by-species basis, which was a great help in writing some texts, and Charlotte Harris computerized the data from our *First Atlas* maps. Irene Morrell typed in many of the records that had been submitted on paper.

John Bannon generously shared his professional knowledge on publishing.

The photographers and artists whose contributions enhance the pages of this book have all donated their work, and the credit is given alongside each image. Andy Harmer initially contacted the photographers and Ray Scally organized the artwork.

In the early days of planning the project, useful contributions were made within CAWOS by Sheila Blamire, Tony Broome, David Cogger, Mike Crawley, Andy Harmer, Bob Harris, Charles Hull, Colin Lythgoe, Michael Miles, Phil Oddy, Hugh Pulsford, Clive Richards and Steve White.

The Atlas Steering Group, four people plus the author, was deliberately kept small to ensure efficient working and communication. David Cogger performed an invaluable role as the primary contact with all fieldworkers, especially in organizing the fieldwork and the return of data, plus handling the individual sponsorship of species. Steve Barber acted as the main interface with Area Coordinators and performed the major tasks of checking data and liaising with the database manager, and also provided useful information from the county rarities panel and other aspects of CAWOS records. Peter Twist acted as the project's business manager, handling the financial planning, corporate sponsorship, grant proposals, especially the major proposal to Heritage Lottery Fund, and the publishing tenders and contract; Peter also coordinated the provision of all the illustrations. Bob Harris provided perspective from Lancashire and North Merseyside, contributing his experience in organizing local BTO members in survey work and liaising with the BTO on the abundance calculations.

Several people commented on draft texts where they had specialized knowledge: Steve and Gill Barber, Malcolm Calvert, John Elliott, Bob Harris, Brian Martin, Richard May, Michael Miles, Stuart Newson, Clive Richards, Paul Slater, Tony Wilkinson and Steve Williams.

The following generously provided extra information: Brian Martin, on Cheshire and Wirral Swifts, Grey Herons and Black-necked Grebes; Andy Webb (Joint Nature Conservation Committee), for maps of Common Scoter distribution in Liverpool Bay; Nick Aebischer (Game & Wildlife Conservation Trust), Mark Greenhough, Ben Gregory and Connor O'Gorman (British Association for Shooting and Conservation) for advice about releases of gamebirds.

Those responsible for surveying one or more tetrads

John Ackroyd, Rob Adams, Andrew Aldridge, Dorothy Alston, Bob Anderson, Andy Ankers, Mark Arnold, Steve Atkins, Rod Atkinson, Andrew Bailey, Margaret Bain, Brian Baird, Neil Baker, Mathilde Baker-Schommer, Mick Ball, John Bannon, R.E. (Bob) Baptist, Ian Barber, Steve and Gill Barber, Marion Barlow, Roger Barnes, Susan Bastin, Paul Beacock, Paul Bebbington, David Beer, Bill Bellamy, Di Bennett, Paddy Bennion, Derek Berry, Christine Bertera, Ray Bertera, Steve Binney, Rob Bithell, Rob Black, Irene Blagden, Sheila Blamire, Richard Blindell, Peter Blud, Alan Booth, Molly Bostock, Iona Bowden, Roy Bowden, Jack Bower, David Bowman, Jeremy Bradshaw, Paul Brewster, Dave Briddon, Dave Bromont, Tony Broome, Douglas Buchanan, Nicole Buckley, Jean Bulmer, Brian Burke, Stuart Burnet, Eric Burrows, Gordon Bushell, Pat Bushell, Colin Butler, Chris Butterworth, Cynthia Cadman, Ron Cadman, Roberta Cameron, Andrew Campion, Jack Canovan, Joe Carroll, Paul Cassidy, Jeff Clarke, Robert Cleeves, Valerie Cleeves, Chris Clowes, Hilary Clowes, John Clowes, Trevor Clowes, Tony Coatsworth, Carol Cockbain, Rob Cockbain, David Cogger, Ralph Cole, Kim Connolly, David Cookson, Barbara Cooper-Poole, Ian Copley, Paul Corner, Andy Coxon, James Coyne, Tony Crane, Reg Crawford, Bob Cunningham, Judy Cunningham, John Davies, Peter Day, Paul Dean, Betty Devereau, David Dewsbury, Sue Dewsbury, Tony Dickinson, Alan Doherty, Alan Douglas, Sheila Downs, Peter Dowse, John Drake, Chris Driver, Mike Dye, Alison Dyke, Brian Dyke, Frank Earle, Heather Eddowes, Mark Eddowes, David Egerton, John Elliott, Richard Elphick, Jean Emsley, David Esther, Ray Evans, Roy Eyres, Laurie Fairman, Howard Fearn, Neil Fergusson, Harold Fielding, Valerie Fielding, Henry Finch, Andy Firth, George Fisher, David Fletcher, George Fletcher, Tony Ford, Andrew Foulkes, Richard Fox, Nick French, Neil Friswell, Richard Gabb, Cliff Gibson, Pam Gibson, Tony Gillam, Frank Gleeson, Dave Goff, Mary Gold, Roy Goodier, Andrew Goodwin, Mike Gough, John Goulding, Marc Granville, Lee Greenhough, Paul Greenslade, John Gregory, Janet Grice, Brian Grieve, Paul Griffiths, Paul and Jane Grimmett, Bob Groom, Ted Groves, Nick Hall, Pete Hall, Tim Halliday, Doug Hambleton, Jan Hanby, Chris Hancock, Andy Harmer, Bob Harris, Mike Hart, Rodger Harvey, Graham Haspey, John Headon, Andrew Hearn, Christian Heintzen, Sue Heintzen, Chris Herbert, Pauline Herbert, Carole Herbstritt, Graham Hewitt, Paul Hill, Paul S. Hill, Steve Hind, Gordon Hodgson, Mike Holmes, Steve Holmes, Chris Honer, Brian Hughes, David Hughes, Paul Hughes, Dave Hughston, Charles Hull, David Hulse, Tom Hunt, Heather James, Martin James, Cynthia Johnson, Alec Johnston, Christine Johnston, Colin Jones, David Jones, Glyn Jones, Les Jones, Mike Jones, Norman Jones, Steve Kemp, David Kennerley, Alan Kimber, David King, John Kirkland, Virginia and Rieks Kuijt, Ian Landucci, Hugh Langford, John Langley, Tracy Langley, Hazel Lawson, Dave Leeming, Karen Leeming, Roy Leigh, Hugh Linn, Andy Livermore, Ted Lock, Rob Lyne, Colin Lythgoe, John MacDonald, Ian Macpherson, Mike Maher, Ian Marshall, Brian Martin, Clive Martindale, Keith Massey, Peter Mathews, Peter Mayers, Ian McGeorge, Dave McMaster, Michael Miles, Simon Miles, Jane Mockford, Paul Morris, Jason Mossman, Viv Mountford, David Nadin, Steve Nichols, David Norman, Roger Nutter, Simon O'Connor, Phil Oddy, Joe O'Hanlon, Paul Oldfield, Derek Owen, John Oxenham, Eric Paalman, Graham Palmer, Roy Palmer, Tony Parker, Richard Parkinson, Chris Parry, Don Pawlett, Brian Payne, Mark Payne, Chris Pearce, Bryan Perkins, Derek Pike, Ed Pilkington, John Power, Catherine Price, Chris Price, Brian Prince, Mary Prince, Hugh Pulsford, Nick Pumphrey, Ann Pym, Craig Pym, Brian and Hazel Raw, John Rayner, Peter Rhodes, Clive Richards, Alan Riley, Brian Rimmer, Idris Roberts, Bernard Robinson, Dave Robinson, Geoffrey Robinson, Margaret Robinson, Hannah Rowland, Peter Royle, Peter Russell, Sheila Ryde, Edwin Samuels, Colin Schofield, Mike Scott, Norman Scott, Ron Shewring, Paul Slater, John Smith, Mark Smith, Richard Smith, Rob Smith, Rodger Smith, Christine Smyth, Pete Spilsbury, Martyn Stanyer, David Steel, Hugh Stewart, Nigel Stones, Chris Stott, Alan Straw, Roger Stringer, Mark Stubbs, Jack Swan, Barry Taylor, Ian Taylor, Stephen Taylor, Stuart Taylor, Matt Thomas, John Thompson, John M. Thompson, Phil Thompson, Tricia Thompson, Ray Thorp, Joan Tilbrook, David Tolliday, Brian Tollitt, Clive Totty, Jane Turner, John Turner, Marie Turner, Mark Turner, Michael Twist, Peter Twist, Bob Unsworth, Tony Usher, Derek Venables, Jon Wainwright, Peter Walton, Elizabeth Watson, John Watson, Ken Webb, Brian Webber, Colin Wells, David Whitehead, Mike Whiteside, Stan Wildig, Roger Wilkinson, Keith Williams, Peter Williams, Steve Williams, John Wilson, Simon Wood, Hilary Woodhead, Noel Woodhead, Phil Woollen, John Wright, Eric Yarwood, Geoff Yarwood, Stephen Young.

The following groups or organizations contributed records directly for the Atlas

BTO Breeding Bird Survey
BTO Heronry Census
BTO Waterways Breeding Bird Survey
BTO Wetland Bird Survey (WeBS) Dee & Mersey Estuaries & Inland
Broxton Barn Owl Group
CAWOS Database and Bird Reports 2004–06
Cheshire Swan Study Group
Eastham Country Park Bird Log (Terry Patrick)
Hilbre Bird Observatory
Merseyside Ringing Group
Mid-Cheshire Barn Owl Conservation Group
Moore Biological Recording Group
Nantwich Natural History Society (Charles Hull)
Rostherne Mere National Nature Reserve Reports (Bill Bellamy, Steve Barber and Jack Canovan)
The RSPB, Macclesfield Local Group Garden Bird Survey (Margaret Hayter and Graham Palmer)
The RSPB, Macclesfield Local Group 'Latest News' (Gordon Howard and David Tolliday)
South Cheshire Barn Owl Group
South East Cheshire Ornithological Society (Colin Lythgoe)

South Manchester Ringing Group (Clive Richards)
Wilmslow Guild Garden Bird Survey
Wirral Barn Owl Trust
Woolston Eyes Conservation Group (Brian Martin)

Contributors of supplementary records

The following contributed supplementary records to the Atlas and are not included in the list of tetrad surveyors:

Terry Ashton, Gillian Cameron, Richard Castell, Allan Conlin, John Dawson, Lee Dunkley, Alan Eyres, Mrs Fennell, Alan Garner, Tom Gibbons, Dave Gregson, Steve Harris, Kevin Hayes, George Hill, Neville Jones, Chris Koral, Geoff Lightfoot, Len Mason, Richard May, Alastair McCreary, Darren Morris, Tony Mossman, Terry Patrick, Neville Powell, Dennis Price, Barbara Punchard, Dave Riley, Lynn Ritchie, Mike Roberts, Allan Rustell, John Shaughnessy, R.W.H. Smith, John Spottiswood, Noel Stubbs, Ian Summerfield, Brian Swann, Melissa Thornton, Derek Todd, Jeremy Weston, Tony Wilkinson, Bernard Wright.

Some records from the following groups or organizations were extracted from the CAWOS database for use in the Atlas

Alderley Park and Radnor Mere Bird Report
Arclid Sand Quarry Bird Report
Bar Mere Bird Report
Birdcall
Birdguides
Birding North West
Bosley Reservoir Bird Report
BTO BirdTrack (formerly Migration Watch)
CAWOS House Martin Survey
Dee Estuary Birding website–latest sightings
Dee Estuary RSPB Nature Reserve Report
Deer Park Mere Bird Report
Fiddler's Ferry Reserve Report
Frodsham Marsh Bird Log
Gayton Sands RSPB Reserve Report
Hurleston Reservoir Bird Log
Inner Marsh Farm RSPB Reserve Bird Log
Pickering's Pasture Local Nature Reserve Report
Risley Moss Reserve Bird Log
Sandbach Flashes Bird Log
Seaforth Bird Report
Witton Area Conservation Group

Area coordinators

SJ18	Steve Williams
SJ27	Colin Wells
SJ28	Richard Smith
SJ29	Colin Schofield
SJ35	Neil Friswell
SJ36	Neil Friswell
SJ37	Ian Copley (to October 2004); Phil Woollen
SJ38	Edwin Samuels
SJ39	Colin Schofield
SJ44	Neil Friswell
SJ45	Neil Friswell
SJ46	Joe O'Hanlon
SJ47	Andy Ankers
SJ48	Rob Cockbain
SJ54	Charles Hull
SJ55	Charles Hull
SJ56	Peter Twist
SJ57	Mark Payne (to September 2005); David Cogger
SJ58	Tony Parker
SJ59	Steve Kemp
SJ64	Charles Hull
SJ65	Charles Hull
SJ66	David Cogger
SJ67	Paul Hill (to April 2005); David Cogger (to January 2006); Howard Fearn
SJ68	David Bowman
SJ69	Rob Smith
SJ74	Colin Lythgoe
SJ75	Colin Lythgoe
SJ76	Colin Lythgoe
SJ77	Tony Usher
SJ78	Tony Coatsworth
SJ85	Colin Lythgoe
SJ86	Marc Granville (to September 2006); David Cogger
SJ87	Steve Barber
SJ88	Brian Dyke
SJ96	Alan Kimber
SJ97	Ray Evans
SJ98	Phil Oddy (to May 2006); Steve Barber
SK06/07	John Power (to December 2004); Ray Evans

Financial support

Cheshire and Wirral Ornithological Society acknowledges the Heritage Lottery Fund for its award of a 'Your Heritage' grant towards the costs of financing this five-year project. The grant also supports the subsequent educational programmes to be operated by our partners to the HLF award, Cheshire Wildlife Trust and Halton Borough Council, who are developing their curricula utilizing the Atlas as an important learning tool.

We are very grateful to our other major sponsors, who gave financial support and whose logos appear on the cover of this book: Cheshire County Council, Forestry Commission, Macclesfield Borough Council, Natural England, Shell UK, United Utilities, Vale Royal Borough Council and the Zoological Gardens Chester.

Many individuals have supported the Atlas through sponsoring bird species, and their names are given alongside each species text.

Substantial in-kind support was also provided by the British Trust for Ornithology, including the Breeding Bird Survey and Wetland Bird Survey, AstraZeneca and Halton Borough Council. The RSPB also contributed towards the Atlas.

List of abbreviations

To avoid too much repetition, several abbreviations are used extensively throughout the book.

'The county'	Cheshire and Wirral
'twenty years ago'	Used to refer to our *First Atlas* period, 1978–84
BAP	Biodiversity Action Plan
BBS	Breeding Bird Survey
BTO	British Trust for Ornithology
BTO Second Atlas	The BTO national breeding bird Atlas, 1988–91: *The New Atlas of Breeding Birds in Britain and Ireland: 1988–1991*, ed. D.W. Gibbons, J.B. Reid, & R.A. Chapman (London: T. & A.D. Poyser, 1993)
BTO Winter Atlas	The BTO national wintering bird Atlas, 1981/82–1983/84: *The Atlas of Wintering Birds in Britain and Ireland*, ed. P.C. Lack (Calton: T. & A.D. Poyser, 1986)
BWP	*Birds of the Western Palearctic*, volumes I-IX, ed. S. Cramp *et al.* (Oxford: Oxford University Press, 1977–94)
CAWOS	Cheshire and Wirral Ornithological Society
CWBR	*Cheshire and Wirral Bird Report*, published annually by CAWOS; until 1987 the reports were known as *Cheshire Bird Report* but, for continuity, no such distinction is made in this book. Synonyms of 'county bird report' or 'annual county bird report' are frequently used in the text. Titles include the year to which the records refer, rather than the year of publication of the report. A brief history of bird-recording in Cheshire is given in the *First Atlas*.
First Atlas	The first breeding bird Atlas of Cheshire and Wirral, 1978–84: *The Breeding Bird Atlas of Cheshire and Wirral*, J.P. Guest, D. Elphick, J.S.A Hunter & D. Norman (CAWOS, 1992)
LBAP	Local Biodiversity Action Plan
Migration Atlas	*The Migration Atlas: movements of the birds of Britain and Ireland*, ed. C.V. Wernham *et al.* (London: T. & A.D. Poyser, 2002)
'national population index'	Figures calculated by the BTO from various annual breeding surveys, published as *Breeding Birds in the Wider Countryside: their conservation status 2007* (BTO Research Report No. 487), S.R. Baillie *et al.* (Thetford: BTO, 2007)
Ramsar site	Site designated under the Convention on Wetlands of International Importance especially as Waterfowl Habitats (Ramsar, Iran, 1971)
RSPB	Royal Society for the Protection of Birds
SPA	Special Protection Area under the European Birds Directive
SSSI	Site of Special Scientific Interest
WeBS	Wetland Bird Survey

Overview of this Atlas

During the three breeding seasons 2004–06 and three winters 2004/05–2006/07, Cheshire and Wirral Ornithological Society (CAWOS) organized more than 350 volunteers to survey all of the county, trying to find every species of bird that was breeding or wintering. The basis for survey was the 2 × 2 km square of the Ordnance Survey grid, a standard recording unit for many local biological Atlases with an area of 4 km², called a tetrad. There are 670 tetrads in the county for the breeding season and 684 for winter, the latter including some offshore areas with no permanent land area, thus being unsuitable for breeding birds but occupied by seabirds and waterfowl at various states of the tide. Fieldworkers recorded birds throughout Cheshire and Wirral, covering every suitable habitat within each tetrad. This is the county's second breeding bird Atlas, starting 20 years after the end of the previous Atlas for which fieldwork ran from 1978 to 1984, but there has been no previous survey in winter at the tetrad scale.

In the breeding season, species were observed carefully and their behaviour noted according to a hierarchy of 16 codes indicating different levels of breeding status: these translated into categories of possible, probable or confirmed breeding (see overleaf). Surveyors were urged to try to achieve as high a level of breeding status as possible, with the ideal being one of the 'two-letter' codes representing a variety of behaviour consistent with proof of breeding. A total of 34,516 unique records (only one record of a species per tetrad in any of the three years) were collected, of 153 species.

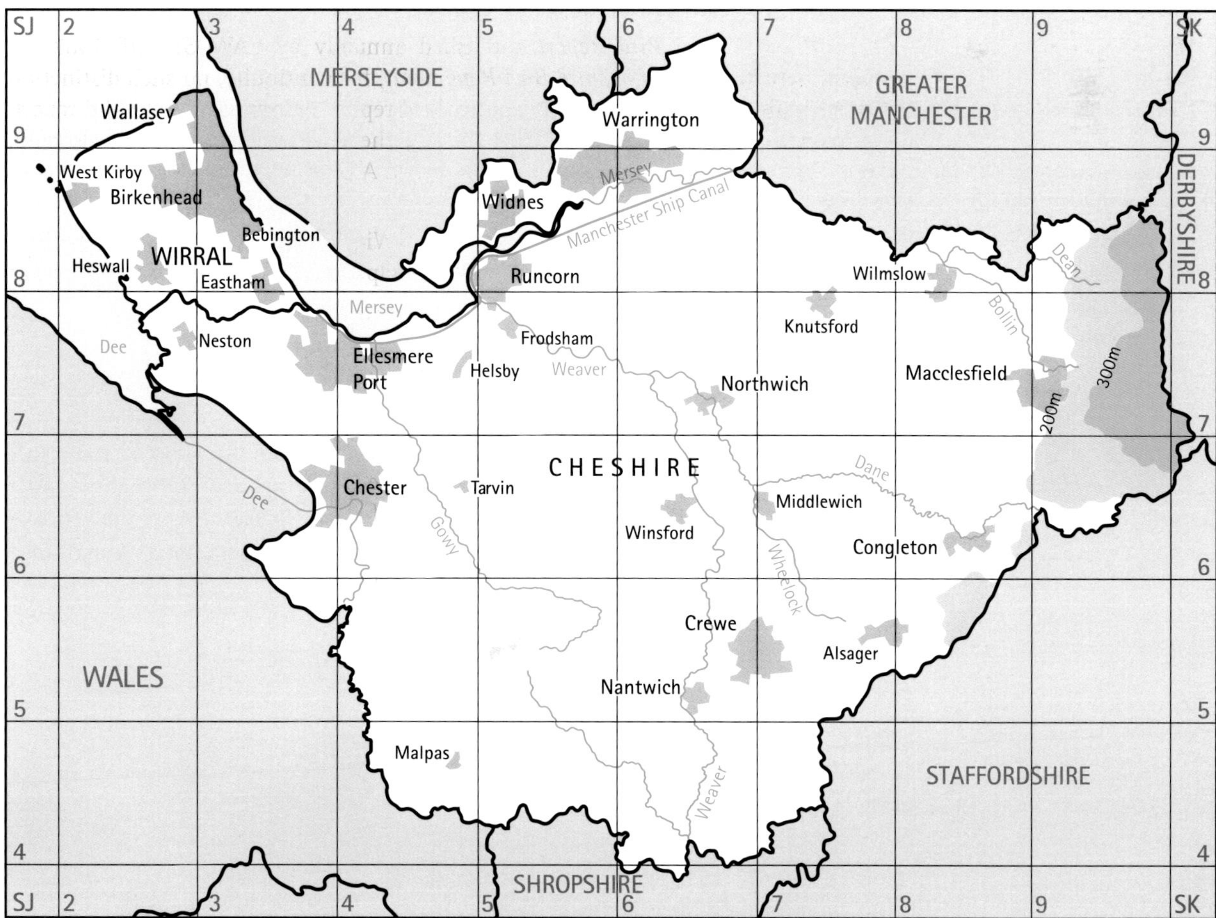

Cheshire and Wirral, showing the main conurbations, rivers and canals, and land lying above 200 m and 300 m in altitude.

Tetrad nomenclature

Every 10 × 10 km square of the Ordnance Survey national grid can be divided into 25 tetrads, each allotted a letter of the alphabet from A to Z, omitting O, as in the square below. The full reference for a tetrad consists of the two-letter Ordnance Survey label for the 100 × 100 km square—which is SJ for all of Cheshire and Wirral apart from the two easternmost tetrads which lie in SK—followed by the two-digit designation from the easting and northing 10 km gridlines and finally the tetrad letter.

E	J	P	U	Z
D	I	N	T	Y
C	H	M	S	X
B	G	L	R	W
A	F	K	Q	V

For instance, Thornton Manor Lake, Wirral, is in tetrad SJ28V, Reaseheath College is in SJ65M and Pott Shrigley in SJ97P. This key is also provided on the breeding and wintering maps for each species.

In winter, the aim was to record every species that was using the tetrad, where possible including some additional information on the size of flocks or roosts; birds flying over but not using the tetrad were excluded from the Atlas. The winter period was intended to avoid periods of migration and breeding and, to make an Atlas sensible, to cover the time when most birds were settled in one area. Having the same dates for all species, regardless of their biology, inevitably entails a compromise, and 'winter' was defined as 16 November to the end of February. In winter, 34,237 unique records (only one record of a species per tetrad in any of the three winters) were submitted, of 183 species.

To increase the value of the data for conservation, habitat information was also collected, with observers for every record, breeding or winter, allocating one or more habitat codes according to the standard system devised by the British Trust for Ornithology (BTO). This is, we believe, a feature that has not been incorporated into previous Atlases, but proved to be straightforward to do and has provided much new information of great interest for many species. The section 'Cheshire and Wirral and its habitats for birds' includes a listing of these codes and discussion of the county's habitats.

As well as recording distribution and habitats, it was felt important to measure the abundance of the county's birds. For the scarce breeding species it usually proved possible either to count the known nest sites or to assess from the number of occupied tetrads. For the more

Breeding status codes

Recording of breeding birds requires observation of a bird's behaviour and attribution to one of a number of breeding status codes. For some fieldworkers this meant a new approach to birds—putting the 'watching' back into 'birdwatching'. For the last couple of decades, much of the emphasis has focused on identification of species, usually via the minutiae of feather detail, and some surveyors had not been used to listening to birds' song or calls, or to observing their behaviour. Some people also have an abhorrence of approaching birds' nests. But there is no need to disturb a nest to record confirmed breeding, as most of the two-letter codes are indirect measures showing that a bird has eggs or chicks.

Category	Code	Description
Not breeding (not mapped)	**O**	Bird **O**bserved (seen or heard); no more knowledge of the species' status or of habitat suitable for breeding
Possible breeding (mapped with small dots)	**H**	Species present in suitable nesting **H**abitat; no other indication of breeding
	S	**S**inging male heard, or breeding calls heard
Probable breeding (mapped with medium dots)	**P**	**P**air observed in suitable nesting habitat
	D	**D**isplay or courtship
	N	Bird visiting a probable **N**est site
	B	Birds seen **B**uilding a nest, carrying nesting material, or excavating nest cavity
	A	**A**gitated behaviour or anxiety calls from adults suggesting a nest or young nearby
	I	Active brood patch on trapped bird, probably **I**ncubating
Confirmed breeding (mapped with large dots)	**DD**	**D**istraction **D**isplay or injury-feigning from adults
	UN	Recently **U**sed **N**est (used this season), or eggshells
	ON	**O**ccupied **N**est in use (e.g. high nest or nest hole whose contents cannot be deduced)
	FY	Adults carrying **F**ood for **Y**oung
	RF	**R**ecently **F**ledged young, still dependent on parents
	FS	Adults carrying **F**aecal **S**ac away from nest site
	NE	**N**est with **E**ggs, or adult sitting on nest
	NY	**N**est with **Y**oung, or downy young of nidifugous species

common and widespread species we achieved estimates of breeding population from results of the Breeding Bird Survey (BBS) in the county. This is a simple system based on observers walking two 1 km transects twice during the breeding season, counting every bird seen or heard. The BBS scheme was devised by the BTO to monitor year-to-year changes in bird populations, and has been used nationally since 1994 at more than 3,500 sites. In Cheshire and Wirral, the results from BBS in 2004 and 2005 have been used to calculate, in collaboration with the BTO, breeding populations for 65 species. This is the first time that this technique has been used at a county level. A further unique feature of this work is that maps of abundance across the county have been generated for 35 species.

The population figures are expressed as the number of individuals. The relationship between this figure and that for breeding pairs depends on the birds' behaviour, and differs between species depending on the relative detectability of males and females and the proportion of non-breeders (Newson *et al.* 2008). The populations are quoted with the statistical confidence limits in brackets, within which there is a 95% probability that the true value lies.

We had hoped to be able to assess the abundance of birds in winter but this is a much more difficult task—most birds are not territorial, many of them flock and many are silent—and there is no established methodology. So, this was the one aspect of the original objectives that was not fulfilled. However, 63% of winter records were accompanied by a count of the largest flock seen, allowing for the first time realistic estimates of populations of some of the wintering birds in the county.

Species accounts make up the bulk of this book. They concentrate on putting the Atlas results in context, describing the species' distribution within the county and, where possible, their abundance; changes in breeding distribution from our *First Atlas*; national changes in population and distribution; and links to habitat and conservation. For the breeding season, the former status in the county has been well described in our *First Atlas* and is not repeated here. As this is the first wintering bird Atlas of Cheshire and Wirral, the winter texts place the present results against the background of previous published work in the county.

Although the subject is birds, this is a 'People's Atlas'! All of the participants were amateurs, volunteering to do this work in their spare time; the term 'citizen science' is better established in the USA than in Britain, but endeavours like this Atlas are perfect examples of the engagement of citizen scientists. Even though every surveyor was an amateur, we have tried to maintain the highest professional standards in the work, and we believe that this Atlas stands alongside the best of all local projects to date.

More of the results of this Atlas are given in the following chapters, and more detail of the organization and methodology of the Atlas is given in Appendix 1.

PETER TWIST

This Atlas aimed to provide a complete record of birds in every area of Cheshire and Wirral in the breeding and wintering seasons.

PETER TWIST

Cheshire and Wirral and its habitats for birds

Situated in the north-west of England, Cheshire and Wirral spans 84 km (52 miles) from east to west and 58 km (36 miles) from north to south, a land area of about 2,498 km^2, which happens to be about 1% of the area of the UK (244,820 km^2). The human population, at the 2001 census, was almost 1.3 million.

Administratively, English counties have undergone substantial changes in the last 35 years. There was a major revision of local authorities in 1974, which included creation of the Metropolitan Borough of Wirral. Halton and Warrington were formed as Unitary Authorities in 1998, and the remainder of Cheshire is to be split into two new Unitary Authorities, Cheshire East and Cheshire West and Chester, from 2009.

Despite these changes in local authorities, thankfully, 'ornithological Cheshire and Wirral' has remained the same since our *First Atlas*, those recording boundaries having been agreed and set in 1978.

It is not just the boundaries that have undergone extensive modification by man. As with most of England, there is little or no 'natural' habitat left in Cheshire and Wirral. Broadly speaking, the county has an agricultural south-west, urban and industrialized north, and heavily grazed higher land in the east. According to the most recently available land-use statistics, from the year 2000 (Haines-Young *et al.* 2002), 72% of the land area of Cheshire and Wirral is grassland or arable, 8% woodland and 16% developed, with the remainder estuarine and coastal (3%), inland fresh water (0.7%) and heath or bog (0.5%).

The underlying geology consists mainly of Triassic sandstones, with the eastern hills of Millstone Grit. The hill country, roughly east of Macclesfield and Congleton, is mostly Carboniferous grits and shales, cut by several steep rivers, and is mainly farmed as unimproved grassland. The high plateau in the far east of Cheshire consists mostly of grassland, cotton-grass or heather moorland. Elsewhere in the county the only high land is where the red Bunter sandstone forms outcrops, such as the Sandstone Ridge from Bickerton to Helsby and Frodsham Hills; other lines of ridges define the Wirral, with obvious outcrops at Red Rocks and Hilbre. Most of Cheshire and Wirral is low-lying, however, with 85% of tetrads within 100 m of sea level.

Flooding of the Cheshire Plain 220 million years ago laid down large beds of minerals in the centre of the county, now being worked for the nationally important resources of salt and silica sand. Natural dissolution of the salt probably led to formation of some of the county's meres, and the subsidence of old salt excavations caused the flashes. In agricultural terms, the parts of the Plain overlain with Boulder clay, mainly to the south and west, have mostly been farmed as improved grassland; a notable feature is the many thousands of 'marl-pits', ponds formed about two centuries ago where slightly calcareous subsoil was dug out to fertilize farmland, helping the county to its position as the pond capital of Europe. The better-drained areas to the north and midwest of the county have proved suitable for arable cropping, while the very sandy soils across the centre of the county, from Delamere to Congleton, have been difficult to farm and are dominated by forestry plantations or sand quarries. The areas of the highest grade of agricultural land are mainly where former mosses have been destroyed by drainage, especially along the Mersey valley and parts of the 'Meres and Mosses country' of central southern Cheshire.

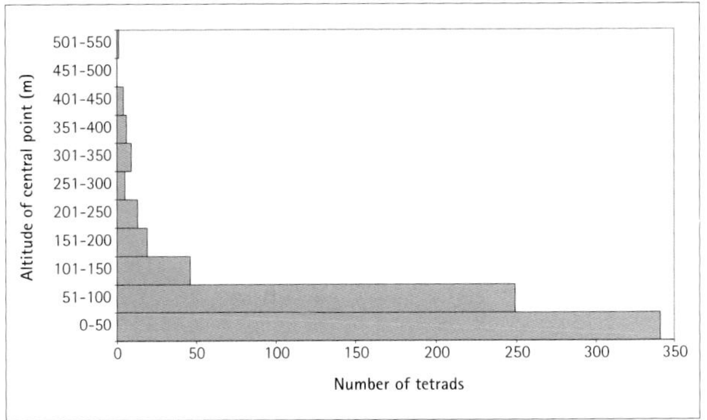

Tetrads by median altitude.

The remainder of this chapter presents some statistics, maps and images of some, but by no means all, of Cheshire and Wirral's habitats for birds.

The habitat distribution maps are compiled from the CEH 'landcover 2000' data (Haines-Young *et al.* 2002); the key at the bottom left of each map indicates, using square symbols of decreasing size, the proportion of this type of habitat in each 1 × 1 km square.

Habitat codes

The habitat coding system, as used for all bird surveys organized by the BTO, follows a straightforward hierarchy, with a letter for the primary habitat type and a number giving more detail. Observers could use as many habitat codes for each species as they felt appropriate. It was emphasized that the habitat is determined mostly by where the birds find their food, rather than the nest site, and that it is helpful to look at the habitat from the birds' point of view.

A Woodland

A1 Broad-leaved
A2 Coniferous
A3 Mixed (10% of each)
A4 Broad-leaved–waterlogged (carr)
A5 Coniferous–waterlogged (carr)
A6 Mixed–waterlogged (carr)

B Scrubland

B1 Regenerating natural or semi-natural woodland
B3 Heath scrub
B4 Young coppice
B5 New plantation
B6 Clear-felled woodland with or without new saplings
B7 Other

C Semi-natural grassland/marsh

C2 Grass moor (unenclosed)
C3 Grass moor mixed with heather (unenclosed)
C5 Other dry grassland
C6 Water-meadow/grazing marsh
C7 Reed swamp
C8 Other open marsh
C9 Salt-marsh

D Heathland and bogs

D1 Dry heath
D2 Wet heath
D3 Mixed heath
D4 Bog
D6 Drained bog
D7 Bare peat

E Farmland

E1 Improved grassland
E2 Unimproved grassland
E3 Mixed grass/tilled land
E4 Tilled land
E5 Orchard
E6 Other farming

F Human sites

F1 Urban
F2 Suburban
F3 Rural

G Waterbodies (fresh water)

G1 Pond (less than 50 m^2)
G2 Small waterbody (50–450 m^2)
G3 Lake/unlined reservoir
G4 Lined reservoir
G5 Gravel-pit, sandpit, etc.
G6 Stream (less than 3 m wide)
G7 River (more than 3 m wide)
G8 Ditch with water (less than 2 m wide)
G9 Small canal (2–5 m wide)
G10 Large canal (more than 5 m wide)

H Coastal

H1 Marine–open shore
H2 Marine shore–inlet/cove/loch
H3 Estuarine
H4 Brackish lagoon
H5 Open sea

I Inland rock

I1 Cliff
I2 Scree/boulder slope
I4 Other rock outcrop
I5 Quarry
I6 Mine/spoil/slag-heap

J Miscellaneous

The missing numbers (B2, C1, etc.) are for specialized habitats not found in the county–chalk downland, breckland, machair, limestone cliffs and caves. After the first year of fieldwork, we added three further farmland codes:

E7 Farmland–stubble (the remains of last season's crop left in the ground, not ploughed)
E8 Farmland with hedge–taller than about 2 m (a little above head height)
E9 Farmland with hedge–shorter than about 2 m

Very little of the county is managed specifically to benefit birds, with the notable exception of the RSPB reserve at Inner Marsh Farm (SJ37B), south Wirral.

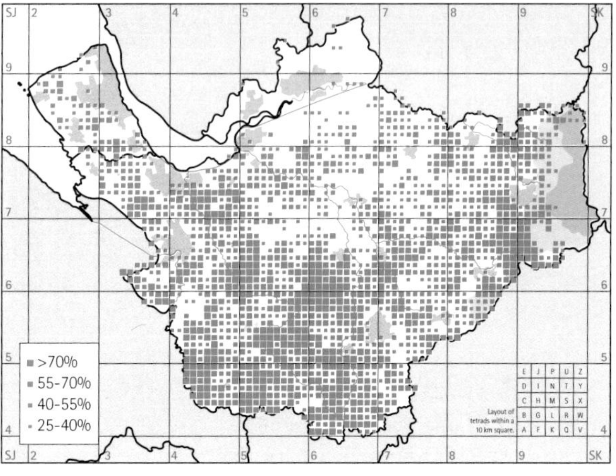

More than 38% of the county's land area is 'improved' grassland, where the adjective refers to improvement for agricultural purposes, with large input of fertilizers and other chemical treatments; from the point of view of the birds, this is not an improvement. Most of this land is grazed by dairy cattle. Although rather few breeding birds are found in such fields, they can hold wintering corvids, Snipe, Meadow Pipits, thrushes and sometimes Golden Plovers.

PETER TWIST

Taller hedges (E8) are much preferred by most birds to shorter hedges (E9). In the breeding season they are more likely to provide suitable nest sites, and harbour more insects on the growing shoots. In winter, they are more likely to have berries and provide better shelter.

PETER TWIST

Hedgerow trees form important song-posts, but their use by corvids can also inhibit Lapwings and Skylarks from nesting in the fields.

PETER TWIST

A mixture of habitats—grassland, hedgerow, scrub, trees and streams—allows the maximum diversity of bird species to use farmland.

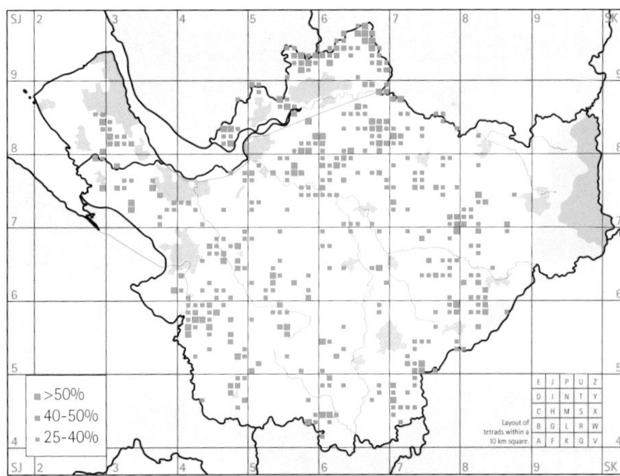

Some 21% of the county is classed as arable, with 12% used for cereals and 9% for horticulture. Parts of the Mersey valley are amongst the few areas of high-grade agricultural land in the county. Corn Buntings are fast disappearing, as are Yellow Wagtails.

HALTON BOROUGH COUNCIL

ANDY HARMER

Overgrown marl-pits usually hold a pair of resident Moorhens, and perhaps Reed Buntings.

PETER TWIST

The fodder needs of livestock significantly shape the Cheshire landscape. Few farms now produce hay, silage being the dominant method of cropping grass, and maize growing is widespread.

Most stubbles in the county are maize, not particularly good for small birds except when flooded or slurried. They are frequented more by larger species such as corvids, pigeons and occasionally geese.

Farm buildings provide nest sites especially for Swallows and House Sparrows.

The vegetation cover for the county's well-drained sandstone was naturally heath, but little of this habitat can be found nowadays. Most of the remaining heath is in the Peak District at the east of Cheshire.

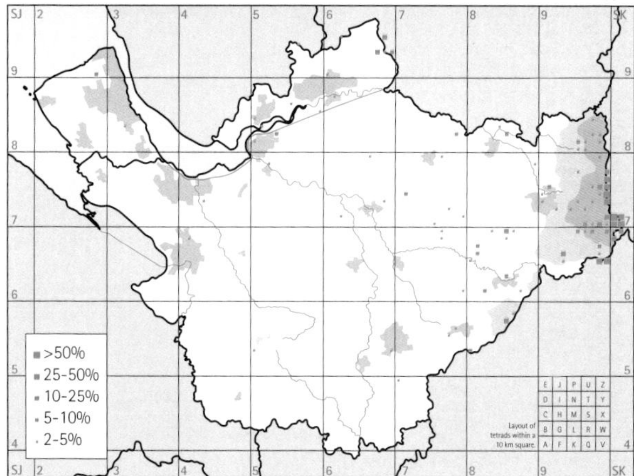

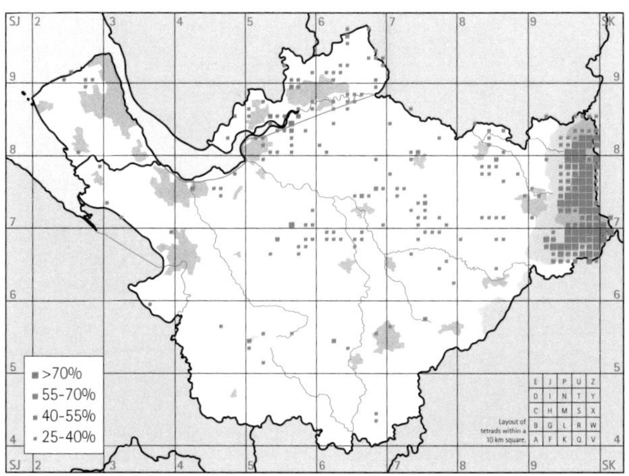

Unimproved grassland comprises 12% of the county, mostly in the eastern hills. Elsewhere, land that has not been intensively managed for a few years can hold high numbers of Skylarks, with perhaps Grey Partridges nesting under the hedges.

Several species are only found in the eastern hills, such as breeding Wheatear, Ring Ouzel and Golden Plover, with others reaching highest densities here including Curlew and Stonechat.

Meadow Pipits and Skylarks are among the commonest breeding birds of the edge of the Peak District, with Red Grouse where there is enough heather; the latter is one of the few species there in winter.

STEVE HOLMES

Cheshire's canals provide breeding and wintering sites for Moorhens, Little Grebes and Mallards, and feeding areas for Grey Herons, even amongst heavy traffic of narrow boats.

PETER TWIST

ANDY HARMER

By-products of the county's largest canal, the Manchester Ship Canal, the dredging deposit lagoons at Woolston and Frodsham hold some relatively scarce birds. The eutrophic waters attract breeding Black-necked Grebe, Gadwall, Pochard, Shoveler and other scarce species, with thousands of wintering dabbling ducks. The adjacent damp scrub and reed-beds are ideal for Reed and Sedge Warblers and Reed Buntings amongst other species.

ANDY HARMER

HALTON BOROUGH COUNCIL

Large areas are covered by industrial estates and warehouses, as ugly from the air as they are from the ground, but adjoining areas of scrub, woodland and wetland will still be used by birds. The site in the foreground, Manor Park, Runcorn (SJ58M), holds a colony of 30 pairs of Grey Herons, with Grasshopper and Sedge Warblers, Whitethroats and Reed Buntings breeding in the damp scrub.

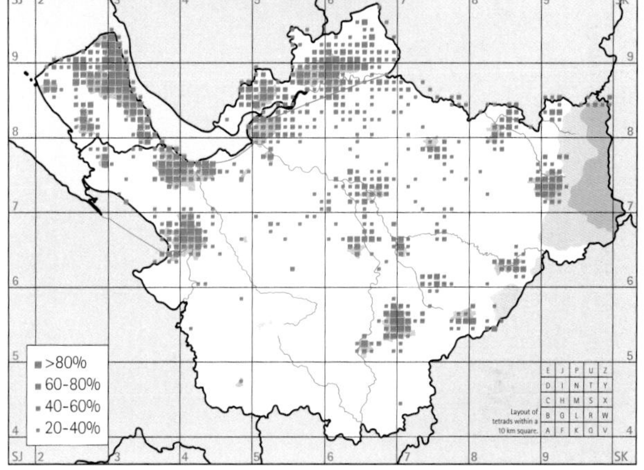

ANDY HARMER

Landfill sites sustain most of the county's inland gulls, especially in winter.

PETER TWIST

The older buildings in Cheshire villages are constructed of red sandstone. House Martins and Pied Wagtails are typical bird species, with perhaps Swifts.

PETER TWIST

PETER TWIST

PETER TWIST

PETER TWIST

Actively worked sand quarries provide nest sites for most of the county's Sand Martins, as long as suitable vertical faces are left. Little Ringed Plovers may breed on the flat areas, and a Pied Wagtail's nest is usually to be found somewhere amongst the machinery. In winter, large numbers of gulls roost in those quarries that have breached the water-table.

PETER TWIST

Most worked-out sand quarries are returned to agriculture or forestry. Opportunities for nature conservation are being lost.

HALTON BOROUGH COUNCIL

Although they both have extensive areas of intertidal mud-flats and salt-marshes, the county's two great estuaries are very different in shape and character. The Dee has a classic estuarine form, gradually widening from inland to seaward, with man's influence in the straightened section from Chester to around the Welsh border but mainly natural beyond there. The Mersey is constrained by major sandstone outcrops at its outer (Liverpool-Birkenhead) and inner (Runcorn-Widnes) ends, at its widest in between, with industrial development beside most of its length including the Manchester Ship Canal along its southern edge. The Canal also blocks the free access to the sea of the Gowy and the Weaver, whose flood plains are but a fraction of their former size. In the Mersey estuary, birds are squeezed between industry and agriculture. The salt-marsh around Hale Duck Decoy (SJ48Q) is part of the internationally important SSSI, SPA and Ramsar site.

RICHARD SMITH

The Dee estuary has been designated a European Special Area of Conservation under the Habitats Directive, as well as an SSSI, SPA and Ramsar site. Much of the salt-marsh at the south end, seen here with the Welsh hills in the background, is part of the RSPB reserve, and the combination of mud-flats and salt-marsh suits tens of thousands of waders and wildfowl.

RICHARD SMITH

The open shores of the north Wirral hold many feeding waders at low and medium tides, with most of the county's seabirds passing at high tides.

Hilbre is unique—the Cheshire island—and especially comes into its own for seabirds, some wildfowl and waders.

RICHARD SMITH

ANDY HARMER

The upland reservoirs hold fewer dabbling ducks than the lowland waters but seem as attractive to most diving species.

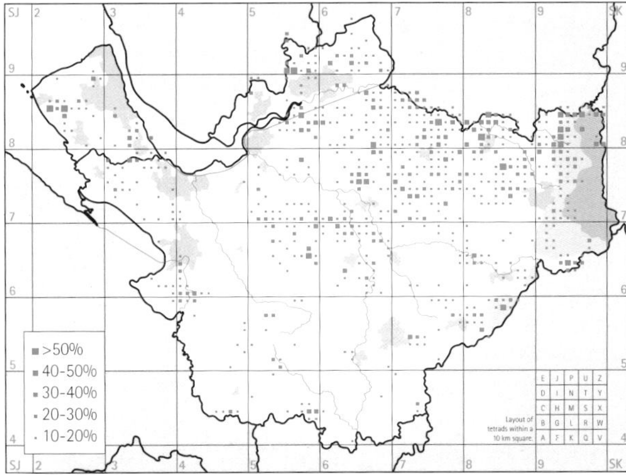

There is relatively little old broad-leaved woodland in Cheshire and Wirral. Nuthatch and Treecreeper are amongst its characteristic species, with Redstart and Pied Flycatcher especially in the east of the county.

ANDY HARMER

ANDY HARMER

The Wych valley is one of the oldest wooded parts of the county and is among the few strongholds of Marsh Tits.

ANDY HARMER

A succession of bird communities use newly planted woodland as it matures.

PETER TWIST

Coniferous woodland makes up 1% of the area of the county, mainly in the plantations of Delamere and Macclesfield Forests, holding Crossbills, Siskins and Lesser Redpolls, as well as the 'A2 habitat' specialists, Coal Tit and Goldcrest. The reflooded area of Blakemere (above) in the centre of Delamere Forest was rapidly colonized by what is currently Cheshire's largest Black-headed Gull colony, with the county's first breeding Mediterranean Gulls amongst them.

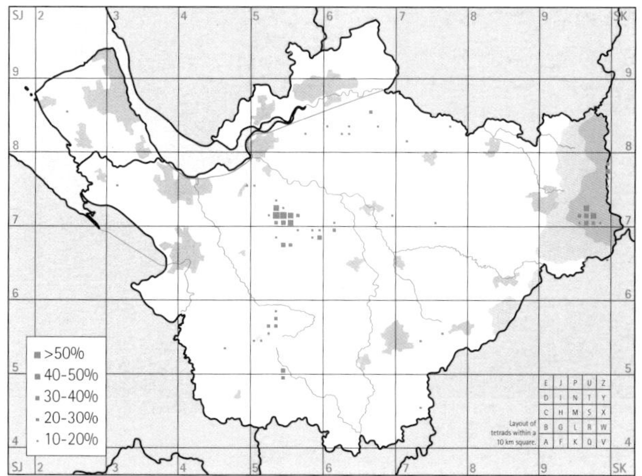

PAT WARING

ANDY HARMER

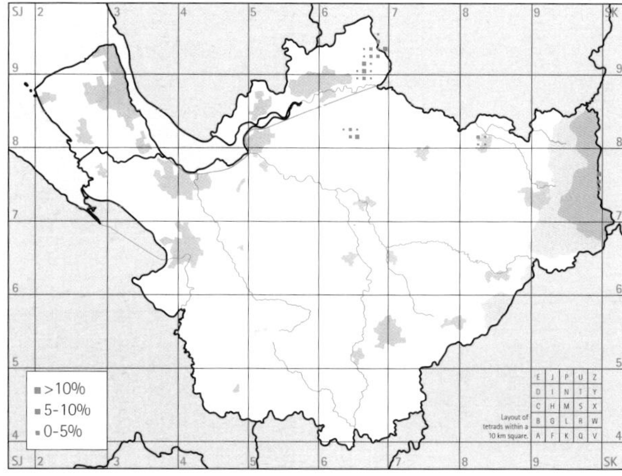

The small amount of bog in the county is botanically interesting but is too acidic for many birds.

Gorse is frequented by many breeding birds, especially Linnets.

ANDY HARMER

Wet fields and grazing marsh are likely to be the best places for breeding Lapwings.

STEVE HOLMES

Although picturesque on the now-occasional day of hard frost, in such conditions the flashes offer few feeding options for birds.

SHEILA BLAMIRE

ANDY HARMER

Any of the relatively undisturbed waters is suitable for breeding grebes and other waterfowl.

ANDY HARMER

PETER TWIST

Phragmites reed-beds fringe many of the county's waters.

The birds of Cheshire and Wirral

Even within a relatively small area like Cheshire and Wirral, there can be large differences in the numbers of species from one tetrad to another, depending obviously on the diversity of habitats present. Figure 1 shows the tetrads allocated by their total number of species in the breeding season, in any of the three categories of confirmed/probably/possibly breeding, displayed in nine bands with equal numbers of tetrads in each. In the breeding season, tetrads vary from holding four breeding species up to 86, with the regions of greatest avian diversity in the north-east and south-west of Cheshire, and isolated hotspots elsewhere, including most of the county's well-watched bird sites in the top two bands. The most impoverished areas are the highest parts of the eastern hills and a band running from south Cheshire to the north Wirral. The urban areas, especially of Halton and eastern Wirral, hold fewer species; indeed few parts of the Wirral, with its paucity of rivers and waterbodies, reach the higher levels of diversity.

In winter, tetrads hold from four to 107 species, with still generally higher numbers in the north-east and south-west of Cheshire, but at this season the south Mersey, north-west Wirral and some of the meres and flooded sand quarries come into prominence. Figure 2, plotting the number of species present in each tetrad in winter, shows that the areas of lowest bird diversity include the extremes of altitude, the eastern uplands

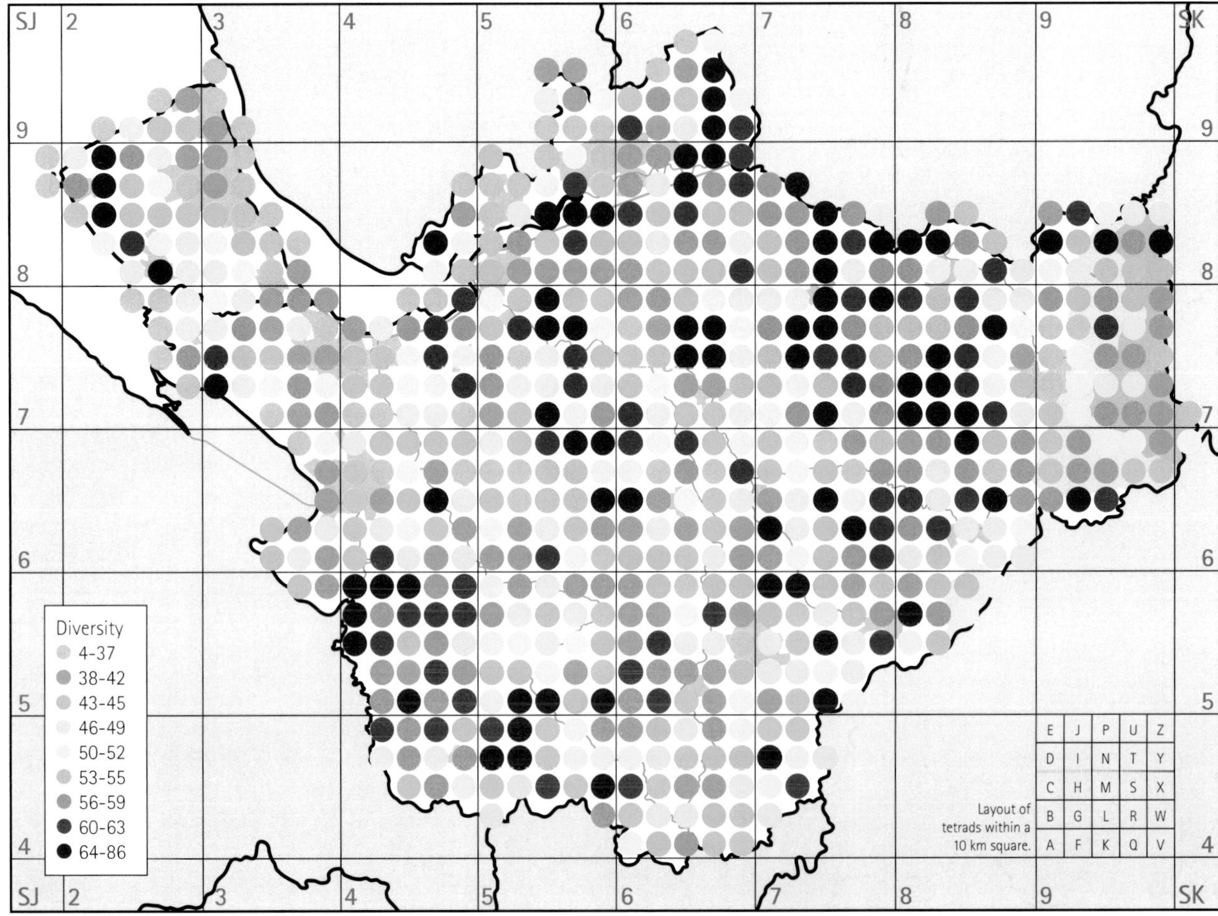

Figure 1: Species richness in the breeding season.

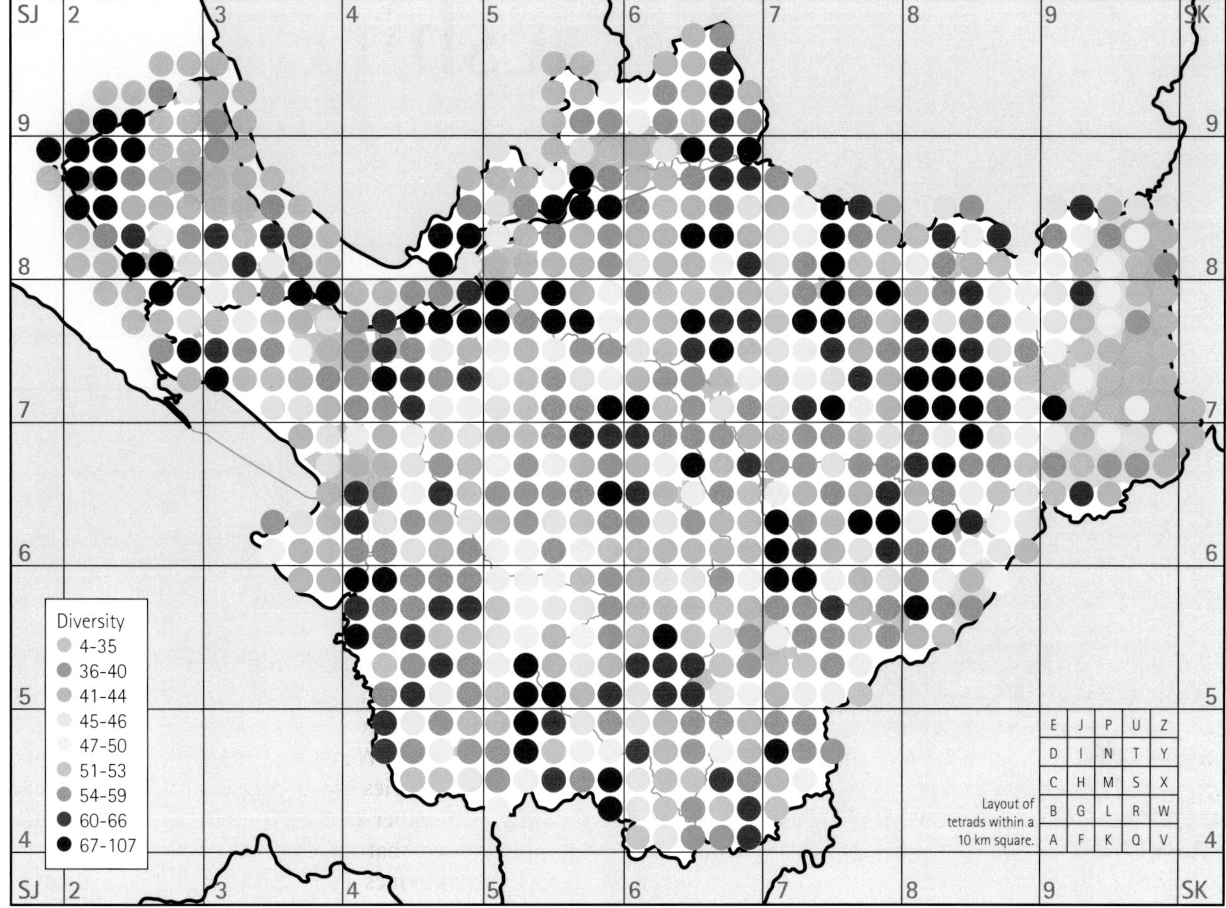

Figure 2: Winter species richness.

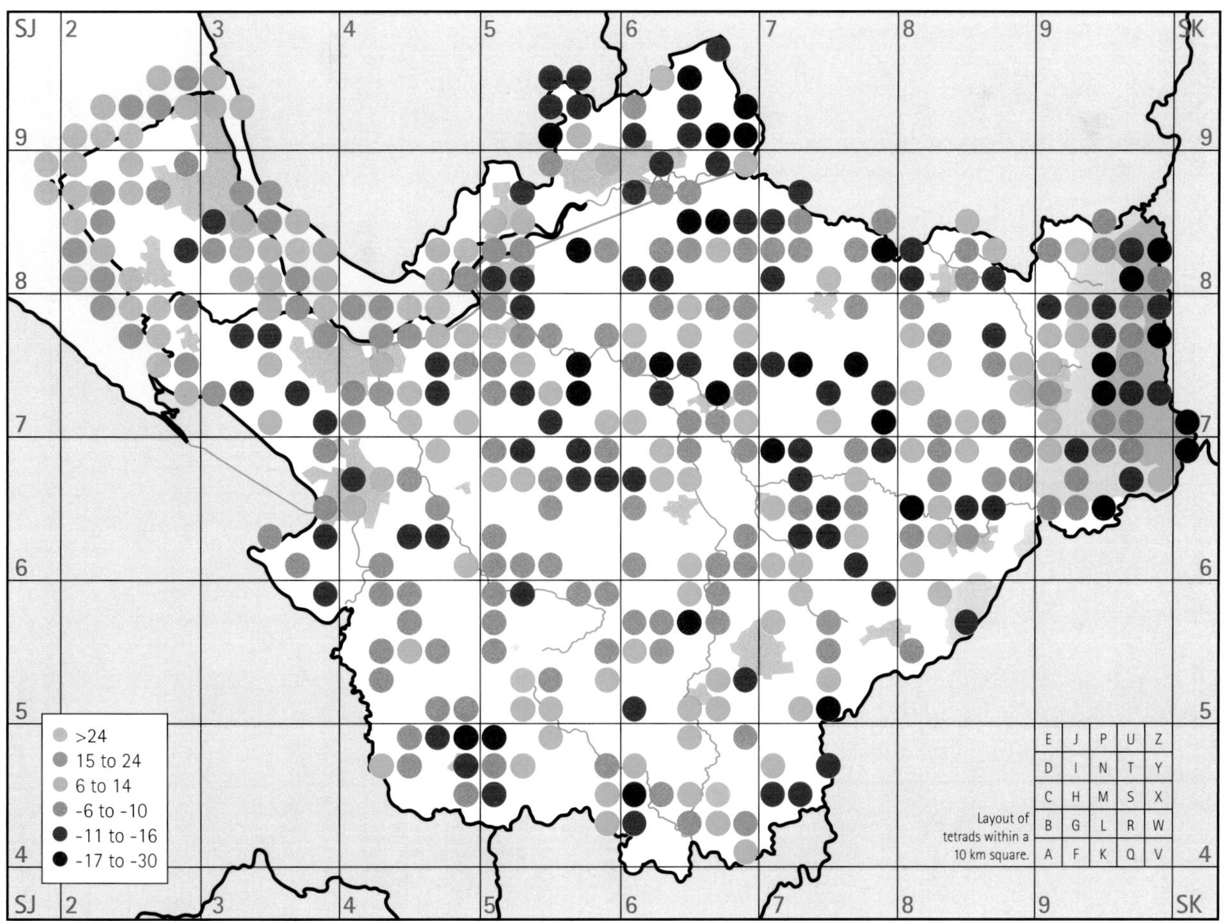

Figure 3: Winter minus breeding.

and the estuarine intertidal tetrads, with generally fewer species in the northern and western areas of Cheshire.

Fortuitously, very similar numbers of records were received for the two seasons, 34,516 unique records in the breeding season and 34,237 in winter, although of more species (183) in winter, compared to 153 breeding. A straightforward subtraction of the number of species breeding from those present in winter yields Figure 3. More species were held in 270 tetrads in winter, with 30 the same in both seasons and 384 tetrads holding fewer in winter than breeding. A further 295 tetrads held similar numbers of species, in the range from five more to five fewer, and these are not plotted on this map. The map graphically shows the shift in bird distributions from breeding to winter seasons, well known to birdwatchers, from the hills to the coast, and winter is the season in which the Wirral comes into its own for birds in the county.

While these maps relate to all species, more sophisticated analyses can be performed of the distribution of various groups of birds.

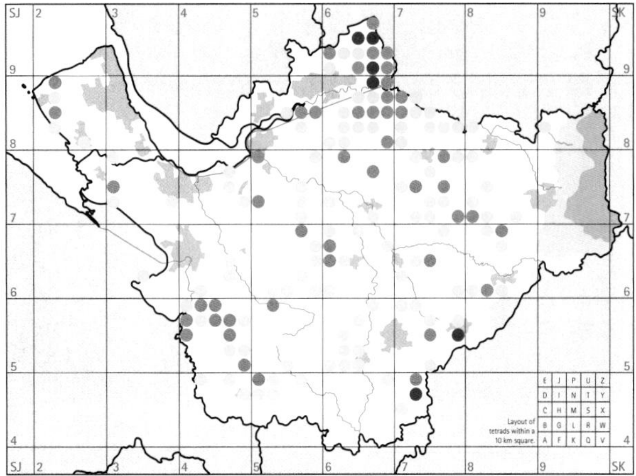

Figure 4: Farmland Red-listed species.

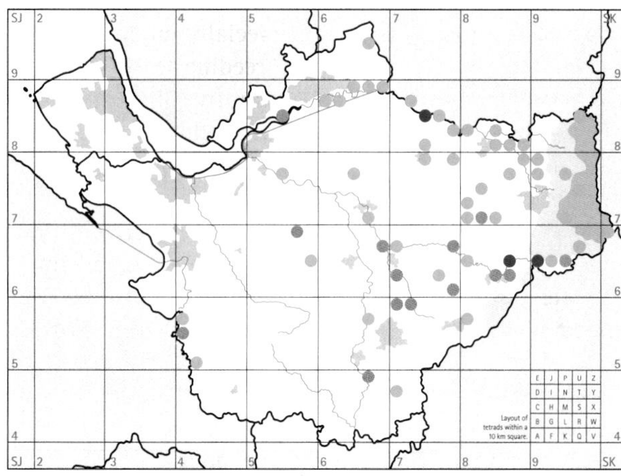

Figure 5: River species.

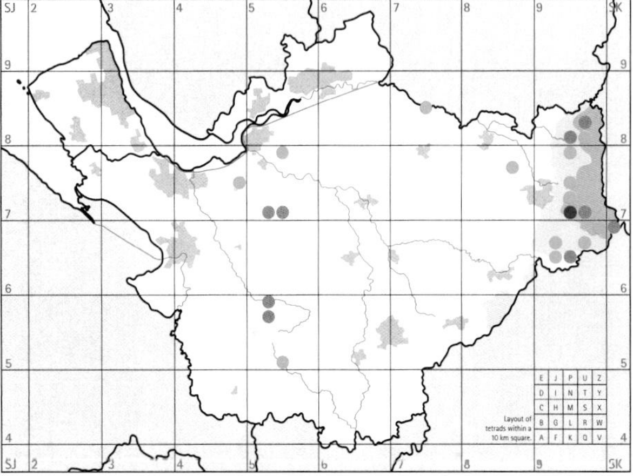

Figure 6: Deciduous woodland specialists.

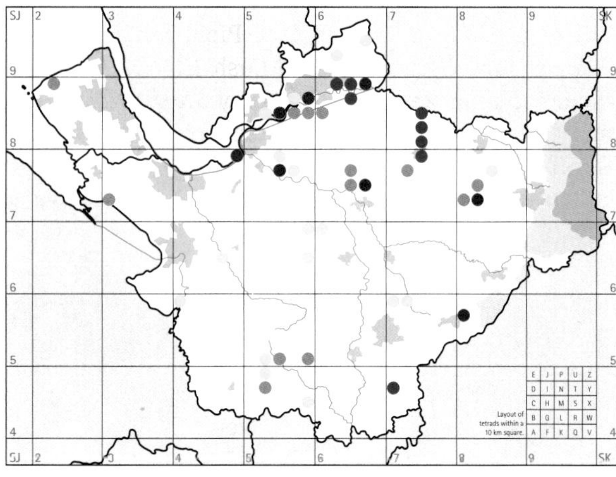

Figure 7: Wetland breeders.

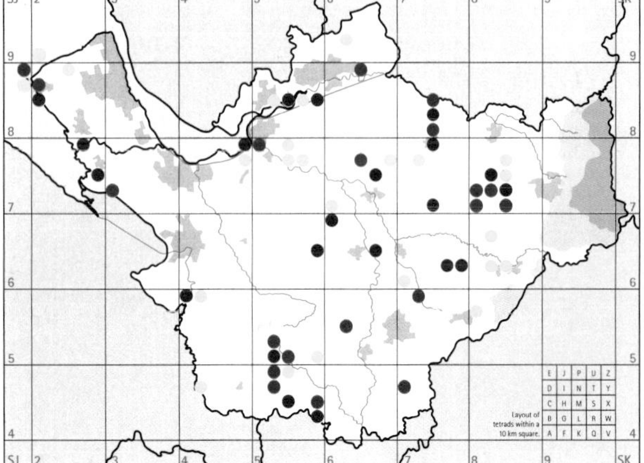

Figure 8: Winter waterfowl.

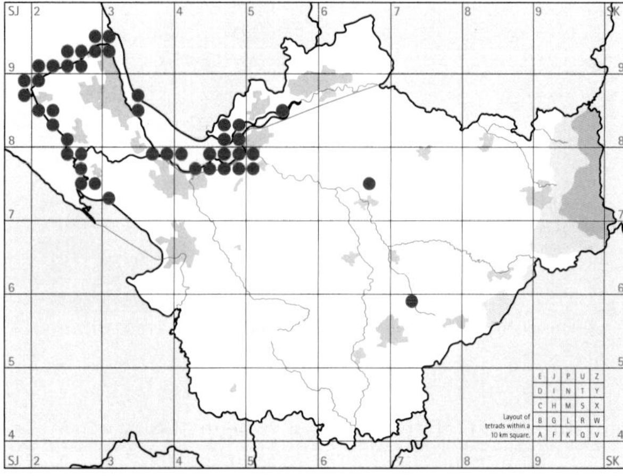

Figure 9: Wintering waders.

Figure 4 depicts tetrads with breeding season presence of six (yellow), seven (orange) or eight (brown) of the Red-listed species of conservation concern that mainly frequent farmland: Grey Partridge, Skylark, Tree Sparrow, Linnet, Bullfinch, Yellowhammer, Reed Bunting and Corn Bunting; the almost-ubiquitous Song Thrush, Starling and House Sparrow are omitted. The concentration around Warrington in SJ68, SJ69 and SJ78 is striking, corresponding to the main areas of arable agriculture in the county. There are other hotspots around Blakenhall (SJ74I/J) and Alsager (SJ75X), although too much should not be made of the presence or absence of just one or two species. The mainly pastoral areas of south-west Cheshire are also especially important.

Figure 5 shows tetrads with breeding season presence of three (green), four (orange) or five (brown) of the six species Goosander, Common Sandpiper, Kingfisher, Sand Martin, Grey Wagtail and Dipper. Apart from three tetrads on the river Dee, all of the important sites are in the east of Cheshire, with the Dane the premier river system in the county. This Atlas shows a mixed picture for the county's river birds: Goosanders have started breeding in the last twenty years and Grey Wagtails have increased greatly, but Dippers and Common Sandpipers have declined, with Kingfishers showing varied fortunes.

The county does not have much high-quality woodland, so the range of some specialist species is restricted. Figure 6 shows tetrads holding three (green), four (orange) or all six (brown) of the six breeding species Green Woodpecker, Tree Pipit, Redstart, Wood Warbler, Pied Flycatcher and Marsh Tit. Other obvious woodland birds are omitted as they are so widespread, such as Great Spotted Woodpecker, Nuthatch and Treecreeper. The best tetrad for these special woodland birds is clearly Langley (SJ97K), with other concentrations in the same area and also Delamere Forest (SJ57 F/K), Peckforton (SJ55I/J) and Lyme Park (SJ98).

The major wetlands for breeding birds are shown by Figure 7, which depicts tetrads holding six (yellow), seven (orange), eight (red) or nine, ten or eleven (brown) of the eleven species Mute Swan, Greylag Goose, Canada Goose, Mandarin, Gadwall, Shoveler, Pochard, Ruddy Duck, Little Grebe, Great Crested Grebe and Black-necked Grebe. The main areas are along the Mersey valley from Woolston (SJ68J/P/U) to Astmoor (SJ58H), Tatton/Rostherne (SJ77P/SJ78K/L/M) and Doddington (SJ74D), with other important areas including Frodsham Marsh (SJ47Z), the lower Weaver valley (SJ57N/P/T), Anderton/Marbury (Great Budworth)/Neumann's Flash (SJ67M/N/S), Chelford Sand Quarries (SJ87), Astbury Mere (SJ85D) and the south Cheshire meres on the Cholmondeley estate (SJ45/55). The only Wirral tetrads to feature are those including Inner Marsh Farm (SJ37B) and Meols (SJ28J). Note that this Atlas is based on tetrads, not sites, and some individual sites appear to have greater prominence than others if they happen to span more than one tetrad.

Although it does not show on a map like this, one notable result of this Atlas has been the extension of breeding onto smaller waters by several waterfowl, especially Canada Goose, Greylag Goose, Coot and Tufted Duck; Moorhen and Little Grebe may have suffered from this intrusion into their domain.

SIMON BOOTH

Reed Bunting is a Red-listed species that is quite widespread on the county's farmland.

Far more waterfowl winter in the county, and most tetrads hold a few species, so Figure 8 depicts tetrads with 13 or 14 species (yellow), 15 or 16 species (red) or 17–26 species (brown), highlighting the well-known areas of the estuaries, with inland meres, sand quarries and dredging deposit grounds.

Those tetrads with nine or more wintering wader species are shown in Figure 9. The only tetrads away from the vicinity of the estuaries are Neumann's Flash (SJ67S) and Sandbach Flashes (SJ75J).

Table 1: Top 30 most widespread breeding species, ranked by number of tetrads with breeding season presence.

Position	Species	Number of tetrads
1	Wren	660
2=	Blackbird	655
2=	Robin	655
2=	Woodpigeon	655
5	Blue Tit	654
6	Chaffinch	653
7	Magpie	650
8	Great Tit	649
9	Dunnock	647
10	Carrion Crow	644
11=	Greenfinch	639
11=	Song Thrush	639
13	Goldfinch	637
14	Swallow	636
15	Mallard	635
16	Starling	631
17	House Sparrow	629
18	Chiffchaff	615
19	Collared Dove	612
20	House Martin	606
21	Blackcap	605
22	Pied Wagtail	602
23	Long-tailed Tit	593
24	Moorhen	591
25	Great Spotted Woodpecker	588
26	Mistle Thrush	583
27	Kestrel	565
28	Buzzard	560
29	Jackdaw	559
30	Pheasant	556

Table 2: Top 30 most widespread wintering species, ranked by number of tetrads in which they were recorded.

Position	Species	Number of tetrads
1=	Robin	656
1=	Blue Tit	656
3=	Wren	655
3=	Magpie	655
3=	Blackbird	655
6	Carrion Crow	654
7	Great Tit	653
8	Chaffinch	650
9	Dunnock	644
10	Woodpigeon	643
11	Mallard	624
12	Long-tailed Tit	622
13=	Starling	621
13=	Song Thrush	621
15	Greenfinch	617
16	Pied Wagtail	616
17	House Sparrow	614
18	Mistle Thrush	606
19	Redwing	603
20	Collared Dove	599
21	Kestrel	597
22	Goldfinch	589
23	Moorhen	585
24	Great Spotted Woodpecker	578
25	Buzzard	576
26	Fieldfare	574
27	Jay	567
28	Jackdaw	553
29	Pheasant	543
30	Sparrowhawk	533

Species league tables

The 'league tables' of species in this Atlas, and comparisons with our *First Atlas* for breeding species, make interesting reading.

The most widespread breeding species obviously are those with catholic habitat preferences (Table 1). Thirteen species are found in the breeding season in 95% of the county's tetrads, and 21 species in 90% of the tetrads. The top thirty are mainly passerines, making up nine of the top ten (the only non-passerine being Woodpigeon), and 17 of the top twenty (with Mallard and Collared Dove as the other non-passerines). The vast majority are land-birds, plus the two aquatic species that utilize almost any waterbody, Mallard and Moorhen. Nearly all are residents, with just four summer migrants in the list. The ranking of the top twenty summer visitors is shown in detail in Table 7.

Table 2 shows that almost all of the top thirty most widespread wintering species are residents, although the local population may be augmented by continental immigrants, with only Redwing (nineteenth) and Fieldfare (twenty-sixth) exclusively winter visitors. There are few significant changes in position between the lists for breeding and wintering seasons.

Comparing the rankings for abundance with those for distribution (Table 3), in general, colonial breeding species are placed higher on the abundance ranking—House Sparrow, Starling, Jackdaw, Linnet, Feral Pigeon

Table 3: Top 30 most numerous breeding species, from the population estimates derived as detailed in Appendix 1.

Position	Species	Breeding population (individuals)
1	House Sparrow	211,490
2	Blue Tit	195,250
3	Chaffinch	185,450
4	Blackbird	182,810
5	Robin	147,520
6	Woodpigeon	129,890
7	Wren	129,370
8	Great Tit	104,180
9	Starling	72,240
10	Dunnock	71,680
11	Greenfinch	49,950
12	Swallow	43,620
13	Long-tailed Tit	37,670
14	Mallard	35,630
15	Jackdaw	32,610
16	Carrion Crow	30,640
17	Goldfinch	30,440
18	Collared Dove	26,650
19	Pied Wagtail	20,120
20	House Martin	19,630
21	Linnet	17,830
22	Song Thrush	17,200
23	Whitethroat	16,890
24	Chiffchaff	15,800
25	Magpie	14,190
26	Blackcap	12,910
27	Feral Pigeon	12,710
28	Rook	9,910
29	Pheasant	9,420
30	Skylark	9,010

and Rook, but not Swallow or House Martin—indicating that they are not widespread but are numerous where they occur. Most of the larger birds are lower in rank order for abundance—Woodpigeon, Carrion Crow and Magpie—as they are conspicuous and widespread but space themselves at lower densities than most smaller birds.

The importance of Cheshire and Wirral in national terms

One measure of the importance of the county in national terms is the proportion of the UK's breeding bird population that is in Cheshire and Wirral, bearing in mind that the county covers 1% of the land area of the UK. Using the same methodology as for the county population, national population estimates have been derived (Newson *et al.* 2008) and Table 4 ranks species in terms of the percentage of the UK population. There are quite large error bars on these proportions and the fine differences should not be taken too literally, but they do indicate some general trends.

The importance of the county for Grey Heron is explained in the species text: with two of the country's five largest heronries and the most ponds per county, it is not surprising that this species ranks so highly. Most of the other species that breed on small waterbodies are also disproportionately present in Cheshire and Wirral, including Canada Goose, Mallard, Moorhen and Coot in this list. The preponderance of livestock in the agricultural scene probably accounts for the presence of several of the species that feed on flying insects, Swift, Swallow, House Martin and Pied Wagtail. The pastoral landscape may also be reasonably good for birds that take earthworms and other soil invertebrates, including Lapwing, Blackbird, Mistle Thrush and perhaps Kestrel, Starling and Jackdaw. But the presence of others on this list is puzzling and would repay in-depth study. Nuthatch and Treecreeper are unexpected in our relatively unwooded county, as is the presence of three warblers in this list.

At the other end of the range, species with a low proportion of the national totals include Coal Tit and Goldcrest, which are much more numerous in the parts of the country with coniferous forests.

The Wren is our most widespread breeding species.

RICHARD STEEL

BEN HALL

Small insectivorous resident species such as Long-tailed Tits have considerably expanded their range and population since our *First Atlas*.

Table 4: The proportion of the UK breeding population in Cheshire and Wirral. From the population estimates derived as detailed in Appendix 1, this table lists the top 30 species in terms of the percentage of the UK total. The figures were calculated to two decimal places but are rounded here to one decimal place for presentation.

Position	Species	Percentage of UK breeding population
1	Grey Heron	4.2%
2	Nuthatch	3.9%
3	Long-tailed Tit	3.6%
4	Lesser Whitethroat	3.4%
5	Canada Goose	2.8%
6	Jay	2.6%
7	Kestrel	2.6%
8	Lapwing	2.5%
9	Moorhen	2.2%
10=	Chiffchaff	2.2%
10=	Swift	2.2%
12	Mallard	2.2%
13	House Sparrow	2.0%
14	Treecreeper	2.0%
15	Pied Wagtail	2.0%
16=	Coot	1.9%
16=	Swallow	1.9%
18	Blackbird	1.8%
19	Great Tit	1.8%
20	Robin	1.8%
21	Blue Tit	1.7%
22	Dunnock	1.6%
23	House Martin	1.6%
24	Wren	1.6%
25	Goldfinch	1.6%
26	Carrion Crow	1.5%
27	Starling	1.5%
28	Mistle Thrush	1.4%
29	Garden Warbler	1.4%
30=	Collared Dove	1.3%
30=	Jackdaw	1.3%

Table 5: The net increase in the number of tetrads occupied in the breeding season in this Atlas compared to our *First Atlas*. This table lists the top 30 species that have increased their ubiquity in the county.

Position	Species	Net gain
1	Buzzard	548
2	Canada Goose	197
3	Chiffchaff	166
4	Mute Swan	151
5	Long-tailed Tit	139
6	Goldcrest	137
7	Barn Owl	134
8	Pheasant	130
9	Hobby	119
10	Nuthatch	114
11	Raven	97
12	Sparrowhawk	96
13	Oystercatcher	94
14	Greylag Goose	89
15	Great Spotted Woodpecker	86
16	Red-legged Partridge	81
17	Goldfinch	78
18	Coot	77
19	Blackcap	72
20	Grey Wagtail	69
21	Tufted Duck	63
22	Jackdaw	61
23=	Mandarin	59
23=	Greenfinch	59
25	Shelduck	58
26	Mallard	57
27=	Jay	50
27=	Cormorant	50
29	Collared Dove	44
30	Whitethroat	42

The county's changing bird-life

There are a number of common factors amongst the species that have increased their spread across the county (Table 5). Most raptors have fared well (Buzzard, Hobby, Sparrowhawk), with Raven in a similar category. Most waterfowl have spread (Canada Goose, Mute Swan, Greylag Goose, Tufted Duck, Mandarin, Shelduck, Mallard and Coot). The introduced gamebirds are more widespread (Pheasant, Red-legged Partridge). Small insectivorous resident species have risen spectacularly (Long-tailed Tit, Goldcrest), as have the short-distance summer migrants, species which mostly winter around the Mediterranean (Chiffchaff, Blackcap). Two of the common finches are even more common now (Goldfinch, Greenfinch).

There are some common factors amongst those that have decreased their range (Table 6). Several farmland seed-eaters are on this list (Grey Partridge, Corn Bunting, Tree Sparrow, Yellowhammer, Linnet, Skylark, Turtle Dove, Reed Bunting and Bullfinch), as are the 'brown tits' (Marsh Tit and Willow Tit) and most of our breeding waders (Woodcock, Curlew, Snipe, Lapwing). Trans-Saharan migrants feature disproportionately (Spotted Flycatcher, Turtle Dove, Cuckoo, Yellow Wagtail, Willow Warbler, Tree Pipit, Wood Warbler and Whinchat).

Most of those on the 'loss' list are species of conservation concern nationally, indicating that it is not just

Some Skylarks flock together in winter, especially during periods of frost.

JEFF CLARKE

Cheshire and Wirral where they are decreasing. Of the 30 birds lost from the most tetrads, 13 are on the Red List (Grey Partridge, Corn Bunting, Willow Tit, Spotted Flycatcher, Tree Sparrow, Yellowhammer, Linnet, Skylark, Lesser Spotted Woodpecker, Turtle Dove, Marsh Tit, Reed Bunting and Bullfinch) and 12 on the Amber List (Cuckoo, Yellow Wagtail, Lesser Redpoll, Willow Warbler, Woodcock, Curlew, Snipe, Lapwing, Tree Pipit, Wood Warbler, Meadow Pipit and Mistle Thrush), with five unlisted (Tawny Owl, Treecreeper, Little Owl, Garden Warbler and Whinchat).

Summer migrants make up a decreasing proportion of our breeding avifauna (Table 7). Only the first six in the table are found in more than half of the county's tetrads, and there is a big gap in ubiquity between them and the rest.

Tables 8 and 9 showing the top thirty breeding species in this Atlas and our *First Atlas* reveal some interesting changes. Not much should be inferred from changes of a few positions, which may mean only a few tetrads difference, but several species have shown dramatic changes. Two of the top four species in 1978–84 have dropped significantly—Starling and House Sparrow—as have House Martin and Mistle Thrush, which had not been commented upon as declining. Others that were formerly widespread are no longer in the top thirty: Willow Warbler, Skylark, Linnet, Yellowhammer, Reed Bunting and Cuckoo. Substantial rises have been shown by several commensal birds, Greenfinch, Goldfinch, Mallard and Collared Dove. Chiffchaff, Long-tailed Tit and Great Spotted Woodpecker have spread spectacularly. But all are eclipsed by the Buzzard.

Over the past 30 years, since the start of fieldwork for our *First Atlas*, some of the most extreme changes in the county's breeding birds have been the gains and losses of some species. The timeline in Table 10 illustrates this for the regularly breeding species.

The Swallow is Cheshire and Wirral's most widespread summer visitor.

ANDY HARMER

Table 6: The net decrease in the number of tetrads occupied in the breeding season in this Atlas compared to our *First Atlas*. This table lists the top 30 species that have decreased their ubiquity in the county.

Position	Species	Net loss
1	Cuckoo	-305
2	Grey Partridge	-270
3	Yellow Wagtail	-259
4	Lesser Redpoll	-227
5	Corn Bunting	-223
6	Willow Tit	-221
7	Spotted Flycatcher	-206
8	Tree Sparrow	-202
9	Yellowhammer	-200
10	Linnet	-161
11	Skylark	-150
12	Lesser Spotted Woodpecker	-147
13	Turtle Dove	-142
14	Tawny Owl	-136
15	Marsh Tit	-130
16	Reed Bunting	-115
17	Willow Warbler	-109
18=	Woodcock	-91
18=	Curlew	-91
20	Snipe	-90
21	Lapwing	-82
22	Tree Pipit	-69
23=	Wood Warbler	-68
23=	Treecreeper	-68
25	Bullfinch	-65
26	Meadow Pipit	-56
27	Little Owl	-52
28=	Mistle Thrush	-46
28=	Garden Warbler	-46
30	Whinchat	-43

Table 7: Top 20 most widespread summer visitors, ranked by number of tetrads with breeding season presence.

Position	Species	Number of tetrads
1	Swallow	636
2	Chiffchaff	615
3	House Martin	606
4	Blackcap	605
5	Whitethroat	543
6	Willow Warbler	533
7	Lesser Whitethroat	263
8	Garden Warbler	253
9	Cuckoo	229
10	Spotted Flycatcher	226
11	Sedge Warbler	210
12	Swift	150
13	Reed Warbler	137
14	Yellow Wagtail	126
15	Hobby	119
16	Sand Martin	88
17	Grasshopper Warbler	83
18	Little Ringed Plover	47
19	Redstart	44
20	Pied Flycatcher	40

Table 8: Top 30 most widespread breeding species in this Atlas compared to our *First Atlas*, ranked by number of tetrads with breeding season presence.

Position	Position in *First Atlas*	Species	Number of tetrads in this Atlas
1	3	Wren	660
2=	2	Blackbird	655
2=	7	Robin	655
2=	11	Woodpigeon	655
5	5=	Blue Tit	654
6	15=	Chaffinch	653
7	5=	Magpie	650
8	12=	Great Tit	649
9	9=	Dunnock	647
10	9=	Carrion Crow	644
11=	22	Greenfinch	639
11=	12=	Song Thrush	639
13	28	Goldfinch	637
14	8	Swallow	636
15	23	Mallard	635
16	1	Starling	631
17	4	House Sparrow	629
18	42	Chiffchaff	615
19	25	Collared Dove	612
20	15=	House Martin	606
21	31	Blackcap	605
22	20	Pied Wagtail	602
23	40	Long-tailed Tit	593
24	19	Moorhen	591
25	33	Great Spotted Woodpecker	588
26	17=	Mistle Thrush	583
27	27	Kestrel	565
28	108	Buzzard	560
29	36	Jackdaw	559
30	45	Pheasant	556

Table 9: Top 30 most widespread breeding species in our *First Atlas* compared to this Atlas, ranked by number of tetrads with breeding season presence.

Position	Present position	Species	Number of tetrads in *First Atlas*
1	16	Starling	663
2	2=	Blackbird	661
3	1	Wren	659
4	17	House Sparrow	657
5=	5	Blue Tit	655
5=	7	Magpie	655
7	2=	Robin	654
8	14	Swallow	653
9=	9	Dunnock	652
9=	10	Carrion Crow	652
11	2=	Woodpigeon	651
12=	11=	Song Thrush	647
12=	8	Great Tit	647
14	33	Willow Warbler	642
15=	20	House Martin	638
15=	6	Chaffinch	638
17=	35	Skylark	631
17=	26	Mistle Thrush	631
19	24	Moorhen	608
20	22	Pied Wagtail	595
21	44	Linnet	587
22	11=	Greenfinch	581
23	15	Mallard	578
24	49	Yellowhammer	571
25	19	Collared Dove	568
26	34	Lapwing	566
27	27	Kestrel	564
28	13	Goldfinch	560
29	43	Reed Bunting	542
30	58	Cuckoo	535

Loss	Year	Gain
	1978	
	1979	
Nightjar	1980	
	1981	Gadwall
	1982	
	1983	
	1984	
Dunlin	1985	
	1986	
	1987	Black-necked Grebe
	1988	
	1989	Peregrine
Twite, Hawfinch	1990	
Whinchat	1991	Raven
	1992	
	1993	
	1994	
	1995	Goosander
	1996	
	1997	
	1998	Hobby
	1999	
Turtle Dove	2000	
	2001	
	2002	Avocet
	2003	Lesser Black-backed Gull
	2004	Cormorant, Little Egret, Mediterranean Gull, Siskin
	2005	
	2006	

Table 10: This timeline shows the gains and losses amongst regularly breeding species in the county, indicating the last year of breeding of those lost, and the first year of regular breeding of those gained. Inevitably, there is an element of subjectivity in such a plot and it is not intended to contain every detail of recorded breeding in the last 30 years. Several other species have bred for a few years and then been 'lost' again (Common Tern, Great Black-backed Gull, Bearded Tit); others have bred sporadically, probably being underrecorded (Short-eared Owl, Merlin, Goshawk, Herring Gull); some have bred once only (Marsh Warbler, Black-winged Stilt, Black Redstart, Firecrest); and several of the colonizing species bred once several years before the major colonization (Black-necked Grebe, Siskin, Cormorant, Little Egret).

The county's changing bird-life: some common trends and reasons

A variety of key factors underlie the changes demonstrated by this Atlas, and these are summarized here, building on the summary in our *First Atlas* and a previous analysis by the author (Norman 1999). The natural world is complex, and the fortunes of many species are probably affected by a combination of causes, so the divisions given here are undoubtedly an oversimplification.

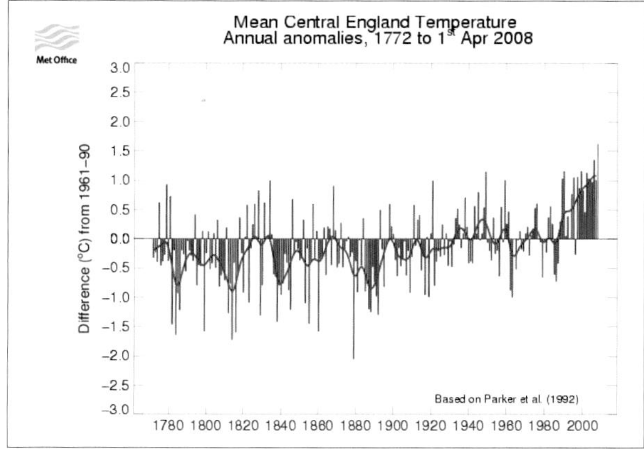

Figure 1: Annual surface air temperatures for central England (a roughly triangular area enclosed by Bristol, Lancashire and London) from 1772 to the present, with the red line the 10-year running mean (http://www.metoffice.gov.uk/research/hadleycentre/obsdata/cet.html).

Climatic change in Britain

We are now in the warmest period on record since the Industrial Revolution, illustrated by the graph of mean temperatures (Figure 1).

With this warming trend, it is perhaps not surprising that the county has been colonized by several species with a southerly distribution, such as Hobby, Little Egret, Avocet and Mediterranean Gull. Others have continued to spread northwards, including Reed Warbler, and the increased range of the Red-legged Partridge has probably been helped by the warmer weather. It would be too naive, however, to assume that southerly species are thriving and several have declined considerably, notably Turtle Dove, Tree Pipit and Wood Warbler, with Nightjar showing little sign of recolonizing the county. And, further confounding the picture, Siskin has now spread from the north to establish itself as a regular breeder in Cheshire.

At least as big an effect of the changing climate has been in winter, where the graph of winter temperatures (Figure 2) particularly shows the lack of hard weather since 1986. This has changed the habits of some birds during winter itself, and also throughout the year. In winter, since the mid-1980s there have been no significant hard weather movements of species like Lapwing, some waterfowl and some thrushes. The milder winters have probably contributed to the increasing numbers

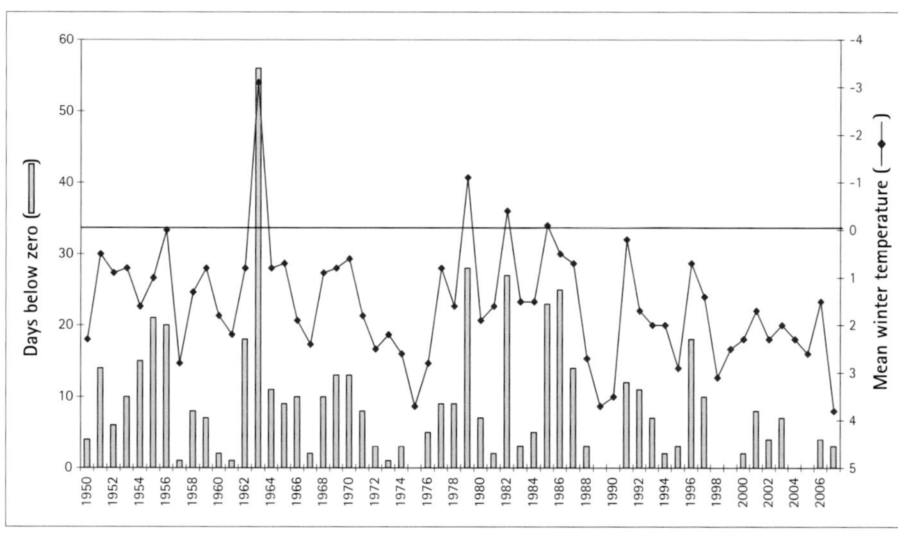

Figure 2: Winter (December to February inclusive) seasonal average temperature and the number of subzero days for central England from 1949/50 to 2006/07 (http://hadobs.metoffice.com/hadcet/).

of wintering warblers, especially the regular Chiffchaff and Blackcap, and must help the survival of rare wintering birds such as Swallow, Pallas's Warbler and Yellow-browed Warbler, all recorded during this Atlas. The wintering numbers and distribution in the county of partial migrants such as Stonechat, Goldfinch and Reed Bunting have undoubtedly increased.

Severe winter weather used to limit the populations of a range of resident species, which have not been restricted by this cause for over 20 years. The breeding numbers of fish-eating birds of fresh water, such as Grey Herons, are now at their highest recorded level in Cheshire and Wirral. Small insectivorous species have undoubtedly benefited from the mild winters: Long-tailed Tit and Goldcrest are much more widespread in the county than in our *First Atlas*, and Wren is the most ubiquitous breeder. Grey Wagtails have probably prospered from the same cause.

Climatic change outside Britain

Many trans-Saharan migrants are decreasing in range and numbers, at least in part owing to conditions experienced on migration and in their winter quarters. The widening Sahara and reduced rainfall in western Africa, particularly from 1968 to 1984, severely reduced the overwinter survival, especially of species that winter in the Sahel including Sand Martin, Sedge Warbler and Whitethroat, but they have largely adapted to their changed winter conditions and the latter two species are slightly more widespread now than during our *First Atlas*.

The Cheshire and Wirral breeding populations of several species that winter in West Africa have declined greatly, such as Turtle Dove, Yellow Wagtail, Whinchat, Redstart, Garden Warbler, Willow Warbler and Pied Flycatcher. Most of the longer-distance migrants have also decreased their numbers or range, notably Cuckoo, Tree Pipit, Wood Warbler and Spotted Flycatcher all dropping substantially, with House Martin also occupying fewer tetrads than in 1978–84. The reasons for these declines are not well understood and urgently need more study.

The warming climate is apparently allowing more Chiffchaffs and Blackcaps to winter around the Mediterranean and not cross the Sahara, benefiting them in earlier spring returns and nesting, and both species are present in considerably more tetrads now than twenty years ago.

A similar effect is applying to some of our wintering birds, notably with a tendency for waterfowl to winter closer to their breeding grounds. Birds from the east, especially those breeding in Siberia, are reaching here in smaller numbers, such as Bewick's Swan, Pochard and Grey Plover. On the other hand, the numbers of some of the species breeding to the north-west (Iceland, Greenland and Canada) are increasing here, as fewer winter in continental Europe, such as Knot, Black-tailed Godwit and Redshank.

Another effect of climate change is an increasing frequency of extreme weather events including more strong winds. Perhaps the weather pattern in November and December 2006 in the Bay of Biscay, driving some seabirds out of their winter quarters, is an example.

Agricultural changes

The effects of modern agriculture on British bird-life are probably the best documented of all links between habitats and birds. 'Cleaner' fields, with more pesticides and herbicides but fewer weeds and insects, allied to a reduction in winter stubble and the practice of planting arable crops in the autumn, have led to massive falls in the numbers and distribution of many farmland species. In Cheshire and Wirral, many of those breeding species that have declined the most since our *First Atlas* are birds that mostly eat small weed seeds throughout the year, with invertebrates essential for their chicks: Grey Partridge, Corn Bunting, Tree Sparrow, Yellowhammer, Linnet, Skylark, Turtle Dove and Reed Bunting have all been lost from 100 or more tetrads in 20 years.

There are some signs of a turn-round in the fortunes of some of these species in recent years where some farmers have taken up options under Countryside Stewardship or Environmental Stewardship, and the UK government is committed to halting the long-term decline in the index of farmland birds by 2020. Incidentally, these species need mapping at the tetrad scale to see the fine detail of their distribution; although Skylark, Linnet and Lapwing, for instance, have shown a large population decline, their distribution has not noticeably contracted at the 10 km square scale, indicating that they remain widespread but at lower density (Fuller *et al.* 1995), a finding that also holds good in Cheshire and Wirral.

Other aspects of agricultural management have adversely affected birds. Drainage has left fewer damp areas suitable for Lapwing, Curlew, Snipe and Yellow Wagtail, all of which have declined in the county. Early, and repeated, cutting of grassland for silage means insufficient time for any species to nest in the fields, especially Lapwings and Skylarks. Pesticides now kill many of the farmland invertebrates, probably hitting the food supplies of species like Mistle Thrush, Rook and Starling.

Thankfully, the agricultural chemicals are now extensively tested and none is known to be a direct poison to birds. The organochlorine seed-dressing used in the 1950s and 1960s hit birds like Stock Doves and accumulated up the food chain to cause breeding failures in species including Peregrines and Sparrowhawks. The rise in these raptors since our *First Atlas* is evidence that the pollutants are now only at low levels in the countryside.

Provision of food and protection

Shortage of nesting sites is seldom a problem for most birds, but provision of nest-boxes has certainly helped a few species. These include Pied Flycatchers, who return from Africa after the resident tits have appropriated most suitable holes, and Dippers, who may struggle to find a site; nest-boxes may be used for breeding and for roosting in during winter.

Provision of food in gardens and feeding stations elsewhere may have helped with overwinter survival of some species, and perhaps encouraged wintering Blackcaps. Especially with finches, which otherwise

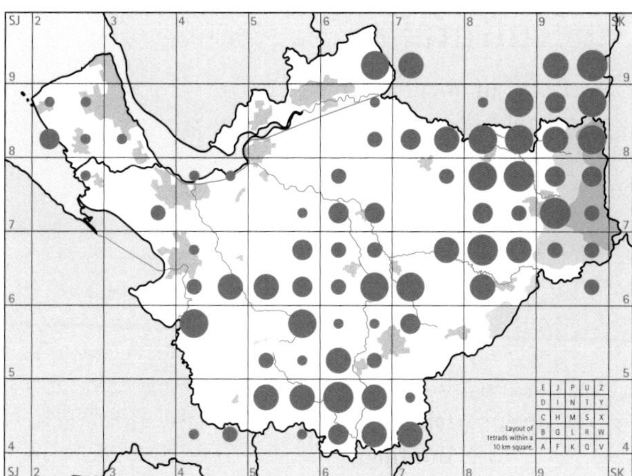

Six pioneering epiphytic lichens, 1992.

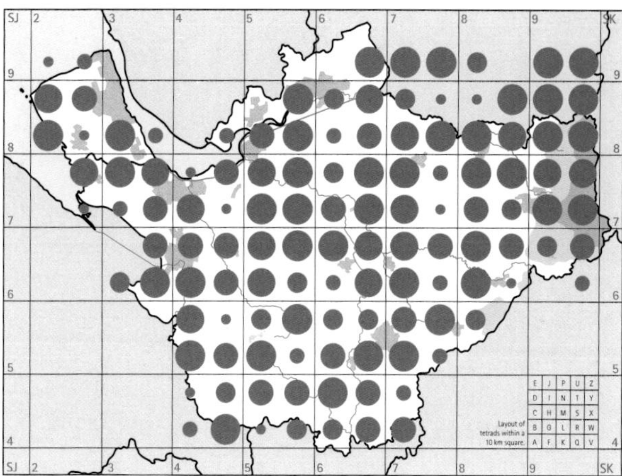

Six pioneering epiphytic lichens, 2002.

have to delay breeding until there is sufficient natural seed available, man's actions may be allowing some to breed earlier, and could have assisted the increased range of Greenfinch and Goldfinch in the county.

Some of the largest winter concentrations of farmland species of conservation concern, such as Tree Sparrow, Reed Bunting and Yellowhammer, have been found in planted areas of wildbird seed crops, an industrial-scale example of food provision.

Reduction in persecution

Several species, particularly raptors and corvids, used to be held way below their natural population level by human persecution. Corvids, especially Carrion Crows and Magpies, were trapped or shot on many farms and estates, but fewer are taken these days; both species have spread to breed closer to man. These two species were already amongst the top ten most widespread breeding species in 1978–84, and have consolidated that position now in the breeding and wintering seasons. In the last twenty years, Peregrines and Ravens have become established as breeding birds in the county, and Buzzard, Raven and Sparrowhawk are all in the top twelve of the table showing increases in the number of tetrads with breeding presence since our *First Atlas*.

Ironically, now that some of these species are achieving a more widespread status, some individuals and organizations are arguing for predatory birds to be killed, often invoking the false equation between nests being robbed or small birds being killed and population declines amongst some prey species.

Improved water and air quality

Pollution is now better understood as a hazard to humans and wildlife, and most pollutants are much reduced. The birds at the top of the aquatic food chain have prospered in the last twenty years, with Grey Heron populations rising enormously, and Cormorant and Little Egret now breeding in the county. Goosanders have also moved in and established themselves as breeders on three of Cheshire's river systems. On the other hand, Dippers have contracted their distribution in the county, and some watercourses are declining in quality. Cleaner air has allowed lichens to spread in the Mersey valley and north Wirral, as shown in the maps taken from *The Lichen Flora of Cheshire & Wirral* (Fox & Guest 2003), with nesting Chaffinches and Long-tailed Tits moving in.

Unknown reasons

In a sense, understanding the decline in most farmland birds has been easy, with relatively straightforward prescriptions for action. Other groups of birds, however, are also dropping in population or decreasing their range, especially woodland species and summer migrants. Much less attention has been paid to them and more research is urgently needed to understand the causes of their declines.

This Atlas shows that a number of species associated with lowland woods have decreased in the county, including Woodcock, Lesser Spotted Woodpecker, Spotted Flycatcher, Marsh Tit, Willow Tit and Lesser Redpoll. Although they all use woodland, their specific habitat requirements differ greatly and it is likely that different factors, probably acting in combination, are responsible. Fuller *et al.* (2005) identified seven probable causes, needing further study: (i) pressures on migrants during migration or in winter; (ii) climate change on the breeding grounds; (iii) general reduction in invertebrate food supplies; (iv) impacts of land use on woodland edges, habitats adjacent to woodland and hedgerows; (v) reduced management of lowland woodland; (vi) intensified habitat modification by deer; and (vii) increased predation pressure from Grey Squirrels, Great Spotted Woodpeckers and corvids. Six of these national factors could apply here, but probably nowhere in Cheshire and Wirral has yet suffered significant pressure from deer (Cheshire Mammal Group 2008), contrasting with some other parts of England where much woodland understorey has been lost, and comparisons between the county and elsewhere in England could be fruitful.

Another group of migrant species especially found in the western Atlantic oakwoods–Tree Pipit, Wood Warbler, Redstart and Pied Flycatcher–are also in decline, for reasons that are largely unknown.

Suggestions for future work

It has been traditional for PhD theses to include a section on 'suggestions for future work', in part to encourage the student to think how the research could be extended, and partly as a humbling recognition that, no matter how good the thesis, it was not the last word on the subject. Similarly with this Atlas: it has been the most comprehensive multispecies survey ever carried out in Cheshire and Wirral, but it should be regarded as a beginning, not the end, and much of it raises more questions than answers. Some of the species texts give examples of projects that could be carried out, by individuals or groups, to fill some of the gaps and further our understanding of the county's birds, and readers will doubtless come up with their own ideas for study. Some of those suggestions are gathered here, to stimulate the reader and to challenge the county's conservation and bird-recording societies. This Atlas has shown that there are hundreds of people interested in participating in systematic bird survey work in Cheshire and Wirral, and more studies ought to be organized locally, as happens in most other counties.

Some of the work of most value for the birds themselves will be to use this Atlas as the basis for local, and possibly national, conservation designations for sites. The results herein should form the basis of a review of the criteria for Local Sites (Sites of Biological Interest or SBIs); in Cheshire and Wirral, SBIs have mainly been designated because of their botanical interest, and the status of birds on existing SBIs should be appraised, with new sites possibly proposed. The preliminary Atlas results, on distribution and population, have already been used to help to set targets for the most recent revision of Local Biodiversity Action Plans: thorough survey work will be necessary periodically to monitor progress.

Direct conservation action can help some species, as shown dramatically for Barn Owls and Mute Swans. Provision of nesting sites can make a difference to birds as diverse as Common Terns and Spotted Flycatchers although not yet, apparently, in Cheshire and Wirral. Can we manage the county's woodland and scrub to meet the needs of Marsh Tits, and the carr habitats to Willow Tits' liking, before it is too late?

Many simple observations are worthwhile. What is the sex ratio in the wintering Wigeon and Pochard flocks? Does it vary from one year to another? What do the inland Shelducks feed on? Has the habit of stealing food from Coots spread to the Gadwall in Cheshire? Even recording the species of tree that different birds use for nesting, feeding or roosting will be valuable: with a worrying number of diseases afflicting a variety of tree species, we have little knowledge of their likely effects on birds in the county.

More and more birds are being colour-marked, often in professionally led studies, and careful observation could help to prove the origins of, for instance, the county's Whooper Swans, Barnacle and Brent Geese. With the advance of molecular and isotopic analysis, even cast-off feathers can be useful. The call of Bitterns is as distinguishable to their ears as a human voice is to ours, so a recording of any booming bird can help in monitoring their spread. Amongst smaller birds, many Dippers and Stonechats are colour-ringed and reports will help to fill in gaps in our knowledge. To be of any value, records should be submitted to CAWOS and the BTO and not just kept in private notebooks or pagers.

PETER TWIST

Meres are a characteristic part of the Cheshire landscape: Nunsmere in summer (left) and winter (opposite).

Some surveys would take a little more effort. Are the Goosanders wintering on the south Cheshire meres and the eastern hill reservoirs the same birds, making circadian movements? Coordinated counts and a few observers on their flight-lines could probably provide an answer. Golden Plovers often visit the same wintering areas every year, with some sites used over long periods of time: how about surveying all the places mentioned by Coward (a century ago) and Boyd (half a century ago)? Have our Treecreepers learned to excavate their own roosts in the county's introduced redwoods? There are so few trees that an investigation would easily be possible.

This Atlas shows the remarkable spread of Buzzards and Ravens in just the last decade or two. Another breeding survey in five or 10 years' time would be valuable in continuing to monitor their status. On the other hand, Rooks appear to be declining and a coordinated count of the county's rookeries is urgently required.

The gulls breeding in Cheshire and Wirral have been largely ignored, not even being included in the national Seabird 2000 survey. Our breeding population of Black-headed Gulls is probably higher than it has ever been, and a thorough count of all known colonies would be valuable. The habit of rooftop breeding is rapidly developing amongst large gulls and ought to be monitored annually in the county, not least for their potential conflict with man and the likely impact of reduced use of landfill for waste disposal.

Winter roosts are vital for many passerines: in midwinter most birds spend twice as much time in their nocturnal roost as in daytime feeding. Thorough surveys of Jackdaw and Rook roosts across the county would be interesting, as would coordination of counts and mapping flight-lines to Starling roosts.

Much useful survey work could be done close to peoples' homes. Are gardens as overwhelmingly important for breeding Song Thrushes in Cheshire as they have been shown to be in Essex? How does the density and distribution of our urban House Sparrows compare to that in North Merseyside?

Some of the results from this Atlas are not easy to explain and will need more study. Why have our urban Swallows declined? Why have Redstarts contracted in range in Cheshire during a time when the national population is stable or expanding? What has happened in the Cheshire uplands in the last twenty years to cause the loss of breeding Starlings and House Sparrows?

The recording of many seabirds in the county seems to depend on the chance occurrence of winds to drive birds close to the north Wirral coast: how about organizing some 'pelagic trips' in Liverpool Bay to count those species that are probably regularly occurring just out of view from land?

Much of our knowledge of the county's birds depends on regular surveys organized locally as part of the BTO's national network. WeBS counts underpin the conservation designations of all the important wetland sites and annual nest counts in the heronries show Cheshire's status among the most significant areas in Britain for Grey Herons; yet both of these simple surveys depend on just a few people and there is a real danger that the county's sites of national or international importance will not be properly monitored. The annual BBS is vital for measuring changes in bird numbers, and this Atlas shows that Cheshire and Wirral has led the way in applying the same survey results to derive county populations.

Notwithstanding all these suggestions for further studies, each of which will advance the state of ornithological knowledge of Cheshire and Wirral, by far the most important project in the county will be a repeat tetrad Atlas of breeding and wintering birds, probably in around 2024. Make a note in your diaries now!

PETER TWIST

Explanation of maps

There are four main types of map accompanying the species texts in this Atlas.

1. Breeding distribution

The breeding distribution maps in this Atlas show the highest level of breeding status recorded in a tetrad in any of the years 2004–06. They have three different sizes of green dots representing the three categories of breeding status:

Large dot	●	Confirmed breeding
Medium dot	●	Probable breeding
Small dot	•	Possible breeding

All the percentages have been calculated exactly but rounded to whole numbers: occasionally rounding errors mean that the total appears to add up to 99% or 101%.

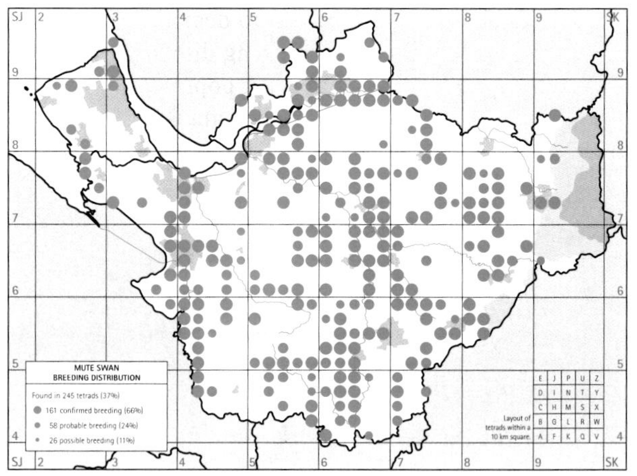

2. Change in breeding distribution

These maps compare the breeding season results of this Atlas with our *First Atlas* of 1978–84. For most species, the comparison only concerns presence during the breeding season, not taking account of which of the three categories of breeding status was recorded. For a small number of species, the main changes are blurred by records of birds on passage or late wintering or immature non-breeders, so 'change' maps are presented of 'confirmed' or 'probable' breeders only. These maps have three colours of dots, all one size:

Green	●	Present during 2004–06, not during 1978–84 ('gain')
Yellow		Present during both Atlases
Red	●	Present during 1978–84, not during 2004–06 ('loss')

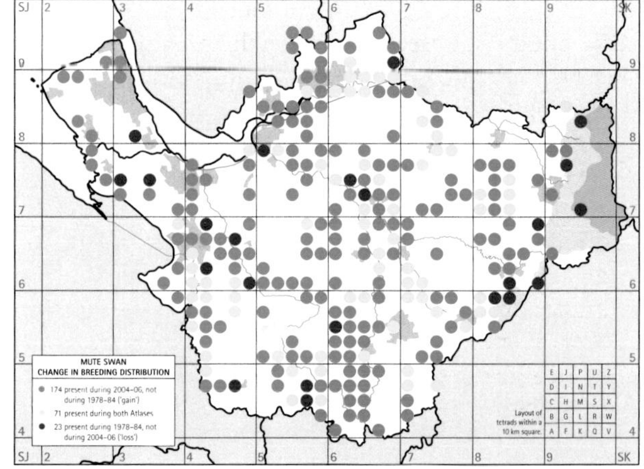

3. Winter distribution

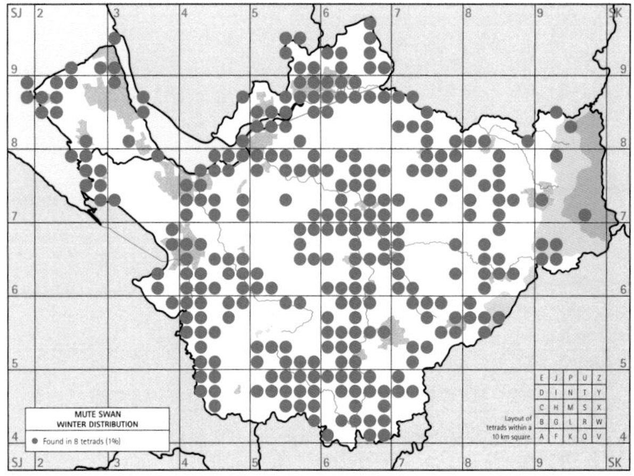

These maps show the species' presence during winter (16 November to end of February) in any of the winters 2004/05–2006/07. These maps have blue dots (●), all one size.

There has been no previous survey in winter at the tetrad scale. The county was surveyed by 10 km squares in 1981/82–1983/84 as part of the national *BTO Winter Atlas*, but there is no species where the comparison at this coarse scale reveals anything, so no 'change' maps are given.

4. Difference between breeding and wintering distribution

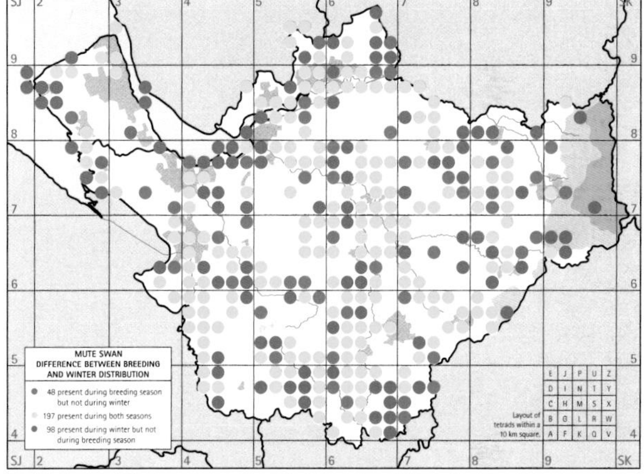

For some species it is instructive to depict the difference between the breeding and wintering distribution during this Atlas. In many cases different populations of birds, from different origins, are involved, and it is not implied that *the same birds* are present in the two seasons. These maps have three colours of dots, all one size:

Green	●	Present during breeding season but not during winter
Yellow	●	Present during both seasons
Blue	●	Present during winter but not during breeding season

Other maps

For the species that bred in the county during our *First Atlas* but do not breed here now, the breeding distribution map is reproduced here with three sizes of brown dots using the same convention as (1) above.

For 35 species, breeding abundance maps are presented, using colours contoured in 10 shades from pale yellow to dark brown. These maps contain a legend giving the species' density in units of birds per square kilometre. This figure can be multiplied by four to give a density in birds per tetrad.

For a few species there are extra maps depicting additional features of interest, such as the differences in the distribution of Lesser Redpoll and Siskin in the three winters, and roosts of a number of winter species with conspicuous communal nocturnal gatherings.

Mute Swan

Cygnus olor

SHEILA BLAMIRE

It is difficult now to recall that, twenty years ago, Mute Swan was among the scarcest birds of Cheshire, with a special census in 1985 finding only 13 breeding pairs, and none in Wirral (Elphick 1985). The cause was simple to diagnose, and easy to remedy. Swans need gravel in their gizzard to grind their vegetable food, and amongst the small stones they were ingesting lead weights carelessly discarded, or lost, by anglers. The resulting poisoning killed many swans. Responsible fishermen voluntarily changed to non-toxic weights, and legislation banning the use of lead became effective on 1 January 1987. The Cheshire Swan Study Group (CSSG) was formed in 1988 and monitored the recovery of the population, topping 100 pairs in the county in 1996, and by the year 2000 the local numbers had outstripped the capacity of CSSG to cover the whole county (Cookson 1993, *CWBRs*).

Even uninterested people find it hard to ignore Britain's heaviest bird, and the Atlas map must be accurate. However, only 66% of occupied tetrads furnished proof of breeding, and about one-quarter of pairs—usually birds in their first year together—do not nest in any one year. Most swans first breed at three or four years old; a few females start at the age of two; but, especially when population levels are high and there is fierce competition for territories, some adults may never breed (Birkhead & Perrins 1986). Pairs normally stay together for life, with divorce being rare, but bereaved swans do find another mate, contrary to the romantic myth.

Their population is probably limited only by the availability of suitable nesting sites. They have few natural predators, the size and fearless nature of the birds being sufficient to deter almost any attack, and their only significant threat is vandalism by hooligans throwing stones at the nest, destroying eggs and occasionally killing an adult. The habitat codes reported in this survey showed that 67% of our swan records are on standing waterbodies (G1–5), with 10% on flowing water (G6–8), 21% on canals (G9–10) and 1% on coastal water on the Dee. They are mostly on larger waters, as would be expected, but swans will nest on small ponds and narrow streams and ditches. Mute Swans eat almost any type of aquatic vegetation (to a metre deep), especially crowfoot, pondweeds and soft grasses. They will also graze on land, and occasionally take insects, molluscs and small amphibians, although it is not known if those are by choice or just because they were caught up in the submerged vegetation. If there is insufficient food for the chicks, adults will lead them, walking overland if necessary, to suitable water sometimes up to a kilometre distant, possibly into an adjacent tetrad.

Mute Swans are now to be found breeding everywhere in the county where there is suitable water with submerged vegetation. Thus, they are absent from the higher ground in the east of Cheshire—they avoid the dystrophic hill reservoirs—and the Sandstone Ridge, and they are scarce on Wirral. The BTO analysis of Cheshire and Wirral BBS data (2004–05) gave a county population of 1,470 birds (470–2,460) in the breeding season. This survey did not distinguish between territorial pairs and non-breeding flocks. Most tetrads hold only one pair, although some have more, and the present population is likely to be around 200–250 pairs breeding, with around 1,000 non-breeding birds. Boyd (1946), never one to shrink from making value judgments on birds, wrote in his newspaper column in 1939 that 'in my opinion they are becoming far too plentiful, and usurp the territory and food of other and more interesting fowl'. What would he think now?

Sponsored by Cheshire Swan Study Group

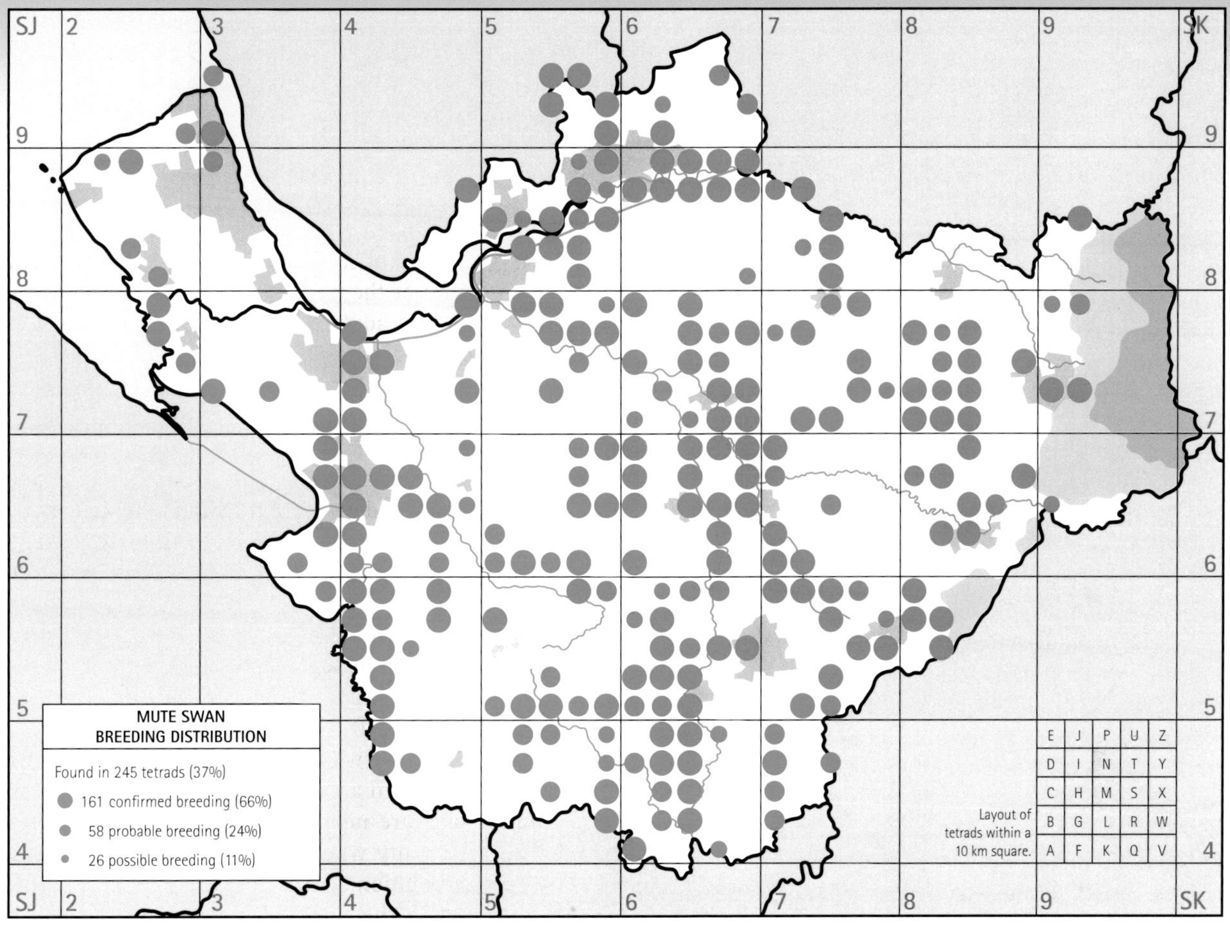
SJ
SK
2
3
4
5
6
7
8
9
MUTE SWAN
BREEDING DISTRIBUTION
Found in 245 tetrads (37%)
161 confirmed breeding (66%)
58 probable breeding (24%)
26 possible breeding (11%)
Layout of tetrads within a 10 km square.
E J P U Z
D I N T Y
C H M S X
B G L R W
A F K Q V

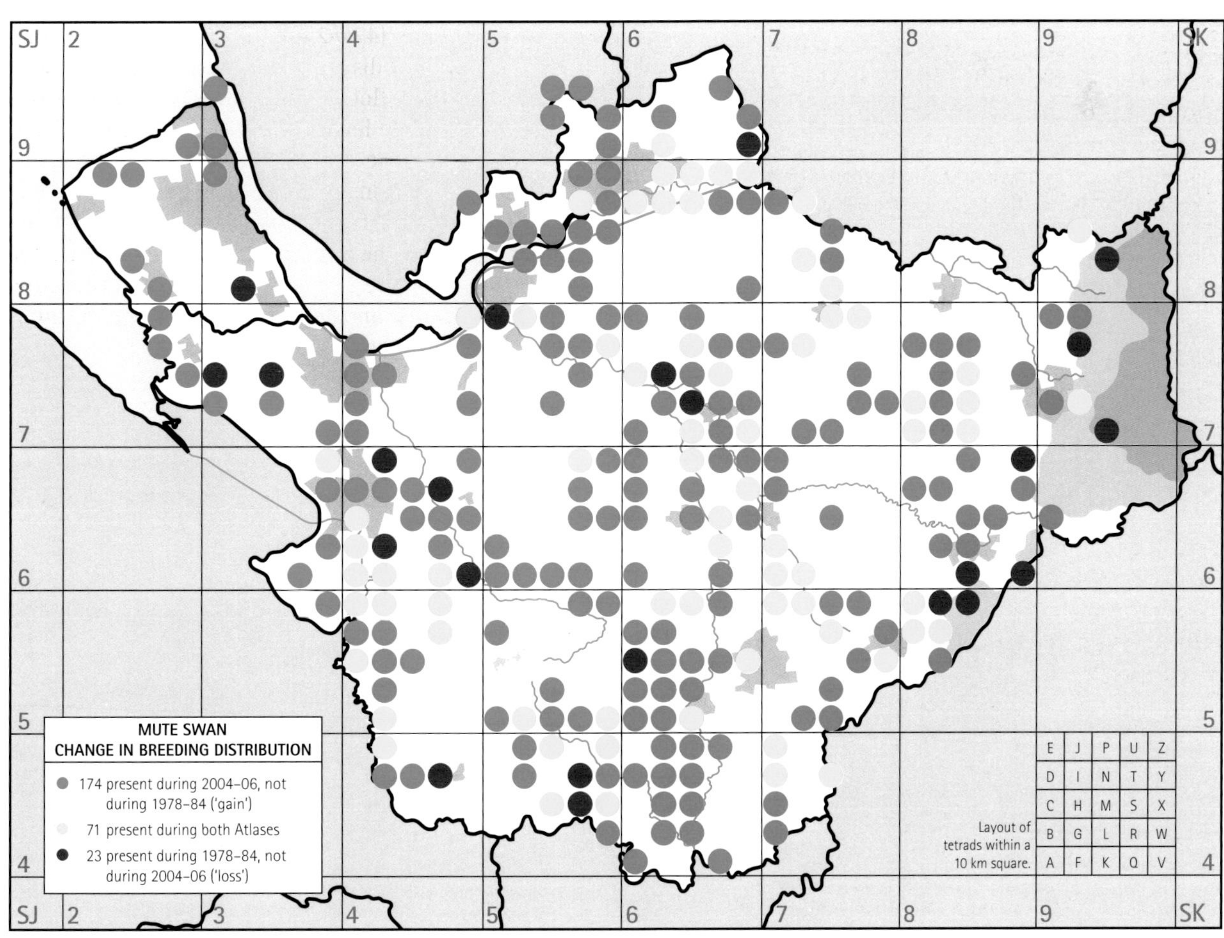
SJ
SK
2
3
4
5
6
7
8
9
MUTE SWAN
CHANGE IN BREEDING DISTRIBUTION
174 present during 2004–06, not during 1978–84 ('gain')
71 present during both Atlases
23 present during 1978–84, not during 2004–06 ('loss')
Layout of tetrads within a 10 km square.
E J P U Z
D I N T Y
C H M S X
B G L R W
A F K Q V

Many Mute Swans maintain their territories throughout the year, so it is surprising that the winter map shows 48 tetrads occupied in the breeding season but vacated in winter. It would be interesting to study what distinguishes those tetrads from those used all year round. In addition, there are 98 extra tetrads with wintering birds. There are many more records on the Dee and Mersey estuaries, and some seasonally flooded fields. The extensive and long-running programme of ringing Mute Swans has shown that there can be significant wanderings, up to around 100 km from their natal site, with exceptional movements to Scotland, Ireland and Gloucestershire, but most Cheshire birds live their lives within the county. There is no immigration from continental Europe.

The other main difference from the breeding season is the large flocks, mostly comprising birds below breeding age. Birds at some sites are often fed by people whose traditional response to any wild creature is to offer bread. The size of these flocks has apparently increased in the last twenty years. The *BTO Winter Atlas* (1981/82–1983/84) mapped only four 10 km squares in Cheshire with counts of 24 or more birds, whereas field-workers for this Atlas reported 33 flocks of that size, in twelve 10 km squares. Four of them exceeded 50 birds, all in 2005/06, with flocks of 56 on the Mersey salt-marsh (SJ47P), 52 on the Manchester Ship Canal (SJ58C), 52 on farmland near Hack Green (SJ64N) and 70 on Redes Mere (SJ87K). Almost half of all counts were of two birds, though, emphasizing the adults' maintenance of their pair-bond, and probably the territory.

Most (79%) of the winter habitat codes were fresh water, with 4% estuarine, 5% semi-natural grassland and marsh, and 9% farmland. More than half were on standing water, with 7% on ponds, 20% small water-bodies and 26% lakes, reservoirs and sand quarries. Linear waterways comprised 26%, equally split between rivers, small canals and larger canals.

Coward and Oldham (1900) dismissed all Mute Swans as 'semi-domesticated'. They noted that they 'may sometimes be seen feeding on the sandbanks and ooze of the Dee estuary, but there is no reason whatsoever to suppose that any of those, shot from time to time on the Dee or elsewhere, are really wild birds'. Boyd (1951) gave no information on the species in winter, and Bell (1962) noted just two counts, of a flock of 90 on the Weaver estuary in hard weather, and another flock of 30 on Sandbach flashes. It is difficult to know whether the lack of information reflects a continuation of Coward's disdain for the species, but the inference is that their population is much higher nowadays, and that winter flocks in the county have become a feature only in the past fifty years.

SIMON BOOTH

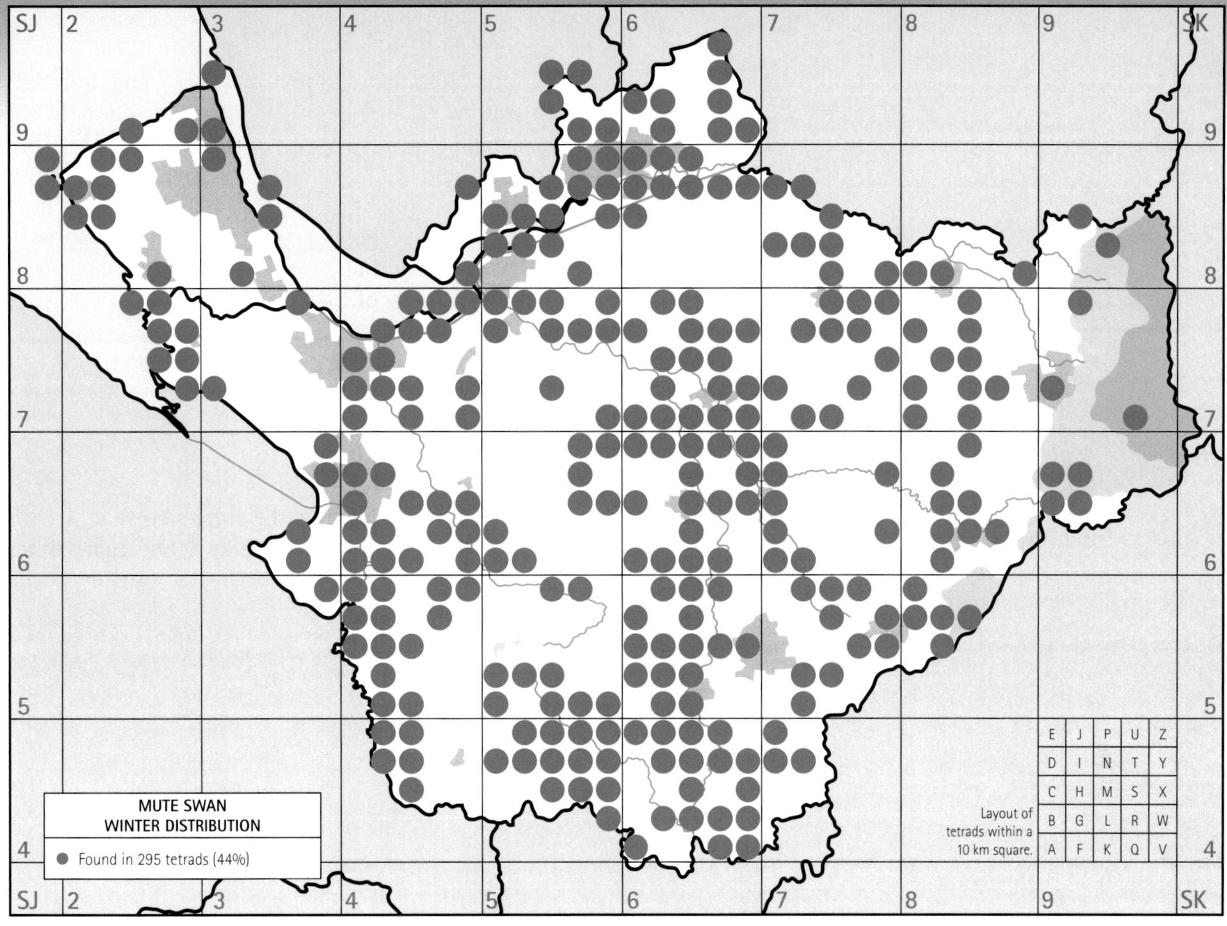
MUTE SWAN
WINTER DISTRIBUTION
Found in 295 tetrads (44%)
Layout of tetrads within a 10 km square.
E J P U Z
D I N T Y
C H M S X
B G L R W
A F K Q V
SJ
SK

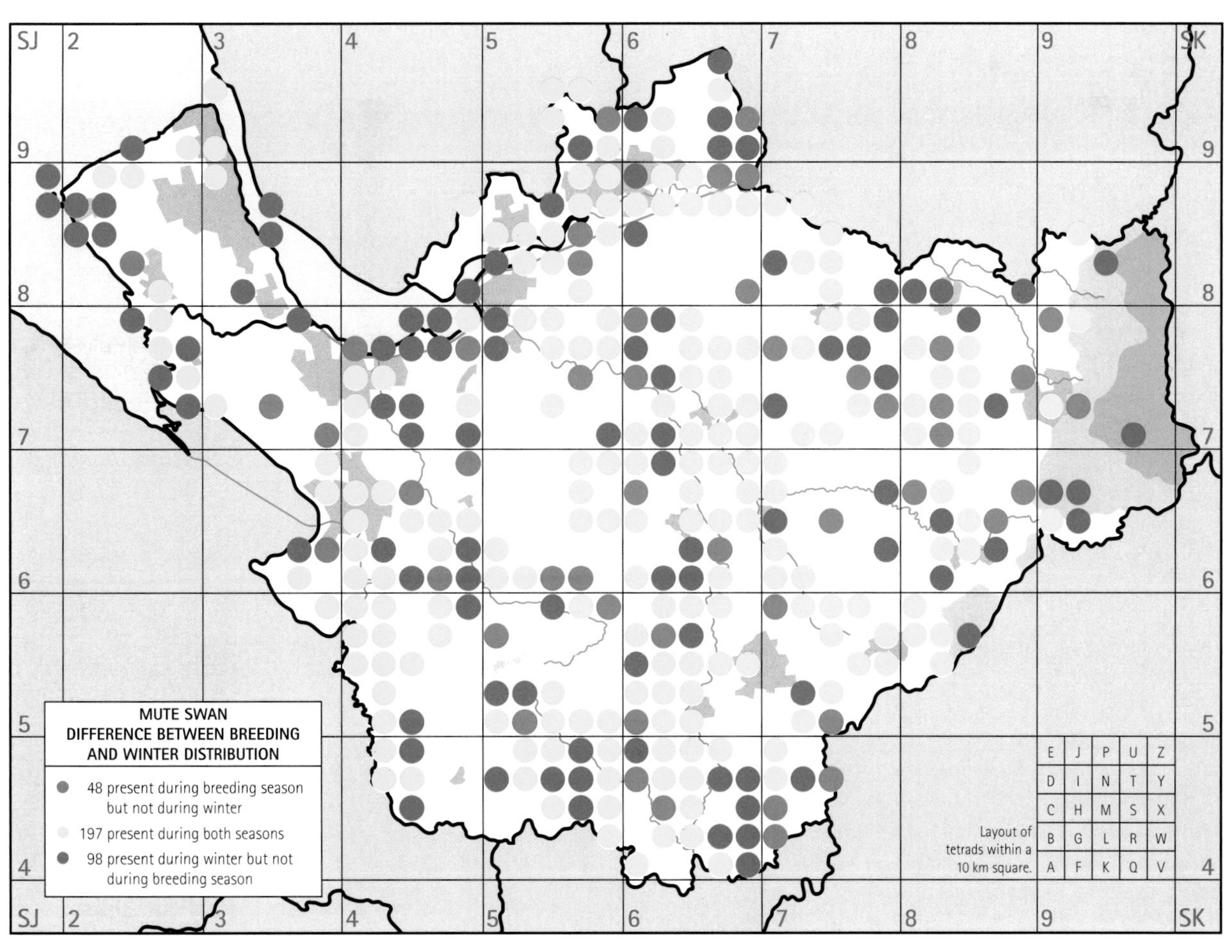
MUTE SWAN
DIFFERENCE BETWEEN BREEDING AND WINTER DISTRIBUTION
48 present during breeding season but not during winter
197 present during both seasons
98 present during winter but not during breeding season
Layout of tetrads within a 10 km square.
E J P U Z
D I N T Y
C H M S X
B G L R W
A F K Q V
SJ
SK

Bewick's Swan

Cygnus columbianus

STEVE ROUND

These small swans breed in Arctic Siberia and winter in north-western Europe, mostly the Netherlands and eastern England. The Wildfowl & Wetlands Trust has been successful in attracting wintering flocks to most of its centres, including Martin Mere in Lancashire. In recent years what are presumably offshoots from this population have taken to wintering on the Dee, and the numbers there make the Dee estuary of national importance for the species. Although these well-known flocks hold the majority of the country's Bewick's Swans, some birds are quite mobile, and colour-marked birds in Cheshire and Wirral have been ringed or seen at Slimbridge in Gloucestershire, the Ouse Washes in Cambridgeshire and Rutland Water in Leicestershire. Occasionally birds are recorded flying across the county, often drawing attention to themselves by their melodious dog-like yelping, but the only records of swans on the ground or water during this Atlas came from four tetrads each alongside our two estuaries. The sum of the maximum tetrad counts submitted for this Atlas, probably with an element of double-counting, amounted to 133 birds in 2004/05, 129 on the Dee and 4 on the Mersey; with no counts submitted for 2005/06 and a maximum in 2006/07 of 142 swans, 121 on the Dee and 21 on the Mersey.

The Dee and Mersey birds are unusual in spending much of their time on the estuarine salt-marsh, whereas Bewick's Swans usually favour freshwater sites. Although they always roost overnight on water, the species has become more terrestrial of late in its feeding habits (Rees 2006). They take copious quantities of leaves and roots of aquatic pondweeds and soft grasses; elsewhere in Britain and Ireland they have learned to favour arable fields, eating root vegetables, but these are seldom found in Cheshire and Wirral.

In the nineteenth century this species was 'apparently a very rare visitor to the Cheshire coast', with only one record, a bird shot on 14 December 1871 (Coward & Oldham 1900). A herd of 27 was found on 15 December 1907 in the Dee estuary (Coward 1910) then Boyd (1951) noted them at Marbury Mere, Great Budworth in eight winters from 1924 to 1950, and they were declared a

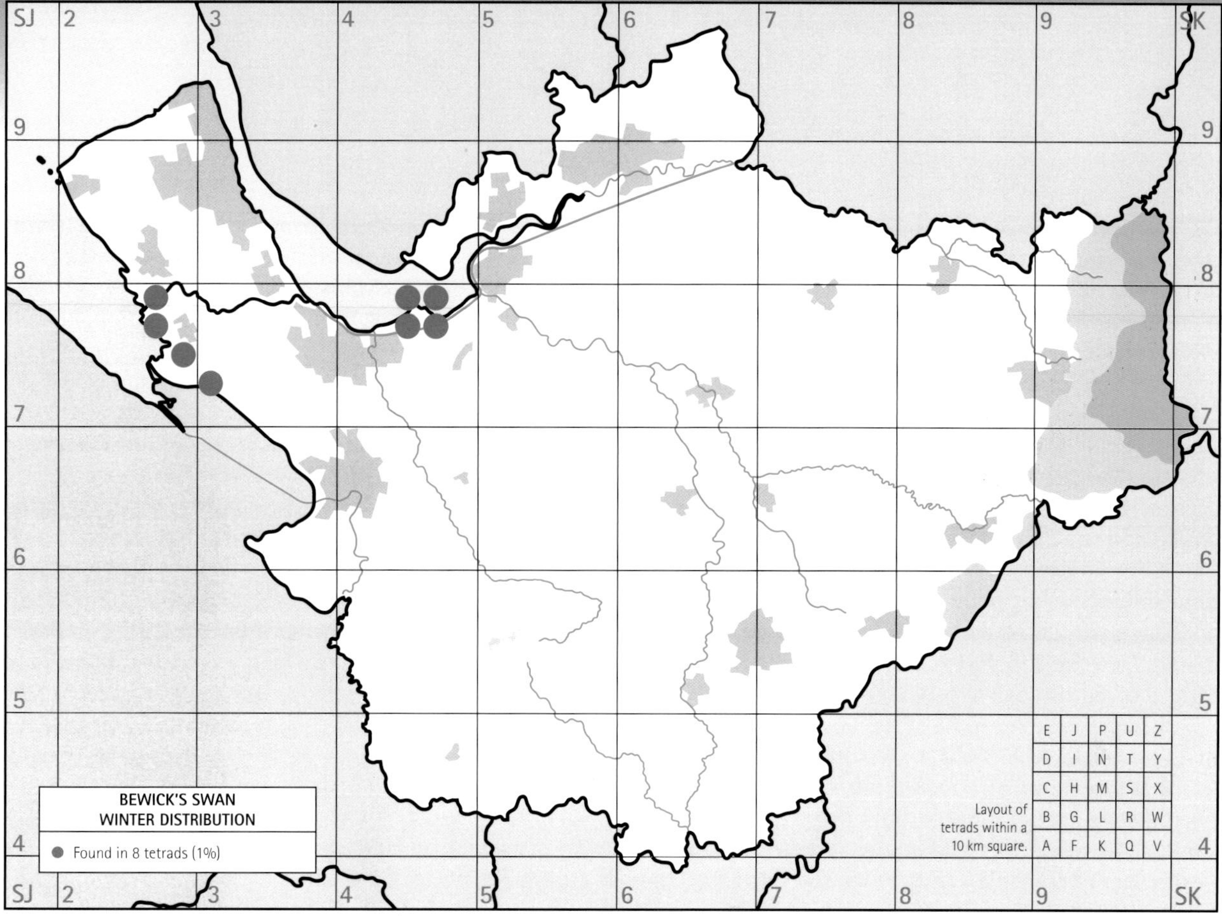

'much more frequent visitor' (than the Whooper). Bell (1962) noted over 60 records between 1938 and 1960, half of them on return passage in March and April. Most parties are small, fewer than 10 birds, and the largest winter flock was Boyd's 1943 record of 27 birds on Marbury Mere, coincidentally seen later the same day on the Mersey.

The annual county bird reports show that, from the 1960s on, flocks were found on the Mersey, several of the meres, flashes and sand quarries, and flooded fields, especially alongside the Dee south of Chester. The Dee estuary salt-marsh was not much used by Bewick's Swans until the RSPB provided large sanctuary areas. Flocks into double figures were first noted in the mid-1970s and continued sporadically until the late 1980s with a leap to 40 birds in 1988/89, 85 in 1992/93 and 110 in 1996/97, fluctuating around that level ever since. These birds usually roost overnight at the RSPB's Inner Marsh Farm reserve; peak counts are in January or February. On the basis of incomplete counts submitted to WeBS, the Dee estuary qualifies as nationally important for this species by virtue of regularly holding 1% or more of the estimated British total (8,100 birds). The numbers in Cheshire and Wirral have lately stopped increasing, and the UK total has dropped by 12% in the last decade (Eaton *et al.* 2007), perhaps because there is now strong evidence that the Bewick's Swan wintering population is shifting eastwards, probably in response to warmer winters.

Whooper Swan

Cygnus cygnus

Probably almost all of the Whooper Swans in the county are from Icelandic stock, as most of these birds winter in Britain and Ireland. Another population breeds in Fennoscandia and Arctic Russia, mostly wintering in continental Europe although there are records of some of these birds in Britain and Ireland (*Migration Atlas*) and it is well worth examining carefully any colour-marked birds seen for evidence of their origins. The UK wintering total more than trebled in the quarter-century to 2003/04; just over 15,000 were counted in the UK in the five-yearly International Swan Census in January 2005 (Eaton *et al.* 2007). Most of the English birds are at Martin Mere and the Ouse Washes, and there is a lot of within-winter movement between Britain and Ireland (*Migration Atlas*), some of these birds passing through Cheshire and Wirral.

During this Atlas, most of the records are odd birds or small flocks. There was a maximum of 26 swans at Inner Marsh Farm in 2006/07 but otherwise the only tetrads with double-figure counts were the four on the south shore of the Mersey estuary, and the annual total in the county is a little under 100 birds. The sum of the maximum tetrad counts submitted for this Atlas, probably with an element of double-counting, amounted to 83 birds in 2004/05, 63 of them on the Mersey; 63 birds in 2005/06, 45 of them on the Mersey; and a maximum in 2006/07 of 166 swans. This higher figure, however, includes a flock that was mobile between four tetrads on the Mersey; eliminating this double-counting leaves a total of 88 for the winter. No site has approached the level for national importance.

Coward and Oldham (1900) noted the Whooper Swan as '... a not infrequent visitor in winter to the Dee and Mersey estuaries', although birds apparently stayed mostly on the mud-flats, as Coward (1910) said that the species 'seldom ascends as high as the marshes'; he mentioned flocks of 16, 40, 21 and 25 birds. Their scarcity inland was shown by Boyd, writing in 1951, who could quote only two winter records, more than 30 years old, from 1918/19 and 1919/20. Bell (1962) concurred, saying that 'in recent times birds have occurred in most years in the estuaries in varying numbers' but the records on inland waters averaged one every few years.

It seems from the old accounts that at some stage during the second half of the twentieth century they switched their distribution, with Whooper Swan now being the bird most likely to be found inland, although

SIMON BOOTH

Sponsored by Ray and Liz Anslow

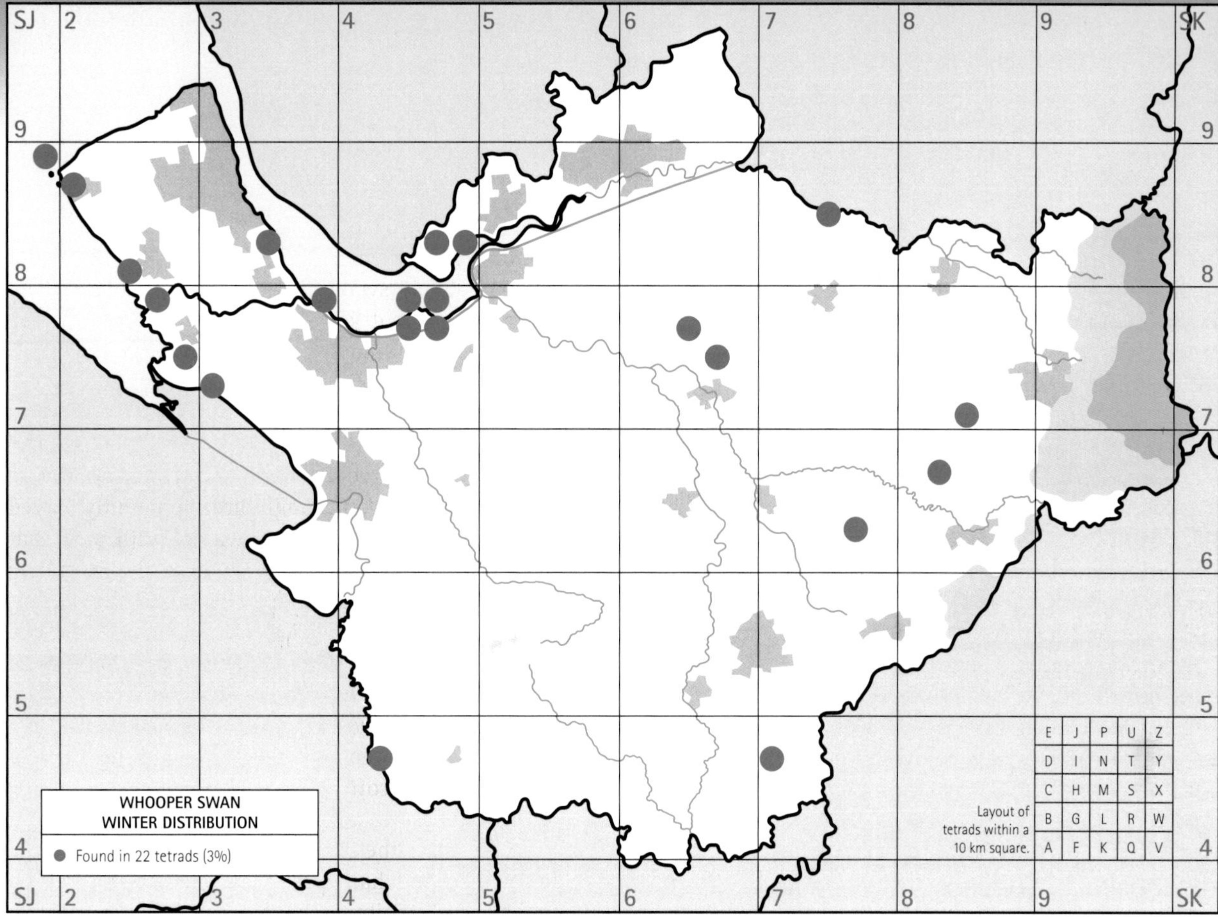

the two winter swans are still both predominantly estuarine birds in the county. It is not clear from the annual bird reports, however, when this happened: from 1964 onwards Whooper Swans have been recorded at from zero to six inland (non-estuarine) sites each winter, with year-to-year fluctuations but no significant change over 40 years. This Atlas map, aggregating three winters' records, exaggerates their annual status in showing birds present in 14 estuarine and 8 inland tetrads.

Underwater plants are their traditional food, and Whoopers are not as agile on land as Bewick's Swans, but flocks will graze grass and winter cereals. Almost all of the county's birds are on water, with odd records on potato fields and stubbles.

Pink-footed Goose

Anser brachyrhynchus

ANDREW MART

Pinkfeet may be seen flying over many parts of the county, sometimes in spectacularly large skeins, but the Atlas map shows only those birds using a tetrad, found on the ground or water. They breed in Iceland, with a few in eastern Greenland, and winter mostly in northern Britain, with up to three-quarters of them in Scotland (*BTO Winter Atlas*). Their main wintering areas in England are Lancashire and Norfolk, and there are normally few records south of Cheshire.

The Atlas map exaggerates the species' status in any one year. Most of the records are of odd birds or of small groups comprising up to seven birds, often consorting with Canada Geese and arousing suspicion of their origins. There were just 12 submitted records of flocks, from 41 to 200 birds, eight of them along the edge of the Dee estuary. The others were from the Dee flood plain (SJ44I), two tetrads in the Sandbach flashes in January 2005 when Andy Firth noted that 'several skeins of up to 250 flew over but a few landed and stayed a while', and from the Toft area (SJ77N) in winter 2004/05 when 120 birds fed on stubble. Apart from this one record on stubble, all the rest were on grassland (either semi-natural or improved agricultural land), salt-marsh or large waterbodies.

The present picture is probably little different from the species' historical status in the county, although the size of the population now is much larger and shooting pressure much reduced. Many nineteenth-century records of geese are clouded by doubt over the species' identity, but Coward and Oldham (1900) gave a few examples from the Dee in the last years of the nineteenth century. They commented that Pink-footed Geese were not often noticed farther inland, and their only examples are two records of birds shot at Tattenhall. A decade later, confidence in identification had obviously advanced and Coward (1910) declared that 'the Pink-footed Goose is undoubtedly *the* goose of the Dee estuary'. The bird was formerly common in the Mersey but was seldom seen on the estuary at the time of their writing; Coward does not mention it, but the opening of the Manchester Ship Canal in 1894 must have made a substantial difference to conditions in the Mersey estuary.

Boyd (1946) commented that they seldom go far from the coast, and noted the perennial problem in 1938 when he was fooled by an escaped aviary bird into thinking it was wild. Bell (1962) gave no records from the first half of the twentieth century but listed roughly annual records of birds seen in flight in the 1950s, especially over Hilbre and Wirral. The records in the annual county bird reports from 1964 onwards are almost all of overflying flocks with only odd others, as now.

The notable exception was a significant influx in freezing weather in January/February 1979, the hardest winter for 16 years and the first since the Lancashire population of Pinkfeet had grown so large (Forshaw 1979). Many of the 20,000 birds quit Lancashire as their feeding areas were blanketed with snow, and 1,150 moved into the Dee estuary, feeding by day in barley stubbles south of Burton and roosting on the estuarine salt-marsh at night. After a week half of these birds left, but more arrived after a few days and the flock built up to 1,500 by mid-February. It was interesting that some of the species' old Dee haunts were revisited after a long absence. Lesser flocks were also found elsewhere in the county, notably 227 on fields at Bartington Heath (SJ67D) for a week.

Sponsored by Altrincham and District Natural History Society

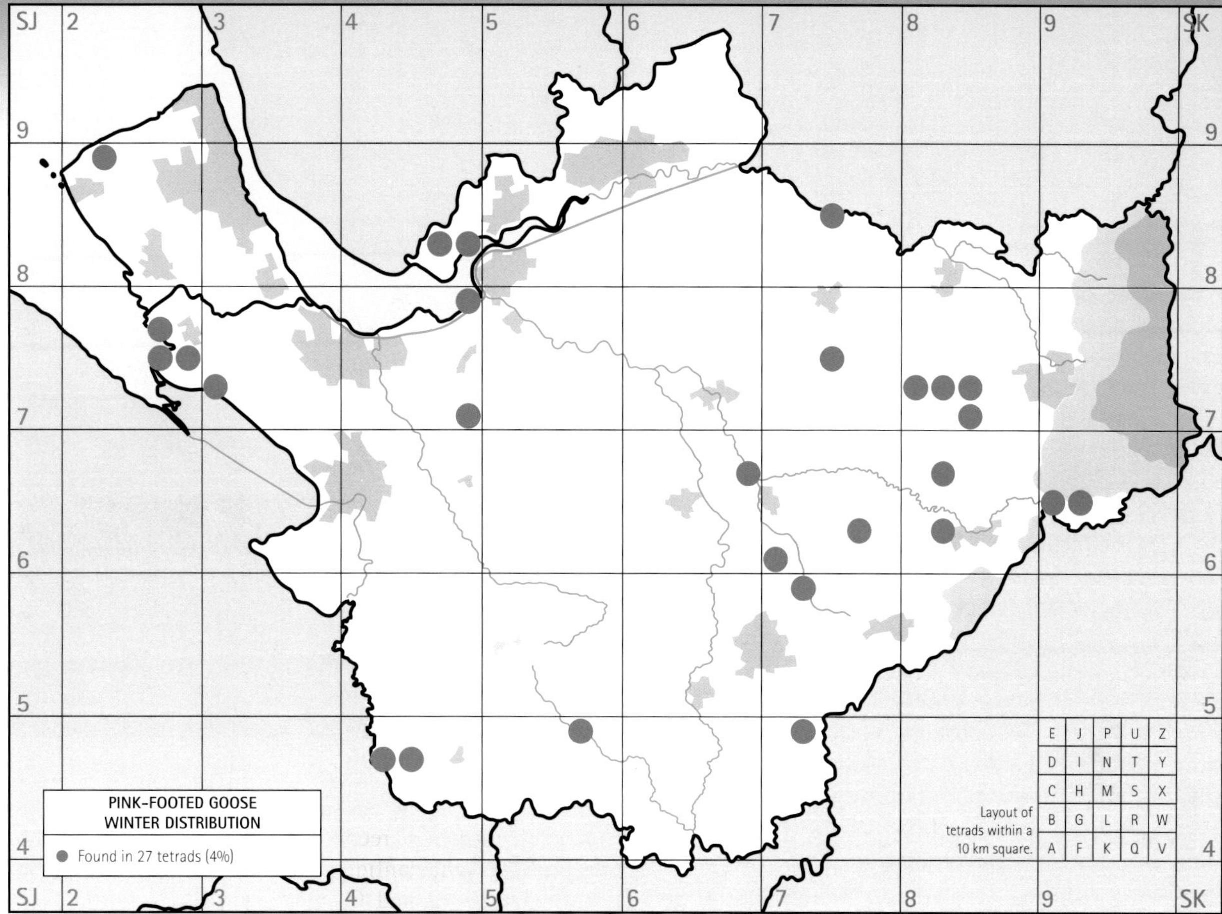

Concentrations, usually fewer than 100 birds, were noted feeding in the county in hard weather during the 1980s, but the 1983 bird report summed up the species' overflying status with the comment 'as usual, few flocks considered our pastures green or pleasant enough to make them want to land!'

Greylag Goose

Anser anser

This Atlas has revolutionized our knowledge of breeding Greylag Geese in the county. Our *First Atlas* showed birds present in 31 tetrads, with breeding proven in 10 and probable in a further 8. But since then, presumably because of many birdwatchers' usual scorn for introduced/escaped species, annual bird reports have contained almost no information. From 1985 to 1994 there were no published breeding records whatsoever, and in the nine years from 1995 to 2003 observers submitted reports of just 12 breeding attempts in total. The picture revealed by fieldwork for this Atlas shows Greylag Goose with breeding season presence in 119 tetrads, out of which breeding was proven in 29, probable in 69 (mainly records of pairs) and possible in 21 tetrads.

SIMON BOOTH

They have increased greatly in numbers and range since our *First Atlas*, spreading out from their original stronghold on the Eaton Estate to colonize most of south and west Cheshire, the mid-Cheshire sand quarries, parts of the south Manchester fringe and western Wirral. Their status in the county appears commensurate with the picture elsewhere. From 1991 to 2000 the national population grew at a rate of 9.4% per annum, giving a doubling in eight years (Austin *et al.* 2007). The Cheshire and Wirral population is not known, but is likely to be more than 200 breeding pairs.

The national surveys show that the greatest increase in Greylag Geese came from an expansion into lowland habitat with some water cover. Most of the county's birds are in low-lying areas, but they were reported at all altitudes from the lowest to the highest waterbodies in the county (Lamaload Reservoir). The dystrophic upland reservoirs are not very suitable for waterfowl breeding, though. The submitted habitat codes show no obvious habitat separation from Canada Geese, although Greylag have a tendency to use larger waters: 48% of Greylag Geese were on G3, G4 or G5 compared to only 31% of Canada Geese. Of the submitted habitat codes, 82% were fresh water (74% on ponds, lakes, meres and reservoirs and 8% on linear watercourses, mostly rivers and large canals); most of the remainder (11%) were agricultural grassland.

They only need sufficient water to provide a nesting site safely away from predators, especially foxes, and somewhere for them to retreat to overnight. The geese and their goslings feed mostly by grazing short-cropped grass but head for the water whenever danger threatens. They usually nest in April, on the ground, preferably on an island if at all possible. Greylag Geese typically lay 5–7 eggs, incubated by the female for four weeks. From the moment they hatch, their downy young can walk, swim and feed themselves but it is seven to nine weeks before they can fly. This long season gives fieldworkers ample time to find the species and the low proportion of confirmed breeding records (only 25%) is probably explicable by their delayed maturity, Greylag Geese not normally breeding until three years of age, with consequent large numbers of non-breeding subadult birds.

Sponsored by an anonymous CAWOS member

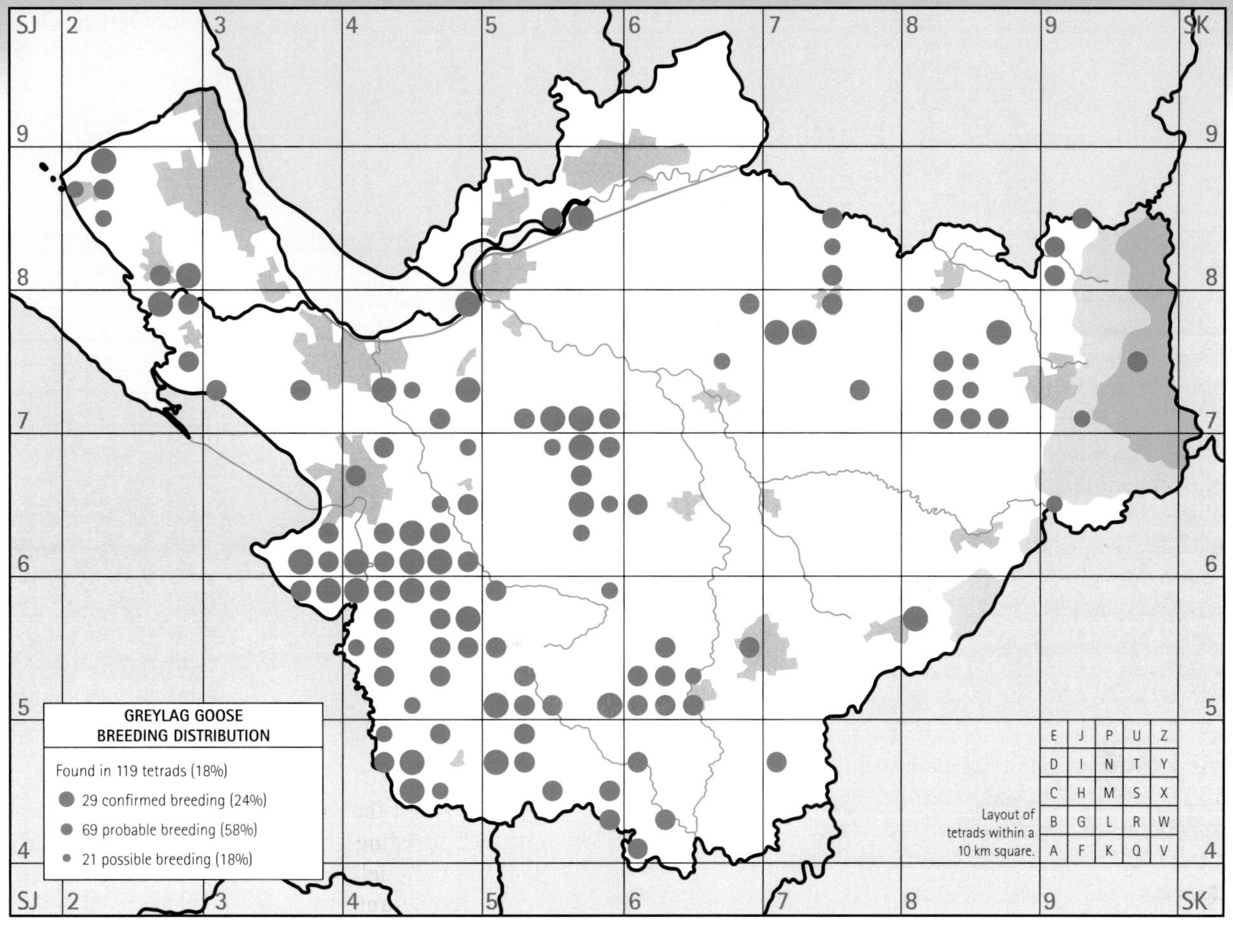
GREYLAG GOOSE
BREEDING DISTRIBUTION
Found in 119 tetrads (18%)
29 confirmed breeding (24%)
69 probable breeding (58%)
21 possible breeding (18%)
Layout of tetrads within a 10 km square.
E J P U Z
D I N T Y
C H M S X
B G L R W
A F K Q V
SJ
SK

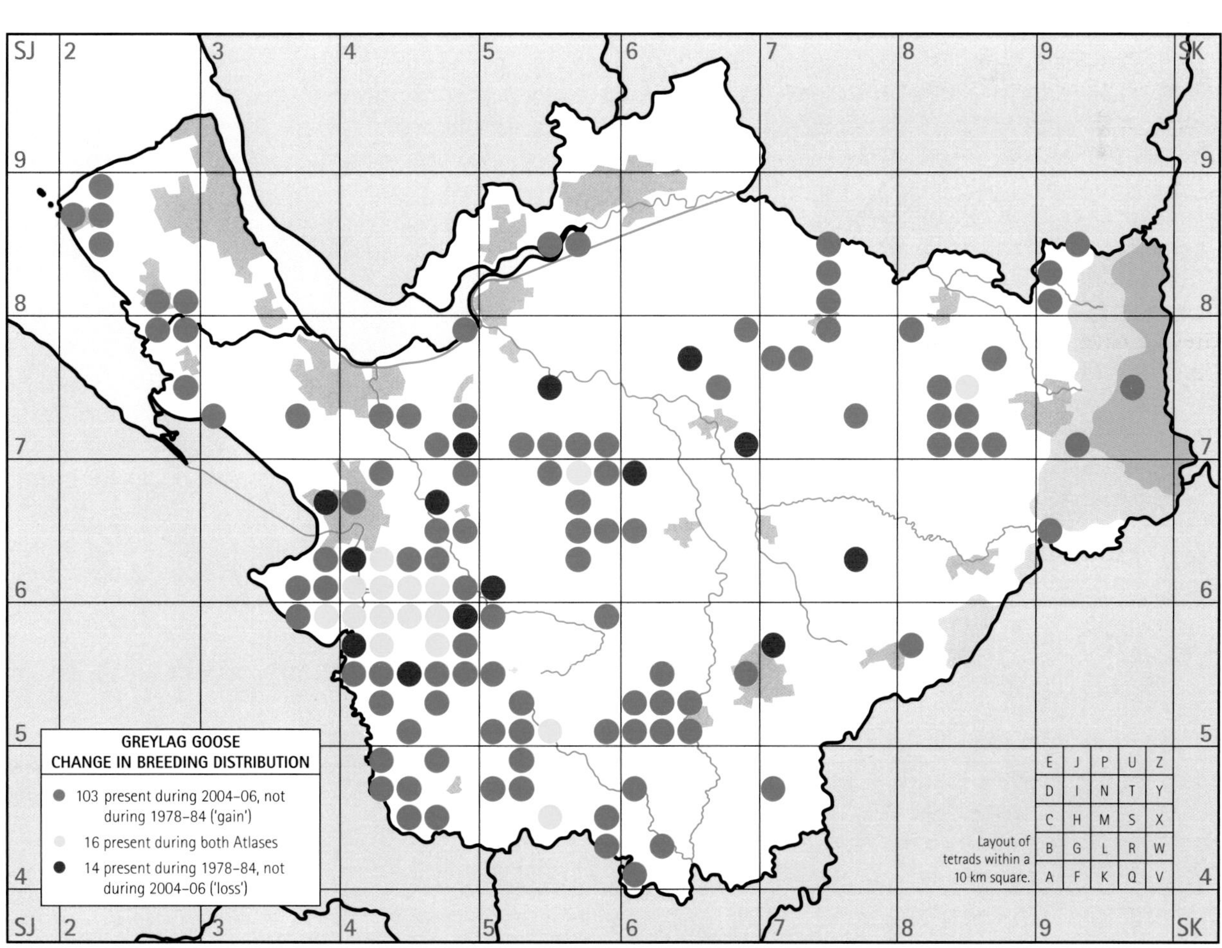
GREYLAG GOOSE
CHANGE IN BREEDING DISTRIBUTION
103 present during 2004–06, not during 1978–84 ('gain')
16 present during both Atlases
14 present during 1978–84, not during 2004–06 ('loss')
Layout of tetrads within a 10 km square.
E J P U Z
D I N T Y
C H M S X
B G L R W
A F K Q V
SJ
SK

The map shows that the winter distribution of Greylag Geese is similar to that for the breeding season, suggesting that they are not likely to move far. Indeed, a characteristic of some flocks of Greylags is that they can be found from week to week in exactly the same spot. Some birds do move around, though, and there were 49 tetrads newly occupied in winter, as well as 53 with the species present in the breeding season only; observers also submitted 22 records of birds in flight, not mapped in this Atlas.

They feed on any plant material, including roots, tubers, shoots and leaves, both in water and on land, but are seldom far from a waterbody on which to take refuge. There are a few records on the Dee and Mersey salt-marshes but they are less likely than Canada Geese to move onto estuarine waters outside the breeding season. The winter habitat codes showed 57% of records on fresh water, almost all of them small waterbodies, meres and sand quarries, with only four records on rivers and canals; 28% on farmland, all on improved or unimproved grassland apart from two records on stubble; and 10% on grazing marsh or salt-marsh.

The species' growth in the county has paralleled a steady climb in their national population. The WeBS index for the re-established population of Greylag Geese was at its highest ever in 2004/05, having risen almost fivefold in 20 years (Banks *et al.* 2006). Nationally, 30 sites had five-year peak means over 500, and 46 sites over 400, but none in Cheshire and Wirral has reached those levels. By far the largest flocks were on the Dee floods above Chester, with the maximum exceeding 500 birds in 2004/05 and 2005/06. At the other extreme, half of the flocks counted for this Atlas were of 10 birds or fewer, possibly just one family.

The previous scarcity of Greylag Geese was emphasized in the county avifaunas. Coward and Oldham (1900) remarked on the species' great rarity: they knew of only three records during the nineteenth century. Bell (1962) traced 16 published records from 1910, usually of single birds or small skeins of less than 10, most of them between November and February, but commented that, as the species is commonly kept in captivity, the possibility of escapes cannot be ignored. Later, Bell (1967) could find no breeding or wintering records ascribable to genuinely wild birds. All of the present population derived originally from captive birds, but most of them now are living in the wild.

RICHARD STEEL

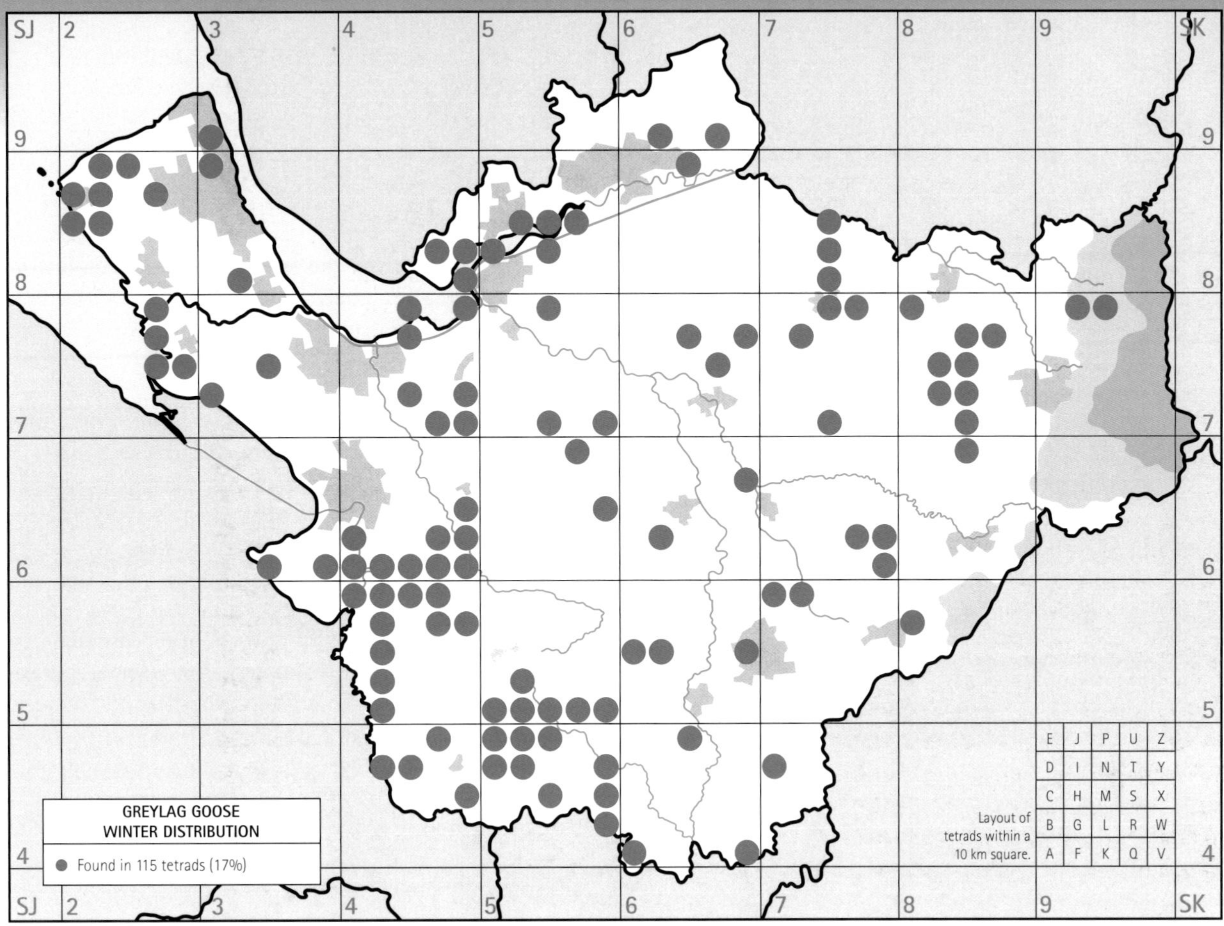
SJ
SK
GREYLAG GOOSE
WINTER DISTRIBUTION
Found in 115 tetrads (17%)
Layout of
tetrads within a
10 km square.
E J P U Z
D I N T Y
C H M S X
B G L R W
A F K Q V

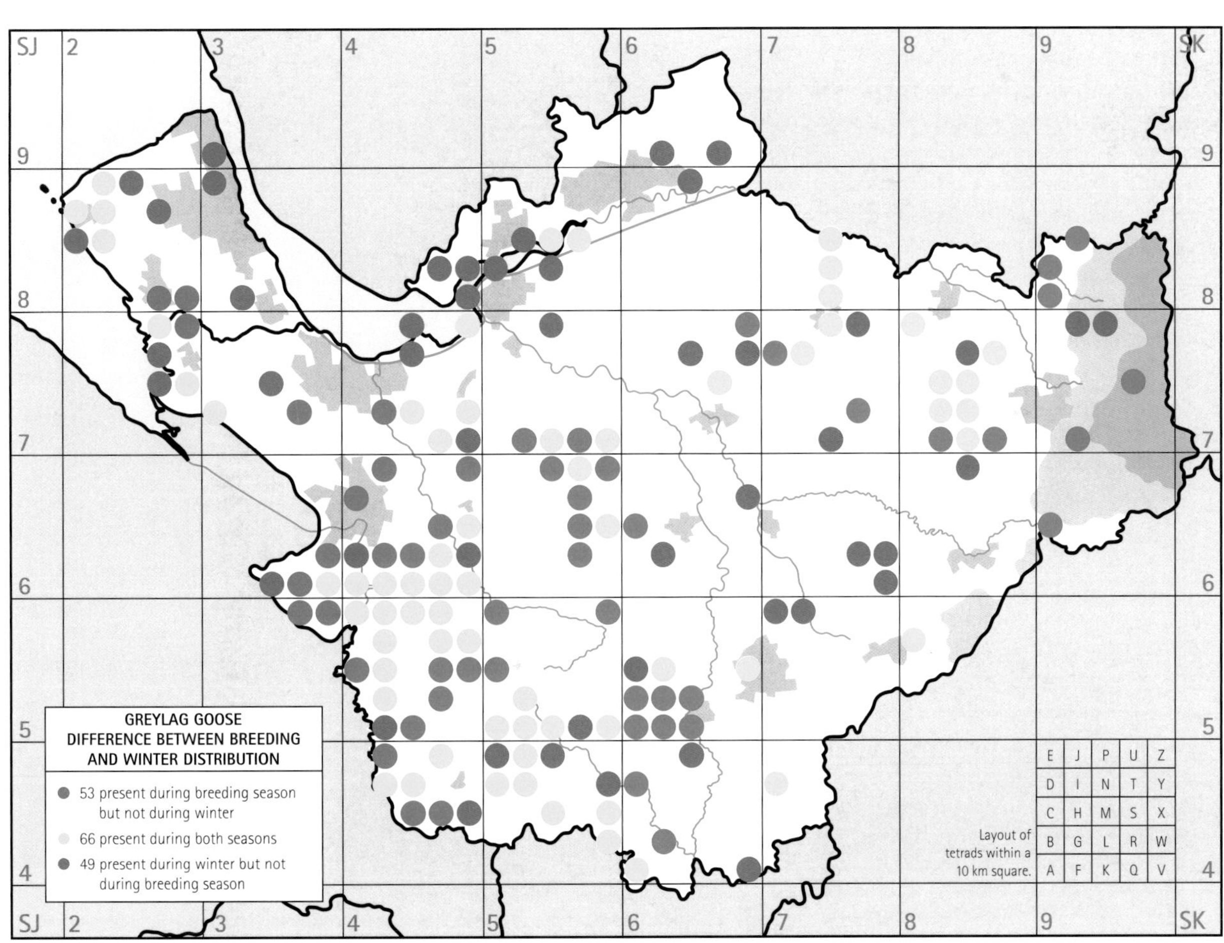
SJ
SK
GREYLAG GOOSE
DIFFERENCE BETWEEN BREEDING
AND WINTER DISTRIBUTION
53 present during breeding season but not during winter
66 present during both seasons
49 present during winter but not during breeding season
Layout of
tetrads within a
10 km square.
E J P U Z
D I N T Y
C H M S X
B G L R W
A F K Q V

Canada Goose

Branta canadensis

SIMON BOOTH

Canada Geese have greatly extended their presence in the county: they are now present in 80% more tetrads than in our *First Atlas*, and were proven breeding in more than twice as many. They have spread to breed on some very small waterbodies, often where water barely shows up on the map such as on drainage ditches and farm ponds. As expected, most (80%) of the submitted habitat codes were fresh water, with 12% on agricultural grassland. They were overwhelmingly on static water; 349 on ponds, lakes, meres and reservoirs and 43 on linear watercourses, mostly rivers and large canals. Most birds were on quite small waters: 22% of those on standing water (G1–5) were on ponds smaller than 50 m^2 in area, with 47% on small waterbodies up to 450 m^2 and 31% on larger waters.

This agrees with the results of national surveys, in which from 1991 to 2000 the population grew at a rate of 9.3% per annum, giving a doubling in nine years (Austin *et al.* 2007). The increase since 1991 occurred mainly in habitats that had previously held low goose population densities, particularly small areas of water. Although densities are still relatively low in this habitat, because of its extent it supported more than half of the total British Canada Goose population in 2000.

In Cheshire and Wirral, the BTO BBS analysis shows that the breeding population in 2004–05 was 6,310 birds (1,460–11,160), an average of about 15 birds per tetrad in which they were recorded. Canada Geese do not breed until three years of age, so some of this total will be non-breeding immature birds, but it nevertheless represents a large rise from the estimate in our *First Atlas* of 600–700 pairs. At 2.8% of the UK total, Cheshire and Wirral holds a disproportionately large population of Canada Geese.

Twenty years ago, most Canada Geese were breeding at sites in a band from the south-west to north-east of Cheshire, with only a dozen tetrads with proven breeding north-west of a line from Chester to Rostherne, and just three of them in Wirral. They have now expanded their distribution to colonize every habitable area in Wirral, the Mersey valley, and all suitable areas of agricultural Cheshire. They are content to breed alongside man, in urban parks, and altitude is no bar to them, being found on the highest waters in the county.

More than two-thirds of records were two-letter codes, confirmed breeding. Their nests are large and obvious, and adults with their young are conspicuous, either on the water, spread out feeding on grassland or sometimes walking long distances, with a line of chicks led by mother at the front, father bringing up the rear. Where breeding numbers are high, young birds flock together in crèches, guarded by some of their parents, as at Frodsham Marsh where sometimes more than 100 birds gather on the Manchester Ship Canal. Most of the probable breeding records on the map came from observations of pairs of geese.

Sponsored by Knutsford Ornithological Society

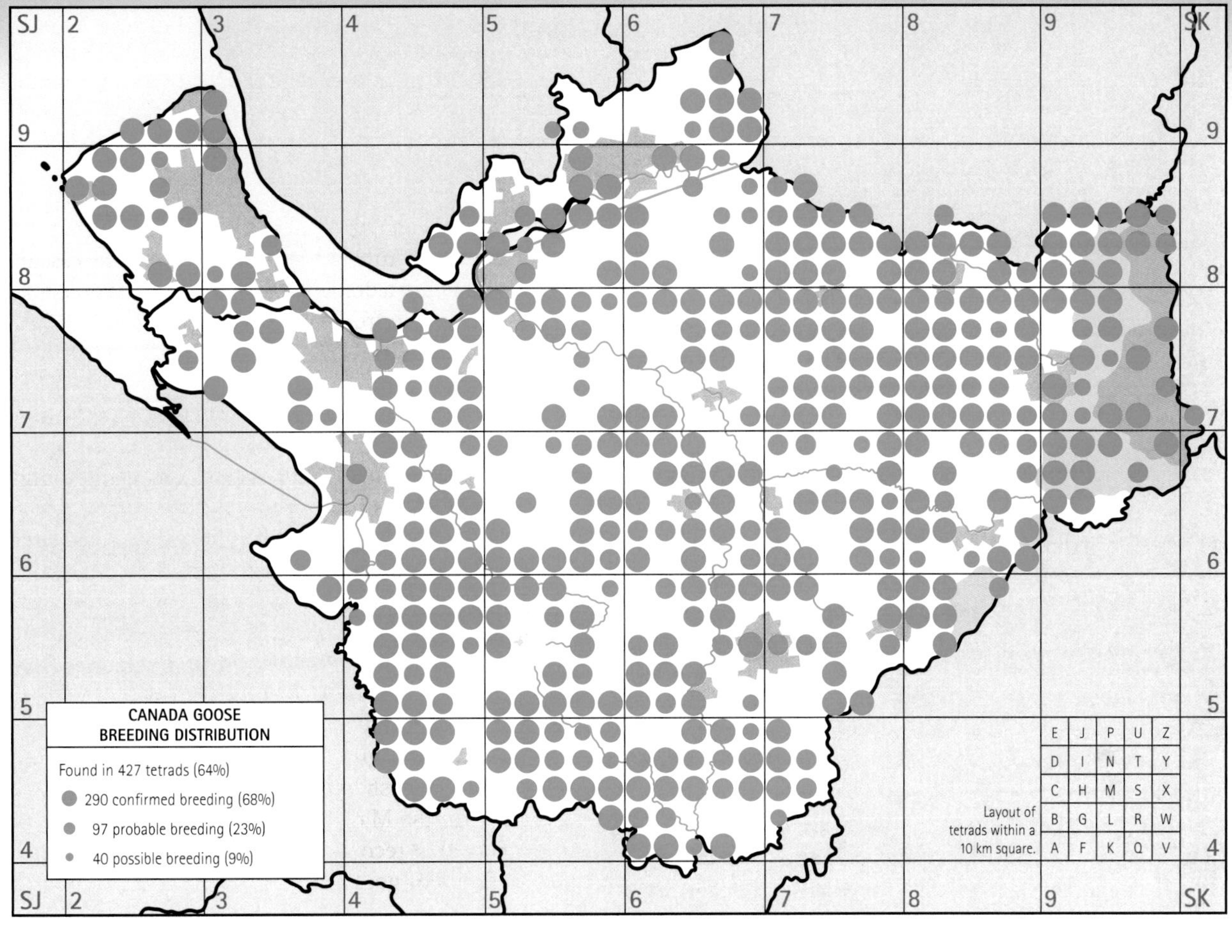
CANADA GOOSE
BREEDING DISTRIBUTION
Found in 427 tetrads (64%)
290 confirmed breeding (68%)
97 probable breeding (23%)
40 possible breeding (9%)
Layout of tetrads within a 10 km square.
E J P U Z
D I N T Y
C H M S X
B G L R W
A F K Q V
SJ
SK

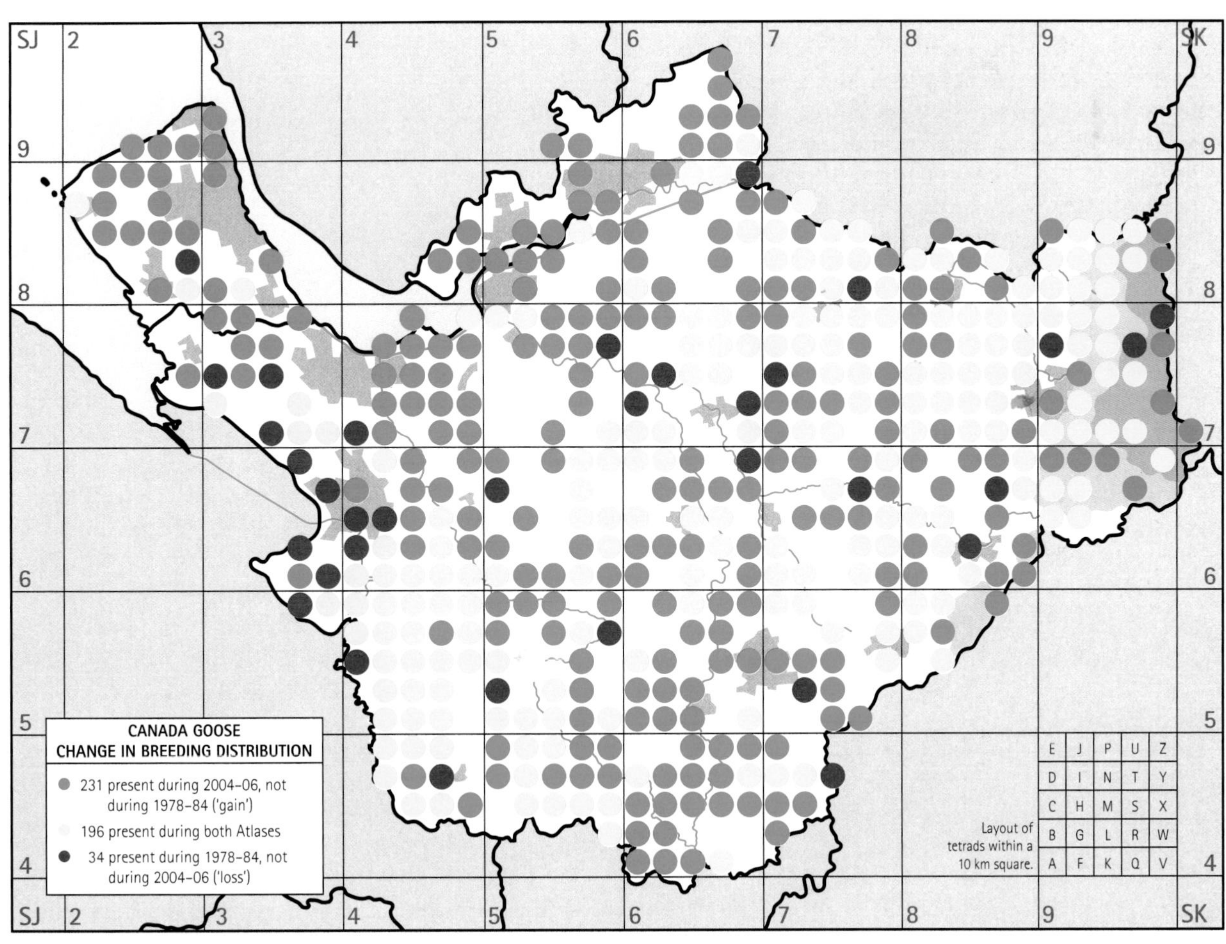
CANADA GOOSE
CHANGE IN BREEDING DISTRIBUTION
231 present during 2004–06, not during 1978–84 ('gain')
196 present during both Atlases
34 present during 1978–84, not during 2004–06 ('loss')
Layout of tetrads within a 10 km square.
E J P U Z
D I N T Y
C H M S X
B G L R W
A F K Q V
SJ
SK

The winter distribution of Canada Geese is broadly similar to that in the breeding season, although they generally gather into flocks and move to larger waters; some birds also spread out into the estuaries. Incomplete counts of the flock on the Dee, up to a maximum of 2,500 in October 2002, place it at the top of the national list of sites for wintering Canada Geese (Banks *et al.* 2006) while the moulting flock on the Mersey, peaking in July and averaging 1,300 birds, puts the estuary in third position on the national table. Winter monitoring by WeBS shows a continuing long-term increase (Banks *et al.* 2006), and the national population, from midwinter WeBS counts, was estimated at 56,000 birds in 2004/05.

Canada Geese were found in some 56 fewer occupied tetrads in winter than during the breeding season (361 winter and 417 breeding season), perhaps explicable by the species' gathering into larger flocks for the winter. More than 50 tetrads recorded birds in flight but not on the ground or water and clearly birds move around a lot within the county. There is, thus, much double-counting of some mobile flocks, but as many as 87 tetrads recorded flocks of 100 or more geese, of which 15 were larger than 500 and five flocks were counted at more than 1,000 birds. Canada Goose numbers have clearly increased greatly since Boyd (1951) commented on 'good flocks' numbering up to 50 birds! Coward and Oldham (1900) treated all introduced or escaped birds with disdain. They wrote that the Canada Goose 'has been long naturalized and today exists in a perfectly wild state in Cheshire, breeding on many of the meres ... in winter it is not unusual to see flocks, varying from half a dozen to two or three hundred birds, feeding in the fields or flying from one sheet of water to another'.

Birds mainly feed on grass. Of the winter habitat codes 29% were farmland, overwhelmingly grassland, and there were only three records of Canada Geese on stubble fields. Most of the habitat codes were fresh water (61% of records), comprising 8% of the total on ponds, 20% small waterbodies, 23% meres, reservoirs and sandpits, and 9% rivers and canals. Three per cent of records were estuarine and 5% on grazing marsh and salt-marsh.

BEN HALL

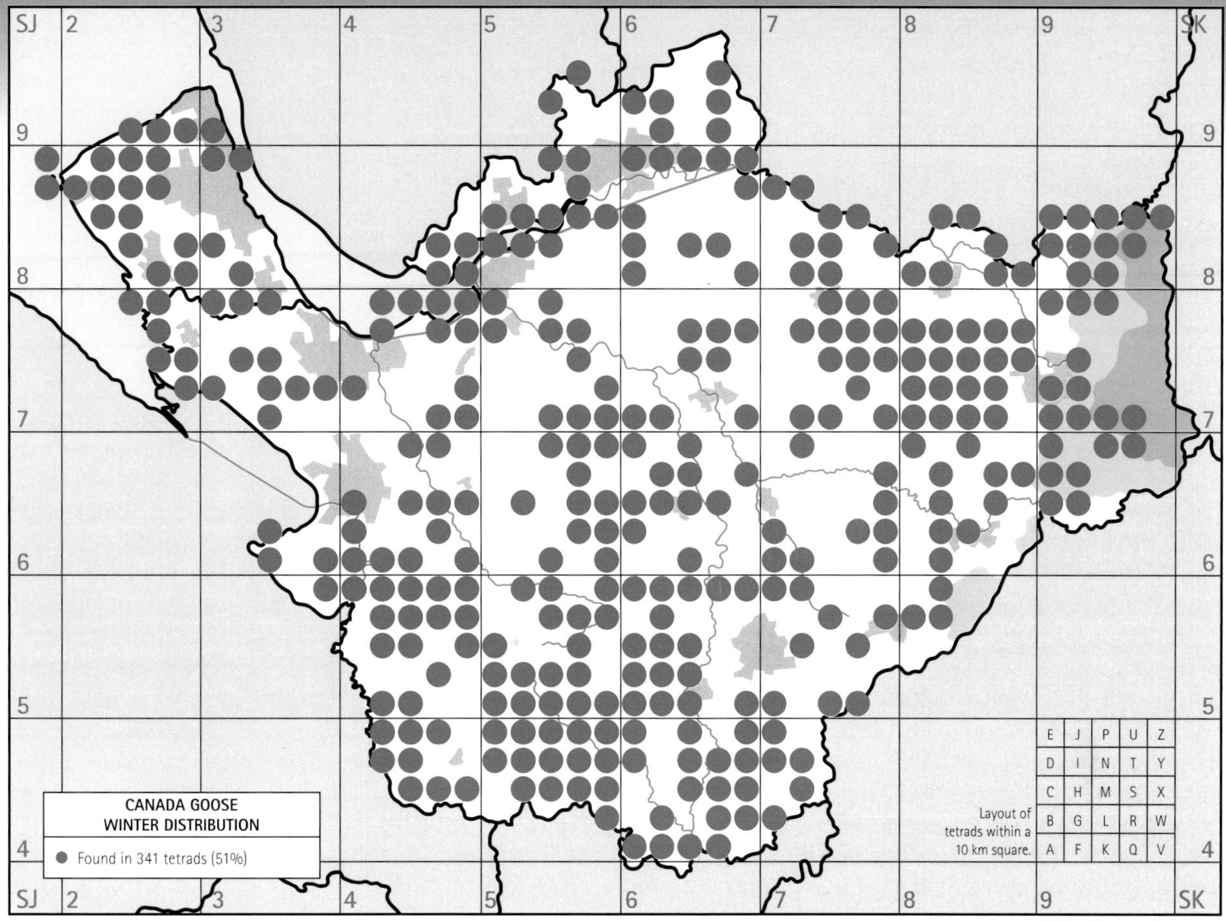
SJ
2
3
4
5
6
7
8
9
SK
9
8
7
6
5
4
CANADA GOOSE
WINTER DISTRIBUTION
Found in 341 tetrads (51%)
Layout of
tetrads within a
10 km square.
E J P U Z
D I N T Y
C H M S X
B G L R W
A F K Q V

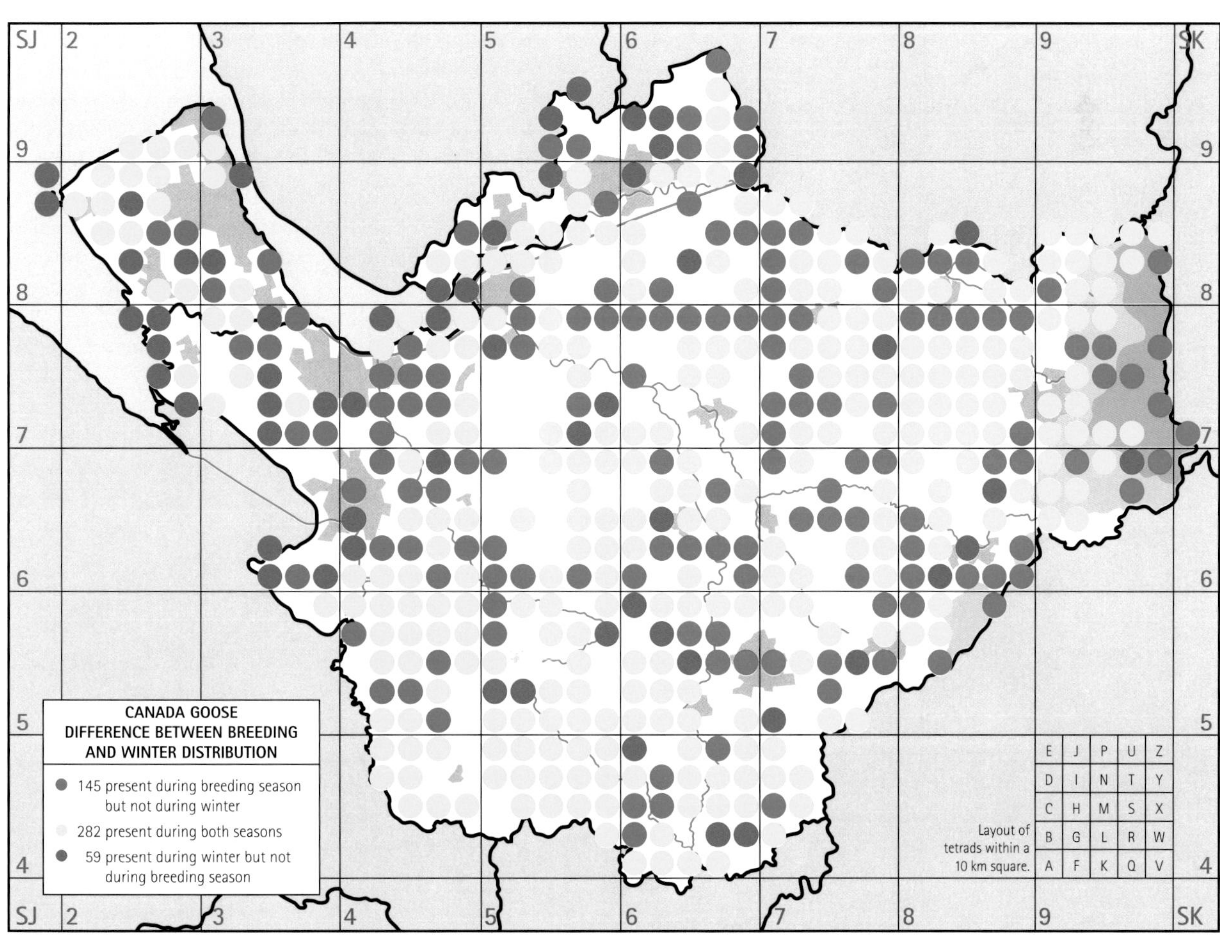
SJ
2
3
4
5
6
7
8
9
SK
9
8
7
6
5
4
CANADA GOOSE
DIFFERENCE BETWEEN BREEDING
AND WINTER DISTRIBUTION
145 present during breeding season but not during winter
282 present during both seasons
59 present during winter but not during breeding season
Layout of
tetrads within a
10 km square.
E J P U Z
D I N T Y
C H M S X
B G L R W
A F K Q V

Barnacle Goose

Branta leucopsis

More than one hundred years ago, wild Barnacle Geese used to winter on the Dee estuary, but now the only birds seen are likely to have originated from wildfowl collections. There seems just an outside possibility that the single mapped bird at the coast could have been wild.

There are three isolated populations of Barnacle Geese, breeding in Greenland, Svalbard and western Siberia, with no interchange between them. The first two winter exclusively in the British Isles, Greenland birds on the western seaboard of Scotland and Ireland, and the Svalbard flock on the Solway Firth. The Siberian breeders winter in the Netherlands.

In the nineteenth century, the winter distribution of Barnacle Geese was obviously very different. Brockholes (1874) stated that 'prior to 1862, this species was very common on the Dee Marshes, now it is very scarce; sometimes a whole winter passes without any being seen'; Coward (1910) wrote that 'Barnacles deserted the locality when the marshes carried so many sheep'. Eight near Hilbre on 2 March 1886, and one shot near Burton Marsh on 29 September 1901 were worthy of comment. There were also considerable numbers on Morecambe Bay as late as 1879, and it was plentiful on the Ribble marshes as recently as 1909 (Oakes 1953).

The retreat of the wild stock almost coincided with the start of records of birds considered to be feral; Barnacle Goose appears to be one of the species most likely to have escaped from, or been released from, wildfowl collections. Bell (1962) notes odd birds in 1911, 1912, 1921/22, 1947, 1961 and 1962 at Radnor Mere and Tabley, but birds off Hilbre might have more authentic pedigrees: three on 3 April 1940 and singles on 5 and 6 December 1942 and 31 December 1961. Since then, the annual county bird reports have included birds in the body of the report rather than the 'escapes' section, but often with comments about their likely provenance. Given that wild Barnacle Geese are gregarious, almost exclusively coastal and amongst the most nervous of all wildfowl, the status of birds inland in Cheshire, many of them associating with Canada or Greylag Geese, can easily be guessed at. They should, nevertheless, be comprehensively recorded: what if they became the Canada Goose of the future?

However, as with the changes in the nineteenth century, we should note that modern wildfowl populations are proving to be quite adaptable in their habits, especially as population figures are so high and likely to be putting pressure on resources at their traditional sites. In recent years, a wintering flock of Barnacle Geese has become established at the Dyfi estuary in mid-Wales, with 140 birds there in 2004/05. They associate with Greenland White-fronted Geese and it is assumed that these Barnacle Geese are from the Greenland breeding population rather than the Svalbard one. Also, the Svalbard birds seem mostly to keep to one large group while the Greenland birds are more prone to forming smaller, scattered, flocks. It seems possible that birds from the Dyfi flock could be found in our area, and perhaps the occasional coastal record derives from this population. Birdwatchers should keep a careful eye open for any colour-marked birds, or even try to collect a cast-off feather: with scientific analysis in its advanced state, it could be possible to prove their origin, rather than merely speculate!

Traditionally, Barnacle Geese have fed on saltmarshes and coastal pastures, but more recently their requirement for short-cropped sward has been met by intensively managed grasslands. They eat grasses, herbs, leaves, stolons and seeds, as well as barley and oat stubbles, spilt grain and undersown grass.

PHIL JONES

Sponsored by Brian Grieve

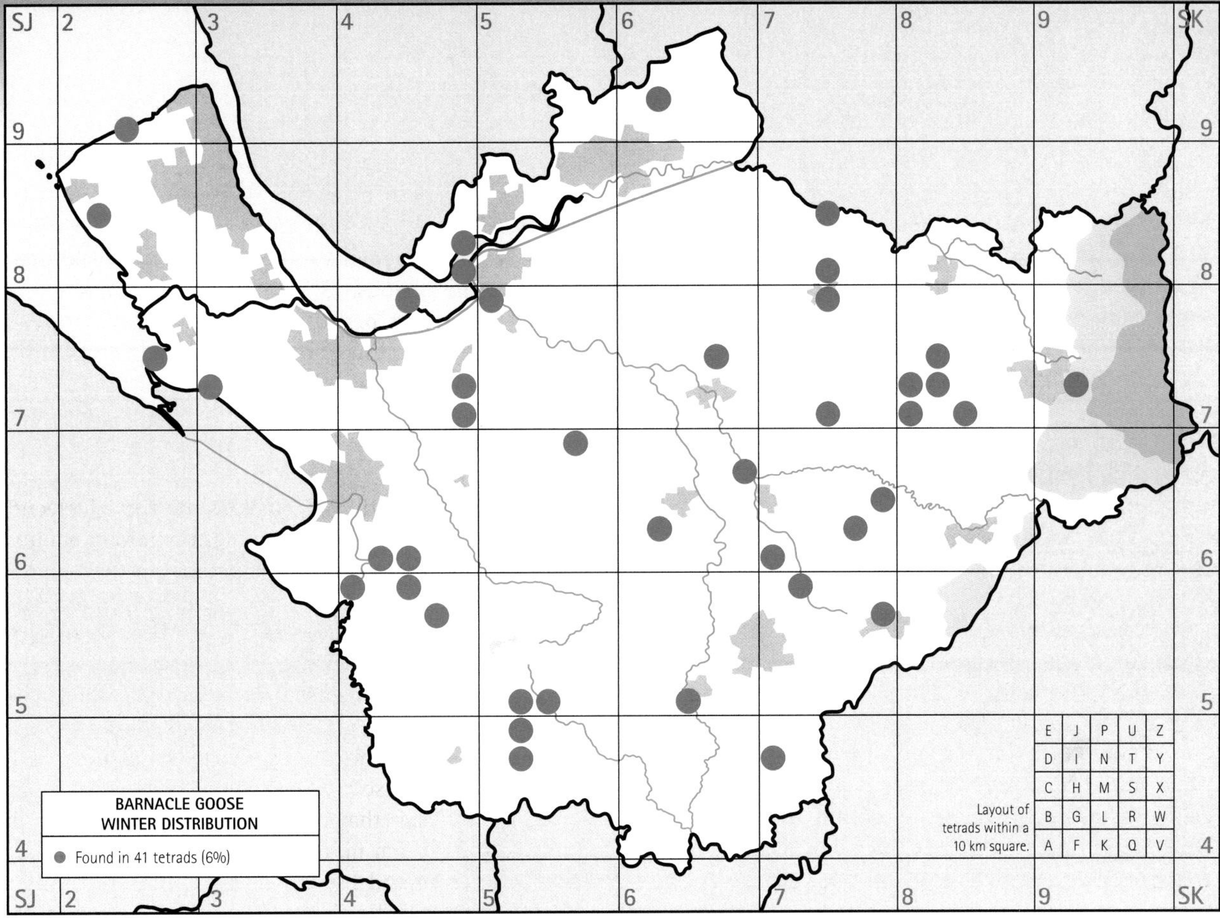

WeBS counts attempt to come up with estimates for the naturalized population of Barnacle Geese in Britain, with recent figures of almost 1,000 birds (Musgrove *et al.* 2007). The Cheshire and Wirral figure might be in the range of 10–20 birds.

● Barnacle Geese were reported in the breeding season in nine tetrads, seven of them single birds and one pair that moved between the Chelford area sand quarries (SJ87A/F), but with no higher evidence of breeding. Birds bred in the county at Radnor Mere (SJ87M/N) in four years 1992–95 and at Tatton Park (SJ78K) in 2001 and 2002. The feral breeding population of the UK was at least 106 pairs in 2004, spread across nine counties (Holling *et al.* 2007b).

Brent Goose

Branta bernicla

During this Atlas period there were more Brent Geese in the county than for at least a century, as it seems that a wintering flock of this species is gradually establishing a presence on the Dee, spilling over from their traditional Irish wintering sites.

There are three distinct components to the British population. Light-bellied Brent Geese *Branta bernicla hrota* breed on islands in the Canadian Arctic and northern Greenland, and migrate through Iceland to winter mostly in Ireland. Another population of the light-bellied form breeds in Svalbard and winters mainly at Lindisfarne (Northumbria). Birds of the nominate dark-bellied race *Branta bernicla bernicla* breed on the tundra in Arctic Russia and winter in the Netherlands and south-east England. Apart from the obvious colour phases, birds from the different populations are not individually identifiable in the field, but their fidelity to wintering areas makes assignment to origin straightforward.

The Canadian population is now at its highest, over 30,000 individuals, having doubled in a decade between the mid-1990s and mid-2000s. As the ice starts to close in on their breeding grounds, they undertake one of the longest wildfowl migrations, staging in Iceland on the way, and arriving in Strangford Lough (Northern Ireland) during October/November where they feed on eelgrass *zostera*. As they deplete this marine grass, the geese change diet to a wide range of estuarine foods including algae and salt-marsh grasses, and might move a little way inland to find grasslands or cereal crops. They also disperse during the winter, mostly to sites in southern Ireland, but some cross the Irish Sea to spend time at estuarine sites in England and Wales, including Anglesey, Morecambe Bay and the Dee. There are relatively few birds at each site, but numbers have been increasing, especially during the twenty-first century, perhaps driven by the rise in population and pressure on feeding grounds at their traditional Irish sites.

The flock on the Dee usually peaks in midwinter, with a maximum total of 121 on the January 2005 WeBS count (Banks *et al.* 2006). As in the Atlas map, they are mostly found near to Hilbre, occasionally along the north Wirral coast or extending up the Dee estuary, apparently feeding on algae and seaweeds found on the rocks. A few dark-bellied geese, in single figures, are noted every winter, often associating with the light-bellied flock, but confusing the inference about the birds' origins. Light-bellied Brent Geese are subject to intense study including satellite tracking from Ireland back to their breeding grounds. A female, colour-ringed in Iceland in May 2005, was on Hilbre for 12 days in November 2005 before moving to spend the winter in Hampshire with a flock of dark-bellied birds, and was seen again in Iceland on spring migration in 2006. She was next reported in Northern Ireland in October 2006, and again on Hilbre for a longer stay, 29 November 2006 to 16 January 2007, pausing briefly on Anglesey on her way back to Iceland, where she was seen in spring 2007 with a possible mate. Proof of her breeding grounds came from Canadian researchers who saw her on Bathurst Island in July 2007, with another stopover in Northern Ireland in October 2007 before revisiting Hilbre from 15 November 2007 onwards. One could hardly have wished for more information from one

RAY SCALLY

Sponsored by Hilbre Bird Observatory and Ringing Station

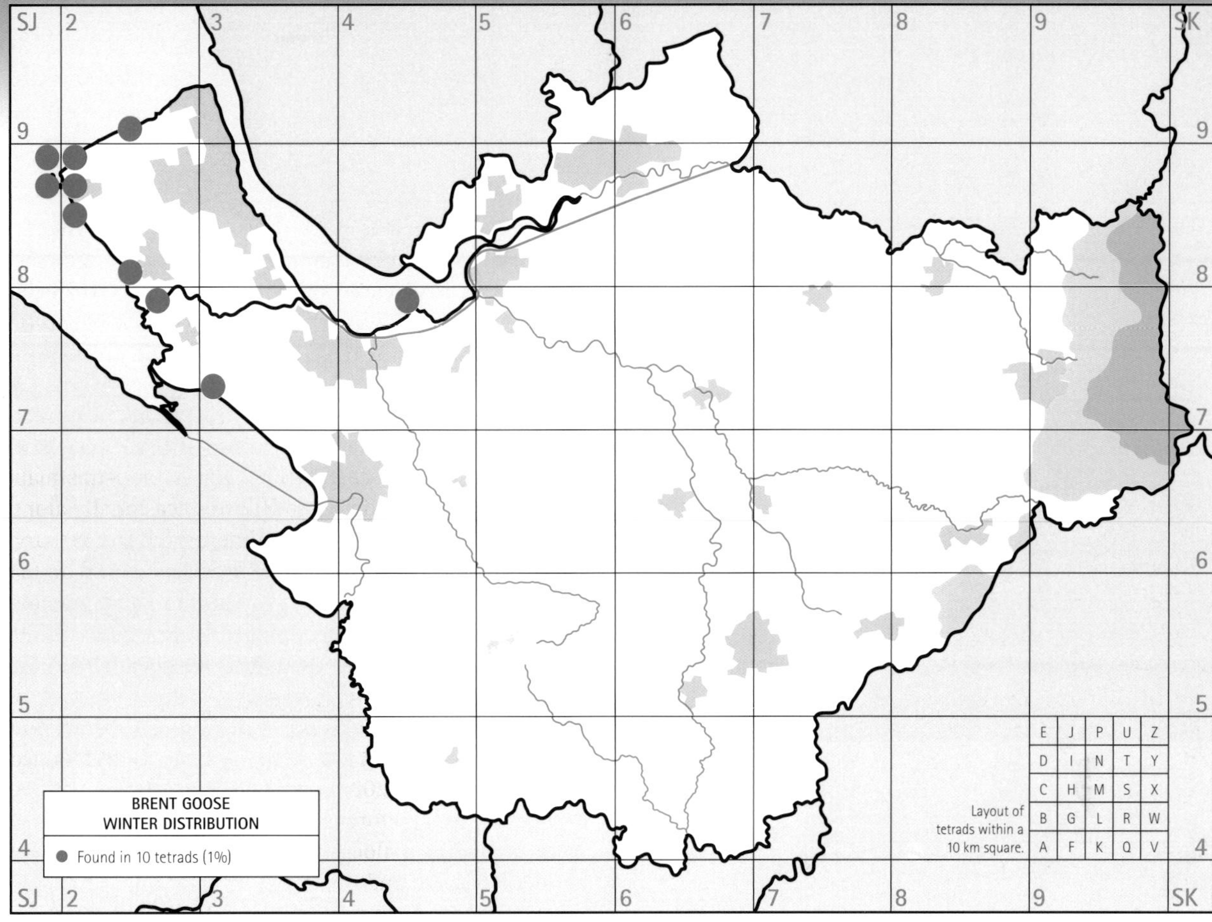

bird: evidence of breeding and wintering areas, spring and autumn passage sites, mixing of the two races then recurrence in winter quarters.

Brent Geese have never been common in the county. In the nineteenth century, Coward and Oldham (1900) wrote that Brent Geese visited the Dee estuary in winter 'in considerable numbers', although the only record of more than an odd bird that they quoted was about 200 seen on 7 February 1888. By 1910 Coward revised the description to read that 'The Brent Goose visits the Dee estuary almost every winter in small numbers. As a rule the flocks are not large ...'. For instance, in winter 1904/05 the largest party was 18 birds. The Brent has only ever been a rare visitor to the Mersey: in February 1895 one was killed on Ince Marsh. Bell (1962) noted 40 on the Dee on 26 February 1916, then six at Gayton on 16 November 1916, but no further records until 1928, after which occurrences were logged almost every year but almost invariably in numbers less than 10 and all from the Dee estuary. Numbers of all three Brent Goose populations crashed in the 1920s and 1930s, in part because of a loss of eelgrass through a parasitic infection: perhaps the few seen in Cheshire were wandering birds, trying to find suitable food. The duration of their visits in practically all cases was said to be very short, with most of the records in the period November to February but occasionally in October. Until recently, most reports do not give the colour form. Fortunately, fewer Brent Geese are kept in captivity than most other species of wildfowl, with consequently fewer confusing records of feral birds.

Bell (1967) noted that three, probably dark-breasted, on a flash at Sandbach on 18 March 1964 were probably the first inland record since one was shot at Comber Mere on 5 November 1895. Unusually, a flock of 39 dark-breasted was seen off Hilbre on 17 January 1960. The county bird reports of the last 40 years show that the species remained a scarce annual visitor, often just odd birds and nearly all in the Dee estuary, until the mid-1990s. There were more records, but usually still in single-figure flocks, during the rest of that decade, until the winter of 2000/01 saw an influx of long-staying birds, with up to 43 birds on the January Dee WeBS count. Similar numbers were found each winter until 2004/05 when there was a big jump to over 100 birds, a level that has been maintained each winter since.

As well as changes in status, the races of Brent Geese have undergone several changes of English name. In Coward's books, the colour forms are not mentioned; Bell referred to them as dark-breasted and light-breasted; the national bird recording organizations, British Ornithologists' Union, BTO and the Wildfowl & Wetlands Trust have used the terms dark-bellied and light-bellied for the last fifty years, but in some bird books, and *CWBRs*, the latter are called 'pale-bellied'! Whatever they are called, their recent increase is interesting and their status in Cheshire and Wirral should be carefully monitored.

Shelduck

Tadorna tadorna

SIMON BOOTH

Shelducks have considerably changed their behaviour in recent years. Ancestrally a coastal breeder, they now occupy more tetrads inland than at the coast, and from 1993 onwards they have abandoned their traditional postbreeding moult migration to the Heligoland Bight and up to 20,000 birds gather in July to moult on the Mersey estuary, the largest flock in Britain (Wells & Friswell 1998).

Shelducks were confirmed or probably breeding in 59 tetrads in our *First Atlas*; this has risen to 98 tetrads in those categories now. The 66% increase is almost entirely in inland areas, more than 2 km from tidal waters, as the species has spread across lowland Cheshire. Following occasional previous records, inland breeding in the county has been annual since 1977. The habit rapidly took hold and there were seven inland tetrads with confirmed and 12 with probable breeding in our *First Atlas*, and 12 tetrads confirmed and 47 probable in this survey. Shelducks also now nest on Hilbre: they just missed out on our *First Atlas*, nesting in 1985 but not during 1978–84.

In the estuaries, birds feed on the flowing tidal water, but not much around high or low tides, mostly sieving the mud for the tiny snail *Hydrobia* which forms the overwhelming majority of their diet. They also eat shrimps, small clams *Macoma* and ragworms; it is not known on what the inland breeders are feeding.

Breeding Shelducks establish and defend territories of around 1 ha in size, in which pairs do most of their feeding, but these territories do not contain the nest site, nor do they bring their brood to the same area. Non-breeding birds stay in flocks until they are two or three years old. The female chooses a nest site, most often in a rabbit burrow, but they will use a variety of suitable holes including in trees, crevices in haystacks, nest-boxes (as suspected in the Wybunbury area, SJ65V), and even in man-made structures. A female laid eight eggs in the hide at Hale Duck Decoy in 2003. Colin Schofield saw a pair fly out of a dockside building in Birkenhead (SJ39F) on 9 June 2004, and even in such incongruous surroundings it is likely that they had at least been prospecting for a nest site, or may have already had a nest inside.

Eggs are normally laid from mid-April onwards, into June, although young had hatched by 23 April 1995 at Budworth Mere. Typical clutches contain eight to 10 eggs, sometimes up to 12, but there may be more where another female has dumped some eggs into the nest. The female alone incubates, for about 30 days, with the male avoiding the nest for this time, but he knows when the chicks are hatching and returns to guard them and his mate. Despite being accompanied by both parents, many chicks, perhaps two-thirds of the brood, die, usually in the first week or so of life, often from predation by large gulls, but it is seven weeks before they have grown enough to fly. Some pairs look after their offspring throughout this period, but many chicks gather into crèches, with a few adults watching over groups of 20 or more youngsters (Patterson 1982). Crèches of 66 and 41 young were counted in Stanlow Bay in 1999 and a massive crèche of 149 chicks was seen off Ince on 2 July 2000 (*CWBRs*).

Nearly all of the records of confirmed breeding in this Atlas came when fieldworkers spotted a pair with their delightfully plumaged chicks, 11 being the largest brood noted. There were five tetrads where a bird was seen visiting a probable nest site, and a further five with pairs displaying, but the vast majority of probable breeding records refer to pairs seen. Such paired birds are not necessarily intending to breed but may be prospecting the area for future years.

With their wide range of nesting areas, Shelducks were catholic in their choice of habitat. Almost all of the inland birds were on standing waterbodies, of all sizes, with birds often seen spreading out into adjacent grassland, either semi-natural or agricultural land, and sometimes into tilled crops.

Some of the most favoured estuarine tetrads held tens of pairs, and surveys in 1998 of the Mersey estuary led to a population estimate of over 100 pairs (*CWBR*). Few inland tetrads held more than one or two pairs, however, and the county population is likely to be around 200 pairs, considerably more than the estimate twenty years ago of 25–50 pairs.

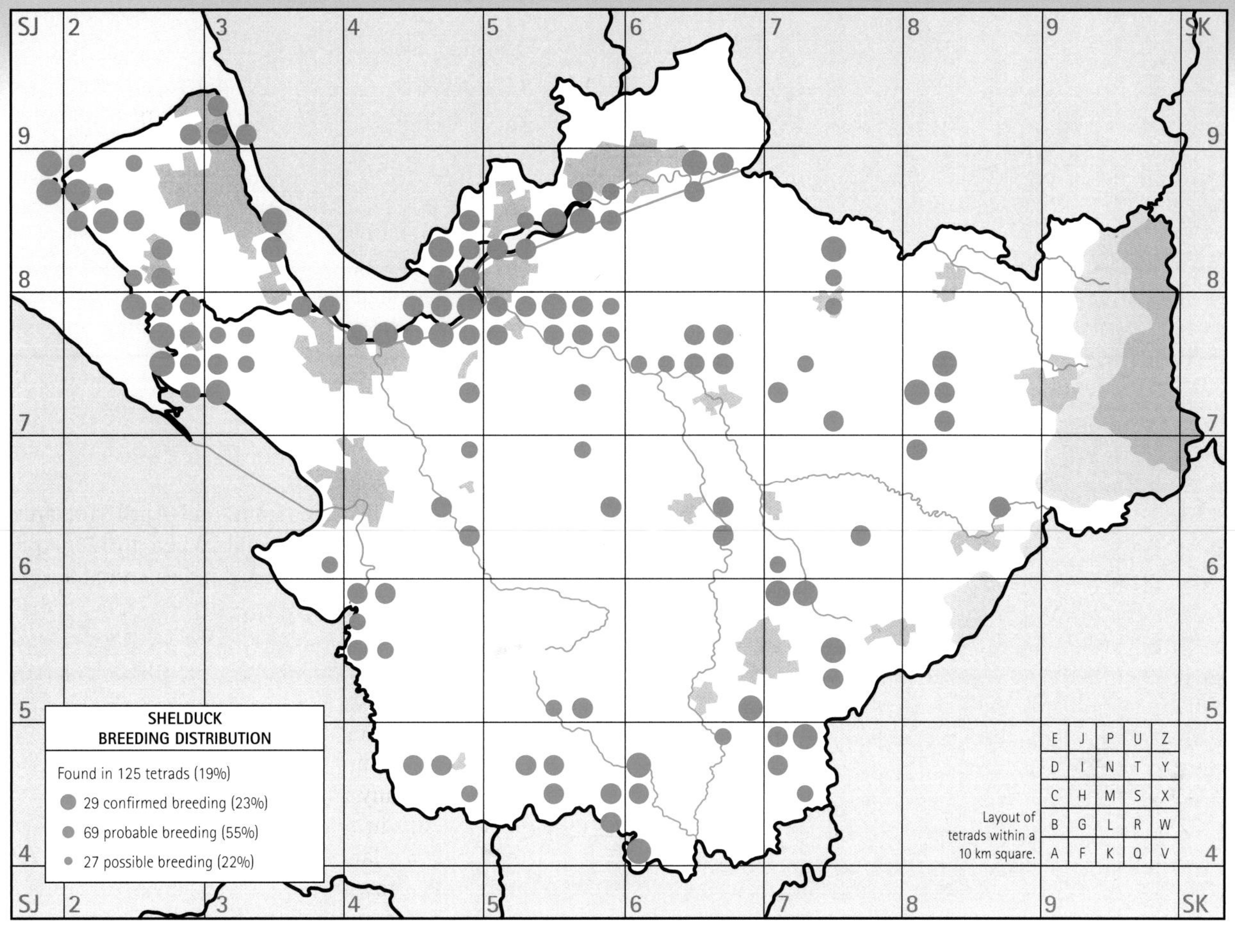

SJ
SK
SHELDUCK
BREEDING DISTRIBUTION
Found in 125 tetrads (19%)
29 confirmed breeding (23%)
69 probable breeding (55%)
27 possible breeding (22%)
Layout of tetrads within a 10 km square.
E J P U Z
D I N T Y
C H M S X
B G L R W
A F K Q V

SJ
SK
SHELDUCK
CHANGE IN BREEDING DISTRIBUTION
77 present during 2004–06, not during 1978–84 ('gain')
47 present during both Atlases
19 present during 1978–84, not during 2004–06 ('loss')
Layout of tetrads within a 10 km square.
E J P U Z
D I N T Y
C H M S X
B G L R W
A F K Q V

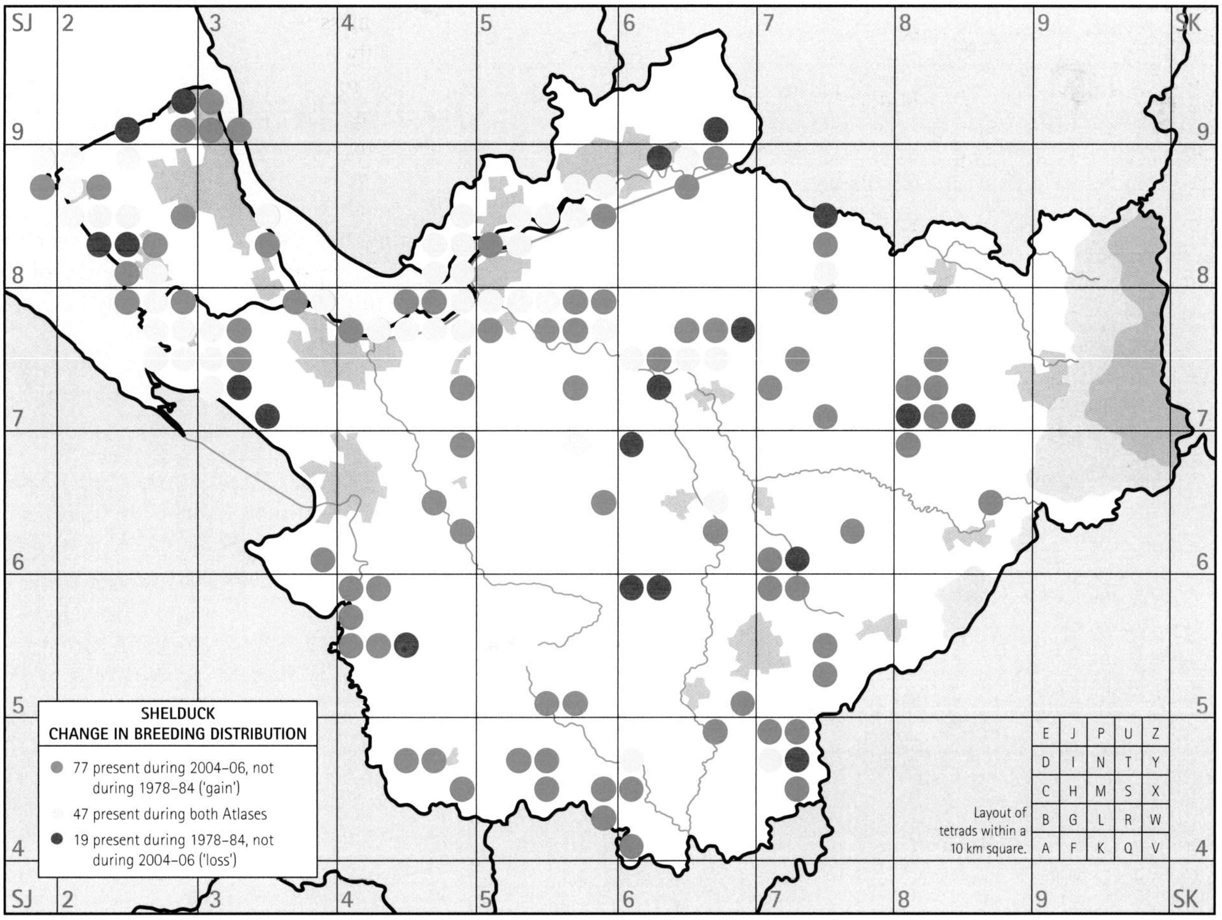

WeBS counts show that our two estuaries are the top sites in Britain for Shelducks, with five-year peak mean figures far exceeding the threshold for international importance of 3,000 birds, averaging 14,500 (Mersey) and over 11,000 (Dee). This status is based on the moulting flock on the Mersey, peaking in July or August, and the maximum on the Dee, usually in October. Midwinter totals are much lower, typically 4,000 on the Dee. The numbers actually staying to winter on the Mersey have dropped considerably since the moulting flock became established, previously reaching 4,000–5,000 birds, but since the late-1990s seldom above 3,000: could it be that the pressure of the huge moulting flock actually depletes the food available until the *Hydrobia* reproduce again in the spring?

Most of the Shelducks wintering here are thought to be British breeders, perhaps with some immigrants from Scandinavia and continental Europe (*Migration Atlas*). The origins of our birds were nicely illustrated by two ringed females found within three weeks of each other in 1990/91: one, caught during an overnight ringing session on the drained New Brighton Marine Lake had been hatched the previous summer on the edge of the Solway in Cumbria, and the other, found dead at Frodsham, was a bird-of-the-year from 1989 ringed at Slimbridge, Gloucestershire so those two made movements of around 160 km in opposite directions to converge on the Mersey.

Although the map shows that they are quite widely distributed, there are few birds wintering inland and the vast majority of the county's birds are in the estuaries. The only non-estuarine tetrads with flocks counted in three figures were Frodsham Marsh no. 6 bed (SJ47Z), with a maximum of 220 birds and Fiddler's Ferry (SJ58M) with up to 100 birds. Both of these are feeding and loafing sites adjacent to the tidal Mersey, however, and only two truly inland sites registered a flock of more than 10 birds: Sandbach Flashes (SJ75E/J) with up to 45 birds, and flooded fields alongside the river Weaver at Aston (SJ57N).

A century ago, Coward (1910) wrote of large flocks frequenting the banks of the Dee and Mersey estuaries, but his 'large flocks' were of hundreds, rather than the thousands of the present day: the largest counted was more than 800 strong, near Denhall on the Dee in February 1906. Bell's assessment was much the same in 1962: 'the numbers wintering in the estuaries are variable, and are difficult to assess over these areas, but may number several hundred'. More quantitative information came from the wildfowl counts, forerunners of WeBS, with, for instance, more than 2,000 at Gayton and 660 on the Mersey at the same time on 16 February 1969. Numbers wintering on the Mersey rose spectacularly to reach 12,000 in 1980/81, then gradually levelled out over the next decade to the figures quoted above, around 4,000–5,000 birds on each estuary.

Their diet is much the same as in the summer, predominantly mud-snails and tubifex worms, although they are also attracted to grain, but in winter Shelducks have to spend more than half of their time feeding. As the winter passes, adult birds become more restless, and during February aggression amongst the flock members increases as they anticipate the coming season.

STEVE ROUND

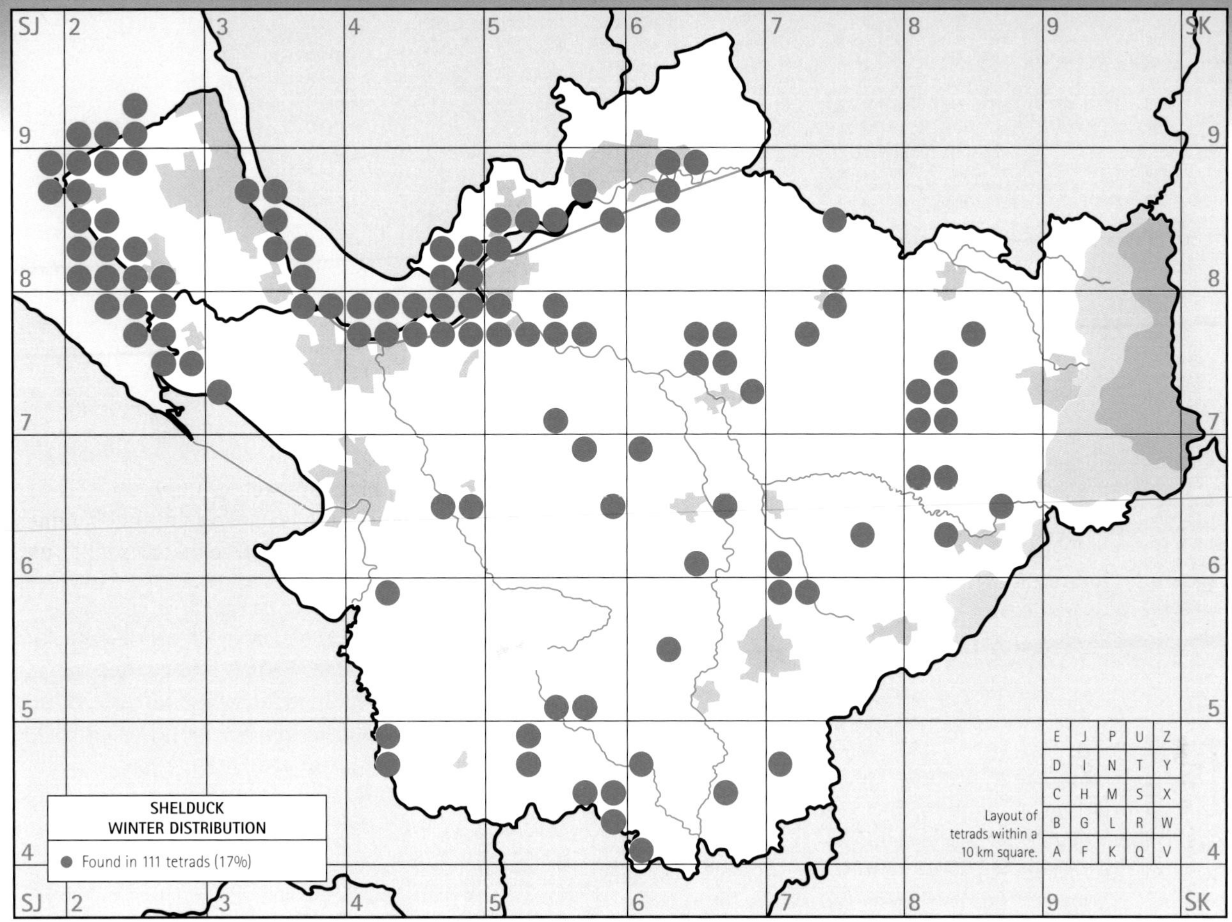
SJ
SK
SHELDUCK
WINTER DISTRIBUTION
Found in 111 tetrads (17%)
Layout of
tetrads within a
10 km square.
E J P U Z
D I N T Y
C H M S X
B G L R W
A F K Q V

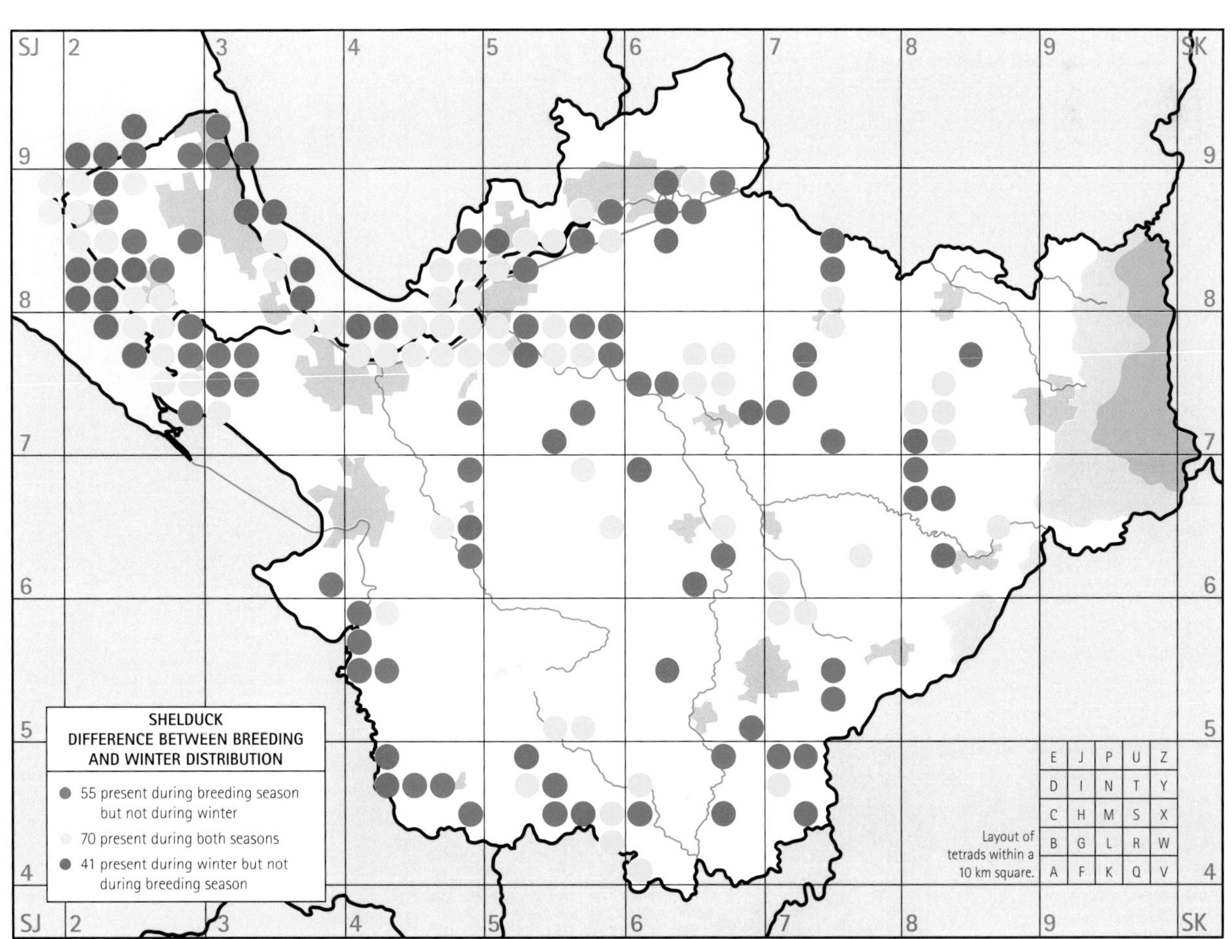
SJ
SK
SHELDUCK
DIFFERENCE BETWEEN BREEDING
AND WINTER DISTRIBUTION
55 present during breeding season
but not during winter
70 present during both seasons
41 present during winter but not
during breeding season
Layout of
tetrads within a
10 km square.
E J P U Z
D I N T Y
C H M S X
B G L R W
A F K Q V

Mandarin Duck

Aix galericulata

ANDREW MART

Mandarins have spread amazingly since our *First Atlas* to become, in terms of confirmed breeding, our third most widespread duck. Twenty years ago they were found in 12 tetrads, with breeding confirmed in four, probable in four and possible in four; during this Atlas they were found in 71 tetrads, with breeding confirmed in 26, probable in 22 and possible in 23. They used to be confined to the vicinity of the Eaton Estate south of Chester, but now are present in most of south-west Cheshire, all suitable waters in Wirral and parts of east Cheshire including the Langley (SJ97K) and Trentabank (SJ97Q) reservoirs in the uplands, possibly using nest-boxes there that were put up for Goldeneyes.

They nest in a hole so the female needs a suitable tree, or a nest-box, not far from water. They usually prefer densely wooded areas near wetlands, especially with a wealth of rhododendron undergrowth (Lever 1977). They feed mostly at night, mainly on insects in spring, and plants, especially *Polygonum*, and frogs in summer.

Most eggs are laid in late April. A normal clutch is nine to 12 eggs, but Mandarins are prone to egg-dumping, where ducks lay their eggs in other females' nests, leading sometimes to enormous clutches of as many as 40 eggs. In one study in Berkshire, at least 56% of clutches were parasitized, and probably many more (Davies & Baggott 1989a, 1989b). It seems that some females reject clutches to which extra eggs have been added, and do not incubate them: they may well still reproduce by retaliating and themselves laying elsewhere. The eggs hatch, after about five weeks' incubation, in early June. In some natural sites where the core of the tree has decayed, the nesting cavity may be many metres deep, but the ducklings still manage to climb to the outside, leap to the ground below and follow the duck to water.

Fieldworkers in 23 tetrads saw females with young, with broods varying from one to eight chicks. Frank Gleeson's observation in SJ28X highlighted one of the hazards facing ducklings when he saw one of a brood of eight young grabbed by a Grey Heron, although it was reprieved when the heron was startled by a dog and dropped the chick.

Recording the habitat of this species is not straightforward because of its dependence on woods and waters. In 39 tetrads they were found on lakes and other waterbodies, with 28 on linear watercourses (streams and rivers), a higher proportion of the latter (42%) than any other duck except Goosander.

The Mandarin Duck is a native of north-east Asia and Japan, introduced to British collections at the beginning of the twentieth century. The birds were first brought here for people to admire the plumage of the gaudy male, especially the golden-orange 'sails' sticking up from his back, although it is the purple-green crested head that gives the species its name, the Latin *galericulata* meaning 'hooded'. The female, although drabber, is striking in her own way, with delicately mottled shades of grey. The Cheshire and Wirral birds originally came from a collection, but the population is now clearly self-sustaining. It seems to be filling a vacant ecological niche, as a tree-perching duck, and is now clearly flourishing in the wild in our county. Observers reported up to four pairs in some tetrads. An average of two pairs per tetrad with confirmed or probable breeding would give a county population of 100 pairs.

Sponsored by Chester and District Ornithological Society

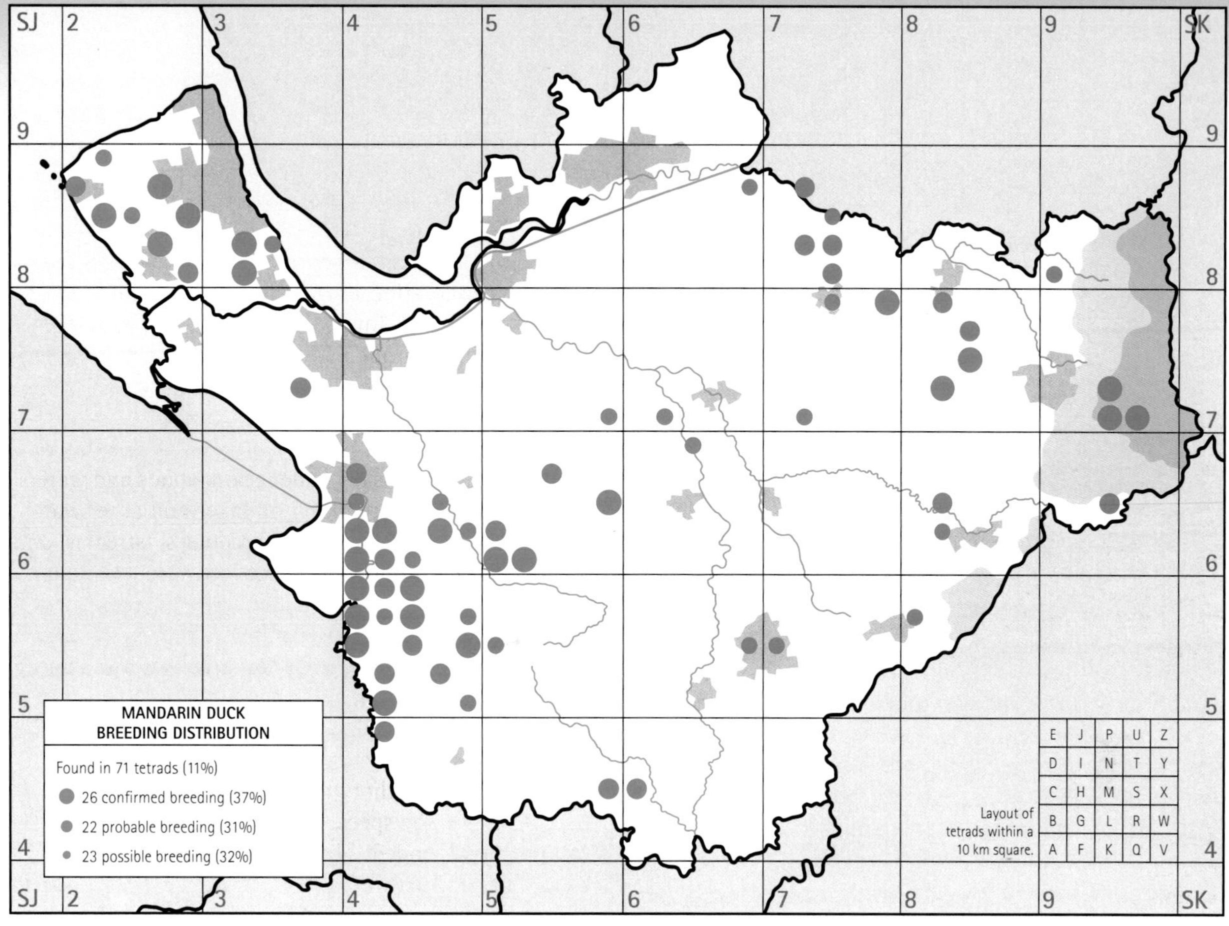
SJ
SK
MANDARIN DUCK
BREEDING DISTRIBUTION
Found in 71 tetrads (11%)
26 confirmed breeding (37%)
22 probable breeding (31%)
23 possible breeding (32%)
Layout of
tetrads within a
10 km square.
E J P U Z
D I N T Y
C H M S X
B G L R W
A F K Q V

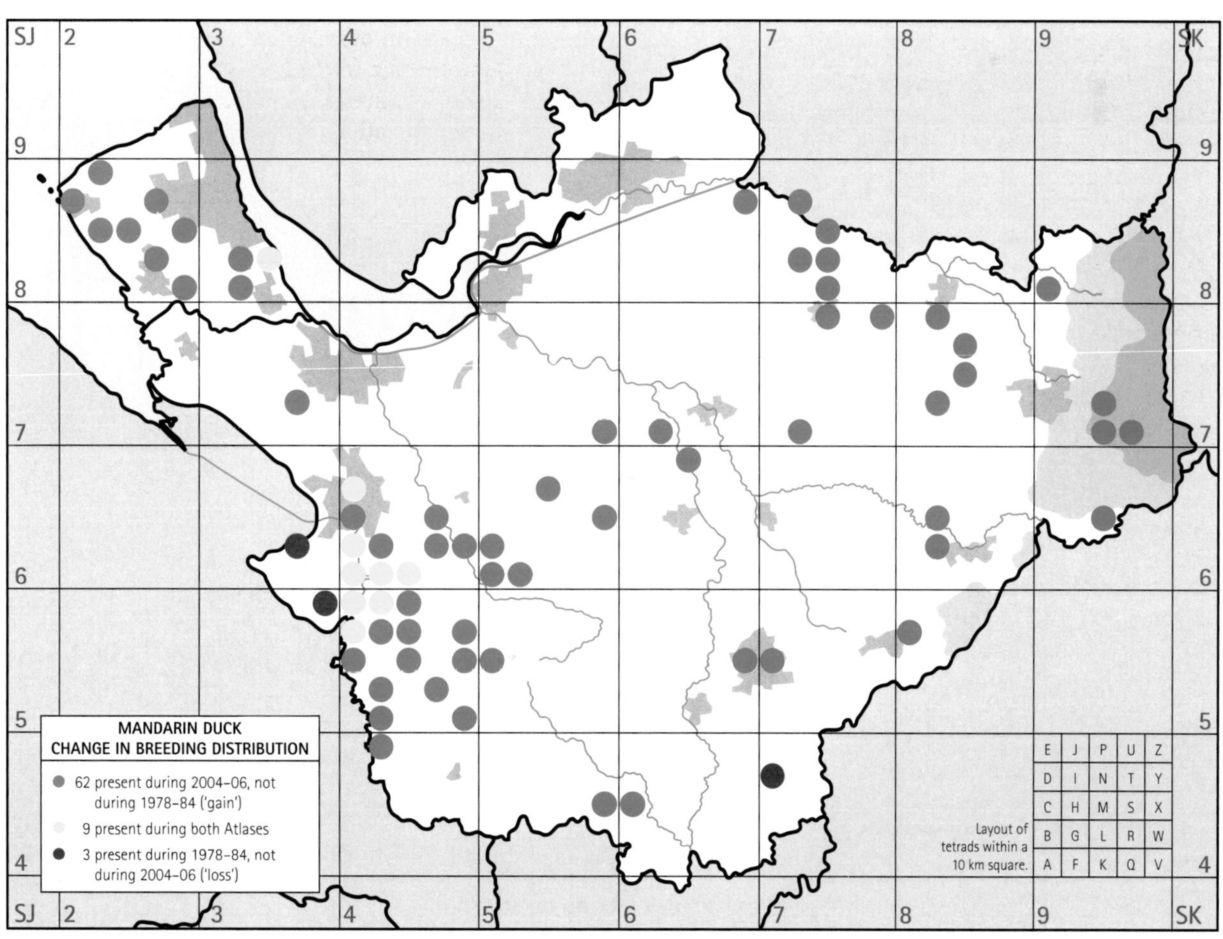
SJ
SK
MANDARIN DUCK
CHANGE IN BREEDING DISTRIBUTION
62 present during 2004–06, not during 1978–84 ('gain')
9 present during both Atlases
3 present during 1978–84, not during 2004–06 ('loss')
Layout of
tetrads within a
10 km square.
E J P U Z
D I N T Y
C H M S X
B G L R W
A F K Q V

Most of Mandarins' early breeding activities take place in the first half of winter. Almost as soon as males emerge from their eclipse plumage in late September or early October, they start displaying, and the majority are paired by the end of the year. Although they are mostly paired, it seems that they are not yet on territory, as many of the breeding tetrads are not occupied in winter; 24 tetrads with breeding season presence did not have birds recorded in winter. This is the same behaviour as is recorded in the core of its British range in southern England, with breeding areas being deserted from late summer until the following spring (*BTO Winter Atlas*).

As well as a concentration onto fewer sites, many birds shift habitat. In contrast to the situation when breeding, few birds in winter were found on linear watercourses: in 38 tetrads they were recorded on lakes and other waterbodies, with only six on linear watercourses (streams, rivers and large canals). Mandarins have been using our largest waters, and at the other extreme, two birds visited a garden pond at Capenhurst (SJ37R). They are not normally an estuarine duck, but a male was swimming with drake Mallards at high tide on the river Mersey near Mount Manisty (SJ37Z) on 24 November 2004. They especially like to feed on nuts, particularly acorns, chestnuts and beechmast.

This species has not been studied in Cheshire and Wirral, and no detail is known of their movements. It is described as 'rather sedentary in nature' but clearly makes local seasonal movements (Brown & Grice 2005). At a site in Berkshire, no more than 30 birds were seen at a time on a lake, yet over 500 birds were ringed there in a two-year period (Davies 1988). Obviously there must be some dispersal to enable them to colonize new sites and, as an extreme, a bird ringed in Britain has been recovered near St Petersburg in Russia, perhaps having been caught up in a return movement with other migratory species (*Migration Atlas*).

Mandarins do not usually congregate in large flocks. Gatherings of 10 birds or more were found in the area south of Chester from Eaton to Churton (SJ45D/E and SJ46A), including the largest flock counted in this Atlas period, 32 birds on a fishpond on 13 January 2005; near Bickerton (SJ55C), where 10 males and 8 females were on a pond with many dead trees; at Little Budworth (SJ56X); and on Trentabank Reservoir (SJ97Q). The largest winter flock ever in the county appears to have been 63 birds at Aldford Brook on 17 December 2001, when all the lakes were frozen.

This Atlas has given us the best picture yet of Mandarins in Cheshire and Wirral, but many accounts of the species emphasize its secretive nature, so they may well be underrecorded.

RICHARD STEEL

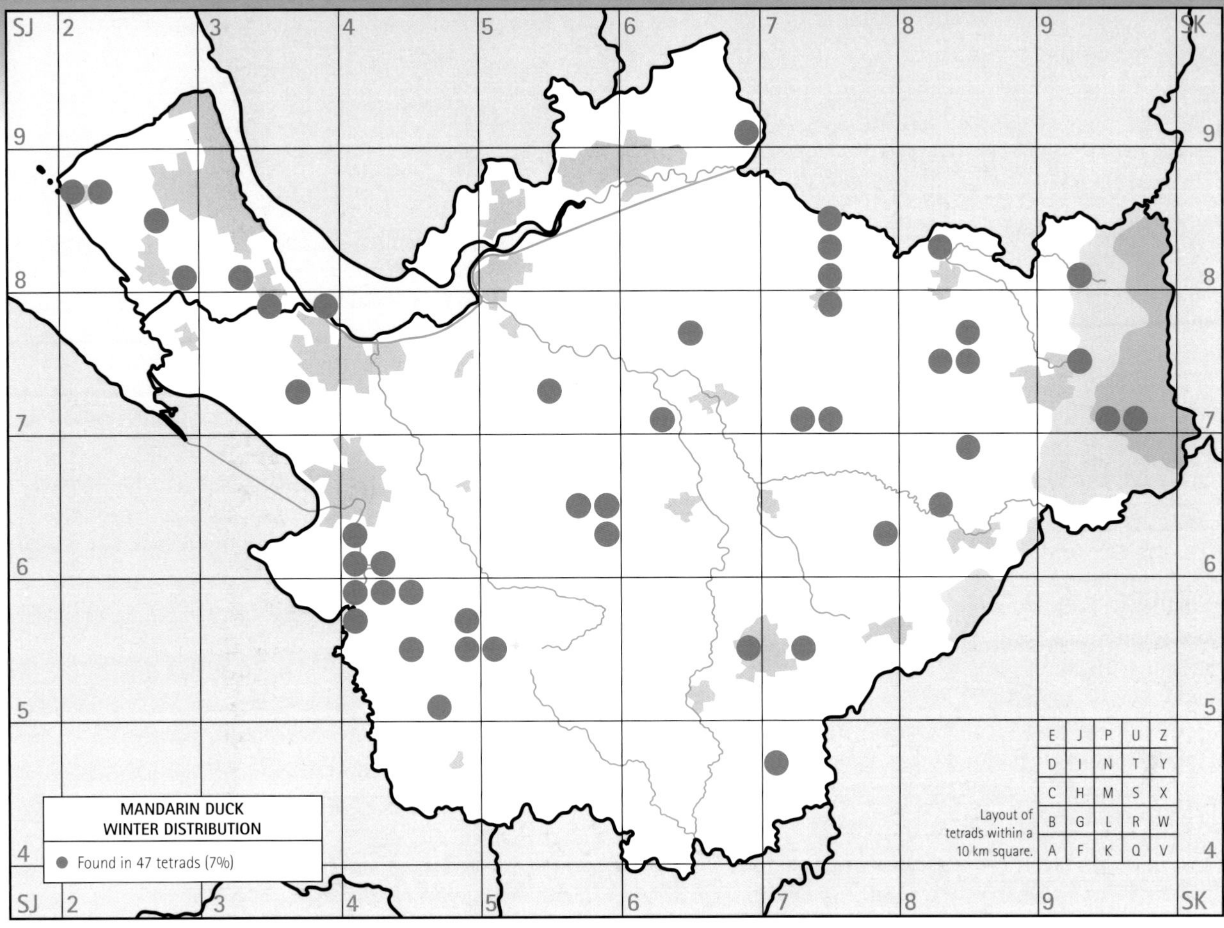
MANDARIN DUCK
WINTER DISTRIBUTION
Found in 47 tetrads (7%)
Layout of tetrads within a 10 km square.
SJ
SK
E J P U Z
D I N T Y
C H M S X
B G L R W
A F K Q V

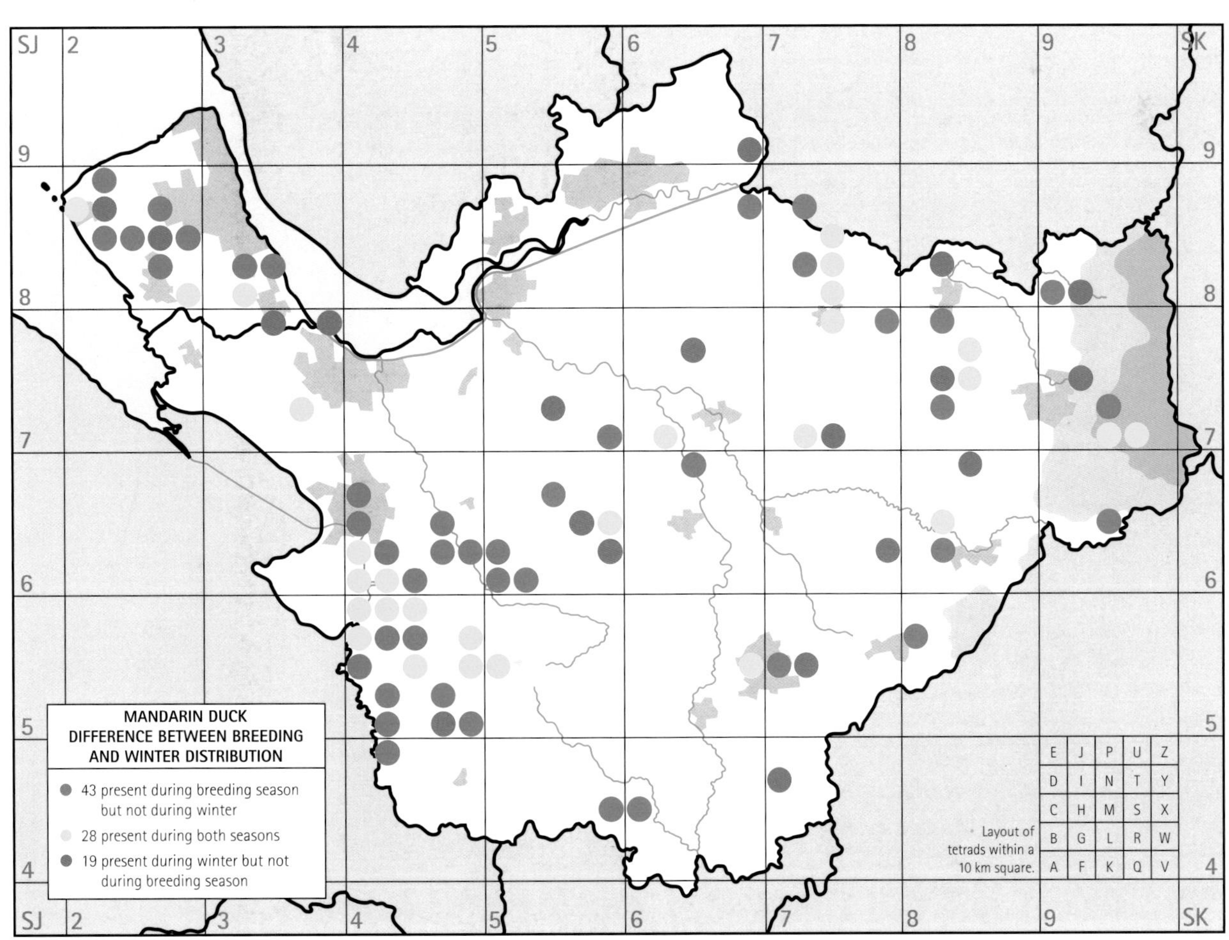
MANDARIN DUCK
DIFFERENCE BETWEEN BREEDING AND WINTER DISTRIBUTION
43 present during breeding season but not during winter
28 present during both seasons
19 present during winter but not during breeding season
Layout of tetrads within a 10 km square.
SJ
SK
E J P U Z
D I N T Y
C H M S X
B G L R W
A F K Q V

Wigeon

Anas penelope

There is no evidence that Wigeon has ever bred in the wild in Cheshire and Wirral, and the records in this Atlas survey were typical of those in many other years. Single birds were present in the breeding season at a number of sites, with some waters holding several birds. Of course, any sighting of a lone male duck in the breeding season should be followed up in case he has a nesting female hidden away, but none of them gave any hint of that. This vegetarian species is the wildfowlers' favourite, and a few summering Wigeons over the years are birds with 'pricked' wings, unable to fly well enough to migrate. Four tetrads had records of pairs in suitable breeding habitat, including birds displaying at Inner Marsh Farm (SJ37B), all counting as 'probable breeding', but nowhere has a nest ever been found or chicks seen.

This story is typical of most counties in Britain. Wigeon is a scarce enough breeding bird for its fortunes to be monitored by the Rare Breeding Birds Panel, and their report for 2004 shows that birds were summering in many counties, and pairs often present, but there were only 20 pairs confirmed breeding in England, in Essex (one pair), Northumberland (four pairs) and Yorkshire (15 pairs) (Holling *et al.* 2007a).

The *Second BTO Atlas*, covering 1988–91, showed that most of the British breeding Wigeons were in the north Pennines and Scotland. They were mainly nesting on the shores of upland lakes and bogs, and their breeding season requirements are little understood although they noticeably avoided acidic waters. The few sporadic breeders in East Anglia use habitats more akin to those in Cheshire. During this survey birds were recorded mostly on medium and large waters, with one pair on salt-marsh pools and others in water-meadows and reed-beds.

RAY SCALLY

Sponsored by Dr Bill Bellamy

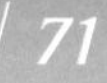

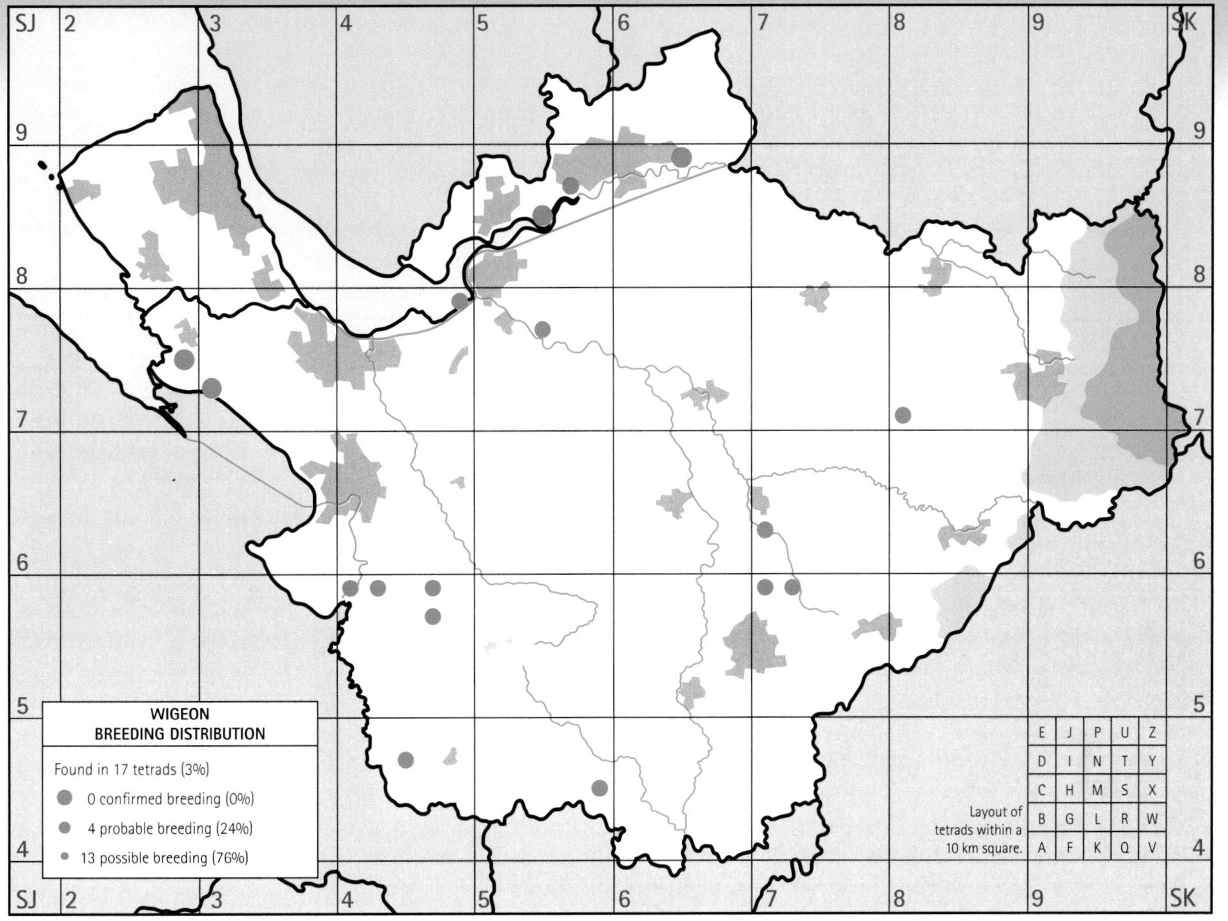

SJ
SK
2
3
4
5
6
7
8
9
WIGEON
BREEDING DISTRIBUTION
Found in 17 tetrads (3%)
0 confirmed breeding (0%)
4 probable breeding (24%)
13 possible breeding (76%)
E J P U Z
D I N T Y
C H M S X
B G L R W
A F K Q V
Layout of tetrads within a 10 km square.

SJ
SK
2
3
4
5
6
7
8
9
WIGEON
CHANGE IN BREEDING DISTRIBUTION
14 present during 2004–06, not during 1978–84 ('gain')
3 present during both Atlases
5 present during 1978–84, not during 2004–06 ('loss')
E J P U Z
D I N T Y
C H M S X
B G L R W
A F K Q V
Layout of tetrads within a 10 km square.

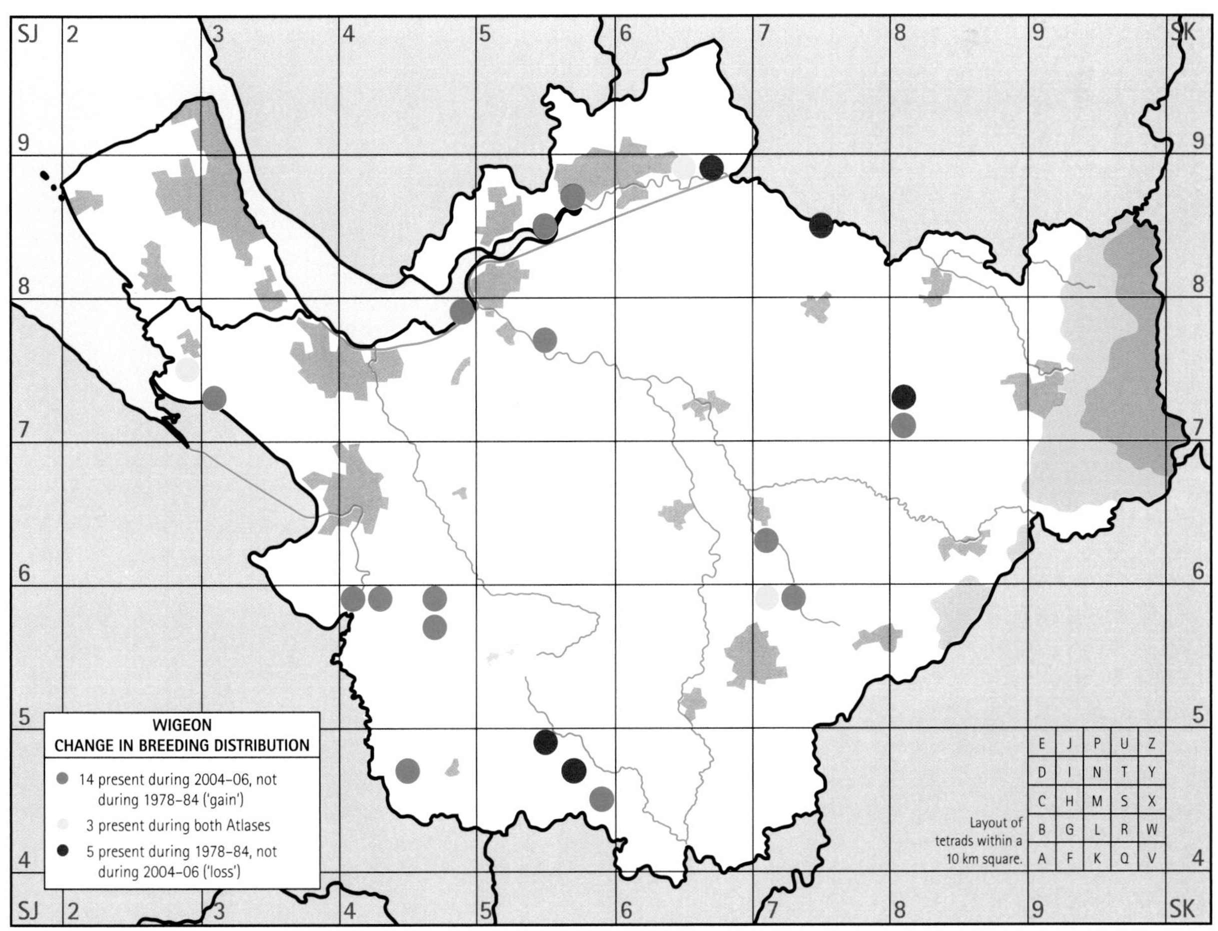

Wigeon were present in winter in 177 tetrads, just over one-quarter of the county. Coward would be surprised to see these figures, and this distribution map. Until the 1940s the great majority of the country's Wigeon was found feeding in intertidal areas, but then switched so that they now obtain most food from freshwater habitats. In 1910, Coward noted that 'during the winter months great numbers of Wigeon frequent the estuaries, and although the bird is less common inland it frequently visits the meres'. He gave no numbers for the estuaries but mentioned 50–60 birds on Rostherne Mere, 11 December 1908, implying that this was a large flock there. By Bell's time, Wigeon preferred the Mersey to the Dee, with the peak counts over 3,000 at Ince in January 1956 and February 1957, while the highest count on the Dee was 1,400 on 22 November 1959. It was also a regular visitor to many inland localities, among its main haunts being Rostherne, with a maximum count in the 1950s of 200 birds, Tatton (160), Comber Mere (370) and Doddington (150) (Bell 1962).

Wigeon come to Britain from breeding grounds in Iceland, Fennoscandia and Russia to at least 90°E; probably many of those in Cheshire and Wirral are from Iceland (Owen & Mitchell 1988). Overwhelmingly the most important site in Britain is the Ribble estuary, with around 80,000 birds, and there may well be interchange with the Dee and Mersey. The Mersey estuary used to be internationally important for the species but numbers have dropped rapidly from 9,150 in winter 2001/02 to only around 2,000 two years later, and continuing at that level during this Atlas period. In 2005/06 the five-year peak mean for the Mersey dropped below the 4,060 threshold for national importance. The Dee estuary maintains its nationally important status with a long-term average of around 4,700, although numbers there have fluctuated greatly, for instance from 2,464 in 2004/05 to 6,695 in the following winter.

Away from the estuaries, Wigeon can be found on almost all waterbodies although they are seldom recorded on the upland waters. The largest flocks reported during this Atlas were 800 on the Dee flood meadows near Worthenbury (SJ44I); 700 at Sandbach flashes (SJ75J); 550 grazing in a field at Handley (SJ45T); and 500 loafing on Frodsham Marsh (SJ47Z). As many as 40 tetrads had flocks of 100 or more, but the median flock size across all occupied tetrads is just 35. Males usually noticeably outnumber females in these flocks, and it would be an interesting exercise to quantify that statement.

Wigeon need to forage for about 14 hours a day to maintain condition during winter, so they feed day and night (Brown & Grice 2005). They are predominantly grazers and estuarine birds feed especially on the saltmarsh, eating copious amounts of the grass *Puccinellia maritima*. On the Mersey estuary, in recent years they have turned to eating seeds by day, much the same as Teal, and grazing by night. At inland sites they feed on any suitable short-cropped grass in areas with an open aspect and no trees nearby, including agricultural grassland, often around marl-pits and field ponds, as well as the edges of meres and other waters. As a grazing bird, Wigeons behave more like geese than other ducks, and in inland sites are often in association with flocks of Canada and Greylag Geese.

The submitted habitat codes show these preferences, although there are far more records from aquatic than

SIMON BOOTH

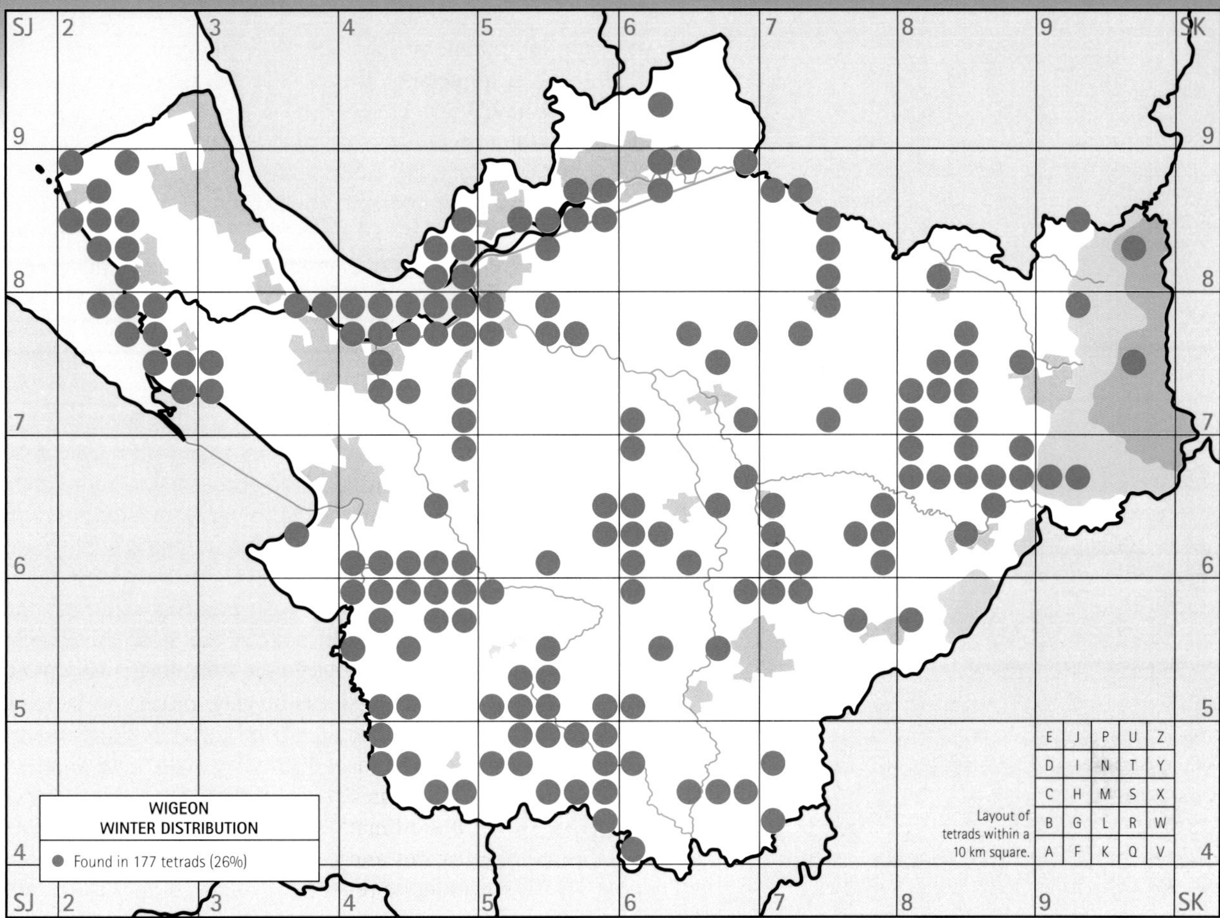

grassland habitats, presumably reflecting their preference for loafing on water by day and feeding at night when fieldworkers were seldom present. The inland habitats recorded include 11 records of wet semi-natural grassland (water-meadow/grazing marsh or reed swamp) and 14 on agricultural improved grassland, with birds on any size of standing water: 10 on ponds smaller than 50 m^2, 43 on small waterbodies and 76 on lakes, reservoirs and sandpits. Only four records came from linear watercourses, with only small numbers apart from on the upper river Mersey.

Gadwall

Anas strepera

Recent recruits to birdwatching are amazed to learn that Gadwalls had never bred in Cheshire until 1981, when they first nested at Woolston, but they are now widespread along the inner Mersey valley, and steadily spreading from there to other suitable waters. Probably all of the birds breeding in Britain derive from man's intervention. The first nesting in England was in the mid-nineteenth century in Norfolk, when a wild wintering pair was trapped, pinioned and later released to breed. These acted as the nucleus of a growing population, but the species did not spread beyond East Anglia. In the mid-twentieth century, birds started breeding at a variety of sites elsewhere, mostly near to wildfowl collections, and wildfowlers released captive-reared birds as well. The origin of the Cheshire birds is not known, but could be the Wildfowl & Wetlands Trust's centre at Martin Mere in Lancashire.

Whatever their source, Gadwalls have found several sites in the county to their liking, and the population is steadily growing. This is still a scarce species nationally, and its numbers are monitored by the Rare Breeding Birds Panel. In 2004, the Cheshire and Wirral population was reported to the RBBP as 31 pairs, clearly an underestimate, out of a national total of 1,520 pairs (Holling *et al.* 2007a). Most of the county's birds are at Woolston: at least 20 broods from an estimated minimum of 30 pairs; 20 broods again in 2005 and 15–17 broods in 2006.

Gadwalls forage almost exclusively on the green parts of plants, particularly emergent and subemergent macrophytes. This food is of such poor nutritional quality that the ducks have to eat vast amounts and so have to be able to feed undisturbed for long periods. They tend only to breed in areas where the biomass of food plants is high, predominantly in eutrophic waters. On deeper waters, such as gravel-pits and reservoirs, Gadwall steal food from Coots which bring up macrophytes from deeper water normally inaccessible to the dabbling Gadwall. Food obtained in this way can account for such a high proportion of their intake that this habit has allowed them to colonize waters that would otherwise be unsuitable for them. Kleptoparasitism from Coots does not seem to have been recorded in Cheshire and Wirral, however, and it would be interesting to record its occurrence and spread.

In this survey, Gadwalls were reported using a range of wet habitats: two-thirds were on lakes, reservoirs and sand quarries, but one pair was on a small pond in Tatton Park (SJ78L) and in six tetrads they were using small waterbodies, two of them holding broods of chicks. Breeding birds were also found on the river Weaver Bend (SJ57E) and at two sites on the Manchester Ship Canal, although perhaps the birds had nested elsewhere nearby. Four were found in wet grassland (C6, C7, C9) including, unusually, a pair on a Dee salt-marsh pool; they are almost invariably birds of fresh water. The actual nesting site may be well away from water, however: nests at Woolston have frequently been found in the dry centre of no. 4 bed, about 500 m from water. The females lead their chicks to the pools, with the first hatching from about late May, and new broods of chicks still being seen into early July.

Sponsored by James Coyne

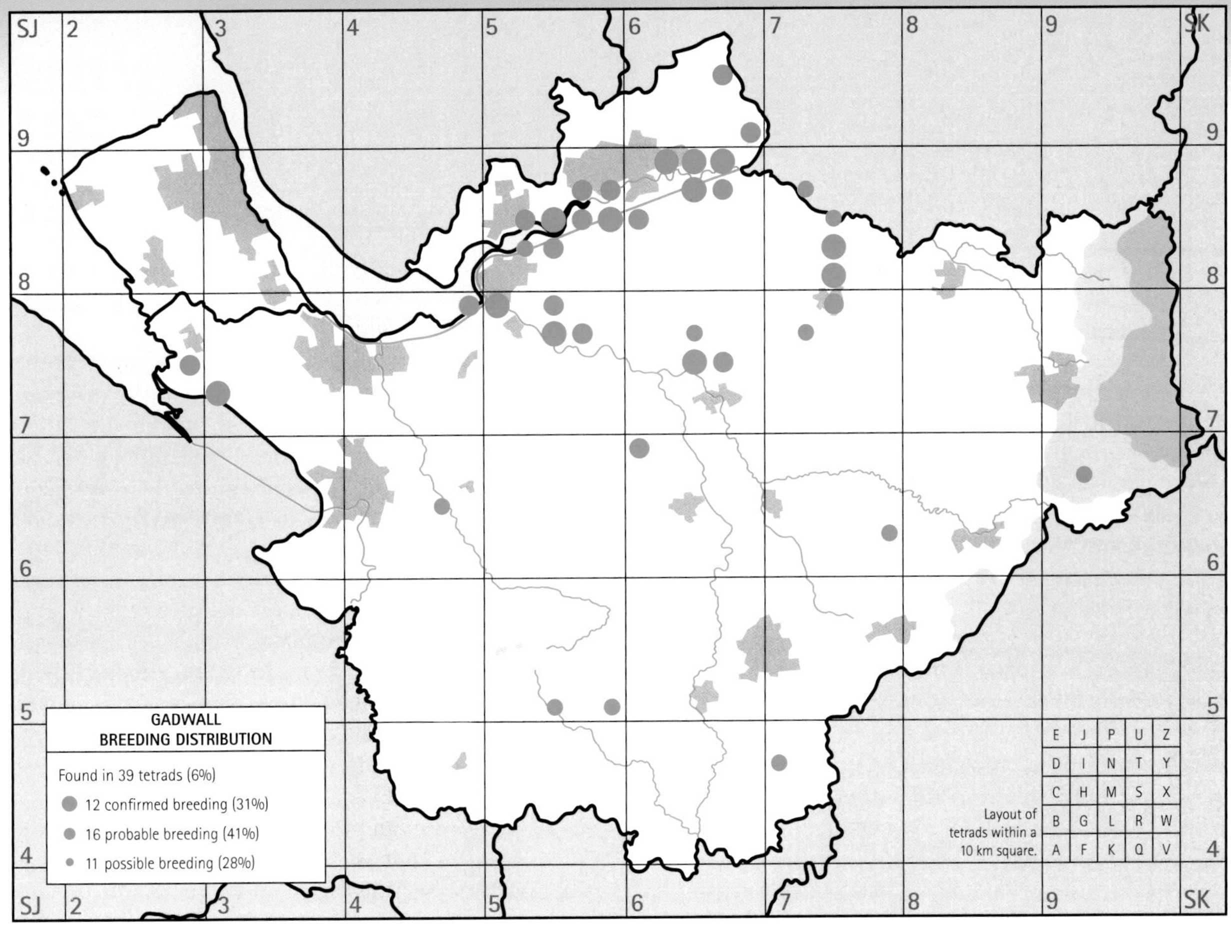
SJ
2
3
4
5
6
7
8
9
SK
GADWALL
BREEDING DISTRIBUTION
Found in 39 tetrads (6%)
12 confirmed breeding (31%)
16 probable breeding (41%)
11 possible breeding (28%)
Layout of
tetrads within a
10 km square.
E J P U Z
D I N T Y
C H M S X
B G L R W
A F K Q V

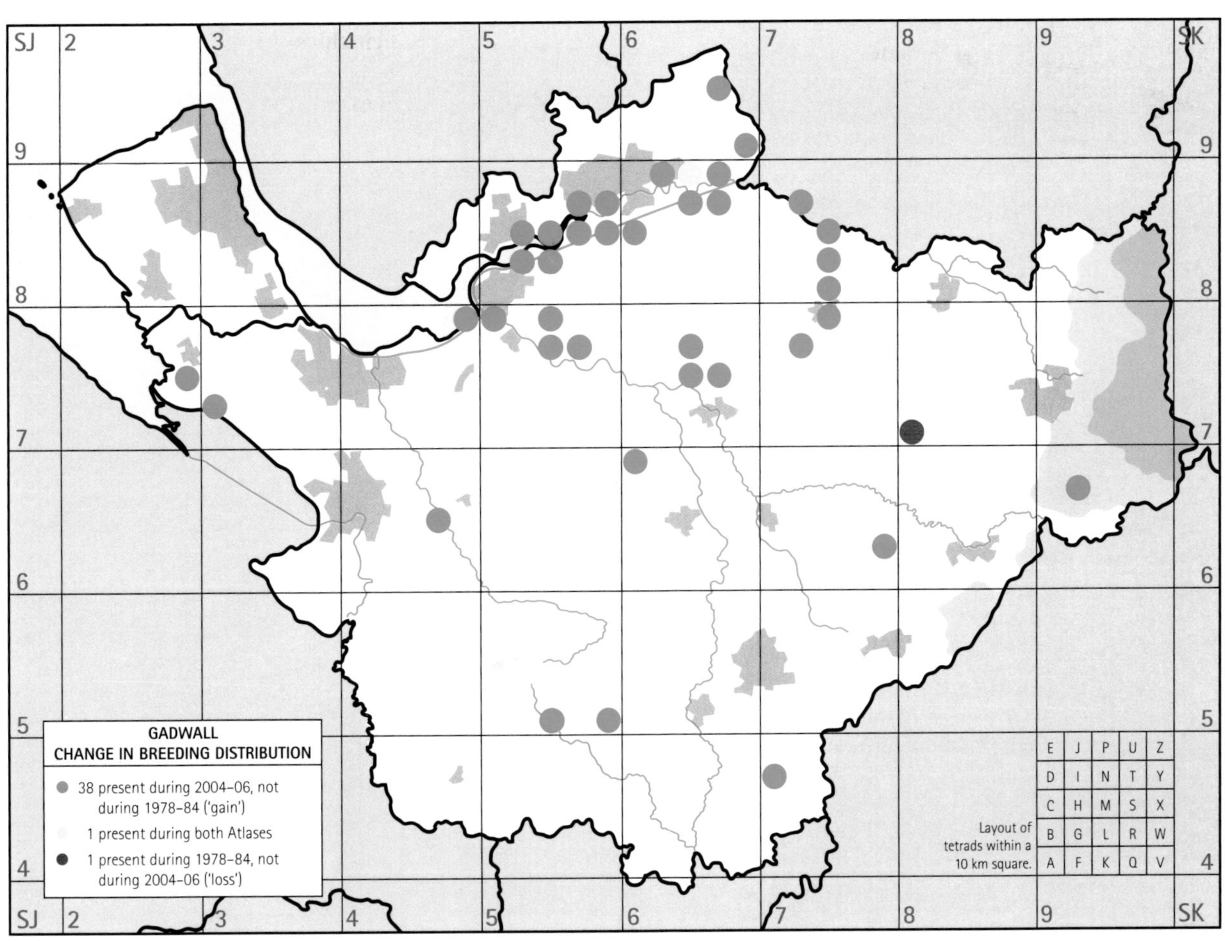
SJ
2
3
4
5
6
7
8
9
SK
GADWALL
CHANGE IN BREEDING DISTRIBUTION
38 present during 2004–06, not during 1978–84 ('gain')
1 present during both Atlases
1 present during 1978–84, not during 2004–06 ('loss')
Layout of
tetrads within a
10 km square.
E J P U Z
D I N T Y
C H M S X
B G L R W
A F K Q V

Gadwalls were found wintering in 54 tetrads, rather more than the 39 with birds recorded during the breeding season, the extra sites being especially in the west and south-west of Cheshire, and SJ86 and SJ87 in the east. Birds were recorded in similar habitats to the breeding season, with 59% on lakes, reservoirs and sandpits, although with a higher proportion (21%) on ponds or small waterbodies perhaps suggesting that, without the demands of a growing brood, even ponds and small waters can provide the food to satisfy their needs. Two birds seen on the Mersey in SJ37Z and in SJ58G were the only estuarine birds.

Between one-third and a half of the Gadwalls wintering in Britain and Ireland originate in eastern Europe, normally as far as the Baltic States, supplementing the largely resident breeding birds and their progeny (*Migration Atlas*). However, the movements of Cheshire and Wirral birds are not known and perhaps some of them could, like Icelandic and Scottish breeders, winter in Ireland.

The British wintering population has risen tenfold in the last 40 years, leading to frequent revisions in the qualifying figures for the national or international importance of a site. Nowhere in the county currently approaches the threshold for international importance of a five-year peak mean of 600 birds, but Woolston is in the top thirty British sites and is nationally important. This species, however, seems to have a history of erratic fluctuations in numbers at a site, with WeBS counts sometimes rising or falling dramatically from one year to another, for reasons that are not understood (Banks *et al.* 2006).

It was only in 1989 that the first three-figure count was recorded anywhere in the county, at Woolston and at Rostherne Mere, and Rostherne was Cheshire's premier Gadwall wintering site until 1997 as Woolston no. 3 bed recovered from the drainage in 1991, emphasizing both the vulnerability of birds being too concentrated on one site, and the value of having alternative suitable refuges. Numbers at Woolston usually peak in August or September, averaging around 250 (Banks *et al.* 2006)—the 470 on 19 September 2004 was a county record—but the highest count during this winter Atlas was 160 birds on 8 February 2006, most of them on the Loop of no. 4 bed, an area specially created for nature conservation. Other than parts of the Woolston complex, the only sites with significant counts, just over 50 birds each, were Moore Nature Reserve (SJ58X) and Abbots Moss (SJ56Z).

These numbers would have been unthinkable to Cheshire's early ornithologists. Coward described Gadwall as a rare visitor to the Dee estuary, and knew of only two records, in March 1845 and October 1908. It appears that the first in winter was one at Rostherne on 5 December 1936 (Boyd 1946). Bell traced over 50 records after 1944 in every month except June, but mainly in April, September and October, and they were only present in very small numbers, with the maximum ever seen together just four birds (Bell 1962).

STEVE ROUND

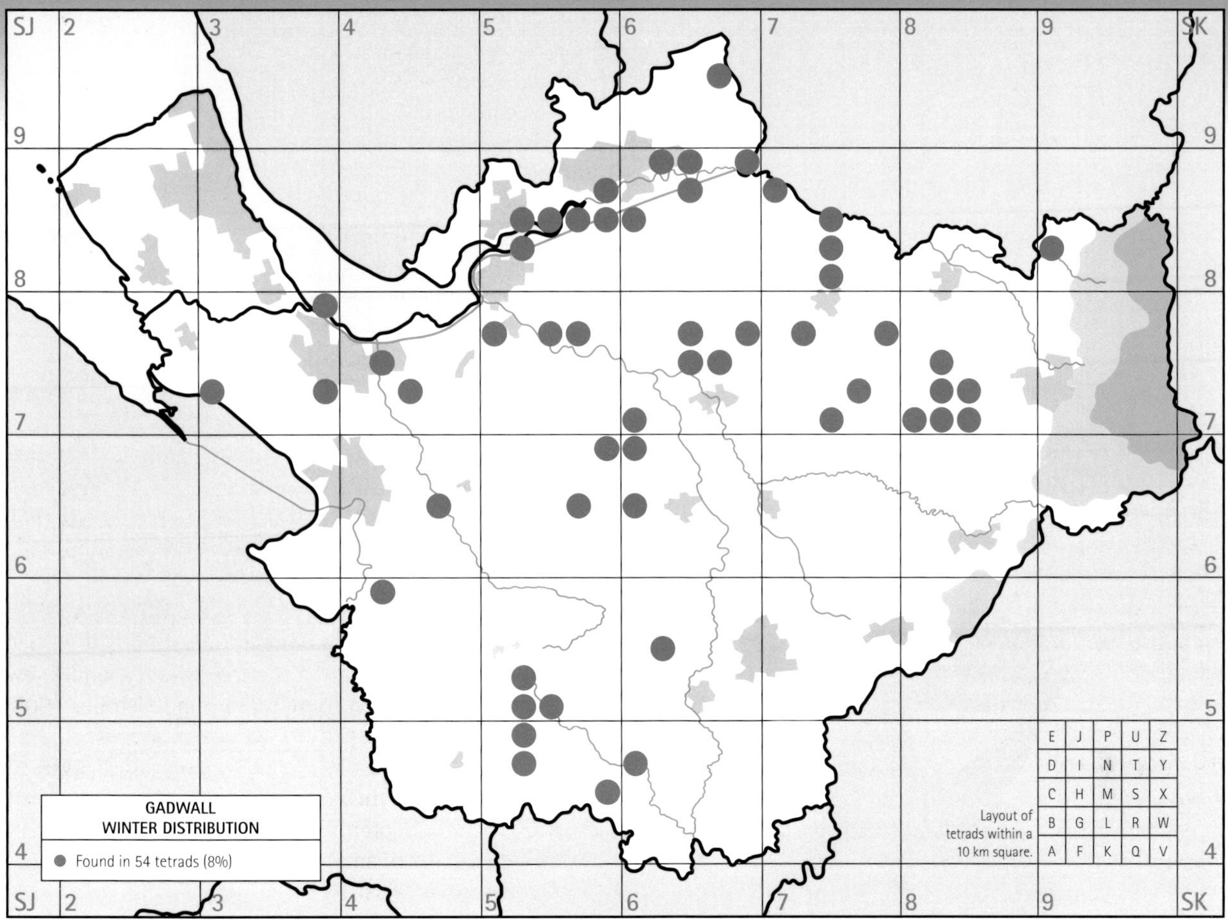
SJ
SK
GADWALL
WINTER DISTRIBUTION
Found in 54 tetrads (8%)
Layout of
tetrads within a
10 km square.
E J P U Z
D I N T Y
C H M S X
B G L R W
A F K Q V

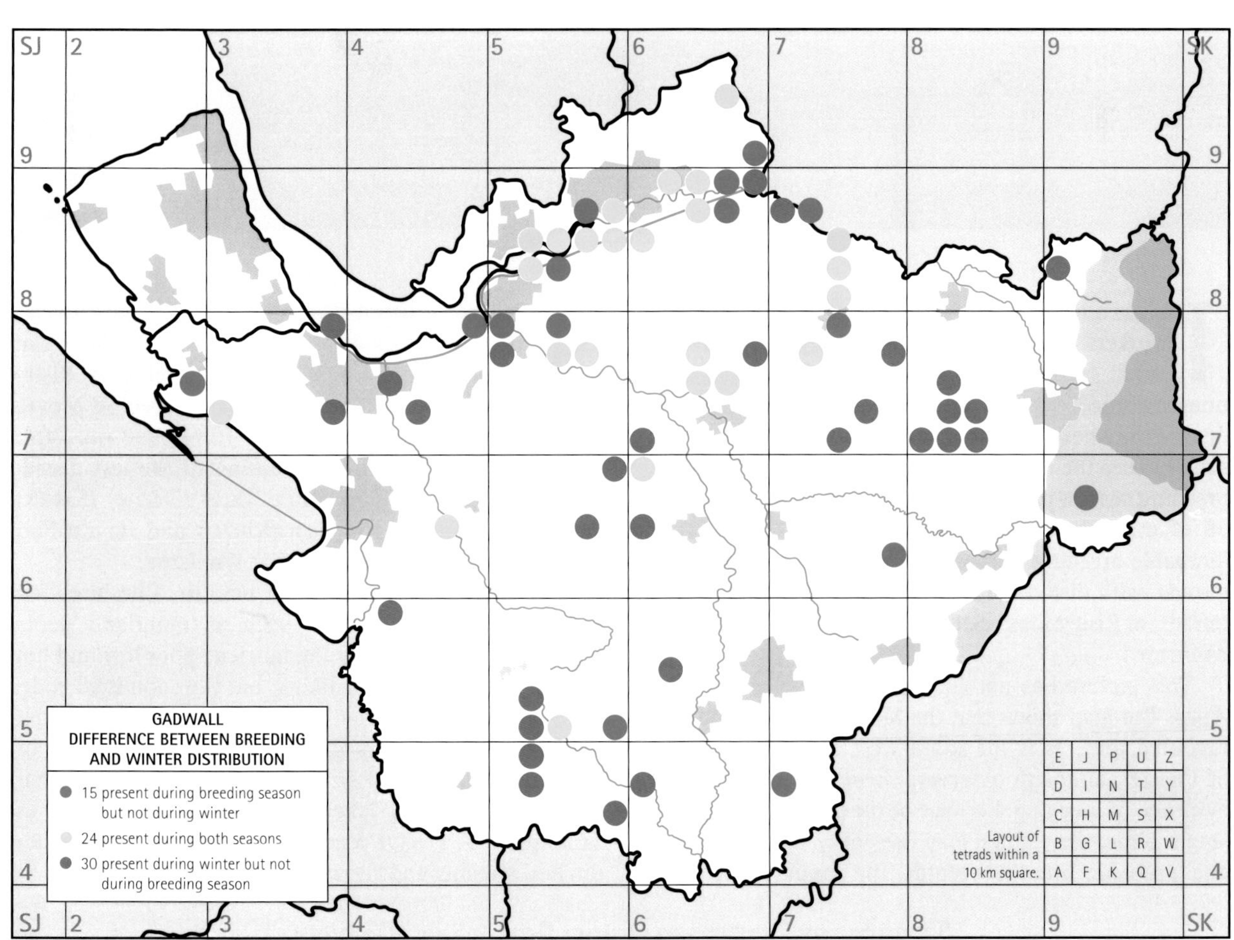
SJ
SK
GADWALL
DIFFERENCE BETWEEN BREEDING
AND WINTER DISTRIBUTION
15 present during breeding season but not during winter
24 present during both seasons
30 present during winter but not during breeding season
Layout of
tetrads within a
10 km square.
E J P U Z
D I N T Y
C H M S X
B G L R W
A F K Q V

Cheshire and Wirral may well be the premier county in Britain for wintering Teal, as nowhere else has three sites with conservation designations for the species. The total county population is probably around 25,000 birds, about one-sixth of the total wintering in Great Britain. The Mersey estuary has been, since the mid-1970s, the most important British site for wintering Teal, although overtaken lately by the Somerset Levels. The Mersey's five-year peak mean is almost 10,000 birds, double the threshold for international importance and a significant part of the estuary's status as a European Special Protection Area and Ramsar site. Nationally important totals are also found on the Dee estuary, averaging 4,400 Teal, of which about 3,000 are usually in Cheshire and Wirral, and at the Woolston Eyes, with around 2,000 birds.

Counts exceeding 1,000 Teal were also made at Rostherne (SJ78M), and flocks of more than 500 birds were recorded at Aldford (SJ45J), the upper Mersey at Astmoor (SJ58H) and Fiddler's Ferry (SJ58M), and Elton Flash (SJ75J). Teal are not just concentrated at those major sites, however, and this Atlas shows that in winter, this is our second most widespread duck, being recorded in half of the county's tetrads. Despite the emphasis on large numbers at specially protected sites, more than 500 counts were submitted during the three years of this Atlas and half of them were of flocks smaller than 25 birds.

Their widespread distribution arises largely from their ability to use small patches of water, and they are often found on marl-pits and farm ponds. The habitat codes submitted by observers showed birds spread across all types of waters, although they clearly avoid canals, which presumably provide little food in winter. Seventy-eight records were G1 (pond less than 50 m^2), 77 G2 (small waterbody 50–450 m^2), and 76 G3 (lake/unlined reservoir). The map shows that they are not found on the upland reservoirs. Fifty-three were on flowing water: 25 on rivers and 28 on narrow streams or ditches. Fourteen records came from waterlogged woodland, far more than any other waterbird. Records came from 35 estuarine tetrads.

Teal feed by day and night in shallow water, by dabbling or up-ending, taking mainly plant seeds and some animal matter such as chironomid larvae and small snails. The mud-flats, creeks and salt-marshes of the estuaries provide this combination in profusion, with the Mersey, especially along the south shore where the Teal mostly congregate, in addition offering welcome protection from the prevailing winds and a slightly warmer microclimate from the local industry. On both estuaries, the seeds of salt-marsh plants are taken, especially glasswort *Salicornia* and orache *Atriplex*; at Woolston the highest numbers of Teal have come when the operations of the Manchester Ship Canal Company have flooded no. 2 bed, flushing especially

RICHARD STEEL

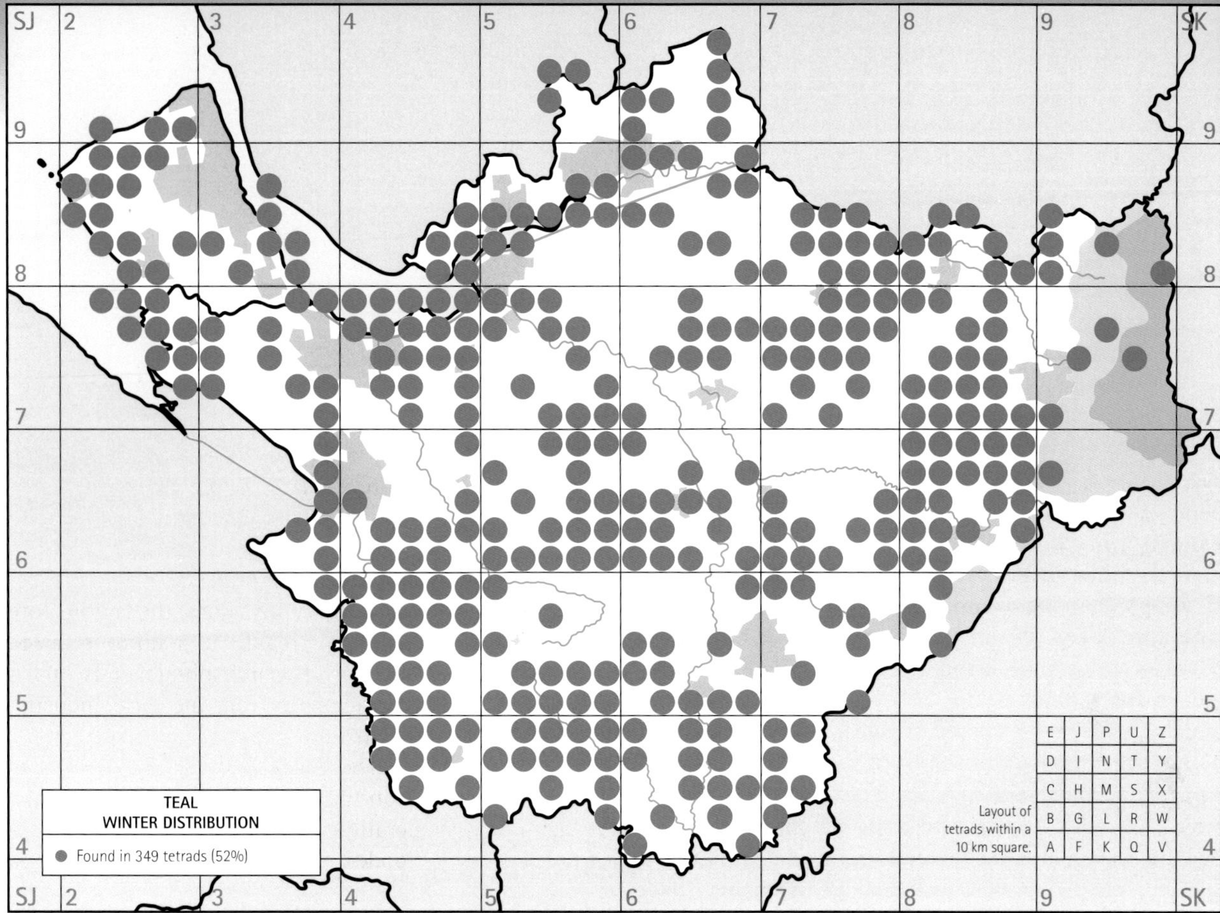

seeds of fat-hen *Chenopodium album* and redshank *Polygonum persicaria* into the water. On occasion thousands of birds have been seen flying into the site at dusk to gorge on the abundant food.

The status of Teal in the county has clearly changed in the last hundred years. Coward (1910) wrote that on the estuaries it was more abundant as a bird of passage than a winter resident. Bell (1962) noted that this species had become much commoner, particularly in winter, since the beginning of the twentieth century. At that time, Rostherne was the inland water with by far the largest counts, exceeding 3,000 at the peak, with similar numbers on the Mersey, even then recognized as their preferred estuarine site.

Thanks to the work of Merseyside Ringing Group, mainly Rob Cockbain at Hale Duck Decoy, we have a very good picture of the origins of our wintering Teal, which arrive here in autumn, from late August onwards, from breeding grounds to the north-east, especially in Finland and northern Russia as far east as the Pechora River. This small duck can be especially susceptible to hard weather, when shallow pools freeze. On 13 December 1981, one of the coldest days of the late twentieth century, the Mersey WeBS counters were treated to the ornithological spectacle of a lifetime when a minimum of 35,000 Teal were gathered in Stanlow Bay: all inland waters were frozen and birds had flown to the estuary to find food. If driven by frost, some Teal move to Ireland, with smaller numbers to France; this is the opposite of the picture for southern England, where almost all hard-weather movements are across the Channel. Similarly, few of the birds ringed in Cheshire have wintered farther south in later years, again contrary to the national figures, and there is clearly a north-south divide in the habits of this species.

The numbers of Teal at a site can vary greatly from month to month. The British total peaks in December and January, showing that some movement continues during the winter. An extreme example of mobility was provided by one unlucky Teal ringed at Hale on 4 September 1979 at 13.00 hours that was shot the same evening on the Humber, having flown across the country during the afternoon.

Mallard

Anas platyrhynchos

This is the most widespread and successful duck in the world, and also probably the bird best known to everyone in Britain from the age of two or three onwards. It is now almost ubiquitous in Cheshire and Wirral, present during the breeding season in 635 of the 670 tetrads, by far the most extensive distribution of any waterbird and the fifteenth most widespread species. In the twenty years since our *First Atlas* it has spread into a further 57 tetrads, having filled all of the major gaps, on Hilbre and north-west Wirral, a broad swathe through the centre of the county and at the highest points of the eastern hills. It is probably only missing from parts of urban east Wirral, as in our *First Atlas*, and a few upland tetrads.

They were proven breeding in more than three-quarters of the tetrads, nearly all by observers seeing the female Mallard with a brood of ducklings. She is ignored by her drake as soon as she is incubating the clutch of eggs, as he then tries to mate with any spare female. They can breed at any time from March, normally to August, but a brood of week-old chicks was seen at Quaker's Coppice, Crewe, as late as 18 November 1996. The nest itself may be well away from water, Mallards frequently featuring in local newspapers for their choice of odd sites from which the mother leads her ducklings across land to reach water. Perhaps because of their semi-domesticated origins, many birds seem quite at home in the presence of humans. Nests were reported in farm buildings and in a house roof space 5 m high, although most nests are in undergrowth on the ground. The typical clutch is 10 eggs, allowing for large losses from the brood of ducklings. Many observers commented on high levels of predation, of chicks and adults, by mink, rats and red-eared terrapins. The higher success rate of nests on islands probably reflects the importance of nocturnal safety from foxes.

Mallards can utilize almost any type of water. The submitted habitat codes comprised 163 G1 (pond less than 50 m^2); 195 G2 (small waterbody 50–450 m^2); 100 G3 (lake/unlined reservoir); 7 G4 (lined reservoir); 25 G5 (gravel-pit, sandpit, etc.); 45 G6 (stream less than 3 m wide); 41 G7 (river more than 3 m wide); 26 G8 (ditch with water less than 2 m wide); 43 G9 (small canal 2–5 m wide); and 38 G10 (large canal more than 5 m wide); as well as other habitats such as waterlogged woodland, reed-beds and salt-marsh. Some fieldworkers noted their propensity to occupy recently created ponds: in urban Runcorn (SJ58K), with little standing water, Mallard was the last species that I found in the tetrad, breeding in 2006 on a small pond so new that it does not appear on the Ordnance Survey maps. The key food for chicks is hatching chironomid midges, so the best waters have an abundance of insect-rich shallows.

MIKE ATKINSON

During the 1990s *CWBRs* contained a number of comments about birds breeding for the first time at well-watched sites, and the population at others has climbed steadily. The three years of this Atlas saw record numbers of broods at Woolston: 55, 58 and 53 breeding in 2004, 2005, 2006. Birds there were widespread across the site, including all parts of the dredging deposit grounds, the Manchester Ship Canal and the river Mersey.

The BTO analysis of BBS results shows that the breeding population of Cheshire and Wirral in 2004–05 is estimated at 35,630 birds (with 95% statistical confidence limits of 22,440–48,830). This figure, an average of almost 60 birds per tetrad with confirmed and probable breeding, amounts to 2.2% of the UK total of birds in just 1% of the UK's area, showing that Cheshire and Wirral is especially significant for breeding Mallard. The county's status as the 'pond capital of the UK' must underlie that importance.

This total dwarfs the estimate of 'around 1,500 pairs' given in our *First Atlas*. The national breeding population rose by one-third in the period between our two Atlases, but the *First Atlas* figure must surely have been a substantial underestimate. It is suggested that a large part of the increase in breeding numbers may be attributable to releases of Mallard for shooting (Marchant *et al.* 1990). Unfortunately, there is no information collated on releases of captive-reared Mallard in Cheshire and Wirral. Nationally, 14% of the shoots submitting data to the National Gamebag Census released reared Mallard in 1984, but it is not known how this has changed in the last twenty years (Tapper 1999).

Sponsored by Mark Greenhough

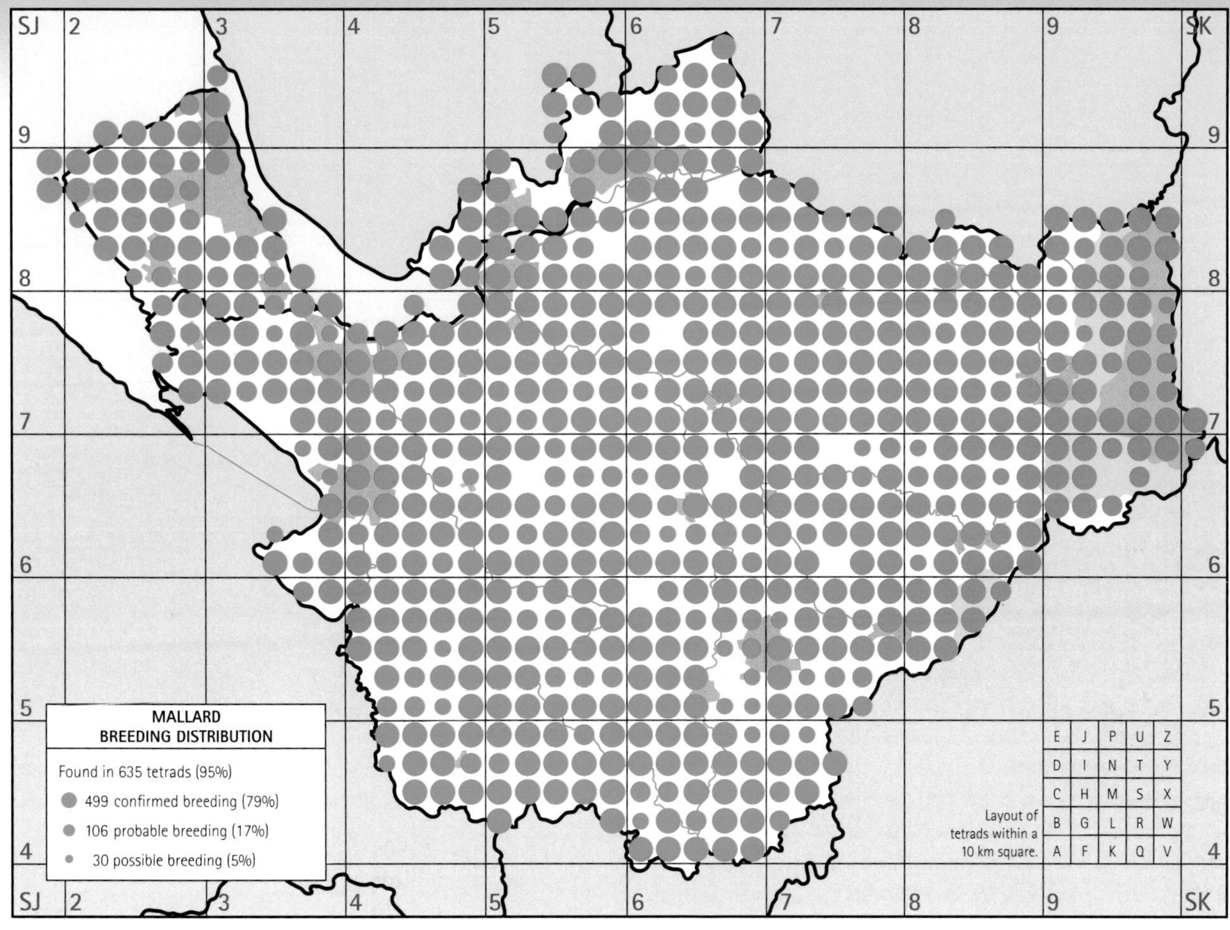
MALLARD
BREEDING DISTRIBUTION
Found in 635 tetrads (95%)
499 confirmed breeding (79%)
106 probable breeding (17%)
30 possible breeding (5%)
Layout of tetrads within a 10 km square.
E J P U Z
D I N T Y
C H M S X
B G L R W
A F K Q V
SJ
SK

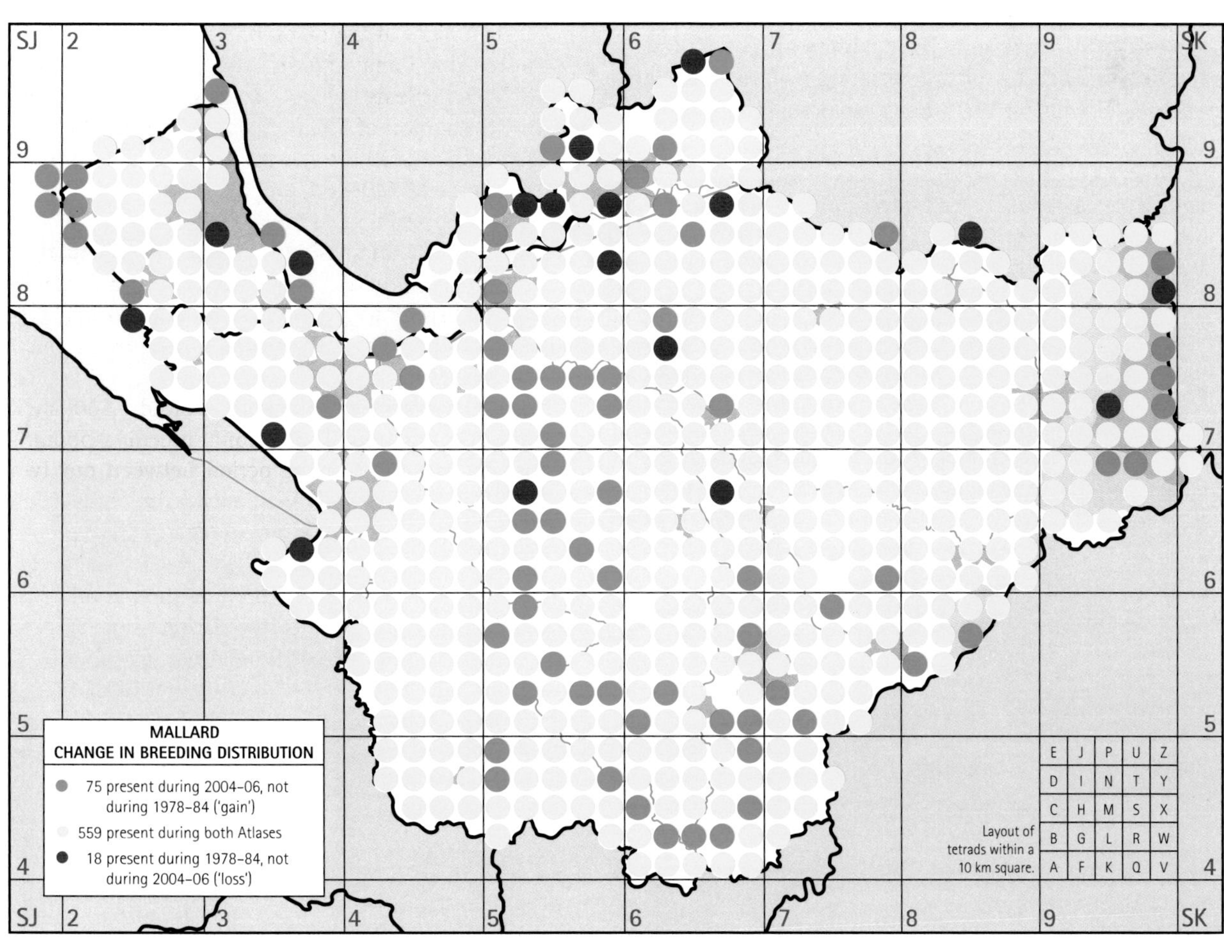
MALLARD
CHANGE IN BREEDING DISTRIBUTION
75 present during 2004–06, not during 1978–84 ('gain')
559 present during both Atlases
18 present during 1978–84, not during 2004–06 ('loss')
Layout of tetrads within a 10 km square.
E J P U Z
D I N T Y
C H M S X
B G L R W
A F K Q V
SJ
SK

In contrast to the burgeoning breeding population, wintering numbers of Mallard have been dropping since the late 1970s (Banks *et al.* 2006), apparently because of a decrease in immigration from continental Europe. Our breeding Mallard are quite sedentary, with a median distance of movement of 22 km (*Migration Atlas*). A few birds fly to continental Europe, including a chick ringed at Frodsham in 1968, shot in the Netherlands in winter 1979/80: almost all of the emigrants are males. Birds have come here especially from Finland and southern Sweden, with smaller numbers from all other countries from Russia to France. The proportion of immigrants in the British wintering population has declined greatly, from 50–60% in the 1950s and 1960s and 40% in the 1970s to only about 15% in the 1990s (*Migration Atlas*).

WeBS counts show that Mallards are widely distributed across many sites, such that only at the Ouse Washes do the numbers exceed 1% of the British total of 350,000 birds and thus qualify as nationally important for the species. The picture in Cheshire and Wirral has clearly changed in the last 40 years, particularly at Rostherne Mere. Coward (1910) noted that on Rostherne, one of the deepest and latest to freeze of the meres, there were often thousands of Mallards when the shallow and more exposed waters were frost-bound. In the first volume summarizing national counts of wildfowl (Atkinson-Willes 1963), numbers of Mallard at Rostherne Mere were 'larger than on any inland water in England', with peak totals of 4,000 in the early 1960s. At that time, Comber Mere and Doddington were the county's next most important sites with counts of 600 and 410 in January 1966 (Bell 1967).

Nowadays the picture is very different. The largest wintering numbers are on the estuaries, with the highest WeBS counts during the three winters of this Atlas of 1,117 on the Dee (including sites outside Cheshire and Wirral) and 883 on the Mersey. Other sites with peak monthly counts in winter exceeding 300, as listed in the *CWBRs*, were Chelford Sand Quarries with 885, Hurleston with 367 and the Sandbach Flashes with 315. The largest individual tetrad counts were 476 at Doddington (SJ74D) on a WeBS count in 2004/05 and 450 in the Gowy flood plain (SJ47G) in 2004/05. Sadly, 206 birds was the maximum at Rostherne, in December 2006, about one-twentieth of the figure 45 years previously.

The Atlas map shows Mallards present in winter in 624 tetrads compared to 635 in the breeding season. Birds were recorded in most estuarine tetrads, in the shallow waters close to shore, but quit 40 in which they were present during the breeding season, including some of the highest eastern tetrads. All of the freshwater habitats were occupied in similar proportions to the breeding season, but with a small shift away from the ponds and smaller standing waters to lakes and rivers, and 32 estuarine/salt-marsh tetrads. Even in the winter flocks, many birds have one eye on the coming breeding season and they seem to keep more or less in pairs, the male following the female closely. Mallards shift to a more vegetarian diet during winter but take a very wide variety of foods. On water they dabble, up-end and occasionally dive in shallow water for seeds and invertebrates. Provided that they feel safe enough, some will feed well away from water, on stubble and other agricultural waste, fruit and of course the inevitable offers of bread from the great British public.

RICHARD STEEL

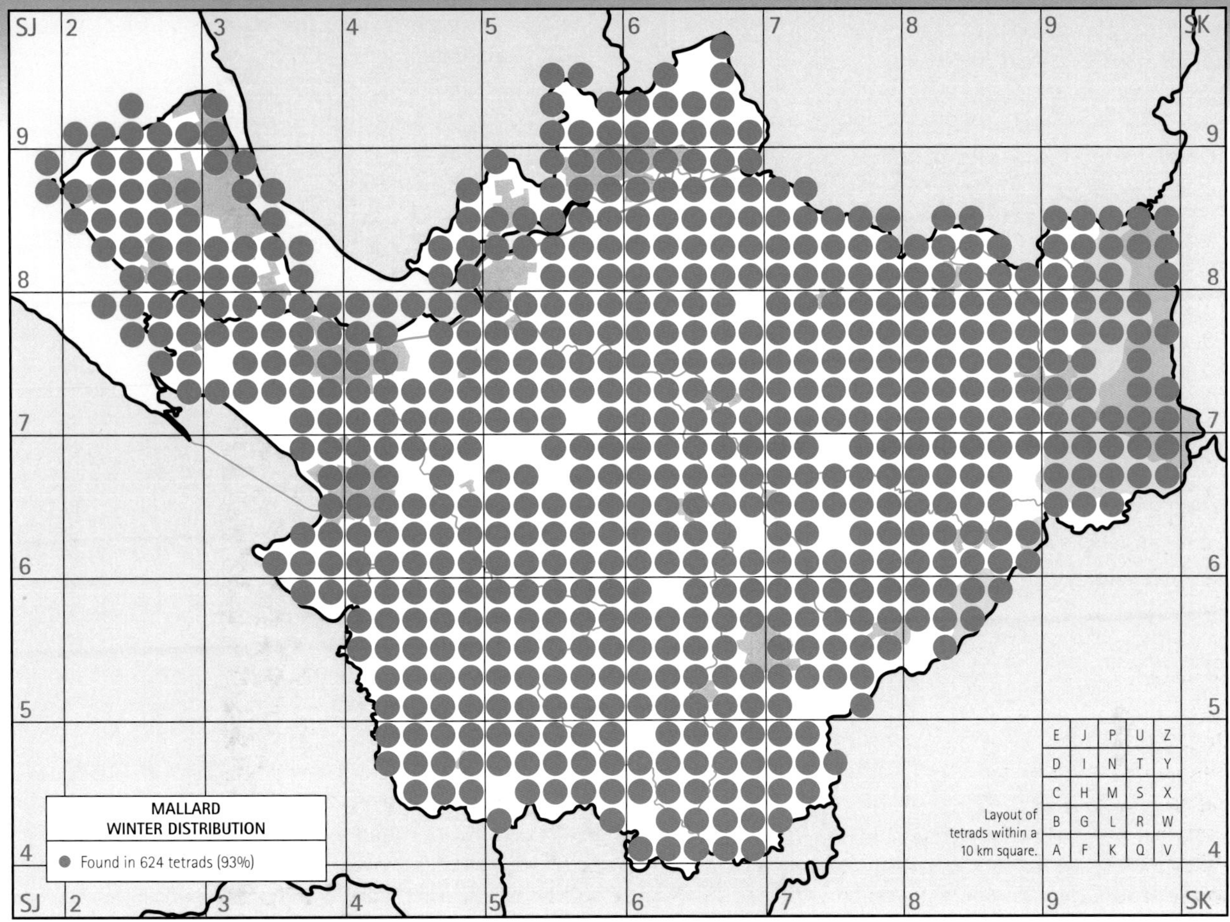
SJ
2
3
4
5
6
7
8
9
SK
9
8
7
6
5
4
MALLARD
WINTER DISTRIBUTION
Found in 624 tetrads (93%)
E J P U Z
D I N T Y
C H M S X
B G L R W
A F K Q V
Layout of tetrads within a 10 km square.

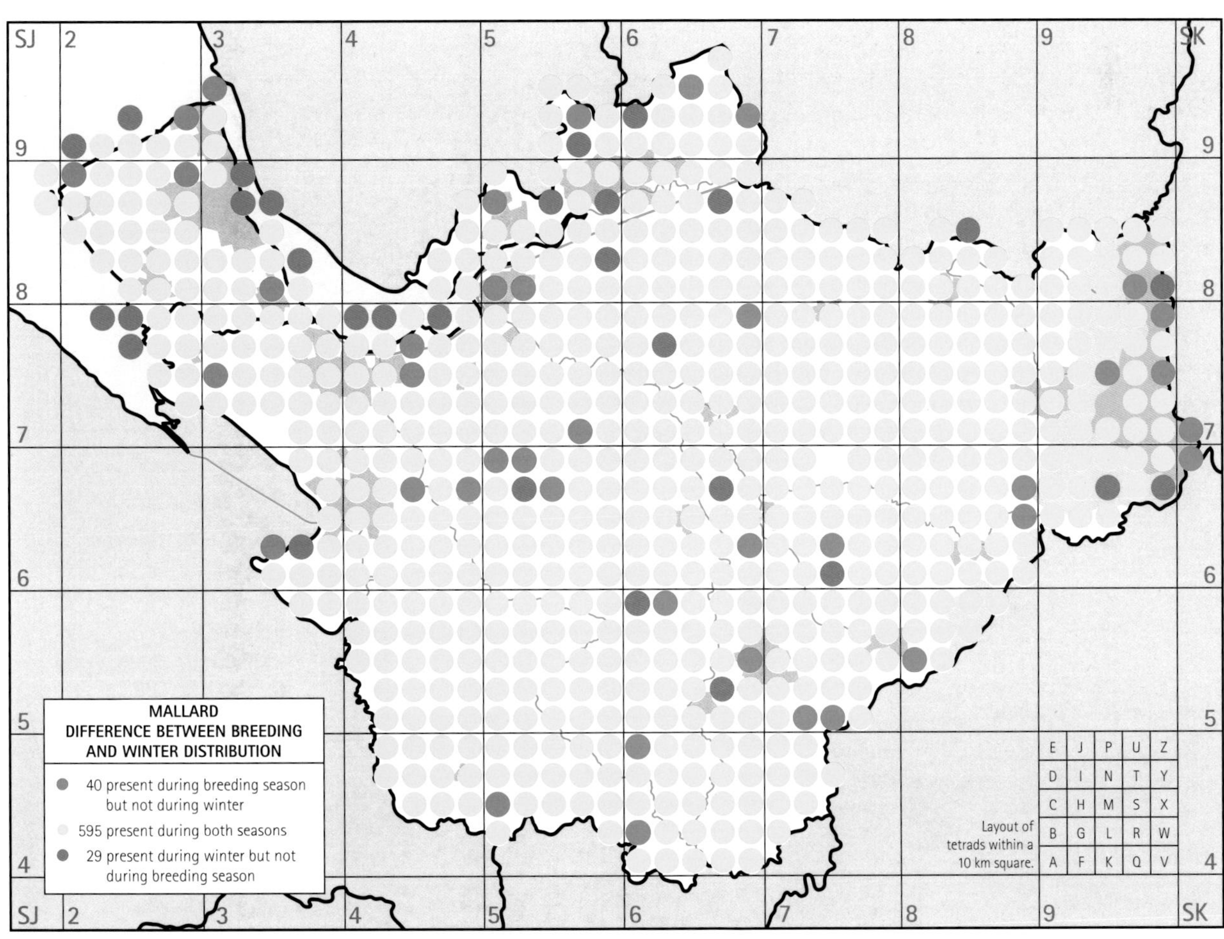
SJ
2
3
4
5
6
7
8
9
SK
9
8
7
6
5
4
MALLARD
DIFFERENCE BETWEEN BREEDING AND WINTER DISTRIBUTION
40 present during breeding season but not during winter
595 present during both seasons
29 present during winter but not during breeding season
E J P U Z
D I N T Y
C H M S X
B G L R W
A F K Q V
Layout of tetrads within a 10 km square.

Pintail

Anas acuta

RAY SCALLY

The records submitted for this Atlas were typical of any of the last 35 years. Pintails have not been found breeding in the county since a female seen with young at Frodsham Marsh in 1969. In many years pairs are present, sometimes displaying, as during this Atlas period. There were no records in 2004. In 2005 a pair was found near the river Weaver at Aston (SJ57N); the male went into eclipse plumage in July. In 2006, three pairs displayed at Inner Marsh Farm (SJ37B), another pair was present at Aldford (SJ45J) and a single female summered in Runcorn Town Park Lake (SJ58L).

Their few breeding sites in Britain are mostly open grassy areas adjacent to shallow eutrophic freshwater or brackish coastal pools, with a copious supply of invertebrates, especially small mud-snails. The national total of breeding birds was only 12–22 pairs in 2004 (Holling *et al.* 2007a).

Sponsored by www.deeestuary.co.uk

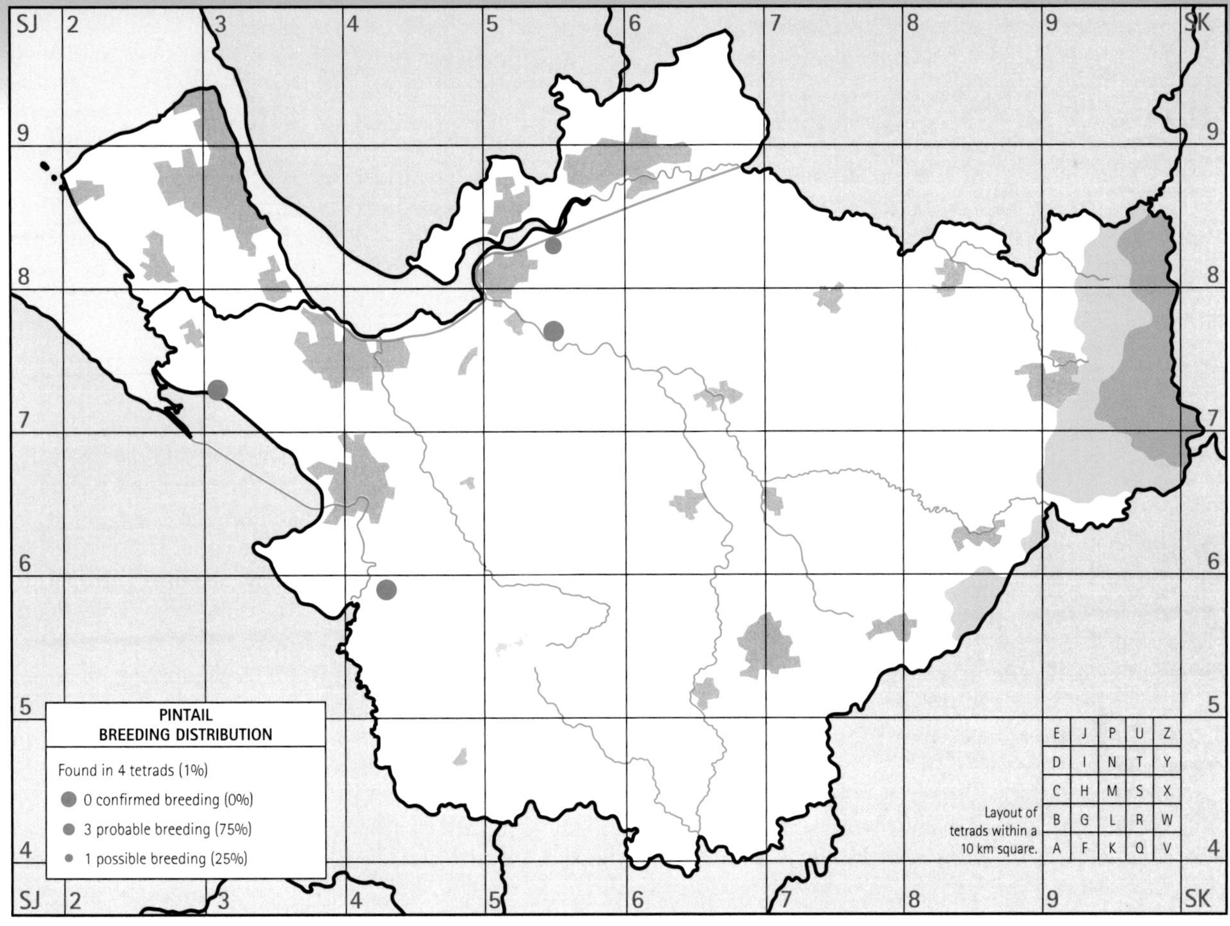
SJ
2
3
4
5
6
7
8
9
SK
PINTAIL
BREEDING DISTRIBUTION
Found in 4 tetrads (1%)
0 confirmed breeding (0%)
3 probable breeding (75%)
1 possible breeding (25%)
Layout of tetrads within a 10 km square.
E J P U Z
D I N T Y
C H M S X
B G L R W
A F K Q V

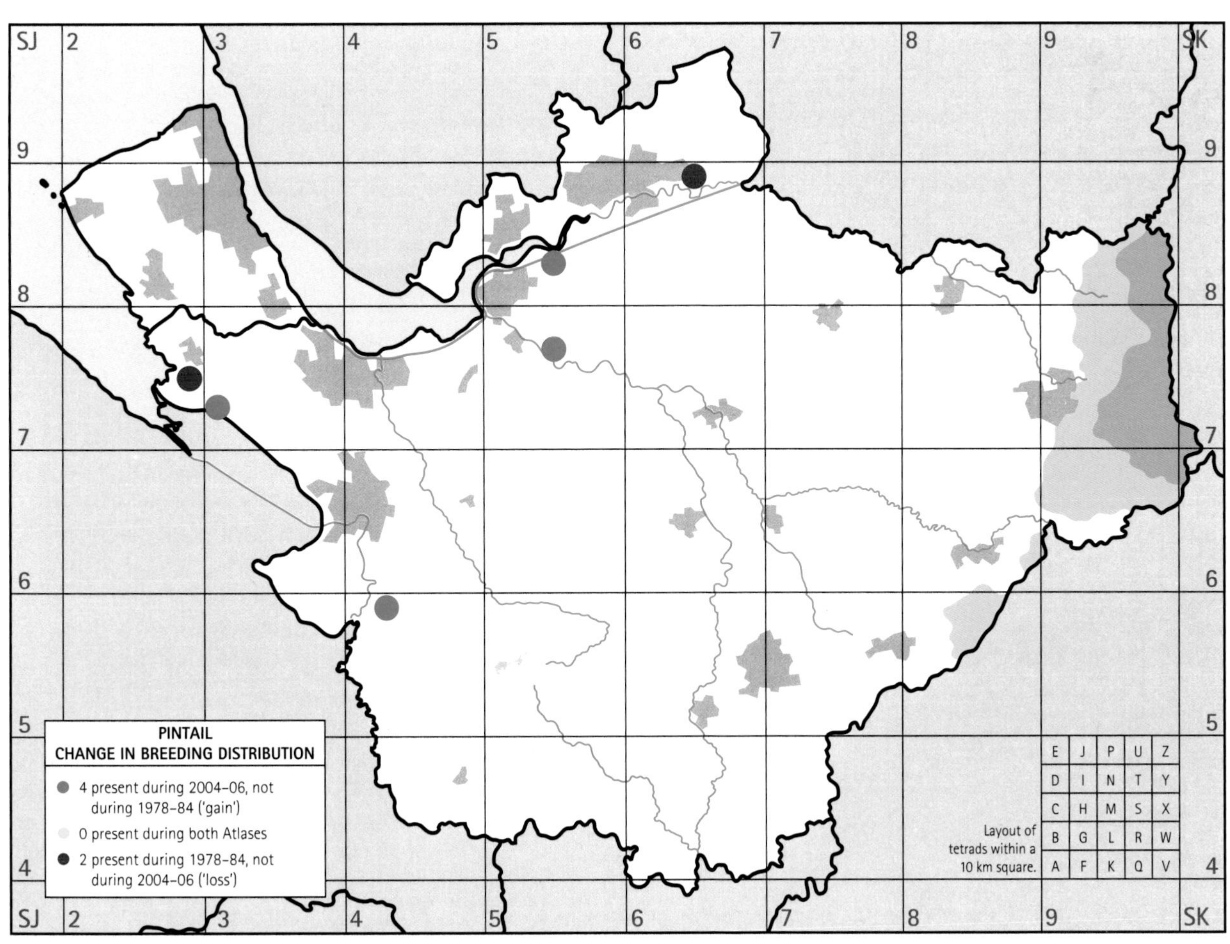
SJ
2
3
4
5
6
7
8
9
SK
PINTAIL
CHANGE IN BREEDING DISTRIBUTION
4 present during 2004–06, not during 1978–84 ('gain')
0 present during both Atlases
2 present during 1978–84, not during 2004–06 ('loss')
Layout of tetrads within a 10 km square.
E J P U Z
D I N T Y
C H M S X
B G L R W
A F K Q V

Our two estuaries have been of paramount importance for Pintail for much of the last century, but have experienced contrasting fortunes. The Dee is currently the premier site in the country, internationally important with a five-year peak mean of around 5,800, almost 10% of the international flyway population; virtually all of these birds are in Cheshire and Wirral. Establishment of the RSPB Gayton Sands reserve at the south end of the Dee has been crucial to them.

The Mersey used to be the supreme site for Pintails: from 1973 to 1984, counts exceeded 10,000 in most winters, and the maximum of 18,450 in November 1980 represented over three-quarters of the British total. But from 1985 onwards, numbers have fallen steadily and in 2004/05 the five-year peak mean fell to as few as 240 birds, below even the 279 necessary for registration as of national importance. The reasons for this are not understood but are clearly related to the site rather than the species as there has been little change over the years in the total visiting Britain. More than half of the British wintering Pintails are on the Irish Sea estuaries of the Dee, Solway, Ribble and Morecambe Bay, and indeed this is the most important region for them in north-west Europe (Brown & Grice 2005).

Going farther back in time, the numbers on the estuaries have clearly varied over the years. Coward (1910) knew the Pintail as a 'fairly plentiful' winter visitor to the Dee estuary, with increasing numbers on the Mersey especially using Hale Duck Decoy as a safe retreat in daytime. Up to about 1940 flocks on the Dee estuary varied from 500 to 1,000 but by 1957 the figures were 1,000–3,000, with the estuary holding the largest numbers in the British Isles, between half and three-quarters of the national wintering total. Far fewer birds visited the Mersey, with notable counts of 150 and 195 in March 1954 and 1956 (Bell 1962). During the 1960s birds apparently shifted from the Dee to the Mersey, with peak counts in 1965/66 of 1,200 on the Mersey but only 300 on the Dee. Up to 600 were on the Dee floods at Aldford at the same time (Bell 1967).

Pintails can be extremely mobile during the winter, taking advantage of habitats which are only temporarily available through flooding, and the Dee flood meadows above Chester also qualify as internationally important with mean counts of 600–700, peaking at 900 birds in winter 2006/07 near Worthenbury (SJ44I), with 250 at Aldford (SJ45E) in 2004/05. The only other three-figure flocks at non-estuarine sites were 250 on a small lake at Frodsham Marsh (SJ47Z) in 2004/05, and up to 180 at Inner Marsh Farm (SJ37B).

Although this species is said usually to be found in large flocks, in fact half of the 117 counts submitted over the three winters were of groups comprising fewer than 10 birds. The habitat codes show that almost all of the county's Pintails were on medium to large standing

RICHARD STEEL

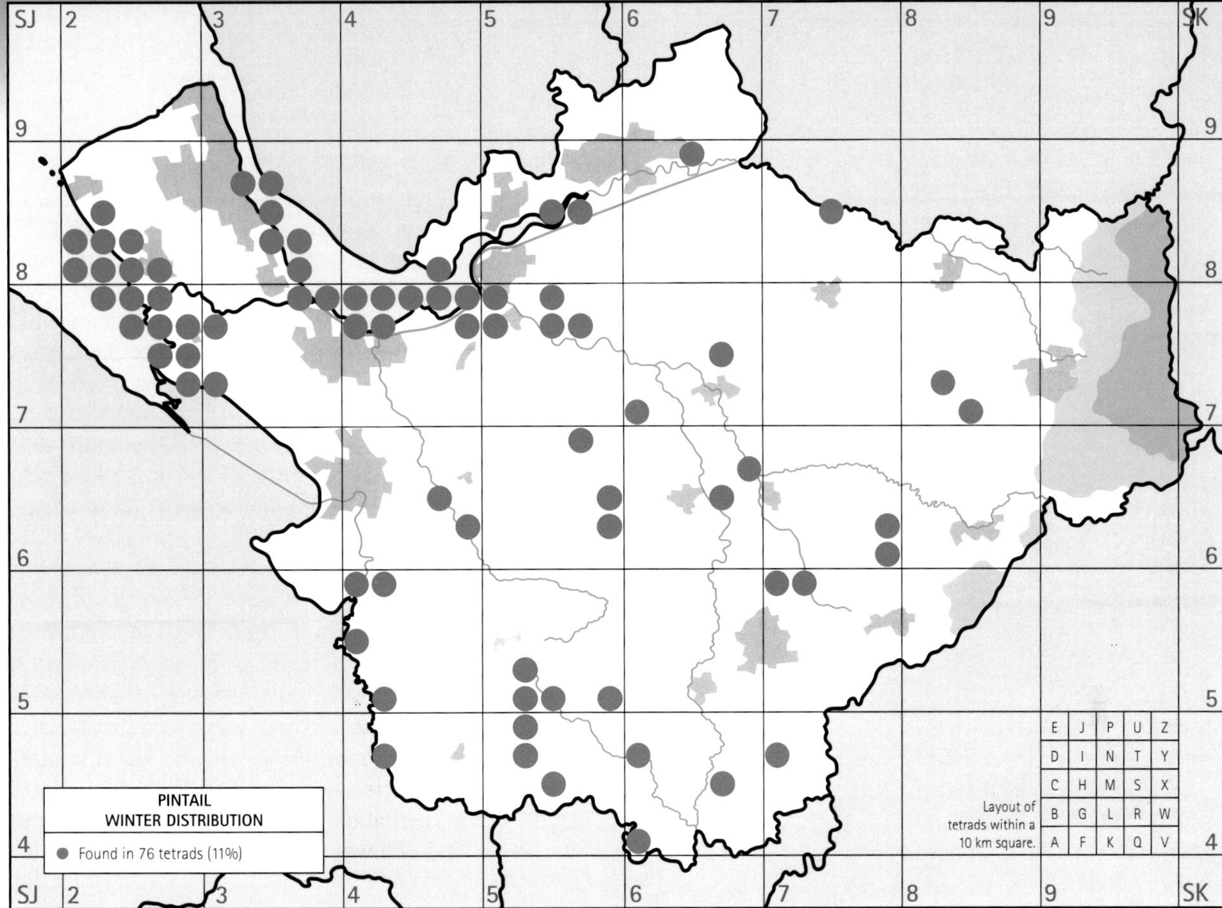

freshwater bodies, or salt-marsh/estuarine areas. Despite their long necks, this species prefers to feed mainly in shallow water, dabbling and up-ending to take invertebrates and seeds. On the estuaries, they depend largely on small *Hydrobia* snails, but on inland grazing marshes seeds are by far the most important food (Owen *et al.* 1986). One examined in studies following the August 1989 Mersey oil spill had been eating blackberries, presumably overhanging or fallen into an inland feeding site.

The winter distribution map has probably not changed much over the last 30 or 40 years. Small numbers are present at most of the meres and lowland waters, but they avoid the uplands.

Pintail come here for the winter from breeding areas in Siberia, Fennoscandia, the Baltic States and Iceland. A bird ringed as a chick in Estonia in 1972 was shot that winter by a wildfowler on the Dee.

Garganey

Anas querquedula

SUE & ANDY TRANTER

This, our only summer-migrant duck, is here close to its north-western limit in Britain. The tiny breeding population in Britain, a minute fraction of the estimated one million pairs in Europe, is found principally in central and eastern England. Garganeys breed in shallow waters with extensive emergent vegetation, their ideal sites being in open marshland dissected by a network of lushly vegetated ditches and open freshwater pools. They nest in dense patches of aquatic plants such as reed-mace *Typha* or common reed *Phragmites australis*, and occasionally in damp areas up to 50 m away from the water. Their main food during the breeding season is animal matter: snails, chironomid and other insect larvae, worms, leeches, crustaceans, frog-spawn and tadpoles.

They spend the winter in trans-Saharan Africa in the seasonal wetlands across the Sahel. Widespread degradation of their wetland habitat, both in breeding and wintering areas, has led to a significant population decline and Garganey is listed as a species of conservation concern across Europe.

Garganeys are early migrants, with many records in March, and occasional drakes in February, but new birds appear to turn up throughout the spring and summer, and their presence at any site does not necessarily indicate that they bred there (Brown & Grice 2005). In some years the seasons seem to merge and the county bird report finds it impossible to differentiate late spring from early autumn birds.

Climate change is likely to shift more birds farther north to breed in Britain. As with most species at the edge of their range, the numbers seen vary greatly from year to year. The Atlas maps appear to show more birds being recorded in Cheshire and Wirral nowadays than during our *First Atlas*, although the annual bird reports show that many observers did not include their sightings of Garganey amongst their *First Atlas* records; despite frequent exhortations to CAWOS members, the same happened during this survey but records submitted for the bird reports have been pooled with the Atlas data. Such 'observer effects' make it difficult to tell whether more Garganeys are visiting the county than twenty years ago.

Most observers provided details of the sex of the birds: the only female noted was displaying with two males at Inner Marsh Farm in 2006. The frequent occurrence of odd birds throughout the breeding season led the Rare Breeding Birds Panel to tighten their criteria in 2002 to exclude from their report 'single birds ... which are probably doing little more than just passing through a locality'. Out of the 13 tetrads with records in this Atlas period, probably only those at Inner Marsh Farm in 2006 would qualify for reporting by the RBBP. They are secretive birds and not easy to prove breeding, but, with so few females noted in the county it seems unlikely that Garganeys bred here during this Atlas.

Breeding has only rarely been proven in the county. The most recent year with recorded behaviour suggesting breeding was 1998, when a pair was present in mid-Cheshire from late March to early June, the female disappearing from view for periods of 29 and 22 days, perhaps making two failed nesting attempts.

Sponsored by Michael S. Twist

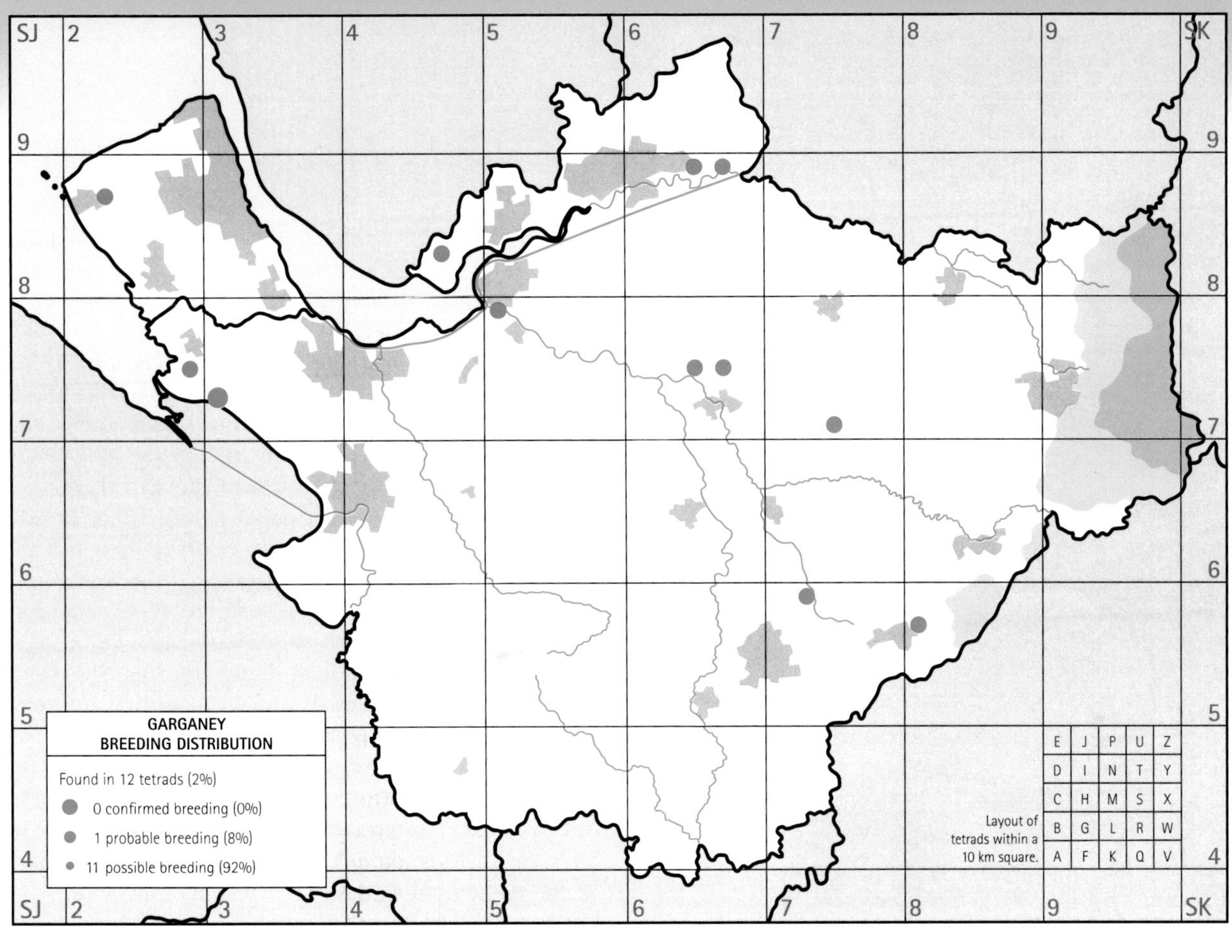
GARGANEY
BREEDING DISTRIBUTION
Found in 12 tetrads (2%)
0 confirmed breeding (0%)
1 probable breeding (8%)
11 possible breeding (92%)
Layout of tetrads within a 10 km square.
E J P U Z
D I N T Y
C H M S X
B G L R W
A F K Q V
SJ
SK
2 3 4 5 6 7 8 9
4 5 6 7 8 9

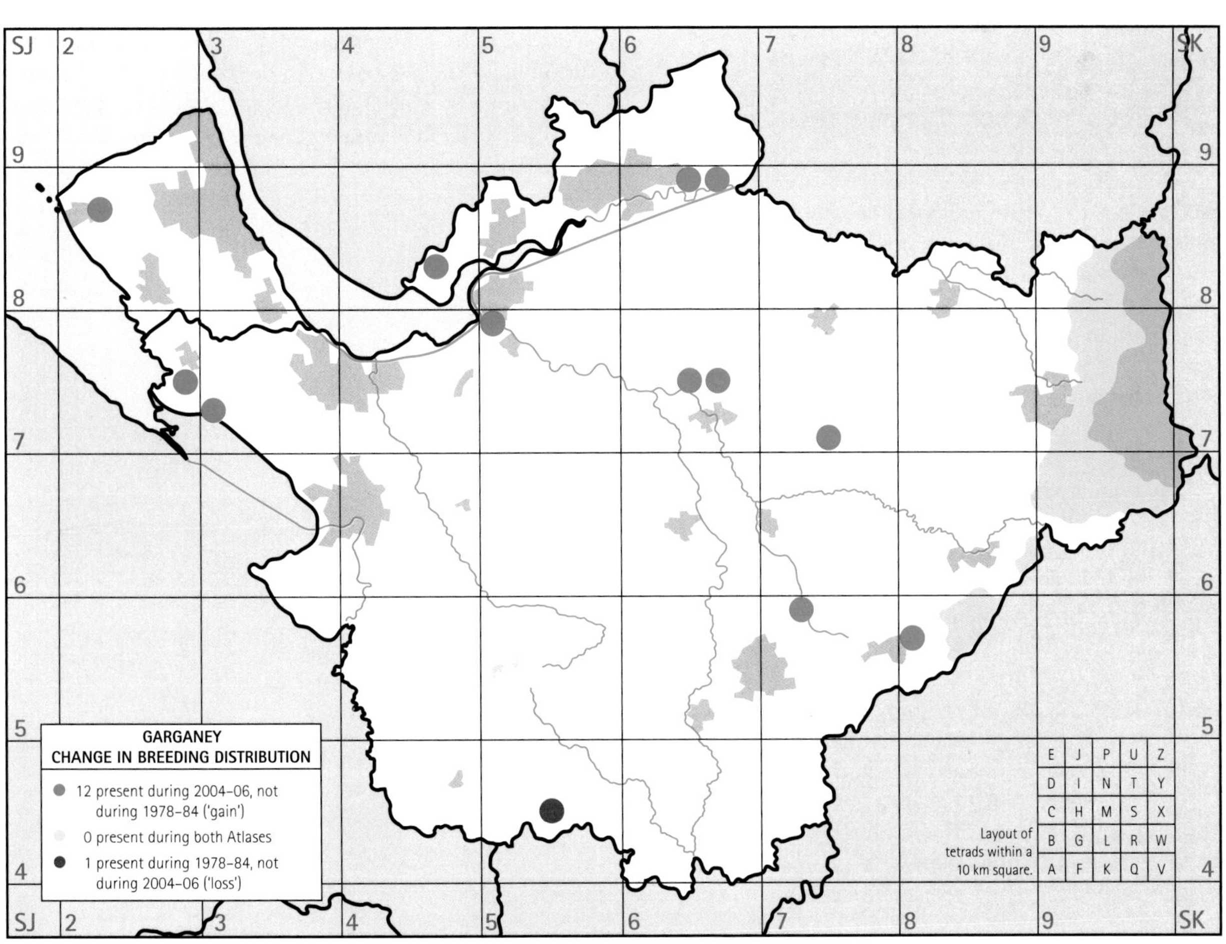
GARGANEY
CHANGE IN BREEDING DISTRIBUTION
12 present during 2004–06, not during 1978–84 ('gain')
0 present during both Atlases
1 present during 1978–84, not during 2004–06 ('loss')
Layout of tetrads within a 10 km square.
E J P U Z
D I N T Y
C H M S X
B G L R W
A F K Q V
SJ
SK
2 3 4 5 6 7 8 9
4 5 6 7 8 9

Shoveler

Anas clypeata

REN HATHWAY

For many years in Britain, Shovelers seem to have been contracting their breeding range and increasingly concentrating on a limited number of sites, especially nature reserves and others with nature conservation designations (*BTO Second Atlas*). This also seems to be true in Cheshire and Wirral. As in our *First Atlas*, the species' stronghold is the Mersey and lower Weaver valleys, and Shovelers were found in slightly more tetrads than twenty years ago (49 compared to 40), but with significantly fewer providing proof of breeding (3 compared to 11). Females were seen with ducklings in SJ57N in the lower Weaver valley, at Woolston (SJ68J) and Risley Moss (SJ69Q). Birds were recorded visiting a probable nest site or displaying in a further three tetrads, SJ27X on the Dee salt-marsh, Inner Marsh Farm (SJ37B) and Woolston (SJ68P), with pairs seen in 23 more tetrads.

In the 19 years between our two Atlas periods (1985–2003), the annual county bird reports have logged confirmed breeding in 16 of the 19 years, but never at more than three locations in a year. All of the sites have been in the north of the county: Woolston (15 years), Frodsham Marsh (four years), Gatewarth SF (four years), Fiddler's Ferry (two years), Astmoor (two years), St Helens Canal (two years) and Risley Moss (one year).

The species' habitat requirements are defined by its remarkable bill, from which it gets both its common and scientific names (*clypeata* = shield-shaped). The prominent projections (lamellae) on its upper and lower mandibles strain material taken in through the tip of the bill, allowing it to feed on tiny particles including plankton. With this method of feeding, they mainly choose shallow eutrophic waters with nutritious material in suspension, and may well lose out in competition with fish.

Unusually for a dabbling duck, breeding Shovelers are territorial, the males defending a feeding territory for the pair. The female nests in vegetation, usually not far from the water's edge, in late April, and incubates the eggs for just over three weeks while the drake stays nearby on the water. Any furtive-looking single male Shoveler in May should be watched carefully in case he has a duck on a nest in the vicinity: she comes off the nest to feed in bouts adding up to three or four hours a day, more than other ducks. With these aspects of behaviour, a briefly observed male or pair could actually be nesting. Broods of up to 12 chicks have been seen, but 8 or 9 is more normal, and many of the males accompany their female with the brood.

Nationally, there were estimated to be over 1,000 breeding pairs in Britain in 1988–91 (*BTO Second Atlas*), but Shoveler has now (2007) been added to the list of species monitored by the UK Rare Breeding Birds Panel because of its perceived scarcity. The county population is unlikely to be more than five pairs breeding.

The 'possible breeding' records of single birds are not included on the 'change' map.

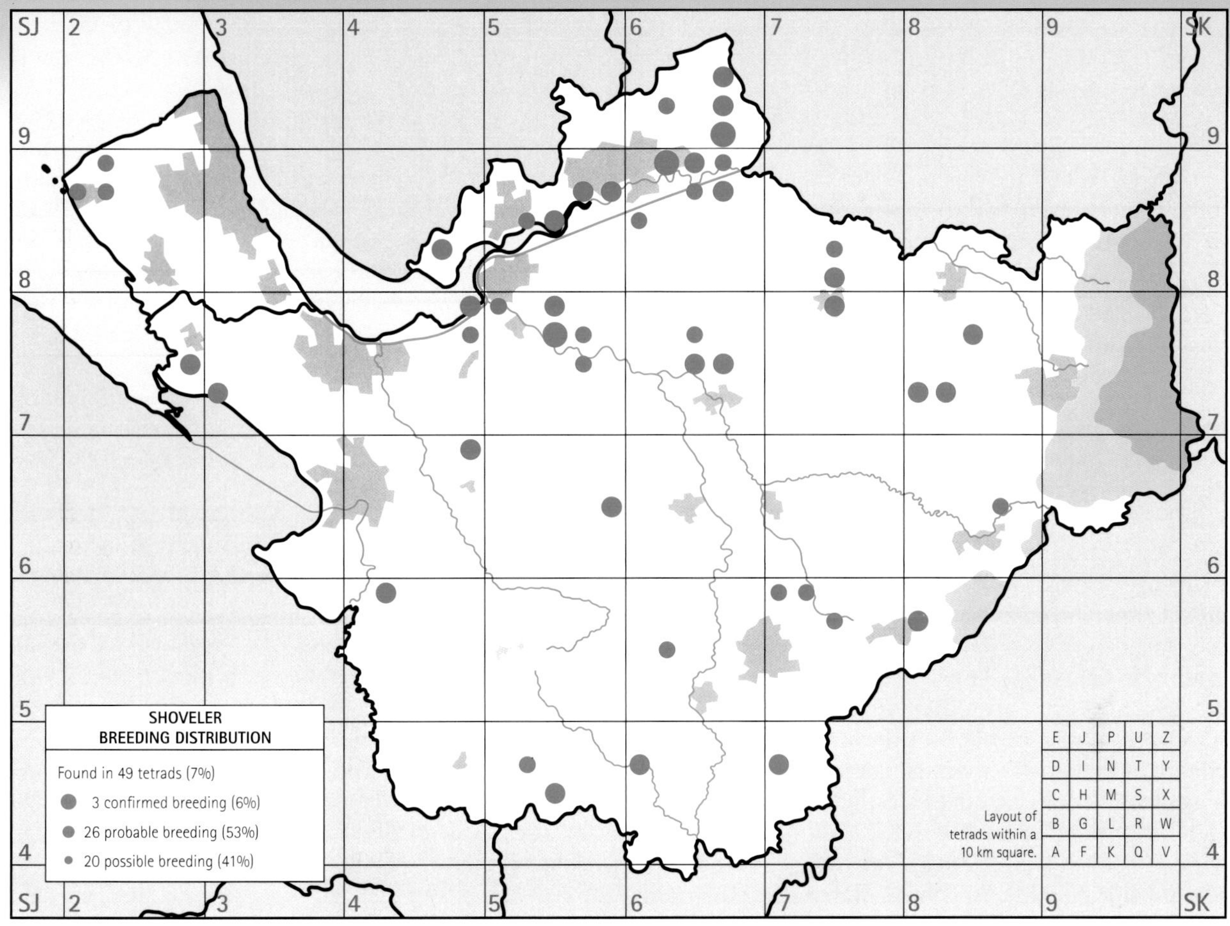
SJ
SK
SHOVELER
BREEDING DISTRIBUTION
Found in 49 tetrads (7%)
3 confirmed breeding (6%)
26 probable breeding (53%)
20 possible breeding (41%)
Layout of
tetrads within a
10 km square.
E J P U Z
D I N T Y
C H M S X
B G L R W
A F K Q V

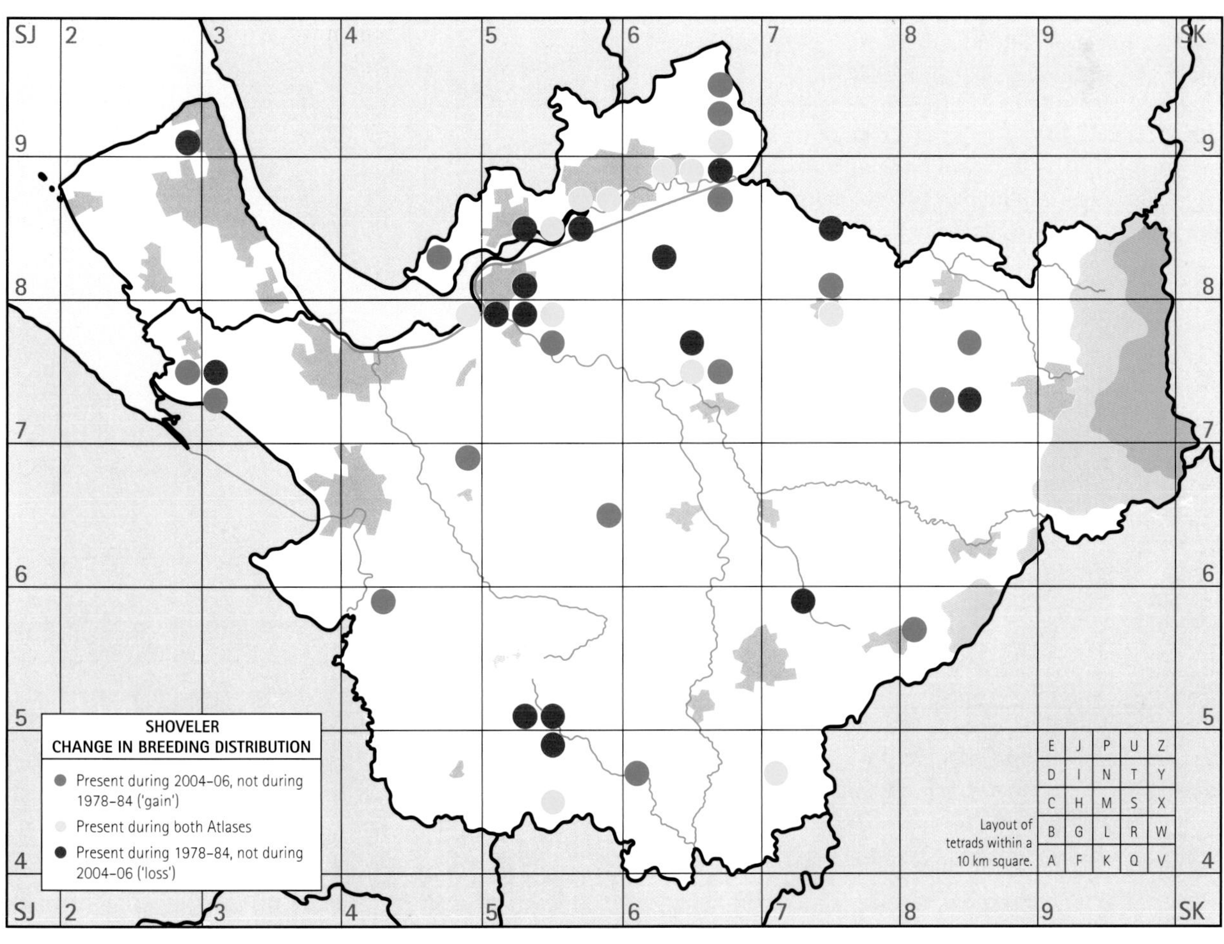
SJ
SK
SHOVELER
CHANGE IN BREEDING DISTRIBUTION
Present during 2004–06, not during 1978–84 ('gain')
Present during both Atlases
Present during 1978–84, not during 2004–06 ('loss')
Layout of
tetrads within a
10 km square.
E J P U Z
D I N T Y
C H M S X
B G L R W
A F K Q V

The Atlas map shows that almost every site (40 of the 49) in the county with breeding season presence also has Shovelers in winter, but they are not the same individuals. Most British birds move out, being found anywhere from Denmark to Iberia, but mainly in western France and Spain. A bird ringed as a fledgling at Runcorn in June 1976 was shot that September in Essex, no doubt on its way to the continent. The Shovelers wintering here come from the east, most of all from Russia (*Migration Atlas*), and the species is found in an extra 67 tetrads which did not have birds in the breeding season.

As in the breeding season, Shovelers find most of their food on or near the water surface. They more commonly feed while swimming than other dabbling ducks, and less often up-end. Groups can often be seen swimming in a line or in circles, each dabbling in the water disturbed in the wake of the one in front. Much of their diet is animal material, mainly freshwater snails, crustaceans and insect adults and larvae: Shoveler is the most carnivorous of the dabbling ducks at the Ouse Washes in Cambridgeshire (Owen *et al.* 1986).

That Shovelers are different from other ducks is illustrated by the locations of the largest flocks in the county in winter, all on waters that tend not to hold the biggest gatherings of other species: 108 on Bar Mere (SJ54I/J), 94 on Tabley Mere (SJ77I), 78 on Deer Park Mere, Cholmondeley (SJ55K) and 60 on Neumann's Flash (SJ67S). Although large waterbodies tend to hold the most birds, wintering Shovelers are often to be found on small waters. In six tetrads they were on ponds, with 26 on small waterbodies compared to 65 on lakes, reservoirs and sand quarries. The map shows that they do not visit the upland reservoirs and, apart from some on the Dee salt-marsh in SJ27X, this is not a bird of the estuaries; until 2004/05 the Dee estuary had been included as a site of national importance for Shoveler on the basis of inclusion of birds at Inner Marsh Farm.

The shallow waters that are its preferred habitat are the first to freeze in hard weather, at which times most Shovelers fly to France or Spain. In some of the hard winters of the 1970s and 1980s, the county bird reports show that they were noticeably scarce.

The species has obviously become much more common in the last hundred years. To Coward and Oldham (1900) Shoveler was known as a winter visitor to the neighbourhood of Chester and to the Dee Marshes, but 'in other parts of the county this duck has not often been observed'. Coward was most familiar with Shovelers as passage migrants, and summarized their status as a regular visitor on migration to the estuaries and inland waters. It was never numerous on the tidal waters but 'occasionally a few were seen with Mallards and Pintails; as a rule it rests during the day on ponds' (Coward 1910). In winter Coward had seen birds, in most cases singly, on the meres.

Boyd (1951) noted that the species had shown a marked increase in the last 30 years and was then seen on the meres in every month. He wrote that the largest numbers on the mid-Cheshire meres are present in winter from October to January, with 20–25 at Arley and Tabley, where they often rested on the ice. Bell (1962) said that 'outside the breeding season it is found in all months on certain meres, such as Rostherne, Tatton, Tabley, Sandbach Flashes and others'. The maximum quoted at Rostherne was about 50 between September and January, with all the other large flocks listed by Bell at the migration seasons.

RICHARD STEEL

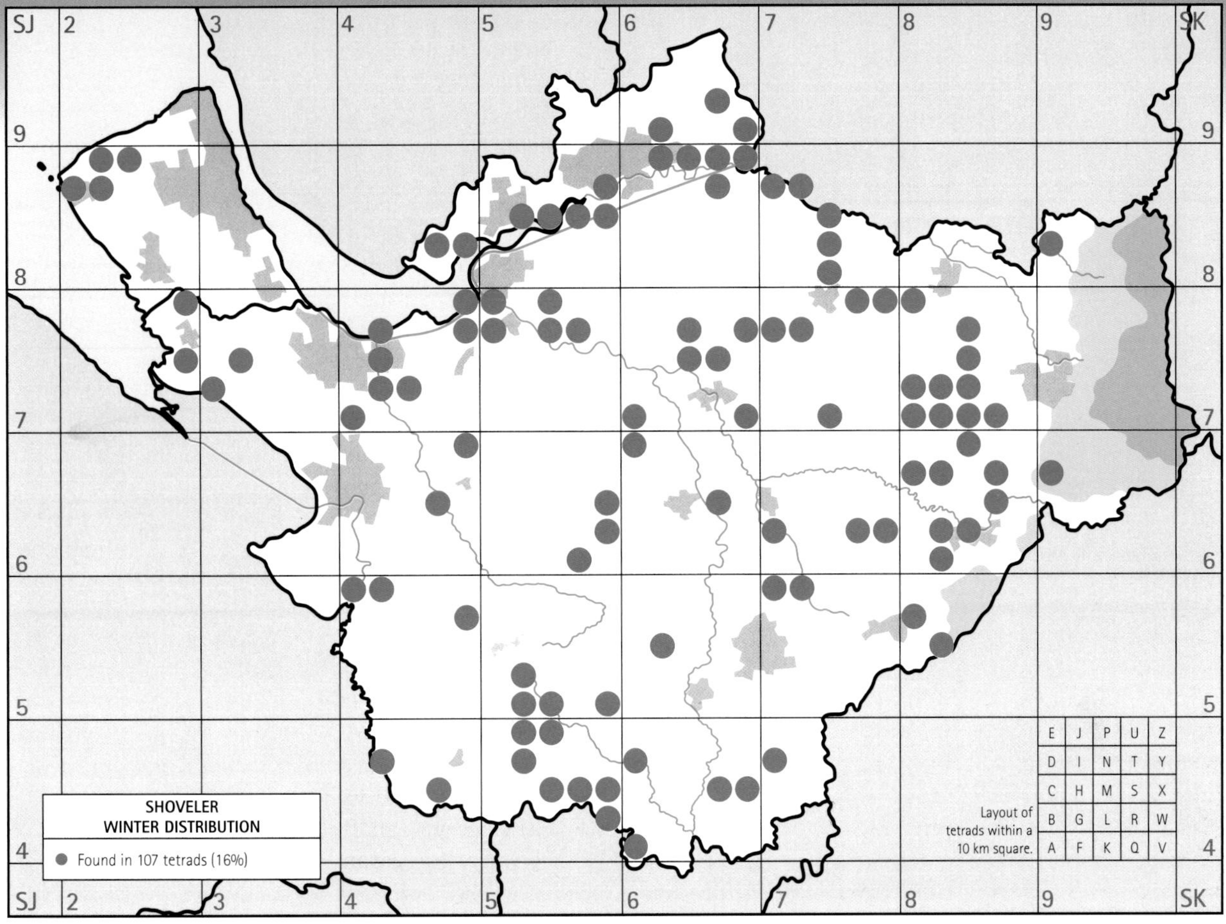
SHOVELER
WINTER DISTRIBUTION
Found in 107 tetrads (16%)
Layout of tetrads within a 10 km square.
E J P U Z
D I N T Y
C H M S X
B G L R W
A F K Q V
SJ
SK

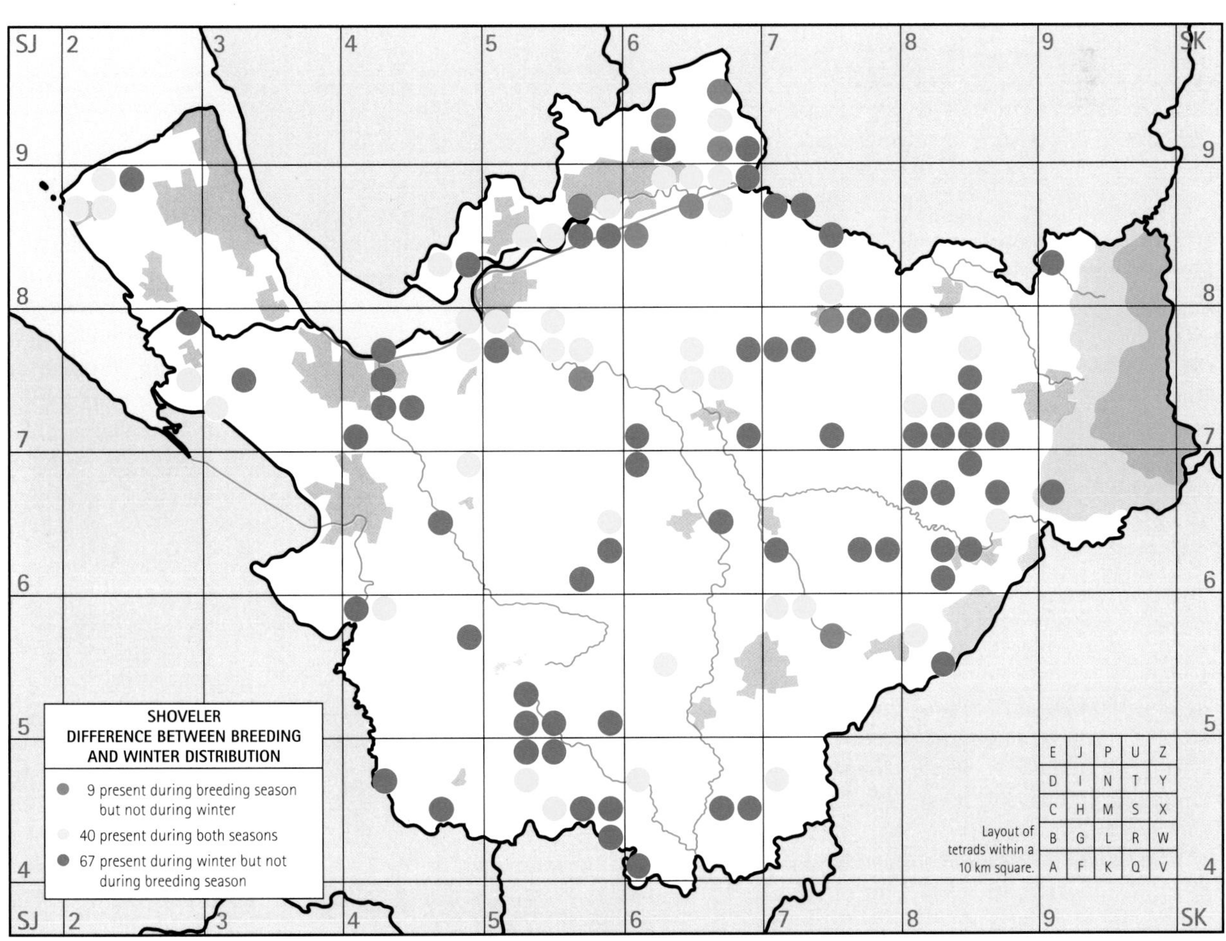
SHOVELER
DIFFERENCE BETWEEN BREEDING AND WINTER DISTRIBUTION
9 present during breeding season but not during winter
40 present during both seasons
67 present during winter but not during breeding season
Layout of tetrads within a 10 km square.
E J P U Z
D I N T Y
C H M S X
B G L R W
A F K Q V
SJ
SK

Pochard

Aythya ferina

STEVE ROUND

Pochard is such a scarce breeder nationally that its numbers have been monitored by the Rare Breeding Birds Panel since 1986. Their latest report shows that, in 2004, the Cheshire and Wirral population was 15 pairs out of a national total of 482 pairs (Holling *et al.* 2007a). There are only seven counties with more breeding birds. It is misleading, however, to use the word 'county' here, because all of our regularly breeding birds are at just one site, Woolston Eyes, as they have been for more than twenty years. As was commented in our *First Atlas*, the Pochard's breeding status in Cheshire depends mainly on the state of the Woolston sludge-beds, and the citation for the SSSI status of Woolston was amended in March 2004 to recognize the site's value for nationally important numbers of breeding Pochard. There were at least 15 broods there in 2004, 22 broods in 2005 and 13–16 broods in 2006.

Their stronghold is clearly along the Mersey valley. In our *First Atlas* they were proved breeding only at Woolston and Doddington (SJ74D); now, twenty years on, breeding was confirmed only at Woolston (annually, in three tetrads) and Fiddler's Ferry (in 2006), with pairs of Pochards found in a further four tetrads. The Atlas map shows that there were single birds at a further eight sites but clearly few sites in the county provide their needs: Pochards are primarily vegetarian, diving for their food in shallow water with abundant plant-life, although they do take some small invertebrates. All of the birds were on standing water, and they can use quite small waterbodies; of the eight probable or confirmed records, one was on a pond less than 50 m^2 (G1) and three on small waters up to 450 m^2 (G2).

Pochards are fairly obvious when pairing, but females then withdraw to nest in dense emergent vegetation, and single males should be carefully watched. The earliest birds at Woolston start nesting in mid-April. Laying the typical clutch of eight to 10 eggs, followed by 25 days incubation, leads to hatching in late May, with new broods from later birds emerging into July.

The 'possible breeding' records are omitted from the 'change' map.

Sponsored by Tony and Margaret Hayter

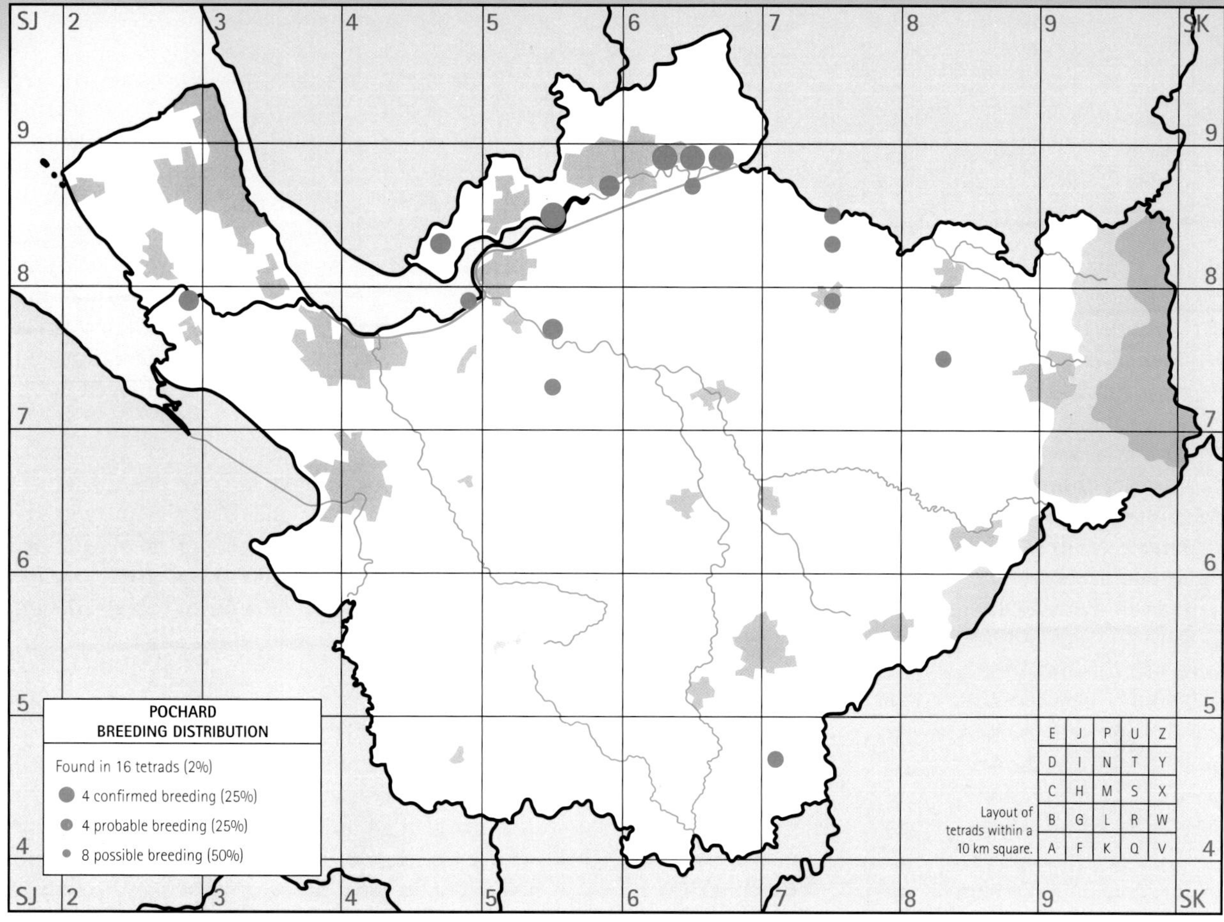
SJ
2
3
4
5
6
7
8
9
SK
9
8
7
6
5
4
POCHARD
BREEDING DISTRIBUTION
Found in 16 tetrads (2%)
4 confirmed breeding (25%)
4 probable breeding (25%)
8 possible breeding (50%)
E J P U Z
D I N T Y
C H M S X
B G L R W
A F K Q V
Layout of tetrads within a 10 km square.

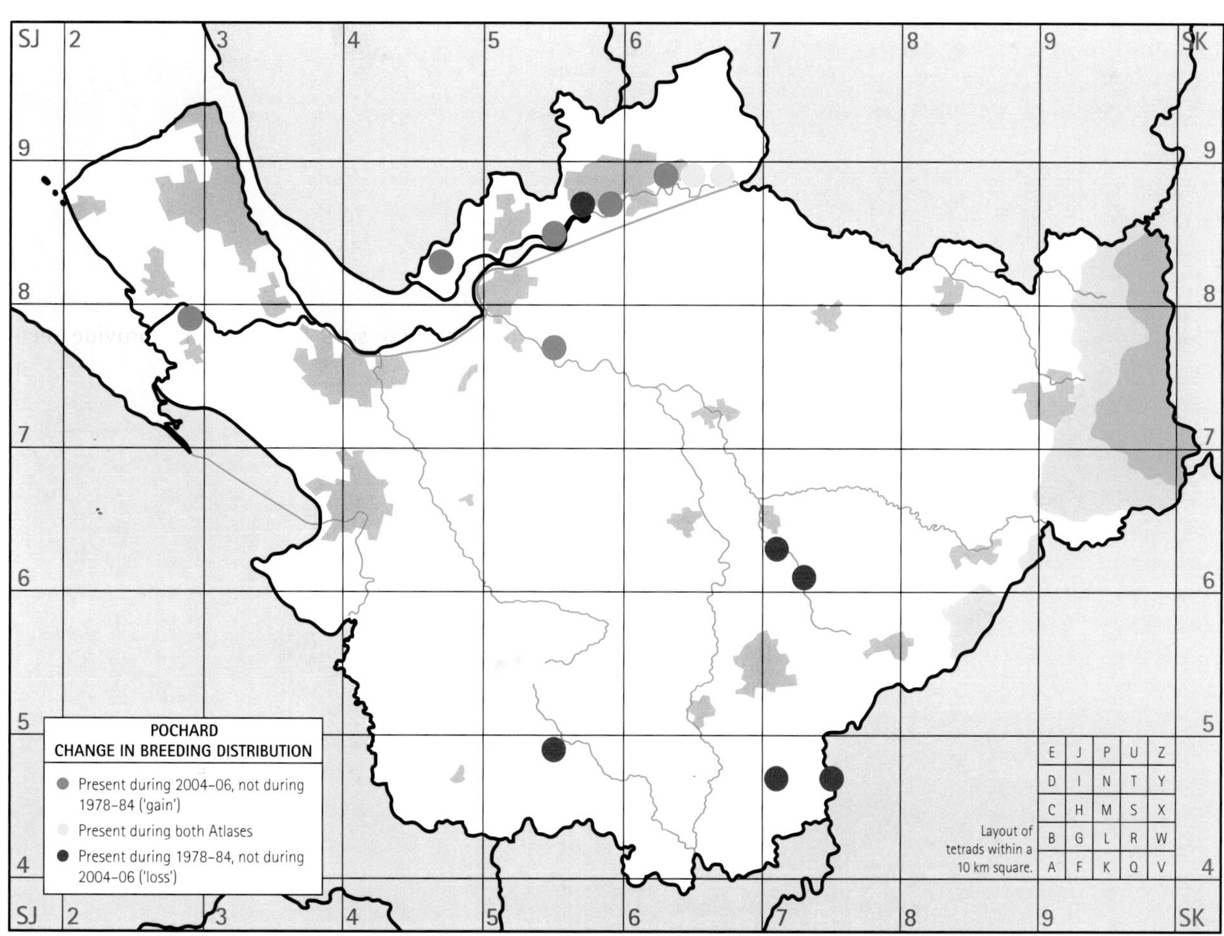
SJ
2
3
4
5
6
7
8
9
SK
9
8
7
6
5
4
POCHARD
CHANGE IN BREEDING DISTRIBUTION
Present during 2004–06, not during 1978–84 ('gain')
Present during both Atlases
Present during 1978–84, not during 2004–06 ('loss')
E J P U Z
D I N T Y
C H M S X
B G L R W
A F K Q V
Layout of tetrads within a 10 km square.

The UK breeding total is around 500 pairs but the British wintering total is currently estimated at 59,500 birds as large numbers arrive here from breeding grounds in the east, reaching as far as 60°E in Russia. Their long movements are explicable because the shallow, eutrophic waters that they favour are likely to be the first to freeze. The numbers reaching Britain have, however, dropped considerably in recent years as the warming climate allows more lakes and rivers in eastern Europe and Russia to remain ice-free, so Pochards do not need to move as far.

There is strong differential migration with females moving farther south, probably because of aggression from the earlier-migrating males. However, where both sexes share a site, the females can hold their own and do not lose out on feeding opportunities. Across Britain as a whole, the wintering population is about 70% males and 30% females, a more imbalanced sex ratio than any other wintering duck, but it varies with latitude from about 8:1 in the north of Scotland to 3:2 in southern England (*Migration Atlas*). The preponderance of males in the county was commented upon by Bell (1962), although by 1967, Bell's own records show that it had declined. He gave no figures, however, and quantification of the sex ratio in the wintering Pochard flocks in Cheshire and Wirral would be an interesting subject for study.

Their distribution is obviously determined largely by the availability of suitable food. Pochards sometimes up-end like dabbling ducks, but mostly feed by diving, to an average depth of about a metre, where they take especially spores of algae and the seeds from pondweed. For several years in the late 1980s Salford Docks was discovered to be an important night-time feeding site for Pochards, and flocks were seen leaving Rostherne and Woolston to fly there at dusk, returning at dawn.

The map shows a striking absence from our estuaries: throughout its range, Pochard is largely an inland species. In the mid-twentieth century, Pochard were said to frequent most of the major meres, with flocks usually between 100 and 200 at Rostherne (Bell 1962). They are mainly birds of the larger waters: almost three-quarters of the winter habitat codes were G3 or G5, lakes, reservoirs and sandpits.

Currently Woolston is the most important site in the county, and the only one ranking as a site of national importance for wintering Pochard, holding (on average over five years) more than 1% of the UK population—595 birds. Rostherne Mere (SJ78M) has now dropped out of the list of sites of national importance for the species, but has been an especially important refuge in times of hard weather, when its deep water remained largely ice-free. In January 1997, cold weather concentrated many Pochards there, and the WeBS count totalled 2,616, by far the largest flock on record in the county; counts in January 2002 and 2003 were close to 900 and 1,000 respectively, but annual peaks since then have not exceeded 200.

During this Atlas period, other favoured sites within the county included Frodsham Marsh (SJ47Z), with a peak count of 150, a count of 53 at Doddington (SJ74D), the meres at Cholmondeley (SJ55K) with up to 52, and an unusually high total of 50 on Astbury Mere, Congleton (86L). However, despite these sizeable flocks gathering at a few sites, the majority of Pochards wintering in Cheshire and Wirral are found in small numbers, up to 20 at most, dispersed widely across the county.

RAY SCALLY

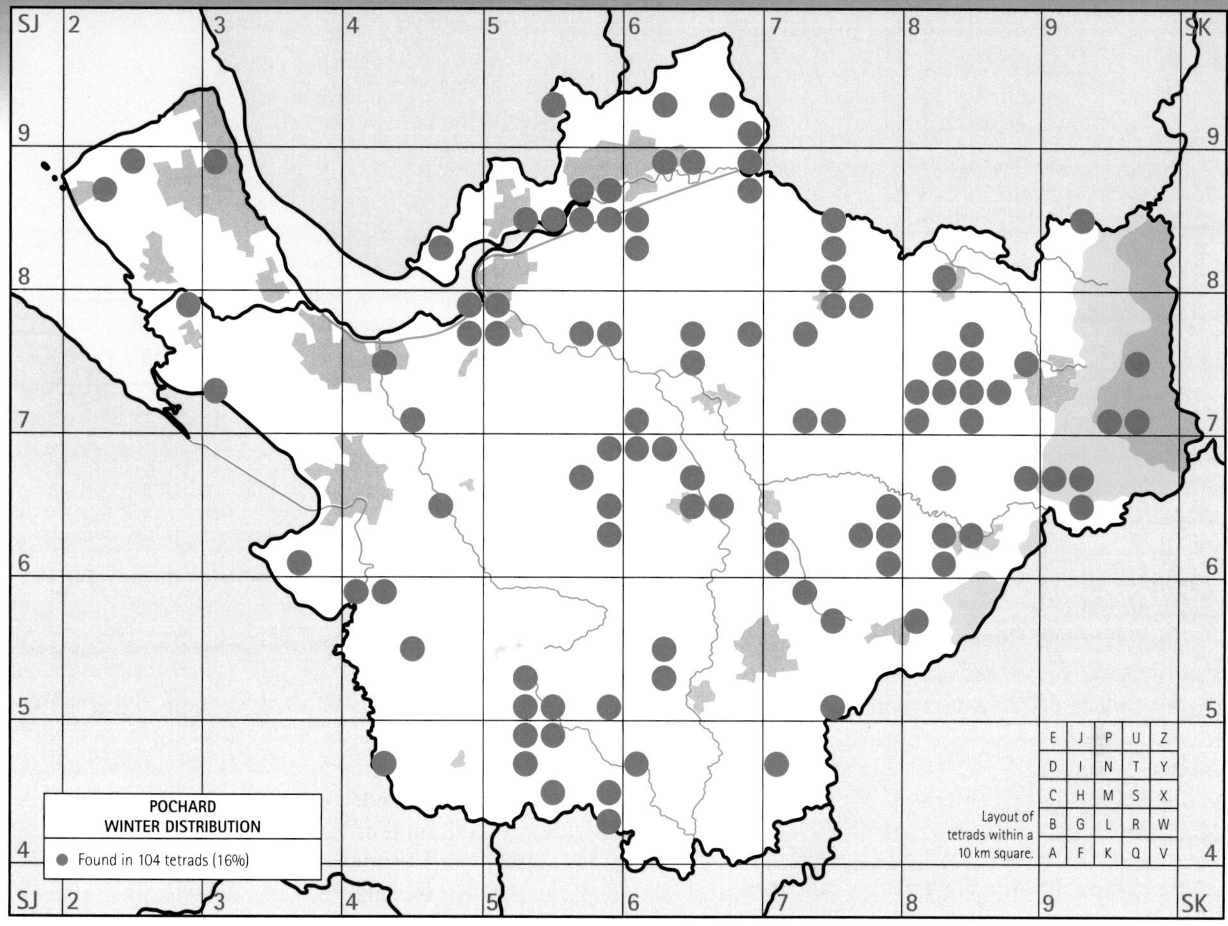
SJ
SK
2
3
4
5
6
7
8
9
POCHARD
WINTER DISTRIBUTION
Found in 104 tetrads (16%)
Layout of tetrads within a 10 km square.
E J P U Z
D I N T Y
C H M S X
B G L R W
A F K Q V

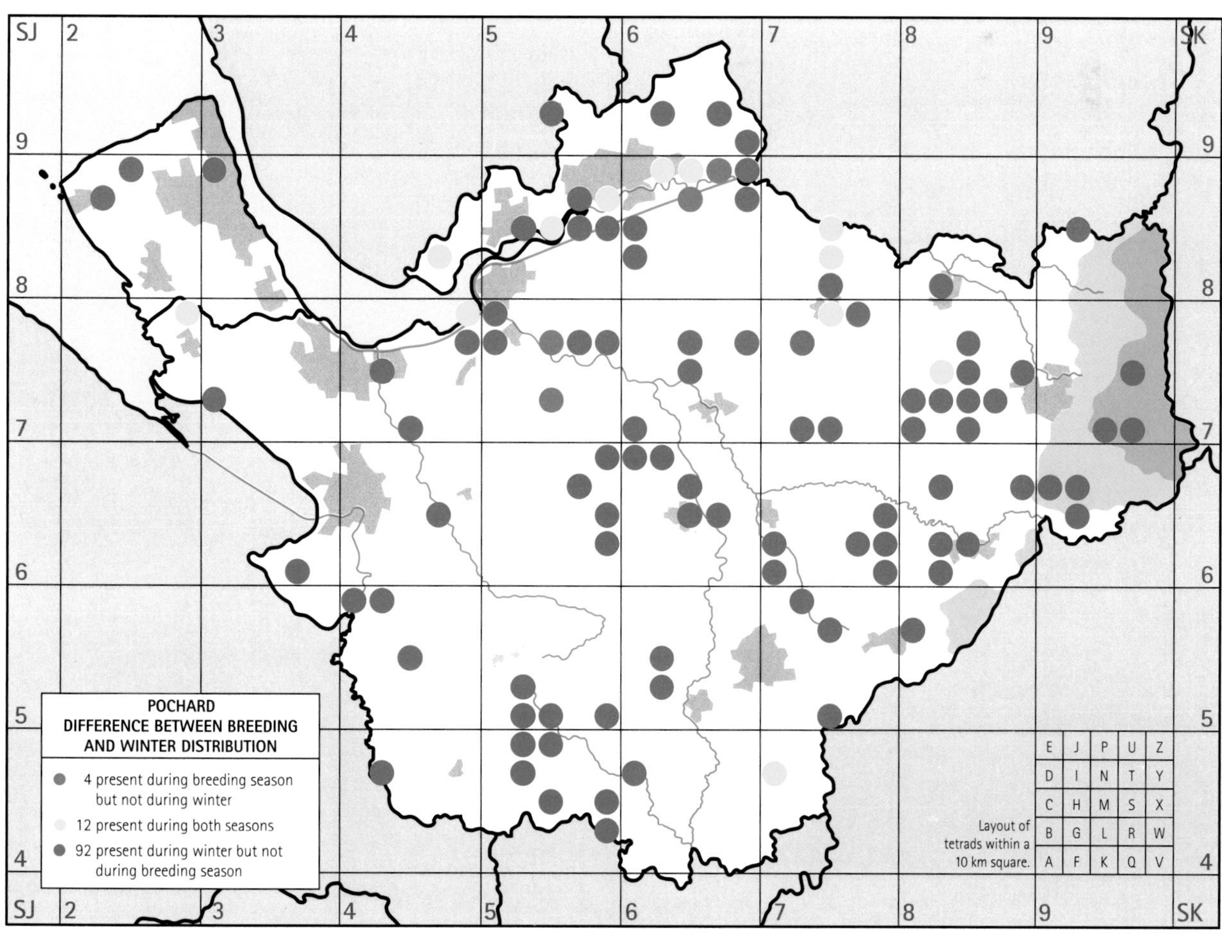
SJ
SK
2
3
4
5
6
7
8
9
POCHARD
DIFFERENCE BETWEEN BREEDING AND WINTER DISTRIBUTION
4 present during breeding season but not during winter
12 present during both seasons
92 present during winter but not during breeding season
Layout of tetrads within a 10 km square.
E J P U Z
D I N T Y
C H M S X
B G L R W
A F K Q V

Tufted Duck

Aythya fuligula

Tufted Ducks have expanded greatly since our *First Atlas*—in twenty years the number of tetrads with confirmed or probable breeding has risen from 108 to 171—and there are now few sizeable waters without the species. They were first proved to breed in the county only in 1908, with a slow expansion to 11 sites by 1938. Now, the distribution map shows that they are our second most widespread breeding duck and can be found almost anywhere in Cheshire, although only at a few Wirral sites. This is one of the few species of waterfowl that apparently thrives on the upland reservoirs of east Cheshire.

They need waters with rich bottom mud to provide the ducklings with abundant small larvae and emerging flies (Owen *et al.* 1986). Although this seems like quite an exacting requirement, the submitted habitat codes for this Atlas show birds on every type of aquatic habitat, and it seems that the population expansion has included use of suboptimal sites including a move onto some very small waters. Most (78%) of the codes were of small waterbodies, lakes or sand quarries, but 18 were described as ponds smaller than 50 m^2 (G1) and 17 were on streams, rivers and canals, including even narrow streams and ditches.

It is very easy to prove breeding of this species by seeing a brood of chicks, chocolate-brown bundles of fluff, following their mother and diving for their own food as soon as they leave the nest. A surprisingly high proportion of records were sightings of a pair (probable breeding), however, perhaps attributable to fieldworkers not visiting tetrads later in the season after the eggs have hatched. In this late-breeding species, chicks are seldom seen before mid-June.

Tufted Ducks are widespread enough to be recorded on a number of BBS transects. The BTO analysis of BBS results shows that the breeding population of Cheshire and Wirral in 2004–05 is estimated at 1,270 birds (with 95% statistical confidence limits of 20–2,530). This figure gives an average of 7 birds per tetrad with confirmed and probable breeding.

From reports at well-watched sites there appear to be about half as many broods seen as the number of pairs recorded, perhaps an indication of the level of nest losses. Some large breeding totals have been included in the annual county bird reports: 12 broods at New Platt Wood Sand Quarry (SJ77K) in 1994, 10 broods at Doddington (SJ74D) in 1995 and 8 broods at Inner Marsh Farm (SJ37B) in 1997. At Woolston (SJ68P) there were at least 16 broods in 2004, a record 27 broods in 2005 and 22 broods in 2006. Tufted Duck broods typically contain 7–9 chicks, but observers often comment on their rapid depletion, attributed to predators including mink, pike and Lesser Black-backed Gulls.

RICHARD STEEL

Sponsored by Michael Thompson

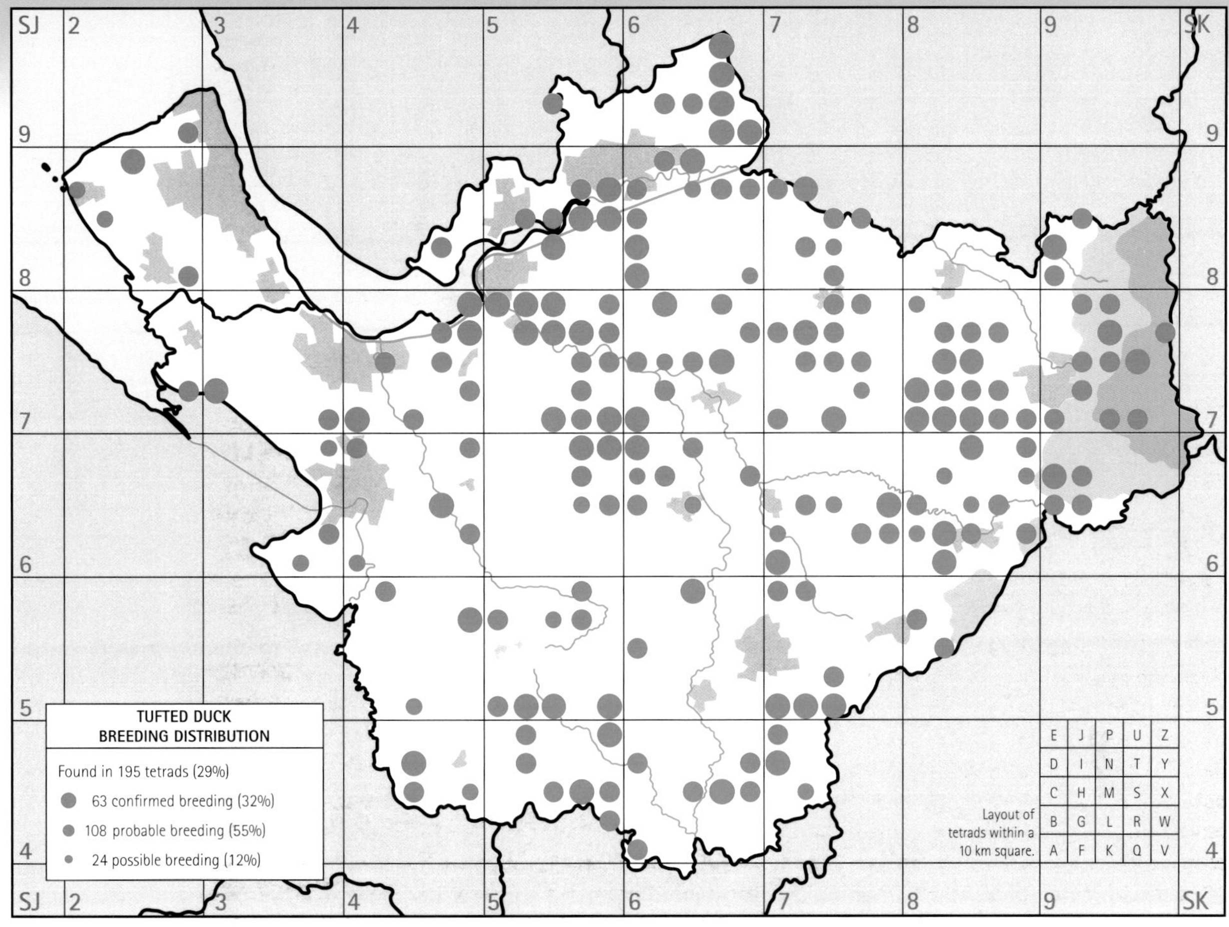
TUFTED DUCK
BREEDING DISTRIBUTION
Found in 195 tetrads (29%)
63 confirmed breeding (32%)
108 probable breeding (55%)
24 possible breeding (12%)
Layout of tetrads within a 10 km square.
E J P U Z
D I N T Y
C H M S X
B G L R W
A F K Q V
SJ
SK

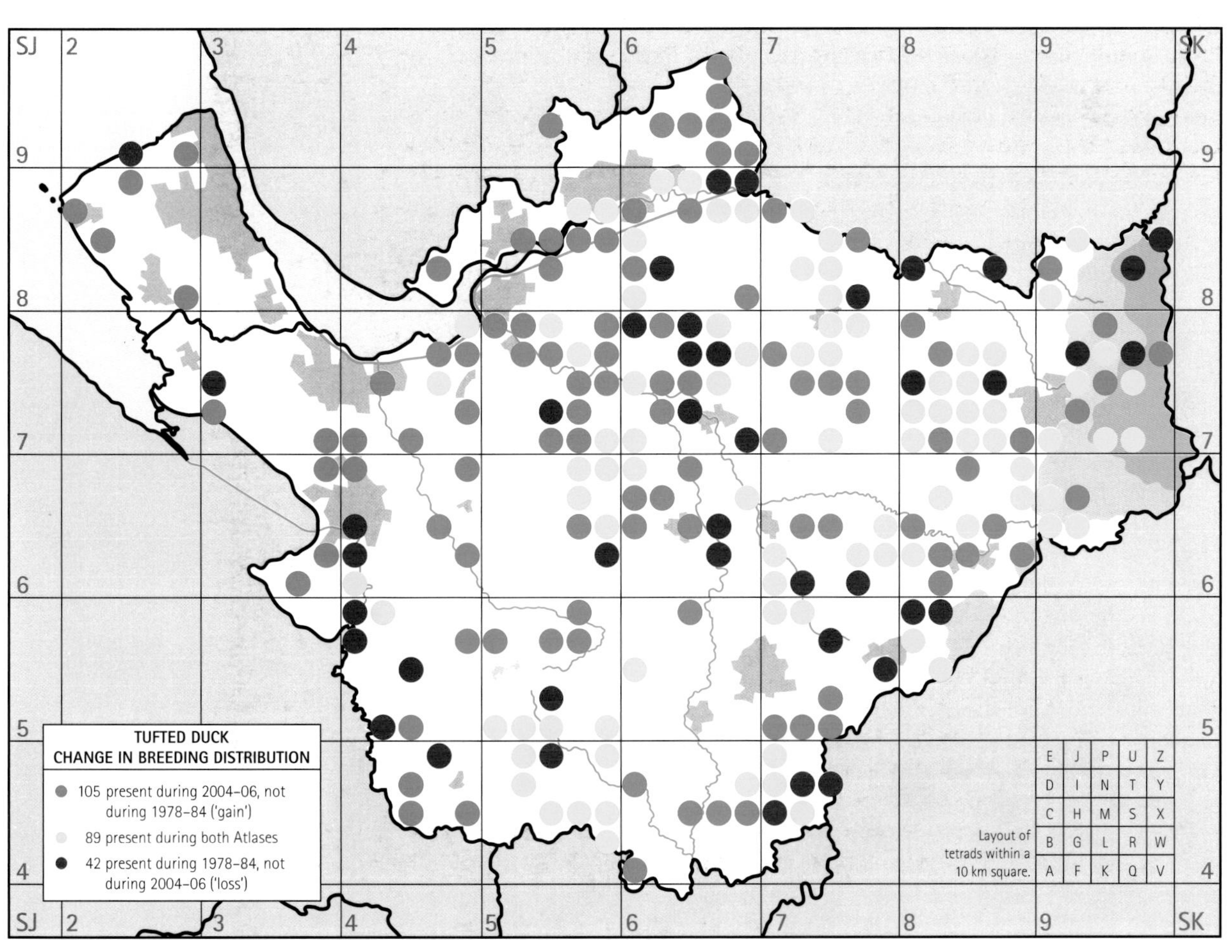
TUFTED DUCK
CHANGE IN BREEDING DISTRIBUTION
105 present during 2004–06, not during 1978–84 ('gain')
89 present during both Atlases
42 present during 1978–84, not during 2004–06 ('loss')
Layout of tetrads within a 10 km square.
E J P U Z
D I N T Y
C H M S X
B G L R W
A F K Q V
SJ
SK

The Tufted Duck is separated ecologically from other diving ducks by having a largely carnivorous diet, mainly molluscs. They find most of their food on the bottom of lakes, and some rivers, up to 5 m deep, diving frequently, typically twice a minute for 15–20 seconds at a time, although males dive deeper and stay submerged for longer than females (Owen *et al.* 1986).

Despite these apparently quite precise requirements, wintering Tufted Ducks are widespread in the county, appearing on almost one-third of tetrads, twice as many as Pochard. They achieve this largely by being able to exploit smaller waters: more than 30% of birds were on ponds or small waterbodies, and 9% of records were on flowing waters, rivers and canals. The largest flock in the county, up to 500 Tufted Ducks, is at Woolston, often on the river Mersey rather than on the dredging deposit beds themselves. As with Pochard, Tufted Ducks seldom use our estuaries.

Tufted Ducks breeding in Scotland mostly move to Ireland for the winter, with a small proportion coming to our area as well; by contrast, those from southern England largely stay within England, with some flying to the Netherlands and some cold-weather movements to Ireland (*Migration Atlas*). The behaviour of the breeding birds and their offspring from Cheshire and Wirral, lying in between, is not known. Most of the Tufted Ducks in Britain in the winter are visitors from more northerly latitudes in Fennoscandia and European Russia. A bird ringed as a chick in Latvia in 1977 was shot in Cheshire in January 1982, and adult birds trapped at Rostherne have been reported from as far north as Lapland and as far east as the river Ob at 65°E, beyond the Ural mountains in Siberia (Wall 1982). One bird ringed at Rostherne was recovered in Iceland; Icelandic breeding birds mainly winter in Ireland, but some mix with the others in Britain. Once here, birds may well move around between sites, but two-thirds of known movements within a winter are short distance, less than 20 km (*Migration Atlas*).

The British wintering population of Tufted Duck has been increasingly slightly for many years, and is now around 90,100 birds (Banks *et al.* 2006). Nowhere in the county holds nationally important numbers, only Woolston coming at all close with figures of 600–700 birds. Other sites with three-figure winter counts during this Atlas included Rostherne Mere (SJ78M), the Chelford Sand Quarries (SJ87B), Redesmere (SJ87K), the Cholmondeley Meres (SJ55K), Frodsham Marsh (SJ57E), Pickmere (SJ67Y) and Astbury Mere (SJ86L), and flocks at Doddington Pool (SJ74D) and Tabley Mere (SJ77I) numbered in the nineties. Half of the mapped tetrads held groups smaller than 10 birds, however: Bell's statement still holds good, that numbers of Tufted Ducks are seldom as large as the Pochard flocks (Bell 1962).

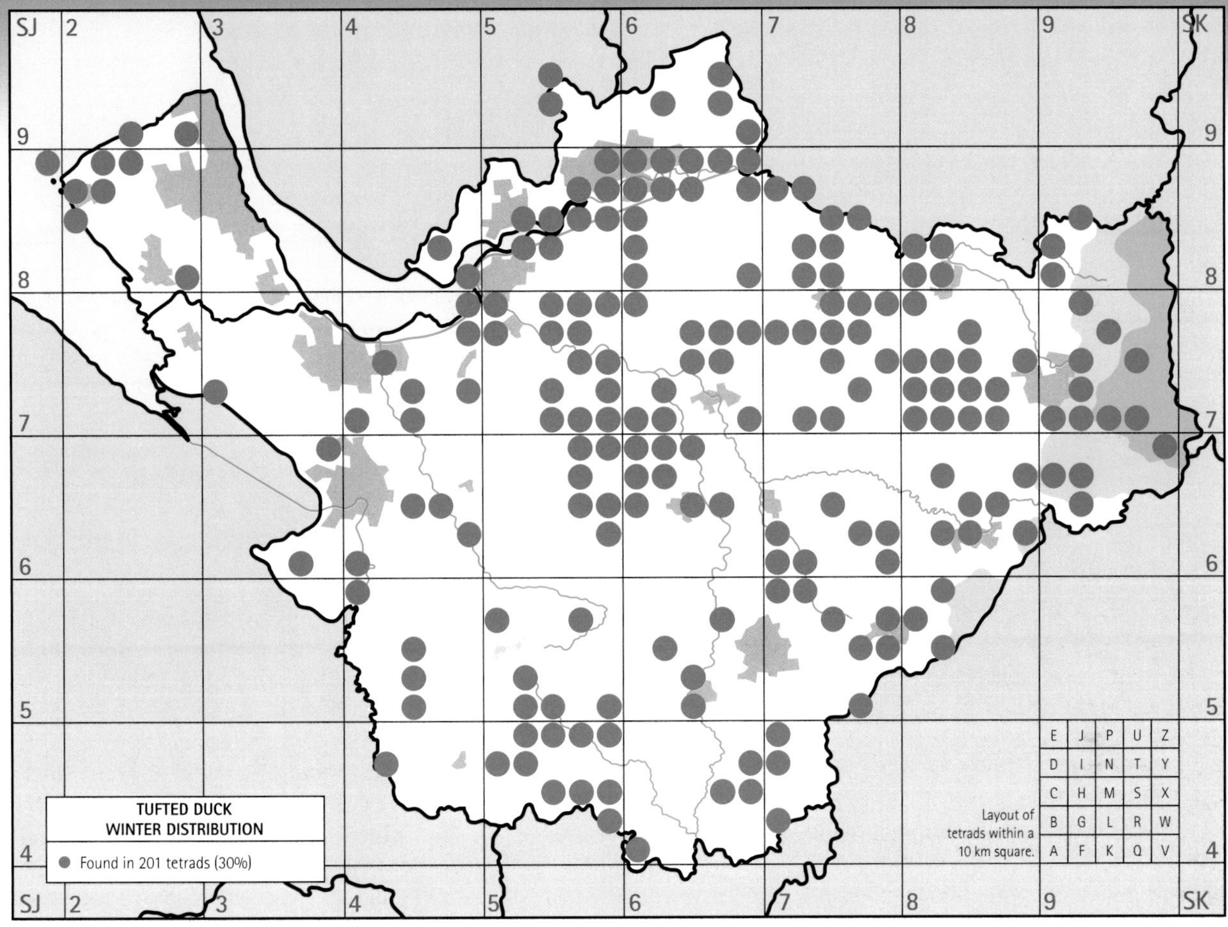
SJ
2
3
4
5
6
7
8
9
SK
9
8
7
6
5
4
TUFTED DUCK
WINTER DISTRIBUTION
Found in 201 tetrads (30%)
E J P U Z
D I N T Y
C H M S X
B G L R W
A F K Q V
Layout of tetrads within a 10 km square.

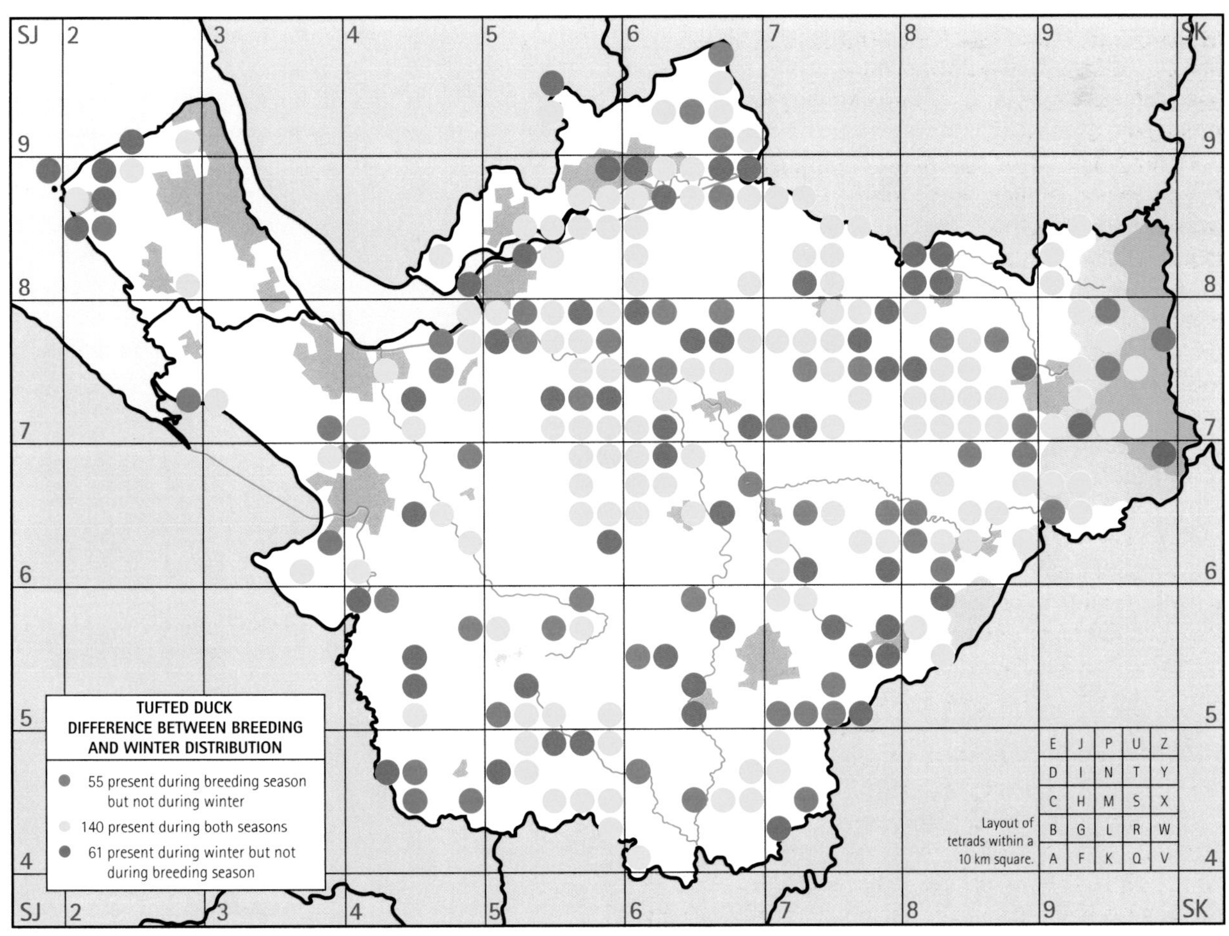
SJ
2
3
4
5
6
7
8
9
SK
9
8
7
6
5
4
TUFTED DUCK
DIFFERENCE BETWEEN BREEDING AND WINTER DISTRIBUTION
55 present during breeding season but not during winter
140 present during both seasons
61 present during winter but not during breeding season
E J P U Z
D I N T Y
C H M S X
B G L R W
A F K Q V
Layout of tetrads within a 10 km square.

Scaup

Aythya marila

RAY SCALLY

Scaup is the most marine of our diving ducks, feeding mostly at night and often elusive even if encountered by day. Their diet is dominated by molluscs, but also includes dead fish and grain, which they obtain by diving, preferring water 6–12 m deep, but frequently reaching 30 m. They visit here mostly from breeding sites in Iceland, and the north Wirral has always seen most of the birds. A century ago, small numbers were found in winter in Liverpool Bay and the estuaries, mostly around the Dee mouth (Coward 1910). Bell (1962) wrote that the Scaup comes here annually but in variable numbers, and it is frequently found in small numbers at inland localities, mostly single birds but occasionally two, and rarely more than five together.

Large wintering flocks in the past have included 300 off West Kirby in 1938/39, and during the winters from 1946 to 1949 there were estimated to be 2,000 off Hoylake and Leasowe. In early 1949 the numbers were nearer 5,000, but since then there do not appear to have been any comparable flocks (Bell 1962). For a while the flock on the Dee, mostly located between Caldy Blacks and Tanskey Rocks (SJ28E), was the only regular wintering haunt of Scaup in western England. The county bird reports note flocks of up to 300 or 400 from the 1960s into the 1980s, but their occurrence was erratic and in some winters there were very few. For instance, in early 1973 the maximum count was 15, leading the editor of the bird report to suggest that they may well disappear completely; but the next year there were up to 250 again. Numbers like this continued until 1983, then in 1984 'the winter flock off Caldy seems to have vanished', but in 1985 there was an 'exceptional' influx of around 200 again, with over 400 in 1986. From the late 1980s the numbers dwindled to maxima below 100, and Hilbre became the most likely place from which to see the species. Counts have continued to decline, although with large annual fluctuations and occasional influxes such as 188 on 23 November 2001.

During this Atlas, the largest flock was counted at 47, with several gatherings of 25 birds, all found off the north or north-west of the Wirral, as far up the Dee as Dawpool Bank off Heswall (SJ28F) where 19 were on a Dee WeBS count. Elsewhere, there were up to four birds at Rostherne Mere in 2004/05, and one or two on all the other waters mapped.

Sponsored by Syngenta CTL

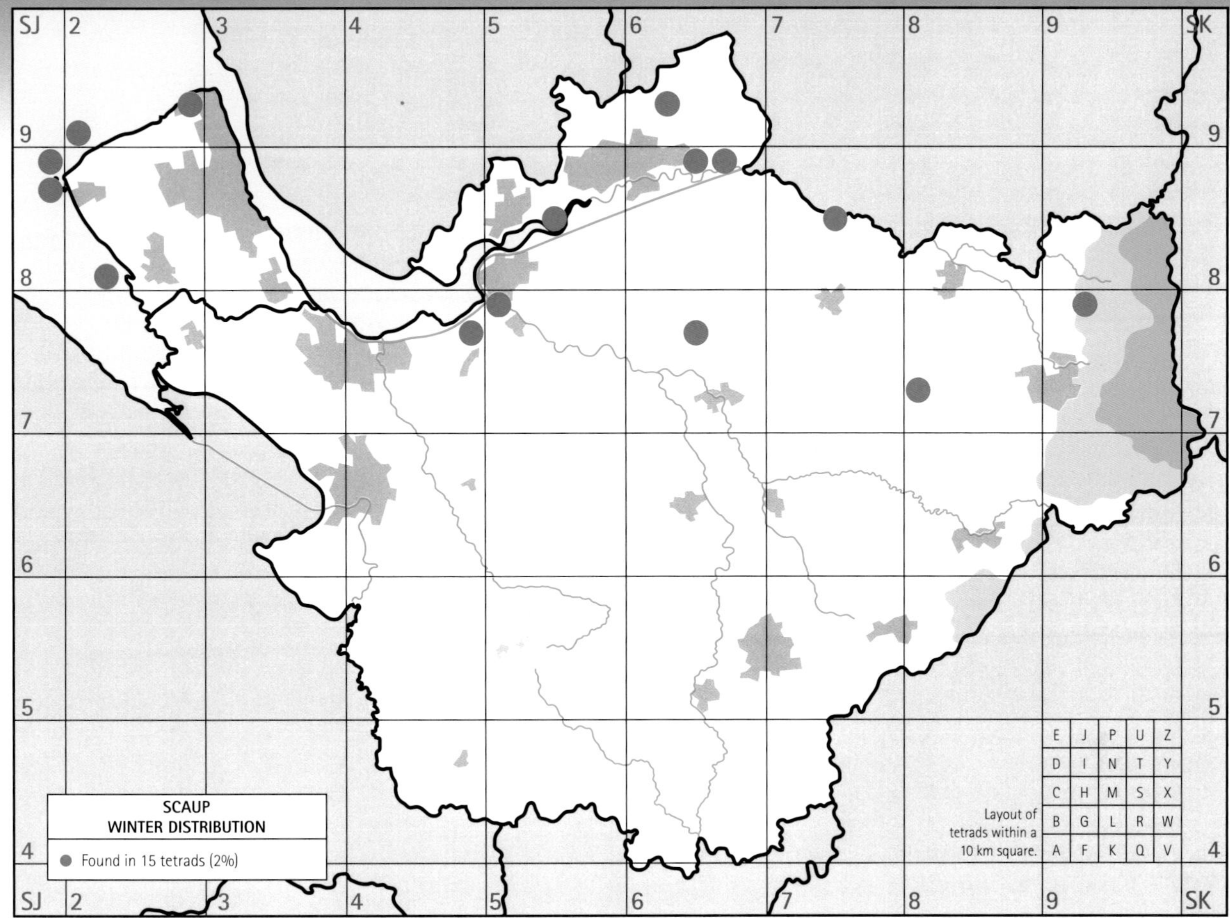
SJ
2
3
4
5
6
7
8
9
SK
SCAUP
WINTER DISTRIBUTION
Found in 15 tetrads (2%)
Layout of
tetrads within a
10 km square.
E J P U Z
D I N T Y
C H M S X
B G L R W
A F K Q V

Eider

Somateria mollissima

Happily, Eiders are no longer threatened with extinction, as they were in the eighteenth century, by collection of their down for use as human bedding. The birds feed in relatively shallow coastal waters, up to about 3 m deep, diving to take molluscs and crustaceans from the seabed, especially Common Mussels *Mytilus edulis* and other bivalves, plus periwinkles, whelks, starfish, crabs, sea urchins and other slow-moving invertebrates. Eiders pair during the winter, the male taking responsibility for watching for predators or competitors whilst his mate feeds and builds up the body reserves necessary for a successful breeding season; females which pair after midwinter usually lay late or fail to breed (*BTO Winter Atlas*).

This sea duck has become more common in the county in the last fifty years. Coward (1910) knew of only one on the coast, seen by Oldham in the lea of the sea-wall at Leasowe on the bitterly cold day of 31 December 1905, with a bizarre flurry of three inland records in 1894 and 1895, at Saighton, near Nantwich and at Aldford. Bell (1962) could trace no further records until 1939, when it started to become more frequent, and was found roughly every other year from 1951 to 1960. Bell (1967) and the county bird reports show that from 1960 Eiders have become almost annual at the coast, most often near Hilbre, with less frequent records from anywhere along the north Wirral. Birds farther up the Dee estuary, such as the female at Parkgate on 11 January 2005, mapped in this Atlas, are as rare as inland records, of which the last was in 1999.

There is no direct proof from ringed birds, but it is tempting to link the rise in sightings in Wirral waters to the foundation of the breeding colony on Walney Island, Cumbria, the most southerly breeding site on the west coast of Britain, which was colonized in 1949, and has been occupied ever since.

The Atlas map shows their typical winter distribution. The only double-figure counts were 14 off Hilbre on 6 December 2006, with 10 off Hoylake Shore in winter 2004/05.

RAY SCALLY

Sponsored by Geoff Blamire

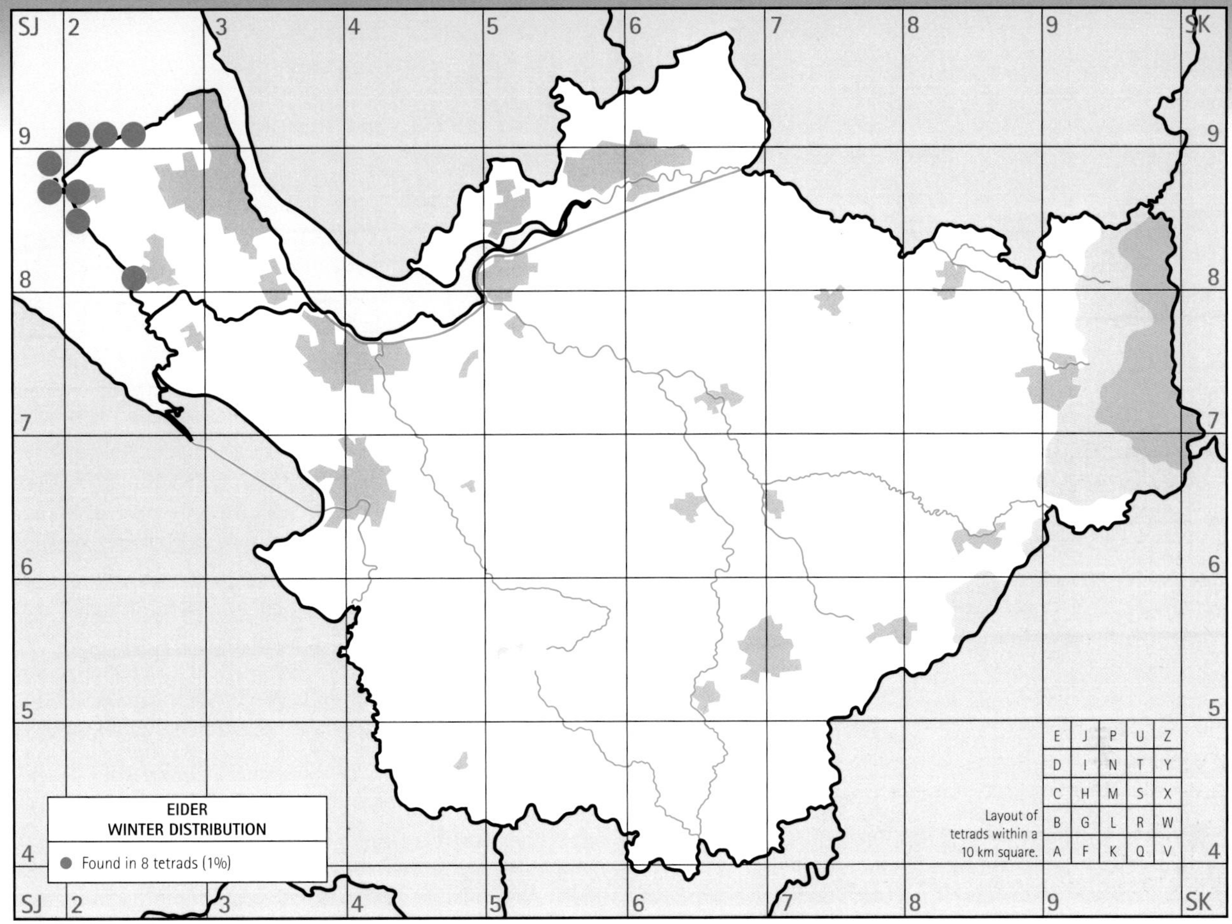
SJ
2
3
4
5
6
7
8
9
SK
9
8
7
6
5
4
EIDER
WINTER DISTRIBUTION
Found in 8 tetrads (1%)
Layout of
tetrads within a
10 km square.
E J P U Z
D I N T Y
C H M S X
B G L R W
A F K Q V

Long-tailed Duck

Clangula hyemalis

RAY SCALLY

A few thousand of this marine species visit Britain every winter, thought to be from the northern Norway and Russia part of their circumpolar breeding distribution, but they nearly all stay in Scottish waters. Like other sea-ducks they dive for their diet of molluscs, especially the Common Mussel *Mytilus edulis*, but also take other bivalves such as cockles and clams, and gastropods such as periwinkles and whelks. When they visit inland sites they probably eat crustaceans and fish such as sticklebacks.

They have always been scarce in Cheshire and Wirral. Coward (1910) wrote that they were seldom met with on the west coast of England, but occasionally immature birds have been obtained in autumn and winter in the Dee estuary. He was able to list just four winter records, from December 1839, December 1886 and November 1900 (two birds). Bell (1962) thought that this understated their true status, since from 1950 on it had been recorded each year in very small numbers, usually singly, 'and this is substantially true for the earlier years from at least 1930'.

Since then, the annual county bird reports show about 48 coastal records, of around 77 birds, in the 40 winters from 1964/65 to 2003/04. They were recorded in 24 of the 40 winters. Inland occurrences have become much more frequent. Bell (1962) knew of only six inland winter records in 60 years, but the annual county bird reports show about 29 records, of up to 40 birds, in the 40 winters from 1964/65 to 2003/04. They are never common, however: apart from a flurry of records from 1979/80 to 1981/82, there have seldom been inland records at more than one site in a winter.

The records during this Atlas represent an increase on those in recent years; all but one were in winter 2004/05 so this is not an effect of aggregating three winters. Inland, two birds were on the river Weaver (SJ57P) on 28 February 2005 and the Chelford Sand Quarries (SJ87A/B) provided the home for two different overwintering birds, a male and a female, throughout winter 2004/05. A feature of inland Long-tailed Ducks has often been their propensity to stay for long periods, and these two were true to form. In their more normal coastal habitats, single birds were seen in both of the tetrads at Hilbre (SJ18Y/Z), one of the species' most regular haunts, and two birds were off the north Wirral shore at Hoylake (SJ29A). Finally, from mid-February 2005, a drake was on West Kirby Marine Lake (SJ28C/D), continuing its long association with the species first recorded 70 years ago when Farrer wrote 'nowadays a walk along West Kirby Promenade during the winter months will generally result in a view of long-tails fishing in the Marine Lake' (Farrer 1938).

Sponsored by Charlotte Twist

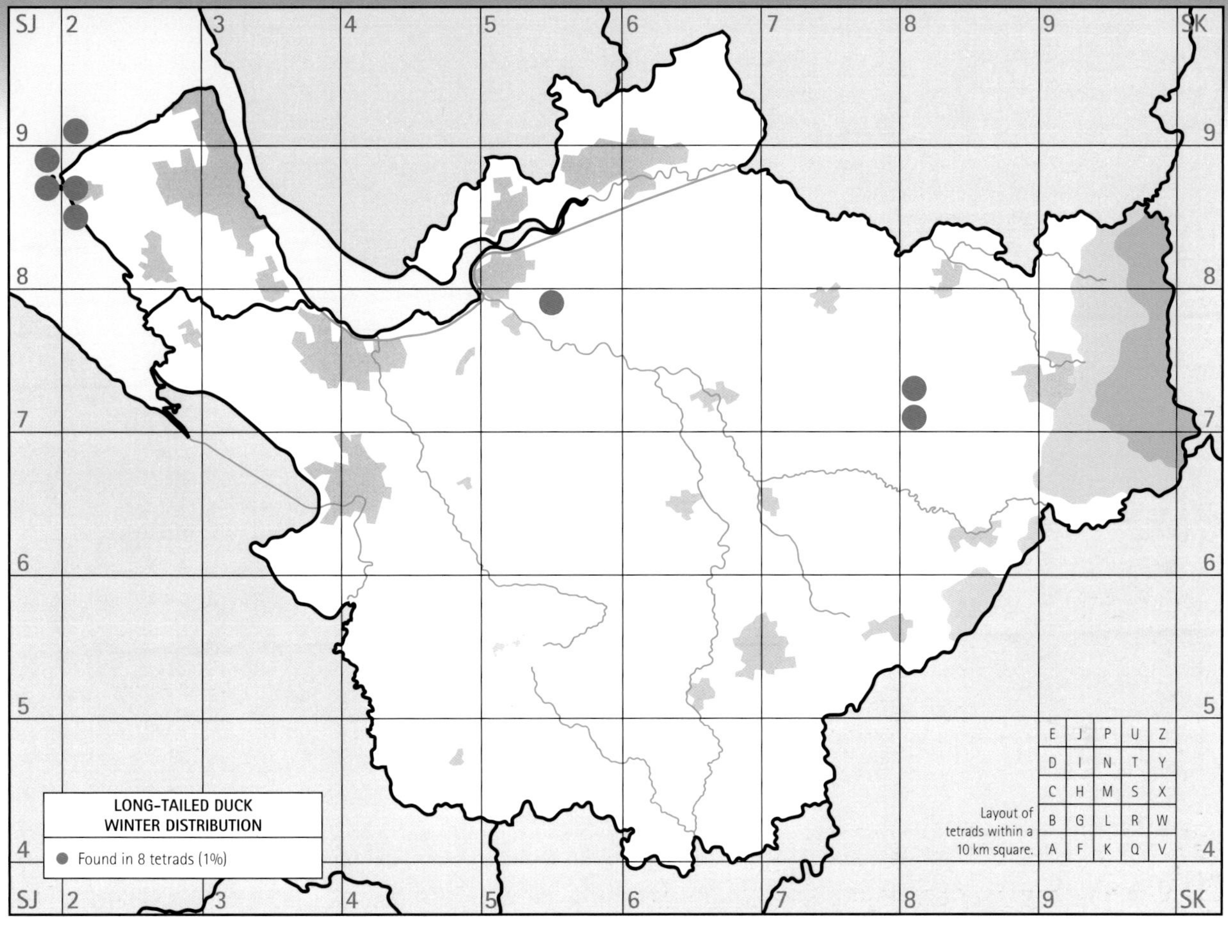
LONG-TAILED DUCK
WINTER DISTRIBUTION
Found in 8 tetrads (1%)
Layout of
tetrads within a
10 km square.
E J P U Z
D I N T Y
C H M S X
B G L R W
A F K Q V
SJ
SK
2
3
4
5
6
7
8
9

Common Scoter

Melanitta nigra

ANDREW MART

We now know that the Common Scoters seen from the north Wirral shore, often at the limits of telescope vision even for dedicated sea-watchers, are just a small part of the vast concentrations in Liverpool Bay. Aerial survey work since 2000/01 has shown that an average of 51,000 Common Scoters spend the winter in the Irish Sea between the North Wales coast and the Solway Firth, the biggest gathering anywhere in Britain (Banks *et al.* 2006). Their main concentrations are on the Shell Flat, offshore from Blackpool, and in Colwyn Bay, but another important wintering site is off the north Wirral coast, an area roughly 4 km in diameter centred just over 3 km north-west of Meols, shown in the map of the aerial survey results (Webb *et al.* 2004). Almost all these birds are within the 10 m water depth contour where they dive to find molluscs, mainly mussels, on the sandy seabed.

Unfortunately, these surveys have been triggered by the potential threats to scoters from the construction of offshore wind farms: it is this species' misfortune to favour the shallow sandbanks that are also the preferred construction sites for turbines. However, the new awareness of the importance of this area has prompted consideration of all of the important areas of Liverpool Bay, including those off the north Wirral, as a marine Special Protection Area.

For such a marine species, the flocks that came close enough inshore to be recorded for this Atlas are the 'tip of the iceberg'. The largest counts submitted were 43 off Hilbre (SJ18Y/Z), 190 and 150 off Hoylake shore (SJ29A and SJ29E respectively) and 80 birds offshore from Meols (SJ29F/G). Much easier to see, and much less common, was the only inland record during this Atlas, a female at Arclid Sand Quarry (SJ76W) on 11 January 2005.

The distribution of Common Scoters in the county has most likely not changed for centuries. Byerley (1856) knew it as 'very abundant about the sandbanks' and Brockholes (1874) wrote that it was 'an abundant duck at sea off the north of Wirral'. It seems that this is one species for which Coward (1910) probably got it wrong. He wrote that 'during the winter months the Common Scoter occurs in considerable numbers in the Dee and Mersey estuaries' although he added that 'as a rule the scoter does not ascend the estuaries to any great distance', and noted that the shallow waters near Hilbre were their favourite feeding grounds. Birds had been noticed occasionally on inland waters, but most

Sponsored by Liverpool University Press

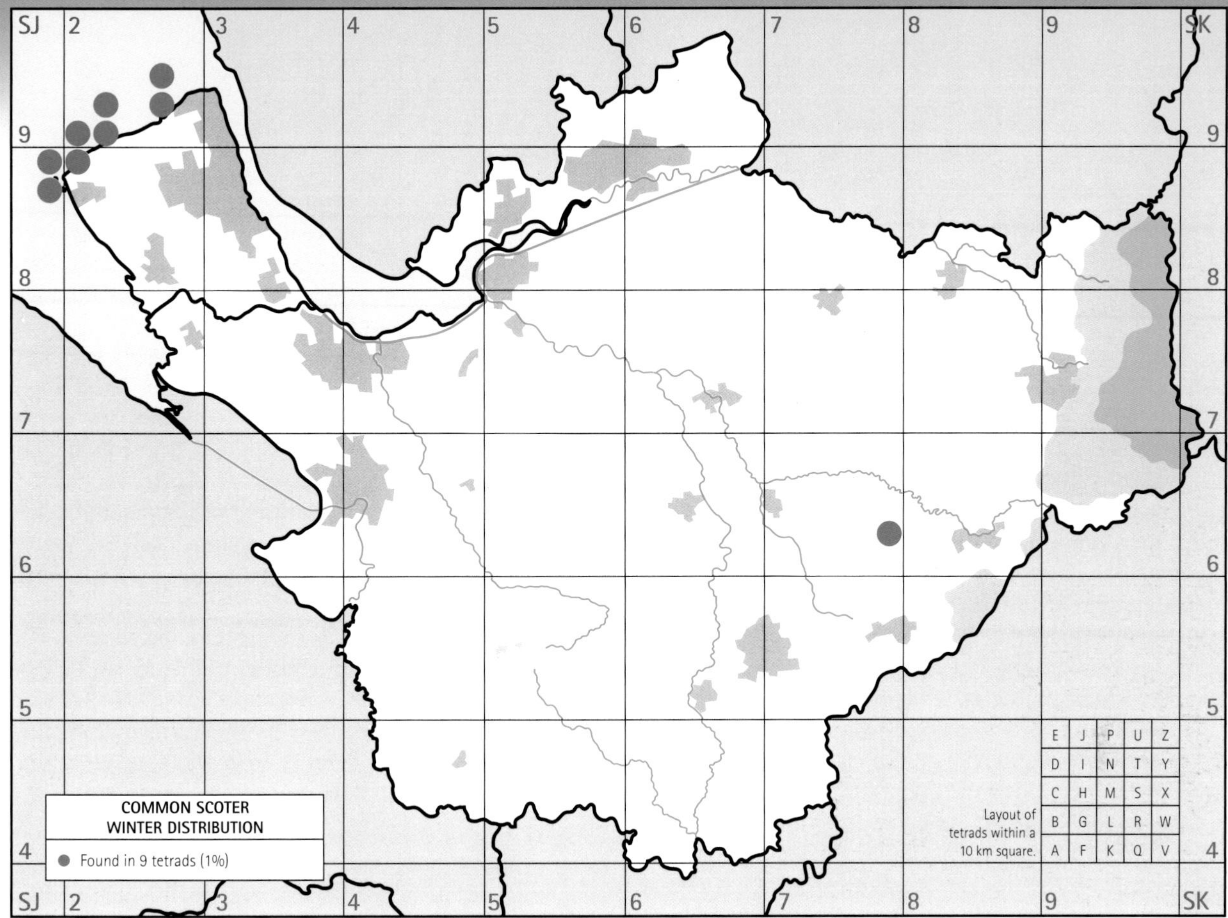

of the records listed are at passage times. Bell (1962) remarked that Coward's description would not fit the twentieth-century picture, with no indication of large estuarine flocks. They were still common in the Dee estuary and could be seen in all months, but numbers in the 1950s rarely exceeded 40 birds. Inland records were almost annual in very small numbers.

Since then, *CWBRs* confirm the status at the mouth of the Dee and north Wirral coasts. Mersey records are very unusual, as are inland birds in winter, with only about three records in the last decade. The Atlas map, therefore, gives a reasonable snapshot of the species' distribution.

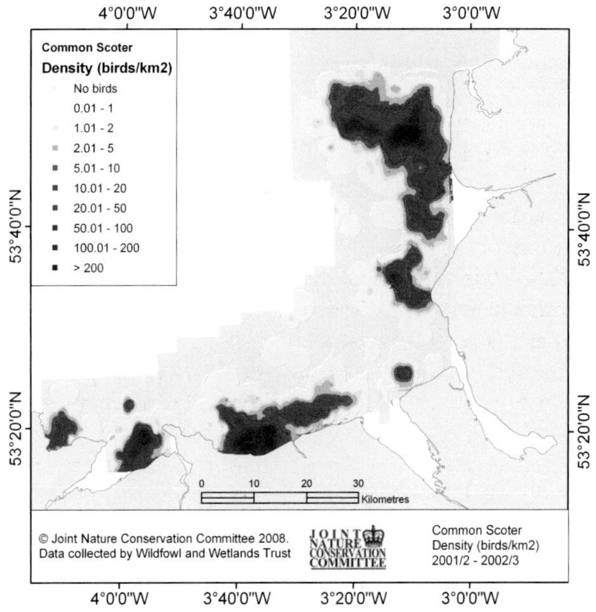

Common Scoter density in Liverpool Bay.

Goldeneye

Bucephala clangula

Goldeneyes come here to spend the winter, mostly from breeding sites in Sweden; Finnish birds tend to leapfrog these and winter in Ireland (*Migration Atlas*). This diving duck feeds in deep water, especially on water beetles with other insects, molluscs and crustaceans.

Although there are year-to-year fluctuations, the annual county bird reports for the last forty years paint a similar picture to that found during this Atlas. Indeed, the general assessment of its status has not changed much for a century or more. Coward (1910) noted that it occurred frequently at the periods of migration, and was met with occasionally during the winter months. Bell (1962) wrote that Goldeneyes had a distinct predilection for Oakmere, Marbury, Tatton and the Langley Reservoirs where, so long as the water remained unfrozen, birds could be found throughout the winter. He added that the species is equally at home on salt water, and may be found from autumn to spring particularly in the Dee estuary in parties up to 20 birds.

Records for this Atlas show Goldeneyes almost exclusively on the larger waters, present in 61 tetrads on lakes, reservoirs and sandpits, but only one on a small waterbody. Three records came from the widest rivers and one from the Manchester Ship Canal, with seven estuarine and two open sea habitat codes. They are found mostly on the deep-water meres—although those noted by Bell are less often visited—and this is one of the ducks that especially seems to favour the upland reservoirs in east Cheshire. On salt-water sites, there were no records from the Mersey, where they are scarce, but birds were found all along the Dee, where they seem particularly to like West Kirby Marine Lake.

There were no large counts and nowhere approaches the threshold figure for national importance (249): it is doubtful whether a flock of even 100 birds has ever occurred in the county. Of the 120 counts submitted during this Atlas, only 26 were in double figures. The highest were at sites that tend not to feature in the lists for other ducks: 39 at Farmwood Pool (SJ87B), 32 on Deer Park Mere (SJ55F/K); 22 at Redes Mere (SJ87K) and 21 at the river Weaver Bend (SJ57E). The total wintering in the county probably does not exceed 400 birds.

SIMON BOOTH

Sponsored by Graham and Dorothy Palmer

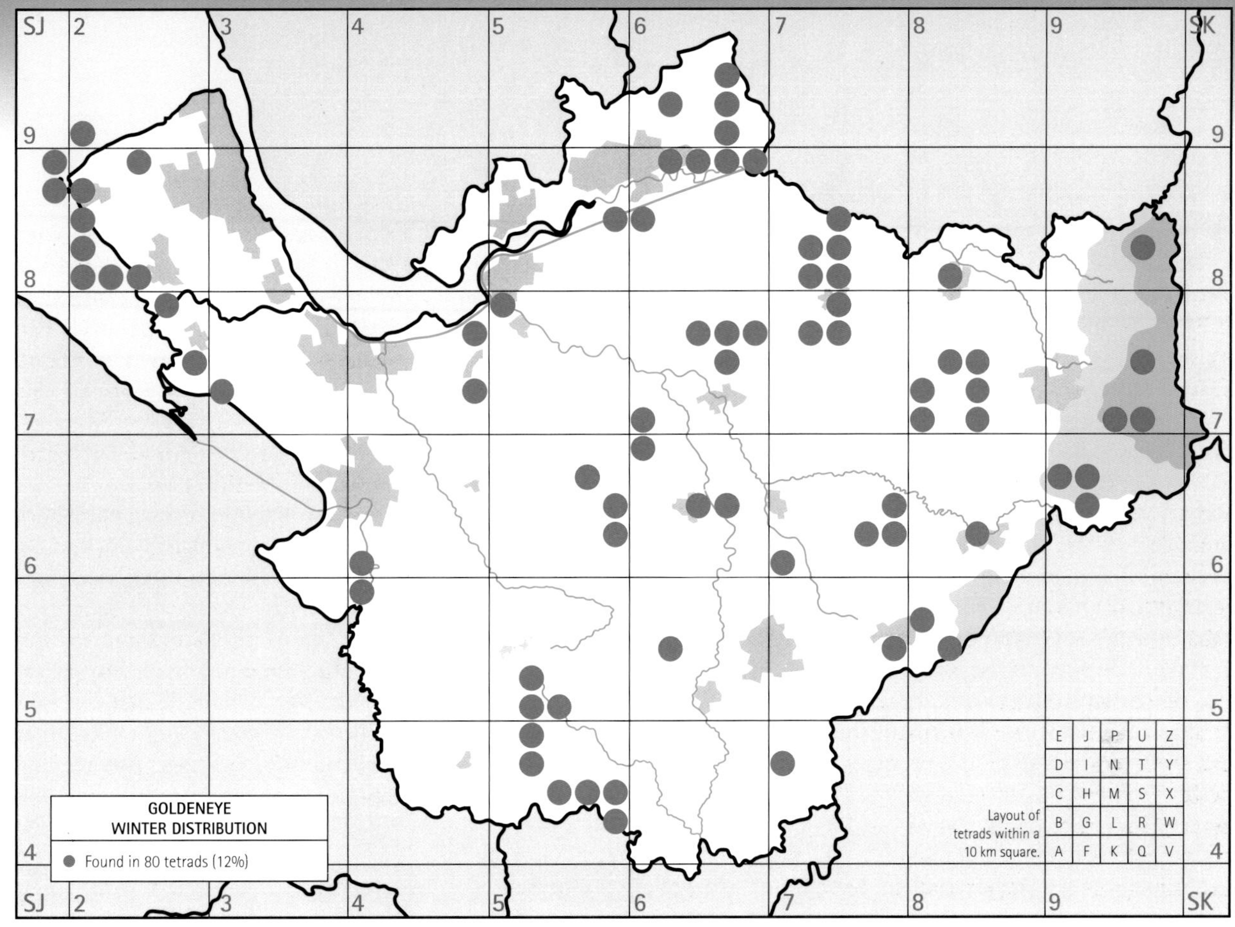
GOLDENEYE
WINTER DISTRIBUTION
Found in 80 tetrads (12%)
Layout of tetrads within a 10 km square.
E J P U Z
D I N T Y
C H M S X
B G L R W
A F K Q V
SJ
SK

Smew

Mergellus albellus

Smew is the rarest sawbill in Cheshire and Wirral. Although the species was found in 11 tetrads during this Atlas, there were only seven birds recorded in the three winters, with no more than one bird present at a time. Two of the meres visited span tetrad boundaries: Chapel Mere (SJ55F/G/K) and Tatton Mere (SJ77P/78K), and one bird accounted for all four tetrads in the eastern hills, a male in February 2006 moving between Bosley Reservoir (SJ96D/H/I) and Tegg's Nose, Bottoms and Ridgegate Reservoirs (SJ97K), apparently finding sufficient fish in the oligotrophic upland reservoirs. This is probably fewer birds in the county than in any three-year period for many years. Although never numerous, most Smews are found here during icy weather, when the thousands of birds wintering in the Netherlands are driven west or south, but the mild winters of late have meant that few birds have had to move this far. The species undertakes only a relatively short-distance migration from its breeding grounds in the boreal zone of Fennoscandia and Russia.

All of the mapped birds were on inland waters; estuarine records are unusual in the county, with the latest being on the Dee salt-marsh for one day each in 1995 and 1999, while the most recent coastal bird, at Leasowe in 2002, appears to have been the first since one off Hilbre in 1980. In eastern Europe Smew winter largely at sea, but in the western part of their range they use inland waters (Tucker & Heath 1994). Coward (1910) summarized the species' status as 'a rare winter visitor to the coast and inland waters', and Craggs (1982) lists five records at Hilbre from 1942 to 1980. There appears to be no justification for Bell's statement that there were 'many records from the estuaries' (Bell 1962).

It seems that Smew now arrive earlier in the winter than previously. Bell (1962) said that they did not usually arrive until the latter part of December, and frequently were not seen until January. The county bird report for 1984, noting the unprecedented arrival of three birds in November, commented that there had been only about nine previous records in the twentieth century, but November birds have been seen in roughly every other year since then. The record for early arrival was set by a male that came to Inner Marsh Farm on 7 October 1999 and stayed until 3 March 2000; this could have been the same bird that had been there for the previous three winters. Smews in Cheshire often seem to have a run of years at the same location and one has to suspect recurrence of certain individuals, although there never has

RAY SCALLY

Sponsored by Syngenta CTL

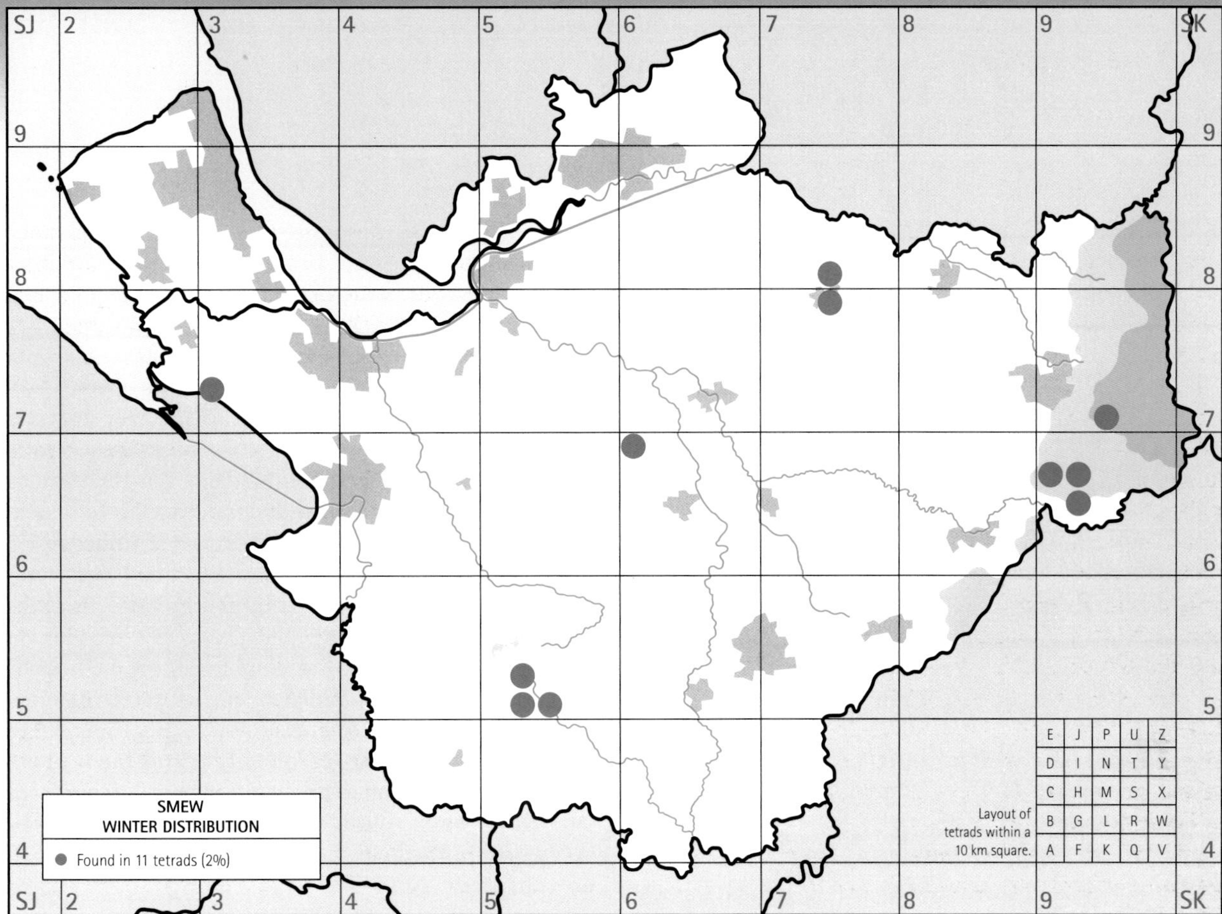

been any proof. One or two females appeared regularly at Tatton Mere, every winter for 10 years throughout the 1970s, and a male was at Inner Marsh Farm for six winters from 1999/2000 to 2004/05.

Three of the seven birds found during this survey were the strikingly marked drakes. They are normally in the minority, being outnumbered by females and immatures in their 'red-head' plumage. The male's eclipse plumage appears identical to the 'red-head' garb, but most birds have moulted into adult male plumage before arriving here. This moult is quite quick, taking about three weeks: a red-head present at Inner Marsh Farm from 9 November 1996 had moulted into 'full adult' male plumage by 30 November that year, and another red-head at the same site from 8 November 1997 had become a smart male by 1 December.

Red-breasted Merganser

Mergus serrator

MIKE ATKINSON

Red-breasted Merganser is now, and always has been, the sawbill of the tidal waters. Coward (1910) knew it as 'a not uncommon winter visitor to the estuaries; rare inland'. Bell (1962) summarized its status as 'today a regular winter visitor to the coast and estuaries from October to April'. Inland, Bell could trace only seven records in winter, from 1893 to 1966, mostly singles but up to four birds for 18 days in 1942 (Bell 1962, 1967).

This Atlas map typifies its present status, with birds in winter in 18 coastal and estuarine tetrads, and two inland, at the Weaver Bend (SJ57E) on 23 and 29 January 2005 and at Hurleston Reservoir (SJ67H) on 7 January 2006, making Hurleston the only site to have recorded both Red-breasted Merganser and Goosander during this winter Atlas period.

The largest flock in one tetrad was 28 birds roosting at Parkgate (SJ27U) on a Dee WeBS count in 2004/05, with 25 birds off Heswall (SJ28K) in 2006/07 and 22 on West Kirby Marine Lake (SJ28C/D) in 2004/05. These figures are typical of the wintering counts in recent years, although more birds are present at passage times, especially in March and April. Nowhere in the county approaches the criterion for national importance (1% of the population) of 98 birds. The Dee probably was more important for them in the 1960s, when it was realized that their main feeding area was the mid-channel of the estuary off Caldy. This is too far away from land for accurate observation, but unprecedentedly high counts were made of around 90 in late February 1965, rising to a maximum of about 250 on 5 March 1965, eclipsing the previous record of only 26 (Bell 1967). Since then, Red-breasted Mergansers have become much more numerous nationally, but not in Cheshire and Wirral. The WeBS index for birds wintering in Great Britain rose steadily, almost quadrupling between the mid-1960s and the mid-1990s, but has since dropped, perhaps as warmer winters reduce the numbers of continental immigrants.

Red-breasted Mergansers swim part-submerged, then dive for their prey, often hunting cooperatively in small flocks. Their serrated bill is well adapted for gripping fish, and they take especially sticklebacks and gobies, with other small marine prey including flatfish, shrimps and lugworms. Most of the habitat codes recorded in this Atlas were H3 (estuarine; 11 tetrads) with five H5 (open sea).

The origins of our wintering Red-breasted Mergansers are not known, but British-breeding mergansers probably stay here for the winter, mixing with birds from continental Europe and Iceland, with some possibly from east Greenland (*Migration Atlas*). A few breed in North Wales, as close as 25 km to Cheshire, but they are never known to have bred in the county. A bird was reported to have built a nest at Oakmere in 1962, but no eggs were laid.

Sponsored by Linda Evans

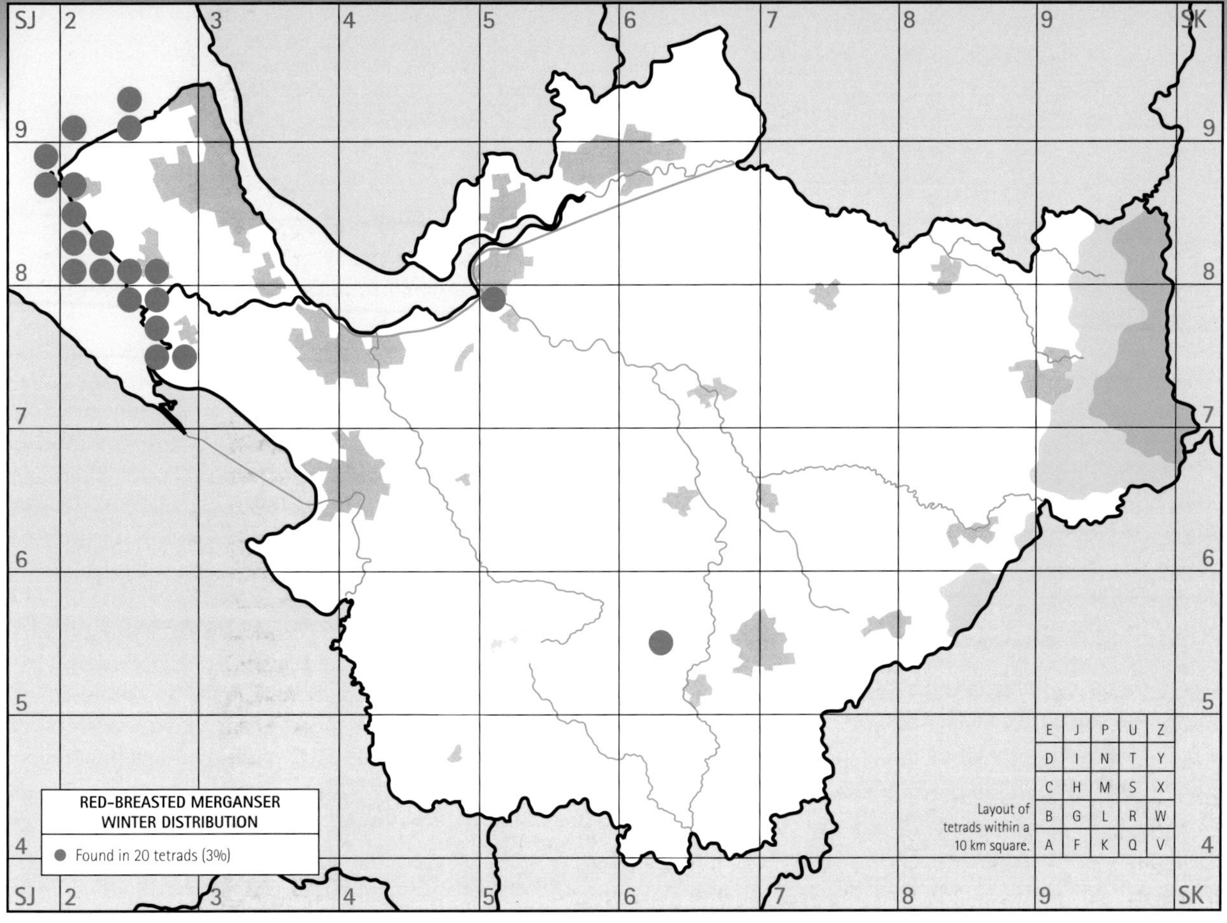
RED-BREASTED MERGANSER
WINTER DISTRIBUTION
Found in 20 tetrads (3%)
Layout of
tetrads within a
10 km square.
E J P U Z
D I N T Y
C H M S X
B G L R W
A F K Q V
SJ
SK

Goosander

Mergus merganser

This species was not even mentioned in our *First Atlas* as there had never been any hint of its presence in the breeding season in the county. It was a bird of Scotland and northern England, first recorded breeding in Northumbria in 1941 and Cumbria in 1950. The national *BTO Second Atlas*, with fieldwork in 1988–91, showed that Goosanders had spread greatly since the *BTO First Atlas* (1968–72) and they have been converging on Cheshire from all sides. To the west, the Welsh population rose rapidly from one pair in 1968–72 to 10 pairs by 1977 and 100 pairs by 1985, and they spread over the English border to Shropshire in 1987. In the Pennines they had reached Lancashire by 1973 and first bred in Derbyshire in 1981.

In the context of this speedy expansion of range, it was perhaps a surprise that the first breeding in Cheshire was not until 1995, when a nest with eggs was found in a hollow tree in the east of the county (Higginbotham 1995). According to the county bird reports, the same site was occupied in 1996 and 1997, then a pair was present, but with no confirmed breeding, from 1998 to 2000, and no indication of breeding at all in 2001. In 2002 unfledged juveniles were noted on the river Dane, Congleton, in late May and in 2003 'the usual records came from the river Dane during the breeding season with a female and four chicks on the river by the Macclesfield Canal aqueduct (SJ96C)'.

This Atlas spurred more recording. Although no confirmed breeding was reported in 2004, pairs were found on two more river systems, the Dee on the Welsh border and the Weaver in central Cheshire. Goosanders were not proven to breed on the river Weaver, but a pair was present near Stapeley (SJ64U) for about two weeks in the breeding season of 2006, frequently visiting an old poplar tree alongside the river, with the female seen entering a hole.

Birds were proven breeding on the Dane in SJ76Y in 2005, and in SJ76N and SJ96C in 2006, and on the Dee near Crewe-by-Farndon (SJ45G) in 2006. In all four tetrads, surveyors found a female with a brood of chicks, a delightful experience whose effect was nicely summarized by Ann Pym: 'Fantastic!! Observed a female swimming with 11 young, quite well grown. In next few weeks saw three more times.' Young chicks eat aquatic invertebrates, graduating to small fish as they grow. They are tended alone by the female; as soon as their

RAY SCALLY

Sponsored by Phil Oddy

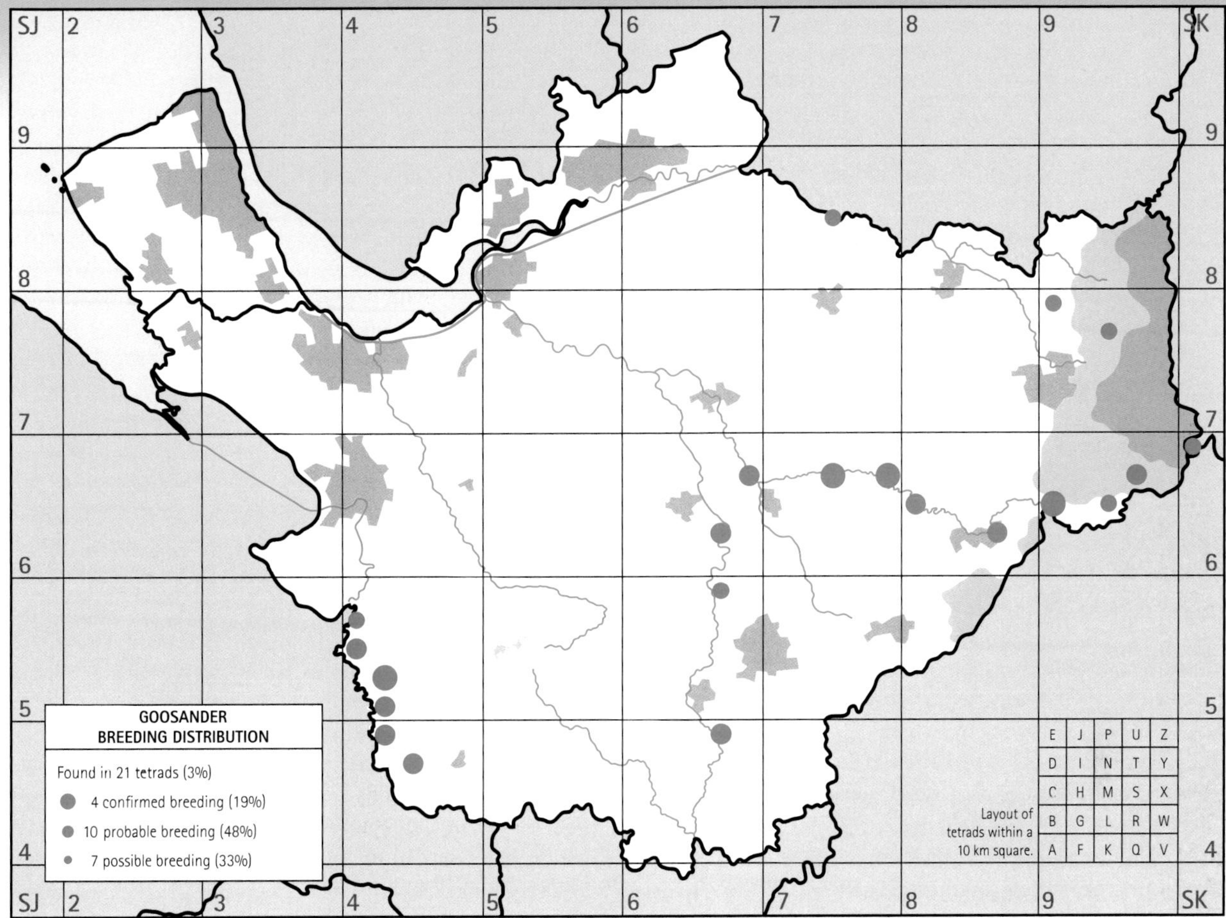

mates are incubating eggs, the drakes migrate to moult in northern Norway, not returning until November (*Migration Atlas*).

The county population is only four pairs confirmed and 10 pairs probably breeding, but with birds on three of Cheshire's river systems the Goosander seems firmly established as a breeding species. In other parts of Britain Goosanders have been encouraged by provision of nest-boxes, and discouraged by illegal shooting by anglers, but neither is known to have occurred in Cheshire.

This is by far the most widespread and numerous sawbill wintering in the county, being found in this Atlas in 102 tetrads, compared to 20 for Red-breasted Merganser and 12 for Smew. The female and immature 'red-heads' usually considerably outnumber the distinctive adult males. Goosanders are almost all found inland, especially in the south and east of Cheshire, as was the case one hundred (Coward 1910) and fifty (Bell 1962) years ago. Records from Hilbre, and sometimes other Dee sites, have been almost annual, especially in migration periods, and Hilbre had one or two on single dates in three of the four winters from 2000/01 to 2003/04, but none during this Atlas. The map shows that Inner Marsh Farm (SJ37B) and Frodsham Marsh (SJ47Z) are the nearest that Goosanders got to the estuaries during the three years of this winter survey. The origins of those wintering in Cheshire are unknown, but the birds are likely to comprise some from northern Britain and some from continental Europe and Fennoscandia (*Migration Atlas*). After completing their moult, British Goosanders return from Norway late in the year, few birds being seen before November.

The largest gatherings of Goosander during this Atlas period were on waters not normally featuring at the top of the lists for wildfowl flocks: 59 birds on Oulton Park Lake (SJ56X), 52 at the Chelford Sand Quarries (SJ87A/B/G), 35 roosting at Bosley Reservoir (SJ96H/I), 30 on Radnor Mere (SJ87M/N), a maximum of 23 on the Dee floods near Worthenbury (SJ44I) and 20 on Chapel Mere (SJ55F/K). More than half of the Atlas records were of just one or two birds.

In contrast to the breeding season, when three-quarters of habitat codes were G7 (river), with 20% on small waterbodies and just one bird on a mere (Rostherne), in winter two-thirds of the birds were using standing water, mostly meres and reservoirs, with the rest on rivers, streams and small canals. They feed almost exclusively on coarse fish, mainly small specimens up to 7.5 cm long.

Some Cheshire waters have been particularly favoured by Goosanders. Bell (1962) wrote that they were liable to visit any of the meres between November and March but they seldom stayed except at Doddington Pool, where they were usually present throughout the winter so long as the water remained open. The maximum count there was 76 in January 1958, although 30 was more normal. He suggested that their predilection for Doddington would provide an interesting subject for research by a hydrobiologist (Bell 1967): 40 years on, still little is known about the species' winter ecology. The annual county bird reports show that a count of around 100 at Doddington in January 1969 was probably the largest flock ever seen in Cheshire. During the 1970s this was still their preferred site when quiet, but was suffering increasing disturbance. From about 1980 onwards the Cholmondeley meres took over as Goosanders' favoured spot, although numbers were low during much of the 1980s. Goosanders often use different waters at night from their daytime haunts (Brown & Grice 2005) and in 1990 a night-time roost was discovered at Lamaload Reservoir, later found to move between there and the upland reservoirs at Bosley and Trentabank. The normal annual maximum count was 50 or 60 birds, reducing to 30 or 40 from the year 2000 onwards. There have been suggestions that those on the south Cheshire meres and the eastern hill reservoirs are in fact the same birds, making circadian movements. It would be a worthwhile, if challenging, task to test this hypothesis, perhaps using radio-tracked birds, coordinated counts and a team of observers on their flight-lines.

RAY SCALLY

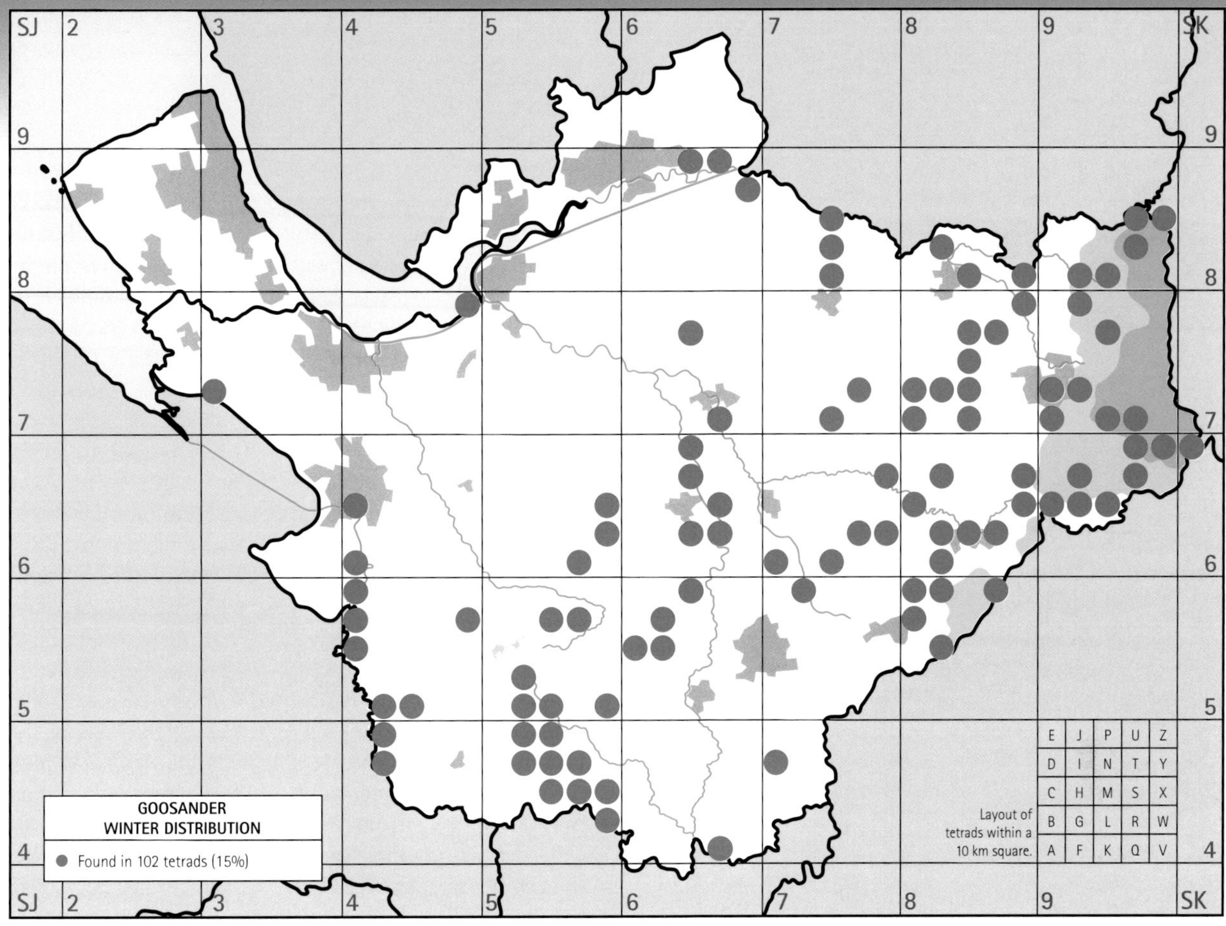
GOOSANDER
WINTER DISTRIBUTION
Found in 102 tetrads (15%)
Layout of tetrads within a 10 km square.
E J P U Z
D I N T Y
C H M S X
B G L R W
A F K Q V
SJ
SK
2
3
4
5
6
7
8
9

Ruddy Duck

Oxyura jamaicensis

SUE & ANDY TRANTER

Our *First Atlas* text concluded with the sentence 'There is no doubt that most of the Cheshire meres provide ideal breeding sites for the Ruddy Duck and have played an important part in its colonization of Britain'. Since then, they have spread further and Ruddy Ducks have now bred on most of the county's lowland waters. The 'change' map shows that in the last twenty years they have expanded into the Wirral and along the Mersey valley, although birds have been lost from many sites across the rest of Cheshire.

The submitted habitat codes show that nearly all birds were found on standing waters, mostly the larger ones, with some waterside vegetation in which to hide their nest. These are the last ducks to breed each year, with chicks seldom appearing before July, and broods hatching sometimes into early September. Males in the breeding season indulge in conspicuous display, but they are not territorial and many mate promiscuously without forming stable pair bonds with females. The typical size of their single clutch is 6–10 eggs, although observations at Woolston show that some Ruddy Ducks lay one or more eggs in another species' nest, usually Tufted Duck or Pochard, but occasionally Mallard, leaving their offspring to be raised by another female. There can be large annual fluctuations in numbers of Ruddy Duck broods, often related to changes in water levels through the season: at Woolston only 5 broods were seen in 2004, 12 broods in 2005 and 10 broods in 2006.

It is impossible to discuss this species nowadays without mentioning 'the cull'. The Ruddy Duck is closely related to the White-headed Duck *Oxyura leucocephala*, but their conservation status is very different: Ruddy Ducks are common and widespread across their native North America, with a population of half a million or more, but White-headed Ducks are endangered, with fewer than 15,000 birds spread across their range of Spain, North Africa and Asia. Measures to protect and restore habitats and ban hunting have helped the Spanish population to rise from 22 in 1977 to 2,500 in early 2003 but the critical threat to this species was identified as hybridization with immigrant Ruddy Ducks from Britain.

A group of UK conservation organizations spent many years, starting in 1992, researching the issues and eventually concluded that the only solution was to eradicate the Ruddy Duck from Britain in order to prevent possible extinction of the White-headed Duck. This proposal to cull Ruddy Ducks, agreed by the UK Government in March 2003, aroused some impassioned debate amongst nature conservation and animal welfare organizations, and professional ornithologists and amateur birdwatchers, with journalists and economists pitching in, and even some political activists complaining that it is 'racist' to try to preserve a species. The UK Ruddy Duck eradication programme started in autumn 2005. By midwinter 2006/07, the UK population had been reduced to about 2,000 birds, just one-third of the level in January 2000.

The two species would not have met if Ruddy Ducks had not been introduced to waterfowl collections here, mainly by the Wildfowl & Wetlands Trust. Sir Peter Scott obviously had an inkling that they could cause problems, and it is worth quoting in full from his foreword to Lever (1977): 'Having been carelessly responsible myself for allowing the North American Ruddy Duck to escape and build up to what seems like a small but viable population in England, I am in no position to pass judgment on others. To be sure the Ruddy Duck is decorative and apparently harmless but no one can know what insidious effect it may have on the ecological web. I really should not have allowed them to fly out into the countryside—although they look delightful in flight.'

Some observers have not submitted records to the annual county bird reports in protest at the cull, and it is not known if any have withheld records from this Atlas.

Sponsored by Anne Morris

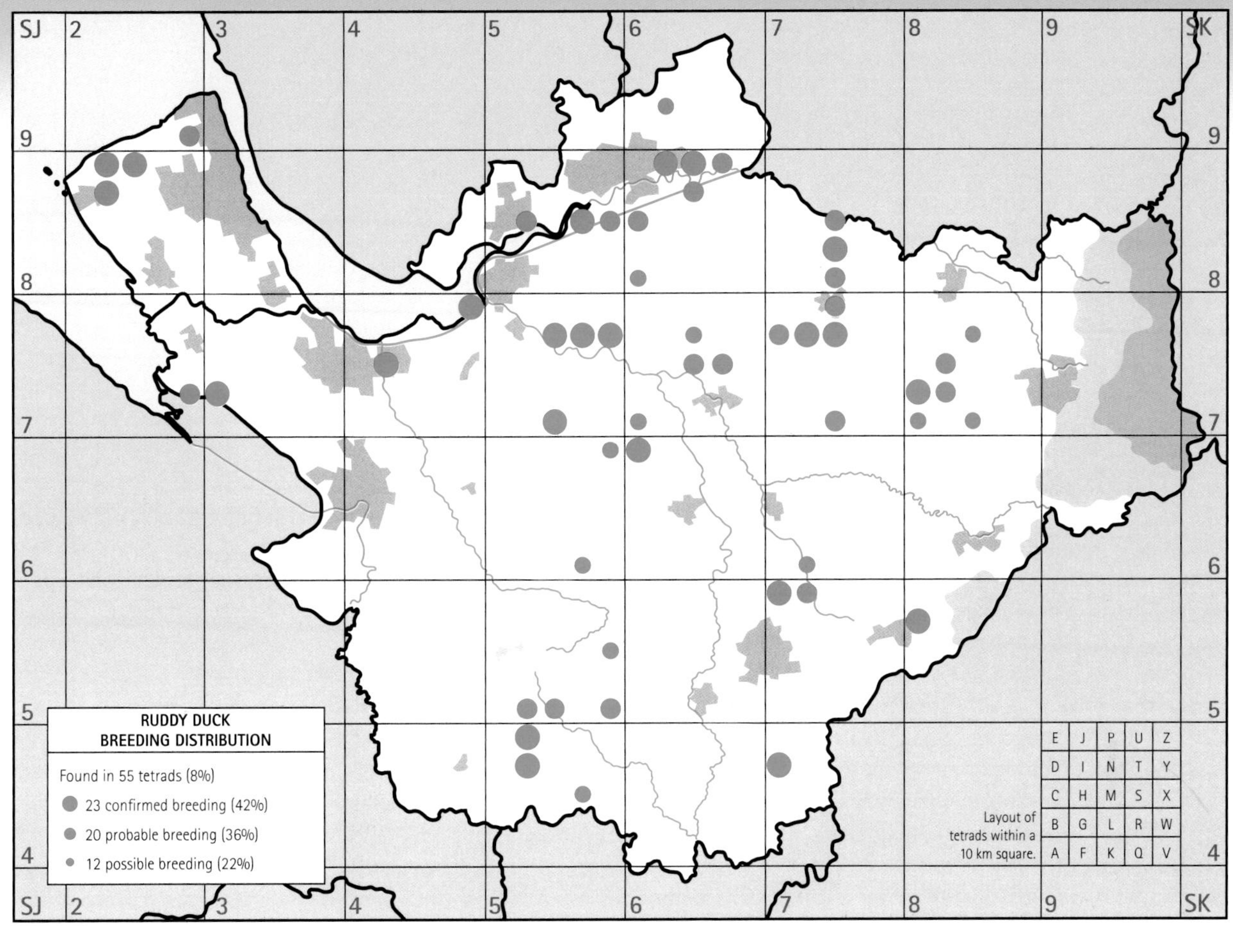
RUDDY DUCK
BREEDING DISTRIBUTION
Found in 55 tetrads (8%)
23 confirmed breeding (42%)
20 probable breeding (36%)
12 possible breeding (22%)
Layout of tetrads within a 10 km square.
E J P U Z
D I N T Y
C H M S X
B G L R W
A F K Q V
SJ 2 3 4 5 6 7 8 9 SK
9 8 7 6 5 4

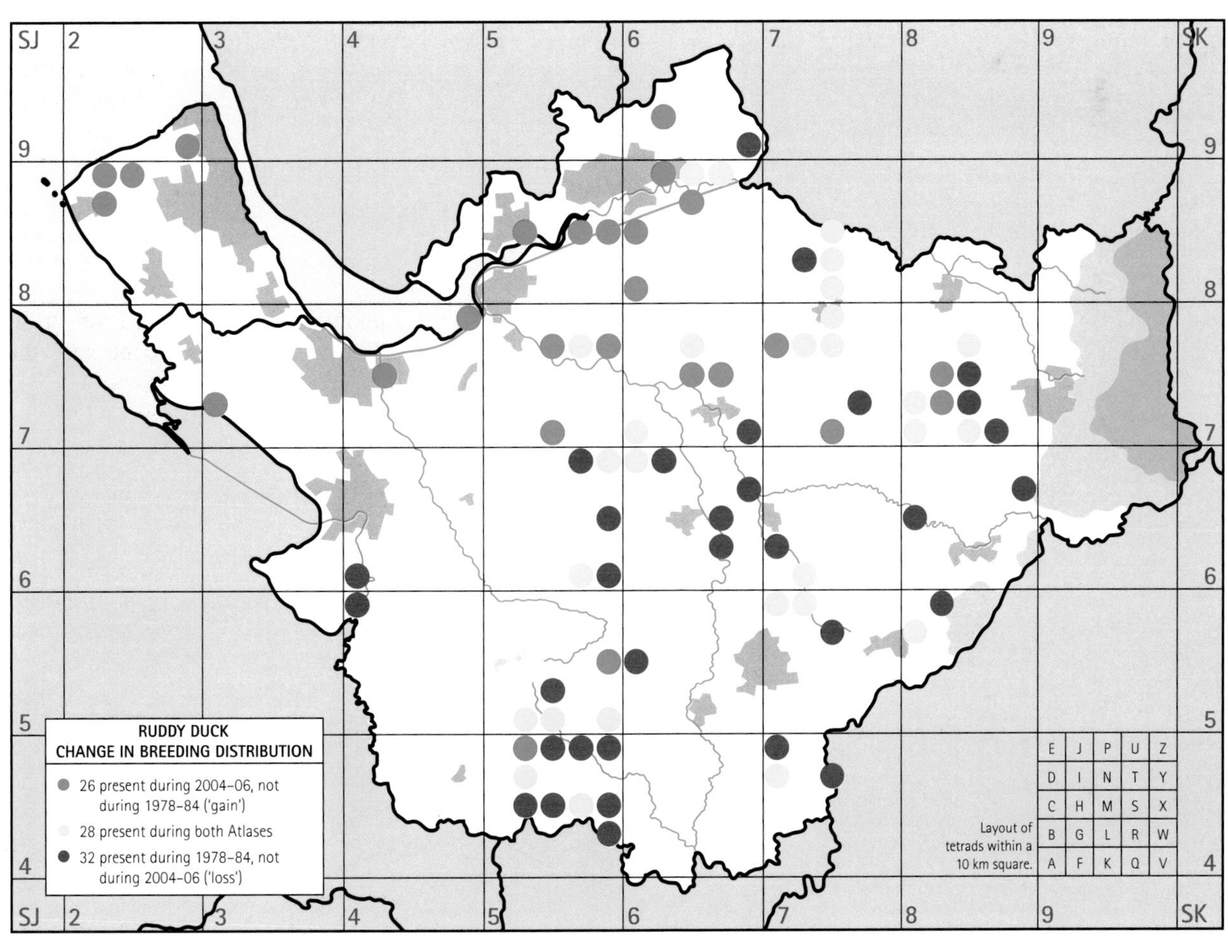
RUDDY DUCK
CHANGE IN BREEDING DISTRIBUTION
26 present during 2004–06, not during 1978–84 ('gain')
28 present during both Atlases
32 present during 1978–84, not during 2004–06 ('loss')
Layout of tetrads within a 10 km square.
E J P U Z
D I N T Y
C H M S X
B G L R W
A F K Q V
SJ 2 3 4 5 6 7 8 9 SK
9 8 7 6 5 4

The winter distribution of Ruddy Ducks in Cheshire and Wirral is similar to that in the breeding season, but they spread out somewhat to occupy a few more sites, and most birds leave their main breeding sites in the county. At three of the winter tetrads the observer found birds in February and commented on an early return to a breeding haunt. In North America, Ruddy Ducks are migratory, undertaking long journeys to the warmer waters of the west coast and Mexico in winter, but comparatively little is known about the introduced British population. Observations show that birds tend to congregate in large flocks on reservoirs, especially in the Midlands and south-east England.

The habitat codes show clearly this move to larger waterbodies: in the breeding season 13 (out of 58) were on G1 or G2 whereas in winter there were only four on G2 (out of 55). They feed mostly by diving and swimming along the bottom, and favour eutrophic waters with plenty of nutrients to supply their varied diet of pondweeds, algae, seeds and some aquatic insects and crustaceans.

In the compilations of national WeBS counts, Houghton Green Pool (SJ69G) and Woolston Eyes (SJ68P) are the only Cheshire sites listed with five-year (2000/01–2004/05) peak mean counts of more than 30 birds (38 and 31 respectively) (Banks *et al.* 2006). More than half of the Atlas records were of single-figure flocks and, apart from Houghton Green Pool, only two other sites registered counts over 20 birds: Frodsham Marsh (SJ57E) with 50 birds in 2004/05 and Appleton Reservoir (SJ68C) with 23 birds on 19 November 2006.

Owing to the secretive nature of female Ruddy Ducks when breeding, the best population estimates are made in winter. These show the rapid rise, by 81% in ten years from 1993/94 to 2003/04 and by as much as 569% from 1978/79 to 2003/04 (Eaton *et al.* 2007). The present cull is just as rapidly reversing their numbers.

ANDREW MART

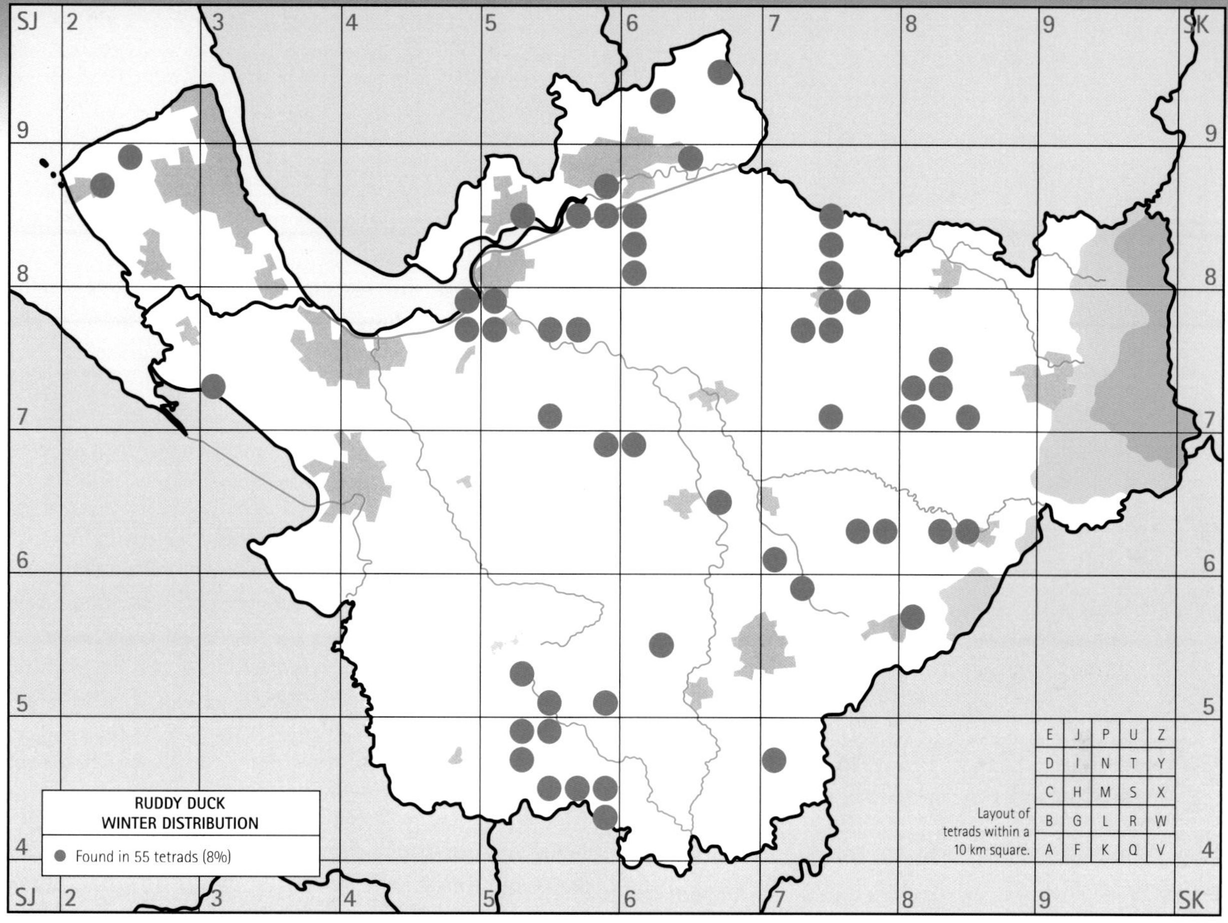
SJ
2
3
4
5
6
7
8
9
SK
RUDDY DUCK
WINTER DISTRIBUTION
Found in 55 tetrads (8%)
E J P U Z
D I N T Y
C H M S X
B G L R W
A F K Q V
Layout of tetrads within a 10 km square.

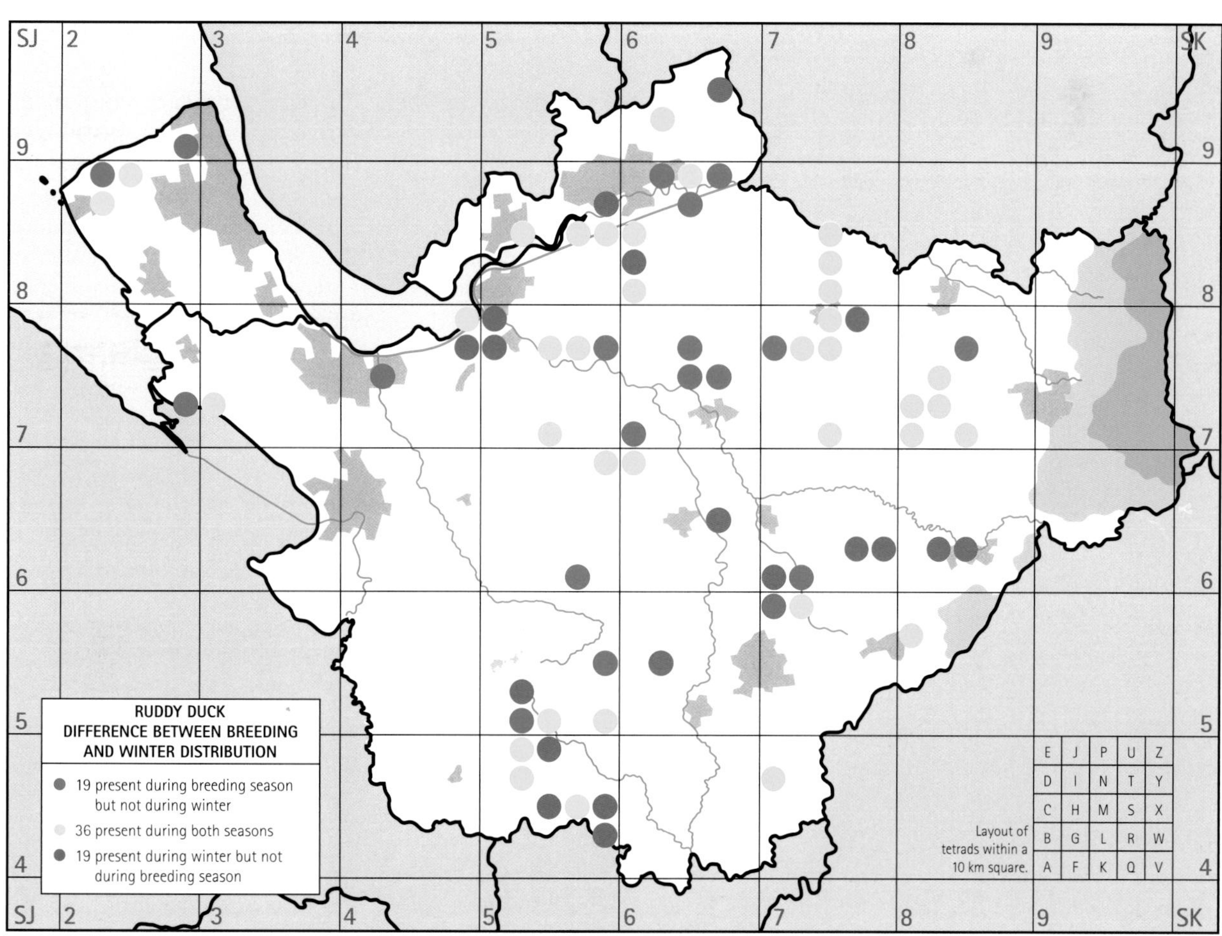
SJ
2
3
4
5
6
7
8
9
SK
RUDDY DUCK
DIFFERENCE BETWEEN BREEDING AND WINTER DISTRIBUTION
19 present during breeding season but not during winter
36 present during both seasons
19 present during winter but not during breeding season
E J P U Z
D I N T Y
C H M S X
B G L R W
A F K Q V
Layout of tetrads within a 10 km square.

Red Grouse

Lagopus lagopus

STEVE ROUND

This is *the* characteristic species of the heather-clad moorland of the Peak District: there can be days in the hills when the only birds to be found are Red Grouse and Meadow Pipits. This seems fitting, because the unique landscape of large parts of upland Britain arises from management to arrest the vegetational succession, solely to benefit grouse.

During this survey, Red Grouse were recorded in 11 tetrads in the breeding season, as in 1978–84, three gains being balanced by three losses. The loss of birds from three tetrads on the edge of their distribution suggests that their range has contracted somewhat. However, a gain comes from a major heather regeneration scheme on High Moor and Piggford Moor (SJ96U): this started in 1990 and by 2001 was suitable for the introduction of some Red Grouse (May 2004, 2005a, 2005b). The population is self-sustaining and the hard work has been rewarded with increasing April counts of 13 pairs (2004), 25 pairs (2005) and 35 pairs (2006).

Because of their importance for the economy of British uplands, this species has received probably more scientific study than any other, mainly by the Game & Wildlife Conservation Trust. However, Red Grouse are now on the Amber List of species of conservation concern because of their long-term national population decline. The causes are said to be poorer moor management through fewer keepers, overgrazing, increasing incidence of disease, increased predation and loss of habitat. Not mentioned in this list, but surely likely to become more significant, is climate change: Red Grouse, the British race of the cosmopolitan Willow Grouse, is a northerly species here at the southern limit of its range and the present warming trend is likely to affect them adversely.

Red Grouse are herbivores, feeding almost exclusively on heather (ling) *Calluna vulgaris*, especially the new growth from plants two to four years old. They do also eat, according to availability, other moorland plants including bilberry, cranberry and cotton-grass. The autumn fruits are favoured, but at any time of year grouse eat the leaves, stalks and flowers. To grind up these hard fibrous materials in their gizzards they need to ingest small sharp pieces of stone, of which there is no shortage in the millstone grit hills of the Dark Peak. Like other gamebirds, chicks need invertebrate food, especially during their first 10 days of life, and females often lead their chicks to areas such as bog flushes that are rich in insects like flies, beetles and sawfly larvae.

A thorough survey of all suitable land in Cheshire led to a population estimate for 2002 of 273 pairs, an average of about 7 pairs per square kilometre: this is quite a high figure (Oxenham 2002). The natural density of Red Grouse is thought to be 4–5 birds per square kilometre, but this is uneconomic; figures of 10–15 breeding pairs per square kilometre are needed to sustain driven shooting and pay for the necessary investment in effective control of predation, disease limitation and heather management. Following the rise in population on High Moor and Piggford Moor, the Cheshire total in 2006 might be 300 pairs.

Grouse numbers are naturally cyclical, peaking roughly every four or five years, mostly because of periodic disease from *Strongylosis*, caused by a parasitic nematode worm; high levels of infection can reduce grouse breeding success and also cause direct mortality, with badly infected birds less able to escape mammalian predators. During this Atlas survey period, monitoring of grouse moors in northern England showed 2004 to be a peak year, followed by a population crash. The high grouse numbers in autumn 2004, together with wet and mild weather, allowed large increases in parasite burdens, and half of all adults died during the 2005 breeding season, compared to 14% in 2004. Combined with lower breeding success (an average of 1.56 young grouse per surviving adult compared with 2.38), the number of Red Grouse at the end of the 2005 breeding season was just 40% of the figure twelve months before.

Sponsored by Richard May

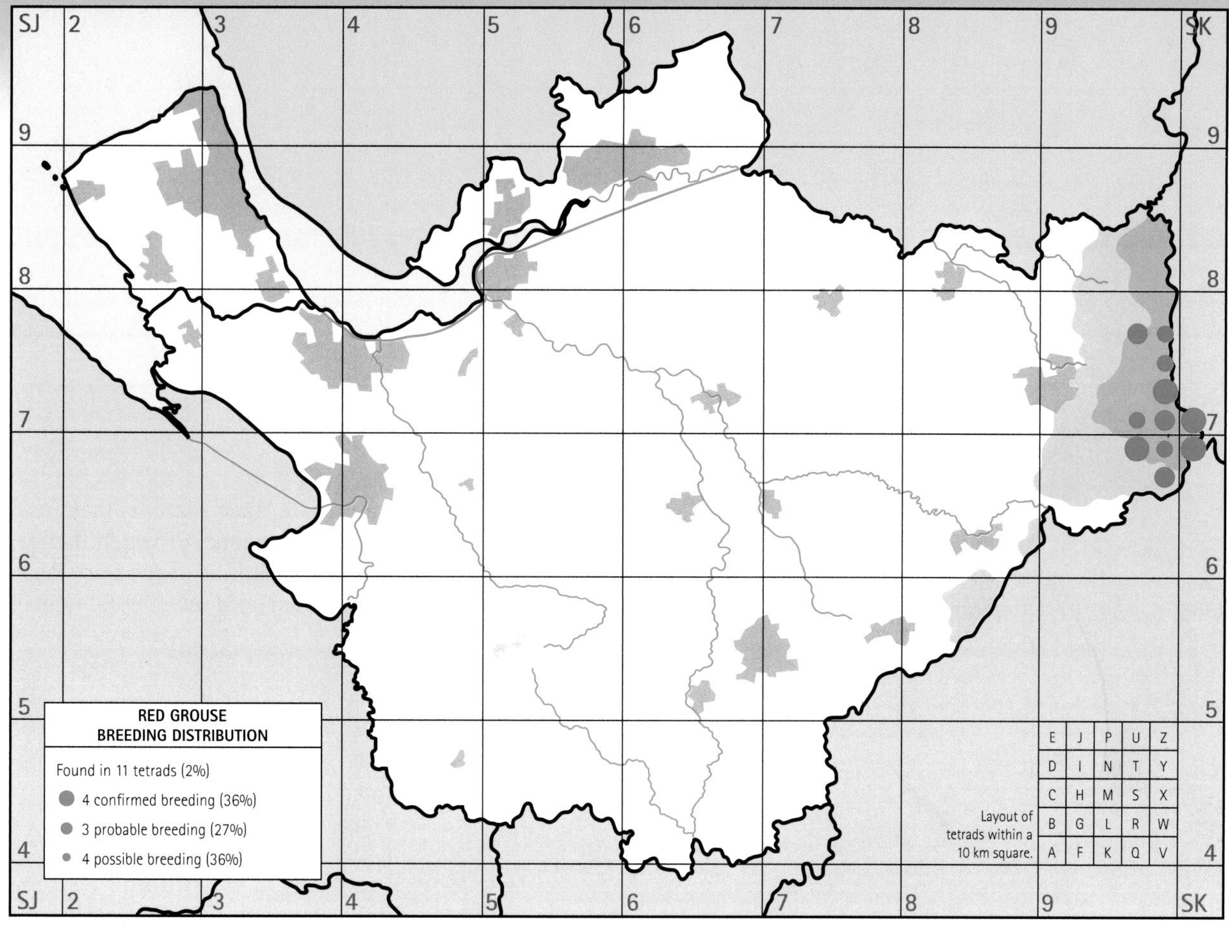
SJ
2
3
4
5
6
7
8
9
SK
RED GROUSE
BREEDING DISTRIBUTION
Found in 11 tetrads (2%)
4 confirmed breeding (36%)
3 probable breeding (27%)
4 possible breeding (36%)
Layout of tetrads within a 10 km square.
E J P U Z
D I N T Y
C H M S X
B G L R W
A F K Q V

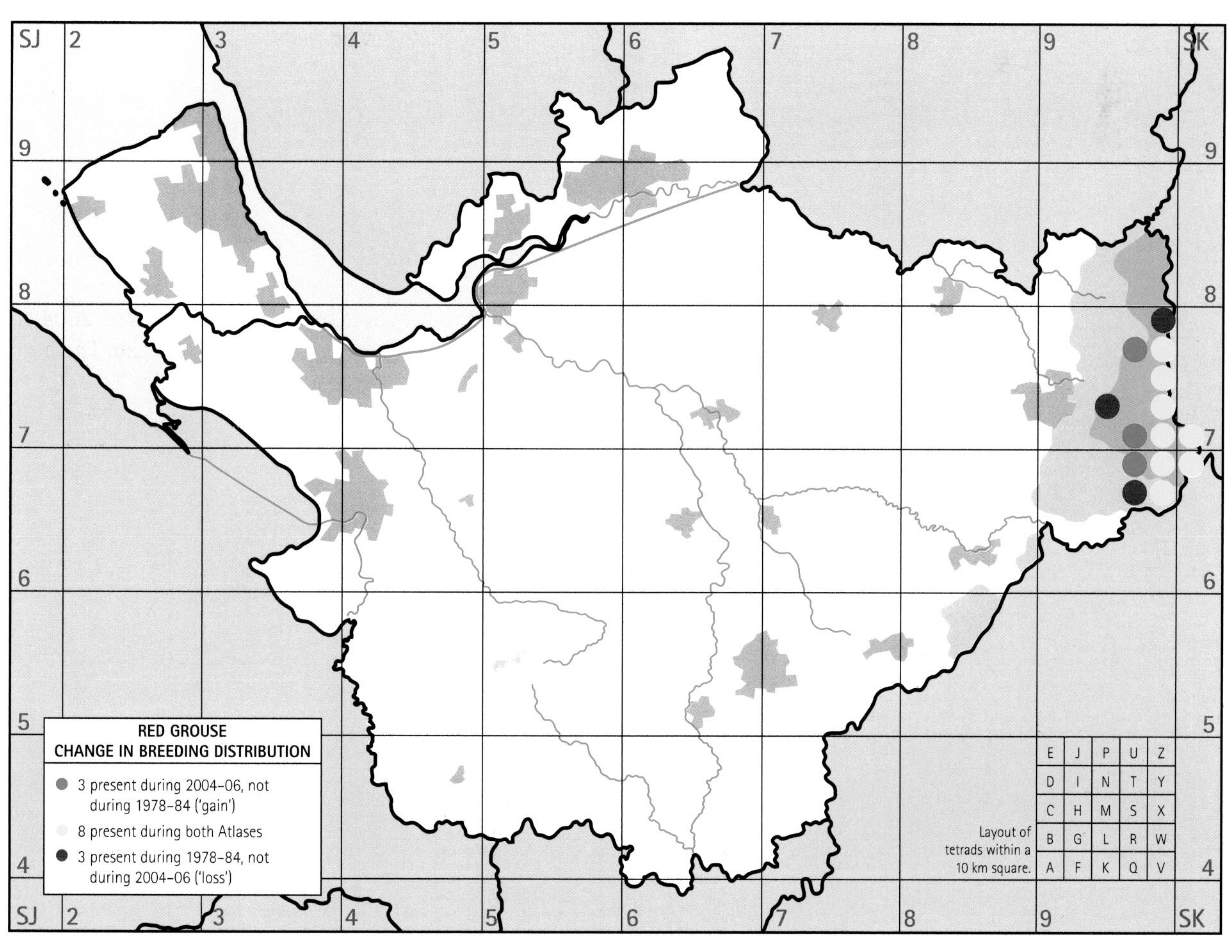
SJ
2
3
4
5
6
7
8
9
SK
RED GROUSE
CHANGE IN BREEDING DISTRIBUTION
3 present during 2004–06, not during 1978–84 ('gain')
8 present during both Atlases
3 present during 1978–84, not during 2004–06 ('loss')
Layout of tetrads within a 10 km square.
E J P U Z
D I N T Y
C H M S X
B G L R W
A F K Q V

The winter distribution map is very similar to that for the breeding season, as would be expected, for this is a very sedentary species, and 80–90% of grouse die within about a mile of their natal site. Red Grouse is the only species that inhabits these moorlands throughout the year, staying put even in the bleakest and most exposed situations. During very hard weather, with deep lying snow, some Red Grouse may travel quite long distances—even onto farmland—to find food; but such conditions are exceptional in the Cheshire hills.

Although their population has probably reduced considerably, the distribution of Red Grouse in Cheshire is much the same as a century ago. Coward and Oldham (1910) wrote that 'thousands of acres on the hills are devoted to the preservation of the Red Grouse and on many of the moors large bags are obtained', although most of their comments apply to the Longdendale part of what was then Cheshire. Bell (1962) found nothing to say except that it was 'common' in the heather-clad hills, the rest of his account being of ancient records of odd birds elsewhere in the county.

Although the season extends until 10 December, most estates finish shooting much earlier as male Red Grouse try to establish territories in the autumn. They hold domain over an area of 1–10 ha of prime habitat, and successful birds survive the winter far better than those in the roaming flocks. A good territory contains a variety of well-managed heather, young plants providing better food and older heather offering better cover. Most mortality is of non-territorial birds in the poorer habitats. They are short-lived birds: nearly two-thirds die in their first year, irrespective of shooting, which takes the harvestable surplus which would die anyway. Those that are not shot experience reduced competition and thus better survival rates.

During the long winter nights Red Grouse normally roost in packs on the ground, identifiable by the collection of their droppings. They sometimes venture forth to feed on bright moonlit nights.

RAY SCALLY

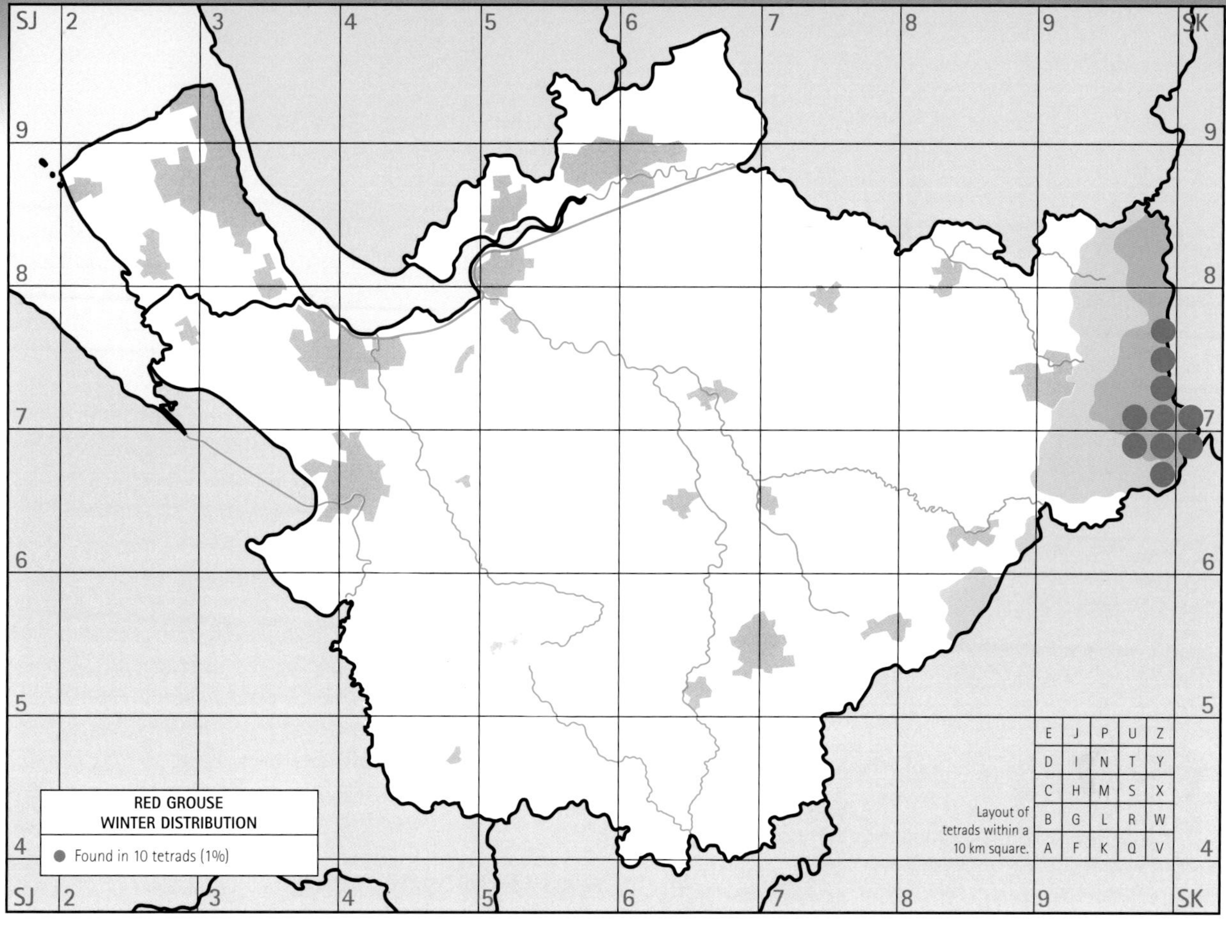

RED GROUSE
WINTER DISTRIBUTION
Found in 10 tetrads (1%)
Layout of tetrads within a 10 km square.
E J P U Z
D I N T Y
C H M S X
B G L R W
A F K Q V
SJ
SK

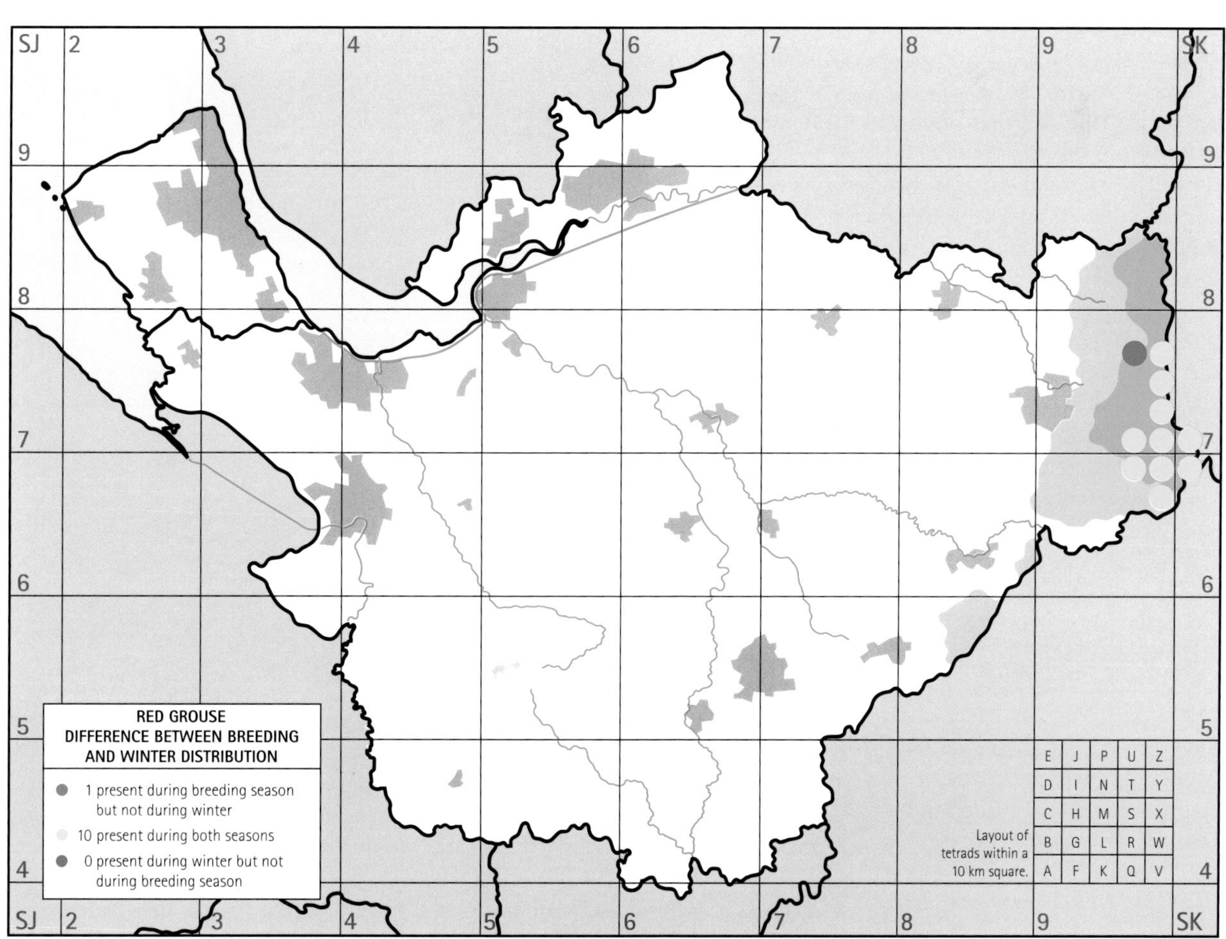

RED GROUSE
DIFFERENCE BETWEEN BREEDING AND WINTER DISTRIBUTION
1 present during breeding season but not during winter
10 present during both seasons
0 present during winter but not during breeding season
Layout of tetrads within a 10 km square.
E J P U Z
D I N T Y
C H M S X
B G L R W
A F K Q V
SJ
SK

Red-legged Partridge

Alectoris rufa

SUE & ANDY TRANTER

This partridge is essentially a south-easterly bird in Britain with Cheshire on the edge of its range, so it is interesting that this survey shows it now to be widespread in several parts of Cheshire, and to have established itself widely in Wirral as well. An indication of its range is well illustrated by the figures for the Atlases of nearby counties: 70% of tetrads in Shropshire (1985–90), 23% in this Atlas, 17% in Lancashire and North Merseyside (1997–2000) and 3% in Cumbria (1997–2001). Red-legged Partridges are usually reported to favour warm and dry areas, and lowland Cheshire fits within the 870 mm annual isohyet and the 19°C isotherm for average maximum July temperature that define their normal climatic requirements. Perhaps their spread in the county, with presence in 127 new tetrads and 46 losses since our *First Atlas*, has been encouraged by the warming climate.

This species was introduced to England in the eighteenth century from its native southern Europe and numerous sporadic attempts to import birds into Cheshire failed to establish a self-sustaining population here. Now, the county map appears to show four main clumps of population, and it is tempting to think that they have spread out from the sites where there have been large-scale releases of birds. The *First Atlas* mentioned releases in the 1970s and 1980s at Betley (SJ74), Withington (SJ87) and Dibbinsdale (SJ38), and more recently others have been 'put down' at Bolesworth and Tilston (SJ45).

All gamebirds suffer high rates of nesting failure. Their open nests, on the ground, are vulnerable to predation throughout their relatively long periods of egg-laying and incubation. Red-legged Partridges attempt to counter this by their unusual habit of double-clutching. Females frequently lay eggs in one nest, leave them unincubated and lay a further set in a second nest. She then incubates the second clutch whilst the male returns to the first nest and incubates them. The two broods, if they survive, are raised separately. This strategy is only partially successful, however, because the first clutch is left unattended for about three weeks and is at greater risk of predation. They also tend to leave their eggs uncovered during laying, while Grey Partridges cover theirs with grass or leaves. Perhaps the low productivity was suggested in this survey by only 29 tetrads having records of confirmed breeding; half of the records were of pairs seen, and others were located by their loud calls, said to resemble small steam-engines.

Analysis of the BTO BBS transects shows that the breeding population of Cheshire and Wirral in 2004–05 was 2,880 birds (820–4,950), an average of 25 birds per tetrad with confirmed or probable breeding: the Red-legged Partridge now exceeds the Grey Partridge in both abundance and distribution. There is no evidence of any direct interaction, however: Grey Partridges dominate Red-legged in any disputes, and Red-legged are more susceptible to predation. However, newly hatched Red-legged Partridge chicks can feed on weed and grass seeds, as well as insects, and it may be that they are less vulnerable to the indirect effects of pesticides than Grey Partridge chicks (Green 1984): this could be a reason why Red-legged survive in areas where Grey Partridges do not.

Famland comprised 92% of habitat codes, with 32% improved grassland, 12% unimproved grassland, 12% tilled land and 26% mixed grassland and tilled land. Elsewhere in Britain, Red-legged Partridges are said to be much more tolerant of wooded landscapes than the Grey yet more restricted to areas of arable crops (*BTO Second Atlas*), but there is no evidence of either of these traits in Cheshire.

Red-legged Partridge abundance.

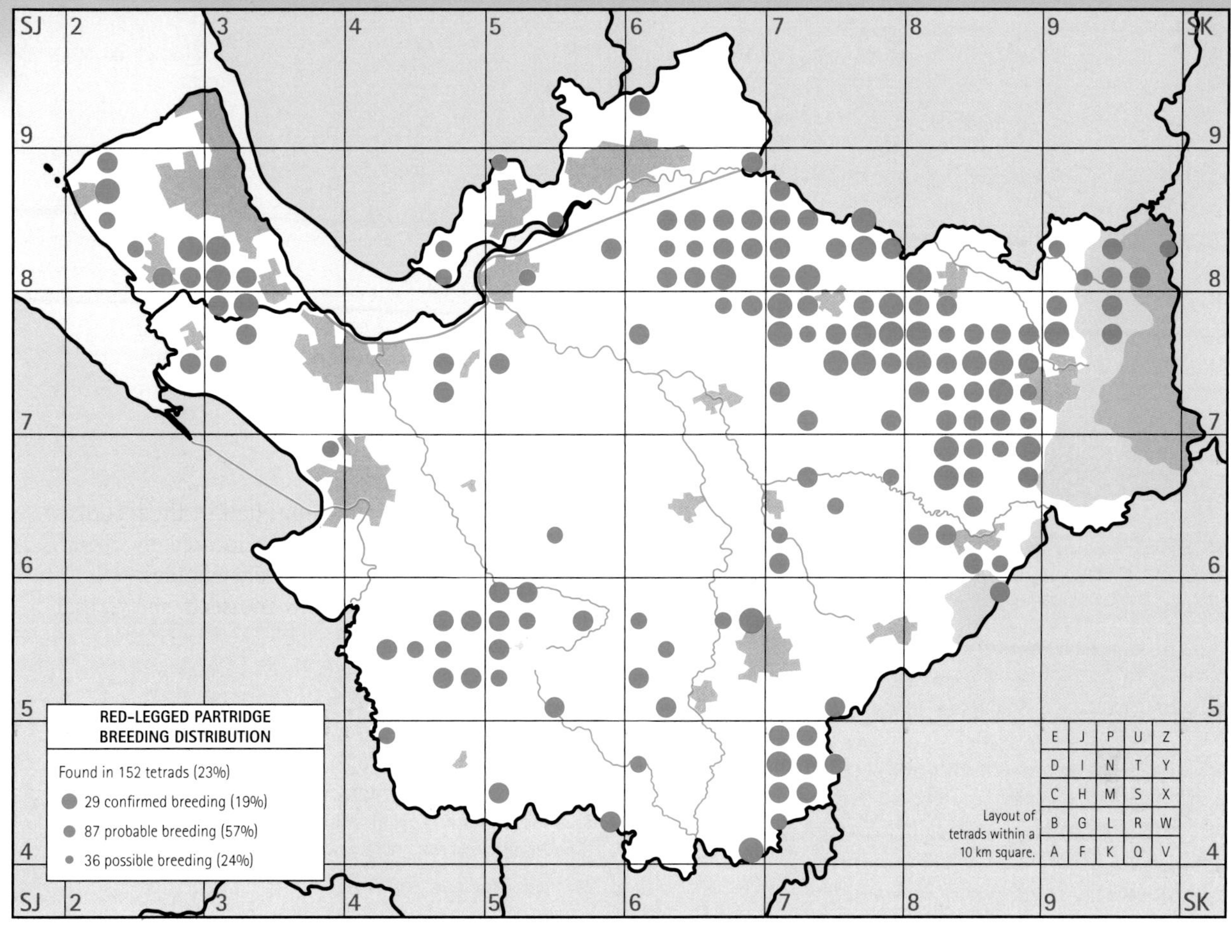
RED-LEGGED PARTRIDGE
BREEDING DISTRIBUTION
Found in 152 tetrads (23%)
29 confirmed breeding (19%)
87 probable breeding (57%)
36 possible breeding (24%)
Layout of tetrads within a 10 km square.
E J P U Z
D I N T Y
C H M S X
B G L R W
A F K Q V
SJ
SK
2
3
4
5
6
7
8
9

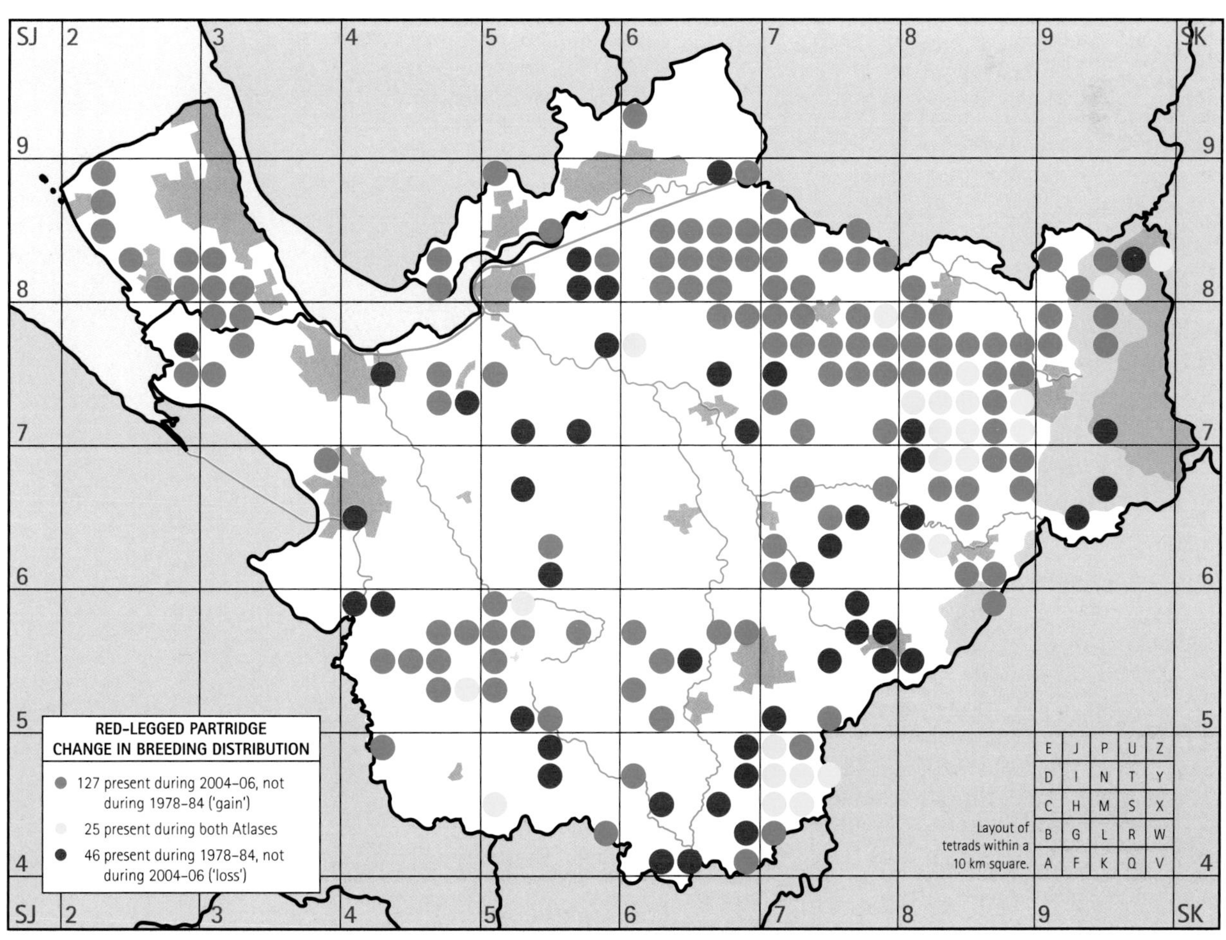
RED-LEGGED PARTRIDGE
CHANGE IN BREEDING DISTRIBUTION
127 present during 2004–06, not during 1978–84 ('gain')
25 present during both Atlases
46 present during 1978–84, not during 2004–06 ('loss')
Layout of tetrads within a 10 km square.
E J P U Z
D I N T Y
C H M S X
B G L R W
A F K Q V
SJ
SK
2
3
4
5
6
7
8
9

For such a sedentary species, there would be expected to be little difference between the breeding and wintering distribution maps, but 67 tetrads held Red-legged Partridges in the breeding season only, and 31 in winter only. This could be explained by birds gathering into flocks for the winter, but they normally stay together as family groups, typically two to five adults and their young (Brown & Grice 2005). This species differs from the Grey Partridge in that young males stay with the family party and it is the young females that disperse to avoid inbreeding: only about one-quarter of young males move more than 0.5 km, while about three-quarters of yearling females do so (*Migration Atlas*). The 'difference' map shows that almost all of the tetrads occupied in winter only were adjacent to one with breeding season presence, and only three tetrads were more than 5 km away. The loss of birds from some of the more isolated breeding sites is difficult to explain, however.

Winter habitat records show 91% on farmland, with similar proportions to the breeding season, 34% improved grassland, 7% unimproved grassland, 13% tilled land and 13% mixed grassland and tilled land. The hedge categories make up much of the remainder, but 7% of records were on stubble. Their winter diet is much the same as that of Grey Partridge, mainly seeds of grain and weeds, especially *Polygonum*, but birds increasingly turn to green food as seed becomes scarcer through the winter, particularly the shoots of winter-sown cereals.

Half of the submitted counts were of four birds or fewer, with 21 records of 10 birds or more. The largest was 35 birds at High Legh (SJ78B), with 28 near Marton in SJ86J, both in 2005/06. The same winter, 20 birds walked casually through Alan Straw's rural garden near Mow Cop (SJ85U).

RICHARD STEEL

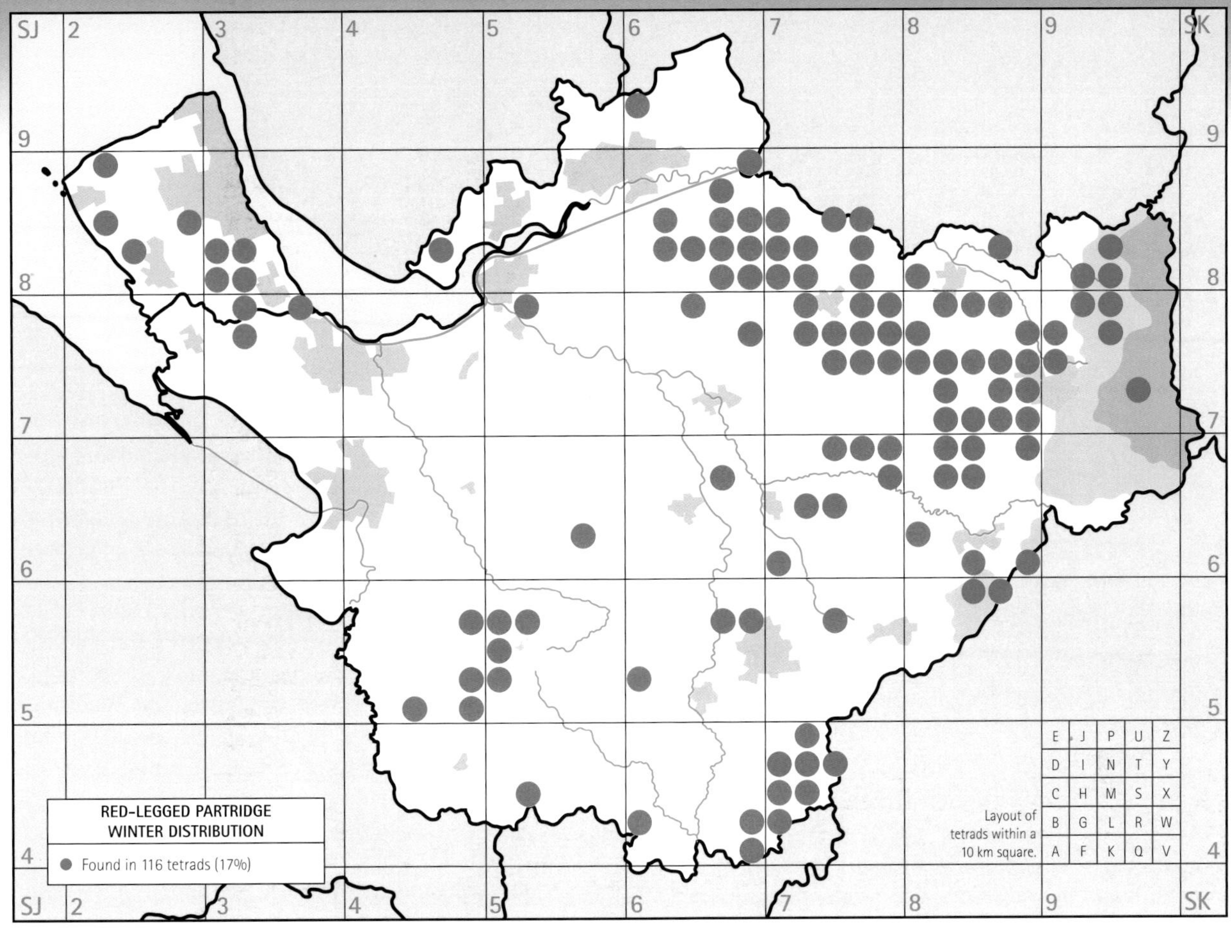
RED-LEGGED PARTRIDGE
WINTER DISTRIBUTION
Found in 116 tetrads (17%)
Layout of
tetrads within a
10 km square.
SJ
SK

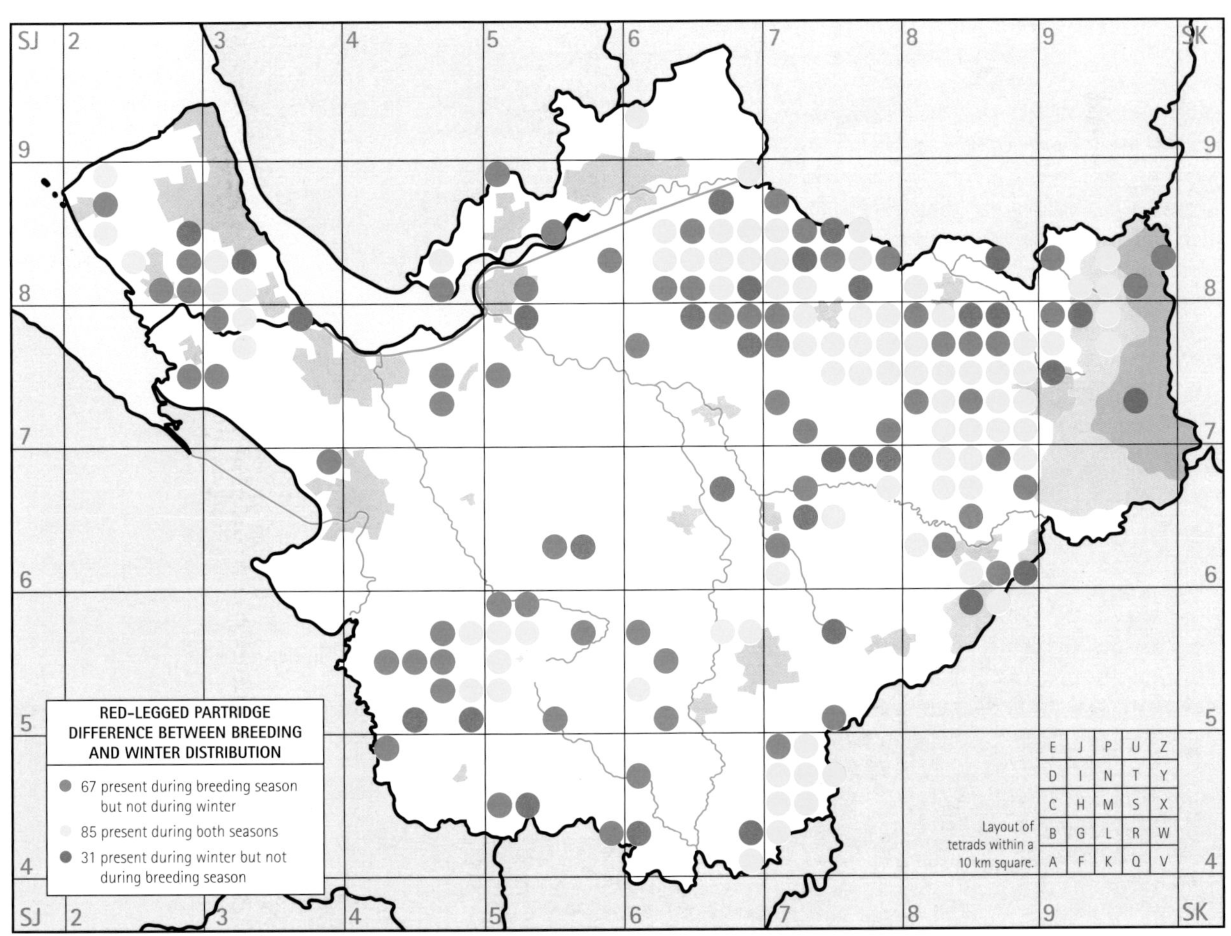
RED-LEGGED PARTRIDGE
DIFFERENCE BETWEEN BREEDING
AND WINTER DISTRIBUTION
67 present during breeding season
but not during winter
85 present during both seasons
31 present during winter but not
during breeding season
Layout of
tetrads within a
10 km square.
SJ
SK

Grey Partridge

Perdix perdix

The Grey Partridge is one of the farmland species whose population has crashed in the last quarter-century. Their distribution in the county reflects that decline, and they have been lost from two-thirds of their breeding areas since the *First Atlas*, down from 420 tetrads to 149. Any species that feeds on weeds, their seeds, and farmland insects will surely have a tough time in an intensifying agricultural régime.

The presence of Grey Partridges is easy to detect at dawn or dusk by the far-carrying 'creaking' calls, but it is not easy to prove breeding except by finding adults with chicks, which often surprise observers by flying short distances well before they are fully grown. The nest is well hidden in long grass, usually under a hedge. During 25 days of incubation the female conscientiously broods her large clutch, averaging 14 eggs, leaving the nest only three times a day, and less often if the weather is wet. This devotion to the nest can carry a heavy price, and up to one-quarter of hens are killed on the nest, mostly at night by foxes.

Adults teach their newly hatched chicks to find invertebrates, especially plant bugs *Hemiptera* and larvae of sawflies and beetles. Such food forms 80–90% of their intake in the first two weeks of life, as their usual vegetable food provides insufficient nutrition for the energy-intensive early stages of growth: low chick survival has been the key to the species' decline. The main food of adults and fledged young is seeds, of grasses and most of the broad-leaved weeds, with invertebrates taken only incidentally. When they can find them, preferred seeds include *Cerastium* and *Stellaria* chickweeds, fat hen *Chenopodium spp.* and hemp-nettle *Galeopsis tetrahit*, all of which were recorded as common in the *Flora of Cheshire* (Newton 1971). On arable land, if available, they favour undersown crops, which contain much higher densities of invertebrates (Shrubb 2003).

As expected, observers found most birds on farmland (83% of records), with 24% improved grassland, 12% unimproved grassland, 27% mixed grassland and tilled land and 8% tilled land. Compared to Red-legged Partridge, relatively fewer were recorded on improved grassland, with more on semi-natural grassland (6% of records) and in the edges of scrub (3%).

National population indices show a drop of 85% from 1978 to 2004, and there is still no sign of a recovery, despite years of research and the application of a BAP (Aebischer & Ewald 2004). The breeding population of Cheshire and Wirral in 2004–05 was 2,020 birds (650–3,390), an average of about 14 birds per tetrad in which they were present. According to Potts (1986), under modern agriculture around four pairs per square kilometre would be expected on optimum ground and two pairs per square kilometre on suboptimum land, with higher densities expected if suitable management is undertaken. The Cheshire figure is below even the suboptimum density, doubtless owing to the low proportion of arable farming in our predominantly pastoral county. The abundance map shows that the area north of Warrington, where much of Cheshire's arable farming is concentrated, holds the highest densities of Grey Partridges. Since the polarization of England into the pastoral west and the arable east, Cheshire can never have been a key county for Grey Partridges, but it is a species being given special conservation effort, under the Farmland Birds LBAP, and it is important that we monitor its local status.

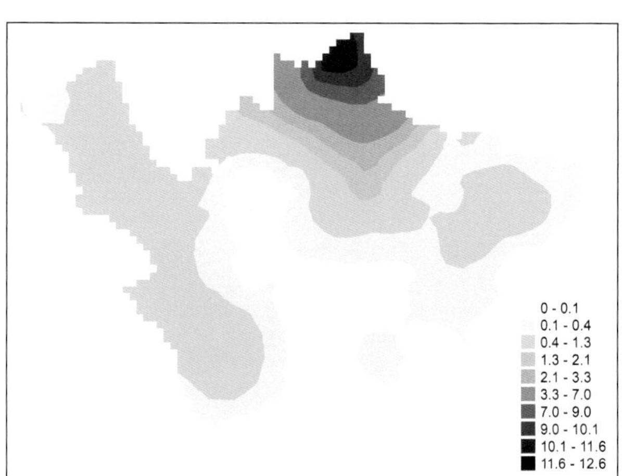

Grey Partridge abundance.

Sponsored by Altrincham and District Natural History Society

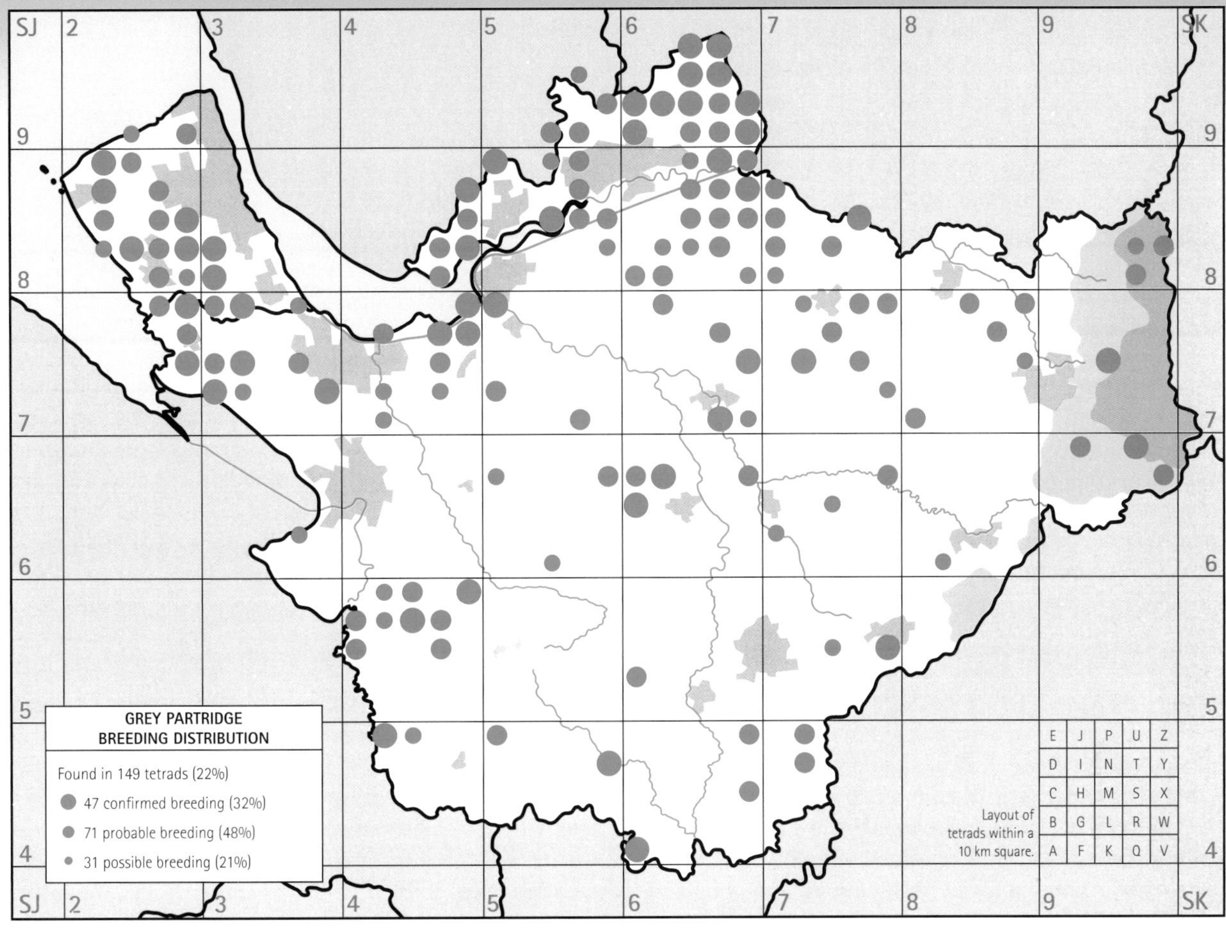
GREY PARTRIDGE
BREEDING DISTRIBUTION
Found in 149 tetrads (22%)
47 confirmed breeding (32%)
71 probable breeding (48%)
31 possible breeding (21%)
Layout of tetrads within a 10 km square.

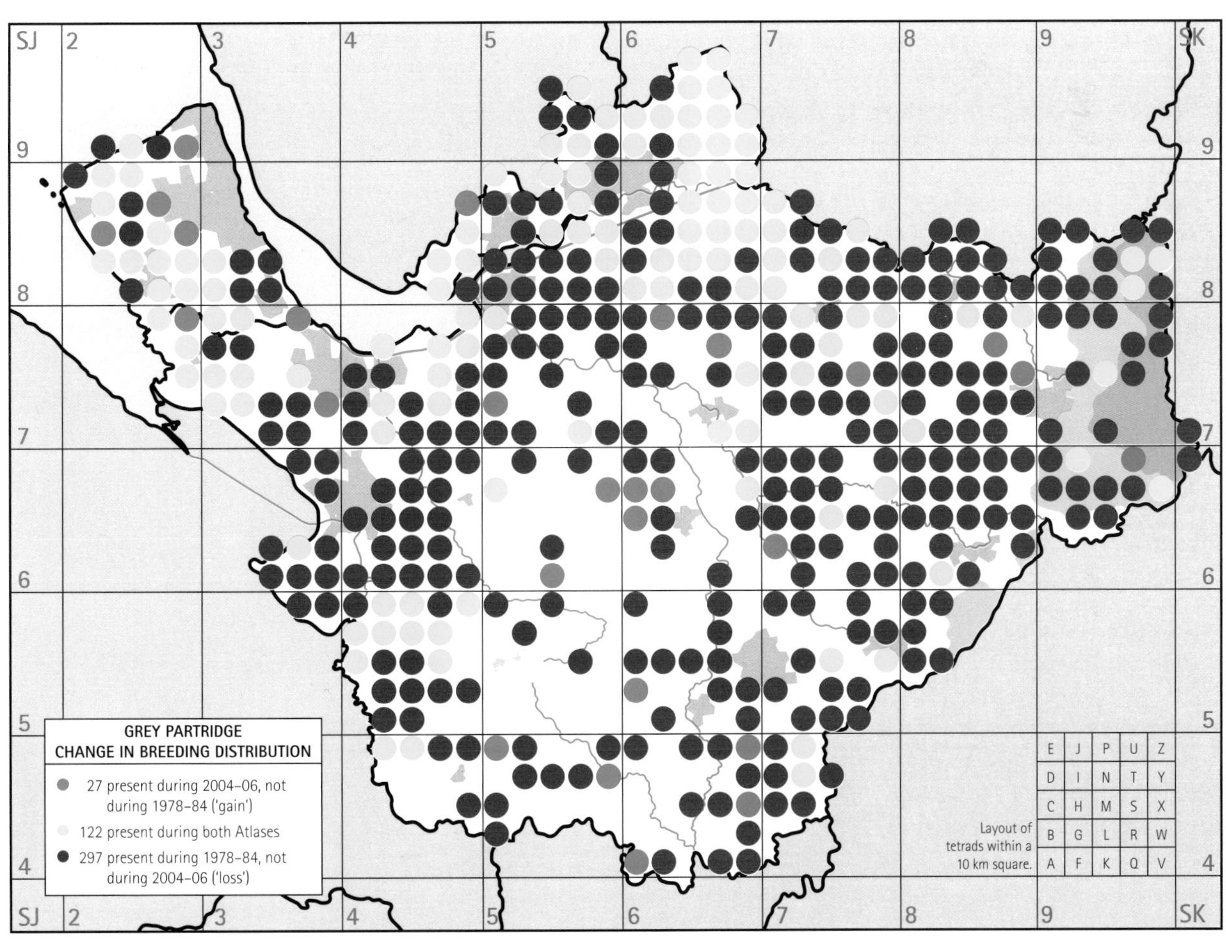
GREY PARTRIDGE
CHANGE IN BREEDING DISTRIBUTION
27 present during 2004–06, not during 1978–84 ('gain')
122 present during both Atlases
297 present during 1978–84, not during 2004–06 ('loss')
Layout of tetrads within a 10 km square.

As expected for a sedentary bird, there is not much difference between the breeding and wintering distribution of Grey Partridges. They appear to quit the eastern hills in winter, and there might be some altitudinal migration, as has been suggested also in Northumbria (Day & Hodgson 2003). Even in the lowlands they will undertake small-scale local movements, and they were found in 42 tetrads in winter where there was no breeding season record, although not found in 67 where they had been present in a breeding season. Farmland made up the great majority of habitat records (88%), with 23% improved grassland, 12% unimproved grassland, 19% mixed grassland and tilled land and 13% tilled land, with 11% on stubble.

None of the twentieth-century Cheshire ornithologists (Coward, Boyd, Bell) makes any significant comment on the winter status of Grey Partridges, testament to their relative abundance in their lifetimes. This is, however, one of the best-studied birds in the world, owing to its economic importance as a quarry species.

After the breeding season, they gather in family groups or coveys, comprising two to five or more old birds together with their young, which might number on average as few as two or as many as eight depending on the year-to-year fluctuations in productivity (Potts 1986). The females in a covey are mostly sisters, but the young males not their brothers, since they disperse, the natural mechanism that avoids inbreeding. There is usually a surplus of adult males because of the high mortality of hens from predation on the nest. Flocking in coveys helps with guarding against predators, and they take it in turns for one bird, the sentinel, to have its head up whilst the others concentrate on feeding. Coveys usually break up in the New Year as the birds form pairs and prepare for the breeding season. Observers for this winter Atlas reported 24 flocks of more than 10 birds but only six larger than 20, and more than half of counts were of four birds or fewer.

In winter they mainly eat grain and the seeds of grasses and weeds, especially *Polygonum spp.*, knotgrass and black bindweed, but these dwindle during the season and proportionately more green food is taken, especially winter wheat or barley and chickweed. Leaves are much less nutritious, however, and to obtain its energy needs, a partridge in a field of wheat has the daily choice of about 1,000 pecks feeding on grains or 25,000 pecks at the leaves (Potts 1986)!

They roost overnight on the ground, and sites can often be identified by concentrations of their droppings. They tend to choose slight depressions such as a ploughed field or tractor tramlines at the edge of a crop, and sometimes they keep a roost site frost-free by the heat of their bodies, huddled into the ground. Indeed, they appear not to be bothered by the vagaries of British winters, and are well able to survive through periods of frost or snow, even starving for several days in subzero temperatures if food is scarce.

Some Grey Partridges are shot during a season lasting from 1 September to 1 February. With the shootable surplus usually calculated according to guidelines from the Game & Wildlife Conservation Trust, such a bag has no effect on the population level; indeed, many shooting groups maintain partridges at a higher density than in areas where they are not shot, through control of mammalian predators in the breeding season. Despite such measures, numbers continue to dwindle, and members of Frodsham and District Wildfowlers' Club, for instance, have not shot Grey Partridges from 2002 to 2007 owing to their concerns about the decline of the local population.

RICHARD STEEL

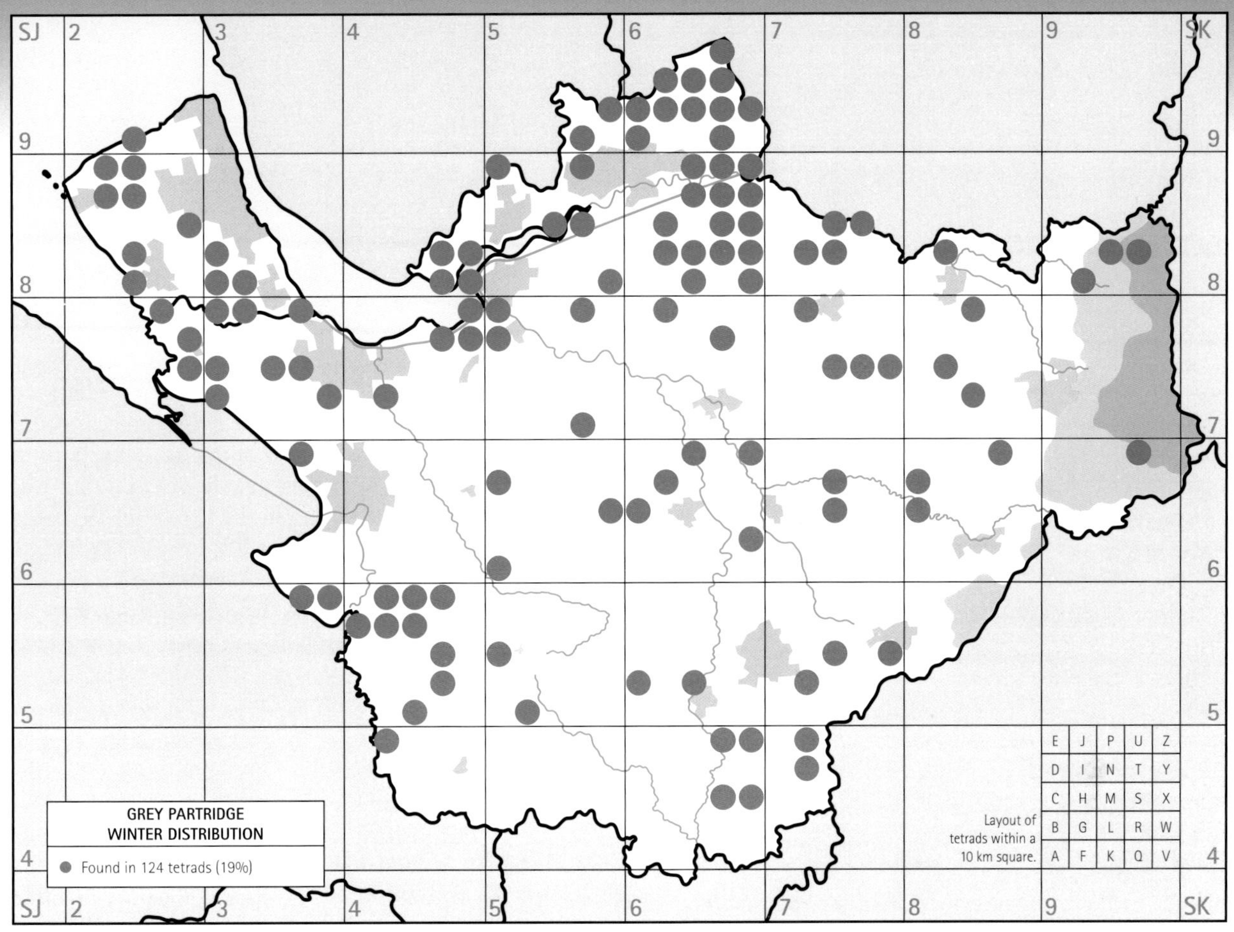
SJ
SK
GREY PARTRIDGE
WINTER DISTRIBUTION
Found in 124 tetrads (19%)
Layout of
tetrads within a
10 km square.
E J P U Z
D I N T Y
C H M S X
B G L R W
A F K Q V

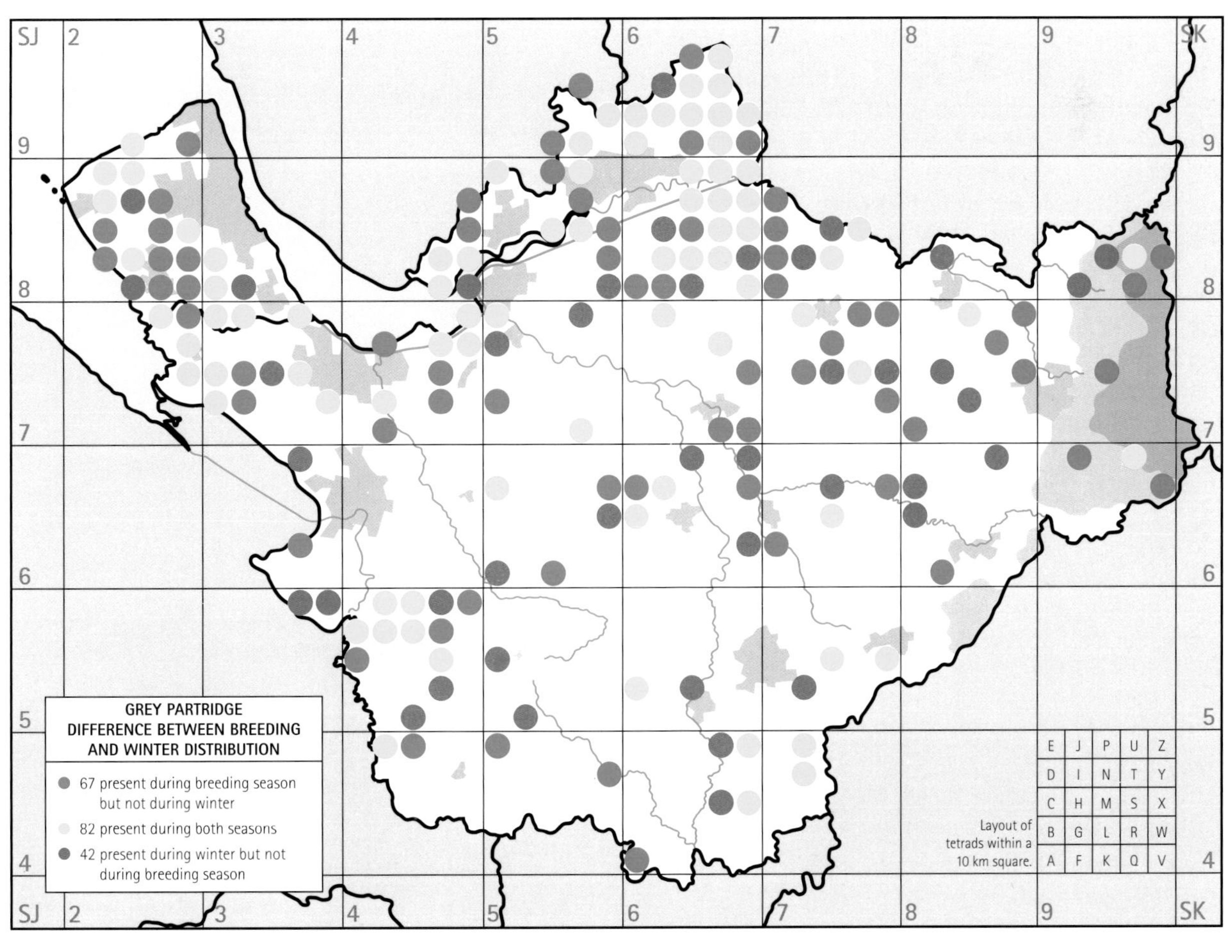
SJ
SK
GREY PARTRIDGE
DIFFERENCE BETWEEN BREEDING
AND WINTER DISTRIBUTION
67 present during breeding season
but not during winter
82 present during both seasons
42 present during winter but not
during breeding season
Layout of
tetrads within a
10 km square.
E J P U Z
D I N T Y
C H M S X
B G L R W
A F K Q V

Quail

Coturnix coturnix

RAY SCALLY

Most Quails are detected when observers hear the distinctive and far-carrying whip-like song, 'wet-my-lips'. This is usually the beginning of a frustrating attempt to find the bird, as they are expert ventriloquists and the call is extremely difficult to localize. When the bird is at very close range a gruff barking call can sometimes be heard, but even then it is difficult to pin it down. Birds tend to call mostly at dawn and dusk, sometimes during the night and occasionally during the day. Several of the Quail on this Atlas map were heard on only one occasion and not on return visits, so an element of luck is needed and the species is probably underrecorded. Males call only very occasionally when mated, and it is difficult to know if a calling bird has found a mate or moved on.

All of the Atlas records were of singing males, apart from one north Wirral tetrad with a pair in 2006 (which had had a singing bird in 2005), and two adjacent tetrads in the south of the county, where one observer found chicks near Bar Mere and Bickley in 2004. They raise a large brood, typically eight or more chicks. Like all gamebirds, they eat mostly seeds on the ground, with invertebrates important for the chicks.

They are mainly found in arable crops or long grass. Two of the Atlas records were on the Dee salt-marsh and 13 of the 16 tetrads had birds in farmland, with seven in habitat code E4 (tilled land): in five of these seven, the observer noted the crop to be barley, quite a scarce plant in Cheshire and Wirral. Modern agriculture is inimical to Quail, and the species has declined greatly in Britain: it is on the Red List of species of conservation concern because of its historical drop in UK population during the period 1800–1995.

Quail have an extraordinary sequential breeding strategy that has evolved to produce the maximum possible number of young. This is the only migratory bird of the 'gamebird' family; they winter around the Mediterranean or in trans-Saharan Africa, an almost unbelievable feat to anyone who has seen how weakly Quail appear to fly. Many of them nest early in spring in North Africa or southern Europe and then migrate further north to have a later breeding attempt. Remarkably, these migrants include young birds from those first broods, which are capable of migrating just two months after hatching and mature sexually at the age of 12–15 weeks (Guyomarc'h *et al.* 1998). The proportion of breeding birds in northern Europe that have been hatched earlier in the same season may be around 50% (*Migration Atlas*).

The first arrival in the county is usually in the second half of May, but new calling birds seem to turn up on any date until early August. Often the new arrivals seem to occur in waves, probably comprising adults and their offspring pushing north for a further breeding attempt. With favourable south-easterly winds, higher numbers reach Britain in some 'Quail years', of which the most recent was in 1989 when 1,655 pairs were estimated possibly breeding, with 50 of them in Cheshire and Wirral. This total seems impressive to us but is only a tiny fraction of the European population of around three million pairs: Quail is a southern species, here at the fringe of its range.

Quails are erratic in their occurrence: they were found in 24 tetrads in our *First Atlas* and 16 in this Atlas, but only one of the tetrads was the same.

Sponsored by Michael S. Twist

QUAIL
BREEDING DISTRIBUTION
Found in 16 tetrads (2%)
2 confirmed breeding (13%)
1 probable breeding (6%)
13 possible breeding (81%)
Layout of tetrads within a 10 km square.
E J P U Z
D I N T Y
C H M S X
B G L R W
A F K Q V

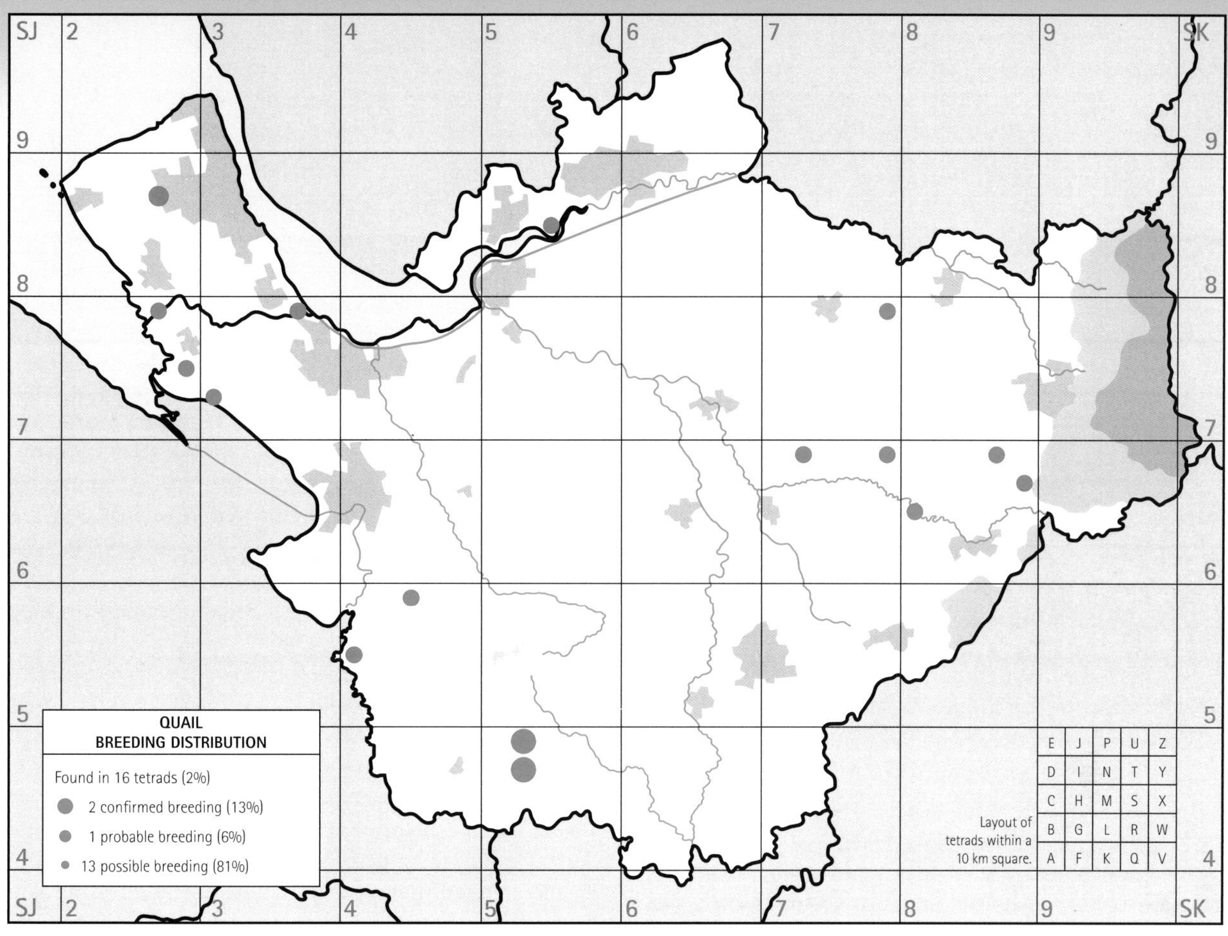

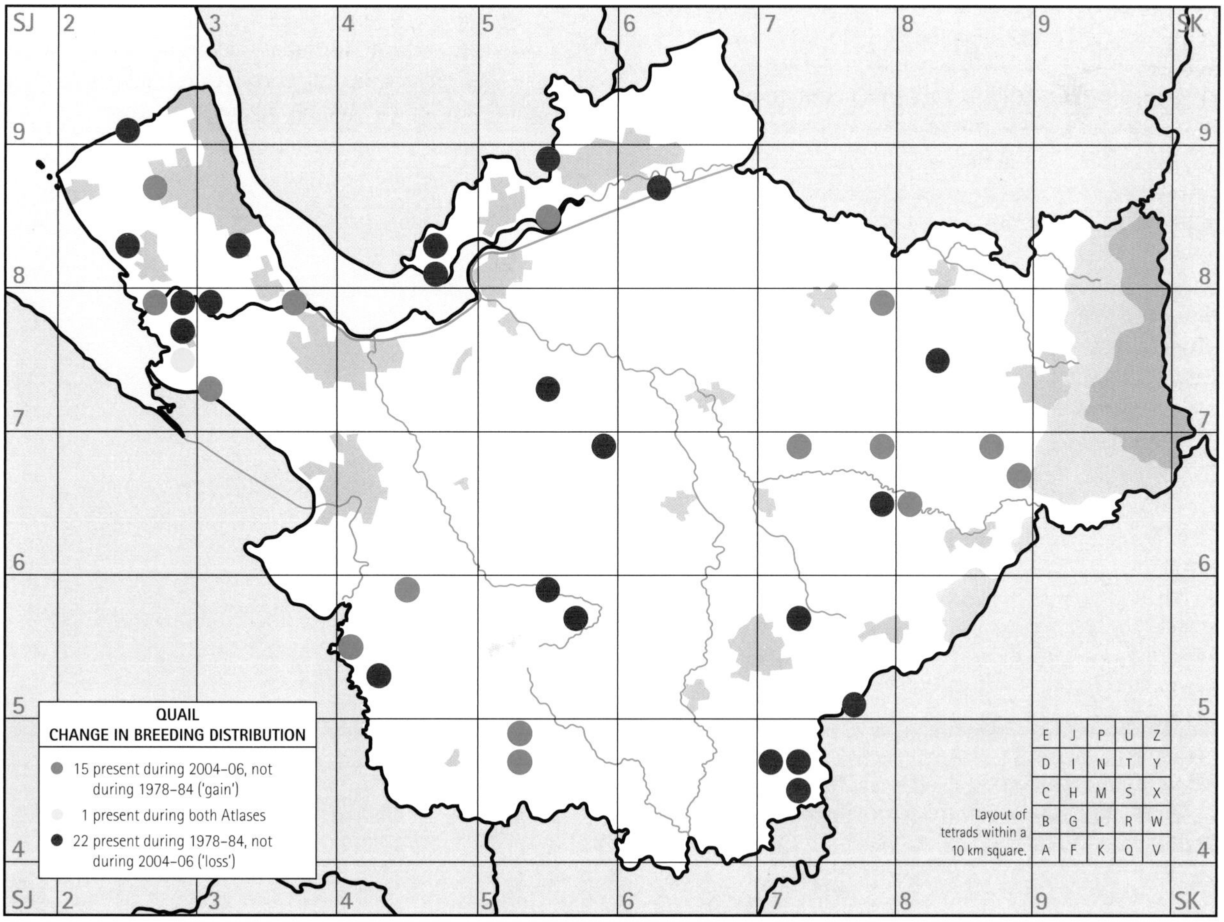

QUAIL
CHANGE IN BREEDING DISTRIBUTION
15 present during 2004–06, not during 1978–84 ('gain')
1 present during both Atlases
22 present during 1978–84, not during 2004–06 ('loss')
Layout of tetrads within a 10 km square.
E J P U Z
D I N T Y
C H M S X
B G L R W
A F K Q V

Pheasant

Phasianus colchicus

BEN HALL

Largely ignored by most birdwatchers, and once voted the most hated bird in Britain, there is a strong argument for saying that Pheasant is in fact England's most important bird as its requirements have shaped much of the English countryside (Marchington 1984). Many wooded areas and hedgerows exist mainly to provide cover for this species. Lest the foregoing be taken as suggesting that the introduction and rearing of Pheasants has had a benign or positive influence on the countryside, however, it should be noted that some authors report potentially negative effects of high Pheasant densities on native UK birds. These include the structure of the undergrowth and woodland field layer and the spread of disease and parasites (Fuller *et al.* 2005). Interspecific competition for food could be an issue as well: at around 1 kg, rather more for males and less for females, the biomass of Pheasants exceeds that of any other British bird.

There are some self-sustaining populations of wild birds but the species' numbers are determined principally by releases of reared birds for shooting: the Game & Wildlife Conservation Trust estimated in the early 1990s that some 20–22 million birds were released in the UK each autumn. This figure has increased fourfold since the mid-1960s (Tapper 1999), and nowadays may well be higher still. About one in 10 of the released birds is expected to survive until spring, when they must form the major part of the breeding population. The corresponding figures for Cheshire and Wirral are not known but the BTO BBS analysis shows that the breeding population of the county in 2004–05 was 9,420 birds (5,810–13,030). Most of those detected on BBS transects were males, which are much more vocal with their far-carrying 'kor-kok' calls, and more visible as the brightly plumaged birds strut about their territories whilst the camouflaged females are hidden on their nests. However, each year roughly half of all males are not breeding because many dominant birds gather a harem of several females, leaving a surplus of unmated, mostly one-year-old males, although some birds do nest as conventional pairs.

The maps show that Pheasants have spread considerably since our *First Atlas*, with a net gain of 130 tetrads, and they are now found almost everywhere apart from urban areas. The most noticeable increases have been in north and west Wirral, east of Macclesfield, and a broad swathe through the centre of Cheshire, roughly following the lines of the rivers Weaver and Gowy. The national population index rose by 57% from 1984 to 2004 and the county population has probably risen substantially from the *First Atlas* estimate of 'from two to five pairs per occupied tetrad'; the current figure corresponds to an average of about 17 birds per tetrad in which the species was recorded. It seems inappropriate to use 'pairs' for a species with such a flexible mating system. Most of the records of confirmed breeding came from observations of one or more adults with a brood of chicks (159 tetrads), but surveyors in 25 tetrads found nests in various stages of occupation.

Pheasants can be found in almost any habitat: two-thirds of the records for this Atlas were farmland, of all types, with woodland (19%), scrub (6%) and semi-natural grassland (4%). They feed in the open, often in field margins, yet remain close to shelter. Favoured areas for cover are protected from wind and weather, and provide suitable nesting areas: most nests are near to the edge of a wood or its internal rides.

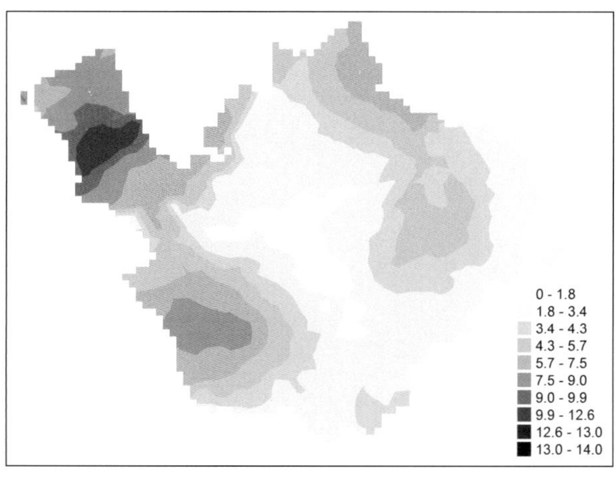

Pheasant abundance.

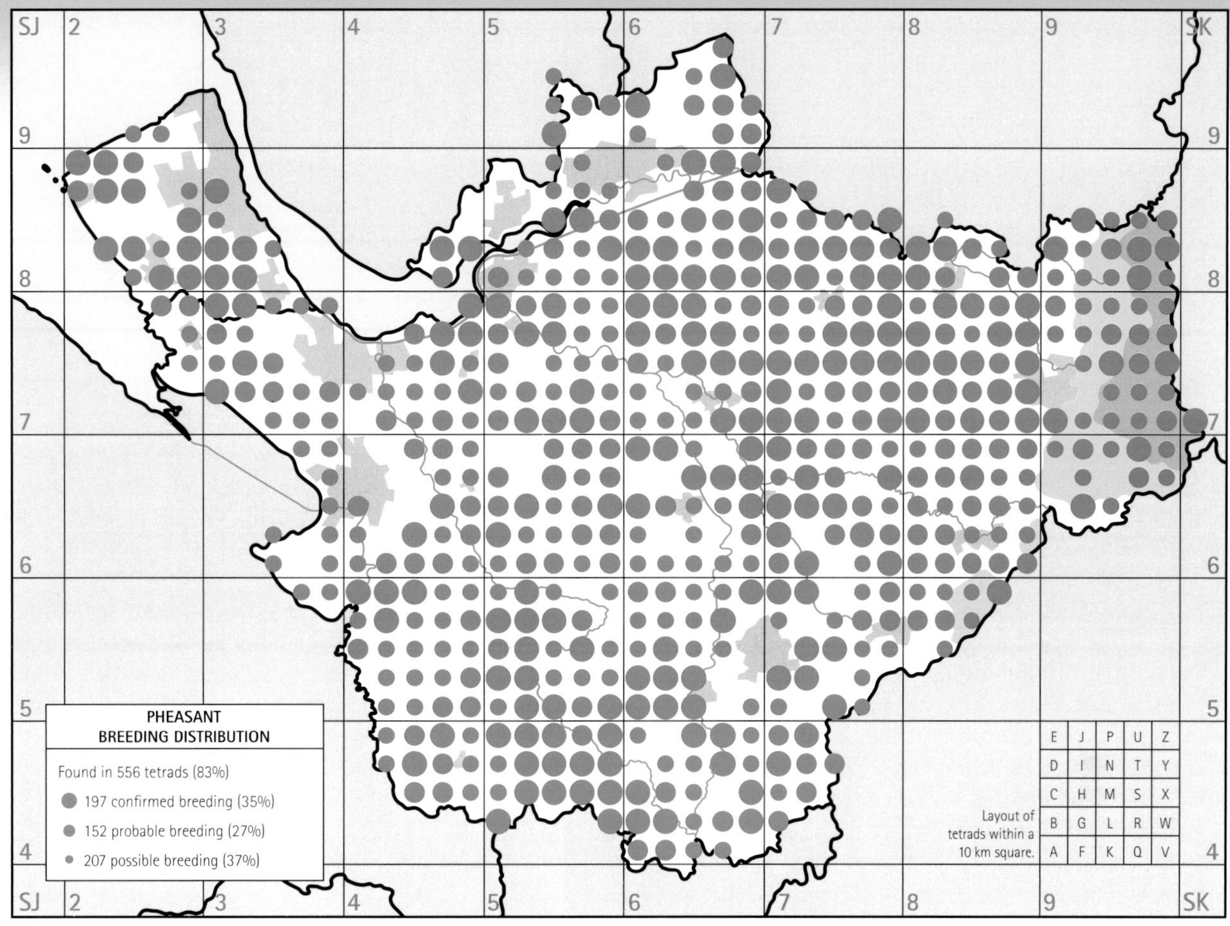
PHEASANT
BREEDING DISTRIBUTION
Found in 556 tetrads (83%)
197 confirmed breeding (35%)
152 probable breeding (27%)
207 possible breeding (37%)
Layout of tetrads within a 10 km square.
E J P U Z
D I N T Y
C H M S X
B G L R W
A F K Q V
SJ
SK

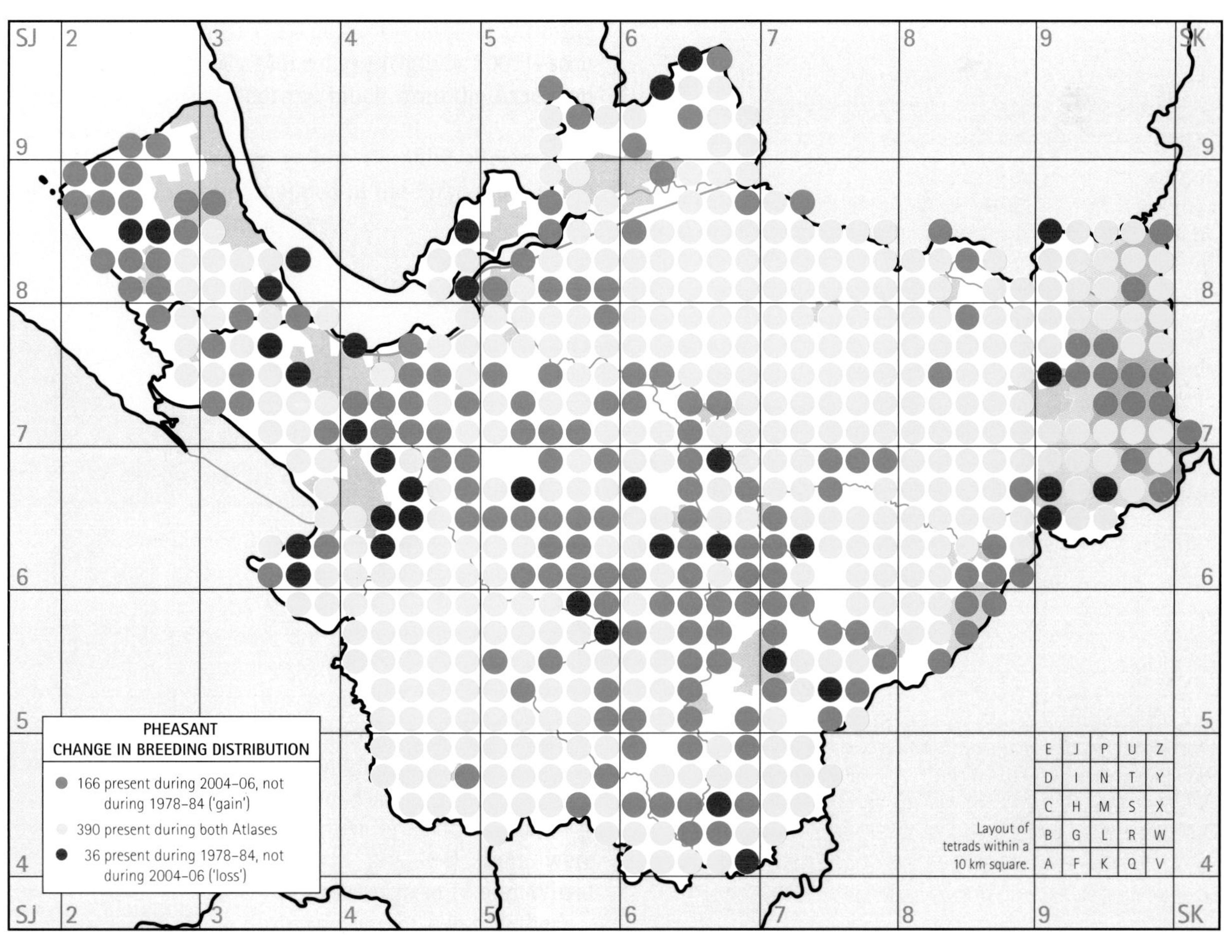
PHEASANT
CHANGE IN BREEDING DISTRIBUTION
166 present during 2004–06, not during 1978–84 ('gain')
390 present during both Atlases
36 present during 1978–84, not during 2004–06 ('loss')
Layout of tetrads within a 10 km square.
E J P U Z
D I N T Y
C H M S X
B G L R W
A F K Q V
SJ
SK

The maps of winter and breeding season distribution are almost identical; Pheasants were found wintering in 43 tetrads where they were not recorded in the breeding season, and were missing in winter from 56 with breeding presence. These differences are most likely to be due to observer effects, perhaps unluckily visiting a location when the resident Pheasant was silent. The females gather into flocks of tens of birds, or more, but even during winter, males are quite aggressive and weaker males, especially the first-year birds, are forced out into suboptimal habitat. Radio-tracking has shown that adult cocks that have previously held a territory move an average of only 80 m to their winter area, compared to about 300 m for birds establishing a territory for the first time (Robertson 1997). This work also showed that they especially favour small woods, seldom moving more than 30 m in from the edge of woodland. They are not fussy about the tree species so long as there is reasonable shelter provided by a good shrub layer. Their use of habitats in this winter Atlas was almost identical to that of the breeding season, with a few birds spreading into human sites and odd records on salt-marsh, although Pheasants do not often go far from cover. They are occasionally found in marshland and reed-beds, often said—wrongly—to be the preferred habitat in their ancestral Chinese homeland from where they have been introduced around the world (Robertson 1997).

In winter Pheasants feed mostly on seeds, often provided for them in woodland grain-hoppers, but also gleaning the remains of cereal crops, and this is one of the few species to be found in maize stubble. Away from woodland, increasing numbers of farms are planting strips of mixed seed-bearing crops intermixed with dense crops such as kale, often known as game cover. Pheasants usually carry substantial reserves of fat and can starve for several days if need be, such as when feeding areas are covered by deep snow; only in prolonged hard weather, such as has not been experienced in the county for 20 years or more, do many birds die from starvation.

One notable feature of Pheasant behaviour in winter is their use of communal roosts. They usually choose a dense tree, walking towards it then noisily flying steeply up into the branches until they reach a height where they feel safe from ground predators, especially foxes. Such roosts are widespread although fieldworkers in only six tetrads recorded them, with the largest estimated to contain 50 and 60 birds. It seems that at least one of the birds is always awake, keeping watch for threats to the whole party.

Many of the comments made by previous chroniclers of the county's birds could equally apply today. Coward (1910) wrote that, except in those parts of the hills east of Macclesfield where there is no suitable cover, the Pheasant is extensively preserved and exists everywhere in a semi-domestic condition. Hand-reared birds are turned down in thousands in woods and coverts, which are maintained and often planted solely for their benefit. Boyd (1951) summed up the traditional birdwatchers' view in saying that it was difficult to think of them as really wild birds, but they are found throughout the area in a perfectly wild state. Bell (1962) linked the fortunes of the Pheasant in the county almost entirely to the birds keepered on large estates, but also noted that, even during the Second World War when there was little or no gamekeeping, a stock of wild birds did manage to hold their own despite severe poaching.

SIMON BOOTH

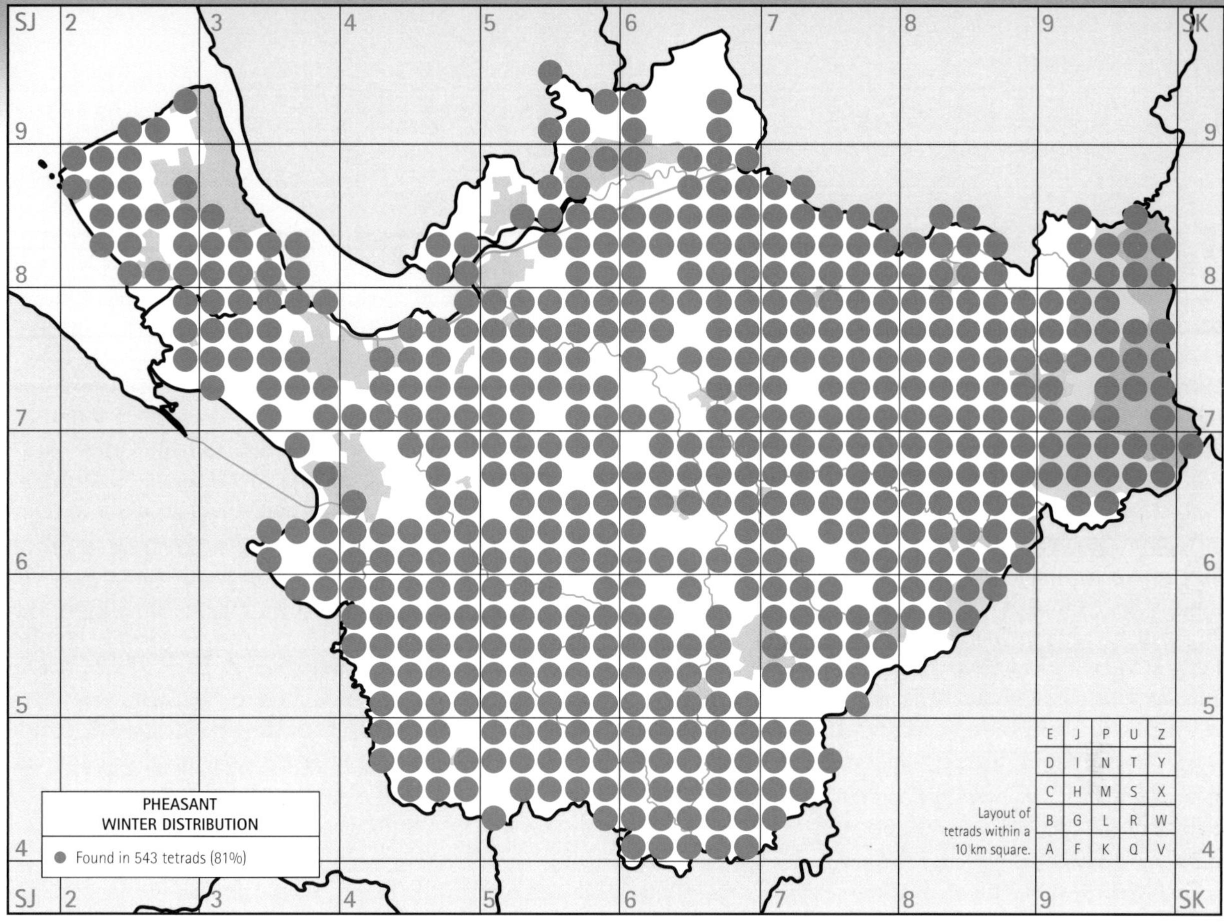
SJ
SK
2
3
4
5
6
7
8
9
PHEASANT
WINTER DISTRIBUTION
Found in 543 tetrads (81%)
Layout of tetrads within a 10 km square.
E J P U Z
D I N T Y
C H M S X
B G L R W
A F K Q V

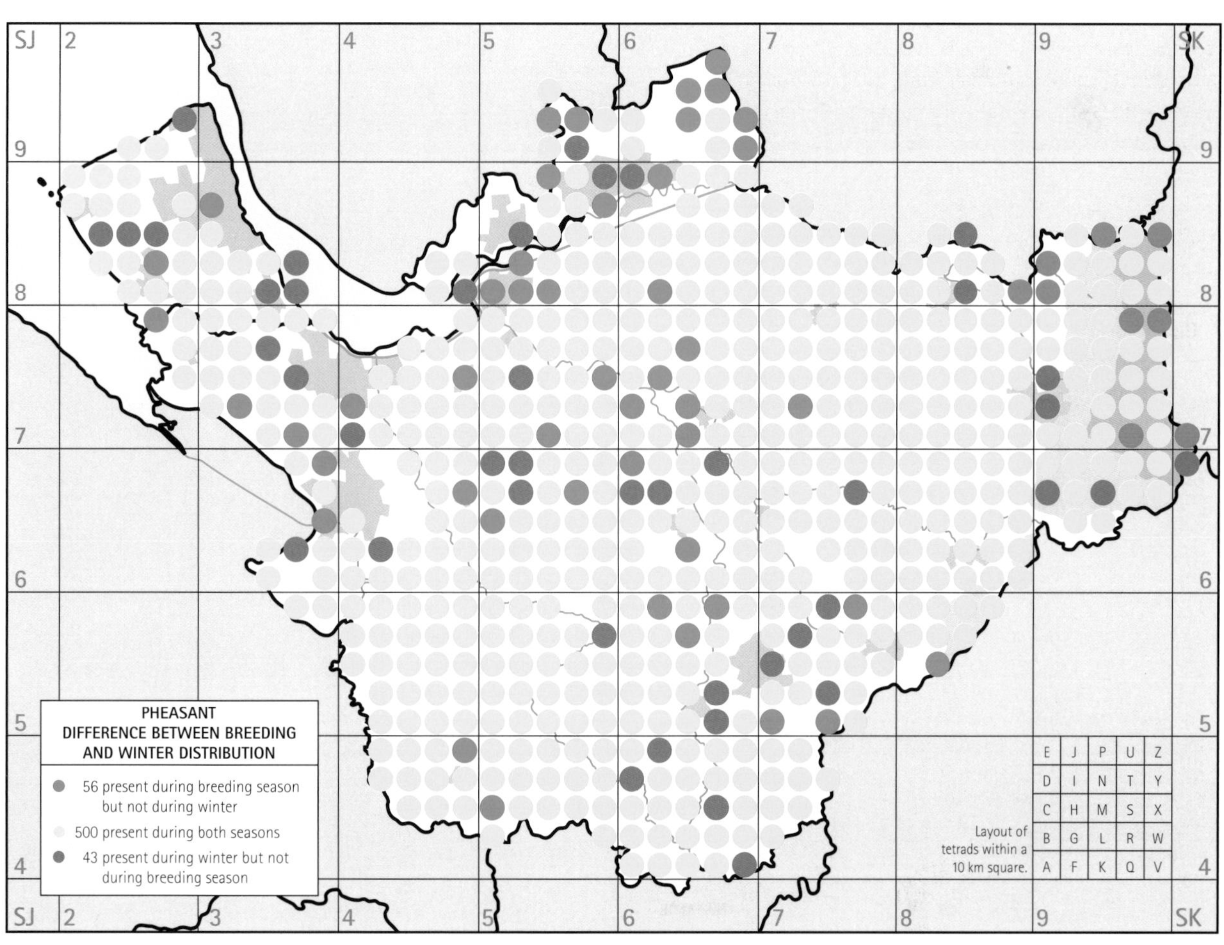
SJ
SK
2
3
4
5
6
7
8
9
PHEASANT
DIFFERENCE BETWEEN BREEDING AND WINTER DISTRIBUTION
56 present during breeding season but not during winter
500 present during both seasons
43 present during winter but not during breeding season
Layout of tetrads within a 10 km square.
E J P U Z
D I N T Y
C H M S X
B G L R W
A F K Q V

Red-throated Diver

Gavia stellata

Red-throated Divers mostly spend their winters in the open sea, where they find their food of sand eels, crustaceans, sprats and other fish, so shore-based observations can only sporadically hint at their true presence and numbers. Aerial survey work since 2000/01, triggered by research and proposals for offshore wind farms, has shown that there may be 1,200–1,500 divers in Liverpool Bay in winter, nearly all of them Red-throated Divers (Banks *et al.* 2006, Musgrove *et al.* 2007). As a result of these findings of internationally important numbers, all of the significant areas of Liverpool Bay, including those off the north Wirral, are now being considered as a marine Special Protection Area for divers and Common Scoters. Almost all of the Red-throated Divers are in waters up to 10 m deep, this contour stretching about 10 km offshore from Anglesey to the Fylde. Divers are most frequently found off the Welsh coast west of Abergele, but another regularly used spot is about 6 km north-west of Hoylake (Webb *et al.* 2004). Has the offshore limit of the Cheshire and Wirral ornithological recording area ever been defined?

The origins of those in Liverpool Bay are unknown, but Red-throated Divers from a wide range of breeding areas appear to mix in winter around the coasts of Britain and Ireland. Ringed birds from Finland and Sweden have been found in the Irish Sea, and birds from the east and west coasts of Greenland have reached the North Sea off south-east England. Birds from Orkney and Shetland mostly winter at sea off Scotland and Ireland; some immatures, which migrate farthest, have been found off Finistère in France, but it is not known if they move through the Irish Sea on their way (*Migration Atlas*).

This Atlas map shows a typical picture of the species' records in recent years, with all birds at or near the north Wirral coast. Most records are of single birds, or a few together, but each winter larger flocks were counted off Hilbre (SJ18Z), with maxima of 50, 60 and 17 reported in the three years of this Atlas. A flock of 27 was on East Hoyle Bank (SJ29A) in the first winter. Mersey records are unusual, and the dot for the New Brighton tetrad (SJ39C) owes its inclusion to a flock of four birds, seen from Seaforth on the Liverpool side, flying out of the river mouth during strong north-westerly winds on the extraordinary seabird day of 9 December 2006.

This has probably always been the commonest diver in the county, although records increased greatly

RAY SCALLY

Sponsored by Derek Pike

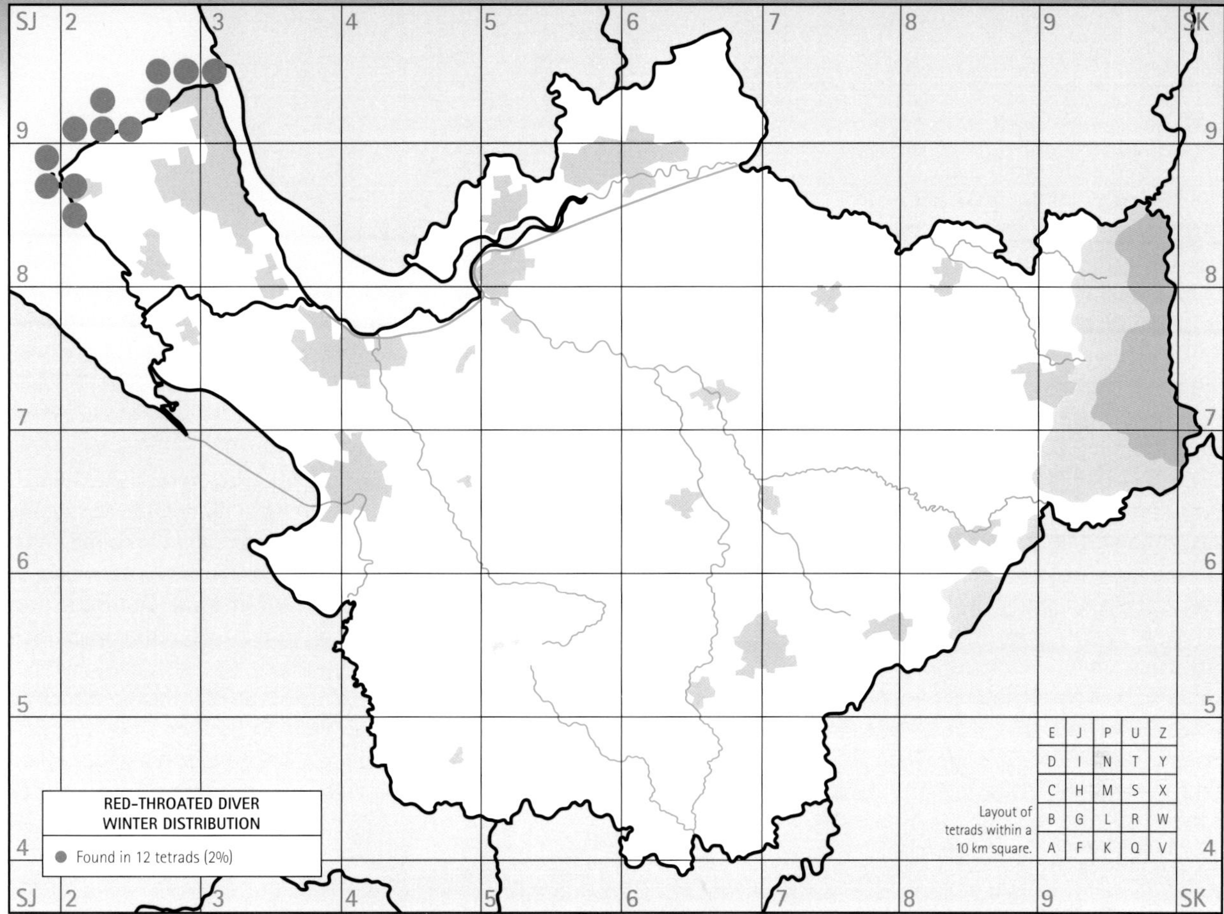

during the twentieth century. Coward (1910) called it 'a wanderer to Cheshire waters in winter' but knew of few records, while Bell's summary was that considerable numbers were sometimes seen between autumn and spring (Bell 1962). The largest numbers are recorded after north-westerly gales, with the highest daily count of 125 logged at Hilbre on 2 January 1965 (Craggs 1982). The annual county bird reports show most sightings from Hilbre, with other records from Red Rocks and Hoylake. Winter counts for winters from 1981/82 onwards vary from maxima of four in 1981/82 to a peak in 1989/90 when 67 flew west past Red Rocks on 28 January. Red-throated Divers are seldom found inland in winter, with the last records in 1995/96 including two that showed that birds can subsist on our meres and rivers, one staying at Rostherne and Tatton Park from 4 to 20 January and it, or another, living at the Weaver Bend from 27 February to 25 June (*CWBRs*).

Great Northern Diver

Gavia immer

This species is scarce on Irish Sea coasts, most birds being found in Ireland and the north and west of Scotland (*BTO Winter Atlas*). All of the UK sites with WeBS counts in double figures are in Scotland. This north-westerly distribution reflects the origins of the wintering population. Their breeding grounds are unknown, but those in our waters must include birds from Iceland, Greenland and northern Canada. Great Northern Divers spend the winter in deeper water, farther offshore than the other divers, and are also less susceptible to being blown towards land, so this species is difficult to record at the coast. Paradoxically, though, this is the most likely diver to be found inland.

Coward (1910) wrote of the Great Northern Diver as 'an occasional winter visitor to the coast and inland waters, and birds passing northward have been met with in spring'. Bell (1962) thought that that statement of status 'would hold good up to the present time', noting that 'it is nowadays seen in most years off Hilbre, particularly since about 1950 when that area has been very fully watched'. That assertion was quantified during the period 1957–77 with a total of 50 bird-days from mid-November to February (Craggs 1982). Daily records rarely exceeded two but a remarkable eight were noted on 24 December 1961. Boyd (1946) seems to have overstated the position when he wrote in his newspaper column in 1936 that Great Northern Divers appeared almost every winter on the Cheshire meres, and he was probably influenced by a run of such records during the 1930s. There was another coincidence of inland birds in late 1963 when Great Northern Divers made stays of various lengths at Tatton, Comber Mere and Budworth Mere, with sightings at all three on 1 December (Bell 1967).

In the 30 winters since 1977/78 the county bird reports list sightings in 23, with both coastal and non-coastal records in eight winters, 10 winters with coastal records only and five winters with only inland records.

RICHARD STEEL

Sponsored by Steve Kemp

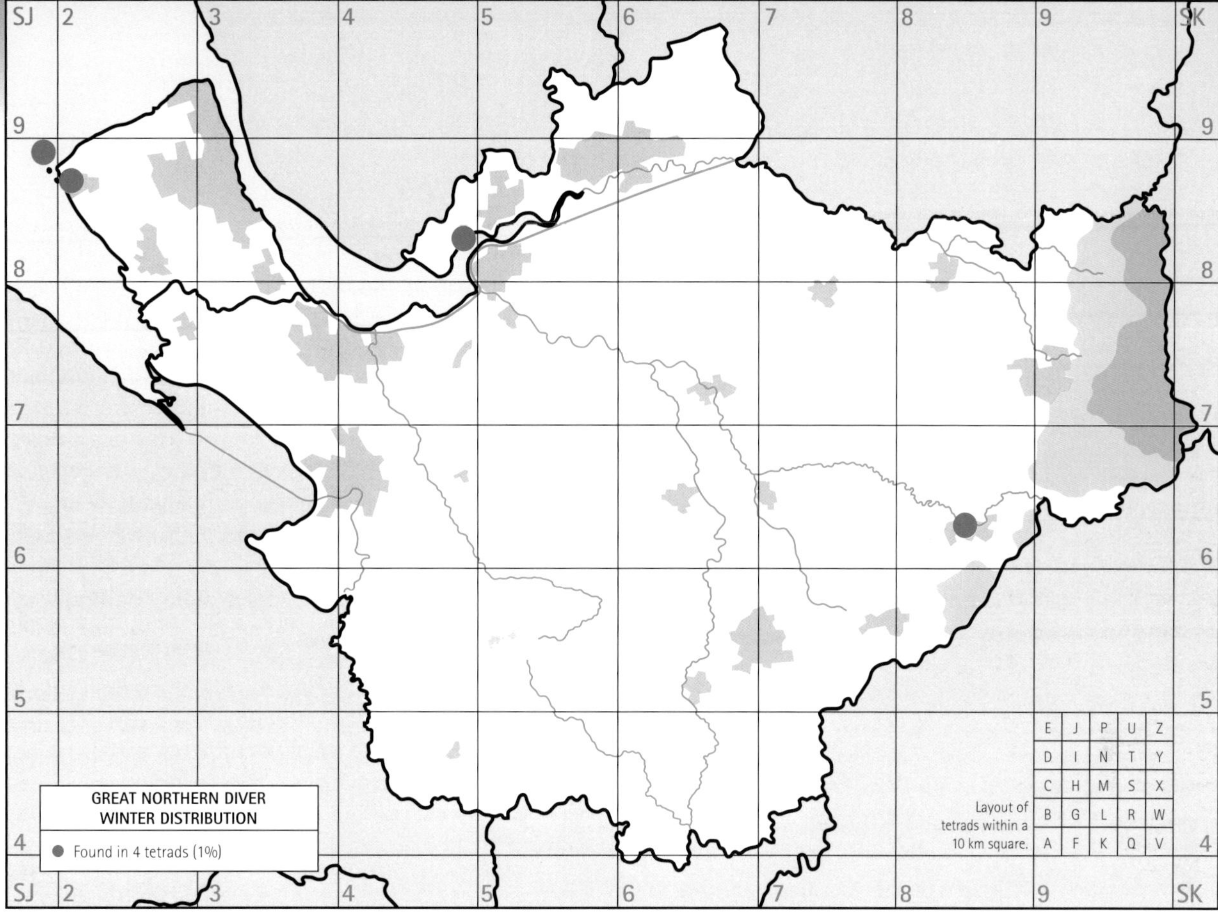

The sightings are sparse, however, from one to four per winter, with most records of solitary birds and the only multiple sightings from Hilbre, two birds in three winters and three birds on 12 January 1986. Most birds are seen from Hilbre, but there are coastal records from New Brighton to the mouth of the Dee off Caldy. Birds are more random in their choice of inland waters but they have appeared in three winters at both Budworth Mere (SJ67N/T) and Farmwood Pool (SJ87B). A feature of this species' inland visits is that they usually tend to stay at a site for a week or more, with the record held by one that remained at Farmwood Pool from 13 November 1982 to 5 February 1983. As with all divers, they feed mostly on small fish and crustaceans and their diet is not tied to marine organisms.

Thus, the records during this Atlas were fairly typical, in distribution and numbers. No birds at all were reported in winter 2004/05, with just one in 2005/06, at Hilbre. Four records came in 2006/07, at Hilbre, one on West Kirby Marine Lake for about two weeks, one seen on the river Mersey at Hale (SJ48W) and one that visited Astbury Lake, Congleton (SJ86L) for a morning.

Little Grebe

Tachybaptus ruficollis

SIMON BOOTH

The decline in breeding Little Grebes was one of the surprises of this survey, as it had not been noticed or commented upon previously. Compared to the *First Atlas*, the species has been lost from many of its former breeding sites in central and south Wirral, south of Chester and the region from Northwich to Congleton. There have been gains in scattered sites across the county, and a noticeable increase in occupied tetrads in the eastern hills; in some areas there appear to have been minor redistributions from one tetrad to another, but the net effect is a loss of 19 tetrads from twenty years ago.

There could be several reasons for the decline in breeding records of Little Grebe. Their food—mainly aquatic invertebrates, especially larvae, and small fish—puts them in competition with the larger fish favoured by anglers, so ponds that have been taken over by fishermen are often inimical to this species, overstocked with fish and denuded of marginal vegetation. Also, their favoured smaller waters are perhaps those most affected by unsympathetic water use—river engineering, pollution, agricultural run-off and overabstraction. Brown and Grice (2005) note that the future of the Little Grebe is inexorably linked to the appropriate management of our lowland wetlands and that we should make greater efforts to monitor trends in breeding numbers: this comment should surely apply to Cheshire and Wirral.

As the Little Grebe has declined, Great Crested Grebes have spread, but there does not seem to be direct competition between them. Bell (1962) said that Dabchicks (as Little Grebes were usually known then) were on many waters which were too small for Great Crested Grebes but Boyd (1951) had 'never seen a nest on the little marl-pits as are occupied by Moorhens'. In this survey, 66 tetrads had records of Little Grebe and not Great Crested; 64 tetrads had records of Great Crested Grebe and not Little; and 60 tetrads had records of both species. The submitted habitat codes show clearly the Little Grebe's bias towards smaller standing waters: 12 pond; 50 small waterbody; 48 lake/unlined reservoir; 4 lined reservoir; 14 sandpit, etc.; and 5 on linear watercourses.

Little Grebes are secretive, but their far-carrying trilling 'song'—a high-pitched whinnying—readily betrays their presence. It seems that some observers were not familiar with the birds' trilling calls, however, so perhaps some birds were missed, and a disappointingly high proportion of records was of birds seen in suitable habitat only. Little Grebes return to their breeding areas in the New Year and have a protracted breeding season (February to September) although most eggs are laid from late April to late June (Moss & Moss 1993). The nest, on a floating platform of vegetation concealed in emergent vegetation, is vulnerable to fluctuations in water level, either flooding following heavy rain, or being left stranded in drought. Once the chicks have hatched the birds tend to become more visible, and 55 out of the 61 two-letter codes were sightings of adults with young. The striped chicks are often carried on the adults' backs, although less frequently than in the larger grebes, and some parents build brood platforms for their young.

Nationally, the species has declined rapidly on linear waterways but the wider populations (including birds on small still waters) are healthy. In Cheshire and Wirral, some tetrads hold more than one pair and the county population may lie in the range of 150–200 pairs. With the large number of waters in the county, Cheshire would perhaps be expected to hold an even larger population of this species. A thorough survey of breeding numbers would be useful.

Sponsored by Joe O'Hanlon

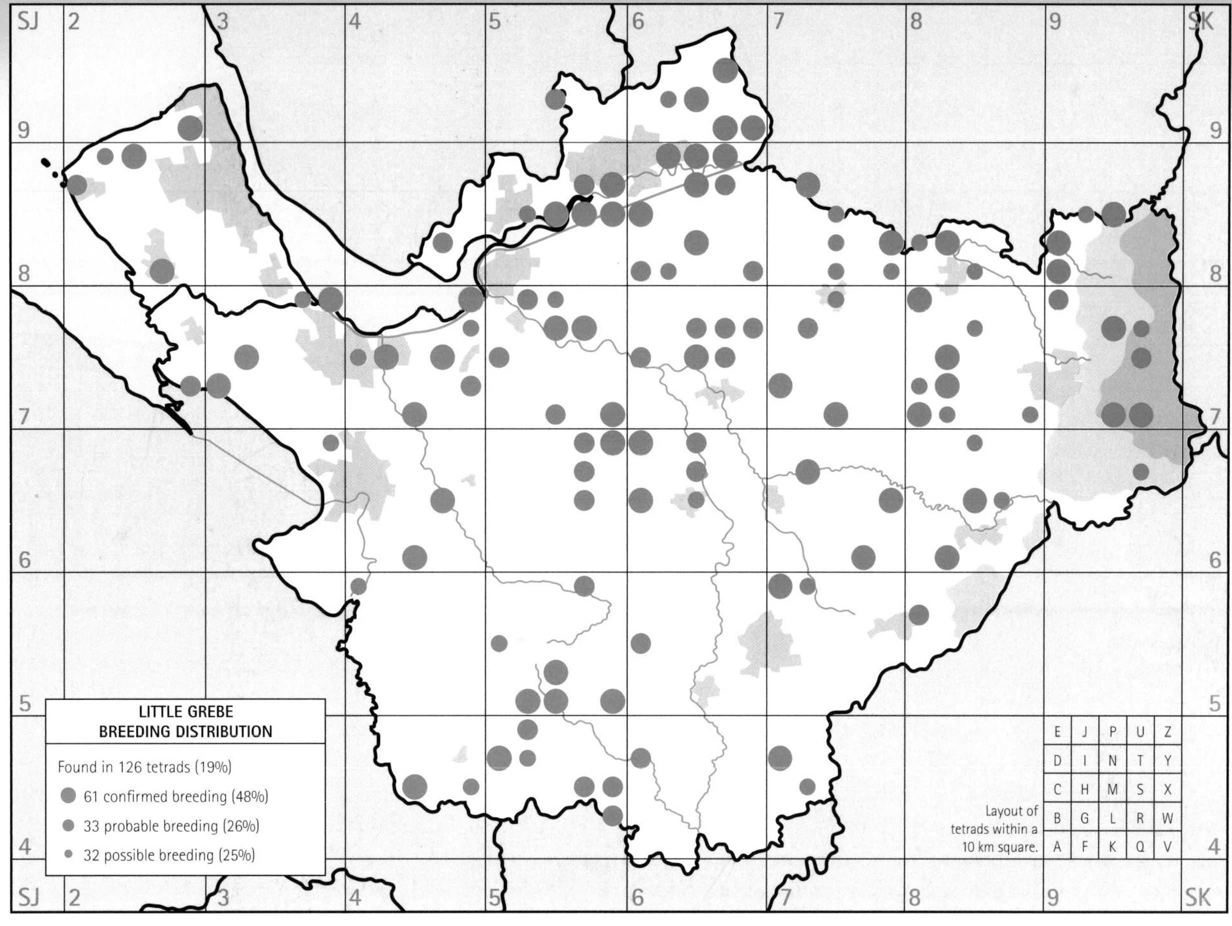

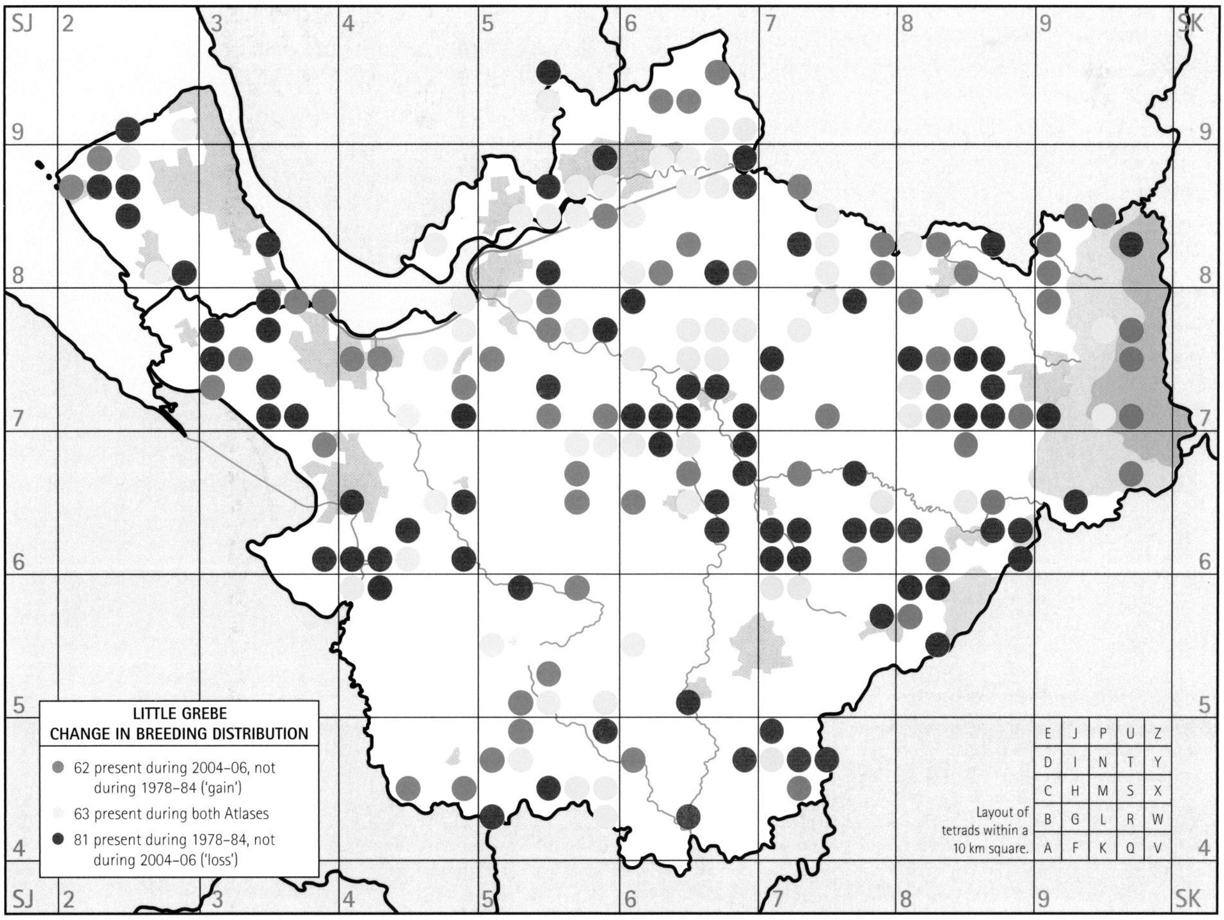

LITTLE GREBE
CHANGE IN BREEDING DISTRIBUTION

- 62 present during 2004–06, not during 1978–84 ('gain')
- 63 present during both Atlases
- 81 present during 1978–84, not during 2004–06 ('loss')

E	J	P	U	Z
D	I	N	T	Y
C	H	M	S	X
B	G	L	R	W
A	F	K	Q	V

Layout of tetrads within a 10 km square.

There is a clear shift in habitat and distribution of this species in winter. More than a century ago, Coward and Oldham (1900) noted that 'The Little Grebe is widely distributed throughout the Cheshire lowlands in the breeding season, and in winter is often seen on waters where it does not nest. At this latter season, even when the ponds and meres are not frozen, it occurs on swift-flowing streams and rivers.' This summary holds good today, and is well demonstrated by the habitat analysis. In the breeding season, there were 12 records on ponds and 50 on small waterbodies, 66 on lakes, meres and reservoirs with just five on rivers and canals; in winter there is some withdrawal from the smallest waters, with six on ponds and 43 using small waterbodies, with a major increase to 35 on linear watercourses, 23 on streams and rivers and 12 on canals. As Coward had commented, there was no freezing weather during our Atlas period to force the birds to move.

The winter map shows birds present in 72 tetrads that were empty in the breeding season, with an obvious increase especially on the Dee and Weaver, but they were recorded in only two estuarine tetrads: contrary to the suggestions from Vinicombe (1982) that birds breeding inland disperse to the coasts, there is no evidence for this in Cheshire and Wirral (or in the *Migration Atlas*). Eighty-five tetrads were occupied in both seasons, with their early return to the breeding areas doubtless accounting for some of the 'winter' records, such as a pair trilling on Trentabank Reservoir (SJ97Q) on 29 January 2005. The 41 tetrads with breeding season presence that were unoccupied in winter were scattered across the county with no obvious pattern.

Anderson (1993) noted a decline in the wintering population of Little Grebes on the river Weaver in Nantwich, from figures of 12–31 in January to mid-March 1986 to counts of four to six in the same period of 1993. It was difficult to ascribe reasons for this, but the decline paralleled the arrival of Mink and the loss of Water Voles, although numbers of Moorhen and Mallard in the area were not affected. Up to 1986, double-figure winter counts were recorded in *CWBRs* from at least six sites, but since that year, no site other than the Weaver Bend had reported a double-figure count. This suggests a long-term and widespread drop in numbers. During this Atlas survey most counts were of just two birds and only three tetrads registered flocks larger than eight Little Grebes: 30 were counted at Frodsham Marsh (SJ57E) by Peter Twist in 2005/06, 22 at the north Wirral clay pits (SJ28P) were logged by Jeremy Bradshaw in 2004/05, and a maximum of 12 was present at Doddington Pool (SJ74D) in two winters.

Little Grebes are seldom seen on migration, and few are ringed, so the extent of immigration from the continent is unknown, but there are two foreign-ringed birds in winter elsewhere in Britain, from Denmark and Latvia. The maximum total WeBS counts account for only about one-quarter of the supposed British and Irish breeding population, and many wintering birds must be on small waters and rivers not covered by WeBS.

RICHARD STEEL

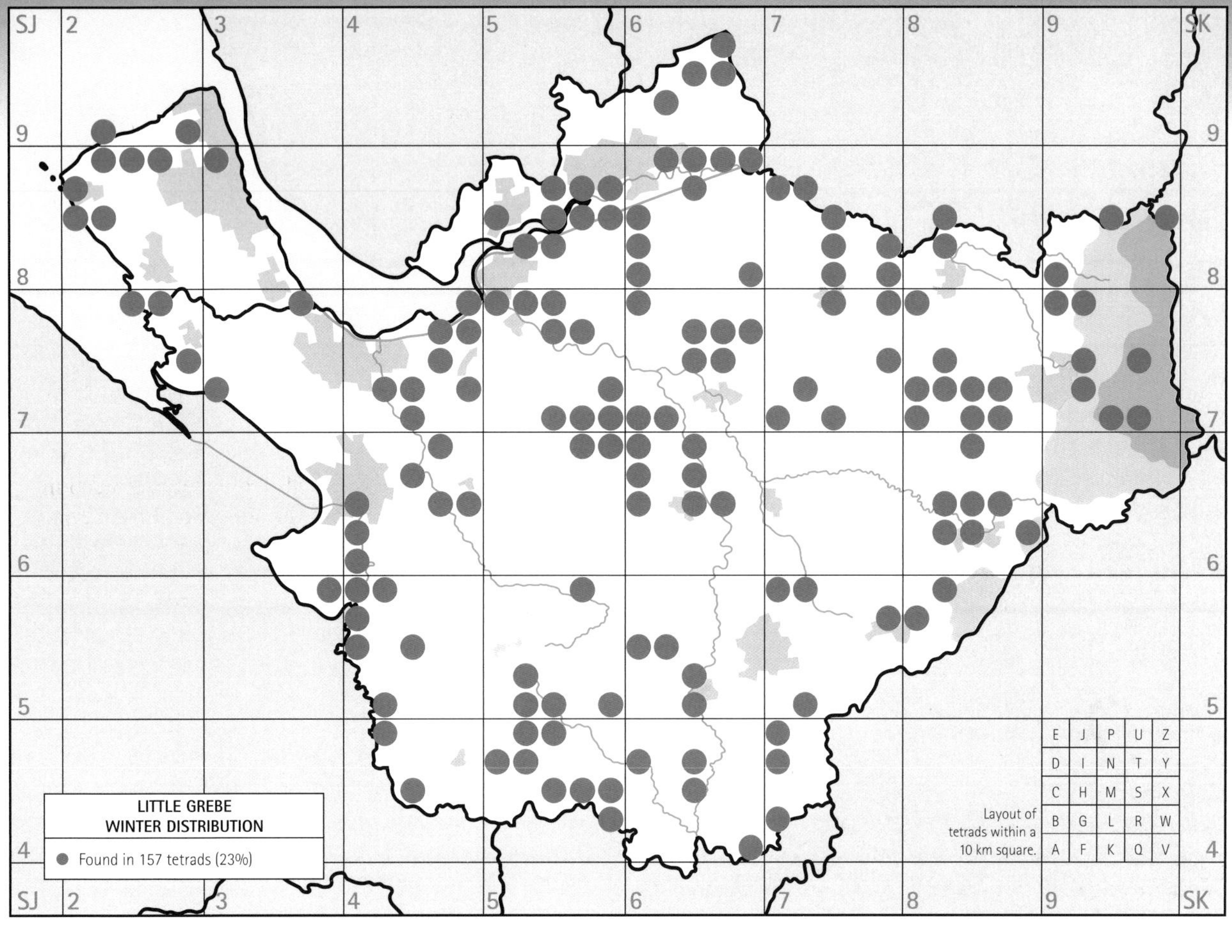

SJ 2 3 4 5 6 7 8 9 SK

E J P U Z
D I N T Y
C H M S X
B G L R W
A F K Q V

Layout of tetrads within a 10 km square.

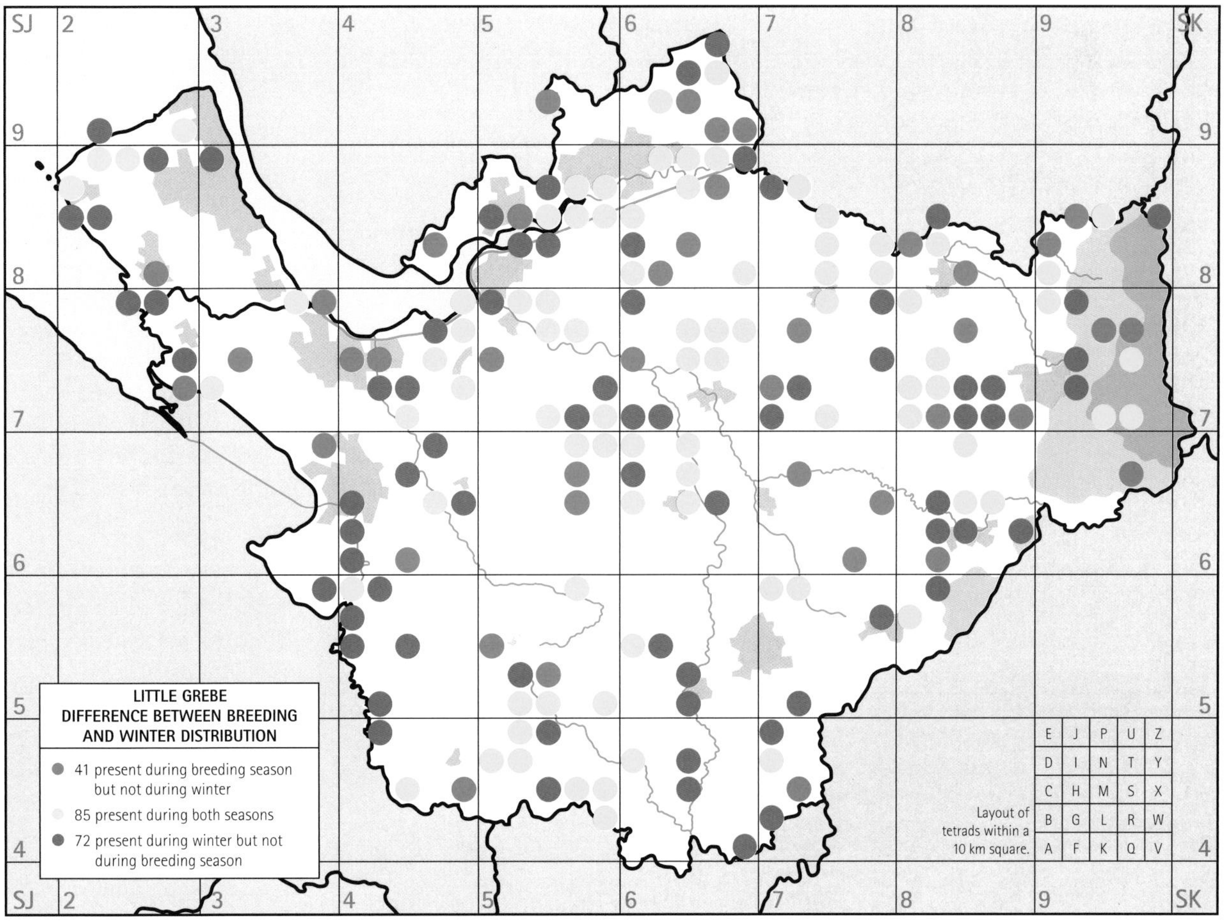

LITTLE GREBE
DIFFERENCE BETWEEN BREEDING AND WINTER DISTRIBUTION

- 41 present during breeding season but not during winter
- 85 present during both seasons
- 72 present during winter but not during breeding season

Great Crested Grebe

Podiceps cristatus

This Atlas confirms a significant increase in Great Crested Grebes. The 'change' map shows a net gain of 24 tetrads with the species, 50 gains and 26 losses. The latter are scattered across the county, with no consistent pattern, and the gains are especially in the Mersey valley, around Northwich and on the upland reservoirs, with grebes consolidating their previously tenuous hold on Wirral. With most of the gains being in or near urban areas, it is tempting to suggest that improvements in water quality underlie their rise.

The distribution map illustrates their clear easterly bias in the county, with only six of the 124 tetrads with records west of the SJ50 longitude line. This mostly follows the presence of large waterbodies. The submitted habitat codes show clearly their preference for the county's larger standing waters: 1 pond; 12 small waterbody; 76 lake/unlined reservoir; 3 lined reservoir; 21 sandpit, etc.; 7 river; and 3 large canal. Their diet is mostly coarse fish up to about 20 cm in length, caught by diving. At Woolston, most nests are on the river Mersey or the Manchester Ship Canal, rather than on the dredging deposit beds themselves, probably reflecting the availability of fish. The oligotrophic eastern reservoirs have obviously become more suitable for them in the last twenty years.

BEN HALL

This is a conspicuous bird—even when out of sight, their distinctive croak can betray their presence—and most fieldworkers found it easy to obtain a two-letter code. As in our *First Atlas*, 72% of records were confirmed breeding. In 68 tetrads observers found adults with their stripy chicks, often carried on their parents' backs, and a further 21 tetrads held occupied nests or nests with eggs. Pairs were found in another 21 tetrads, with nest material in three of them and in seven of them fieldworkers saw them engaged in their spectacular displays. There is plenty of time to record breeding: they can have an extended season, starting in February in some years, with a month of incubation and 10 or 11 weeks before chicks can fly. Some of the early breeders might have a second brood, although most raise just one family of two or three chicks in a year. The latest chicks in the county may still be dependent on their parents into November.

There were 110 tetrads with confirmed or probable breeding, and several sites held multiple pairs, headed by Rudheath (SJ77K) and Woolston (SJ68P) with eight pairs reported at each site: the county population is at least 150 pairs. In the *First Atlas* it was thought unlikely to exceed 100 pairs in any one year. In the mid-nineteenth century the secluded Cheshire meres were vital in saving Great Crested Grebes from extinction in the period of persecution for their 'fur' and ornamental feathers, and even now the county holds an above-average proportion of the national population: there are around 4,000 pairs in Britain (Brown & Grice 2005).

Sponsored by Lymm Ornithology Group

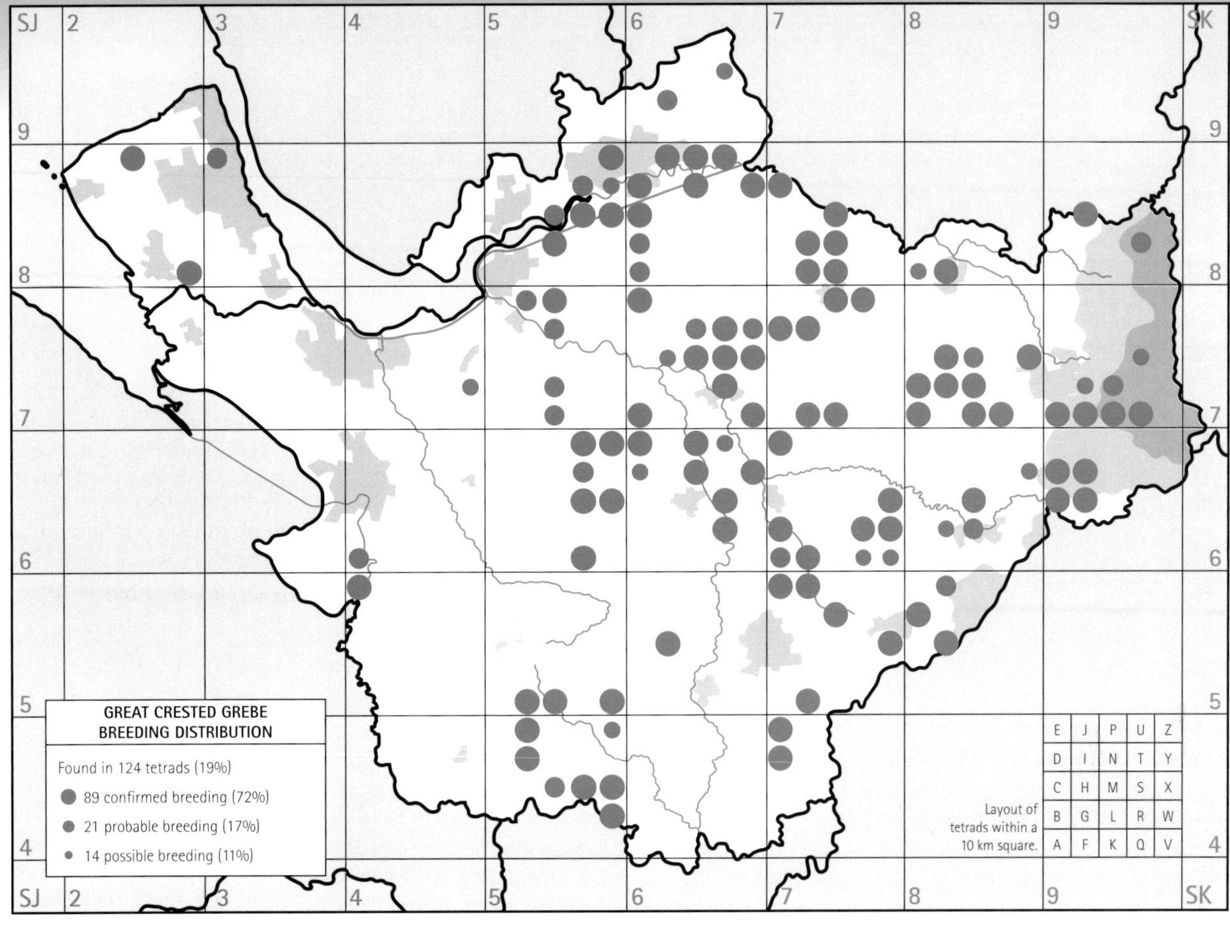
GREAT CRESTED GREBE
BREEDING DISTRIBUTION
Found in 124 tetrads (19%)
89 confirmed breeding (72%)
21 probable breeding (17%)
14 possible breeding (11%)
Layout of tetrads within a 10 km square.
SJ
SK

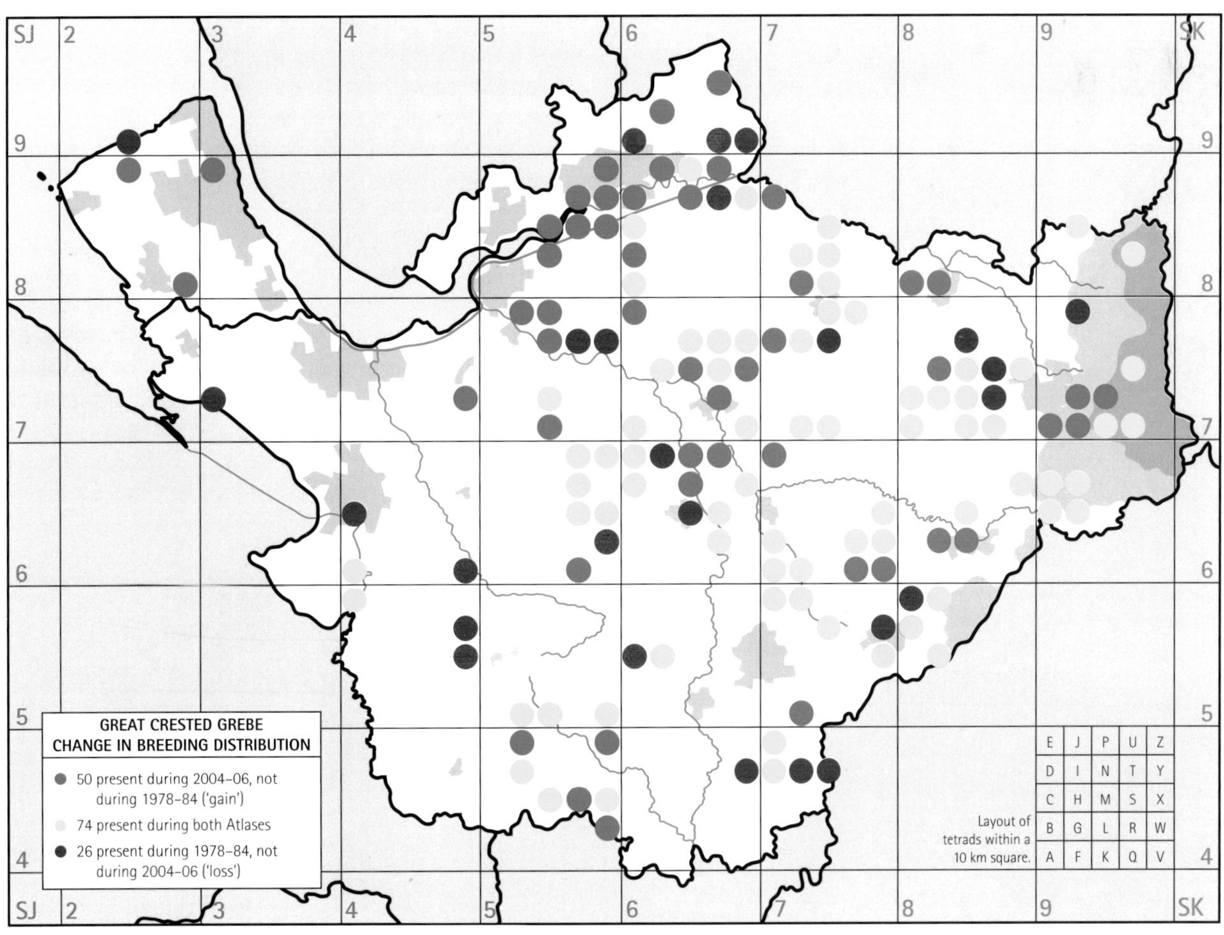
GREAT CRESTED GREBE
CHANGE IN BREEDING DISTRIBUTION
50 present during 2004–06, not during 1978–84 ('gain')
74 present during both Atlases
26 present during 1978–84, not during 2004–06 ('loss')
Layout of tetrads within a 10 km square.
SJ
SK

In winter most (96 out of 124 tetrads) of the Great Crested Grebes' breeding areas are also occupied, probably by the same individuals, with the birds either remaining resident year-round or returning to make an early start to the breeding season; a century ago Coward (1910) noted that '... in autumn and early winter the numbers on the meres are frequently less than at the end of the breeding season, but in January and February, especially after gales, there is often a marked increase'. They usually pair during mid- to late-winter, Simon Wood seeing courtship display on 7 January 2007 at Rudheath (SJ77K). Of the 28 that were vacated in winter, 20 of them are tetrads newly occupied since the *First Atlas*, perhaps suggesting that they are more marginal sites and that it was their unsuitability in winter that left them unused previously.

In addition, 62 tetrads were occupied in winter only, most of them off the north Wirral coast and in the estuaries, where they favour the deeper waters in the centre of the channel. The salt-water habitats were adjudged to be 2 open shore, 9 open sea, 1 brackish lagoon (West Kirby Marine Lake) and 31 estuarine. There was little difference from the breeding season in the freshwater habitats submitted: 1 pond; 9 small waterbody; 71 lake/unlined reservoir; 7 lined reservoir; 18 sandpit, etc.; 6 river; 1 small canal and 3 large canal. Their diet is much the same all year round, fish that they catch by swimming underwater.

The north-west corner of the Wirral is the place to find the highest numbers of Great Crested Grebes. There were 120 off Hoylake (SJ29A) in 2004/05 with 100 off Hilbre (SJ18Z) in 2005/06, but these were trumped by an amazing flock off Dove Point, Meols (SJ29A/F) on 7 February 2007, counted by Richard Smith at 458 birds and probably the largest flock ever in the county. Otherwise, the median count from the 232 submitted counts was just four birds, and only 29 flocks were in double figures. The largest inland flocks were on Marbury (Budworth) Mere (SJ67N), peaking at 36 birds in 2006/07. Nowhere in the county approaches the threshold for national importance by regularly holding 159 birds each winter.

WeBS counts show that many British sites record large differences in numbers of Great Crested Grebes from one winter to another, for reasons unknown. Similarly the migrations of grebes are poorly understood (*Migration Atlas*) although some birds from continental Europe have been found in southern England. Nothing is known of the movements of Cheshire and Wirral birds.

STEVE ROUND

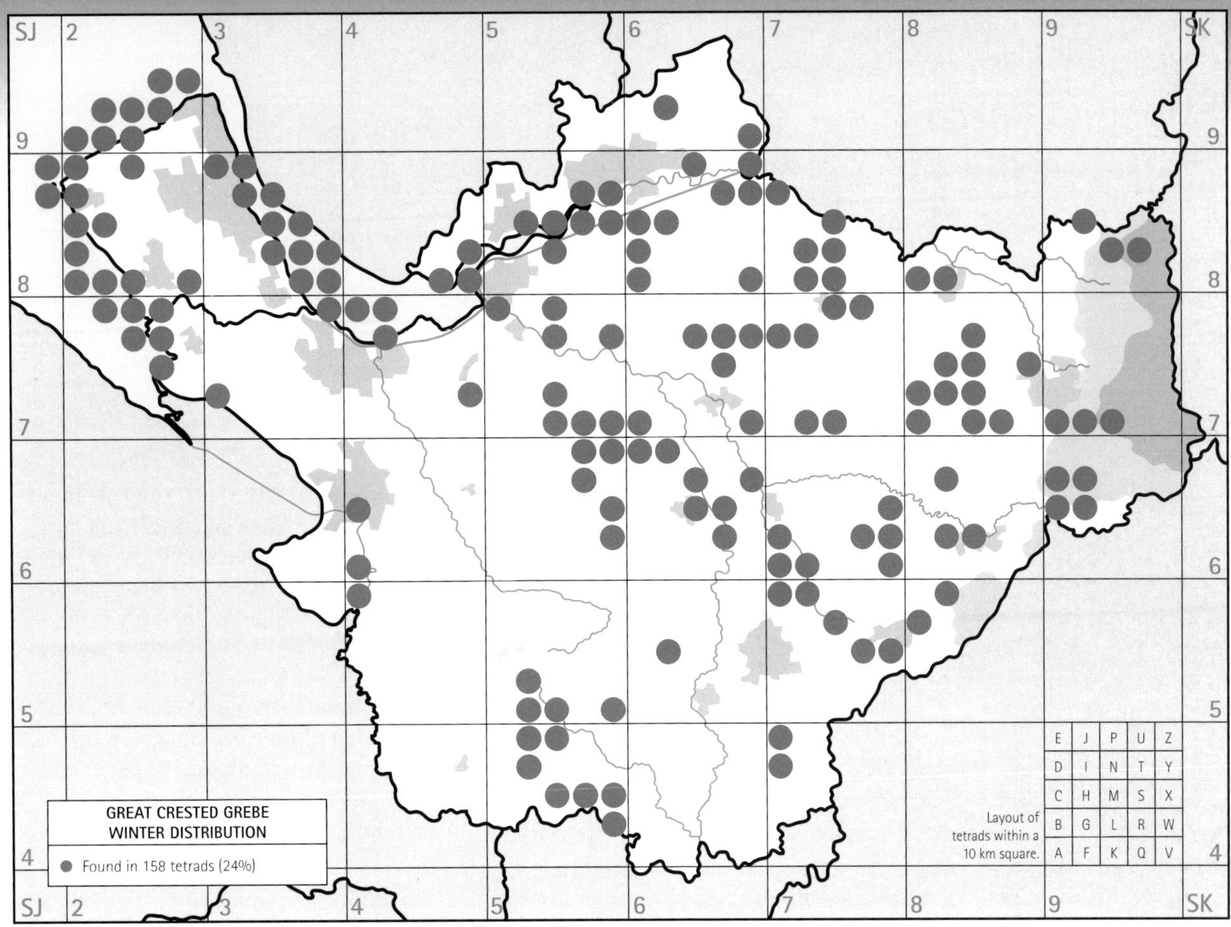
GREAT CRESTED GREBE
WINTER DISTRIBUTION
Found in 158 tetrads (24%)
Layout of tetrads within a 10 km square.
E J P U Z
D I N T Y
C H M S X
B G L R W
A F K Q V
SJ
SK

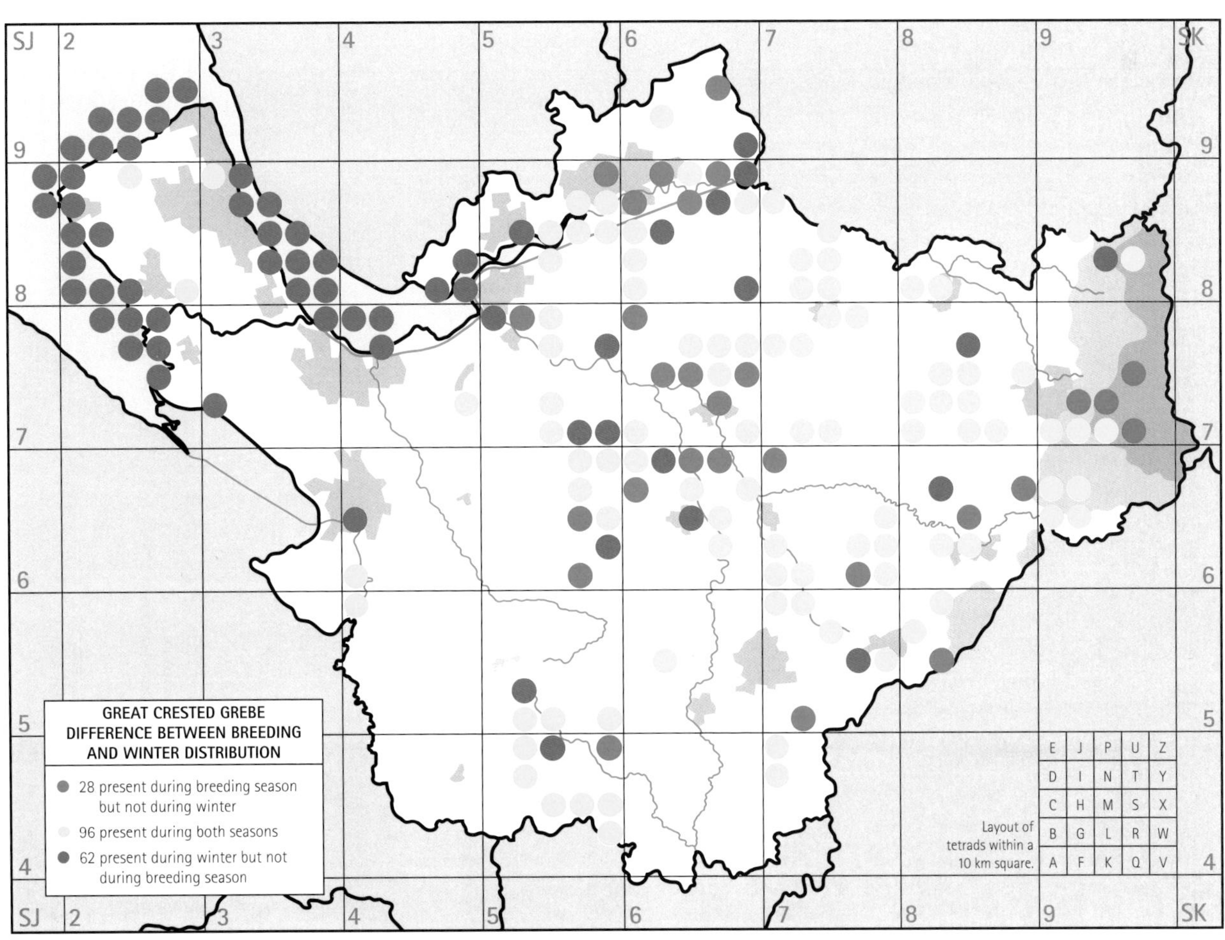
GREAT CRESTED GREBE
DIFFERENCE BETWEEN BREEDING AND WINTER DISTRIBUTION
28 present during breeding season but not during winter
96 present during both seasons
62 present during winter but not during breeding season
Layout of tetrads within a 10 km square.
E J P U Z
D I N T Y
C H M S X
B G L R W
A F K Q V
SJ
SK

Black-necked Grebe

Podiceps nigricollis

SUE & ANDY TRANTER

Cheshire featured strongly in the twentieth-century history of Black-necked Grebes in the UK, so it is fitting that, during the period of this survey, the county held the largest colony of Black-necked Grebes in the country (Holling *et al.* 2007a).

As well as the colony at the Woolston Eyes SSSI, which includes parts of three tetrads (SJ68J/N/P), during this Atlas survey pairs with young were seen at the Moore Nature Reserve (SJ58X/Y), and single birds stayed at three other sites in the northern part of the county. Despite thorough survey work during this Atlas, no Black-necked Grebes were found in the Delamere area, the species' favoured location during earlier colonization of the county in the 1940s, 1950s and 1980s: Blakemere, with its large gull colony, appears to be eminently suitable, but the birds obviously think otherwise. A prominent feature of most, but not all, successful Black-necked Grebe colonies is their association with nesting Black-headed Gulls, which must give some measure of protection from aerial predators. On the other hand, such a congregation of easy prey might attract other killers such as mink.

Their favoured habitat is shallow, eutrophic waters, usually with extensive fringing vegetation and often floating aquatic plants, and a site preferably sheltered from strong winds. Black-necked Grebes mainly eat insects and their larvae, occasionally other invertebrates or small fish, mostly caught by diving for 20 or 30 seconds, but some of which they gather with their charming habit of skimming the water surface and turning their head from side to side, using their slightly upturned bill in the manner of an Avocet.

After a typically elaborate 'grebe-type' display, pairing seems to be rapid and breeding at Woolston is often much earlier than normally recorded elsewhere. The first chicks are usually seen in late May, with most pairs apparently rearing two young, and one adult looking after each chick; the stripy-plumaged youngsters often ride on an adult's back. In occasional years, including 2004, some late broods hatch in July, presumed to be from second clutches of eggs, although their success rate is poor.

This species has a well-merited reputation for rapidly colonizing and—just as quickly—abandoning breeding waters, so we should enjoy them whilst we may. The history of the breeding numbers at Woolston since the time of our *First Atlas* is shown in the graph.

Concerns are often expressed about the low productivity, averaging only about one fledged chick per pair, but it appears to be sufficient to maintain stable or slowly increasing numbers. Unfortunately, apart from the numbers breeding, very little is known about the population dynamics of the British Black-necked Grebes: How long do they live? When do they first breed? Do the young birds return to the UK? Is it a 'closed' population or is there interchange with other European birds? Neither is much known about why Woolston is such a good site for them, and studies of habitat, the density of aquatic invertebrates, the presence of fish (either as predators of chicks or as competitors for food), water chemistry and predation would help to provide prescriptions for their conservation, both at Woolston and other sites.

Much of the information on the species' biology comes from work in North America, where the species (known there as the Eared Grebe) is abundant. These birds, however, have some exceptional physiological adaptations that do not apply to European stock—such as reducing their pectoral muscles so much that

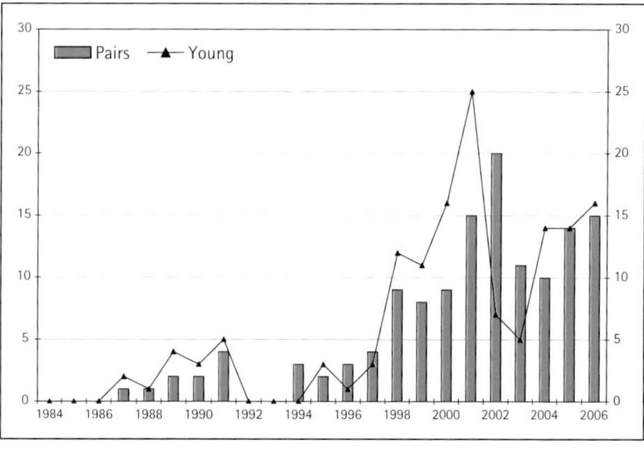

Black-necked Grebe breeding numbers at Woolston.

Sponsored by Woolston Eyes Conservation Group

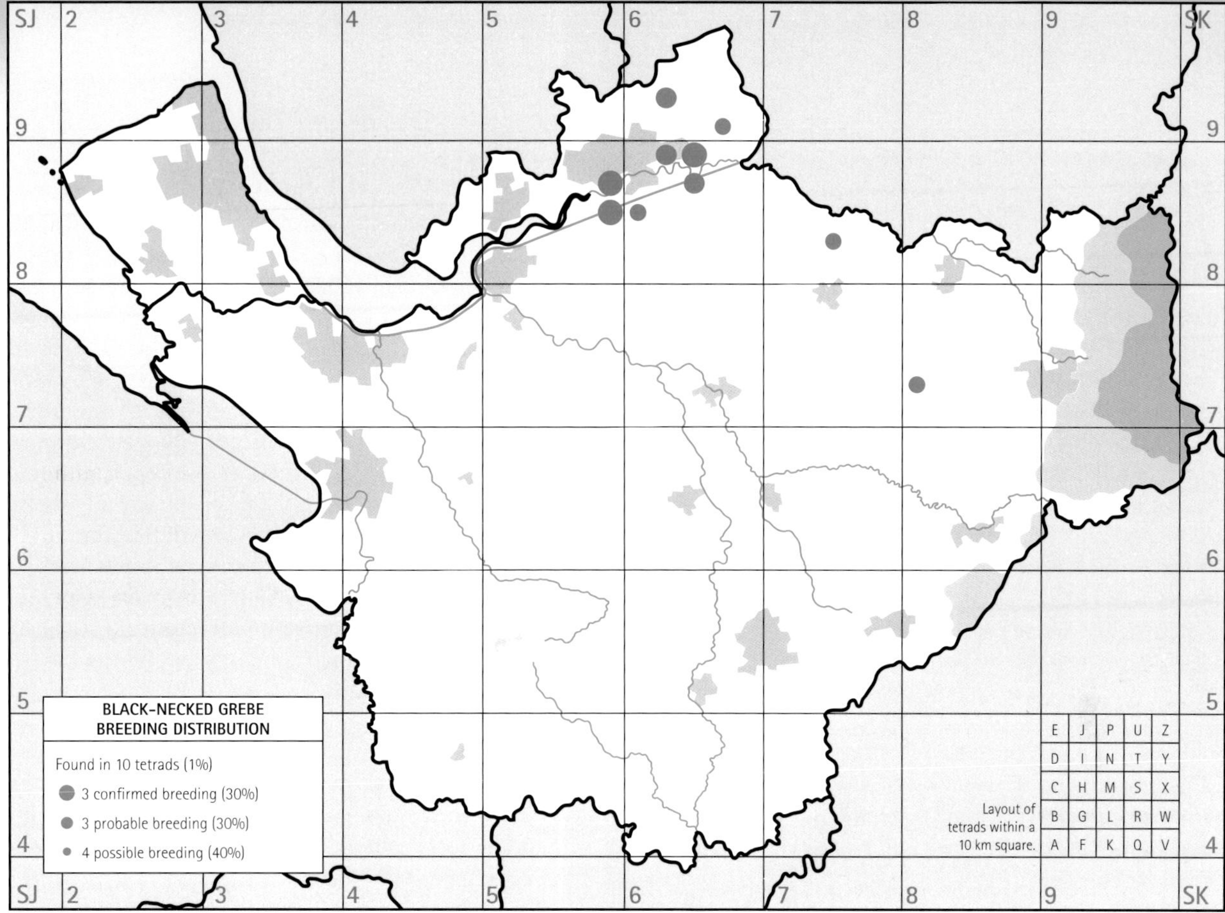

they cannot fly whilst they gorge themselves on brine shrimps at California's Mono Lake (Ogilvie 2003)—so it is perhaps not wise to borrow much from the American studies.

Breeding was proven at one Cheshire site in 1984 but the species was not mapped in the *First Atlas*, so no 'change' map is presented here.

● During the wintering Atlas survey, Black-necked Grebes were recorded in three tetrads, all of them also having breeding season records, and they may well be late autumn migrants rather than truly wintering birds. It is not known where British Black-necked Grebes spend the winter; as nocturnal migrants, they are seldom seen on migration. The species extends as far south as trans-Saharan Africa, and there has been some speculation, from the coincidence of their spring arrival dates at Woolston with the first summer migrants, that the grebes might have undertaken similar journeys from southern Europe or perhaps beyond. On the other hand, Brown and Grice (2005) suggest that it is likely that birds that breed in Britain overwinter in this country. The known numbers wintering in British waters, around 120 birds (*BTO Winter Atlas*, Baker *et al.* 2006) and thought to contain birds from continental Europe (*Migration Atlas*), would nowhere nearly account for all of the British breeding stock.

In the *BTO Winter Atlas* (1981–84) there were records from six 10 km squares in Cheshire and Wirral (five records of single birds and one of two together).

Manx Shearwater

Puffinus puffinus

A Manx Shearwater within sight of the Wirral coast in winter is in the wrong place, in location and habitat: in that season, most of them are in the southern hemisphere and way offshore beyond the continental shelf (*BWP*, *Migration Atlas*). All of those recorded during this Atlas were on 21 November 2006 or 9 December 2006, the two days during which an unusual combination of winds also brought record numbers of winter Leach's Petrels to our coast.

The normal status of Manx Shearwater in Cheshire and Wirral is as a coastal visitor, most often seen during strong onshore winds from April to September, with largest numbers from June to August. These are adult birds finding food, away from their nests in burrows on offshore islands. About 80% of the world population nests in the British Isles but, despite the species' name, only 34 pairs nest on the Calf of Man. Our nearest colonies are at Copeland, Northern Ireland (nearly 5,000 pairs) and Bardsey Island, Gwynedd (16,000 pairs), but it would only be a relatively short flight for a bird from the largest Welsh colonies, 102,000 pairs on Skomer and 46,000 pairs on neighbouring Skokholm in Dyfed (Mitchell *et al.* 2004). Those from the world's largest colony, the 120,000 pairs on Rum off the Scottish west coast, normally head west to forage off the Atlantic shelf. The two parents take it in turns to keep the single egg warm throughout the seven-week incubation period, and in bringing food to the chick during the 10 weeks before it fledges. They may well be away for several days at a time, some Skokholm birds being known to fish for sardines in the Bay of Biscay up to 1,000 km from their nest. When the chick fledges in September, the adults and juveniles leave and fly rapidly, perhaps covering 750 km a day, to winter in the Atlantic off South America. But, crucially for their position in this Atlas, small numbers stay in the Bay of Biscay (*Migration Atlas*).

These few Manx Shearwaters thus share similar wintering quarters to some of the Leach's Petrel population, and were presumably caught up in the same pattern of winds from mid-November 2006, when gale-force south-westerly winds apparently blew some birds

STEVE ROUND

Sponsored by Noel and Hilary Woodhead

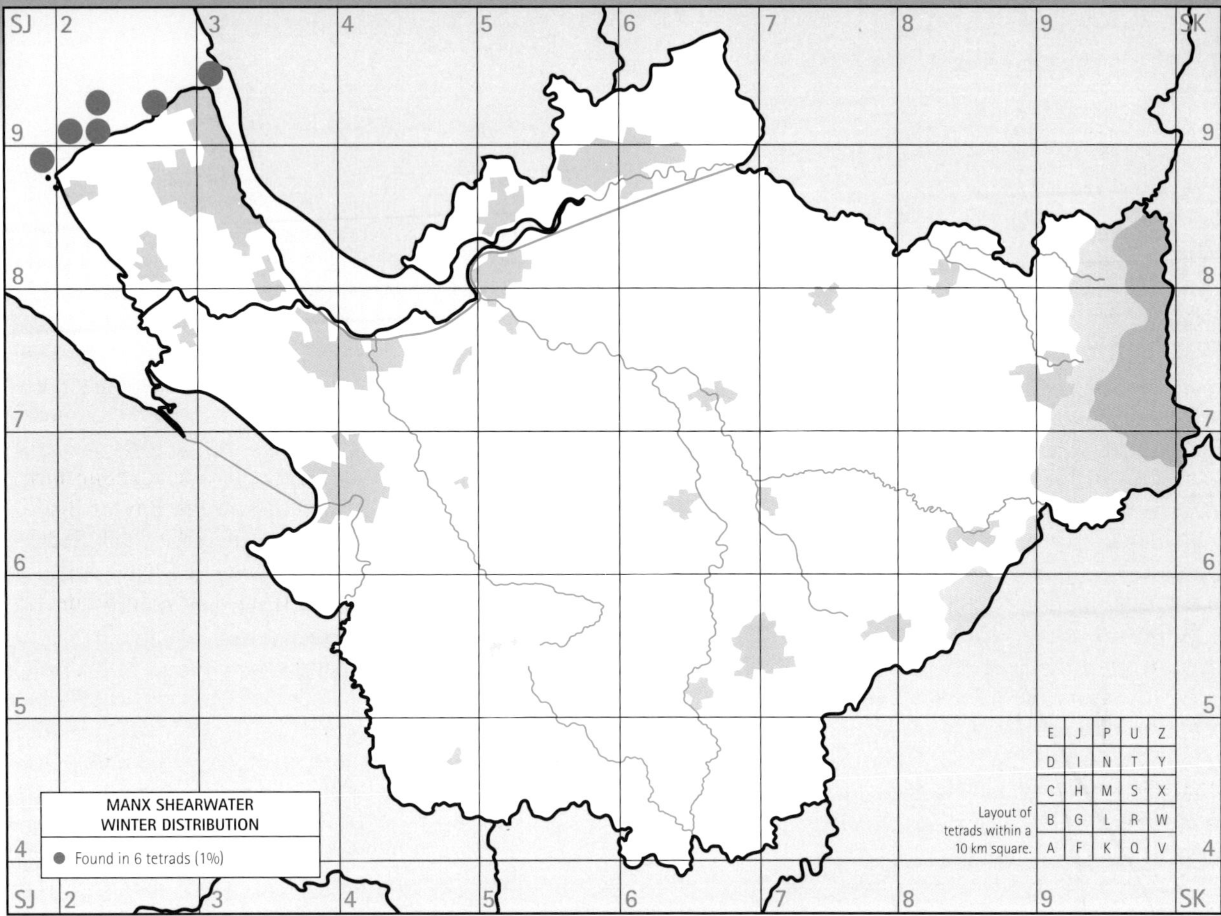

back north from their wintering areas into the Irish Sea. When the winds changed to north-westerly the seabirds were driven within sight of observers on land, first on 21 November 2006 when one Manx Shearwater was seen off Hilbre Island and later on 9 December when the species was reported from a further five tetrads. No more than one bird was seen at any one time but it is impossible to tell how many were present on that remarkable day. One observer, Colin Jones, reported a Manx Shearwater from three different tetrads off the middle of the north Wirral coast (SJ29F/G/R) and, from the times and places of observation and the movement of the birds, believes that they were three different birds. The records at the ends of the north Wirral, Hoylake shore (SJ29A) and the bird seen flying out of the Mersey at New Brighton (SJ39C), could have been different again, making a total of anything from one disoriented individual to a maximum of five birds.

The extraordinary nature of these records is illustrated by reference to the ornithological literature. Coward (1910) knew of no winter birds, but later had the good fortune to see a party of seven near the Liverpool Bar lightship on 30 January 1931 (White *et al.* 2008). Hardy (1941) used the throwaway line 'occasionally at Mersey and Dee mouths in autumn and winter' but without any detail it is impossible to know what support there was for that statement. A bird off Hilbre on 28 November 1984 (*CWBR*) appears to be the only documented record of a Manx Shearwater ever seen from land in Cheshire and Wirral during winter prior to those in 2006.

Looking outside the county, there was only one record of the species in England (off Filey, Yorkshire) during the winters 1981/82–1983/84, with two sightings in Wales, groups of one and five off Anglesey (*BTO Winter Atlas*). The *Birds of Lancashire and North Merseyside* contains the statement that 'it is doubtful if any Manx Shearwater has ever occurred in Lancashire in a healthy state during winter' (White *et al.* 2008). The state of health of those seen in late 2006 is not known, but none was known to have been found sick or dead.

Leach's Petrel

Oceanodroma leucorhoa

It had seemed unlikely that this species would feature in this Atlas other than as the logo of CAWOS, but the weather of November/December 2006 changed all that.

Leach's Petrels migrate west of Ireland between their breeding sites, on remote islands off Scotland and Iceland, and wintering areas thought to include the Bay of Biscay and farther south in the Atlantic as far as the equator. They feed on marine macro-zooplankton—especially lanternfishes and crustaceans including krill—that are forced close to the ocean surface by upwelling along the steep edge of the continental shelf. Their preferred habitat is thus way offshore over deep oceanic water, from 200 m to 2,000 m deep, but north-westerly gales in September and October drive some birds into the Irish Sea and some of these reach the mouth of the Mersey, the north Wirral coast and Hilbre. This offers the only opportunity for many bird-watchers to see this most pelagic of species, and many visit the Wirral at such times. This passage is over by the end of October, and usually before.

However, in mid-November 2006 gale-force south-westerly winds apparently blew some Leach's Petrels back north from their wintering areas into the Irish Sea. Seven were seen flying past Hilbre Island on 21 November when the winds changed to north-westerly and brought some birds inshore. Winds remained southerly into early December when a severe gale on 3 December blew many more petrels into the Irish Sea. Birds were reported from many south-westerly facing coasts but only one, on 6 December, from our area. Then, winds veering north-westerly again forced Leach's Petrels near to the north Wirral coast and counts totalling 25 and 78 were made on 8 and 9 December. One was blown inland and seen on Radnor Mere on 10 December, and single birds were recorded on the north Wirral on 10 and 11 December, then this remarkable event was over (Smith 2006).

These birds that are blown off course are often doomed, although some Leach's Petrels can apparently survive in the shallow inshore waters off our coasts, possibly finding edible items at the sea surface such as molluscs, offal and other detritus by using their sense of smell as well as sight. Apart from one reported freshly dead in West Kirby on 12 December, it is not known how many other dead petrels were found in December 2006.

The rarity of this incident is indicated by there being only three or four previous winter records of single birds in our area. On 8 December 1886 in Chester and 16 December 1907 in Ellesmere Port, birds were found sick or dead, and Boyd (1946) saw one swimming and flying on Marbury Mere (Great Budworth) on 26 December 1942. The *BTO Winter Atlas* (1981/82–1983/84) included one bird seen in the 10 km square SJ39, spanning Cheshire and Wirral and Merseyside.

SUE & ANDY TRANTER

Sponsored by Hilbre Bird Observatory and Ringing Station

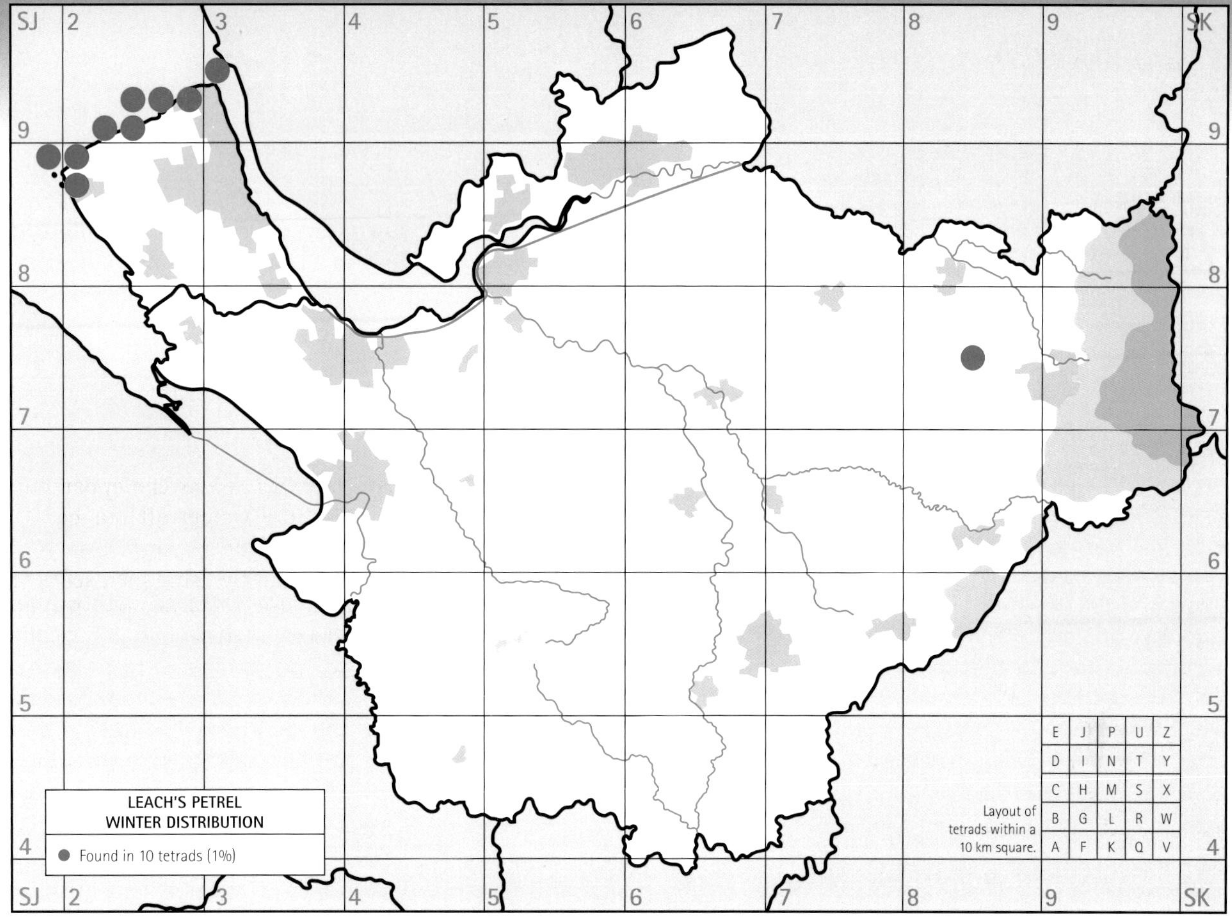
SJ
SK
LEACH'S PETREL
WINTER DISTRIBUTION
Found in 10 tetrads (1%)
Layout of
tetrads within a
10 km square.
E J P U Z
D I N T Y
C H M S X
B G L R W
A F K Q V

Cormorant

Phalacrocorax carbo

After years of hanging about in the county, occasionally building nests that came to nothing (including a pair laying eggs on a platform at Fiddler's Ferry in 1999), Cormorants marked the start of this Atlas in 2004 by their first successful breeding in Cheshire. Amazingly, this happened simultaneously at four widely spaced sites—Frodsham Marsh, Fiddler's Ferry, Rostherne Mere and Trentabank Reservoir. What triggered this breeding is not known, but it seems that they just needed that stimulus, and three of these sites now host significant colonies.

The Cormorant was almost exclusively a coastal breeder in the UK until 1981, but has since established colonies in many inland areas of England. The species account in the 'Seabird 2000' book (Mitchell *et al.* 2004) seems especially prescient, concluding with the comment 'Many of these new inland colonies have been established at sites used as winter roosts. Given the large number of roost sites and the availability of suitable feeding areas nearby, further expansion of the inland-breeding habit in England (and beyond) seems inevitable.' All of the Cheshire breeding sites indeed hosted substantial winter roosts, and at Frodsham and Trentabank there is a clear association with an established heronry.

There has been much speculation about the origins of the birds, and it is impossible to mention breeding Cormorants without hearing the word '*sinensis*'. Cormorant is a cosmopolitan species, breeding in every continent except South America and Antarctica, with probably six races/subspecies (del Hoyo *et al.* 1992). The nominate race *carbo* nests on rocky cliffs from eastern North America, through Greenland and Iceland to the British Isles and Norway. The *sinensis* race is found from China (as its name implies) through India and across continental Europe where they usually nest in trees. *Sinensis* are smaller and greener in colour, normally with more white on the throat and with more

RICHARD STEEL

Sponsored by A.M. Broome

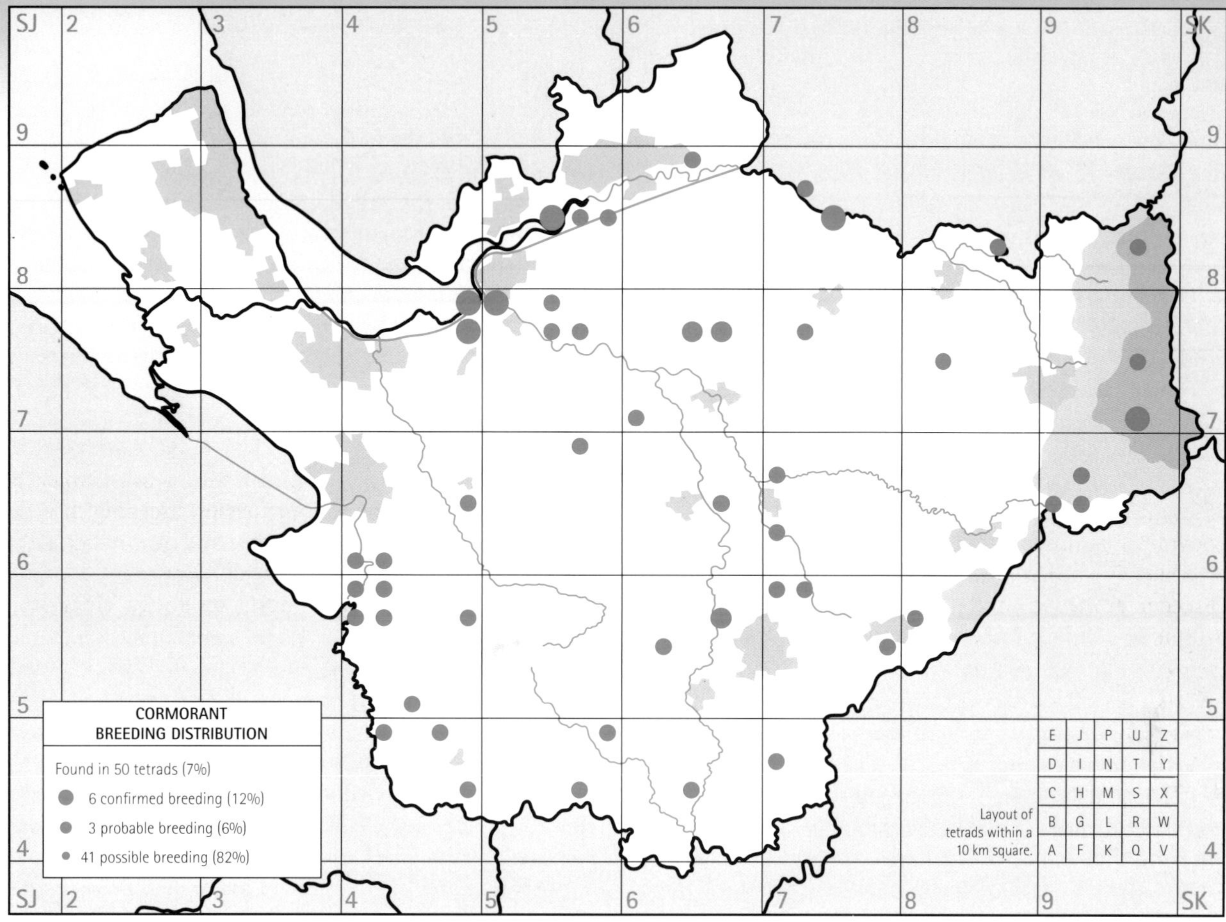

filoplume feathers on the neck, but there is much individual variation and some old *carbo* show a lot of white on the head, so racial attribution on the basis of appearance or behaviour is not as straightforward as some birdwatchers believe.

Cormorants have occasionally nested inland in Britain for centuries, but this habit really took off in 1981. In the quarter-century to 2005, breeding had been recorded at 58 inland sites, and the inland population rose to at least 2,096 pairs, exceeding the coastal total of 1,564 pairs (Mitchell *et al.* 2004, Newson *et al.* 2007). Detailed study (Newson *et al.* 2007) at colonies in eastern and central England, including observations of colour-ringed birds and DNA sampling, suggests that inland breeding has probably been sparked by birds of the continental race *sinensis* from the Netherlands and Denmark, but many *carbo* chicks from coastal colonies in Wales and England have also moved to inland sites to breed. The proportion of *carbo* increases in longer-established colonies, suggesting that inland colonies might be founded by *sinensis* but more and more *carbo* then join them. Cormorants are faithful to their natal colony, but as a site nears its carrying capacity an increasing proportion of mostly younger birds breeds elsewhere, either by moving to existing colonies or founding new ones.

Although Cheshire's nests have not been studied, Cormorants normally lay three or four eggs and the parents share incubation for 28–31 days. Chicks are in the nest for around seven weeks before fledging. Research elsewhere shows that inland-breeding Cormorants achieve significantly higher rates of productivity (2.3–3.0 chicks per pair) than coastal breeders (1.8–2.4) (Mitchell *et al.* 2004). Some more in-depth study of the Cheshire colonies would be valuable, including searching for rings or colour-rings on the adults, monitoring the productivity of the nests, taking DNA samples from the birds and observations of food items.

The map appears somewhat to exaggerate their status because the nests at Frodsham span three tetrads. This survey found birds displaying in trees next to the river Weaver (SJ65T). Birds often display, carry sticks and occasionally build nests in years before they successfully establish a new breeding site, so all such observations are worth recording. There are also records of non-breeding Cormorants from many waters in Cheshire. They normally start breeding from the age of three to five years (occasionally two), so there are many immature birds present all summer.

This winter Atlas map would have come as a great surprise to earlier generations of ornithologists. A century ago it was something of an event to record a Cormorant inland, although they were regular non-breeding residents at the coast (Coward 1910). Writing in 1951, Boyd noted that 'thirty years ago Cormorant was seldom seen on the meres, but it has become a much more regular visitor in the last ten years in every month of the year'. The largest inland flock known to Bell (1962) was 44 birds at Tatton, but he thought that numbers had not increased since the 1940s. They must have not reached east Cheshire because a single bird seen in February 1961 on Langley Reservoirs was suggested as indicating an extension of range (Bell 1962). Bell (1967) noted a rise in numbers at Rostherne since the National Trust took over Tatton, and a count at Rostherne of 28 birds in April 1963 was thought noteworthy. Although the move inland drew most comment, Bell (1967) pointed out that they were seen throughout the year at the coast, with highest numbers in autumn and winter, with up to 500 at Hilbre in winter 1957/58 as an exceptional count.

This Atlas map shows Cormorants to be widespread across the county, at the coast, both estuaries, the major rivers and most of the meres and lakes, including regularly in small numbers on the upland reservoirs. The shift inland is illustrated by the submitted habitat codes, showing that only one-quarter of the occupied tetrads were marine or estuarine, with three-quarters of them fresh water. The latter comprised about one-third on linear waterways and two-thirds on meres, sandpits and other waterbodies. However, the largest numbers are still in the Dee estuary, where the WeBS counts show a five-year peak mean of almost 700 birds, the fourth highest for any site in the UK (Musgrove *et al.* 2007). Cormorants often gather into large flocks, but of the 314 counts submitted for this Atlas, half of them were of four birds or fewer. There were just 20 counts of 50 or more, with the largest flocks 420 birds off Hilbre (SJ18Z) in 2006/07 and 300 birds in SJ28C (off Caldy) in 2004/05. Cormorants do not need to spend much of their time fishing, and many of the larger counts came from their diurnal roosts, birds perching prominently on trees (often dead ones) or electricity pylons, or standing on a sandbank. The roost at Rostherne (SJ78M) numbered 212 birds in 2004/05, almost 10 times the figure of 40 years before.

Our wintering birds are mostly from colonies around the Irish Sea (*Migration Atlas*). Outside the breeding season, adults may move 100 km or more from their colony, and immature birds, below breeding age, disperse similar distances or farther. The index of wintering numbers in Britain, from WeBS counts, has shown a steady increase from the mid-1980s to 2003/04, but might have levelled off in recent years.

Cormorants' diet is almost exclusively fish, with a few crustaceans and amphibians, perhaps taken incidentally. At sea, they stay close to land and mostly take flatfish, sand eels and cod. Inland, they especially favour roach and perch. The Cormorants' move to breeding and wintering inland in the UK is an apt metaphor for man's abuse of the environment. Man has overfished the seas and overstocked some inland waters; it is not surprising that this adaptable seabird has responded.

RAY SCALLY

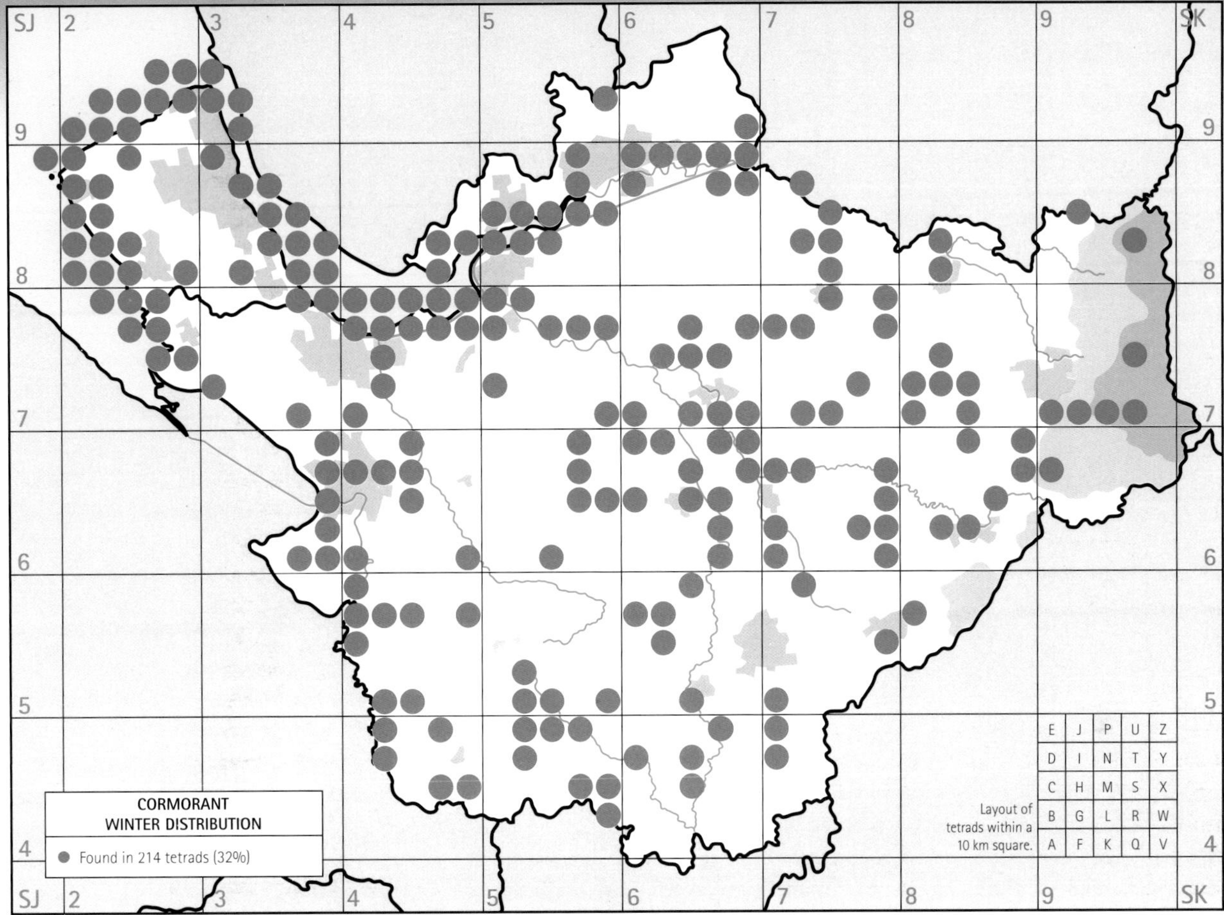

With such a fish-based diet, however, some of the birds have made a nuisance of themselves by fishing in areas where angling clubs have stocked the waters, and some anglers have campaigned to be allowed to kill Cormorants, stigmatizing them with the name 'Black Plague'. In recent years the UK Government's Department for Environment, Food and Rural Affairs has issued some licences for shooting Cormorants. Their guidance states that a shooting licence will only be issued to reinforce the effects of scaring measures being carried out at a site where: there is clear evidence that serious damage is being caused by Cormorants, or on recent past evidence, that it is likely to occur; other non-lethal measures have been found to be ineffective or impracticable; other factors are not likely to be responsible for the serious damage; shooting will be successful in reducing the damage, and there is no other satisfactory solution.

Shag

Phalacrocorax aristotelis

SHEILA BLAMIRE

Most wintering Shags prefer rocky shores, tend not to move far from their breeding sites and seek rocky cliffs and islands for overnight roosts. With that set of requirements their range in Cheshire and Wirral is bound to be limited, although the offshore sea defences and marine lakes make up for some of the natural deficiencies.

Their nearest breeding sites are on Anglesey and the Isle of Man. Adults stay close to breeding sites; most of the Shags in our area are immatures, which may disperse up to 100 km or more in the first four or five months after fledging (*Migration Atlas*). Their main diet elsewhere is fish, especially sand eels in the breeding season and gadoids (cod, haddock, and hake) in winter, but their food in the Irish Sea in winter is unknown.

Shags seem to have become somewhat more common in the county in recent years. A century ago the species was described as 'an occasional wanderer to the estuaries and meres' (Coward 1910) and fifty years ago it was 'an occasional and, to some extent, an accidental visitor to the county' (Bell 1962). At Hilbre, Craggs (1982) said it was 'generally a scarce bird' yet the annual county bird reports show more records from Hilbre than anywhere else. In the 1980s sightings appear to have been made in the county on up to 25 dates each year, and from 1990 to 2001 birds were recorded on between just four and 24 dates. A significant increase in the number of records followed with birds being seen on 38 to 91 dates from 2003 to 2006, probably the highest ever annual figure. Some of the largest winter counts on record are during this Atlas, five birds off Hilbre on 25 January 2005 and three on West Kirby Marine Lake (SJ28D) in winter 2004/05 and 2006/07, with three also on Bird Rock, Red Rocks (SJ28E) in the intervening winter.

The Atlas map shows their typical distribution of recent years. As well as these counts, Shags were reported from Hilbre (SJ18Y/Z) in each winter, with maxima of five, two and four birds. Single birds were on Hoylake shore (SJ29A), Leasowe shore (SJ29W) and New Brighton Marine Lake (SJ39C).

This species is prone to occasional 'wrecks' when many birds, mostly immatures, are blown inland. Such events are much more common on the east coast, but one was recorded in Cheshire in January 1912, when Shags turned up in extraordinary places including six birds on an *araucaria* (monkey-puzzle) tree at Ashton

Sponsored by Syngenta CTL

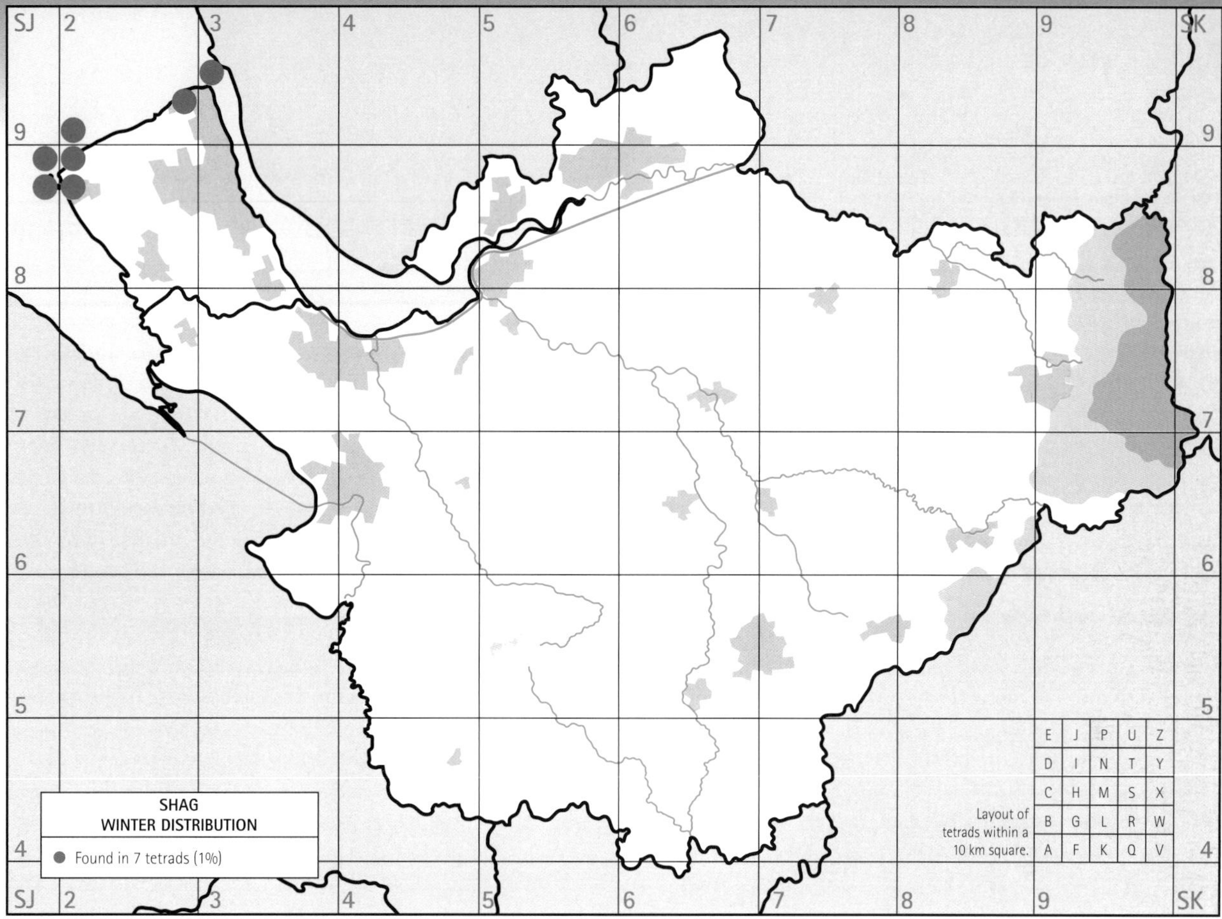

Hayes and another on the tower of Nantwich Church. However, inland records are scarce, with just nine in 40 years from 1967. Five of them, all single birds, were in winter, on the river Dee at Chester, Sutton Reservoir, Budworth Mere and Astbury Mere (twice) (*CWBRs*).

Bittern

Botaurus stellaris

Bitterns are never found away from *phragmites* reed-beds, where they patiently stalk their favourite food of eels, with some fish, amphibians and aquatic invertebrates, and occasional birds and small mammals if they come within reach. Some British birds, especially immatures, disperse from their breeding sites and the population is augmented by winter arrivals from the continent, with ringed birds having been recorded in Britain from Sweden, Germany, the Netherlands, Belgium (*Migration Atlas*) and France. One of the two from Germany was actually reported in Cheshire, a bird ringed as a chick at Königswartha, Saxony on 23 May 1931 and found dead here on 2 January 1932; and another Bittern chick ringed in Norfolk on 16 May 1950 was found in Nether Alderley on 6 November 1950. These examples nicely show the possible origins of birds wintering in Cheshire. In recent years Bitterns have regularly frequented three sites—Rostherne Mere (SJ78L/M), Budworth Mere (SJ67N) and Moore Nature Reserve (SJ58Y)—and it is no surprise that the Atlas map shows these, plus Deer Park Mere, Cholmondeley (SJ55K), where a bird was found on 17 February 2007. Two birds were found at Budworth Mere during 2004/05 and 2006/07, and up to three birds were at Moore in 2005/06.

In the nineteenth century, Bitterns were persecuted to extinction as a breeding bird in Cheshire and Wirral and a century ago, Coward (1910) reported that most wintering birds were killed: of 38 records, at least 28 of them were shot. Birds fared better in the twentieth century, but were very scarce, with an average of about one a year recorded (Bell 1962). The annual county bird reports have documented an increase in records in the last forty years. Bitterns were found in five of the years from 1967 to 1975, then in every year except 1987. There were no winter records until 1970/71 but then birds were seen in 10 of the 17 winters to 1987/88 and in every winter since then. The rise is also illustrated by their more widespread occurrence: in the seven winters from 1988/89 to 1994/95 there were reports from one to three sites, while the nine-year period 1995/96–2003/04 saw birds noted annually from up to seven sites. Movements around the county are impossible to assess but the frequency of sightings from Budworth Mere and

JEFF CLARKE

Sponsored by Matthew and Liz Bannon

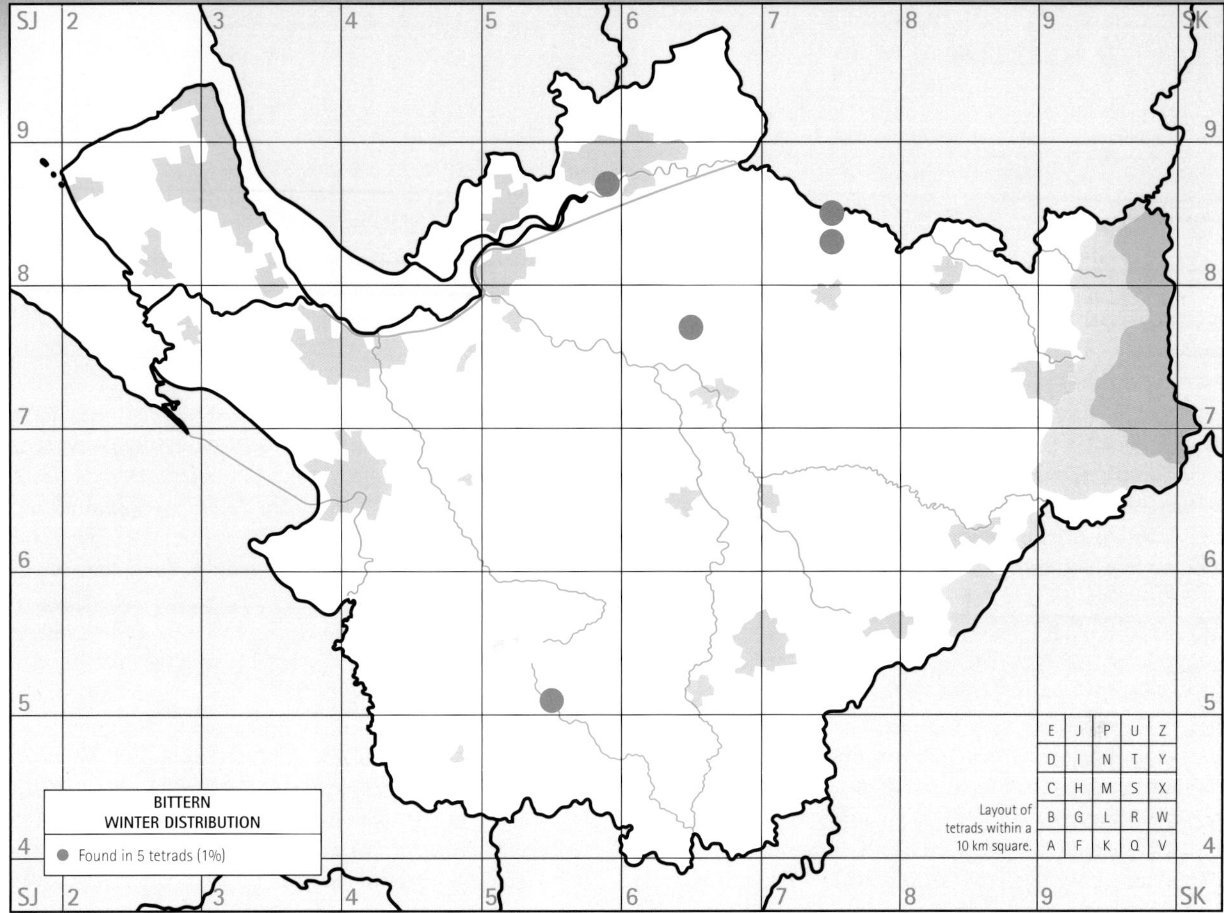

Moore suggests that birds have often been present at both sites, and there have probably been five or more birds present in Cheshire and Wirral on occasion.

Bitterns are susceptible to hard weather, especially if their food is locked away beneath ice. In the exceptional frost of the first quarter of 1963, the warden at Rostherne Mere captured one Bittern, thought to have been starving, and fed it on liver for seven weeks; another bird managed to survive in the wild there at the same time, however. The next really cold winter, 1978/79, brought a widespread influx of continental birds to Britain and was probably responsible for records at Neston Reed-bed, Doddington Pool and Tabley Mere.

● The only records showing any breeding intent in the county were of males giving their characteristic far-carrying booming 'song' at Knutsford Moor on 19 March 1995 and at Budworth Mere on 6 May 1995. During this Atlas period a bird was heard booming 'on at least one occasion' in the early months of 2006 at Moore: Bitterns are individually identifiable by their sonogram spectrum, and observers should attempt to record any future booming birds (Gilbert *et al.* 2002). Others were seen at Rostherne Mere on several dates in 2004 from 29 June onwards, and in 2005 from 10 July to 14 September, presumably examples of early dispersal from breeding sites elsewhere.

The species is responding to the UK Biodiversity Action Plan but the breeding population is still small (55–69 booming males in 2004, Holling *et al.* 2007a) and concentrated mostly in eastern England, where some two-thirds of the population is threatened by sea level rise. Conservation action to create suitably large reed-beds in Cheshire and Wirral would help to safeguard the Bittern's future.

Little Egret

Egretta garzetta

This species offers a striking recent demonstration of birds' mobility and adaptability. Little Egrets used to be rare visitors to Britain and until 1991 records were considered by the British Birds Rarities Committee. This was changed by an influx in 1989, starting in July, amounting to more than 100 birds, probably postbreeding dispersal from colonies in north-west France (Combridge & Parr 1992).

They first bred in 1996 in Britain at two sites, one in Dorset and one in Cornwall, and since then have built up to a number of substantial colonies spread across most of southern England, with continued northward expansion. Most, but by no means all, breeding Little Egrets are associated with Grey Heron colonies in tall trees; being later breeders, the egrets join an active heronry and benefit not only from the social interaction but also from an element of communal defence. The report of the Rare Breeding Birds Panel shows that the UK breeding population in 2004 was 354–357 pairs at 36 sites in 16 counties (Holling *et al.* 2007a), of which the birds in Cheshire and Wirral were the farthest north.

In Cheshire the first authenticated record was in 1982, followed by others in 1984, 1988 and 1990. All of these sightings were during May, typical of spring overshoots from breeding sites in continental Europe; the national influx in autumn 1989 brought single birds to Clwyd and Derbyshire but not Cheshire and Wirral. In 1992 a bird was seen on the Dee in July/August and from 1993 onwards Little Egrets were found much more often in the county, in different months and staying longer, with several birds together on occasions. In 1995 two birds at Frodsham Marsh collected twigs and reeds and tried to construct a nest within a flooded hawthorn hedge, a year before Little Egrets first bred in southern England.

That attempted breeding would now count as 'probable' under the definitions used for this Atlas. In the following years, birds were seen in ever-increasing numbers and more widely spread across the county until 2001 when one pair of Little Egrets bred at Frodsham Marsh, raising one chick in a nest in a flooded hedge just one metre below an active Grey Herons' nest (Morton 2001). No more birds bred in Cheshire and Wirral until the start of this Atlas period in 2004 when a pair nested in Chester Zoo, one of the birds being a ringed individual that had originally escaped from the zoo in 1998 and had flown around the county for six years before pairing with an apparently wild bird.

ANDREW MART

Sponsored by Roy Eyres

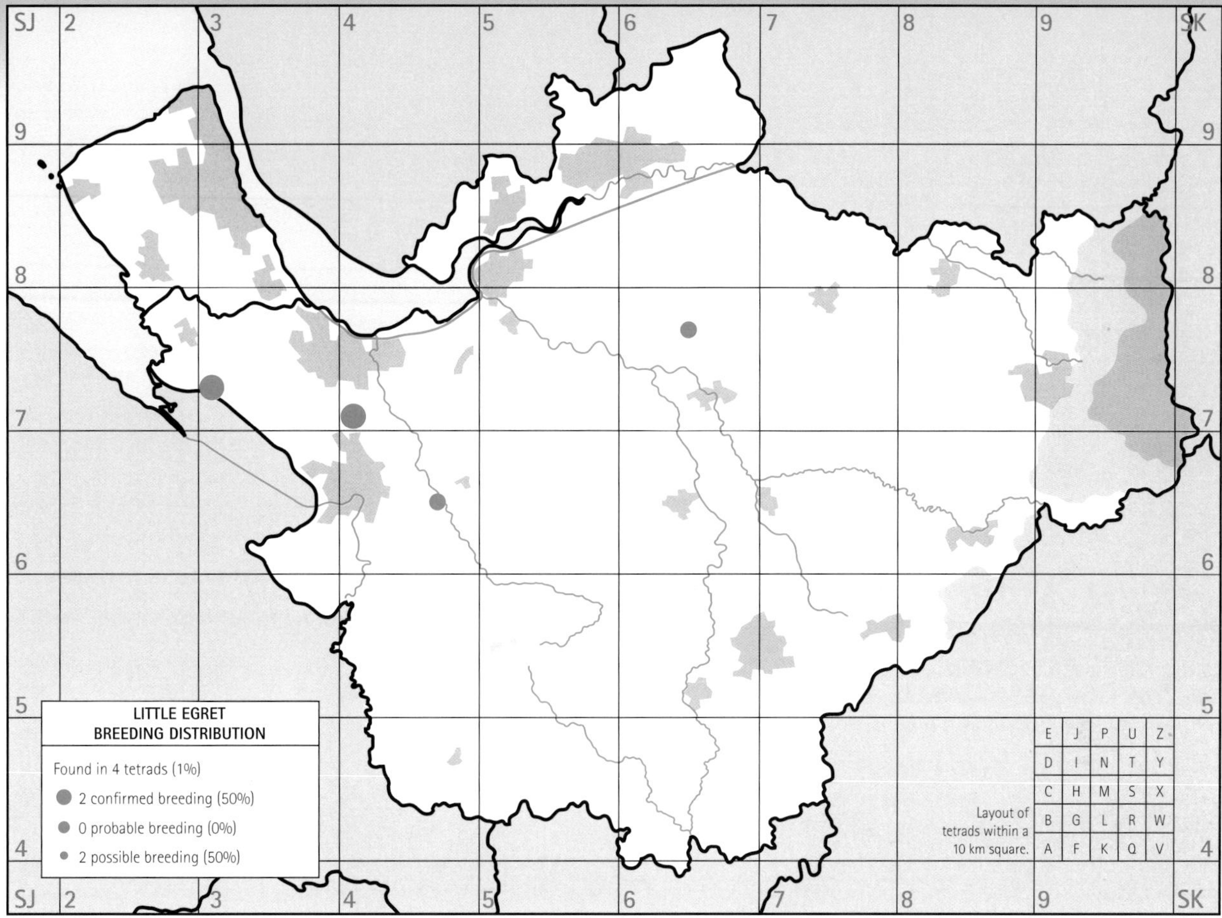

As at Frodsham, nesting at Chester Zoo was not repeated in the following year but 2005 saw the start of an egret breeding colony in the county when birds nested in private woodland near to Inner Marsh Farm RSPB reserve (Wells 2005). The birds were not studied in detail at their nests, but from observation of family parties it is thought that four pairs nested, fledging 15 young. These numbers increased in 2006 to 10 pairs fledging 40 young. In the first five years of establishment of breeding colonies at various sites in southern England, the average productivity was two or three chicks per pair (Brown & Grice 2005) and the phenomenally high figures from the Dee estuary site presumably indicate perfect feeding conditions. Their diet is likely to be, as elsewhere in Europe, mostly small fish and eels up to about 6 cm in length; they also take plenty of insects, crustaceans and frogs but the energy content is low compared to fish (Voisin 1991).

RICHARD STEEL

The seasonal occurrence of Little Egrets has changed considerably in the short time that they have been regular members of the county's avifauna. They have shifted from being overshooting spring birds to autumn postbreeding dispersers then, from 1997/98 onwards, birds have been seen throughout winter, mostly in the Dee estuary. The numbers have shot up during this decade, with peak counts, either feeding or at their night-time roost, in the six winters from 2001/02 to 2006/07 of 21 (November 2001), 30 (October 2002), 32 (November 2003), 70 (December 2004), 112 (October 2005) and 169 (same total on 8 September and 9 October 2006).

This Atlas map shows Little Egrets reported from 30 tetrads during the three winters of this survey, with a clear westerly bias and mostly on or near the estuaries. All of the submitted counts away from the Dee were of single birds apart from one flock of six feeding in creeks on Ince Marsh (SJ47P) in 2006/07. More than half of the recorded habitat codes (19 out of 36) were estuarine or salt-marsh, with four from reed-beds and a variety of freshwater habitats (two on small waterbodies; three on lakes/reservoirs), and records from streams or ditches in the areas of Chester (SJ36Y), Hockenhull Platts (SJ46S/X) and Fowle Brook next to Maw Green tip (SJ75D). There is no reported change in their diet in winter.

The residence or migratory status of the birds in Cheshire and Wirral is not known. Apart from the single escaped bird from Chester Zoo, no ringed bird is known to have been reported in the county. Birds from continental Europe usually migrate south for winter, some staying around the Mediterranean but most crossing the Sahara. They cannot tolerate hard weather, and birds that wintered in France in the 1980s have died *en masse* in freezing conditions (Voisin 1991). However, this is an adaptable and responsive species and by the late 1990s the French wintering population numbered more than 20,000. It has been suggested that the higher numbers and northward penetration along the west coast of Britain, which is milder than the east, is a reflection of their sensitivity to hard weather (Musgrove 2002).

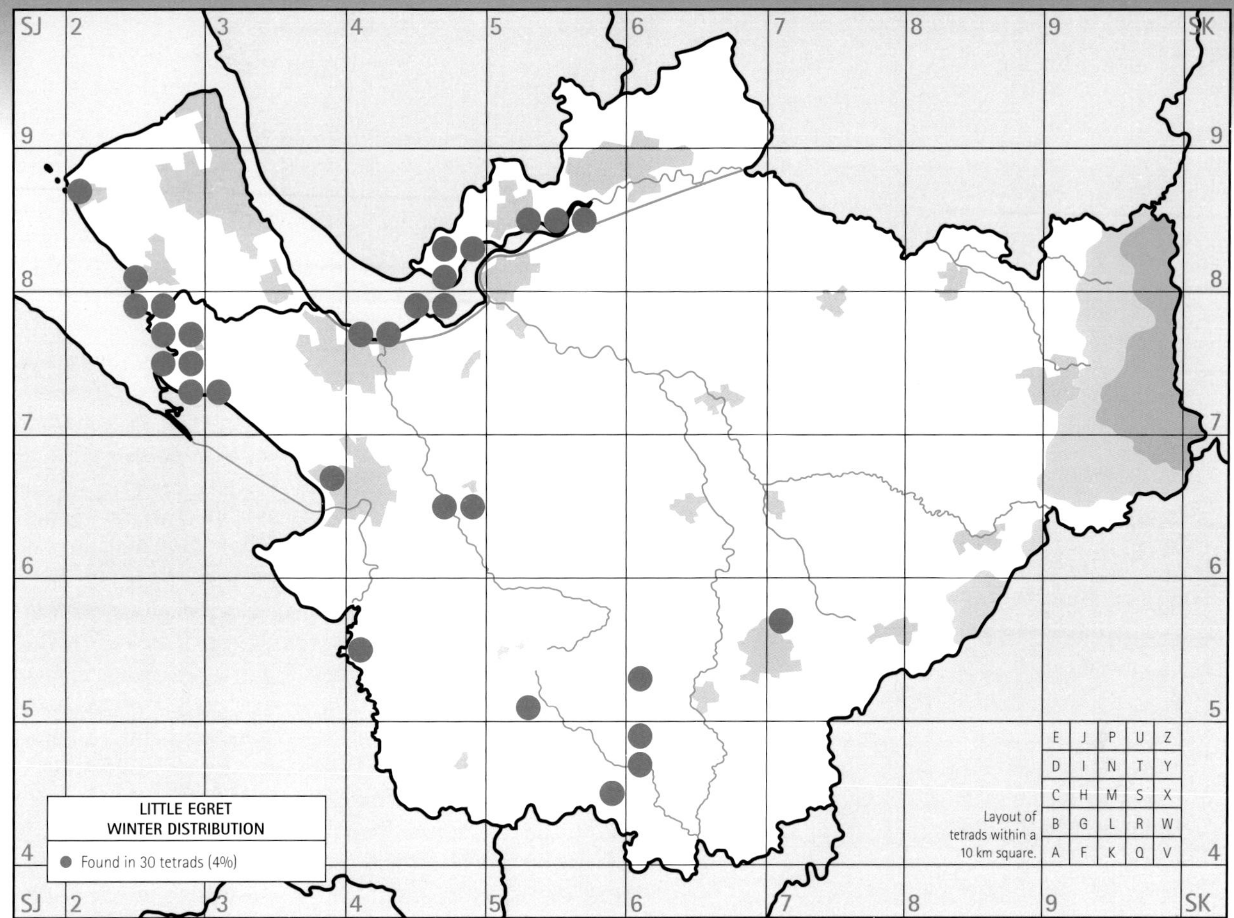
LITTLE EGRET
WINTER DISTRIBUTION
Found in 30 tetrads (4%)
Layout of
tetrads within a
10 km square.
E J P U Z
D I N T Y
C H M S X
B G L R W
A F K Q V
SJ
SK
2
3
4
5
6
7
8
9

Grey Heron

Ardea cinerea

RICHARD STEEL

Cheshire is the pond capital of Britain, and it is not surprising that it is the heron capital as well. Two of the five largest heronries in Britain are in Cheshire and Wirral, and the county holds more than one in 20 of Britain's birds. The county's major heronries are all in tall trees at secluded sites. Grey Herons use a wide variety of species of tree, whichever are tall enough; those recorded in the county since 1980 are Scots pine, Corsican pine, oak, horse chestnut, alder, birch, larch, sycamore, poplar, beech, ash, elm, willow and hawthorn. There can be many nests in the same tree, up to 18 in one alder at Radnor Mere in 1999. They usually nest at heights of 12–20 m or more, and the nests in the tallest trees in the wood are presumably the most desirable because they are the first to be occupied each year. Less usual nesting sites are on or near the ground, as with an odd nest in *Phalaris*/willow at Woolston in 1999 and 2000, and up to 14 nests in the flooded hawthorn hedges in no. 6 bed deposit lagoon at Frodsham Marsh, where some have been only a metre above the water level as pumping operations proceeded, and herons have faced competition from Canada Geese!

All of the county's known heronries are counted annually as part of the national census started in 1928, surveyors going into the woods in April or May, mapping the trees and assessing the occupation of nests: the total of apparently occupied nests (AON) in Cheshire and Wirral in the three years of this Atlas was 629, 678 and 616. Nesting numbers in the county have risen substantially in the last twenty years: the mean during the three years of this Atlas of 641 AON is more than three times the low point in 1986 of about 193. The British total of around 10,600 AON in 1986 rose nowhere nearly as sharply, by 27% to 13,430 in 2003 (Baker *et al.* 2006). The private wood on the north side of Marbury (Budworth) Mere (SJ67N) currently holds the largest colony of Grey Herons in Britain, 180 AON in 2005, and that at Eaton Hall (SJ45E)—in existence since at least 1874—is the third largest with 149 nests.

Their numbers are restricted, locally and nationally, by mortality in harsh winters, and the warming climate must have assisted their rise, probably along with a long-term improvement in the aquatic environment. The long-running programme of nest-recording and ringing by Merseyside Ringing Group has shown that, as the county population has risen, the number of chicks fledged per nest has fallen, in a clear example of density-dependence: the Grey Heron population is limited by the carrying capacity of the ecosystem.

The Grey Heron population of Cheshire and Wirral, assessed from the BBS transects in 2004–05, was 3,050 birds (with wide confidence limits of zero to 7,940). The number of breeding adults is about 1,300 so this figure implies more non-breeders than breeders: most Grey Herons do not nest until two or three years of age, so there are large numbers of immature birds present, and BBS fieldworkers might also have counted some early fledged juvenile birds. The county figure is 4.2% of the national total of 57,220 birds (Newson *et al.* 2008).

Grey Herons breed early, some birds returning to their nests around Christmas, and many are sitting on eggs or chicks during the worst of the winter weather. On the other hand, some, perhaps first-time breeders or others replacing a lost clutch or brood or maybe adults having a rare second brood, may be nesting late in the season and there can be chicks in the nest for almost half of the year, from February to August.

At the top of the aquatic food chain, Grey Herons eat almost anything that they can find, mostly fishing in ditches and ponds; birds nesting in woods alongside lakes seldom seem to fish in the lake itself, and adults can fly at least 10 km from the nest to find food (Lowe 1953). Most feeding is concentrated around dawn and dusk, and chicks get half of their daily intake in the first two hours of daylight. Herons often raid ornamental ponds for goldfish but their staple food in Cheshire appears to be coarse fish, especially perch, roach and sticklebacks, with occasional amphibians and spawn. Birds near the estuaries eat numerous eels.

The Atlas map only shows the heronries. Birds were reported during the breeding season from almost everywhere in the county, but are not mapped. These could be breeding birds foraging for their chicks, immature

Sponsored by Macclesfield RSPB Members Group

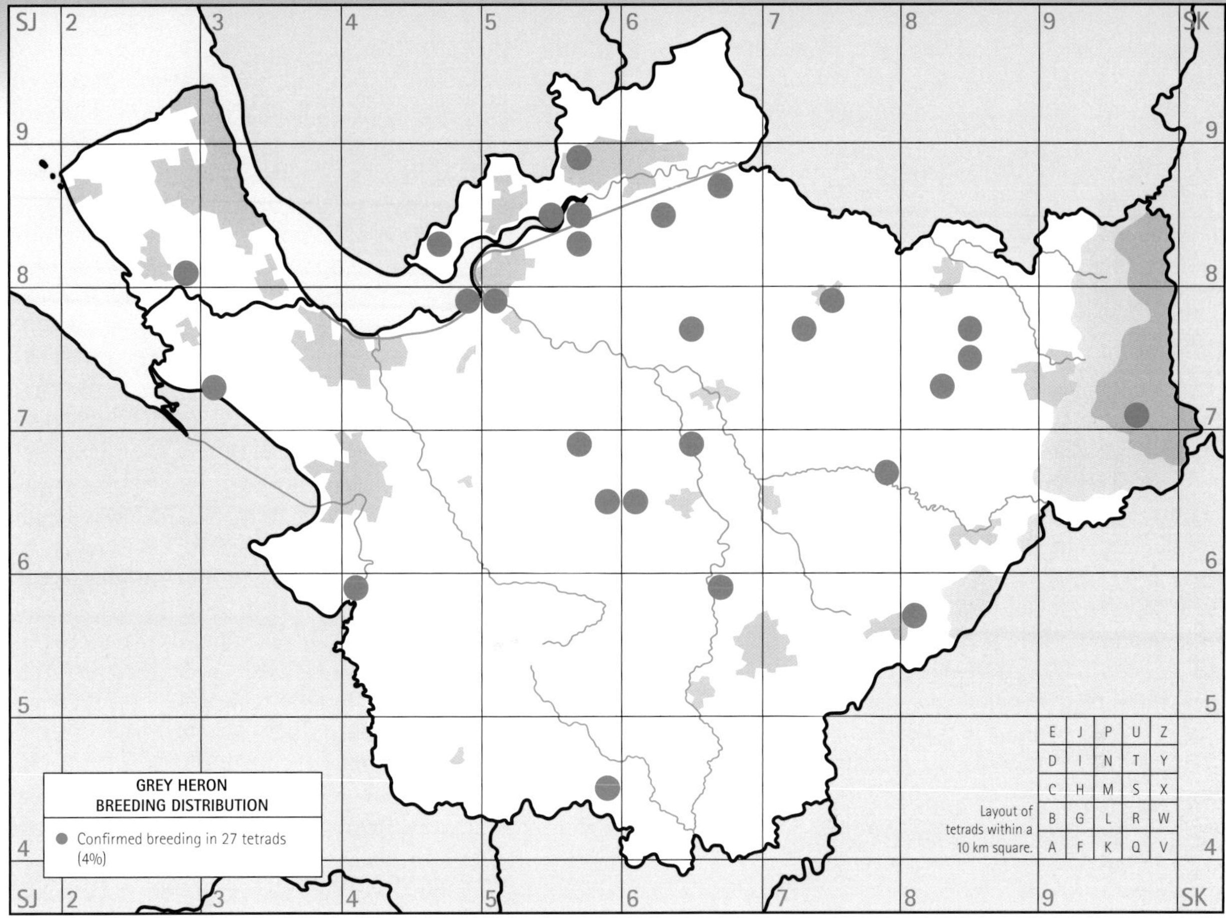

non-breeders and early fledged young herons. Juveniles are not tended by their parents once they leave the colony, although they may return to the nest for supplementary feeds. They can disperse rapidly: an extreme illustration is the bird ringed as a chick in its nest at Budworth Mere on 29 March 1997 that probably fledged during April and by 27 May was found dead on Humberside, 175 km away.

There are some gaps in the map, especially towards the west of the county, where there could conceivably be other birds breeding—Grey Herons can be surprisingly inconspicuous from the outside of a wood—but it is unlikely that many are not known about. Four new nesting sites were discovered during this Atlas survey, each of them holding just one or two pairs.

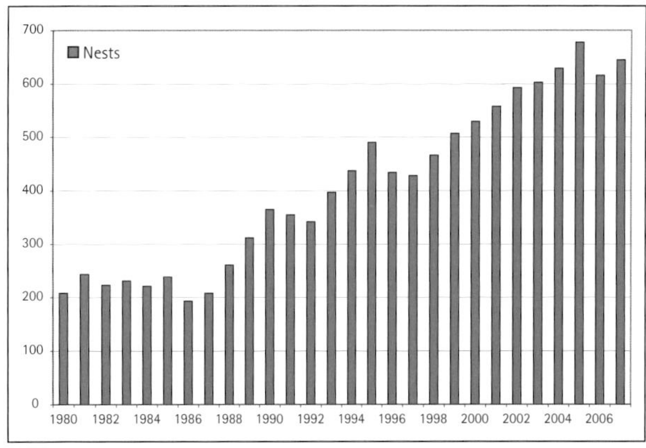

The total of apparently occupied Grey Heron nests in Cheshire and Wirral, 1980–2007.

This is a bird with two distinct characters: when breeding, they form large groups, nesting colonially at the tops of tall trees; in winter, they are solitary birds in flat, open areas. This is emphasized by the records submitted: of 529 counts of Grey Herons, half of them were of single birds. There were only 23 counts in double figures, most of them of birds back at their breeding sites after the New Year, with just a few gatherings at daytime loafing or roosting areas: some birds spend much of their day in a sheltered spot, often alone but sometimes in small groups, by far the largest of which was 47 birds at Inner Marsh Farm.

In a lot of places, especially on linear watercourses and ponds, a Grey Heron can be seen regularly and detailed studies have shown that many birds return repeatedly to specific feeding sites, with the better ones defended against other herons. In winter Grey Herons continue with their diet of any aquatic food but most larger fishes move to deeper waters as the temperature drops so herons broaden their intake to include a wider range of prey, with, famously, Water Rails on the Dee salt-marshes, and on occasion rabbits, rats, squirrels and water voles, but they show their opportunistic nature by also spending time catching worms in flooded fields. The numbers on the Mersey estuary built up rapidly as water quality improved and more fish were present: from single figures in the 1970s, WeBS counts built up to 53 in 1990/91.

The map shows Grey Herons to be widespread in winter, present in 486 tetrads. They were recorded flying over another 30 tetrads, not mapped. They were found in a wide range of habitats: estuarine and salt-marsh codes were submitted from 42 tetrads, with 367 freshwater records. Their distribution suggests a preference for the county's smaller waters, either standing or flowing: 77 pond; 74 small waterbody; 68 lake/unlined reservoir; 4 lined reservoir; 14 sandpit, etc.; 44 stream; 38 river; 19 ditch; 14 small canal; and 15 large canal. There were 103 records of farmland habitat codes, mostly grassland: the versatility of herons is such that they will exploit almost any damp area. In winter, many Grey Herons utilize built-up areas although, surprisingly, there were only 35 records from human habitats; they are wary birds, often visiting in the semi-darkness and leaving at the first sign of disturbance, so are probably underrecorded.

Most British birds are said to be resident (*BTO Winter Atlas*), but the median distance of juvenile dispersal is around 50 km and three birds ringed as chicks in Cheshire colonies have been reported from overseas in their first winter. One from the Oakmere heronry in 1990 was reported on 4 February 1991 in Iceland, the only British-ringed bird to be found in that country where herons are rare migrants. Another from the Runcorn area heronries was shot in Denmark

RICHARD STEEL

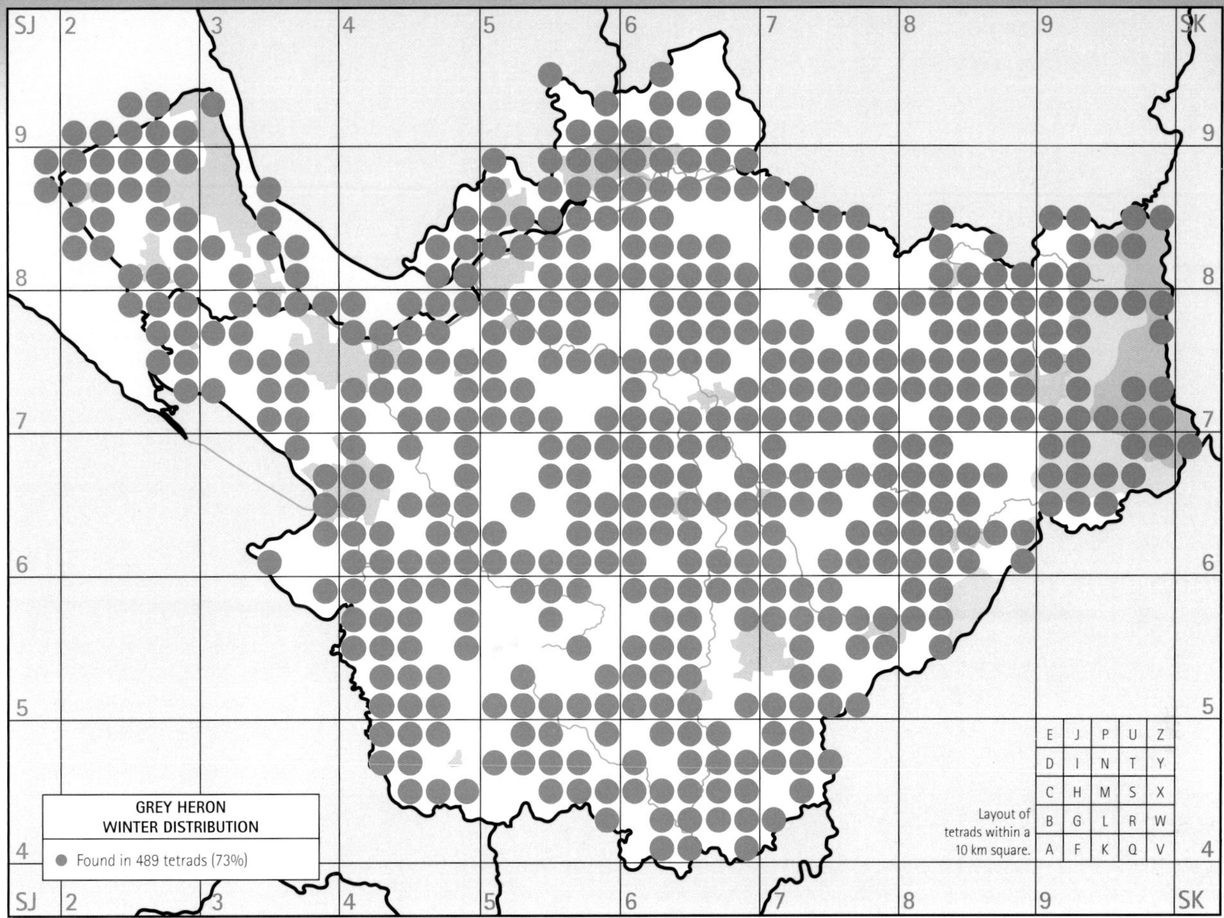

on 24 November 1990, only the second British-ringed Grey Heron there, and a third was in county Louth in Ireland in December 1973. The wintering population is boosted by an unknown number of immigrants, mostly from Scandinavia, where Grey Herons have to leave to find unfrozen feeding areas (*Migration Atlas*). In hard weather in Britain, some herons concentrate in coastal areas but many stay on inland fresh water, often moving to flowing waters; if subzero temperatures persist for more than a few days, many Grey Herons die, especially immature birds, and winter weather is the main factor affecting their population. During this Atlas period the winter of 2005/06, not particularly severe but with more days of frost than any year since the mid-1990s, had a noticeable effect on breeding totals, most Cheshire and Wirral heronries seeing a drop of around 10% in the numbers of nests.

Marsh Harrier

Circus aeruginosus

Marsh Harriers have not yet been known to breed in the county—our *First Atlas* predicted that 'future breeding seems unlikely'—but they are considerably expanding their range and numbers, and occur frequently on spring passage. Several birds have been recorded in suitable breeding habitat, including three during this Atlas period. The closest approach to breeding so far appears to have been in 2005 when an adult female was present at a site in the north of the county during June and the first half of July, carrying prey into a marshy area. Close inspection, under a Schedule 1 licence, revealed no nest but a regularly used food-caching site, with recognizable prey items including Coot, Moorhen and Mallard. No male Marsh Harrier was ever seen.

After coming back from the brink of extinction as a British breeding bird, with only one pair nesting in 1971, their population has grown rapidly. A dedicated national survey in 1995 found a total of 156 breeding females, and the follow-up census in 2005 reported 360 breeding females, an increase of 131%. Females are counted rather than pairs, because about one-fifth of nests result from polygny, usually one male with two females but occasionally three females sharing one male; such nests are just as successful as those of monogamous pairings (Underhill-Day 1998).

Along with the growth in numbers, Marsh Harriers have extended their distribution. They colonized Leighton Moss in north Lancashire in 1987 and have bred there annually since then, but this is the only regularly occupied site in western Britain.

Their typical nesting habitat has been extensive *Phragmites australis* reed-beds, comprising 86% of more than 500 nests recorded during 1983–90 and 1995. All but two of the rest were in cereal crops, mostly oilseed rape and winter wheat, this habit growing rapidly since it was first recorded in 1982 (Underhill-Day 1998).

Many Marsh Harriers pass through the county in spring and autumn, and it is probably only lack of suitable habitat that restricts the breeding population.

Sponsored by David Kennerley

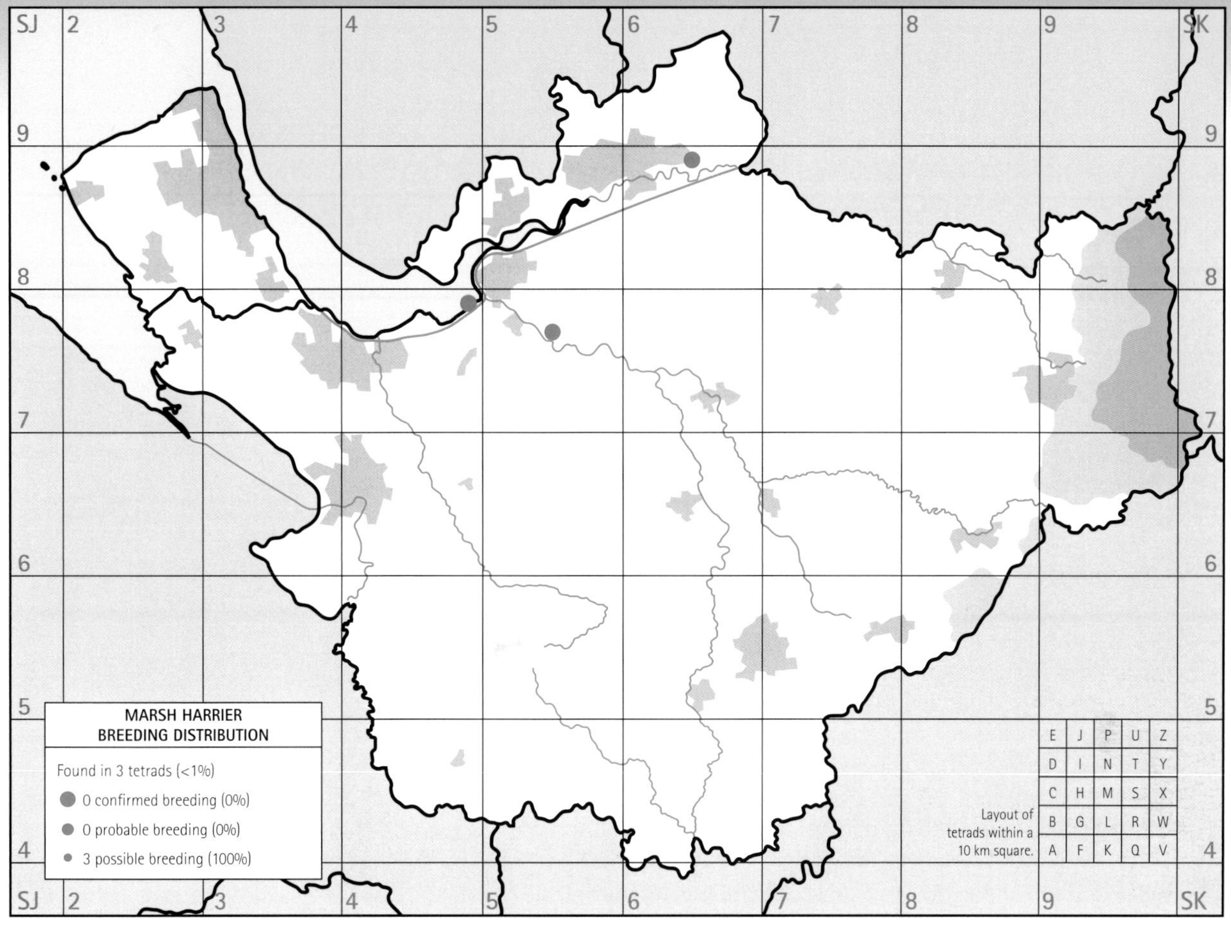
SJ
2
3
4
5
6
7
8
9
SK
9
8
7
6
5
4
MARSH HARRIER
BREEDING DISTRIBUTION
Found in 3 tetrads (<1%)
0 confirmed breeding (0%)
0 probable breeding (0%)
3 possible breeding (100%)
E J P U Z
D I N T Y
C H M S X
B G L R W
A F K Q V
Layout of tetrads within a 10 km square.

As the British breeding population has risen, so have the number of birds wintering in the country. Probably no more than 10 wintered in Britain in 1981/82–1983/84 (*BTO Winter Atlas*), and Clarke (1995) thought that 'the number wintering in Britain as a whole probably does not exceed thirty'. Ten years later, several small roosts, containing up to 20 birds each, had become established in eastern and south-eastern England (Brown & Grice 2005).

Cheshire and Wirral has shared in that rise in numbers, especially on autumn passage, with occasional birds on late dates that bring them into our defined winter Atlas period, and some that seem to have been genuinely wintering here. This habit has clearly become more common recently, and the period of this Atlas, with five records, referring to four birds, shows the highest known winter total for the county.

The first on record in the county seems to be a bird on 1 December 1946 at Thelwall, followed at intervals of twenty years by another on 30 January 1966 at Wallasey, and then on 18 November 1987 at Moore. After just three birds in forty years there were two during the 1990s, on 1 December 1994 at Fiddler's Ferry and 22 November 1996 at Great Sankey, then annually from 2001 onwards: 10 December 2001 at Bar Mere, then a long-staying bird on the Dee salt-marsh, seen from 19 to 27 December 2002 and again on 20 January 2003, usually going to roost with a Hen Harrier off Parkgate Old Baths. As with some of the others, one on 16 November 2003 at Heswall was probably just a late migrant, but the bird on 1 February 2004 on the Mersey at Ince was not (Bell 1967, *CWBRs*).

Marsh Harriers normally migrate south for the winter, reaching southern Europe at least, with some in Africa including roosts of hundreds seen in Senegal (Clarke 1995, *Migration Atlas*). There is significant sexual dimorphism in this species, and most of those attempting to winter here are the larger females. They feed especially on waterfowl, up to the size of large ducks, but will take any suitable prey including carrion.

RAY SCALLY

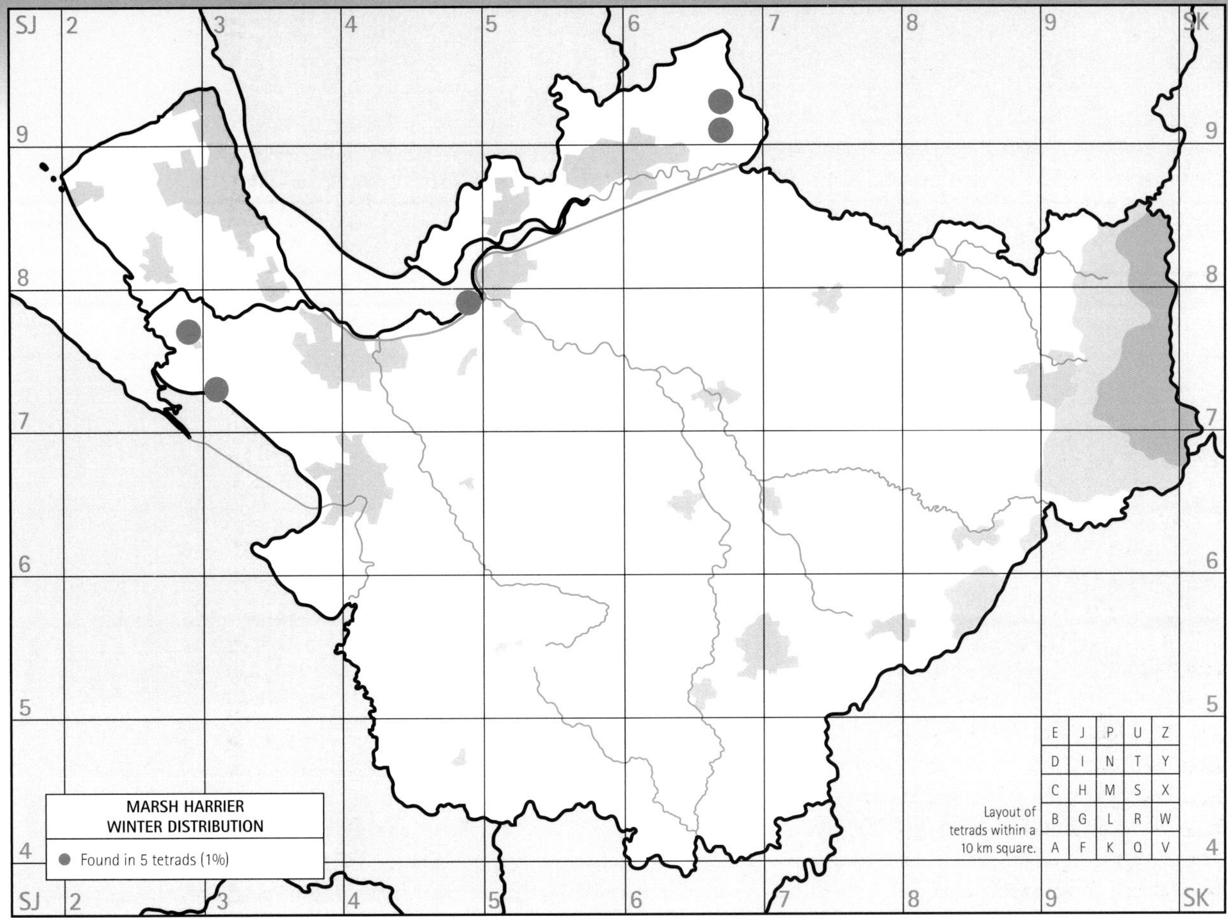
MARSH HARRIER
WINTER DISTRIBUTION
Found in 5 tetrads (1%)
Layout of tetrads within a 10 km square.
E J P U Z
D I N T Y
C H M S X
B G L R W
A F K Q V
SJ
SK

Hen Harrier

Circus cyaneus

NORMAN RICHARDSON

Hen Harriers come down from their breeding sites on the moors of Scotland, northern England and North Wales to spend the winter in the lowlands, especially alongside estuaries and in other open areas with low vegetation. Their diet consists of a wide range of small mammals and birds, but their winter habits are overwhelmingly linked to the abundance of field voles; indeed, an American book on the Marsh Hawk, the Nearctic race of this species, is memorably subtitled 'The Hawk that is ruled by a mouse' (Hamerstrom 1986). When hunting, the harriers quarter the ground, keeping an eye on any movement below, then stall and drop onto their prey. They frequently associate with Merlins, sometimes apparently cooperating in flushing small birds, but other times disputing a catch.

Female Hen Harriers weigh half as much again as the males and are able to take larger prey, including rabbits and hares. They are also better able to withstand hard winter weather, so many females stay all year round on their breeding territory in the Scottish strongholds; males tend to move towards the coast. Even amongst the inexperienced birds, most of them do not move far. Detailed wing-tagging studies have shown that 53% of sightings of tagged males and 65% of sightings of tagged females were reported within Scotland during their first winter, these figures rising to 70% and 75% for older birds (*Migration Atlas*). Thus, the birds that winter in England tend to be males, especially immature birds; first-year males move farther south than older, more experienced birds (Etheridge & Summers 2006). There is direct evidence for the origins of some of our wintering birds from reports of wing-tagged birds. First-year males that had been marked as nestlings in the Scottish Borders were seen on Frodsham Marsh in 1996 and on the Dee estuary in 1998, and another wing-tagged bird in 1999 was 'thought to have originated from the Forest of Bowland', according to the annual bird report. A first-year female from the North Wales breeding population was seen in winter on the Dee (Etheridge & Summers 2006).

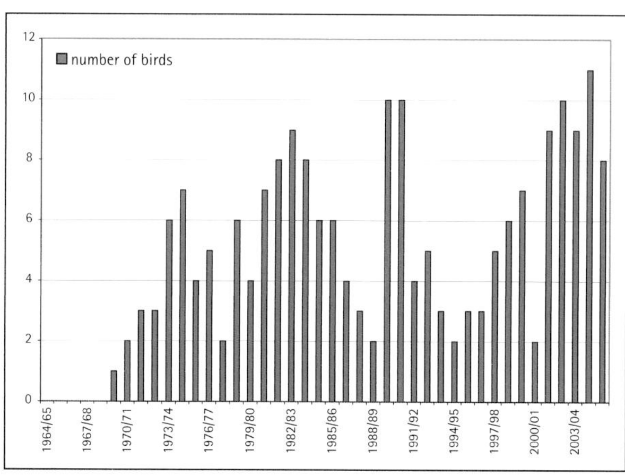

Hen Harrier wintering numbers.

Sponsored by John Wright

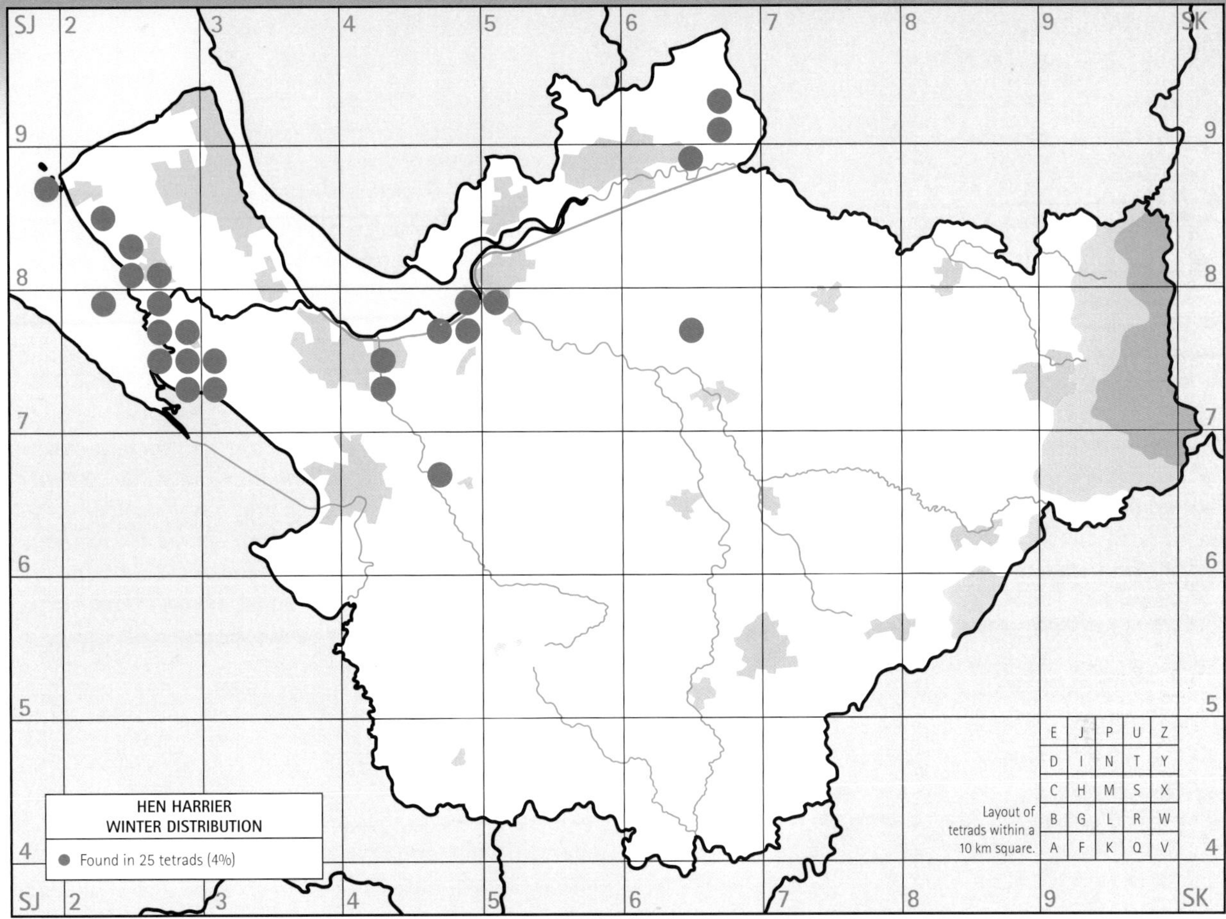

According to the books of Coward (1910), Boyd (1946) and Bell (1962), there were about 20 records of Hen Harriers in Cheshire to the early 1960s. The dates of most of them indicate birds passing through, but five or six of them were within our defined winter period. This scarcity continued in the early years of *CWBRs*, from 1964, with numbers gradually increasing during the 1970s, as shown in the bar chart. A communal roost in *spartina* cordgrass on the Dee estuary was first noted in 1980/81, around the time that many such roosts were discovered (Clarke & Watson 1990), with numbers fluctuating from year to year up to a maximum of seven birds.

Most of the records were on the Dee estuary, on the south side of the Mersey at Frodsham Marsh, and at Risley Moss, with a few scattered observations elsewhere, exactly the picture shown by this Atlas map.

● There were no breeding season records during the period of this Atlas survey. In several years they have bred in Derbyshire, with birds occasionally recorded hunting in Cheshire during 1990, 1997 and, notably, in 2003, when a pair was displaying on four dates.

Goshawk

Accipiter gentilis

There have long been rumours of Goshawks breeding in the county, most reports coming from the vicinity of the dense conifer plantations of Macclesfield and Delamere Forests. Published records are few, however: submissions are assessed by the county rarities panel, and sightings are frequently not described to their satisfaction. Goshawks are big birds, with many females being larger than Buzzards. Their sexual size difference means that males are not much more than half the weight of a female, but even so, a male Goshawk is considerably larger than any female Sparrowhawk, and three times their weight (Marquiss & Newton 1982).

Knowledge is sketchy, but the current status in the county is probably much the same as during our *First Atlas*, when breeding was confirmed at three sites, at one of which the nest contents were regularly taken by man. RSPB reports show that even now, Goshawks are close to the top of the list of species illegally targeted by egg-collectors, would-be falconers and gamekeepers.

At least some of the county's Goshawks have escaped or been released from captivity. Deforestation and persecution led to their extinction as a British breeder in the 1880s and there was no known natural breeding in England in the first half of the twentieth century until resurgence of interest in falconry in the 1960s and 1970s led to the import of large numbers of birds from central Europe and Fennoscandia. The accidental and intentional release of some of these birds and their captive-bred descendants provided a foundation for the current feral breeding population (Marquiss & Newton 1982). The origin of birds currently seen in Cheshire is unknown but the median recovery distance of 47 km (*Migration Atlas*) could encompass dispersing birds from nests in the South Pennines or Wales.

Goshawks display prominently over their woodland territory but these may be unpaired individuals as there is a significant pool of prospecting first-year birds: they can breed at one year of age, although not very successfully. Birds start breeding early in the year, often nest-building in February. There is not much suitable habitat in the county, Goshawks occupying extensive areas of mature woodland. They favour more open stands of woodland than Sparrowhawks, with a mean distance between trees from 2.5 m up to 6 m or more, presumably because their larger wingspan means they need wider flyways (Newton 1986). The smaller bird uses the denser woods, thus achieving ecological separation. Goshawks do not tolerate Sparrowhawks, frequently killing them, and Sparrowhawks instinctively avoid areas with the larger bird present. So, in a naturally balanced environment, Goshawks act to limit the population of Sparrowhawks. They probably also keep in check the burgeoning corvids, although their main prey is pigeons, gamebirds, rabbits and squirrels.

ANDREW MART

Sponsored by Syngenta CTL

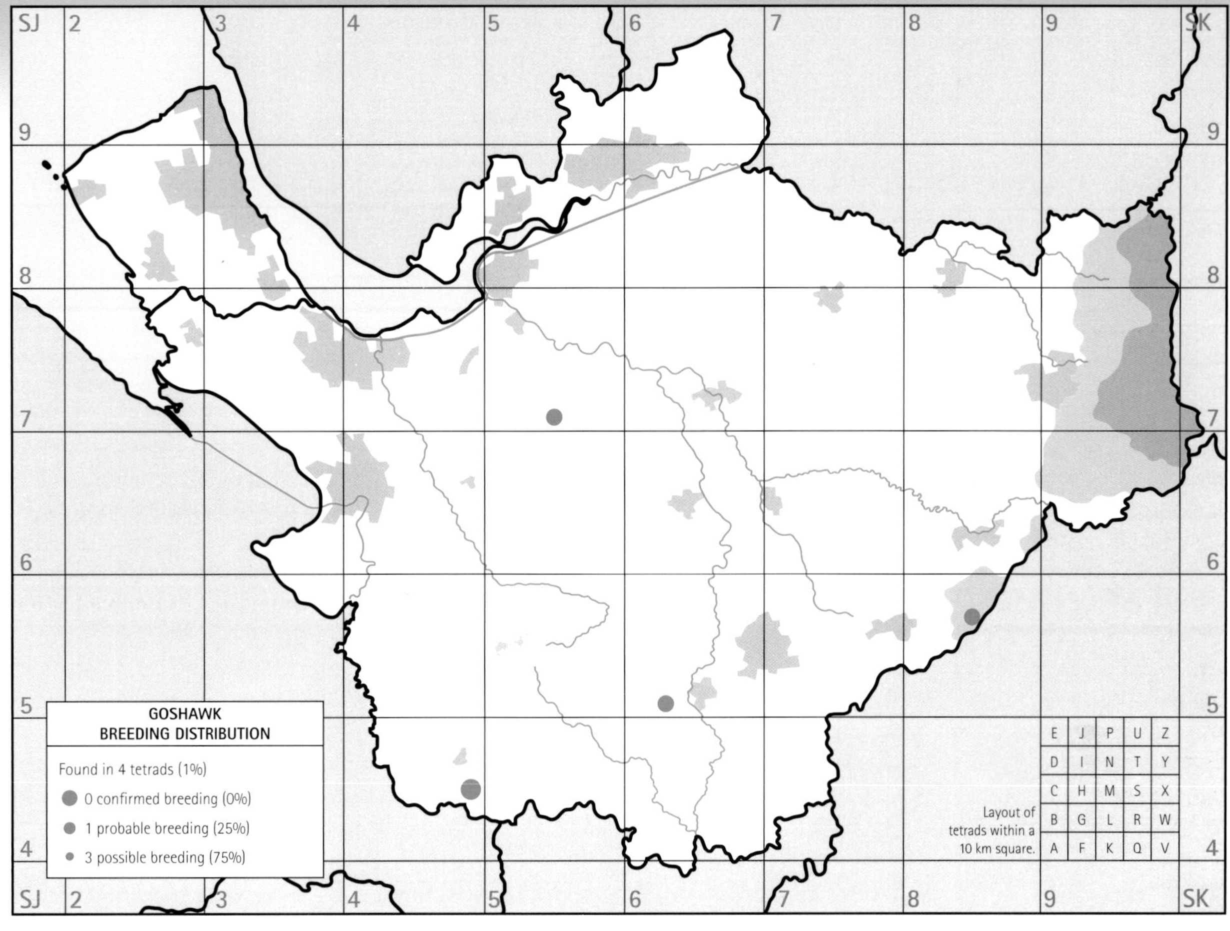
GOSHAWK
BREEDING DISTRIBUTION
Found in 4 tetrads (1%)
0 confirmed breeding (0%)
1 probable breeding (25%)
3 possible breeding (75%)
Layout of tetrads within a 10 km square.
SJ
SK

PETER SMITH

'Goshawks are rarely seen in Britain and Ireland, even in those areas where there are established populations': so began the text for the *BTO Winter Atlas*. Thus, it is no surprise that there are few records on the winter Atlas map of Cheshire and Wirral. In only four tetrads were observers able to provide a description that satisfied the county rarities panel, the four birds being an adult and immature of the two sexes. None of these tetrads had a breeding season record, despite this species' sedentary nature and early display, perhaps another measure of their secretive nature. The extent of underrecording can be quantified from the tetrad Atlases of Northumbria, where there were at least 50 pairs breeding producing more than 100 young a year (Day *et al.* 1995). So, fieldworkers are well used to seeing Goshawks, but only 70 birds were recorded in the three seasons (1996/97–1998/99) of the county's wintering Atlas (Day & Hodgson 2003).

However, despite the difficulty in recording the species, Goshawks are unlikely to be common or widespread in Cheshire and Wirral because they need substantial areas of woodland. In winter this requirement is relaxed somewhat and birds spend more time hunting in open areas. The observers of these four records provided seven habitat codes, all different: broad-leaved and coniferous woodland; scrub–'regenerating natural or semi-natural woodland'; dry semi-natural grassland, unimproved agricultural grassland and mixed grassland/tilled land; and dry heath. These indicate the wide range of area over which Goshawks can be found.

Wherever they are, Goshawks should have no difficulty in finding food in a Cheshire winter. As well as large birds–of the size of Woodpigeons, Moorhens, corvids and the like–they also prey on the larger thrushes, especially Fieldfares, and regularly eat medium-sized mammals, mainly squirrels and rabbits.

The ornithological history of Goshawk in Cheshire and Wirral appears straightforward but for the last quarter-century is clouded by rumour, doubts over identification and caution on publishing records. Coward and Oldham (1900), and Boyd (1946), make no mention of the species. Bell's (1962) only reference is to one seen on Christmas Day in 1955, which was such an unusual record that it was published in *British Birds*. The annual county bird reports contain few records from the winter period, excluding the occasional cryptic references to 'well-known resident pairs' and those known to be escaped captive birds. The plot shows a mean of only one per winter, and a maximum of four birds in any of the 30 years before this winter Atlas; thus, the four birds recorded in the three winters of this project is about average.

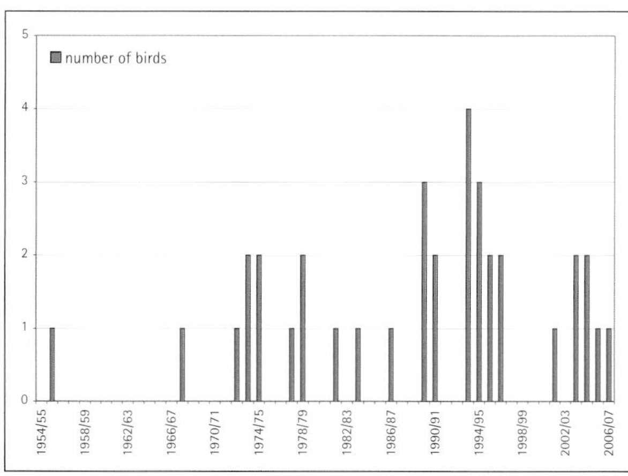

Goshawk wintering numbers.

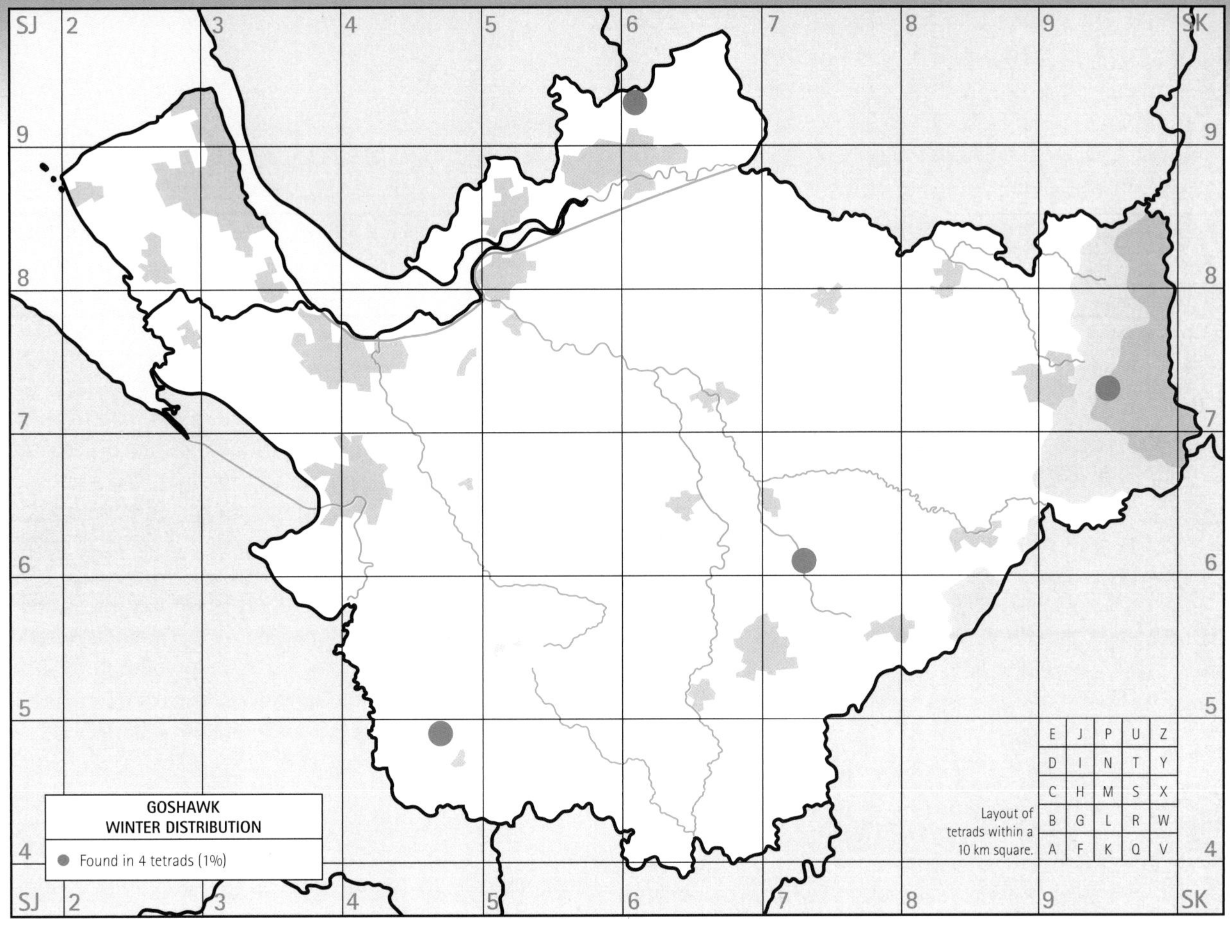
SJ
2
3
4
5
6
7
8
9
SK
9
8
7
6
5
4
GOSHAWK
WINTER DISTRIBUTION
Found in 4 tetrads (1%)
Layout of
tetrads within a
10 km square.
E J P U Z
D I N T Y
C H M S X
B G L R W
A F K Q V

Sparrowhawk

Accipiter nisus

SHEILA BLAMIRE

This survey shows that Sparrowhawks are much more widespread than they were twenty years ago, when the species was still recovering from the effects of organochlorine pesticides. In our *First Atlas* they were found in 382 tetrads, 97 of them with confirmed breeding and 84 with probable breeding; the equivalent figures in this Atlas have risen to 478, 130 and 105. They nest only in trees, especially in the largest available woods, but otherwise they use parks and large gardens as they have spread into the areas of densest human population, including the Mersey valley and north Wirral, and across much of agricultural south-west Cheshire. The main areas of absence are the treeless areas of the highest land (where they seem to have withdrawn from several tetrads in which they were found in the *First Atlas*) and the estuarine salt-marsh, along with the Gowy valley and scattered parts of central Cheshire. Although Sparrowhawks always nest in woodland, they often hunt in other areas, and the reported habitat codes reflect this: 49% woodland, nearly all of them broad-leaved or mixed, 4% scrub, 31% farmland and 13% human sites.

The size difference between the sexes is greater than in any other raptor, female Sparrowhawks being around twice the weight of males, allowing the pair to exploit a very wide range of prey (Newton 1979). Their diet is exclusively birds, up to their own body weight or even more. Males especially take tits and finches, and species up to the size of Blackbirds. Females can catch much larger prey, tackling anything from Woodpigeons downwards. In the breeding season Sparrowhawks mostly catch fledglings, and they time their own breeding to be later than that of most of the smaller woodland birds, so that maximum numbers of prey are available to feed their own young. They will fly a long way from their nest to find food, typically up to 3–4 km in good habitat and 4–6 km in poorer areas, thus overlapping their hunting range with other Sparrowhawks (Newton 1986). There is inevitably, therefore, a chance that records of birds seen hunting, or carrying food for their young, belong to an adjacent tetrad. Observers found nests in 46 tetrads, with adults carrying food providing the bulk of confirmed breeding records (65), and 19 observations of recently fledged young, chicks spreading out through woodland whilst still obviously showing flecks of down amongst their plumage. In seven tetrads birds were seen building or visiting a probable nest site (B or N) and in eight tetrads surveyors reported the agitated 'kek-kek-kek' calls of adults; however, half (51) of the probable breeding records came from fieldworkers seeing display, one or both adults circling on stiff wings high above their territory, with 35 reports of pairs.

The Sparrowhawk population nationally is now about double that at the start of our *First Atlas* in 1978, but we do not have a good quantitative estimate of the county population because Sparrowhawks are only sporadically recorded on BBS transects. The hunting range of male birds in the breeding season may be as little as 30 ha, mostly woodland, at low elevations, but more than 250 ha at 200 m altitude (Newton 1986). These figures suggest that a density of one or two pairs per tetrad is sustainable in reasonable habitat. With this Atlas survey showing 235 tetrads with confirmed or probable breeding the Cheshire and Wirral population is likely to be in the range 300–400 pairs, more than twice the figure in our *First Atlas*, but only half the total for Kestrels. The national estimate for the British population is 38,600 pairs of Sparrowhawks, very similar to that for Kestrels (35,400) (Baker *et al.* 2006); Cheshire and Wirral is a less well-wooded county than many, so it is not surprising that our total of breeding Sparrowhawks is lower than that for Kestrels.

Sponsored by James Quinn

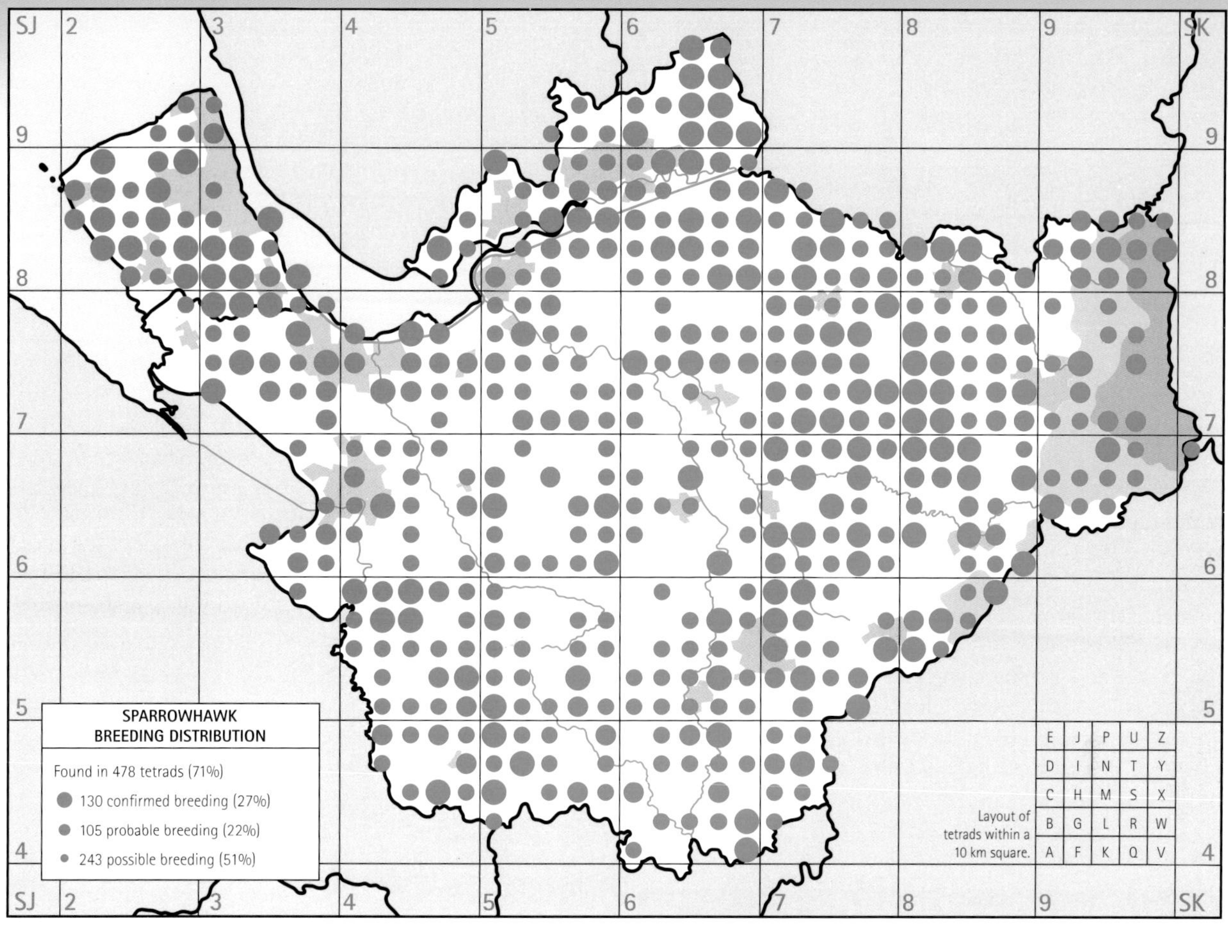
SPARROWHAWK
BREEDING DISTRIBUTION
Found in 478 tetrads (71%)
130 confirmed breeding (27%)
105 probable breeding (22%)
243 possible breeding (51%)
Layout of tetrads within a 10 km square.
E J P U Z
D I N T Y
C H M S X
B G L R W
A F K Q V
SJ
SK

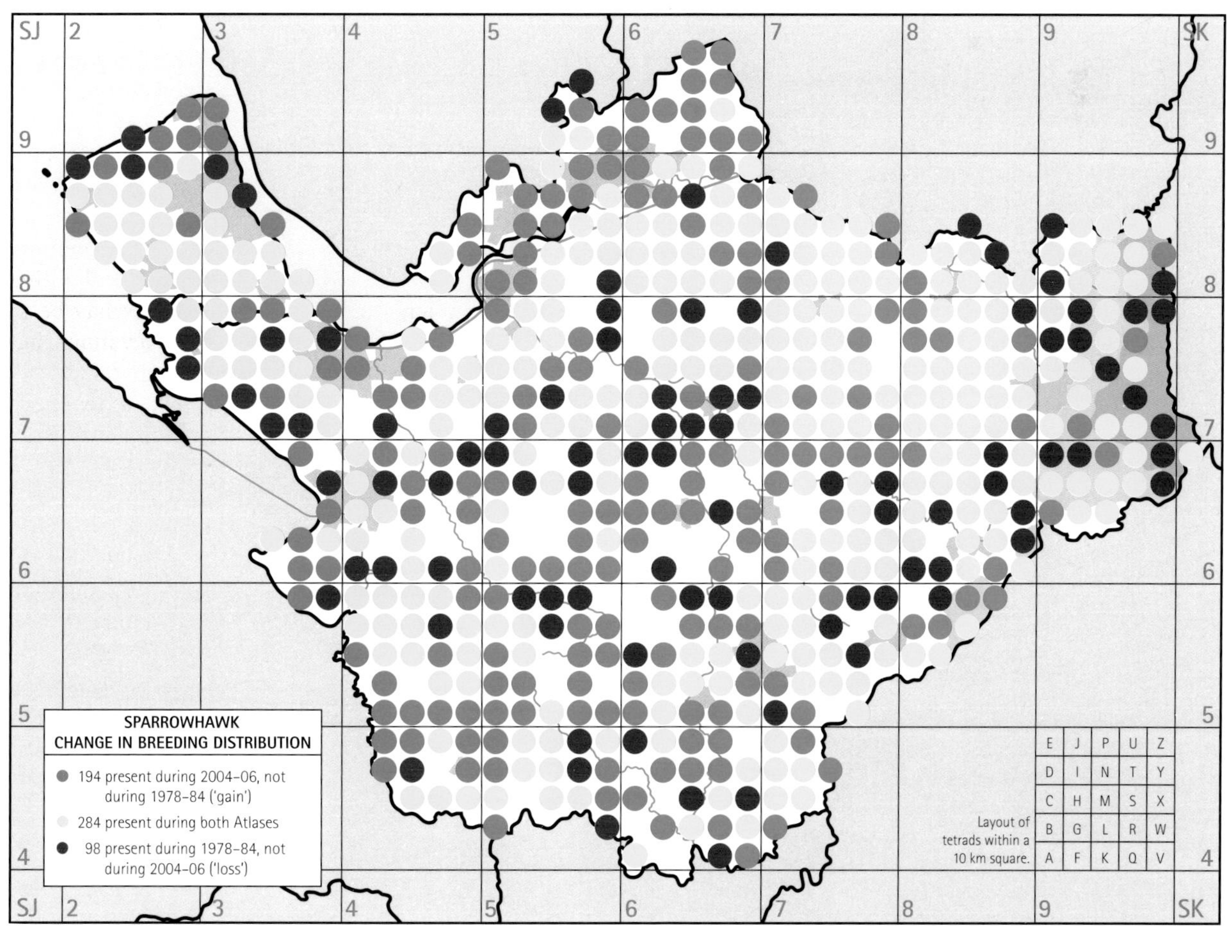
SPARROWHAWK
CHANGE IN BREEDING DISTRIBUTION
194 present during 2004–06, not during 1978–84 ('gain')
284 present during both Atlases
98 present during 1978–84, not during 2004–06 ('loss')
Layout of tetrads within a 10 km square.
E J P U Z
D I N T Y
C H M S X
B G L R W
A F K Q V
SJ
SK

Most Sparrowhawks which have good quality territories remain in them all year round, while those on low-grade territories tend to move away, whether they have successfully bred or not. First-year birds spend much of the winter trying to find a suitable territory, although not many succeed, fewer than 20% of birds breeding at one year of age. There is also an influx in winter of migratory birds, mostly from Norway and Denmark (*Migration Atlas*). There is thus no reason why the winter distribution map of Sparrowhawk should be similar to that for the breeding season, but it is: the species is widespread but missing from the sparsely wooded areas of central Cheshire and not found in some of the bleakest upland tetrads.

In winter, there is less reason for the apparent correlation with woodland because the sexes tend to separate, males hunting mostly in woodland and females more often in open country. This is dictated partly by their size and manoeuvrability, allied to the likely habitat preferences of their favoured prey. In summer, their prey is overwhelmingly the naïve fledglings but by wintertime, the easy pickings have gone and birds are more difficult to catch. The range over which Sparrowhawks have to hunt to fulfil their daily needs increases greatly, to a mean of 350 ha at low elevations—10 times the breeding season figure—and more than 800 ha (two tetrads) at 200 m altitude (Newton 1986); these figures are for male birds, with females travelling perhaps twice as far, covering four times the area. The greater variety of habitats covered in winter is shown by the recorded habitat codes, with 27% woodland, 5% scrub, 2% semi-natural grassland and marsh, 44% farmland and 21% human sites.

When they have no chicks to feed, Sparrowhawks hunt mainly in the first three hours of daylight, then are inactive for large parts of the day, usually from late morning onwards. There is a late-afternoon flurry, especially by first-year hawks, as some of them attack birds coming into roosts. I have found, in 23 years of ringing birds roosting at Norton Priory, Runcorn, a significant correlation from year to year between the total of thrushes ringed and the number of Sparrowhawks caught: in years with more thrushes roosting, there are likely to be more hawks visiting.

Coward and Oldham (1900) noted that 'in winter the Sparrowhawk frequents the more open country. It hunts over a regular beat as a rule, passing a given spot about the same time day after day'. To Boyd (1951) the species was a fairly common resident, but by Bell's time (1962 and 1967) they had become very scarce, as the lethal impact of organochlorine pesticides hit Sparrowhawks hard. The present county population may well be the highest in recorded ornithology.

STEVE ROUND

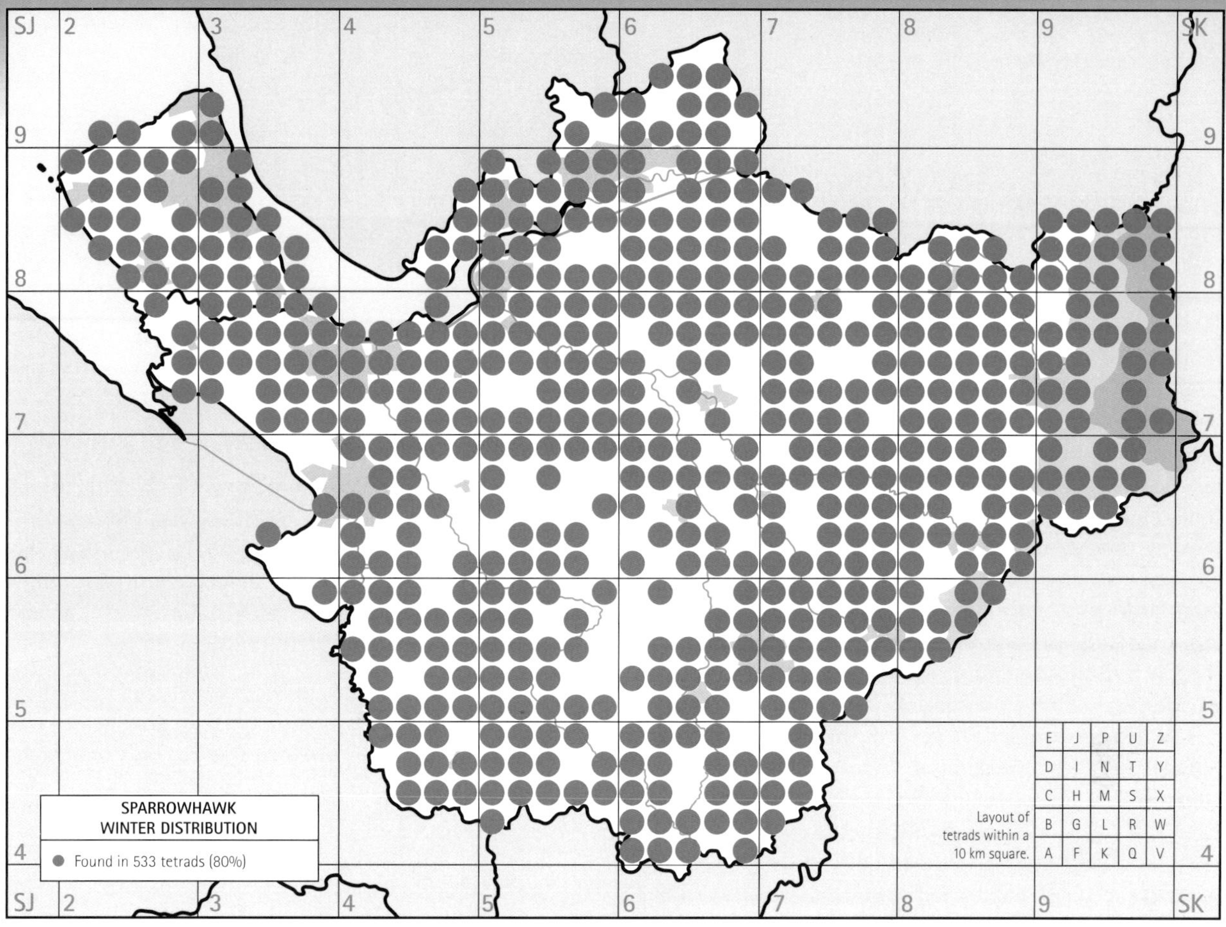
SPARROWHAWK
WINTER DISTRIBUTION
Found in 533 tetrads (80%)
Layout of tetrads within a 10 km square.
E J P U Z
D I N T Y
C H M S X
B G L R W
A F K Q V
SJ
SK

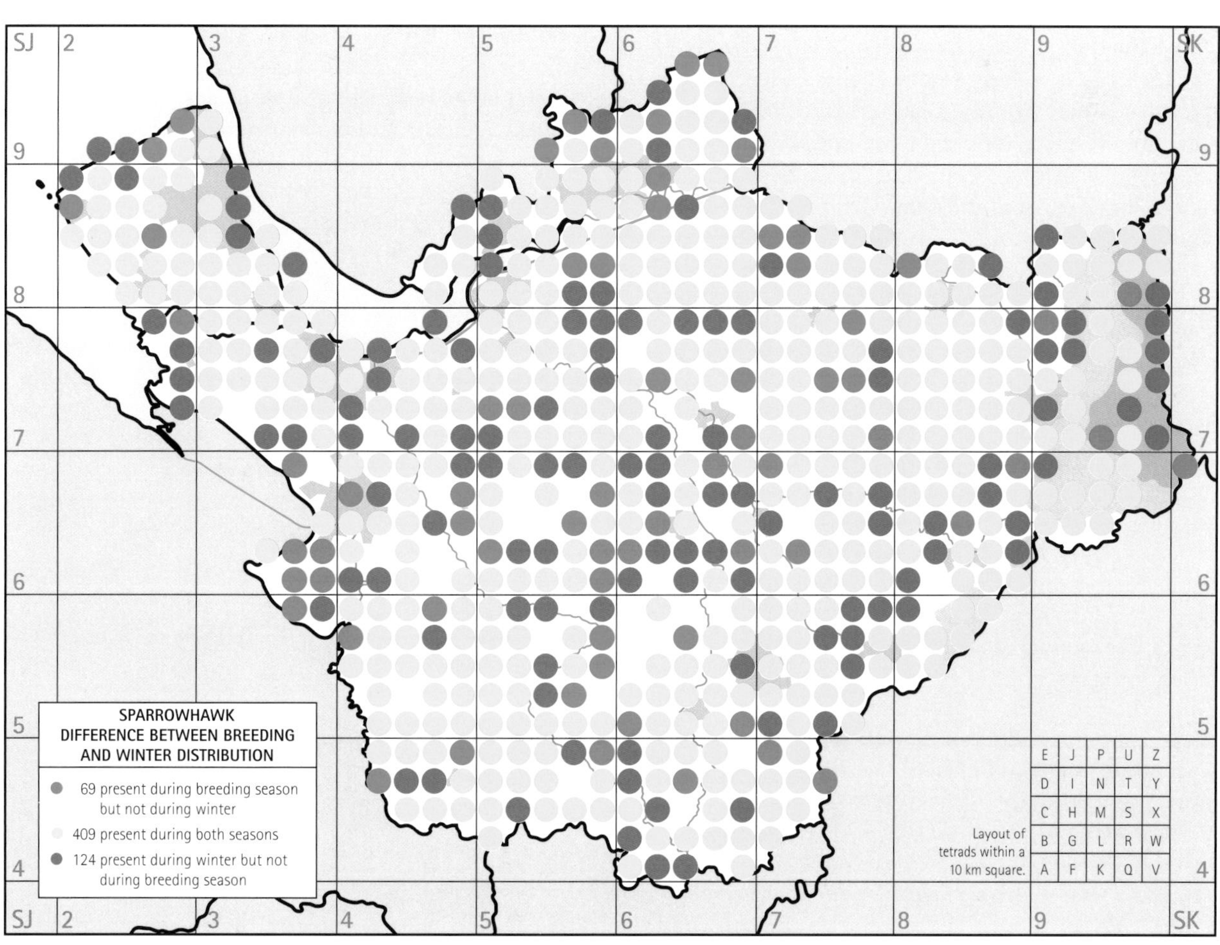
SPARROWHAWK
DIFFERENCE BETWEEN BREEDING
AND WINTER DISTRIBUTION
69 present during breeding season but not during winter
409 present during both seasons
124 present during winter but not during breeding season
Layout of tetrads within a 10 km square.
E J P U Z
D I N T Y
C H M S X
B G L R W
A F K Q V
SJ
SK

Buzzard

Buteo buteo

The rapid spread of the Buzzard is an amazing success story, from being one of the scarcest to one of the commonest raptors in the county in just a few years. The Atlas map shows that they are now absent only from the most built-up areas and the treeless coastal, estuarine and hill tetrads. Most birds were recorded in woodland (47%) or farmland (45%). Buzzards feed in open fields or in woodland and mostly take small mammals, especially rabbits, but also catch birds and reptiles, actively flying after relatively slow-moving prey or taking recently dead carrion. They also walk or run and, especially on bare ground, Buzzards take large numbers of beetles and earthworms. There is no shortage of food for such a generalist feeder and their breeding population does not fluctuate annually as does that of the vole specialists.

Buzzards have always been common in Wales, and have undertaken a substantial eastward range expansion starting in the late 1980s. The increase nationally has been associated with improving nesting success, perhaps through reduced persecution and a resurgence in rabbit numbers as their population stabilized with myxomatosis (Clements 2002). In our *First Atlas*, there were two tetrads with confirmed breeding and 10 with possible breeding from the seven years of fieldwork (1978–84). As their numbers in Cheshire and Wirral were obviously increasing, two surveys were organized by CAWOS and the Cheshire & Wirral Raptor Study Group: in 1994 there were five confirmed and 14 probable breeding pairs, in 18 tetrads, and the rapid growth of the population was shown six years later, when the 1999/2000 census found 56 confirmed and 128 probable breeding pairs in 145 tetrads (Barber & Hargreaves 1999).

With a long breeding season from display in March to fledging in July, a large nest and a common bird, it is not surprising that fieldworkers found nests in 85 tetrads. A characteristic behaviour of nesting Buzzards is to decorate the nest with green leaves, usually visible from the ground and a sure sign of an occupied nest. Adults were seen carrying food for their young in a further 24 tetrads, but the most common method of proving breeding, in 101 tetrads, was RF—surveyors seeing recently fledged chicks with their parents, who regularly feed their chicks for up to two months after they leave the nest. Most broods are of two or three chicks, the average apparently decreasing as the population has grown and the productivity of each pair has dropped. Most of the 220 records of probable breeding came from observers recording pairs, or display, which was the main method of counting during the 1994 and 1999/2000 surveys.

The BTO BBS analysis shows that the population of Cheshire and Wirral in 2004–05 was 1,650 birds (710–2,600). Buzzards do not normally breed until three years of age, so perhaps half of the birds seen were non-breeders. With the BBS counts in early mornings in April and May meaning that only one bird was seen from each pair of Buzzards, this figure would give a county population of 835 pairs which is perhaps a reasonable upper limit for the current estimate.

SIMON BOOTH

Such a total corresponds to two pairs per tetrad with confirmed or probable breeding, an average density of 0.5 pairs per square kilometre. How does this compare with other figures? The prime habitat of the New Forest in the 1960s supported Buzzards with a mean territory size of 0.55 km^2, equivalent to 1.8 pairs per square kilometre (Tubbs 1974). In a 75 km^2 study area of north Somerset, Robin Prytherch found that Buzzards increased from 13 pairs in 1982 to 84 pairs in 2001, over 1.1 pairs per square kilometre (quoted by Clements 2002). In the 1999/2000 survey of Cheshire and Wirral, the area of greatest breeding density, covering 160 km^2, held an average of 0.22 pairs per square kilometre (Barber & Hargreaves 1999). As the population grows, the birds' territory shrinks, they tend to nest closer and closer together and produce fewer young per pair until eventually equilibrium is reached. That has not yet happened in Cheshire and Wirral and another survey in a few years' time would be worthwhile.

Sponsored by Frank Gleeson

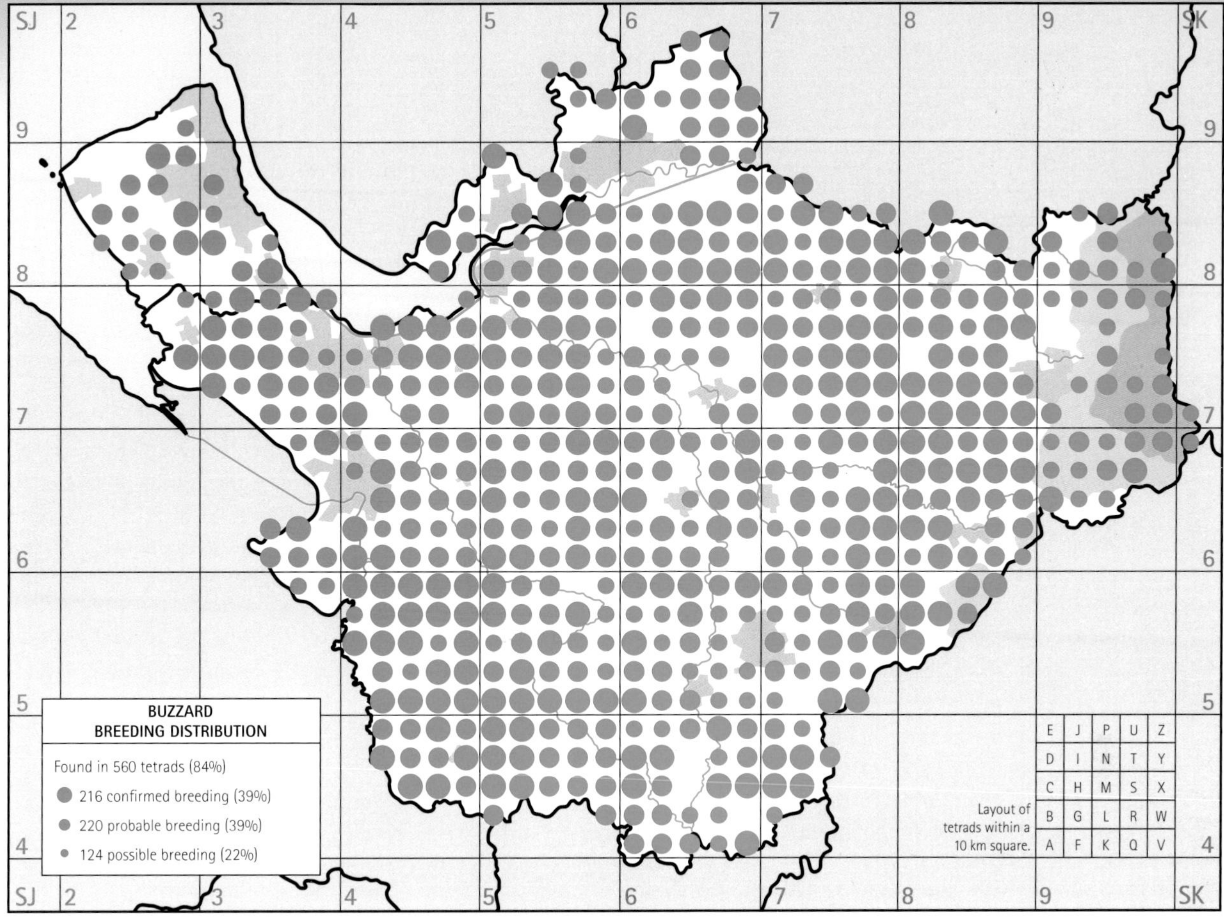
SJ
SK
BUZZARD
BREEDING DISTRIBUTION
Found in 560 tetrads (84%)
216 confirmed breeding (39%)
220 probable breeding (39%)
124 possible breeding (22%)
E J P U Z
D I N T Y
C H M S X
B G L R W
A F K Q V
Layout of tetrads within a 10 km square.

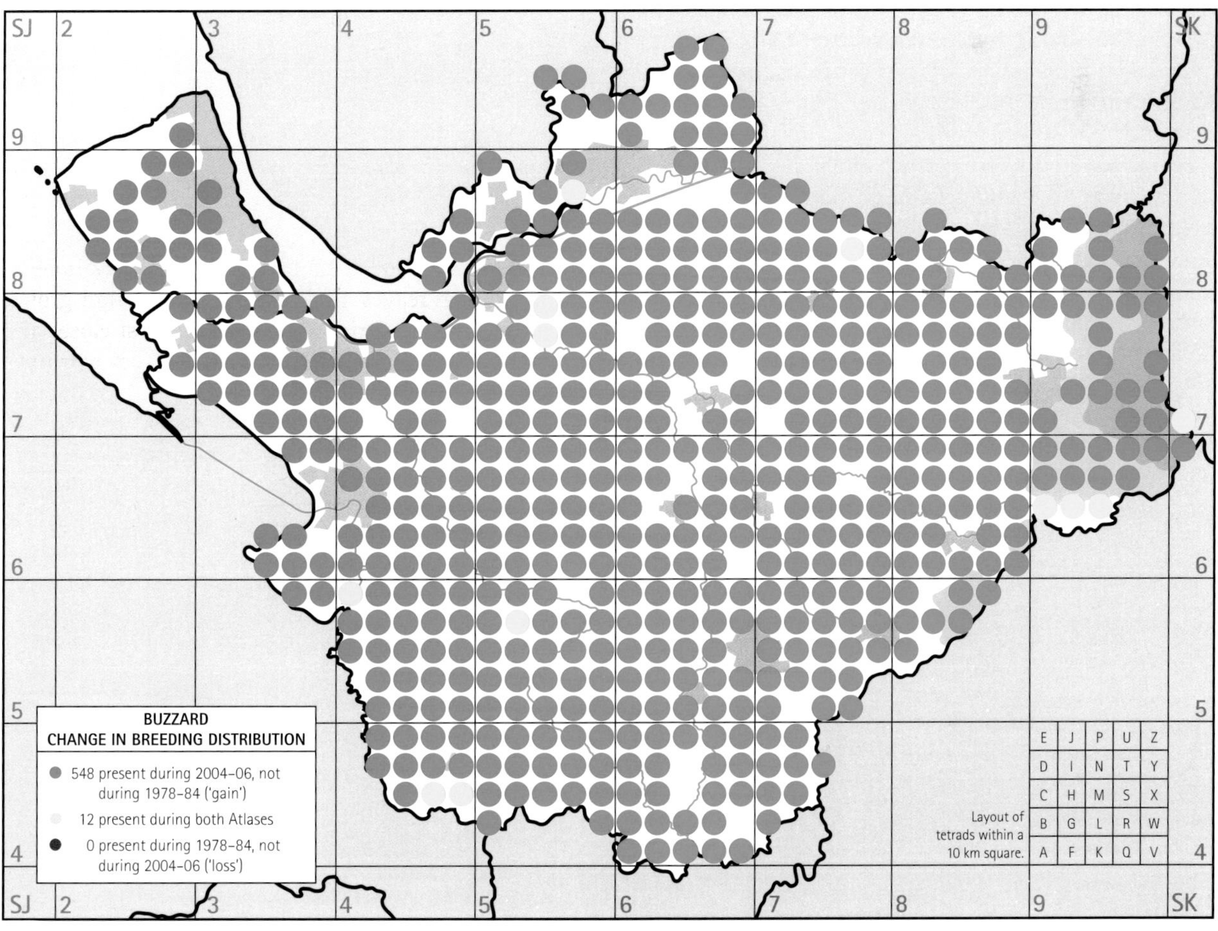
SJ
SK
BUZZARD
CHANGE IN BREEDING DISTRIBUTION
548 present during 2004–06, not during 1978–84 ('gain')
12 present during both Atlases
0 present during 1978–84, not during 2004–06 ('loss')
E J P U Z
D I N T Y
C H M S X
B G L R W
A F K Q V
Layout of tetrads within a 10 km square.

SIMON BOOTH

The Buzzard's winter distribution differs little from that of the breeding season, except that the requirement for trees is relaxed, allowing the species to use almost every part of the county apart from the most urban areas. The winter habitat codes show, compared to the breeding season, a substantial shift out of woodland (30%) into farmland (59%), with more birds in human sites (4%) and in a range of types of semi-natural grassland and marsh (4%). Adults usually remain on their territories throughout the year. Young birds, becoming independent during their first autumn, have to try to establish themselves between the ranges of surviving pairs. During the early winter, when boundaries are not defended so vigorously, they may be tolerated within a territory, but are driven away as soon as the adults recommence breeding behaviour. Some young birds do wander far during the juvenile dispersal stage, doubtless accounting for their turning up in odd places, including occasionally flying over town centres. Radio-tracking of juveniles has shown that 40% of birds stayed in their natal area during the first winter, and 72% of those that dispersed returned to the vicinity in the following breeding season (Brown & Grice 2005).

In winter, they tend to hunt more from a perch, rather than flying after their prey. Their diet becomes dominated by invertebrates, mainly earthworms, with rabbits when they can get them; but birds become harder to catch and small mammals are scarcer than in the breeding season. An average young rabbit provides about two days' worth of sustenance for a Buzzard, so they are sought after even when not abundant (Brown 1976). Female Buzzards are about 10% larger than the males, but this does not lead to any significant difference in food choice or hunting technique.

The species' former status in the county was as mainly a rare visitor during autumn and winter. Their rarity is well illustrated by the ornithological chroniclers. Coward (1910) gives the species' status as 'a wanderer to Cheshire, more frequently met with in the west than elsewhere', suggesting that birds seen in Cheshire are from the Welsh population. He lists a few examples, one every few years on average, almost every bird being shot or trapped. Boyd (1946) noted that at least 18 occurrences of the Buzzard in Cheshire were recorded between 1924 and 1936, the majority seen or shot between October and March, with quite a number of them seen in east Cheshire. In his diary for 3 October 1941, Boyd wrote 'any Buzzards I have seen in Cheshire have been dead ones, trapped or shot by the ignorant, but I still hope to see a living one in the county': it is not known if he ever did. Bell (1962), as usual, copied Coward's comments, saying that 'most of the published reports come from the Wirral peninsula, although single birds may occur anywhere, especially in the spring and autumn'.

The number of records grew during the 1960s, although most birds were in autumn and the annual *CWBRs* contain few winter reports. In 1968 the County Recorder was apparently so concerned at the number of Buzzard records received (eight) that he urged observers to consider fully the possibility of their being misidentified Honey Buzzards or Rough-legged Buzzards! Throughout the 1970s and 1980s, even when the species started to breed in Cheshire, the number of wintering birds recorded was still in single figures, and it was only from about 1993/94 onwards that the numbers became uncountable.

It would be a rare day's birdwatching now without encountering a Buzzard in the county: what a change!

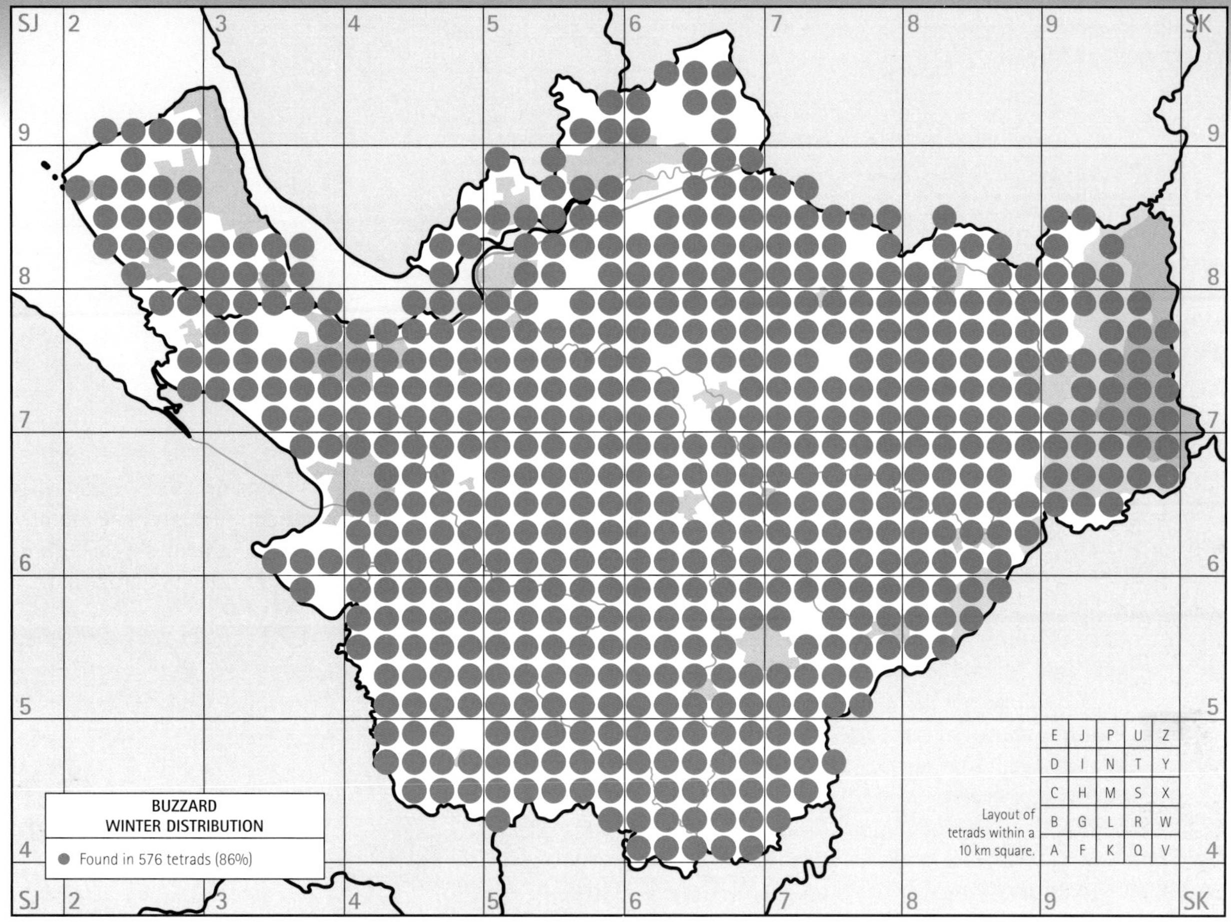

BUZZARD
WINTER DISTRIBUTION
Found in 576 tetrads (86%)
Layout of tetrads within a 10 km square.
E J P U Z
D I N T Y
C H M S X
B G L R W
A F K Q V
SJ
SK

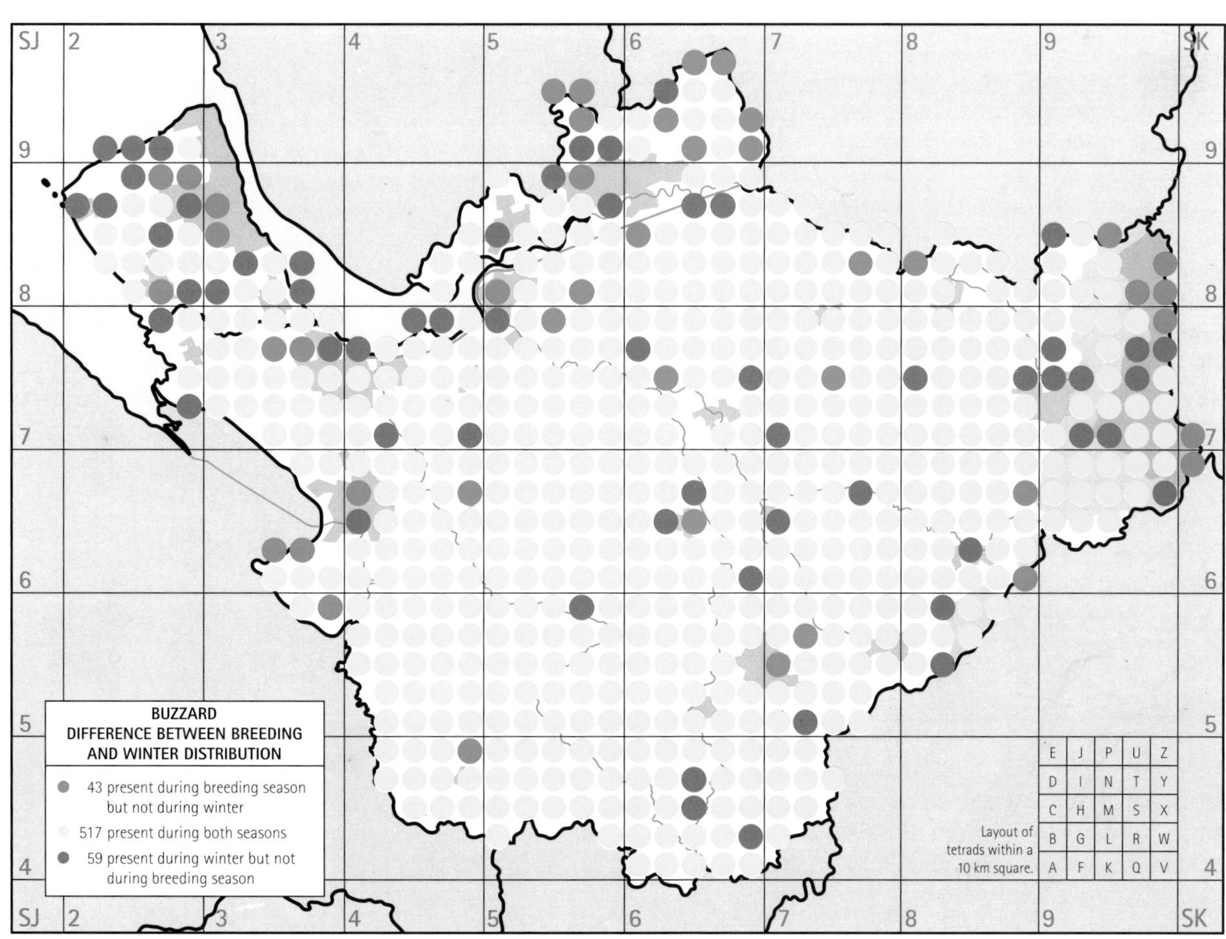

BUZZARD
DIFFERENCE BETWEEN BREEDING AND WINTER DISTRIBUTION
43 present during breeding season but not during winter
517 present during both seasons
59 present during winter but not during breeding season
Layout of tetrads within a 10 km square.
E J P U Z
D I N T Y
C H M S X
B G L R W
A F K Q V
SJ
SK

Kestrel

Falco tinnunculus

Breeding Kestrels are found at any altitude and almost every habitat. The habitat codes recorded were mostly farmland (63% of records), especially grassland areas, with 15% woodland, 12% human sites, 4% scrub and 3% semi-natural grassland and marsh. They occupy much the same number of tetrads as twenty years ago, but the 'change' map shows that their distribution has altered significantly. In our *First Atlas*, Kestrels were present in almost every tetrad in Wirral, Halton and Warrington, and around Northwich and Chester; whereas now there are substantial gaps in their presence in those areas. On the other hand, the species has spread into much of central, southern and south-western Cheshire where it used to be missing. The net effect is a shift in habitat, with a reduction in urban Kestrels and an increase in rural birds.

This loss from many urban areas has not previously been noted in the county and merits more research as it is not readily explicable. The spread in rural Cheshire is perhaps linked to changed agricultural practices, including the widespread adoption of Environmental Stewardship with uncropped field margins and sympathetically managed hedges. These measures have been vital in Barn Owl conservation, but are benefiting Kestrel which is the diurnal equivalent, filling the same ecological niche.

Their most successful and best-known hunting technique is hovering, facing into the wind and keeping stationary by tilting the tail, scanning the ground below for some movement. But hovering is energy-intensive and Kestrels often switch to three other methods of hunting: perching, dropping onto prey below; walking on the ground, sometimes looking into mammal-runs in grass, or taking invertebrates; and a low flight, like a Sparrowhawk, used to catch small birds. Some Kestrels take mainly field voles, and their breeding population varies cyclically according to the abundance of their prey. During this Atlas, 2004 and 2005 were average years, with 2006 a year of very low field vole numbers, and in well-studied areas of Cheshire only about one-third of the normal number of Kestrels nested. Urban Kestrels take more mice, rats and birds, up to the size of pigeons, usually fledglings. Females are larger than males, and there is some difference in their diet. Males take more insects, especially beetles, and females take more earthworms. Males are more proficient at catching birds, with young Starlings especially a favoured target.

Their wide range of nesting sites gives them an unfettered choice of tetrad: large holes in trees, old corvid nests, ledges on any type of human artefact and nest-boxes are all readily taken. They usually start laying around the end of April, but can be a month earlier in years of plenty, or delay by a month (or not breed at all) if food is scarce. They take no particular steps to conceal their nests, and observers found nests in 77 tetrads, with adults carrying prey for their young in a further 55 and recently fledged chicks, often with tufts of down visible, confirming breeding in another 51 tetrads.

SIMON BOOTH

The BTO BBS analysis shows that the breeding population of Cheshire and Wirral in 2004–05 was 1,300 birds (650–1,960). Kestrels can breed at one year of age, but only 20–40% of females do so, and half that proportion of males, never successfully (Shrubb 1993), so some of those counted on BBS transects will have been non-breeding immature birds. Assuming that 400 were non-breeders and that, in most cases, only the male of each pair was seen—the female being occupied with incubation—the Cheshire and Wirral total of Kestrels is likely to have been in the range of 600–800 pairs. This is double the estimate of 350 pairs in the *First Atlas*, partly because that figure now appears to be too low, and partly because the local population has risen. The BBS figure amounts to 2.6% of the UK population, suggesting that Cheshire and Wirral provides particularly good habitats for Kestrels.

Sponsored by S.C. Nichols

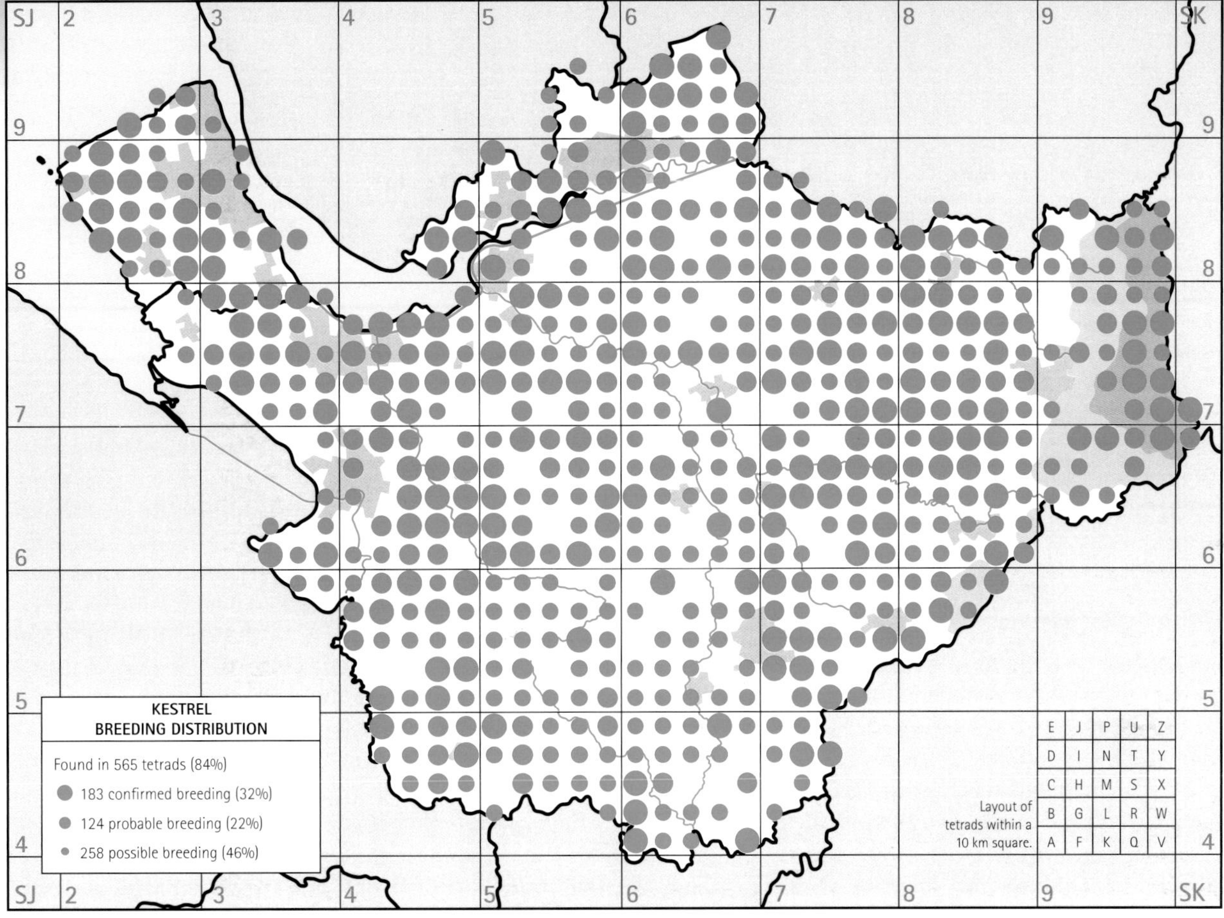
SJ
SK
2
3
4
5
6
7
8
9
KESTREL
BREEDING DISTRIBUTION
Found in 565 tetrads (84%)
183 confirmed breeding (32%)
124 probable breeding (22%)
258 possible breeding (46%)
E J P U Z
D I N T Y
C H M S X
B G L R W
A F K Q V
Layout of tetrads within a 10 km square.

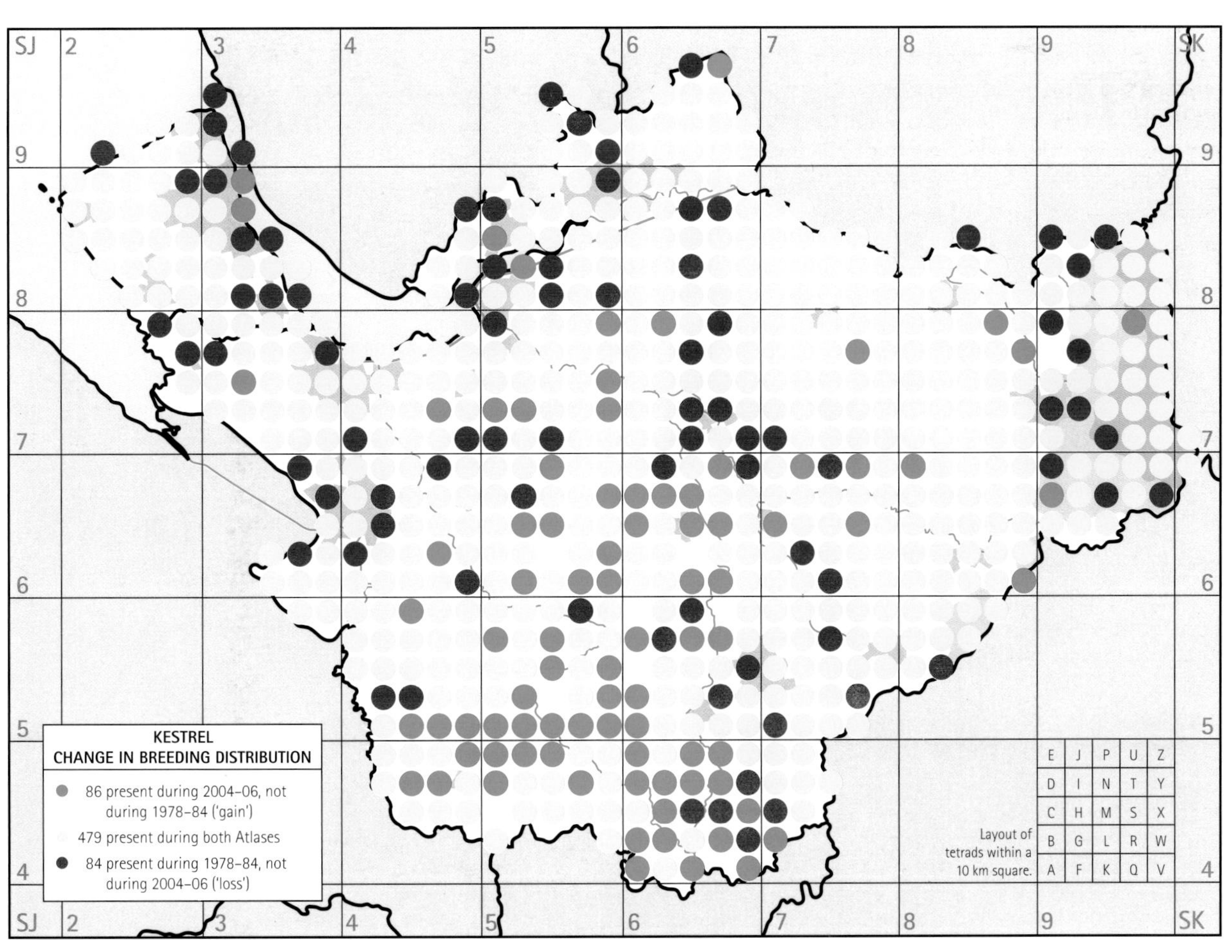
SJ
SK
2
3
4
5
6
7
8
9
KESTREL
CHANGE IN BREEDING DISTRIBUTION
86 present during 2004–06, not during 1978–84 ('gain')
479 present during both Atlases
84 present during 1978–84, not during 2004–06 ('loss')
E J P U Z
D I N T Y
C H M S X
B G L R W
A F K Q V
Layout of tetrads within a 10 km square.

The winter distribution map is similar to that for the breeding season, with a few records in areas where they were not found to breed, and a few gaps where the species was unluckily missed in winter. Kestrels exhibit a variety of strategies for coping with winter. Some pairs remain together on their breeding territory; others split up, with the male staying and the female moving off to defend a separate winter territory, probably re-forming the pair-bond in spring; some first-year birds squeeze into areas between occupied territories; and others migrate long distances, including Scandinavian birds coming to Britain, some of them making it to the west coast and Ireland. British birds breeding in the lowlands are mostly sedentary while those in the uplands tend to move south, and to lower altitudes (Brown & Grice 2005). Birds fledging late in the season are much more likely to travel far from the nest (*Migration Atlas*). This mixture of approaches means that Kestrels can probably be found in winter anywhere with sufficient food, and that certainly applies in Cheshire and Wirral. Although inhospitable uplands are deserted for the winter (*BTO Winter Atlas*), the east of Cheshire obviously offered enough food and shelter during this Atlas survey for Kestrels to be found in almost every tetrad.

The winter habitat codes show significant shifts from the breeding season. Farmland comprises an even higher proportion (72% of records), with only half as many in woodland than during the breeding season (7%), fewer in human sites (8%), 5% scrub and a doubling to 6% of the fraction of semi-natural grassland and marsh.

The 'home range', the area over which an individual hunts, is at its minimum size in autumn, when first-year birds are finding space for themselves; this is probably tolerable because autumn is the time of maximum vole numbers. In grassland areas, Kestrels in autumn use about 1–2 km^2 each but this virtually doubles by late winter as some birds die and others move out (Village 1990).

Whilst Kestrels are most often noticed when hovering, especially over roadside verges, they only do so within a certain range of wind speeds; it is too difficult, or energetically costly, in calm conditions or when the wind is very strong. Birds then usually resort to sitting on perches, especially telegraph poles and the like, dropping onto prey. Kestrels seem to avoid hunting in rain if possible, and may spend hours sitting in a sheltered site.

It can be difficult to tell on what they are feeding, and no observer for this Atlas commented on prey in winter. Small mammals seem to be the staple if they can be found: Kestrels can detect vole urine, visible in ultra-violet light, and probably use this faculty to select areas with high concentrations of the mammals. Bank voles, wood mice and harvest mice are less strictly nocturnal during winter, and thus more likely to be available to Kestrels. Fewer birds are taken in winter in upland areas, reflecting the scarcity of small- to medium-sized avian prey there, but on farmed land with flocks of seed-eaters, birds may form the majority of Kestrels' winter food (Shrubb 1993). Some Kestrels attack passerine roosts.

Apart from a respite from persecution, there has probably been little change in the Kestrel's status for a century or more. Alfred Newton's *Dictionary of Birds* (1893–96) described the Kestrel as 'almost entirely a summer migrant', but Coward (1910) helpfully comments that 'in Cheshire the bird is as frequently met with in winter as in summer', a phrase that holds good today. There is a hint that the species has changed its habits, however, with Coward and Oldham deeming worthy of special comment the fact that Brockholes (1874) stated that they 'sometimes breed in a hollow tree'.

RICHARD STEEL

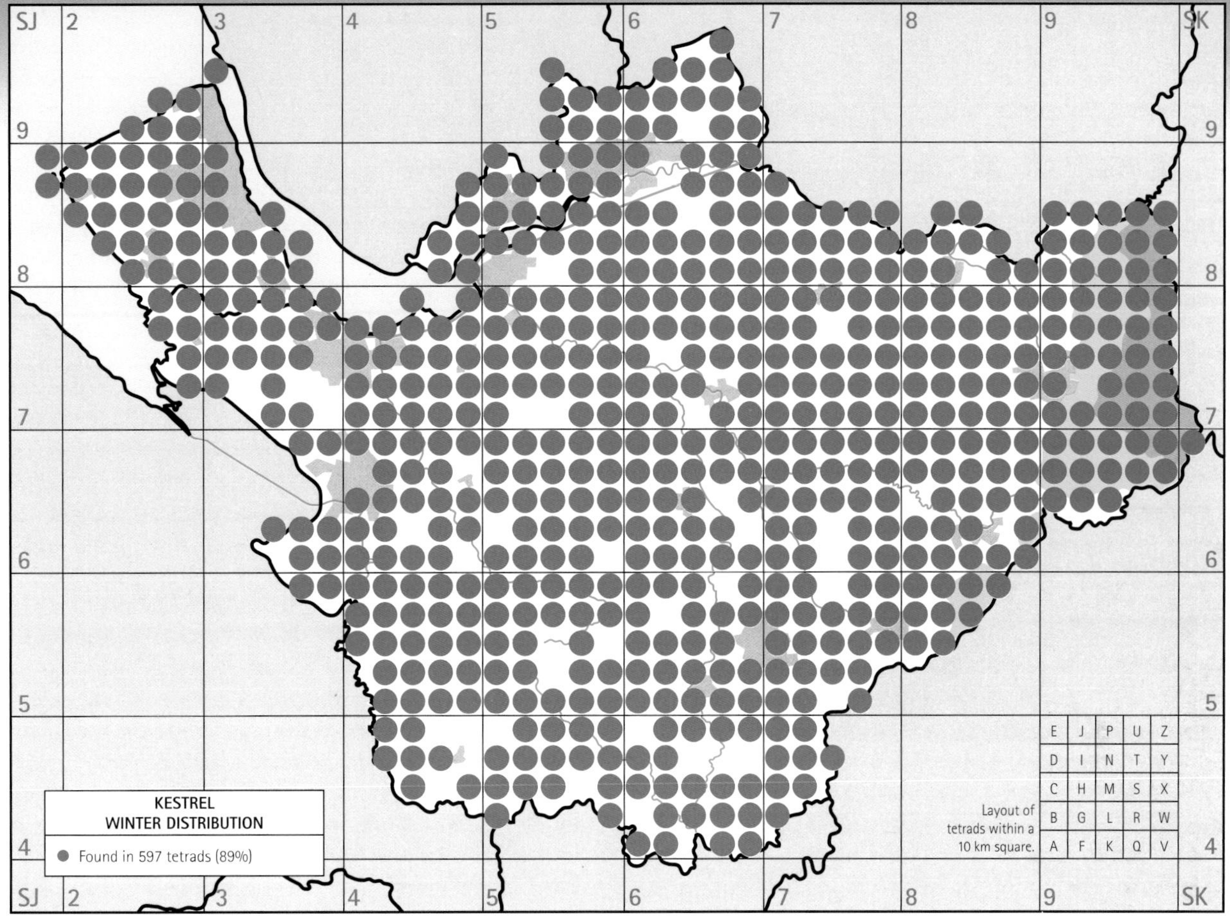
SJ
2
3
4
5
6
7
8
9
SK
KESTREL
WINTER DISTRIBUTION
Found in 597 tetrads (89%)
Layout of
tetrads within a
10 km square.
E J P U Z
D I N T Y
C H M S X
B G L R W
A F K Q V

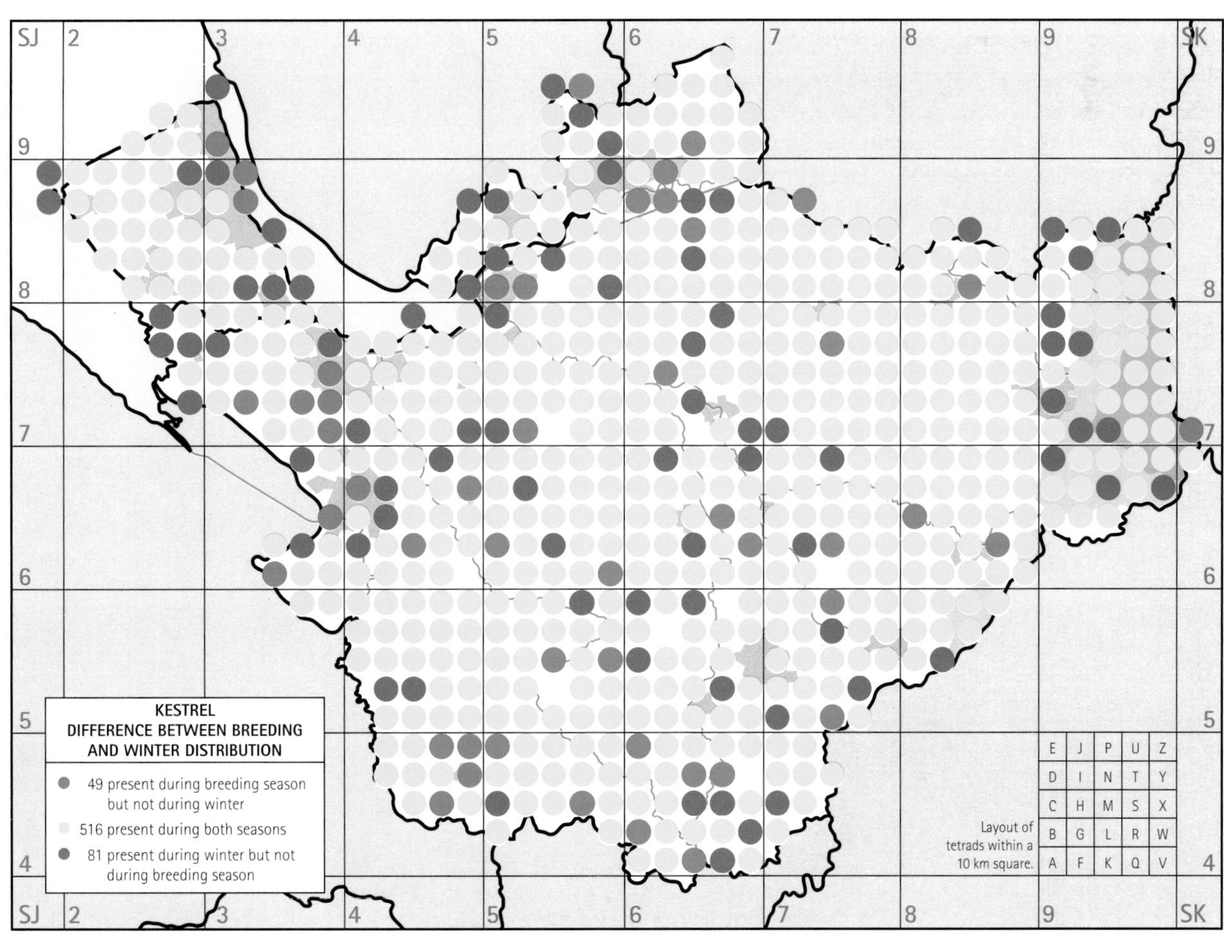
SJ
2
3
4
5
6
7
8
9
SK
KESTREL
DIFFERENCE BETWEEN BREEDING
AND WINTER DISTRIBUTION
49 present during breeding season but not during winter
516 present during both seasons
81 present during winter but not during breeding season
Layout of
tetrads within a
10 km square.
E J P U Z
D I N T Y
C H M S X
B G L R W
A F K Q V

Merlin

Falco columbarius

JOHN POWER

The Merlin is one of a group of predatory birds—with Hen Harrier and Short-eared Owl—that breeds on the fringe of Cheshire and might or might not actually nest in the county. During this Atlas survey, one was seen carrying food to chicks in 2004, the first confirmed breeding within the existing county boundaries for at least 70 years.

It is not at all clear when breeding last took place. Bell (1967) noted a nest in 1951 and 1952 in Longdendale, not now part of Cheshire, and Bell (1962) said that 'during the last 25 years there is no evidence of it having bred in the hills', implying that it did so before then, but giving no further substantiation. Coward and Oldham (1900) wrote that 'possibly an odd pair of Merlins may succeed in rearing their brood on the moors east of Macclesfield, as they undoubtedly do just beyond the Staffordshire border'.

The Merlins of the southern Peak District, of which Cheshire forms a small part, have been well studied for the last half-century. A population of 45 pairs in the 1950s suffered a catastrophic decline to near extinction by 1980, after which the number of occupied nesting areas in the South Pennines increased from two (in 1980) to 66 (in 1992) (Newton *et al.* 1981, Brown & Stillman 1998). Their decline had probably been caused—as has been well documented for another bird-eating falcon, the Peregrine—by accumulation of organochlorine pesticides. Merlins feed almost exclusively on small passerines, especially Meadow Pipits which can make up half of their diet. The population recovery followed the gradual cessation of use of these pesticides, aided by a reduction in persecution and egg-collecting.

The records published in Cheshire and Wirral annual bird reports track the recovery. There were odd records in suitable habitat in 1970, 1987, 1989, 1990, 1991, 1993, 1994, 1995, 1996, 1997, 2000 and 2001, and a pair was seen in three years, 1966, 1972 and 2003; breeding is difficult to prove in casual visits, however. Their favoured habitat is moorland with scattered shrubs. The Peak District birds nest mostly on gently sloping ground in heather, less commonly in old Crow nests in trees, avoiding areas of high recreational pressure.

Sponsored by John and Debbie Bannon

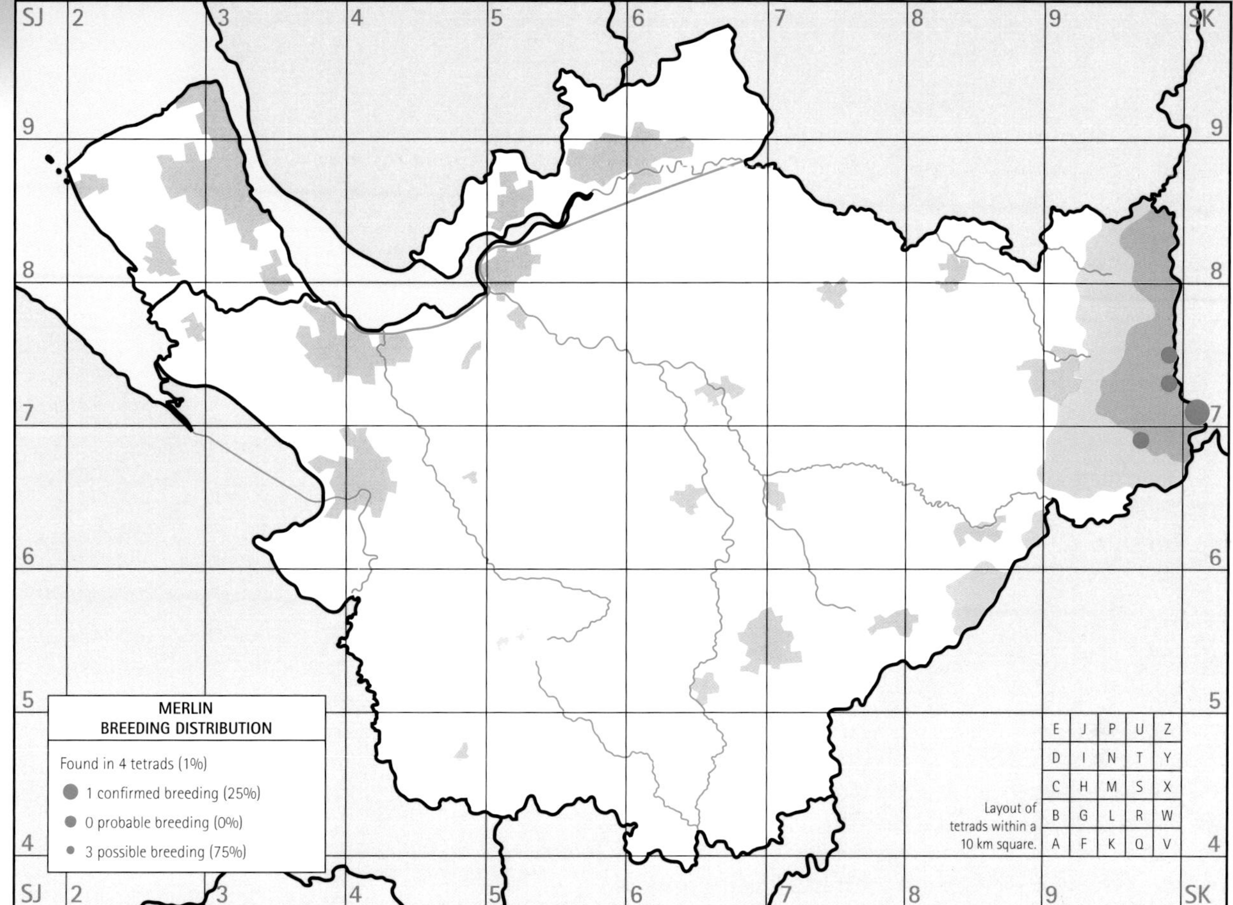
MERLIN
BREEDING DISTRIBUTION
Found in 4 tetrads (1%)
1 confirmed breeding (25%)
0 probable breeding (0%)
3 possible breeding (75%)
Layout of tetrads within a 10 km square.
E J P U Z
D I N T Y
C H M S X
B G L R W
A F K Q V
SJ
SK

Merlins have always been much more common in Cheshire and Wirral in winter. Coward and Oldham (1900) quoted Brockholes (1874) saying that a few birds remained through the winter in the Dee marshes, where they sometimes prey upon the Feral Pigeons which feed there. In Coward's time the bird was occasionally encountered in winter in the marshes of the Mersey estuary, near Thornton and Ince, and less commonly on the plain. Boyd (1951) knew the Merlin as an infrequent winter visitor, seen one at a time, to areas around his Frandley home.

This Atlas map bears out that same general description today. The main concentrations are along the estuarine edges but an odd bird can be found almost anywhere in the lowlands. One bird showed an early return to the eastern hills. Compared to Hen Harriers and Short-eared Owls, there are proportionately more in the rough grassland around the Mersey than along the Dee salt-marshes, which may reflect the Merlins' dependence on small passerines rather than mammals and larger birds. In winter Merlins mainly hunt for passerines but also take small waders up to the size of Redshank, usually skimming low over the ground and surprising their prey. They sometimes appear to cooperate with another Merlin or a different raptor, especially a Hen Harrier, in flushing prey. The submitted winter habitat codes reflect their use of open areas. Farmland comprised 47% of records, mostly grassland with 5% of stubble—birds presumably trying to surprise a feeding passerine—with 25% on grazing marsh or salt-marsh and 15% in estuaries.

The majority of British Merlins remain within Britain all year, with a median distance of 99 km between the breeding season and winter and movements being generally southerly and to lower altitudes. One ringed as a nestling in North Yorkshire was found dead near Warrington in its second winter in 1998. Most Icelandic birds winter in Ireland and western Britain so surely some of our wintering Merlins are of the Icelandic race *Falco columbarius subaesalon*. They are slightly larger and somewhat darker in plumage, but usually not safely distinguishable in the field, not least because northern British Merlins, from Shetland, Orkney and northern Scotland, are mainly within the Icelandic size range (*Migration Atlas*).

There were records submitted of 20, 28 and 26 Merlins in the three winters of this Atlas project.

RAY SCALLY

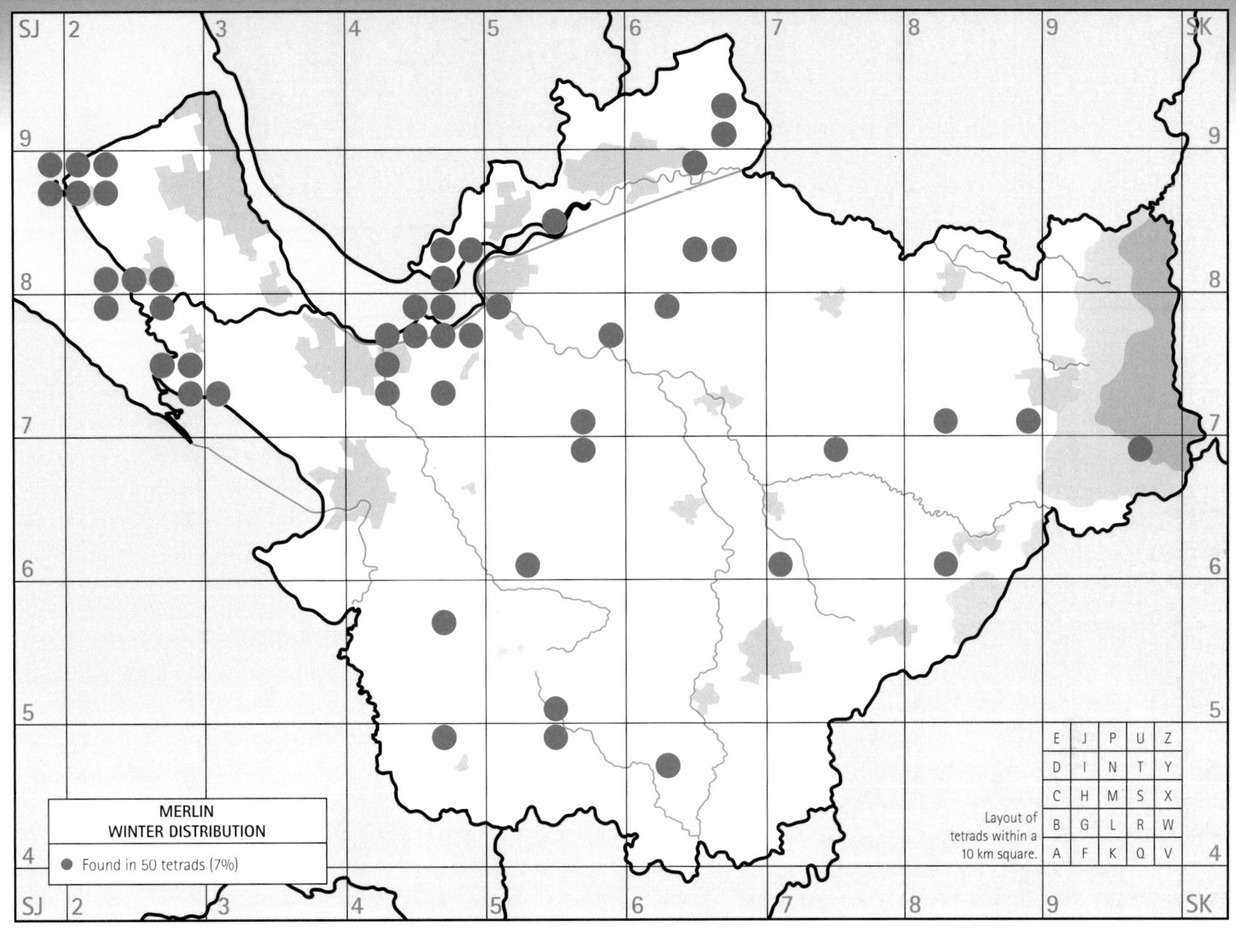
SJ
SK
MERLIN
WINTER DISTRIBUTION
Found in 50 tetrads (7%)
Layout of
tetrads within a
10 km square.
E J P U Z
D I N T Y
C H M S X
B G L R W
A F K Q V

Hobby

Falco subbuteo

STEVE ROUND

Cheshire has shared in the northern spread of this spectacular bird of prey and its county population is now larger than at any time in the history of ornithological recording. Hobbies bred occasionally during the nineteenth century, when most birds seen were shot, but the only nests known to Coward (1910) were in 1895 and 1898. The next proven breeding came exactly a century later in 1998, following an increasing number of summer sightings during the 1990s; occasional records had strongly hinted at breeding, including a pair which nested successfully in 1996, and probably in 1995, about 200 m outside the county boundary. Since then they have increased greatly and the fieldwork for this Atlas shows that there may be as many as 50 pairs breeding in the county.

Several suggestions have been put forward to explain their increase and northward spread in England, including the similar expansion of several dragonfly species (Prince & Clarke 1993); greater availability of corvid nests because of reduced persecution (Chapman 1999); and mechanized farming meaning fewer humans in the countryside (Messenger & Roome 2007). For a bird so closely associated with warm summer days, climate change is surely implicated, as well.

Hobbies are one of the latest breeding species and most arrive back from their southern African wintering grounds—believed to lie in the Zambezi basin between 10°S and 20°S—during May. On arrival in the nesting territory in spring, the male calls frequently and flies conspicuously over the woodland canopy, or the former nesting area; it is surprising that no D (display) records were submitted as breeding status codes. They nest anywhere with a good view, typically 15 m above ground in a hedgerow tree or an open area on the edge of woodland. The frequently cited preference of Hobbies for nesting in Scots pines is erroneous, a result of their being the commonest trees in the southern English heathlands where earlier studies were performed (Fiuczynski & Nethersole-Thompson 1980). In Derbyshire, 84 out of 106 known nests were in oak (Messenger & Roome 2007). More than 90% of Hobbies use an old Crows' nest, about half of them from earlier in the same season, the Crow chicks having already fledged before the Hobby's arrival. The female usually lays three eggs and starts incubating from mid-June whilst the male provides her with food, an average of 2.6 birds per day. Incubation lasts for four weeks, followed by a fledging period of four to five weeks.

Hobbies fiercely defend their nest area against potential predators such as Kestrels, Buzzards and corvids (Chapman 1999). Woodpigeons often choose to nest near to a Hobby, even in the same tree, as was noted in the first breeding in the south-east of Cheshire (Stubbs 2001). This is probably a symbiotic relationship, the pigeons gaining from the raptor's defence against predators, and the Hobbies having another species alerting them to threats.

In Cheshire, Hobbies are a farmland bird, settling wherever there is sufficient prey. Two-thirds of submitted habitat codes were farmland, mostly improved grassland (32%), unimproved grassland (11%) and mixed grassland/tilled land (19%), with 18% woodland. They catch their food on the wing. Moths, butterflies and dragonflies are mainly taken and eaten by the adults themselves, although if they are superabundant, the male brings lots of insects to his brooding mate. Their favoured avian prey is hirundines. Sand Martins dread visits to their colonies by this species more than any other raptor: colonies return to normal within a minute or two of an attack by Sparrowhawk or Kestrel, even if successful, whereas they often take 10–15 minutes to recover from a Hobby's visit. They have evolved a special alarm call, as have Swallows, different from that given for other aerial predators. This is obviously innate, as was demonstrated at Cheshire Sand Martin colonies in the 1990s that had never previously experienced Hobby attacks. They have been recorded taking at least 70 different species in Europe (*BWP*), and various English studies have found them taking at least 36 species, including almost every small- or medium-sized bird of open habitats: Swifts, larks, pipits, tits, sparrows, finches and buntings, as well as noctule bats (Chapman 1999).

The submissions for this Atlas total 37 tetrads with confirmed or probable breeding and a number of other

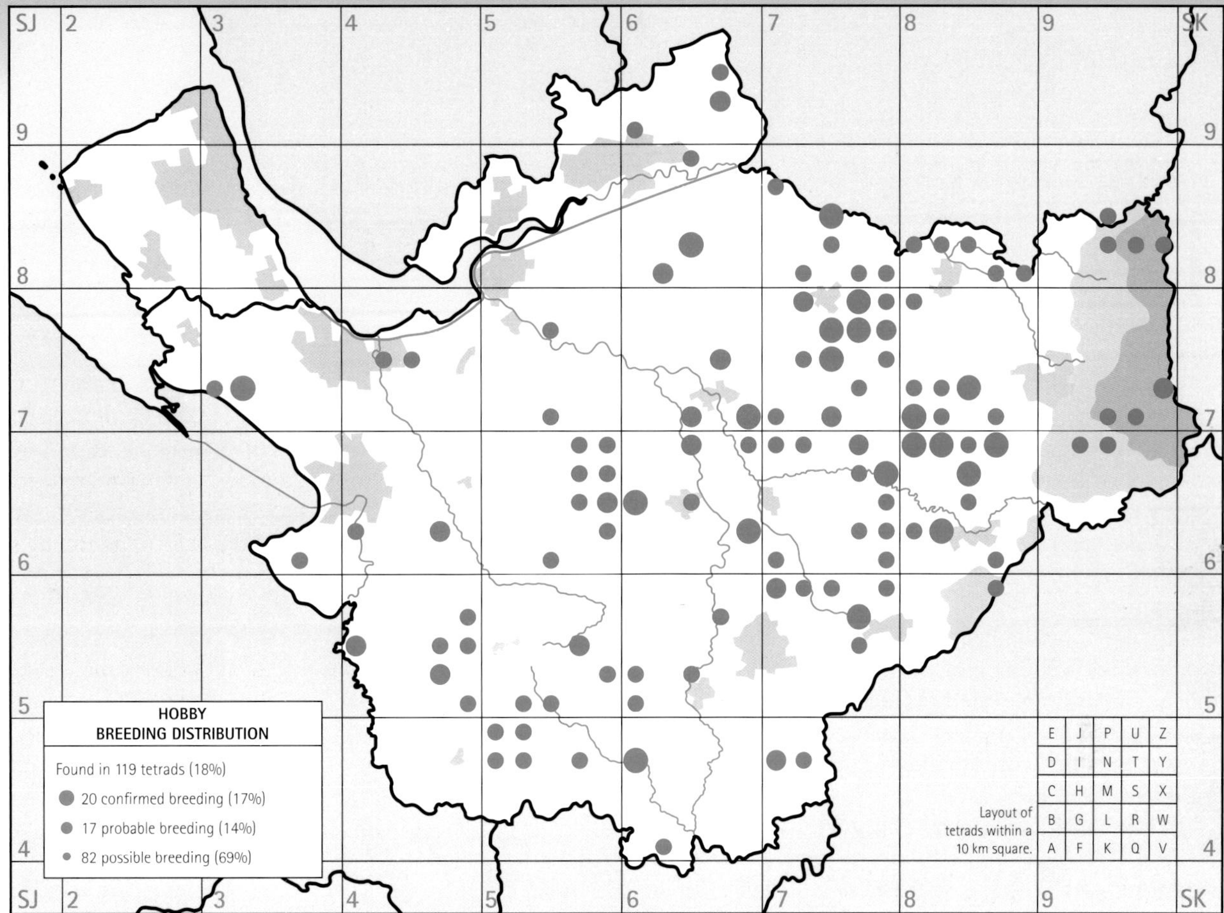

areas with clusters of records. A few of the records might refer to a pair moving across tetrad boundaries, either within a season or from year to year, but there must have been other pairs that were missed, bearing in mind that this is a difficult species in which to prove breeding. Hobbies do not normally breed until two years of age and some of the odd birds that turn up could be non-breeders. Nevertheless, the county total must surely lie in the range 40–50 pairs, probably towards the upper end of that band.

There are several ways of expressing the territory size or nesting density of Hobbies. In prime habitat a pair of Hobbies keeps a home range of about 750 ha, an area of almost two tetrads; the nearest-neighbour spacing between nests averages 4.5 km, ranging from 1.5 to 7.3 km; and a number of English studies find a mean of 1.3–4.9 breeding pairs per 100 km^2 (Chapman 1999). Based on these figures and the Atlas map, some parts of eastern Cheshire must now have reached their carrying capacity and be 'full' of Hobbies, a remarkable position less than a decade after their recolonization of the county.

Peregrine

Falco peregrinus

The Peregrine has been a welcome addition to the county's breeding avifauna since our *First Atlas*, and it is probably only a shortage of nesting sites that inhibits its further expansion. The first breeding in Cheshire was in 1989 after several years of display, on the sandstone cliff of Beeston Castle (SJ55J), followed in 1993 by the county's other major natural site at Helsby (SJ47X). Since then Peregrines have also used a range of industrial structures—oil refinery, power station, railway bridges, a tower on an urban station and a chemical works. The latter site is next to a conveyor belt loading 1,200 tonnes a day of limestone into the plant, with the concomitant noise and dust all day and night. It was singled out for comment in the BTO's 2002 national Peregrine survey (Crick *et al.* 2003)—'Is this the most unusual/inhospitable site for a nesting Peregrine?'—but it has been occupied every year from 1997 onwards. Some other sites have been used for several years then not again.

JEFF CLARKE

The spread into Cheshire and Wirral has been part of the rise of the national Peregrine population, which is now probably larger than it ever has been. The number of UK breeding pairs recorded in the decennial census has grown as follows: 385 pairs in 1961; 489 pairs in 1971; 728 pairs in 1981; 1,283 pairs in 1991; and 1,402 pairs in 2002 (Ratcliffe 1993, Banks *et al.* 2003). The species has largely recovered from the detrimental effects of organochlorine pesticides in the 1950s and 1960s, which manifested themselves especially in thin eggs that broke before hatching. Unhatched eggs from Cheshire nests have been taken, under licence, for analysis and show just 'background' levels of these chemicals, with shells of normal thickness (Norman & Lythgoe 1997).

Most Peregrines return to the breeding area during winter, certainly by February. Adults may well pair for life, but the attachment is to the nest site rather than to each other. The nest in the chemical works mentioned above has been known to have been used by the same female—a distinctively plumaged brown bird—from at least 2000 to 2007, and she has raised 27 chicks during that time, a very high annual average. The birds' usual breeding cycle is to lay four eggs in late March, with the female laying every other day then incubating for about 32 days so that eggs hatch in early May. The male (tiercel) provides most of the food during this time, as he does for the first 10 days or so after the chicks hatch, during which time they cannot regulate their own body temperature and are brooded by their mother. After about 10 days of age the chicks (eyasses) grow their second coat of down and the female leaves the nest ledge to share hunting duties with her mate, returning to feed the chicks, and brood them during rain and overnight. Chicks fledge five to six weeks after hatching, in mid-June, followed by two or three months of decreasing dependence on their parents as they learn the skills needed to catch their own food. At this time chicks can be found in unusual situations, including gardens occasionally.

Recorded Peregrine prey from British eyries includes almost every species of bird from Shelduck to Goldcrest (Ratcliffe 1993). Food items found at Cheshire nests are mainly Feral Pigeons, but Starlings and waders feature regularly, and the remains of a Swift—a rarely recorded prey species—were identified once. They often share nesting sites with potential prey items but appear to declare a truce with their near neighbours, although sometimes chasing them in 'low-intensity' pursuit where it seems that the Peregrine has no intention of killing the target (Ratcliffe 1993).

There are normally five pairs of Peregrine breeding in the county. First-year birds disperse widely, and they do not breed until at least two years of age, so there are likely to be immature birds anywhere in the county during the breeding season; one of the breeding birds had been ringed as a chick in North Yorkshire and moved over 100 km to settle here. There also appear to be several 'spare' adults or pairs, as illustrated in 2001 when the female of the resident pair at Beeston died and was subsequently found to have a tumour in her intestine. Even while she was still alive, but must have been ailing, another female was present, who then immediately moved in with the widowed male. The shortage of suitable nest sites is probably limiting their numbers; an imaginative programme of placing nest-boxes on tall buildings and utility structures would surely benefit Cheshire Peregrines.

Sponsored by Roy Bircumshaw

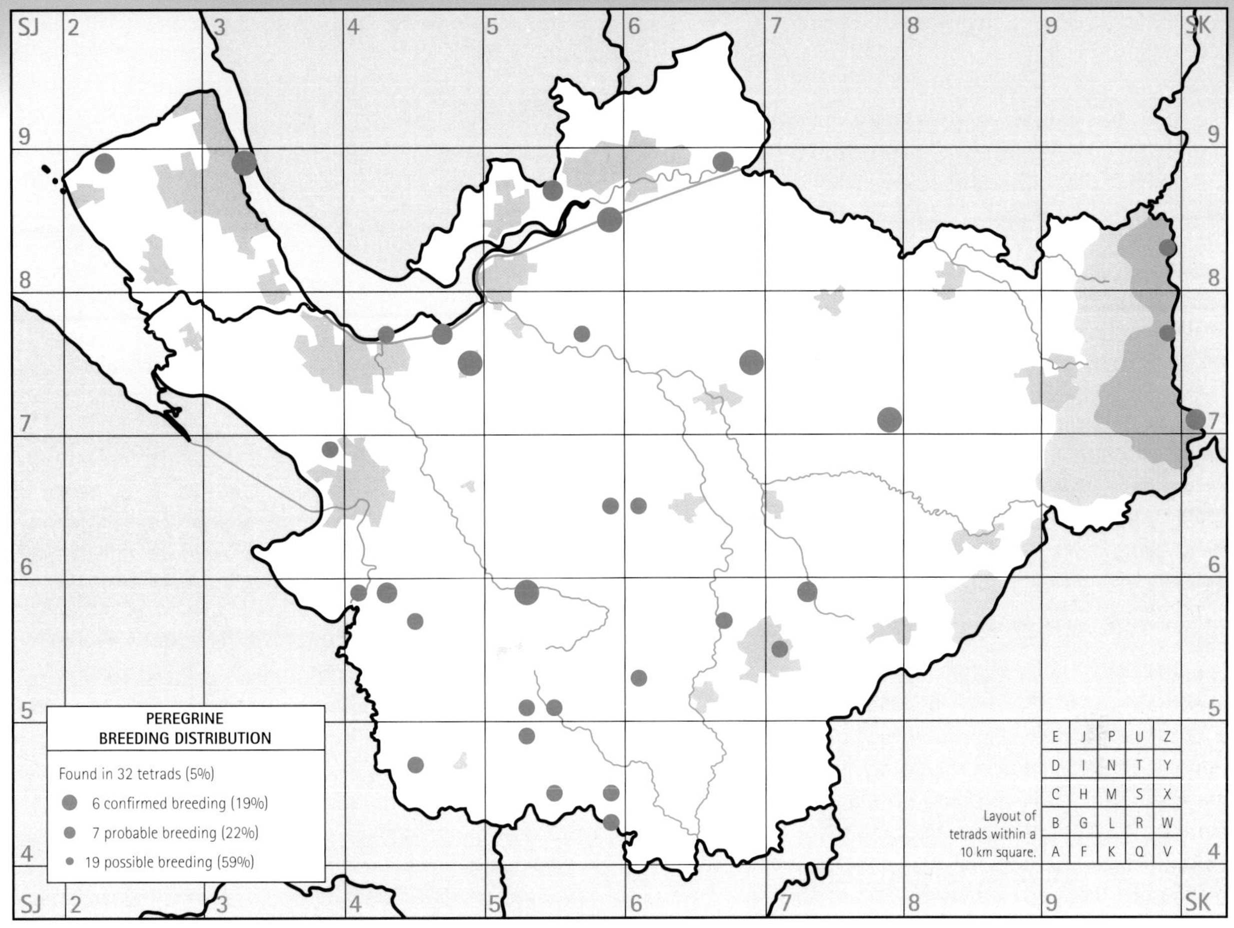

SJ
SK
2
3
4
5
6
7
8
9
PEREGRINE
BREEDING DISTRIBUTION
Found in 32 tetrads (5%)
6 confirmed breeding (19%)
7 probable breeding (22%)
19 possible breeding (59%)
Layout of tetrads within a 10 km square.
E J P U Z
D I N T Y
C H M S X
B G L R W
A F K Q V

There are more Peregrines in the county now than have ever been recorded before, with birds found in winter in almost one-quarter of tetrads. Coward (1910) wrote that one or two annually frequent the Dee estuary, often pursuing the wildfowl and pigeons crossing the water. They were also found in the south-west of the county, apparently feeding on Redwings. Most of the birds known to Coward were shot, and in the hill country 'scarcely a winter passes without one or more being killed on the grouse moors'. Boyd (1951) knew it as an occasional winter visitor to mid-Cheshire.

Peregrines could now potentially be found almost anywhere in the county in winter. Large concentrations of waterfowl obviously attract them, with the Dee and Mersey estuaries and the Dee floods showing on the Atlas map with clusters of occupied tetrads, but they can find food anywhere. Winter Atlas surveyors reported them using a wide range of habitats. Farmland (47% of records) was most common, followed by semi-natural grassland and marsh, mostly salt-marsh, with 13% and human sites on 12%, mostly suburban. Water habitats comprised 9% fresh water and 10% marine, with even woodland and scrub recorded for 7% of tetrads. They take a wide range of prey, almost entirely birds and especially those species that flock, including Woodpigeons, gulls, ducks, waders, gamebirds and Fieldfares. Moorhens must be particularly unlucky as they often feature in lists of Peregrine diet although they do not seem to fit the normal profile of their prey. Urban Peregrines may well subsist almost entirely on Feral Pigeons and Starlings. Many birds are killed by the spectacular stoop, the Peregrine diving from on high and using its advantage of height and speed to knock its prey to the ground, but they also catch birds by flying after them almost in the manner of a Sparrowhawk, or flushing prey as a harrier does. Some birds are taken on the ground as well (Ratcliffe 1993). As with all falcons, the female is bigger than the male, half as heavy again, and she is more likely to take heavier prey. Peregrines occasionally dispossess another raptor of its prey, but Neil Friswell saw the tables turned at Tattenhall (SJ45Z) on 26 January 2005 when a male was chased off its kill by a Raven.

Breeding birds mostly stay in their territories, although a pair may temporarily split up and cover a larger area between them, but young birds disperse in the autumn and the winter birds in the county could have a range of origins. The median distance of movement is 45 km, but some ringed birds have been found more than 200 km from their natal site, although few Scandinavian Peregrines reach the west of Britain (*Migration Atlas*).

The winter population of the UK was estimated as 4,000 birds in the early 1980s (*BTO Winter Atlas*), since when the breeding population has doubled. In the three winters of this Atlas, fieldworkers recorded 95 birds in 74 tetrads in 2004/05, 85 birds in 66 tetrads in 2005/06 and 97 birds in 78 tetrads in 2006/07. Most individuals will range over several tetrads, and there will obviously be much double-counting, but fewer than half of the county's tetrads were visited each winter, and there may well be as many as 50 Peregrines in the county during winter.

STEVE ROUND

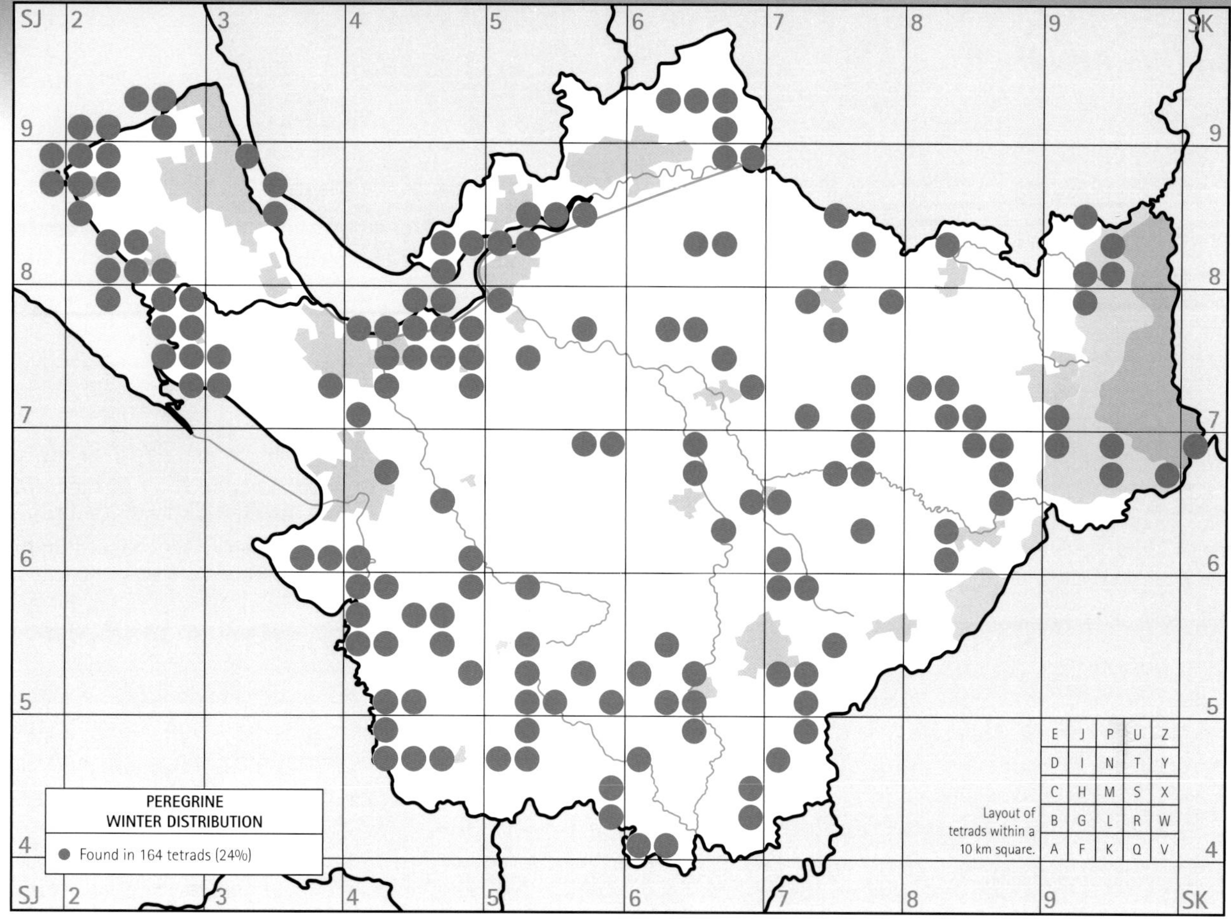
PEREGRINE
WINTER DISTRIBUTION
Found in 164 tetrads (24%)
Layout of tetrads within a 10 km square.
E J P U Z
D I N T Y
C H M S X
B G L R W
A F K Q V
SJ
SK

Water Rail

Rallus aquaticus

STEVE ROUND

This elusive species is seldom seen and birds were most often detected by sound, especially at night when their weird collection of calls—some apparently borrowed from pigs and steam trains—can be heard from a long distance. Fieldworkers found birds in all types of standing water, from small ponds to large meres, and in all of the damp categories of semi-natural grassland, with most recorded in areas of rushes, sedges and *phragmites* reeds. A detailed study of the species' habitat preferences found that they were significantly more abundant in areas of *phragmites* in standing water (Jenkins & Ormerod 2002),

Water Rails were proven to breed in eight tetrads, more than ever before in the county. In all of these cases, observers saw adults with chicks: they have been reported from early May to August, presumably indicating two broods. All of the definite or probable breeding tetrads were towards the north of the county, and the sites at which breeding was confirmed read like a roll-call of the county's main wetlands: Woolston Eyes, Risley Moss, Rostherne Mere, Fiddler's Ferry (the first breeding there) and Neumann's Flash. Water Rails have colonized the north Wirral since our *First Atlas*, with alarm calls heard in 2004 and 2005 from birds in Red Rocks Marsh (SJ28E) where they were first proven to breed in 2001. The species has not been recorded in the east of Cheshire since they favour the eutrophic lowland waters. They mainly eat aquatic invertebrates but will also take vegetable matter and occasionally fish and amphibians.

Water Rails were reported in 31 tetrads during the three years, with breeding confirmed in eight and probable, through recording of pairs, display or alarm calls, in a further four. Nineteen tetrads were logged with possible breeding through observers seeing individuals or hearing breeding calls. Eight of the tetrads had also had breeding season records during our *First Atlas*, with 'gains' in 23 tetrads and 'losses' from 18. Work elsewhere has shown that thorough surveying of areas of suitable habitat, including playback of the birds' calls (Jenkins & Ormerod 2002), usually reveals many more birds than were previously suspected. At least nine pairs and two single birds were found in 2002 in an RSPB census of *phragmites/scirpus/juncus/typha* reed-beds at Neston, Burton Point and Inner Marsh Farm (Wells 2002). The breeding population of Cheshire and Wirral is likely to be at least 20 pairs.

The national total is unknown, but Brown and Grice (2005) suggest a figure for England probably in excess of 1,000 pairs. Water Rail has now (2007) been added to the list of species monitored by the UK Rare Breeding Birds Panel because of its perceived scarcity. There has been some concern over the species' status and conservation, causing it to be placed on the Amber List, not least because their breeding range contracted significantly between the two national Atlases (1968–72 and 1988–91).

Sponsored by Marc Granville

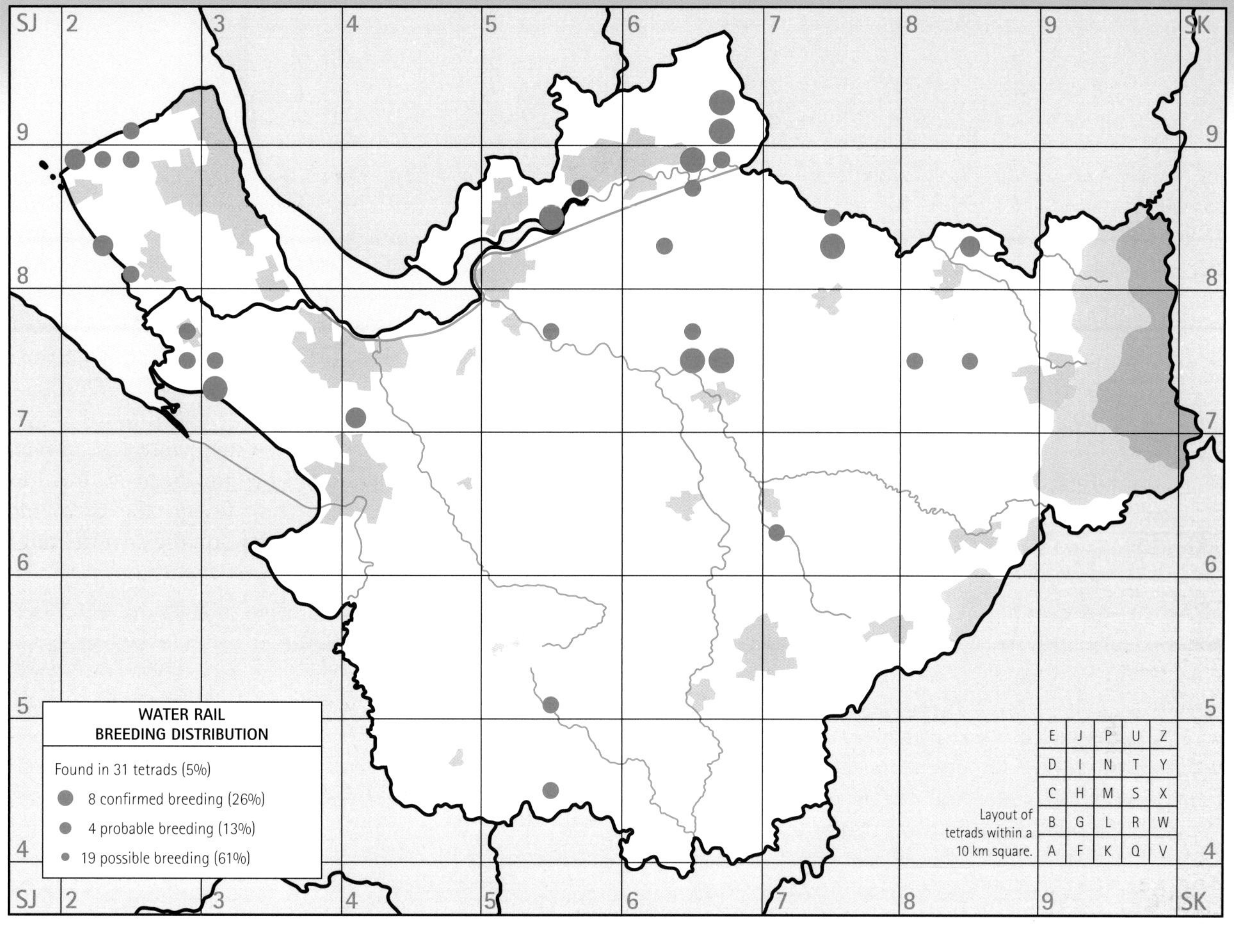

SJ
2
3
4
5
6
7
8
9
SK
WATER RAIL
BREEDING DISTRIBUTION
Found in 31 tetrads (5%)
8 confirmed breeding (26%)
4 probable breeding (13%)
19 possible breeding (61%)
Layout of tetrads within a 10 km square.
E J P U Z
D I N T Y
C H M S X
B G L R W
A F K Q V

SJ
2
3
4
5
6
7
8
9
SK
WATER RAIL
CHANGE IN BREEDING DISTRIBUTION
23 present during 2004–06, not during 1978–84 ('gain')
8 present during both Atlases
18 present during 1978–84, not during 2004–06 ('loss')
Layout of tetrads within a 10 km square.
E J P U Z
D I N T Y
C H M S X
B G L R W
A F K Q V

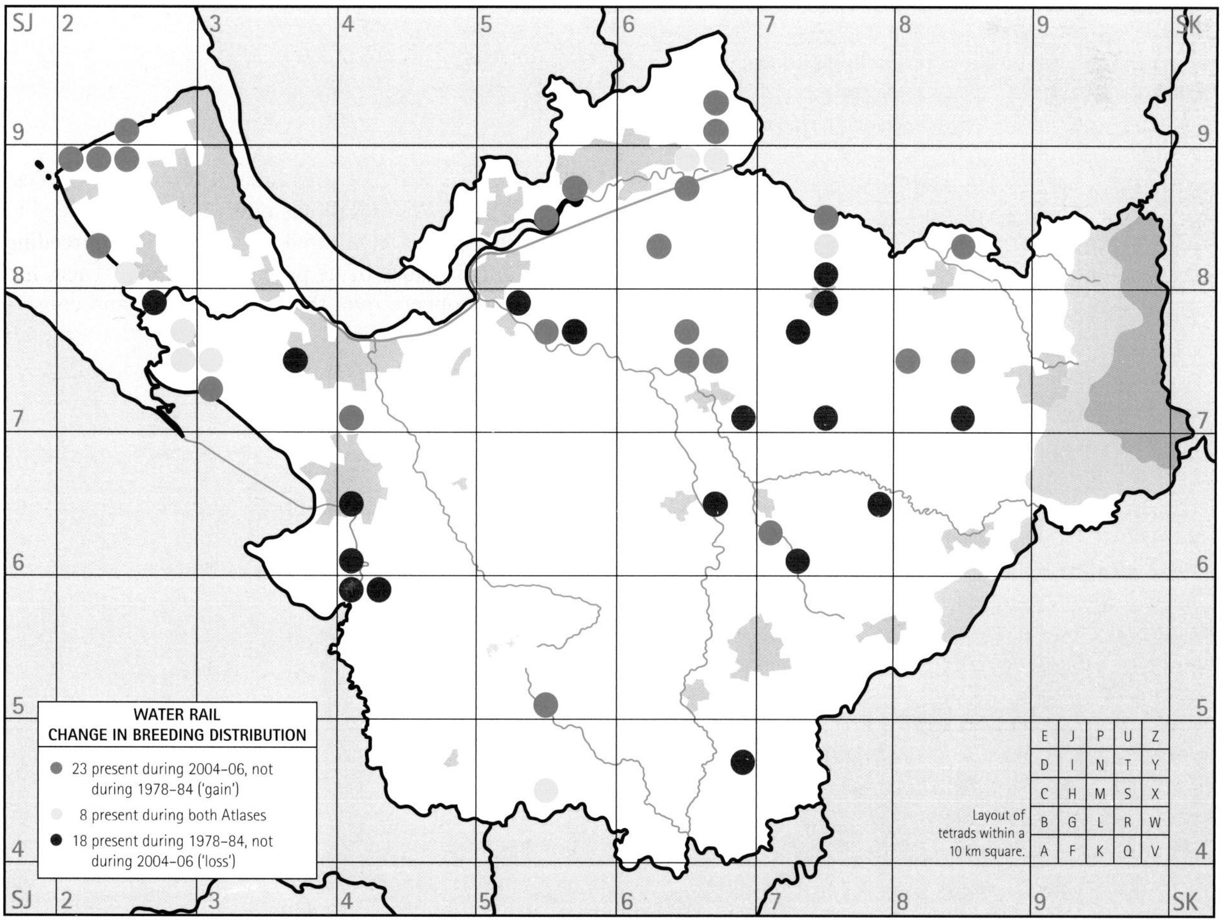

Water Rails are much more numerous in winter, when resident birds are joined by immigrants from northern and north-eastern Europe, especially Germany and Denmark (*Migration Atlas*). As is illustrated by the preponderance of blue dots in the 'difference' map, Water Rails become much more widespread in winter. The species occurred in both seasons in 21 tetrads, was found in 10 during the breeding season but not in winter, but was recorded in 63 tetrads during winter only. Despite this impressive total, Water Rails may be underrecorded as they can be difficult to detect and are usually silent in winter.

Because they can be hard to find elsewhere, it has long been traditional for birdwatchers to travel to Parkgate to see Water Rails flushed from the salt-marsh by high tides, although sometimes they have to be alert if they wish to see the rails alive; for instance, eight were simultaneously being eaten by Grey Herons in February 1974, and ten were seen there on 11 January 1997, of which seven were killed and eaten by Great Black-backed Gulls. Numbers in the Dee salt-marshes have much reduced from the 140 counted in February 1974, perhaps a result of warmer winters making inland fresh waters more suitable. Sixteen has been the maximum recorded on a WeBS count there this decade, with 30 birds the highest Dee count on any winter day during this three-year Atlas, in SJ27U in 2006/07.

Such congregations are unusual, with the Dee flock nationally renowned, and normally Water Rails are solitary or only loosely gregarious during the winter months (*BTO Winter Atlas*): half of the submitted records for this Atlas were of single birds only. The total of 11 birds, counted in overgrown ditches near West Kirby (SJ28I) in 2004/05, was exceptional, with figures of six at Woolston and five at Rostherne the next highest inland counts. There are usually far more birds present than are seen, however, as illustrated by the total of 17 birds trapped by ringers at Woolston during winter 2001/02. An idea of the density attainable is shown by the finding of seven Water Rails using a small Welsh reed-bed only 0.5 ha in extent, birds maintaining loose winter territories within the site (Jenkins *et al.* 1995). Their winter diet is much the same as in the breeding season: aquatic invertebrates from insects and larvae to shrimps and molluscs; any animals that they encounter, including frogs and newts; plus some vegetable matter, especially the nutritious roots and rhizomes. When food is hard to find, they turn to carrion and killing their own prey, including small mammals and birds. Birds leave inland waters if they freeze over, but are likely to return to the site, even to the same part of the water, when it thaws (Jenkins *et al.* 1995).

Compared to the breeding season, Water Rails were much more likely to be found on larger waters, 21 of the 46 records on fresh water being on lakes, meres and reservoirs, with only 10 on small waterbodies or ponds; 15 were on the flowing water of rivers, streams and ditches and none on canals. By far the most commonly recorded habitat code was C7 (reed swamp).

Coward (1910) wrote that more were seen in winter than summer, but he wondered how much of this was due to its skulking habits rather than to any increase in numbers. Bell (1962) recognized that many wintering birds were likely to be immigrants, and said that it was seen and heard not only in the reed-beds around the meres, but was a regular visitor to suitable habitats both in the Dee and Mersey estuaries. There were just two records of single birds on the Mersey during this Atlas.

GARY BELLINGHAM

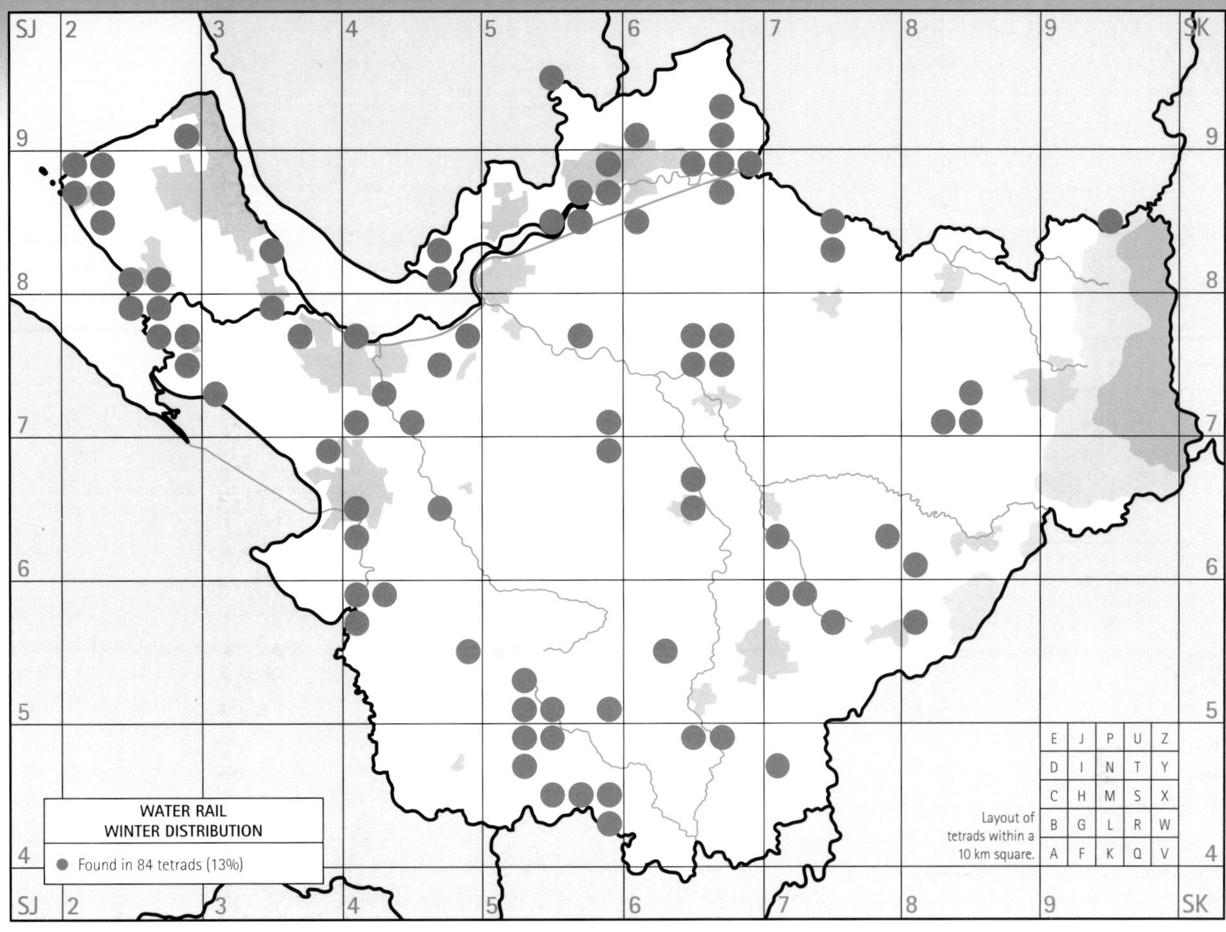
SJ
2
3
4
5
6
7
8
9
SK
9
8
7
6
5
4
WATER RAIL
WINTER DISTRIBUTION
Found in 84 tetrads (13%)
E J P U Z
D I N T Y
C H M S X
B G L R W
A F K Q V
Layout of tetrads within a 10 km square.

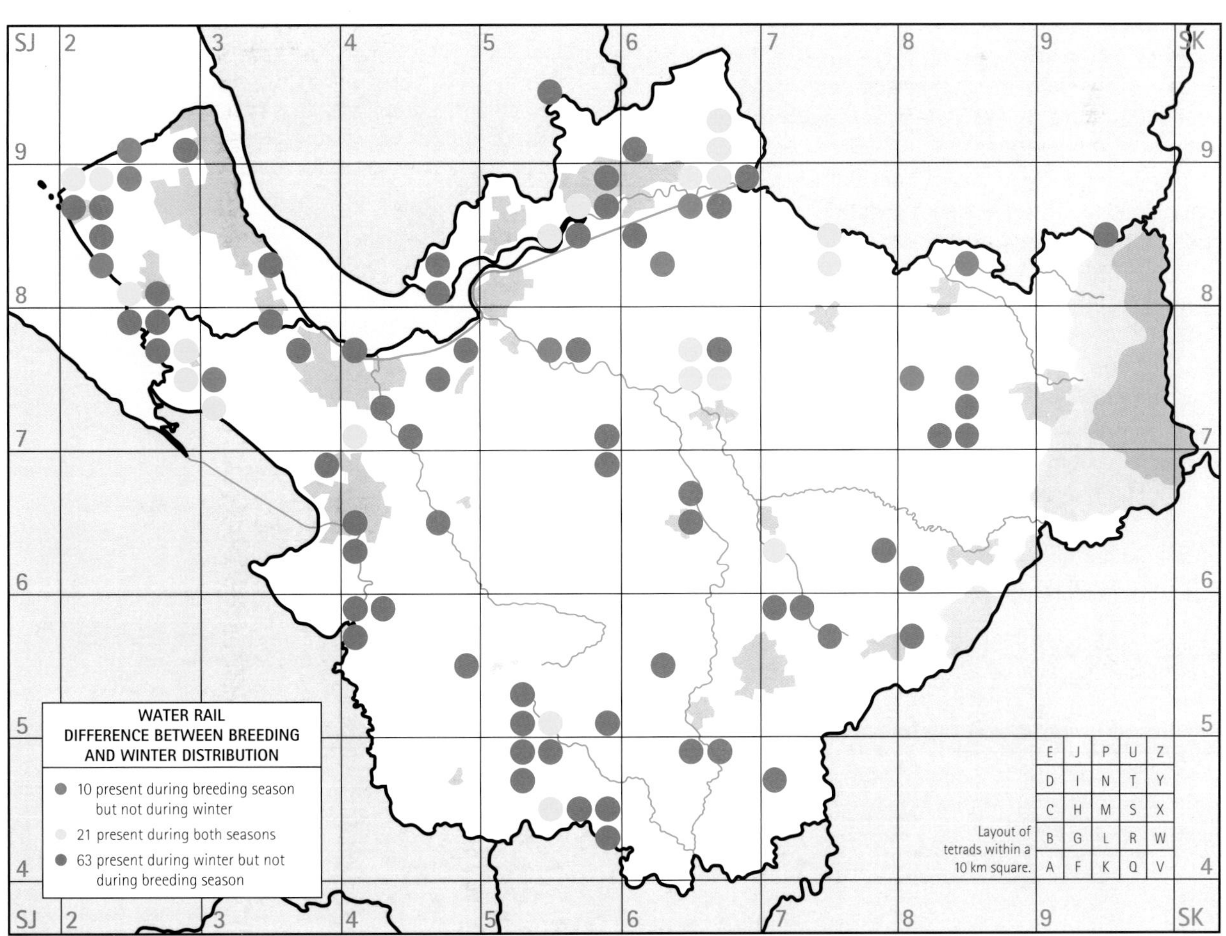
SJ
2
3
4
5
6
7
8
9
SK
9
8
7
6
5
4
WATER RAIL
DIFFERENCE BETWEEN BREEDING AND WINTER DISTRIBUTION
10 present during breeding season but not during winter
21 present during both seasons
63 present during winter but not during breeding season
E J P U Z
D I N T Y
C H M S X
B G L R W
A F K Q V
Layout of tetrads within a 10 km square.

Moorhen

Gallinula chloropus

Moorhens are present in the breeding season almost everywhere in Cheshire and Wirral up to an altitude of about 250 m in the eastern hills. This is our second most widespread breeding waterbird, headed only by Mallard. There has been a small net loss of 17 tetrads relative to our *First Atlas*, possibly from an element of underrecording, but perhaps birds have been displaced from some areas by the move of many Coots to smaller waters. Richard Elphick and Mike Scott, however, recorded Moorhens 'nesting amicably in a small pool with nesting Coots' near Alderley Edge (SJ87T). This species needs waters with some fringing vegetation, and readily suffers from unsympathetic riparian management.

They build their nest from the broad leaves of aquatic plants, the female laying an average of six eggs and sharing the three weeks of incubation with the male. They sometimes surprise observers by nesting in trees, using an old nest of a corvid or other species. Proof of breeding was obtained in 83% of the tetrads in which they were recorded, mostly (426 out of 488) from observers seeing chicks during an extended season lasting from mid-April onwards, often into September. The adults often build one or more 'brood platforms', rudimentary nest-like structures on which the chicks can rest, wait for food to be brought to them, roost overnight and perhaps escape predation from pike. Mink are a big problem for them, however, as can be cats when they spread out onto waterside meadows and lawns. Moorhens usually raise two broods of chicks, sometimes even three, and adopt an unusual breeding strategy in which the first-brood chicks help to feed their younger siblings from the second nest, thus helping to relieve the burden on their parents and giving themselves some practice for their own breeding attempts in the next year. Some nests hold more than the normal size of clutch, either from egg-dumping by neighbouring females, or because of cooperative nesting when two, three or four females were paired to the same male (*BTO Second Atlas*). In cooperative nesting, the females share the parental duties along with the male; where studied in detail, the females have been shown to be mother and daughter.

Moorhens were frequently noted nesting on ponds in gardens, farms and on golf courses. The recorded habitats show 35% on ponds and 33% on small waterbodies, with only 15% using the larger meres, lakes and reservoirs; 17% of breeding Moorhens were on linear watercourses, mostly canals, where they seem content to co-exist with traffic from holidaying narrow boats. A count in 1996 found seven nests along a 6 km stretch of the Bridgewater Canal near Warrington and in 1998 ten pairs were reported on 4.3 km of the Shropshire Union in south Cheshire (*CWBR*).

The BTO analysis of the Cheshire and Wirral BBS data shows that the breeding population in 2004–05 was 7,940 birds (5,420–10,460), corresponding to an average of about seven pairs per tetrad with confirmed or probable breeding. This is one of the few species where this survey gives a population figure significantly lower than the estimate from our *First Atlas*, which was 6,000 pairs. It is not known if this represents a real drop or an overestimate of the 1984 total. Nationally, the breeding population of Moorhen has been fairly stable, dropping in years following extra mortality in hard winters. Reductions in the number and quality of farmland ponds, and the spread of mink along watercourses, have been suggested as possible causes of decline.

Nevertheless, 7,940 birds is more than 2.2% of the British population, showing that the county is disproportionately important for the species.

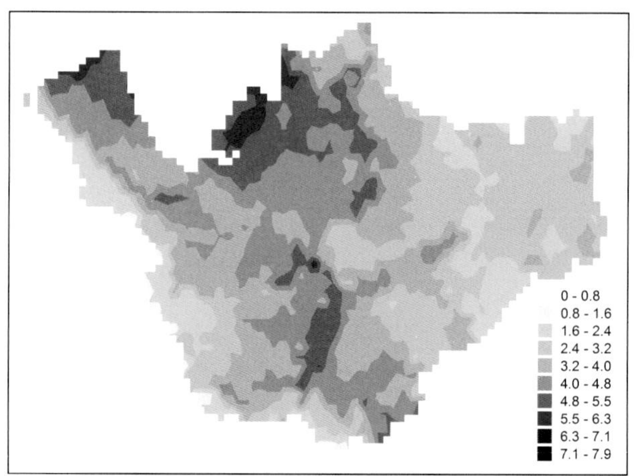

Moorhen abundance.

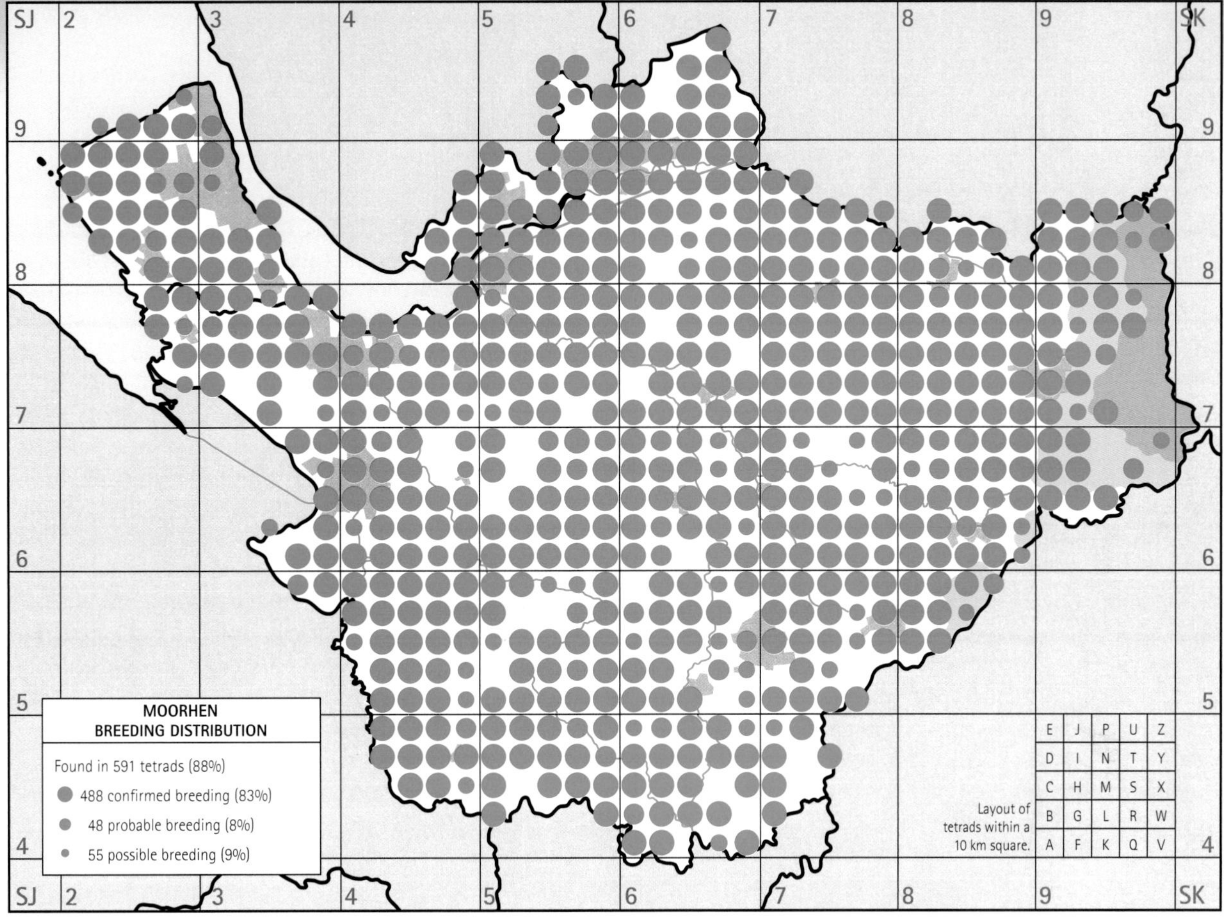
SJ
SK
MOORHEN
BREEDING DISTRIBUTION
Found in 591 tetrads (88%)
488 confirmed breeding (83%)
48 probable breeding (8%)
55 possible breeding (9%)
Layout of tetrads within a 10 km square.
E J P U Z
D I N T Y
C H M S X
B G L R W
A F K Q V

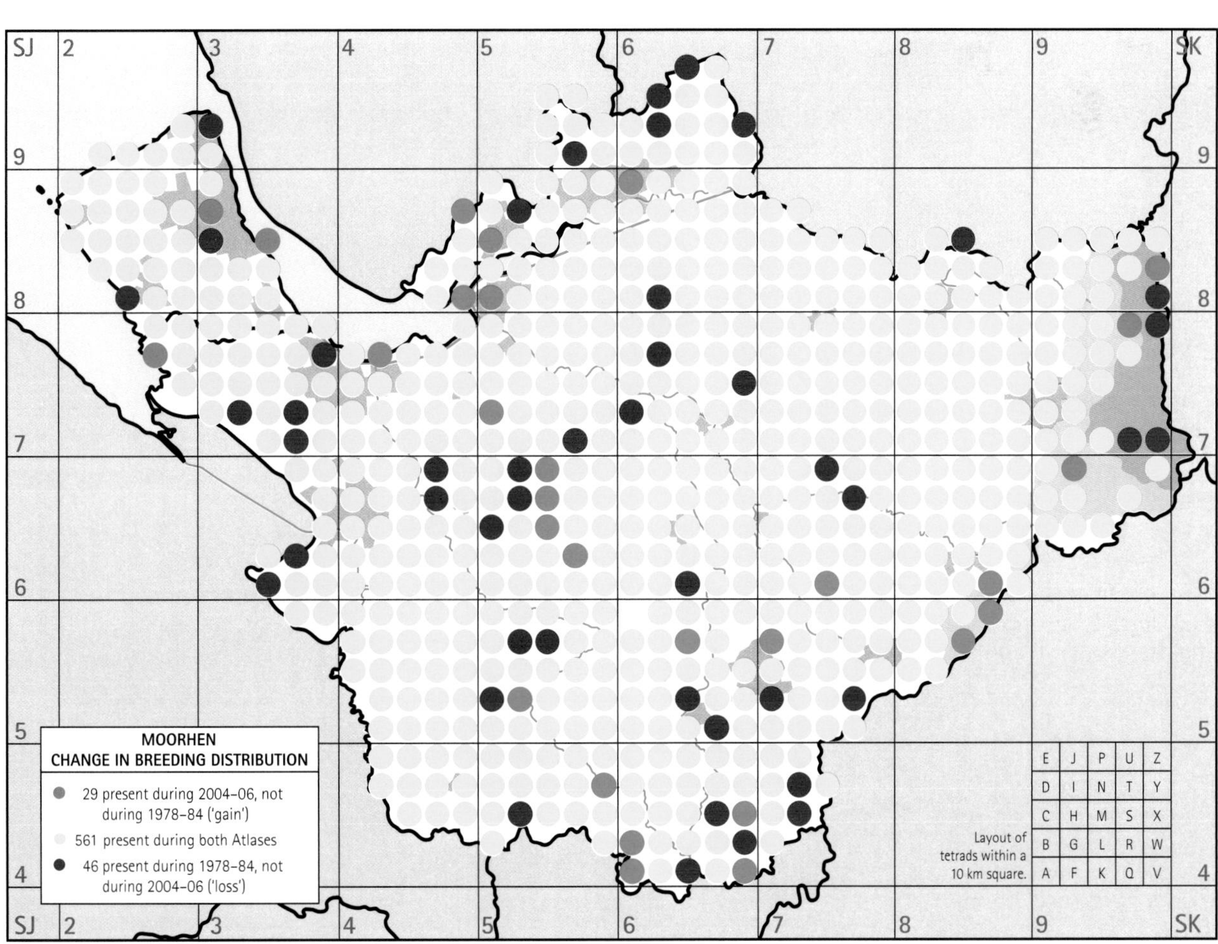
SJ
SK
MOORHEN
CHANGE IN BREEDING DISTRIBUTION
29 present during 2004–06, not during 1978–84 ('gain')
561 present during both Atlases
46 present during 1978–84, not during 2004–06 ('loss')
Layout of tetrads within a 10 km square.
E J P U Z
D I N T Y
C H M S X
B G L R W
A F K Q V

British Moorhens are highly sedentary, but are joined in winter by migrants from continental Europe, especially the Netherlands, Germany and Denmark (*Migration Atlas*). A bird ringed at Woolston in February 2007 was found in Denmark in October 2007.

As expected for a sedentary species, there was little difference between the breeding and wintering distribution. They were recorded in both seasons in 547 tetrads, in 38 in winter only, and in 44 in the breeding season only, half of these in a relatively small area in the centre of the county: the apparent absence in winter in parts of SJ56 and SJ66 merits further investigation. Moorhens normally avoid the highest ground (*BTO Winter Atlas*) but, oddly, birds were found in four tetrads in the highest eastern hills where they did not breed. An interesting comment on its behaviour in one upland tetrad, near Oakgrove (SJ96J), where the species does breed, came from Steve and Gill Barber: 'on a cold morning after a heavy frost we watched this bird as it grazed an area of short (sheep-grazed) grass high on a gorsey hillside'.

Moorhens eat a variety of plant and insect food, collected from in or near water, including seeds, fruit, pondweeds, worms, fish and carrion. More than one-third of records came from the smallest ponds, and in winter they stay on the small ponds but tend to retreat from other standing waterbodies, perhaps because of competition from flocks of waterfowl. The proportion on linear watercourses (G6 to G10) grew from 17% in the breeding season to 24% in winter, spread evenly across ditches, streams, rivers and canals. A century ago, Coward (1910) noted that 'in winter, when the ponds are frozen, it resorts to running water' and evidently some birds shift habitat even in the warmer climes of today. Moorhens quite frequently venture out of water, especially in damp grassy areas, and observers in 55 tetrads recorded them on agricultural grassland; they scamper back to the safety of water when alarmed, sometimes submerging with just the tip of the bill showing.

This bird is mostly a creature of fresh water, although a few gather on the Dee salt-marsh, 25 being flushed by high tide in winter 2006/07 at Gayton Sands (SJ27U). They seldom gather in large flocks and it is estimated that waters covered by WeBS counts hold only 1% of the British population (Brown & Grice 2005). In this Atlas, more than half of counts were of just one or two birds, and 90% of them were of 10 birds or fewer. The largest flock was 71 at Gilroy Road Nature Reserve, West Kirby (SJ28I), counted by Chris Butterworth, double the next highest counts, 35 by Mary Prince and Susan Bastin on the Shropshire Union Canal at Christleton (SJ46M) and the same total by Alan Booth at Redes Mere (SJ87L).

RICHARD STEEL

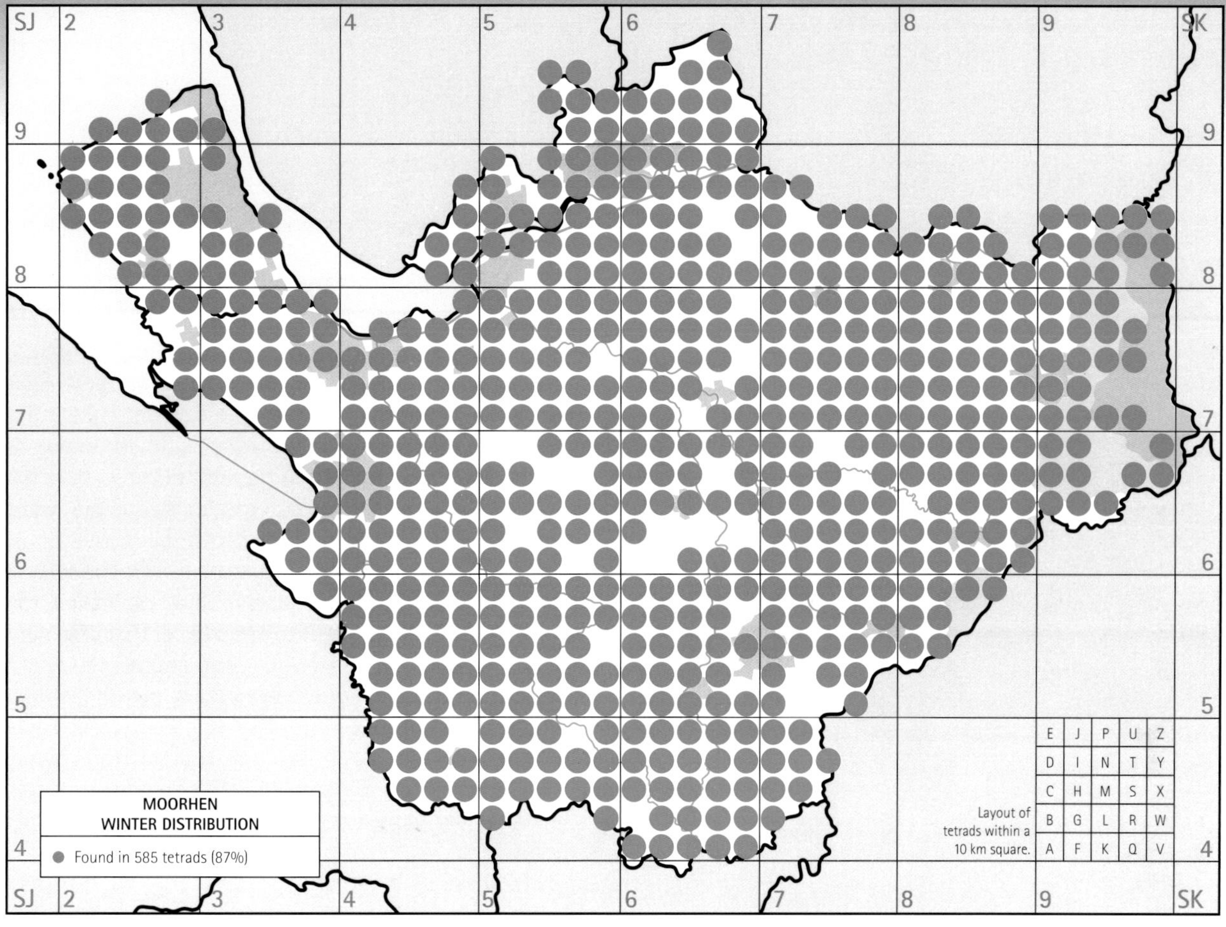
SJ
2
3
4
5
6
7
8
9
SK
MOORHEN
WINTER DISTRIBUTION
Found in 585 tetrads (87%)
Layout of
tetrads within a
10 km square.
E J P U Z
D I N T Y
C H M S X
B G L R W
A F K Q V

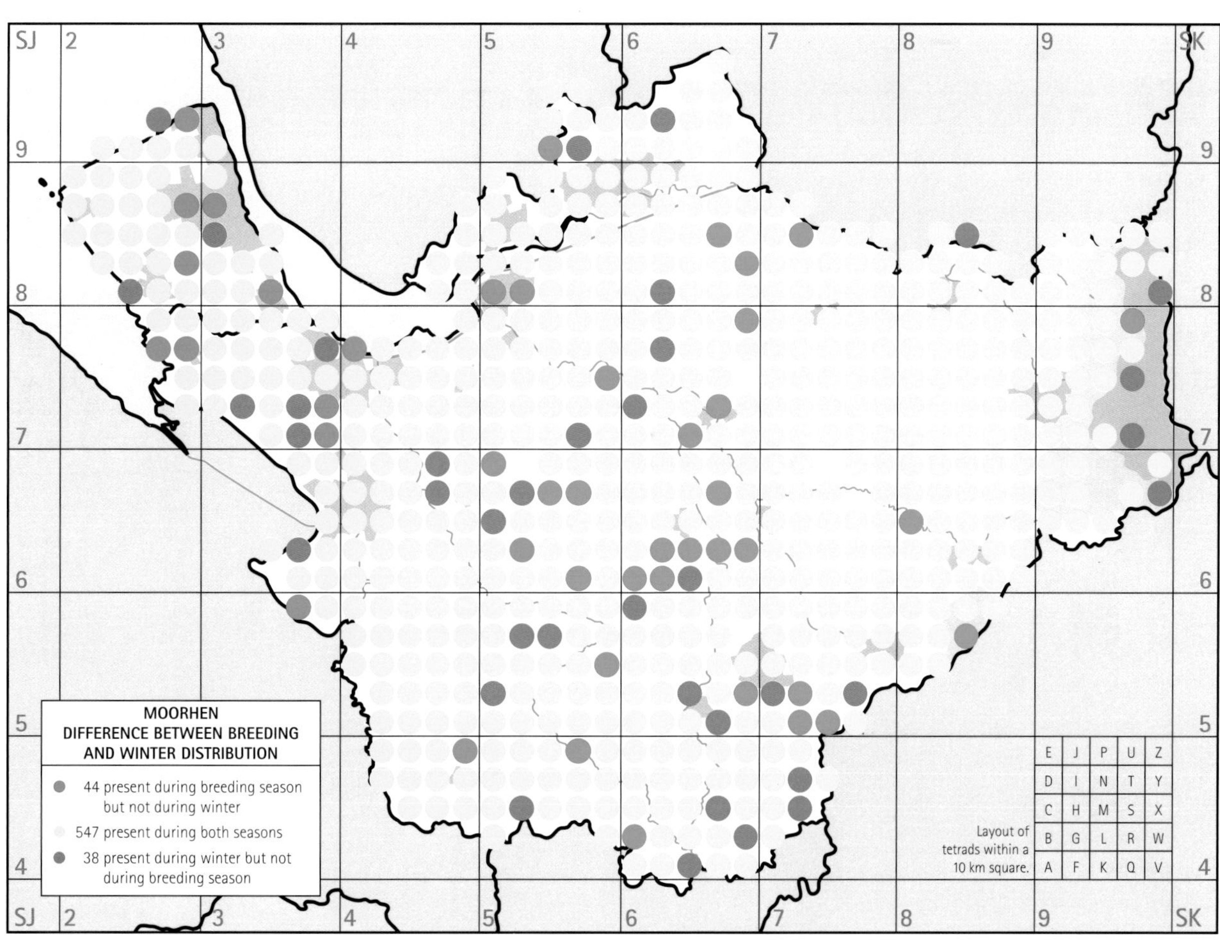
SJ
2
3
4
5
6
7
8
9
SK
MOORHEN
DIFFERENCE BETWEEN BREEDING
AND WINTER DISTRIBUTION
44 present during breeding season but not during winter
547 present during both seasons
38 present during winter but not during breeding season
Layout of
tetrads within a
10 km square.
E J P U Z
D I N T Y
C H M S X
B G L R W
A F K Q V

Coot

Fulica atra

BEN HALL

'A typical bird of all but the smallest waters in the county' were the first words of the text for Coot in our *First Atlas*, but in the last twenty years they have spread to smaller waters and this has allowed them to extend their distribution by as many as 77 extra tetrads. The recorded habitats show 20% on ponds and 41% on small waterbodies, with 31% using meres, lakes and reservoirs; 8% of breeding Coots were on linear watercourses, mostly canals. The species is now widespread across Cheshire but Coots are missing from much of the highest land, in the east of Cheshire and in the Delamere area: they need water with abundant supplies of floating or submerged vegetation to provide the diet for themselves and their chicks. They have spread to most of north Wirral but are scarce on the rest of the peninsula, in line with the sparsity of inland waters there, and have abandoned parts of Ellesmere Port and Neston district that were occupied in the *First Atlas*.

Since then, the national population index for Coot has risen substantially, by around two-thirds in the BTO's general breeding bird surveys although by much less on linear waterways. The BTO analysis of the county's BBS transects shows that the breeding population of Cheshire and Wirral in 2004–05 was 4,430 birds (2,000–6,850), corresponding to an average of more than six pairs per tetrad with confirmed or probable breeding. This is about 1.9% of the British population, showing that the county is disproportionately important for the species. Some locations hold quite high numbers of Coots. In the last decade, at least 10 broods in a year have been recorded at many of the county's well-watched sites: Chelford Sand Quarries, Radnor Mere, Sandbach Flashes, Budworth Mere, Moore Nature Reserve and Inner Marsh Farm. High counts were 21 broods at Rostherne in 2000, at least 19 nests seen on Frodsham no. 5 bed on 13 May 2000, and at least 49 broods at Woolston in 2004, the highest total there for twenty years.

This is an easy species to prove breeding, with 80% of records being two-letter codes. Most of these (267 out of 326) came from observers seeing Coot chicks, but the conspicuous nature of their nests is illustrated by as many as 59 tetrads for which the highest level of proof was an adult on eggs: their bulky nest may be hidden in a reed-bed, but often is clearly visible.

In February or March, Coots switch behaviour from their winter flocking to become aggressively territorial as the breeding season approaches. Disputes with neighbours can turn into fights, birds using their sharp claws to strike at each other, sometimes causing injury. Most Coots do not breed until two years of age, so there can be a lot of immature birds to test territory boundaries. The typical clutch of six eggs, maybe up to ten, is incubated by the female for three weeks with the male nearby.

The chicks start out with spiky red down and only gradually change to look like their parents during the two-month fledging period; they are fed by their parents, who often split the brood and care for two or three chicks each. Coots usually rear only one brood, but may have multiple nesting attempts until they are successful, so the breeding season can extend from March to July. Their nests and chicks are vulnerable to predation, perhaps especially by mink: Sheila Blamire recorded the mustelid equivalent of chutzpah when she saw a mink asleep in an empty Coot's nest at Mere (SJ78F)!

Sponsored by Roger and Kay Millen

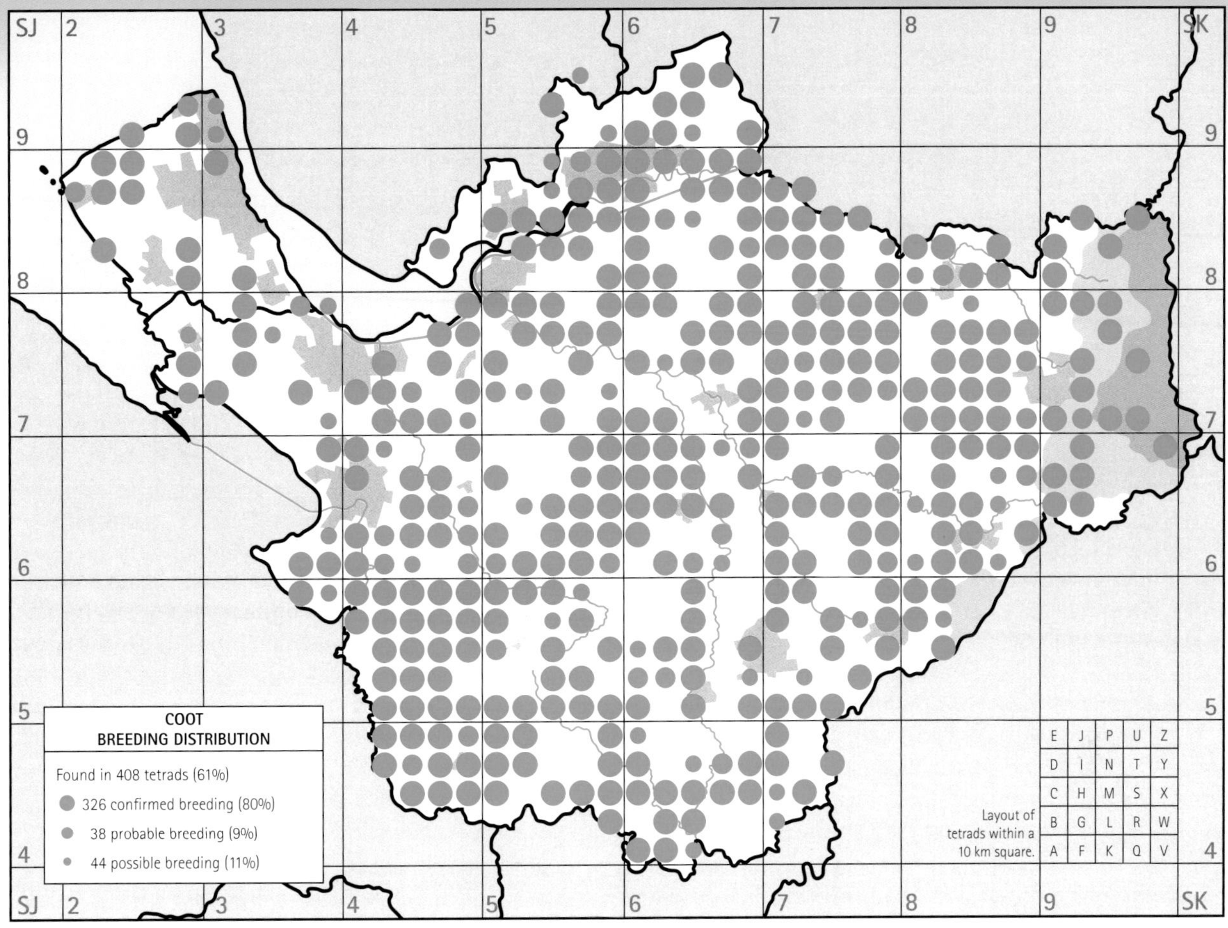
SJ
SK
COOT
BREEDING DISTRIBUTION
Found in 408 tetrads (61%)
326 confirmed breeding (80%)
38 probable breeding (9%)
44 possible breeding (11%)
Layout of
tetrads within a
10 km square.
E J P U Z
D I N T Y
C H M S X
B G L R W
A F K Q V

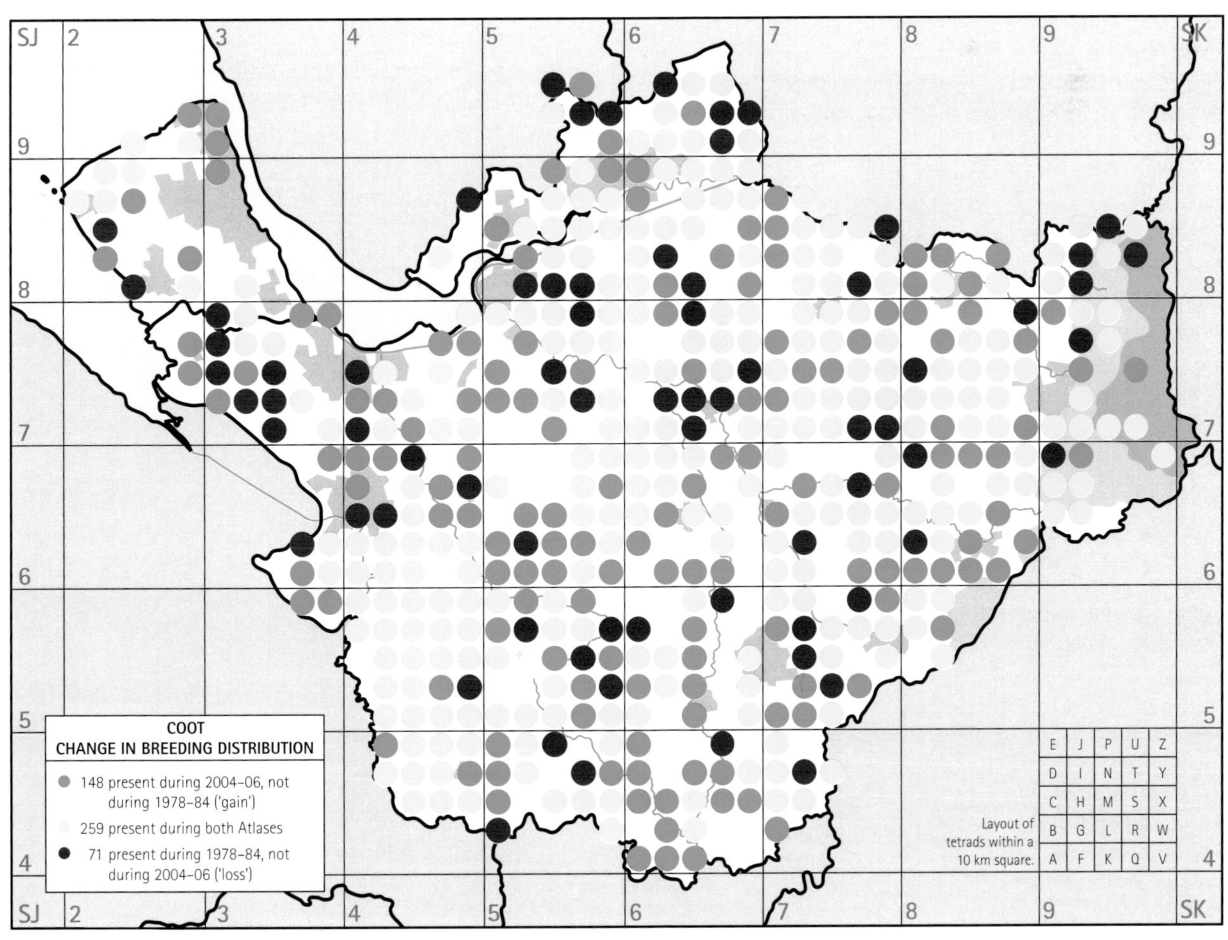
SJ
SK
COOT
CHANGE IN BREEDING DISTRIBUTION
148 present during 2004–06, not during 1978–84 ('gain')
259 present during both Atlases
71 present during 1978–84, not during 2004–06 ('loss')
Layout of
tetrads within a
10 km square.
E J P U Z
D I N T Y
C H M S X
B G L R W
A F K Q V

After the breeding season, Coots abandon their territoriality and gather into flocks, where our resident birds are joined by immigrants from continental Europe (*Migration Atlas*). Birds are seldom seen in flight, however—they mostly migrate at night—and little is known about the origins of Coot wintering in Cheshire and Wirral. They abandon some of their breeding tetrads for the winter: this Atlas shows that they were found in both seasons in 313 tetrads, with 95 occupied in the breeding season but not in winter, and 56 used in winter but not for breeding.

The major site for Coots in Cheshire and Wirral is Doddington Pool (SJ74D), where 884 birds were counted in November 2004, not far short of its record winter flock of 1,300 in November 2001. The Doddington gathering was more than twice the size of the next largest reported flock during this Atlas period, 400 on Redes Mere (SJ87K), and Deer Park Mere (SJ55F/K) was the only other site holding flocks more than 200 strong. Other sites that have sporadically recorded more than 200 birds in the last decade include most of the larger lowland waters: Budworth Mere, Chelford Sand Quarries, Houghton Green Pool, Sandbach Flashes, Radnor Mere, Moore Nature Reserve, Rostherne Mere and, briefly, Frodsham Marsh no. 6 bed when pumping of dredgings from the Manchester Ship Canal first started in 1995/96. No site in the county approaches the threshold for national importance, currently set at 1,730 birds.

Several of those sites have long been favoured by Coots: Bell (1962) lists Radnor Mere, Doddington, Rostherne 'and particularly Tabley, where flocks of up to 400 have occurred'. Doddington Pool was the most frequently mentioned location in the early years of the *CWBRs*, holding 400 or more birds in the mid-1960s. The sizes of the large flocks have grown over the years, and their national winter population index on sites monitored by WeBS has also increased, by about one-third in the last 20 years (Banks *et al.* 2006).

The habitats used by Coots during winter are much the same as in the breeding season, although there is a small shift away from the smallest standing waters (G1 and G2) to linear watercourses (G6 to G10) whose proportion rises from 8% to 13%: most of these birds are on canals. This is a freshwater bird and there was only one estuarine record, two birds in the Mersey (SJ48V): the three-figure totals in the Dee WeBS come from the inclusion of birds on the pools at Inner Marsh Farm with those of the estuary. Coward (1910) reported that Coots were common in the Dee estuary in severe winters. This, however, has not been borne out by any records published thereafter (Bell 1962). In periods of hard weather in recent years, birds have flocked together on unfrozen waters, including the deeper meres and rivers, especially the lower Weaver.

SIMON BOOTH

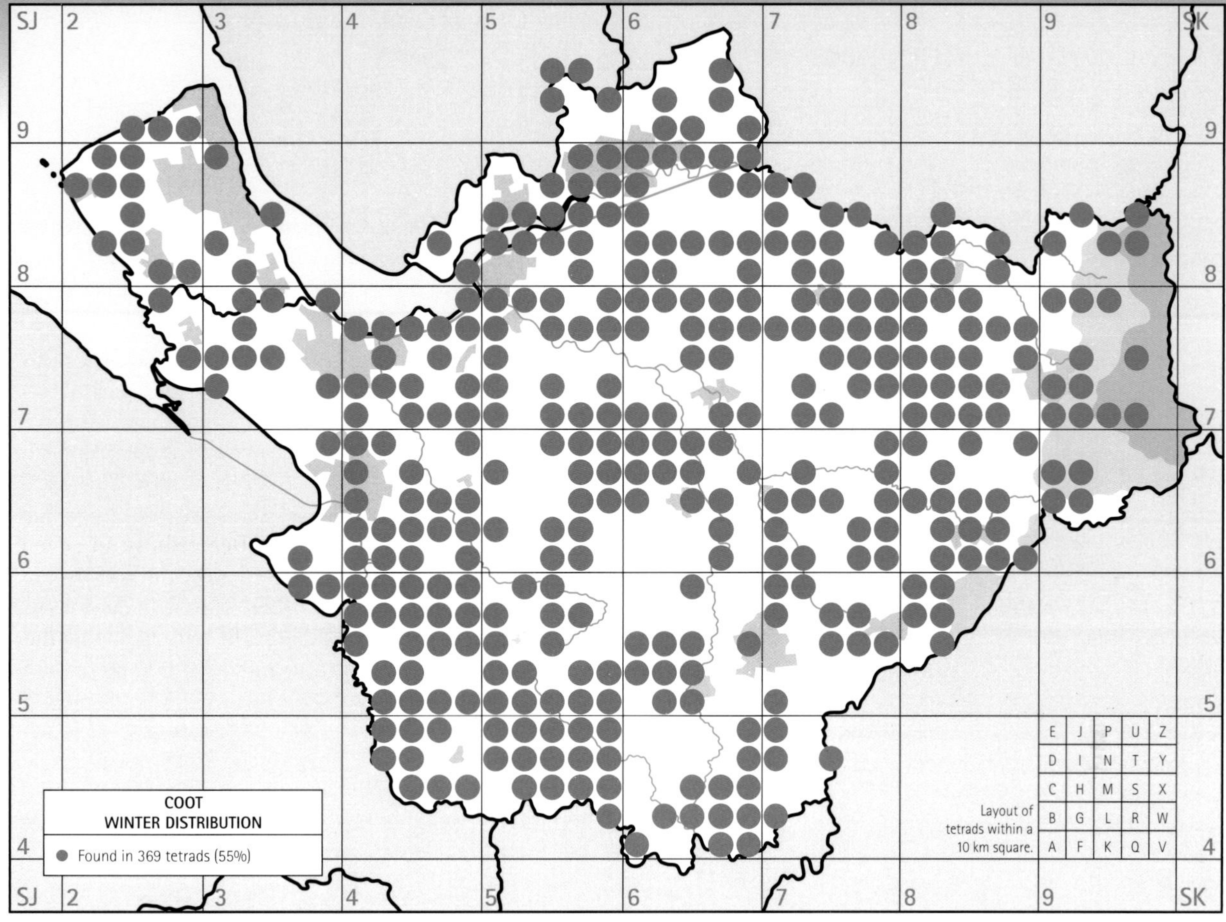
COOT
WINTER DISTRIBUTION
Found in 369 tetrads (55%)
Layout of tetrads within a 10 km square.
E J P U Z
D I N T Y
C H M S X
B G L R W
A F K Q V
SJ
SK

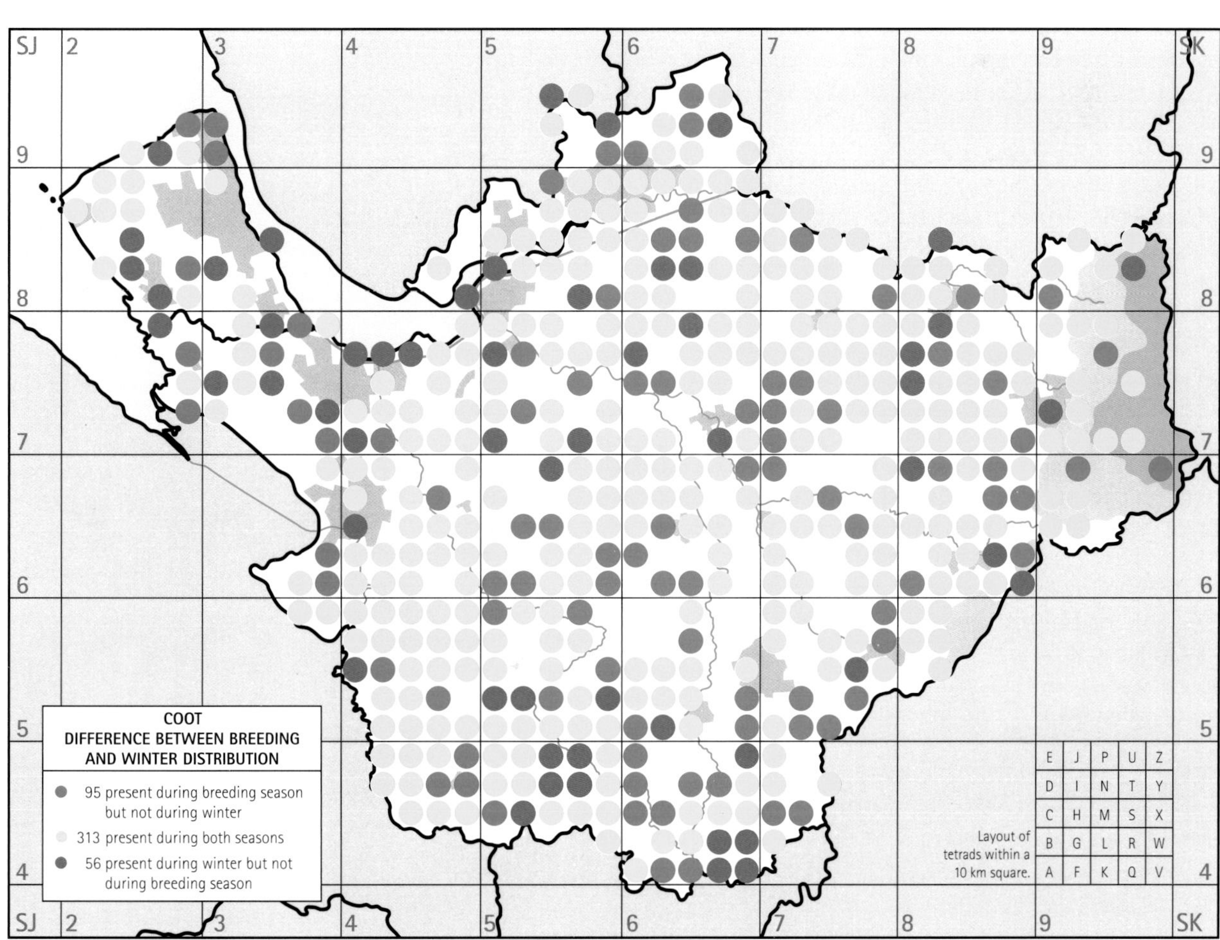
COOT
DIFFERENCE BETWEEN BREEDING AND WINTER DISTRIBUTION
95 present during breeding season but not during winter
313 present during both seasons
56 present during winter but not during breeding season
Layout of tetrads within a 10 km square.
E J P U Z
D I N T Y
C H M S X
B G L R W
A F K Q V
SJ
SK

Oystercatcher

Haematopus ostralegus

SIMON BOOTH

Breeding Oystercatchers have undergone dramatic changes in the last twenty years. There were only 25 tetrads where Oystercatchers were present in the breeding season during our *First Atlas* and this Atlas, with 116 newly occupied and the species lost from 22. The 'change' map shows a major expansion of range inland, especially in the eastern half of Cheshire, and in the south of the county, around Delamere, along the river Dee south of Chester and along the west coast of Wirral. At the same time there are obvious losses especially along the lower reaches of our two main rivers, the Dee and the Mersey. The spread inland parallels what has happened in the rest of north-west England. They started breeding inland on gravel banks in rivers early in the twentieth century, colonizing the Eden in Cumbria in 1920, the Lune in north Lancashire in 1928, the Ribble in 1934 and the remainder of the Lancashire rivers during the 1950s and 1960s, then, from the 1970s, moved onto agrarian habitats. Birds breeding in farmland have so many advantages that it is easy to see how the habit rapidly spreads: they nest a month earlier than on the coast, suffer lower predation and fledge twice as many young per pair than coastal or riparian breeders (Briggs 1984).

Their normal nest is on the ground, amongst shingle or rubble, and inland often on bare earth in the middle of fields, with three eggs incubated for nearly four weeks. In Scotland some birds nest in the tops of rotting fence posts and a similar habit has taken hold amongst Oystercatchers alongside the Manchester Ship Canal at Frodsham Marsh (SJ47T/Z) where up to four pairs now nest in the tops of wooden jetties, surrounded by, and a metre or more above, the water of the canal. This is the only British wader where the adults feed their chicks: for the inland breeders, this means a diet mostly of earthworms. Most habitat codes (76) were from farmland (33 improved grassland, 8 unimproved grassland, 22 mixed grass/tilled land and 13 tilled land), with 62 alongside freshwater bodies and 12 on damp semi-natural grassland including 6 on estuarine salt-marsh.

Oystercatchers are long-lived birds, with some known to have reached the age of 30, and females do not breed until at least three years of age, with males delaying until five years or older. There seem to be few immature birds in the county during the breeding season and it must be supposed that they spend the summer elsewhere, probably on their wintering grounds in France and Iberia (Brown & Grice 2005).

The Oystercatcher breeding population of Cheshire and Wirral in 2004–05 was large enough to be sampled on Breeding Bird Survey transects, and is estimated at 510 birds (with a confidence range from zero to 1,220), at least a tenfold increase on the figure of 20 pairs suggested in our *First Atlas*. The abundance map shows that their highest density is inland, in eastern Cheshire.

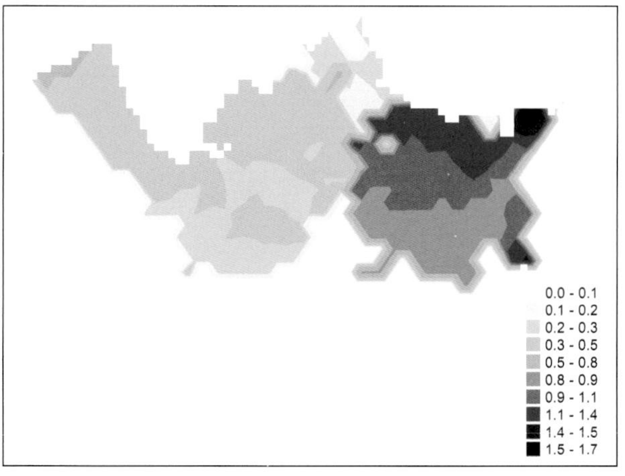

Oystercatcher abundance.

Sponsored by Dee Estuary Voluntary Wardens

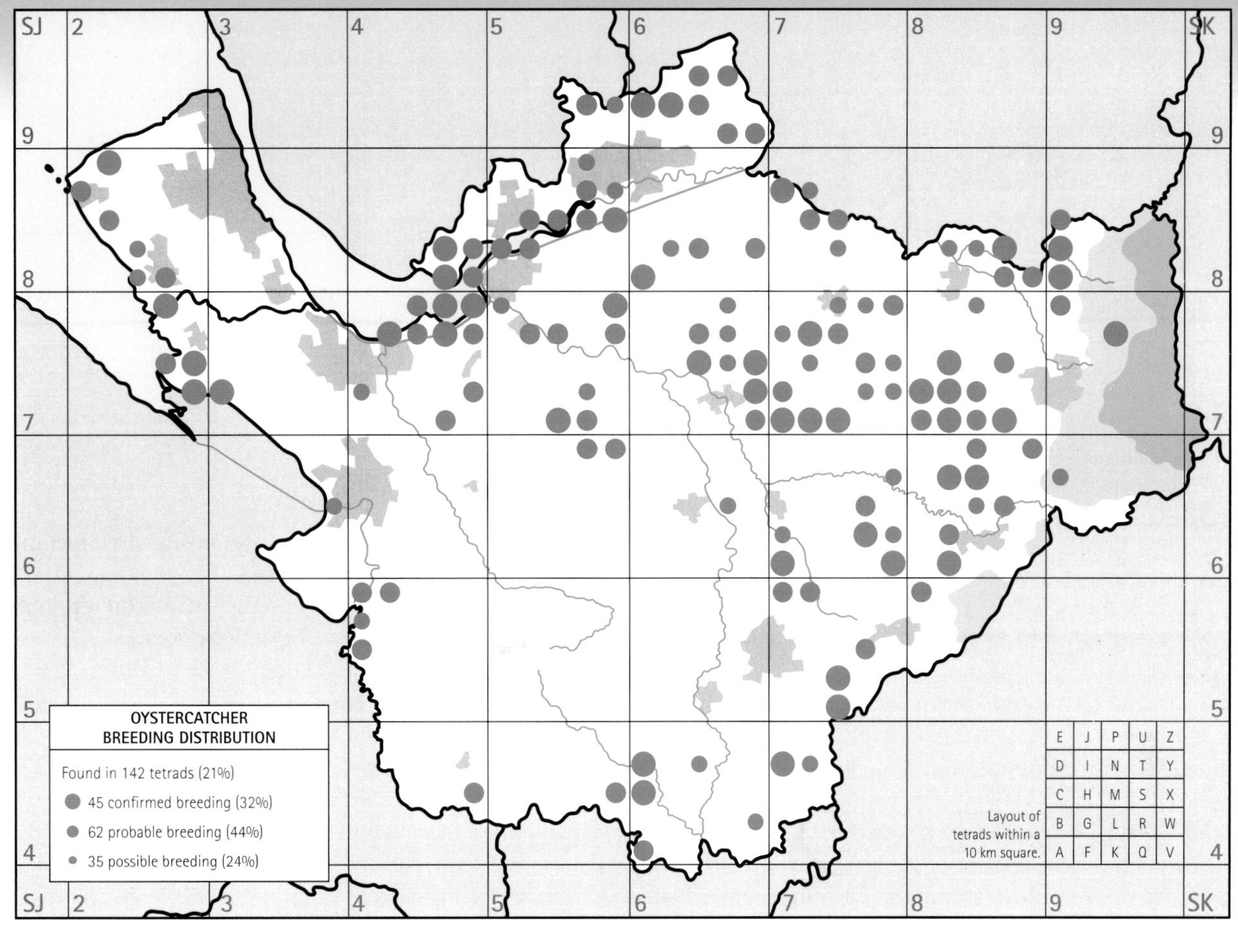
OYSTERCATCHER
BREEDING DISTRIBUTION
Found in 142 tetrads (21%)
45 confirmed breeding (32%)
62 probable breeding (44%)
35 possible breeding (24%)
Layout of tetrads within a 10 km square.
E J P U Z
D I N T Y
C H M S X
B G L R W
A F K Q V
SJ
SK

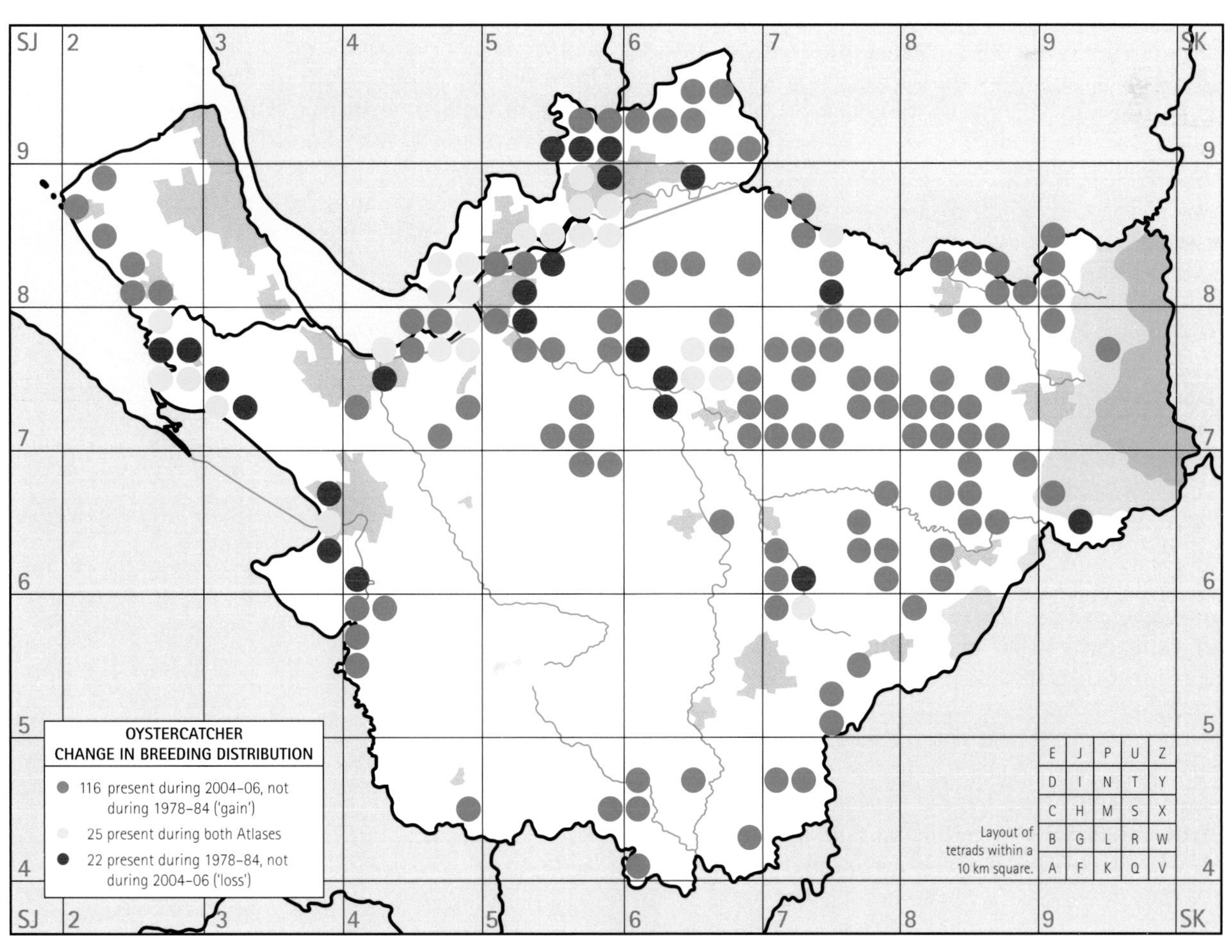
OYSTERCATCHER
CHANGE IN BREEDING DISTRIBUTION
116 present during 2004–06, not during 1978–84 ('gain')
25 present during both Atlases
22 present during 1978–84, not during 2004–06 ('loss')
Layout of tetrads within a 10 km square.
E J P U Z
D I N T Y
C H M S X
B G L R W
A F K Q V
SJ
SK

The winter influx of Oystercatchers comes from the north: Scotland and northern England, the Faeroes (whose national bird it is), Iceland and Norway. They come here to feed on the abundant shellfish, especially cockles and mussels, with *Macoma* as a backup. No other wader is capable of opening the bivalves, and Oystercatchers have evolved two specialized methods, with appropriately different types of bill. Some have short, blunt bills and hammer their prey through the shell, while others have longer, pointed bills and prise the two shells apart.

Although the winter map shows birds in almost every tetrad in both estuaries, and inland across parts of eastern Cheshire and much of Wirral, the key area is the Dee estuary, which is internationally important for the species and ranks third amongst British sites on the basis of WeBS counts (Musgrove *et al.* 2007). The five-year peak mean total is nearly 25,000 birds, more than 10% of the winter population of Britain, although sometimes half of the Dee birds are in Wales rather than in Cheshire and Wirral. The Irish Sea is the key area for wintering Oystercatchers, with four of the top five sites: Morecambe Bay, Solway estuary, Dee estuary and the Ribble estuary.

Coward (1910) noted that, although most abundant as a bird of passage in spring and autumn, 'considerable numbers of Oystercatchers remain in the Dee and Mersey as winter residents'. At all seasons it was more plentiful near the mouth of the Dee than higher up the estuary. Some quantitative information came from Hardy (1941), that winter flocks at Hilbre may reach from 300 to 1,000, and from Bell (1962) that several thousand winter at the mouth of the Dee, but it was not until the start of the Birds of Estuaries Enquiry that hard figures were obtained, with sample figures of 11,208 in December 1972, 22,489 in January 1976, 30,360 in December 1983 and 35,775 on 18 November 1990. From then onwards, Oystercatcher numbers declined quite rapidly, reaching 12,506 in 1999/2000 against a background of stable regional and national populations, which is puzzling as adult birds are normally site faithful, although immature birds move to new areas (*BTO Winter Atlas*).

This decline caused concern, including amongst the secretariat that administers the Ramsar Convention for internationally important wetlands which included the Dee estuary in the 'Montreux Record', the subset of Ramsar sites in need of priority conservation attention. Harvesting of cockles was one of the site impacts listed, and the UK Environment Agency imposed Britain's first cockling ban on the Dee estuary beds in 1997, lifted for a few days in most years since. The Dee estuary cockles are particularly valuable commercially, said to contain more meat than those from any other fishery, and the Environment Agency is seeking new by-laws to restrict the number of cocklers and the methods they use. The decline in Oystercatcher numbers is not directly linked to the cockle fishery, but the population has recovered to around 25,000 birds wintering across the whole site.

Some large flocks were recorded during this Atlas but half of the 160 records with a count were of 10 birds or fewer. There were 33 four-figure flocks and two five-figure counts, 10,000 birds off West Kirby (SJ28C) in 2004/05 and 12,000 off Heswall (SJ28K) in 2005/06. Occasionally some significant gatherings feed inland on fields, such as the 285 birds counted by Roy Palmer on 12 January 2006 between Heswall and Barnston (SJ28R). Numbers are small away from the Dee. Although Coward (1910) mentioned the Mersey in the same sentence as the Dee, he gave no further information and there are no documented records of the Mersey ever having been important for the species; the largest count in the Mersey during this Atlas was 210 birds near Stanlow Point (SJ47I). Inland, no more than five birds were reported from any site in the eastern half of the county. Indeed, many of the Oystercatchers in inland areas were seen as pairs, and in 10 inland tetrads, observers specifically commented that the birds recorded in the Atlas 'winter' period were early-returning breeders, usually around mid-February. All previous authors had emphasized its scarcity inland—Boyd (1951) knew just two winter records in the 25 years from 1926 to 1950 in the Great Budworth area—and Oystercatchers are probably more often seen inland nowadays than ever before.

RICHARD STEEL

Most Oystercatchers were reported in estuarine (31 tetrads) or open shore (9) habitats in winter, but elsewhere they were found in a range of habitats including various types of fresh water (28), agricultural land (35, mostly grassland) and semi-natural grassland (19, mostly salt-marsh or grazing marsh).

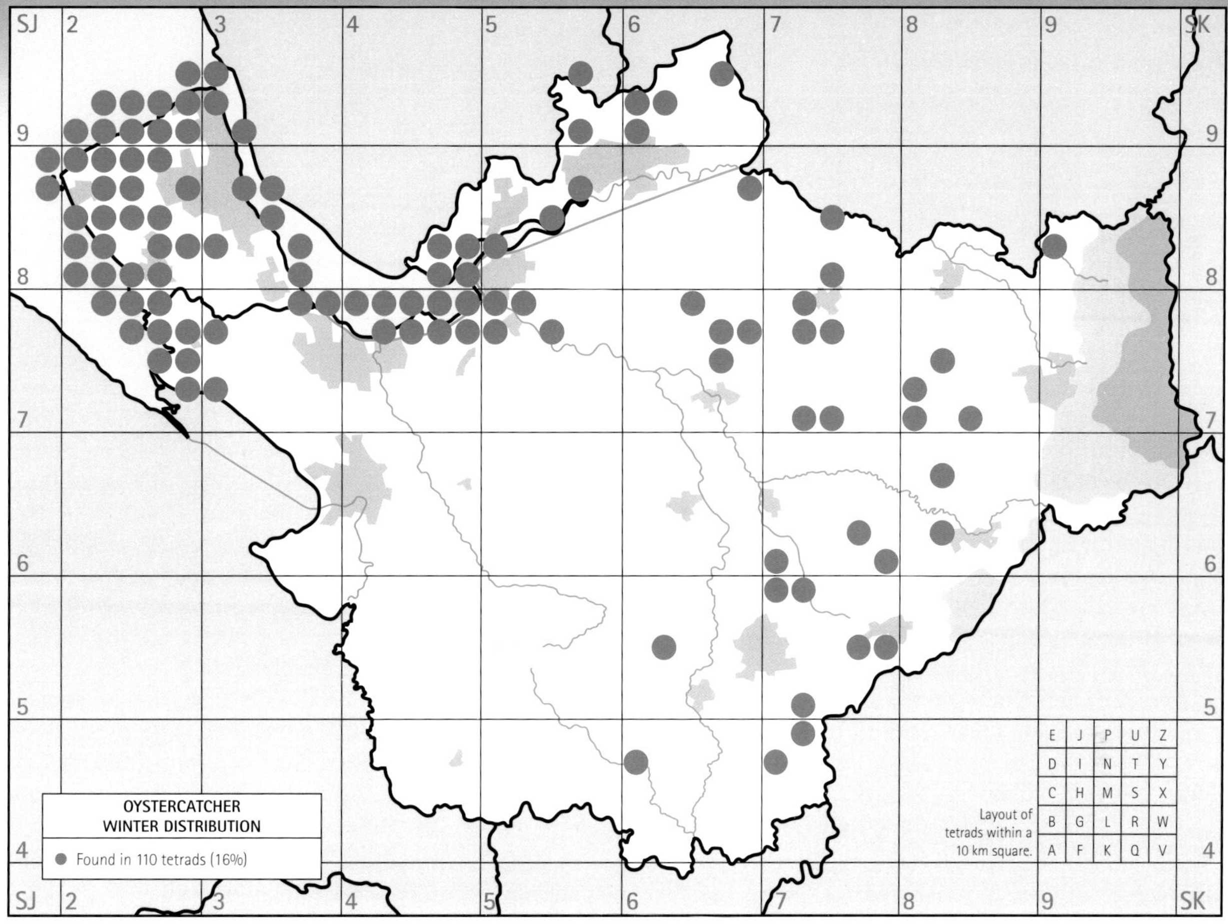

OYSTERCATCHER
WINTER DISTRIBUTION
Found in 110 tetrads (16%)
Layout of tetrads within a 10 km square.

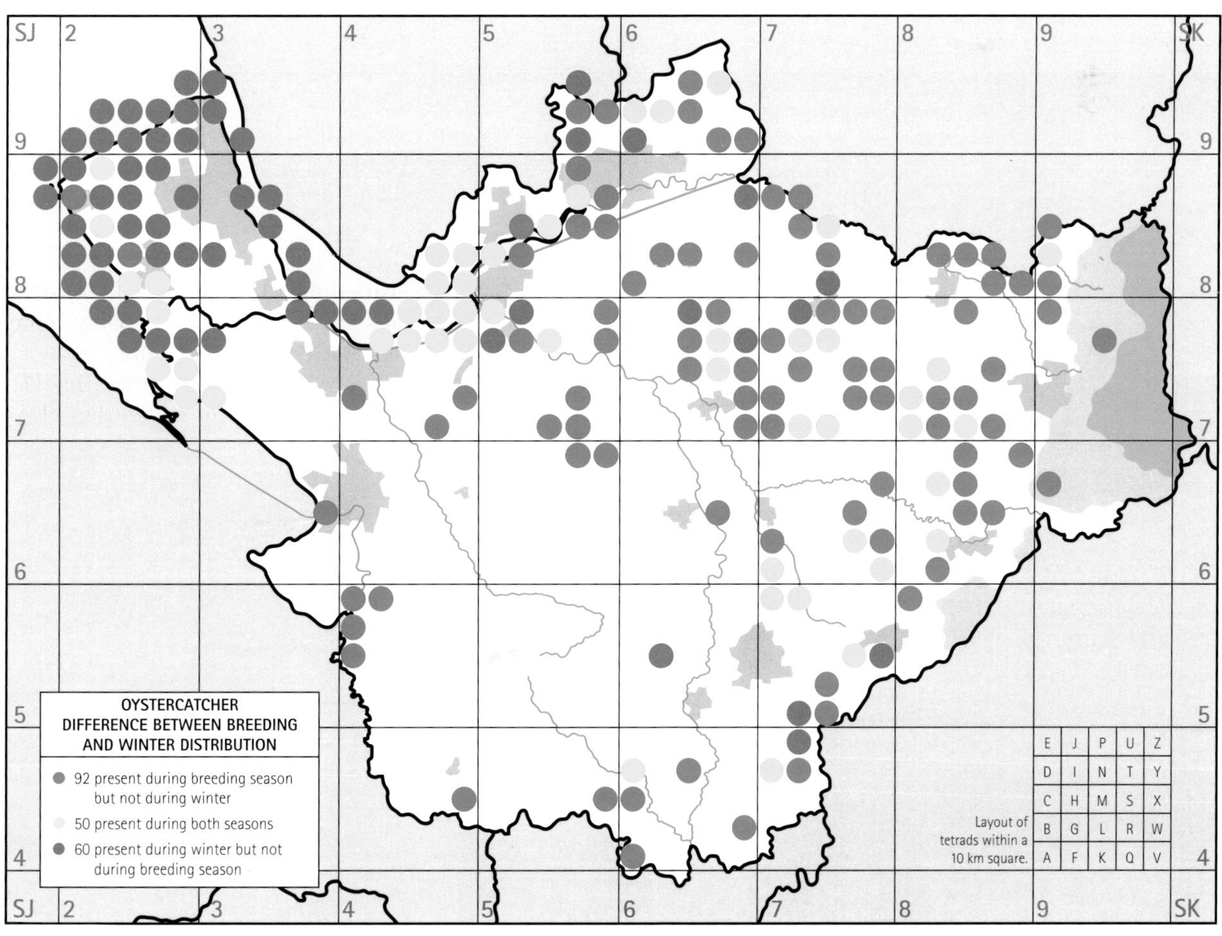

OYSTERCATCHER
DIFFERENCE BETWEEN BREEDING AND WINTER DISTRIBUTION
92 present during breeding season but not during winter
50 present during both seasons
60 present during winter but not during breeding season
Layout of tetrads within a 10 km square.

Avocet

Recurvirostra avosetta

This much sought-after wader, the emblem of the Royal Society for the Protection of Birds, has been extending its range for many years. Avocets have regularly bred in Suffolk since 1963, Norfolk since 1977, Kent since 1986 and Yorkshire since 1994. There were sporadic breeding records in the 1990s in Dorset and inland in London, Cambridgeshire and Leicestershire (Brown & Grice 2005). Then in 2001 came the first breeding record in north-west England, when a pair bred at Leighton Moss, north Lancashire; their first attempt failed, but they persevered with a second clutch of three eggs, two of which hatched and one chick fledged. By 2004, the Lancashire population was up to 24 pairs and Avocets were breeding in 13 counties in England and Wales (Holling *et al.* 2007a).

Cheshire and Wirral shared the excitement of the species' exploration of new sites. In 1999, two appeared at Sandbach Flashes on 1 May, displaying and copulating to 6 May, but did not nest and then left. It seemed like that was that: in 2000, there were just two records of single birds in the Frodsham Marsh area, and the species was not even recorded in the county in 2001.

Then, in 2002 a pair was present for four weeks at Inner Marsh Farm (SJ37B), displaying, copulating and nest-scraping but not laying any eggs there. However, during their periodic absences from the RSPB reserve, they had taken a liking to a disused ICI lagoon adjacent to the Weaver Bend (SJ57E) and laid an egg in a scrape there. They abandoned this egg during cold, wet and windy weather at the beginning of May and returned to Inner Marsh Farm for 10 days. The pair finally went back to Weston Lagoon on 11 May and laid four eggs from which the chicks hatched on 6 June. On 14 June the adults obligingly took them into public view on the bank of the river Weaver, where they remained until all four young fledged, first flying on 11 July, a perfect outcome celebrated with two of the chicks and one of their parents starring on the front cover of that year's *Cheshire and Wirral Bird Report*. The family party went back to Inner Marsh Farm for a day at the end of July then left the county (Platt 2002).

In 2003 three pairs bred at the same site, at least six chicks hatched but all the young birds were predated by Magpies and gulls. During this Atlas period, in 2004 up to six birds were present from 2 March to 8 April, with seven on one day, and one pair stayed in the vicinity of the Weaver Bend throughout the breeding season until 10 July. They were seen copulating and nest-scraping on Frodsham Marsh no. 6 bed (SJ47Y) but no eggs were laid. In 2005, up to six birds were at the Weaver Bend from 20 to 28 March after which they deserted the site and left the county, but three birds were at Inner Marsh

DAVID PLATT

Sponsored by Graham Hewitt in memory of Ian May, a fellow rambler, ornithologist and good friend

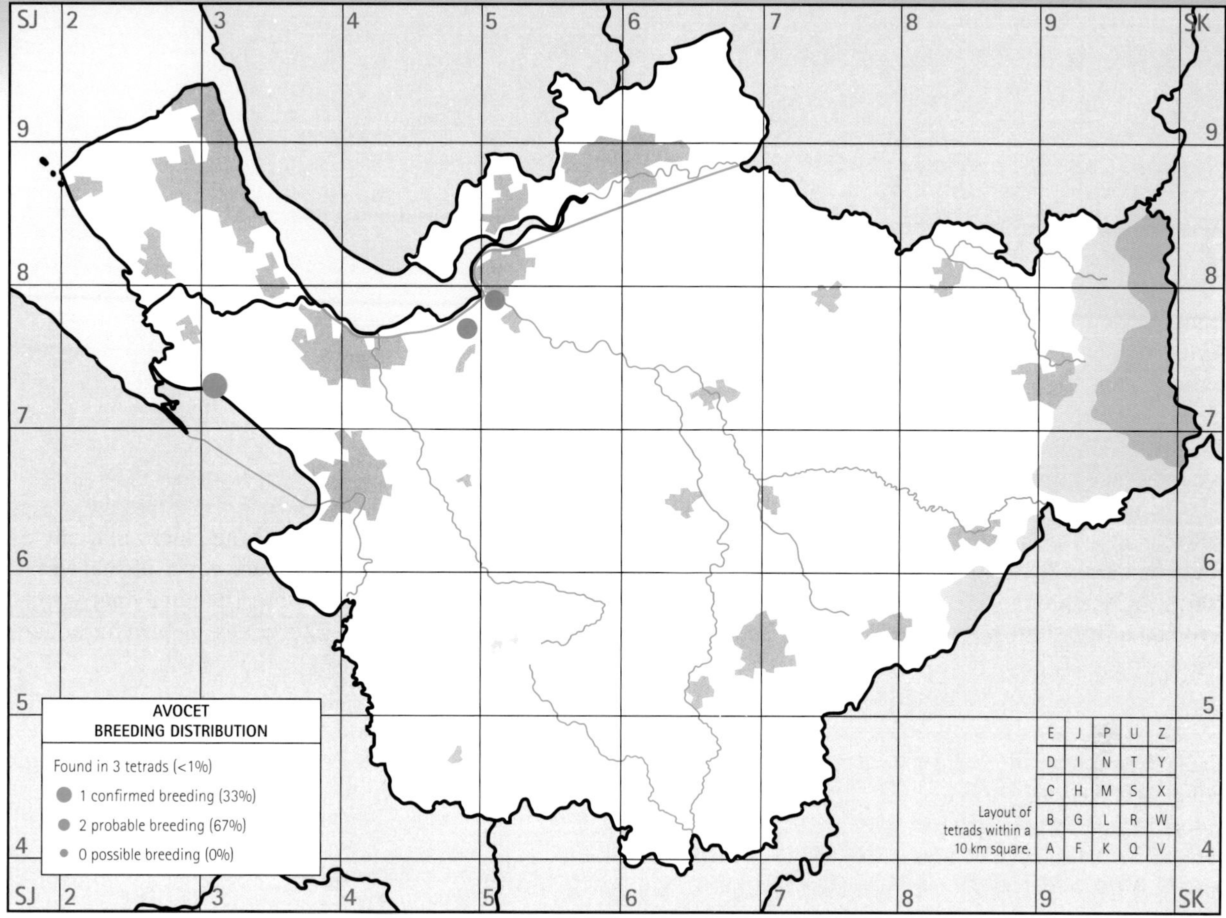

Farm from 13 May to 2 June. In 2006 the RSPB was rewarded with a pair nesting at their reserve, four chicks hatching by 21 May and three of them fledging by 27 June.

It is not known where these birds have wintered. Increasing numbers of British birds use south coast estuaries, where they are joined by some birds from continental Europe, but others migrate as far as France, Portugal or south of the Sahara to Senegal and Guinea. Avocets have occasionally been recorded in the county during winter, most recently on the Dee off Heswall from 18 December 1994 to 1 January 1995.

For many years it had been thought that the habitat and food requirements of Avocets were stringent, the adults and chicks needing shallow saline lagoons that did not dry out during the summer. Perhaps they have changed their habits, but it is now clear that they can use a variety of freshwater pools provided that grazing or flooding maintains sparse or low vegetation; they need water up to 15 cm deep over soft sediments rich in aquatic invertebrates. This more relaxed requirement has allowed them to expand widely across England and Wales. Avocets normally do not breed until two or three years of age but immature birds may prospect new sites, and once they have bred at a location, adults tend to return in subsequent years (*BTO Second Atlas*). These features of their breeding biology, along with their colonial nature, have led to Cheshire and Wirral being able to enjoy Avocets' presence during the last decade.

Little Ringed Plover

Charadrius dubius

In Britain, Little Ringed Plovers are birds of unvegetated industrial and postindustrial land. This is a transient habitat and breeding sites are seldom occupied for more than a few years. The large sand quarries may provide newly exposed areas year after year, but other sites tend to become too overgrown and thus unsuitable for this species. It is no surprise that there is a high proportion of red dots on the 'change' map: they were recorded in 57 tetrads in our *First Atlas* and 47 in this survey, but only 21 of the tetrads had birds present in both Atlases. Many of the gains and losses appear to be randomly scattered, although they have colonized north Wirral and it is noticeable that several non-industrial sites are now being used amongst agricultural land, and there are far fewer records now than twenty years ago in the Mersey valley, the species' former stronghold.

DAVID PLATT

For a bird that likes such artificial sites it can be tricky to decide on the appropriate habitat codes, and observers submitted a wide variety: 59 records comprising 17 different codes. The majority were category G (fresh water), with 13 G5 (sandpits), 8 G3 (lakes or reservoirs) and 7 G2 (small waterbodies). Few fieldworkers were licensed to approach the breeding area of this Schedule 1 species, but adults or chicks can often be seen from afar without illegal disturbance. Reported nesting areas included several industrial sites with restricted access, some of them hazardous or toxic to humans. As well as sand, nests appeared to be on concrete, rubble, fly ash, lime and crushed limestone. Other sites with successful breeding included a new golf course development, and some on agricultural land, nesting in a 'rubbish strewn area of ploughed field' and on bare ground in crops of *miscanthus*, and sparsely germinated rape. This opportunistic species will use completely dry areas but several observers noted that temporary flooding by heavy rainfall encouraged a pair to nest, but breeding often failed after the transient pool dried up.

The nest is completely exposed on flat ground, the birds relying for concealment on their camouflage and that of their eggs. There can be high losses to predation from foxes and corvids, and Little Ringed Plovers may re-lay two or three times, but true second broods are unusual. At 22 nests that I have found in which the eggs were incubated to hatching, at various Cheshire sites in the years 1982–2004, hatching dates ranged from 24 May to 23 July. As with many species with nidifugous young, production of the eggs requires a tremendous reproductive effort, the normal clutch of four eggs weighing as much as 70% of the female's own weight. The benefit is that the chicks grow well during their 24 days in the egg, with sharp eyesight and their legs almost fully developed from the moment that they hatch. At a few hours of age, chicks run around feeding themselves—picking insects from the surface of damp ground—attended by their parents whose alarm call makes them crouch flat or run into the edge of cover. In 12 tetrads surveyors reported seeing chicks, and at several sites observers reported the 'broken-wing' performance of an adult trying to lure them away from their nest or young, this being one of the classic species employing such a distraction display.

Our *First Atlas* reported that competition with Ringed Plovers had been a problem for this species, its larger cousin often being on territory in March before Little Ringed Plovers returned from their West African wintering areas. Such antagonism appears to have become less of an issue since the mid-1980s, perhaps because only 12 tetrads had records of both species during this Atlas. Little Ringed Plover is believed to be one of the species for which all birds found in the breeding season are probably recorded in the annual county bird reports. From 1985 to 2006 the breeding totals have fluctuated in the range of 14–32 pairs. Bearing in mind that this Atlas map aggregates three seasons' records, and that few observers found more than one pair in a tetrad, the present population is probably around 20 pairs. The last BTO-organized national survey, in 1984, found 21–24 pairs in Cheshire and Wirral, and the results of the 2007 BTO survey will make an interesting comparison. Baker *et al.* (2006) estimated the UK population to be 825–1,070 pairs.

Sponsored by South-East Cheshire Ornithological Society

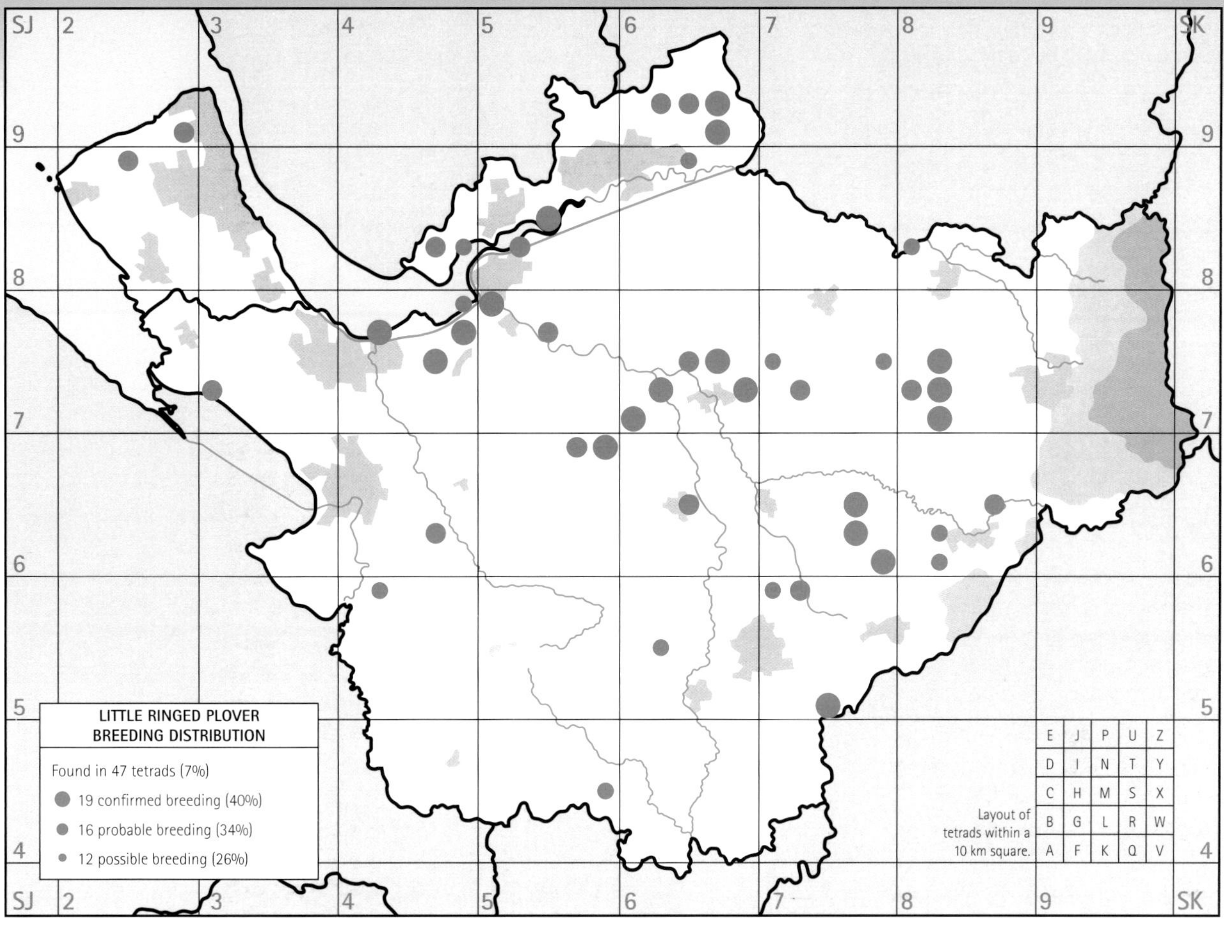

SJ
SK
LITTLE RINGED PLOVER
BREEDING DISTRIBUTION
Found in 47 tetrads (7%)
19 confirmed breeding (40%)
16 probable breeding (34%)
12 possible breeding (26%)
Layout of tetrads within a 10 km square.
E J P U Z
D I N T Y
C H M S X
B G L R W
A F K Q V

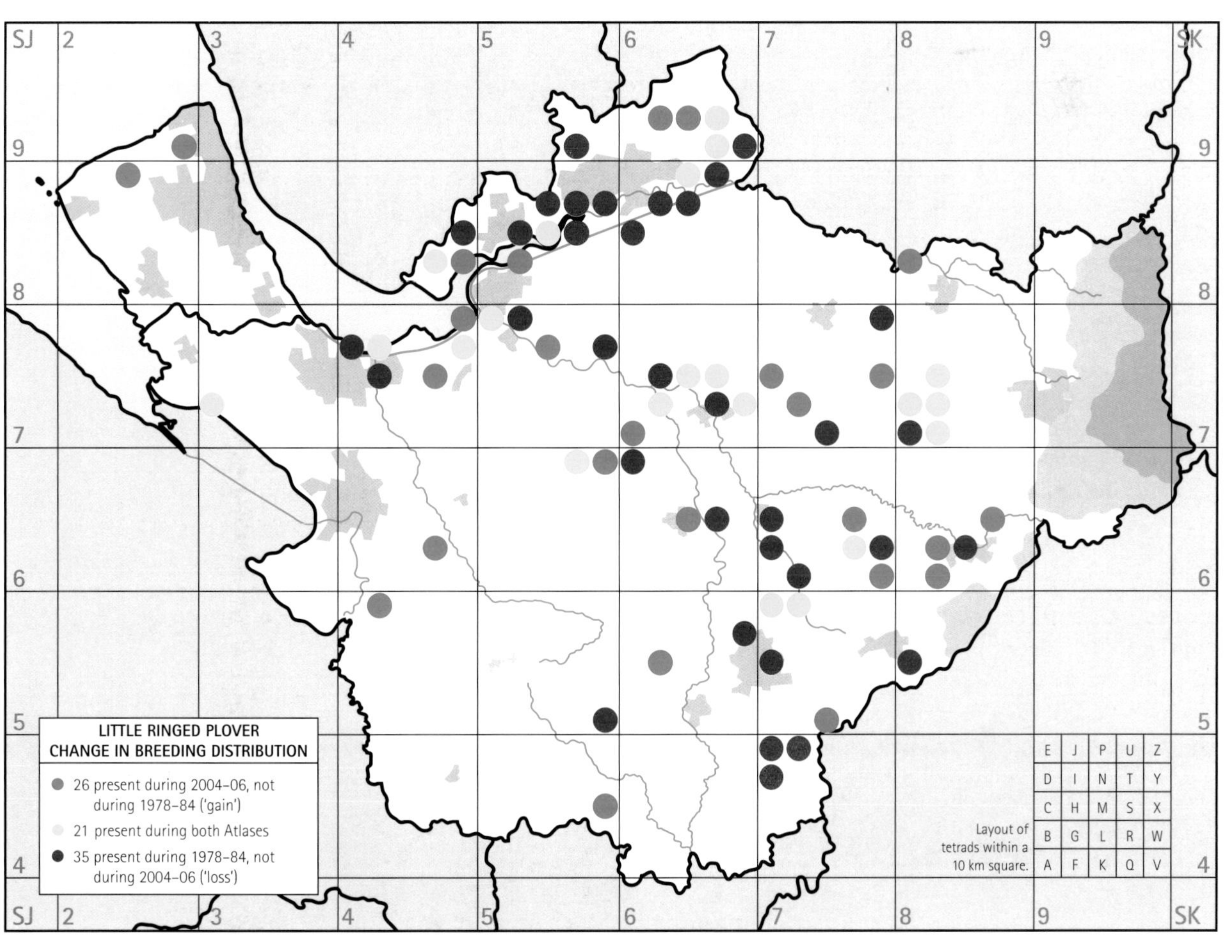

SJ
SK
LITTLE RINGED PLOVER
CHANGE IN BREEDING DISTRIBUTION
26 present during 2004–06, not during 1978–84 ('gain')
21 present during both Atlases
35 present during 1978–84, not during 2004–06 ('loss')
Layout of tetrads within a 10 km square.
E J P U Z
D I N T Y
C H M S X
B G L R W
A F K Q V

Ringed Plover

Charadrius hiaticula

REN HATHWAY

Ringed Plovers in Cheshire and Wirral favour transient habitat, especially postindustrial sites near to the shore, but these are abandoned if they become too vegetated. Birds were found at abandoned or reclaimed docksides, a demolished power station and petrochemical plant, a dry clay pit, flashes, lime beds and canal dredging deposit beds. Their breeding status is much the same as in our *First Atlas* but, as indicated by the 'change' map, few of the sites where they nested twenty years ago are still suitable; only four tetrads held birds in both Atlas periods. Their traditional breeding sites are sandy shores, but the Wirral beaches are far too disturbed and no Ringed Plovers use them now: the two records in 1978 and 1983, during our *First Atlas*, are the last known.

The female lays four eggs in a scrape on the ground, neatly arranged with their pointed ends always in the centre of the nest, and shares the incubation with her mate. After about 24 days the chicks emerge with their legs fully formed and able to run around and find their own food of invertebrates and insects. In the ten tetrads with confirmed breeding, five of them came from observers seeing the gawky youngsters and five with an adult sitting on eggs; three instances of 'probable breeding' arose from pairs seen. The young birds can fly after about another 24 days, and the pair usually has a second brood; I have dates for nests with eggs in Cheshire from 8 April until early July.

The trend in the national breeding population is not well known and the results of the BTO survey of Ringed Plovers and Little Ringed Plovers in 2007 are awaited. The spread away from the coast was noted in the *BTO Second Atlas* (1988–91), and a census in England and Wales revealed an increase of 12% in breeding birds in wet meadows, mostly at coastal sites, between 1982 and 2002 (Wilson *et al.* 2005). The Cheshire and Wirral breeding population at the end of our *First Atlas* in 1984 was at its highest level for well over one hundred years, at 13 pairs. In the years since then, the annual bird reports have seldom recorded breeding anywhere other than at 'river Mersey/Weaver sites' but clearly this Atlas has stimulated more thorough surveying and the county population is probably still around a dozen pairs.

Sponsored by Mike Allsopp

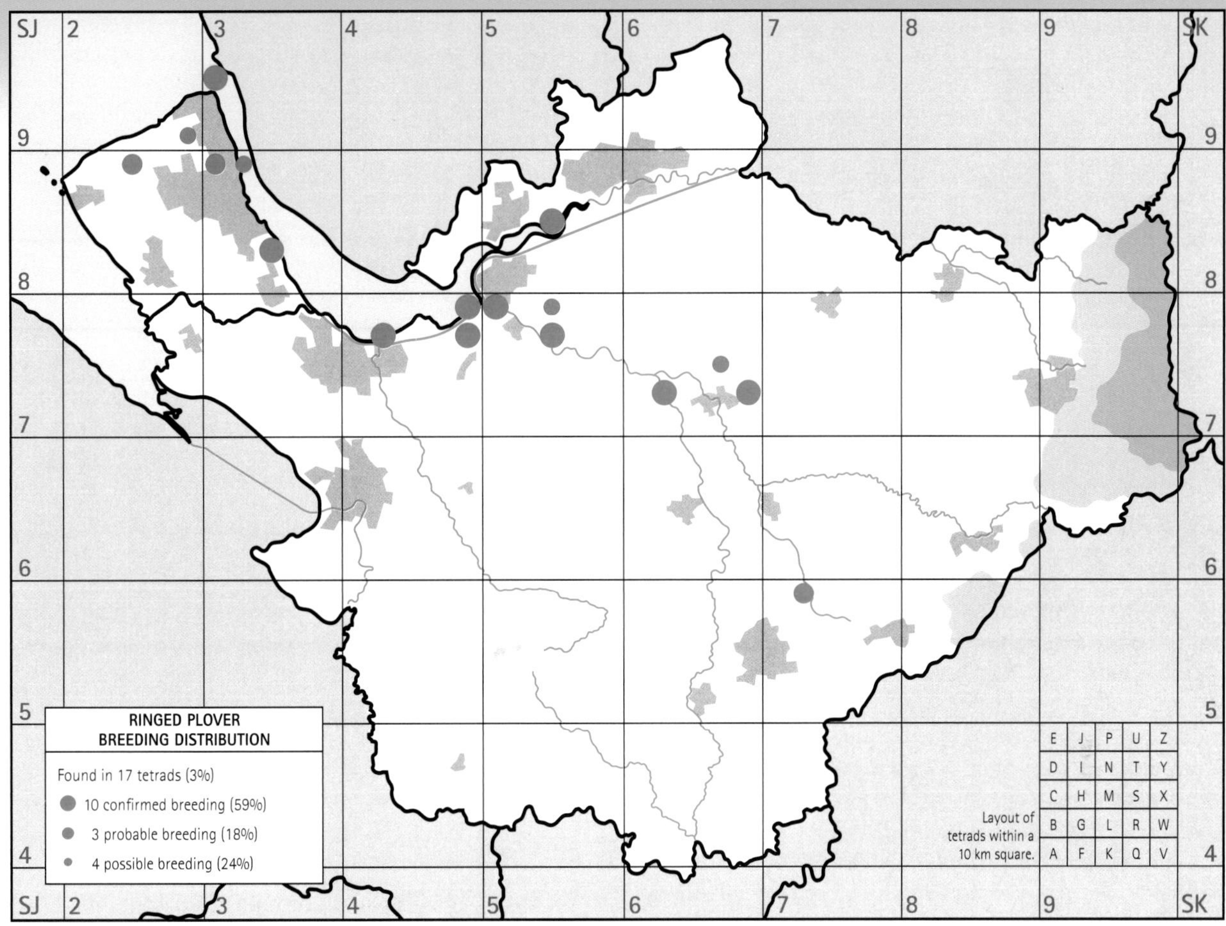
RINGED PLOVER
BREEDING DISTRIBUTION
Found in 17 tetrads (3%)
10 confirmed breeding (59%)
3 probable breeding (18%)
4 possible breeding (24%)
Layout of
tetrads within a
10 km square.
E J P U Z
D I N T Y
C H M S X
B G L R W
A F K Q V
SJ
SK

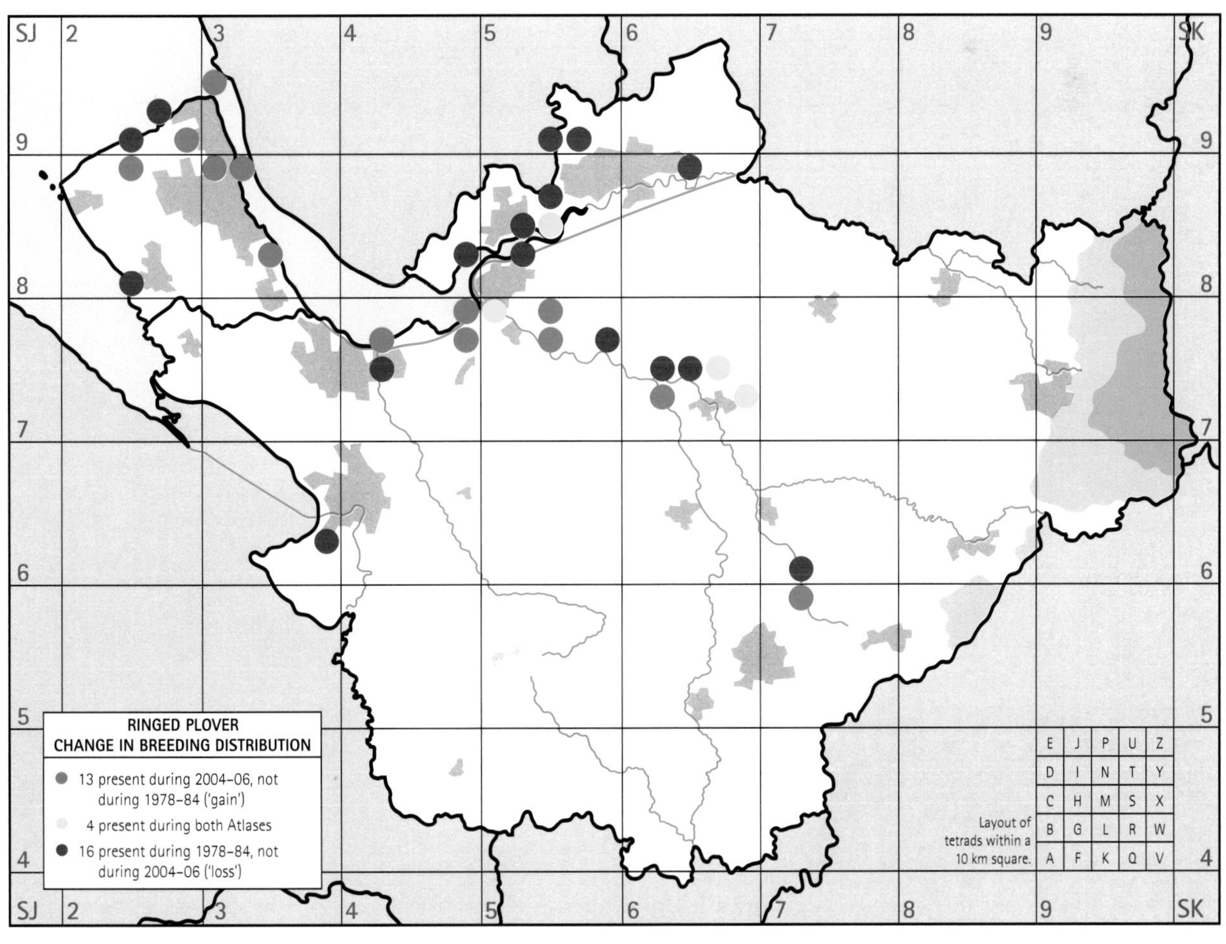
RINGED PLOVER
CHANGE IN BREEDING DISTRIBUTION
13 present during 2004–06, not during 1978–84 ('gain')
4 present during both Atlases
16 present during 1978–84, not during 2004–06 ('loss')
Layout of
tetrads within a
10 km square.
E J P U Z
D I N T Y
C H M S X
B G L R W
A F K Q V
SJ
SK

Large numbers of Ringed Plovers pass through in spring and autumn on their journeys between Greenland and Africa, and both the Mersey and Dee estuaries exceed the national threshold for passage of 300 birds, but far fewer winter in the county and no site is of conservation importance for the species. Most of the wintering birds are of British stock, but there might be some immigrants from continental European breeding sites along the coasts of the Wadden Sea and Baltic. They find their food by watching for movement at or near the sand surface, taking primarily marine worms, crustaceans and molluscs, and they tend to keep towards the top of the beach, away from the tide edge.

The species is Amber listed because of its decline in winter numbers nationally, and those in Cheshire and Wirral have certainly dropped over the last 30 years. At the beginning of the twentieth century the Ringed Plover was a plentiful winter resident, both in the Dee and Mersey, and Coward (1910) had seen 'large flocks consorting with Dunlins and Redshanks in December and January, and in February the numbers are often very great'. Without any numbers quoted, it is impossible to know what these adjectives mean, although they sound much larger than the present figures, as does Bell's assessment of 'common winter resident at the coast', although he later says 'regular in small numbers in the estuaries throughout the winter' (Bell 1962).

By the start of the Birds of Estuaries Enquiry counts in 1970 there were almost 300 Ringed Plovers wintering on the Dee but they were present only in single figures on the Mersey, if at all. The Dee figure of 386 in January 1975 was unusually high, but by the mid-1980s numbers on the Dee had dwindled to less than 100 in most winter months, rising again by the early 1990s to average around 150, a level maintained, with yearly fluctuations, to the present. Most WeBS counts during this Atlas period were low, however, with only the odd winter month exceeding 100 birds.

Otherwise, the only three-figure counts during this Atlas came from the north-west Wirral coast, with 120 at Hilbre in 2005/06 and 100 there in 2006/07, and separate counts of 150 birds in 2004/05 at West Kirby (SJ28D) and Hoylake shore (SJ29A), with 100 at West Kirby in 2005/06. The only other count over 60 was of 90 birds at Frodsham Marsh in 2004/05. Half of the Atlas records were in small groups of 10 or fewer. Ringed Plovers were found in only three sites away from tidal areas: two birds were reported in SJ68R, and two or three birds returned early to breeding sites in the Neumann's Flash area (SJ67S/W).

DAVID PLATT

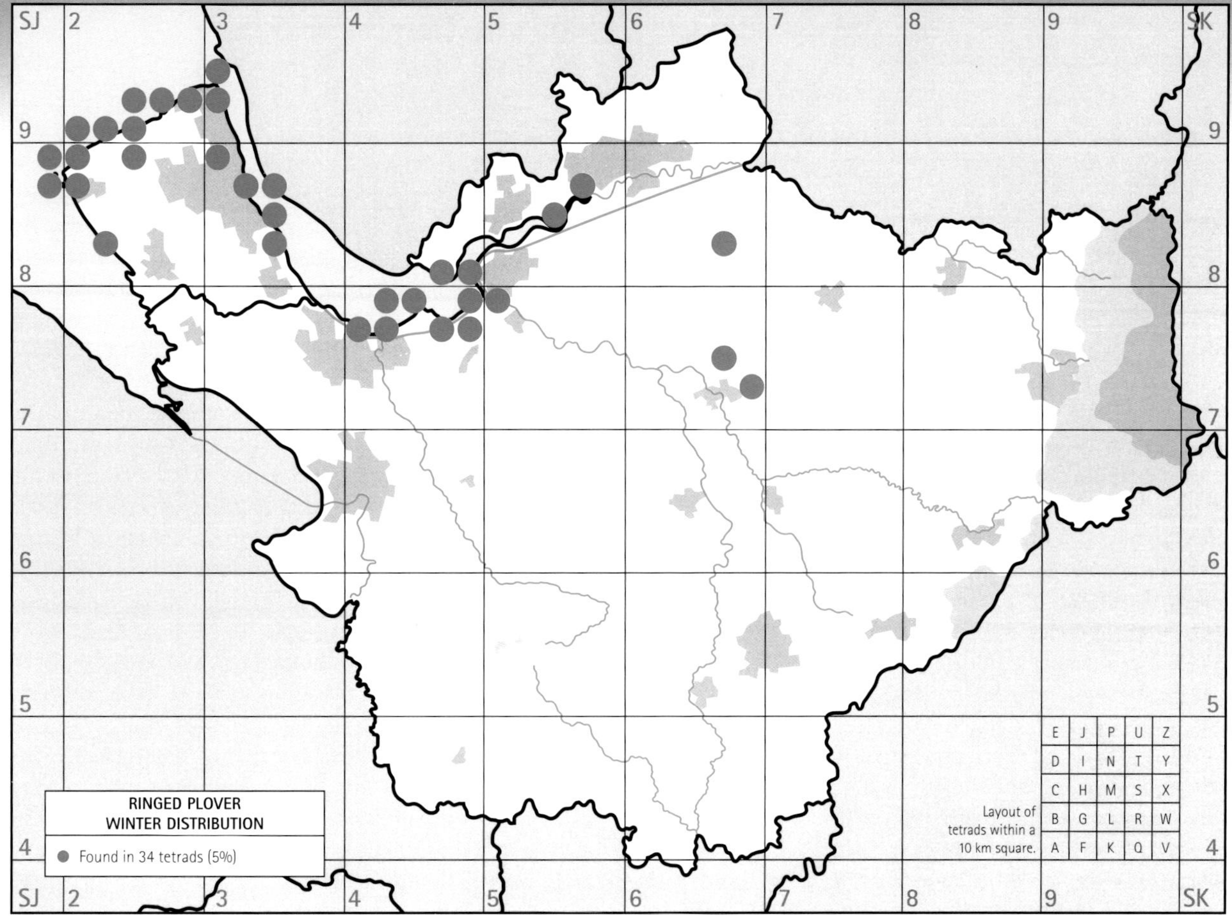
SJ
2
3
4
5
6
7
8
9
SK
RINGED PLOVER
WINTER DISTRIBUTION
Found in 34 tetrads (5%)
Layout of
tetrads within a
10 km square.
E J P U Z
D I N T Y
C H M S X
B G L R W
A F K Q V

Golden Plover

Pluvialis apricaria

Despite concern over their status, and the comment in our *First Atlas* 'that this species is clearly endangered as a breeding bird in the county', Golden Plovers appear to be maintaining their range and numbers in England, although declining significantly in Scotland (Sim *et al.* 2005). Surveys of the South Pennine Moors SPA, of which the Cheshire moors are a part, showed no change between 1990 and 2004–05 in the breeding population of Golden Plovers (Eaton *et al.* 2007). This Atlas map shows that their range has contracted somewhat since our *First Atlas*, when they were present in 14 tetrads, with breeding confirmed in six of them, but an annual total of only seven or eight territories. They have been lost from six of those tetrads, including four at the northern end of the hills, but were recorded in two where they were not seen twenty years ago. Birds were proven to breed in three tetrads, all in 2006, when adults with chicks were seen on High Moor/Piggford Moor (SJ96U); in the Shining Tor tetrad (SJ97W) and in the Birchenough Hill tetrad (SJ96Y). Probable breeding records came when agitated adults were found in SJ97V (above Yarnshaw Hill) and near the Cat and Fiddle (SK07A), with birds displaying near the county boundary near Jenkin Chapel (SJ97Y). All of these tetrads are above 350 m in altitude.

In SJ97R, north of Macclesfield Forest, it is not thought that they breed in the tetrad but since 1999 Steve Atkins has noted flocks of up to 28 birds feeding there from April through to July, with birds seen flying in from the east and displaying in flight. These are probably off-duty birds, especially females as males do much of the daytime incubation of the eggs, who fly up to 10 km from their nest to feed in fields rich in earthworms, tipulid (crane-fly) larvae and other invertebrates. Such fields are as important to their breeding success as is suitable moorland itself (Brown & Grice 2005).

Golden Plovers have been returning to the Cheshire hills noticeably earlier in recent years and breeding earlier in warmer springs, although ultimately the warming climate will probably put an end to their breeding in our area, and they are predicted to be lost completely from England as a breeding bird later this century (Huntley *et al.* 2007). Tipulids are the main food taken by chicks, totalling 60% or 70% of their daily intake, both as larvae (leatherjackets) and adults (daddy-long-legs); timing the breeding cycle to coincide with emergence of the adults is important for chicks to grow well. They also eat beetles, spiders and caterpillars, with a few berries. Adults may move their chicks up to 2 km to find better foraging sites, which include bare peat and small marshy areas (Pearce-Higgins & Yalden 2004).

In prime habitat they can achieve densities of 20–30 pairs per tetrad, with nests every 400 m (*BTO Second Atlas*) but the Cheshire moors are very different: the county bird reports during the 1990s gave annual figures that varied from four to 12 territories. During this Atlas period, John Oxenham thought that there were three pairs in SJ96Y in 2004, and the Cheshire total must be at least six pairs, but a coordinated count would be valuable to arrive at a definitive figure for the Golden Plover population.

RAY SCALLY

Sponsored by Dr J.D. Atkinson

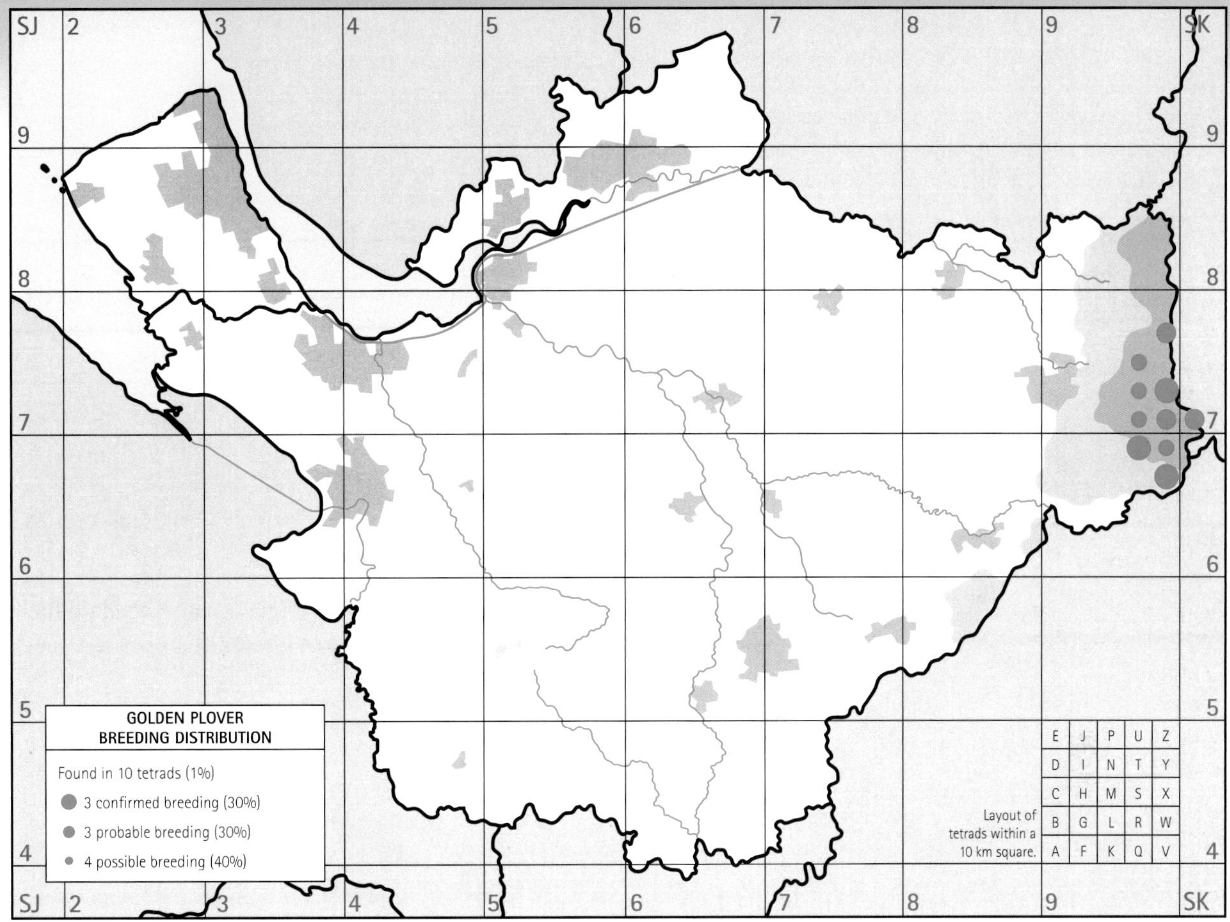
GOLDEN PLOVER
BREEDING DISTRIBUTION
Found in 10 tetrads (1%)
3 confirmed breeding (30%)
3 probable breeding (30%)
4 possible breeding (40%)
Layout of tetrads within a 10 km square.
E J P U Z
D I N T Y
C H M S X
B G L R W
A F K Q V
SJ
SK

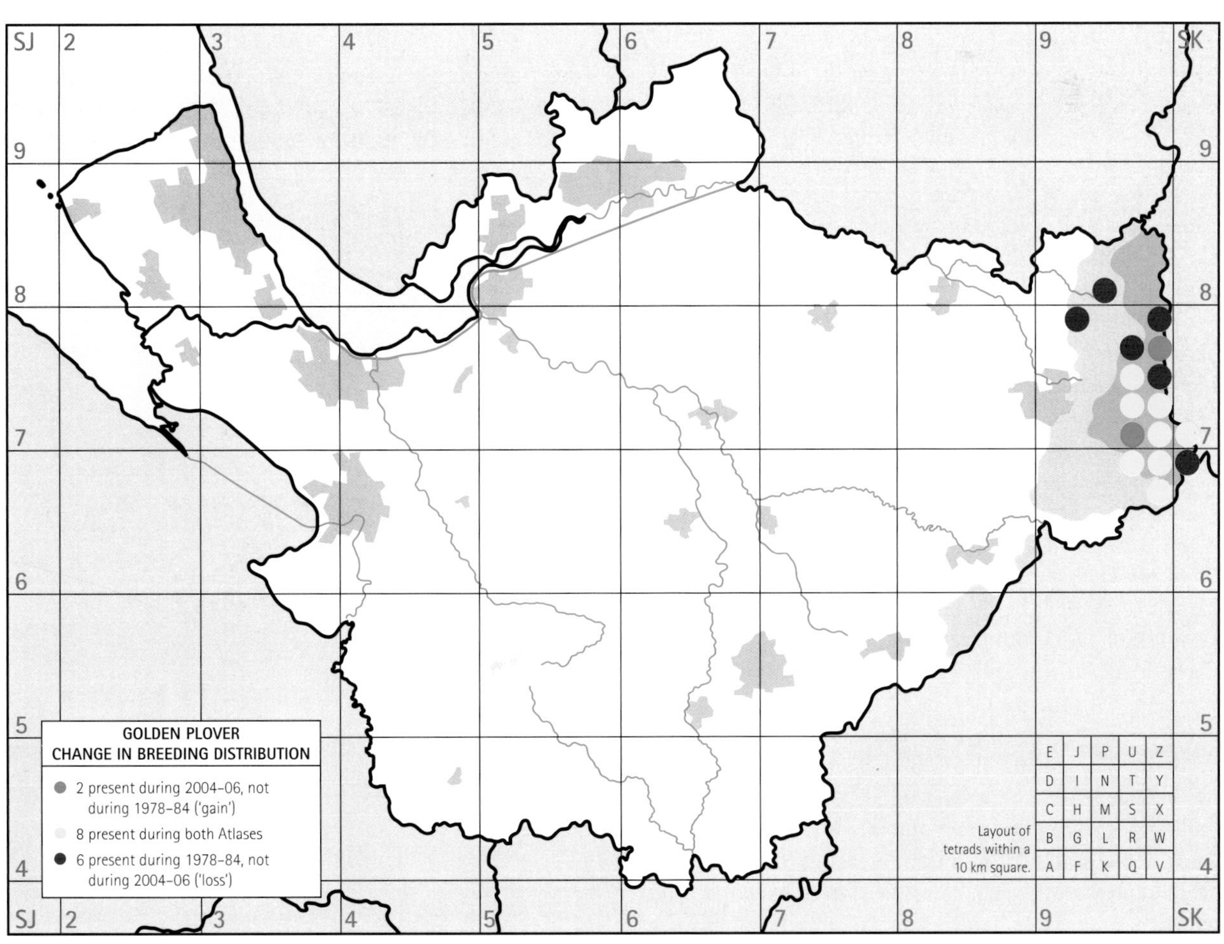
GOLDEN PLOVER
CHANGE IN BREEDING DISTRIBUTION
2 present during 2004–06, not during 1978–84 ('gain')
8 present during both Atlases
6 present during 1978–84, not during 2004–06 ('loss')
Layout of tetrads within a 10 km square.
E J P U Z
D I N T Y
C H M S X
B G L R W
A F K Q V
SJ
SK

The Atlas map shows that Golden Plovers are scattered widely across the county during winter. Local birds leave their breeding grounds and move to the British coasts, France and Iberia, to be replaced by immigrants from Iceland, most of whom winter in Ireland with some in western Britain, and from Scandinavia and possibly Russia (*Migration Atlas*). They have long been known for their propensity to occupy the same groups of fields every winter, and seldom visit other sites (Coward 1910, Boyd 1946). They normally quit the moorland for the winter, and many of the occupied tetrads on the map are from birds that have returned early to their breeding areas. The county bird reports have noted that some Golden Plovers have considerably advanced their return dates, from mid-March during the 1990s to 24 February 2000, 17 February 2001, 9 January 2002, 18 January 2003, 11 February 2004, 9 February 2005 and 10 February 2006.

By far the most favoured site, holding perhaps half or more of the county's birds, is Frodsham Marsh, as it has been for over 40 years; in the 1960s it was not unusual to find winter flocks up to 1,000 birds there (Bell 1967). During this Atlas period, there were reports of seven flocks of 1,000 or more, all in the area of Frodsham or Hale on the opposite bank of the Mersey, with maxima of 1,300 on the north side at Hale Marsh (SJ48W) on 6 February 2005, and 4,000 on the south side at Frodsham Marsh (SJ57E) in January 2006. Elsewhere, the highest counts were 360 birds in 2004/05, roosting next to boats in the Heswall gutter (SJ28K) and 400 birds on 17 February 2005 at Ashley (SJ78S), which was one of their favoured sites mentioned by Coward, still in use one hundred years later. Most birds were in much smaller flocks, with a median size of 40 birds. They often form mixed flocks with Lapwings, and sometimes Fieldfares, but try to avoid Black-headed Gulls who often wait for the plovers to extract worms then rush in to steal the food. This kleptoparasitism drives Golden Plovers and Lapwings to feed at night, provided that there is sufficient moonlight, usually in different fields from their daytime haunts (Gillings *et al.* 2005).

This is not normally an estuarine species, except in hard weather, with only 10–15% of the winter population found on coastal mud-flats (*Migration Atlas*), but they feed in inland fields, mostly on earthworms and other soil invertebrates. Nearly two-thirds of the 71 submitted habitat codes were farmland, 26 of them improved grassland, with only one on unimproved grassland, and six each on stubble, tilled land and mixed grass/tilled land. These proportions are similar to those for Lapwing, except that Golden Plovers are significantly more likely to be found on improved grassland and less likely to be on unimproved grassland than Lapwings: this seems surprising in view of Golden Plovers' adherence to long-established feeding sites, many of them predating the chemical era of modern agriculture and the establishment of lush grass. The remainder of the habitat records were grass moor with heather (C3) in three of the hill tetrads, one on grazing marsh at Inner Marsh Farm, three each of small waterbodies and sand quarries, one open shore (a small flock of four birds at

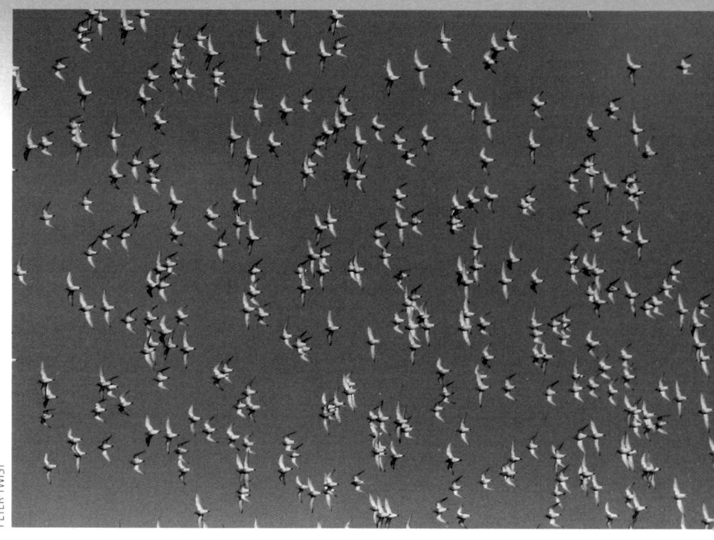

PETER TWIST

Hoylake), and four records of salt-marsh and 11 habitats with estuarine codes.

Since the 1980s there has been a substantial shift of wintering Golden Plovers to the east of England, perhaps in response to the warming climate, with more birds on arable fields and estuaries and fewer on grassland (Gillings *et al.* 2006). There has been little change in the flocks at the county's main site, implying a likely reduction at sites that are not regularly monitored, although this has not been noted in the records submitted to the annual bird reports. Revisiting all the areas mentioned by Coward and Boyd would make an interesting and worthwhile small project.

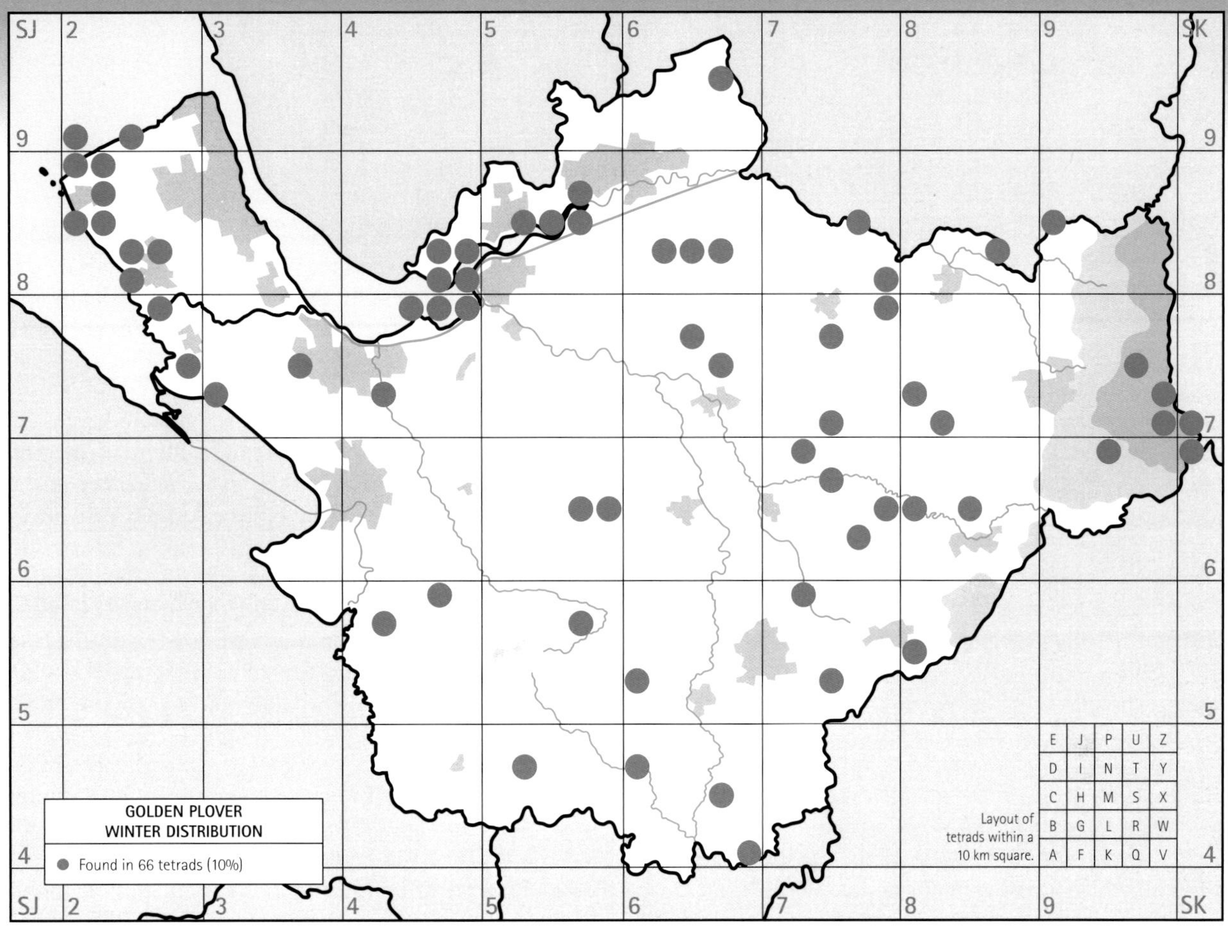
GOLDEN PLOVER
WINTER DISTRIBUTION
Found in 66 tetrads (10%)
Layout of tetrads within a 10 km square.
E J P U Z
D I N T Y
C H M S X
B G L R W
A F K Q V
SJ 2 3 4 5 6 7 8 9 SK

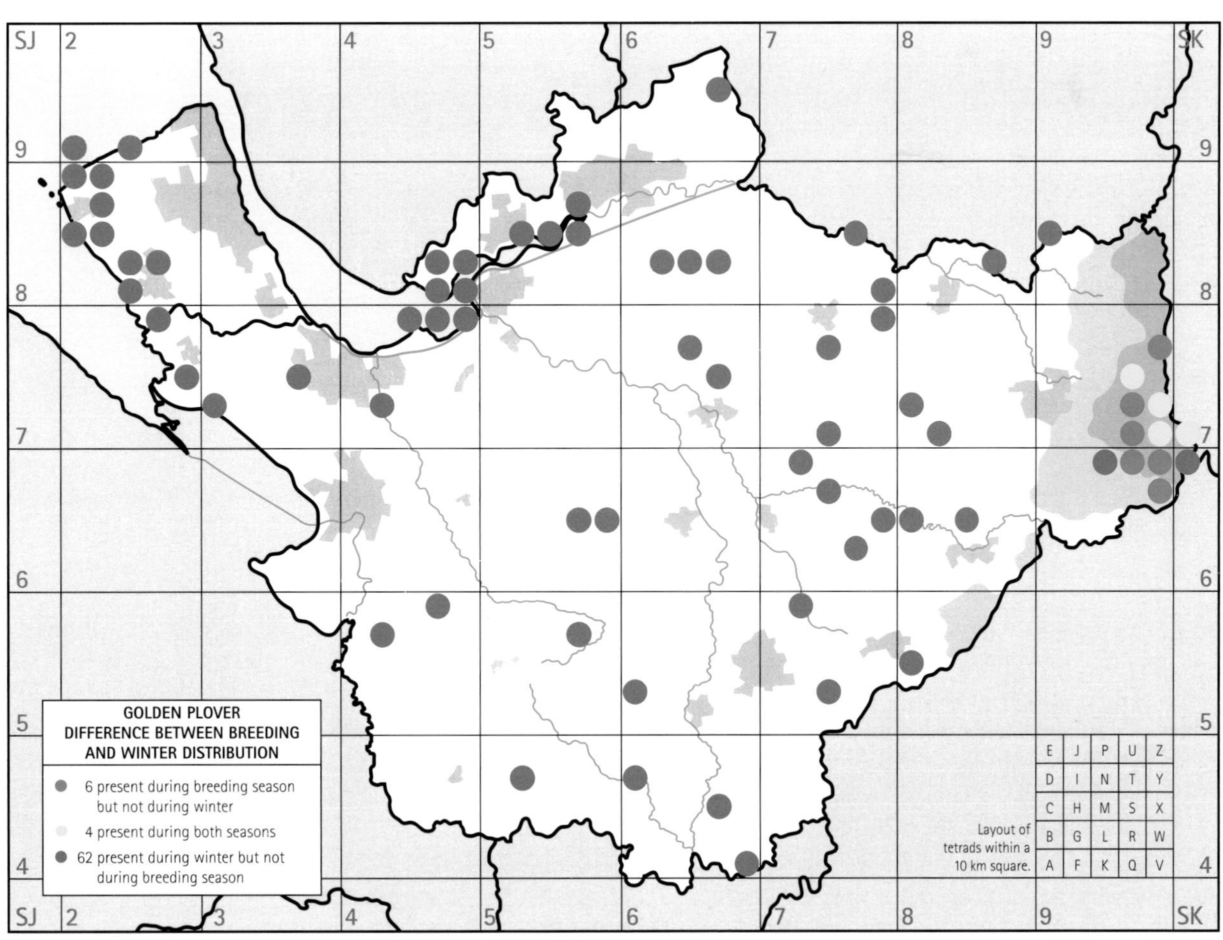
GOLDEN PLOVER
DIFFERENCE BETWEEN BREEDING AND WINTER DISTRIBUTION
6 present during breeding season but not during winter
4 present during both seasons
62 present during winter but not during breeding season
Layout of tetrads within a 10 km square.
E J P U Z
D I N T Y
C H M S X
B G L R W
A F K Q V
SJ 2 3 4 5 6 7 8 9 SK

Grey Plover

Pluvialis squatarola

Grey Plovers migrate here from breeding grounds in the high Arctic, mostly the Taimyr Peninsula of Siberia, and in some winters there are probably now more of them in the county than there have ever been. Coward (1910) knew it as a spring and autumn passage migrant in the estuaries, with a few remaining for the winter, but gave no figures. Hardy (1941) provided useful quantitative information, quoting an average of five to 10 birds, with 40 the biggest flock. Bell's statements were contradictory, writing 'no apparent change since the beginning of the twentieth century' although clearly the numbers had increased: 'flocks exceeding 100 are rare and in many years the maxima are much less, not usually reached until November or December' (Bell 1962). Two unusually large flocks of around 150 were then found, at Red Rocks on 17 November 1962 and Leasowe shore on 16 February 1964 (Bell 1967). Numbers obviously grew rapidly, but unremarked by the annual county bird reports which contained no winter records until a flock of 300 at Parkgate on 12 January 1975 then a massive 1,700 on the Dee in December 1979, of which 1,550 were at Gayton Sands.

Most Grey Plovers winter in estuaries on the east coast of England, and it is probably no coincidence that many of these exceptionally large counts occur in severe weather when the sheltered west coast estuaries offer a temporary lifeline. When it freezes, this is the second most vulnerable wader species after Redshank (*Migration Atlas*). The county's largest ever flock, 2,620 on the Mersey on 17 February 1991, appeared when the east coast of Britain was frozen hard.

Perhaps because of this apparent sensitivity to the weather, the Dee estuary WeBS counts fluctuate greatly, often by a factor of two or three from one winter to the next. The Mersey seems to be a secondary site, with even larger variations in numbers, dropping from 2,100 in 1993/94 to only 60 birds in 2000/01. During this decade the Dee estuary high-tide WeBS counts have averaged around 1,000 birds, with about 200 on the Mersey estuary. Many more birds are found by low-tide feeding counts, however, implying that many birds must roost at sites that are not counted, with maxima of 2,201 at low tide on the Dee in 2001/02 and 597 on the Mersey in 2005/06. The current threshold for national importance is a five-year peak mean of 530 birds.

This winter Atlas map is a good representation of their normal distribution. Grey Plovers are seldom found in winter inland, away from tidal areas, with perhaps one or two birds a decade, usually at Sandbach Flashes, but none during the three years of this survey. They are

GARY BELLINGHAM

Sponsored by Tony and Margaret Hayter

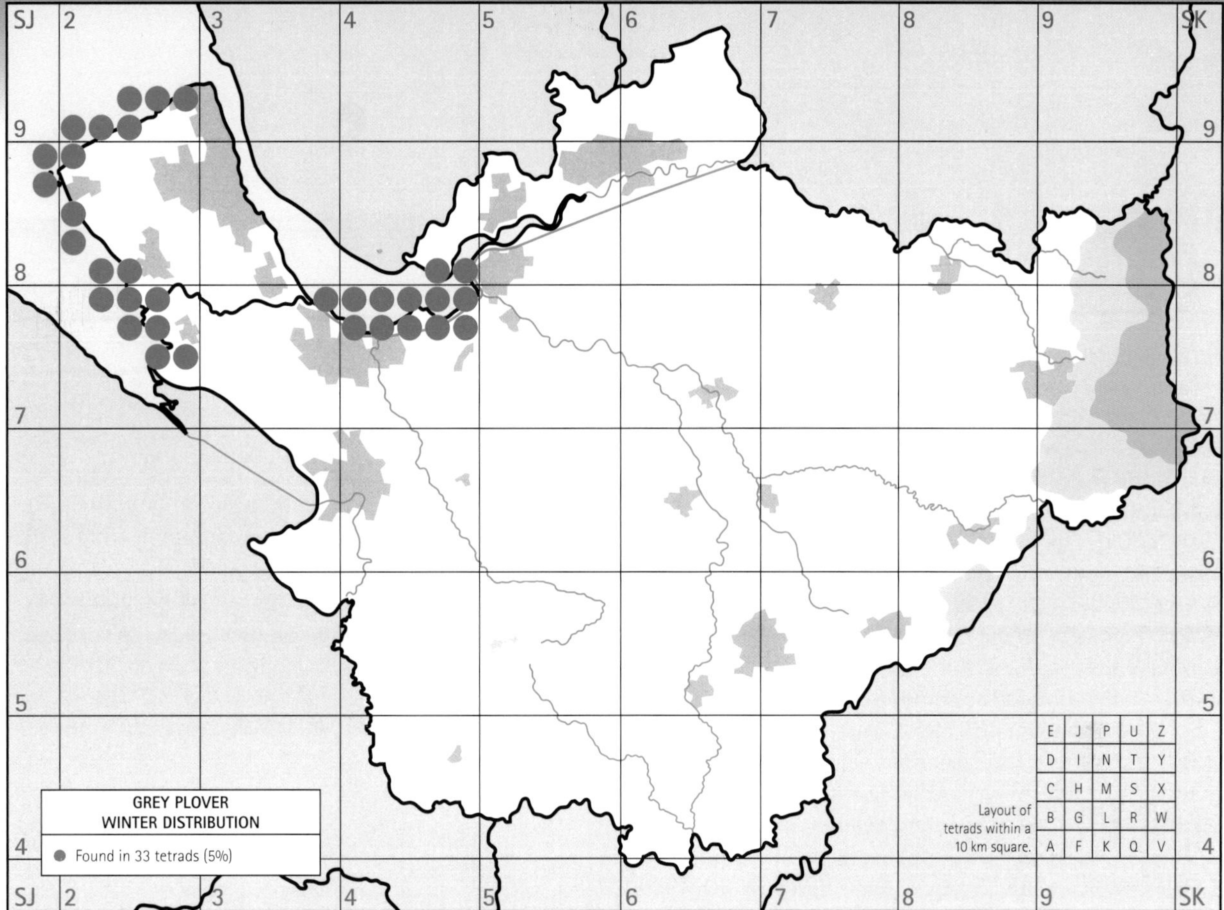

birds of very restricted habitat. The 38 submitted habitat records comprised 23 H3 (estuarine), five H1 (open shore), nine C9 (salt-marsh) and one C8 ('other open marsh'), used to describe the dry area of the dredging deposit lagoon of no. 6 bed at Frodsham Marsh. They feed, loosely scattered across a mud-flat, on a variety of invertebrate prey, especially those that come to the surface or near to it; some birds defend feeding territories, and the majority feed as much at night as by day.

Lapwing

Vanellus vanellus

The Lapwing has been widely publicized as one of the birds that has declined as a result of agricultural changes, and is Amber listed as a result, so the maps for this species have been eagerly awaited. As it happens, breeding Lapwings are probably more widespread than many had feared, being still found in 72% of the county's tetrads. This is one of the species that makes a good case for undertaking surveys at a finer scale than the national Atlases. Although Lapwing has shown a large population decline, their distribution has not noticeably contracted at the 10 km square scale, indicating that they remain widespread but at lower density (Fuller *et al.* 1995). Comparing with our *First Atlas*, they were found in 438 tetrads in both surveys, and have been gained in 45, mostly in a band running north-south through the southern part of Cheshire, but these are outnumbered by the 127 losses, scattered widely across the county. The most obvious factor determining their distribution in this Atlas was their avoidance of urban areas. All of the county's conurbations show up as gaps on the map: east Wirral, Heswall, Ellesmere Port, Chester, Runcorn and Widnes, Warrington, Northwich, Macclesfield, Congleton, Sandbach, Nantwich and Crewe. It seems that they are happy to breed on suitable rough land in industrial areas, such as Birkenhead Docks and the Stanlow petrochemical complex, but not amidst human dwellings.

SIMON BOOTH

The habitat codes show that Lapwing is overwhelmingly a farmland bird, with 84% of the records, especially on tilled land (25% of the total): this is more than twice as many records on tilled land as any other species in this Atlas. Others were on improved grassland (24%), mixed grassland/tilled land (21%) and unimproved grassland (9%). Some birds used semi-natural grassland or marsh, mainly water-meadow/grazing marsh (3% of records) and 'other dry grassland' (2%), and 5% were recorded alongside waterbodies, including sand quarries.

The national population was stable until 1984, coincidentally the last year of our *First Atlas* fieldwork, then dropped by one-half in just 10 years, and has levelled out since then. National surveys in England and Wales showed a 49% population decline between 1987 and 1998, and a 60% fall in north-west England (Wilson *et al.* 2001). The reasons for the decline have been intensively studied. The key factor is that their productivity is too low, with too few chicks surviving to balance adult mortality. Lapwings nest from early April to late June or even July, and some will lay up to three or four times in attempts to raise a brood, but are succeeding far less often these days. On agricultural land, many nests fail owing to predation, mainly by nocturnal mammals. Nests within 50 m of a field boundary have only about half of the chance of survival of those farther away from the edge (Sheldon *et al.* 2007). Although they favour tilled land, as shown by the habitat preferences in this Atlas, they prefer spring-sown crops, especially when adjacent to permanent grassland (Wilson *et al.* 2001); Lapwings often nest in one type of habitat and lead their young chicks, some distance if necessary, to a different type that offers more soil invertebrates. With increasingly specialized modern agriculture, such mixtures of habitats are not often found.

The analysis of BBS transects shows that the breeding population of Cheshire and Wirral in 2004–05 was 7,980 birds (1,310–14,650). This amounts to 2.5% of the UK total, so the number of Lapwings in the county is quite significant in national terms.

Contrary to the decline on lowland farmland, surveys of the South Pennine Moors SPA, of which the Cheshire moors are a part, showed an 80% rise between 1990 and 2004–05 in the breeding population of Lapwings (Eaton *et al.* 2007).

Sponsored by Chris Honer

LAPWING
BREEDING DISTRIBUTION
Found in 484 tetrads (72%)
263 confirmed breeding (54%)
177 probable breeding (37%)
44 possible breeding (9%)
Layout of tetrads within a 10 km square.
E J P U Z
D I N T Y
C H M S X
B G L R W
A F K Q V
SJ
SK

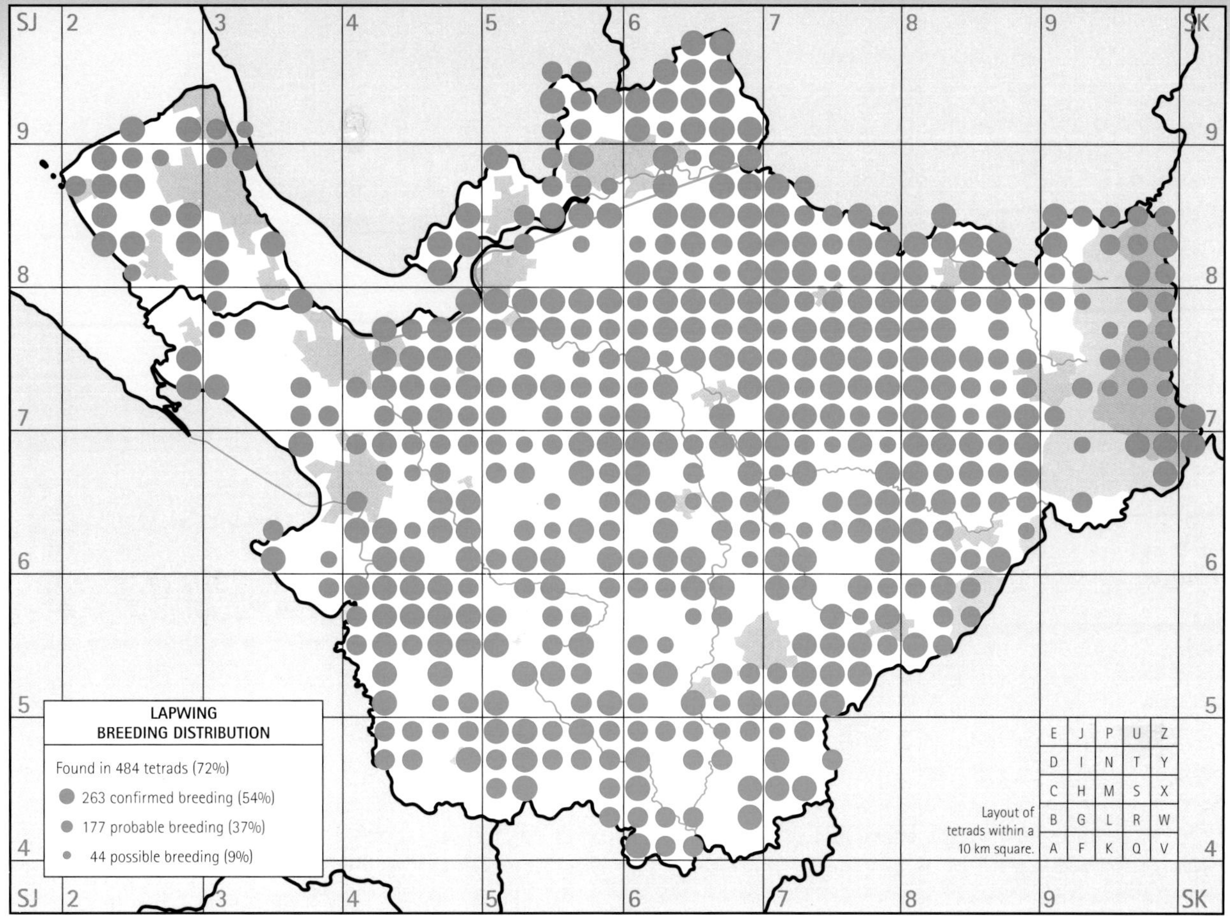

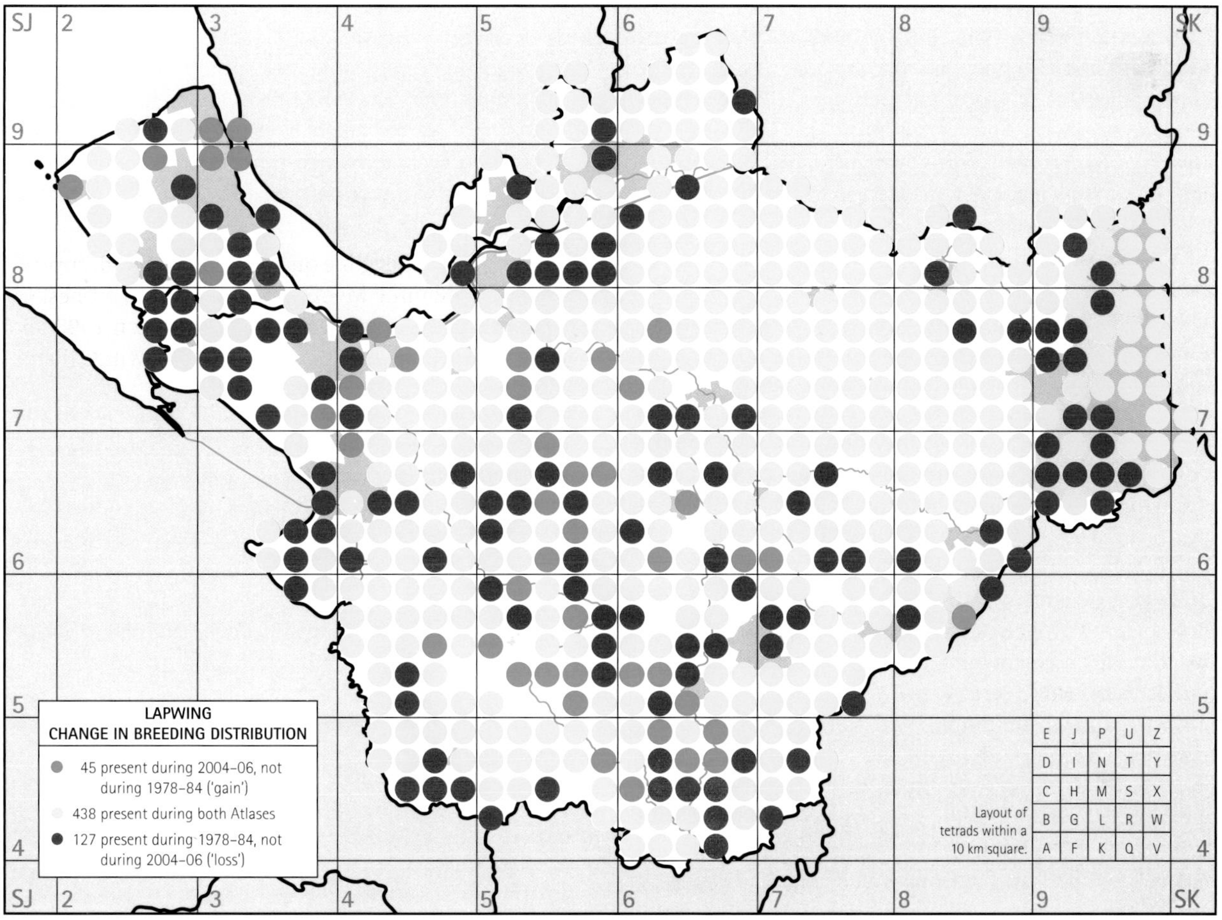

LAPWING
CHANGE IN BREEDING DISTRIBUTION
45 present during 2004–06, not during 1978–84 ('gain')
438 present during both Atlases
127 present during 1978–84, not during 2004–06 ('loss')
Layout of tetrads within a 10 km square.
E J P U Z
D I N T Y
C H M S X
B G L R W
A F K Q V
SJ
SK

PETER TWIST

As soon as breeding is over—in June or even during May for some failed breeders—Lapwings gather together, and spend the rest of the year in flocks. Immigrants from continental Europe, as far east as Russia, come here to join local breeding birds, which tend to move to lowland grassland and the coast. Some British birds go to Ireland or France, but it is only the rare spells when the ground is frozen hard that cause most of them to leave. Previous authors emphasized the hard weather movements of Lapwings: Hardy (1941) noted that flocks went to the coast, and returned inland when it thawed. From the mid-1970s to mid-1980s it was almost an annual occurrence for the county bird report to note thousands of birds on the move, with the county almost deserted in spells of severe frost, as in December 1976, February 1978, January 1979, December 1981, February 1983, January 1984, January 1985 and February 1986, but the hard weather movements of January 1987 are the last on record in the county (*CWBRs*). Perhaps connected with this warming trend, there has been a substantial shift of wintering Lapwings to the east of England, presumably meaning that fewer continental birds are reaching the county (Gillings *et al.* 2006).

The Atlas map shows that most of the breeding areas in the eastern hills are vacated in winter, as are many tetrads throughout the county as birds join flocks at favoured, and regularly used, feeding fields. With 273 tetrads occupied in both seasons, 56 hold birds in winter only, 21 of which are estuarine or coastal, and 211 tetrads are used for breeding only. Most of the records in the hills are of birds returning in January or February to their breeding sites, a characteristic that was noted by Coward (1910) a century ago. He wrote that they usually leave the uplands in October, but in mild winters such as 1897/98 they remained on the moors east of Macclesfield throughout winter. During the relatively clement winters of this Atlas, most upland tetrads were blank, however.

Most Atlas observations of Lapwings were accompanied by a count, showing that half of flocks were of 70 birds or fewer, but there were 43 gatherings of over 1,000 birds. Most of these were on the estuaries or adjacent sites, with 11 four-figure flocks elsewhere, headed by 1,500 on the Gowy flood plain (SJ47G) and at Neumann's Flash (SJ67S). In tidal areas, 6,000 were at Fiddler's Ferry (SJ58M) in 2004/05 and 5,000 on the adjacent salt-marsh in 2005/06, but the largest flock in one tetrad, 8,000 birds on Ince Banks in the Mersey (SJ47P) on 14 January 2005 was rightly described by Andy Ankers as 'a very special sight'. None of these flocks, however, comes close to the 15,000 seen at Witton Flashes—then a favourite winter resort—by Boyd on 25 November 1950, which was probably the largest flock ever noted in Britain (Bell 1962). Modern WeBS counts on the estuaries do not properly represent this inland species, but the five-year peak mean on the Mersey averages over 11,000, and that on the Dee nearly 8,000, usually reaching a maximum in January or February (Musgrove *et al.* 2007).

The submitted habitat codes showed that, as in the breeding season, this is mainly a farmland bird, making up 74% of the tetrads with wintering Lapwings. Most were on improved grassland (35%) but Lapwings favoured tilled land (14%) and stubble (7%) more than most other birds. They visit the estuaries sporadically, comprising 11% of their habitat records, with fresh water (6%) and semi-natural grassland and marsh making most of the remainder (4%). Several observers commented on mobile flocks making use of flooded maize stubble and recently slurried or ploughed fields, from which it was doubtless easy to find their favoured earthworms.

Lapwings often roost by day and feed at night, particularly to avoid having their earthworm prey stolen by Black-headed Gulls. An unusual facet of their behaviour, especially prevalent in north-west England, is the formation of daytime roosts on rooftops of industrial buildings, even in town centres (Calbrade *et al.* 2001). The only example on record in Cheshire and Wirral has been at Handforth (SJ88R), mostly in autumn, but holding 46 birds on 9 January 2000 (*CWBR*). When feeding at night, Lapwings usually frequent different areas from their daytime haunts (Gillings *et al.* 2005), and we should be aware that we are only recording half of their life in winter: despite a recent comprehensive monograph (Shrubb 2007), there is still more to learn about the species.

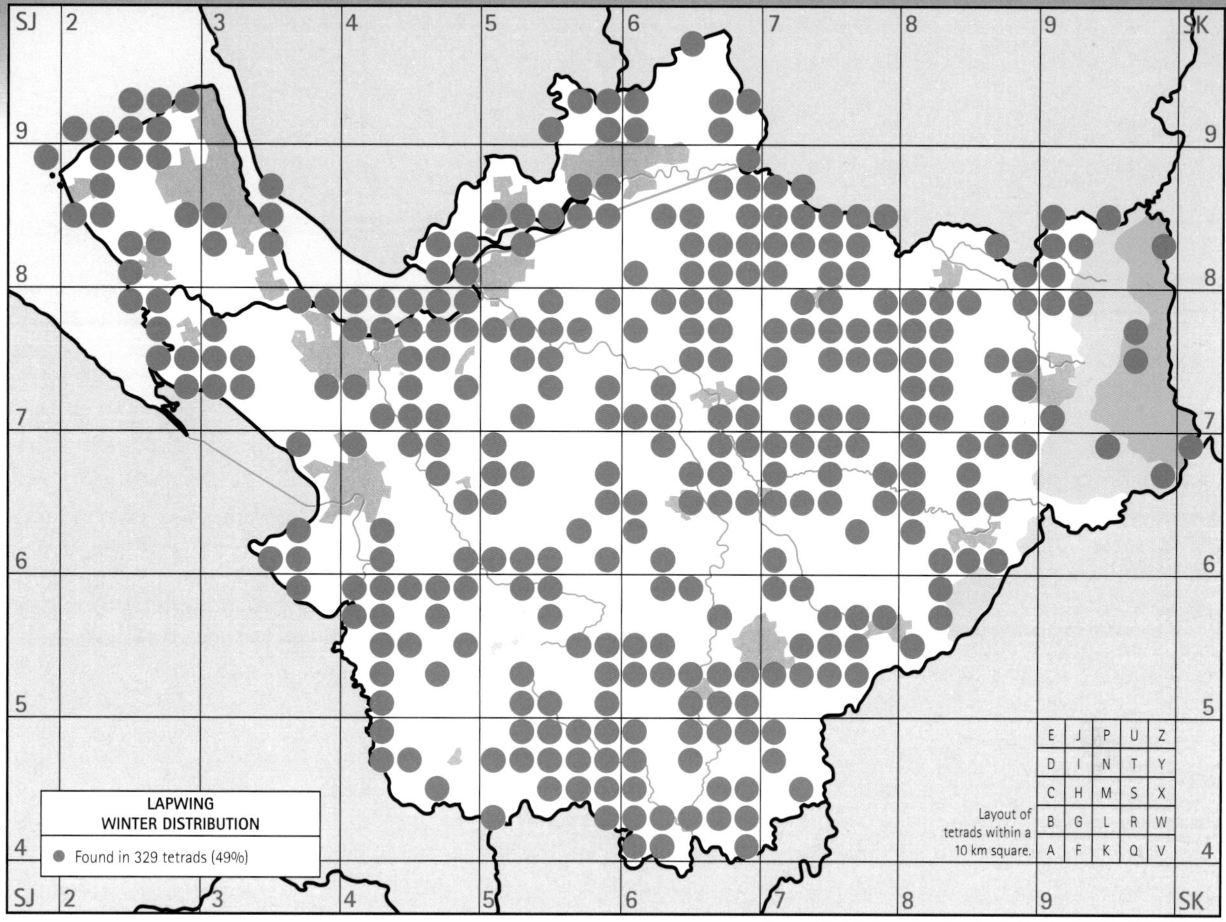
SJ
SK
LAPWING
WINTER DISTRIBUTION
Found in 329 tetrads (49%)
Layout of tetrads within a 10 km square.
E J P U Z
D I N T Y
C H M S X
B G L R W
A F K Q V

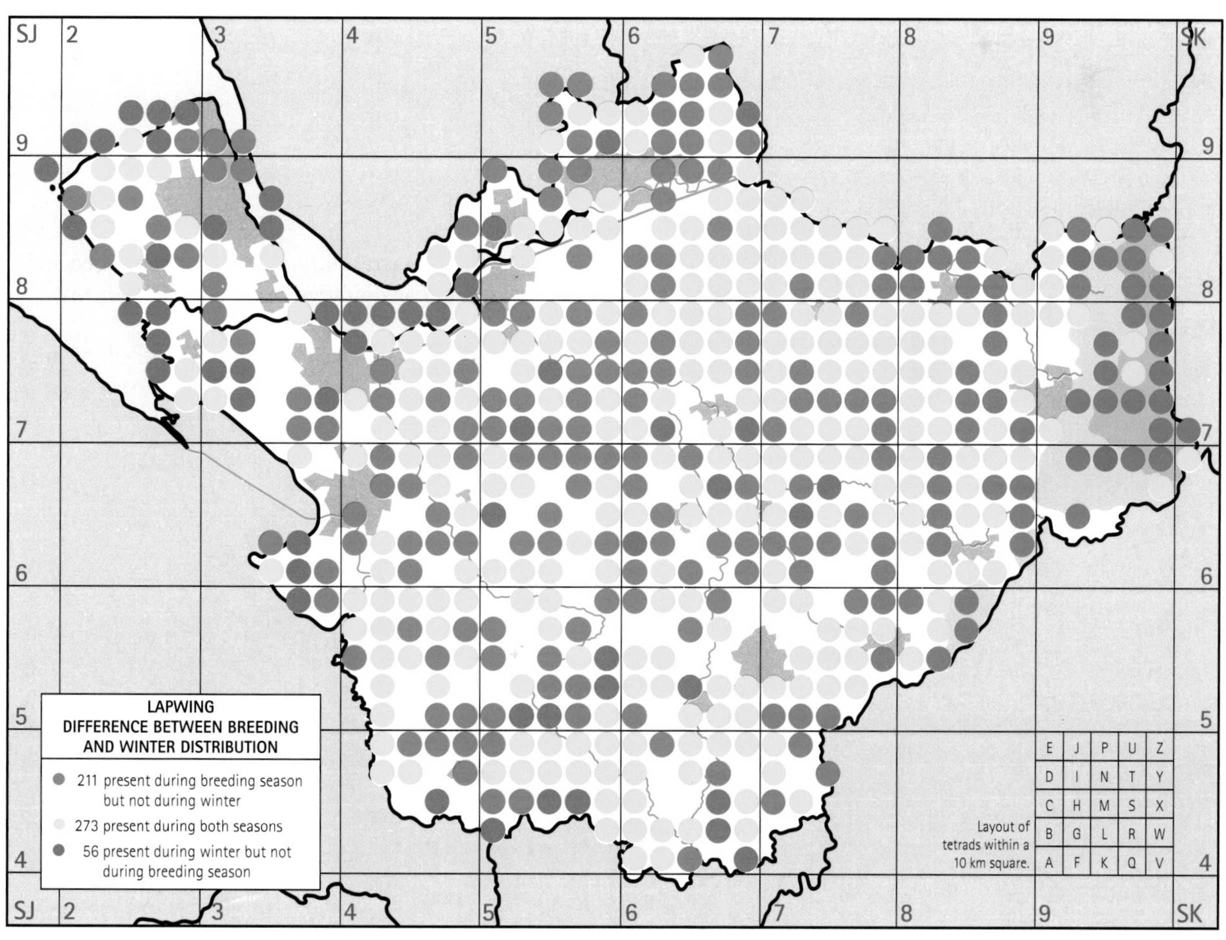
SJ
SK
LAPWING
DIFFERENCE BETWEEN BREEDING AND WINTER DISTRIBUTION
211 present during breeding season but not during winter
273 present during both seasons
56 present during winter but not during breeding season
Layout of tetrads within a 10 km square.
E J P U Z
D I N T Y
C H M S X
B G L R W
A F K Q V

Knot

Calidris canutus

Eric Hardy, in his 1941 book *The Birds of the Liverpool Area*, evoked the image of Knot on Hoylake shore by describing 'the flocks attaining cloud size and nearly a mile long at times'. This graphic depiction gives us no idea of numbers but the birds roosting on Hilbre and Little Eye were famous and attracted photographers including, over 20 times from 1946 onwards, Eric Hosking who mentioned a single pack of Knots numbering 50,000 (Hosking 1970). On 13 November 1965 'about 100,000 at Red Rocks was considered a very conservative estimate' (*CWBR*) but in the early 1970s the Knot population wintering in Britain roughly halved within three or four years, probably because of a series of unproductive breeding seasons from which they never recovered (*BTO Winter Atlas*).

Before that drop in the British wintering population, the Dee flocks were already suffering human disturbance and in 1969 the annual bird report noted that 'for some years past the huge numbers of Knot in the Dee estuary had taken to "flying out" the peak of the very high tides', circling over the estuary rather than roosting on the small areas of land remaining. The pressure increased, day and night, from walkers, dogs, horses and sea anglers but the birds put up with it for more than 10 years until, in 1980/81, Knots feeding in the Dee suddenly switched to flying to the Alt estuary to roost (Mitchell *et al.* 1988). The feeding areas of the Dee, mainly Dawpool Bank off Heswall (SJ28F) and Mockbeggar Wharf off Leasowe (SJ29R) were obviously so productive—especially of their favourite food, the bivalve mollusc *Macoma*—that the Knots were still attracted to them, but they used extra energy flying a round trip of up to 40 km twice a day to find a safe roost. Both sites, the Dee and the Alt, are vital for the species' conservation and both have SSSI and SPA status for Knots.

Since the 1980s the Dee Estuary Voluntary Wardens have run a major campaign to try to educate those disturbing the birds and more Knots now stay to roost on the north Wirral shore off Hoylake, but, for reasons unknown, they have not returned to the Hilbre Islands. On the highest tides, when there is least beach left, they

STEVE ROUND

Sponsored by David and Fran Cogger in memory of Sam

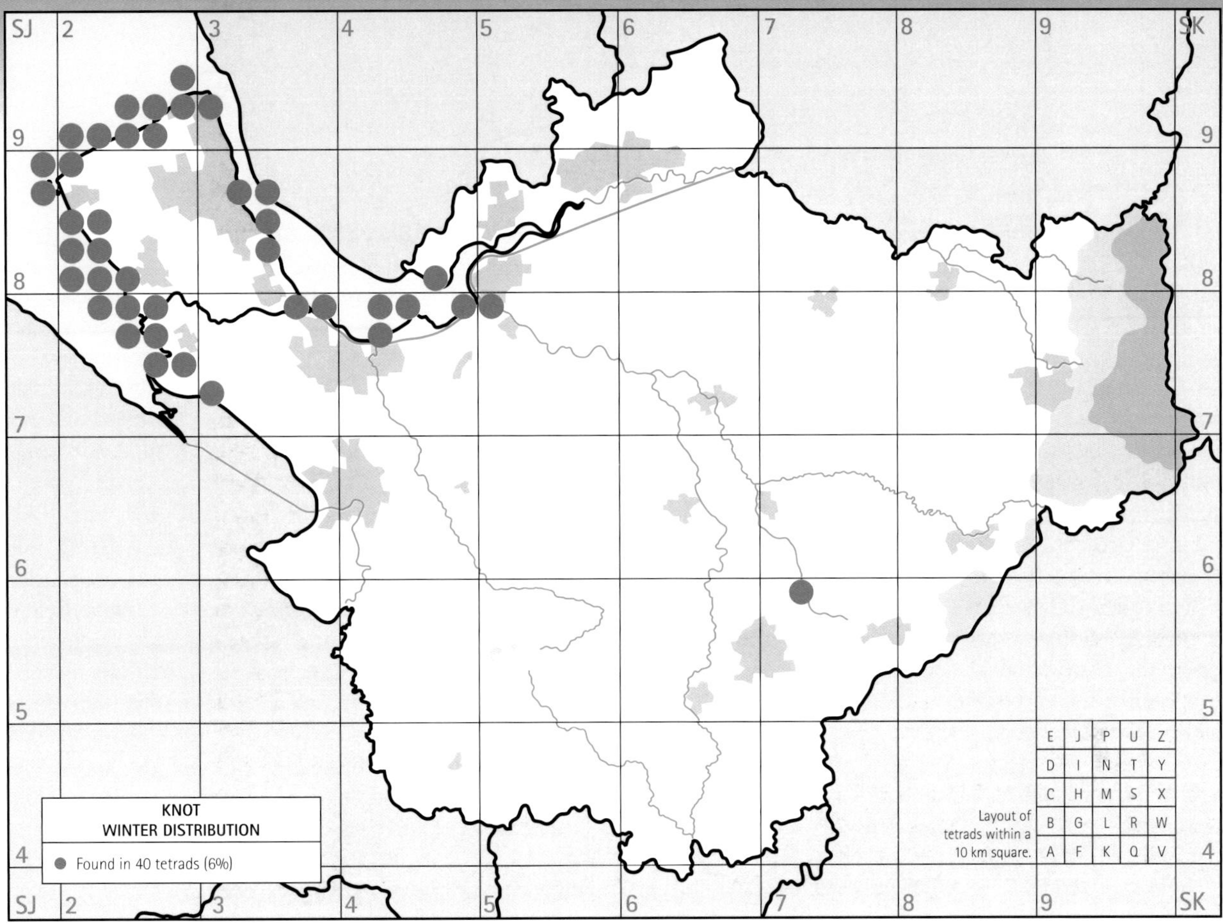

still normally fly to the Alt. On the basis of WeBS counts the Dee estuary currently ranks sixth in the UK, with a five-year peak mean of over 30,000 birds (Musgrove *et al.* 2007), although the figures fluctuate wildly from one year to another, from 5,000 to 50,000, depending on whether the feeding or roosting birds were counted. Some of these figures seem almost unbelievable but, when roosting during high tides, Knot can pack into very tight flocks at amazing densities: I have calculated mean densities of 20 birds per square metre in some flocks caught for ringing.

The Atlas map shows Knots present in every tetrad in the Dee estuary and the north Wirral coast: the largest flocks were 22,400 in SJ29R in 2005/06 and 20,000 off the south of Hilbre (SJ18Y) in the same winter, with the same total also reported in 2004/05 from West Kirby shore (SJ28D) and Hoylake shore (SJ28E). Away from the Dee and north Wirral, Knots were found in 13 tetrads in the Mersey, but numbers are very much lower. The peak Mersey count was 200 birds on Stanlow Banks (SJ47I) and about 100 in the Bromborough/New Ferry areas (SJ38L/M). Knot is a rare bird inland, and there was just one record of a single bird, on 20 and 21 November 2004, at Elton Hall Flash, Sandbach (SJ75J).

The Knots that spend the winter here are of the *islandica* race that crosses the Atlantic to breed far to the north-west, even in '*ultima Thule*' as with the bird ringed at West Kirby on 30 November 1970, found dead on 29 May 1972 in the Thule region of Greenland (76°34′N 68°48′W), 3,694 km away. Merseyside Ringing Group has records of 10 Knots ringed on the Dee and found in Greenland, with another 38 exchanges between the Dee and Iceland, used as a staging ground. One of them was ringed at Hoylake on 11 February 1970 and was in the west of Iceland just four days later, showing that even in mid-February some birds are eager to get back towards their breeding areas, which extend as far as Ellesmere Island, Canada. The UK is of particular importance for the *islandica* Knot, with at least two-thirds, and sometimes up to 90%, of the entire population wintering here; the proportion appears to have been increasing lately owing to redistribution of birds from the Netherlands and Germany, with Knots now tending to winter slightly closer to their breeding grounds. Once here for the winter, birds generally stay put but might move south to France if severe weather closes in, as with the bird ringed at West Kirby beach on 6 November 1964 that was reported from the Vendée, 794 km south, on 31 December the same year.

Sanderling

Calidris alba

Sanderlings are only normally found at the tide edge on sandy shores, for this is the little bird that follows each wave in and out like a clockwork toy, picking small shrimps from the water. At low water they sometimes feed on tiny molluscs and at high tide they may search along the strand line of seaweed for sandhoppers and small flies.

Sanderlings have always been more common on passage in spring and autumn than in winter, but the species has obviously changed its wintering habits quite recently. A century ago it was a scarce winter resident (Coward 1910), and Hardy (1941) wrote of 'a few seen in winter', with Bell (1962) stating that it was irregular in numbers and appearances in the Dee estuary never more than 50 and often considerably fewer. The first mention in a county bird report was in 1971 when 267 Sanderlings were on the Dee in January, so obviously numbers had risen rapidly, with 642 a year later in January 1972, but it was December 1989 before a higher winter count was recorded, of 823 birds. There were then several winters with large flocks, 1,010 on 18 November 1990 and 1,581 on 19 January 1992, but only just over 300 in the following winter: large fluctuations from one year to the next are a feature of this species. After another four-figure maximum in winter 1994/95 numbers fell to a peak usually in the range of 200–400 birds until another winter WeBS count of over 1,000 birds came in 2005/06. It has to be said, sadly, that the *CWBRs* never distinguish how many of the Dee estuary birds were actually in the county, and Sanderlings have often favoured the Welsh side of the river.

The records in this Atlas are, therefore, particularly valuable, with counts on a variety of dates in 2004/05 including 405 at Hilbre (SJ18Z), 1,000 at West Kirby (SJ28C) and 560 on Hoylake shore (SJ28E). The following winter, 2005/06, a large flock of 3,000 was reported from Hilbre, with 600 on Hoylake shore, and in 2006/07 600 were counted at Hilbre. Birds are concentrated mostly around the north-west corner of Wirral, with the highest count farther east being just 40 birds at New Brighton (SJ29W). Birds away from the north Wirral shore are unusual, including the flock of 20 seen by Michael Miles feeding on the Mersey shore off Hale Lighthouse (SJ48Q) on 27 January 2006.

Sanderlings breed on the Arctic tundra, with birds visiting western Europe from north-east Greenland, Svalbard and Siberia. Many birds end up wintering in Africa but the origins and movements of the different populations are still not clear, although it is thought that birds from the north-west just pass through on passage and that those from Svalbard and Siberia are likely to winter here (*Migration Atlas*). The picture is further complicated by some individuals that arrive here in July or August and moult before moving on, some of these birds often staying into the early part of winter in the second half of November. The winter population of the Dee has been little studied but Merseyside Ringing Group has many distant records from birds ringed on passage through the estuary, from Russia and Iceland to the north to Malta and 15 birds in Africa, the farthest south being two in Ghana.

Despite the enormous year-to-year fluctuations detailed above, which are seen at many sites in Britain, birds are said to be very faithful to wintering and passage sites (*Migration Atlas*), suggesting that changing proportions of juvenile birds might account for the variations in numbers. The Dee estuary consistently holds more than 1% of the British wintering population of Sanderlings (210 birds) and thus qualifies as nationally important for the species, but it would be good to have more understanding of the winter habits of this enigmatic bird.

RICHARD STEEL

Sponsored by Sheila Blamire

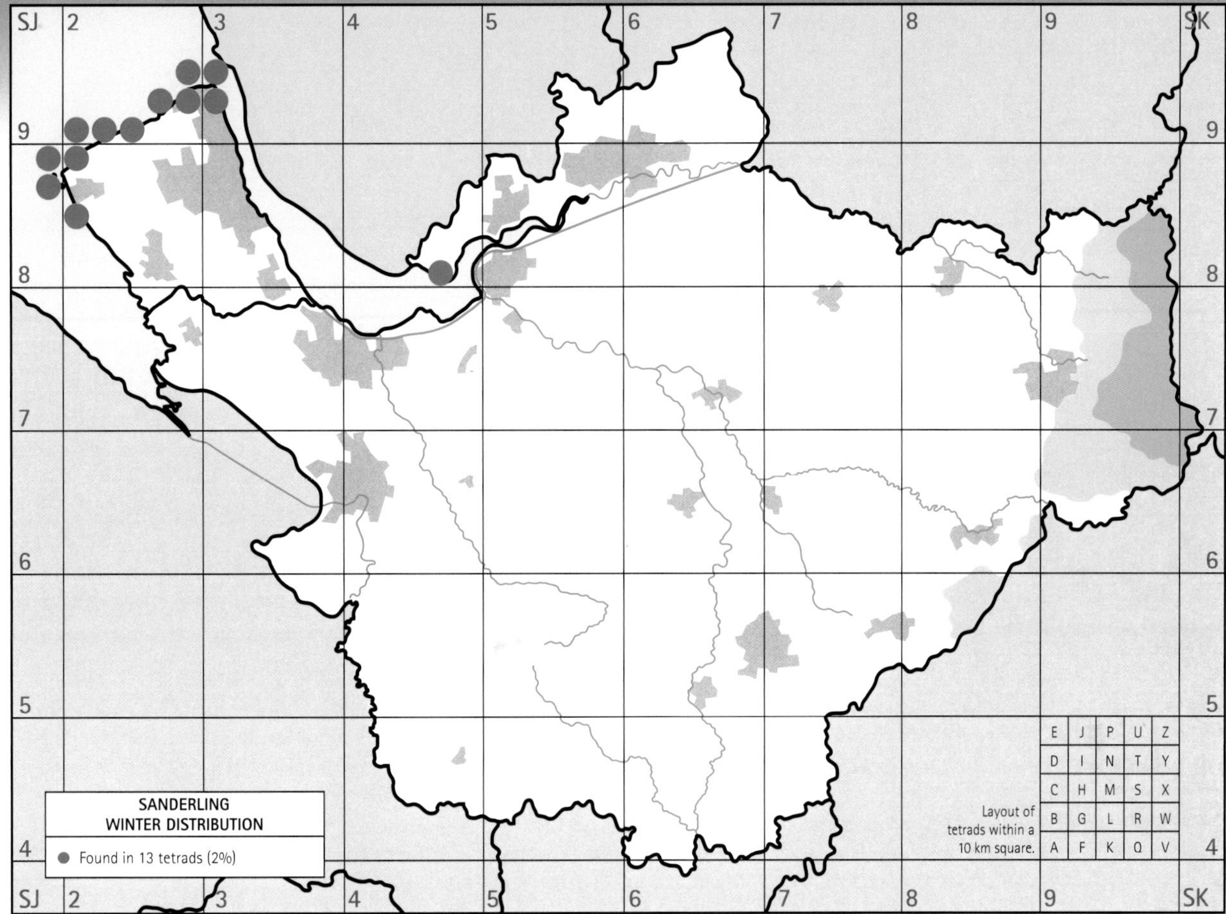
SANDERLING
WINTER DISTRIBUTION
Found in 13 tetrads (2%)
Layout of tetrads within a 10 km square.
E J P U Z
D I N T Y
C H M S X
B G L R W
A F K Q V
SJ
SK
2
3
4
5
6
7
8
9

Little Stint

Calidris minuta

Little Stint is one of several waders that mainly occur here on autumn passage, especially when easterly winds blow inexperienced young birds off course, with appearances in winter and spring becoming more common in recent years. They breed on the high Arctic tundra from northern Sweden eastwards across Russia, with most of the population in Siberia, and one million or more winter in trans-Saharan Africa, with perhaps 10,000 in Europe, mostly in the Mediterranean Basin (BirdLife International 2004). Britain is at the extreme northern edge of the wintering range, and there were fewer than 30 wintering in Britain and Ireland during the early 1980s (*BTO Winter Atlas*). Numbers have increased to an estimated 100–400 in Ireland during the late 1990s but still so few in Britain that they were not listed in the pan-European collation (BirdLife International 2004).

The Atlas map shows a reasonable reflection of the species' status in Cheshire and Wirral, although the aggregation of three winters exaggerates the picture somewhat. Five of the seven Atlas dots come from single birds, with two birds on Frodsham Marsh no. 6 bed (SJ47Y) on 7 January 2006, and a flock of at least 12 birds on the northern part of the same site (SJ47Z) in 2006/07. Frodsham Marsh and the adjacent river Mersey has been the favourite site for Little Stints in winter in the county for at least the last 35 years, with Inner Marsh Farm (SJ37B) and the Sandbach Flashes (SJ75J) the next most likely to be visited.

Apparently the first winter record in the present recording area was at Frodsham Marsh on 28 November 1954 (Bell 1962), followed by one at Burton in December 1957. The county's third wintering Little Stint was ringed at New Ferry (SJ38M) on 31 December 1958 and found in Friesland, the Netherlands, on 9 April 1959, giving interesting information on the timing and route of return towards the breeding grounds. Bell (1967) knew of wintering birds in each year since 1961, including five remaining at Sandbach Flashes until 25 November 1962. Since then, the annual bird reports show Little Stints present in the county in almost every winter since 1972/73. In some winters sightings have been only occasional and numbers small, while in others birds have been present throughout. Frodsham Marsh is the favoured winter site with overall monthly maxima of 30 in December, 25 in January and 26 in February, with these peak counts all in the period 1998/99–2001/02. Higher numbers wintering tend to follow the largest influxes in autumn, usually September, and that in September 1998 was the largest on record (Brown & Grice 2005). As well as being Cheshire's main site for the species in winter, during 1981/82–1983/84 the 10 km square including Frodsham Marsh was one of only five in Britain to have held more than three birds (*BTO Winter Atlas*).

Little Stints feed mostly by picking insects and crustaceans from the surface rather than probing into mud, and probably cannot cope well with freezing weather. The warming climate presumably accounts for the increased numbers wintering here, although they are but a tiny proportion of the species' population.

Sponsored by Keith A. Leggett

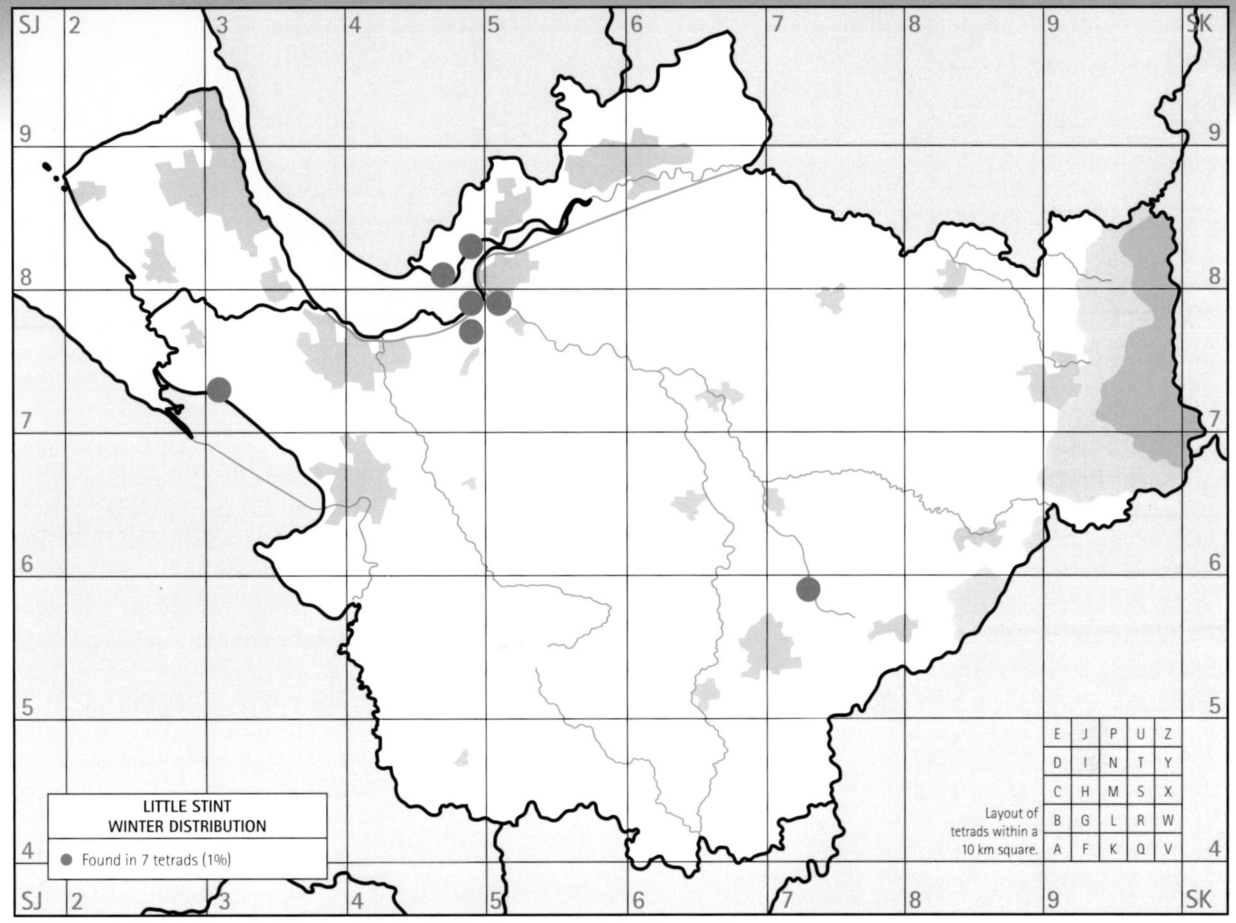
LITTLE STINT
WINTER DISTRIBUTION
Found in 7 tetrads (1%)
Layout of tetrads within a 10 km square.
SJ
SK

Purple Sandpiper

Calidris maritima

Purple Sandpipers are the most northerly wintering waders in the world, with the birds in Britain at the southern edge of their range. Some remain to winter in their breeding areas in Greenland and Norway provided that the shore stays ice-free, and those that breed in Iceland are all resident. The sandpipers work up and down the tide edge, feeding throughout the daylight hours on molluscs, especially winkles, dog-whelks and mussels, with some crustaceans, small worms and algae. As a bird of rocky shores, Purple Sandpiper is never going to be widespread in Cheshire and Wirral, but this Atlas map shows all its usual haunts.

For as long as records have been kept, Hilbre has been their main site in Cheshire and Wirral. Counts of around 20 birds on the island were reported by Coward (1910) and Hardy (1941) but numbers then rose during the 1950s to between 30 and 50, with up to 100 present in the 1959/60 winter (Bell 1962). Further increases were implied by Craggs (1982) who stated that numbers varied, year to year, from 50 to 100. There can be considerable fluctuations but, according to figures in the annual county bird reports, since 1969/70 there does appear to have been a gradual reduction in the numbers wintering (November to February) at Hilbre, with the range of winter maxima for 10-year periods being 40–83 birds in 1969/70–1978/79; 34–56 birds in 1979/80–1988/89; 32–55 birds in 1989/90–1998/99; and 24–45 birds in 1999/2000–2006/07, including 29 in 2004/05 as the maximum during this Atlas period. Is this another effect of a warming climate, allowing more birds to winter on or near their northern breeding grounds?

The Purple Sandpipers have been closely studied over the years by Hilbre Bird Observatory, with an early colour-ringing project—continuing to the present day—adding much to our knowledge of the species' migration and site fidelity, birds being seen at the same site up to eight years after ringing (Craggs 1982). One of

RICHARD STEEL

Sponsored by Hilbre Bird Observatory and Ringing Station

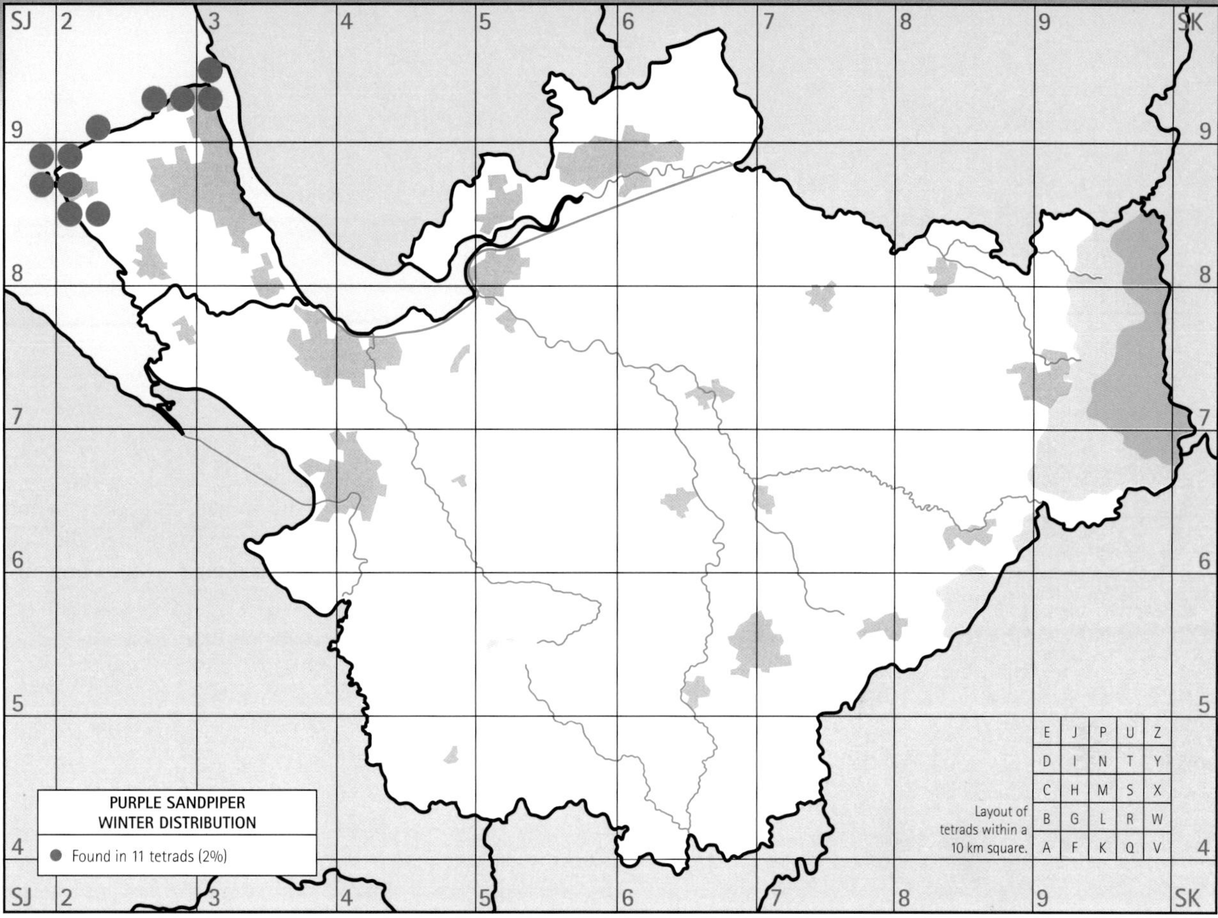

the first birds caught on Hilbre (7 February 1959) was later found in southern Greenland, but their movements are complex and the biometrics of ringed birds have been important in sorting out the origins and wintering areas of the species. Even this is complicated, females being larger than males, but birds breeding in Norway are substantially smaller than those from other areas and these are mostly found in winter on the east coast of Britain. Longer-billed birds predominate in the north of Scotland and along the west coast of Britain, and it is now thought that they are from breeding grounds in the north of Canada. The Hilbre-ringed bird in Greenland, found there on 27 October 1964, was probably not a local breeding bird but a Canadian one on passage through Greenland (*Migration Atlas*). To confuse the picture further, Purple Sandpipers from different breeding areas probably intermix somewhat during winter, and two colour-ringed birds from Hilbre have been seen in Northumberland!

As well as the Hilbre flock, over the years Purple Sandpipers have been located at almost every suitably rocky spot around the north Wirral coast and most of them appear on this Atlas map for holding a bird or two at some stage during the three winters of this survey. The rocks between Caldy and Thurstaston, by West Kirby Marine Lake, Tanskey Rocks offshore from there, Red Rocks, the sea defences at Leasowe and New Brighton, New Brighton Marine Lake and the Mersey shore from Wallasey to New Ferry have all held birds on occasion. There are usually fewer than 10 at these sites but 20 were counted at Red Rocks on 23 January 2003 and 14 were at Wallasey on 27 November 2004, with the largest flock away from Hilbre during this Atlas period being 16 birds on a groyne at New Brighton on 30 December 2005.

This is clearly a fascinating bird whose small population wintering on Wirral deserves continued study.

Dunlin

Calidris alpina

The Dunlin has been on its way out as a breeder in the county for many years, and our *First Atlas* remarked that it had only the slenderest of toeholds here. The last on record was the year after fieldwork finished for our *First Atlas*, in 1985, when the stark 'one or two pairs bred in the Cheshire hills' in the annual county bird report does not, with hindsight, do justice to the occasion.

The decline in breeding Dunlins is not restricted to Cheshire. Between the first two BTO national Atlases (1968–72 and 1988–91), they were lost as a breeding bird from many of their southernmost 10 km squares, in the Pennines, Wales, the Scottish borders and Ireland. The *BTO Second Atlas* has birds 'seen', the equivalent of possible breeding, in three 10 km squares in Cheshire (SJ58, SJ68 and SJ69) but the instructions for that Atlas made no requirement for birds to be in suitable breeding habitat, and it is certain that birds in those 10 km squares had no intention to breed there.

Many possible reasons have been put forward for the decline in breeding birds of the uplands across Britain, including habitat deterioration and loss, perhaps through overgrazing or drainage; increased predation following reductions in gamekeeping; disturbance by ramblers; and increased afforestation. Climate change is implicated for many other northern species, and presumably Dunlin as well. It is not clear to what extent, if at all, these varied factors have operated in the Cheshire part of the Peak District, but Dunlins would struggle to find much of their preferred wet moorland habitat, especially with areas of cotton-grass *Eriophorum latifolium* that they favour.

A survey of the South Pennine Moors SPA, of which the Cheshire moors are a part, showed a 32% drop between 1990 and 2004–05 in the breeding population of Dunlins and none was found south of Kinder Scout in SK08 (Eaton *et al.* 2007).

There is still a substantial spring passage of Dunlins through the estuaries, with odd birds at other sites, but none in suitable breeding habitat although they sometimes sing on spring migration. Dunlin was recorded as possibly breeding in two of the Dee salt-marsh tetrads

Sponsored by www.deeestuary.co.uk

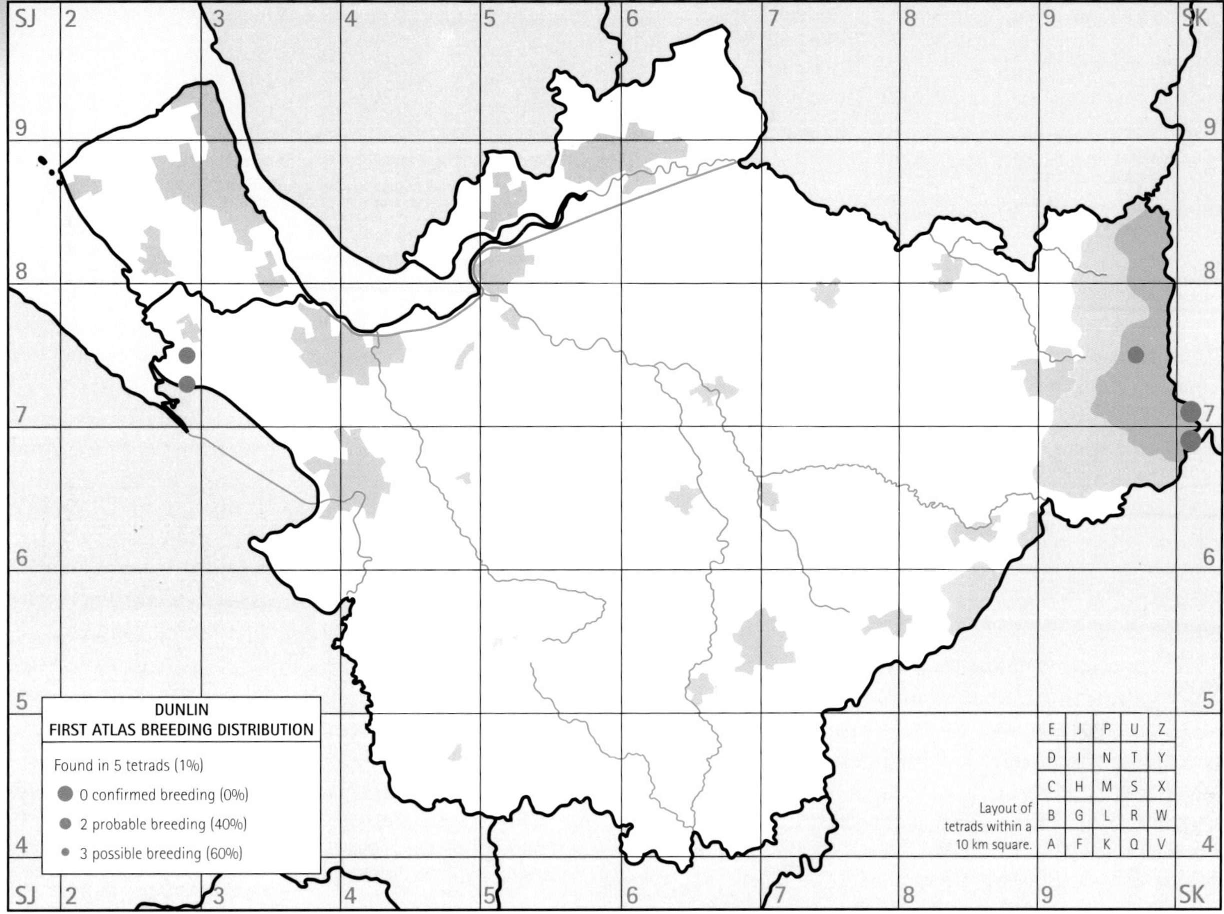

during our *First Atlas*, and the species probably bred in this habitat during 1997–2000 on the Ribble and Morecambe Bay (Pyefinch & Golborn 2001).

The birds in England and Wales are the most southerly breeding Dunlin in the world, and the species is predicted to be lost completely as an English breeder later this century, as climate change takes effect (Huntley *et al.* 2007).

This is the most abundant coastal wader wintering in Europe, with totals of 1.3 million in western Europe, about half a million in Britain and up to 70,000 of them in Cheshire and Wirral. Both of our estuaries are internationally important for the species, with the Mersey estuary the second site in the UK ranking because of its five-year peak mean of almost 45,000 birds, and the Dee estuary in fourth place with a five-year peak mean of nearly 27,000 birds, only about 5,000 of these being in Wales (Musgrove *et al.* 2007). The totals on both estuaries have been dropping in recent years, along with those elsewhere in Britain, and the national total in 2005/06 was at its lowest level since 1970. This decline is mirrored by a rise in the Netherlands, suggesting that birds migrating here from the north-east—the origin of most of our wintering Dunlin—are stopping in the Wadden Sea, aided by warmer winter weather. As sea levels continue to rise, especially in south-east England, and squeeze coastal habitats, it will be interesting to monitor how the Dunlin populations respond.

Three races visit the county, with *schinzii* passing through in spring and autumn between winter quarters in Africa and breeding grounds in Iceland, south-east Greenland and Britain, accompanied by small numbers of *arctica* on their way to and from north-east Greenland from the same wintering areas. The birds that come here for the winter are *alpina*, the larger, longer-billed race that breeds from northern Scandinavia to Russia. One ringed at Hoylake by Merseyside Ringing Group (MRG) was found in May on a Hull-based trawler fishing off Bear Island, Svalbard, well within the Arctic Circle at 74°N, and others have been ringed or caught on Great Ainov Island in the Murmansk region of Russia; the MRG files contain details of 25 birds between here and Finland and 82 movements involving Sweden. Once birds are here for the winter, they are faithful to a site and seldom move more than a few kilometres during the season; they also usually return to the same area in subsequent winters. This site fidelity does make them vulnerable to coastal zone development, oil spills and other man-made hazards.

Our knowledge of Dunlin races and migration has advanced since Hardy (1941) wrote that the majority of winter Dunlin were *schinzii*, although he had found *alpina* amongst birds killed by hard weather in January 1940. No previous Cheshire ornithologists have given any numbers, but Coward (1910) described Dunlin as an abundant winter resident and Bell (1962) wrote that it was common in both estuaries.

The Atlas map shows that Dunlins were recorded in every tidal and adjacent tetrad with suitable habitat. WeBS counters logged enormous concentrations in some tetrads, with the largest totals in the Mersey being 28,000 birds on their main low-water feeding ground, Stanlow Banks (SJ47E), in 2004/05 and 37,000 at the

RICHARD STEEL

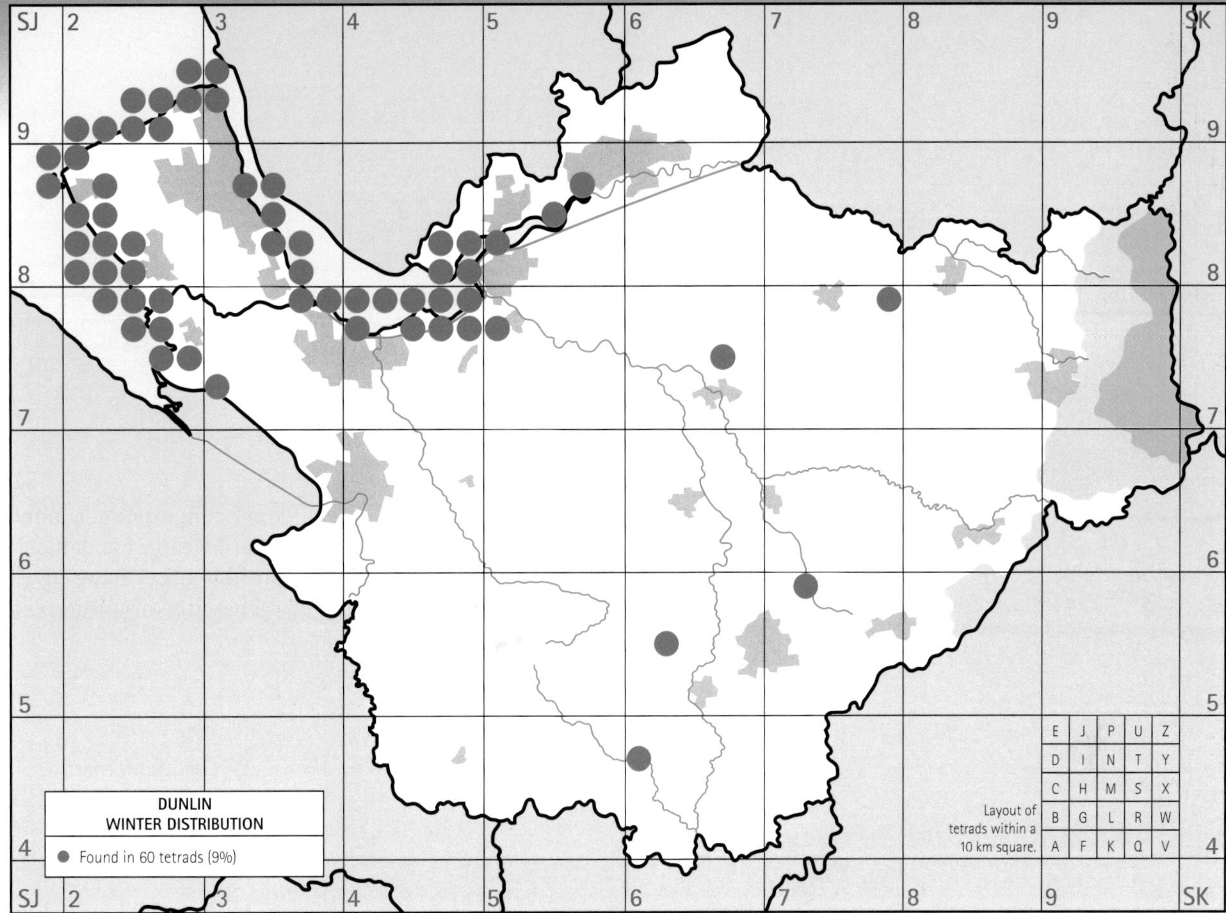

high-tide roost on Ince Banks (SJ47U). Birds on the Dee tend to spread out over a larger area, with fewer huge flocks, but even so, a maximum of 21,000 birds massed on Hoylake Shore (SJ28E). By contrast, the five inland tetrads recorded only one or two birds at a time.

Dunlins feed on a wide variety of invertebrates, especially ragworms and *Hydrobia* snails, probing into the mud to reach their prey. When winter storms disturb the estuarine mud-flats, it is noticeable that sometimes the Dunlin flocks shift their preferred feeding areas according to the sediments and the worms they contain. In hard weather, and sometimes at roost sites on salt-marshes or inland fields, they feed on earthworms and other soil invertebrates.

Ruff

Philomachus pugnax

RICHARD STEEL

Coward (1910) only knew Ruff as 'a bird of passage in spring and autumn, both on the coast and inland; never abundant' but Bell (1962) wrote that 'during the last 25 years it has become well established as a winter visitor in small numbers, particularly around the Mersey marshes in the Frodsham and surrounding areas'. Numbers wintering rose considerably during the 1960s and into the 1970s at sites near the Mersey estuary, particularly Frodsham Marsh. Sixty were there in December 1965, 110 in December 1974 and a peak of 150 in January 1977. The birds were quite mobile, also being seen on Frodsham Score and across the river at Hale where 120 on 29 January 1979 is the last three-figure count in the county at any season. Subsequently the highest winter count in the Mersey estuary vicinity is just 18, at Frodsham Marsh in January 1998. In the winters of 1979/80 and 1980/81, Woolston held the largest numbers with December maxima of 29 and 43 respectively. In almost every subsequent winter the largest numbers have been found at Sandbach Flashes where maxima have ranged from eight in December 1982 to 42 in December 1992. Ruffs have been present at Inner Marsh Farm in every winter from 1988/89 with a maximum of 20 in February 1993, but otherwise the species is scarce on Wirral. Elsewhere in the county there are sporadic winter records.

Thus, this winter Atlas map presents a typical picture of Ruff, although the aggregation of three years' records probably overstates the position. Most groups were from one to four birds strong, with the largest flocks of 20 at Sandbach Flashes (SJ75J) and nine at Inner Marsh Farm (SJ37B), both in 2004/05. Up to five were noted on the Dee salt-marsh (SJ27X) but all other Ruffs were on inland freshwater sites, in three tetrads on wet agricultural grassland and the rest in areas whose habitat was categorized as C6 (water-meadow/grazing marsh).

Most Ruffs breed in northern Fennoscandia and Russia and winter in seasonal wetlands in trans-Saharan

Sponsored by Mrs J.C. Bell

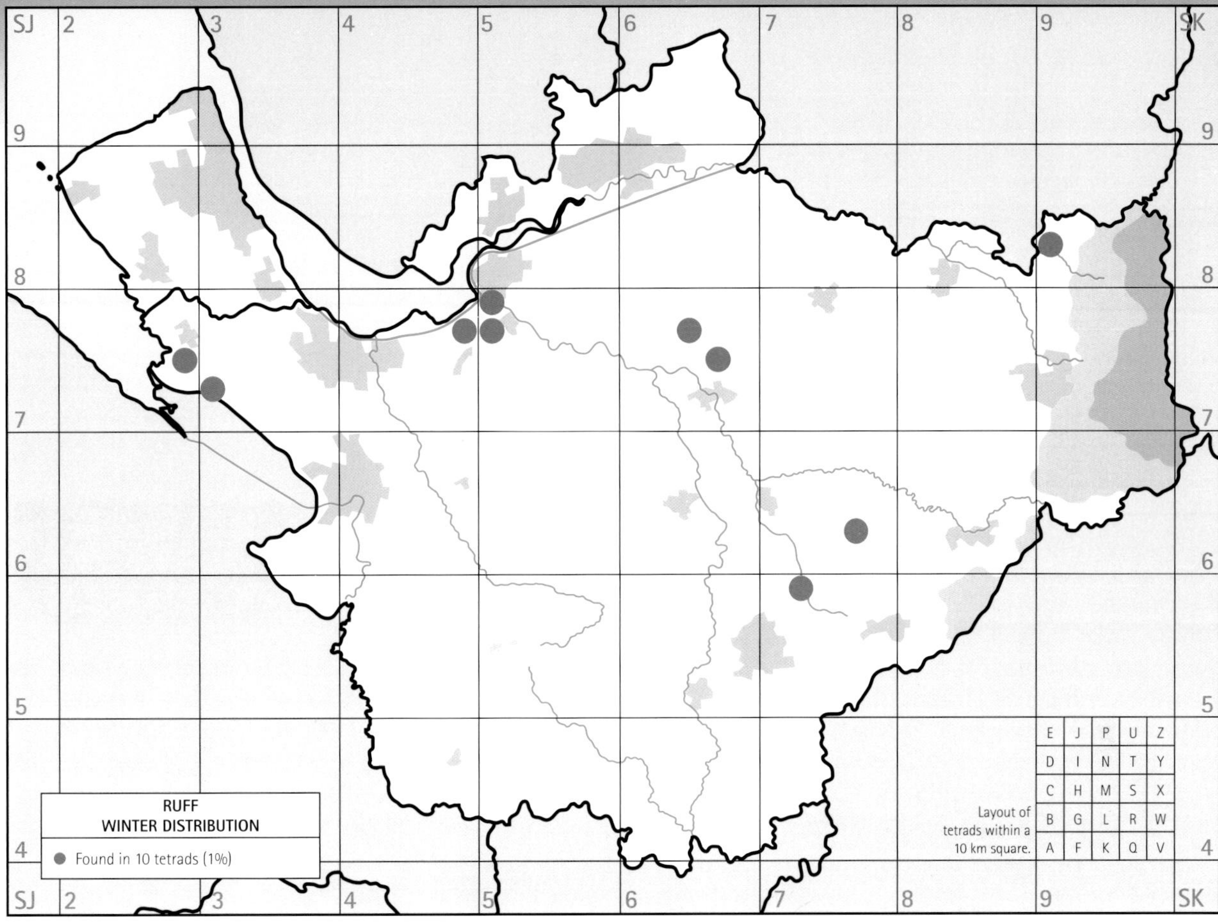

Africa. They mostly feed on mud-dwelling invertebrates, but some of the hundreds of thousands of birds wintering in Senegal have taken to gorging themselves on rice, making themselves a tastier target for the locals who can trap or shoot them. A tiny proportion of the population, probably birds breeding in eastern Siberia and predominantly the much larger males (*Migration Atlas*), spend the winter in western Europe. Wintering in Britain was first recorded in 1934, with numbers increasing to more than 1,000 during the 1970s, then falling to only a few hundred (*Migration Atlas*): clearly, at times, Cheshire and Wirral used to hold a significant fraction of the British total, but not now. WeBS counts have shown an increased tendency for Ruffs to winter in Britain since the late 1990s, with eight sites, all in England, now having five-year peak mean figures of more than 50 birds. That for the Dee, including Inner Marsh Farm, is 14 birds (Musgrove *et al.* 2007).

● Ruff has never bred in Cheshire and Wirral. Birds were reported during the breeding season from four tetrads—Inner Marsh Farm (SJ37B), Ashton's Flash (SJ67S), Sandbach Flashes (SJ75J) and a farm with a flooded field near Aston (SJ64D)—but it is debatable if they offer suitable breeding habitat and whether the records should be classed as H or O: the first three of these sites also had winter records of the species. Although some of them are males in breeding plumage with the eponymous ruff around the neck, and Sandbach Flashes (SJ75J) were visited by a male and female on 3 May 2006, most birds do not stay and move on quickly. To breed, female Ruffs need the stimulus of a communal display (lek) by several males. Three or more males have been noted displaying in the county occasionally, as in 1949 (Boyd 1951), 1963, 1991, 1997 and 1998 (*CWBRs*). This is one of the rarest breeding waders in Britain and the reports of the Rare Breeding Birds Panel show its scarcity: a handful of birds nested in Scotland in 2003 and 2004, but the previous record of confirmed breeding was in 1996 (Holling *et al.* 2007a). They have bred or attempted to breed in Lancashire, in 11 years from 1969 to 2002, at three different sites (White *et al.* 2008), so any spring gathering of Ruffs in Cheshire and Wirral should be carefully monitored.

Jack Snipe

Lymnocryptes minimus

The casual records submitted to the county bird reports in the last twenty years have found Jack Snipe at 12–30 sites annually, many of them on autumn or spring passage. This Atlas provides a much more comprehensive view of the species' widespread distribution, showing it present in 61 tetrads during the three years. This is very much a bird of the lowlands: all but three birds were below 100 m in altitude, with only one above 200 m, in the Birchenough Hill tetrad (SJ96Y) at around 400 m.

Although they are often thought to share feeding areas with Snipe, and only four of the 61 tetrads did not hold the larger species as well, the habitat analysis reveals major differences. The main habitats for Jack Snipe were semi-natural grassland or marsh (48% of habitat records), with far fewer in farmland (13%): for Snipe the proportions are 21% and 39% respectively. In more detail, birds in semi-natural grassland or marsh were in water-meadow/grazing marsh (22%), reed swamp (10%), other open marsh (10%) and salt-marsh (5%). On farmland, there were only eight records (13% of the total of habitat codes submitted), with four of them on flooded stubble fields and only three on grassland. In six tetrads they were reported from bog (10% of the total), an interesting result considering the tiny amount of this habitat in the county, only 0.1% of the land area of Cheshire and Wirral. Freshwater habitats accounted for 24% of records, mostly standing waterbodies (17%) of any size. Jack Snipe are highly crepuscular, usually sitting out the day on a favourite tussock, often the same one from one day to another. They feed mainly on larvae, insects and sometimes seeds, feeding from the surface more than Snipe, perhaps because of their shorter bills.

RAY SCALLY

Previously in the county, Coward (1910) knew the species as a regular winter resident, less plentiful than Snipe in most parts of Cheshire. Boyd (1951) called it 'distinctly uncommon' in the Great Budworth area: he had never seen more than four together but shooting parties had occasionally reported larger numbers. Bell's general comments do not accord with the present picture: he wrote that their 'chief haunts are in marshes bordering Dee and Mersey estuaries but only in small numbers. Elsewhere in the county it is exceedingly local and scarce' (Bell 1962). As now, he noted that Jack Snipe were very unusual in the eastern hills, and 'on the plain it favours certain localities where it is fairly regular'.

Ringing studies in Britain have indeed shown that some birds turn up again at the same site from winter to winter, and that they are relatively sedentary within a winter at their favoured localities (*Migration Atlas*). Jack Snipe migrate here from their breeding areas in Sweden, Finland, the Baltic States and Russia, and, if forced by hard weather, some move on to France, Iberia and as far as North Africa.

Its combination of characteristics—cryptic coloration, reluctant to flush, usually silent, crepuscular habits—makes the Jack Snipe very difficult to count. The vast majority of records were of one or two birds. Two substantial counts came from the area of Coddington Brook/Aldersey Brook (SJ45N) where Neil Friswell flushed 12 birds from *juncus* rushes on 5 February 2007, and Keith Massey counted 14 at Fiddler's Ferry (SJ58M) in 2005/06. The sum of counts submitted in the three winters was 60, 49 and 71 birds, allowing, since not all tetrads were visited each year, an estimate of around 100 birds present each winter: this is probably the first time that a population estimate for the county could be achieved.

Sponsored by John Wilson

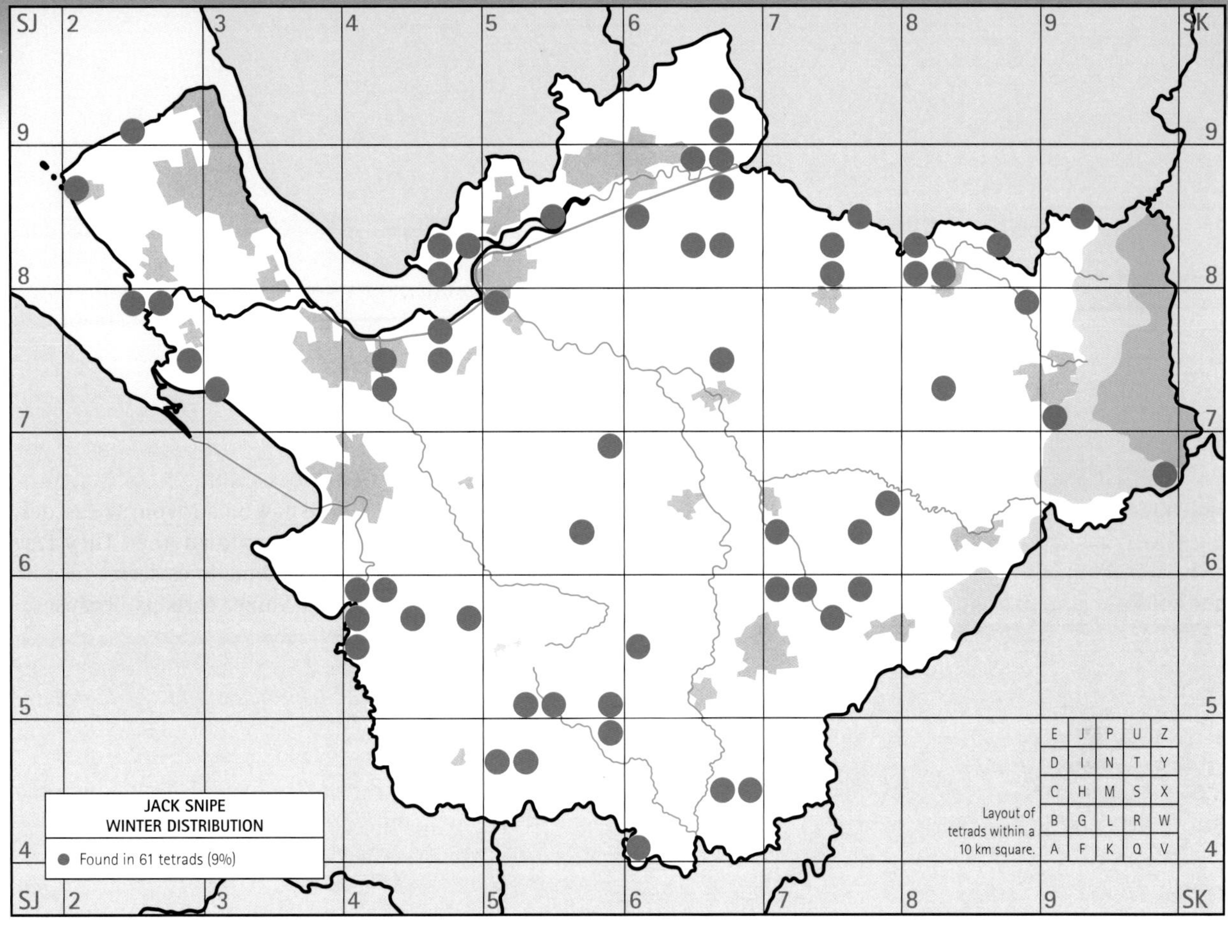
JACK SNIPE
WINTER DISTRIBUTION
Found in 61 tetrads (9%)
Layout of tetrads within a 10 km square.
E J P U Z
D I N T Y
C H M S X
B G L R W
A F K Q V
SJ
SK

Snipe

Gallinago gallinago

STEVE ROUND

Breeding Snipe have declined considerably since our *First Atlas* and the species now has just a tenuous hold on the county. The picture is confused in a standard Atlas map by 59 tetrads with H records, almost all of which were late-wintering birds observed in April; these were scattered across Cheshire, with Inner Marsh Farm the farthest into Wirral. There were only nine tetrads with evidence of breeding (apart from H). Records of 'possible breeding' in this Atlas are omitted from the 'change' map.

It is difficult to track the decline of the last twenty years because, as with many species, as soon as fieldwork for our *First Atlas* finished, few observers recorded breeding birds. From 1985 to 2003, the annual county bird reports contain records of confirmed breeding in only six years, with just one pair each year: 1988 'one bird flushed away from a nest' at an unnamed location; 1989 'confirmed at one site in the eastern hills'; 1990 'a pair appears to have bred successfully on Frodsham Marsh'; 2000 'bred Risley Moss' with no further details; 2001 'one pair bred Risley Moss'; and in 2003 two adults with a well-grown young bird were at Aldford Brook Meadows (SJ45J) on 30 June. During this Atlas, there were three occupied nests in 2005 at Risley/Rixton Moss (SJ69Q) and in 2006 broods of chicks were seen in two tetrads (SJ69Q/R) at Risley Moss.

Most other evidence of breeding comes from observers seeing, and hearing, the male birds' unusual displays, either 'drumming', flying over a territory and splaying his outer tail feathers during descent, making a peculiar throbbing noise or, whilst perched on a post or in flight, giving a repeated 'chipper-chipper-chipper-chipper' call. Some observers recorded these as S (breeding calls heard) and others as D (display or courtship) so little emphasis should be placed on the apparent differences between 'possible' and 'probable' breeding. Drumming and chippering can be given by sole male birds so they indicate no more than 'possible' breeding, but a paired male continues with these displays, even on moonlit nights, whilst his mate incubates their eggs. During this Atlas, Snipe were displaying in June in three upland tetrads, and heard drumming in four more.

They are on the Amber List of species of conservation concern because of their UK population decline. National surveys of waders breeding on wet lowland grasslands in England and Wales, conducted in 1982 and 2002, showed a 62% drop in breeding Snipe, with most of the country's birds concentrated onto a small number of damp, protected sites, with cattle and sheep grazing (Wilson *et al.* 2005). The main reason for their decline in the lowlands is drainage of farmland. Snipe need damp areas in which they can probe for worms, with some insects, crustaceans and molluscs, using the sensitive and flexible tip of their bill to feel for food, much of which they take at night.

The trend in the upland and moorland strongholds of the species is not fully known, but surveys in the South Pennine Moors SPA, of which the eastern hills of Cheshire is a part, have shown a 16% rise between 1990 and 2004–05 in the breeding population of Snipe (Eaton *et al.* 2007). The decline in the Cheshire hills is puzzling.

SNIPE
BREEDING DISTRIBUTION
Found in 68 tetrads (10%)
2 confirmed breeding (3%)
3 probable breeding (4%)
63 possible breeding (93%)
Layout of tetrads within a 10 km square.
E J P U Z
D I N T Y
C H M S X
B G L R W
A F K Q V
SJ
SK

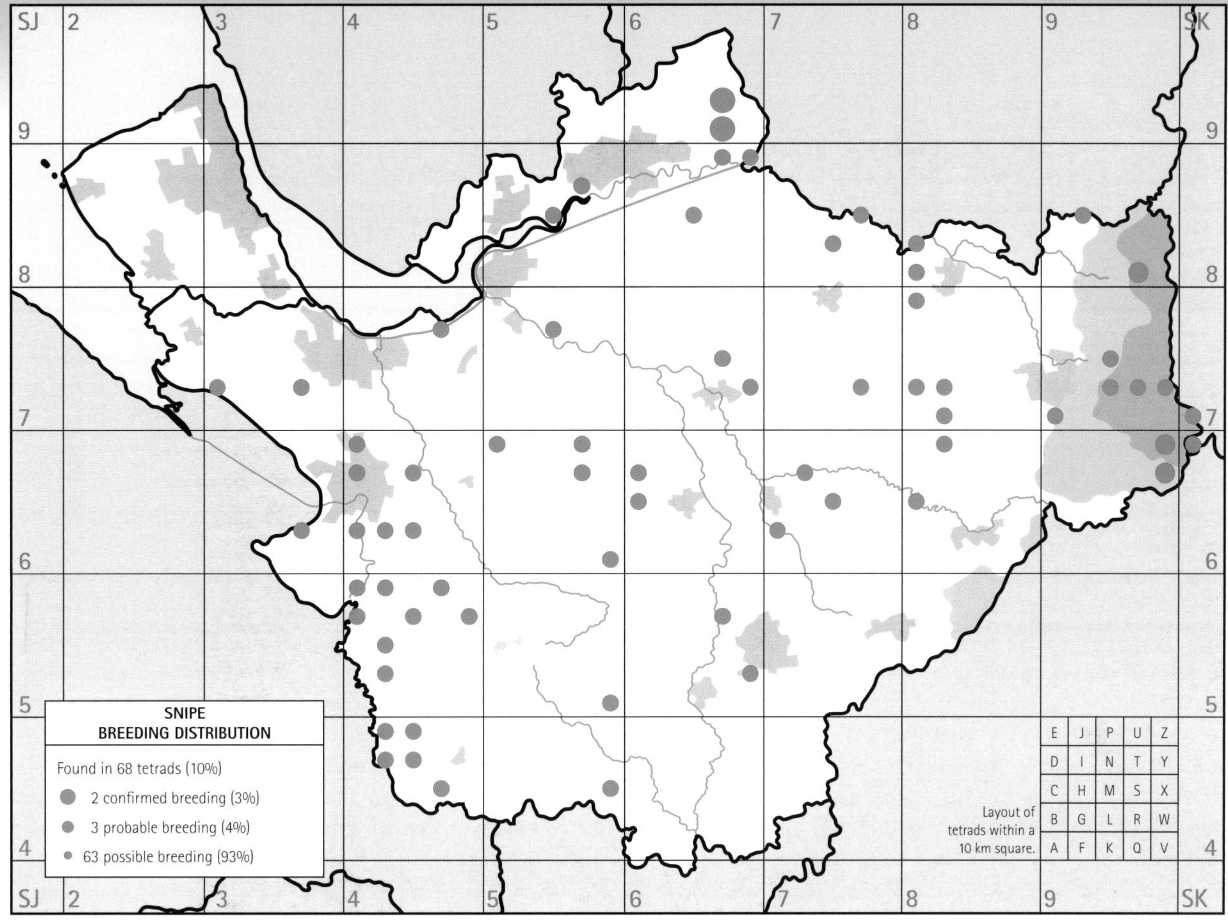

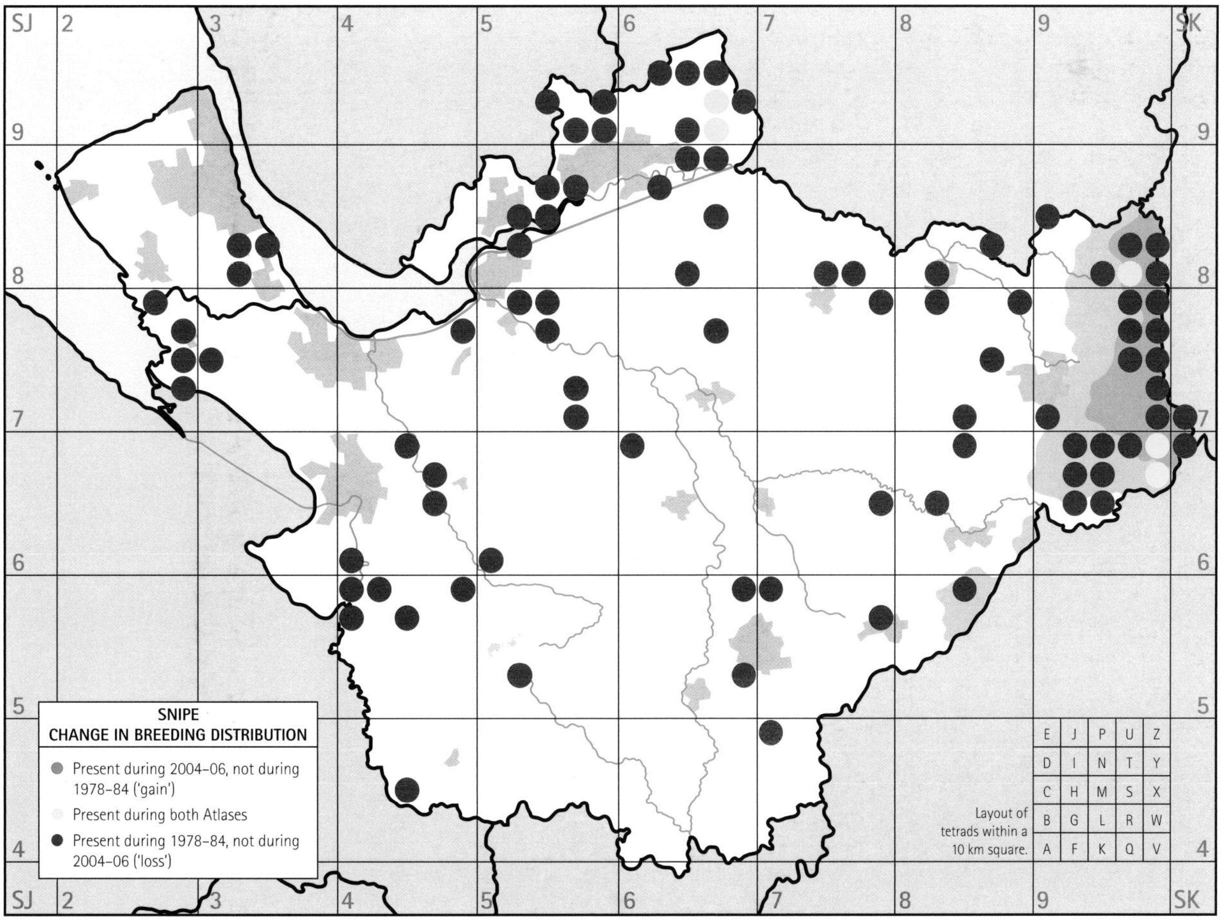

SNIPE
CHANGE IN BREEDING DISTRIBUTION
Present during 2004–06, not during 1978–84 ('gain')
Present during both Atlases
Present during 1978–84, not during 2004–06 ('loss')
Layout of tetrads within a 10 km square.
E J P U Z
D I N T Y
C H M S X
B G L R W
A F K Q V
SJ
SK

Although most of the county's farmland dries out too much to provide suitable breeding conditions for Snipe, it stays sufficiently wet during winter for Cheshire and Wirral to hold significant numbers of birds. They were recorded in 327 tetrads, almost half of the winter tetrads. They clearly avoid built-up areas, and were scarce in the higher land in the east of Cheshire. In the rural lowland parts of the county, many Atlas fieldworkers expressed surprise at how widespread they were, and how easy to find: any suitably damp area was likely to hold Snipe, well camouflaged but easily detected, if flushed, by their rasping 'zip' call and characteristic zigzag flight.

Snipe used a wide range of habitats. Observers recorded farmland in 39% of occupied tetrads, most on improved or unimproved grassland, with 5% in flooded stubble fields. Freshwater habitats made up 33%, mostly standing waterbodies (25%) of any size from pond or marl-pit to mere, with almost all of the rest on narrow ditches or streams. Semi-natural grassland or marsh accounted for 21% of habitat records (10% water-meadow/grazing marsh, 6% reed swamp, 3% salt-marsh and 2% other open marsh) with 2% in bogs. They tend to rest by day and feed at night, eating more vegetable matter and seeds during winter, perhaps taken incidentally to their main diet of earthworms and tipulid larvae, with beetles, flies and their larval stages (*BTO Winter Atlas*).

They tend to form loose flocks when feeding or loafing. More than three-quarters of records were accompanied by counts, showing that the median flock size was six birds. There were 16 counts of over 50 birds and four over 100, all in the last winter, 2006/07. The largest flock in the submitted Atlas records was near Statham (SJ68T), where David Bowman flushed an exceptional total of 166 birds on 20 December 2006, with other groups of 121 and 112 at Risley Moss (SJ69Q/R), and 104 at Aldford Brook Meadows (SJ45J). The wintering population of the county certainly exceeds 2,000 birds, and may be considerably more.

There is a substantial migratory movement of Snipe across Europe, with perhaps one million birds wintering in Britain and Ireland. Snipe from Iceland winter in the Western Isles and Ireland, and our wintering population comprises birds from Finland, Sweden and elsewhere in northern Europe as far east as Russia. Many of the Snipe breeding in Britain move south or depart for winter to Ireland, France and northern Iberia, to be joined, during hard weather, by some immigrants that had started the winter in Britain (*Migration Atlas*).

The species' winter status has probably not changed much in one hundred years. Coward (1910) wrote that 'during the winter months the Snipe is generally distributed throughout the county, frequenting pit-sides and damp meadows, often singly or in couples, but sometimes in wisps of considerable size'. Boyd (1951) had notes of 50–100 or more during mild weather in each of the months November to February. He commented that 'hard frost scatters them ... many leave the district, and the few that remain pop up from any deep unfrozen ditch or spring which they rarely visit at other times'. Bell (1962) summarized the species as an 'abundant winter visitor ... birds found in all suitable localities during the winter'.

STEVE ROUND

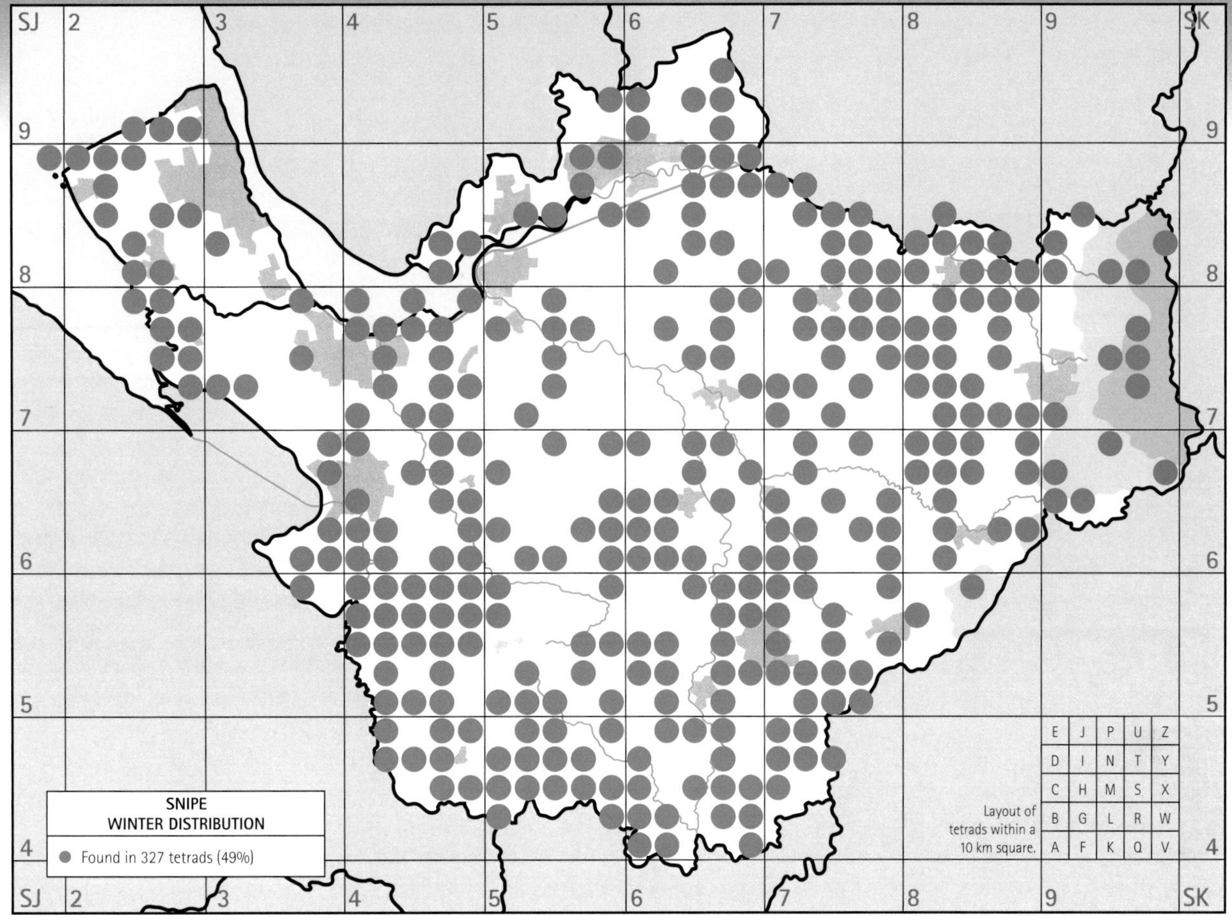
SJ
2
3
4
5
6
7
8
9
SK
9
8
7
6
5
4
SNIPE
WINTER DISTRIBUTION
Found in 327 tetrads (49%)
Layout of tetrads within a 10 km square.
E J P U Z
D I N T Y
C H M S X
B G L R W
A F K Q V

Woodcock

Scolopax rusticola

Woodcock has declined substantially as a breeding bird in the last twenty years. The map showing change from our *First Atlas* reveals that they were present in just 15 tetrads in both surveys, with birds in 10 new tetrads now, and lost from 101 occupied during 1978–84. This is not an easy bird to census. BTO Common Birds Census (CBC) results show decreases every year from its peak in 1974 until the end of the CBC in 1999, with a 76% drop in that quarter-century. From the end of our *First Atlas* fieldwork period in 1984 there has been at least a 60% fall in the national population, so it is not surprising that this Atlas shows a substantial contraction in range, and Woodcock is now almost entirely a bird of eastern Cheshire.

Most of the Atlas records were of birds in May or June roding, their peculiar display flight in which males fly in circuits just above the woodland canopy in the half-light of dawn or dusk, emitting low-pitched grunting noises and loud shrill disyllabic whistles. The sounds can carry up to 300 m and probably attract the attention of a female, which in turn entices the male to the ground. Woodcocks are polygynous, with a few older, dominant males roding for the longest each day and obtaining most of the matings with females, whereas first-year males only rode for short periods. Birds were recorded for this Atlas roding in eight tetrads, with a bird visiting a possible nest site in another and one observer reported pairs in another two tetrads. The only confirmed breeding record came from Daresbury Firs (SJ58R) where a bird was inadvertently flushed off eggs at the base of a fir tree in a heathland regeneration area. According to the annual county bird reports, this appears to be the first proven breeding since 1984. Although they are probably underrecorded, it seems unlikely that the county population will be more than 20–30 breeding females, a substantial drop from the estimate of 150 just twenty years ago.

Birds were recorded for this Atlas in a range of woodland types: broad-leaved (nine tetrads), coniferous (two), mixed (six), waterlogged (carr) broad-leaved (two) and waterlogged coniferous (two). Their preferred breeding habitat is deciduous or mixed woodland, with conifer plantations used up until they become too dense; at least some understorey and damp earthworm-rich soils are important, as are wide rides and small clearings (2–4 ha) in larger woods. Their current breeding distribution corresponds roughly with the most wooded parts of the county.

Woodcocks probably merit a place on the Red List of species of conservation concern, but are currently Amber listed until specialized surveys have ascertained their true status as a British breeding bird. The reasons for the species' decline are not well established, but the hypotheses include recreational disturbance, the drying out of natural woodlands, overgrazing by deer and the maturation of new plantations (Fuller *et al.* 2005).

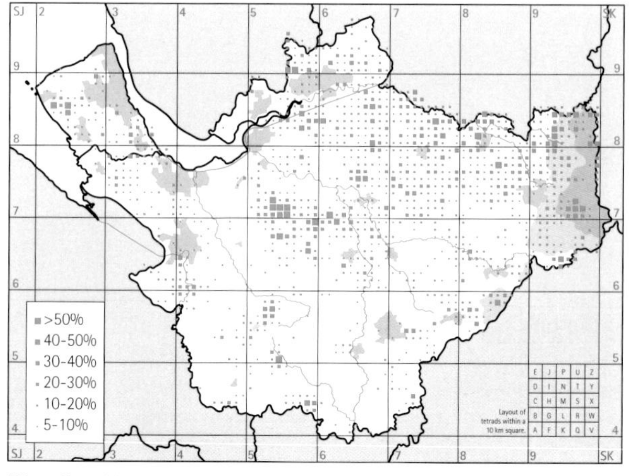

Woodland land cover.

Sponsored by John E. Ashworth

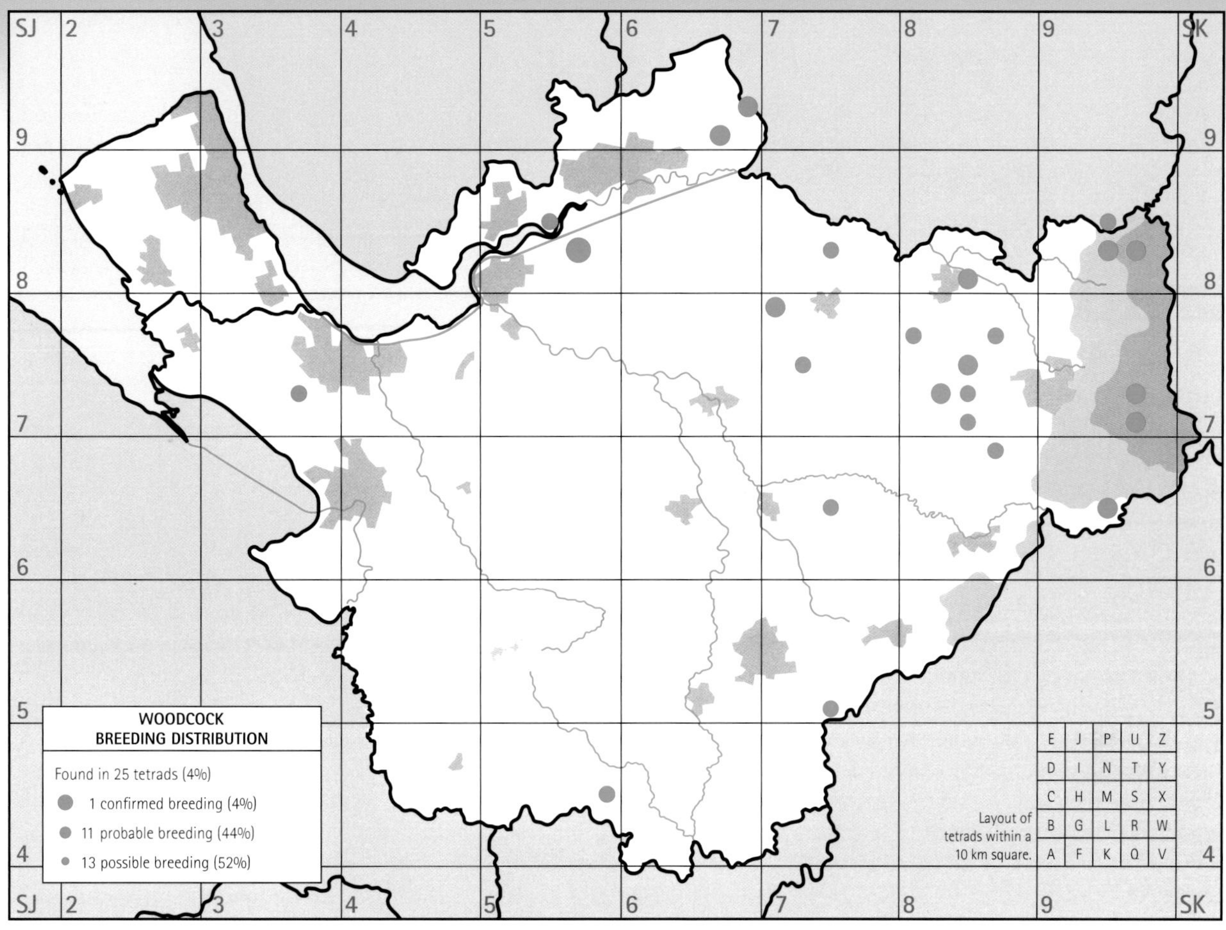
WOODCOCK
BREEDING DISTRIBUTION
Found in 25 tetrads (4%)
1 confirmed breeding (4%)
11 probable breeding (44%)
13 possible breeding (52%)
Layout of tetrads within a 10 km square.
E J P U Z
D I N T Y
C H M S X
B G L R W
A F K Q V
SJ
SK
2
3
4
5
6
7
8
9

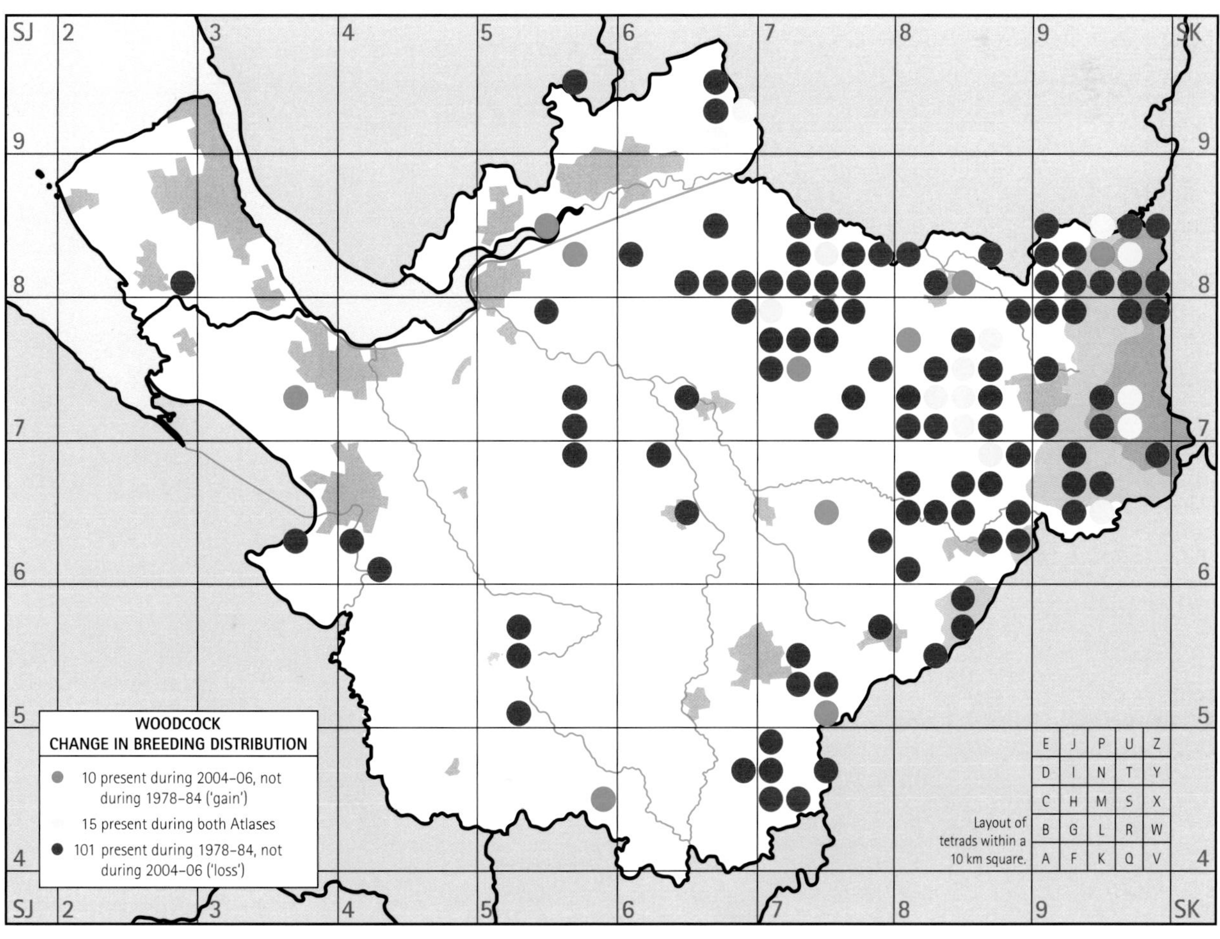
WOODCOCK
CHANGE IN BREEDING DISTRIBUTION
10 present during 2004–06, not during 1978–84 ('gain')
15 present during both Atlases
101 present during 1978–84, not during 2004–06 ('loss')
Layout of tetrads within a 10 km square.
E J P U Z
D I N T Y
C H M S X
B G L R W
A F K Q V
SJ
SK
2
3
4
5
6
7
8
9

Most British Woodcocks are sedentary, but their numbers are dwarfed in winter by those of birds from the north-east, with migrants outnumbering residents by about 13:1 in midwinter (*Migration Atlas*). Birds generally arrive on the November full moon, mainly from Fennoscandia and the Baltic states, with a few from Russia; one ringed in Lithuania was shot at Thurstaston (SJ28M) on 24 November 2003. When they first come in overnight, Woodcocks are prone to turning up in odd places including, in foggy weather, flying into tall buildings. Amongst those recorded in this survey were birds brought into a veterinary surgery in Birkenhead and caught by a cat in Tarporley, both released unharmed. The Atlas map shows them widely distributed across Cheshire, at all altitudes, although avoiding urban areas and sparse on Wirral.

In winter, Woodcocks mostly feed in fields at night, mainly eating earthworms and preferring areas with permanent, frost-free pasture or long-rotation grass leys because these offer the highest density of invertebrate foods. During the day they rest within woodland or scrub within about a kilometre of the feeding sites, and their winter distribution is determined mainly by the availability of suitable nocturnal feeding areas rather than diurnal cover; these relaxed habitat requirements mean that they are found in a much wider range of woodland than in the breeding season, with even some quite small patches of scrub often holding Woodcock during the day.

Because they leave the woods after sunset and return before sunrise, most birds are recorded in their daytime loafing areas rather than where they feed, and the submitted habitat codes reflect this bias. As many as 59% of the records were in woodland, including 12% in waterlogged carr, with 10% in scrub, mostly regenerating natural or semi-natural woodland. There were odd records from wet pastures and rushy fields, with 5% in bogs, 7% on farmland (mostly grassland or stubble) and 6% in freshwater sites (mostly narrow watercourses). Woodcocks are susceptible to cold winters when the ground freezes, and then tend to seek unfrozen areas in ditches or alongside small streams.

Most birds were found singly, accounting for two-thirds of the Atlas records, and they spread out in separate areas when feeding although several can share a favoured daytime site: there were three records of four birds, three of five and two of six, all eclipsed by the figures of up to 20 counted in Moss Wood on the Cholmondeley estate (SJ55K). Some large totals are occasionally reported from shooting estates. Figures from the Game & Wildlife Conservation Trust show an average of about 1.5 birds shot annually per square kilometre of estate area, with little change in this number from the beginning of the twentieth century.

Coward (1910) knew the species as a winter resident in varying numbers, occurring in all parts of Cheshire, and Bell (1962) suspected that it was underrecorded and wrote that 'as a winter visitor it must be much commoner than the records indicate'. That comment probably still applies nowadays, and an element of luck is needed to find Woodcocks, but this Atlas map shows them to be widespread and is probably the most comprehensive ever assessment of their winter distribution in the county.

RAY SCALLY

WOODCOCK
WINTER DISTRIBUTION
Found in 173 tetrads (26%)
Layout of tetrads within a 10 km square.
E J P U Z
D I N T Y
C H M S X
B G L R W
A F K Q V
SJ 2 3 4 5 6 7 8 9 SK
9
8
7
6
5
4

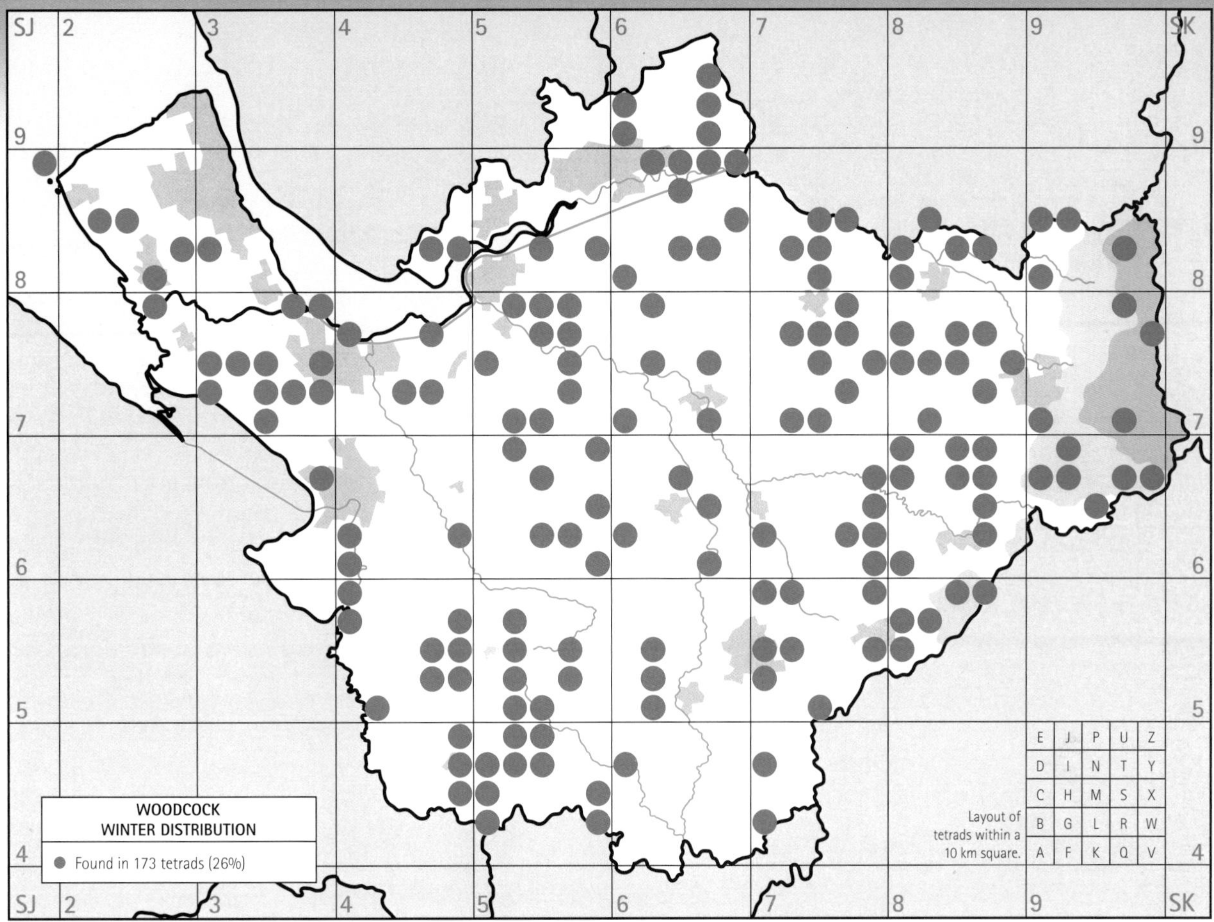

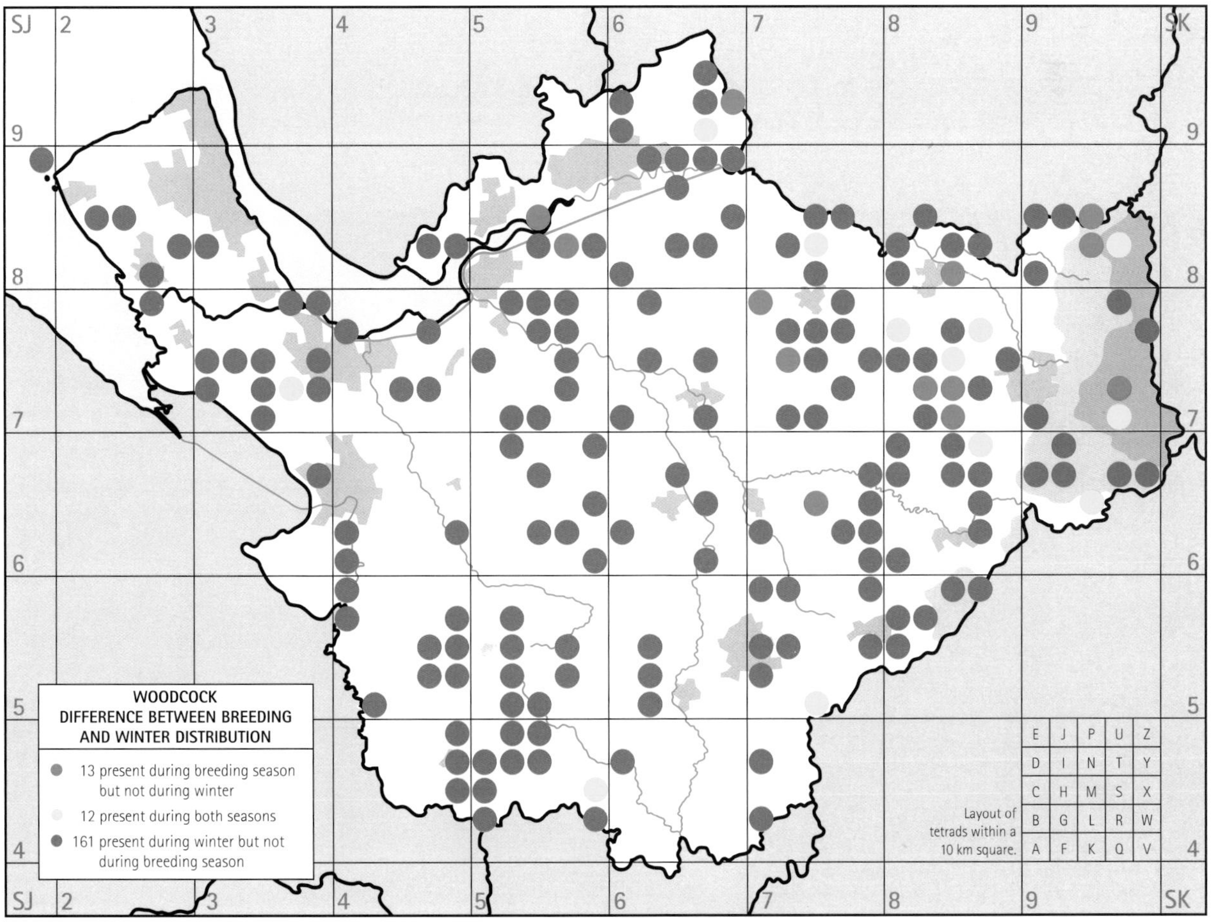

WOODCOCK
DIFFERENCE BETWEEN BREEDING AND WINTER DISTRIBUTION
13 present during breeding season but not during winter
12 present during both seasons
161 present during winter but not during breeding season
Layout of tetrads within a 10 km square.
E J P U Z
D I N T Y
C H M S X
B G L R W
A F K Q V
SJ 2 3 4 5 6 7 8 9 SK
9
8
7
6
5
4

Black-tailed Godwit

Limosa limosa

Black-tailed Godwits have increased greatly during the last century. To Coward (1910) they were only known in Cheshire as a rare visitor on migration. By the time of Bell's 1962 avifauna, the species was a regular passage migrant in varying numbers and to some extent a winter visitor. Wintering birds had been reported since at least 1939 when one was at Bromborough Dock from 12 November to 12 December, followed by a flock of 15 at Hoylake on 10 January 1947 and records of wintering in five of the 10 winters from 1949/50 to 1958/59. The 1960s saw a large change in the species, with flocks at Burton Marsh up to 70 on 20 November 1960, with 40–50 still present two weeks later, there having been no previous evidence of any such numbers in the Dee. It was also a regular visitor to the south shore of the Mersey estuary, with a flock of 45 at Ince in mid-November 1961. Bell (1967) reported that 60–70 birds wintered, with their favourite localities continuing to be the Dee estuary and the Mersey around Frodsham and Ince.

The Black-tailed Godwit's preferred habitat is muddy estuaries, the areas with fine sediments rather than sand, in which they use their long bills to extract lugworms and ragworms, and by the late 1960s it was realized that hundreds of birds were feeding far offshore in the Dee, only being driven within view by the highest spring tides. The first BoEE counts found over 600 throughout winter 1970/71, with 1,471 in February 1973, although with great variation from month to month and year to year. The Dee figures were usually over 1,000 during the 1980s, and topped 2,000 on some counts in the 1990s. From the 2000/01 winter onwards, numbers exceeded 3,000 and rapidly surpassed the 4,000 mark. Very few were on the Mersey until 1984/85 when 150 were recorded, but totals remained at a relatively low level until rising rapidly from 1995, topping 1,000 in 1996 when 1,429 were counted on 24 November 1996, and 2,086 in January 1998. This was the first winter in which the Mersey WeBS figure was higher than that for the Dee, although often the majority of the Dee birds were in Wales, but no county recorder or bird report editor has tackled the presentation of true figures for Cheshire and Wirral.

After the species' remarkable rise, nationally and locally, the Dee is second in the national ranking on current WeBS figures, with a five-year peak mean of 4,700 birds. The large numbers on the Mersey in autumn, around 2,500, reduce to an average of 500 over winter, just exceeding the threshold for international importance of 470. The main factor driving the increase seems to be a large rise in the Icelandic breeding population, possibly through climatic amelioration or changes in land use (Brown & Grice 2005).

During this Atlas, there were several instances of four-figure flocks within a single tetrad, headed by 2,250 in SJ27T and 1,500 in SJ27S, both on the edge of the Dee estuary salt-marsh. The other high counts were also in contiguous squares along the Dee shore, 750 off West Kirby (SJ28C), 800 off Thurstaston (SJ28G) and 580 off Heswall (SJ28K). The highest counts in the

PETER TWIST

Sponsored by www.deeestuary.co.uk

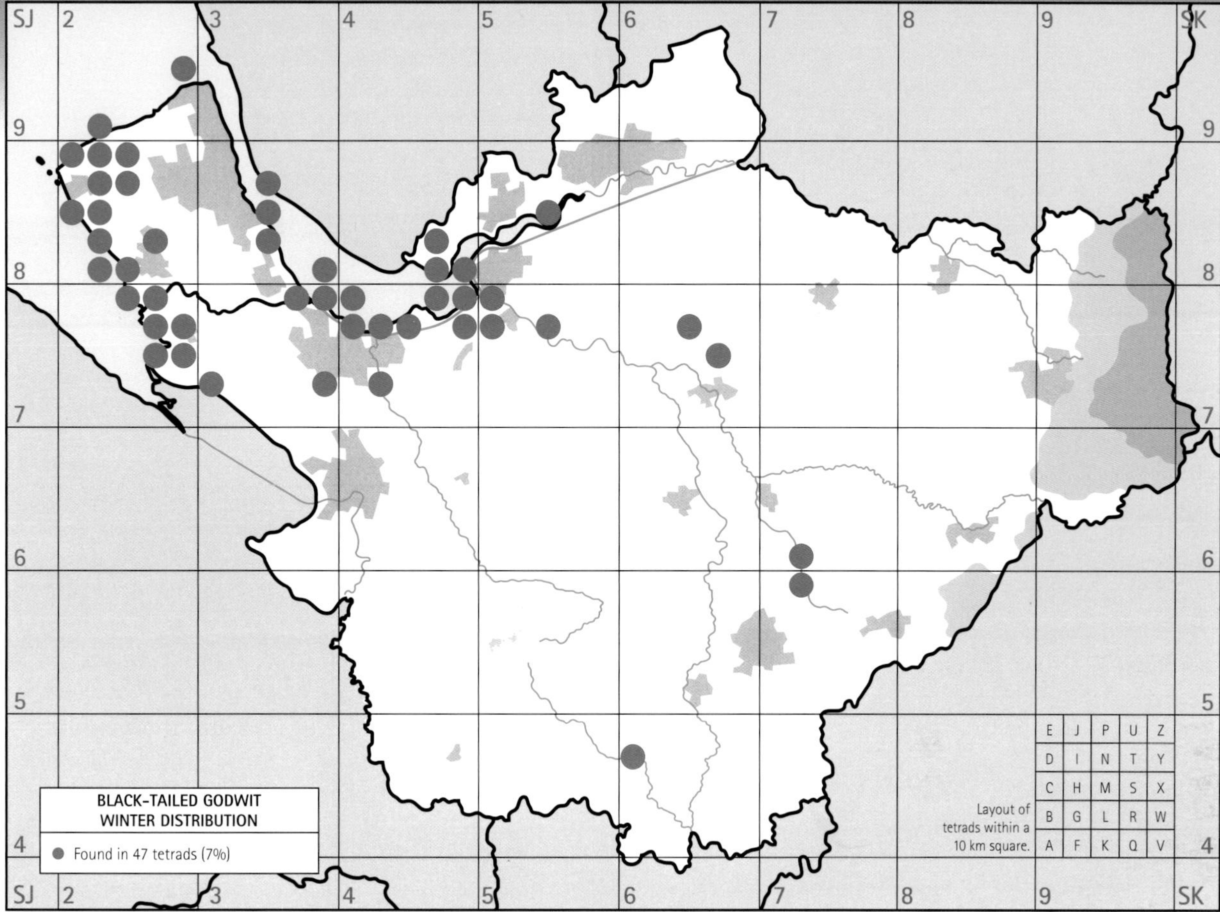

Mersey tetrads were 418 in SJ47D and 400 in SJ47I, both in Stanlow Bay. The freshwater sites adjacent to the estuaries are important for the species where they can supplement their diet with earthworms—Inner Marsh Farm (SJ37B) (which held a maximum of 700 birds in 2006/07) and Frodsham Marsh—and there is considerable interchange between the flocks at these two sites. There were few Atlas records of birds away from the estuaries and adjacent sites, with 50 on a flooded field alongside the river Weaver near Aston (SJ57N) in 2005/06 but elsewhere birds were only in single-figure groups.

The Black-tailed Godwits visiting the county are of the race *islandica*, breeding in Iceland and larger, but shorter-billed, than the nominate race that breeds in continental Europe. Sightings of colour-ringed birds have shown fascinating detail of their movements (Smith *et al.* 2008).

● Black-tailed Godwits were reported in the breeding season from 15 tetrads, some of them being in breeding plumage and some of the sites providing potentially suitable breeding habitat of wet meadows; but none of the birds was displaying or otherwise showing breeding intent and many of them were likely to be immatures, this species not breeding until at least two years of age. They have never bred in Cheshire and Wirral and Black-tailed Godwit is a rare breeder in Britain, with the Rare Breeding Birds Panel reporting that 63–75 pairs bred at 15 sites in 11 counties in 2004, the majority of these at the Ouse Washes in Cambridgeshire but including two sites in Lancashire (Holling *et al.* 2007a). Intriguingly, these, including the Lancashire birds, are all thought to be of the *limosa* race from continental Europe (Holling *et al.* 2008).

Bar-tailed Godwit

Limosa lapponica

STEVE ROUND

Bar-tailed Godwits are record-breaking long-distance migrants, with satellite-tracked birds from the Alaskan breeding race flying non-stop for eight days, more than 11,000 km across the Pacific to winter in New Zealand. Those that we see in Cheshire and Wirral have not undertaken such prodigious journeys, but nevertheless have come here for the winter from breeding areas far to the north-east. A bird ringed at West Kirby in winter 1965/66 was shot on 20 May 1967 near Arkhangelsk in Russia (65°50′N 44°17′E), 2,922 km away and still probably on its way to its breeding grounds on the Taimyr peninsula of Siberia.

The Atlas map shows that the main areas for them in the county are the north Wirral coast and the outer parts of the Dee estuary. Mockbeggar Wharf off Leasowe (SJ29R) is usually the most important feeding area for Bar-tailed Godwit, but the largest flocks recorded in a tetrad were 3,000 each on Hoylake Shore (SJ28E) and East Hoyle Bank (SJ29A), just offshore from there, in 2004/05. Away from the north Wirral, Bar-tailed Godwits are scarce, with a maximum during this Atlas of seven birds in the south Dee estuary, 21 in the Mersey estuary (SJ47I) and 10 at Fiddler's Ferry (SJ58M). They are seldom found in winter away from tidal areas, the last records listed in the annual county bird reports being in November 1996 at Neumann's Flash (SJ67T) and Tatton Park (SJ78K).

The Dee estuary is listed in the national WeBS reports as holding the eighth highest total of Bar-tailed Godwits, with a five-year peak mean of almost 2,800 birds (Musgrove *et al.* 2007), but this is a meaningless figure because it averages one year's low-tide feeding flocks (12,163 birds in 2001/02) with four years of roost counts ranging from 1,209 (2003/04) to as low as 127 birds in 2002/03. For feeding birds, the Dee and the north Wirral shore may well be the most important site in Britain, or perhaps in second place behind the Wash.

The explanation for this is just the same as for Knot. Until 1979/80, Bar-tailed Godwits used to spend all winter on the Dee, with a maximum count of 11,149 in February 1977, but in 1980/81 the birds feeding on the Dee suddenly shifted to roost on the Alt estuary to avoid

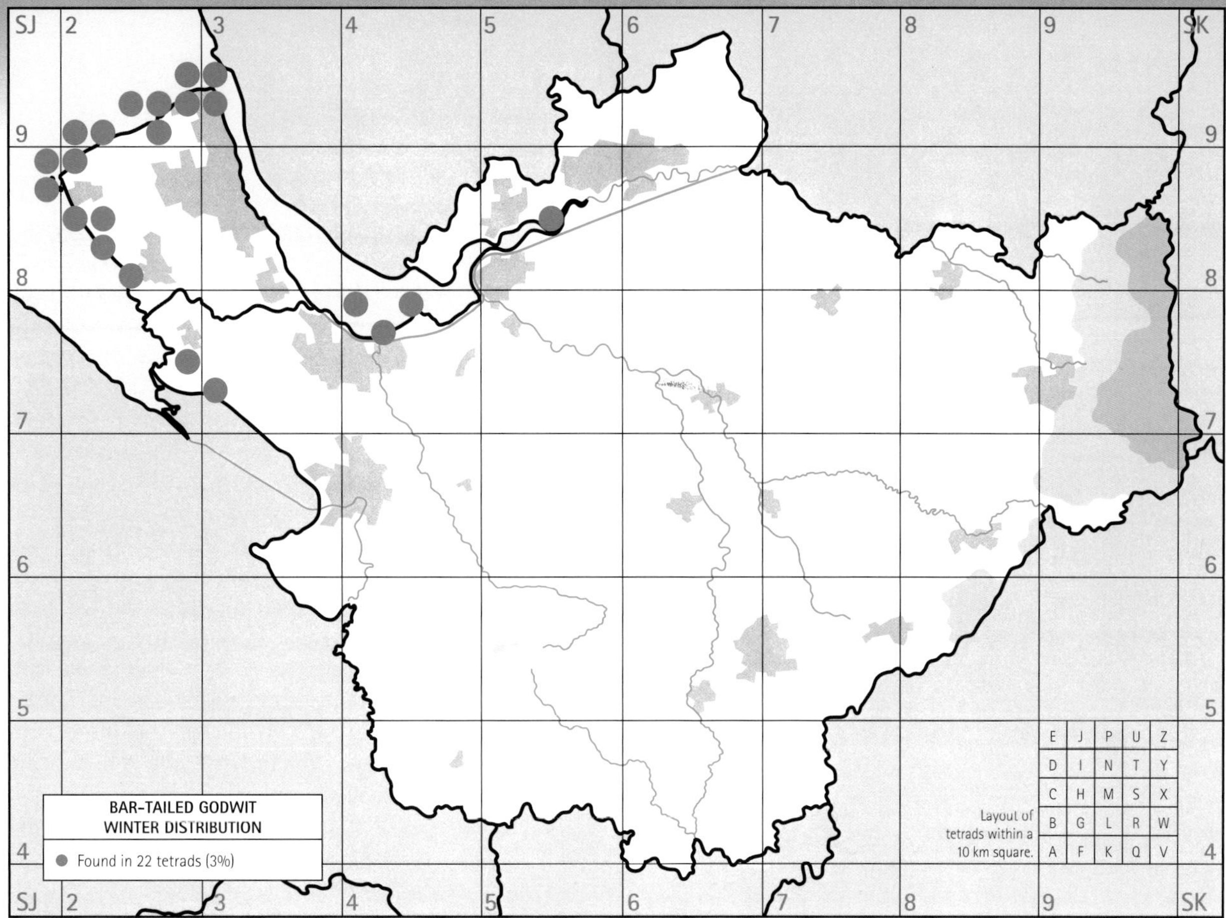

the frequent disturbance from dog-walkers, horse-riders and anglers (Mitchell *et al.* 1988). Even with the area patrolled by the Dee Estuary Voluntary Wardens, the godwits have never come back to roost on high tides on the Dee, although clearly the feeding is good and foraging birds are around in near record numbers.

Female Bar-tailed Godwits are larger, with longer legs and bills, and feed in deeper water: they monopolize the better quality foraging areas along the tide edge, leaving males to feed more on the exposed intertidal mud-flats. The species' favourite prey is lugworms *arenicola*, which tend to be found in the sandier areas, not used as much by other waders. These burrow too deep even for the godwits' long bills to reach, so they wait for them to come to the surface then run to probe in the newly formed worm-cast. They also take large ragworms *nereis*, with some smaller worms and *Macoma* molluscs.

Curlew

Numenius arquata

SIMON BOOTH

In the last century, the Curlew has waxed and waned as a breeding bird in the county, but is now definitely waning. Their breeding areas used to be only the eastern hills, but from about 1940 to 1965 they occupied much of south-west and central Cheshire as well. By the time of our *First Atlas* they may have been decreasing, and the 'change' map shows that, in the last twenty years, they have been lost from large parts of the county: almost all of Wirral; around Chester; much of the agricultural south of Cheshire; and many tetrads in the vicinity of Wilmslow and Congleton in the east. In terms of breeding season presence, there is a net loss from 91 tetrads. The picture is probably worse than that figure suggests, however, because almost half of the tetrads have only a small dot on the map ('possible' breeding) because the only evidence was one or more birds seen in potentially suitable habitat. In many instances there was no sign of the species later in the season—some of these will have been one-year-old birds, too young to breed—and observers felt sure that Curlews had not bred in the tetrad. The number of tetrads with confirmed or probable breeding is now only 67, a 55% drop from the figure of 149 in the *First Atlas*. Observers proved breeding in only 14 tetrads (a big fall from 61 tetrads twenty years ago) when birds with chicks were seen in 10 tetrads, with adults performing distraction display in a further four. Probable breeding was recorded in 53 tetrads (down from 88) with 12 instances of birds showing agitated behaviour, 19 of display and 22 tetrads with pairs present.

The reasons for their decline across much of Cheshire probably lie in changes in agricultural practice, especially early cutting of grass for silage, and continued drainage. The habitat codes in the 67 tetrads with confirmed or probable breeding show the species' dependence on farmland: 37 were recorded as E1 (improved grassland), 17 E2 (unimproved grassland) and six E3 (mixed grass/tilled land), with six on grass moor and three on heath or bog. This is a higher proportion of records on unimproved grassland than any other species in the county.

Curlews were lost from much of lowland southern England between the national breeding Atlases of 1968–72 and 1988–91, and surveys in England and Wales revealed a decrease of 39% in breeding birds in wet meadows between 1982 and 2002 (Wilson *et al.* 2005). On the other hand, the breeding population of the South Pennine Moors SPA, of which the Cheshire moors are a part, showed a 31% rise between 1990 and 2004–05 (Eaton *et al.* 2007). The analysis of BBS transects shows that the Curlew breeding population in Cheshire and Wirral during 2004–05 was 180 birds (with a wide confidence range of zero to 420), a considerable drop from the estimate in our *First Atlas* of 250–350 pairs. The abundance map shows that the highest densities of Curlew are in the eastern hills.

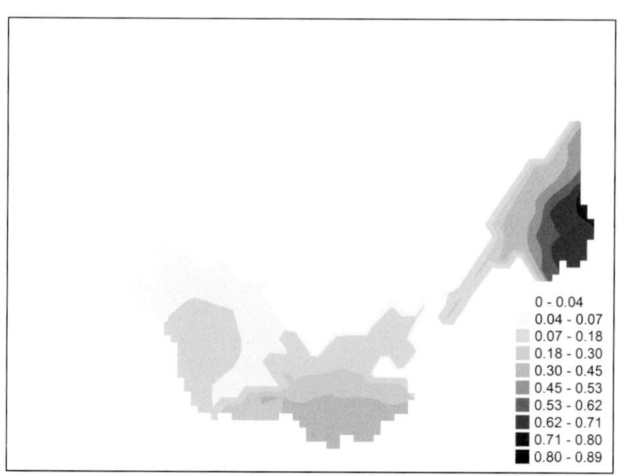

Curlew abundance.

Sponsored by Peter Mathews

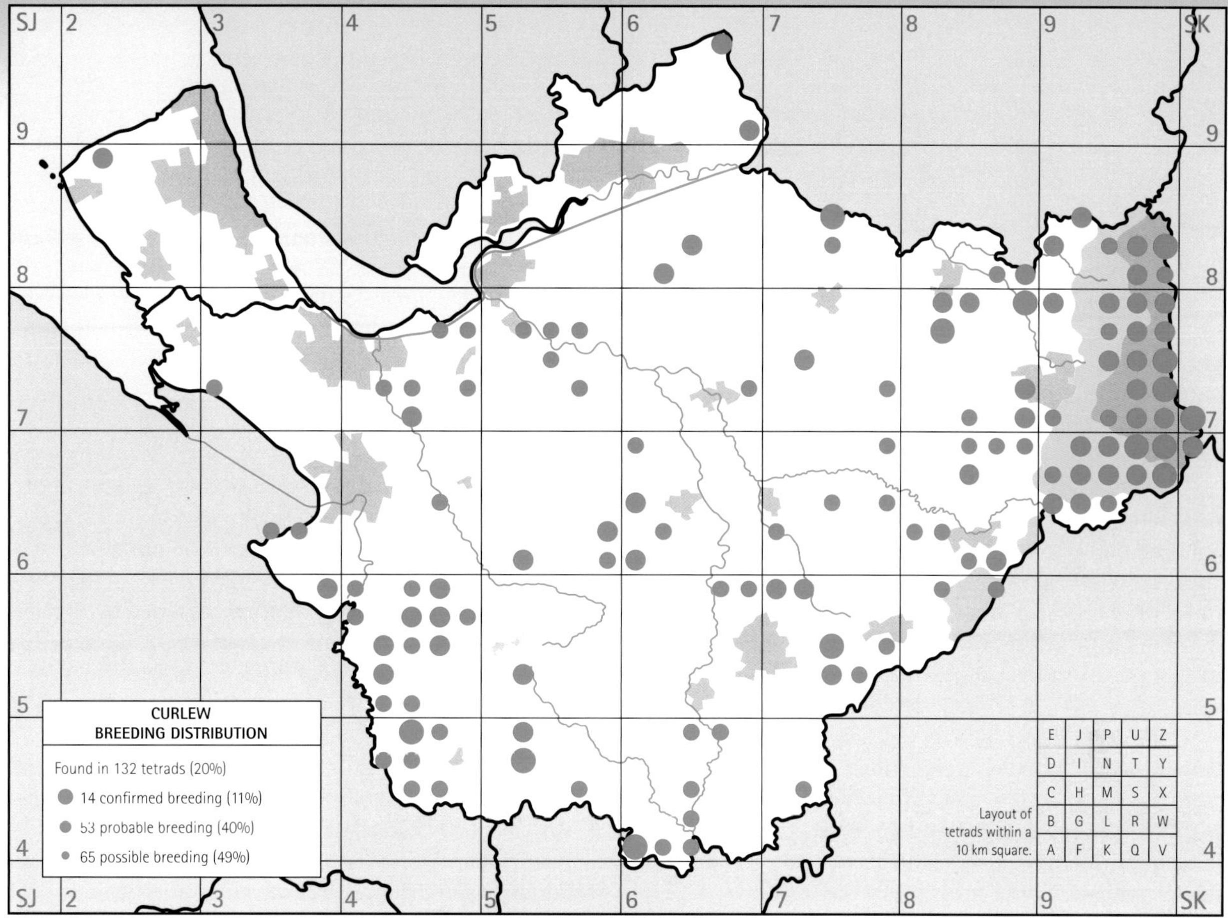
CURLEW
BREEDING DISTRIBUTION
Found in 132 tetrads (20%)
14 confirmed breeding (11%)
53 probable breeding (40%)
65 possible breeding (49%)
Layout of tetrads within a 10 km square.
E J P U Z
D I N T Y
C H M S X
B G L R W
A F K Q V
SJ
SK

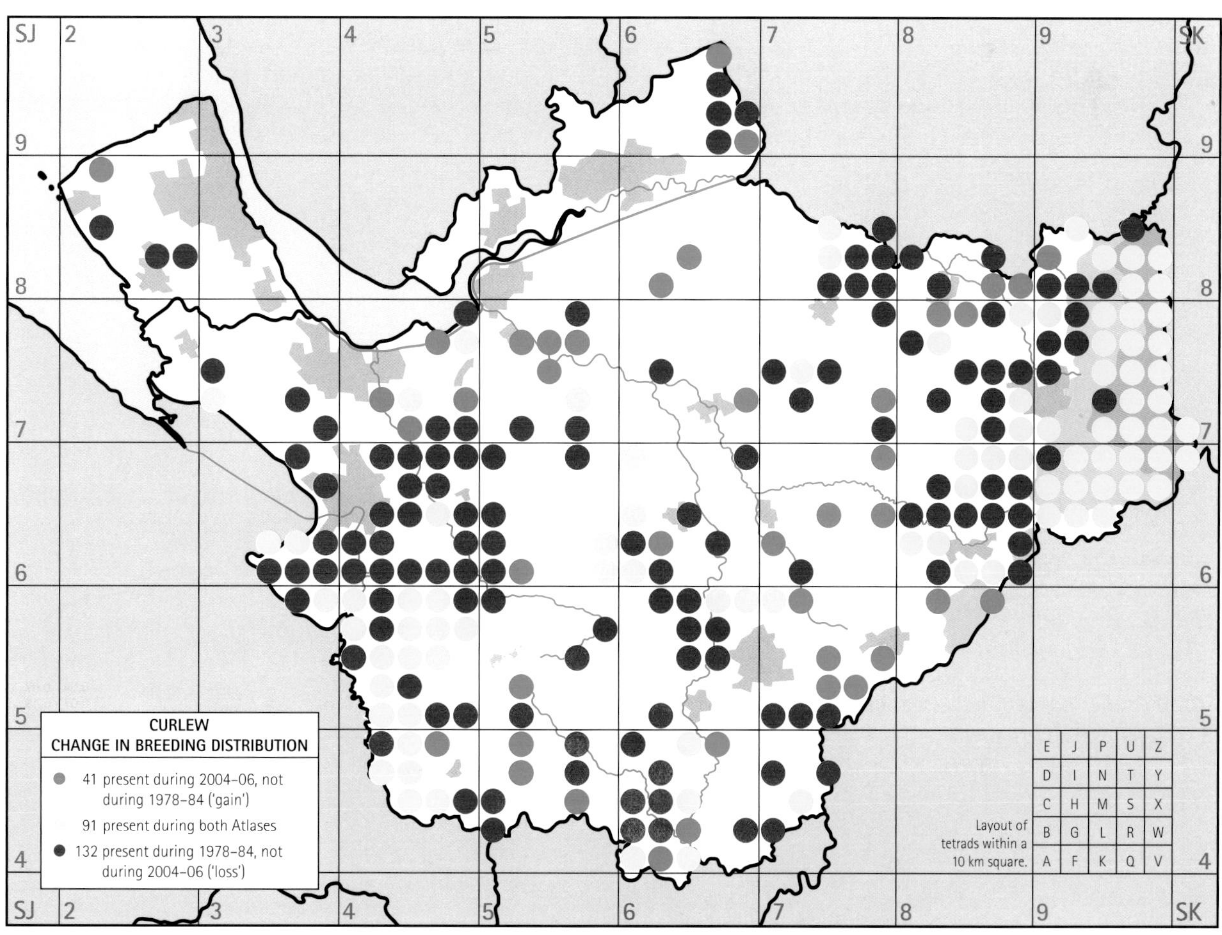
CURLEW
CHANGE IN BREEDING DISTRIBUTION
41 present during 2004–06, not during 1978–84 ('gain')
91 present during both Atlases
132 present during 1978–84, not during 2004–06 ('loss')
Layout of tetrads within a 10 km square.
E J P U Z
D I N T Y
C H M S X
B G L R W
A F K Q V
SJ
SK

The winter distribution of Curlew is almost the opposite of that in the breeding season, with birds in both estuaries and adjacent areas, and concentrations east of Northwich and towards Sandbach, whilst they are absent from most of agricultural Cheshire and the eastern hills; some of the records in the latter areas were noted by the observer to be from birds in February returning to their breeding sites. There are only 25 tetrads with birds present in both seasons, compared to 107 with birds only in the breeding season and 118 with Curlews in winter only. They are different birds. Most British-breeding birds move out, to the west coast, south-west England, the south of Ireland or France, while there is a large influx of birds from the north-east, especially Finland (*Migration Atlas*).

The habitat codes showed that 56% of the tetrads with wintering Curlews were farmland, mostly improved (34%) or unimproved (11%) grassland, with few on tilled land. Most of the rest (34% of the total) were on tidal sites or salt-marsh. Although there were more records of Curlews on farmland, the large flocks are in tidal areas so that most of the birds are on the estuarine mud-flats where they feed on worms such as ragworm, and crabs and molluscs. Especially in hard weather, ragworms burrow deeper and the shorter-billed males cannot reach them as easily, so the sexes often form separate flocks, with the females at the coast and males tending to feed inland, but there is considerable movement between the tidal areas and inland fields, often daily.

On the estuaries, this is one of the easiest birds to count as Curlews often fly past in long lines or are scattered across the mud-flats, and this is one of the few species for which the county avifaunas give any numbers. Coward (1910) wrote that they were most abundant on passage, but at all seasons Curlews may be seen on the mud-flats and sandbanks of the estuaries of the Dee and Mersey. In winter he had observed flocks, generally from 50 to 100 birds, scattered all over the miles of banks exposed at low tide. Bell (1962) said that, on the Dee estuary, numbers built up in September and October and into the winter. As many as 3,000 were in the Mersey estuary in December 1933 and flocks of varying sizes up to 2,000 were common in the Dee estuary at any time during winter. Nowadays, WeBS counts show that four-figure flocks are present in every winter month on the Dee, and in at least one or two of the winter months on the Mersey. Both of the estuaries are nationally important for Curlew, with five-year peak mean figures of 3,750 and 1,500 respectively, the maximum usually being recorded in November or December (Musgrove *et al.* 2007). The national totals for wintering Curlew have shown a shallow long-term increase, in which the county's estuaries have shared.

It is not just WeBS participants who enjoy counting Curlews, and almost every record for this Atlas was accompanied by a number. The median flock size was 40 birds, with the largest gatherings counted by Richard Smith in 2005/06, 960 off Heswall (SJ28K) and 900 on Hoylake shore (SJ28E), while the largest flock in a Mersey tetrad was 730 birds off Stanlow Point (SJ47I) in 2006/07. Flocks of up to 200–300 birds can often be found in Wirral fields. Away from the tidal areas and adjacent fields, 200 were estimated at Billinge Green (SJ67V) and 177 on 29 January 2006 in fields north of Lach Dennis (SJ77B). Many Curlews were found in traditional sites, and observers noted the tendency for birds to frequent the same fields from week to week and indeed from one winter to another.

From records submitted to the annual county bird reports, the inland roosts, which used to be a feature of the county in the 1970s and 1980s (Elphick 1979), now seem to be occupied in autumn but not into winter. The habits and movements of our largest wader would repay further study.

PHIL JONES

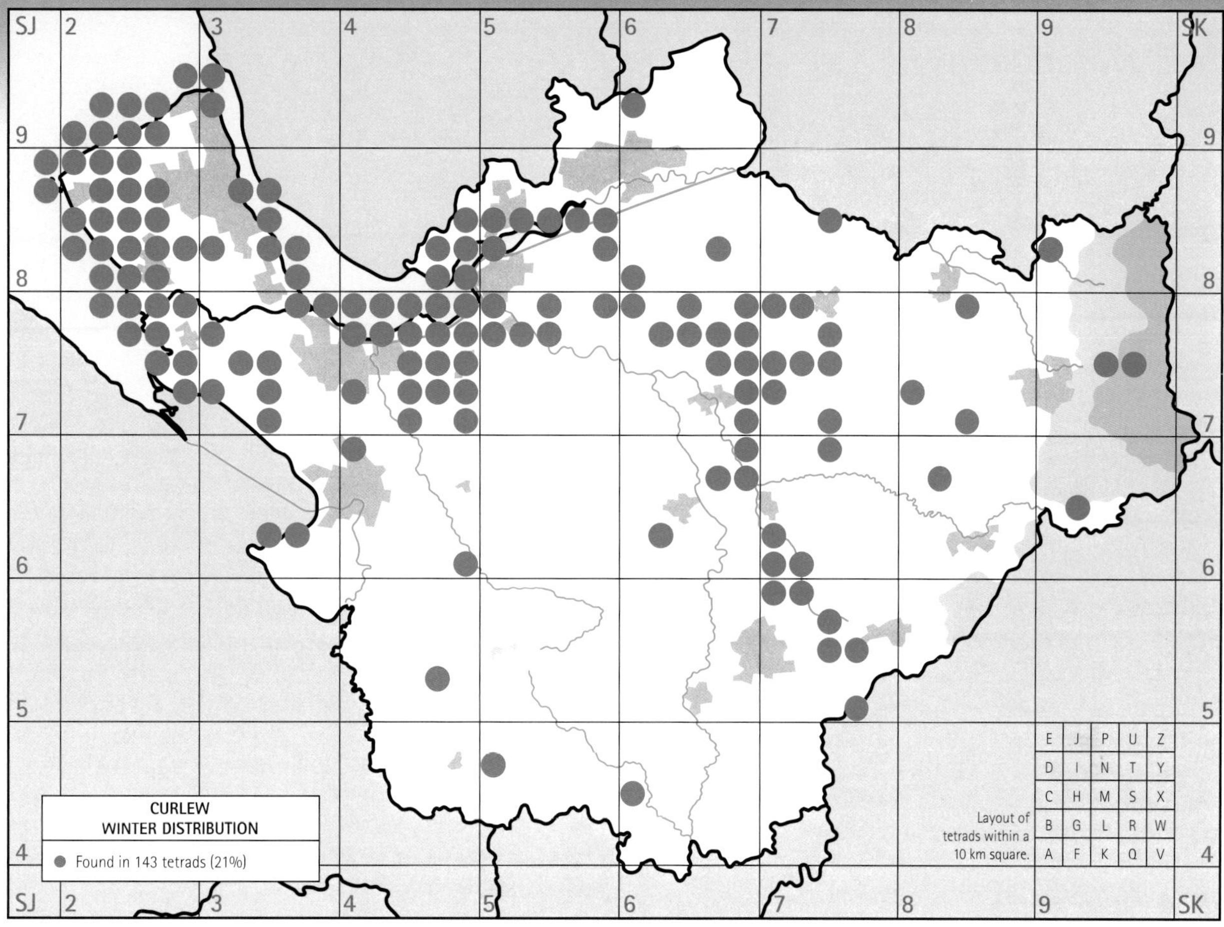
CURLEW
WINTER DISTRIBUTION
Found in 143 tetrads (21%)
Layout of tetrads within a 10 km square.
E J P U Z
D I N T Y
C H M S X
B G L R W
A F K Q V
SJ
SK

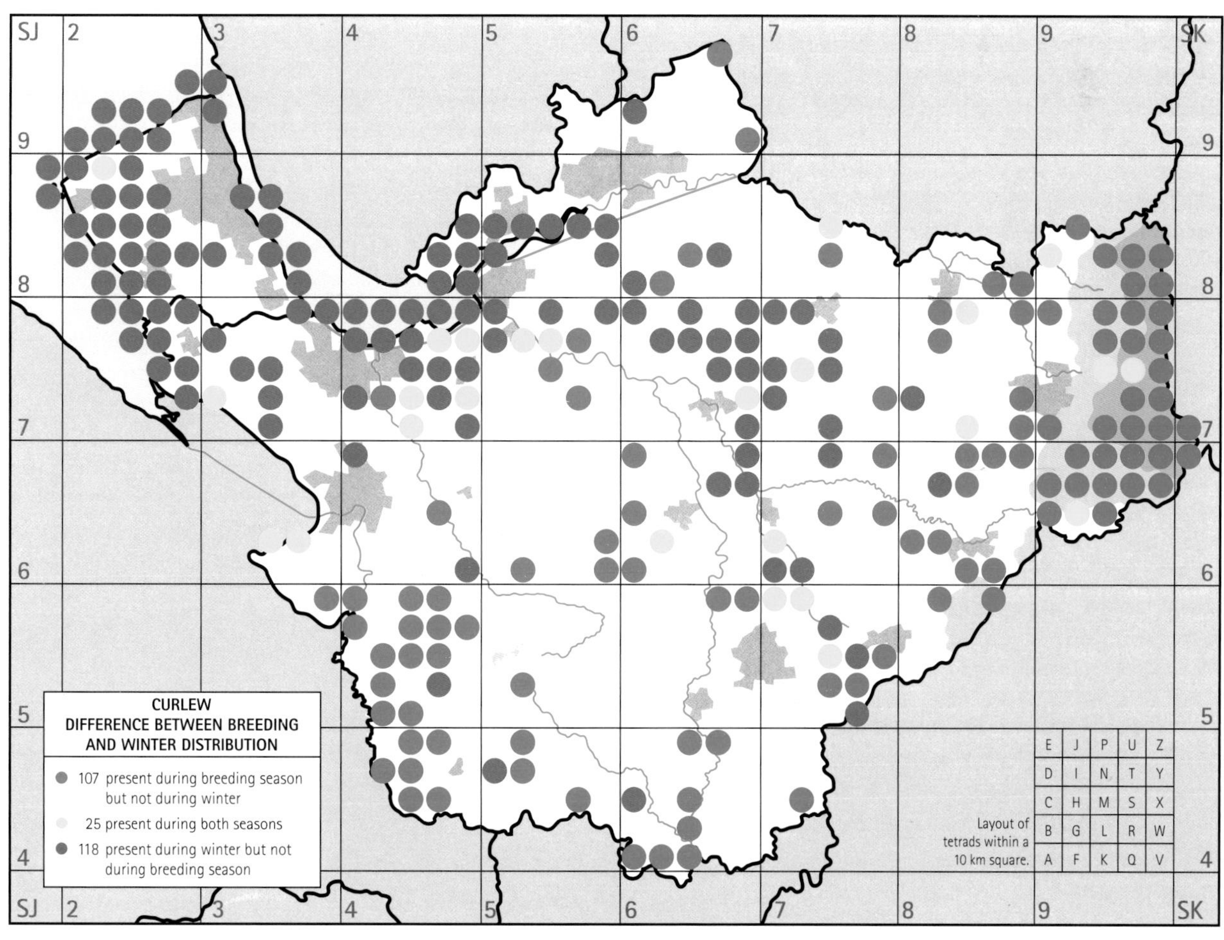
CURLEW
DIFFERENCE BETWEEN BREEDING AND WINTER DISTRIBUTION
107 present during breeding season but not during winter
25 present during both seasons
118 present during winter but not during breeding season
Layout of tetrads within a 10 km square.
E J P U Z
D I N T Y
C H M S X
B G L R W
A F K Q V
SJ
SK

Common Sandpiper

Actitis hypoleucos

STEVE ROUND

Birdwatchers are familiar with Common Sandpipers turning up on spring passage at locations where they do not breed. Many of these are potentially suitable breeding sites thus meriting an H status code and mapping in this Atlas as 'possible' breeding. Most move on rapidly, usually within a day, but some favoured sites attract two or more birds and have been recorded as P, probable breeding. In practice, true breeding behaviour is very noticeable. Adults are very demonstrative whilst they are establishing territories and attracting a mate, although they go quiet for three weeks whilst the female incubates the four eggs. After hatching in early June, their vocal defence of their chicks makes it easy to confirm breeding, and the fact that only one tetrad furnished proof in this Atlas suggests that the county breeding population is very low: in the *First Atlas*, breeding was confirmed in 14 tetrads. Females often leave their mates when the chicks are half-grown, and males quit the breeding areas almost as soon as the young can fly. Common Sandpipers are recorded widely on return passage, with failed breeders and females from June onwards, and males and independent young birds in July. A few enthusiastic observers also included such birds as H in their Atlas submissions, and they are mixed with others on the map. The 'possible breeding' records are omitted from the 'change' map, however.

It is clear that the map gives an inflated impression of the species' now-tenuous toe-hold on Cheshire. This is an easy species in which to demonstrate at least probable breeding, and birds only 'present in suitable nesting habitat' are likely to have been on passage (Dougall *et al.* 2004). This also applies to some of the P records: disregarding H and P records, observers in only three tetrads found evidence of breeding: a pair with chicks in 2004 at Acre Nook Sand Quarry (SJ87F), a pair displaying in 2005 alongside the river Dee in SJ45C and two pairs at Lamaload Reservoir (SJ97S) in 2005 'defending territory with much calling'. Common Sandpiper is normally regarded as one of the characteristic breeding birds of upland hill streams, but none was found in such habitat during this survey; in fact all but three of the habitat codes recorded—in SJ45 and SJ47—were standing water, especially sand quarries and the upland lakes or reservoirs.

Nationally, the BTO's Waterways Bird Survey, albeit based on small samples, shows a population decline of 37% from 1984 to 2004. Derek Yalden, writing in our *First Atlas*, noted that recruitment barely balanced adult mortality in his Peak District study area, and birds there were badly hit by an April snowstorm in 1989, from which they did not recover to their former levels; this could have been caused by poorer breeding success or reduced survival of first-year birds over winter in West Africa (Holland & Yalden 2002). However, surveys of the South Pennine Moors SPA showed that the breeding population of Common Sandpipers more than doubled between 1990 and 2004–05, so the drop in Cheshire is likely to have been caused by some local factors (Eaton *et al.* 2007).

It is not clear when the Cheshire decline started as the records submitted annually for *CWBRs* depend on the vagaries of recording effort. Immediately after the end of concerted effort for the *First Atlas*, when the national population was probably at its peak, the county bird report for 1985 noted that records were submitted from only four sites with no proven breeding, and commented that 'if this reflects the true situation, then the species is in danger of becoming extinct as a breeding bird in the county'. The call for 'more relevant records' was not heeded immediately but during 1988–92 from nine to 15 pairs were confirmed or probably breeding, at Acre Nook and Arclid Sand Quarries and the reservoirs in the eastern hills. The recorded population then dropped and from 1995 onwards (apart from 2001 when there could have been up to nine pairs present) the maximum in any year has been four pairs.

Sponsored by Mike Allsopp

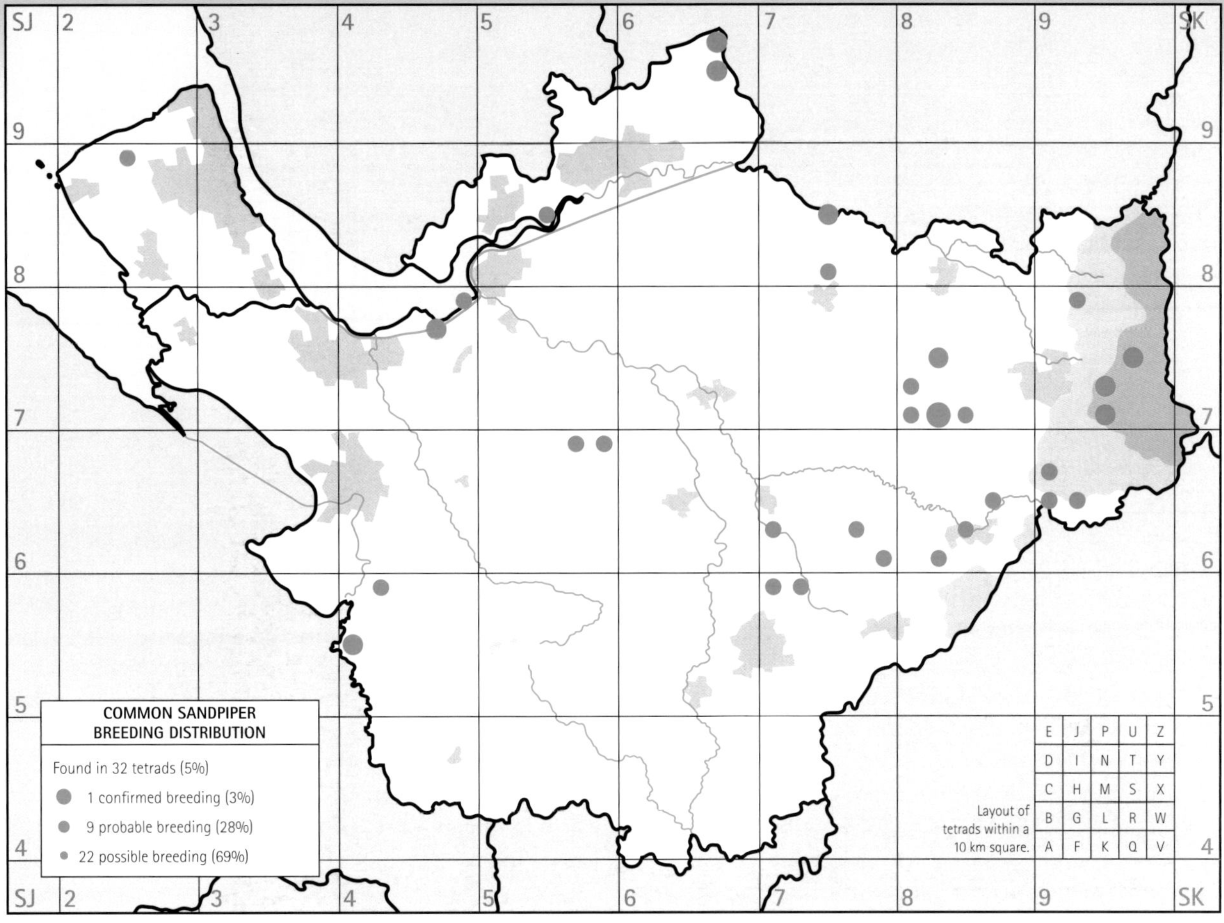

SJ
SK
COMMON SANDPIPER
BREEDING DISTRIBUTION
Found in 32 tetrads (5%)
1 confirmed breeding (3%)
9 probable breeding (28%)
22 possible breeding (69%)
Layout of tetrads within a 10 km square.
E J P U Z
D I N T Y
C H M S X
B G L R W
A F K Q V

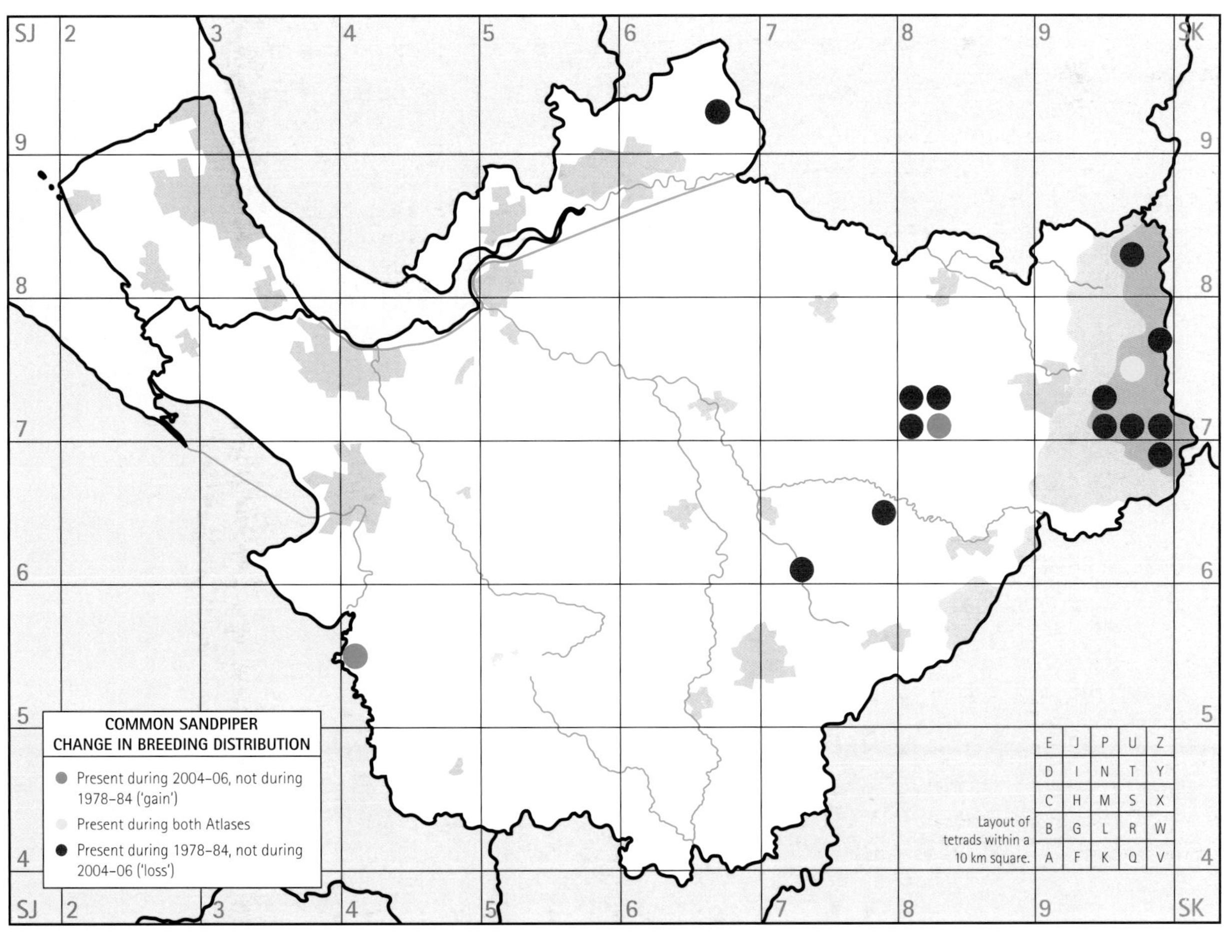

SJ
SK
COMMON SANDPIPER
CHANGE IN BREEDING DISTRIBUTION
Present during 2004–06, not during 1978–84 ('gain')
Present during both Atlases
Present during 1978–84, not during 2004–06 ('loss')
Layout of tetrads within a 10 km square.
E J P U Z
D I N T Y
C H M S X
B G L R W
A F K Q V

Most Common Sandpipers migrate to West Africa but odd birds are found here in winter. There is no evidence to show whether or not it is birds of our breeding population that remain here, but it is most likely that the wintering birds are breeders from farther north, or continental immigrants. The Fennoscandian breeding population numbers some half a million pairs (Hagemeijer & Blair 1997), and they migrate in a south-south-westerly direction in autumn, bringing some of them to England (*Migration Atlas*).

The *BTO Winter Atlas* (1981/82–1983/84) found about 100 Common Sandpipers annually, with half of them in south-west England. It was noted that the national distribution of wintering birds was almost an exact reversal of their breeding situation, with virtually no overlap in the ranges. The same applies here at a local level, with none of the wintering birds found in the eastern areas of the county where they breed. Indeed, all of the winter records are close to sea level, five of them along the Manchester Ship Canal and the other next to the river Mersey. This also indicates a habitat shift, with almost all of the breeding birds being alongside standing water (lakes, reservoirs and sand quarries) but the wintering records on flowing water.

The split is not as absolute as this description makes it sound, however, and in the last 20 years birds have been found in winter at several of the inland waters including Rostherne Mere, Pickmere, Hockenhull Platts and Arclid Sand Quarry, with occasional individuals along the river Dee.

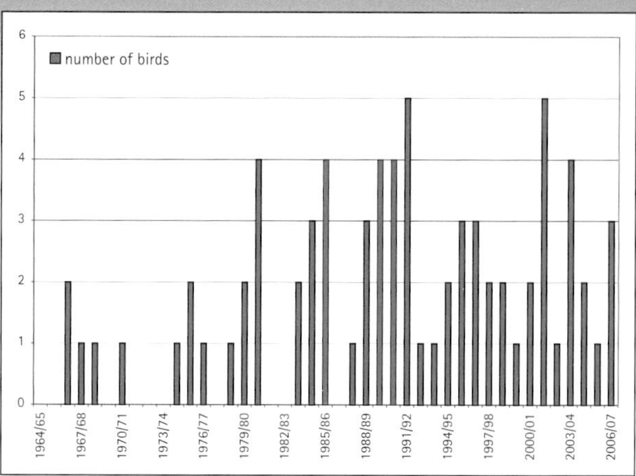

Common Sandpiper wintering numbers.

Most Common Sandpipers in winter are solitary, but occasionally two or three can be found on the same stretch of canal, when they might defend a feeding territory. As in the breeding season, their diet comprises terrestrial and freshwater small invertebrates collected from the water's edge. In both of these respects they are the opposite of most waders, flocking in large numbers on estuarine sites.

RICHARD STEEL

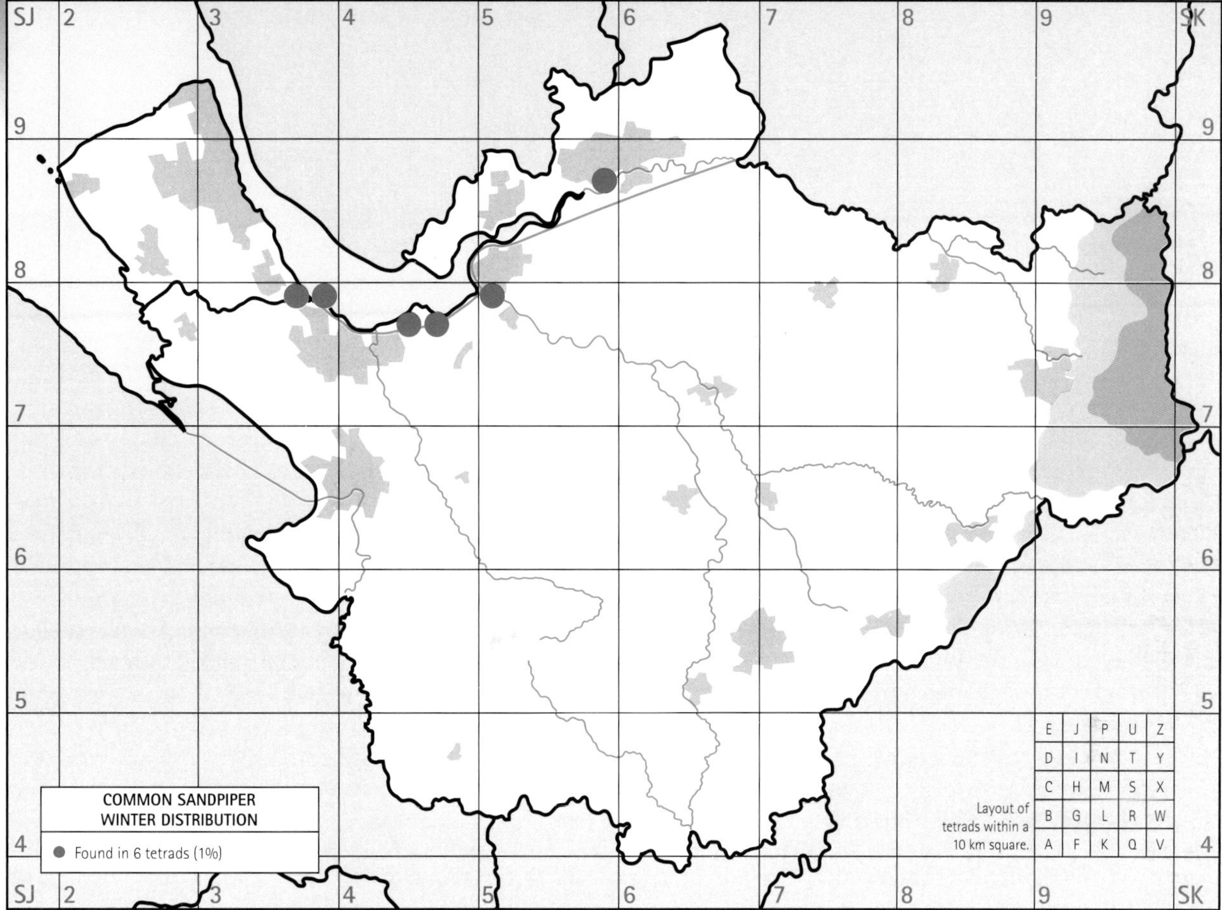

It would be expected that more birds would winter here in mild weather but so far there is no evidence of a correlation with winter temperatures. Records submitted to the annual *CWBRs* over 43 winters from 1964/65 to 2006/07 show that wintering Common Sandpipers have totalled from zero to five. The figures suggest that such records have become more common, but considering the increase in observers and their mobility, and the improvement in quality of optical equipment, the change in numbers of birds found does not seem striking.

Green Sandpiper

Tringa ochropus

The status assessment for this elusive species, published annually in *CWBRs*, is 'scarce autumn migrant, rare in winter and spring', meaning an average of one to five birds each winter, so it was a surprise that Green Sandpipers were recorded in 50 tetrads during the three winters of this Atlas. The map shows them to have been scattered widely across the county, but not in east Cheshire or Wirral beyond Inner Marsh Farm (SJ37B). During the *BTO Winter Atlas* (1981/82–1983/84) birds were found in all three 10 km squares SJ96, SJ97 and SJ98, but now they seem to be confined to the lowlands. There were at least 31 birds in 2004/05, 22 birds in 2005/06 and 19 birds in 2006/07. Most occurred on their own, but seven tetrads had two, one held three birds and five were counted at Mere Farm Quarry (SJ87H) on 20 November 2005 when smaller waters were iced over in a cold spell.

All of the Green Sandpiper's habitats are damp, with 41 of the 60 submitted codes being category G (fresh water) but they especially make use of small wet areas. One-quarter of the total (15) were narrow watercourses (streams or ditches) with a further four on small ponds. All other types of freshwater habitat were represented, but there was only one record from a canal, showing a clear differentiation in winter habitat between this species and Common Sandpiper. A further seven records were in C6 (water-meadow) or C7 (reed-swamp), and nine in agricultural grassland (E1 or E2) including flooded areas and seasonal flashes.

Their main food is aquatic invertebrates, mostly from near the surface, Green Sandpipers rarely probing into the ground. Birds at a Hertfordshire site were actively feeding 80% of the time in daylight, and flew to roost at a gravel-pit 3.2 km away. They foraged for food from 16% to 40% of the time at night, increasing according to how cold it was (Smith *et al.* 1999).

Perhaps half a million pairs breed in eastern Europe, most of them in Finland and Russia, wintering mainly in southern Europe and Africa, many of them crossing the Sahara. There is no definitive evidence of the origins of British wintering birds, but they are likely to be from the northern parts of their breeding range (*Migration Atlas*).

The national wintering total in the *BTO Winter Atlas* was estimated as 500–1,000 Green Sandpipers annually. This figure is likely to have increased and

ANDY HARMER

Sponsored by David and Fran Cogger in memory of Tina

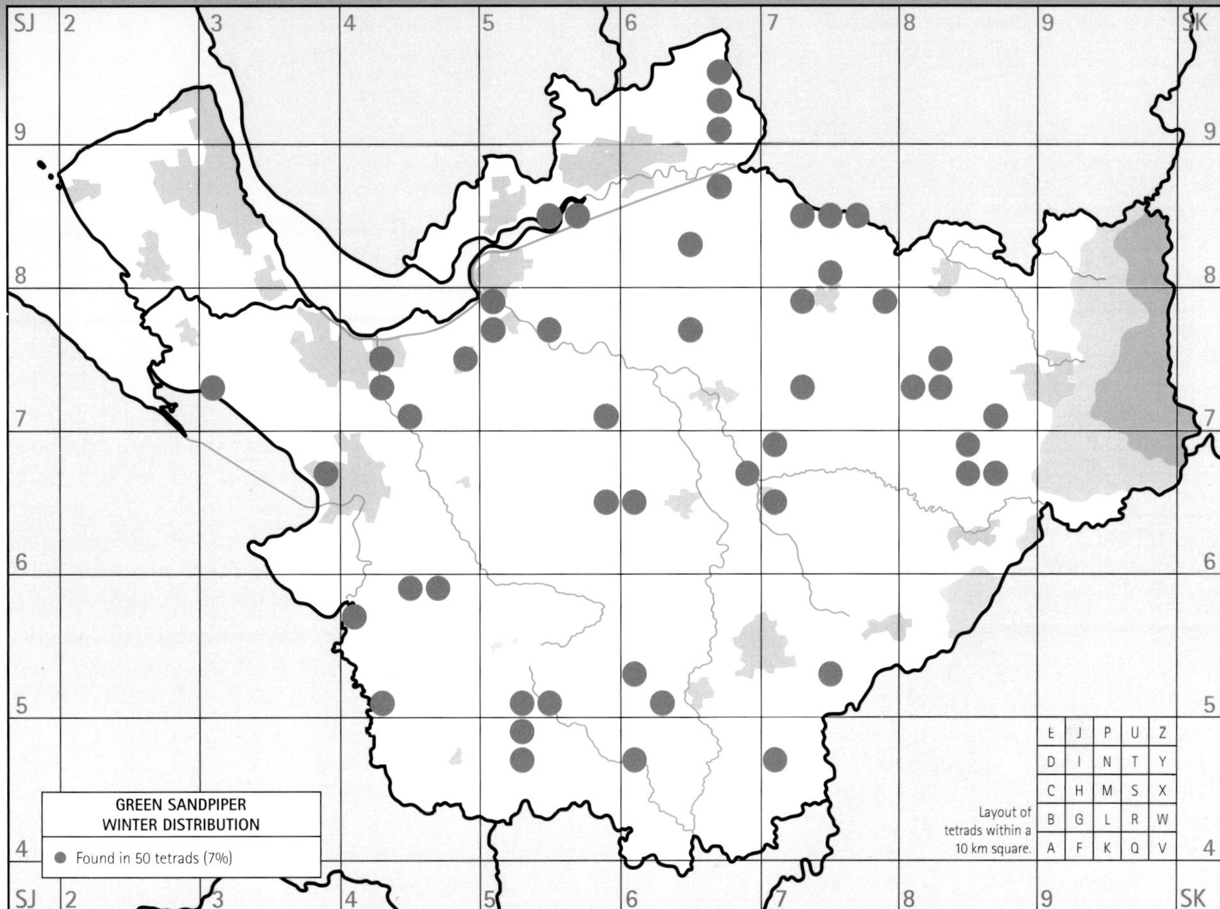

certainly wintering Green Sandpipers in Cheshire and Wirral have become much more common in the last forty years, as shown by the county annual bird reports. During the 1960s, the maximum appears to have been four birds at three sites, with some winters having no records at all.

Through the 1970s the numbers clearly rise but are impossible to follow because the annual reports jumble the early and late winter periods; by 1978 the report declares that it 'probably occurs on all our river systems during the winter months' (*CWBR*). From 1982/83 onwards, quantitative records show presence of an average of 14 birds at 10 sites, fluctuating by a few either side of those figures, a level that seems to have been maintained, probably with a gradual increase, until this Atlas prompted more extensive fieldwork.

Intensive study of marked birds elsewhere shows that an individual may return to the same wintering areas for a number of years, and some Cheshire sites have become 'regular' for this species, some clocking up 10 or more successive years with a Green Sandpiper present in winter. However, there can also be much movement between sites during the course of the winter, particularly during periods of severe weather, and it is difficult to establish true population levels.

Spotted Redshank

Tringa erythropus

RAY SCALLY

Spotted Redshank is chiefly a passage migrant in the county, mainly in autumn on its way from breeding areas in northern Europe to wintering quarters in West Africa. Birds on spring passage and in winter have become more frequent in the last thirty years. Those recorded during this winter Atlas were typical, in numbers and distribution, of recent years: winter birds occur exclusively in the tidal Dee or Mersey or adjacent sites. Most birds were seen singly, but two or three birds were together in the West Kirby and Hoylake tetrads (SJ28D/E) in 2004/05 and Inner Marsh Farm (SJ37B) had peak counts of four birds in the first two winters, with five in 2006/07. Possibly the same birds were at Boathouse Flash (SJ27U) in 2004/05. It is difficult to avoid double-counting, but there could have been up to eight birds on the Dee in 2004/05, and one on the Mersey (one seen at Pickering's Pasture (SJ48W) on 15 December 2004 and possibly the same, or another, on the Ince Banks salt-marsh (SJ47U) on 16 January 2005). Groups of Spotted Redshanks can be spectacular to see as they feed together in deep water, even swimming on occasion, to catch insects, small crustaceans, molluscs, worms, fish and amphibians.

Apparently the first known Spotted Redshank in winter within the current county boundaries was one at Hilbre in hard frost on 4 January 1941 (Hardy 1941). By 1962 it was 'an almost regular winter visitor to the estuaries' and Bell knew of records on the Dee and Mersey in every month except June, with wintering birds from November to February reported in very small numbers in most years since about 1954 (Bell 1962). Since then the annual county bird reports show some large autumn flocks, peaking at 110 in early October 1974 and 127 on 22 September 1978, but autumn numbers then decreased, with maximum autumn counts through the subsequent decades of 7–47 in the 1980s, 6–14 in the 1990s and 6–19 since 2000.

In winter, the largest count on record was of 25 on Burton Marsh in December 1979 following large numbers present that autumn, but otherwise the winter counts in the 1970s and 1980s ranged from one to nine. Subsequently the span has been from two to 15. All the birds have been on the Dee or Mersey or nearby sites. Although Spotted Redshanks had been recorded in the 1930s wintering at Altrincham Sewage Farm (now Greater Manchester) before it was modernized, it appears that there has never been an 'inland' record in the present recording area during the winter period.

The numbers in the winter months, especially at Inner Marsh Farm (SJ37B), the most regularly used site, usually peak in February, perhaps suggesting an early return of birds wintering elsewhere. The spring migration of Spotted Redshanks in central Europe has become significantly earlier during the period 1966–2002, especially following warmer winters (Anthes 2004).

Perhaps 1–2% of the total population winters in Europe, mostly in Mediterranean countries, with an estimate of 138 birds in the UK, 1994–99 (BirdLife International 2004). These are the most northerly of all wintering Spotted Redshanks, and would be expected to be sensitive to climate change.

Gifted to Peter F. Twist

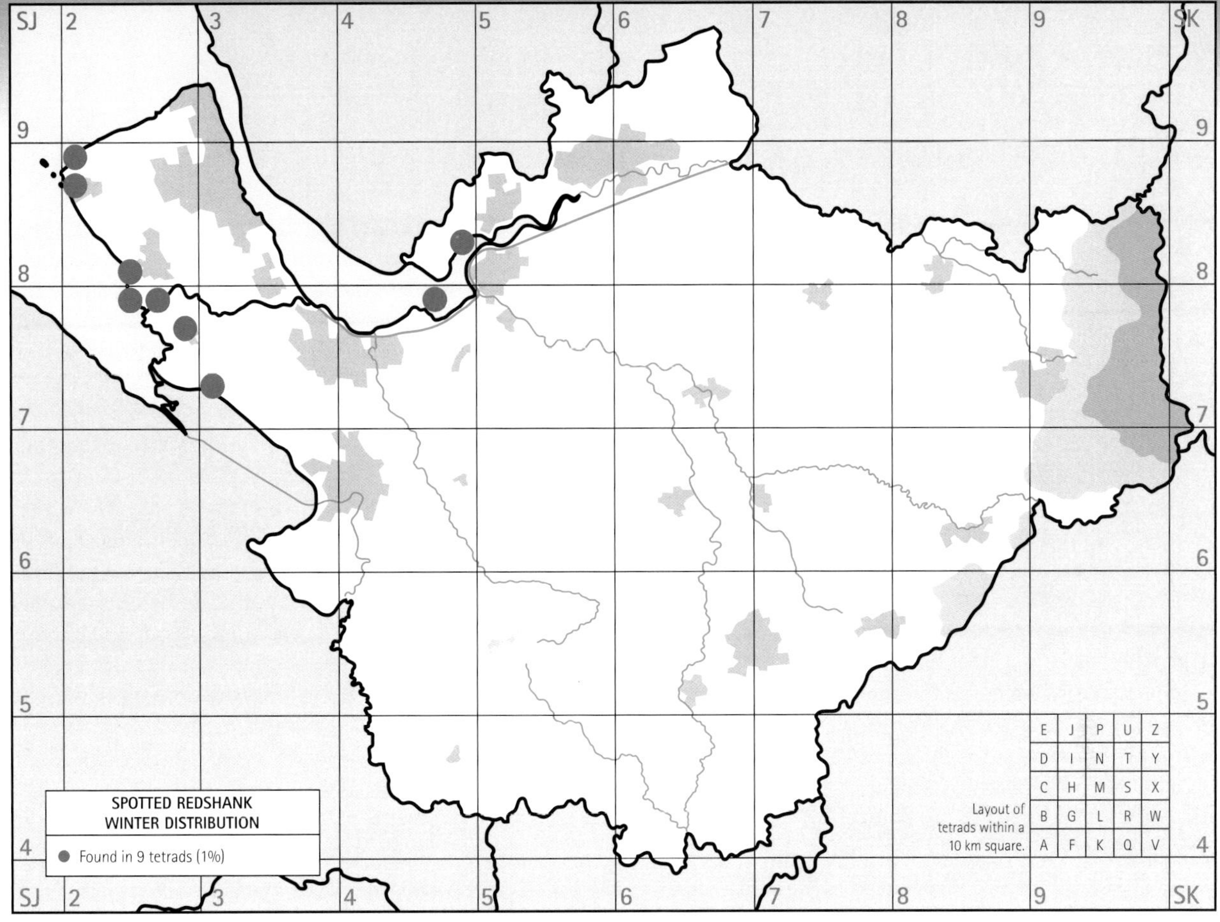
SPOTTED REDSHANK
WINTER DISTRIBUTION
Found in 9 tetrads (1%)
Layout of tetrads within a 10 km square.
E J P U Z
D I N T Y
C H M S X
B G L R W
A F K Q V
SJ
SK

Greenshank

Tringa nebularia

The Atlas map shows clearly that the edges of the Dee, and possibly the Mersey, are the places to see this scarce wintering wader and hear their strident 'chu-chu-chu' call. Aggregating three years' worth of records does, however, overstate the occurrence of Greenshanks, as there were records from just two tetrads in 2004/05, one in 2005/06 and three in 2006/07. Three of them were recorded as estuarine habitat (H3), with others as salt-marsh (C9), water-meadow/grazing marsh (C6) and small waterbody (G2). They feed more on fish than any other British wader, often chasing through the shallows apparently dancing with wings raised, and also take shrimps, worms and crabs, prey more likely to be found in the water than buried in mud (*BTO Winter Atlas*).

Greenshanks breed in the high arctic taiga, mainly in marshy pools amongst forest or scrub. In Scotland, around one thousand pairs (in the range 720–1,480) breed in the open, peaty landscape of the 'Flow Country' (Hancock *et al.* 1997). The species winters mostly in West Africa south of the Sahara, but a tiny proportion, estimated at 3,000 birds, perhaps 1% of the population, overwinter in western Europe. These are overwhelmingly found in the milder climate along the western seaboard, with those in the British Isles predominantly in Ireland and the western and southern coasts of England and Wales (*BTO Winter Atlas*).

Most Greenshanks appear in Cheshire and Wirral on passage in autumn, with a few in spring. Wintering birds are rare, but have clearly become much more frequent in recent decades. Coward (1910) knew of just two winter records, in 1890 and 1904. Bell (1962) summarized its status at this season with the comment 'its recent occurrences in winter are rare'. Greenshanks had been found in the county in 1932/33, 1933/34, 1951/52, 1952/53, 1954/55, 1959/60 and 1961/62; all of them were single birds, and only one of them was seen on more than one date (Bell 1962, 1967).

According to the annual county bird reports the next winter record was of two on 13 December 1970 at Sandbach (SJ75J) and subsequently birds have occurred in the county in every winter except for three of the

STEVE ROUND

Sponsored by Joan and David Howe

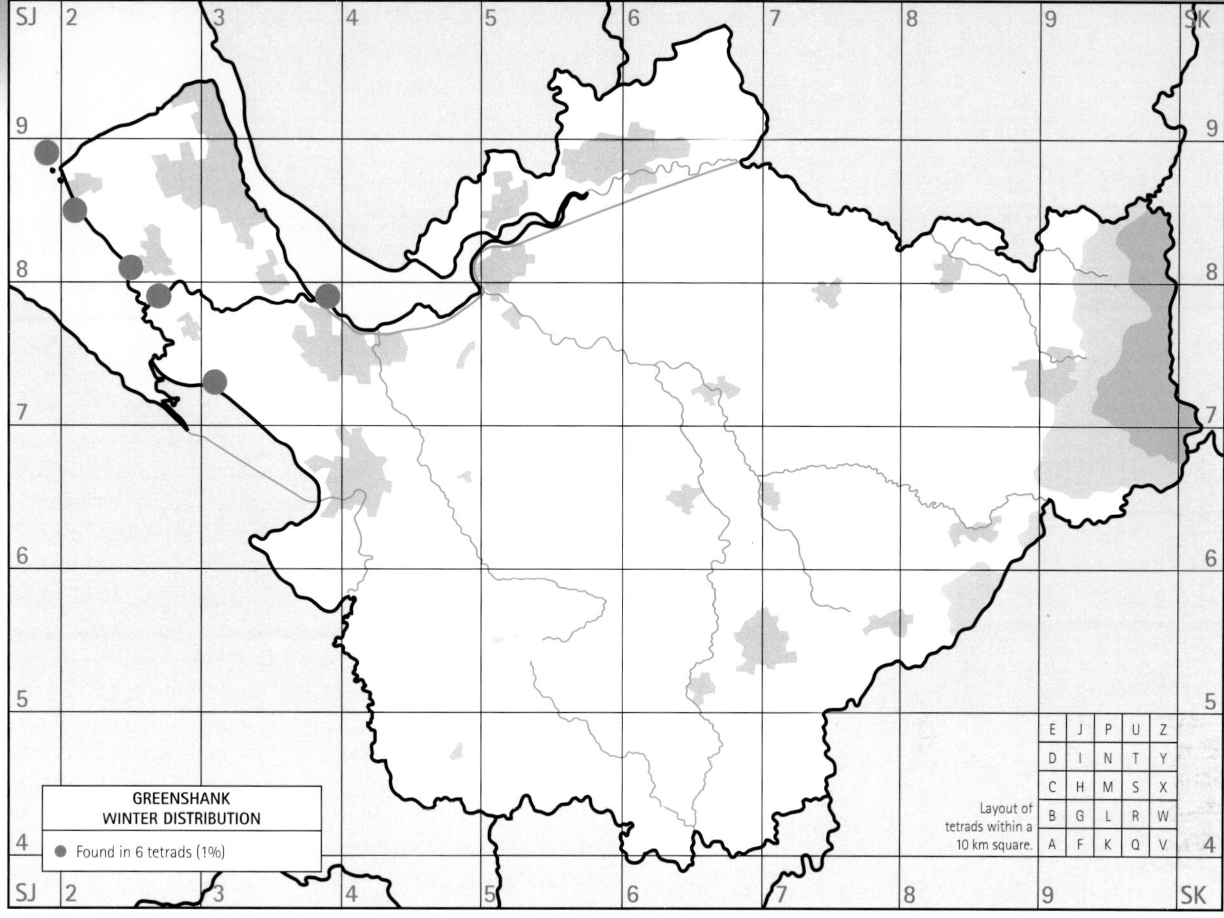

four winters from 1978/79 to 1981/82: it may not be a coincidence that these included some of the harshest winters of recent times. The vast majority of the sightings are of birds on the Dee Marshes, probably including some in Wales, but birds have certainly been present on the Cheshire side of the Dee in at least 22 of the 34 winters from 1970/71 to 2003/04, with favoured sites being Inner Marsh Farm and the marshes off Heswall and Parkgate.

The frequency of Greenshank sightings varies from year to year but there is a fairly even split between winters when birds were seen on up to three dates and those with birds apparently staying throughout the winter. Most records are of single birds but larger numbers have occurred and include up to seven seen in the Parkgate area during high tides in the early part of 1975, while Inner Marsh Farm held four on 17 November 1991 and again on 22 November 2000 and three there on 13 December 2000. The marshes of the Mersey and Frodsham have had single birds on single dates in five winters during this period with sightings in each month. The area of the north Wirral coast from Leasowe to Meols held a bird in seven of the 10 winters from 1994/95 to 2003/04, often for lengthy periods, and probably accounted for sightings in two winters at Red Rocks and Hoylake; three were at Meols on 2 January 2001. Hilbre has recorded a bird on three winter dates before this Atlas. Greenshanks inland in winter are unusual (*BTO Winter Atlas*) and the only county records in recent years are the two at Sandbach in 1970 and singles on single dates at Woolston (SJ68P) in 1985/86, Kingsley (SJ57T) in 1992/93 and Bar Mere (SJ54I/J) on 10 December 2003.

The increase in wintering Greenshanks is presumably a result of the ameliorating climate.

Redshank

Tringa totanus

Land managed in a way that suits Redshanks is in short supply these days, and their breeding distribution has contracted considerably since our *First Atlas*, with them being proven to breed now in only seven tetrads. Their key requirements are a high water-table with local soil saturation, open landscapes with lookout posts, moderately dense tussock vegetation (preferably grass or sedge) of intermediate height, and nearby wetlands for feeding (Tucker & Heath 1994). In saline areas they mostly eat small crustaceans, molluscs and polychaete worms, and inland breeders take earthworms and tipulid (crane-fly) larvae.

Redshanks have occupied three types of site in the county during our *First Atlas* or since: salt-marsh, primarily along the Dee estuary, with a few birds in the Mersey; riverside flooded meadows; and other sites, especially alongside sand quarries or flooded agricultural grassland. However, Redshanks breeding in the second have now disappeared in Cheshire, whereas twenty years ago they were proven to breed in two tetrads along the lower river Weaver, with possible breeding alongside the non-tidal section of the river Dee, from where there were no records at all in this survey. Thirteen of the 25 tetrads with confirmed or probable breeding were estuarine salt-marsh, with the other birds in a variety of habitats, most on the edges of large waterbodies, sand quarries or the Frodsham Marsh deposit grounds, or in water-meadows/grazing marshes.

The seven tetrads with confirmed breeding came from observers seeing adults with chicks in five cases, with an occupied nest observed on the Dee salt-marsh and birds performing their distraction display, trying to lure the observer away from their nesting area, in a Mersey tetrad. The 18 instances of probable breeding arose from seven observations of agitated behaviour (A), seven of display (D), and four sightings of pairs of birds.

With the expected 'coastal squeeze' from sea level rise and development close to the sea, the areas of salt-marsh and coastal grasslands will reduce, and Redshank has been taken as an indicator species for research (Smart & Gill 2003). Salt-marsh supports the most breeding Redshanks, followed by coastal grassland, then inland grassland; but on salt-marsh and coastal grassland, few young survive because of predation and tidal flooding washing away nests, whereas on inland grasslands, half of the pairs in the East Anglian study areas produced at least one fledgling.

The county population, as in our *First Atlas*, depends crucially on estimates of the numbers on the Dee salt-marshes, with at most 10–15 pairs elsewhere. RSPB surveys of their land in SJ27 during 1996 and 2000 show that Redshanks vary greatly according to the intensity of grazing, with perhaps 100 pairs or more in the whole area. Redshanks are on the Amber List of species of conservation concern, partly because of their UK population decline. National surveys of waders breeding on wet lowland grasslands were conducted in 1982 and 2002, revealing a 29% drop in breeding Redshanks, and showing that nature reserves were by far the best sites for them, with cattle and sheep grazing and flooding managed to benefit breeding waders (Wilson *et al.* 2005). Although no action targeted at their conservation is yet in place, there are national and local Biodiversity Action Plans for coastal and flood plain grazing marsh, that ought to benefit breeding Redshanks. The only local action on these habitats so far has been at the Gowy Meadows (SJ47H/M), however, where the species has not been recorded for many years; at least 50 pairs nested there in 1907 and it would be good to see a return (Coward 1910).

Sponsored by www.deeestuary.co.uk

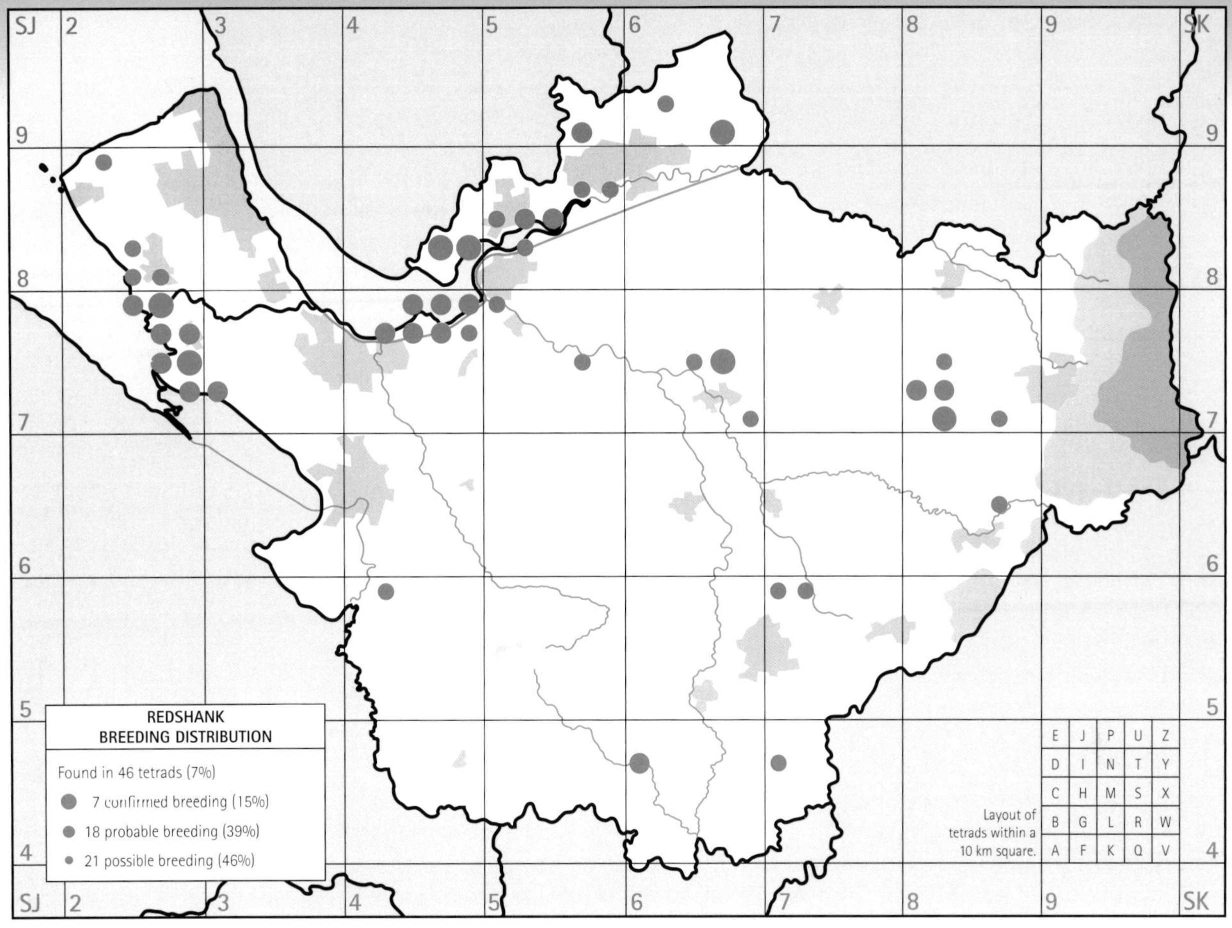

SJ
2
3
4
5
6
7
8
9
SK
REDSHANK
BREEDING DISTRIBUTION
Found in 46 tetrads (7%)
7 confirmed breeding (15%)
18 probable breeding (39%)
21 possible breeding (46%)
Layout of tetrads within a 10 km square.
E J P U Z
D I N T Y
C H M S X
B G L R W
A F K Q V

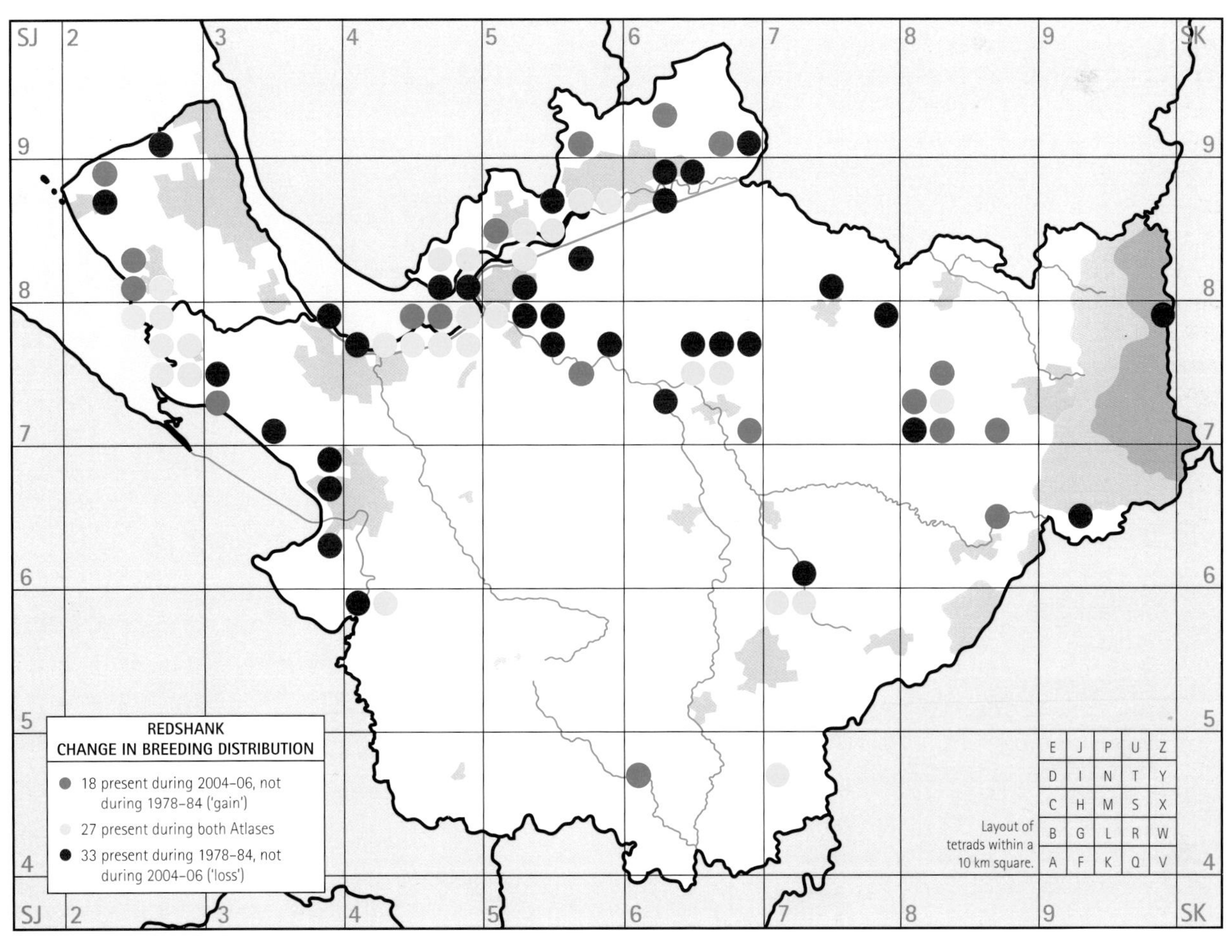

SJ
2
3
4
5
6
7
8
9
SK
REDSHANK
CHANGE IN BREEDING DISTRIBUTION
18 present during 2004–06, not during 1978–84 ('gain')
27 present during both Atlases
33 present during 1978–84, not during 2004–06 ('loss')
Layout of tetrads within a 10 km square.
E J P U Z
D I N T Y
C H M S X
B G L R W
A F K Q V

Cheshire and Wirral is the most important county in Britain for wintering Redshanks, with WeBS counts showing the Dee and Mersey estuaries both in the top five sites in the UK. The Dee figures include birds in Wales and inland at Inner Marsh Farm but our estuaries hold an annual average of around 10,000 birds between them. They both qualify as internationally important, exceeding the 2,800 threshold, and this is one of the species listed among the estuaries' citations for European Special Protection Area and Ramsar status. Redshank is amongst the most frail of waders and is particularly susceptible to freezing conditions, so our relatively warm and sheltered west coast estuaries may be of especial value for them (Norman & Coffey 1994).

The vast majority of these birds are of Icelandic stock, which have longer wings and shorter bills than British birds, typical adaptations for living in colder climates: work on the Mersey birds suggested that about 85% of the adult population were of the Icelandic-breeding race (Norman & Coffey 1994). Merseyside Ringing Group has records of nine birds that have been found in Iceland, including one unfortunate individual that apparently overshot and landed on a fishing boat between Iceland and Greenland, where Redshanks have never been known to breed. Some of our wintering birds are British breeders, including birds moving south from Scotland, but many British birds, especially the juveniles, winter in France.

Redshanks feed singly or in small groups on the mud-flats and in the estuarine creeks, taking small molluscs and crustaceans, with the little marine shrimp *corophium* a favourite, and various worms. At high tides they flock to roost on the edge of the salt-marsh. As with all waders, Redshanks' lives are dictated by the rise and fall of the tides rather than by daylight, and some birds occupy different areas at night, including some unusual sites where they would probably not feel safe by day. Edwin Samuels noted a night-time high-tide roost in a field at Bebington Oval Sports Centre (SJ38H) with up to 200 birds present.

The winter map shows Redshanks present at a few sites away from the estuaries, but only in small numbers. Apart from those roosting at Inner Marsh Farm, up to a maximum of 380 during this Atlas period, few Redshanks were found at any freshwater site, the only double-figure counts being 30 or more on flooded fields alongside the lower river Weaver at Aston (SJ57N) and 20 at Sandbach Flashes (SJ75J).

From the publications of earlier Cheshire authors it is not possible to know whether there has been a change in status of wintering Redshanks. Coward (1910) wrote that 'in December, January and February there are generally a few winter residents about the shores and marshes', but followed that by adding that he had seen 'very large flocks' at the end of December on the Mersey sands near Eastham and Stanlow. Although by 1952 the famous photographer Eric Hosking knew Hilbre as the best place to film vast assemblages of waders, including Redshanks, Bell (1962 and 1967) does not even mention birds wintering on the estuaries, but overemphasizes the small numbers inland.

MIKE ATKINSON

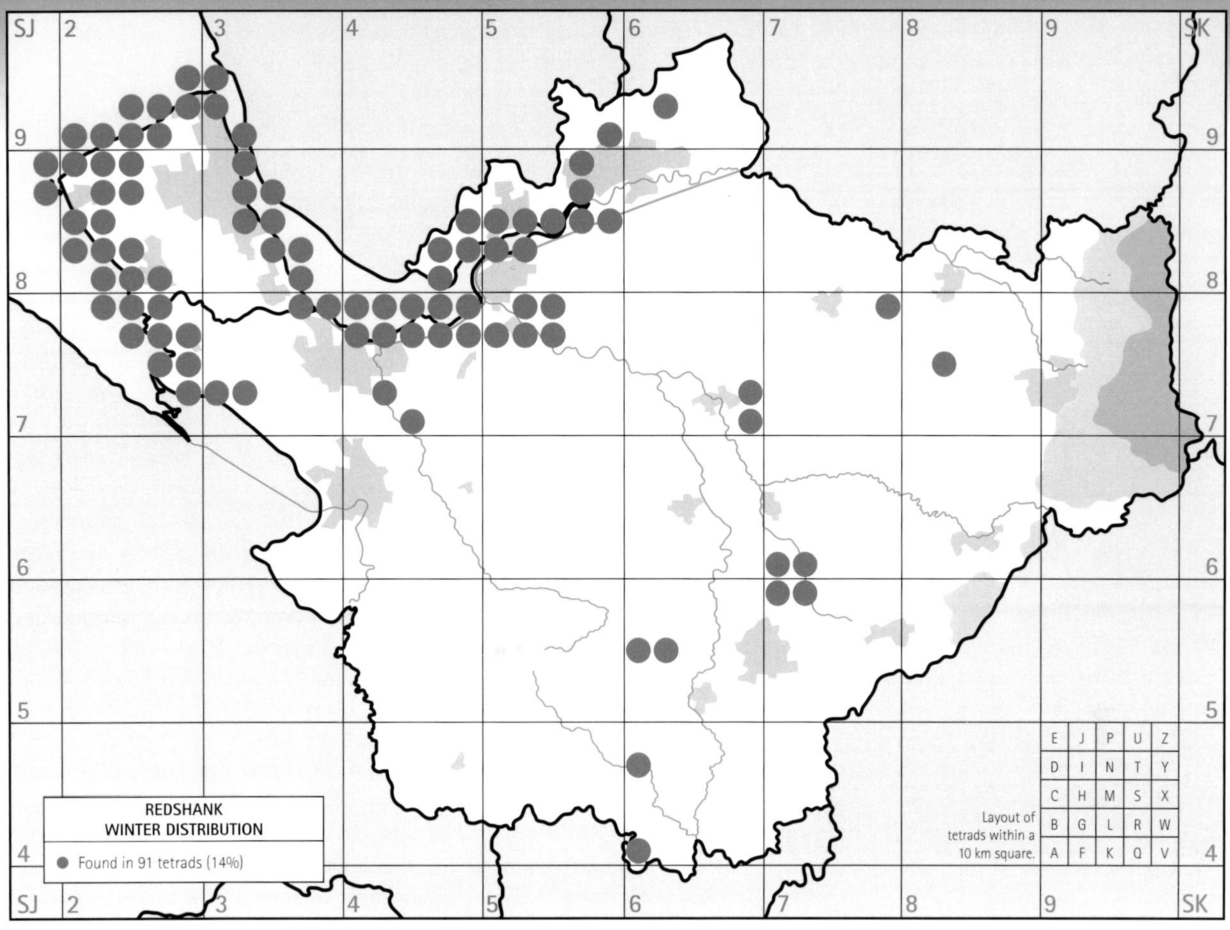
REDSHANK
WINTER DISTRIBUTION
Found in 91 tetrads (14%)
Layout of tetrads within a 10 km square.
E J P U Z
D I N T Y
C H M S X
B G L R W
A F K Q V
SJ
SK
2
3
4
5
6
7
8
9

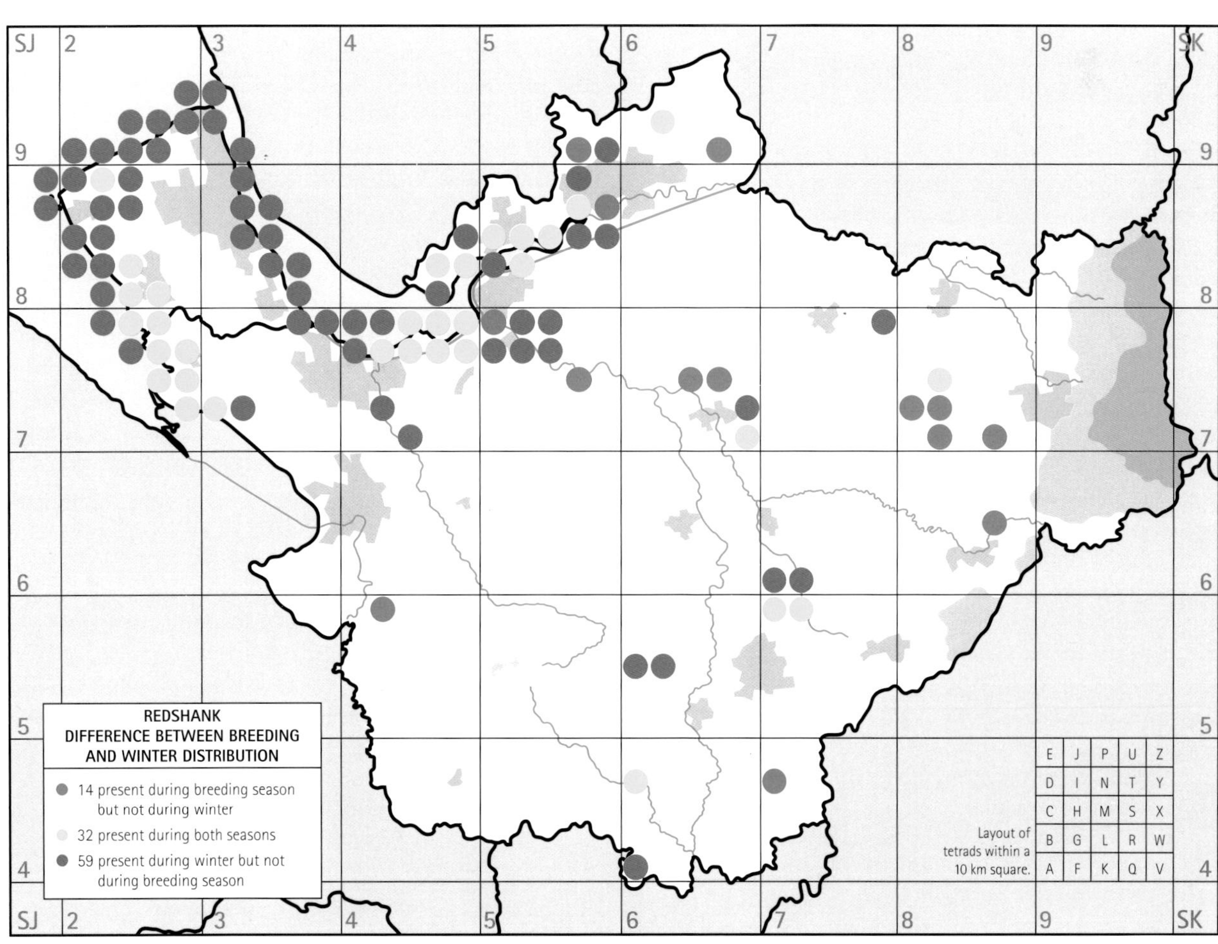
REDSHANK
DIFFERENCE BETWEEN BREEDING AND WINTER DISTRIBUTION
14 present during breeding season but not during winter
32 present during both seasons
59 present during winter but not during breeding season
Layout of tetrads within a 10 km square.
E J P U Z
D I N T Y
C H M S X
B G L R W
A F K Q V
SJ
SK
2
3
4
5
6
7
8
9

Turnstone

Arenaria interpres

RICHARD STEEL

Turnstones breed in the high Arctic, to within 500 miles of the North Pole on Ellesmere Island, Canada, and undertake prodigious migrations to spend every winter within the same small area around our coasts. They are a long-lived bird, and extremely site faithful. During winter 1990/91, for instance, Merseyside Ringing Group caught 339 Turnstones at night roosting on the drained New Brighton Marine Lake (SJ39C) and 43 of them had been ringed on the north Wirral or at Seaforth over 10 years previously, the oldest being three from 1977 returning for at least their fourteenth winter (Norman & Coffey 1994). Two of them were doomed not to return, however, being found dead in July 1996 on breeding grounds in north-west Greenland and in June 1999 in Baffin Island, Canada, the latter in the area normally occupied by Turnstones that winter in the USA.

Turnstones probably have the most varied diet of any wader and have been recorded scavenging many bizarre items on the tideline including dog food, potato peelings, cheese, oatmeal, soap, gull excrement and the flesh of dead animals, including birds, a sheep, a wolf, a cat and a human corpse, culminating in a note in *British Birds* entitled 'What won't Turnstones eat?' to which the answer appeared to be 'almost nothing!' (Gill 1986). Their more natural food comprises shore crabs, mussels, periwinkles and crustaceans, using their strong bill to probe and chisel under stones and seaweed. Turnstones studied on Egremont shore (SJ39B) in 1989 fed almost exclusively on barnacles.

The Turnstone's status in the county has changed considerably in the last one hundred years. Brockholes (1874) said that they were scarce in the nineteenth century, but by the beginning of the twentieth century Coward (1910) regarded the species as not uncommon as a passage migrant, although in winter there were only two records, both from Red Rocks, of a single bird in January 1907 and a flock of six in January 1909. They must have changed their habits markedly in the next 30 years because Hardy (1941) knew the species regularly at Hilbre throughout the winter, counting a flock of 72 on 8 January 1939. Bell (1962) noted that their chief haunt was the Dee estuary, particularly around Hilbre and Hoylake, with flocks of 400–600 birds on autumn passage, but the numbers fell away in October and November to leave up to 100 or so wintering. On the Mersey estuary it was much less common, with small numbers reported from Bromborough, in Tranmere Bay, and Frodsham Marsh.

The county bird reports from 1964 onwards made no mention of Turnstones in winter until a count of 300 at Hilbre in February 1977, and by 1982 the 'resident' population there was usually 200–500 birds (Craggs 1982). This continues to be true of Hilbre Island to the present day, with occasional exceptional figures like the 601 counted in January 1994, although flocks are more normally towards the bottom end of this range. Elsewhere on north Wirral, high counts were also reported from Leasowe Bay, 250 on 9 February 1980 and 550 on 29 December 1982, with the species' versatility again displayed when 400 roosted and fed on school fields at Leasowe on 12 January 1986. During the 1980s New Brighton emerged as another important roost site, and the importance of Egremont shore for feeding was realized by 1988, with around 300 birds there in December 1988, these birds roosting at Leasowe. Low-water counts were instigated in the Mersey Narrows from New Brighton to Egremont, revealing some massive figures including 1,100 in February 1995, the county's record of 1,785 on 5 February 1997 and 1,719 on 30 November 1998, but numbers reduced following construction of three long groynes to stabilize the beach wall, with 678 birds there on 16 January 2000, and *CWBRs* include no further counts although the 2004 report noted that 'good numbers' were present there.

The Mersey Narrows held, at times, the third largest concentration of Turnstones in the UK, but its importance was sadly not recognized for many years because the birds roosted on the north Wirral and all the WeBS counts were lumped in with those for the Dee estuary. The site was eventually designated as an SSSI in August 2000, and the Mersey Narrows and North Wirral Foreshore has been notified to the UK government as a potential Special Protection Area under the European Birds Directive.

Sponsored by Hilbre Bird Observatory and Ringing Station

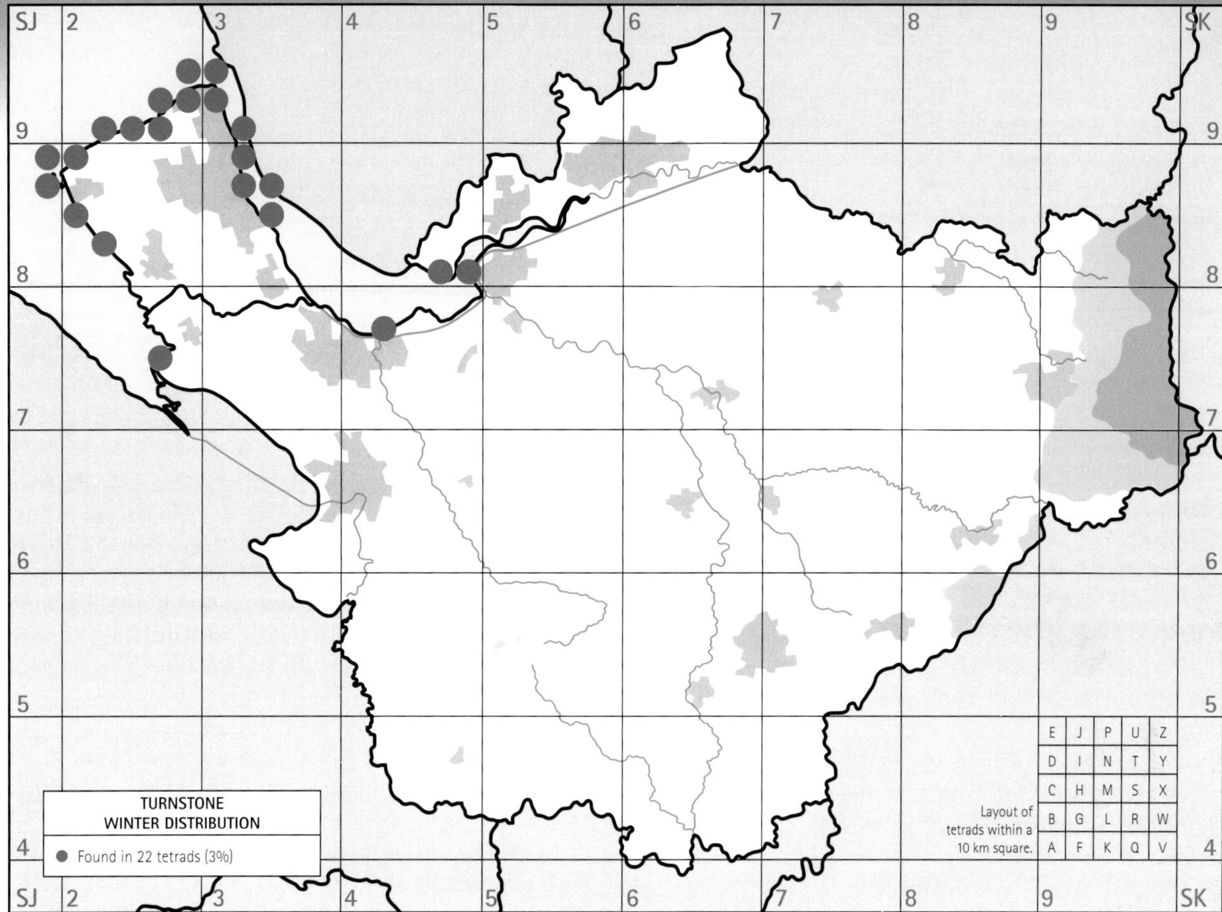

Conservation status for a site cannot, however, make species immune from wider trends and the numbers of Turnstones wintering in England fell considerably during the 1990s, back to about the level of the early 1970s; it appears that the Cheshire and Wirral figures have followed a similar pattern (Brown & Grice 2005).

This Atlas map gives a good depiction of all the places where Turnstones are found in winter: any of the shores with hard substrates, and roost sites often on man-made structures. The largest counts reported during this Atlas period, all of roosting flocks, were on Hilbre (300, 247 and 220 respectively in the three winters), 285 at Leasowe (SJ29R) and 114 on the wall of West Kirby Marine Lake (SJ28D). Although the map shows birds present in several tetrads farther up the Mersey and Dee, the numbers of Turnstone decrease with distance from the north Wirral, with reported maxima of 35 on the shore at Tranmere/Rock Ferry (SJ38I), 16 at New Ferry (SJ38M), 1–3 birds on the three inner Mersey sites and just one in SJ27S in the south Dee salt-marshes.

Great Skua

Stercorarius skua

Adult Great Skuas mostly winter in the Bay of Biscay and off Iberia, where they associate with fishing boats and feed on discarded fish. Some immature birds may mix with them, but others move farther south to winter off African coasts, with some birds crossing the Atlantic to be found off South America or in the USA (*Migration Atlas*). It seems that it was probably Great Skuas from the Bay of Biscay that were caught up in the remarkable gales of November/December 2006 that brought a series of records in the last winter of this Atlas, in a similar way to those for Leach's Petrel and Manx Shearwater. After no records in 2004/05 or 2005/06, the first Great Skuas in 2006 were noted off Hilbre on 4 and 6 December, with two off Hoylake shore on 6 December. There was another report from Hoylake shore (SJ28E) on 9 December, the day of the largest numbers of petrels and shearwaters. It could well have been the same bird that moved farther up the Dee estuary, and certainly one individual was reported to have been responsible for Atlas records in all three tetrads mapped there. On 10 December it was seen on the outer salt-marsh off Burton Point (SJ27S) harassing roosting waders and wildfowl, and was then seen on 11 December off Parkgate (SJ27U) exhibiting the same behaviour before flying out to roost on a sandbank in the centre of the estuary (SJ27J). A final record was added, again from Hoylake shore, on 29 December 2006.

This large predator usually passes through in autumn, accompanying terns and gulls which it harasses until they disgorge their food. Winter birds are rare and the early county records are confused. The earliest documented winter record appears to have been at the end of November 1939, when a correspondent of Boyd saw one at the mouth of the Dee (Boyd 1946). Bell (1967) details the first known dated December record as a bird off Hilbre on 4 December 1961, although Craggs (1982), summarizing Hilbre records for 1957–77, shows none for the period mid-November to February. There seem to be no such queries over birds at Red Rocks on 6 December 1964 and off Ince Bank on 11 December 1966 (Bell 1967).

In the 42 years from Bell's book (1962) to the start of this winter Atlas, Great Skuas have appeared in 15

RAY SCALLY

Sponsored by Bob Anderson in memory of John C. Gittins

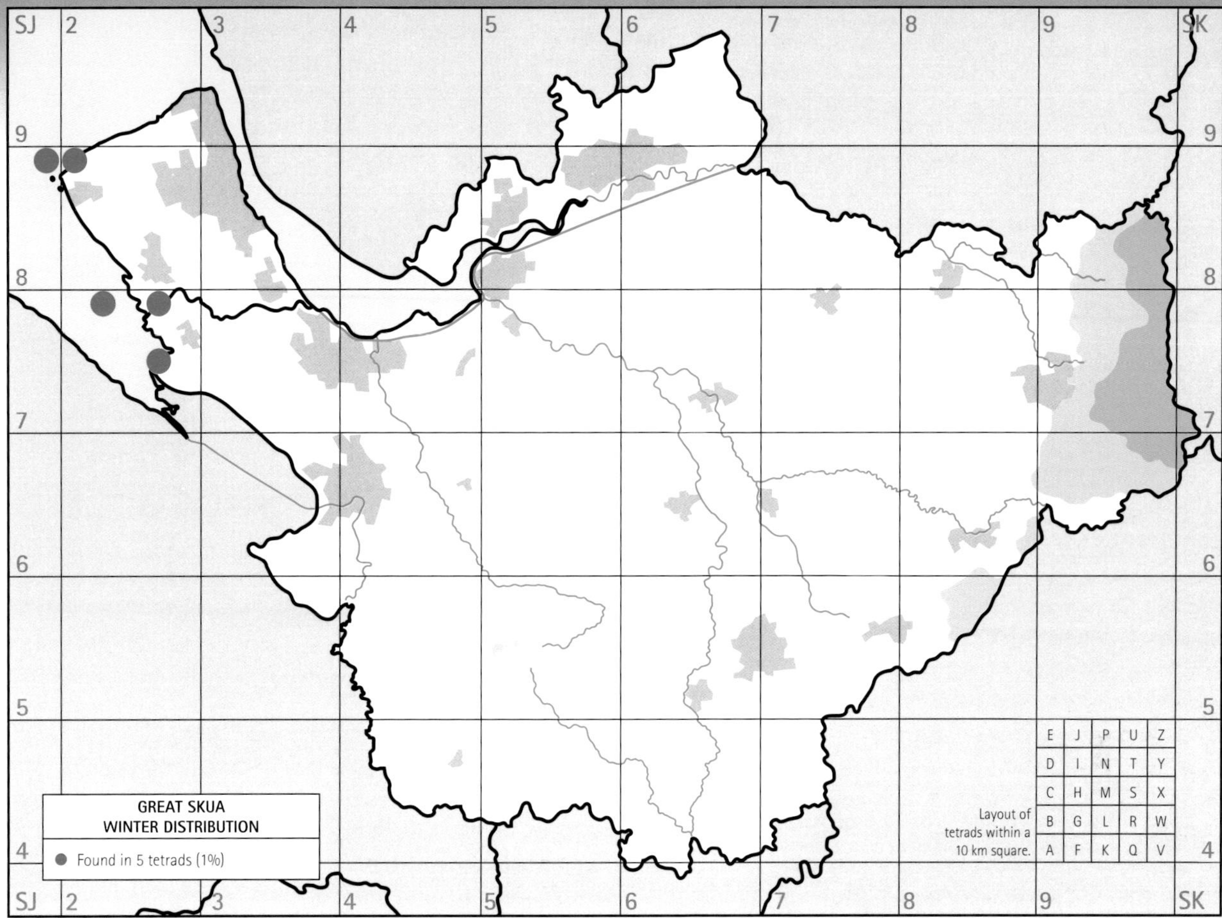

winters, with an even spread of birds in each month from November to February. Although most winters had only odd records, there were multiple sightings in four winters: in 1987/88, single birds were seen on four dates from 3 January to 18 February, 1992/93 had at least two different birds on seven dates from 2 January to 19 February, while 1999/2000 had single birds on three dates from 26 November to 27 December. By far the most remarkable was the winter of 1989/90 when birds were seen from Red Rocks and Hilbre on many days from 27 January into early March. Four birds were off Red Rocks on 28 January, while on 11 February six moved west and two east there. Next day ones and twos were seen at several sites along the north Wirral coast between New Brighton and Hilbre while one was up the Dee estuary off Burton. The majority of all winter sightings are from the north Wirral coast but birds have been seen in four winters in the Dee estuary as far as Inner Marsh Farm and the Mersey estuary to Ince Marshes.

Thus, although the gales of December 2006 were extraordinary in their effect on some seabirds, this winter Atlas map for Great Skua was typical of any recent three-year period.

Kittiwake

Rissa tridactyla

RAY SCALLY

This is the world's most numerous species of gull and, in winter, is the most oceanic. Outside the breeding season, birds from all colonies and countries mix and spread across the whole of the north Atlantic, from Europe to North America, south to about 30°N (*Migration Atlas*). Apart from those that latch on to fishing vessels, they probably feed mainly on planktonic marine invertebrates and often forage by flying daintily just above the water's surface. A few winter birds are visible from shore in Britain, but less than 1% of the total that comes here to breed (*BTO Winter Atlas*). They are usually seen in Cheshire and Wirral during or after gales; this winter Atlas map depicts their typical distribution.

Birds were reported from Hilbre in all three winters, with submitted counts of 5, 2 and 20 birds, but all of the other Kittiwake records came in two periods of extreme weather. The only large numbers were in November 2004 off Hoylake, when a flock of Kittiwakes was feeding offshore after big gales and counts were made of 100 in SJ28E and 1,250 in SJ29A; this was the same period as the largest flocks of Guillemots and Little Gulls. The other extremely windy spell, in November/December 2006, brought the only inland record during this Atlas, a first winter bird on Hurleston Reservoir (SJ65H) on 25 November 2006. Another Kittiwake was not quite on the shore, roosting amongst other gulls on a field at Hoylake Langfields (SJ28J) on 11 December 2006, at the end of the same series of gales, and birds were seen in the other four tetrads off the north Wirral coast during the same spell that also affected several pelagic seabirds (Manx Shearwater, Leach's Petrel, Great Skua).

The early ornithological literature is confusing about the winter status of Kittiwake in the county. In part this is probably because some birds have changed their habits—some returning in midwinter to breeding colonies from the 1960s onwards (*BTO Winter Atlas*)—but probably derives from the sporadic nature of study of the county's seabirds, allied to Kittiwakes' irregular occurrence. Records from 1957 to 1977 for the one site with systematic records of seawatching, Hilbre Island, show that the period from November to March is by far the quietest of the year for this species (Craggs 1982). As with some other seabirds, published reports overemphasize the occasional storm-driven inland birds. Kittiwakes do not willingly venture away from the sea and those found inland are probably weak or ill; they are seldom able to feed adequately on freshwater sites and have to return to the coast or die (*BTO Winter Atlas*).

In the last forty years the county bird reports indicate presence of birds in the mouth of the Dee each winter, but only irregularly in the Mersey. Large flocks, typically up to 200 birds, are found on average every few years, always connected to unusual weather.

In memory of Gail Bunker

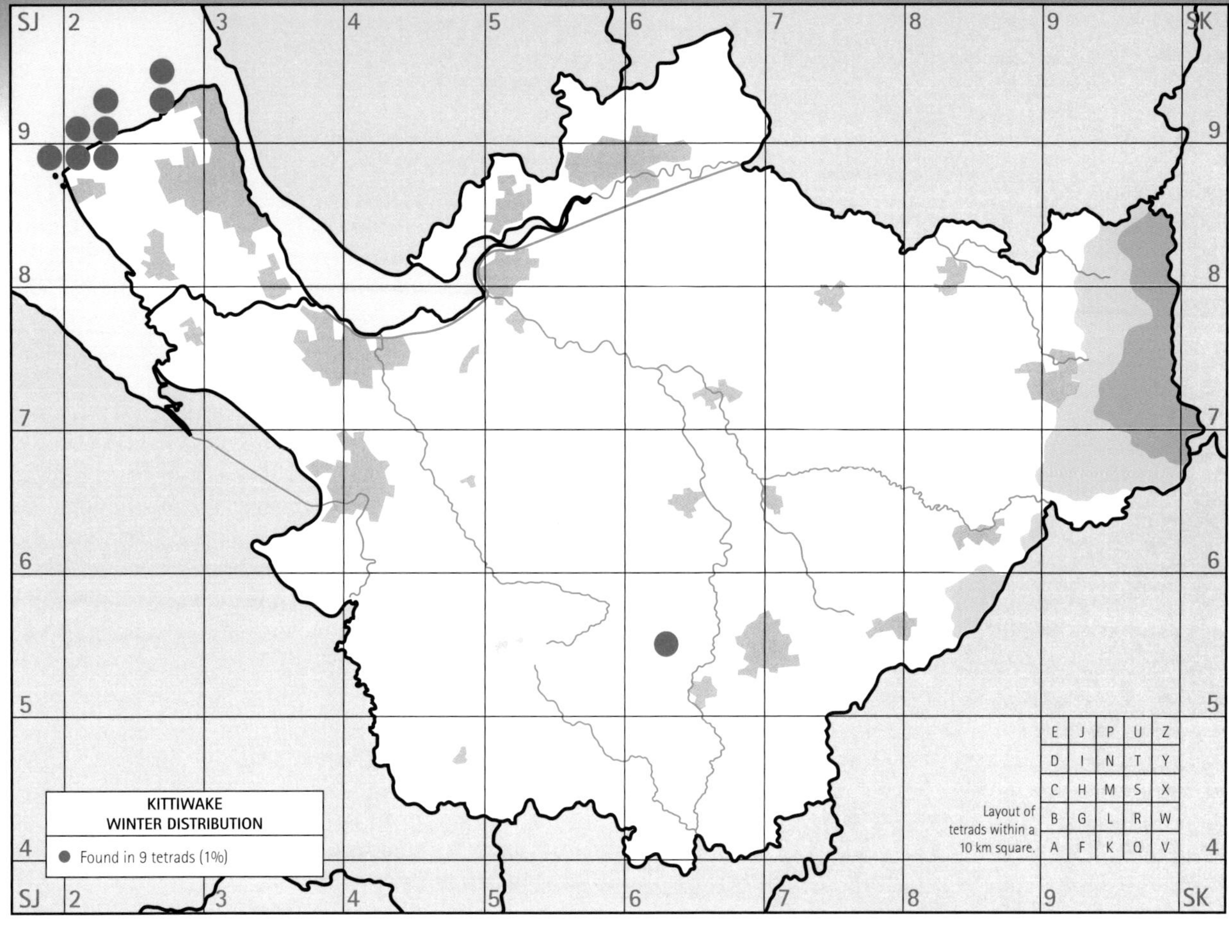
SJ
SK
KITTIWAKE
WINTER DISTRIBUTION
Found in 9 tetrads (1%)
Layout of
tetrads within a
10 km square.
E J P U Z
D I N T Y
C H M S X
B G L R W
A F K Q V

Black-headed Gull

Chroicocephalus ridibundus

ANDY HARMER

There are three substantial Black-headed Gull colonies in the county. It can be difficult to count the numbers but estimates in 2004 were at least 1,000 pairs at Blakemere (SJ57K), 600–800 pairs at Woolston (SJ68N/P) and 650 nests at Inner Marsh Farm (SJ37B); in 2005 the figures were at least 1,000 pairs at Blakemere and 500 pairs each at Woolston and Inner Marsh Farm. With fewer than 10 nests at any other site, the county total lies in the range of 2,000–2,500 pairs. This is the third highest total of inland-breeding Black-headed Gulls of any county in England, with the Cheshire population exceeding 10% of the English total, but unfortunately the county's records were not submitted to the national 'Seabird 2000' survey (Mitchell *et al.* 2004).

Our *First Atlas* noted the historical association of Black-headed Gulls with the Delamere area, going back at least 400 years, which had ceased by 1965. Gulls made sporadic attempts to nest in the area but the crucial event was the decision by the Forestry Commission to abandon tree production in the wettest part of Delamere Forest. In late 1996 the Forestry Commission cut down 46.7 ha of trees and allowed the area naturally to flood, re-creating Blakemere Moss. By 1999 Black-headed Gulls had colonized the lake, with their population rapidly rising and estimates of 200 pairs (2000), 400 pairs (2001), 450 pairs (2002), 800 pairs (2003) and 1,000 pairs (2004–06).

Avoidance of ground predators, mainly foxes and rats, is crucial for breeding Black-headed Gulls, and overflying birds are always alert to the formation of a new island. Most nests are on the ground, amongst grass tussocks, or just above the water level in submerged bushes. Even there, they are not safe from mink, which cause havoc when they go through the colony at Woolston, or Lesser Black-backed Gulls, which in some years have taken a large toll of eggs and chicks at Inner Marsh Farm. No significant predation has been noted at Blakemere, although the site is not watched as regularly as the other two. Availability of food provides little constraint on the location of a colony as they obtain little food from the waters immediately surrounding it, and their diet is mostly terrestrial invertebrates obtained from farmland, especially earthworms and the larvae of tipulids and beetles.

Colonies are occupied from February, with the area filled with noise every second of daylight until the birds drift away in July. The cacophony of a Black-headed Gull colony means that no breeding concentration of any size should have been overlooked, but pairs can nest singly or in small groups anywhere and might have been missed. Most sites were recorded as large waterbodies, with odd birds in water-meadow and bog; off Parkgate they nested on the estuarine salt-marsh. One pair nested in 2004 at Frodsham in the top of a rotting wooden post in the Manchester Ship Canal, copying the Oystercatchers there.

The Black-headed Gull is on the UK's Amber List of species of conservation concern because of its moderate population decline over the last quarter-century and its concentration into a relatively small number of sites, which makes it vulnerable to a localized catastrophe. On the other hand, the Cheshire and Wirral breeding population of Black-headed Gulls is probably higher than it has ever been, and a thorough count of all known colonies would be valuable.

Sponsored by Hazel J. Raw

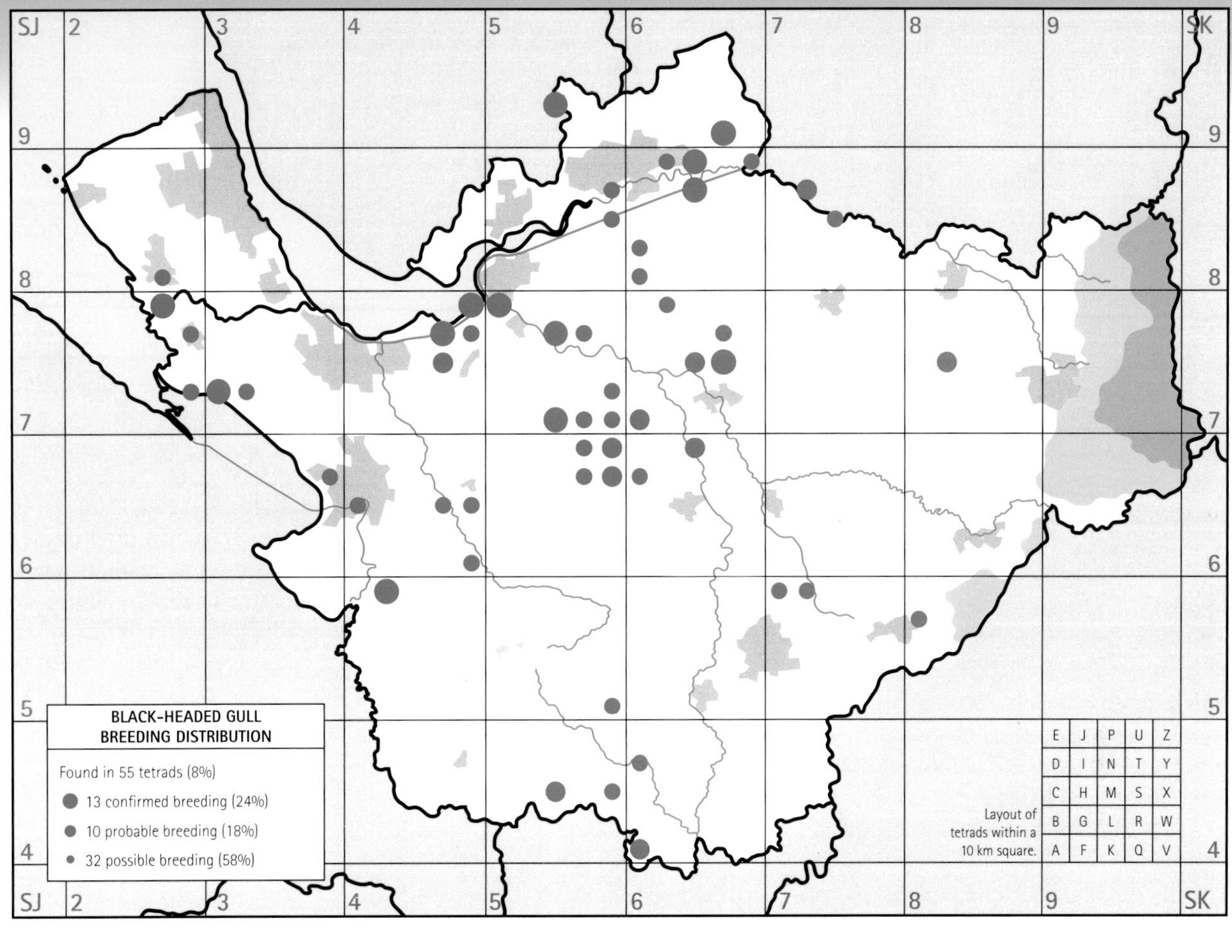
BLACK-HEADED GULL
BREEDING DISTRIBUTION
Found in 55 tetrads (8%)
13 confirmed breeding (24%)
10 probable breeding (18%)
32 possible breeding (58%)
Layout of tetrads within a 10 km square.
E J P U Z
D I N T Y
C H M S X
B G L R W
A F K Q V
SJ
SK
2
3
4
5
6
7
8
9

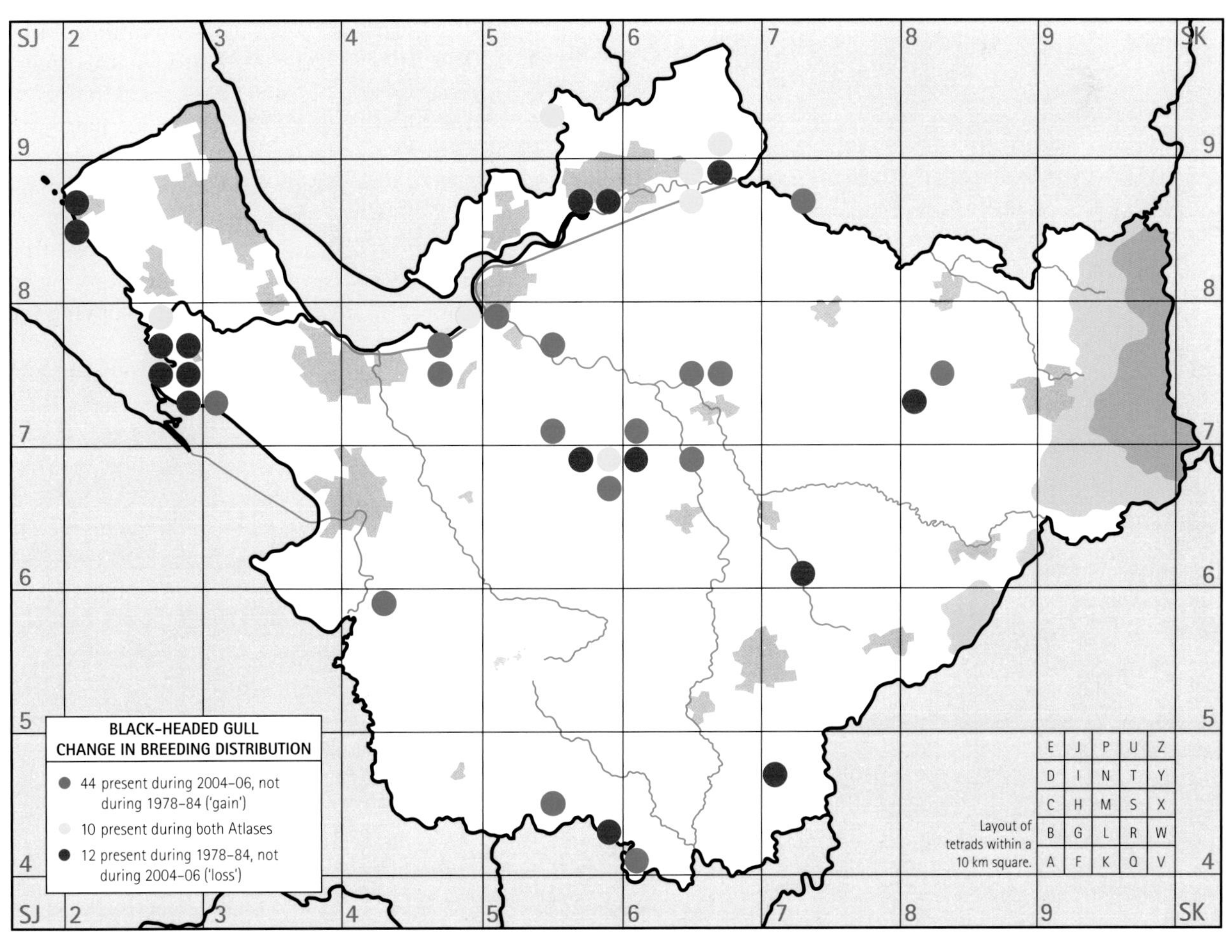
BLACK-HEADED GULL
CHANGE IN BREEDING DISTRIBUTION
44 present during 2004–06, not during 1978–84 ('gain')
10 present during both Atlases
12 present during 1978–84, not during 2004–06 ('loss')
Layout of tetrads within a 10 km square.
E J P U Z
D I N T Y
C H M S X
B G L R W
A F K Q V
SJ
SK
2
3
4
5
6
7
8
9

Black-headed Gull is the most widespread gull in winter, being found in almost three-quarters of the county's tetrads, and seen flying over almost all of them. They avoid the highest land in the eastern hills, and there is a noticeable gap around the environs of Manchester Airport in SJ88, perhaps showing the effects of the airport's bird-scaring manoeuvres. Not only is it the most widespread gull, it is also the most numerous, found in by far the largest flocks. The median flock size was 60 birds and fieldworkers made 288 counts of 100 or more, and 43 counts of 1,000 or more Black-headed Gulls. The largest gatherings were on water, observers reporting loafing or roosting flocks of 20,000 at Hurleston reservoir (SJ65H), 12,000 on Doddington Pool (SJ74D) and a regular roost of 10,000 birds on mud-flats in the river Mersey after feeding at the Arpley landfill site (SJ58T/Y).

Some three-quarters of the wintering population are immigrants. There are movements of ringed Black-headed Gulls between Cheshire and Wirral and breeding grounds in every country around the North Sea, with the most distant over 1,000 km inland in Russia, halfway between Moscow and the Black Sea. On the other hand, some locally bred birds move out for the winter, with a Woolston-ringed chick wintering in Galway City on the west coast of Ireland.

They feed on a wide variety of soil invertebrates, carrion and marine invertebrates taken in intertidal areas, and domestic waste. Of the habitat records submitted for this survey 58% were farmland, with 9% in human sites, 20% on fresh water and 9% in marine areas. Most of the farmland habitats were grassland (42%), with 15% on tilled land or stubble.

They have obviously changed their habits considerably over the years. Until late in the nineteenth century Black-headed Gulls were almost entirely a coastal bird (*BTO Winter Atlas*). Coward (1910) commented on their remarkable increase inland, most notably in the north of the county next to the line of the newly constructed Manchester Ship Canal, which gulls followed along its length. It was worth mentioning that, after 1900, Rostherne Mere had become a regular roosting place for hundreds of birds. Bell (1962) noted that the species was abundant and widespread inland, with 'a vast roost' around Runcorn on the Mersey estuary and major roosts at Rostherne, Doddington and Witton flashes. The Rostherne roost was estimated at 10,000–12,000 in February 1962 (Bell 1967).

RICHARD STEEL

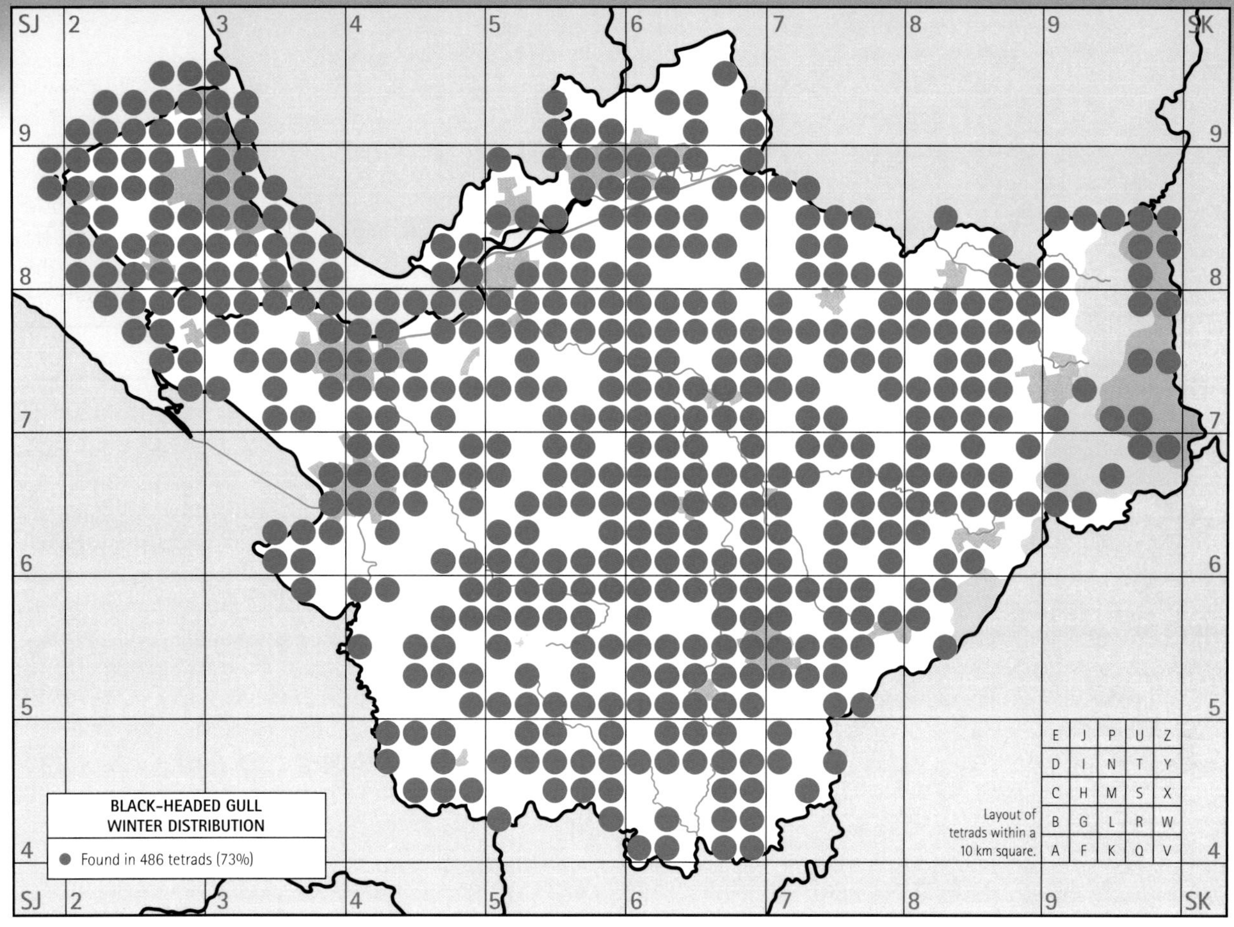

SJ
2
3
4
5
6
7
8
9
SK
BLACK-HEADED GULL
WINTER DISTRIBUTION
Found in 486 tetrads (73%)
Layout of tetrads within a 10 km square.
E J P U Z
D I N T Y
C H M S X
B G L R W
A F K Q V

Little Gull

Hydrocoloeus minutus

The British status of this, the smallest gull in the world, has changed considerably in the last half-century, with the species becoming more common and likely to be found at any season. The turbid water at the mouth of the Mersey has become a favourite feeding area for them to pick invertebrates from the surface, and flocks of several hundred Little Gulls can be present in spring as birds gather on their return to their Baltic breeding grounds. Their rise in numbers from the 1960s is thought to be linked to a substantial increase in the western component of their breeding population in Finland (Hutchinson & Neath 1978), and by the early 1980s the Irish Sea was notable as the main area where winter flocks could be found, although not every year (*BTO Winter Atlas*).

In the early twentieth century, the Little Gull was 'a rare wanderer to Cheshire in winter' (Coward 1910) but from about 1950 onwards they could be found in any month of the year, mostly in the two estuaries with more in the Dee than the Mersey (Bell 1962). That would be a reasonable statement of their status to the present day. Winter numbers and occurrences are very variable in both estuaries and birds are not recorded every winter. Most sightings are in January and February and are in single figures, but the county bird reports for the last 40 years show monthly maxima in the Mersey of four in November, 20 in December, 37 in January and 60 in February. Unusually, in 1975/76 there appeared to be 100 or more birds present for much of the winter and counted occasionally from Hilbre. Away from the coast its occurrences are annual, usually in small numbers, with records widespread across Cheshire in every month over the years since 1967, but mainly from April to September. There have been inland records in the winter period (mid-November to end-February) in 13 of the years since 1967, all of single birds.

This winter Atlas map shows their normal distribution, although rather exaggerating the picture by

RICHARD STEEL

Sponsored by an anonymous CAWOS member

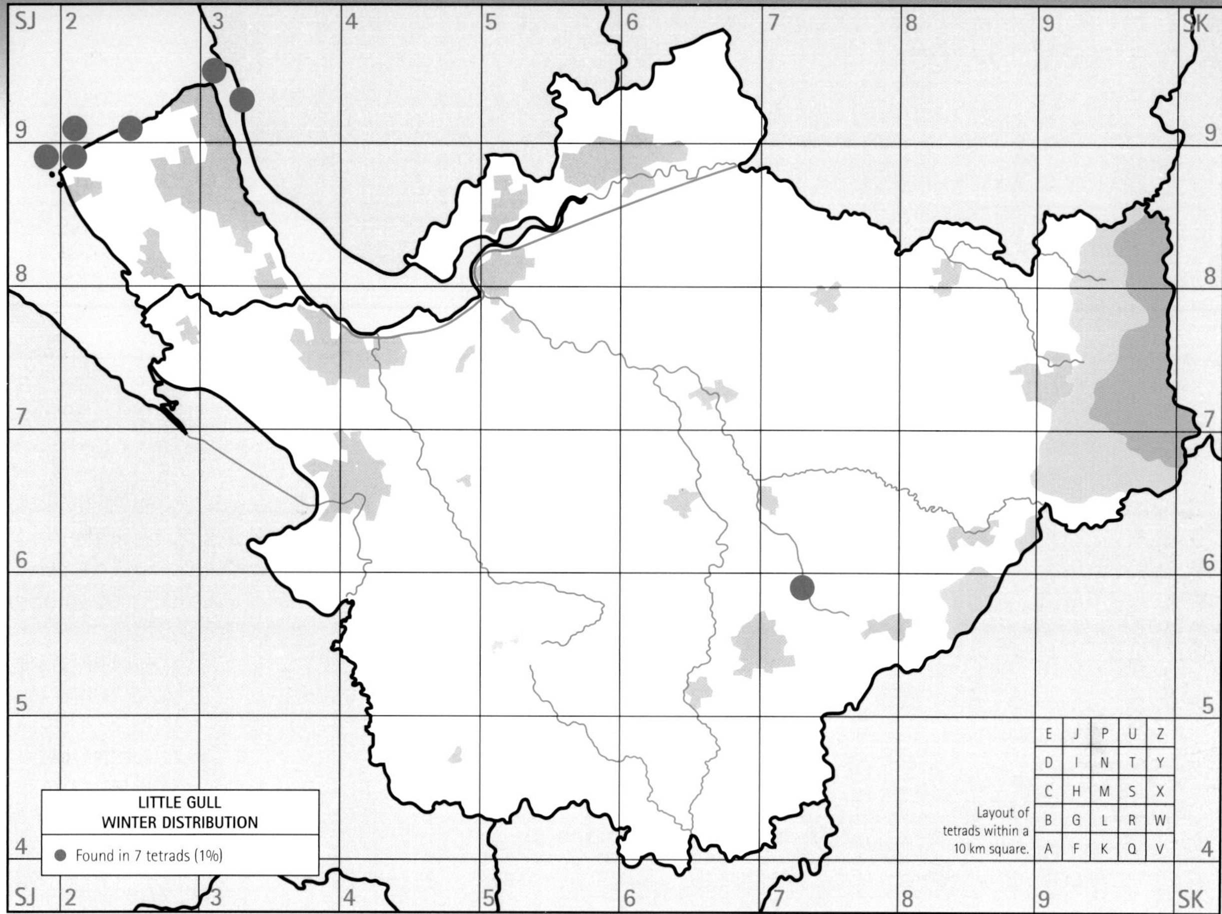

aggregating three years' data. A maximum of six birds was reported at Hilbre, but the largest flocks were on Hoylake shore in November 2004, when nine birds were in SJ28E and a group of 65 birds in SJ29A. One bird inland, at Sandbach Flashes (SJ75J) in January 2006, is typical for a three-year period.

● Little Gulls attempted to breed four times in England, at four different sites and always unsuccessfully, from 1975 to 1987 (Brown & Grice 2005). All four nests were in Black-headed Gull colonies and failed with eggs predated or through human interference. In Cheshire and Wirral there has been no suggestion of breeding but Little Gulls occasionally have visited the gulleries at Woolston, Frodsham Marsh or Inner Marsh Farm. These have nearly always been immature birds but adults in breeding plumage have been seen at Woolston: one or two adults were present from 22 April to 19 May 1985; it was considered possible that an adult remained with a first summer bird from 10 May to 7 June 1988; and two adults were present from 25 to 30 April 2001. During this Atlas period, two adults were present from 15 to 28 April 2006.

Mediterranean Gull

Larus melanocephalus

RAY SCALLY

Mediterranean Gulls marked the start of this Atlas in 2004 with their first breeding in the county; not, as many expected, at Woolston (SJ68P) or Inner Marsh Farm (SJ37B), where birds had displayed to Black-headed Gulls for years, or paired with immature conspecifics, but in the Black-headed Gull colony at Blakemere Moss (SJ57K) in Delamere Forest.

They first bred in Britain, in Hampshire, in 1968 and 1969, but the initial colonization was slow because most of the pioneering birds were males and few female Mediterranean Gulls reached Britain. Many early pairings were with female Black-headed Gulls, sometimes producing hybrid offspring although none of them seems to have been fertile. They next produced chicks in Hampshire in 1976, then in Kent in 1979 but it was the 1990s before they spread, with successful breeding in eight counties during that decade (Brown & Grice 2005). The northward expansion included breeding in Lancashire from 1997 and in Greater Manchester in 2003. By 2004 there were 183–241 pairs breeding at 26 sites in 15 counties (Holling *et al.* 2007a).

Mediterranean Gulls do not normally breed until three years of age, although some two-year-olds try to do so, and they spend much of their time in Black-headed Gull colonies. The build-up to Mediterranean Gulls' breeding in Cheshire and Wirral, as in most counties, is clouded by the behaviour of two-year-old birds and interactions with Black-headed Gulls. In most years from 1995 to 2004 pairings including immature birds and mixed-species displayed and sometimes built nests, at Inner Marsh Farm, Frodsham Marsh or Woolston (*CWBRs*). Breeding finally occurred in 2004 when several adult Mediterranean Gulls visited the county's largest Black-headed Gull colony at Blakemere (SJ57K)—the first time that they had been recorded there—and at least two pairs raised young. Three pairs nested at Blakemere in 2005 and six birds were seen on nests in 2006. It seems that, given the initial stimulus, most of the county's birds with breeding intent now gather at the one site, as there were fewer records at Inner Marsh Farm or Woolston in 2005 and 2006 than for the previous decade.

Most Mediterranean Gull colonies are in tidal lagoons but they seem equally at home on the county's freshwater sites. Their diet should place no restriction on their distribution because their main food during the breeding season appears to be terrestrial invertebrates, especially earthworms, and insects (Mitchell *et al.* 2004).

Sponsored by Peter F. Twist

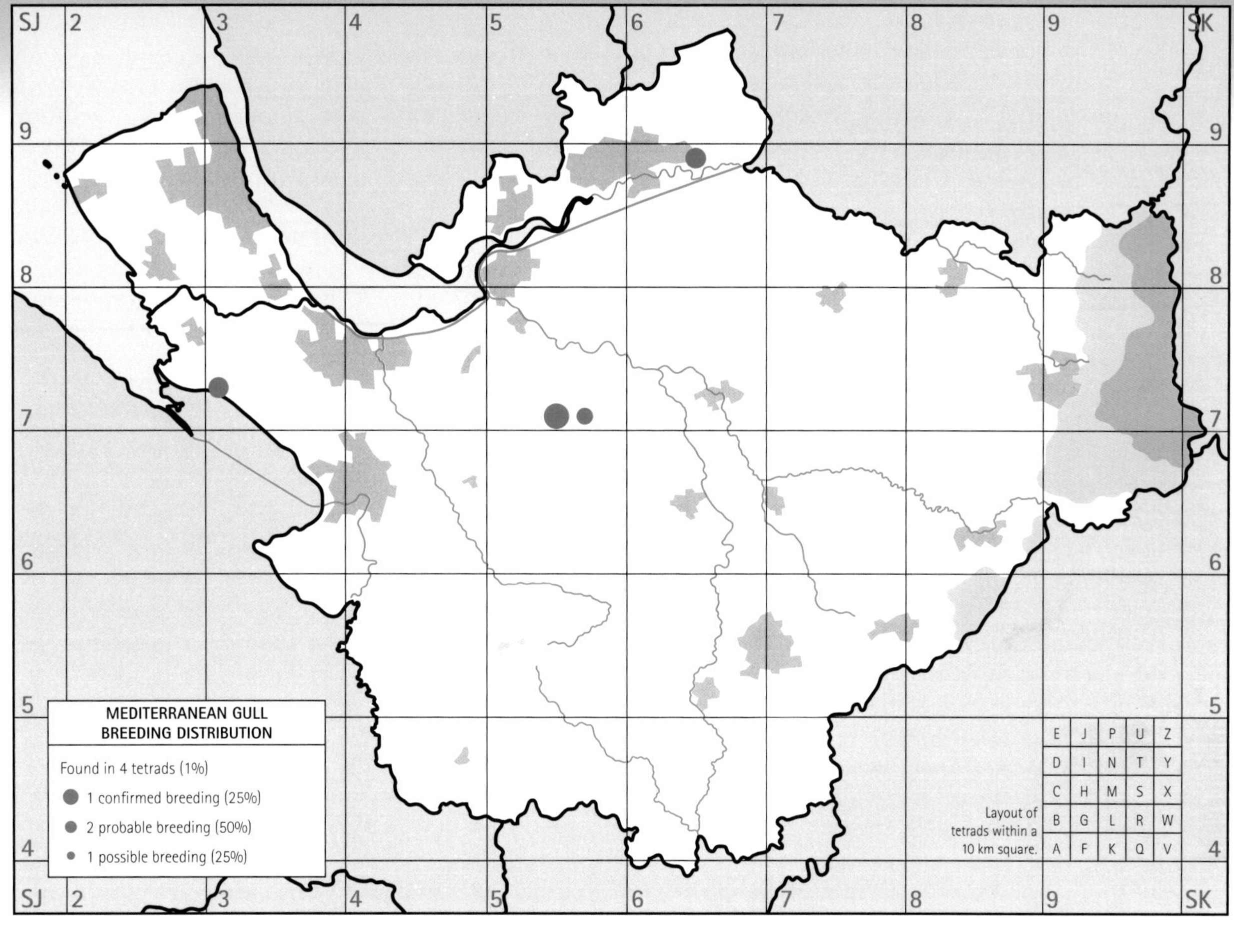
SJ
2
3
4
5
6
7
8
9
SK
MEDITERRANEAN GULL
BREEDING DISTRIBUTION
Found in 4 tetrads (1%)
1 confirmed breeding (25%)
2 probable breeding (50%)
1 possible breeding (25%)
Layout of
tetrads within a
10 km square.
E J P U Z
D I N T Y
C H M S X
B G L R W
A F K Q V

The rise in numbers of this species in Britain has been remarkable. Until 1940 only four or five had ever been recorded, and it remained so rare that records were considered by the British Birds Rarities Committee until 1962. The first in Cheshire and Wirral was identified in 1967 and the species has been recorded every year since. Until about 1994 most records were from the Wirral coast, including the Mersey Narrows, but since then birds have been widespread across the county.

During this Atlas birds were recorded in 29 tetrads, with about a dozen birds each winter of this survey. This is typical of any year in the last ten, since the *CWBR* for 1998 noted that wintering numbers appear to be relatively constant. There is a mixture of site fidelity and nomadism, with some individuals regularly appearing for several years in succession, and others newly arriving and visiting new sites. Several birds have been noted wearing rings indicating that they were hatched in colonies on the north coast of France or Belgium. In Lancashire, where some observers have carefully observed and reported rings, there are also records of birds from eastern Europe–Poland, Czech Republic, Slovakia, Hungary and the Ukraine–showing that some of the Mediterranean Gulls have come from as far as the Black Sea, the heart of the species' distribution (White *et al.* 2008).

The submitted habitat codes indicate the breadth of areas exploited by Mediterranean Gulls, with 10 records of marine habitats (four open sea/shore, six estuarine), 11 fresh water (two small waterbody, eight lake/reservoir/sandpit, one river) and four farmland (three grassland, one stubble). Their winter food is similarly varied: marine fish and molluscs, terrestrial invertebrates and anything edible discarded by man. The only record of two birds together during this Atlas survey was at Meols (SJ29F) where Richard Smith saw them 'feeding on scraps next to a mobile chippy, just over the sea wall from the shore'.

RICHARD STEEL

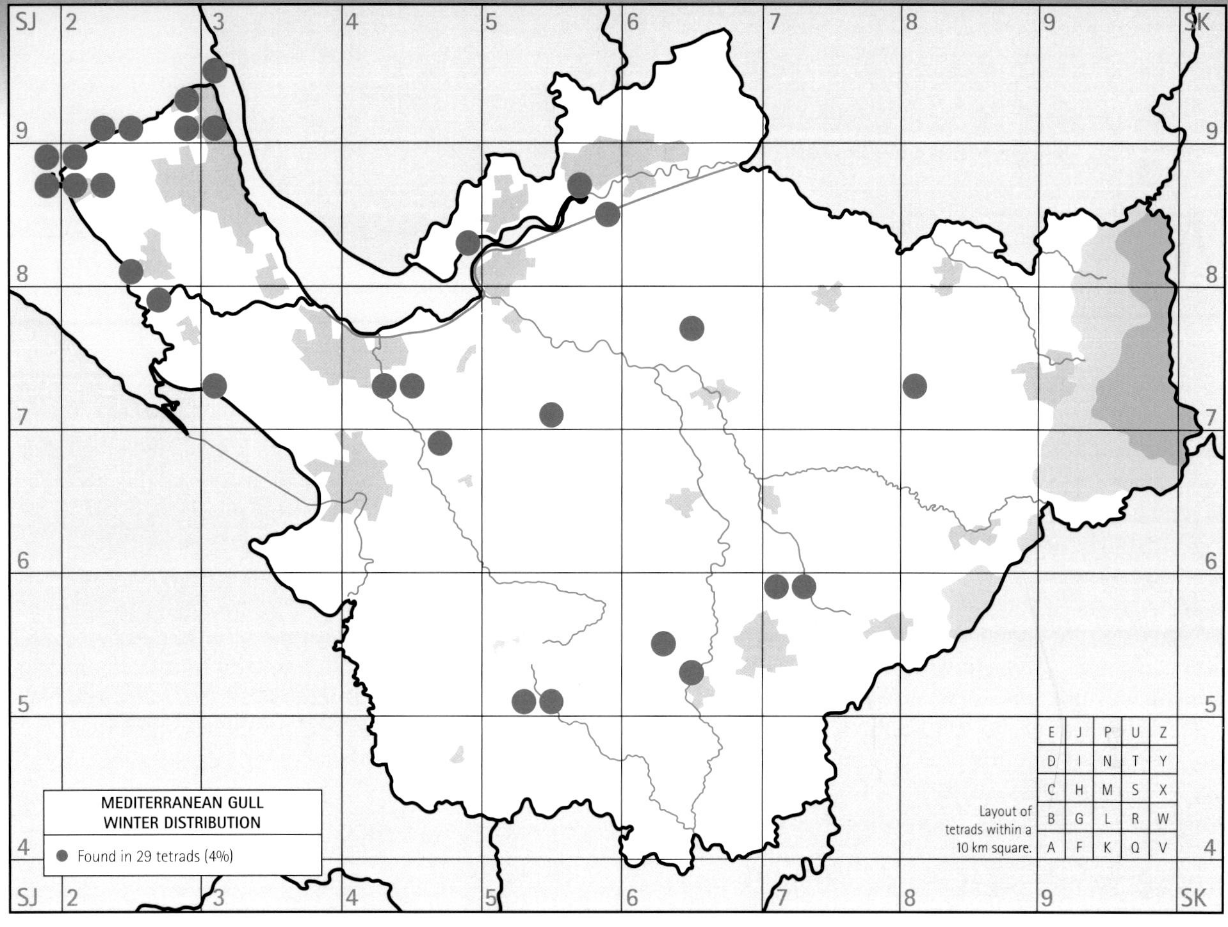
MEDITERRANEAN GULL
WINTER DISTRIBUTION
Found in 29 tetrads (4%)
Layout of tetrads within a 10 km square.
E J P U Z
D I N T Y
C H M S X
B G L R W
A F K Q V
SJ
SK
2
3
4
5
6
7
8
9

Common Gull

Larus canus

Although widespread, reported from almost half of the county's tetrads, the map shows Common Gulls to have a curious distribution. They were recorded all around the coast and estuaries, and tetrads within a few kilometres inshore, and quite widespread in agricultural land in south-west Cheshire. But the species was almost absent from a band running from Warrington through Knutsford to Congleton and sparsely distributed in the east of the county. Across Britain, they tend to avoid land above about 300 m (*BTO Winter Atlas*).

Their main food is earthworms, with other soil invertebrates found incidentally. At the coast, they mainly take molluscs. In some ways this seems to be the purest of the gulls, the one most apt to be feeding on natural foods and least likely to be scavenging the detritus of human life, but this Atlas survey showed no significant difference in habitat codes from Black-headed Gull. Farmland comprised 53% of habitat records, with 8% in human sites and 19% on fresh water. The only differences from Black-headed Gull were that Common Gulls were less liable to be found on tilled or mixed farmland (8% of records compared to 13% for Black-headed Gull), and more likely to favour marine areas (14% of records compared to 9% for Black-headed Gull). In urban areas this is the gull most frequently using the closely mown greenspace areas including playing fields. The experience of Merseyside Ringing Group on visits to Warrington area landfill sites during the 1990s was that Common Gulls were seldom present, and could only reliably be expected during hard weather, and then only in small numbers compared to the other species. However, 1,250 Common Gulls were reported from the Gowy landfill site (SJ47G) during this Atlas survey.

Most Common Gulls were found in small groups, with a median flock size of 20 birds. Observers submitted 84 counts of 100 or more and 10 counts of 1,000 or more birds. The largest was a flock of 3,500 counted by Neil Friswell on mainly flooded maize stubble near Pulford (SJ35U), with another big farmland gathering of 1,800 on a wet field at Tattenhall (SJ55E). The largest marine flocks were 3,000 on Hoylake shore (SJ28E/29A) and 1,800 in the Mersey night-time roost on Ince Banks (SJ47P).

Common Gulls wintering in the county originate from breeding grounds in Scotland and Fennoscandia. Birds have been found here that were ringed as chicks in Norway, Sweden, Finland and the Netherlands.

RAY SCALLY

Sponsored by Esther Reinhard

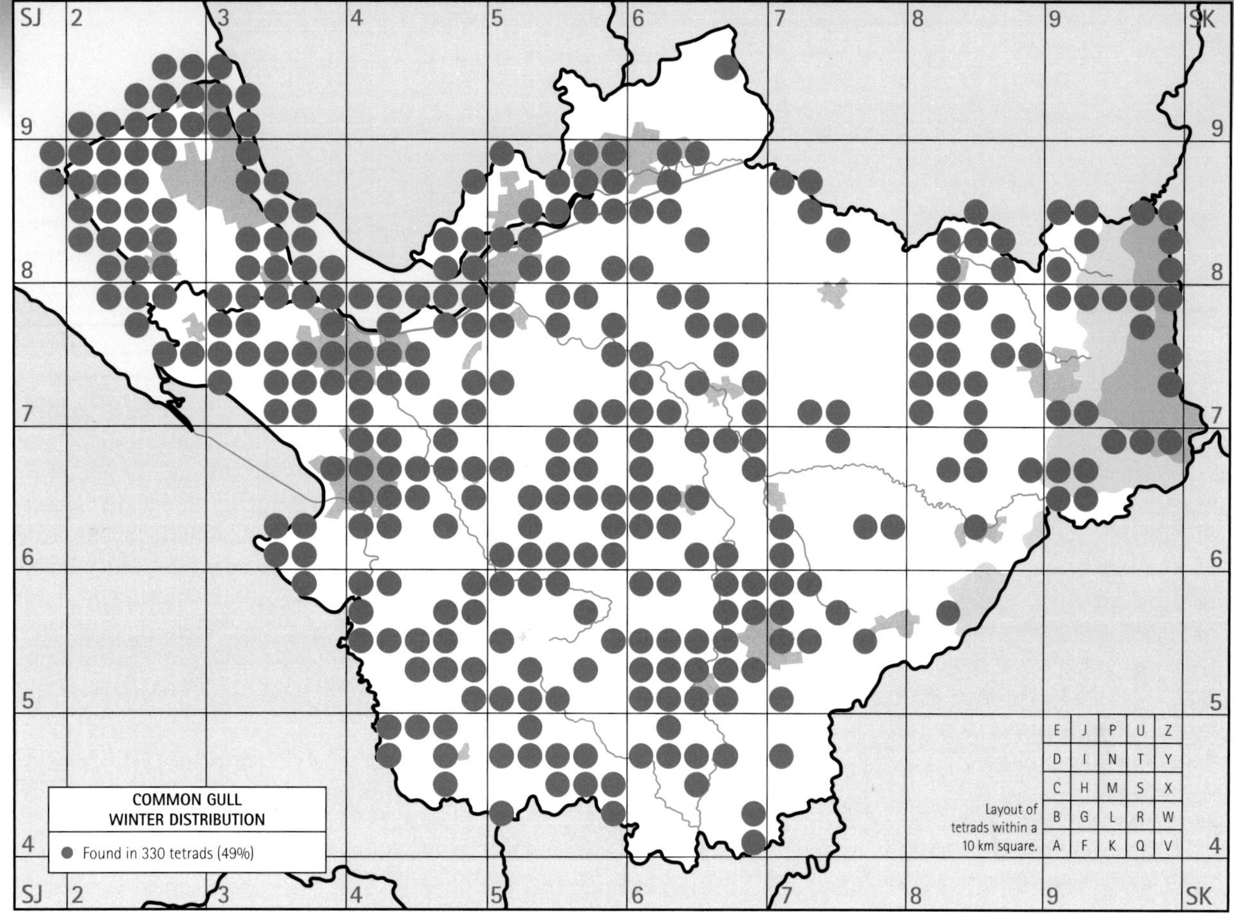
COMMON GULL
WINTER DISTRIBUTION
Found in 330 tetrads (49%)
SJ
SK
Layout of
tetrads within a
10 km square.
E J P U Z
D I N T Y
C H M S X
B G L R W
A F K Q V

Lesser Black-backed Gull

Larus fuscus

MIKE ATKINSON

Lesser Black-backed Gulls normally breed near the coast, nesting on flat ground amongst grasses. Ground predators, including foxes and mink, are their main enemies, and this adaptable species has recently realized that the roofs of buildings provide a safe alternative. The habit of rooftop nesting has spread rapidly in Britain, from 325 nests at 11 colonies in 1976, to 2,501 nests at 63 colonies in 1993–95 and 10,790 nests at 125 colonies in 1999–2002 (Mitchell *et al.* 2004). About 10% of the country's Lesser Black-backed Gulls now breed on rooftops.

In Cheshire, a pair of Lesser Black-backed Gulls nested at Witton flashes (Northwich) in 1943, with three pairs reported nesting on Burton Marsh in 1955 and 1956, and a single pair there in 1978 (*First Atlas*). The annual county bird reports show that a pair held territory, displayed and copulated without nesting, at Inner Marsh Farm (SJ37B) every year from 1996 to 2000, being responsible for substantial predation of eggs and chicks of Black-headed Gulls, Coots and ducks. A pair also held territory at Woolston (SJ68U) in 2000. The year 2003 saw the first nesting in Cheshire and Wirral for a quarter-century, and the start of a significant new development, when a pair raised chicks on the roof of a dockside building in Birkenhead (SJ29V). The same site was used again in 2004, Mike Gough reporting the female sitting tight on the nest in poor weather on 20 June, with the male nearby. During this Atlas period pairs were seen on rooftops elsewhere in Poulton, Birkenhead (SJ39A) and New Brighton (SJ39C), with a single bird possibly breeding in a different area of Birkenhead (SJ38J). Much farther inland, in 2006 in an industrial estate at Landican (SJ28X) Steve Holmes saw recently fledged young and adults behaving in a very aggressive manner to anyone in the vicinity.

Lesser Black-backed Gulls also breed just outside the county boundary on the roof of the Ford/Jaguar building at Halewood (SJ48L); in 2005, there were 40 or more pairs (White *et al.* 2008).

The species was recorded during this survey from many other tetrads with no suitable breeding habitat. It is the dominant species on the county's landfill sites in midsummer, with ringing showing that many of the adult birds are commuting daily from breeding grounds on the Ribble salt-marshes, Lancashire and Walney Island on the Cumbrian coast. There are also many immature birds around: they do not breed until at least four years of age.

Now that some birds have taken to breeding on buildings, there is no shortage of nest sites for them, and an abundance of food, either fish or other marine items, putrefying waste at landfill sites or, increasingly, take-away food discarded by humans in urban areas. In view of the rapid development of rooftop breeding in other urban coastal areas it would be good to monitor thoroughly the progress of this habit in Cheshire and Wirral.

Sponsored by Dave Murray

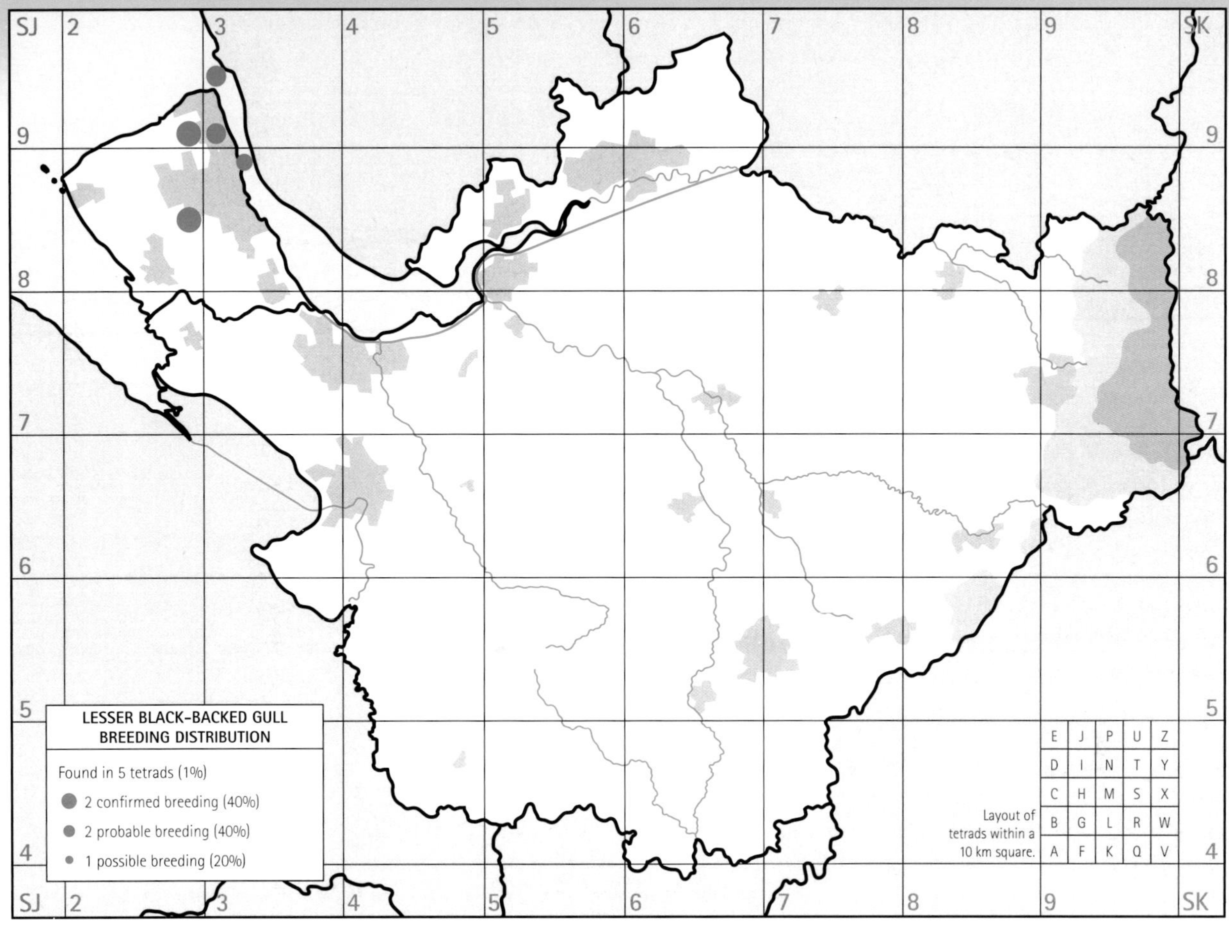
SJ
2
3
4
5
6
7
8
9
SK
9
8
7
6
5
4
LESSER BLACK-BACKED GULL
BREEDING DISTRIBUTION
Found in 5 tetrads (1%)
2 confirmed breeding (40%)
2 probable breeding (40%)
1 possible breeding (20%)
Layout of
tetrads within a
10 km square.
E J P U Z
D I N T Y
C H M S X
B G L R W
A F K Q V

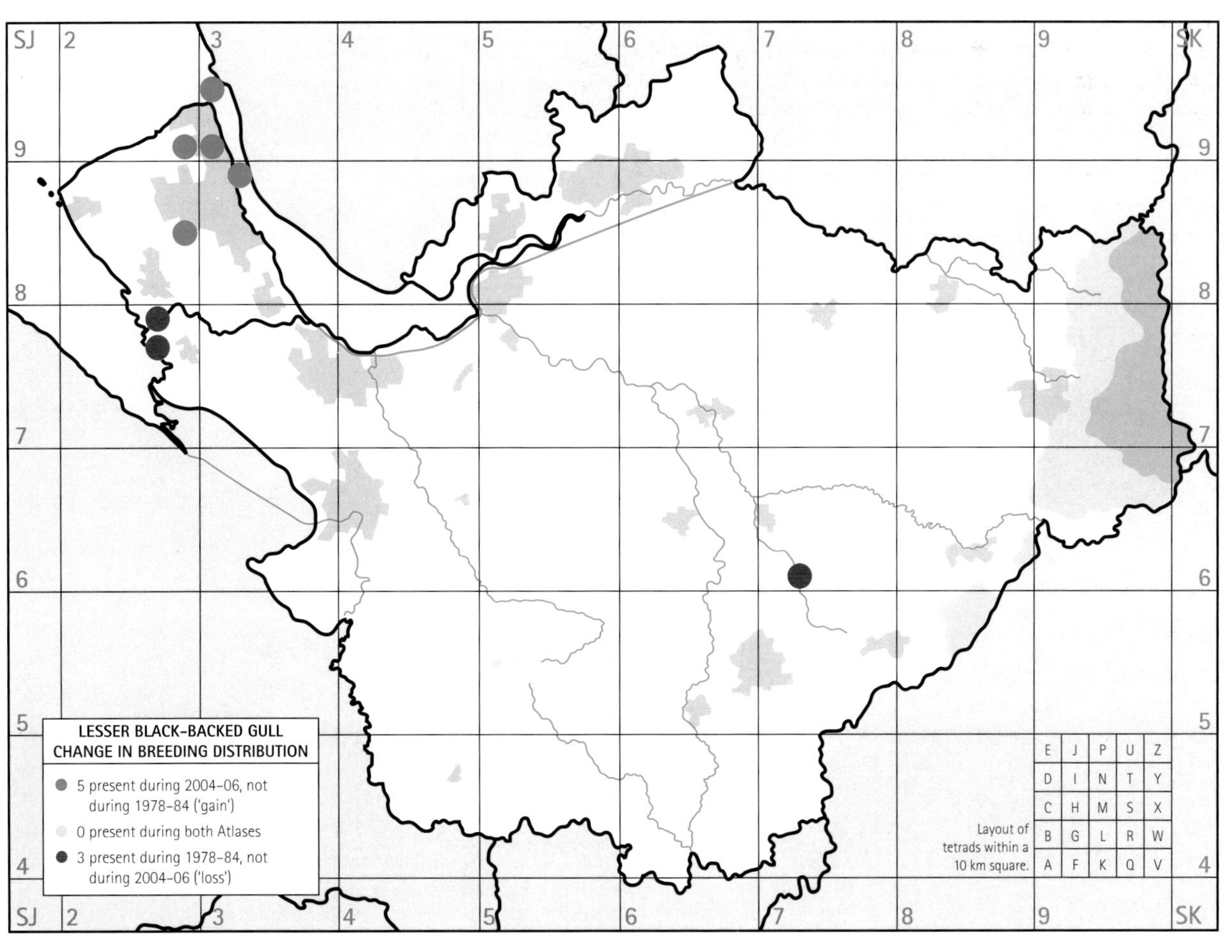
SJ
2
3
4
5
6
7
8
9
SK
9
8
7
6
5
4
LESSER BLACK-BACKED GULL
CHANGE IN BREEDING DISTRIBUTION
5 present during 2004–06, not during 1978–84 ('gain')
0 present during both Atlases
3 present during 1978–84, not during 2004–06 ('loss')
Layout of
tetrads within a
10 km square.
E J P U Z
D I N T Y
C H M S X
B G L R W
A F K Q V

Lesser Black-backed Gulls used to be almost exclusively summer visitors to Britain. Before 1928 Boyd had never seen one in the four winter months, but from then to 1950 he recorded them regularly in November, in December in 14 years, in January in 13 years and in February in 10—sometimes on the ice of the frozen Marbury Mere (Boyd 1951). They have probably adapted to wintering here by being, or becoming, mostly an inland gull, and the sheltered Mersey estuary is unusual in being one of the few places in Britain where substantial numbers have been present on the coast. In the January 1983 national survey, only 13,726 Lesser Black-backed Gulls were recorded at coastal sites, but 10,190 of these were on the Mersey, by far their largest roost in the UK (*BTO Winter Atlas*). The species' rise in wintering numbers is shown by the decennial January surveys of gulls roosting inland. In England there were 165 in 1953, 6,960 in 1963, 15,823 in 1973, 36,154 in 1983 and 27,230 in 1993 (Burton *et al.* 2003), with a preliminary figure of 43,879 in the 2003/04 survey. The Mersey no longer has any special importance, holding only 294 birds on the 2003/04 survey date (17 January 2004), with 250 on the same date inland in south Cheshire at Comber Mere (SJ54X).

The map shows that Lesser Black-backed Gulls spread out widely across the county. They require a large waterbody for a safe overnight roost but otherwise do not need water and more than half (122 out of 218) of the tetrads in which they were reported did not have a freshwater or marine (G or H) habitat code. In their feeding and roosting areas, all of the gulls tend to form mixed flocks, but this Atlas shows that this is the large gull most likely to be found on grassland, comprising 74% of their farmland records compared to 65% for Herring Gull. They especially favour slurried fields and flooded stubble, and take invertebrates, seeds and roots. Landfill sites attract some for an easy meal. Many sightings of Lesser Black-backed Gulls are of odd birds or just small groups, with half of all the submitted counts being of five birds or fewer. There were 33 flocks of 100 or more birds, with the maximum of 3,500 on Hoylake shore. Other four-figure flocks were at Arpley tip, loafing on the nearby Mersey (SJ58T/Y), on Maw Green tip (SJ75E) and the Mersey estuary night-time roost (SJ48J/P).

The Lesser Black-backed Gulls wintering in the county are of the race *graellsii*, which breeds in Britain and Iceland and winters along the Atlantic seaboard southward from Britain to West Africa, with most in Iberia. Each winter a few individuals are seen of the darker *intermedius* race which breed in southern Scandinavia. There has only been one proven record of the nominate race *fuscus* in England, in 1961. They breed in northern Fennoscandia and migrate south-eastwards to winter in eastern Africa.

ANDREW MART

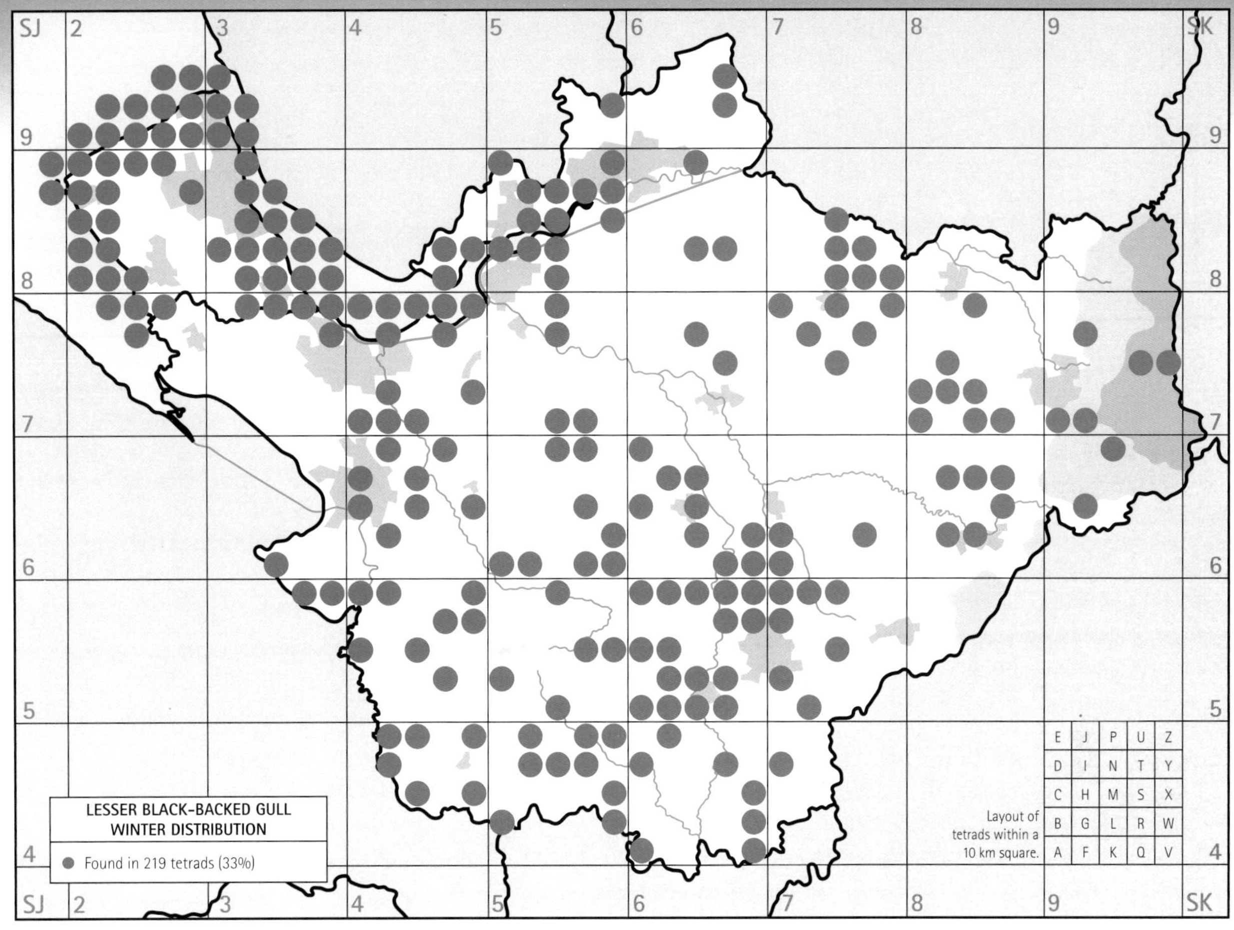

SJ
SK
LESSER BLACK-BACKED GULL
WINTER DISTRIBUTION
Found in 219 tetrads (33%)
Layout of tetrads within a 10 km square.
E J P U Z
D I N T Y
C H M S X
B G L R W
A F K Q V

Herring Gull

Larus argentatus

This well known 'seagull', whose call is recognized by many from its weekly broadcast by BBC Radio 4's *Desert Island Discs*, is becoming increasingly familiar to some residents of north Wirral as the habit of rooftop nesting takes hold. All of the eight tetrads with dots on the map were connected to rooftops in that area, in West Kirby, Hoylake, Birkenhead, Wallasey and New Brighton: one confirmed breeding through a pair with recently fledged young, six probable breeding (two with birds seen building a nest, one pair in courtship display and three records of pairs observed in suitable nesting habitat) and one possible breeding with a bird in suitable habitat.

The few previous records of Herring Gulls nesting in the county were all on Wirral. In 1945 a nest presumed to be Herring Gull was seen on Middle Eye, Hilbre. A pair bred, rearing one chick, on a Hoylake rooftop in 1971 but were deterred by the householder in 1972, and in the 1976 national census of large gulls nesting on buildings there were records of a pair at West Kirby and 'nesting' at Heswall. At Inner Marsh Farm a pair built a nest in 1995 but did not lay eggs, and in 2003 a pair was seen on a nest but it is not known if they bred. The *CWBR* for 2000 records a pair at Hoylake fledging one young, presumably from a rooftop although the site is not mentioned.

Rooftop nesting by Herring Gulls first started in 1910 in south-west England and is now widespread in Britain, accounting for about 11% of the species. Considerable effort and money has been expended in attempts to deter gulls in some places, almost always unsuccessfully (Rock 2005), and the numbers of nests increased by 10% a year in the quarter-century from 1976 to 2001: from 2,944 nests at 63 colonies in 1976, to 10,865 nests at 128 colonies in 1993–95 and 19,953 nests at 218 colonies in 1999–2002 (Mitchell *et al.* 2004). Many householders do not like having gulls breeding on their houses but one of the main reasons that the species is flourishing is the messy habits of mankind. Herring Gulls feed mainly on inshore fish and discards from commercial or recreational fishing, waste sent to landfill sites and edible litter on urban streets.

RICHARD STEEL

In memory of Doreen Botwood

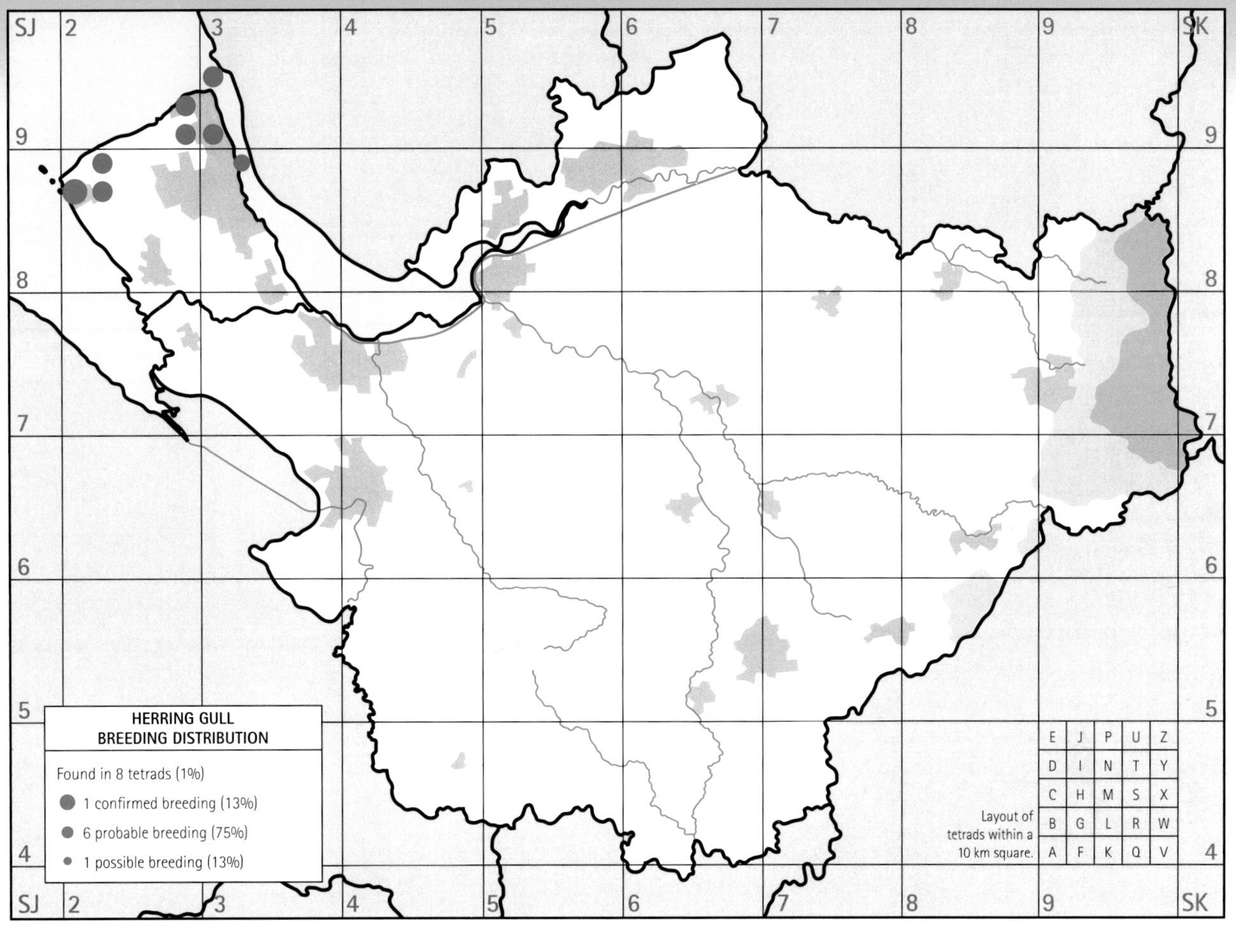
HERRING GULL
BREEDING DISTRIBUTION
Found in 8 tetrads (1%)
1 confirmed breeding (13%)
6 probable breeding (75%)
1 possible breeding (13%)
Layout of tetrads within a 10 km square.
SJ
SK

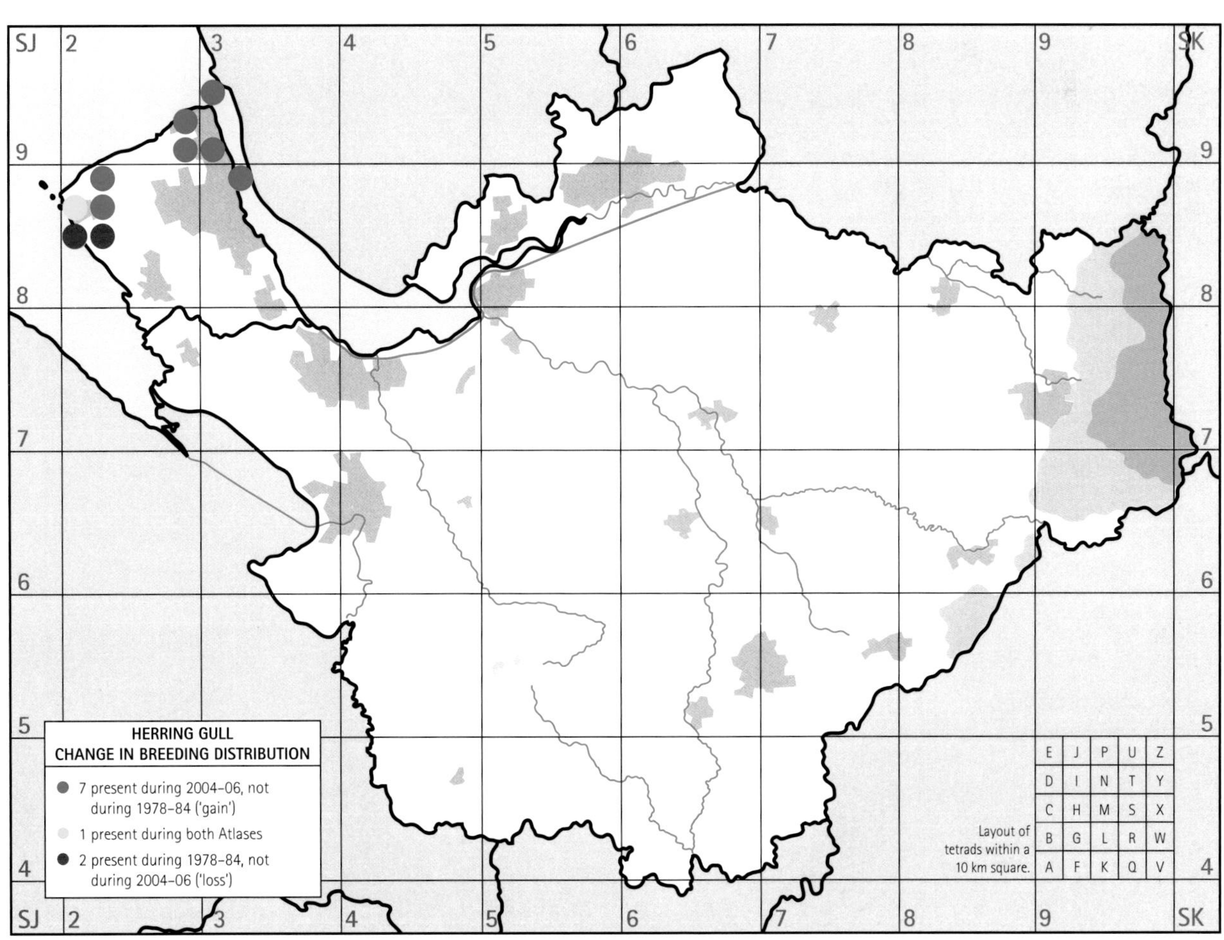
HERRING GULL
CHANGE IN BREEDING DISTRIBUTION
7 present during 2004–06, not during 1978–84 ('gain')
1 present during both Atlases
2 present during 1978–84, not during 2004–06 ('loss')
Layout of tetrads within a 10 km square.
SJ
SK

Herring Gulls were reported in winter from slightly fewer tetrads than Lesser Black-backed Gulls (200 against 219) but they were more numerous and gathered into larger flocks. The biggest gatherings were at the north-west corner of the Wirral, with maxima of 8,000 on Hoylake shore and 5,000 off Hilbre, but the Gowy landfill site attracted many, with 5,000 being estimated loafing on nearby fields (SJ47L). There were many solitary birds and small groups, however, and the median count was only 10 birds.

The old word of 'seagull' probably used to be more appropriate. Bell (1962) wrote that 'the most significant change since Coward's time is probably its winter status inland', and Boyd (1951) noted that Herring Gulls had become much more abundant and widespread, beginning about 1927. The distribution map shows that they occupy more tetrads from SJ57 north-westwards, and obviously fewer in the centre and south-west of the county, than Lesser-black Backed Gulls. Herring Gulls are more likely to be found in human sites than Lesser-black Backed Gulls (12% of records against 8%), especially suburban areas of the Wirral, and on tilled farmland. These gulls are omnivorous. Probably most of them feed at sea, taking fish or invertebrates, but many scavenge on refuse tips and take whatever they can find, even small mammals, from farmland.

The Mersey estuary was the only site in the county to record a roost count exceeding 1% of the British national total (380,000 Herring Gulls) in the January 1993 BTO Wintering Gull Survey when a total of 5,321 was counted (Burton *et al.* 2003). Only 318 were found during the 2004 repeat survey, though.

The *Handbook of Birds of the World* regards the systematics of the Herring Gull and its close relatives as 'one of the most complex challenges in ornithology' (del Hoyo *et al.* 1992). Although excessive prominence is given by some birdwatchers to unusual races, and most of the species' accounts in the annual *CWBRs* are devoted to them, they are rare. Most of the birds from continental Europe concentrate on the east coast of Britain (*Migration Atlas*). The vast majority of our wintering Herring Gulls comes from northern Britain.

STEVE ROUND

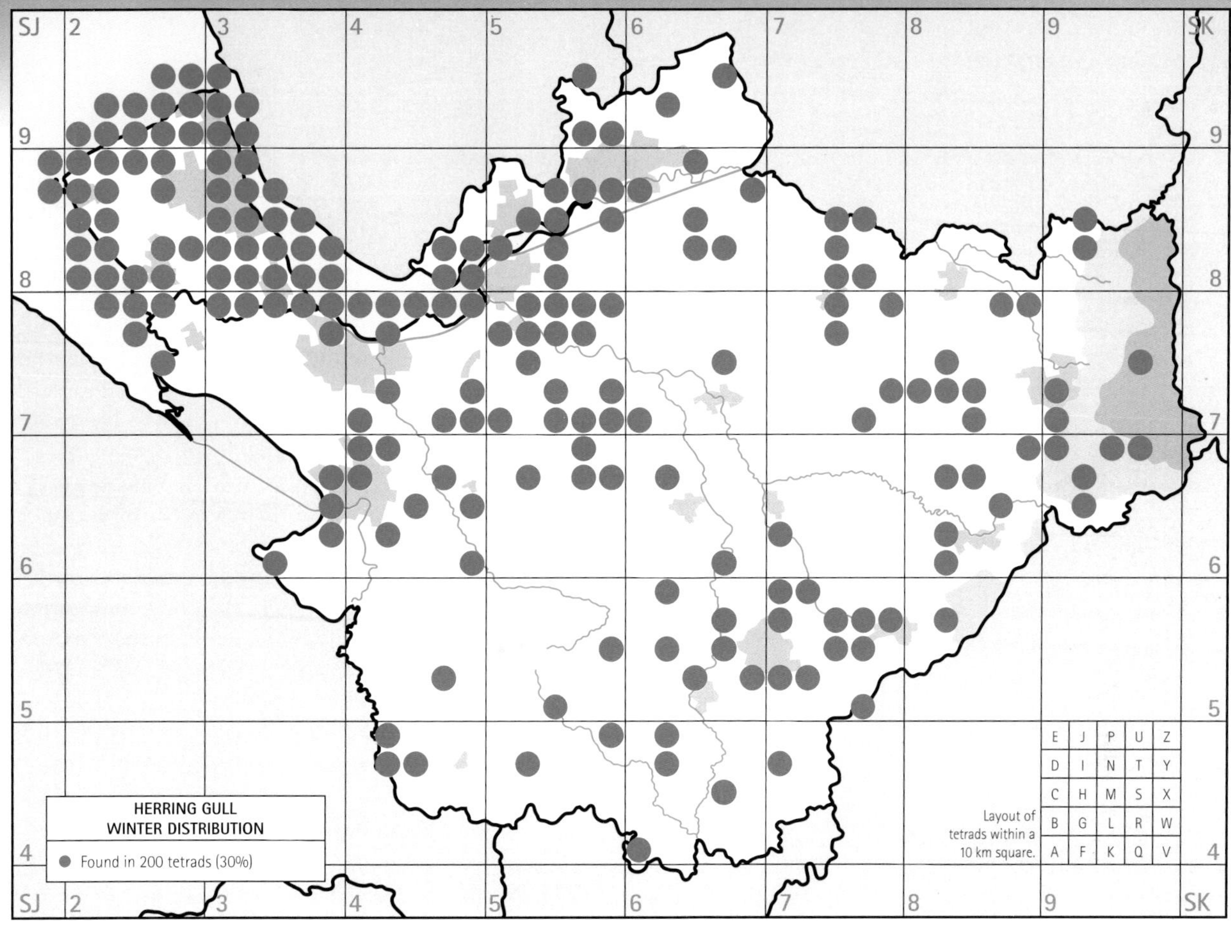
SJ
2
3
4
5
6
7
8
9
SK
HERRING GULL
WINTER DISTRIBUTION
Found in 200 tetrads (30%)
Layout of
tetrads within a
10 km square.
E J P U Z
D I N T Y
C H M S X
B G L R W
A F K Q V

Yellow-legged Gull

Larus michahellis

RAY SCALLY

Yellow-legged Gull is a species that did not exist until part-way through this Atlas survey! Large gulls are obviously in a state of genetic flux and can generate considerable discussion amongst some birdwatchers and much research amongst taxonomists, molecular biologists and behavioural ecologists. The British Ornithologists' Union, the arbiters of the British List, had taken a conservative approach but in October 2005 announced that Yellow-legged Gull would be considered as a separate species.

They breed, mainly at coastal sites and usually on rocky cliffs, around the Mediterranean Sea, where the population is increasing rapidly (Hagemeijer & Blair 1997). Some have spread north along the Atlantic coast of France, and they have bred in Britain from 1995 onwards. There has been little growth in numbers breeding in Britain, however; by 2004 there was only one pure pair, in Dorset, and mixed pairs with Lesser Black-backed Gulls in Bedfordshire and possibly Northern Ireland. Only hybrid young have been raised since 2001 (Holling *et al.* 2007a).

Many Yellow-legged Gulls stay close to their breeding sites all year round, but others, especially immature birds, wander and some reach Britain. Here they mix with the other large gulls and share their habits and feeding areas, especially landfill sites and adjacent areas for loafing. During this winter Atlas most records came from the vicinity of Arpley tip—at Fiddler's Ferry (SJ58M), the river Mersey at Richmond Bank (SJ58T) or Moore Nature Reserve (SJ58X)—with other sightings from the Mersey off Pickering's Pasture (SJ48W) and Sandbach Flashes (SJ75J). Up to three birds were seen at a time.

Boyd recorded the first known 'Yellow-legged Herring Gull' in Cheshire on 3 January 1942 at Witton Flashes (Boyd 1951), but it was 30 years before another was documented, at Neston on 1 September 1972, followed by another at New Brighton on 15 November 1977 (*CWBRs*). Despite uncertainty over their status, the annual county bird reports have included records every year since 1980. The history of these records has inevitably reflected the growing awareness and interest of recorders and knowledge of criteria for identification and ageing. Through the 1980s and 1990s there was a gradual rise of records. Birds were found in every month, with most in the period July to October, but monthly maxima during the winter period of 6 in December, 11 in January and 5 in February. Nearly all sightings were inland in Cheshire, especially at sites along the river Mersey (Fiddler's Ferry, Richmond Bank/Gatewarth, Arpley tip), Neumann's Flash while the nearby tip was still active, and Sandbach Flashes and the nearby Maw Green tip, with a few records from the gull haunts at Arclid Sand Quarry, Chelford Sand Quarries and Witton Flashes. Yellow-legged Gulls were seldom recorded at Wirral sites, but from 2001 onwards there have been more birds reported at Hilbre and the coast from West Kirby to Leasowe. There has also been a wider spread of other sites in the county than in previous decades, with winter records from Hurleston Reservoir, the area of Danes Moss tip and Sutton Reservoir, and Wimbolds Trafford near the Gowy landfill site.

Compared to most recent years, this Atlas map seems to be rather empty: ironically, there have been fewer records since Yellow-legged Gull was declared to be a separate species than previously.

Sponsored by Eric Yarwood

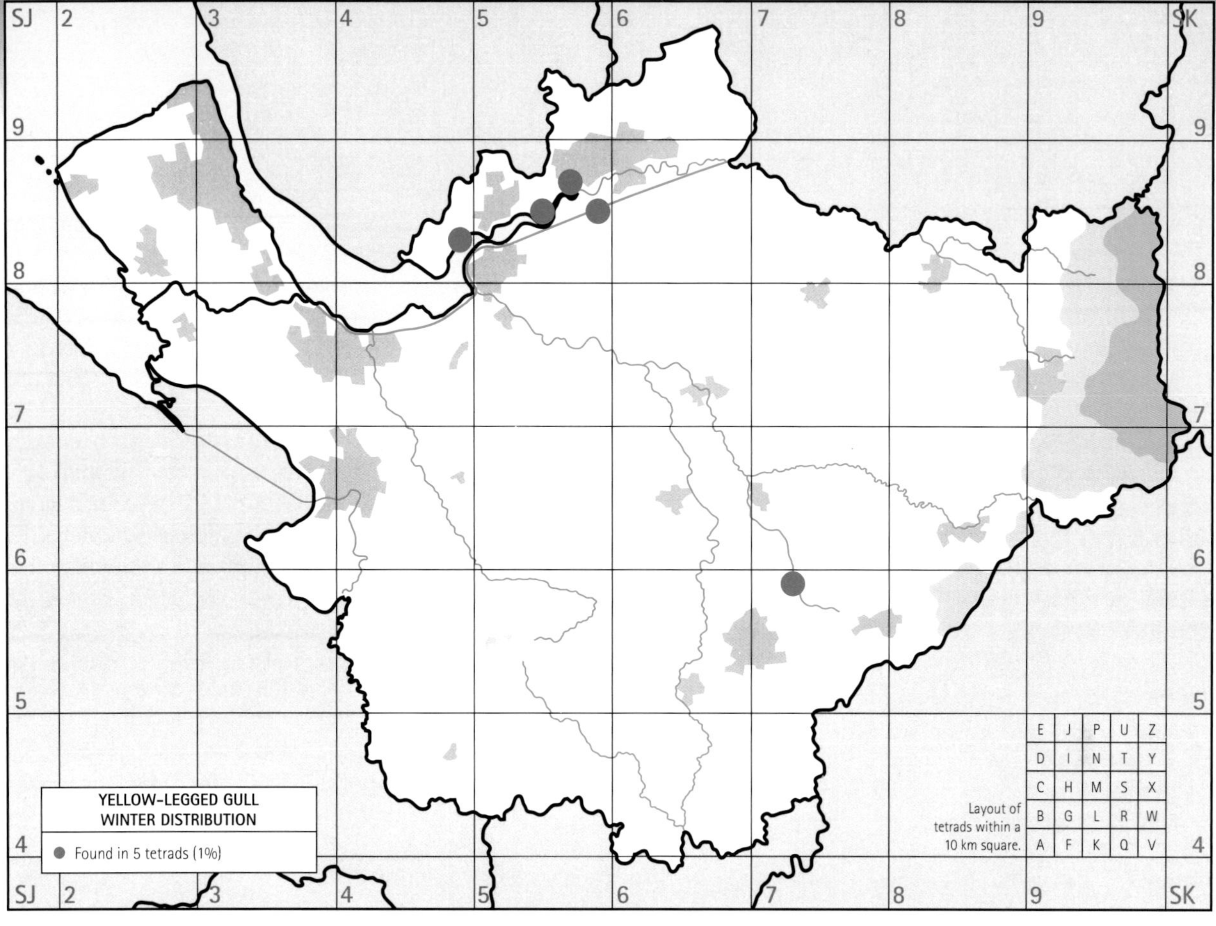

SJ
2
3
4
5
6
7
8
9
SK
YELLOW-LEGGED GULL
WINTER DISTRIBUTION
Found in 5 tetrads (1%)
Layout of tetrads within a 10 km square.
E J P U Z
D I N T Y
C H M S X
B G L R W
A F K Q V

Iceland Gull

Larus glaucoides

Iceland Gulls, confusingly, do not breed in Iceland but up to 100,000 pairs nest along the west and east coasts of Greenland. Most of those from west Greenland are resident or short-distance migrants and it is thought to be birds from east Greenland that move south-east to Iceland and the Faeroes, with some reaching Britain. Typically 100–200 a year winter in Britain, with occasional larger influxes, suggested to be linked to hard Arctic weather pushing more birds south or to poor years in the Icelandic fishing industry (*Migration Atlas*).

There were probably fewer Iceland Gulls in Cheshire during the three winters of our Atlas survey than at any time since the early 1980s. The winter distribution map exaggerates their status, as the records in five tetrads in SJ54 and SJ75 come from only two or three birds. They eat fish and waste food of all kinds, and almost all the records in the county in recent years are from refuse tips and nearby washing pools or roosts. In the 2004/05 winter, birds were seen at the Arpley landfill site (SJ58Y), an adult on 15 January 2005 and a first winter bird a week later. One or more birds were seen in three tetrads in the same area (SJ58M/T/X) in 2005/06, and an adult moved between Maw Green tip (SJ75D) and the adjacent flashes (SJ75E/J) in late February 2006. In 2006/07 one bird was seen on Bar Mere, spanning SJ54I and SJ54J, a first-year bird visited Sandbach Flashes (SJ75J) on 20 December 2006, a second-winter bird was at Fiddler's Ferry (SJ58M) on 21 December 2006, a first-winter bird was at Richmond Bank (SJ58T) on 30 December 2006 and a bird in third-winter plumage was on Sutton Reservoir (SJ97A) a week before the end of this Atlas survey, on 20 February 2007.

Iceland Gulls used to be exceptionally rare, or under-recorded, in the county. A bird was shot at Hoylake, probably during winter 1872/73, and another was off New Brighton on 2 June 1909 (Coward 1910). The next records were in 1955 (Bell 1962) but since then

SHEILA BLAMIRE

Sponsored by Roy Eyres

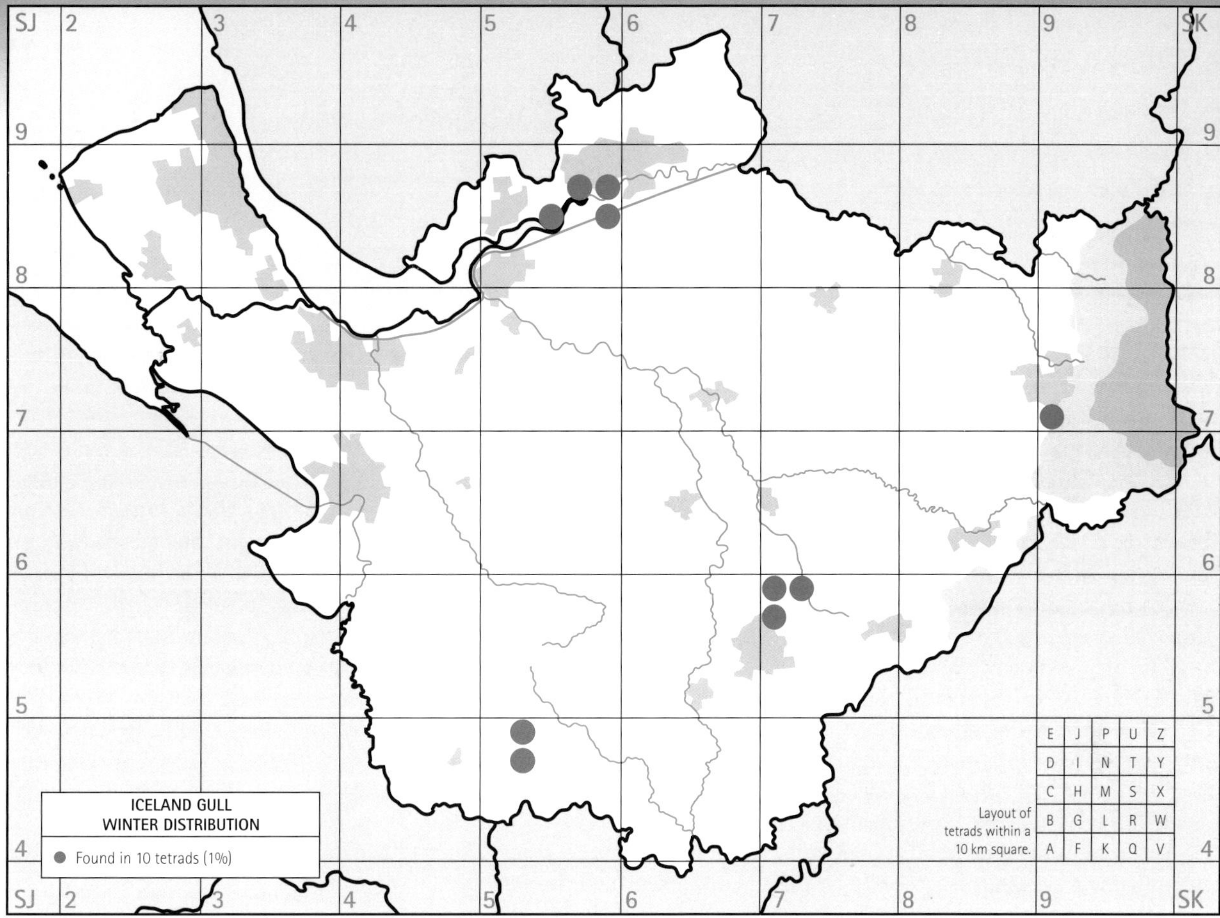

birds have been annual and there have been records in every winter since 1956/57. Initially the status of annual winter visitor depended almost entirely on the return visits to New Brighton of the bird which was first seen in January 1957 when in its third winter and last seen there on 16 March 1985, not long after some birdwatchers had held a thirtieth birthday celebration in its honour. Birds were seen at Ness and Rostherne in the 1961/62 winter but it was only from 1967/68 onwards that annual winter visitor status ceased to be dependent on the New Brighton bird.

It is usually December before birds are seen and are then present in each month through to February in most winters, in variable numbers. Since the demise of the faithful old New Brighton bird there have been coastal records in only six winters and these are limited to one or two birds at one or two sites, usually on a single date. It is difficult to know how much of the rise in records was attributable to changed habits of birdwatchers, paying more attention to gull roosts and, later, to refuse tips and nearby pools where the birds washed and rested. From the 1970s Iceland Gulls were reported fairly regularly at the Rostherne roost, and from the 1980s, at or close to landfill sites such as along the river Mersey between Richmond Bank and Fiddler's Ferry and the Witton and Sandbach Flashes. Cheshire and Wirral shared in national influxes in the 1980s and in the peak years there might have been as many as 12 individuals in the county, although numbers are hard to quantify because of movement between sites, variability in plumage as winter progresses and indeed difficulty in ageing many birds (White *et al.* 2008).

From the late 1990s there has been a drop in records of both Iceland and Glaucous Gulls in the county, and in neighbouring Lancashire and North Merseyside (White *et al.* 2008). If earlier influxes to Britain were driven by severe winter weather, it is tempting to think that the recent decline in wintering Arctic gulls in Cheshire and Wirral is linked to climate change.

Glaucous Gull

Larus hyperboreus

This ghostly visitor from the north has been seen far less often in the last decade in Cheshire and Wirral, and also in adjacent Lancashire and North Merseyside (White *et al.* 2008). The explanation for the decline may well, as with Iceland Gull, be the recent run of warmer winters. This Atlas map typifies their recent distribution, with most records from waste disposal sites or associated loafing areas, or roosts of birds which feed on the tips. Most Glaucous Gulls in Britain used to be at the coast, where they feed on fish and any edible detritus (*BTO Winter Atlas*) but the proportion inland has increased over the years, and the two birds found in three Dee estuary tetrads in this survey were the first wintering coastal records since December 1999.

Glaucous Gulls come here from breeding grounds in Norway, Bear Island (Svalbard) and Iceland, and possibly Greenland (*Migration Atlas*). Most records in Britain are of first-year birds, which often wander widely, or of adults, many of which are thought to return to a favourite site (*Migration Atlas*). They were unknown in Cheshire and Wirral until fifty years ago, but the first bird recorded within the present county boundaries set the tone for this species' typical behaviour. It was initially seen as an immature in the Hilbre-Hoylake area on 15 September 1957. The gull stayed in the vicinity for 18 months, until 8 April 1959—still the longest stay by a Glaucous Gull in the county—and reappeared the following winter almost in adult plumage. It then returned to the same area in each winter until it was last seen in March 1963.

After that first bird in the county, Glaucous Gulls were recorded in every year except 1967, with birds in each winter apart from 1968/69 and 1970/71, although they remained scarce until the late 1970s. It is impossible to tell whether the rise in records from then on was a real reflection of more birds being present, or a shift in birdwatchers' habits to pay more attention to refuse tips and nearby pools, where gulls washed, and to overnight roosts such as Doddington and Rostherne. The national *BTO Winter Atlas* (1981/82–1983/84), probably stimulated more winter recording, and the publication in the early 1980s of some specialist identification guides to gulls and seabirds probably prompted more records as well. Whatever the reasons, the annual bird reports show far more records of Glaucous Gulls in the county in the 1980s and 1990s.

Records in this period are fairly evenly split between coastal and inland sites with the majority of the latter from our defined winter period while most of the coastal ones fall outside it, particularly in spring passage. Of the winter months, January and February have the most sightings, with numbers varying considerably from year to year. In some winters only odd birds are seen while in others, sites such as Fiddler's Ferry/Richmond Bank and the Witton Flashes, both adjacent to large refuse tips, have held several different birds of various ages. Another regular visitor was recorded at Thurstaston: first appearing as an immature bird in October 1981, it returned to the same area each winter until it was last seen in January 1992.

Nearly all of the records during this Atlas survey were in winter 2004/05, with just one bird at Hurleston Reservoir (SJ65H) in January 2006 and none at all in 2006/07. Some birds moved between tetrads whilst other sites were visited by several different birds. An adult was at Little Eye (SJ18Y) and West Kirby (SJ28D) in January 2005. One or two first-winter birds were at Maw Green tip and adjacent flashes (SJ75D/E/J) while three different first-year birds were thought to have been seen at Richmond Bank (SJ58T).

RAY SCALLY

Sponsored by Brian Dyke

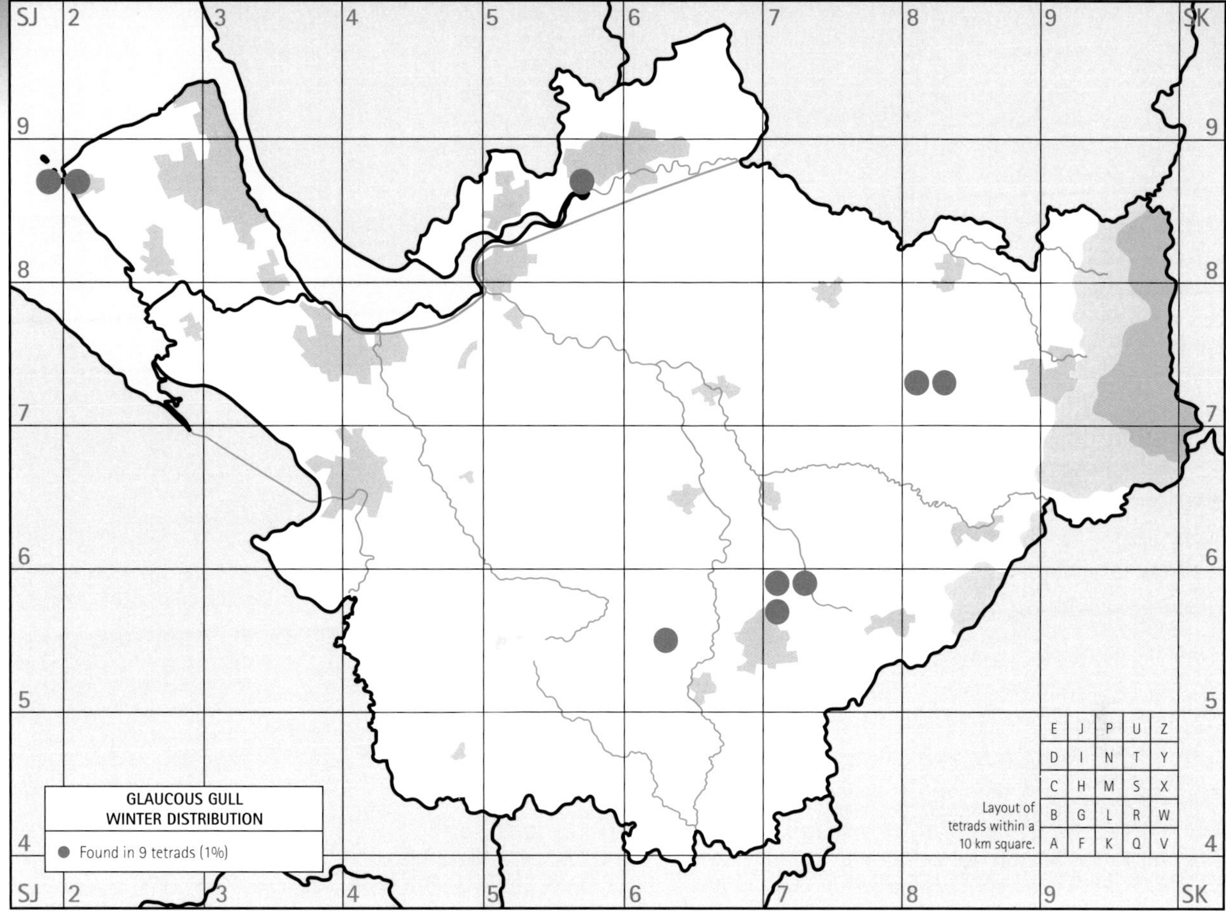

GLAUCOUS GULL
WINTER DISTRIBUTION
Found in 9 tetrads (1%)
Layout of tetrads within a 10 km square.
E J P U Z
D I N T Y
C H M S X
B G L R W
A F K Q V
SJ
SK

Great Black-backed Gull

Larus marinus

RICHARD STEEL

One glance at the winter map for Great Black-backed Gull immediately shows the aptness of its scientific name—the marine gull. A century ago they were virtually unknown inland in Cheshire (Coward 1910): the only instance then on record was that of one shot in Witton Flashes in 1898 and recorded as an albatross! They started to be found inland from the early 1920s, visiting the Flashes and Marbury Mere, mostly from October to February, often only one at a time and very rarely more than three or four together (Boyd 1951). Bell repeated this assessment in his 1962 book, but in his 1967 supplement he wrote that 'indications are that inland occurrences are becoming more frequent and in larger numbers'. This Atlas map shows them now to be probably more widespread than ever before, but still scarce more than a few kilometres away from the tidal Dee or Mersey.

As expected, the submitted habitat records show that more than half of the tetrads with the species included an H (marine) code. There were 23 records on farmland, compared to 85 for Herring Gull and 98 for Lesser Black-backed Gull. Their distribution is noticeably influenced by landfill sites at Maw Green (SJ75E), Danes Moss (SJ97A) and Gowy (SJ47K/L). The effect of these artificial feeding sites should not be exaggerated, however, and they are not numerous compared to other large gulls: cannon-netting by Merseyside Ringing Group at waste disposal sites in the Warrington area during the 1990s caught just nine Great Black-backed Gulls compared to 1,344 Herring Gulls and 1,166 Lesser Black-backed Gulls. The largest flocks during this Atlas period were 250 on Hoylake shore and the same number adjacent to the Gowy landfill site in SJ47G, with about 200 on the Mersey at Richmond Bank, near to the Arpley landfill site (SJ58T). The median count was of only five birds. Great Black-backed Gulls forage mainly on natural marine foods although these gulls can be fearsome predators and scavengers: the

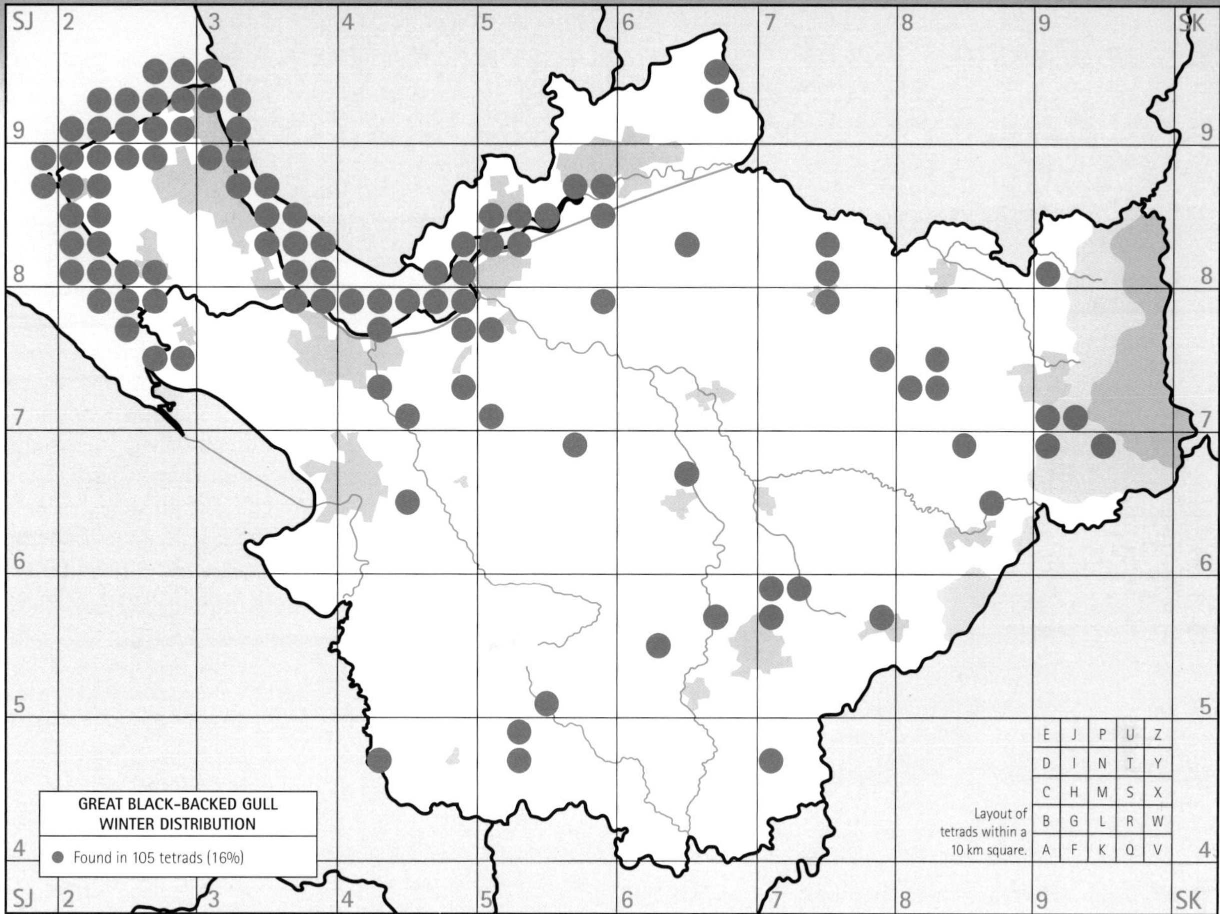

highest-altitude bird, in (SJ96P), was feeding on a sheep carcass.

The birds wintering in the county are thought to be predominantly breeding birds from the Irish Sea coasts, the nearest colonies being on Puffin Island, Gwynedd and the Calf of Man, and from the west of Scotland, which undertake a general southward movement in winter. Females are twice as likely as males to move inland. Norwegian Great Black-backed Gulls—indistinguishable in colour or size—are common along the east coast but rarely penetrate to the west coast of Britain (*BTO Winter Atlas*).

● Great Black-backed Gulls were reported during this Atlas period from three tetrads in the breeding season meriting possible breeding status, with adult birds of breeding age present at Frodsham Marsh (SJ47Y/Z) and Fiddler's Ferry (SJ58M). Until a few years ago these would not have been thought to be suitable breeding habitat but one pair at Frodsham changed that, breeding there for five years from 1998 to 2002. This event was not welcomed with the usual fanfare and descriptive article in the *CWBR* but was nevertheless notable as the first ever breeding in the county and in an unusual site, on the ground on a tiny heap of mud surrounded by water, rather than the species' normal offshore rocky islets.

Common Tern

Sterna hirundo

SUE & ANDY TRANTER

It is amazing to recount that, apart from the south-west peninsula, there are only two counties in England without breeding Common Terns, and Cheshire is one of them (Mitchell *et al.* 2004)! Just 3 km outside the county boundary in the Shotton steelworks is one of the four largest colonies in Britain, having grown from 13 pairs on a raft in its first year (1970) to around 800 pairs nesting on concrete islands (2007), all created by the volunteer members of Merseyside Ringing Group. It is a mystery why none of Cheshire's conservation organizations or numerous bird societies has provided similar secure nest sites, taking up the closing words of the species' text in our *First Atlas*: 'the provision of islets or nesting rafts in sand quarries or meres could encourage Common Terns to breed in the county'.

The birds at Shotton used to nest on the adjacent salt-marsh, where the species had nested frequently from the early twentieth century, almost invariably failing owing to tidal flooding (Farrer 1938). The history of Common Terns breeding on the Cheshire and Wirral part of the Dee salt-marshes is obscured by the sloppy recording practices of the past, where the birds beyond the Welsh boundary were often included in the county bird reports. There was no confirmed breeding in our *First Atlas*, but birds were displaying in three tetrads, and present in two more, all in SJ27. In the twenty years since then, the annual bird reports detail several instances of birds with breeding intent. A pair was present intermittently at Arclid Sand Quarry (SJ76L/R) from 5 to 9 July 1987, too late for breeding although they indulged in some courtship display. Two pairs displayed and made trial nest scrapes at Inner Marsh Farm (SJ37B) in 1989, but no eggs were laid, and in 1992 a pair failed in a breeding attempt there.

In 1996 the first ever inland breeding in our area was confirmed at a mid-Cheshire site where a pair was seen with three half-grown young in late July/early August; it is not known whether they fledged. In 1997 a pair held territory at the same site, with unknown outcome, and in 1998 a breeding attempt there failed. The county bird reports in 1996 and 1997 stated that adults seen elsewhere with dependent juveniles could suggest local breeding, but Common Terns migrate as family parties and some adults feed their young all the way to Africa, so that behaviour is no indication of local provenance.

After 1998, *CWBRs* contained no records suggesting breeding anywhere in the county, until this Atlas period. In 2004, a pair was on a sandbank at the edge of the Winsford flashes (SJ66S) and in 2006 pairs were displaying on small islands in pools on the Dee salt-marsh (SJ27W/X) and at Inner Marsh Farm (SJ37B).

The adaptability of Common Terns has helped them to prosper. Not only will they use a wide variety of nesting areas, but they can adjust their diet to whatever is locally available. Coastal birds mainly catch sand eels, although they switch to other small fish if need be, and inland birds will eat almost anything aquatic including fish and invertebrates.

Sponsored by Merseyside Ringing Group

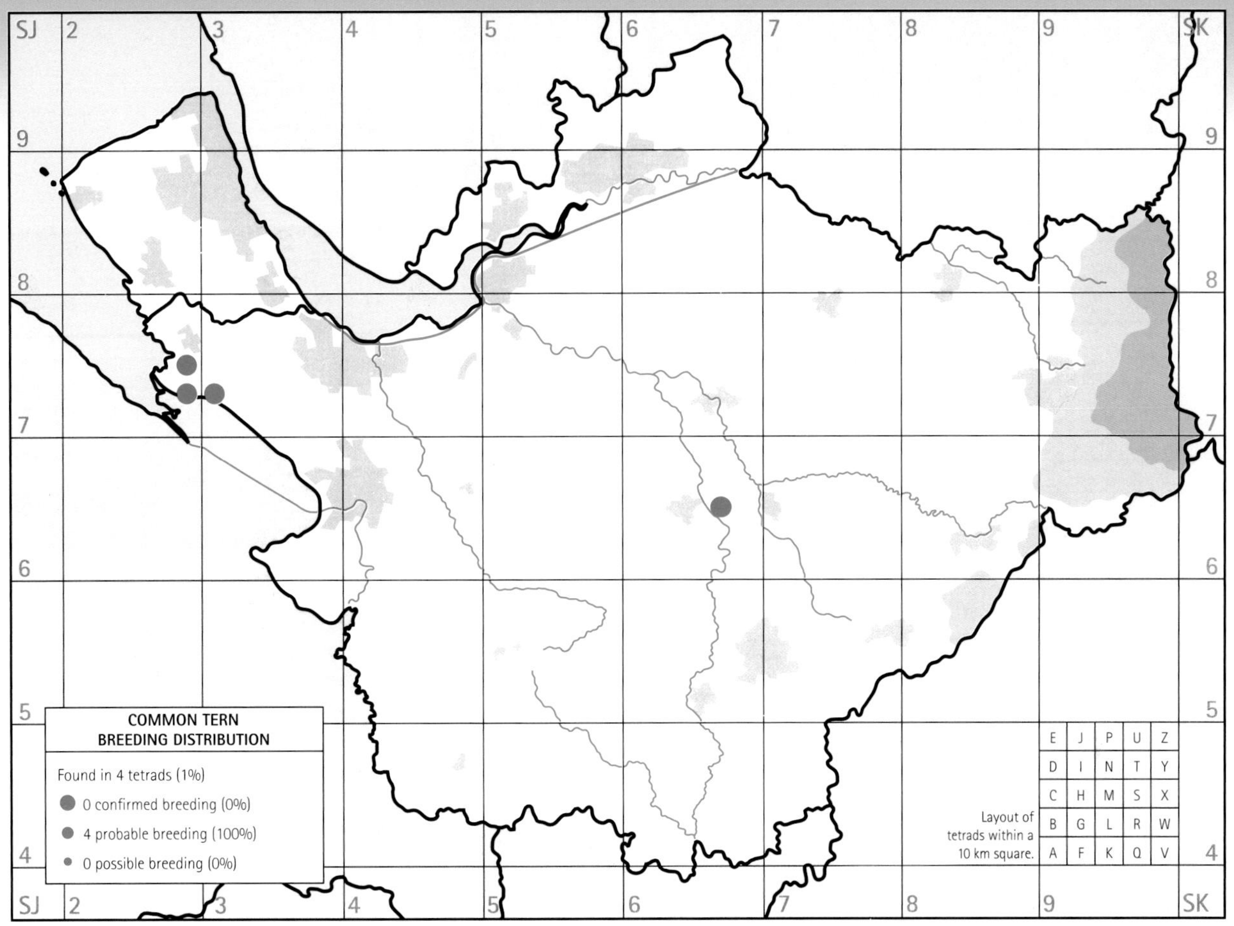
SJ
SK
COMMON TERN
BREEDING DISTRIBUTION
Found in 4 tetrads (1%)
0 confirmed breeding (0%)
4 probable breeding (100%)
0 possible breeding (0%)
Layout of
tetrads within a
10 km square.
E J P U Z
D I N T Y
C H M S X
B G L R W
A F K Q V

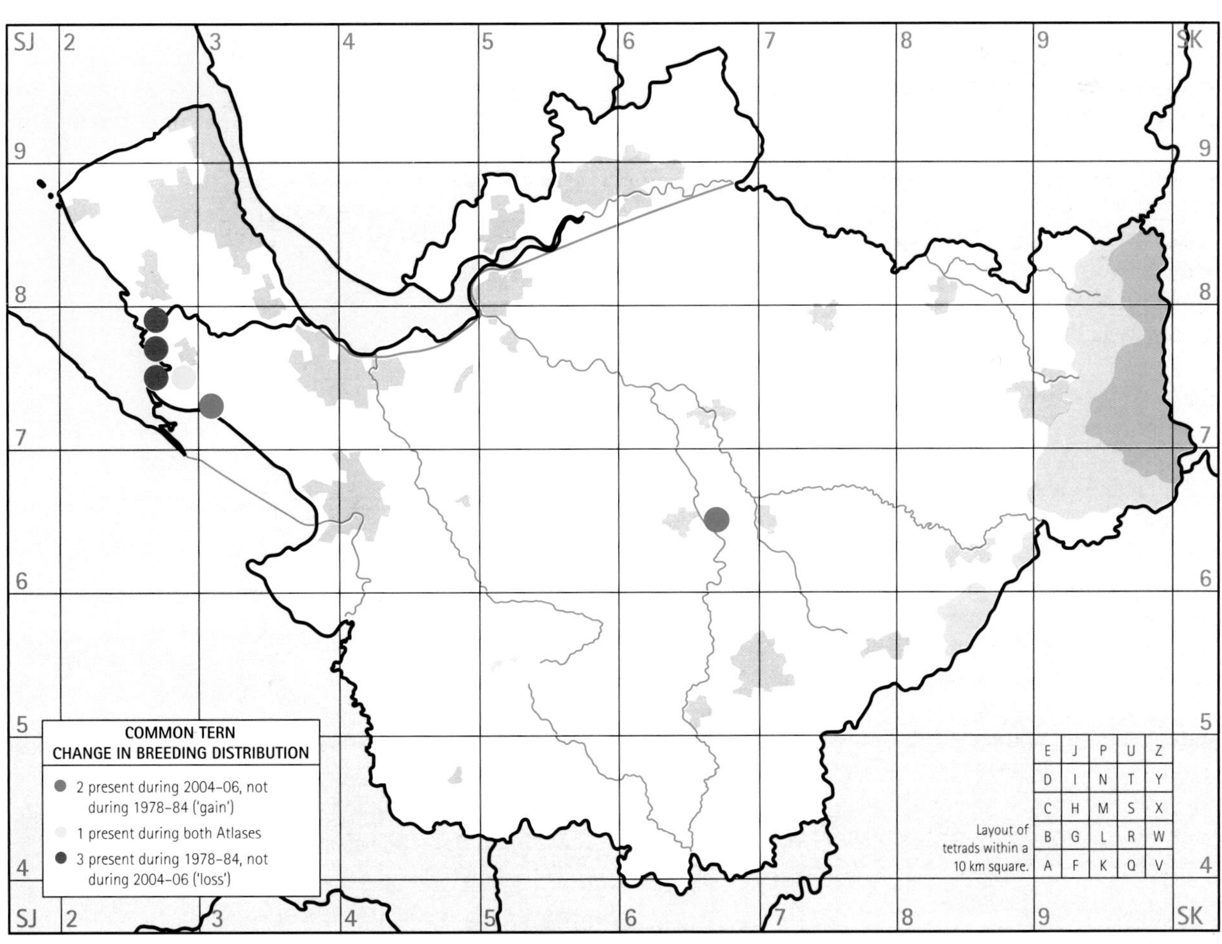
SJ
SK
COMMON TERN
CHANGE IN BREEDING DISTRIBUTION
2 present during 2004–06, not during 1978–84 ('gain')
1 present during both Atlases
3 present during 1978–84, not during 2004–06 ('loss')
Layout of
tetrads within a
10 km square.
E J P U Z
D I N T Y
C H M S X
B G L R W
A F K Q V

Guillemot

Uria aalge

This is the most numerous seabird in Britain and Ireland, with a breeding population of about one million pairs (Mitchell *et al.* 2004). The Guillemots found in winter in our area are most likely to be from colonies in western Britain or Ireland. Immature birds, below the age of five years which is when they normally start breeding, spend the winter significantly farther away than adults, with median distances of around 600 km and 350 km respectively and most birds moving south or east (*Migration Atlas*). Probably most of the birds off our coasts are immature birds, for many adults return to their breeding ledges from October onwards, after the males have finished feeding their chick on the water and as soon as they have regained the power of flight following their autumn moult (*BTO Winter Atlas*).

RICHARD STEEL

The winter Atlas map fairly shows this species' typical distribution in the county, entirely coastal and mainly clustered around the north-west Wirral. Maximum counts of 30, 6 and 66 were submitted from Hilbre for the three winters, and very large flocks of 120 and 450 birds were reported in November 2004 from two tetrads on Hoylake shore (SJ28E and SJ29A), flying west after gales eased. Elsewhere in the outer Dee or north Wirral coast, one or two birds were found in several squares.

Coward (1910) wrote that the Guillemot was plentiful in Liverpool Bay in the summer months, and was often driven close inshore in winter. He noted that dead bodies of the auks could be found lying amongst the tideline debris at any time of year. Bell (1962) described the species as common in small numbers off the coast at any time outside the breeding season. Most birds in winter were alone or in parties of fewer than 10 birds, although strong winds could change the picture, with 44 counted after gales on 6 January 1957. Hilbre records for 1957–77 show an average of about 30 bird-days each winter (Craggs 1982). Most subsequent annual bird reports for the county indicate winter presence in small numbers, although unfortunately few counts are given until 2002; flocks of 25 on 25 November 1984, 50 on 24 December 1991 and 25 on 9 February 2002 were singled out for mention. From 2002 onwards, the monthly maxima at Hilbre were tabulated, with peak figures for each month of 20 in November (2005), 35 in December (2006), 30 in January (2005) and 7 in February (2002), with 85 counted off Hoylake on 27 November 2003. The lack of data in *CWBRs* precludes any comparison with the numbers off the coasts of Lancashire and North Merseyside, where there has been a dramatic decline in sightings of Guillemots since about the mid-1990s, for unknown reasons (White *et al.* 2008).

Away from the north-west corner of Wirral, few birds are found in Cheshire and Wirral. There is only one record in a county bird report at the Mersey end of the Wirral coast, one at New Brighton on 6 February 1983, a date coinciding with one of the biggest recorded incidents of mass mortality of auks in the North Sea and Scotland (*BTO Winter Atlas*). Guillemots occasionally move as far up the Dee estuary as Burton, but inland records are rare, with just five birds found in the last forty years (*CWBRs*). Their preferred diet is squid, pelagic worms and crustaceans, difficult to find away from the sea.

Sponsored by John Gilbody

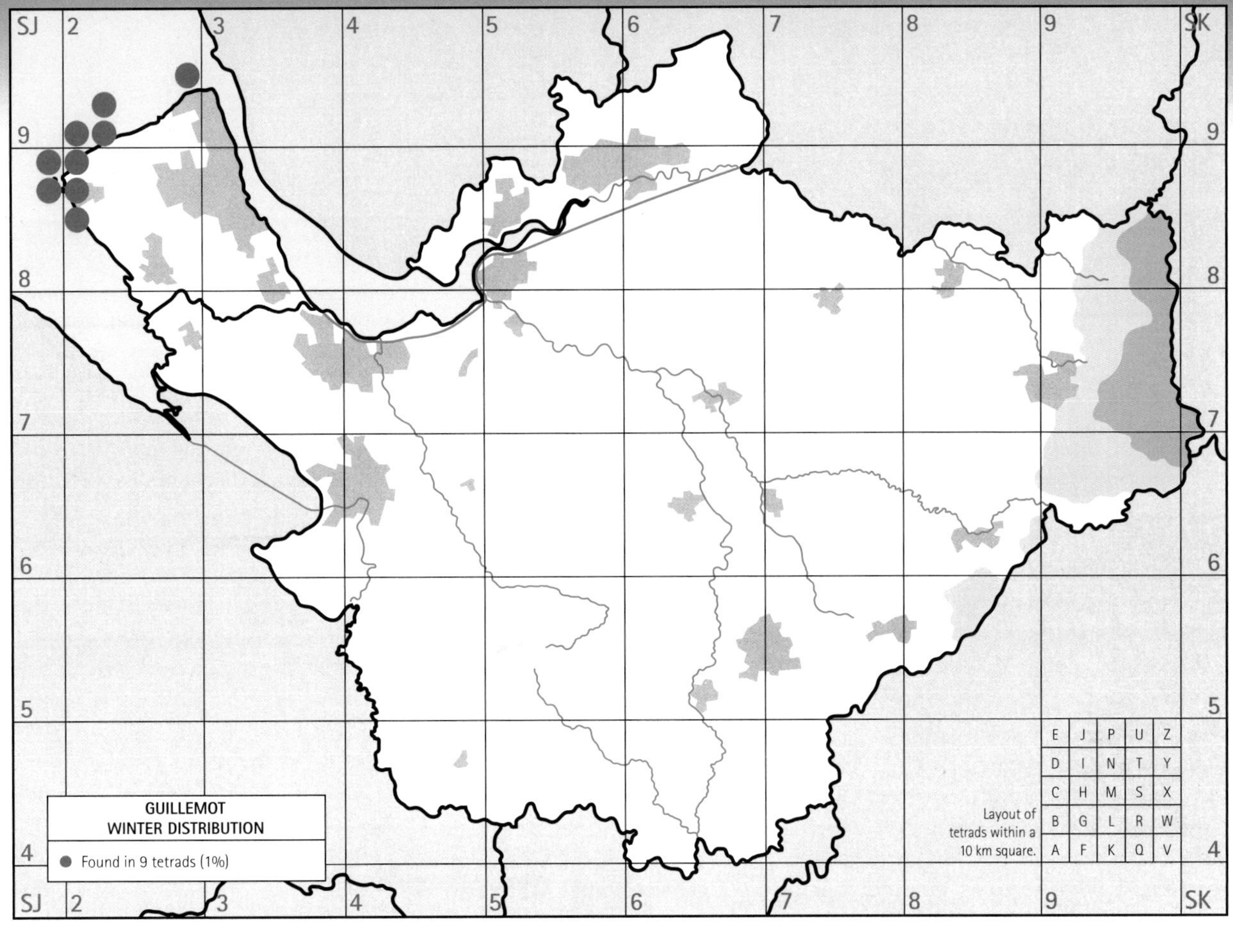
SJ
2
3
4
5
6
7
8
9
SK
GUILLEMOT
WINTER DISTRIBUTION
Found in 9 tetrads (1%)
Layout of
tetrads within a
10 km square.
E J P U Z
D I N T Y
C H M S X
B G L R W
A F K Q V

Feral Pigeon

Columba livia

MIKE ATKINSON

Feral Pigeon holds the curious distinction of being the species most familiar to those who know nothing about birds and most ignored by those who do. It is a bird of two habitats, apparently being equally at home scavenging amongst shoppers' feet in a town centre or foraging for seed in farmland. Their nest is normally on a ledge, often in buildings and under bridges, with many sites holding several nests close together. The 120 tetrads with confirmed breeding included 93 where observers found nests. Sites included farm barns and cowsheds, quarry buildings, a demol ished power station, many railway and road bridges, town centre tower blocks and other artefacts from a Macclesfield gasometer to Bidston Windmill. They seem especially drawn to railway buildings, perhaps because they are tall and open, with copious gantries and ledges to support nests.

Analysis of the habitats shows that 74% of records were in human sites, with Feral Pigeon having the highest proportion of F1 (urban) habitat codes of any species (13%), with 15% suburban and 46% rural. Most of the rest (22%) were farmland. Our *First Atlas* showed them mainly in the north and west of the county, almost ubiquitous on Wirral, with clusters around Chester, Runcorn, Warrington and Northwich but sparsely distributed elsewhere. This map shows a much more even spread, with pigeons lost from many tetrads in their former strongholds but now present across much of the rest of the county: they were gained in 171 tetrads and lost from 140. They have apparently spread to upland areas in SJ96 and SJ97 and altitude is not a bar to their distribution. The *First Atlas* map was said to be 'undoubtedly incomplete' and perhaps this species was not included by all fieldworkers in that survey, but the widespread losses across the north of the county suggest a real decline in population there.

Young birds are able to breed from about six months of age, and Feral Pigeons can nest all year round so their numbers can rise rapidly, but shortage of nest sites limits the population and many birds spend their lives in non-breeding flocks (*BTO Second Atlas*). This large pool of non-breeders, continually topped-up by wayward racing pigeons, militates against many efforts to control their numbers.

It is only since the inception of the BTO's Breeding Bird Survey in 1994 that Feral Pigeon numbers have been monitored alongside all other species. The national data suggest a stable population with, as yet, no obvious trend up or down. The BTO BBS analysis for Cheshire and Wirral in 2004–05 shows that the breeding population was 12,710 birds, although with very wide confidence intervals of 2,010–23,400. This figure averages 56 birds per tetrad with confirmed or probable breeding but an average is likely to hide wide variations. Some conurbations hold 50–100 pairs whilst some farming areas have only a few birds.

Sponsored by Andy Harmer

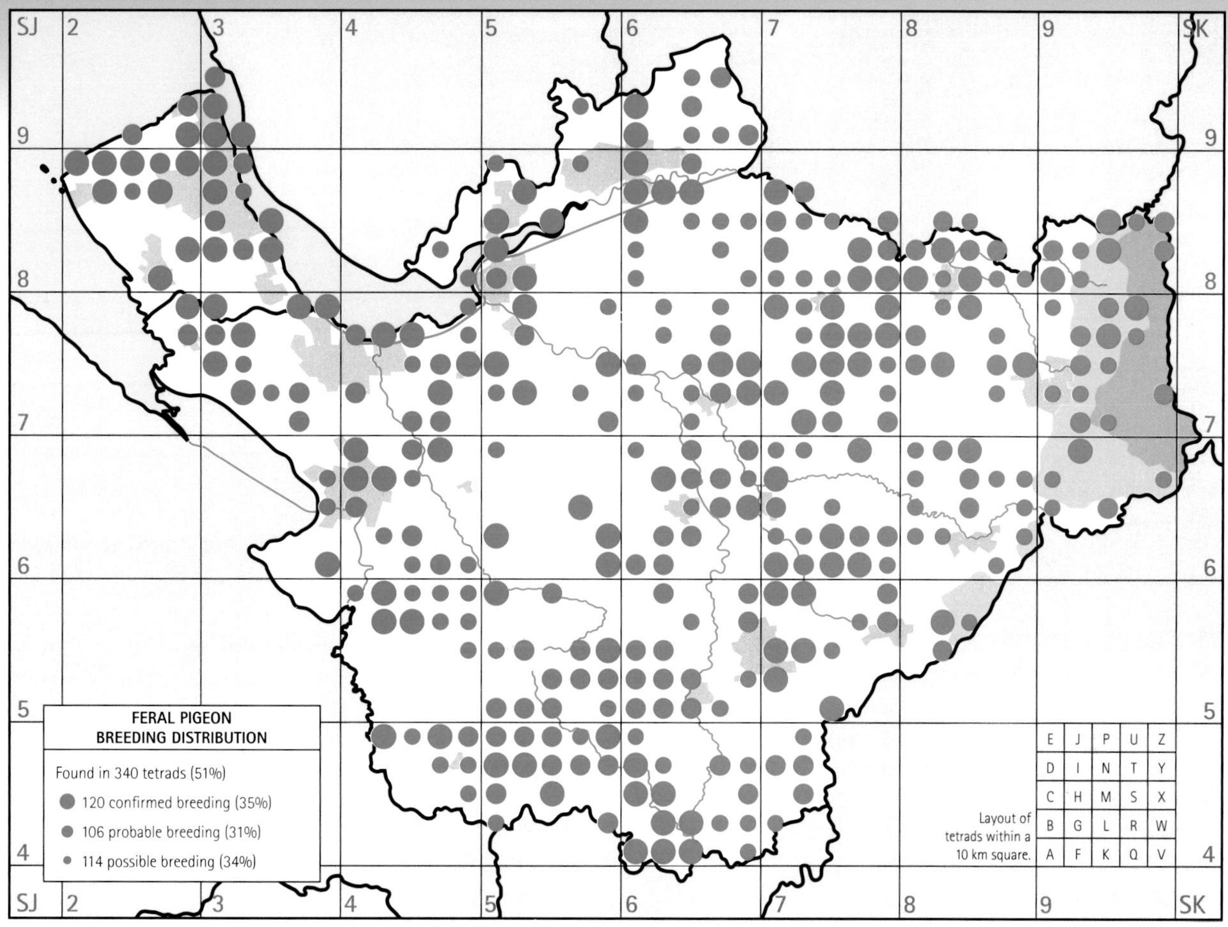
FERAL PIGEON
BREEDING DISTRIBUTION
Found in 340 tetrads (51%)
120 confirmed breeding (35%)
106 probable breeding (31%)
114 possible breeding (34%)
Layout of tetrads within a 10 km square.
E J P U Z
D I N T Y
C H M S X
B G L R W
A F K Q V
SJ
SK

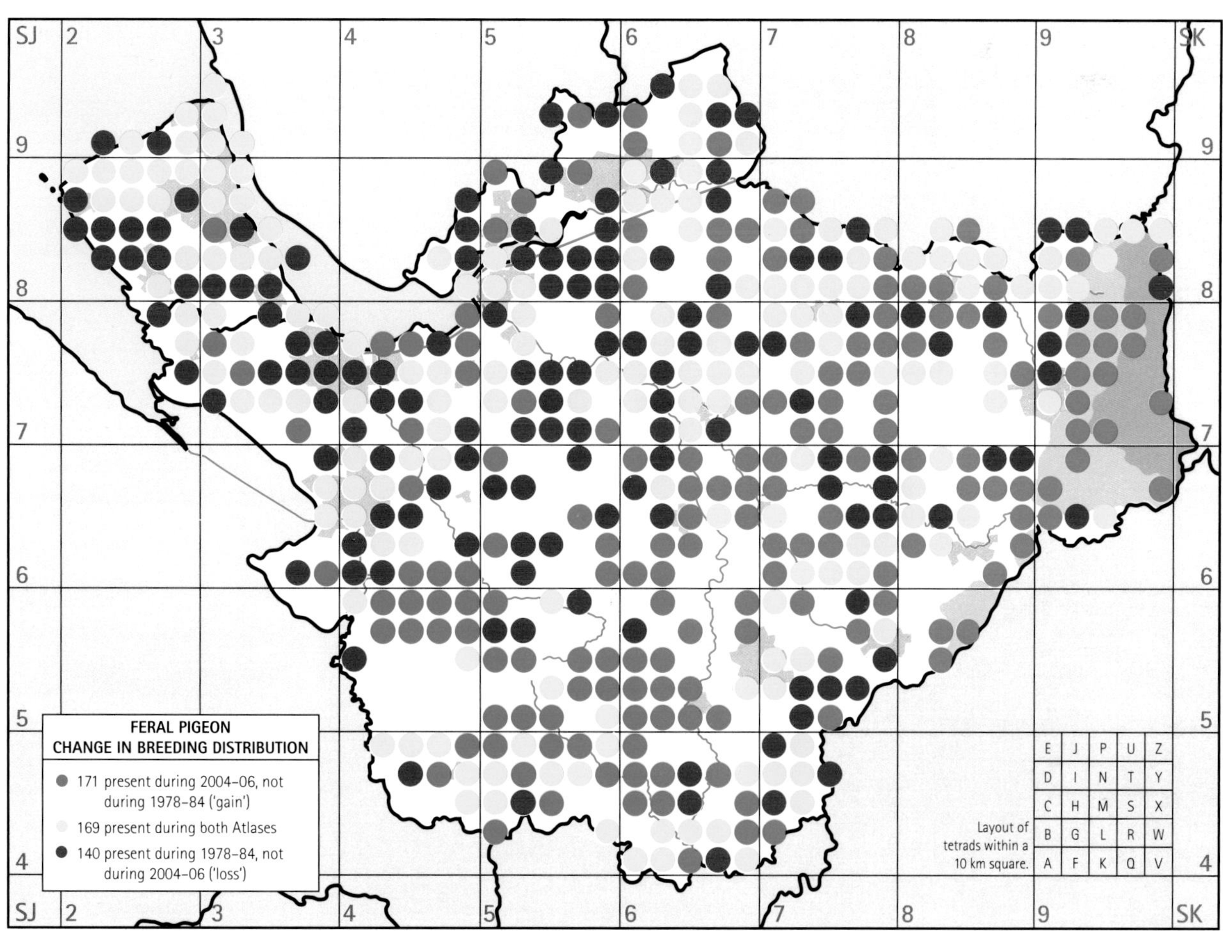
FERAL PIGEON
CHANGE IN BREEDING DISTRIBUTION
171 present during 2004–06, not during 1978–84 ('gain')
169 present during both Atlases
140 present during 1978–84, not during 2004–06 ('loss')
Layout of tetrads within a 10 km square.
E J P U Z
D I N T Y
C H M S X
B G L R W
A F K Q V
SJ
SK

Many Feral Pigeons are resident all year round, some of them indeed breeding in almost any month, and they occupied a similar number of tetrads in both seasons. There appears to have been quite a bit of local movement, however, with 95 tetrads holding birds in the breeding season and not in winter, whilst 102 had birds wintering but not breeding. There is some shift in habitat, with 65% of winter records in human sites and 29% in farmland, and a few in semi-natural grassland or salt-marsh. This suggests that some birds leave their man-made sites, especially in rural (F3) habitats, and flock into agricultural areas. Five per cent of the records were from stubble fields, often of mixed flocks with Woodpigeons and Stock Doves.

Most Feral Pigeons spend their lives in flocks, and Atlas fieldworkers submitted 287 counts, with a median size of 12. Twenty-three gatherings were estimated at 100 birds or more, headed by a maximum of 500 at Fiddler's Ferry (SJ58M) in 2005/06. Pigeons also gather communally to roost in a variety of places including urban buildings and farm barns; they prefer to be underneath a canopy or a bridge to keep the rain off, but in some sites they have to make do with spending the night on an exposed roof. Fifteen roosts were recorded during this Atlas, holding up to a maximum of 200 birds in Crewe (SJ75C).

Feral Pigeons were apparently unknown to Cheshire ornithology until a quarter-century ago. They were not mentioned by Coward (1910), Boyd (1951) or Bell (1962), or in the annual county bird reports until 1981. Since then, some large winter flocks have been reported annually, usually 100 or more in most town centres or stubble or slurried fields. In Arctic weather on 9 January 1988, 1,500 birds took to feeding on the salt-marsh at the Gayton Sands RSPB reserve.

Few of the larger land-birds excite birdwatchers (gamebirds, pigeons and doves and corvids) but they constitute the majority of the country's avian biomass and we should do our best to record as much as we can about them. Feral Pigeons are certainly not everyone's favourite bird, and probably still underrecorded as a result, but this Atlas provides the most comprehensive assessment ever of their status in the county.

DAVID NORMAN

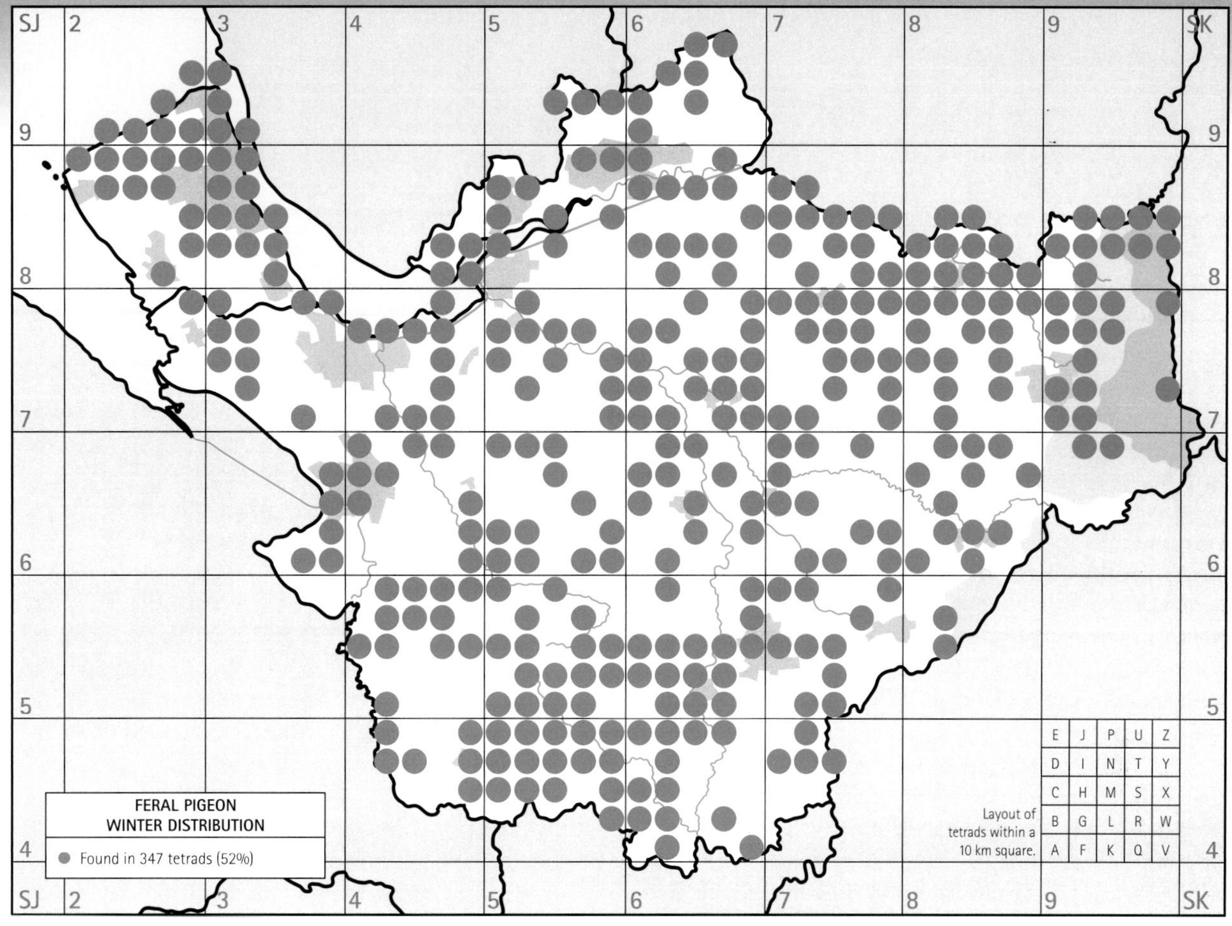
FERAL PIGEON
WINTER DISTRIBUTION
Found in 347 tetrads (52%)
Layout of tetrads within a 10 km square.
E J P U Z
D I N T Y
C H M S X
B G L R W
A F K Q V
SJ
SK

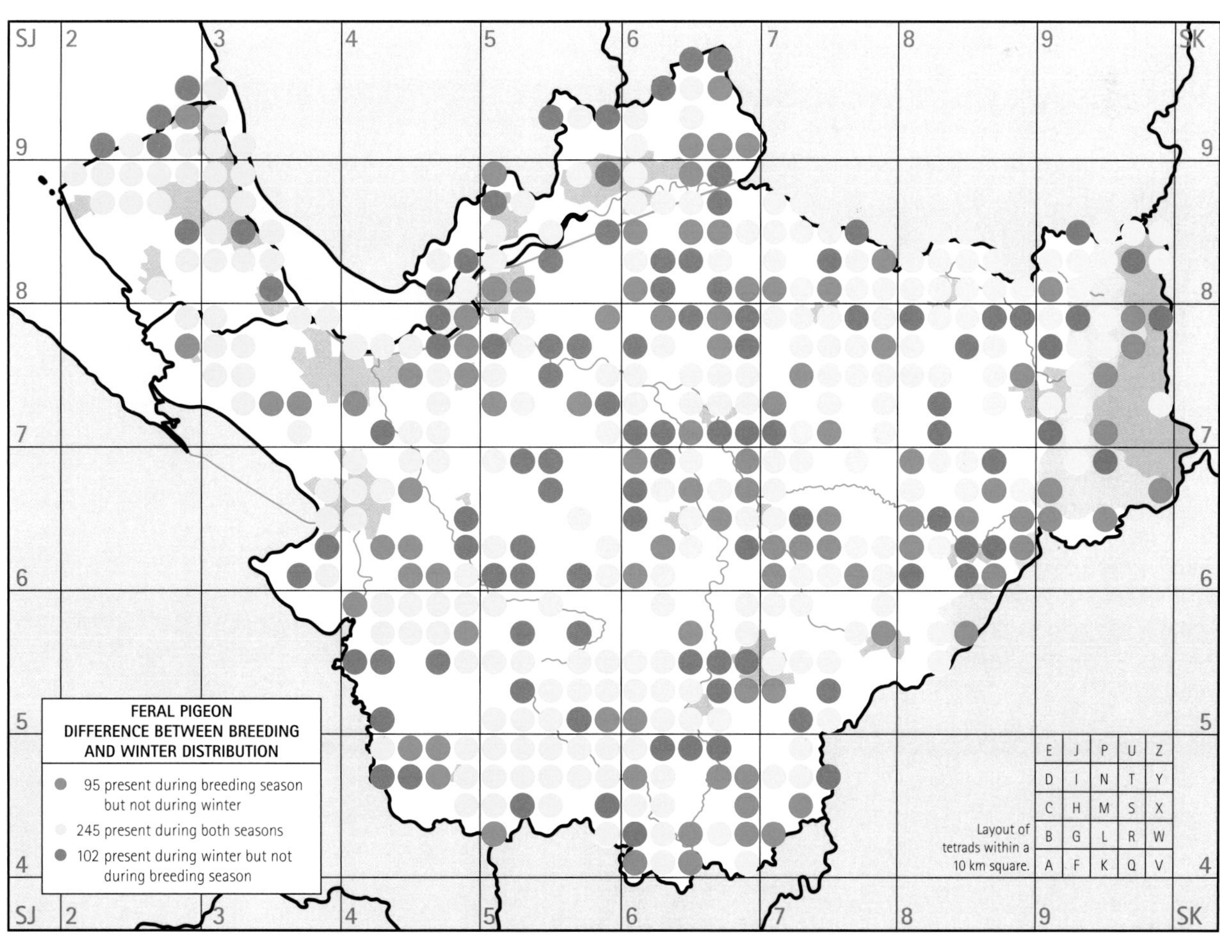
FERAL PIGEON
DIFFERENCE BETWEEN BREEDING AND WINTER DISTRIBUTION
95 present during breeding season but not during winter
245 present during both seasons
102 present during winter but not during breeding season
Layout of tetrads within a 10 km square.
E J P U Z
D I N T Y
C H M S X
B G L R W
A F K Q V
SJ
SK

Stock Dove

Columba oenas

The distribution of Stock Doves has changed little in twenty years. As in our *First Atlas*, they are widely spread across the county, with the gains and losses almost balancing out and no coherent pattern except perhaps for the cluster of eight newly occupied tetrads in SJ69. In some areas they could have been underrecorded, some birdwatchers having a blind spot for pigeons and not recognizing their far-carrying excited 'coo-oo-up' calls. They avoid most urban areas, with gaps around east Wirral, Chester, Widnes, Warrington, Northwich, Congleton and Macclesfield visible on the distribution map. This also shows in the habitat records, with only 6% of codes from human sites, mostly in rural areas, and 54% in farmland, 36% in woodland and 3% in scrub. This is primarily a bird of parkland, the edges of woods and farmland with copses and hedgerow trees.

Their diet of farmland seeds, leaves and buds, meant that they were badly hit in the 1950s and early 1960s by the poisonous organochlorine seed-dressings, but, following the ban on their use, Stock Dove numbers bounced back. Their stable distribution in the county might suggest that their population has levelled out between our two Atlases, and the BTO figures show the national index to be just 16% higher than in 1984. Grazing farmland has deteriorated as a breeding habitat for Stock Doves in recent years, however (Siriwardena *et al.* 2000b). According to the analysis of BBS transects in Cheshire and Wirral, the Stock Dove breeding population in the county in 2004–05 was 2,130 birds (870–3,390), an average of only just over four birds per tetrad in which they were found.

Stock Doves may have several broods in a season lasting from February to September, although most activity is in June. Their nests are completely different from the rest of the pigeon family, in a large tree cavity, so they find themselves in competition with species including Tawny and Little Owls and Jackdaws. They readily take nest-boxes and are in fact the commonest occupant of boxes erected for Barn Owls in the area of west Cheshire covered by the Broxton Barn Owl Group. Oak was the only species of nesting tree recorded during this Atlas. Observers proved breeding in less than one-third of tetrads, mostly by finding nests (123 tetrads), with recently fledged young reported in 20. Birds were found carrying sticks or visiting likely nest sites in a further 27 tetrads, these activities counting as probably breeding.

RAY SCALLY

Sponsored by Syngenta CTL

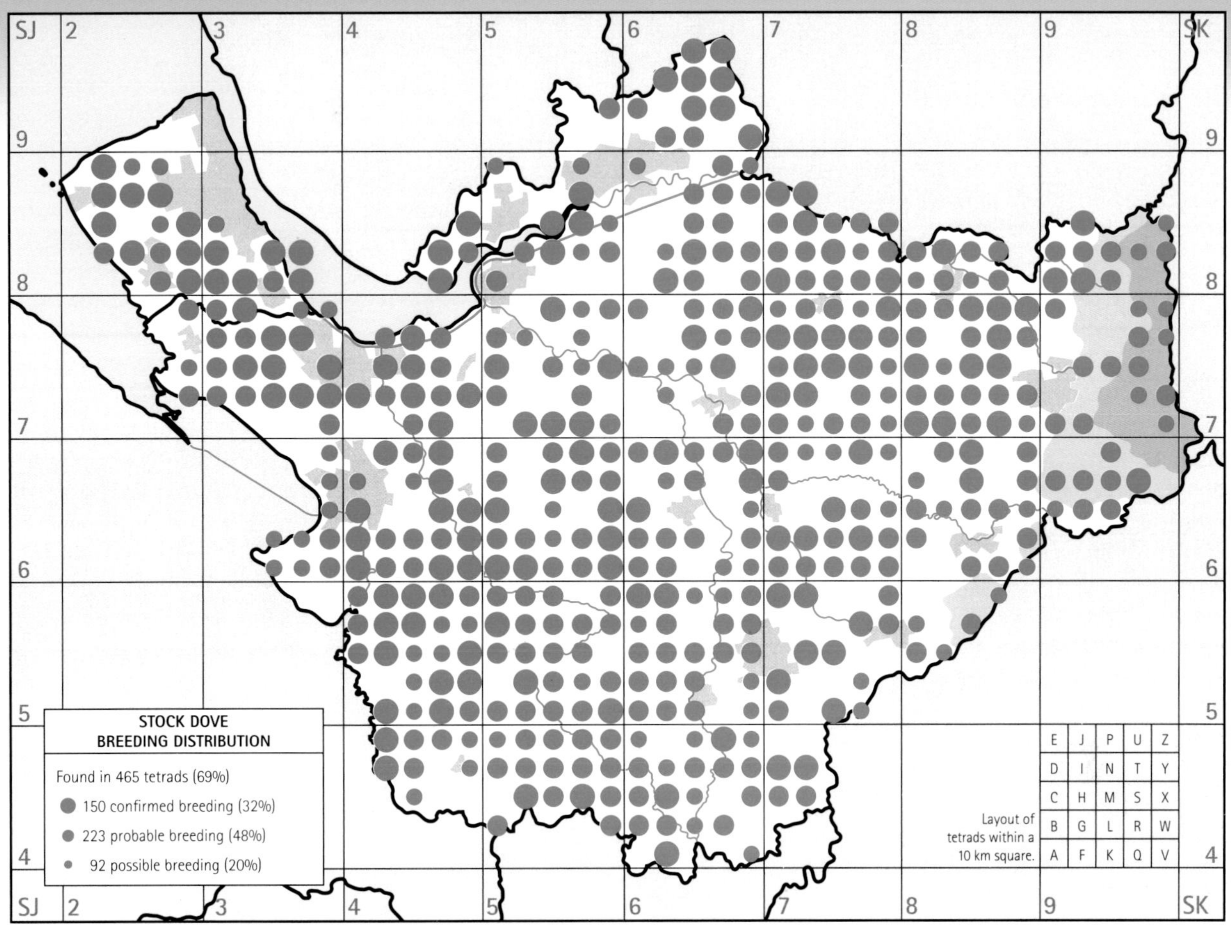
SJ
SK
STOCK DOVE
BREEDING DISTRIBUTION
Found in 465 tetrads (69%)
150 confirmed breeding (32%)
223 probable breeding (48%)
92 possible breeding (20%)
Layout of
tetrads within a
10 km square.
E J P U Z
D I N T Y
C H M S X
B G L R W
A F K Q V

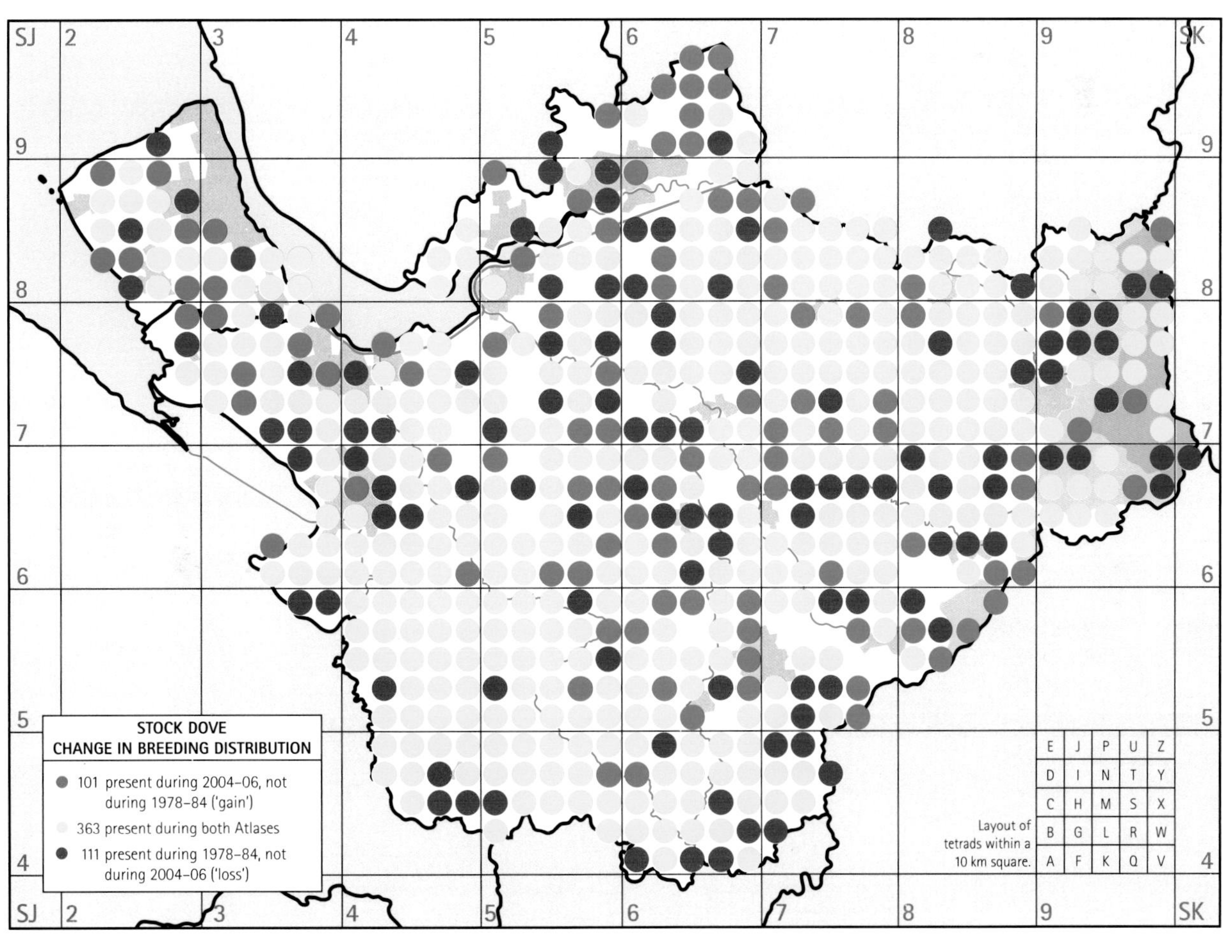
SJ
SK
STOCK DOVE
CHANGE IN BREEDING DISTRIBUTION
101 present during 2004–06, not during 1978–84 ('gain')
363 present during both Atlases
111 present during 1978–84, not during 2004–06 ('loss')
Layout of
tetrads within a
10 km square.
E J P U Z
D I N T Y
C H M S X
B G L R W
A F K Q V

Stock Doves were recorded in 49 fewer tetrads in winter than during the breeding season, perhaps because some birds move to join flocks. There are noticeable gaps in the Wirral peninsula and in the centre of the county around Winsford in SJ66, and they seem to withdraw from the highest altitudes, as was reported in the national *BTO Winter Atlas*. Stock Dove flocks are seldom as large as those of Woodpigeons, although they sometimes join them and form mixed flocks. The median count of Stock Doves was four birds, with 16 flocks of 50 or more, the biggest being 200 at Capenhurst (SJ37R) and Frodsham Marsh (SJ57E). Their roosts are less noticeable, being reported in only three tetrads, two of them in single figures but that at Fiddler's Ferry (SJ58M) holding up to 150 birds. From mid-January onwards, some birds were seen in pairs prospecting suitable nest sites.

In winter, many Stock Doves shift habitats to farmland, which makes up 72% of the winter records, including 9% in stubble. This is one of the few species to take advantage of maize stubble, commented upon by observers in 12 tetrads. Far fewer (20%) were in woodland, with only 3% of codes from human sites and 2% from salt-marsh. Stock Doves feed mainly on weed seeds, although it is almost impossible to see what they are taking when foraging in a field. They especially favour slurried fields and manure heaps, with birds also reported from game cover, rape, sprouts, cattle and horse pastures and paddocks, and a field of improved grassland left to go to seed.

As with Woodpigeon, the migratory status of the winter flocks has been in doubt. Coward (1910) thought that 'apparently the numbers are increased in winter by immigrants', and Hardy (1941) described them as a winter visitor in small flocks. Boyd (1951) said they were sedentary, found throughout the Great Budworth district at all times of year in woods and hedgerows and feeding in the fields, often in company with Woodpigeons. Bell (1962) wrote that there was no evidence of migration, probably meaning that birds were not seen flying past Hilbre, but noted that sizeable flocks, between 50 and 100, had been reported frequently in autumn, and again in February in hard weather. Analysis of the national database of ringed birds now shows that British Stock Doves are indeed sedentary, with a median distance of movement of 6 km, and only four birds have shown movements over 200 km, three of them to France or Spain. Three foreign-ringed birds have been found in south-east England (*Migration Atlas*).

RICHARD STEEL

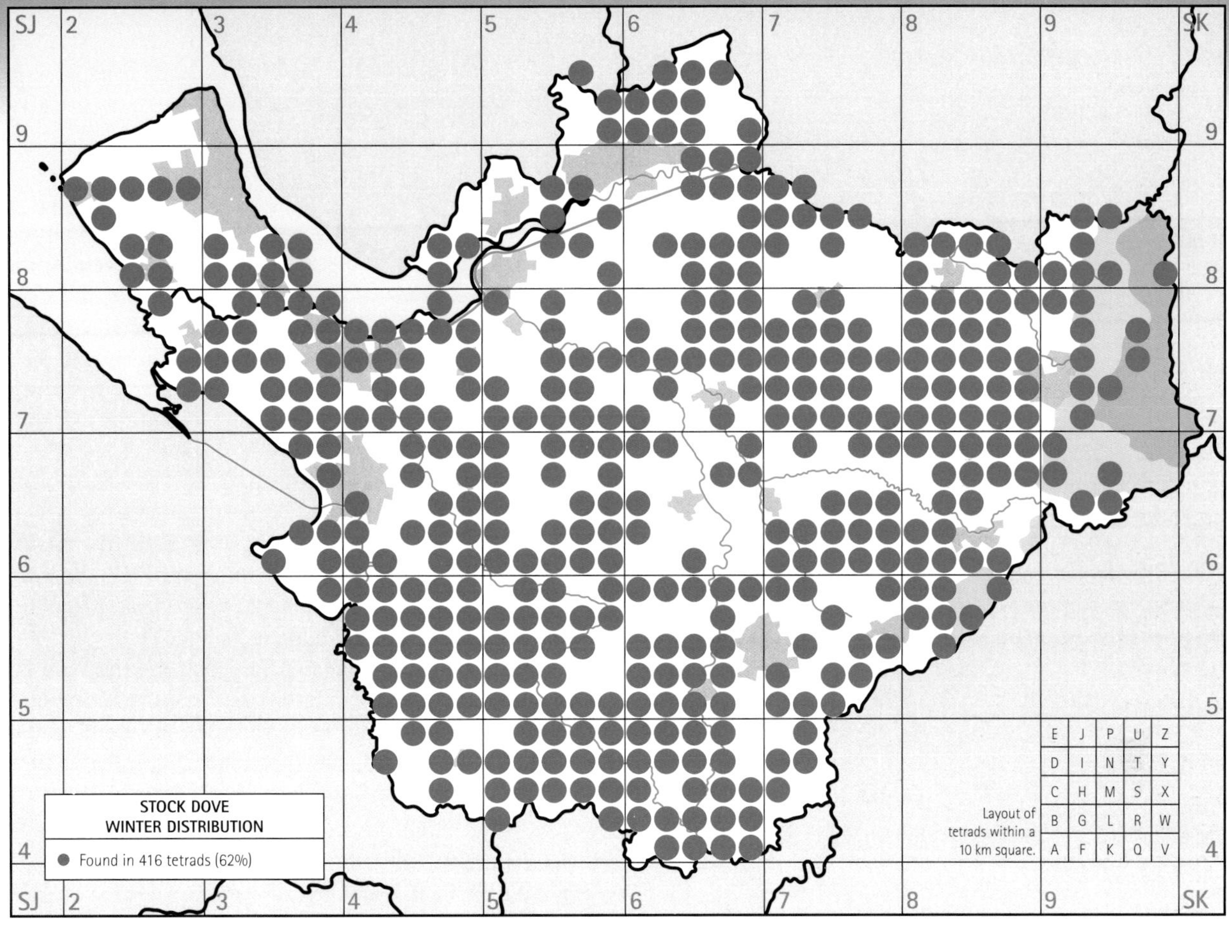
SJ
2
3
4
5
6
7
8
9
SK
9
8
7
6
5
4
STOCK DOVE
WINTER DISTRIBUTION
Found in 416 tetrads (62%)
E J P U Z
D I N T Y
C H M S X
B G L R W
A F K Q V
Layout of tetrads within a 10 km square.

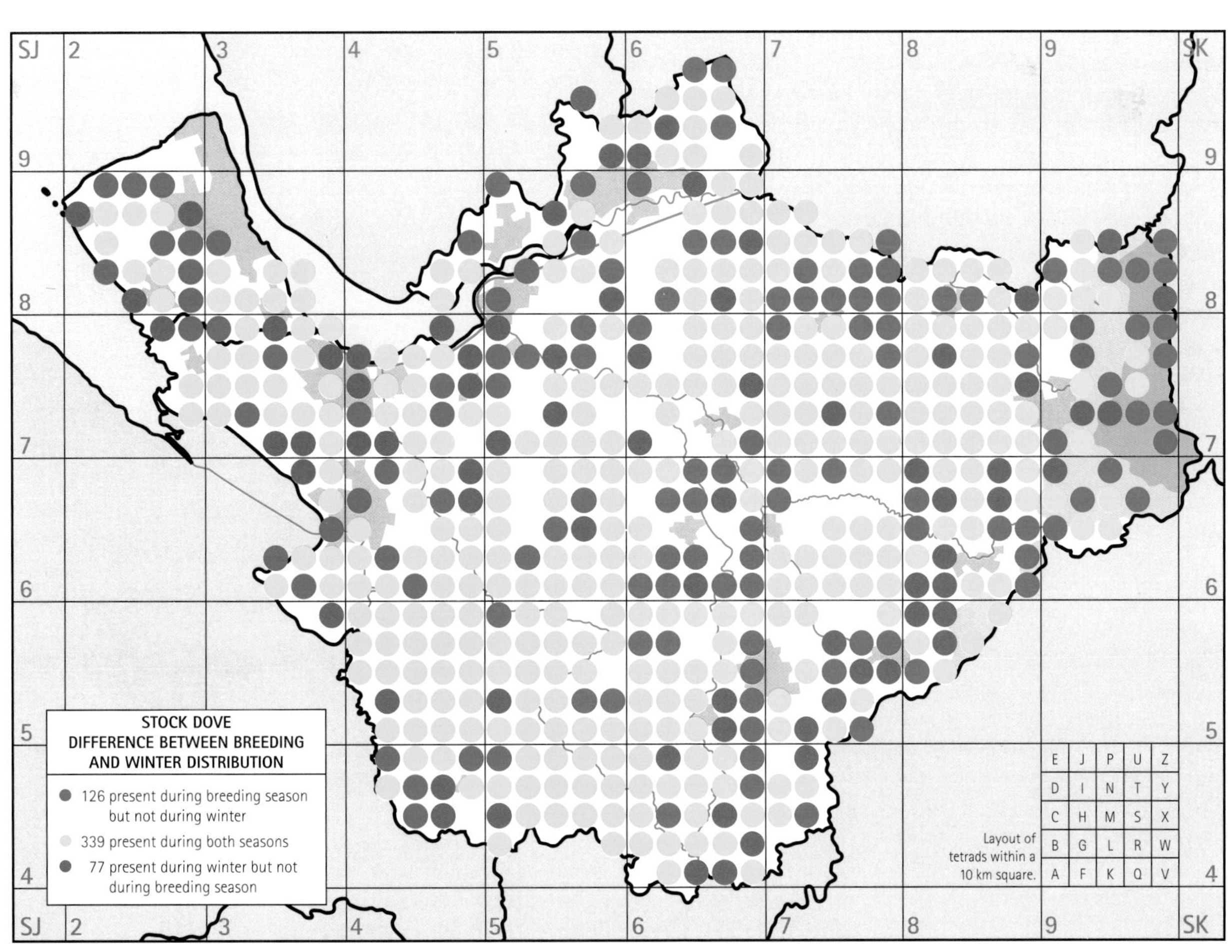
SJ
2
3
4
5
6
7
8
9
SK
9
8
7
6
5
4
STOCK DOVE
DIFFERENCE BETWEEN BREEDING AND WINTER DISTRIBUTION
126 present during breeding season but not during winter
339 present during both seasons
77 present during winter but not during breeding season
E J P U Z
D I N T Y
C H M S X
B G L R W
A F K Q V
Layout of tetrads within a 10 km square.

Woodpigeon

Columba palumbus

Woodpigeon is now the sixth most abundant species in Cheshire and Wirral, with a breeding population in 2004–05 of 129,890 birds (102,450–157,330), corresponding to an average of almost 200 birds per tetrad in which they were found. The abundance map shows that they were least numerous in the eastern hills and in the most wooded parts of the county, in north-east Cheshire and the centre around Delamere, with highest densities in agricultural areas. The distribution map shows that they were present almost everywhere in this Atlas, as they were twenty years ago. Their numbers are probably higher, however, as the national breeding population index has risen steadily year on year, and was up by 60% in the 20 years since 1984.

Their move into suburban and urban areas, first started in about the 1930s, is now complete and modern Woodpigeons appear to have little fear of man. The habitat codes showed 2.5% of records in urban areas and 7.5% in suburbia, with 9% in rural human sites. Farmland habitats made up 37% of records, with 36% in woodland and 6% in scrub.

They have an extended breeding season, at least from April to October, but most successful broods come later in the season, from July onwards, when the nests are better hidden by leaves and there are far more seeds available for the adults to eat (Murton 1965). They may well nest earlier in urban areas but the switch to autumn sowing, and thus earlier ripening, of cereals has helped them advance their breeding season in farmland (O'Connor & Shrubb 1986). The flourishing population in Sefton Park, Liverpool is more akin to farmland birds in its timing, perhaps because they feed especially on oilseed rape, flying at least 6 km away from the nest to fields outside the city (Slater 2001). This strategy obviously works because the nests of those pairs, and perhaps those of similar habit in Cheshire and Wirral, are much more successful in raising young than is found in farmland nests.

Fieldworkers proved breeding in two-thirds of tetrads, usually by finding a nest, sometimes given away by an eggshell on the ground beneath. Henry Finch, whilst surveying near Alvanley (SJ47W), had the unusual experience of recording a nest's contents by seeing an 'obliging' crow remove an egg. Their nests are built of a few twigs, often so flimsy that the eggs can be seen from the ground underneath, birds often drawing attention to them by uttering a soft 'coo' close to the nest. Typical sites are hawthorn hedges and creepers such as ivy, but many birds build in trees, of almost any species. Perhaps a measure of their high density is that nests were found on girders in barns and in industrial sites, more typically the habitat of Feral Pigeons or Collared Doves. An urban myth says that 'you never see baby pigeons' but observers in 88 tetrads found recently fledged youngsters, perhaps none as easily as Marc Granville who had them come into his Holmes Chapel garden (SJ76T) and comically try using his children's climbing frame from which to learn to fly.

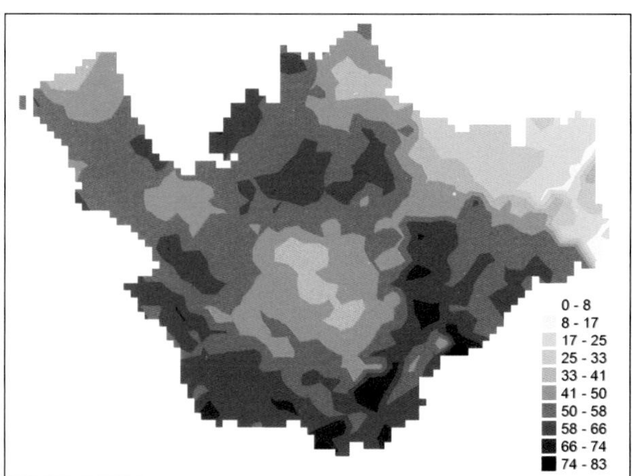

Woodpigeon abundance.

Sponsored by David and Fran Cogger in memory of Jasper

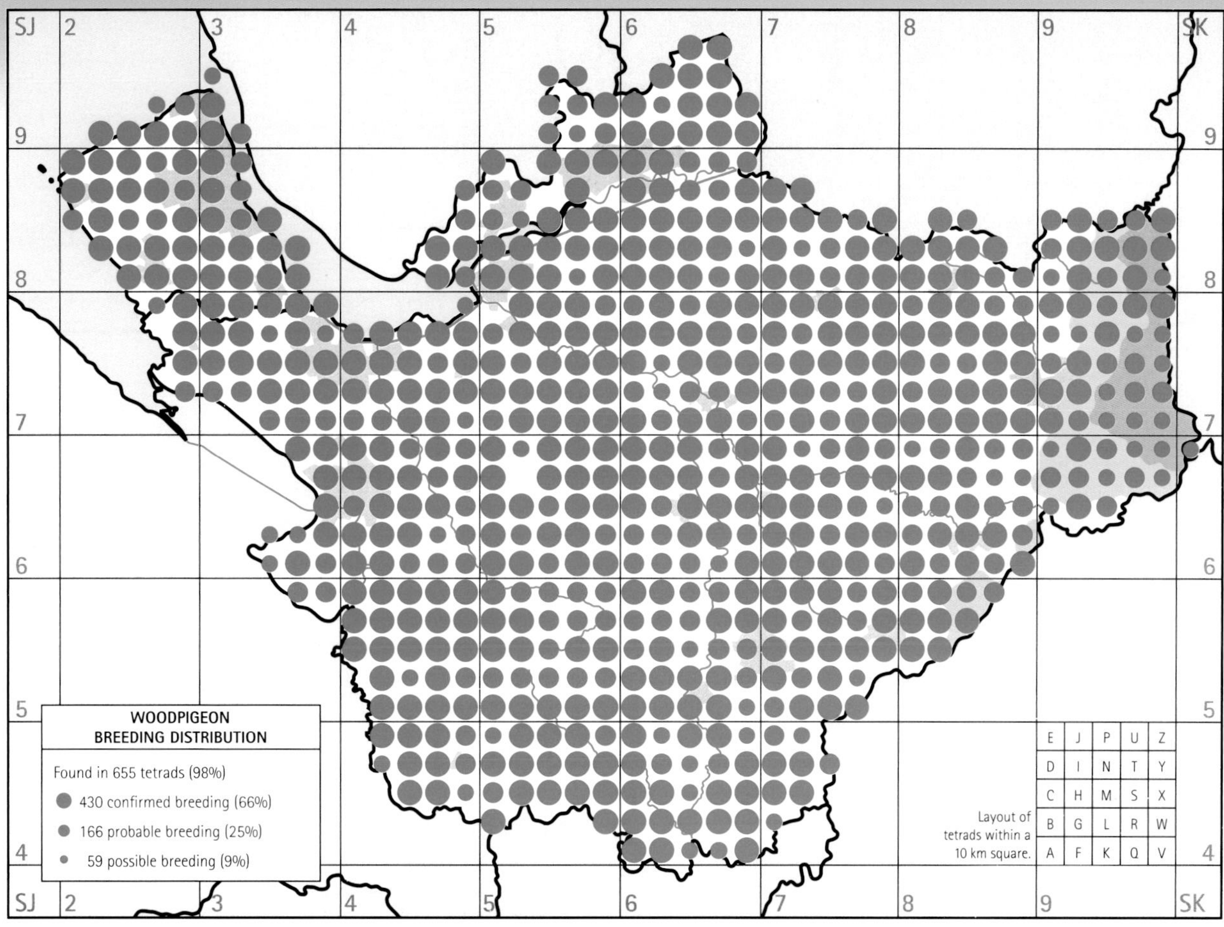
SJ
SK
WOODPIGEON
BREEDING DISTRIBUTION
Found in 655 tetrads (98%)
430 confirmed breeding (66%)
166 probable breeding (25%)
59 possible breeding (9%)
Layout of tetrads within a 10 km square.
E J P U Z
D I N T Y
C H M S X
B G L R W
A F K Q V

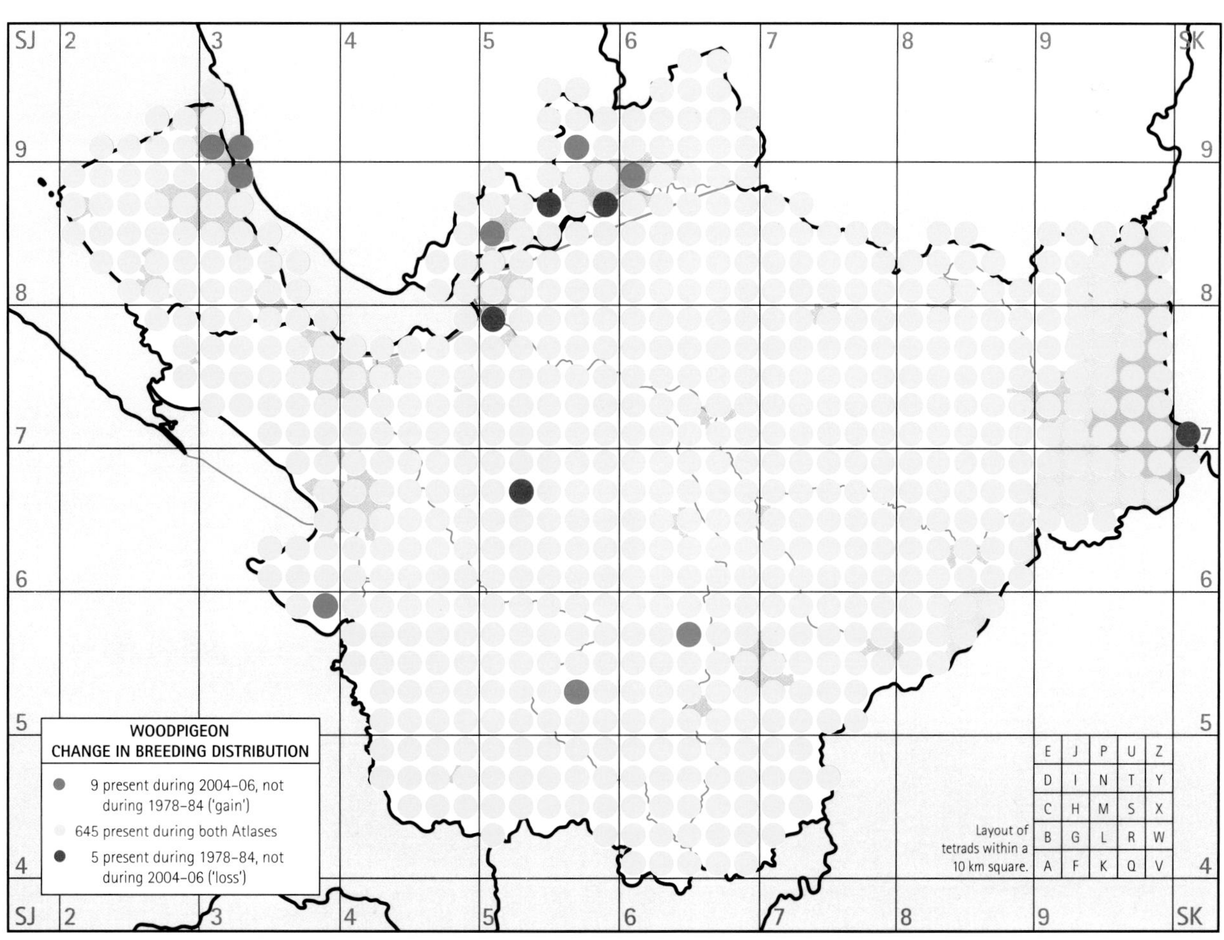
SJ
SK
WOODPIGEON
CHANGE IN BREEDING DISTRIBUTION
9 present during 2004–06, not during 1978–84 ('gain')
645 present during both Atlases
5 present during 1978–84, not during 2004–06 ('loss')
Layout of tetrads within a 10 km square.
E J P U Z
D I N T Y
C H M S X
B G L R W
A F K Q V

The winter survey showed Woodpigeons to be almost ubiquitous, missing only from a few of the easternmost and bleakest tetrads on the Derbyshire border and a few scattered squares elsewhere. Many Woodpigeons change habitats in winter, with more records in farmland (55% of the winter records), including 4% in stubble. Fewer (29%) were in woodland or scrub (2%), with 2% given a range of codes in the semi-natural grassland and marsh group. The changes in occupation of the 'human site' categories were puzzling, with half as many as in the breeding season in urban or rural areas, but much the same numbers in suburbia. They will even enter the smallest gardens if they see suitable food.

Birds were reported feeding on a wide variety of agricultural land, oilseed rape, sprouts, turnips, bare and slurried stubble, ploughed fields, horse paddocks, and improved grassland with sheep grazing. Boyd (1951) undertook a very informative analysis of the number of Woodpigeons he had recorded feeding in different agricultural crops. Their preferred order, judging from the size of the flocks, started with clover, then kale and similar brassicas, grain, newly sown fields, pasture and finally, least favoured, stubble, ploughed land and old potato ground. We do not know how much of each crop was available, or the extent of shooting or scaring, but the main change from today is that little clover is grown now, and oilseed rape is usually their favoured food. However, although oilseed provides Woodpigeons with a more than ample food supply, its nutritional value is low and birds have to consume vast amounts of it and spend long hours each day feeding. Higher quality food such as grain, beechmast or acorns is preferred, if available.

Woodpigeons tend to forage in groups, fieldworkers submitting 726 counts of flocks. The median size was 30 birds, with 184 over 100 and four flocks over 1,000 strong, with a maximum of 2,000 at Caldy (SJ28H) in 2004/05. They also gather to spend the night communally, and 96 records were submitted of flocks going to roost, with half of the counts of 100 birds or more and seven over 1,000, topped by the gathering of 2,500 noted by Pete Hall at Toft (SJ77N) in 2004/05.

All previous authors have commented on winter immigration of Woodpigeons, although there is no evidence for their origins. Coward (1910) wrote that these winter influxes varied from year to year. In keeping with the norm for the time, he gave no numbers, but the winter of 1893/94 saw 'an exceptional invasion', with 'hordes' of the species in Cheshire, correlated with an unusual abundance of acorns. Hardy (1941) described the species as an abundant winter visitor, 'about three times the nesting population', with immense winter flocks roosting in woods, especially pines. Boyd (1951) recorded influxes in November and December, with winter flocks numbering many hundreds and even thousands. Bell (1962) wrote that winter immigration varied from year to year, again sometimes in hundreds or even thousands.

Most British adult Woodpigeons are sedentary, but first-year birds disperse up to a median distance of 30 km in midwinter, returning towards their natal area to breed. Since about 1980, the growing of oilseed rape has influenced their behaviour, with few birds moving away from areas where it is available (*Migration Atlas*). The large flocks that are seen moving south in some years, usually in October, might be from the highly migratory northern European populations, drifted over on their journey to Iberia to feed on the copious acorns there.

ANDREW MART

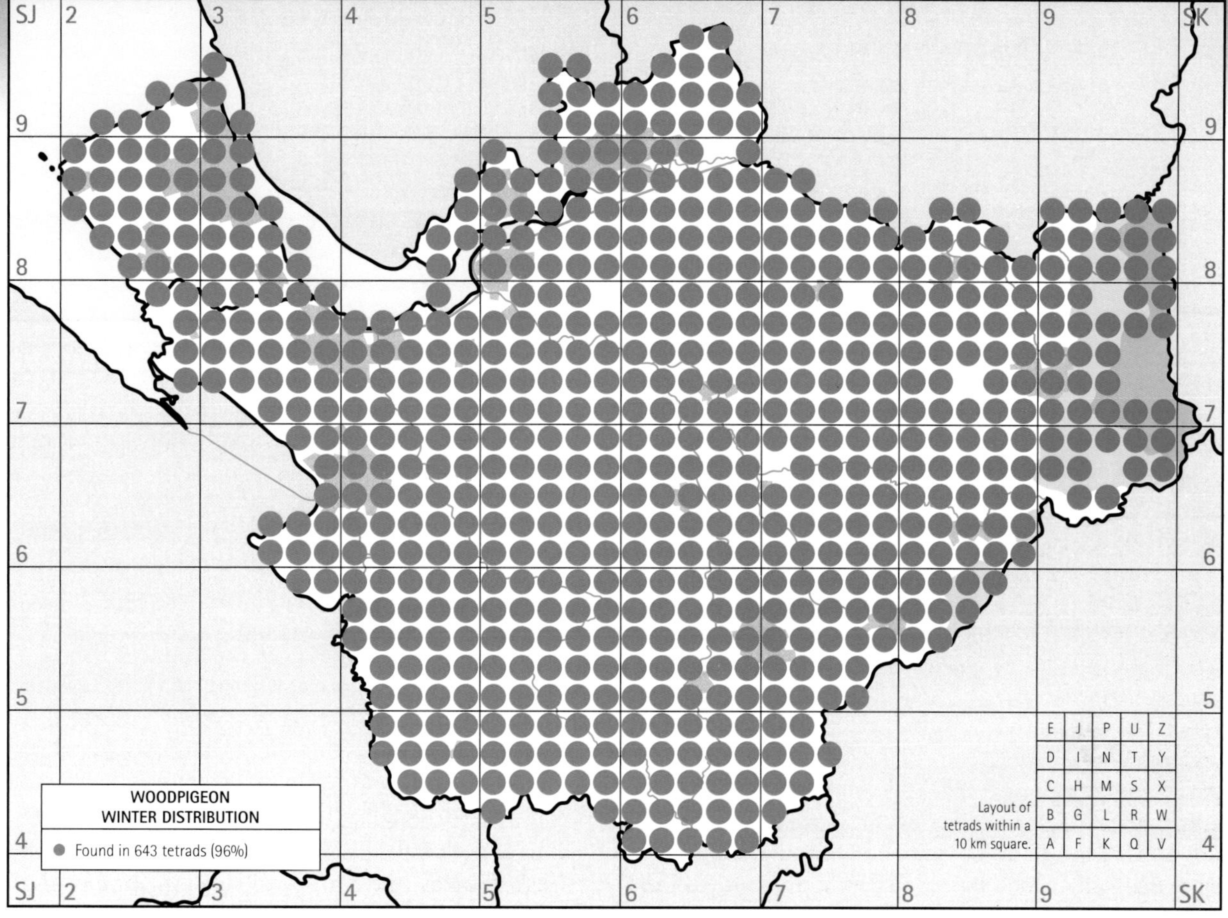
SJ
2
3
4
5
6
7
8
9
SK
WOODPIGEON
WINTER DISTRIBUTION
Found in 643 tetrads (96%)
Layout of tetrads within a 10 km square.
E J P U Z
D I N T Y
C H M S X
B G L R W
A F K Q V

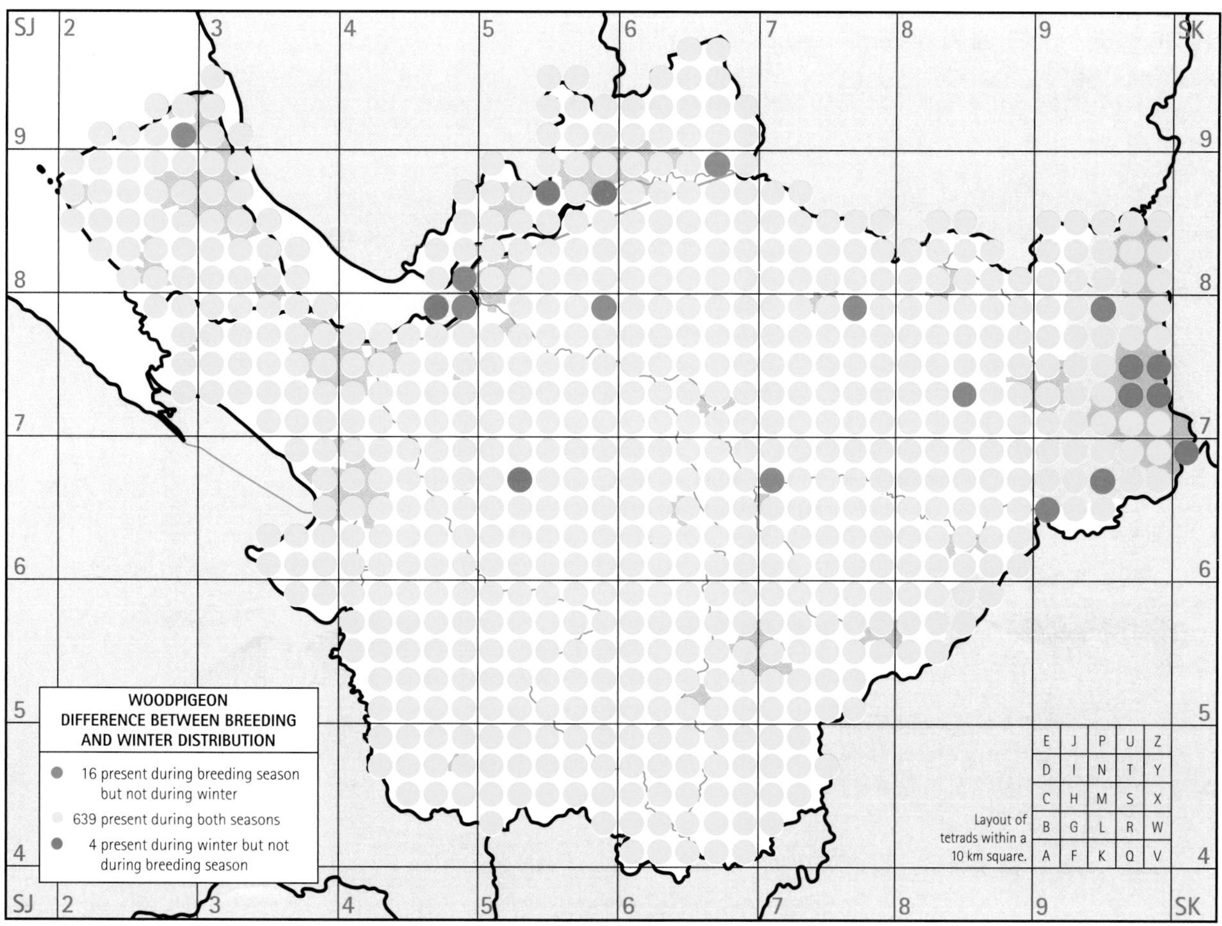
SJ
2
3
4
5
6
7
8
9
SK
WOODPIGEON
DIFFERENCE BETWEEN BREEDING AND WINTER DISTRIBUTION
16 present during breeding season but not during winter
639 present during both seasons
4 present during winter but not during breeding season
Layout of tetrads within a 10 km square.
E J P U Z
D I N T Y
C H M S X
B G L R W
A F K Q V

Collared Dove

Streptopelia decaocto

RICHARD STEEL

It bears repeating that Collared Doves were not recorded in the county until 1960, with first breeding suspected in 1961 as part of their remarkable spread to the north-west from Turkey and the Balkans that started in the 1930s. Most of Cheshire and Wirral had been colonized by the time of our *First Atlas*, but this Atlas map shows some further expansion with a net gain of 44 tetrads with birds present in the breeding season. The 'change' map shows that there is probably no significance to the 26 tetrads from which they have been lost, but they have filled in almost all of the odd gaps across the county, with a notable cluster of newly occupied tetrads around Macclesfield in SJ97.

One of the factors that helped its expansion of range is that it encountered no opposition and has been able to exploit a vacant ecological niche for a medium-sized granivore tolerant of man. The Atlas habitat codes show 72% of records in human sites (5% urban, 19% suburban and 48% rural), with 14% on farmland, 10% in woodland and 3% in scrub. This is not a bird of dense woods, however, and most of the woodland records are from thinly wooded sites with adjacent fields or urban greenspace in which they feed.

Their spread has also been helped by a high reproductive rate. Birds often start nesting in February, or March at the latest, and some carry on into October. They quickly build a flimsy nest and their clutch of two eggs takes only about 16 days of incubation, with chicks fledging about 18 days later, unusually short periods for a bird of its size. Many birds shorten the cycle even further by laying a new clutch whilst still feeding dependent young, allowing most of them to have three broods a year, and some pairs as many as six. They have taken advantage of our horticultural preferences in their nesting, with *leylandii* hedges probably their most-used sites, and fieldworkers recorded other examples of their exploiting man, including a nest in April 2006 at the Cheshire Oaks shopping complex (SJ47C) and nests in two tetrads supported by the bracket holding a domestic satellite television aerial.

Observers reported nests in 201 tetrads, with the remainder of the confirmed breeding records coming from recently fledged youngsters. Whilst they are in the nest and for a few days after, both adults share the task of feeding their brood with 'crop milk', also known as 'pigeon's milk', a secretion from the lining of their crop that is rich in protein and fat. Of the 225 tetrads with probable breeding, 133 of them had pairs recorded, 33 arose from surveyors seeing birds with nesting material or visiting an apparent nest site, and 59 from nuptial display, a male flying high into the air and stalling, dropping with closed wings to impress his mate and deter other doves.

The BTO BBS analysis shows that the breeding population of Cheshire and Wirral in 2004–05 was 26,650 birds (19,430–33,880), an average of 44 birds in every tetrad in which they were recorded. The national index shows an increase of 61% in the 20 years from 1984.

Sponsored by Altrincham and District Natural History Society

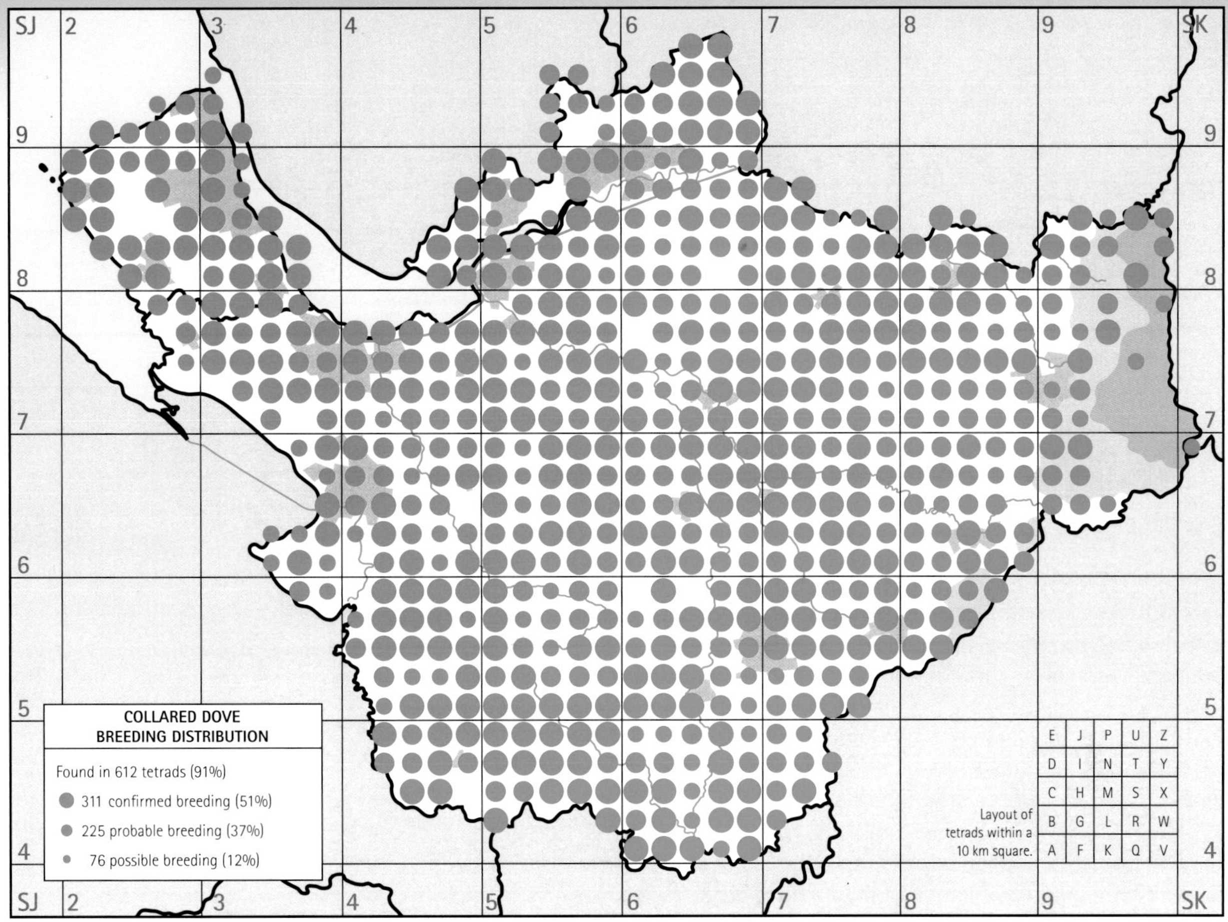
SJ
SK
COLLARED DOVE
BREEDING DISTRIBUTION
Found in 612 tetrads (91%)
311 confirmed breeding (51%)
225 probable breeding (37%)
76 possible breeding (12%)
Layout of
tetrads within a
10 km square.
E J P U Z
D I N T Y
C H M S X
B G L R W
A F K Q V

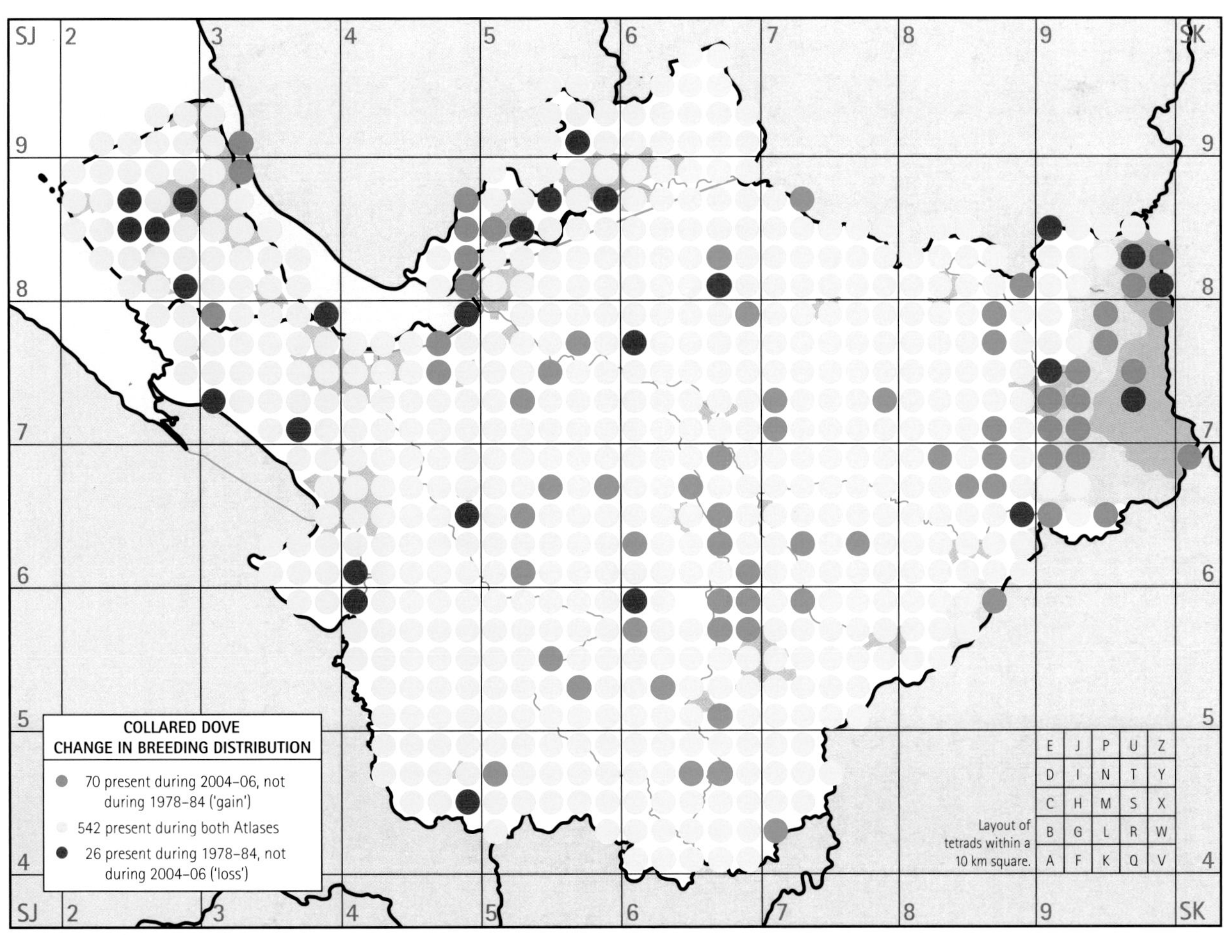
SJ
SK
COLLARED DOVE
CHANGE IN BREEDING DISTRIBUTION
70 present during 2004–06, not during 1978–84 ('gain')
542 present during both Atlases
26 present during 1978–84, not during 2004–06 ('loss')
Layout of
tetrads within a
10 km square.
E J P U Z
D I N T Y
C H M S X
B G L R W
A F K Q V

Now that their great nomadic phase is over—and no-one knows what caused it—Collared Doves appear to be sedentary. Since 1980 the median distance of movement of Collared Doves from the national ringing database is only 1 km (*Migration Atlas*). Prior to that, the archives of Merseyside Ringing Group for the 1960s contain several examples of the species' expansionary phase, with two Belgian-ringed birds caught here and three birds moving on to Ireland, although one that moved to north Germany, the only one on record, confused the picture. A bird ringed at Chester Zoo in 1980, found dead in 1982 in Strathclyde, 312 km north, was the last to exhibit long-distance movement.

Thus, it is no surprise to see from the Atlas map that their winter distribution in the county is essentially the same as in the breeding season. They were present in 574 tetrads in both seasons, being found in 25 tetrads in winter where they were not reported in the breeding season, and absent in winter from 38 with breeding season presence. They can be rather more difficult to find during the middle of winter, especially for surveyors visiting a tetrad, as they tend to be quiet and less obtrusive, but by the end of our winter period most birds are displaying and starting to breed again.

Although all members of the pigeon family are gregarious, Collared Doves tend not to form large flocks as much as the other species, and the median size of the 537 counts was four birds. Where they do flock, it is usually on a copious source of grain. There were only five groups of 50 or more, with by far the largest flock being 180 birds in a farmyard at Aldford (SJ45J) on 8 January 2007, counted by Neil Friswell: this appears to have been the first three-figure winter gathering in the county since 1999 (*CWBRs*). Sixteen communal roosts were reported, up to 80 birds in size, mostly in farm buildings or *leylandii* trees or hedges.

There is no significant difference in the habitats recorded in winter from those used in the breeding season. There were slightly fewer woodland or scrub codes as the association with trees for breeding sites is relaxed, and a handful of birds on winter stubble, but they are seldom found far away from buildings and most birds find all their year-round needs within their breeding area or nearby.

SUE & ANDY TRANTER

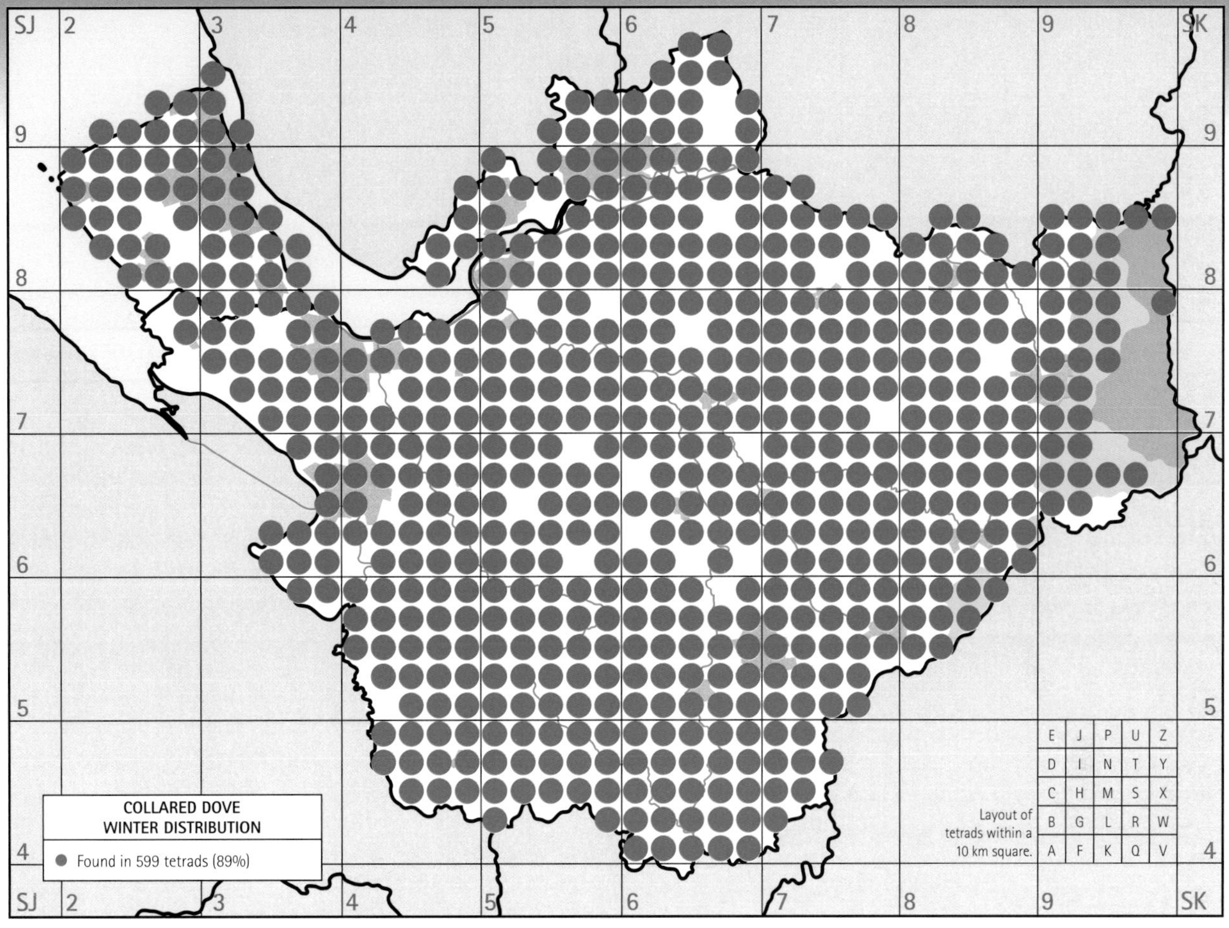

SJ
SK
COLLARED DOVE
WINTER DISTRIBUTION
Found in 599 tetrads (89%)
Layout of tetrads within a 10 km square.
E J P U Z
D I N T Y
C H M S X
B G L R W
A F K Q V

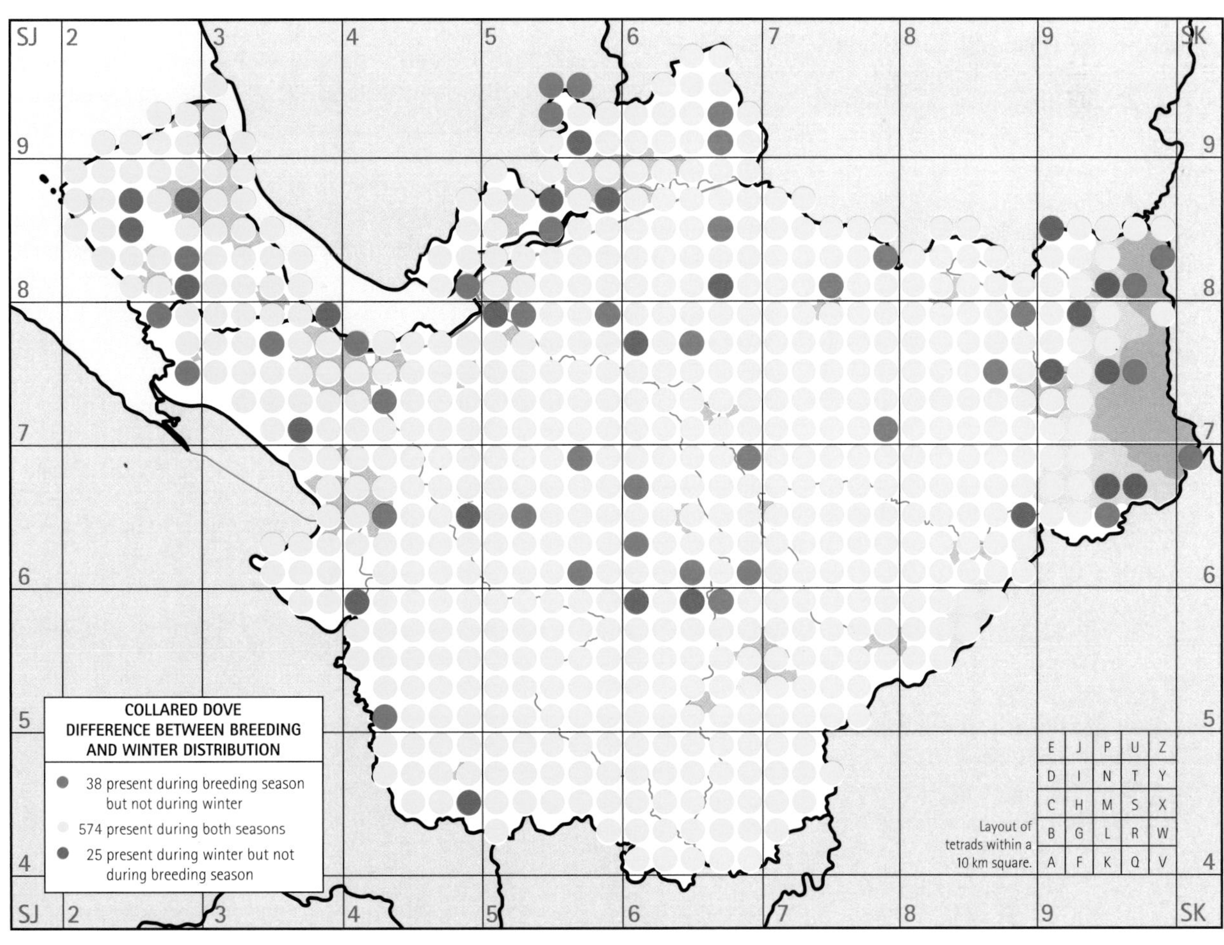

SJ
SK
COLLARED DOVE
DIFFERENCE BETWEEN BREEDING AND WINTER DISTRIBUTION
38 present during breeding season but not during winter
574 present during both seasons
25 present during winter but not during breeding season
Layout of tetrads within a 10 km square.
E J P U Z
D I N T Y
C H M S X
B G L R W
A F K Q V

Turtle Dove

Streptopelia turtur

RICHARD STEEL

This species, our only long-distance migrant in the pigeon family, has recently been lost from the county's breeding avifauna. It would probably come as a surprise to new birdwatchers that just twenty years ago, in our *First Atlas*, Turtle Doves were recorded in 144 tetrads, more than one-fifth of the county, with breeding proven in 20 of them. During this survey there were just two records of single birds in 2004, and one or two birds in 2006 at Risley Moss.

It is not straightforward to track the decline in the county from annual bird reports, in part because its occurrence has been understated as Turtle Doves are not easy to detect in casual birdwatching. Their song, a soporific purring, is mainly heard in the first two hours of daylight; through the rest of the day only 10–20% of birds sing (Calladine *et al.* 1999). Even during the *First Atlas*, whilst tetrad workers were finding it a widespread species, the annual bird reports declared it to be scarce. In 1992 its county status was changed to 'very scarce' (6–10 breeding pairs) and by 1994 it was noted that 'Delamere and surrounding area remains this species' last breeding toe-hold in Cheshire'. Appeals were made from 1997 onwards for submission of all data but there were no breeding records in 1998 or 1999, the species was lost from its Delamere haunts, and the last confirmed breeding was in 2000 at Rixton Claypits. From 2001 to 2004 the annual reports contained records of birds seen in the Rixton/Risley area but nearly all of the published records were of birds flying over just a handful of sites. The species' demise seemed to be complete when there was no mention at all of Turtle Doves in the 2005 *CWBR*.

Their national population index fell by one-third during the period of our *First Atlas* (1978–84) and has dropped by a further 70% from 1984 to 2004. Turtle Doves today have a substantially earlier close to the breeding season and produce barely half the number of clutches and young per pair than in the 1960s, nowhere nearly enough to maintain their numbers (Browne & Aebischer 2005). Along with the decline in population, their range has shrunk considerably. They were recorded in 25% fewer 10 km^2 squares in the national 1998–91 Atlas than in 1968–72 and their retreat to the south-east has continued since then. An indication of its range is well illustrated by the figures for the Atlases of nearby counties: 27% of tetrads in Shropshire (1985–90), 4% in Lancashire and North Merseyside (1997–2000) (and only two records north of the Ribble) and two records of single birds in Cumbria (1997–2001).

Turtle Doves' decline parallels that experienced by many other seed-eating species and probably shares some of the same causes, particularly changes in agricultural practice such as the increased use of herbicides and fertilizers. By migrating across the Sahara for the winter they avoid the shortage of food on British farmland, but they face the additional hazards of deterioration of their African habitat and of being traditionally a favourite target of Mediterranean hunters. In the breeding season they feed on a wide variety of small wild seeds and cultivated grain on rather bare ground: in the Delamere area they used to find the edges of sand quarries especially to their liking. They need dense hedges or woodland for nesting (Browne *et al.* 2004), and for safe cover when disturbed. Turtle Doves are still widespread but declining elsewhere in Europe, where they breed anywhere at low altitude, in habitats including hedges, borders of forest, spinneys, coppices, young tree plantations, scrubby wasteland, woody marshes or scrub, all with agricultural areas nearby for feeding (Tucker & Heath 1994).

Sponsored by Michael S. Twist

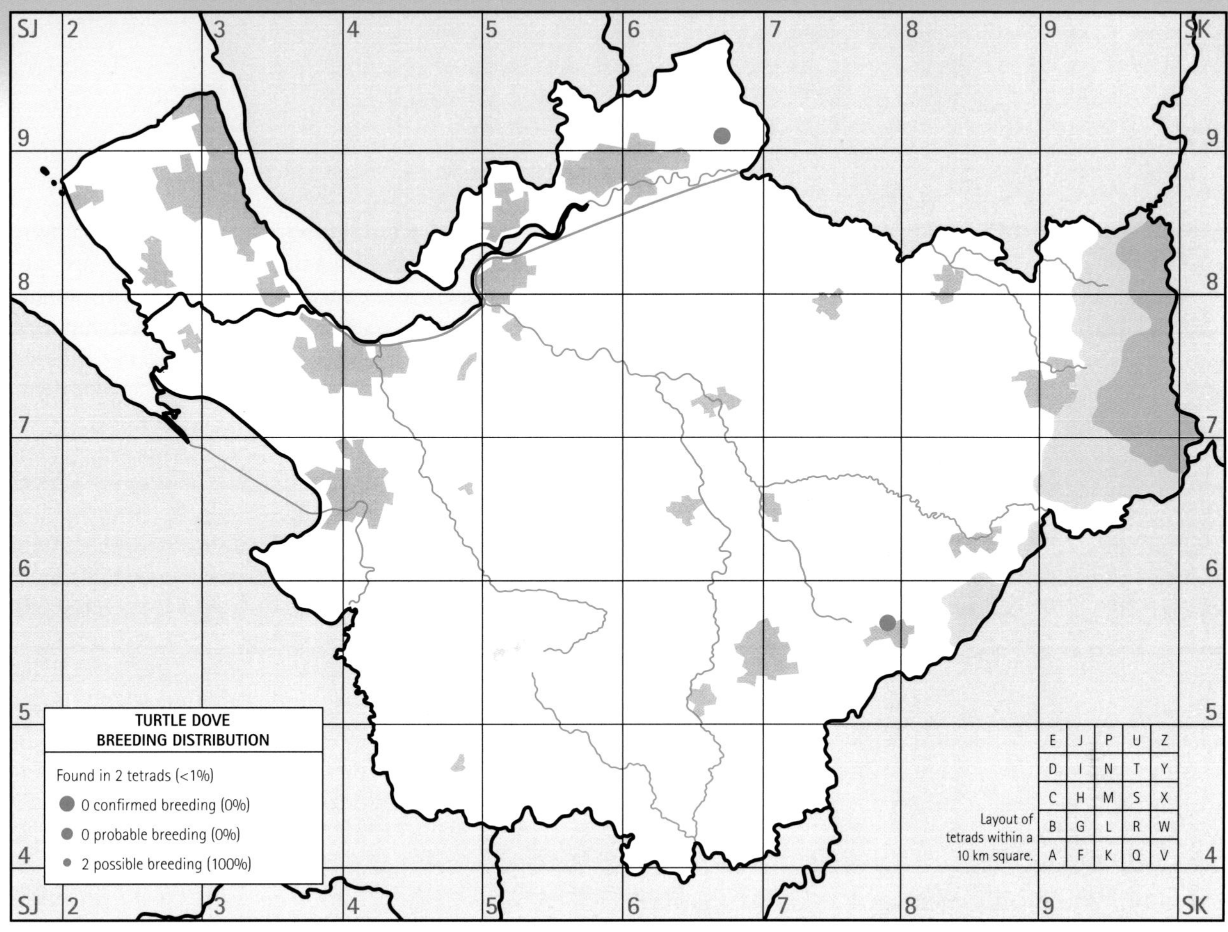

SJ
2
3
4
5
6
7
8
9
SK
TURTLE DOVE
BREEDING DISTRIBUTION
Found in 2 tetrads (<1%)
0 confirmed breeding (0%)
0 probable breeding (0%)
2 possible breeding (100%)
Layout of tetrads within a 10 km square.
E J P U Z
D I N T Y
C H M S X
B G L R W
A F K Q V

SJ
2
3
4
5
6
7
8
9
SK
TURTLE DOVE
CHANGE IN BREEDING DISTRIBUTION
0 present during 2004–06, not during 1978–84 ('gain')
2 present during both Atlases
142 present during 1978–84, not during 2004–06 ('loss')
Layout of tetrads within a 10 km square.
E J P U Z
D I N T Y
C H M S X
B G L R W
A F K Q V

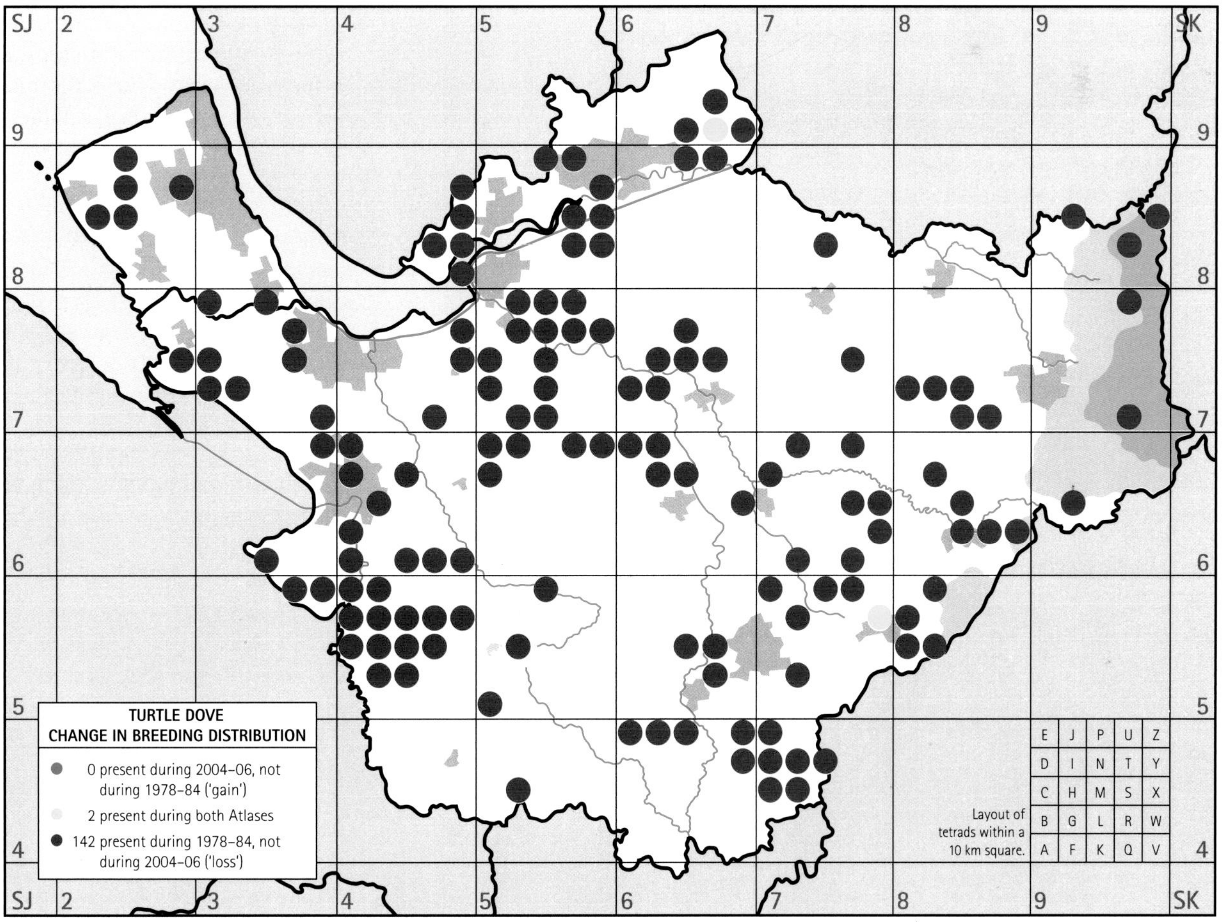

Cuckoo

Cuculus canorus

SIMON BOOTH

The Atlas maps show dramatically that Cuckoos are now found in far fewer places than twenty years ago. Their population in the UK has been in free fall during that time, with the national index dropping by 56% from 1984 to 2004. It is officially on the Amber List of species of conservation concern, and at the next revision will surely be moved to the Red List.

The only British brood-parasite, female Cuckoos lay a single egg in up to 25 other birds' nests each year. Their eggs have a short (about 12-day) incubation period: the Cuckoo chick hatches quickly and then pushes the host's eggs or small chicks out of the nest, so that the host foster-parents devote all their efforts to feeding the Cuckoo chick. Their main hosts are Dunnock and Meadow Pipit. In more south-easterly parts of Britain, the Reed Warbler is a common host for Cuckoos, but this had only been recorded twice in Cheshire before 1988, when nine nests at Rostherne and three at Woolston were cuckolded that year (Calvert 1988, Smith & Norman 1988). Cuckoos were then recorded from at least four Cheshire Reed Warbler sites over the next few years, including annually at Rostherne 1988–93 (Calvert 2005) and at Woolston until 1995 and again in 1998.

There is no definitive explanation for the drop in Cuckoo numbers, but three postulated reasons. First, the two main host species for the Cuckoo have both declined, by around 40% in the last 30 years, so opportunities for cuckoldry have dipped as well. Secondly, many moths are scarcer, including those species, the hairy or brightly coloured poisonous ones, on whose caterpillars adult Cuckoos largely feed (Conrad *et al.* 2004). For instance, the garden tiger moth, whose large black hairy caterpillar is poisonous to all British birds apart from the Cuckoo, has decreased, also by over 40% in the past 30 years. The decline of moths is thought to be caused by higher levels of pesticides in the environment, and the spread of fungi, encouraged by milder and wetter winters, which attack the overwintering caterpillars. Thirdly, conditions on the Cuckoos' African wintering grounds are probably more difficult for them, especially with periodic droughts cutting the invertebrate populations. It is not well known where they winter, but birds migrate to the south-east out of Britain and certainly cross the Sahara.

There is no obvious explanation for the current distribution of county records. They are clearly absent from built-up areas, and seem to be especially scarce from Chester along the length of the Wirral. They are not much restricted by habitat, of which Cuckoos have a catholic choice, and more than 30 different codes were recorded, spanning woodland (20%), scrub (9%), grassland (6%), farmland (54%), human sites (7%), reed-beds (2%) and others (2%).

As well as a major decline in the number of tetrads in which Cuckoos were found—from 535 in the *First Atlas* to 229 now, the biggest drop of any species—there are massive falls in the proportion showing confirmed breeding (from 51 to 4 tetrads) or probable breeding (from 271 to 13 tetrads). The four confirmed breeding records comprised three RF, with chicks, only weakly flying, two being fed by Dunnocks and the third by a group of House Sparrows, and one Reed Bunting nest with a Cuckoo chick. Although a seven-year survey, as our *First Atlas* was, will inevitably achieve a higher proportion of the higher breeding status codes, there are probably some observer effects including the continuing aversion from nest-recording and a reduced familiarity with the female calls, which in itself indicates how scarce the species has become. The males' onomatopoeic 'song' is well-known, but the females' bubbling call, often given after laying an egg, or responding to a male, is much more likely to indicate that the species is breeding in the area. However, many of the Atlas records are of birds present for a day or two only, perhaps on passage; many observers noted that a Cuckoo was heard on just one visit, and daily recording at some sites indeed showed that the majority of the calling males did not apparently stay.

Based on these figures, the Cheshire and Wirral population is unlikely to exceed 50 breeding birds, and may well be less.

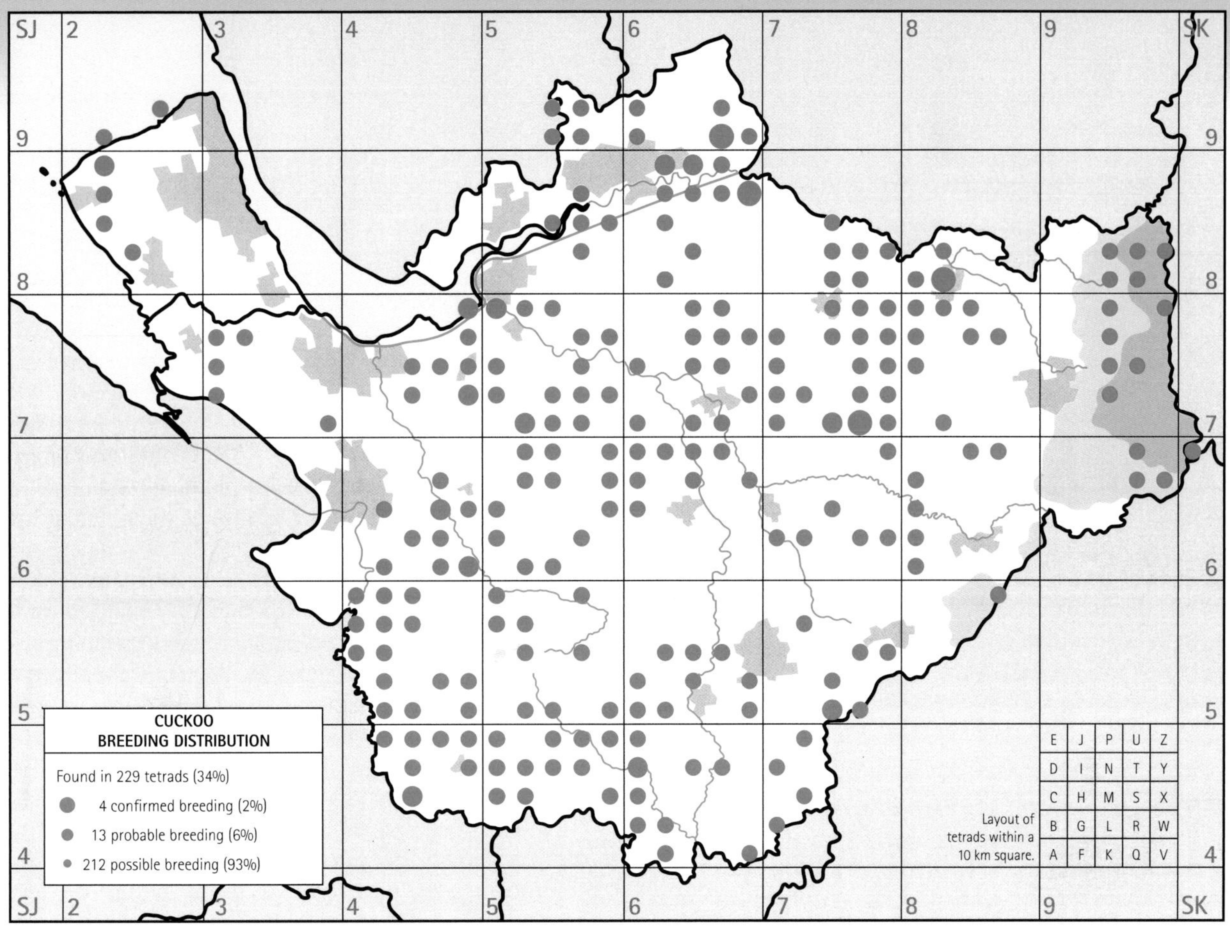
SJ
SK
CUCKOO
BREEDING DISTRIBUTION
Found in 229 tetrads (34%)
4 confirmed breeding (2%)
13 probable breeding (6%)
212 possible breeding (93%)
Layout of
tetrads within a
10 km square.
E J P U Z
D I N T Y
C H M S X
B G L R W
A F K Q V

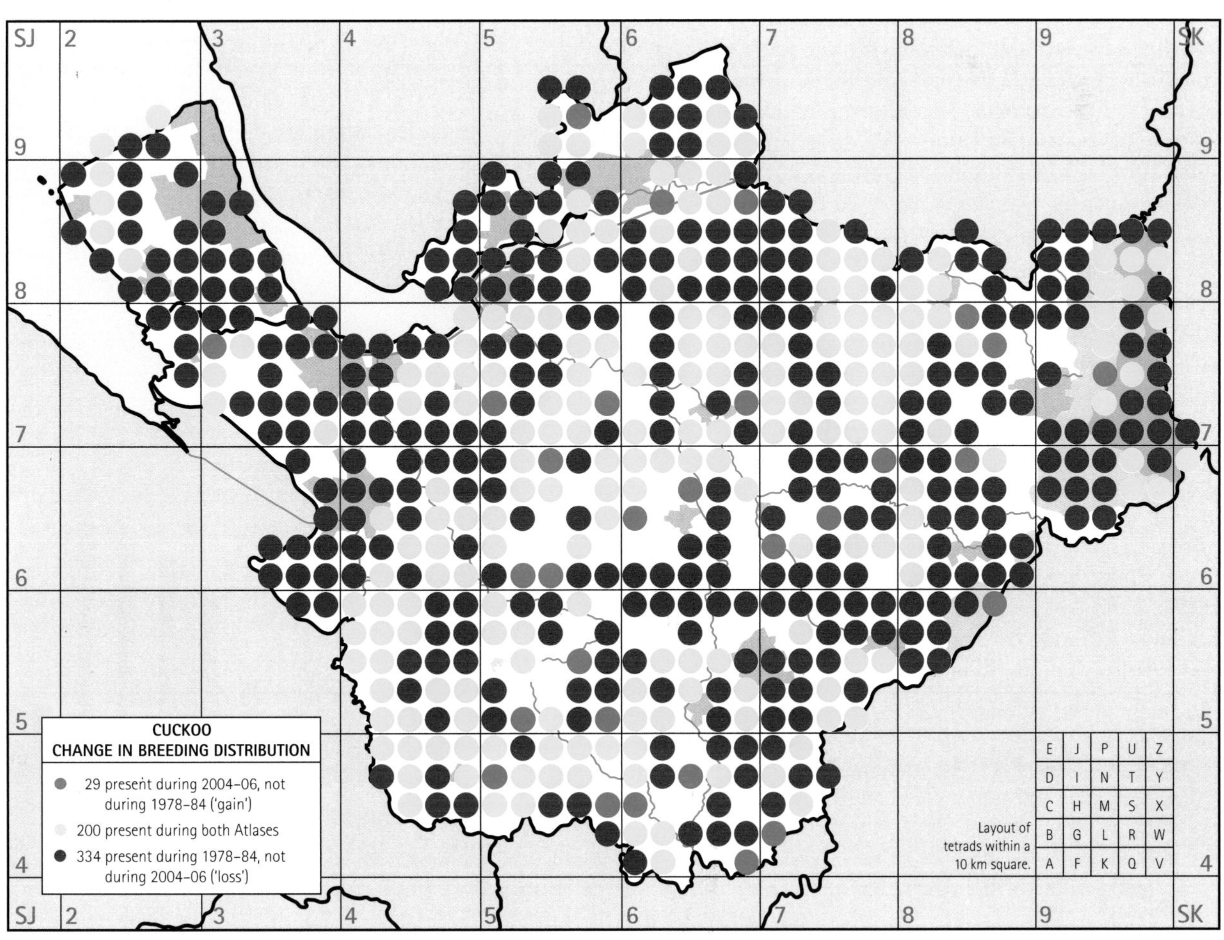
SJ
SK
CUCKOO
CHANGE IN BREEDING DISTRIBUTION
29 present during 2004–06, not during 1978–84 ('gain')
200 present during both Atlases
334 present during 1978–84, not during 2004–06 ('loss')
Layout of
tetrads within a
10 km square.
E J P U Z
D I N T Y
C H M S X
B G L R W
A F K Q V

Barn Owl

Tyto alba

This species' map is a tribute to direct action by Barn Owl conservation groups. National surveys had shown that the Cheshire population was 240 pairs in 1932 but only 35 pairs in 1982–85 (Shawyer 1987), an 85% drop over 50 years in the county, much more severe than the 69% decline across England and Wales as a whole. In 1998 the known county breeding population was only seven pairs. The combination of causes for their decline included agricultural practice, especially the loss of summer feeding habitat, overstocking of land and intensive use of chemicals including rodenticides applied around farmsteads. Direct mortality has risen especially owing to road traffic (Shawyer 1998).

Previously, some people had tried to help Barn Owls by rearing them in captivity and releasing birds into the wild, where they rapidly died. This was outlawed in 1993 and the work of Barn Owl groups has shown that the key to the species' conservation is to interest the landowners and improve the habitat, then put up nest-boxes and the Barn Owls will respond naturally.

The increase in nests in west Cheshire illustrates how well the birds have indeed reacted, and the map shows that they are now widespread. They steer clear of conurbations but find some industrial sites to their liking, especially landfill sites such as the Gowy and Maw Green areas which provide ideal hunting habitat. Barn Owl is a bird of low altitude, with over 90% of nests nationally found below 150 m, and none in Cheshire and Wirral is known to nest above this level.

Their main natural nesting site is in ash, which splits and rots to provide suitable cavities. The species was recorded for 12 of the trees used for nesting during this Atlas: 11 in ash and one in oak. Shawyer (1987) showed that they tend to choose trees in areas of low rainfall, such as Cheshire, and use mainly buildings in counties with high rainfall. Many suitable old barns in the county have been converted for human occupation, and modern metal-framed farm buildings are seldom used, so there are few sites known in buildings in Cheshire and Wirral. The majority of birds nest in boxes provided for them, on poles or in trees, and there are more than 500 such boxes in the county. A breeding pair often uses two adjacent boxes, perhaps on opposite sides of a field, with the male roosting in one of them whilst his mate and their brood use the other.

Although observers reported a wide variety of habitat codes, they were found overwhelmingly in agricultural grassland. They hunt mainly along rough grass margins, and each pair has to bring in 20–30 small mammals a day during the breeding season, which needs a length of 15–25 km of 6 m-wide grassland strips within their normal hunting range of 1–2 km from the nest. This might sound like a lot, but it amounts to only 1% or 2% of the land area, and can easily be provided by suitably managed banks of rivers and other watercourses, or by the unplanted margins of fields, for which farmers can be paid under Environmental Stewardship schemes.

Their favoured prey is short-tailed field voles, which need soft grasses as palatable food and for making their nests, with wood mice and common shrews taken as well. Vole populations, especially, vary cyclically, with a crash every three or four years. Their main predators, Barn Owls and Kestrels, tend to follow with similar cyclical abundance although they mitigate the worst effects by switching to alternative prey including mice, shrews, rats and birds. The large drop in the number of west Cheshire Barn Owl nests in 2006 was caused by the field vole cycle; they rebounded from that, with their breeding total in 2007 even higher than in 2005.

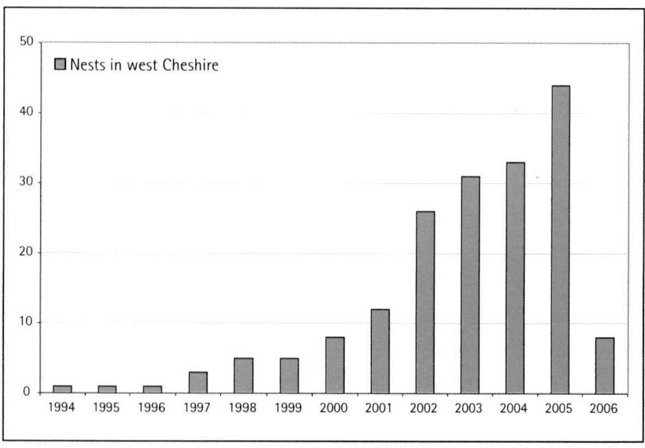

Barn Owl breeding numbers in west Cheshire.

Dedicated by the Cheshire Barn Owl Groups to the memory of George Bramall, founder of the Broxton Barn Owl Group and inspiration to the founding of other Barn Owl groups in Cheshire

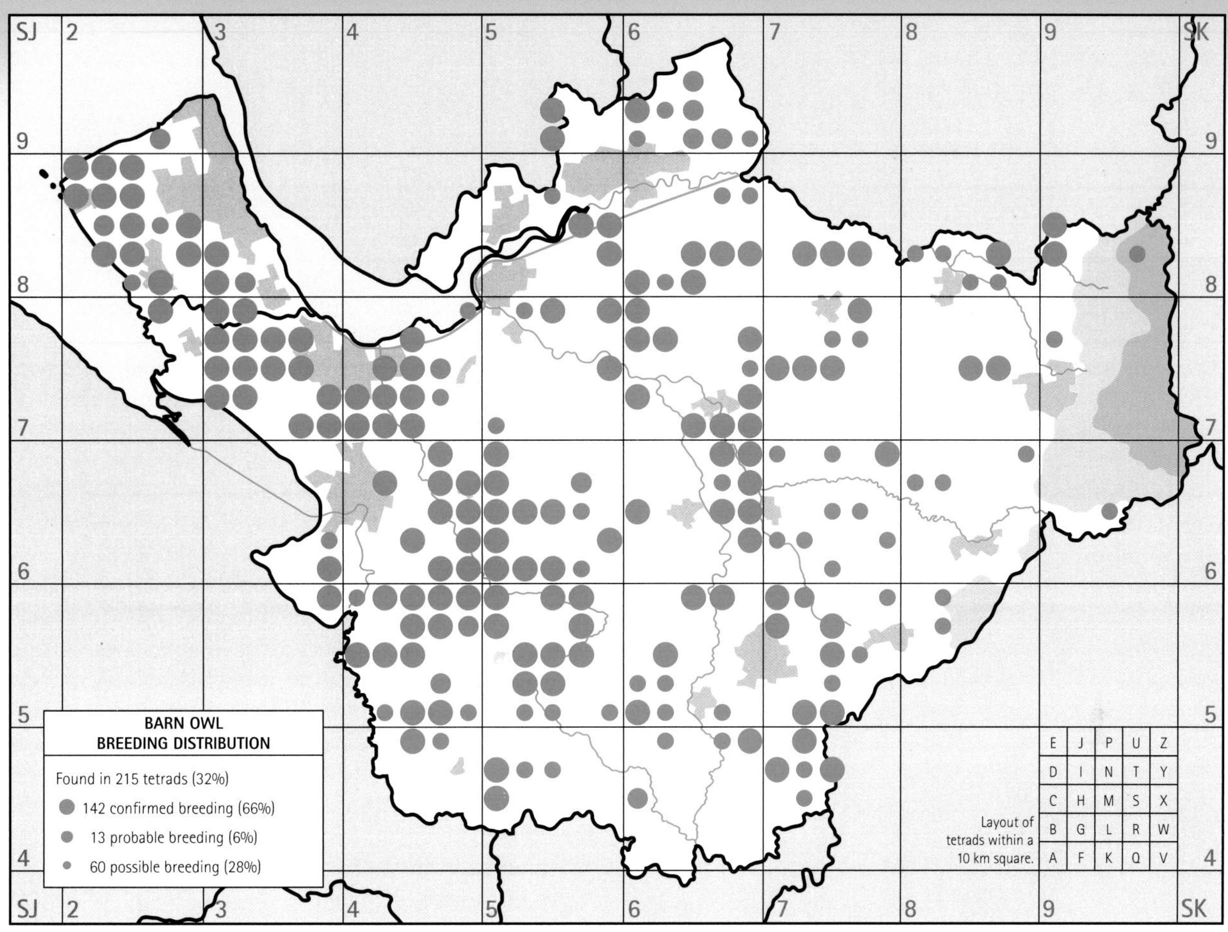

SJ
SK
2
3
4
5
6
7
8
9
BARN OWL
BREEDING DISTRIBUTION
Found in 215 tetrads (32%)
142 confirmed breeding (66%)
13 probable breeding (6%)
60 possible breeding (28%)
Layout of tetrads within a 10 km square.
E J P U Z
D I N T Y
C H M S X
B G L R W
A F K Q V

SJ
SK
2
3
4
5
6
7
8
9
BARN OWL
CHANGE IN BREEDING DISTRIBUTION
180 present during 2004–06, not during 1978–84 ('gain')
35 present during both Atlases
46 present during 1978–84, not during 2004–06 ('loss')
Layout of tetrads within a 10 km square.
E J P U Z
D I N T Y
C H M S X
B G L R W
A F K Q V

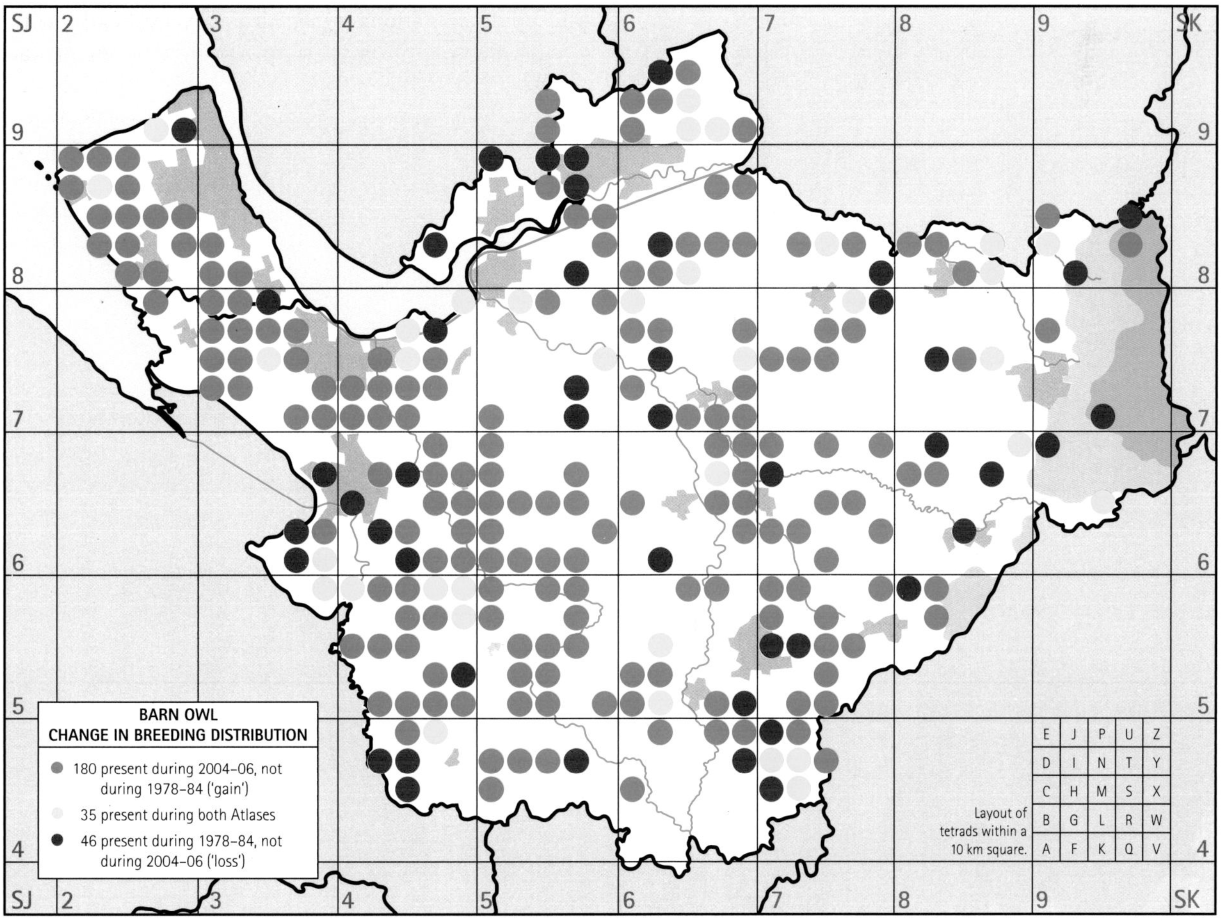

Adult Barn Owls rarely move far from their breeding areas, and the map shows that fieldwork for this Atlas substantially underrecorded them in winter. Apart from a few visits from members of the county's Barn Owl conservation groups, most birds were found by chance. They give few clues, seldom calling in winter, and not eliciting as much mobbing by small birds as other owls and raptors do (Bunn *et al.* 1982). Birds can appear to be secretive, mainly seen unexpectedly when a ghostly bird floats silently past, the paler males especially seeming to be almost white. Although mostly nocturnal, they may often be found active during daylight, especially after a period of wet weather, because they try to avoid hunting in the rain and have reduced success in high winds. Surveyors saw birds hunting near roads in several tetrads. At Davenham (SJ67Q) their presence was proven with a bird found freshly dead on the road, but, more happily, the records in SJ88R came courtesy of Wilmslow Police, whose officers several times saw a Barn Owl from their patrol cars.

SIMON BOOTH

The winter map shows birds present in just 105 tetrads, 39 of them in which Barn Owls were not recorded during the breeding season, but they were not reported from 149 tetrads that were occupied for breeding. They would be expected to have a wider distribution in winter than during the breeding season. Individual birds cover more ground, increasing their typical hunting range from 1–2 km to 4–5 km, and dispersing first-year birds wander about until they can find a territory and a mate for themselves. Ringed chicks typically seem to settle to breed about 5–6 km from their natal site.

Of the 133 habitat records submitted, 92 were farmland (69%), with more unimproved grassland (28) than improved grassland (26) indicating their preference for uncultivated land. Twenty-four were recorded as human sites, with seven semi-natural grassland. Barn Owls' diet, easily examined by analysis of their pellets, inevitably follows the seasonal availability of their prey. Field voles peak in late autumn, perfect for the inexperienced young owls attempting to fend for themselves. Wood mice numbers are at their highest during early winter. Shrews tend to reach maximum numbers in midsummer and rapidly die off in autumn, but they are especially susceptible to Barn Owls during winter and early spring because, eating live prey of insects and invertebrates, they have to remain active and presumably quite visible (Shawyer 1998). Whatever the species of mammal, Barn Owls preferentially go for the largest males in the prey population (Taylor 1994). As well as rain and strong winds, any periods of prolonged snow cover make hunting particularly difficult for them as their targets are hidden, but it is some years since Cheshire experienced such conditions. As a southern species here at the northern limit of its cosmopolitan distribution, Barn Owls can suffer badly in severe winter weather.

Most birds were found singly, with just eight records of more than one bird, several times attributed by observers to family parties. Although this map is for our defined winter period, some Barn Owls are still breeding late in the year and may have a second brood still in their nest; the chicks fledged from one Wirral nest-box in the last week of December in 2004.

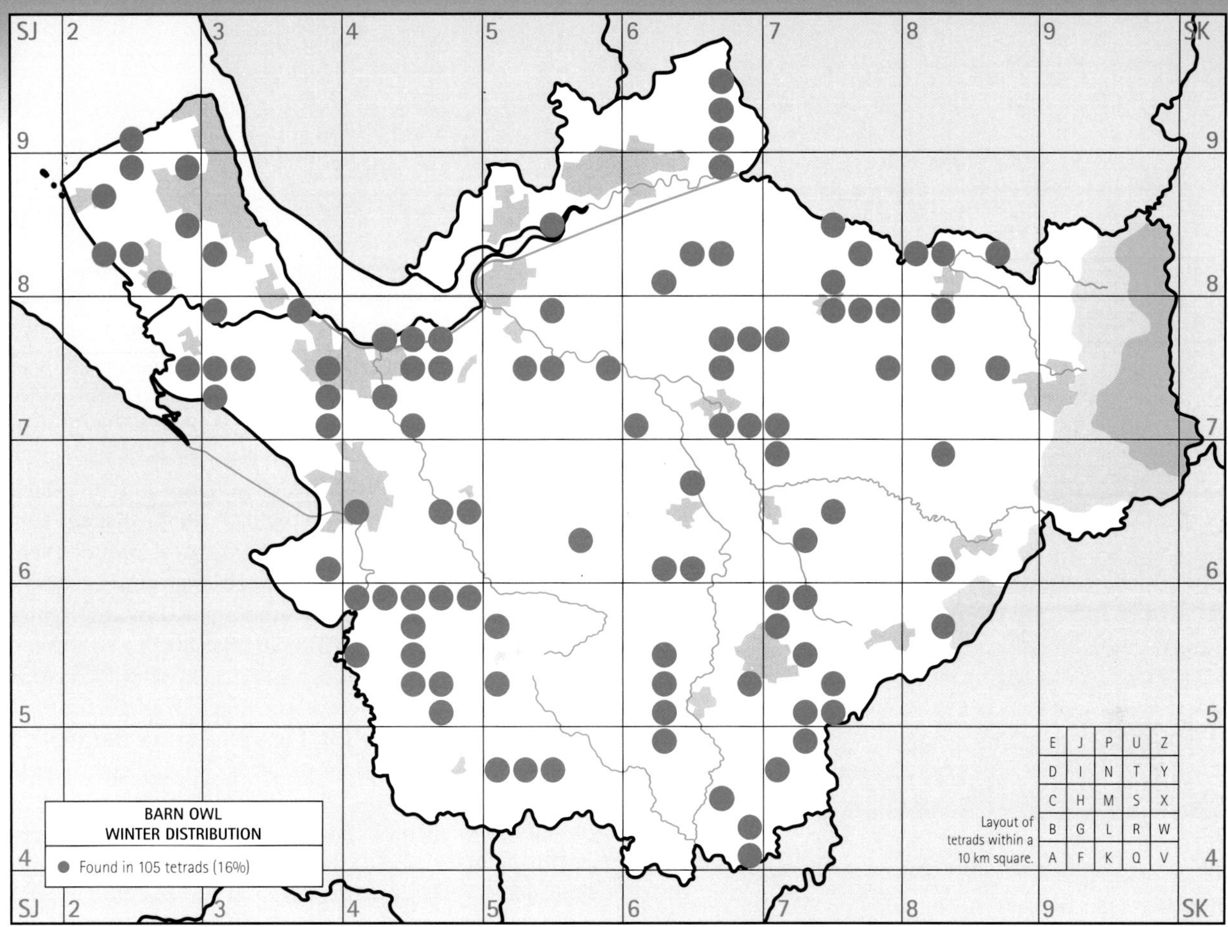
BARN OWL
WINTER DISTRIBUTION
Found in 105 tetrads (16%)
Layout of tetrads within a 10 km square.
E J P U Z
D I N T Y
C H M S X
B G L R W
A F K Q V
SJ
SK

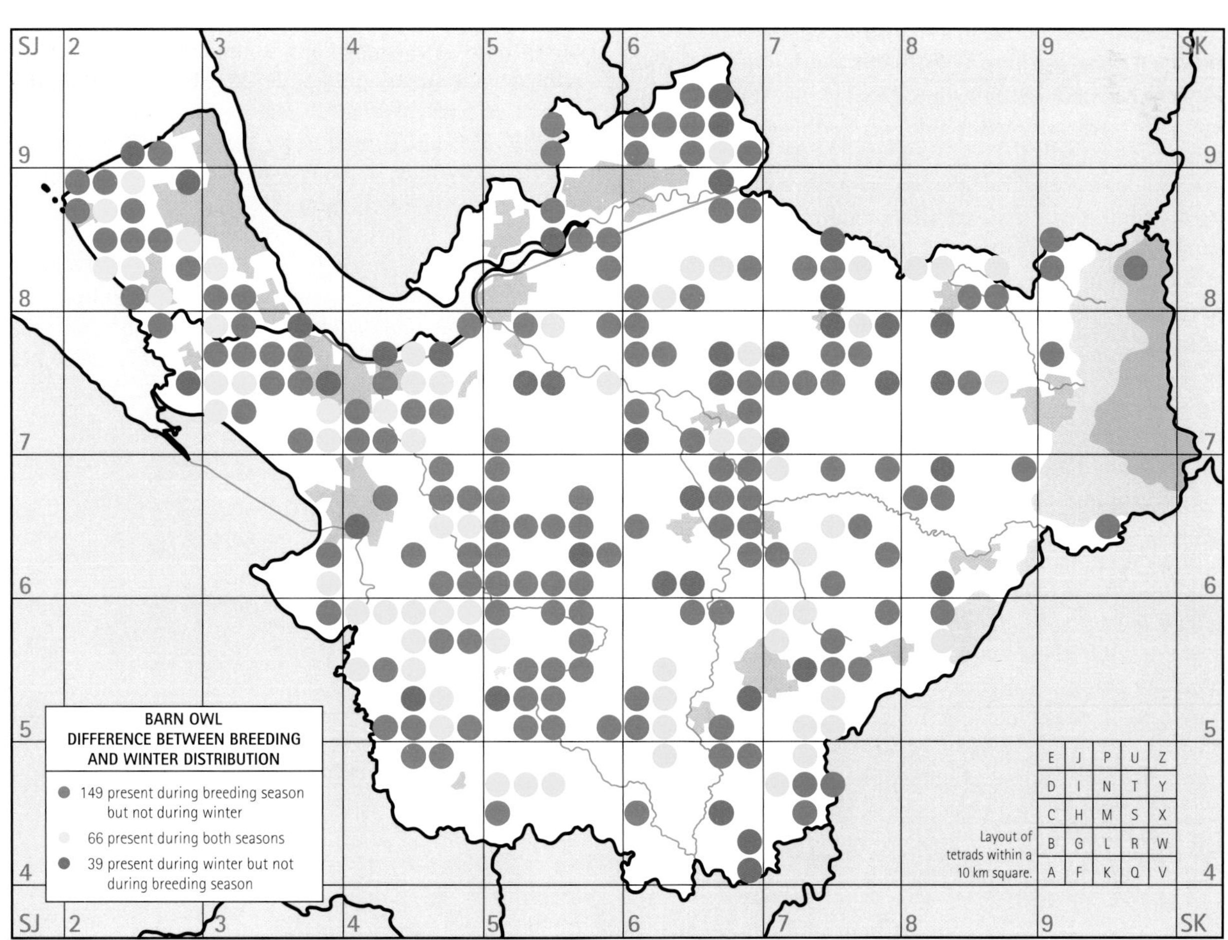
BARN OWL
DIFFERENCE BETWEEN BREEDING AND WINTER DISTRIBUTION
149 present during breeding season but not during winter
66 present during both seasons
39 present during winter but not during breeding season
Layout of tetrads within a 10 km square.
E J P U Z
D I N T Y
C H M S X
B G L R W
A F K Q V
SJ
SK

Little Owl

Athene noctua

STEVE ROUND

The Atlas map confirms that Little Owls' stronghold is the north-east of the county, although in the last twenty years they have disappeared from most of the tetrads on the fringe of Greater Manchester. The species has consolidated its position on the Wirral, in the open areas north of Warrington and in the hills east of Macclesfield. Altitude appears to be no bar to them, and Little Owls are found from the lowest to the highest points of the county. Their avoidance of the major urban areas shows up well on the map, with the largest gaps in its distribution in the east Wirral conurbation, Chester, Runcorn/Widnes/Warrington and Northwich. They are at the bottom of the pecking order amongst raptors, and particularly avoid areas with Tawny Owls if possible, although this is not obvious at the tetrad scale of the Atlas maps. Two observers reported interaction with Kestrels, in one instance the owls being evicted from their chosen nest hole.

The male Little Owl begins to mark its territory from the beginning of February, and their laying season spans mid-March to mid-June, with a mean start date of the end of April. Most clutches are three or four eggs, although from one to seven have been recorded. The female sits for about four weeks, incubation usually starting with the first egg and leading to asynchronous hatching. The owlets leave the nest hole after about 30–35 days and stay nearby for a week or more until they can fly reasonably strongly. Little Owls are normally most active around dawn and at dusk, and will also hunt by day, especially when chicks have to be fed. They tend to hunt in areas without high vegetation, either from conspicuous perches or on the ground. The main food is large insects, especially beetles, along with small rodents. They also take birds during the nesting season, most commonly Starlings, House Sparrows, Blackbirds and Song Thrushes. In Britain the Little Owl is the classic bird of parkland, scattered mature trees in an open landscape. Sixty per cent of the habitat codes submitted in this Atlas were category E (farmland), with 18% each in woodland and human sites.

Hedgerow trees are especially important for them, as are isolated trees in fields. Atlas fieldworkers reported five nests in holes in oak trees, one of them only 2 feet above ground. Other nests were in rabbit burrows and in barns, one of them noted by the farmer to be in potato boxes. Of the 98 tetrads with confirmed breeding, observers found nests in 53, with 36 records of family parties of recently fledged young and 9 of adults carrying food for their young, A further 19 tetrads furnished records of birds visiting a probable nest site (N).

The annual bird population monitoring surveys organized by the BTO show that the national population index for Little Owl peaked at the end of our *First Atlas*, in 1984, and has halved since then, although the results are regarded with caution and not sufficient to trigger listing as a species of conservation concern. The BTO estimate for the Little Owl breeding population of Cheshire and Wirral, based on the 2004–05 BBS data and a detection probability derived from the national dataset, is 550 birds (with wide confidence limits of 110–990). It is not known to how many pairs this figure would correspond. There is not thought to be a great sex difference in detectability (Newson *et al.* 2008), and only 32 of the 161 Atlas possible breeding records were S, suggesting that most birds were detected by sight rather than sound. Thus, the figure of 550 individuals might refer to some 300 pairs, an average of only one pair per tetrad in which they were recorded, and a big drop from the estimate in the *First Atlas* of 700–1,000 pairs. There is little certainty in these figures, however, and a dedicated survey of the county's Little Owls would be welcome.

Sponsored by AstraZeneca, Club AZ Natural History section

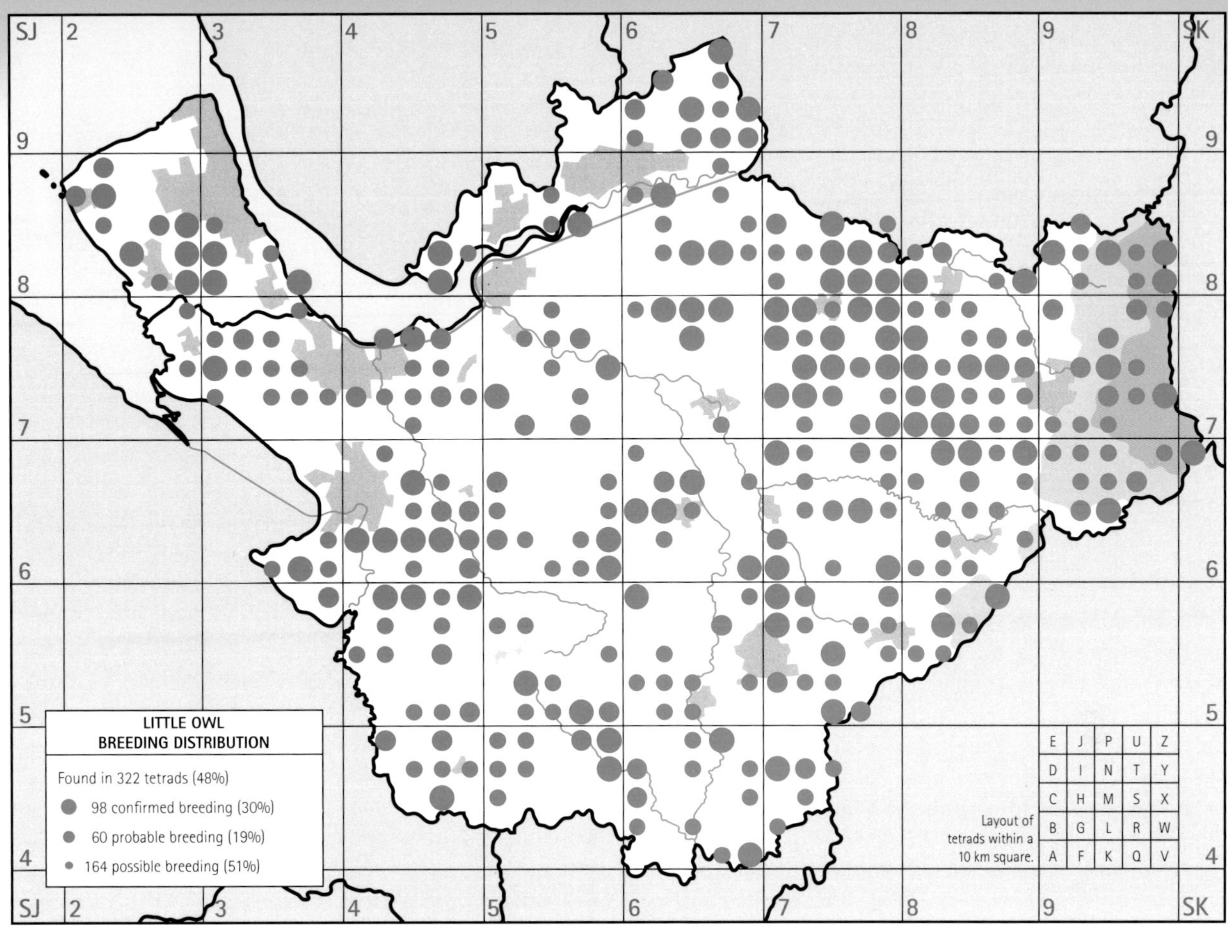
SJ 2 3 4 5 6 7 8 9 SK
9
8
7
6
5
4
LITTLE OWL
BREEDING DISTRIBUTION
Found in 322 tetrads (48%)
98 confirmed breeding (30%)
60 probable breeding (19%)
164 possible breeding (51%)
E J P U Z
D I N T Y
C H M S X
B G L R W
A F K Q V
Layout of tetrads within a 10 km square.

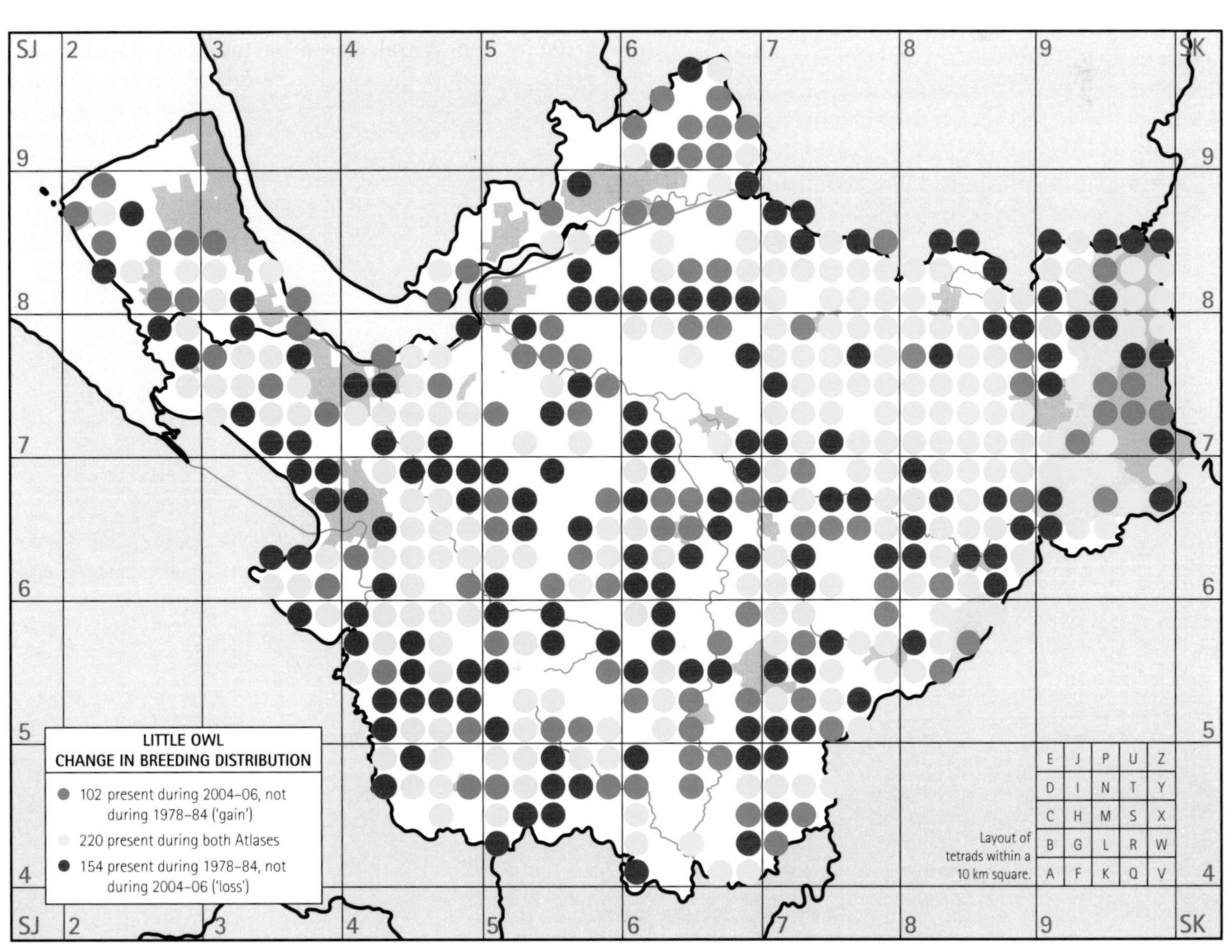
SJ 2 3 4 5 6 7 8 9 SK
9
8
7
6
5
4
LITTLE OWL
CHANGE IN BREEDING DISTRIBUTION
102 present during 2004–06, not during 1978–84 ('gain')
220 present during both Atlases
154 present during 1978–84, not during 2004–06 ('loss')
E J P U Z
D I N T Y
C H M S X
B G L R W
A F K Q V
Layout of tetrads within a 10 km square.

Little Owls were found in 208 tetrads in winter. In 54 of them the species had not been recorded in the breeding season, whilst there were 168 tetrads with breeding season presence where it was not found in winter. There was no consistent pattern to these seasonal changes, except perhaps for a withdrawal from the highest land. These bald statistics seem to counter the normal view that Little Owls are sedentary. Nationally, the median dispersal distances of ringed birds are 2 km for adults and 7 km for birds ringed as chicks (*Migration Atlas*). It could be that birds were underrecorded, but the *BTO Winter Atlas* regards them as being 'more easily located in winter than the other British owls', with birds often seen in daylight and calling frequently, especially in late winter.

The winter habitat codes show 72% of records on farmland, mostly grassland and hedgerows, with 15% human sites and 10% woodland. There were only four records each in scrub or semi-natural grassland, with none on salt-marsh. They depend on trees for winter shelter as much as for nesting, with birds less often occupying isolated buildings and cavities like rabbit burrows, perhaps accounting for their scarcity and absence in winter from many open areas including salt-marsh (*BTO Winter Atlas*). An inability to tolerate prolonged periods of ice and snow cover excludes them from many upland areas.

Fieldworkers submitted 140 counts of Little Owls in winter, mostly of one or two birds, but four records of three birds and three counts of four birds, in 2004/05 at Hockenhull Platts (SJ46S) and in 2005/06 near Burton (SJ37H) and near Tabley (SJ77J).

We have little indication of the Little Owl's former status in the county. Coward and Oldham (1900) treated it with the disdain that introduced species often induce. Boyd (1951) noted their rapid colonization of mid-Cheshire from about 1926, but did not comment on their winter distribution, and Bell (1962) added nothing beyond quoting some 50-year-old records.

SIMON BOOTH

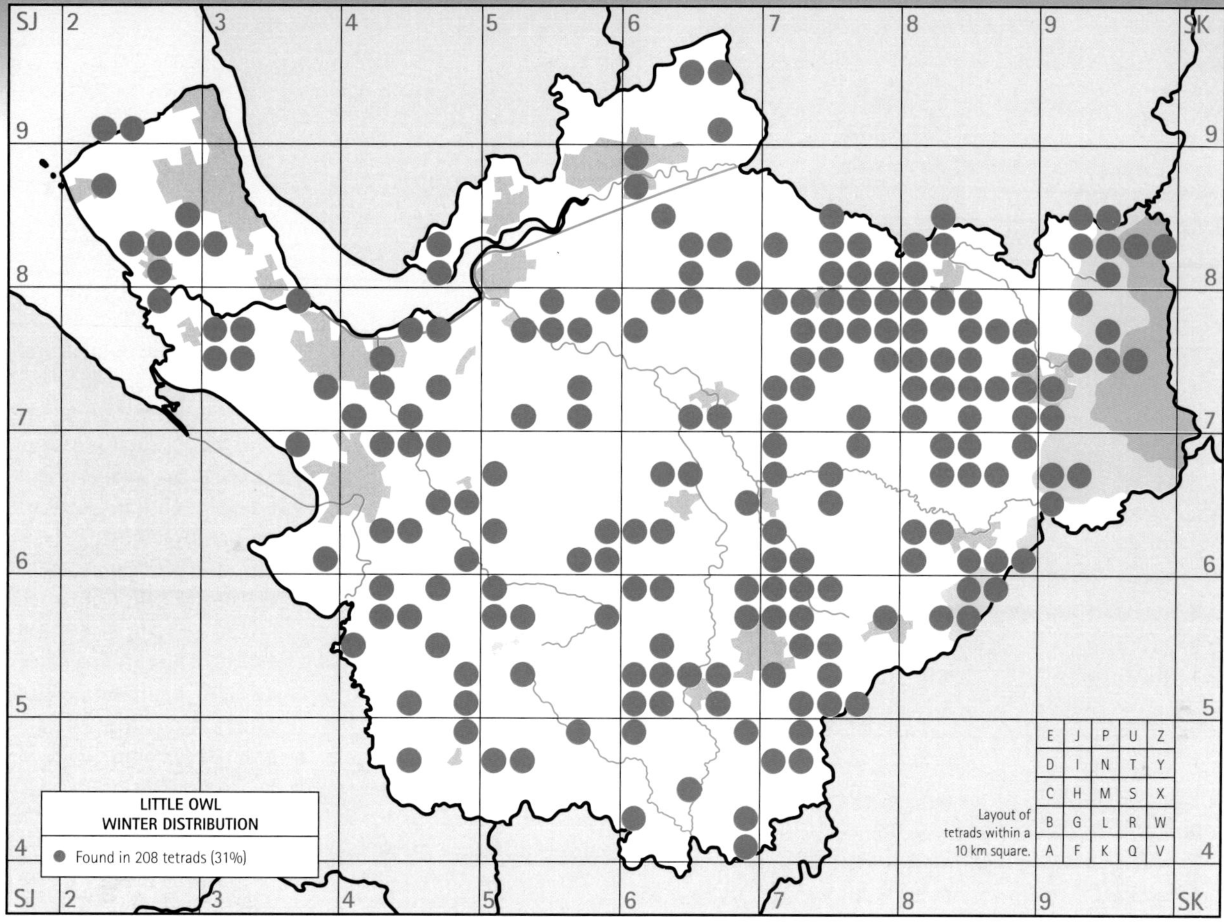
LITTLE OWL
WINTER DISTRIBUTION
Found in 208 tetrads (31%)
Layout of tetrads within a 10 km square.
E J P U Z
D I N T Y
C H M S X
B G L R W
A F K Q V
SJ
SK

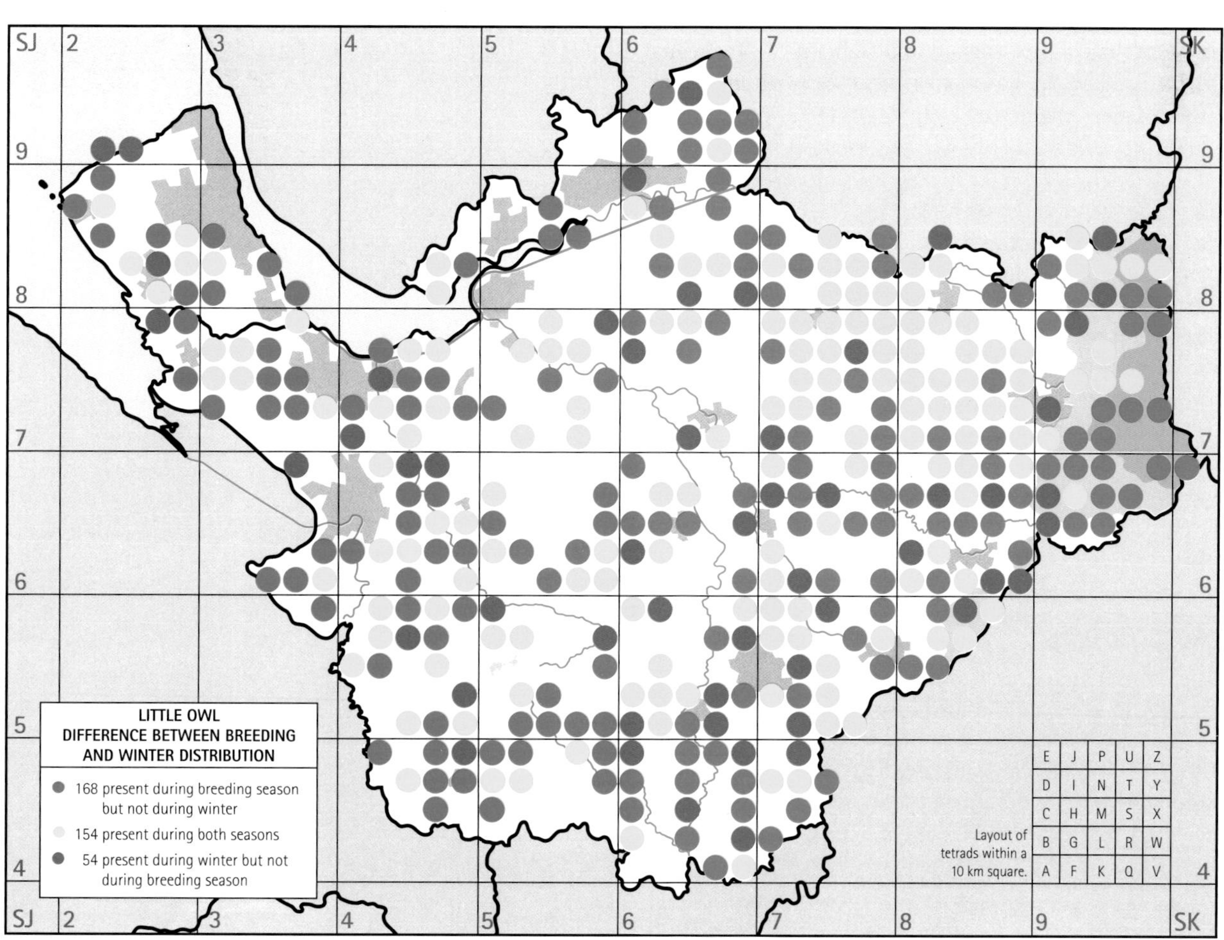
LITTLE OWL
DIFFERENCE BETWEEN BREEDING AND WINTER DISTRIBUTION
168 present during breeding season but not during winter
154 present during both seasons
54 present during winter but not during breeding season
Layout of tetrads within a 10 km square.
E J P U Z
D I N T Y
C H M S X
B G L R W
A F K Q V
SJ
SK

Tawny Owl

Strix aluco

ANDY HARMER

This is *the* woodland owl, and Tawny Owl distribution shows a strong correlation with woodland cover. Two-thirds of the habitat codes submitted were category A (woodland), all but a handful of them A1 (broad-leaved) or A3 (mixed). Provided that there are sufficient trees, even large gardens are occupied in some areas, and in 53 tetrads, habitat codes for human sites were recorded, 5 urban, 25 suburban and 23 rural. The Atlas map shows that Tawny Owls have significantly contracted in range since our *First Atlas*, mainly retreating into their core wooded areas.

Tawny Owls hunt mostly by waiting on a perch then pouncing when they hear some movement below. Their main prey is small mammals, especially wood mice and bank voles, with shrews and moles. Some individuals are adept at catching frogs, and others take a surprisingly high proportion of earthworms and beetles, especially when they have hungry chicks to feed. Birds, of any size from Jay to Wren, may comprise 10% of their diet, with urban and suburban owls taking far more birds than rural ones.

They nest in a hole or ledge, or an old nest of a corvid or raptor, or a squirrel's drey. Nest-boxes are also used, and are perhaps especially good for them, because Tawny Owls often seem to choose a natural site with a shallow entrance from which overadventurous half-grown chicks can fall out of the nest, often with fatal consequences unless the bird can climb back high enough to be safe from predators.

The typical timing is for Tawny Owls to lay their first egg around the third week of March, with chicks hatching 30 days later and fledging around the end of May. Odd pairs may nest much earlier than that, however, and chicks in March are reported every year. The average brood size is two chicks. Two-thirds of the 95 confirmed breeding records came from observers finding recently fledged chicks, often alerted to them by their plaintive hunger calls.

Although all nocturnal species are liable to be underrecorded, the sound of its loud hooting is noticeable and carries a long way. A number of records were passed on to surveyors by interested landowners. Their 'tu-whit, to-whoo' call is unmistakeable, except that many people wrongly think that one sex gives one call and one the other. Most observers initially located Tawny Owls by sound, but some had their attention drawn by a bout of persistent mobbing by small birds who found an owl's daytime roost.

Tawny Owl is poorly covered by the national monitoring schemes, but they suggest a shallow decline, perhaps a 25% drop between our two Atlas periods. Breeding was confirmed in 100 tetrads and probable in a further 34, and many of the 180 tetrads with possible breeding must hold at least one pair of this underrecorded species. Even if there is only one pair per tetrad, and allowing for some double-counting of their far-carrying calls, the county total must be at least 250 pairs. This would be just half of the figure in the *First Atlas* of 550 pairs.

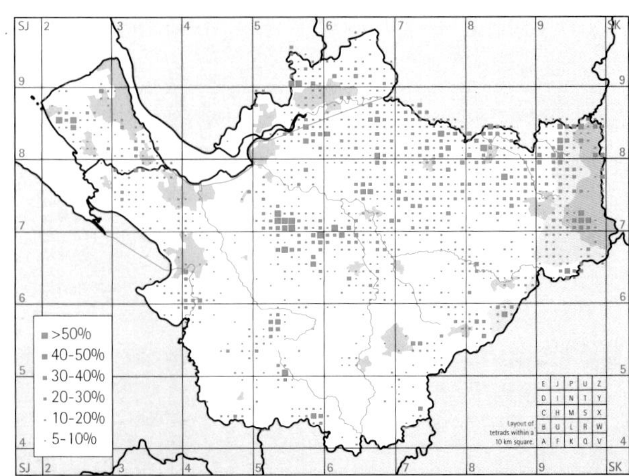

Woodland land cover.

Sponsored by John Patterson

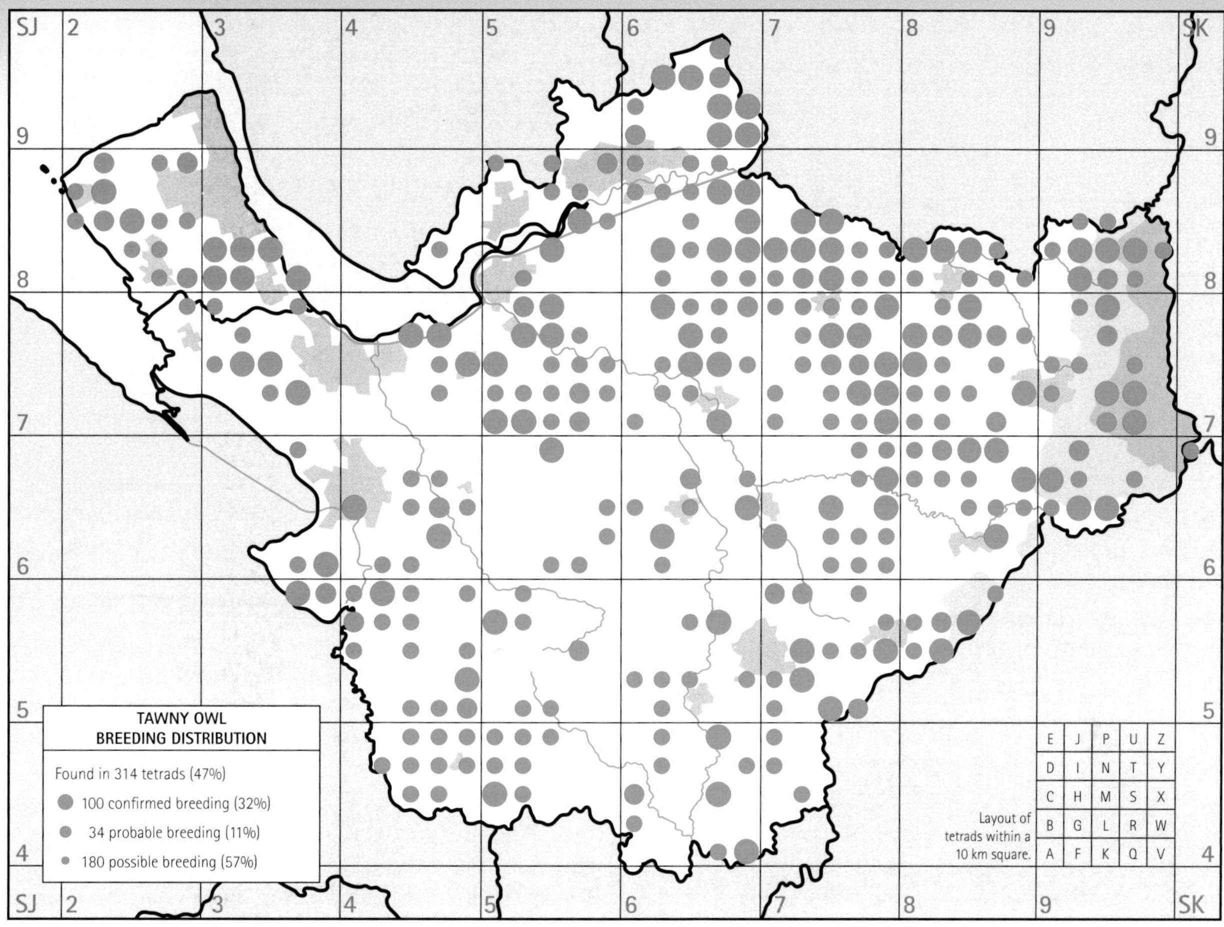

TAWNY OWL
BREEDING DISTRIBUTION
Found in 314 tetrads (47%)
100 confirmed breeding (32%)
34 probable breeding (11%)
180 possible breeding (57%)
Layout of tetrads within a 10 km square.
E J P U Z
D I N T Y
C H M S X
B G L R W
A F K Q V
SJ
SK

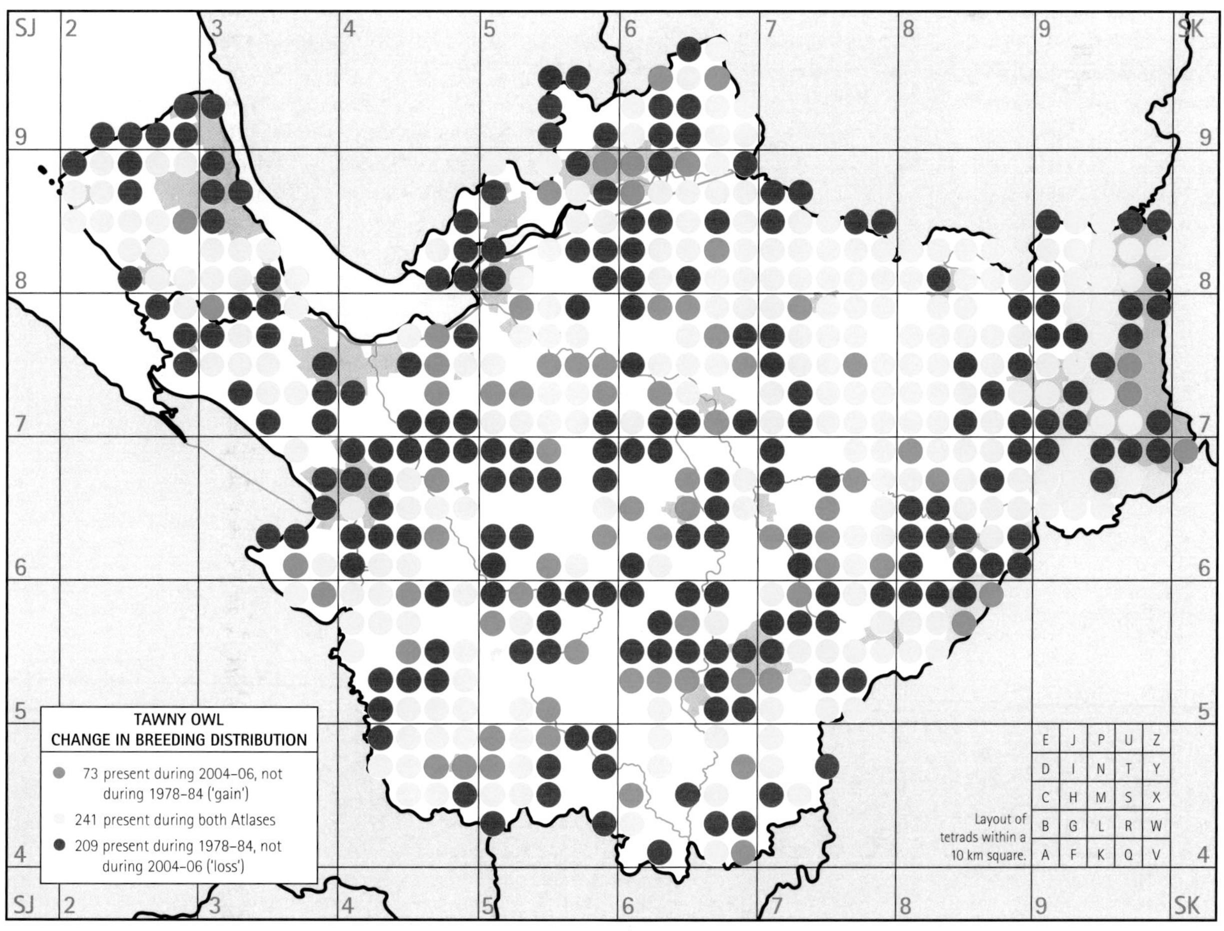

TAWNY OWL
CHANGE IN BREEDING DISTRIBUTION
73 present during 2004–06, not during 1978–84 ('gain')
241 present during both Atlases
209 present during 1978–84, not during 2004–06 ('loss')
Layout of tetrads within a 10 km square.
E J P U Z
D I N T Y
C H M S X
B G L R W
A F K Q V
SJ
SK

Tawny Owls were found in winter in 278 tetrads, but the distribution is puzzling, comprising 193 tetrads with breeding season and winter records, 85 tetrads with a winter record but no breeding season presence, and 111 in the breeding season where it was not found in winter. They are long-lived birds and, after their first autumn, sedentary: an adult male, at least three years old when ringed at Norton Priory, Runcorn (SJ58L) in December 1996 was retrapped in the same place five years later, and a first-year male ringed at Woolston (SJ68P) in November 1990 was retrapped there in May 1996. Some of the 'extra' winter tetrad records may be first-year birds, prospecting for territories after they have been noisily driven out from their parents' territory, usually by October or November: these inexperienced birds may well occupy unusual areas that are unsuitable for breeding, although they will try to breed at one year of age if they can attract a mate.

Nevertheless, the difference between winter and breeding distribution is a surprising result for a species that is normally reputed to be one of the most sedentary of all birds, with the adult birds normally remaining in their territories all their lives, all year round. This discrepancy was obvious even from the first year's records, and observers' attention was drawn to it in the December 2005 Atlas newsletter, with the exhortation to 'please try to get out and visit your tetrad, listening for owls, during this winter, especially if they bred in the area: it only needs a few minutes on a clear night, and a bit of luck, to hear one, and you might pick up some other species as well. And, in those tetrads where the species was found in winter but not in the breeding season, they are likely to be breeding somewhere close, so please try to find where!' After a further two years of fieldwork, however, the stark seasonal differences persist and it remains an open question whether this is a real feature of the species' biology or a recording effect of observer bias.

All but eight of the submitted counts were of one or two birds, with five records of three and three counts of four birds, near Warmingham (SJ76B) in winter 2004/05 and 2005/06, and near Lower Peover (SJ77M) in the first winter. The habitat codes show most records from woodland (58%), but surprisingly high proportions in farmland (17%), with even more in human sites than during the breeding season (68 records, 22% of the total).

Adult Tawny Owls start reinforcing their territory at the beginning of winter, calling frequently. In courtship feeding, from December to February, the male brings extra food to his much larger mate to cement the pair-bond and to build up her condition for an early start to breeding. In some ways, winter might be an easier season for the species, with long nights for their feeding, although the reduced numbers of some prey species causes some owls to shift their diet to feed more on birds, and many roosts of thrushes and finches suffer frequent attention from a Tawny Owl or two.

In autumn 2005 the BTO organized a national survey of Tawny Owls, observers revisiting tetrads covered in the earlier 1989 survey. Publication of the results is awaited.

BEN HALL

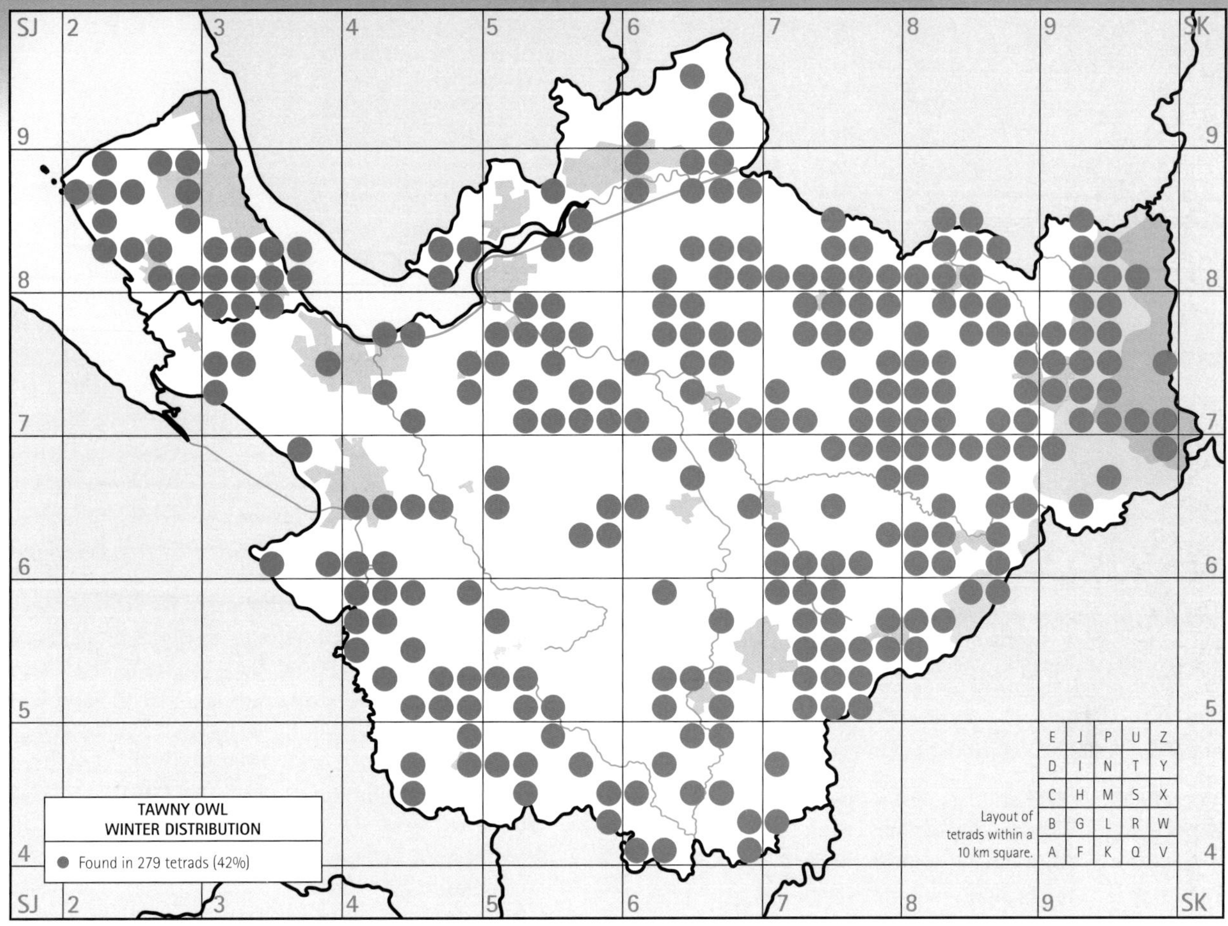

TAWNY OWL
WINTER DISTRIBUTION
Found in 279 tetrads (42%)
Layout of tetrads within a 10 km square.
E J P U Z
D I N T Y
C H M S X
B G L R W
A F K Q V
SJ 2 3 4 5 6 7 8 9 SK

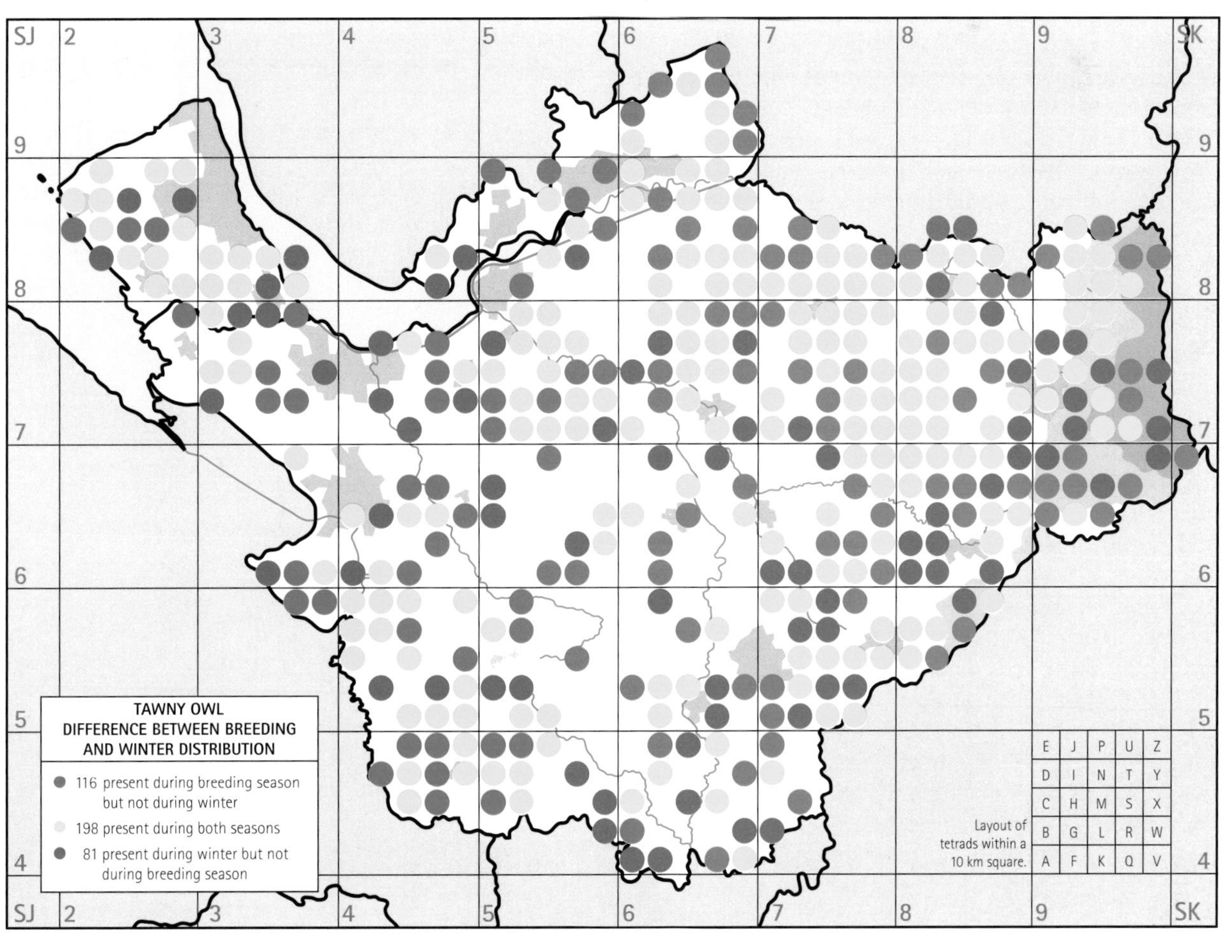

TAWNY OWL
DIFFERENCE BETWEEN BREEDING AND WINTER DISTRIBUTION
116 present during breeding season but not during winter
198 present during both seasons
81 present during winter but not during breeding season
Layout of tetrads within a 10 km square.
E J P U Z
D I N T Y
C H M S X
B G L R W
A F K Q V
SJ 2 3 4 5 6 7 8 9 SK

Long-eared Owl

Asio otus

PETER SMITH

This survey confirmed that the Mersey valley is the only part of the county where this elusive species can regularly be found in the breeding season. They favour dense scrub and young woodland for nesting, with adjacent areas of rough grassland in which to feed. 'Cheshire is blessed with few suitable habitats and most owls occur far away from natural sites. Instead, Long-eared Owls are found on lands largely created inadvertently by man, by-products of various industries and derelict areas. Many of these habitats, some of which have become rich in small mammals, are often temporary, awaiting further development—landfill, housing, mineral extraction, business parks and so on, to name a few' (Lees 1994).

Long-eared Owls hunt almost exclusively at night, with their main method being to quarter an area, flying silently to and fro at a height of about a metre, and dropping onto their prey. British studies have found small mammals to make up most of the diet, headed by field vole, typically half of all items consumed, followed by wood mouse, bank vole, common shrew, brown rat, pygmy shrew and water vole. Odd birds take rabbit, grey squirrel, house mouse and pipistrelle bat. They also take roosting birds, deliberately beating the branches of a bush to disturb their prey; owls often work in pairs using this technique (Scott 1997). House Sparrows are reported to be the bird by far the most commonly taken, but the list extends to at least 50 species.

It is quite difficult to prove the presence of Long-eared Owls and the species has probably been under-recorded. Birds are strictly nocturnal, and their soft, mournful call does not carry far and is mostly given early in the year, typically during February. However, they can be faithful to an area so, once found, it is straightforward to check on them each year. By far the easiest way of finding them, and of proving breeding, is to hear the creaking calls of the young, every few minutes all night long.

Wherever they occur, Long-eared Owls are widespread but thinly distributed, as shown by the figures for occupation of adjacent counties in breeding Atlases. They were found in nine out of 670 tetrads (1.3%) in this survey, 20 out of 870 tetrads (2.3%) in Shropshire (1985–90), 38 out of 931 (4.1%) in Lancashire and North Merseyside (1997–2000) and 12 out of 1844 (0.6%) in Cumbria (1997–2001).

All texts on the species emphasize its vulnerability to competition, even extending to direct attack, by Tawny Owls, and Long-eared Owls flourish in Ireland and the Isle of Man where Tawnies are absent. Now that Tawny Owls have declined in Cheshire, there is potential scope for expansion of Long-eared Owls, if the habitat is right. A century ago, in Coward's day (1910), this was the commonest owl 'in the wooded parts of the Hill Country'.

Lees (1994) noted substantial year-to-year fluctuations in population and estimated a Cheshire total of 11–20 pairs; he wrote that 'Long-eared Owls breed in six of Cheshire's 37 10 km squares and have, in the past, occurred in another five or six at which breeding remains unconfirmed'. This is higher than the distribution shown by this Atlas but, optimistically allowing for an element of underrecording and some undetected pairs, the present total might just be into double figures.

Long-eared Owls were confirmed breeding in 4 tetrads during our *First Atlas*, but the species' distribution was not mapped, so no 'change' map is presented here.

Sponsored by Steve Binney

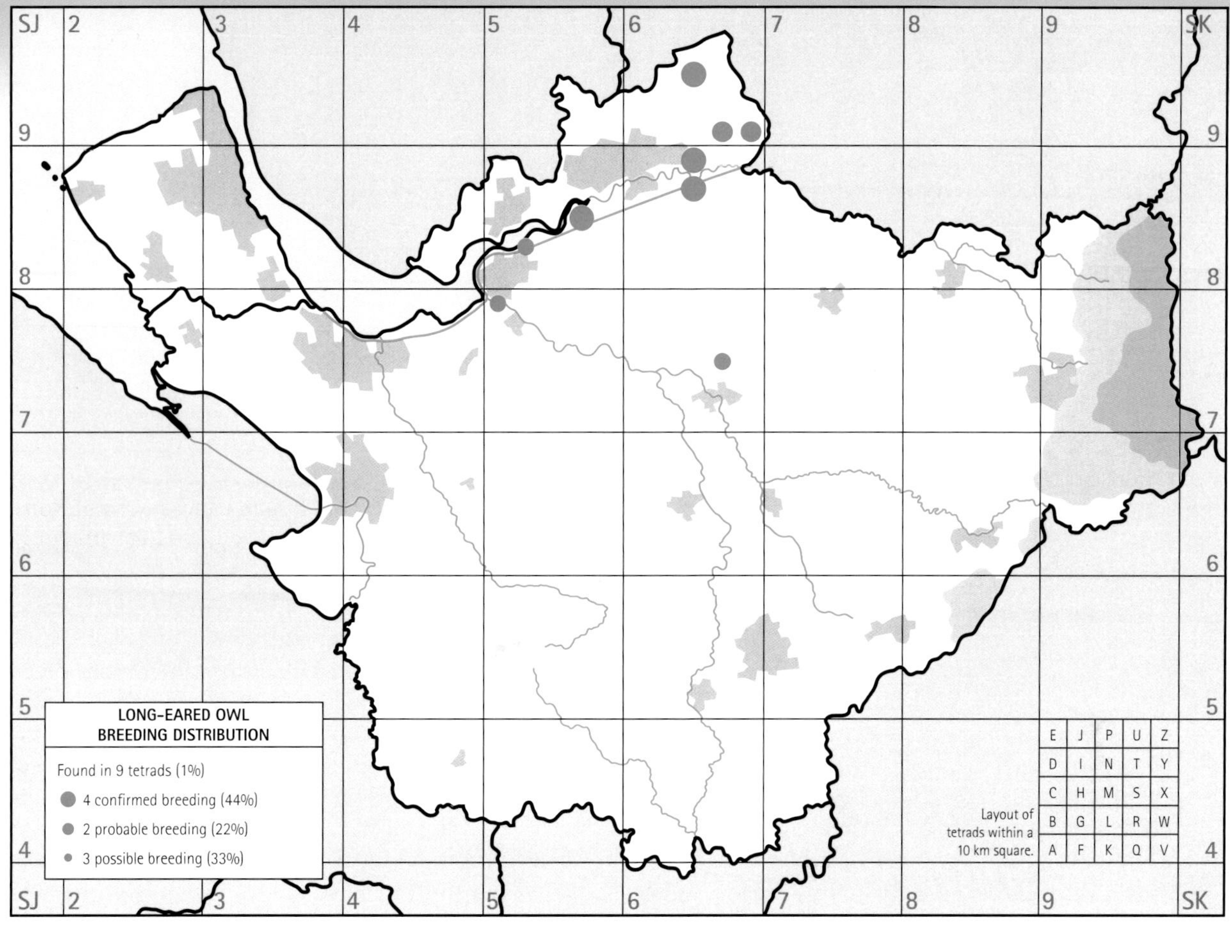
LONG-EARED OWL
BREEDING DISTRIBUTION
Found in 9 tetrads (1%)
4 confirmed breeding (44%)
2 probable breeding (22%)
3 possible breeding (33%)
Layout of tetrads within a 10 km square.
E J P U Z
D I N T Y
C H M S X
B G L R W
A F K Q V
SJ
SK
2
3
4
5
6
7
8
9

Adult Long-eared Owls do not move far from their breeding territory all year round, but immature birds will wander. Lees (1994) reported that dispersal and movements were greatly aided by water-courses where owls can hunt along continuous river banks rich with small mammals, then arrive at suitable overwintering grounds or at potential breeding sites.

It seems surprising that only two of the tetrads with owls present in the breeding season also had a winter record, especially as adults are probably resident and recommence breeding activity during our winter period. They have presumably been overlooked in some sites, and they certainly do little to draw attention to themselves in winter apart from their spectacular gathering at communal daytime roosts. Their feeding behaviour changes little from the breeding season, and Long-eared Owls are seldom seen hunting by day except in very hard weather. They take a similar range of prey items as in the breeding season, but tend to eat a higher proportion of birds, especially wintering thrushes and finches, probably mostly caught at their roosts.

Out of the eight tetrads on the winter map, seven did not have Long-eared Owls reported in the breeding season, and some of these are likely to have been occupied by continental birds. The British wintering population is considerably augmented by immigrants from Fennoscandia, the numbers varying from year to year according to small mammal abundance and the severity of winter weather. Three birds roosted together at Brimstage (SJ38B) in 2004/05, and two birds were at Neumann's Flash (SJ67S) in 2006/07, but the other records were all of singles.

There is little information on wintering Long-eared Owls in the writings of the earlier Cheshire ornithologists, and the annual county bird reports have contained few records from the mid-1980s until recently. Wintering birds are found annually, in variable numbers, from sites along the Mersey valley from Frodsham Marsh to Woolston/Risley. Odd birds are reported sporadically from scattered sites elsewhere in the county, but the only other location with a claim to regular occurrence is Neumann's Flash, with sightings in most of the last 10 winters and, in 1999/2000, a roost of up to nine birds.

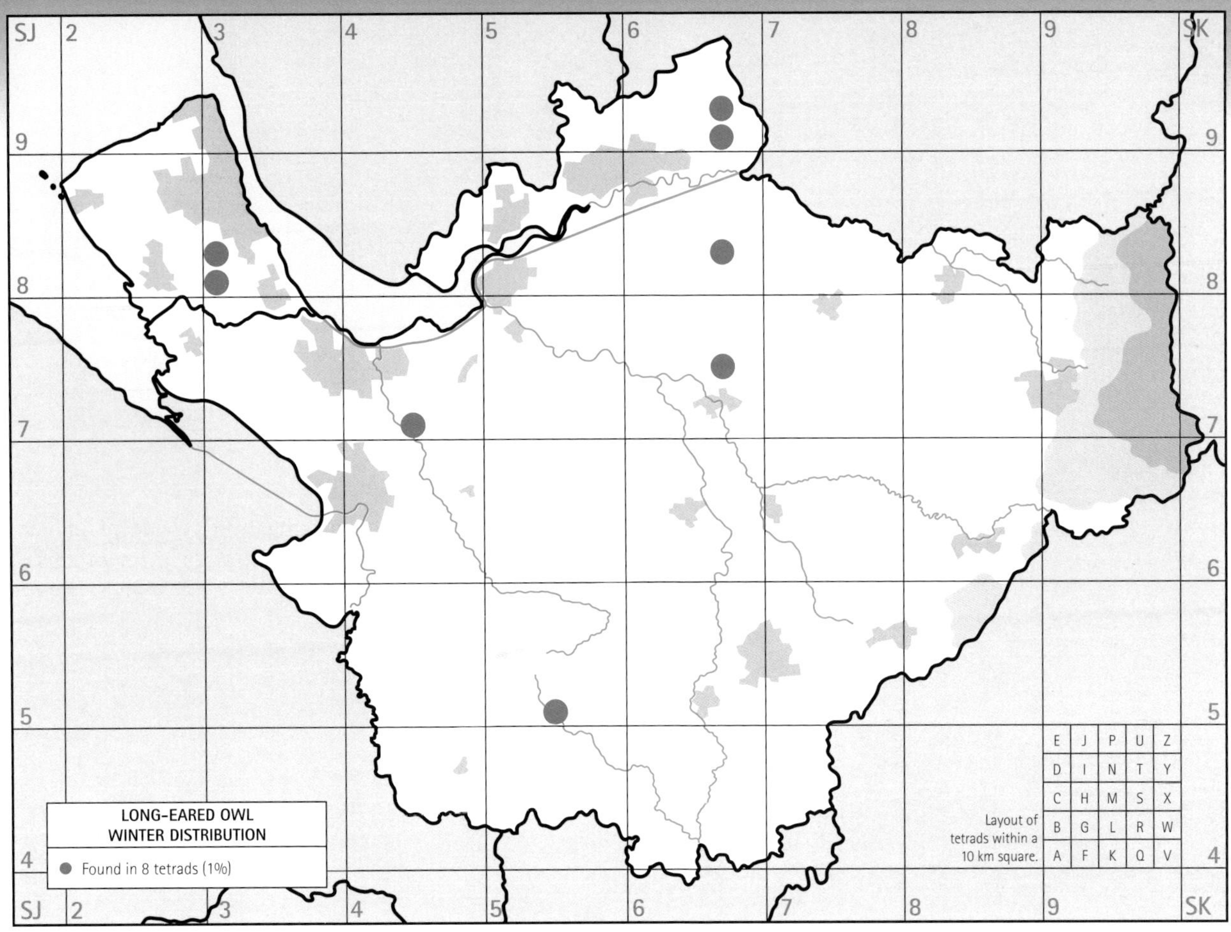
LONG-EARED OWL
WINTER DISTRIBUTION
Found in 8 tetrads (1%)
Layout of tetrads within a 10 km square.
E J P U Z
D I N T Y
C H M S X
B G L R W
A F K Q V
SJ
SK

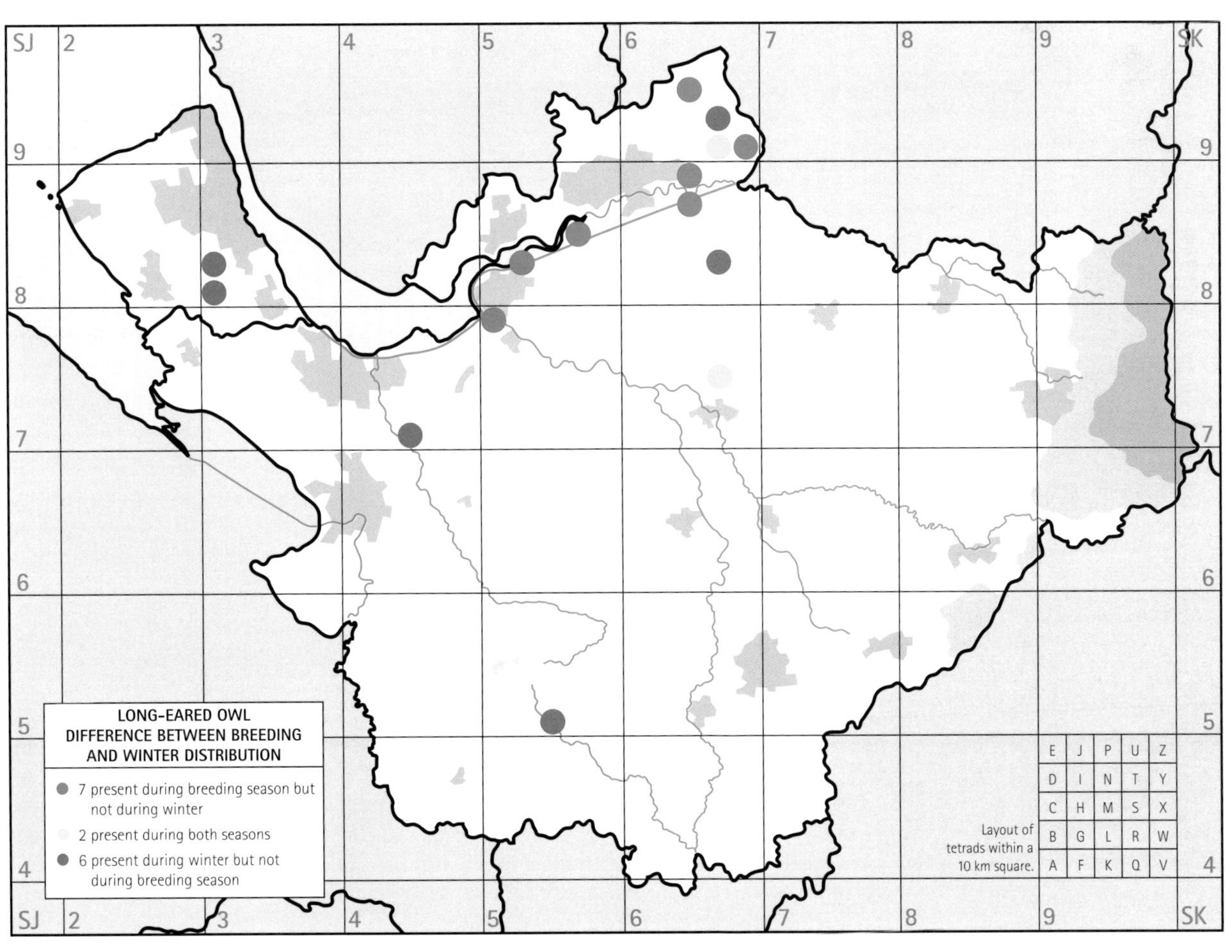
LONG-EARED OWL
DIFFERENCE BETWEEN BREEDING AND WINTER DISTRIBUTION
7 present during breeding season but not during winter
2 present during both seasons
6 present during winter but not during breeding season
Layout of tetrads within a 10 km square.
E J P U Z
D I N T Y
C H M S X
B G L R W
A F K Q V
SJ
SK

Short-eared Owl

Asio flammeus

RICHARD STEEL

This is a bird of two habitats, the upland moorlands and the estuarine edge: Short-eared Owls may be found prospecting for breeding sites around the highest and the lowest points of the county, but nowhere in between. They probably bred in the Frodsham Marsh area for two or three years in the mid-1970s, with a nest found in 1975, and 'a pair is reported to have bred in the county' according to the 1989 annual bird report, but with no detail. Odd sightings of single birds in the breeding season were recorded on the eastern moors in 1990–93, 1996, 1998 and from 2003 onwards. During this Atlas period, pairs were seen in two of the moorland tetrads, with breeding proven in one of them. Surveys of the South Pennine Moors SPA showed a 50% increase between 1990 and 2004–05 in the breeding population of Short-eared Owls, and it seems that the Cheshire moorland fringe has shared in this rise in their fortunes (Eaton *et al.* 2007).

Short-eared Owls nest in open country, in moorland, marsh and bogs, and in young conifer plantations; in recent years they have also been seen prospecting in set-aside fields, and have been known to breed in them elsewhere in England. The adults hunt by day, especially in the afternoons, and at night, quartering the ground with their long winged flight. In the breeding season, they depend especially on field voles which comprise more than 80% of their food items, with the remainder being mice, shrews and birds.

Much of their lives is determined by the abundance of field voles, which varies on a cycle of three or four years. Short-eared Owls can have a protracted breeding season, some birds laying eggs in March while others linger late in wintering areas, even until mid-May in some years. This is the only Palearctic owl that builds a nest, making a scrape lined with dead grasses. They can lay four to nine eggs or more, with most in 'vole years', but clutch size varies with latitude, decreasing at more southerly sites, and figures from Cheshire are unknown. Their ground nests are vulnerable to predation, especially by foxes and crows, and chicks scatter from the nest 12–17 days after hatching to hide in the undergrowth, but cannot fly until 25 days or older.

Sponsored by Dr J.D. Atkinson

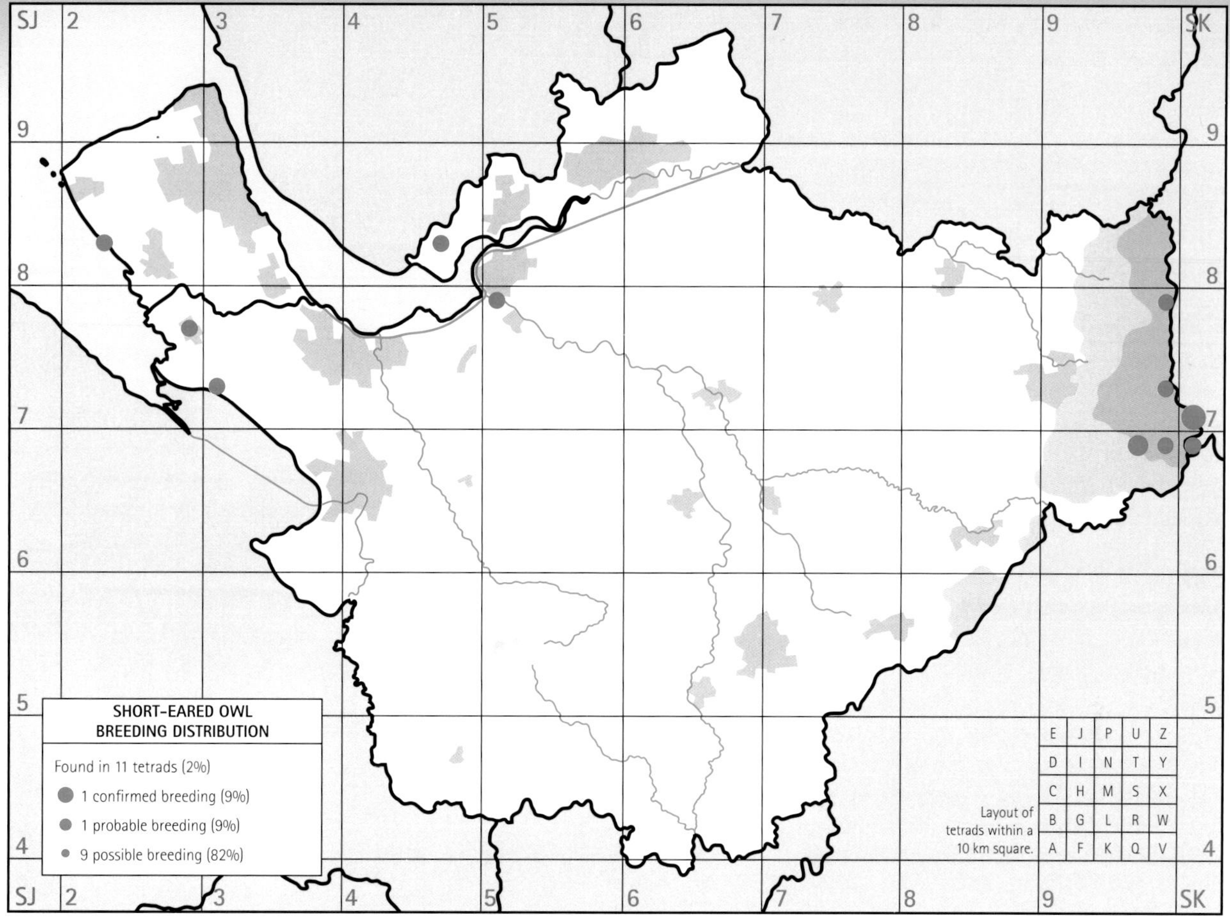
SHORT-EARED OWL
BREEDING DISTRIBUTION
Found in 11 tetrads (2%)
1 confirmed breeding (9%)
1 probable breeding (9%)
9 possible breeding (82%)
Layout of tetrads within a 10 km square.
E J P U Z
D I N T Y
C H M S X
B G L R W
A F K Q V
SJ
SK
2
3
4
5
6
7
8
9

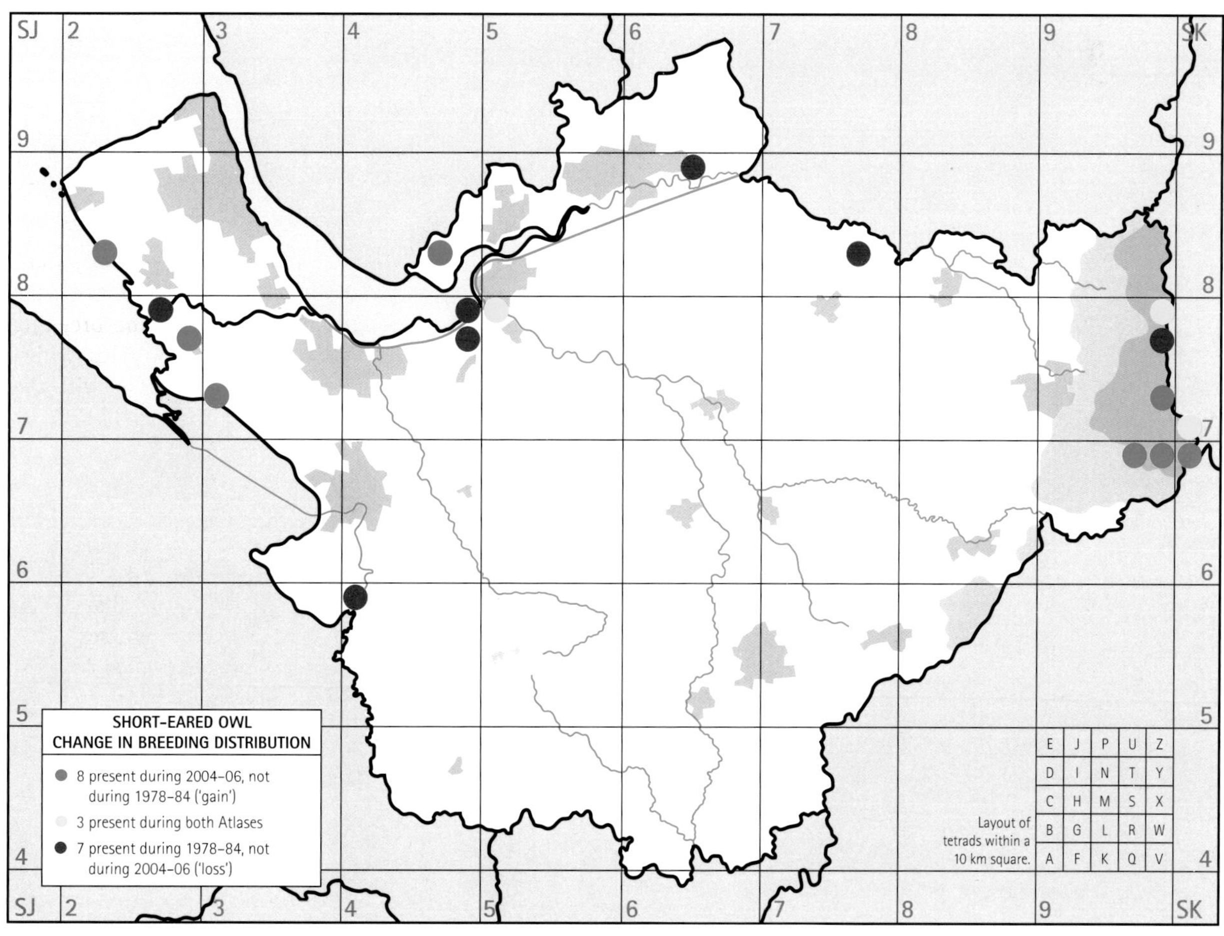
SHORT-EARED OWL
CHANGE IN BREEDING DISTRIBUTION
8 present during 2004–06, not during 1978–84 ('gain')
3 present during both Atlases
7 present during 1978–84, not during 2004–06 ('loss')
Layout of tetrads within a 10 km square.
E J P U Z
D I N T Y
C H M S X
B G L R W
A F K Q V
SJ
SK
2
3
4
5
6
7
8
9

Both of the *Asio* owls undertake long-distance migration, with long sea crossings no barrier to them. Our wintering population is likely to comprise birds from northern England and Scotland, and immigrants from Fennoscandia (*Migration Atlas*). Young birds disperse in all directions, but many recoveries suggest a movement away from upland moors and hills to coastal localities. The Atlas map shows that most of the winter records are along the edges of our estuaries, with a scattering of tetrads visited elsewhere in lowland Cheshire. Apart from one bird making an early return to the eastern hills, their breeding season sites are vacated. The winter habitat codes reinforce the impression of a bird of rough open land. Of the 34 records, 13 are semi-natural grassland and marsh (8 of them salt-marsh), 3 bog, 12 farmland (7 of them unimproved grassland) and 5 estuarine.

In winter, Short-eared Owls take more birds than in the breeding season, also preying on wood mice and brown rats as well as the staple fare of field voles. In some years, large numbers reach Britain following the periodic crashes in abundance of small rodents, especially voles, but there is no evidence that numbers in Cheshire and Wirral fluctuate greatly. Totals of 24, 23 and 21 birds were recorded for the three winters of this Atlas period, similar figures to most winters for the last decade. Where several birds are present, they roost communally on the ground, possibly sharing a site with Hen Harriers. Two areas held most of the birds. Counts from the Dee salt-marsh included five on Heswall Shore (SJ28K) in 2005/06 and nine on Gayton Sands (SJ27U) in 2006/07. Frodsham Marsh (SJ47Y/SJ57E) held groups of four, four and three in the three winters.

Although there is little indication of numbers and their true status before the onset of modern recording, wintering Short-eared Owls might have been more numerous and widespread a century ago, when Coward and Oldham (1900) wrote that 'this well-known autumn visitor is found in open situations in Cheshire, from the coast sandhills to the moors of the East, and is often flushed by shooting parties from its resting place amongst the turnips or in the heather'. Bell's summary in 1962 sounds little different from today: 'the bird is now only an autumn to spring visitor and confined almost entirely to the Mersey marshes around Frodsham, and in West Wirral, where it appears regularly in small numbers'.

RICHARD STEEL

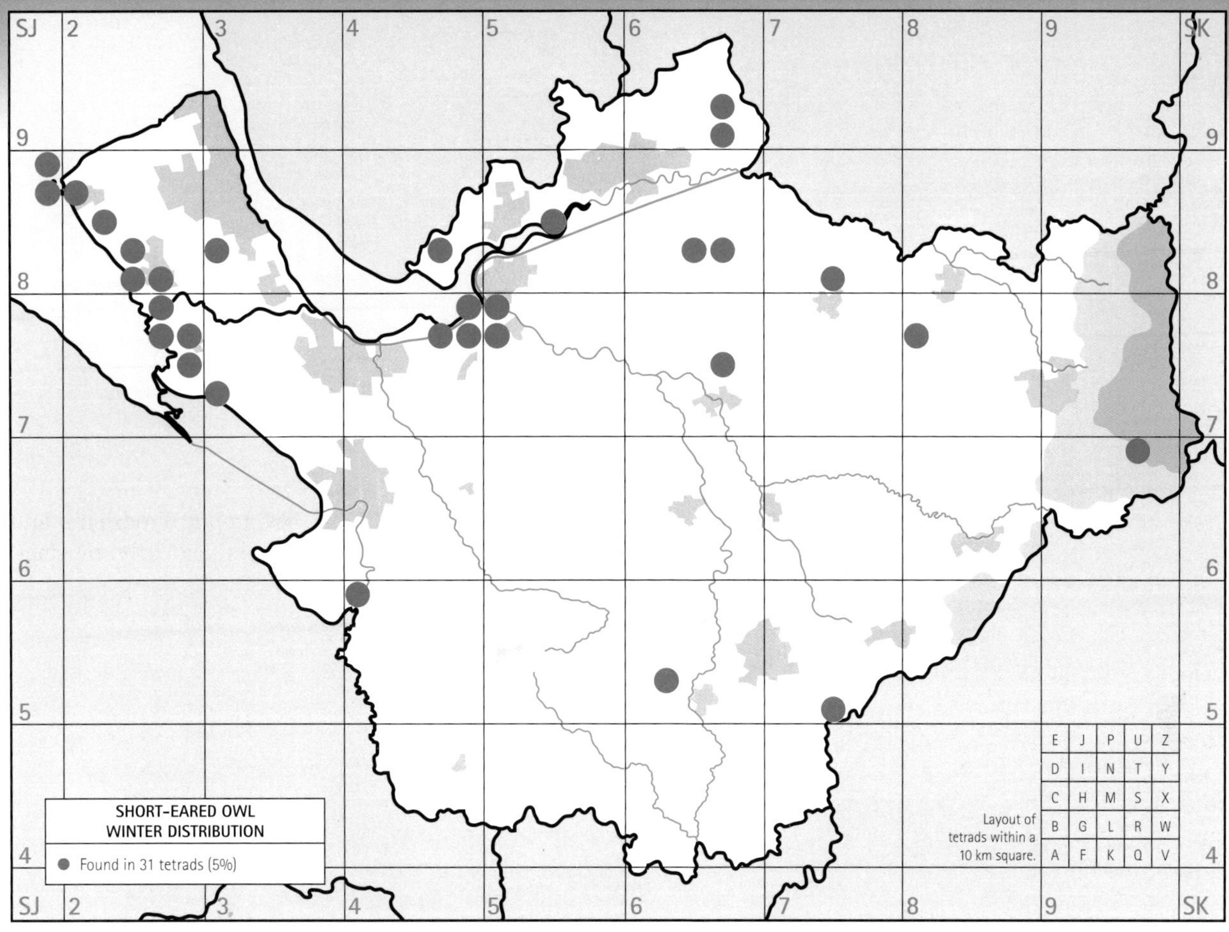
SHORT-EARED OWL
WINTER DISTRIBUTION
Found in 31 tetrads (5%)
Layout of tetrads within a 10 km square.
E J P U Z
D I N T Y
C H M S X
B G L R W
A F K Q V
SJ
SK

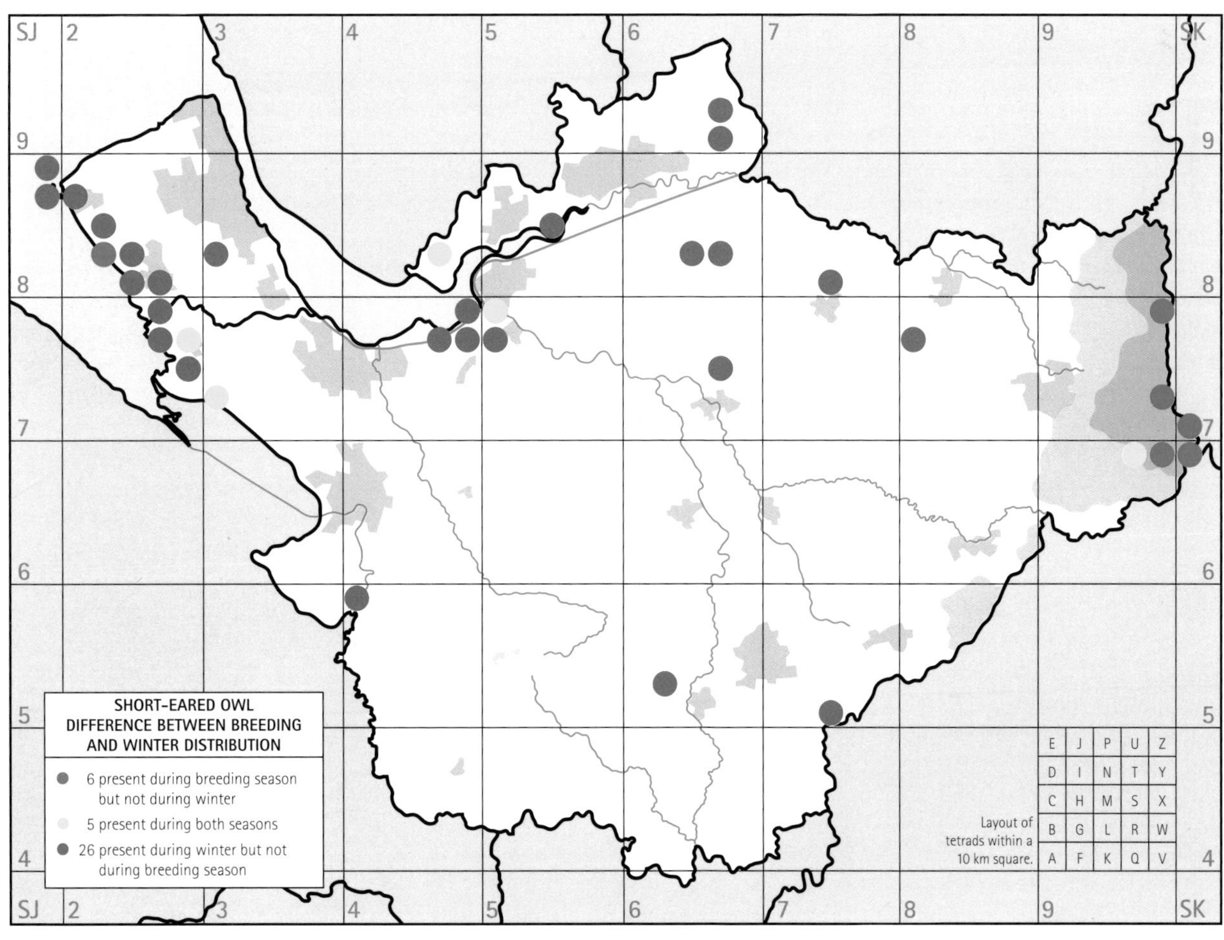
SHORT-EARED OWL
DIFFERENCE BETWEEN BREEDING AND WINTER DISTRIBUTION
6 present during breeding season but not during winter
5 present during both seasons
26 present during winter but not during breeding season
Layout of tetrads within a 10 km square.
E J P U Z
D I N T Y
C H M S X
B G L R W
A F K Q V
SJ
SK

Nightjar

Caprimulgus europaeus

PHIL JONES

This species probably bred in the county during our *First Atlas* period, when birds were at Risley Moss (SJ69Q/R) in 1979 and 1980. The text in the *First Atlas*, and the county bird reports for those years, describe the records as 'pairs' (probable breeding), yet they were mapped as confirmed breeding. No more information is available to reassess these records. Whatever their status, this was the last time that two birds were found together in Cheshire and Wirral.

Since then, the annual bird reports show single males uttering their weird nocturnal 'song' ('churring') for up to three days each year in 1985, 1986, 1993 and 1994, with odd records of single birds present in 1989, 1991 and 1995, and three single birds seen in 2000.

There were two records during this Atlas, both from the north-west Wirral. On 11 May 2004 a male was flushed from private land near Red Rocks Marsh (SJ28E) and a bird was churring from 4 to 7 May 2005 at the Wirral Country Park at Thurstaston (SJ28G).

Nationally, Nightjar is on the Red List of species of conservation concern because of its major contraction in range: the 1988–91 BTO Atlas showed that it had been lost from more than half of the 10 km squares occupied in 1968–72. The population was also thought to have halved between 1972 and 1981. There was then a dramatic reversal in its fortunes, as a national survey in 1992 showed that the population had risen by 50% since 1981, probably due to increased availability of young forest habitat as plantations were felled and replanted (Morris *et al.* 1994). The latest national survey in 2004 found a further 36% increase in the UK population in 12 years (Conway *et al.* 2007).

These apparently contradictory findings indicate that the species is doing well in its core areas, but is being lost elsewhere. The 2004 survey found evidence of population declines and range contractions since 1992, in North Wales, north-west England, and Scotland. Most birds are in southern and eastern England, although there are outlying groups father north, especially in the North York Moors and Dumfries and Galloway. The nearest birds to Cheshire and Wirral are in North Wales and at Cannock Chase, Staffordshire.

The 1997 UK BAP includes a long term target (by 2017) to restore Nightjar to parts of its former range, including in north-west England. There is a Cheshire LBAP for the species, but it has had little action and no success so far. There is little of their favoured heathland habitat in the county, although suitably managed young conifer plantations would meet their needs, provided that there are enough large moths for them to eat.

Sponsored by Paul Brewster in memory of his parents, Pat and Albert Brewster

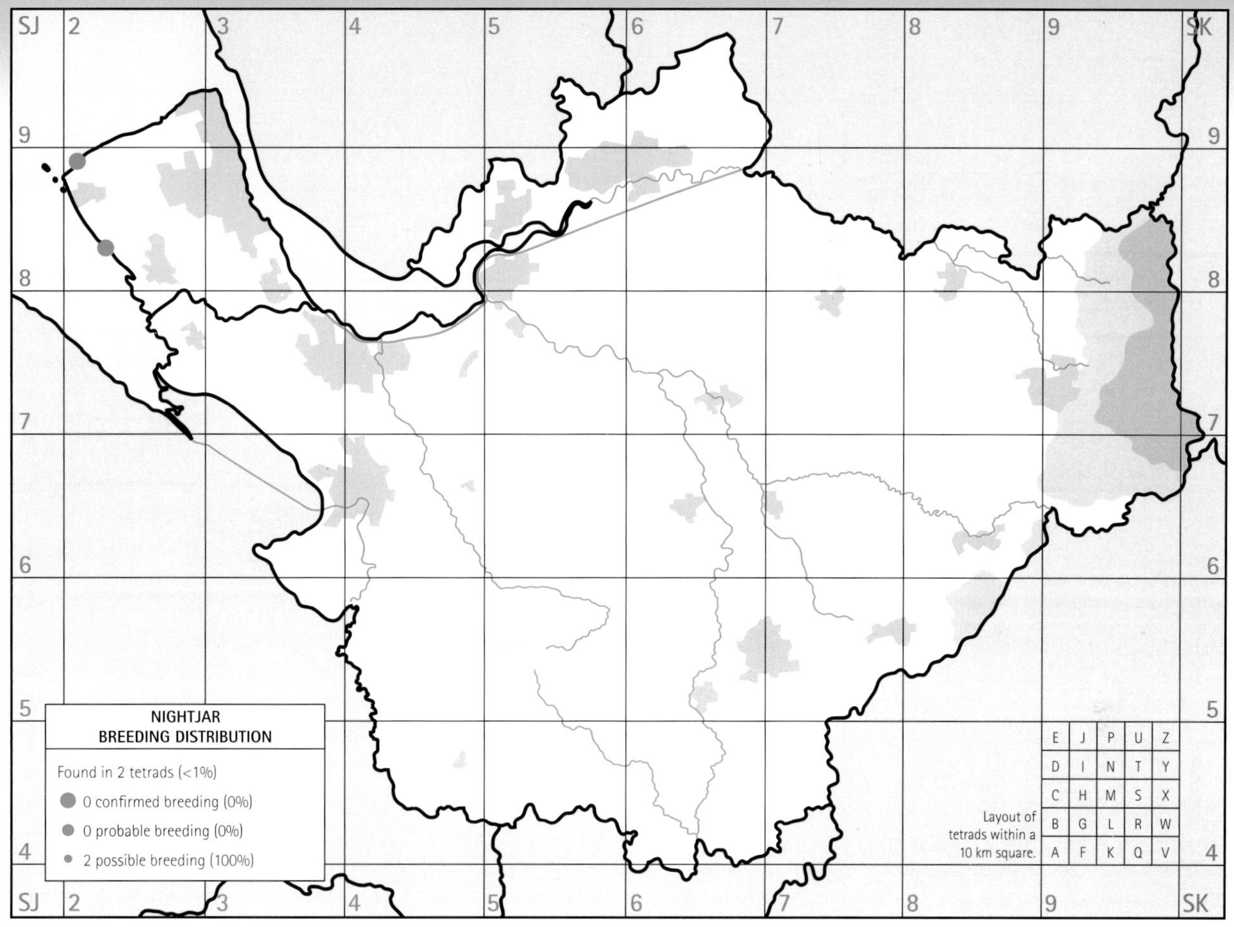
NIGHTJAR
BREEDING DISTRIBUTION
Found in 2 tetrads (<1%)
0 confirmed breeding (0%)
0 probable breeding (0%)
2 possible breeding (100%)
Layout of tetrads within a 10 km square.
E J P U Z
D I N T Y
C H M S X
B G L R W
A F K Q V

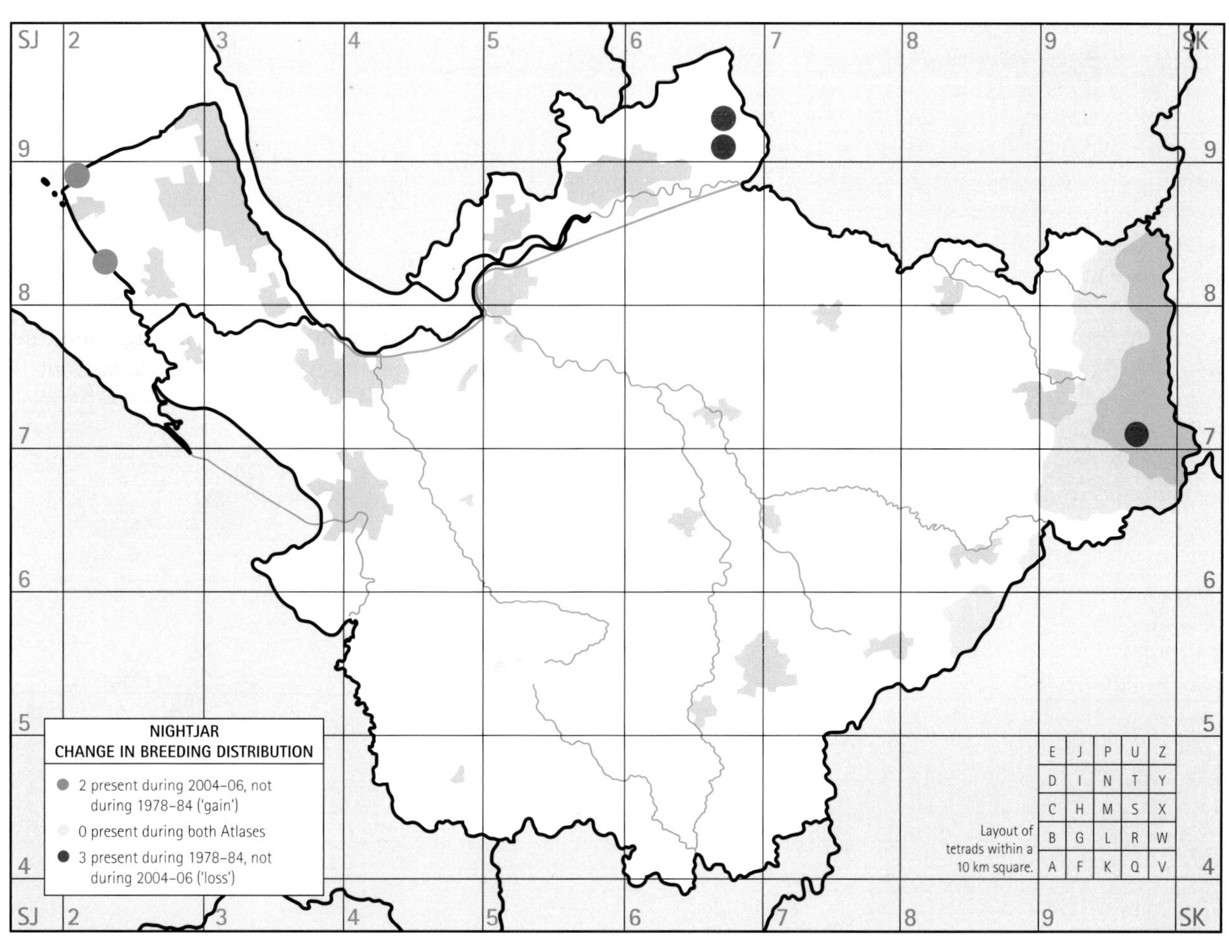
NIGHTJAR
CHANGE IN BREEDING DISTRIBUTION
2 present during 2004–06, not during 1978–84 ('gain')
0 present during both Atlases
3 present during 1978–84, not during 2004–06 ('loss')
Layout of tetrads within a 10 km square.
E J P U Z
D I N T Y
C H M S X
B G L R W
A F K Q V

Swift

Apus apus

MIKE ATKINSON

The *First Atlas* text concluded with the words 'a good census of the county's Swift population would be valuable'. This challenge was accepted by Brian Martin, who led such a project in 1995 (Martin 1997). Swifts are difficult birds to survey. Their normal daily feeding flights probably take them over every tetrad in the county, and they will feed at least 100 miles away from their breeding sites when a summer storm has concentrated their insect prey (Bromhall 1980). Thus, records of birds seen are meaningless for an Atlas of breeding birds, and this Atlas includes, in the distribution and 'change' maps, just records of confirmed breeding and birds visiting probable nest sites (N).

Apart from at their breeding sites, Swifts spend their entire lives—awake and asleep—on the wing, catching nearly all types of flying insects, from minute thrips to large hoverflies, and spiders whisked into the breeze. They feed up to several thousand feet high in the air, and it is often difficult for ground-based observers to see them with the naked eye. On a fine day a pair of Swifts feeding young may catch some 20,000 insects and spiders.

Swifts winter south of the equator in central and southern Africa. They mostly return here in early May, and are conspicuous by their fast flight, and their noisy, screaming flocks. Their ancestral nest sites are probably in trees and caves, but nowadays Swifts entirely depend on man, with their nests exclusively in buildings, mostly houses. They enter the roof space through small gaps under the eaves, and sometimes between tiles. The 1995 survey showed that almost all nests are in properties over 40 years old. Especially favoured are the 1930s council estates and old Victorian and Edwardian houses, and birds are extremely loyal to traditional nesting sites, some of which have held Swifts for the whole lifetime of their human residents (Martin 1997). Not only is the species faithful to established sites, but my study at the colony in Cotebrook Church has shown that most adults use exactly the same nest site from year to year.

The distribution map illustrates clearly the correlation between Swifts and conurbations, and their avoidance of the heavily wooded areas. Despite the comments about site fidelity and stability in a long-lived bird, the maps show substantial changes from the *First Atlas*. There have been gains in urban Wirral, where the species is almost ubiquitous, and around their other strongholds of Warrington, Middlewich, Crewe and Macclesfield, with an intriguing line of new records running north-south to the east of Tarporley. There has been a serious drop in the Chester area and west Cheshire in general, and east of Runcorn and south of Crewe. Much of this appears to have occurred in the decade between the *First Atlas* and the 1995 survey, for the changes from the 1995 survey to this Atlas are less dramatic, but include large-scale losses around Chester, with smaller losses around Northwich, Crewe and Macclesfield.

The 1995 survey found an estimated county total of around 6,500 Swifts (Martin 1997). Almost half of them were in four areas—Crewe, Warrington, Chester and the east Wirral conurbation from Ellesmere Port to Wallasey. It is impossible to translate that figure into pairs, mainly because of unknown proportions of incubating birds and non-breeders prospecting for nest sites. Using a different methodology, the BTO analysis of BBS returns, the breeding population of Cheshire and Wirral in 2004–05 is estimated at 4,300 birds (with very wide statistical confidence limits from zero to 8,660). Swifts were not monitored by any national survey until the start of the BBS in 1994, since when the population index for England has dropped every year, showing a 41% fall from 1994 to 2007. Repeat surveys in other counties have revealed significant drops, often attributed to a reduction in nest sites in modern buildings

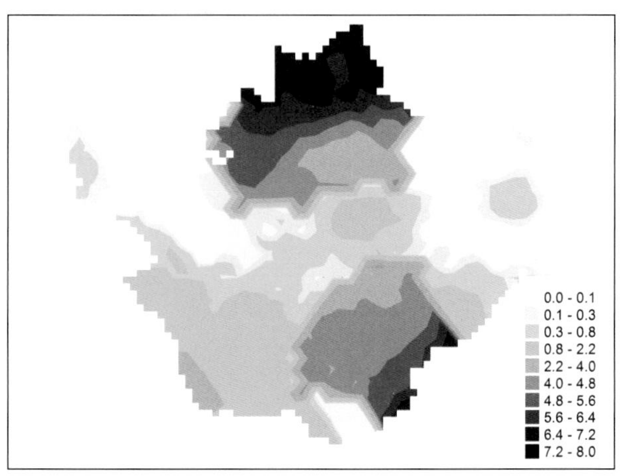

Swift abundance.

Sponsored by Christian and Sue Heintzen

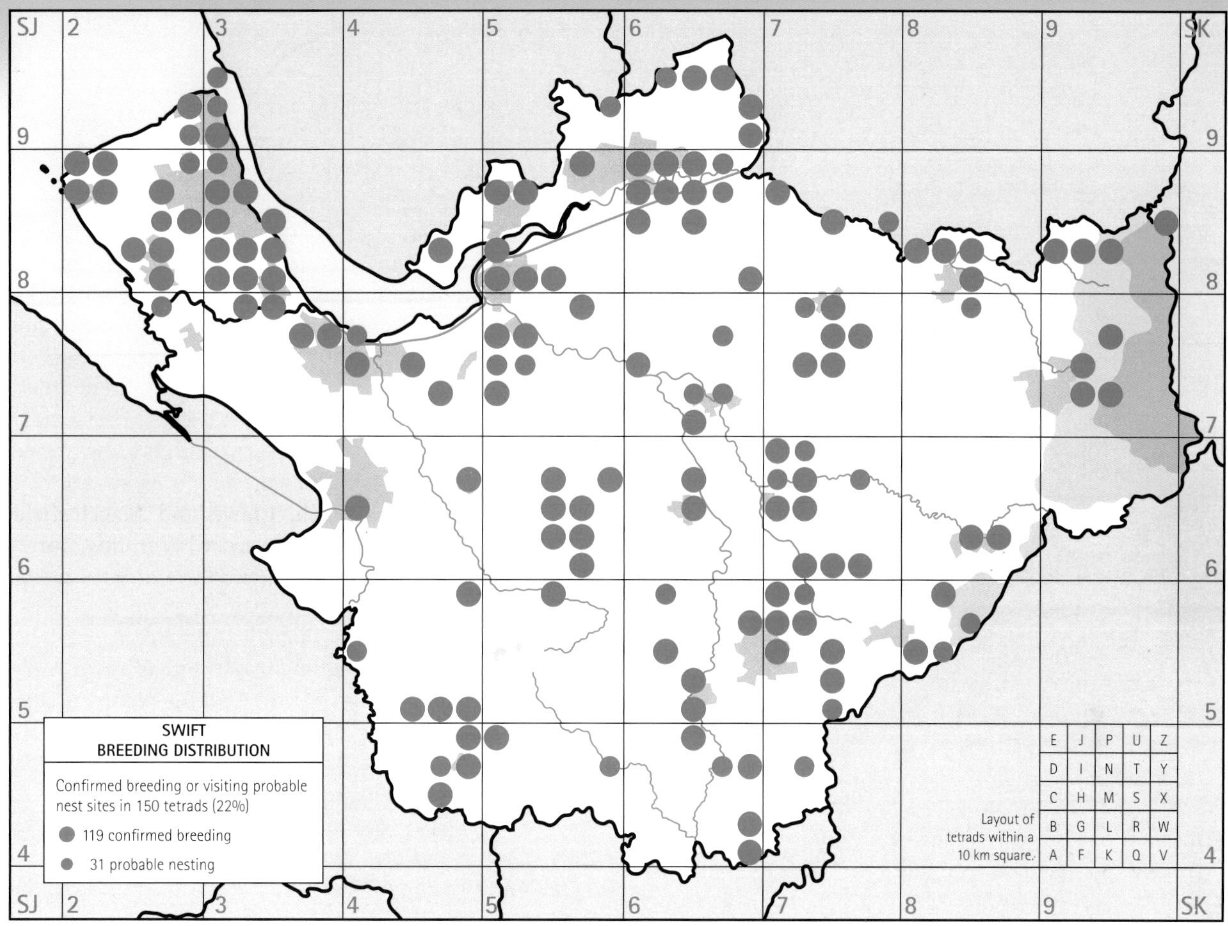

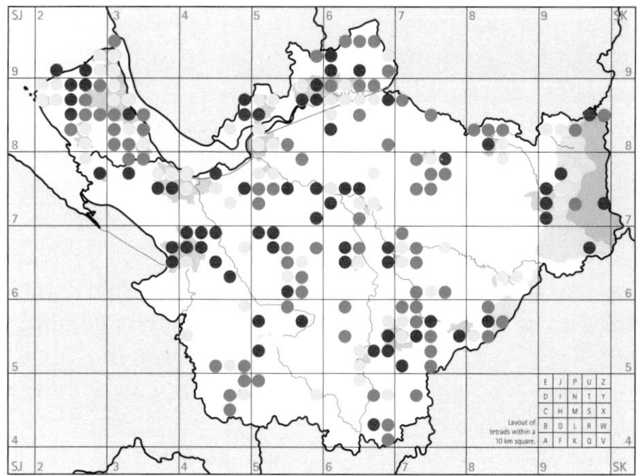

Change in breeding distribution from 1995 survey

- Present during 2004–06, not during 1995 survey ('gain')

- Present during 1995 survey and this Atlas
- Present during 1995 survey, not during 2004–06 ('loss')

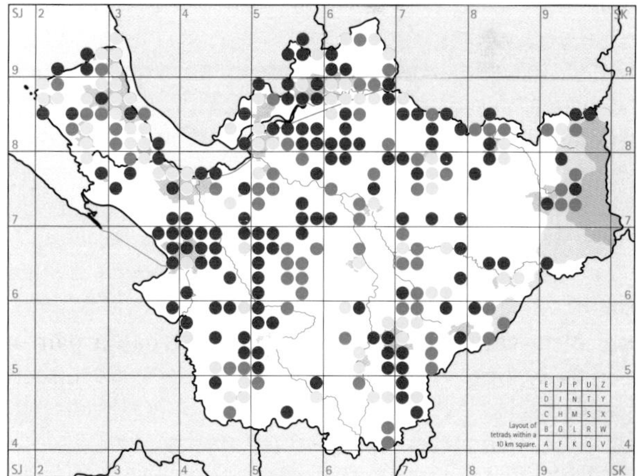

Change in breeding distribution

- Present during 2004–06, not during 1978–84 ('gain')
- Present during both Atlases
- Present during 1978–84, not during 2004–06 ('loss')

and renovation of older properties (Brown & Grice 2005). A local census of south-east Cheshire in 2001 showed a 38% drop in population from 1995/96, with almost every colony showing a decline and the massive west Crewe (SJ65Y) colony down from 450 nests to 120 (Lythgoe 2001).

Kingfisher

Alcedo atthis

SIMON BOOTH

This Atlas map shows that Kingfishers were found in one-quarter of the county's tetrads, slightly fewer than during our *First Atlas*. It is not easy to assess how much the results from this three-year survey would be expected to differ from those of our seven-year *First Atlas*, but a longer survey would surely have increased the proportion of two-letter codes. Many records of Kingfisher require an element of luck and 'being in the right place at the right time', especially in proving breeding through the serendipity of seeing an adult flashing past carrying a fish for its chicks, which is the way that breeding was confirmed in 21 of the 38 tetrads. In seven cases observers saw recently fledged young. Many fieldworkers would envy what Ann Pym described as her 'magical' experience whilst recording near Swettenham (SJ76Y), when she was able to watch two fledglings from 10 yards away, one trying its fishing skills and the other loafing on a branch, just above the water.

Kingfishers have a long breeding season, from March to July, with most pairs having at least two broods and raising an average of 6.5 young per year (Brown & Grice 2005): this high reproductive rate allows them to bounce back from dips in their population, most of which follow hard winters. Surveyors found nests in 10 tetrads, although most fieldworkers only came across a nest by accident, whilst walking along a stream, and were aware that deliberate disturbance of Kingfishers at or near their nest is an offence against the Wildlife and Countryside Act (1981), as the species is specially protected under Schedule 1.

Two Schedule 1 licence-holders have opposing opinions of the fortunes of Kingfishers in Cheshire. One feels that they are doing well, although certainly underrecorded, while the other holds the view that in east Cheshire they are threatened especially by man's activities. It is not difficult to reconcile these views from looking at the 'change' map and dividing the county east and west of the SJ60 longitude line. To the west of this line, the species has been gained in 33 tetrads and lost from 23, a net gain of 10, while to the east, there are 41 gains and 78 losses, a net loss of 37 tetrads. The reasons for this division are not clear, however. This always has been a scarce bird on Wirral and those recorded during this Atlas were the first since 1995 (*CWBR*), but the present position on the peninsula is almost the same as that found twenty years ago.

Kingfishers establish their territories along stretches of running fresh water which is unpolluted, shallow, translucent, partly shaded and not turbulent, with reedy or woody cover at the edges providing plenty of low perches. They feed on minnows, bullheads, roach and other fish 3–7 cm long; occasionally a good feeding area does not contain a suitable vertical face in which they can burrow their nest, so they sometimes fly some distance from the nest, perhaps across dry land, to get food.

Not surprisingly, all of the habitats used contained fresh water, with some observers adding extra habitat codes for the surrounding farmland or human sites. Streams (28%) and rivers (21%) account for almost half of the records, with 18% on lakes/reservoirs, 11% on small waterbodies and 11% on canals. In total, 62% were on linear watercourses and 38% on areas of standing water. They cannot fish well in fast-moving water, so some of the upland rivers are unoccupied, and most Kingfishers are in the lower-lying parts of the county, but they were present in 20 out of the 103 tetrads above 100 m, not significantly different from the proportion at lower altitudes.

The status of the Kingfisher in Britain seems to be reasonably secure; it owes its place on the Amber List of species of conservation concern to a drop in population across Europe as a whole during 1970–90, but the British total has risen since then and now appears to be stable. The county breeding population is likely to be around 150 pairs.

Sponsored by Mid-Cheshire Ornithological Society

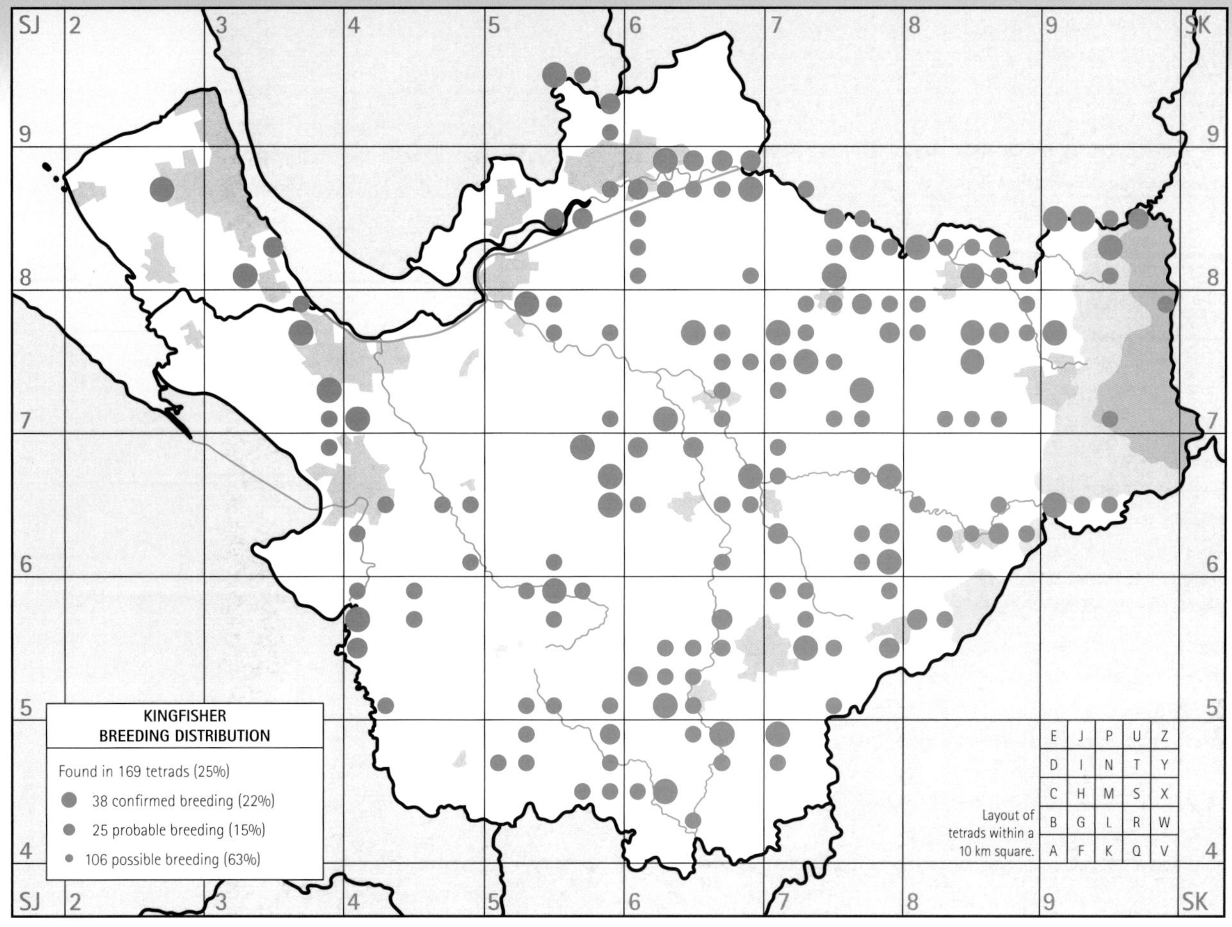
KINGFISHER
BREEDING DISTRIBUTION
Found in 169 tetrads (25%)
38 confirmed breeding (22%)
25 probable breeding (15%)
106 possible breeding (63%)
Layout of tetrads within a 10 km square.
E J P U Z
D I N T Y
C H M S X
B G L R W
A F K Q V
SJ
SK

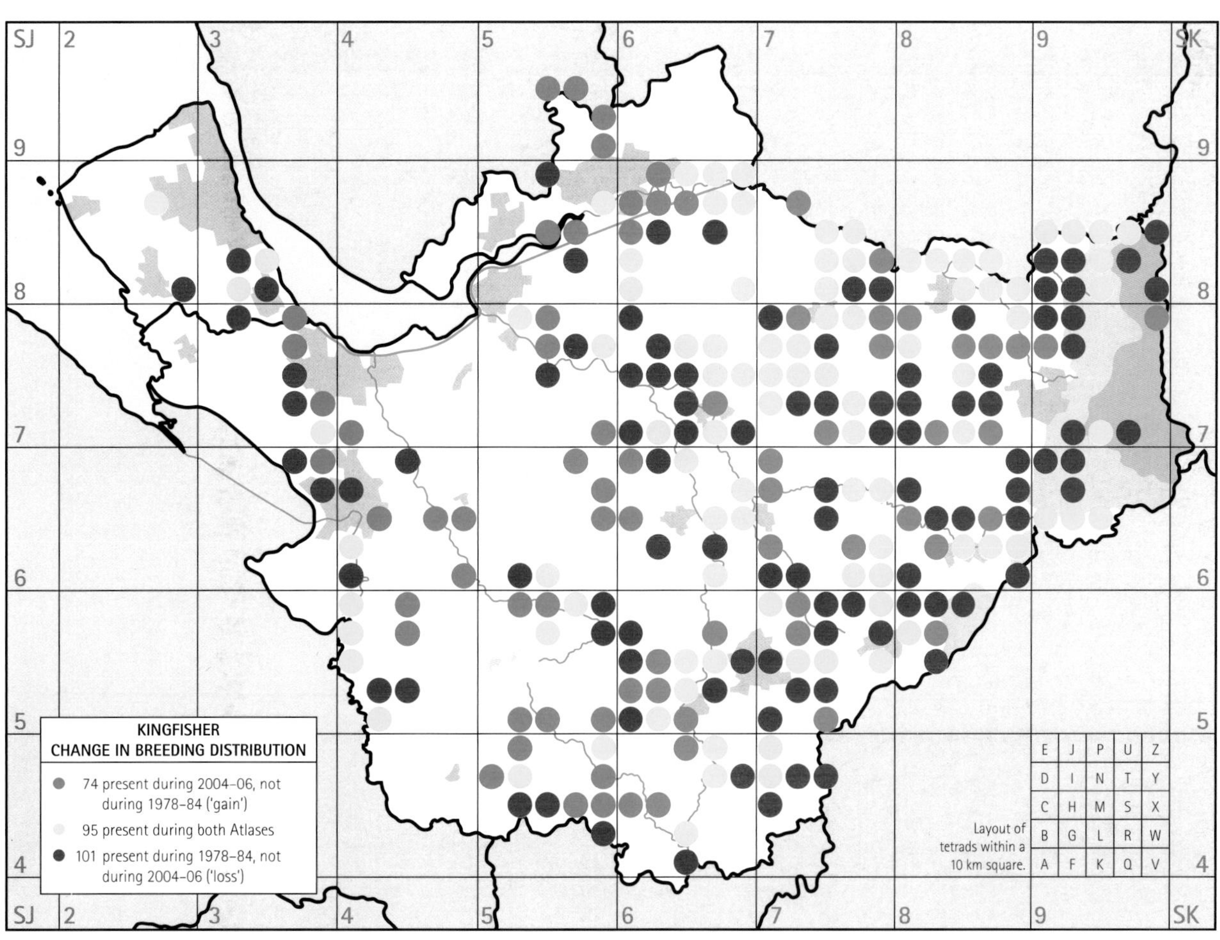
KINGFISHER
CHANGE IN BREEDING DISTRIBUTION
74 present during 2004–06, not during 1978–84 ('gain')
95 present during both Atlases
101 present during 1978–84, not during 2004–06 ('loss')
Layout of tetrads within a 10 km square.
E J P U Z
D I N T Y
C H M S X
B G L R W
A F K Q V
SJ
SK

The winter map shows that Kingfishers are more widespread in winter than when breeding, being present in both seasons in 114 tetrads, in winter only in 93, while they were not recorded in 55 tetrads in which they spent the breeding season. Few birds move very far, but juvenile dispersal may take birds a few kilometres, sufficient to visit almost any suitable water in the county. There are recent examples of ringed young birds in autumn moving 32 km from Congleton (SJ86L) to Woolston (SJ68U) and 11 km from Woolston to Oxmoor, Runcorn (SJ58M), with one exceptional bird ringed at Woolston in June and found six months later 60 km away in Staffordshire.

The wider distribution in winter in part comes from birds occupying a wider range of habitats: they are still tied to water, of course, and need suitable perches from which to look for fish, but they no longer have to find vertical banks nearby. More birds were found using standing waterbodies than in the breeding season, with the ratio of linear watercourses to areas of standing water shifting from 62%: 38% in the breeding season to 55%: 45% in winter. There is a higher proportion on canals (14% in winter, 11% in the breeding season), these often having enough fish but impenetrable brick sides, unsuitable for nesting. All of these differences are relatively small, however, and clearly many Kingfishers live all year round in the same site.

Kingfishers are vulnerable to hard winters, when fresh waters ice over, and many birds die while some move to the estuaries or seashore to find unfrozen fishing areas. Bell (1962) noted that in hard weather they may be driven to the coastal marshes and gutters. There have been no prolonged subzero spells since the 1980s, however, and birds were found in this Atlas in only two tetrads recorded as estuarine, in Stanlow Bay (SJ47D) and Wigg Island (SJ58G) in the tidal river Mersey.

The annual county bird reports mostly seem to receive records from the east of Cheshire and along the river Dee, but this winter Atlas map shows that this is probably an artefact of observers' locations, with Kingfishers widely spread throughout the county, although with the thinnest distribution on Wirral and SJ37/SJ47/SJ57. Individual birds moving along a winter feeding area might exaggerate the picture somewhat, with an extreme example in SJ37S/T/X/Y where Mike Gough noted that one bird wintered on a 1 km stretch of Rivacre Brook which runs through all four tetrads. In some tetrads there may be several birds, although of the 269 records submitted over the three years, only 21 were of more than one bird, illustrating that many Kingfishers maintain territories for winter feeding. There could well be 500 or more birds, widespread across the county in midwinter; the species probably fits Coward's assessment a century ago of 'widely distributed but nowhere abundant' (Coward 1910).

SIMON BOOTH

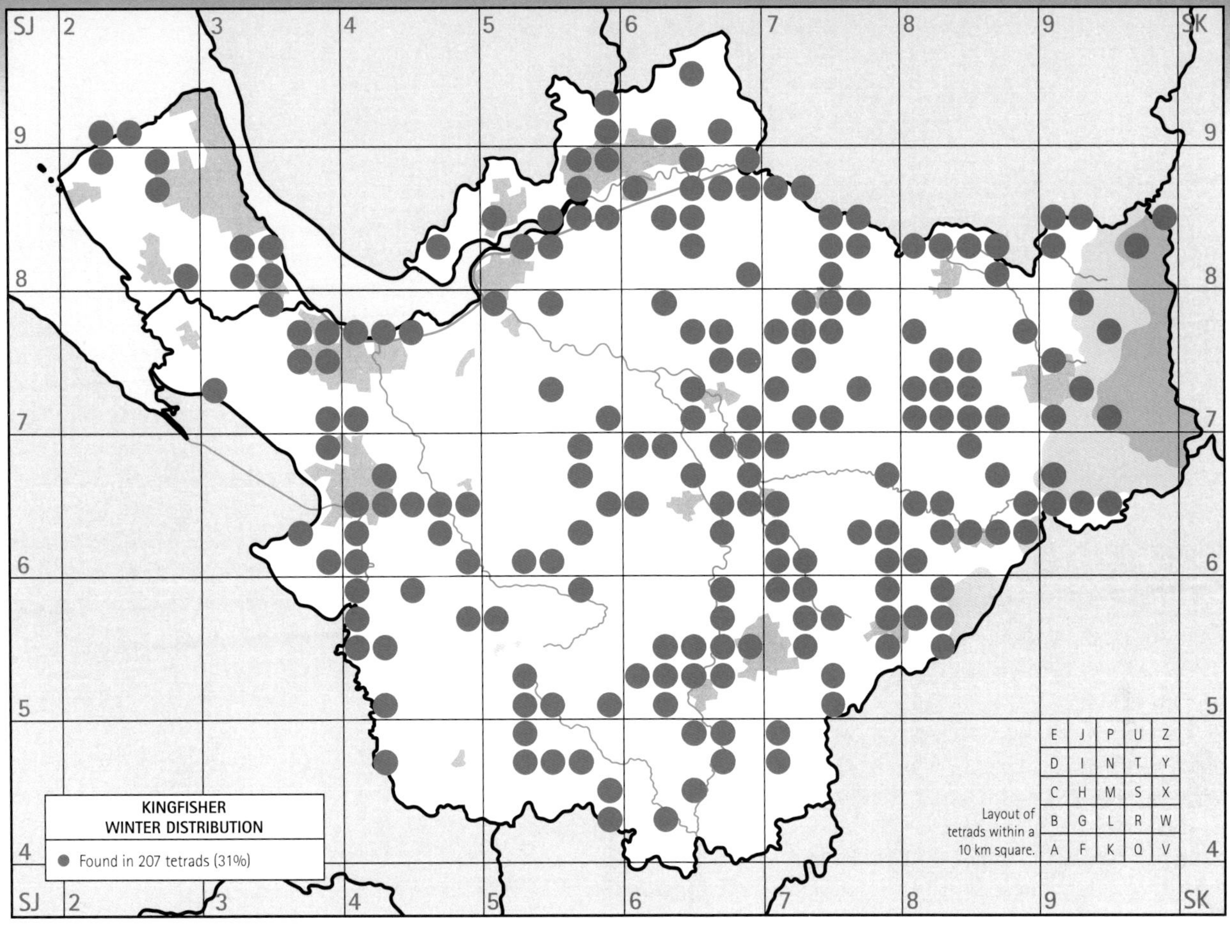
KINGFISHER
WINTER DISTRIBUTION
Found in 207 tetrads (31%)
Layout of tetrads within a 10 km square.
E J P U Z
D I N T Y
C H M S X
B G L R W
A F K Q V
SJ
SK

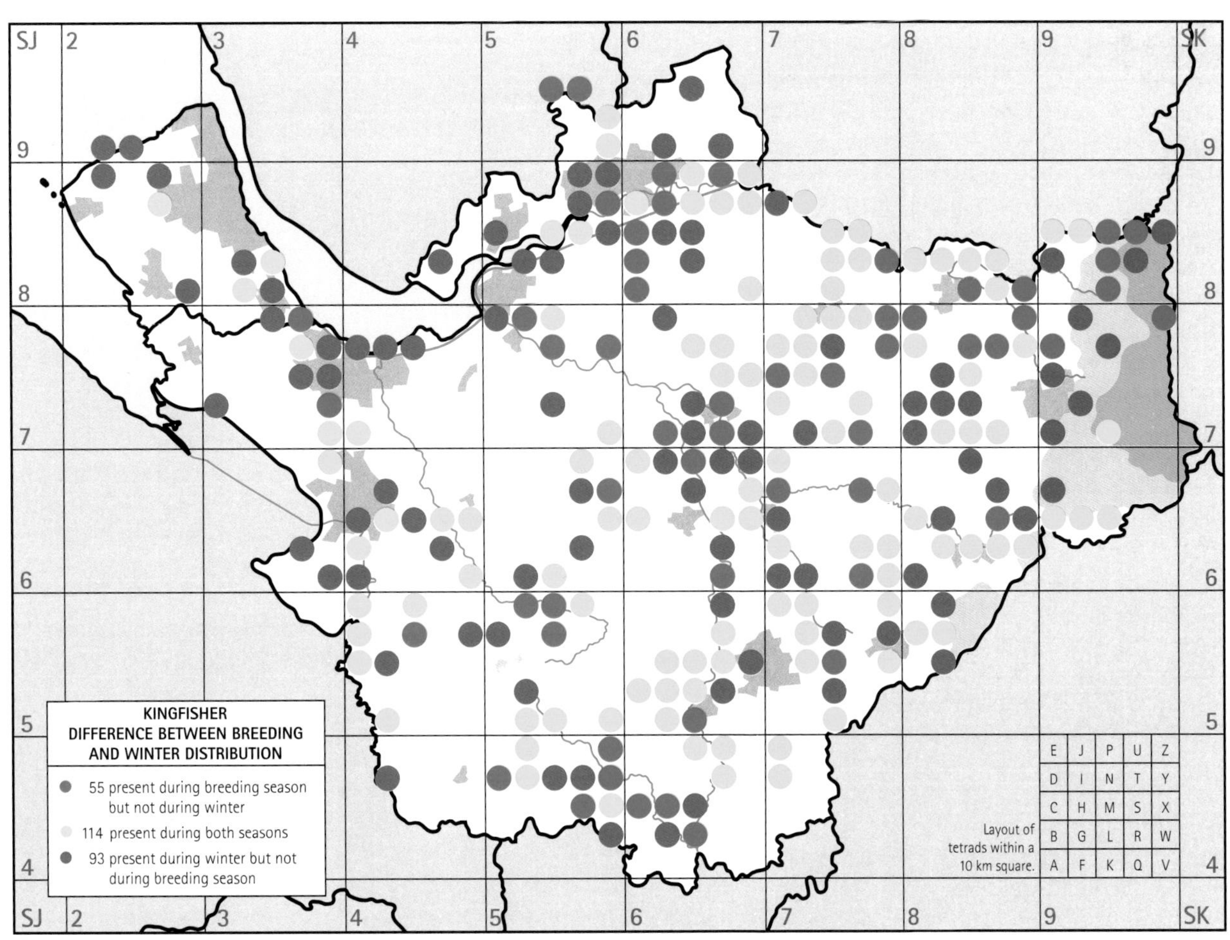
KINGFISHER
DIFFERENCE BETWEEN BREEDING AND WINTER DISTRIBUTION
55 present during breeding season but not during winter
114 present during both seasons
93 present during winter but not during breeding season
Layout of tetrads within a 10 km square.
E J P U Z
D I N T Y
C H M S X
B G L R W
A F K Q V
SJ
SK

Green Woodpecker

Picus viridis

STEVE ROUND

Green Woodpecker numbers have risen widely across Europe and in Britain since the early 1980s, with the British breeding population having more than doubled in the period from 1984 to 2004. The ecological factors underlying the increase have not been established, but this is one of the most vulnerable species in cold weather and their rise in the last twenty years must have been helped by the milder winters. So, against this background it is a surprise that this Atlas shows a contraction of Green Woodpeckers in Cheshire and Wirral, a net loss of 21 tetrads in the breeding season since our *First Atlas*. The map shows clear concentrations around Delamere in the centre of the county, stretching as far as Marbury Country Park (SJ67N) and south of Winsford (SJ66S), and along much of the Wirral peninsula. There are many occupied tetrads south and west of Wilmslow in SJ78/77/87, in a large area of south-west Cheshire centred on Malpas, and also in the lower levels of the eastern hills, although with very few tetrads in these last two localities furnishing other than 'possible' breeding records, many of them detected by the birds' far-carrying 'yaffle' calls. Although the losses have been widespread across the county, there are notable clusters in the areas around the Eaton estate (SJ45E), Audlem (SJ64R) and Congleton (SJ86R), with clear gains in the north of the county, east of Runcorn (SJ58R) and east and south of Warrington (SJ68T).

Like all woodpeckers, this species needs holes in trees for nesting, and they feed their young largely on caterpillars found in woodland; but adult Green Woodpeckers mostly feed on the ground, using their long sticky tongue, armed with barbs at the end, for extracting wood ants. These especially are found in light sandy soils, explaining why the areas of sand outcrops account for much of the Green Woodpecker's distribution.

The Atlas habitat codes show 52% of records in woodland, by some way the lowest figure of the three woodpeckers, and they were almost exclusively in broad-leaved or mixed woodland, with none in coniferous areas and only four records in waterlogged (carr) woodland. The proportions in scrub (6%) and farmland (30%) are more than double those of the black-and-white woodpeckers, with only 7% in human sites. The human sites rarely included habitation, but Green Woodpeckers are associated with two types of man-made sites that can provide good feeding areas for them: golf courses and sand quarries. There were notable records for birds in other feeding areas: grass moor (two records), other dry semi-natural grassland (four), heath (four) and unimproved grassland (12), all of which are more likely to provide their diet of ants than agricultural grassland.

Atlas workers proved Green Woodpeckers breeding in 39 tetrads, in two of them by seeing adults carrying food and in 19 by seeing groups of speckly-looking recently fledged youngsters, who are fed by their parents for a month or so after they leave the nest: in 2004 near Alderley Edge (SJ87I) David Hulse had the enviable experience of seeing three young with a parent on the same branch. In a further 18 tetrads observers found active nests although the species of tree was not recorded for any of them. Analysis of the national nest record collection showed that Green Woodpeckers chiefly nest in oak or ash, and less often in birch, beech and other trees, digging out large nest chambers in the tree trunks (Glue & Boswell 1994). Like the spotted woodpeckers, they used to suffer eviction from nest holes by Starlings, often excavating a nest cavity only to be dispossessed, but since the decline of Starlings in woodland in the last twenty years, eviction of woodpeckers seldom happens, probably another factor that has allowed the species to increase (Smith 2005).

Based on the rising British population, and our *First Atlas* estimate of 150 pairs breeding in 1978, with perhaps 75 pairs in 1982 after a series of hard winters, the present Green Woodpecker total in the county ought to exceed 200–250 pairs. But few tetrads hold more than one pair and breeding was confirmed or probable in only 69 tetrads, so a current estimate is 100–150 pairs.

Sponsored by Dr Paul Brewster and Dr Carys Brewster

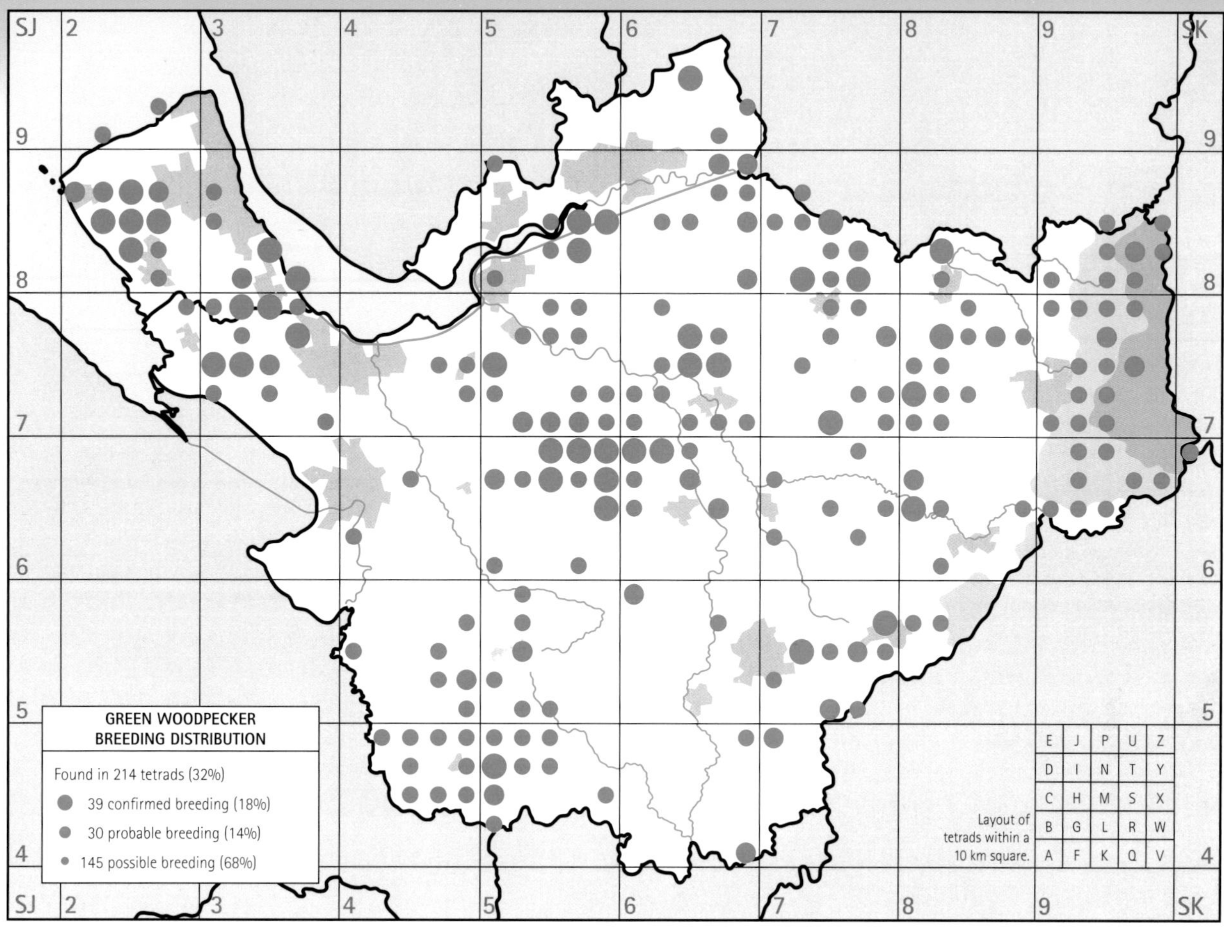
GREEN WOODPECKER
BREEDING DISTRIBUTION
Found in 214 tetrads (32%)
39 confirmed breeding (18%)
30 probable breeding (14%)
145 possible breeding (68%)
Layout of tetrads within a 10 km square.
E J P U Z
D I N T Y
C H M S X
B G L R W
A F K Q V
SJ
SK
2
3
4
5
6
7
8
9

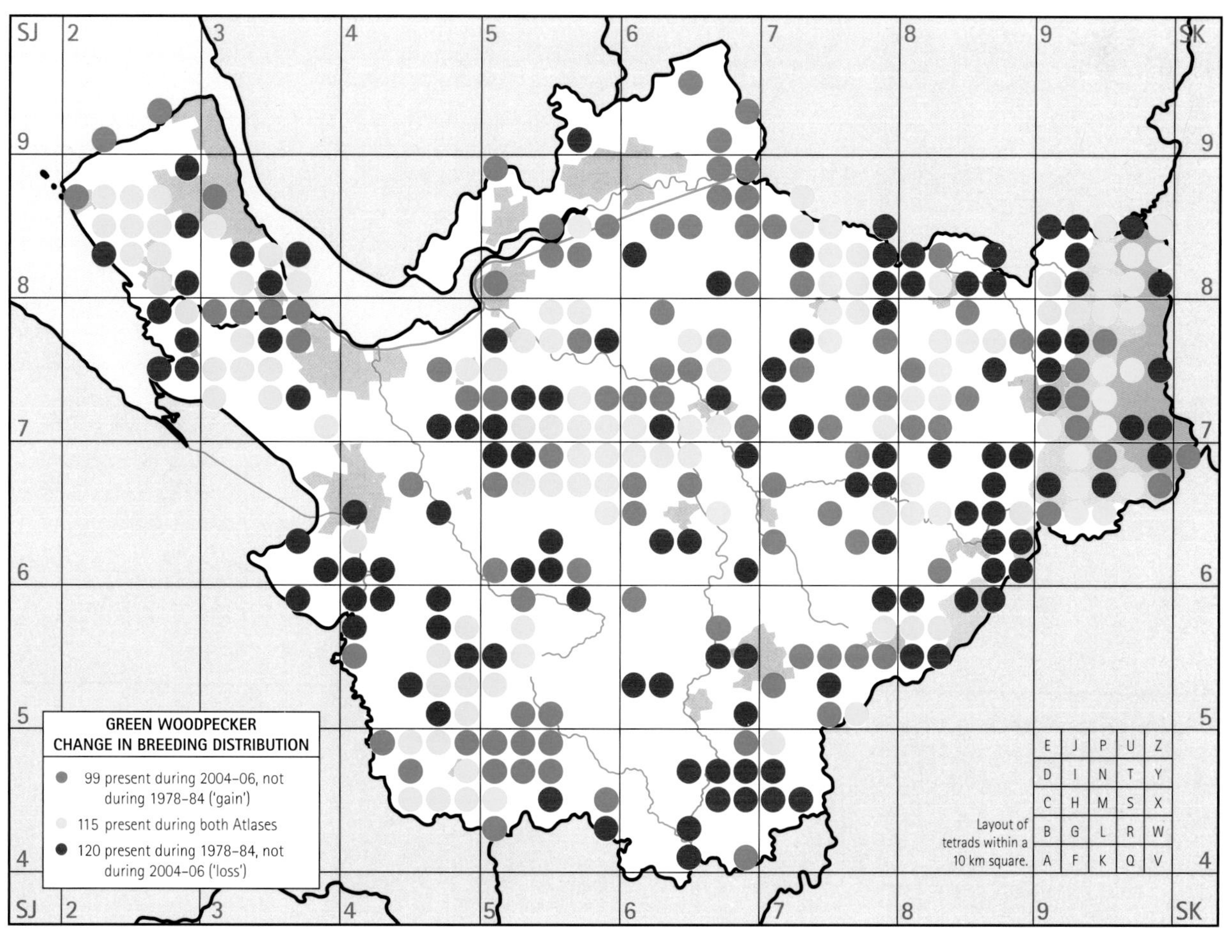
GREEN WOODPECKER
CHANGE IN BREEDING DISTRIBUTION
99 present during 2004–06, not during 1978–84 ('gain')
115 present during both Atlases
120 present during 1978–84, not during 2004–06 ('loss')
Layout of tetrads within a 10 km square.
E J P U Z
D I N T Y
C H M S X
B G L R W
A F K Q V
SJ
SK
2
3
4
5
6
7
8
9

Green Woodpeckers were found in winter in only 148 tetrads, 66 fewer than in the breeding season. The areas with birds missing in winter were widespread across the county, but there were obviously fewer in SJ44, SJ96 and SJ98. Most of the records were of solitary individuals: there were two counts of three birds, 13 of two birds together and 194 of single birds, many of them heard calling.

There is virtually no difference in any of the categories of habitat recorded in winter from the breeding season. They mostly forage on the ground, with adult ants, and their eggs and larvae, remaining a key part of this species' specialized diet all year round, explaining their susceptibility to spells of freezing weather. In 1967, Bell wrote that 'no species has been slower to recover from the exceptional frost of early 1963' (Bell 1967). He had earlier stated that Green Woodpeckers were much commoner in south and central areas than in the north of the county (Bell 1962), no longer true today, but 'its chief stronghold remains in Delamere and surrounding areas where it has always been regarded as abundant'. The present winter Atlas map shows that the largest contiguous group of tetrads is in exactly that part of the centre of Cheshire.

In the Wirral, the species' status has changed markedly. A century ago, it was rare there (Coward 1910). Hardy (1941) knew Green Woodpeckers as occasional winter visitors to Wirral and Bell (1962) wrote that they had noticeably increased during the last 15–20 years. Nowadays, at both seasons, they are widely distributed on the peninsula.

STEVE ROUND

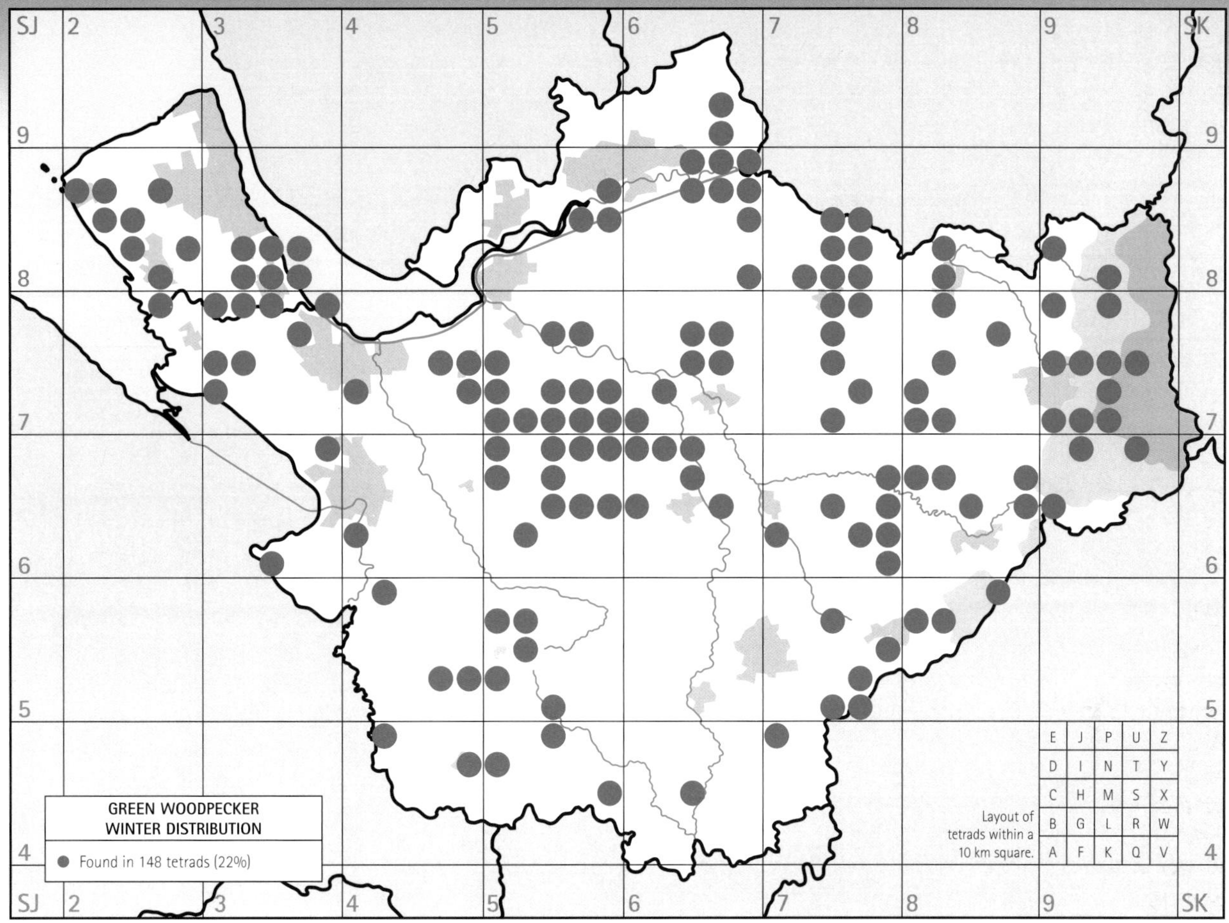
SJ
SK
GREEN WOODPECKER
WINTER DISTRIBUTION
Found in 148 tetrads (22%)
Layout of
tetrads within a
10 km square.
E J P U Z
D I N T Y
C H M S X
B G L R W
A F K Q V

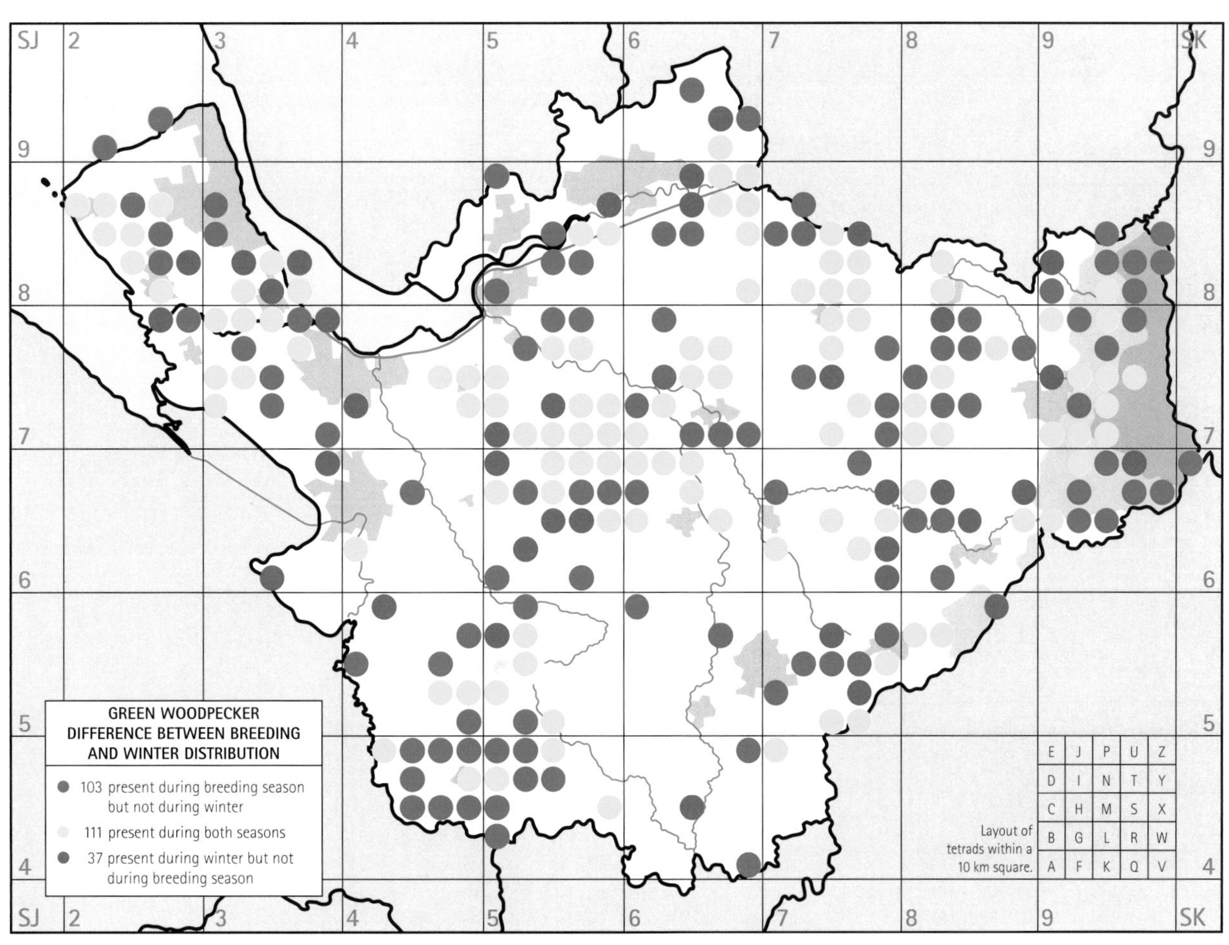
SJ
SK
GREEN WOODPECKER
DIFFERENCE BETWEEN BREEDING
AND WINTER DISTRIBUTION
103 present during breeding season but not during winter
111 present during both seasons
37 present during winter but not during breeding season
Layout of
tetrads within a
10 km square.
E J P U Z
D I N T Y
C H M S X
B G L R W
A F K Q V

Great Spotted Woodpecker

Dendrocopos major

This always has been the most familiar woodpecker but in the last 20 years its numbers have risen considerably, with the UK breeding index almost doubling in the period 1984–2004, and it has expanded its range. During this Atlas Great Spotted Woodpeckers were found in 588 tetrads, a net gain of 86 since our *First Atlas*, and they are now present almost everywhere. There are three main newly occupied areas: in the north of Cheshire, along the Mersey valley; in the eastern hills, where they were found in nine new tetrads, and were absent from only three of the bleakest squares; and widely across the agricultural south of the county. The latter has been possible because many birds have spread out from their core woodland areas and are now are using hedgerow trees.

The habitat codes show more than two-thirds of records (69%) in woodland, nearly all of them in broad-leaved or mixed woodland, with just six records in coniferous and 26 in waterlogged (carr) woodland. Three per cent of records came from scrub, 15% were in farmland and 12% in human sites: urban areas are no bar to this species, as seen from their distribution map.

CAROLYN CHASE

Breeding Great Spotted Woodpeckers go through a cycle of conspicuousness. They are very noticeable when displaying, from early in the new year, making their far-carrying 'drumming' sound by rapidly hammering a suitably resonant piece of timber. Similarly, when excavating their nest holes, the noise draws attention to their activities, but they can be very secretive when laying and incubating. As soon as the chicks hatch, however, they start a continuous racket which carries on throughout daylight hours for the three weeks that they are in the nest, intensifying whenever they hear a parent returning with a beakful of food.

This behaviour means that it is very easy to prove breeding. On a quiet morning in Delamere Forest, I have several times been able to find five or more nests in an hour, just by listening for chicks and moving off in the direction of the next noisy brood, with nests typically spaced from 250 m to 400 m apart, territory sizes of 5–10 ha. They have significantly advanced their breeding season in the last 20 years, from hatching in late May or early June to mid-May in some years nowadays.

Breeding was confirmed in 354 tetrads, and in more than half of them (181) fieldworkers found a nest, although few reported the species of tree: five birch, two oak and one alder. In Delamere Forest they favour birch, particularly trees where the core is being rotted by birch bracket polypore fungi, and Scots or Corsican pine, often using live trees. They normally use the trunk of the tree about 5 m above the ground. Some trees contain several woodpecker holes or trial borings, but birch is seldom suitable two years running as it rots quickly. It is always worth keeping an eye on old woodpecker holes, because they are often used by other species in the next year and Great Spotted Woodpeckers obviously play an important role in woodland ecology.

In 116 tetrads observers noted recently fledged birds, the adults in June often taking their red-headed youngsters on a tour of suitable feeding sites including peanut feeders in gardens. Their natural food is mostly insects hidden under bark or in dead wood, especially the larvae of longhorn beetles, but they also take tree seeds and birds' eggs, often hammering their way into a nest-box occupied by a brood of tits.

The BTO BBS analysis shows that the breeding population of Cheshire and Wirral in 2004–05 was 1,970 birds (930–3,010), corresponding to 3.3 birds per tetrad in which the species was found, or 4.6 birds per tetrad with confirmed or probable breeding. The areas of best woodland habitat often contain five pairs, so to reach that average figure across the county, there must be many suboptimal tetrads with only one pair.

Sponsored by Chester and District Ornithological Society

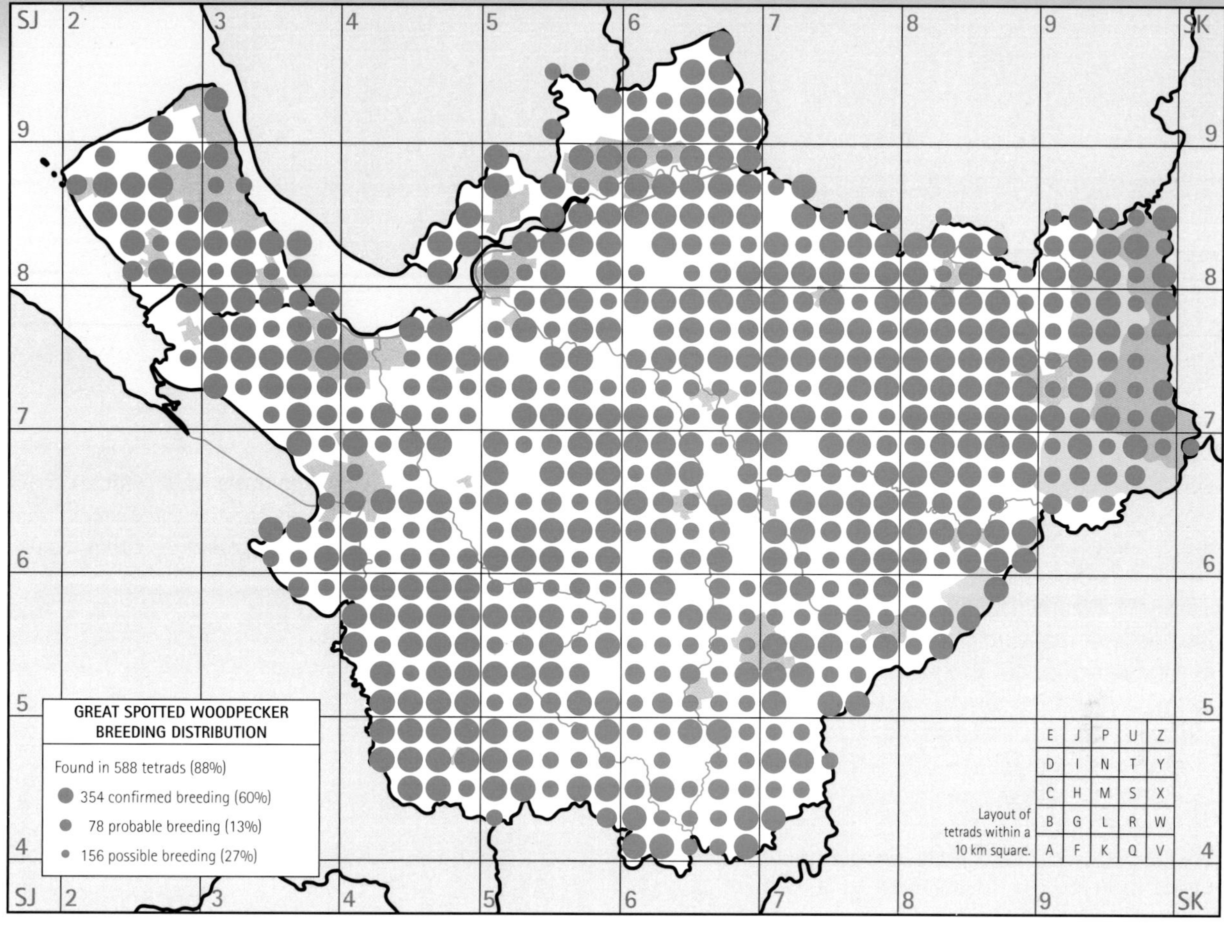
GREAT SPOTTED WOODPECKER
BREEDING DISTRIBUTION
Found in 588 tetrads (88%)
354 confirmed breeding (60%)
78 probable breeding (13%)
156 possible breeding (27%)
Layout of tetrads within a 10 km square.
E J P U Z
D I N T Y
C H M S X
B G L R W
A F K Q V
SJ 2 3 4 5 6 7 8 9 SK

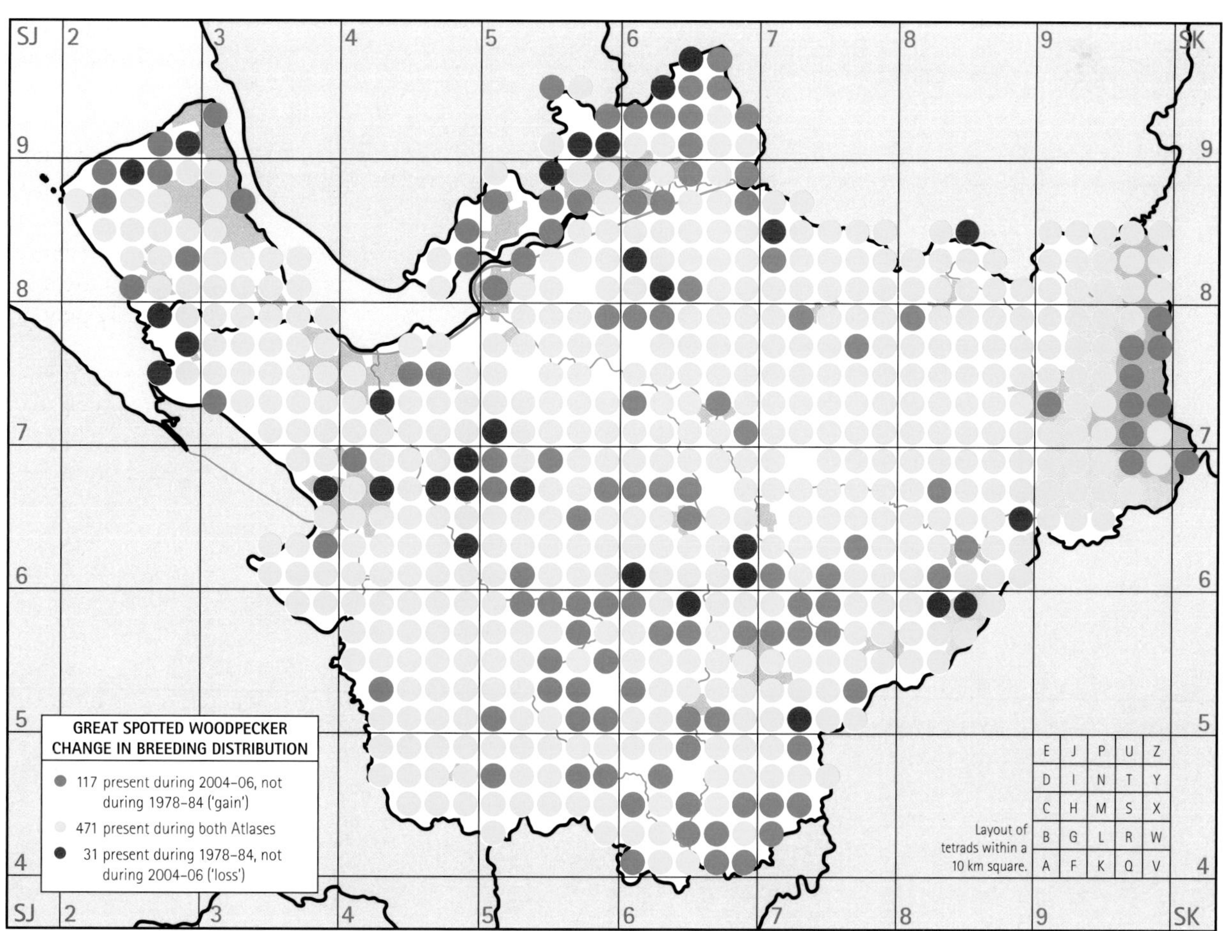
GREAT SPOTTED WOODPECKER
CHANGE IN BREEDING DISTRIBUTION
117 present during 2004–06, not during 1978–84 ('gain')
471 present during both Atlases
31 present during 1978–84, not during 2004–06 ('loss')
Layout of tetrads within a 10 km square.
E J P U Z
D I N T Y
C H M S X
B G L R W
A F K Q V
SJ 2 3 4 5 6 7 8 9 SK

There is little difference between the breeding season and winter distribution of Great Spotted Woodpeckers, with 543 tetrads occupied in both seasons, 45 used in the breeding season but not in winter and 35 with birds in winter only. Perhaps the only significant change is that they were found in winter in a handful of tetrads near the north Wirral coast that had no breeding birds.

Some birds do spread out into new areas in winter. A century ago, when the species was much scarcer and seldom known to breed in Wirral, Coward (1910) wrote that they occurred sparingly during autumn and winter in all parts of the county. Coward also noted that, during the winter months, they will sometimes roost night after night in an old nesting hole. No roosting birds were reported during this Atlas survey, however.

Especially at this season they are most likely to forage on dead wood, but they also take tree seeds (especially beech and other nuts) and a variety of food provided by man including peanuts and fat; they sometimes feed on the ground. Steve and Gill Barber saw two birds foraging on a hillside pasture near Wildboarclough (SJ96Z) in 2004/05. The submitted habitat codes show most records in woodland, but a reduced proportion (59%) compared to the breeding season, with more birds visiting farmland (19%) and human sites (18%).

Most records were of single birds, but they were often recorded as two birds together, possibly a pair. Territorial display starts during winter, with drumming noted from as early as 7 December, and frequent in January and February. There were 45 winter records of three or more birds together, with three counts of six birds including one by Bill Bellamy on 3 December 2006 when he was amazed to see six Great Spotted Woodpeckers perched in a single large oak near Leighton Grange (SJ65T).

SIMON BOOTH

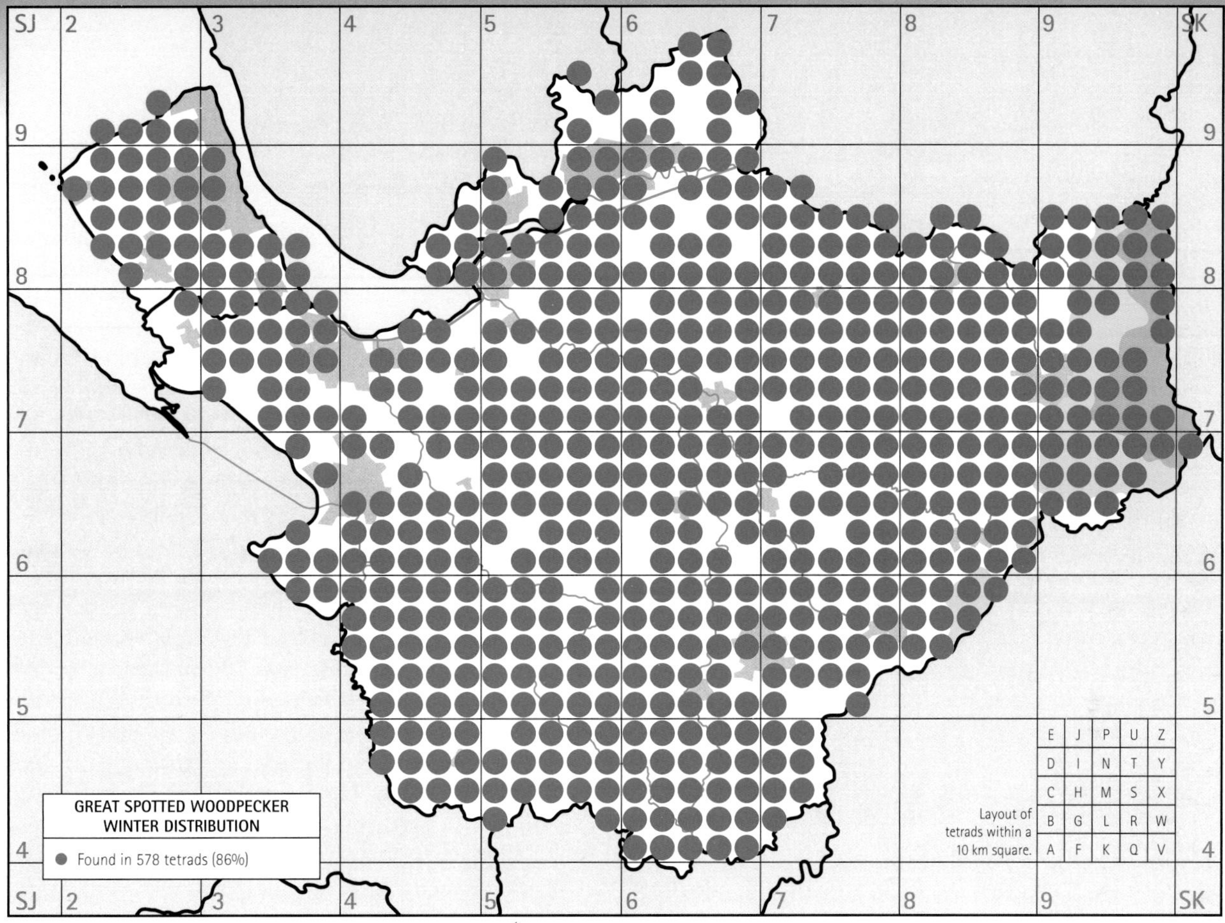
GREAT SPOTTED WOODPECKER
WINTER DISTRIBUTION
Found in 578 tetrads (86%)
Layout of tetrads within a 10 km square.
E J P U Z
D I N T Y
C H M S X
B G L R W
A F K Q V
SJ
SK

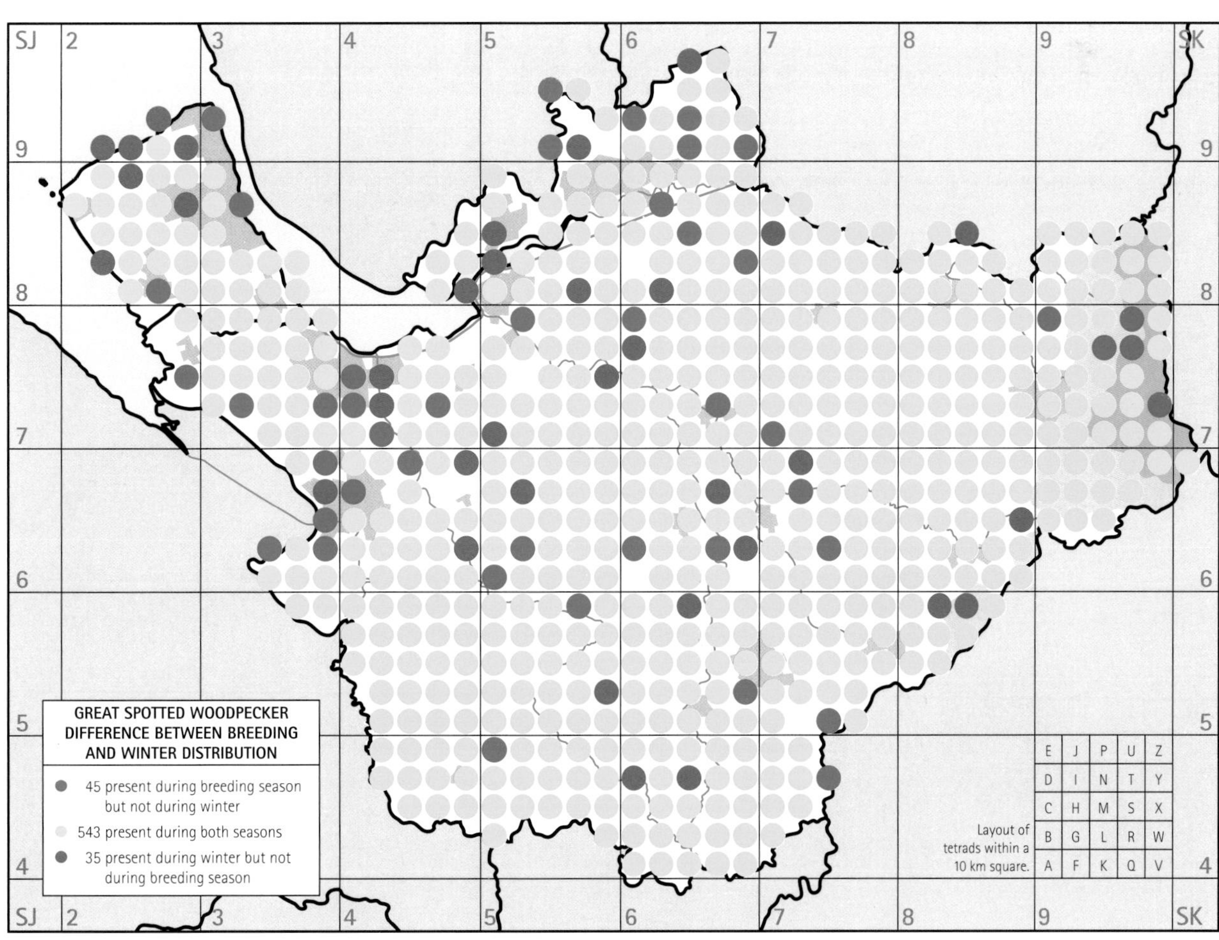
GREAT SPOTTED WOODPECKER
DIFFERENCE BETWEEN BREEDING AND WINTER DISTRIBUTION
45 present during breeding season but not during winter
543 present during both seasons
35 present during winter but not during breeding season
Layout of tetrads within a 10 km square.
E J P U Z
D I N T Y
C H M S X
B G L R W
A F K Q V
SJ
SK

Lesser Spotted Woodpecker

Dendrocopos minor

STEVE FLETCHER

Lesser Spotted Woodpeckers are in trouble. In the last quarter-century, across Europe, they have declined more than any other woodland bird. The British population fell by three-quarters from 1984 to 2000, placing them on the Red List, but then they became too scarce to monitor. It is no surprise to see this Atlas 'change' map dominated by red dots, with 58 tetrads occupied both in our *First Atlas* and now, 34 newly occupied since then and 181 holding them twenty years ago but not now. They have been lost from much of the county, with no obvious pattern; previous strongholds north and east of Chester, in SJ37 and SJ46, are deserted now. This is quite a secretive species and might have been underrecorded, but it is likely that the county population now is in the range of 50–75 pairs, way down on the *First Atlas* estimate of 150–250 pairs.

The reasons for the decline are not well established but include competition with, and predation by, the burgeoning numbers of Great Spotted Woodpeckers, and reductions in small-diameter dead wood suitable for foraging. They occupy large home ranges and perhaps landscape-scale changes in woodland, such as loss of mature broad-leaved woodland, losses of non-woodland trees such as elms, and woodland fragmentation, may also be important (Fuller *et al.* 2005). Here in Cheshire and Wirral, Lesser Spotted Woodpecker is close to the edge of its breeding range, which may be contracting. In the counties in north-west England it was found in 25% of tetrads in Shropshire (1985–90), 14% in this Atlas, 6% in Lancashire and North Merseyside (1997–2000) and 0.4% in Cumbria (1997–2001).

The submitted habitat codes for this Atlas showed 74% of records in woodland, mostly broad-leaved or mixed woodland, with none in coniferous but a significant figure of 11% in waterlogged (carr) woodland—the third highest proportion of any species, behind Willow Tit and Woodcock. Just 3% of records were from scrub, with 12% farmland and 11% human sites. Although they share some habitat characteristics with Willow Tit, the species' distributions in the county are very different.

In the breeding season they are highly territorial, defending a large area of 50–100 ha and individual birds usually show lifelong fidelity to the territory where they first settled. Both sexes participate in the parental duties, with males often taking the larger share. Lesser Spotted Woodpeckers nest late, starting just after oak buds burst, probably because in the breeding season they switch from their normal diet of insect larvae living in dead wood and almost exclusively eat, and feed their chicks on, surface-living insects, especially caterpillars, picked from the foliage and bark of trees (Wiktander *et al.* 2001a).

Proof of breeding was obtained in only 14 tetrads, two from fieldworkers seeing adults carrying food for their young, seven from observations of recently fledged young and five where nests were found. Unfortunately, no-one recorded the species or condition of any of the nesting trees. Especially in view of their major decline, this would be a worthwhile addition to our knowledge, and it would be good for CAWOS to solicit such information with records of Lesser Spotted Woodpeckers. This species depends on dead trees much more than the other two woodpeckers do, with three-quarters of nests in dead wood (Glue & Boswell 1994).

From work in Sweden, the recommendation for conservation of Lesser Spotted Woodpeckers is to have a minimum of 40 ha of woodland dominated by deciduous trees, which may be fragmented over a maximum of 200 ha (half a tetrad) (Wiktander *et al.* 2001b). Few parts of the county approach that prescription.

Sponsored by Peter Day

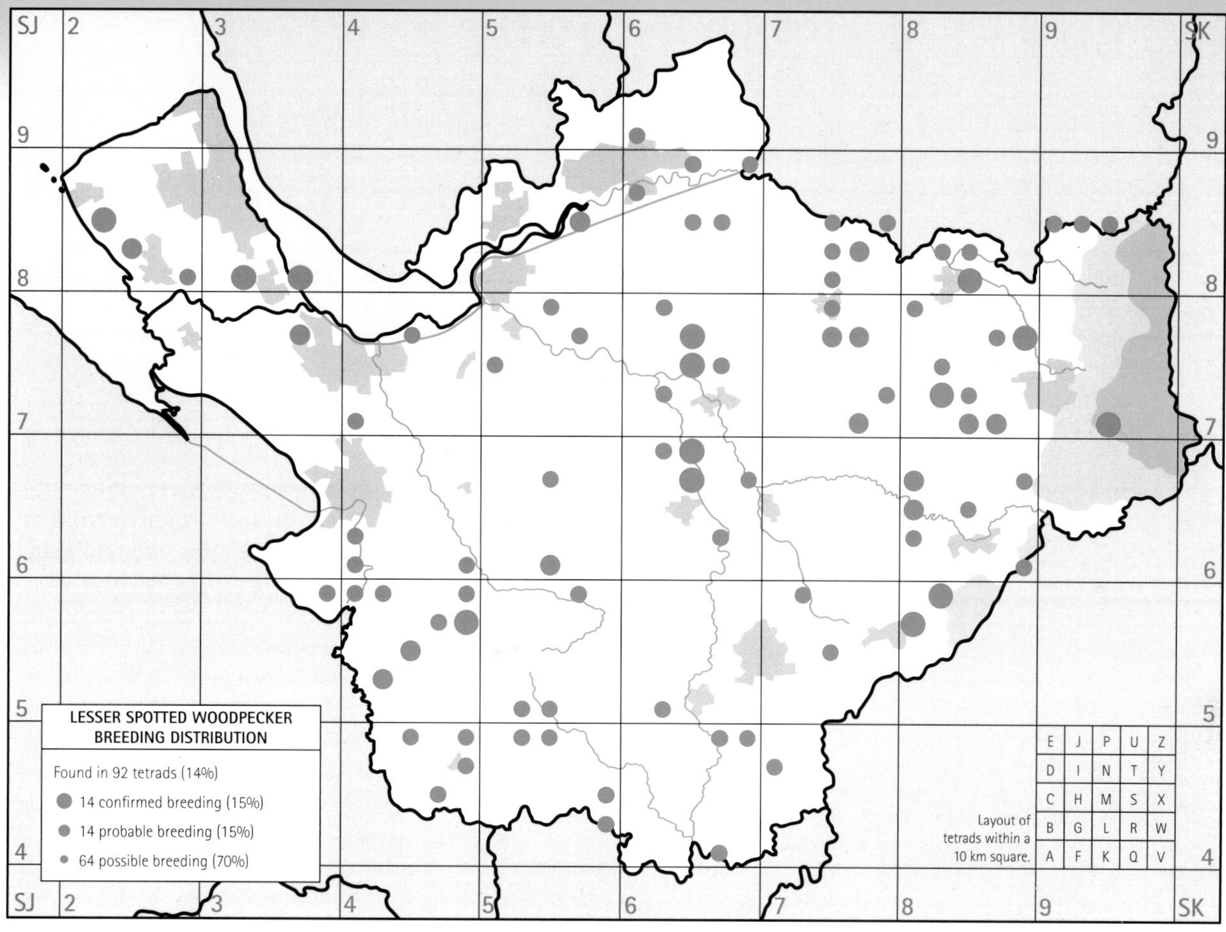
LESSER SPOTTED WOODPECKER
BREEDING DISTRIBUTION
Found in 92 tetrads (14%)
14 confirmed breeding (15%)
14 probable breeding (15%)
64 possible breeding (70%)
Layout of tetrads within a 10 km square.
E J P U Z
D I N T Y
C H M S X
B G L R W
A F K Q V
SJ
SK

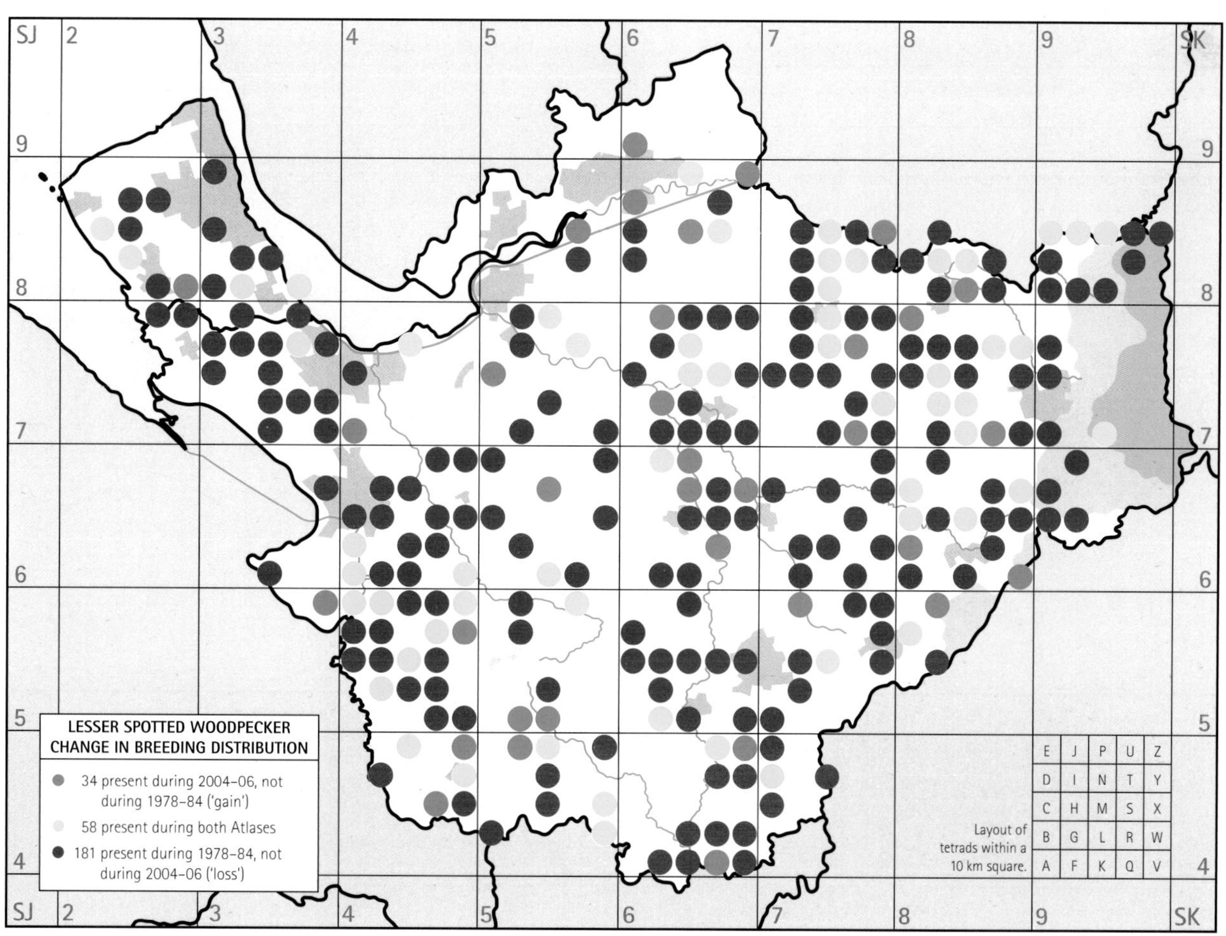
LESSER SPOTTED WOODPECKER
CHANGE IN BREEDING DISTRIBUTION
34 present during 2004–06, not during 1978–84 ('gain')
58 present during both Atlases
181 present during 1978–84, not during 2004–06 ('loss')
Layout of tetrads within a 10 km square.
E J P U Z
D I N T Y
C H M S X
B G L R W
A F K Q V
SJ
SK

This Atlas showed that Lesser Spotted Woodpeckers occupied the same number of tetrads in the two seasons but only 34 had birds present in both, with 58 having breeding season presence only and 57 holding a bird only in winter. Some of this could be the effect of visibility; this is an inconspicuous species, spending much of its time near the treetops and requiring some luck for observers to detect it. Previous authors make the same point, Hardy (1941) describing it as widely distributed but often overlooked, and Bell (1962) echoing those comments and adding that the species had been scarcer in the north but 'now the chances of finding a bird in the north or east appear to be as great as in the south or west of the county'. The winter map shows that Lesser Spotted Woodpeckers are widely scattered, with a big gap in the centre of Cheshire and in the eastern hills, but appearing to have small concentrations in south Wirral, around Knutsford, and Crewe and Nantwich.

Based on studies in Sweden, Lesser Spotted Woodpeckers are solitary outside the breeding season, and these Atlas observations bear that out, with 108 of the 112 winter records of single birds. Just four records were of two together, at least one of which was identified as a pair in February, probably preparing for the forthcoming breeding attempt. Birds roam about a very large home range, centred on their breeding territory and probably covering several hundreds of hectares, more than one tetrad (Wiktander *et al.* 2001b).

In winter, the submitted habitat codes showed most (63%) records in woodland, but with a reduction from the breeding season and a shift to farmland (20%) and human sites (14%). There were noticeably fewer records from carr woodland, just four compared to 11 in the breeding season, and with fewer in scrub as well, hinting that some birds quit these areas for the winter. An alternative suggestion, that observers did not visit these rather unwelcoming habitats as often in winter, does not hold good: for all species there were 465 records from the three categories of waterlogged woodland (A4, A5 and A6) in the breeding season and 411 in winter, not significantly different.

Their winter food is mainly longhorn beetles, adults and larvae, found beneath the bark of dead wood, and this species feeds during winter mainly on thin dead branches. In general, the volume of dead wood in British woods is increasing as many areas are left relatively unmanaged, but Lesser Spotted Woodpeckers do not seem to be benefiting. A possible explanation is that the types of dead wood that are increasing in these woods (large dead limbs and dead wood on the ground) are not favoured foraging habitats for this species. It is also possible, but not proven, that they are now less able to coexist with the high numbers of Great Spotted Woodpeckers principally because of nest site interference and competition (Smith 2007).

RAY SCALLY

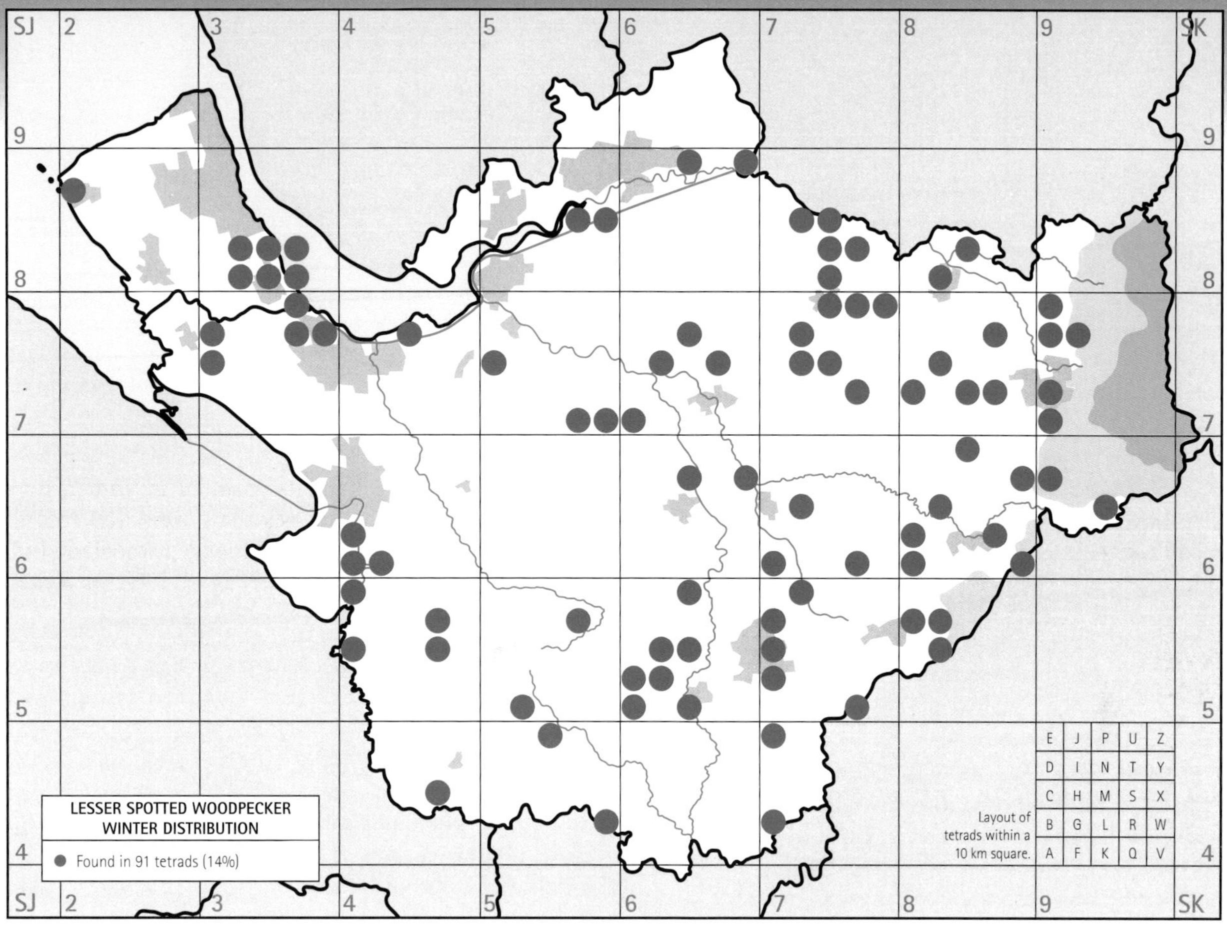
LESSER SPOTTED WOODPECKER
WINTER DISTRIBUTION
Found in 91 tetrads (14%)
Layout of tetrads within a 10 km square.
E J P U Z
D I N T Y
C H M S X
B G L R W
A F K Q V

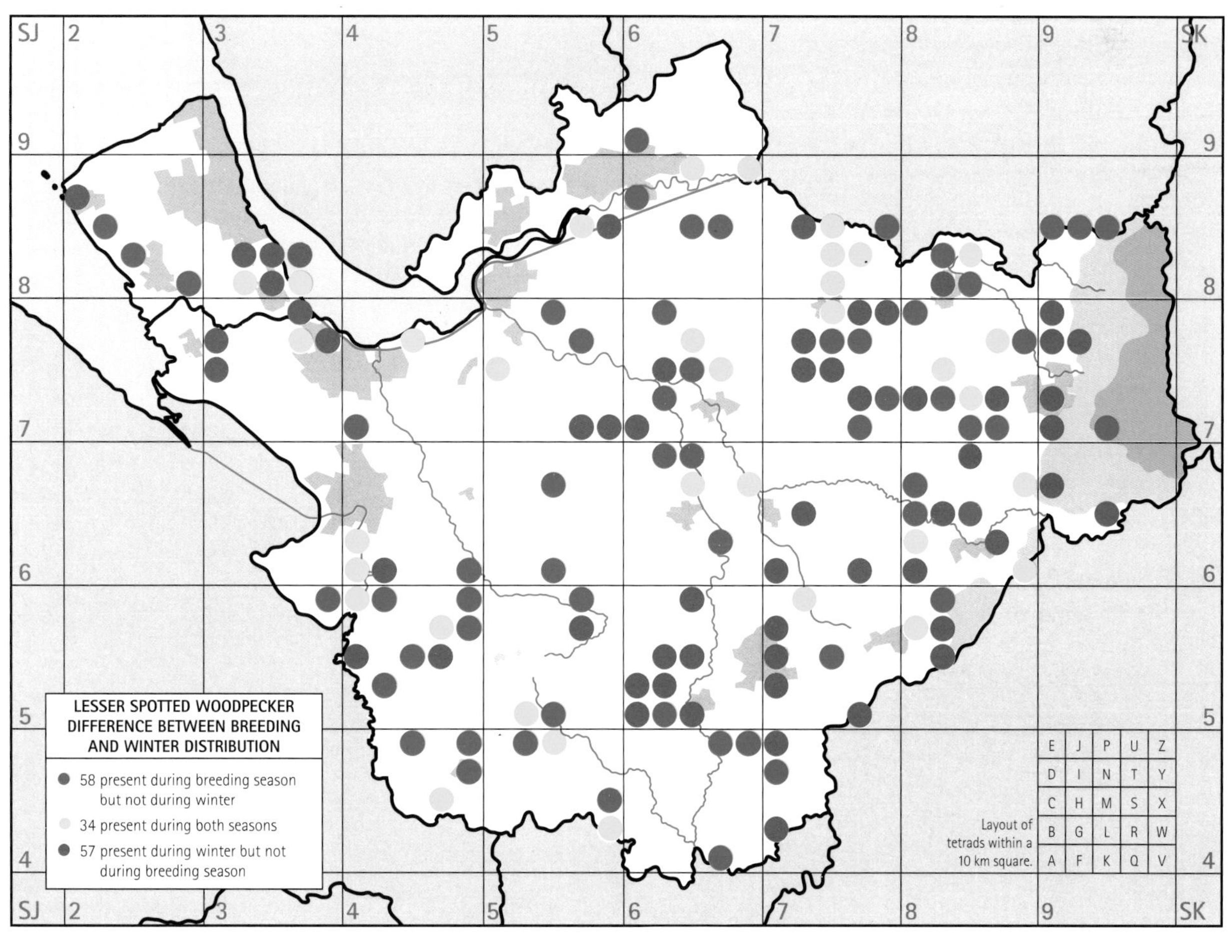
LESSER SPOTTED WOODPECKER
DIFFERENCE BETWEEN BREEDING AND WINTER DISTRIBUTION
58 present during breeding season but not during winter
34 present during both seasons
57 present during winter but not during breeding season
Layout of tetrads within a 10 km square.
E J P U Z
D I N T Y
C H M S X
B G L R W
A F K Q V

Skylark

Alauda arvensis

RICHARD STEEL

The Skylark has become an icon for the effects of industrialized agriculture on our wildlife, so it is depressing to see the extent of loss of this species between our two Atlases. The change map shows Skylarks lost from 172 tetrads, with 17 gains. To put it another way: in 1978–84, there were only 39 tetrads in which the species was not found; in this Atlas, there are 185 blank tetrads. Most of the losses are scattered across agricultural Cheshire, and the distribution map shows several significant gaps, such as the east of SJ87 and the west of SJ46, where Skylarks were present in every tetrad twenty years ago; birds were already patchily distributed in SJ37 in the *First Atlas*, now an obvious blank area. The species has also abandoned Hilbre and most urban areas such as Chester, Ellesmere Port, Northwich, Runcorn and the east Wirral conurbation, although odd birds breed nowadays in derelict brownfield sites in the Birkenhead docklands.

The habitat codes showed, unsurprisingly, that 81% of records were on farmland, with the main categories 33% improved grassland, 15% unimproved grassland, 16% mixed grassland and tilled land and 12% tilled land, so disproportionately high use was made of unimproved and mixed farmland, plus 11% of records on semi-natural grassland and marsh. On improved grassland, high fertilizer applications have led to vegetation that is too tall and dense for nesting, as well as high nest failure rates through trampling by cattle or frequent mowing for silage. Skylarks' ground nests suffer high levels of predation, which they minimize by nesting far away from field edges and having the shortest incubation period of all British birds (11 days), with chicks scattering from the nest about eight days after hatching, well before they can fly. The 79 broods that I have ringed in Cheshire, mostly at Frodsham Marsh, from 1981 to 2007, had hatching dates from 4 May to 12 July. They normally lay a clutch of four eggs, reducing with later attempts: I found a mean brood size of 3.5 chicks in May, 3.4 in June, and 2.9 in July. Skylarks are not choosy about the food they bring to their chicks, taking whatever invertebrate prey is abundant in the area. Adult Skylarks carry large items of food for their chicks, often visible from a distance with the naked eye, and males sometimes sing with a beak full of food! Some Atlas surveyors found the species frustratingly difficult, and many observed just song, although some recorded it as D (display), accounting for the high proportion of 'probable' breeding.

The national population index dropped by 40% during the fieldwork period of our *First Atlas*, 1978–84, and has fallen by another 32% in the 20 years since then. Cheshire can never have been one of the most important counties for Skylark, however, as improved grassland holds the lowest Skylark density of all habitat types (Browne *et al.* 2000).

The BTO BBS analysis for 2004–05 shows that the breeding population of Cheshire and Wirral was 9,010 birds (4,880–13,130), corresponding to an average of about 19 birds per tetrad in which the species was recorded. Probably most of the birds detected on BBS transects are the singing males, so these figures are likely to equate roughly to numbers of pairs. Densities vary enormously across the county, as suggested by the abundance map. In many tetrads, especially in south Cheshire, it was a struggle to find even one Skylark, while some tetrads in the eastern hills, and on Frodsham Marsh, held 20 or more pairs. On the Dee estuary saltmarsh, Skylark breeding densities reach the very high levels of around 120 pairs per square kilometre (around 500 pairs per tetrad) on ungrazed or moderately grazed coastal marshes, but fall to 52 pairs per square kilometre on heavily grazed marshes (Colin Wells, quoted in Donald 2004).

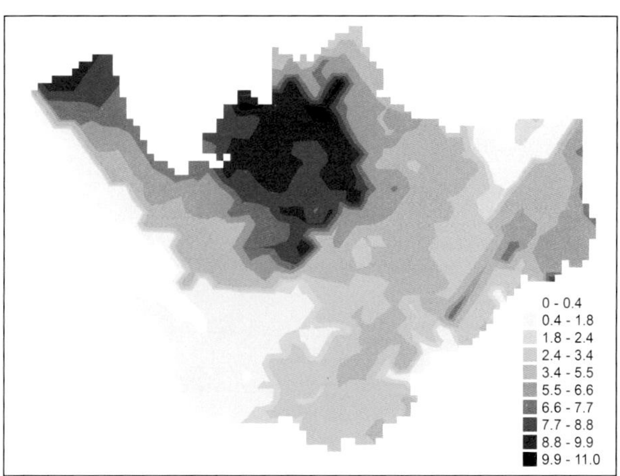

Skylark abundance.

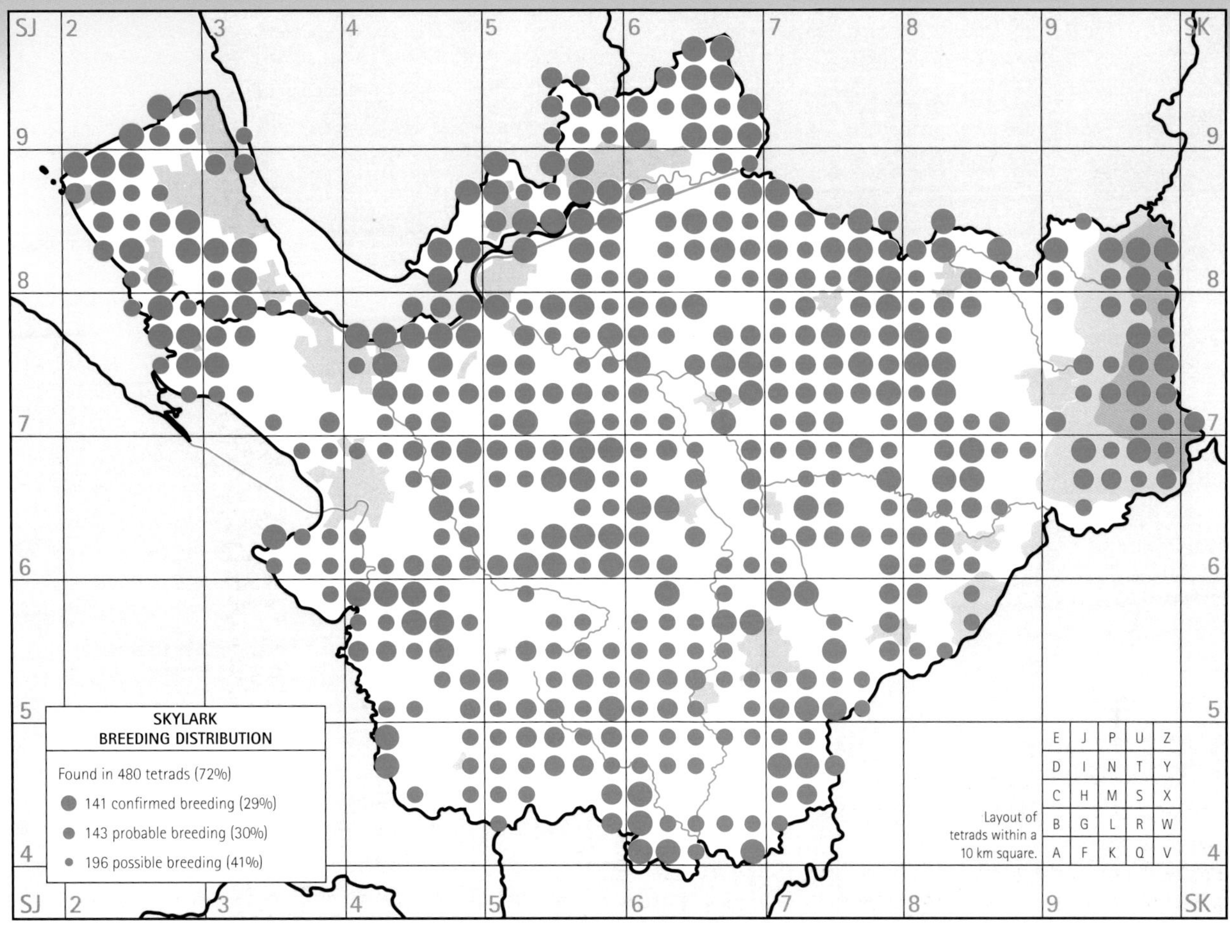
SKYLARK
BREEDING DISTRIBUTION
Found in 480 tetrads (72%)
141 confirmed breeding (29%)
143 probable breeding (30%)
196 possible breeding (41%)
Layout of tetrads within a 10 km square.
E J P U Z
D I N T Y
C H M S X
B G L R W
A F K Q V
SJ
SK

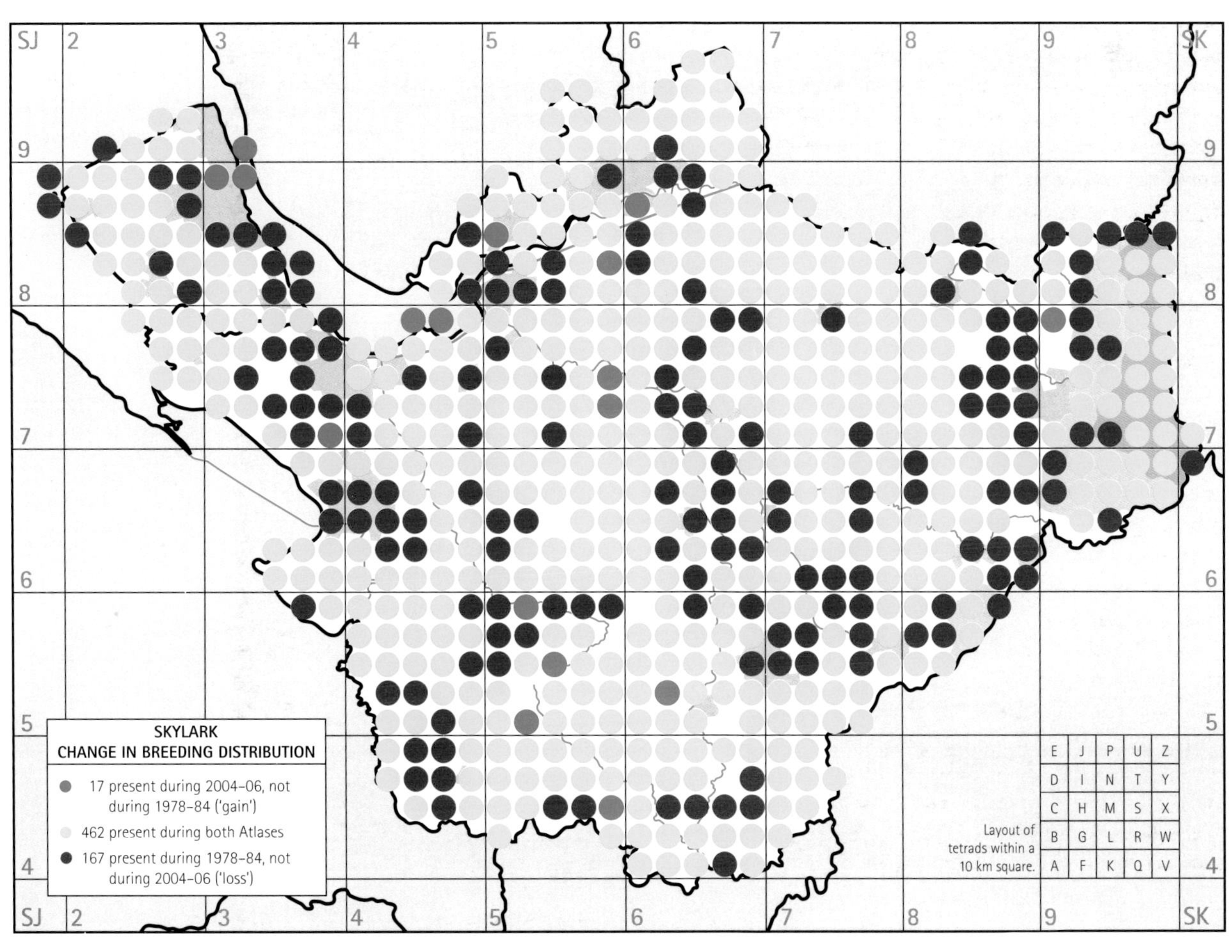
SKYLARK
CHANGE IN BREEDING DISTRIBUTION
17 present during 2004–06, not during 1978–84 ('gain')
462 present during both Atlases
167 present during 1978–84, not during 2004–06 ('loss')
Layout of tetrads within a 10 km square.
E J P U Z
D I N T Y
C H M S X
B G L R W
A F K Q V
SJ
SK

RICHARD STEEL

Many Skylarks remain on their territories in the lowlands all year round. Others leave their breeding areas and join flocks, moving to lower ground or southwards. The winter map shows a similar distribution to that for the breeding season, although the species is everywhere more thinly distributed. Detailed studies have shown that Skylark winter density halves for every 140 m increase in altitude (Donald 2004) and most birds quit the eastern hills: Skylarks were recorded in 30 tetrads above 200 m in the breeding season, but only 10 of them in winter, and six of these 10 were February records with the observers noting song, so probably most of these records were breeding birds returning early to their territories. There were 269 tetrads occupied in both seasons, 211 tetrads had birds in the breeding season but not in winter and 34 tetrads were occupied in winter but not during the breeding season.

As well as the altitudinal move, and some partial migration, Skylarks shift habitats in winter. Grazed grassland, never their favourite habitat in the breeding season, is used even less in winter, and their preferred winter habitats are coastal marshes and weedy cereal stubbles. They are always wary of predators from the field edges, so Skylarks feed only in large fields, avoiding anywhere less than 2.5 ha and selecting fields larger than 7.5 ha, and they favour areas with low hedges and no large trees (Gillings & Fuller 2001). They roost at night on the ground, often where they have been feeding.

Of the winter habitat codes, 85% were farmland and 10% semi-natural grassland and marsh. Observers in 61 tetrads recorded birds in stubble, more than any other species, with amplifying comments indicating seven instances of wheat stubble and four of maize. Most birds were found in singles or pairs, probably the resident birds, and the median flock size was only four. Seventy-two flocks were counted with 10–30 birds, and there were just 33 submitted counts of more than 30 birds in one flock. Seven flocks of 100 or more birds were reported during this Atlas, from widely scattered parts of the county. The largest by far, 1,000 birds, was on the Dee salt-marsh in SJ27U, with others on the Dee in SJ27S and SJ28Q, and the Mersey salt-marsh in SJ47D. Three-figure gatherings on farmland were at Risley (SJ69Q/R), with flocks noted on stubble near Little Leigh (SJ67D) and Blakenhall (SJ74I). Extrapolating from the mean density, there are probably just over 5,000 Skylarks in the county in an average winter.

Outside the breeding season, Skylarks switch to a mainly vegetarian diet (Green 1978): they gain most of their energy from grain and seeds, also taking any arthropods whenever they can find them, but—perhaps because they cannot find sufficient seeds—they often eat copious quantities of leaves. These are of low nutritional value, however, and their digestive system is not adapted to breaking down cellulose. Much of the cause of their population decline is attributable to winter food supplies. On arable land, the shift to autumn sowing of cereals hit Skylarks badly in two ways: the loss of stubble reduces overwinter survival, then, for much of the breeding season, the crop is too tall for them to nest in. High levels of herbicide and insecticide use on farmland have also reduced weed seed and invertebrate food resources.

The general description of the species' status has probably not changed for a century. Coward (1910) wrote that 'in winter it is absent from the bleak moorlands, but frequents the open country of the lowlands in flocks. Especially during hard weather when the inland districts are almost forsaken, great numbers of larks frequent the Dee marshes.' Boyd (1951) noted that 'throughout winter even in the coldest weather many remain in the stubble and old potato ground'. Probably the main aspect of their behaviour that has changed is their hard weather movements, for which Skylark used to be a classic species. Coward (1910) and Bell (1962) wrote about memorable movements of large flocks, and the county bird reports in the 1980s detailed several movements out of the county, or to the Dee, in spells of freezing weather up to December 1989. The only significant episode since then was in January/February 1997 when up to 5,000 were found on the Dee in cold weather. No such event has been recorded in the last decade of mild winters.

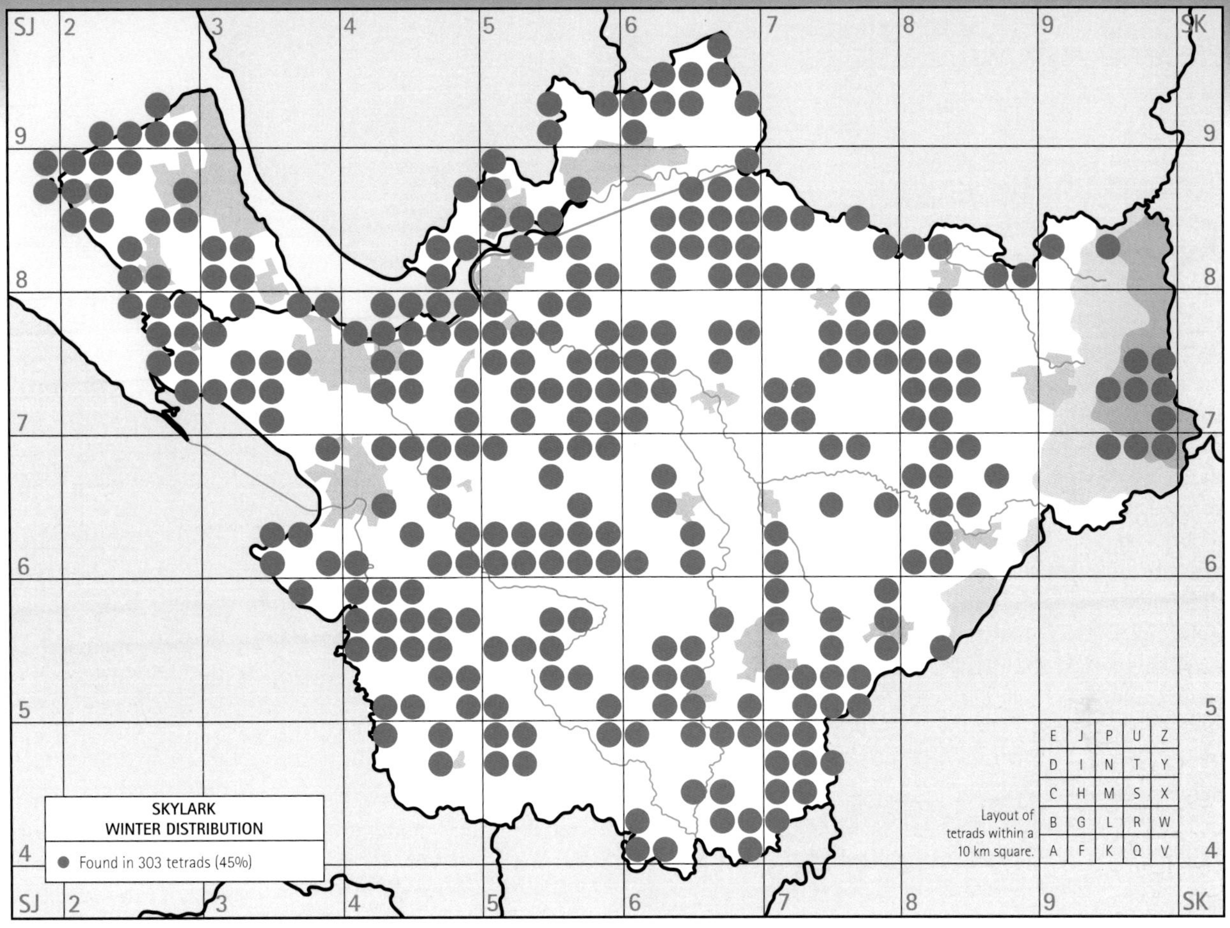
SKYLARK
WINTER DISTRIBUTION
Found in 303 tetrads (45%)
Layout of tetrads within a 10 km square.
E J P U Z
D I N T Y
C H M S X
B G L R W
A F K Q V
SJ
SK

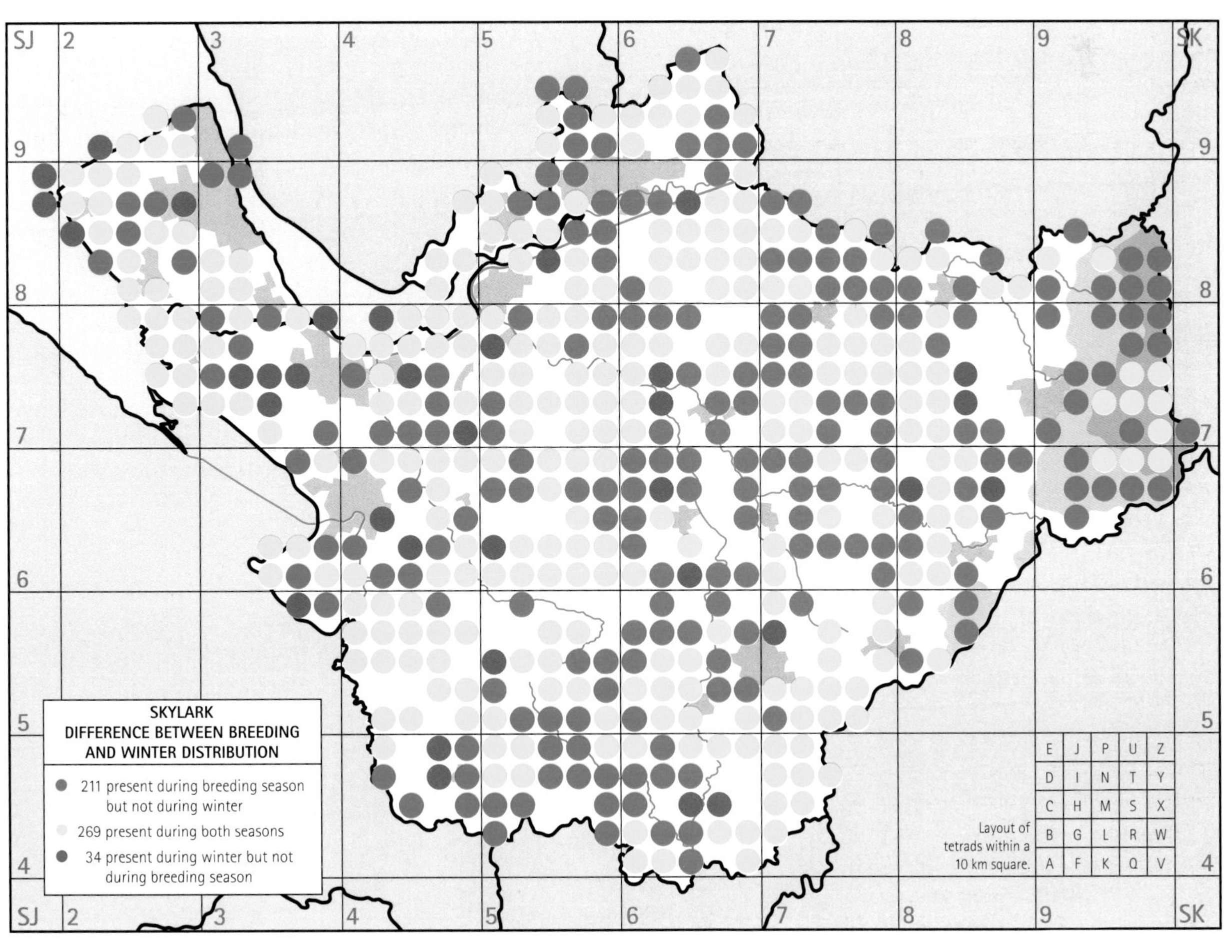
SKYLARK
DIFFERENCE BETWEEN BREEDING AND WINTER DISTRIBUTION
211 present during breeding season but not during winter
269 present during both seasons
34 present during winter but not during breeding season
Layout of tetrads within a 10 km square.
E J P U Z
D I N T Y
C H M S X
B G L R W
A F K Q V
SJ
SK

Sand Martin

Riparia riparia

Sand Martins live up to their scientific name and are much more likely to be near water than the other hirundines. Sand Martins live in colonies containing anything from a few to several hundred pairs, and make their nests by burrowing into vertical faces. The association with water, for feeding and for nesting, is dramatically illustrated by the habitat codes submitted for this survey. Eighty per cent of the Sand Martin records were in class G (fresh water) compared to 3% for Swallow and House Martin. Most of the remainder were for the farmland surrounding a nesting area. The Atlas map clearly shows the lines of the county's major rivers, especially the Dee, Dane and Bollin, plus the Manchester Ship Canal.

Most of the county's Sand Martins, however, are to be found in the main industrial sand extraction sites, where their fortunes often depend on economic or commercial decisions of the quarry operators. The amount of construction sand being quarried, mostly in the Delamere/Sandiway area, largely follows the major building projects and is now only half of the peak in the mid-1990s, and there are fewer exposed sand-faces, many of them being sloping rather than vertical. There are more likely to be suitable breeding sites in the Chelford and Congleton quarries, from where the whiter, sharper silica sand is extracted; there is less fluctuation in its use, for making glass, moulds for foundries and ceramic glazes, and nearly half of the UK's nationally important reserves are in the glacial deposits of east Cheshire.

Sand Martin distribution appears to have contracted compared to the *First Atlas*, with 47 tetrads with confirmed or probable breeding compared to 82 then (B and N regarded as confirmed breeding in our *First Atlas*), but with such a peripatetic species, a three-year survey will inevitably find fewer occupied sites than one spanning seven years. Such a colonial species cannot be reliably monitored by the normal BBS methods, but counts of apparently occupied nest holes provide a good census. Based on annual surveys of the mid-Cheshire quarries, the county's breeding population in an average year is estimated at 1,500 pairs. Their population can swing markedly from one year to another, mainly driven by the level of winter mortality (Cowley & Siriwardena 2005). They migrate to spend the winter in West Africa just south of the Sahara: Cheshire-ringed birds have been reported from the Niger inundation zone in Mali and the Djoudj National Park in northern Senegal. Year-to-year ringing in the mid-Cheshire quarries shows that the annual survival of adult Sand Martins varies from 12% in the worst year (1983–84) to around 50% in the best years, determined almost entirely by the rainfall prior to their arrival in West Africa (Norman & Peach to be published). In the drier years there are too few flying insects to support the population so many birds starve, and they are at increased risk of other hazards such as sandstorms.

This is one of our earliest spring migrants, with the first birds in March, but the main arrival in April is only patchily recorded. In years with cold, wet springs, many birds gather at the county's meres and reservoirs to feed. In dry and warm weather, best for the birds, most of them make their way straight to breeding sites, so birdwatchers at migration points and waterbodies see few Sand Martins and declare it to be 'a poor spring' for the species. Nests can be constructed in a few days, with chicks flying by the end of May in some years. Many pairs will have a second brood, often shifting to a new site, partly to avoid nest collapse as the sand dries out, and to minimize infection by nest parasites such as ticks. The first broods are best for the species because juveniles fledging early in the season survive the immediate postfledging period better (Cowley 2001).

As well as avalanches, which can cause total loss of a colony, their other main hazards are land-based predators, especially foxes, badgers and mink, who dig out the nests and contents. Raptors take some flying birds, Hobbies being especially feared. In the 1990s, as breeding Hobbies started to move into the county, it was interesting to observe that Sand Martins scattered in fright at their special 'Hobby' alarm call, different from that given for other aerial predators, even though they had never previously experienced such attacks at Cheshire colonies.

RAY SCALLY

Sponsored by Syngenta CTL

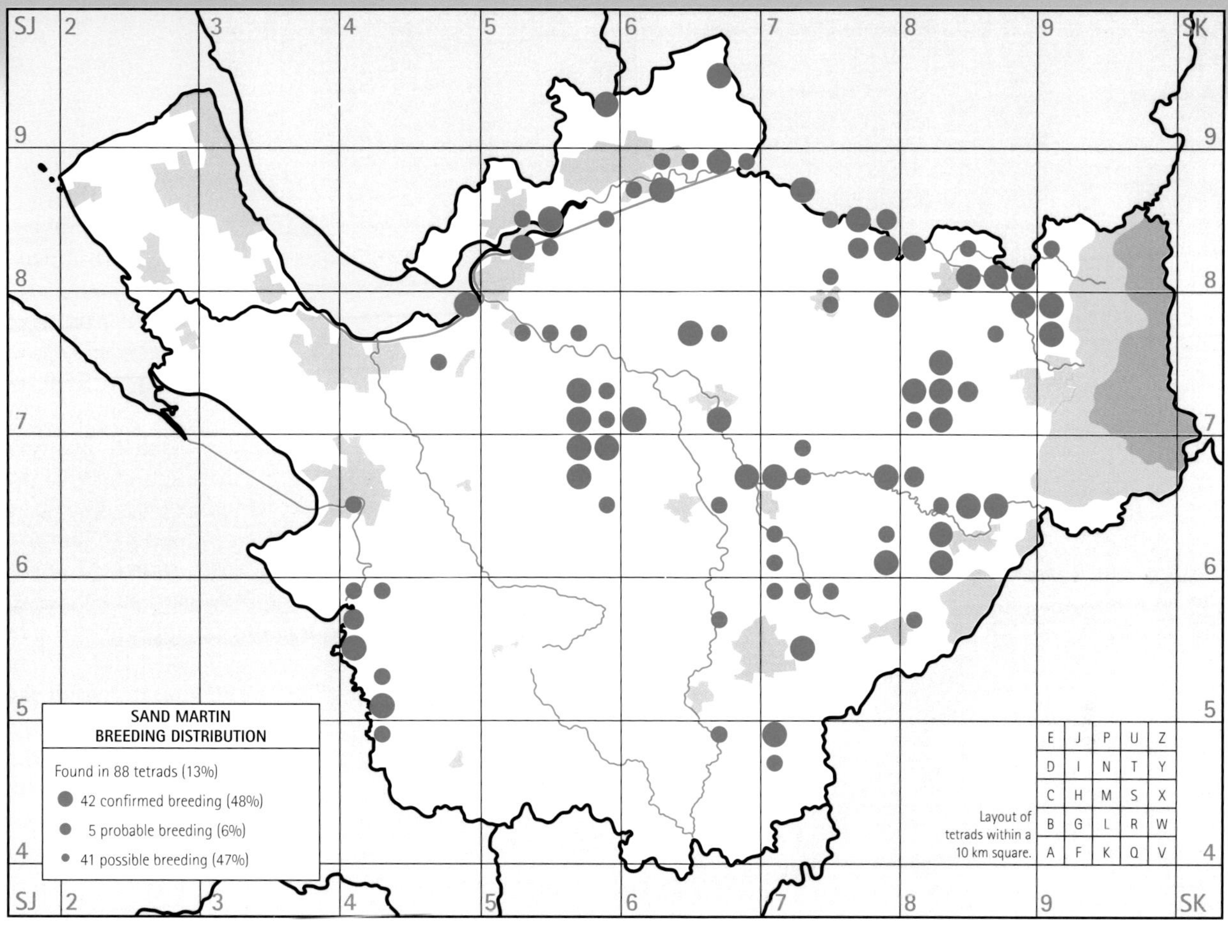
SAND MARTIN
BREEDING DISTRIBUTION
Found in 88 tetrads (13%)
42 confirmed breeding (48%)
5 probable breeding (6%)
41 possible breeding (47%)
Layout of tetrads within a 10 km square.
E J P U Z
D I N T Y
C H M S X
B G L R W
A F K Q V
SJ
SK
2
3
4
5
6
7
8
9

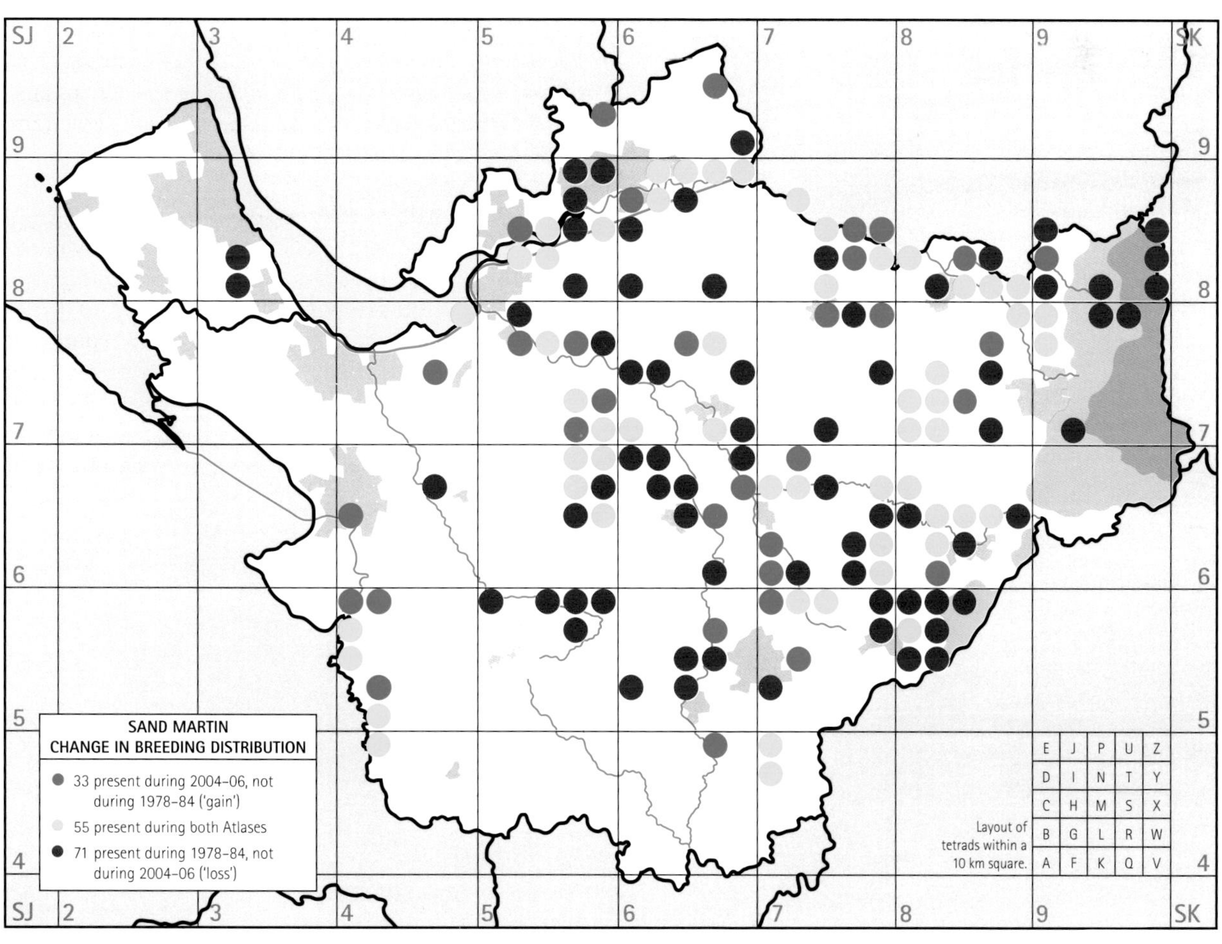
SAND MARTIN
CHANGE IN BREEDING DISTRIBUTION
33 present during 2004–06, not during 1978–84 ('gain')
55 present during both Atlases
71 present during 1978–84, not during 2004–06 ('loss')
Layout of tetrads within a 10 km square.
E J P U Z
D I N T Y
C H M S X
B G L R W
A F K Q V
SJ
SK
2
3
4
5
6
7
8
9

Swallow

Hirundo rustica

Swallow is our most widespread, and most numerous, summer migrant. The maps show that they are almost ubiquitous, but in the last twenty years have been lost from 23 tetrads, notably in built-up areas including the east Wirral conurbation, the Mersey valley towns and Macclesfield; proof of breeding was difficult to obtain in Northwich, Chester and Crewe. There is no explanation for their loss from these sites. Their preferred habitats for feeding are pastures, meadows and areas of water where flying insects are most abundant: nearly all of the habitat codes submitted were farmland, mainly grassland, or human sites, predominantly rural. They especially follow large grazing animals, and in good weather Swallows take roughly one insect every six seconds, preferentially seeking out large flies such as horseflies and hoverflies, which they are well able to distinguish from wasps—quite a feat whilst flying at 25 miles per hour (Turner 2006).

Swallows are conspicuous birds with little fear of man, and it is very easy to prove when they are breeding. Nests are usually in the dark corner of a building, particularly those housing livestock, and it is amazing to watch their aerial prowess as they swoop from a bright summer's day into a dim shippon or stable without apparently pausing, often manoeuvring through narrow gaps such as broken window-panes. Swallows are semi-colonial, and there may be 10 or more pairs at favoured sites. Most pairs have two broods, frequently reusing the same nest, with the first-brood chicks often helping their parents with the later broods including feeding their younger siblings, no doubt good practice for their own future life (Skutch 1987).

Their population fluctuates somewhat, perhaps connected to conditions in the Sahel prior to the birds' spring passage through West Africa on their way back from their South African wintering grounds (Robinson *et al.* 2003). Such variations are rather unlikely to have made much difference to their distribution, because in years with peak numbers, more pairs settle on favoured farms rather than establish new colonies at suboptimal sites (Møller 1983). Since the arable/pastoral polarization of agricultural practice, Swallows have declined in the east and risen in the west of England (Evans & Robinson 2004). The BTO analysis of BBS results shows them at their highest density in the agricultural south-west of the county, with a breeding population of Cheshire and Wirral in 2004–05 estimated at 43,620 birds (28,230–59,020). This figure, an average of 72 birds per tetrad with confirmed and probable breeding, amounts to 1.9% of the national population (Newson *et al.* 2008) and suggests that Cheshire may well be the Swallow capital of England.

● Four Swallows were recorded during the winter Atlas period: Gowy Marshes (SJ47G) on 20 February 2005; Fiddler's Ferry (SJ58M) on 31 January 2005; Hankelow (SJ64S) on 10 December 2006; and Edleston (SJ65F) on 20 December 2006. There are only four birds on record from later in December, with none ever before in the county in January or February. The earliest spring date is 8 March, in 1976 and 2001 (*CWBRs*).

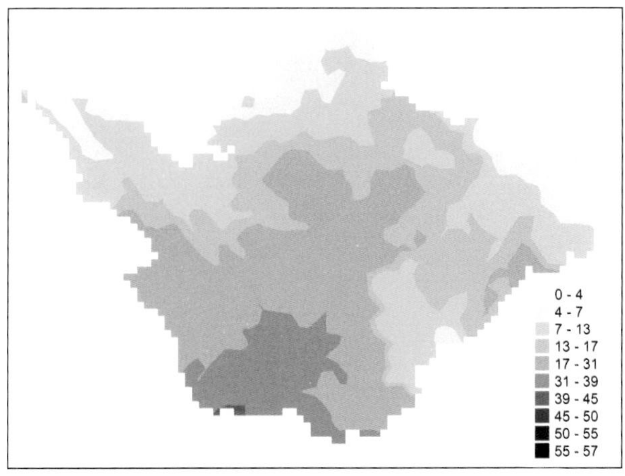

Swallow abundance.

Sponsored by Roy N. Allenby

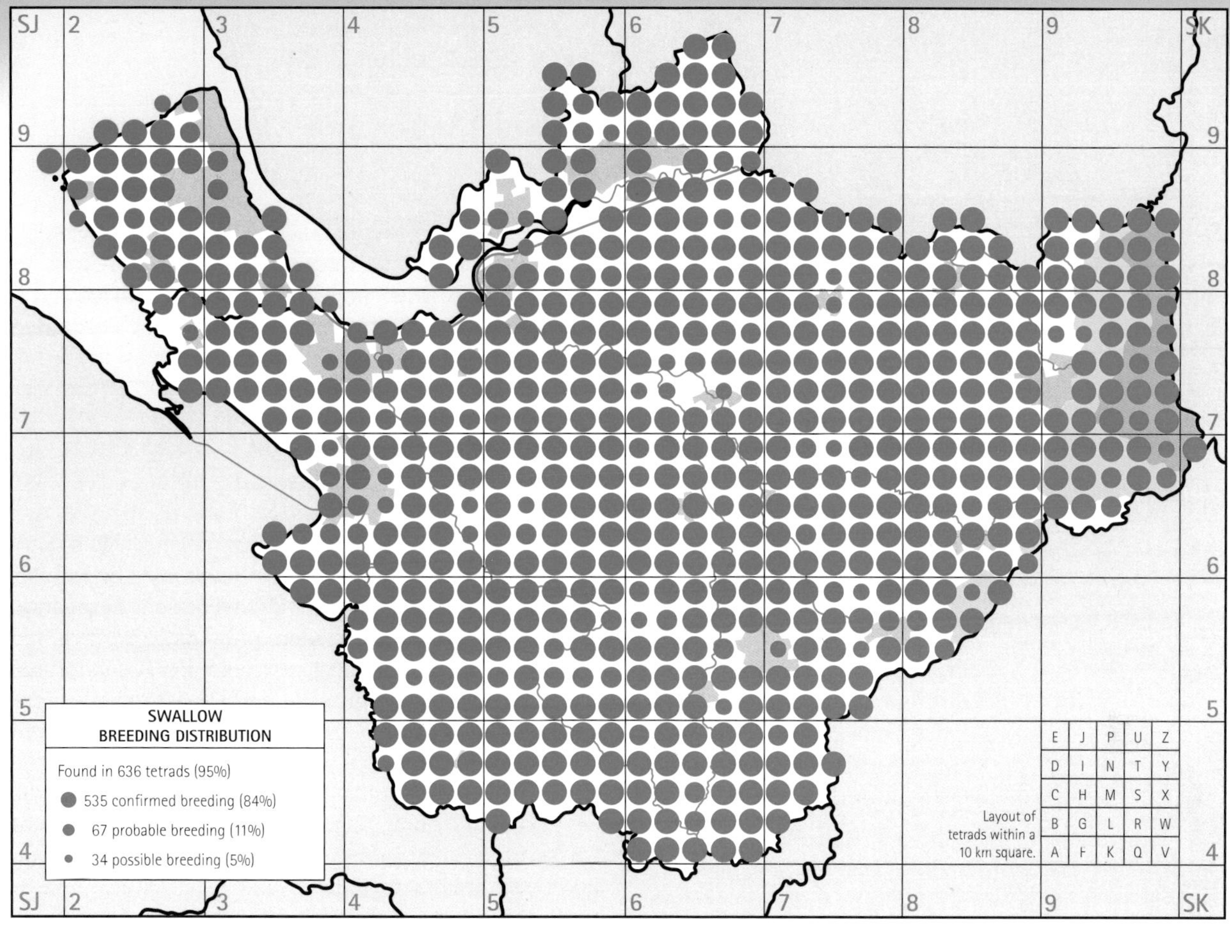
SJ
2
3
4
5
6
7
8
9
SK
9
8
7
6
5
4
SWALLOW
BREEDING DISTRIBUTION
Found in 636 tetrads (95%)
535 confirmed breeding (84%)
67 probable breeding (11%)
34 possible breeding (5%)
E J P U Z
D I N T Y
C H M S X
B G L R W
A F K Q V
Layout of tetrads within a 10 km square.

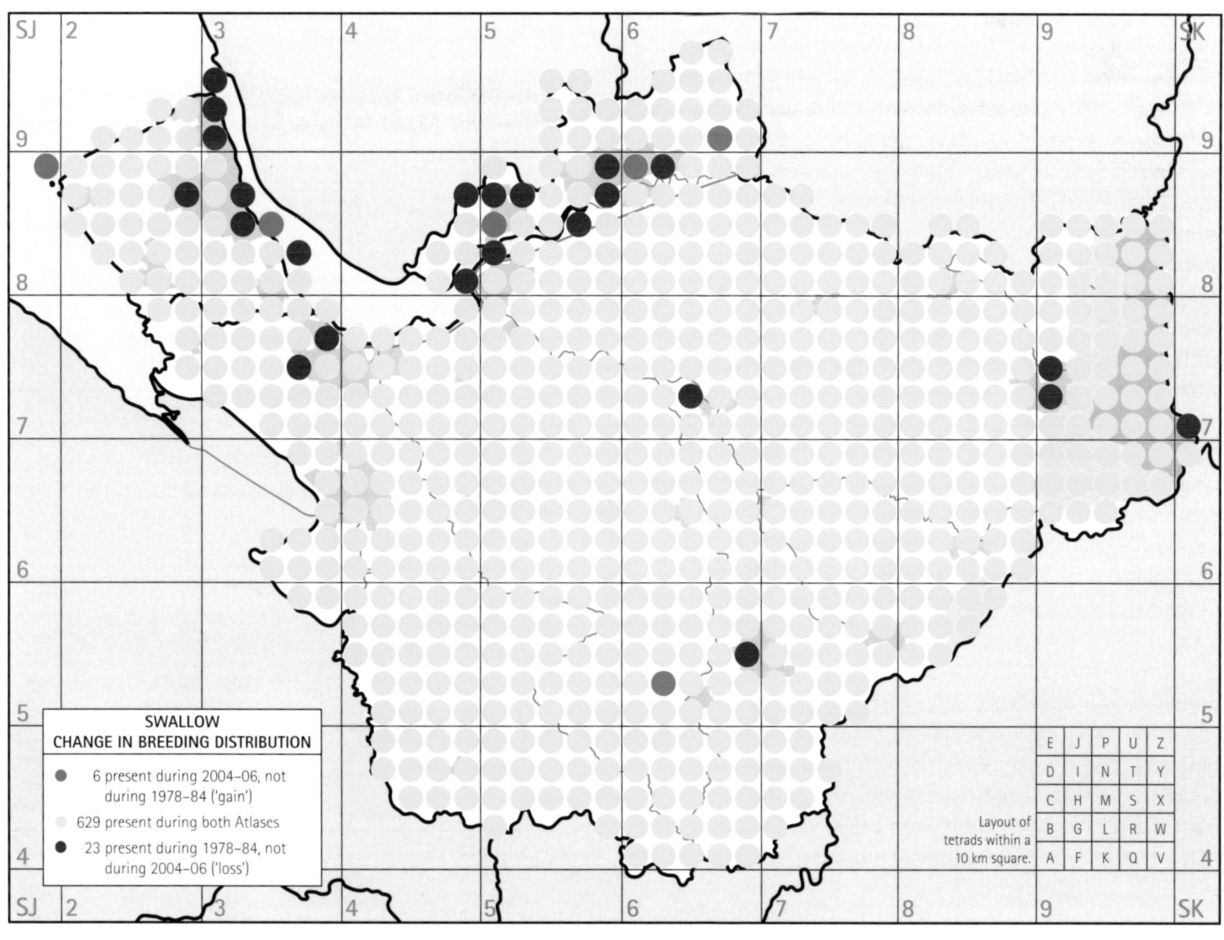
SJ
2
3
4
5
6
7
8
9
SK
9
8
7
6
5
4
SWALLOW
CHANGE IN BREEDING DISTRIBUTION
6 present during 2004–06, not during 1978–84 ('gain')
629 present during both Atlases
23 present during 1978–84, not during 2004–06 ('loss')
E J P U Z
D I N T Y
C H M S X
B G L R W
A F K Q V
Layout of tetrads within a 10 km square.

House Martin

Delichon urbicum

STEVE ROUND

This is surely one of our most familiar commensal birds, all of their nest sites being on man-made structures. Although some House Martins nest singly, most of them group into colonies, which may be obvious, with many nests all on one building, or more dispersed, perhaps covering several streets of houses. Some large colonies have been counted for many years, including at Winick Hospital, Warrington (now demolished) (maximum of 123 nests in 1992); Alderley Park (maximum of 73 nests in 1992); Styal Prison (maximum of 124 nests in 1997) and Toft Hall (maximum of 62 nests in 1999). The colonial birds apparently all join together in feeding flocks, pleasantly twittering, often high overhead, as they catch flying insects, especially flies and aphids.

In this survey, 94% of the habitat codes submitted were in categories E or F (farmland and human sites) exactly the same as for Swallow. House Martins, however, are even more associated with human sites (78% of records compared to 67% for Swallow), and with more of an urban bias (30% of the F codes being urban or suburban, compared to 20% for Swallow). The farmland codes were spread across all categories of farming, but mostly the grassland types where flying insects are most likely to be found.

This Atlas shows that House Martins are almost ubiquitous but apparently missing from the vicinity of Birkenhead, Runcorn, Chester and Northwich, and thinly distributed in the east of Cheshire. They have been lost from a number of tetrads since the *First Atlas*: the 'change' map shows 18 gains but 50 losses, widespread across the county with no discernible pattern. This suggests that the species has become less common than twenty years ago. Participants in the CAWOS House Martin survey report on fluctuations in the number of nests at their site, but unfortunately this tells nothing about the species' population and just reflects the well-known propensity for individual colonies to grow or contract. To establish population changes really requires a thorough survey of all the House Martins in quite a large area.

The BTO analysis of BBS results shows that the breeding population of Cheshire and Wirral in 2004–05 is estimated at 19,630 birds (7,540–31,710). This figure, an average of 19 pairs per tetrad with confirmed and probable breeding, amounts to 1.6% of the national population (Newson *et al.* 2008), making the county much higher than 'average' for House Martin population. Although there is no regular national population monitoring, the BTO has taken a cautious approach and recently added House Martin to the Amber List of species of conservation concern. Many other long-distance migrants are declining; almost nothing is known about the House Martins' wintering areas in trans-Saharan Africa (*Migration Atlas*).

Whilst in Britain, they have no particular hazards to face during the breeding season, although some householders object to their nests and take action to deter the birds, ignoring the folklore that bad luck attends a house deserted by House Martins. Perhaps more of a concern is the use of modern building materials, for the birds cannot build their mud nests on plastic soffits and fascia boards.

Sponsored by Mary Prince and Susan Bastin

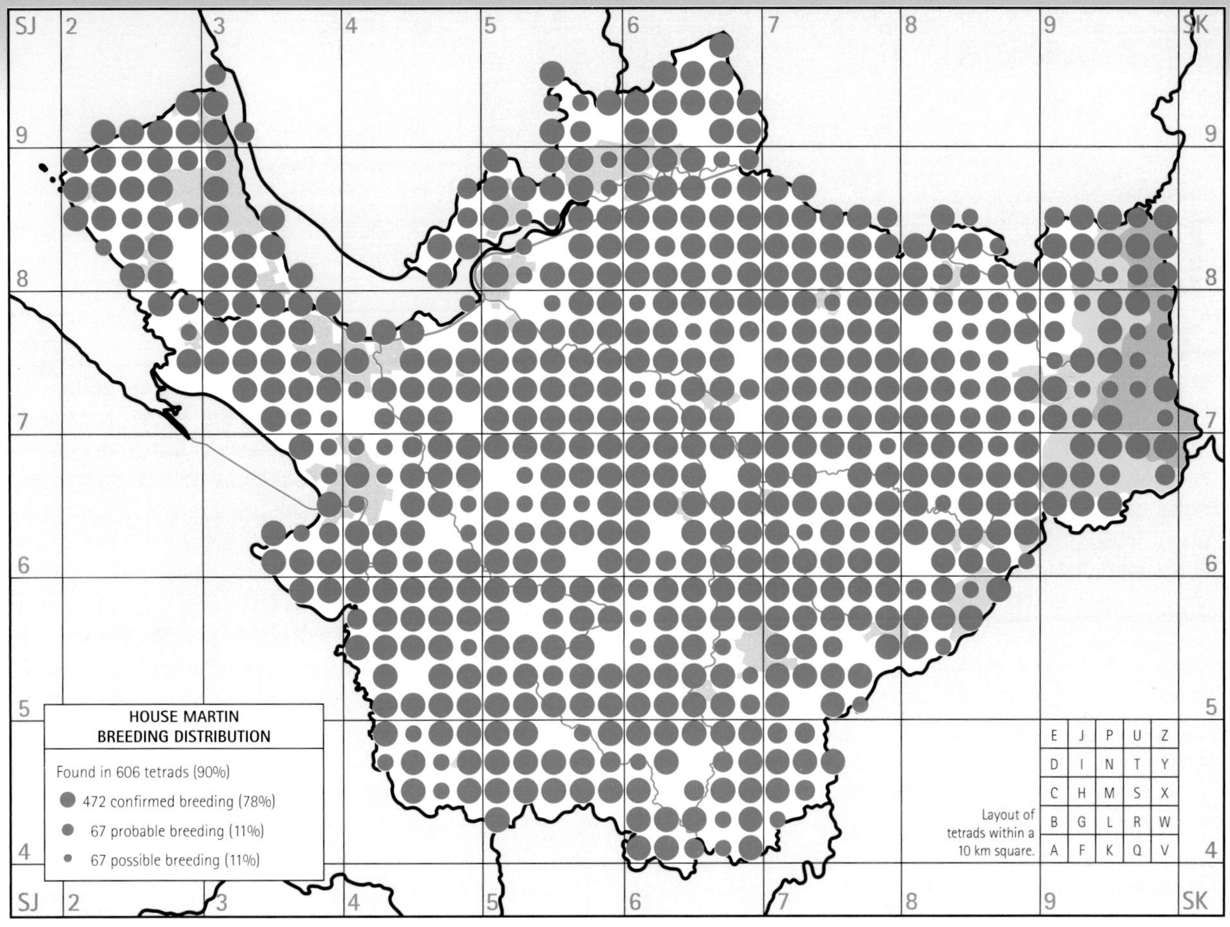
HOUSE MARTIN
BREEDING DISTRIBUTION
Found in 606 tetrads (90%)
472 confirmed breeding (78%)
67 probable breeding (11%)
67 possible breeding (11%)
Layout of tetrads within a 10 km square.
E J P U Z
D I N T Y
C H M S X
B G L R W
A F K Q V
SJ
SK

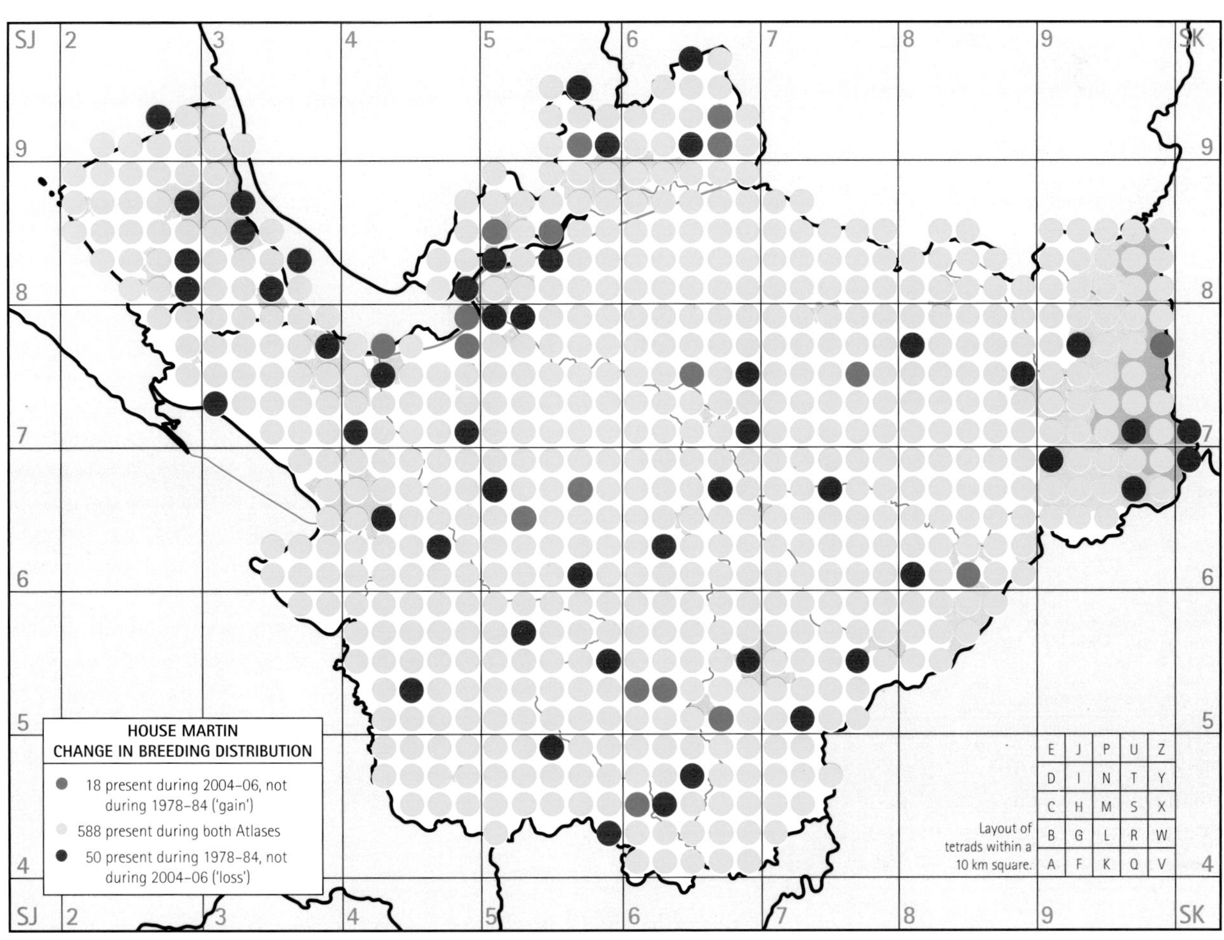
HOUSE MARTIN
CHANGE IN BREEDING DISTRIBUTION
18 present during 2004–06, not during 1978–84 ('gain')
588 present during both Atlases
50 present during 1978–84, not during 2004–06 ('loss')
Layout of tetrads within a 10 km square.
E J P U Z
D I N T Y
C H M S X
B G L R W
A F K Q V
SJ
SK

Tree Pipit

Anthus trivialis

This is now one of our scarcest passerine birds, with probably fewer than 10 pairs breeding in Cheshire. Their county population has crashed, going from 82 occupied tetrads in our *First Atlas* to just 13 now: the only areas where Tree Pipits are normally found are the foothills of the Pennines, and Risley Moss.

The contraction in Cheshire distribution reflects the species' national decline. BTO Common Birds Census (CBC) data show that their population peaked in 1985, and had dropped by 84% to 2005. The reduction in Cheshire was well under way by the time of the national Atlas in 1988–91, when Tree Pipit was lost from as many as 10 of the 10 km squares that had been occupied in the 1968–72 Atlas. The core of their British range is the western Atlantic oakwoods—sometimes dubbed 'Britain's Rainforests'—which have a unique community of birds, especially the migrants Tree Pipit, Wood Warbler, Redstart and Pied Flycatcher, all of which are in decline. These areas were not well surveyed by the CBC, and the uncertainty caused by the sparse coverage means that Tree Pipit is only placed on the Amber List of species of conservation concern, whilst it deserves to be on the Red List. The 'repeat woodland bird survey', in which BTO and RSPB staff revisited in 2003/04 hundreds of woods that had been surveyed 20 years before, also showed drops of 70–85% in Tree Pipit numbers (Amar *et al.* 2006).

The reasons for their population decline are unknown, but have been suggested to be linked to changing forest structure, as new plantations mature, and reduced management of lowland woods (Fuller *et al.* 2005). This explanation does not fit the managed plantations of Delamere Forest, where they used to be found in the early-growth stages but are not there now, even though apparently suitable habitat is readily available. In similar areas of commercial Scots pine and Corsican pine in Thetford Forest, Norfolk, Tree Pipits reach a maximum density when newly planted pines are one to six years old. Birds crowd in, with a minimum territory size of 1 ha in five-year-old stock, but the area is unsuitable for them by the time that the trees are 10–12 years of age. Densities are much higher in the main parts of the forest than in surrounding patches of woodland. The species is limited by the availability of song-posts and the best areas have at least one tall tree left amidst the clear-felled sections (Burton 2007).

As with many of the migrant bird populations that are in decline, perhaps the causes lie outside Britain, on migration or in the African wintering grounds (Sanderson *et al.* 2006). Tree Pipits winter in forest and wooded savannah from Guinea in West Africa as far as South Africa, but the whereabouts of British birds is unknown.

The present state of near-extinction in Cheshire was not mirrored in the local Atlases of Lancashire and North Merseyside (1997–2000) or Cumbria (1997–2001), perhaps for three reasons: they had no previous tetrad survey with which to compare; contractions in range are usually more obvious where a species is at the edge of its distribution; and, probably most importantly, Tree Pipit in Britain is becoming mostly an upland species and the edges of the Pennines and Lakeland provide many more opportunities for them to breed.

As their name suggests, they need trees, but only at low densities. Sparse upland sessile oakwoods are ideal, but the analysis of BTO nest record cards (Rose 1982) and the work of Simms (1992) showed them using an eclectic range of habitats, including grass/heather moorland, grassland, heath and wasteland including old quarries. In this survey the few Tree Pipits found were reported from a wide variety of habitats in woodland, scrub, semi-natural grassland, heath and farmland.

They are often said to be amongst our earlier migrants, with the first arrival in Cheshire and Wirral typically in the first week of April, but this is a misleading statistic as most birds come much later and they are one of the latest to breed, with first-egg dates in mid-May. In this survey there were only two tetrads with proven breeding, both from observers seeing adults carrying insects back to their young, and most records were of birds performing their conspicuous 'parachuting' song-flight.

STEVE ROUND

Sponsored by Paul S. Lewis

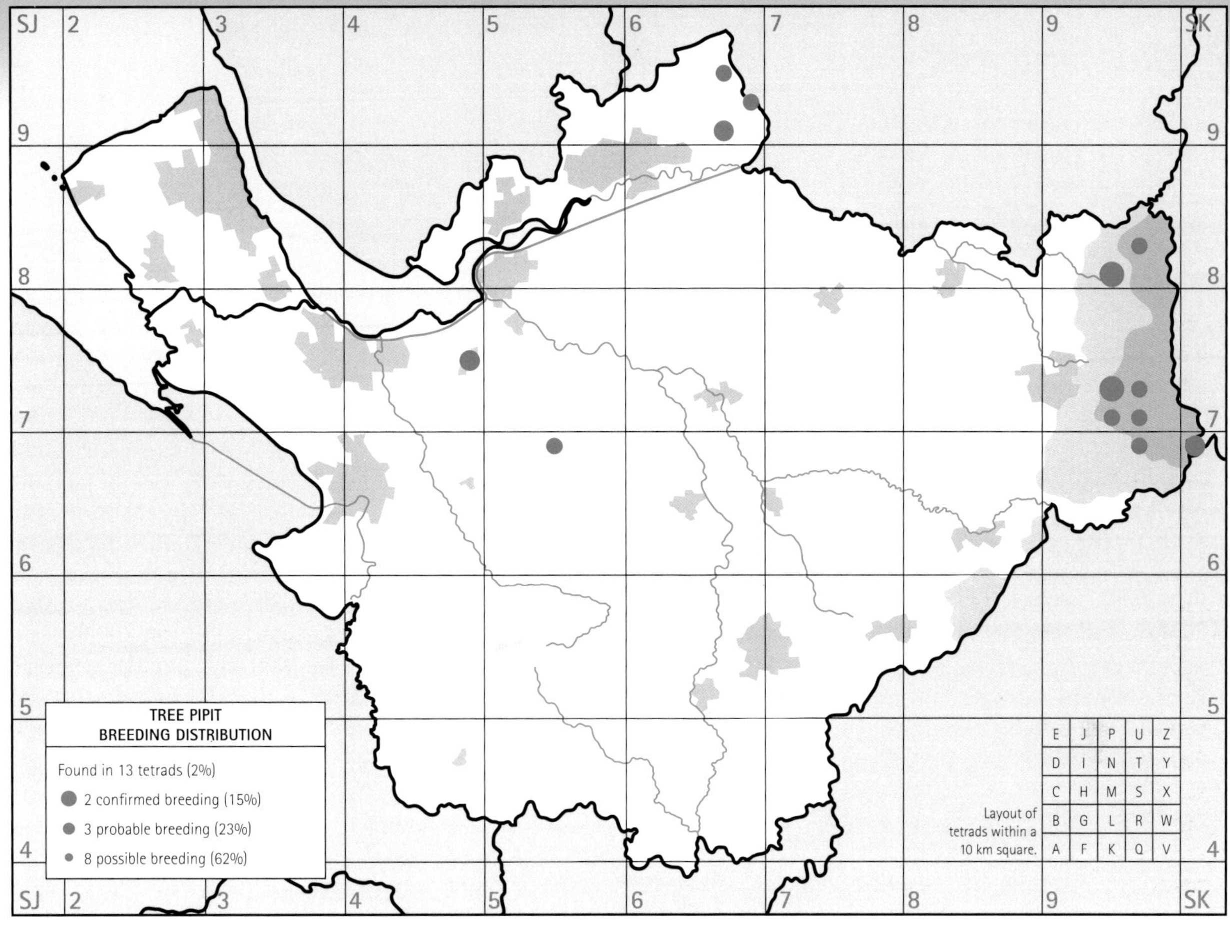
TREE PIPIT
BREEDING DISTRIBUTION
Found in 13 tetrads (2%)
2 confirmed breeding (15%)
3 probable breeding (23%)
8 possible breeding (62%)
Layout of tetrads within a 10 km square.
E J P U Z
D I N T Y
C H M S X
B G L R W
A F K Q V
SJ
SK

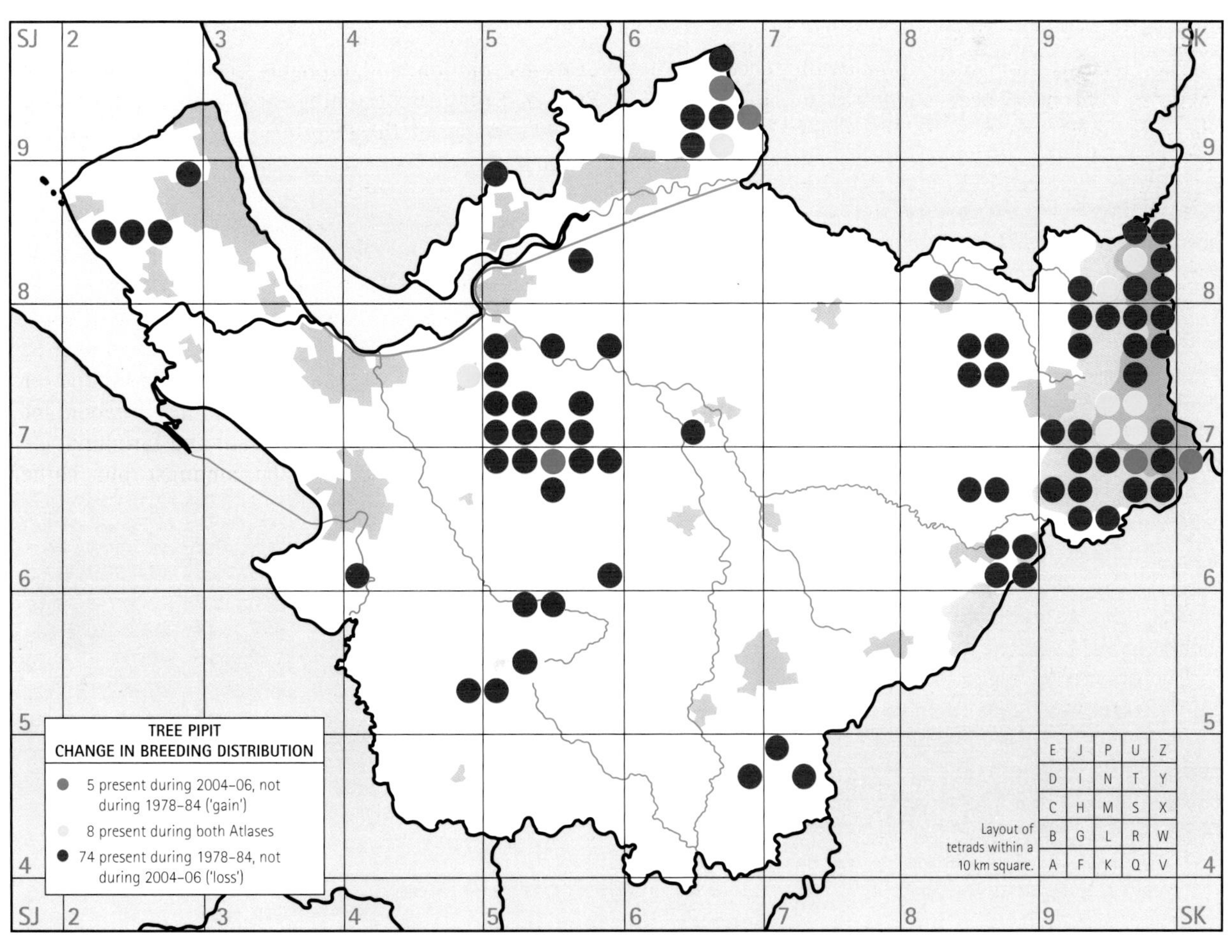
TREE PIPIT
CHANGE IN BREEDING DISTRIBUTION
5 present during 2004–06, not during 1978–84 ('gain')
8 present during both Atlases
74 present during 1978–84, not during 2004–06 ('loss')
Layout of tetrads within a 10 km square.
E J P U Z
D I N T Y
C H M S X
B G L R W
A F K Q V
SJ
SK

Meadow Pipit

Anthus pratensis

This is the commonest bird, and the most obvious, in the eastern hills, but is equally at home in low-lying areas near the coast and on rough land in some sites inland. They seem to favour some post-industrial land, including brownfield sites in peri-urban areas and the edges of sand quarries. Meadow Pipits avoid mature trees and are mainly birds of rough grassland or moorland, but the submitted habitat codes for all birds do not show that, with 102 farmland, 43 semi-natural grassland, 22 on estuarine salt-marsh and 11 heathland and bog. A truer picture is obtained for the tetrads with confirmed breeding only: 24 farmland (11 of which were unimproved grassland, with 9 improved grassland), 22 semi-natural grassland, 15 estuarine salt-marsh and 7 heathland and bog.

The map exaggerates the species' apparent presence during the breeding season. Many of the small dots are probably attributable to passage birds. Spring passage, of birds returning from as far as Iberia and Morocco, is noticeable through March and into April, and birds may be found in apparently suitable breeding habitat for a day or two, males sometimes singing, but they do not stay to breed. Further, half (17 out of 32) of the 'probable' breeding record codes are D (display) and some observers have allotted this code to the characteristic 'parachuting' song-flight of a single bird.

Most birds in the lowlands are paired on territory during April, although they are later at higher altitudes. The 119 broods that I have ringed at Frodsham Marsh, from 1981 to 2007, have hatching dates from 7 May, with the peak of first broods hatching on 18 May. Most females lay five eggs and raise an average of four chicks, and many pairs have a second brood in July, averaging three chicks. They betray the presence of chicks with their anxious 'pit-pit' calls, but the nests can be challenging to find, and only nine tetrads recorded NY or NE, with a further three FS codes as adults sometimes carry their chicks' faecal sacs 100 m or more before dropping them. Meadow Pipits eat, and feed their chicks on, a variety of flies that they find on the ground. They mostly take the flying forms rather than larvae, especially favouring the seasonally abundant crane-flies and mayflies. Adults are obvious when carrying beak-loads of invertebrates for their chicks, and 44 of the 67 confirmed breeding codes were FY. Chicks leave their nests before they can fly properly, and 11 tetrads furnished RF records of chicks fluttering weakly.

The BTO analysis of 2004–05 BBS data puts the breeding population of Cheshire and Wirral as 5,300 birds (with wide confidence limits of 190–10,410). As shown by the abundance map, most of these are in the eastern hills, with the moorland areas holding as many as 68 birds per tetrad. The best habitats can hold local concentrations up to perhaps one pair per hectare (Simms 1992), a density equivalent to 400 pairs per tetrad.

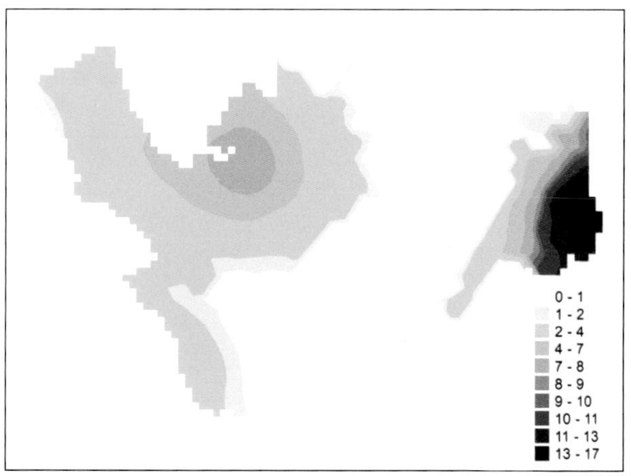

Meadow Pipit abundance.

Sponsored by Jane Turner

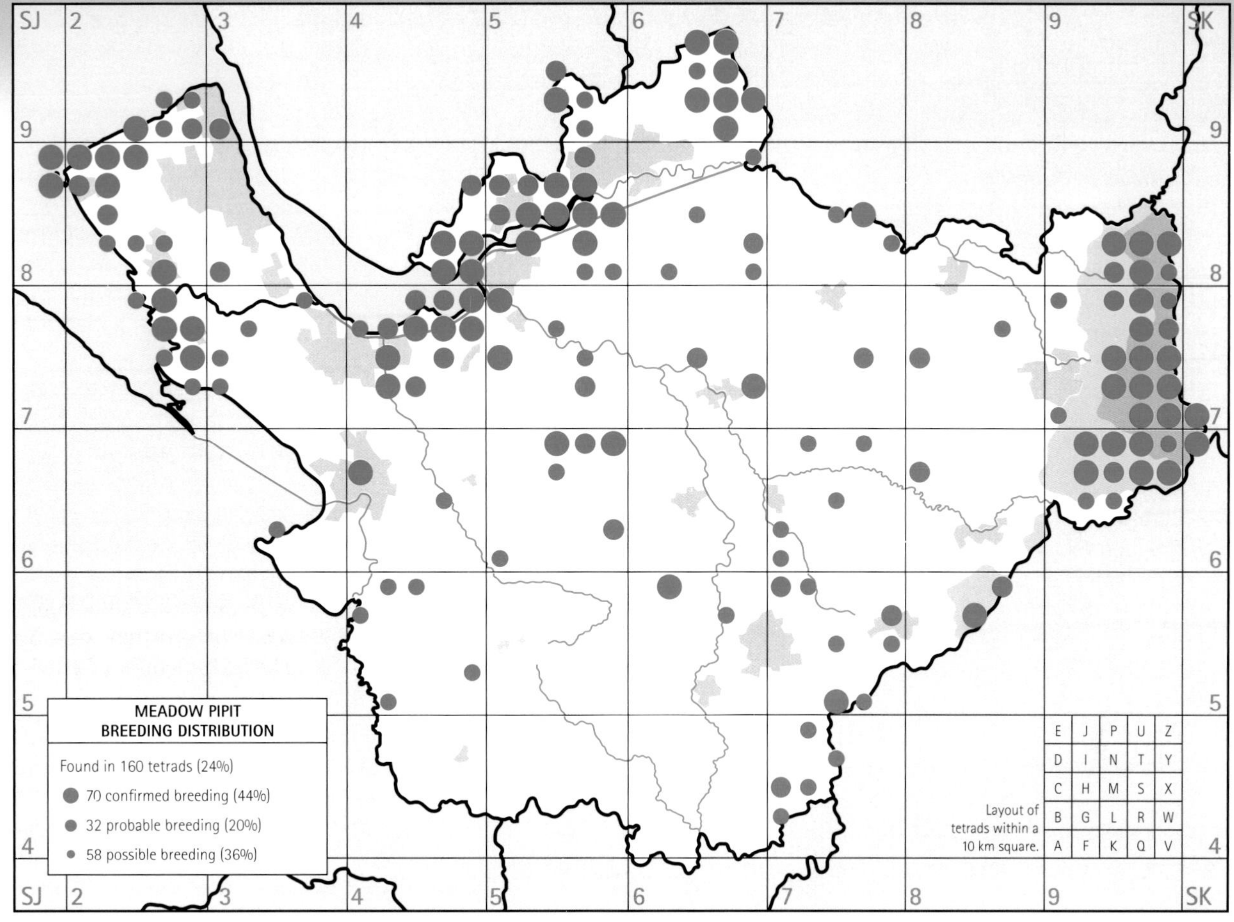
SJ
2
3
4
5
6
7
8
9
SK
MEADOW PIPIT
BREEDING DISTRIBUTION
Found in 160 tetrads (24%)
70 confirmed breeding (44%)
32 probable breeding (20%)
58 possible breeding (36%)
Layout of tetrads within a 10 km square.
E J P U Z
D I N T Y
C H M S X
B G L R W
A F K Q V

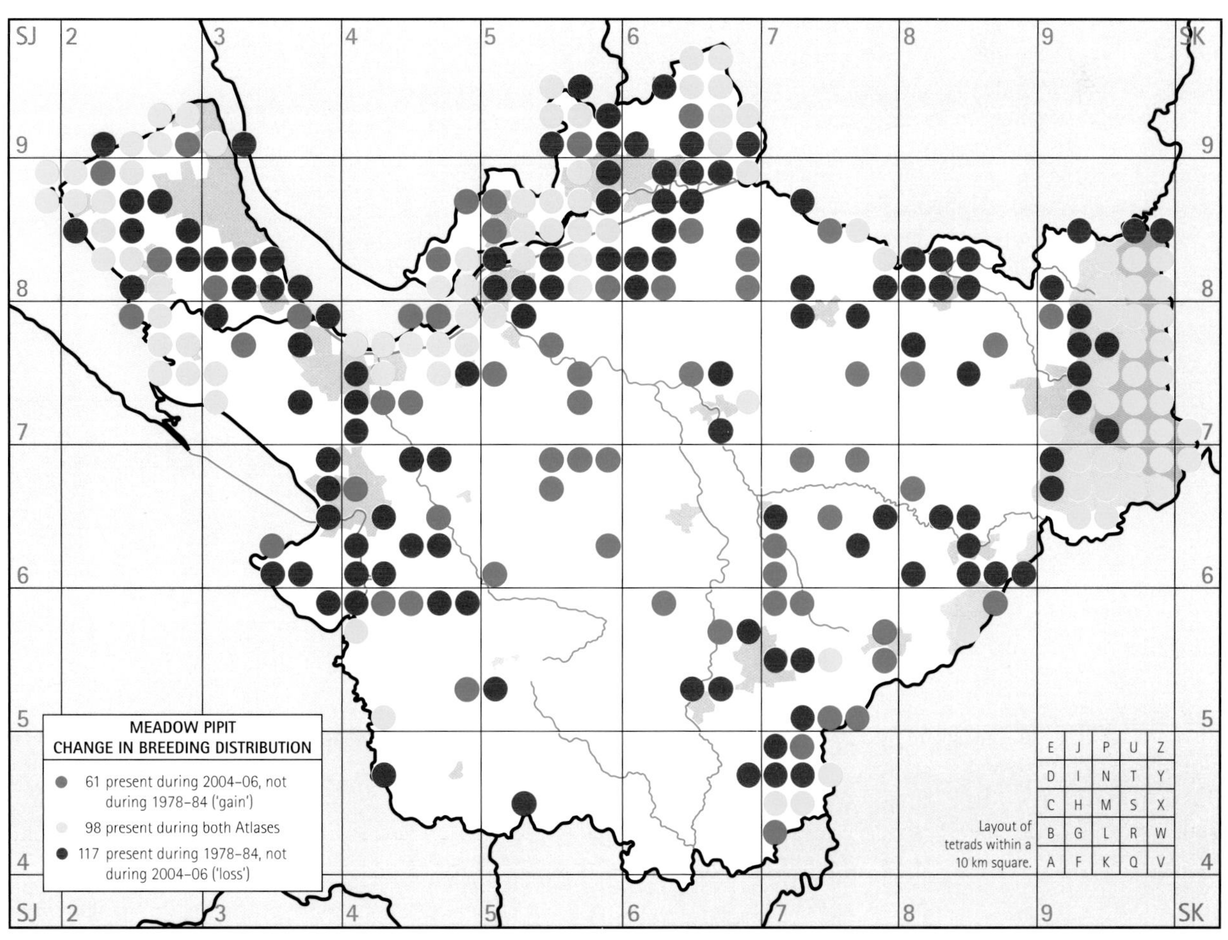
SJ
2
3
4
5
6
7
8
9
SK
MEADOW PIPIT
CHANGE IN BREEDING DISTRIBUTION
61 present during 2004–06, not during 1978–84 ('gain')
98 present during both Atlases
117 present during 1978–84, not during 2004–06 ('loss')
Layout of tetrads within a 10 km square.
E J P U Z
D I N T Y
C H M S X
B G L R W
A F K Q V

The Atlas map shows that wintering Meadow Pipits are distributed throughout the county, and they must be much more widespread now than they used to be. Older ornithologists wrote mainly about their status in freezing conditions. Coward and Oldham (1900) said that in hard winters the moorlands were deserted but a correspondent saw Meadow Pipits on the hills near the Cat and Fiddle in mild weather on 5 January 1899. The species was also absent in winter from many parts of the plain, but on the Dee marshes and in the water-meadows bordering the larger rivers it could be found all the year round. Coward (1910) added that hard weather drove the birds to the marshes, where, in severe frost they were very abundant. Boyd (1946) commented on a Meadow Pipit in January 1945 which lived for five days at the bottom of a ditch, 'usually walking in the shallow water like a tiny wader; an odd choice for a bird which often leaves these islands for Portugal and southern Spain in winter'. Bell (1962) copied Coward's description of the species' seasonal status.

In winter Meadow Pipits seek out invertebrates, especially in sites such as sewage works, farmland slurry pits and the damp corners of fields, but otherwise eat almost any type of small seeds. Their ecology seems similar to that of Pied Wagtails, but pipits are much less likely to use human sites, and the map shows that few of the county's urban tetrads had records of Meadow Pipits. Birds were present in about half of the upland breeding tetrads, some of them noted as returning early in spring, but others found in midwinter, although far fewer than during the breeding season.

With their substantial southward autumn movement, Meadow Pipit is one of the most obvious species for those watching visible migration, and the northern half of Britain—where most Meadow Pipits breed—is only sparsely occupied in winter (*BTO Winter Atlas*). The species' traditional wintering grounds lie as far south as the Mediterranean but the destination of Cheshire and Wirral breeders is not known in our changing climate: as a partial migrant, the proportion staying in Britain is likely to have increased with the milder weather of the last two decades.

The winter habitat codes were scattered thinly across a wide range, but the vast majority (83%) were of farmland, with 7% semi-natural grassland and marsh. Cheshire farmland may be inhospitable for them in the breeding season, but in winter it is able to support Meadow Pipits. Of the total, 41% were improved grassland and 12% unimproved grassland, with 9% stubble. This is the small passerine with the highest number of records in unimproved grassland.

From the counts submitted by surveyors for this Atlas, the median flock size is 10 birds, so the county wintering population of Meadow Pipits is at least 5,000 birds. By chance, this is much the same as the breeding population, but most of the birds are different individuals.

RICHARD STEEL

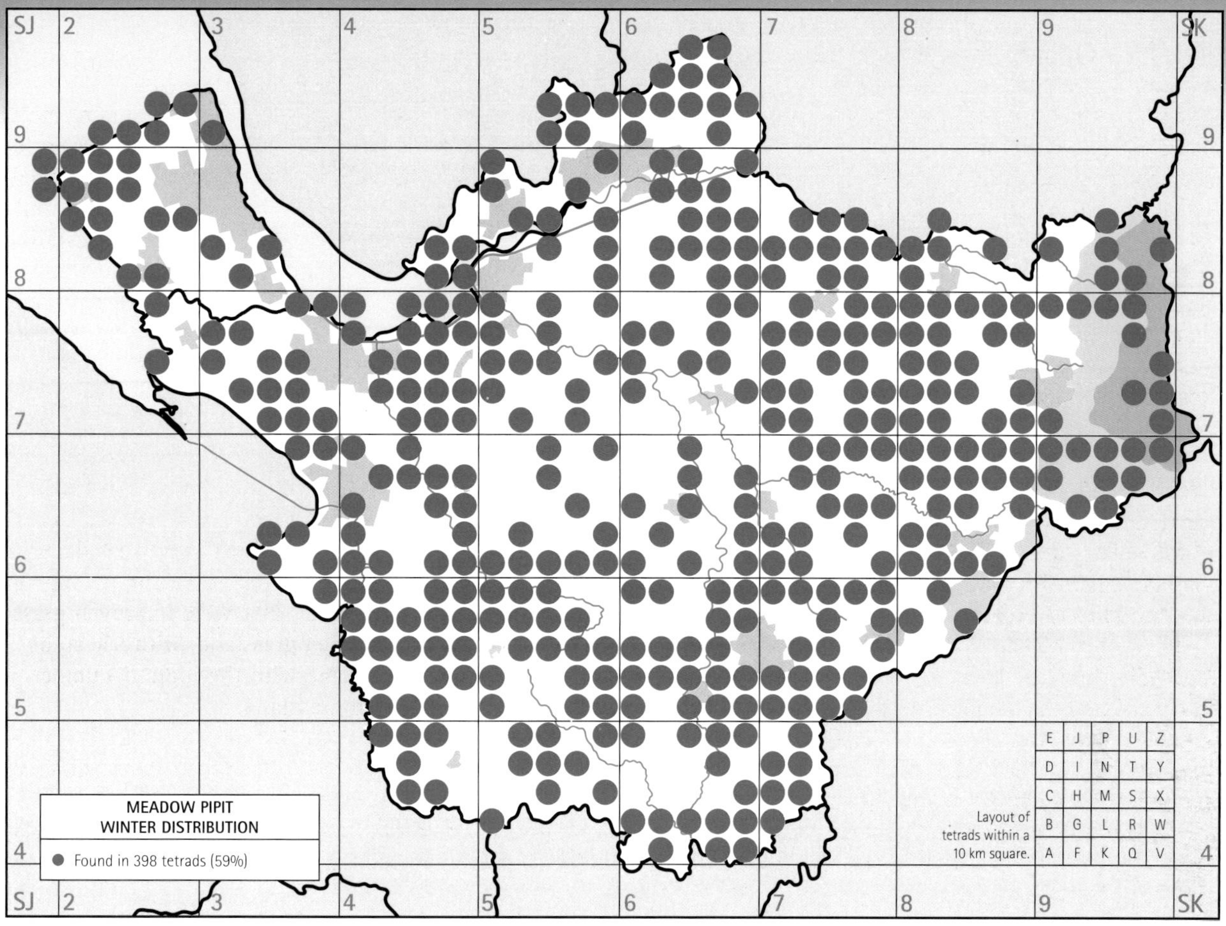

MEADOW PIPIT
DIFFERENCE BETWEEN BREEDING AND WINTER DISTRIBUTION

- 39 present during breeding season but not during winter
- 121 present during both seasons
- 277 present during winter but not during breeding season

Layout of tetrads within a 10 km square.

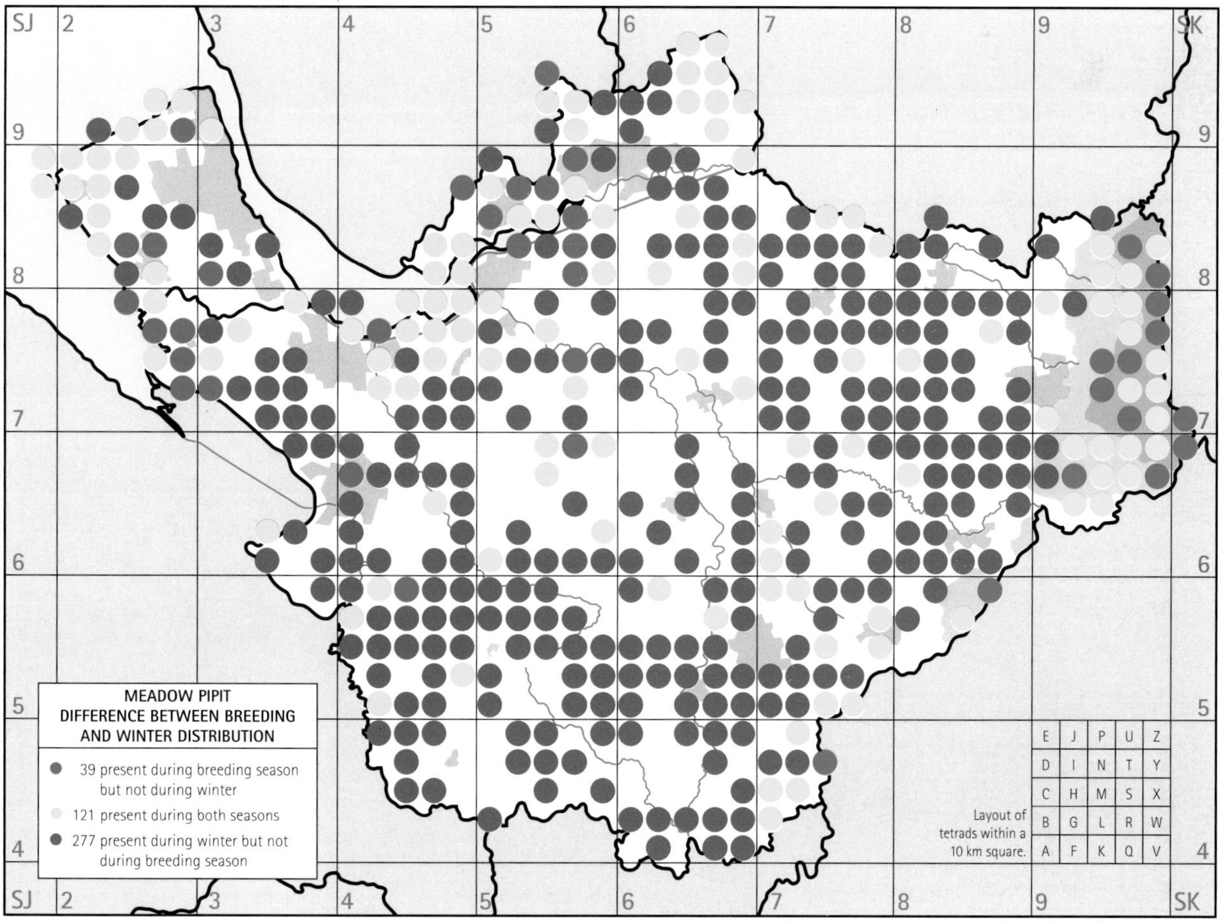

E	J	P	U	Z
D	I	N	T	Y
C	H	M	S	X
B	G	L	R	W
A	F	K	Q	V

SJ 2 3 4 5 6 7 8 9 SK

Rock Pipit

Anthus petrosus

Rock Pipits bred on Hilbre in 1987, and probably in 1985 (*CWBRs*), following other 'old but not well-documented records of breeding' (Craggs 1982). But this species does not normally breed anywhere between Llandudno in North Wales and St Bees Head in Cumbria (*BTO Second Atlas*), and is known in Cheshire and Wirral mainly as a regular winter visitor to the estuarine edges. This Atlas map shows the species more widespread than has previously been reported, in 12 tetrads along the Dee estuary, two on the north Wirral coast and six adjacent to the Mersey estuary. Fieldworkers gave every bird a code of salt-marsh or coastal habitat.

Nothing is known about the origins of the birds wintering in the county. Most British Rock Pipits of the *petrosus* race are sedentary, only odd birds making an exceptional movement of 100 km or more. Large numbers of the race *littoralis* migrate to Britain every year from their breeding grounds in coastal Fennoscandia and the nearby Baltic states. Two Swedish-ringed birds have been found in Anglesey and Cornwall, and one ringed in Norway has reached Ireland, so crossing to the west of Britain is not beyond them (*Migration Atlas*). British Rock Pipits live almost entirely on rocky shores, while *littoralis* birds occur 'commonly on soft coastlines usually devoid of Rock Pipits at other times of year, including sand dunes, harbours and, especially, salt-marshes' (Brown & Grice 2005). Thus, it seems most likely that the birds found annually on the Dee salt-marshes are Scandinavian birds of the *littoralis* race. This race is a county rarity, with no accepted records, not surprisingly as 'single specimens of *petrosus* and *littoralis* cannot be reliably separated in winter' (Alström & Mild 2003).

With the apparent separation between Rock Pipits of the two races in habitats and places where they occur, there is probably a separation in their diet as well. The British birds of the rocky coastline feed mostly in the intertidal zone, mainly eating crustaceans, especially tiny periwinkles and amphipods, a resource not exploited by any other passerine. The continental immigrants in the salt-marsh creeks are probably taking the larvae of chironomid midges and other small insects.

Coward (1910) noted that 'the Rock Pipit is occasionally met with on the shores of the Dee estuary in the winter months'. Bell (1962, 1967) did not comment on its winter status on the coast, but reported inland occurrences, five from the Weaver estuary and one at Altrincham sewage farm. The county bird report for 1980 estimated the wintering population at Gayton Sands reserve as 150–200 birds. In the 1986 *CWBR* it was 'apparently common in the winter months at Gayton Sands but numbers are very difficult to estimate owing to the birds' flightiness and the size of the area', while in the 1988 report '200 were estimated in the salt-marsh creeks'. Otherwise, there are few counts in double figures but the species is frequently noted as underrecorded, with pleas for better information. They are susceptible to hard weather, and most disappeared during the continued frosts of 1981/82, but there have

PHIL JONES

Sponsored by Jane Turner

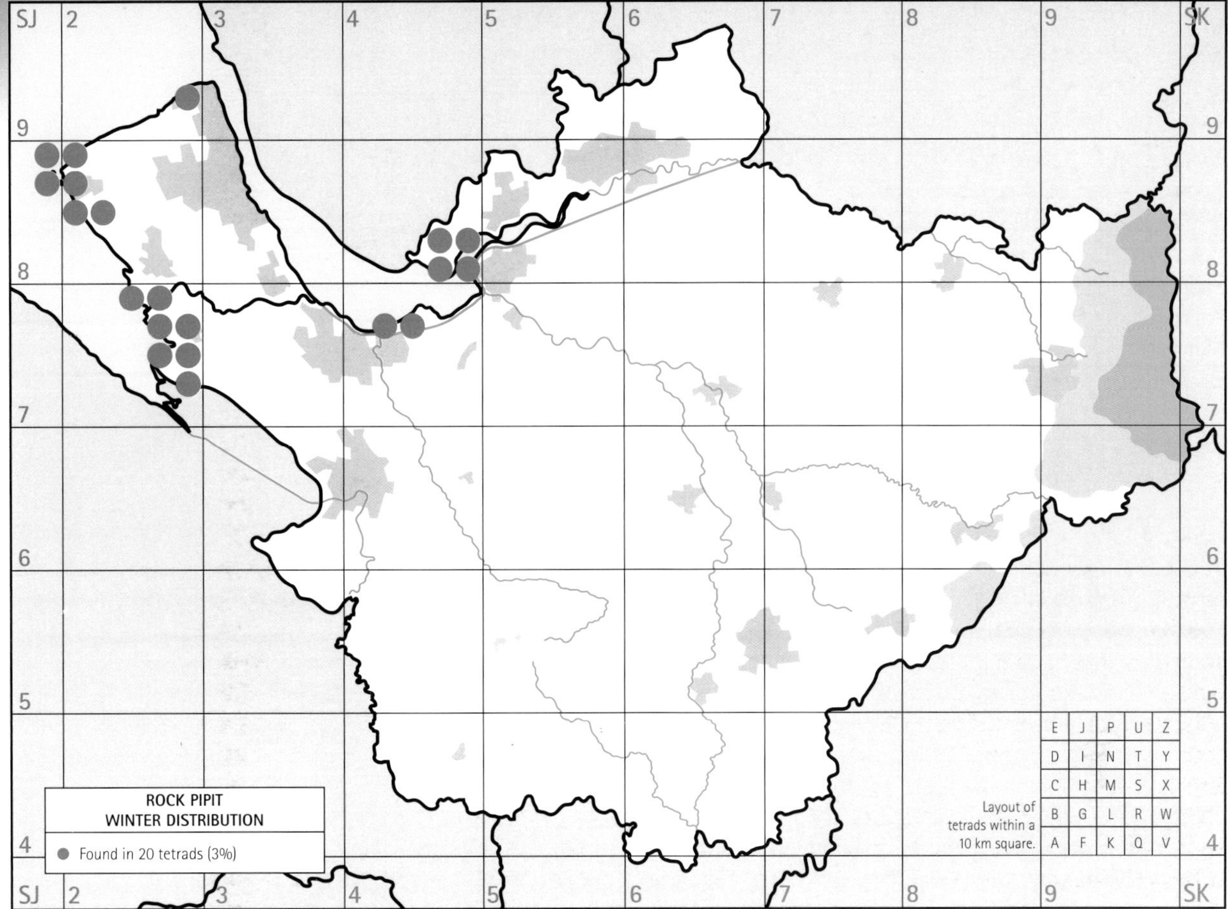

been no extended periods of freezing conditions in the last twenty years. The present wintering population is unknown—the totals of records submitted for this Atlas were 27, 11 and 18 in the three winters—but there is no reason to suppose that it has changed from the 1980s estimates of 200 birds.

There are interesting challenges for the county's birdwatchers to provide reliable figures for the wintering population and for the county's ringers to find out more about the origins and destinations of our Rock Pipits.

Water Pipit

Anthus spinoletta

The county's first Water Pipits were found in breeding plumage by distinguished ornithologists—H.G. Alexander on the Dee marshes near Parkgate on 21 March 1937, and A.W. Boyd at Bar Mere on 3 April 1939—but winter records have been clouded by changing taxonomy and identification criteria. There were three tetrads with records in this Atlas: up to three birds at Neston Old Quay (SJ27Y) on three dates 3 January to 7 February 2005, and one there on 7 January 2007; one on Heswall shore (SJ28K) on 21 January 2006, and one bird at Frodsham Marsh (SJ47Z) on 12 February 2005.

It is most likely that our wintering birds come from breeding areas in the central European mountains; these are deserted in winter as Water Pipits move in all directions, including north, to low-lying land. 'Favoured habitats include ... sewage treatment works, rivers, lakes and flooded gravel-pits, lowland wet grasslands and coastal fresh and brackish lagoons' (Brown & Grice 2005). 'Since Water Pipit is only exceptionally found in typical Rock Pipit habitat, the habitat separation between Rock Pipit and Water Pipit is almost complete' (Alström & Mild 2003). The birds found on the Dee saltmarsh are exceptional and have not read the books.

RAY SCALLY

Sponsored by Jane Turner

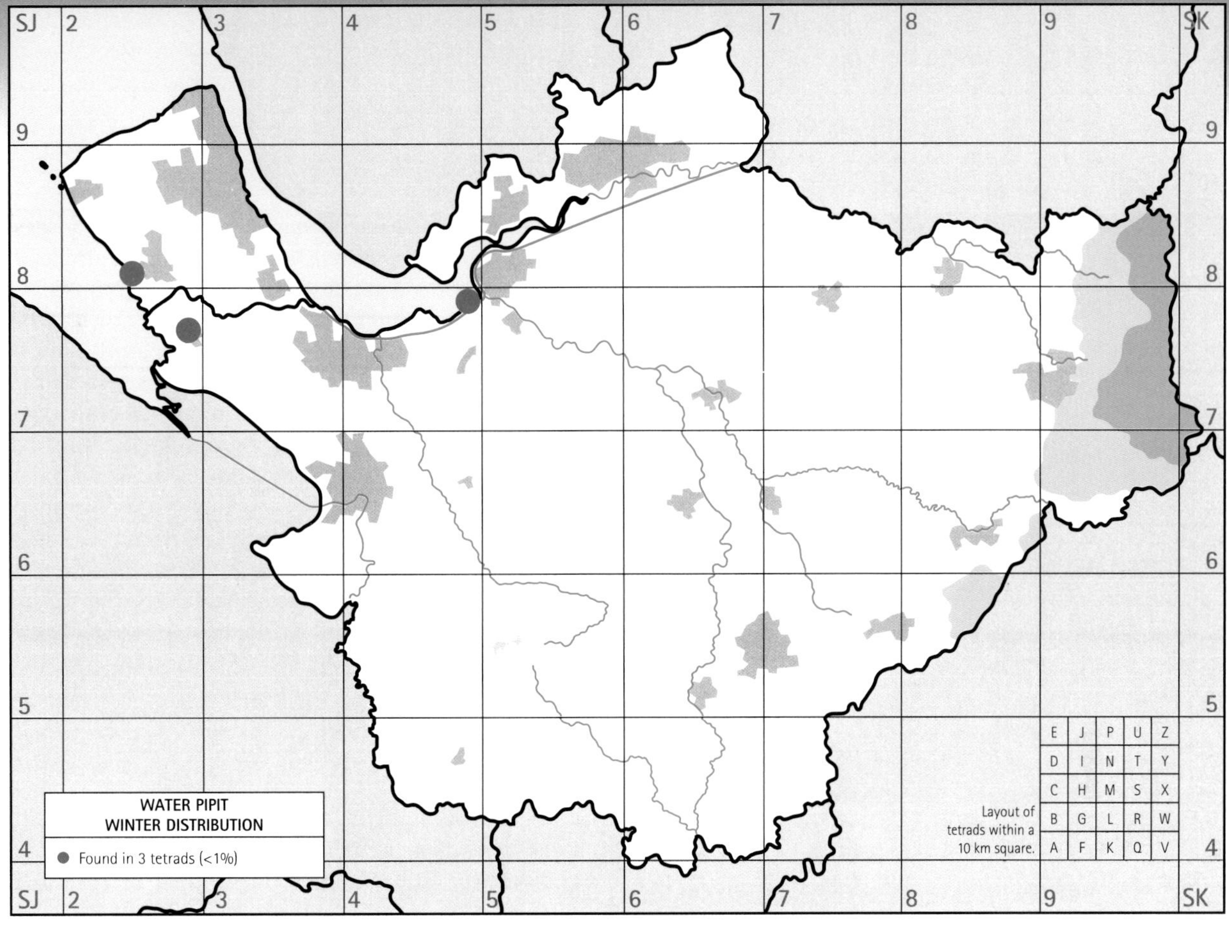

SJ
2
3
4
5
6
7
8
9
SK
9
8
7
6
5
4
WATER PIPIT
WINTER DISTRIBUTION
Found in 3 tetrads (<1%)
Layout of tetrads within a 10 km square.
E J P U Z
D I N T Y
C H M S X
B G L R W
A F K Q V

Yellow Wagtail

Motacilla flava

STEVE ROUND

'Cheshire would appear to be *the* county for the Yellow Wagtail', declared Stuart Smith in his *New Naturalist* monograph (1950) but this claim could never be made today. The Atlas map shows that they are now all but lost from Wirral and the east of the county, and are scarce in most parts of the south-west of Cheshire. They have gone from the south Manchester fringe, including Smith's study area at Gatley, now lost under motorway building and just over the county boundary in Greater Manchester. Nationally, the species is on the Amber List of conservation concern, and due to be Red listed at the next revision, owing to their massive decline. Much of this loss occurred between our two Atlas periods; the BTO's CBC/BBS population index shows a fall of 64% from 1984 to 2004. This is almost the same as the fall in the number of occupied tetrads in Cheshire and Wirral, down 67% from 386 tetrads in 1978–84 to 126 tetrads in 2004–06.

Possible reasons for the reduction have been given as farmland drainage, the conversion of pasture to arable land, the change from spring to winter cereals, and the loss of insects associated with cattle (*BTO Second Atlas*, Nelson *et al.* 2003). British Yellow Wagtails winter in damp habitats in the westernmost parts of trans-Saharan Africa, in similar areas to those in which many other species have suffered population declines.

They take their prey of small invertebrates from on or near the ground, by picking or fly-catching in short sallies. Their traditional association with livestock, birds often feeding around the heels of large animals, no longer seems to hold. Similarly, the Yellow Wagtail's favoured habitat has been damp meadows and marshes, but nowadays it seems to be mainly in agricultural land, especially areas of arable or mixed farming (Brown & Grice 2005). The submitted habitat codes showed 85% of the records in farmland, with 8% in semi-natural grassland/marsh. In 30 tetrads (22% of the records) they were associated with arable land, a higher proportion than for any other species, and there were 31 records in improved grassland and 32 in mixed grassland/arable land. This preference applies at a local scale, but there is, however, no correlation across the county between the distribution of arable land, either cereals or horticulture, and the map of Yellow Wagtails.

They can be conspicuous when feeding chicks, and 37 of the confirmed breeding records were FY, with a further 15 of recently fledged young. An unusually high proportion of records from fieldworkers included comments about the nesting area of Yellow Wagtails. In 12 tetrads birds were reported nesting in agricultural crops: in four of them the nest appeared to be amongst potatoes, with another two in beans. One was in maize, one 'in bare patches in autumn-sown wheat' and four in unnamed 'cereals'. In a further two tetrads with confirmed breeding they were benefiting from set-aside land. They nest on the ground, usually choosing a site under a large leaf, and lay five or six eggs in mid-May. I found that the median hatching date of 14 nests on Frodsham Marsh in the 1980s and early 1990s was 1 June. In the years when they nested earliest, 1988 and 1989, three pairs went on to have second broods in a new nest just five weeks later.

The BTO BBS analysis estimated the breeding population of Cheshire and Wirral in 2004–05 as 550 birds (with wide confidence limits from zero to 1,240), corresponding to an average of three or four pairs per tetrad with confirmed or probable breeding, or two pairs per tetrad in which the species was recorded. This is only about one-third of the estimated total during our *First Atlas*.

The distinctive race *flavissima* (the yellowest) occurs almost entirely in Britain but plumage variations are encountered quite frequently. Most of these aberrants arise from mutations because the species is obviously in a state of genetic flux (Smith 1950). Sometimes such birds are claimed to be of a different race but the county rarities panel received no convincing record of any other than *flavissima* breeding during the three years of this survey.

Sponsored by David Cogger

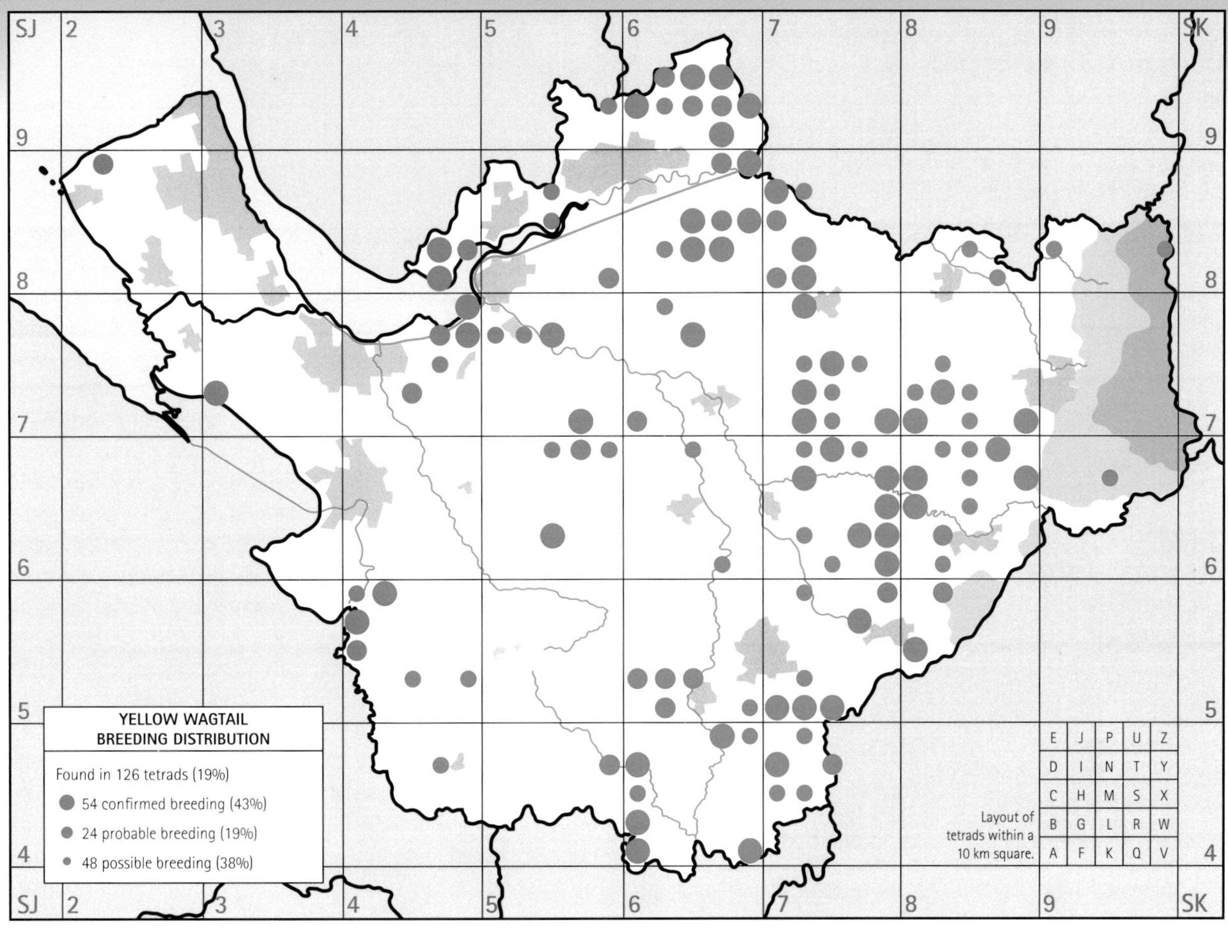

YELLOW WAGTAIL
BREEDING DISTRIBUTION
Found in 126 tetrads (19%)
54 confirmed breeding (43%)
24 probable breeding (19%)
48 possible breeding (38%)
Layout of tetrads within a 10 km square.
E J P U Z
D I N T Y
C H M S X
B G L R W
A F K Q V
SJ 2 3 4 5 6 7 8 9 SK

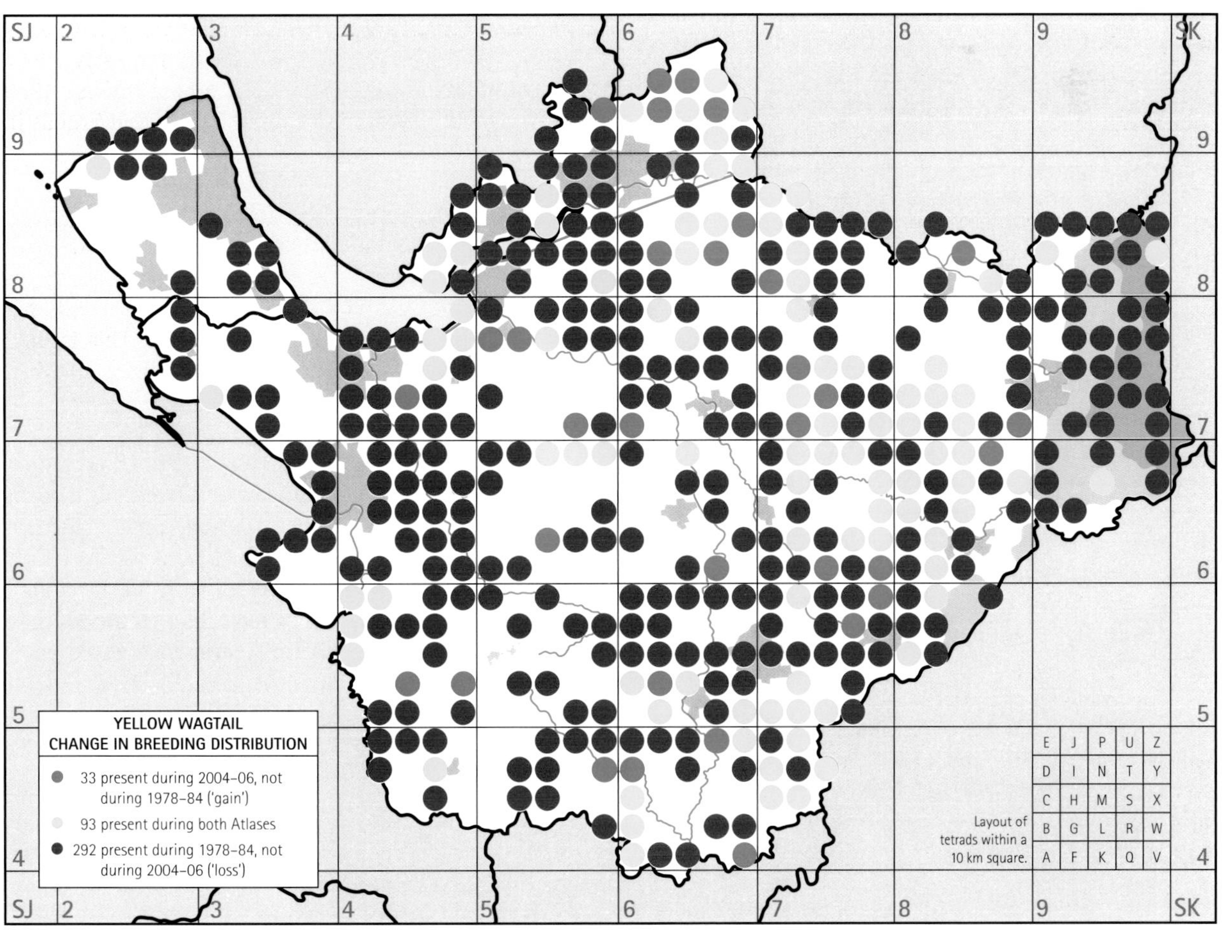

YELLOW WAGTAIL
CHANGE IN BREEDING DISTRIBUTION
33 present during 2004–06, not during 1978–84 ('gain')
93 present during both Atlases
292 present during 1978–84, not during 2004–06 ('loss')
Layout of tetrads within a 10 km square.
E J P U Z
D I N T Y
C H M S X
B G L R W
A F K Q V
SJ 2 3 4 5 6 7 8 9 SK

Grey Wagtail

Motacilla cinerea

RICHARD STEEL

Grey Wagtails have a generally easterly distribution in the county, with a preference for higher altitudes. As in the *First Atlas*, the lines of some of our rivers and canals show up on the Atlas map, notably the Bollin, Dean, Dane and the Mersey/Manchester Ship Canal. But Grey Wagtails have considerably expanded their distribution and have noticeably spread into some urban areas, including Wallasey/Birkenhead and Widnes/Runcorn. Although the general picture is of strong increase in the last twenty years, with 149 tetrads gaining breeding presence and 80 losses, the decline in much of western Cheshire is puzzling.

They used to be confined to sites alongside water, usually fast-flowing, and especially when bordered by native broad-leaved trees, but are now more widespread as a breeder. However, almost three-quarters of the submitted habitat codes are G (fresh water), with the overwhelming majority running water (G6–G10), mostly streams and rivers; the rest are mainly human sites and farmland. Although they are primarily associated with water, their food is mostly flies, caterpillars and spiders of terrestrial origin, so the Grey Wagtail is less susceptible to the effects of stream acidification than species such as the Dipper which share its riparian habitats.

Grey Wagtails make an early start to the breeding season, nesting on a ledge, amongst tree roots or beneath man-made structures such as bridges or culverts from late March and April. Young from second, third or replacement broods may still be in the nest in August. This lengthy season gives observers plenty of opportunity to record high-level breeding status codes, so it is a little surprising that they were proven to breed in only 45% of the tetrads in which the species was found, mainly from records of adults carrying food (37) or observations of recently fledged young (49). Their incessant calls, similar to those of the Pied Wagtail but rather more clipped, readily draw attention to birds with chicks in the nest or nearby.

There were too few registrations of Grey Wagtails on the BBS transects in 2004 and 2005 to produce a robust population estimate for the county, but modelling using a detection probability derived from the national dataset suggests a Cheshire and Wirral total of 870 birds (confidence range of 10–1,740), considerably higher than the estimate in our *First Atlas* of 120–150 pairs. As largely insectivorous residents, their population can be adversely affected by severe winter weather and numbers may vary considerably between years, but the national Waterways Bird Survey index has increased by more than 40% since 1984, and the species has clearly spread into new areas in the last twenty years, so this figure seems not unreasonable. Assuming this to be 435 pairs it corresponds to a density of around 2.5 pairs per tetrad in which breeding was confirmed or probable. Workers studying the species usually quote a linear density, which can vary widely, but averages about 0.5–1 pair per kilometre on a variety of rivers (Simms 1992); the Cheshire and Wirral figure probably lies within this range.

Sponsored by AstraZeneca, Club AZ Natural History section

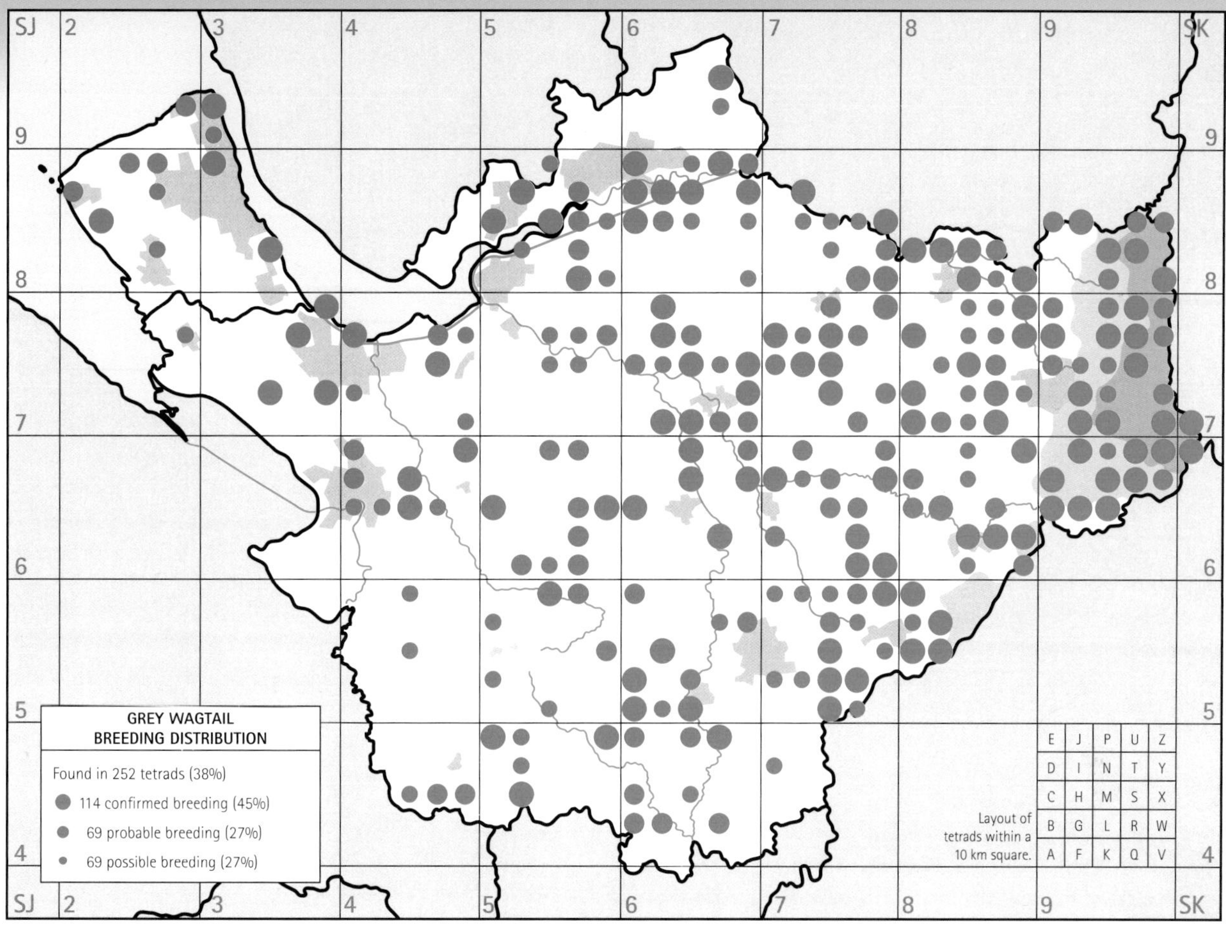
GREY WAGTAIL
BREEDING DISTRIBUTION
Found in 252 tetrads (38%)
114 confirmed breeding (45%)
69 probable breeding (27%)
69 possible breeding (27%)
Layout of tetrads within a 10 km square.
E J P U Z
D I N T Y
C H M S X
B G L R W
A F K Q V
SJ 2 3 4 5 6 7 8 9 SK
9 8 7 6 5 4

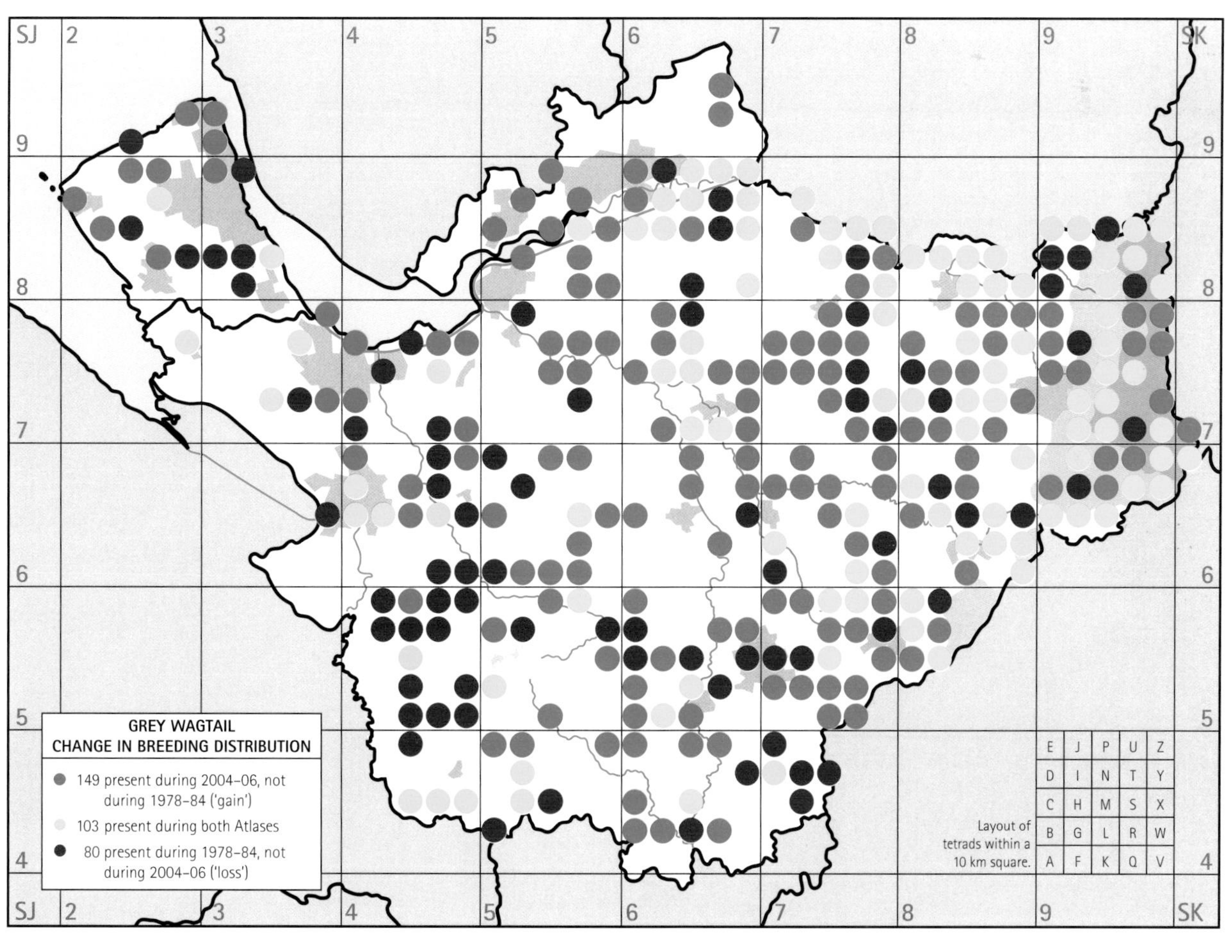
GREY WAGTAIL
CHANGE IN BREEDING DISTRIBUTION
149 present during 2004–06, not during 1978–84 ('gain')
103 present during both Atlases
80 present during 1978–84, not during 2004–06 ('loss')
Layout of tetrads within a 10 km square.
E J P U Z
D I N T Y
C H M S X
B G L R W
A F K Q V
SJ 2 3 4 5 6 7 8 9 SK
9 8 7 6 5 4

In winter, most Grey Wagtails quit their upland and northern areas to move into the English lowlands. Many Scottish birds move to England for the winter, and a few come here from continental Europe (*Migration Atlas*). In Cheshire and Wirral, some stay on their breeding territories while others spread out into a wider range of habitats, not necessarily associated with water. Sewage works, farmyards, slurry pits, canal towpaths and gardens all attract them, and they are a common wintering bird in urban areas. Individuals often seem faithful to particular sites, within a season and from year to year, as Coward (1910) had noted.

The submitted winter habitat codes showed that Grey Wagtails have much less attachment to water (47% of the total, down from 76% in the breeding season), with 22% human sites and 27% on farmland of all types. Observers noted them feeding in slurried fields and in flooded parts of stubble, even in the normally sterile maize fields. They take a wide variety of food: flies, worms and midge larvae when they can find them, small fish and even household scraps.

A century ago, Grey Wagtails left their breeding areas in autumn ... 'the birds descend to the Plain, and from October to March are distributed over the lowlands, where they haunt the meres and smaller streams. In the west, the bird is seldom seen, even in winter. Brockholes (1874) observed it only occasionally in Wirral' (Coward & Oldham 1900). Boyd (1951) described the bird as a winter resident in mid-Cheshire, appearing in October by Marbury Mere and in wet ditches and remaining, often throughout the coldest weather, until March. As now, they were noted visiting farmyard middens and gardens. Bell (1962) echoed these comments, writing that in the autumn the hill streams were deserted and as a winter resident the bird was fairly common along the river valleys and meresides on the plain, returning to the hills between February and April depending on the season.

In this Atlas they were found in 414 tetrads in winter, almost twice as many as in the breeding season. Only 60 of their breeding tetrads were unoccupied in winter, including 11 of those over 250 m in altitude. They are widespread in Wirral and west Cheshire, in areas where they do not breed. It is likely that they would be more restricted in range in hard weather, and the county bird reports over the years link the species' numbers with cold winters. There was no difference between the three years of this Atlas survey, with 211, 201 and 211 tetrads with records: the total numbers counted were incredibly stable at 250, 248 and 252 in the three winters.

Ten birds were seen in one group with eight Pied Wagtails in 2004/05 at Maw Green (SJ75D), and two flocks of six birds were reported elsewhere, but almost three-quarters of counts submitted were of single birds. Grey Wagtails sometimes join Pied Wagtails in their communal roosts, or form a single-species gathering on their own, usually in small numbers. Up to 40 were reported in 1993/94 in a tree growing out of a wall at The Groves, Chester, and a maximum of 17 at Poynton Pool in winter 1995/96. The regular autumn roost at Arclid Sand Quarry from 1985 to 2003 sometimes held a dozen or more birds into the start of the winter period, and occasionally lasted through the winter, with up to 10 birds in 1989/90 and eight in 1992/93. There were, however, no roosting birds reported anywhere in this survey.

STEVE ROUND

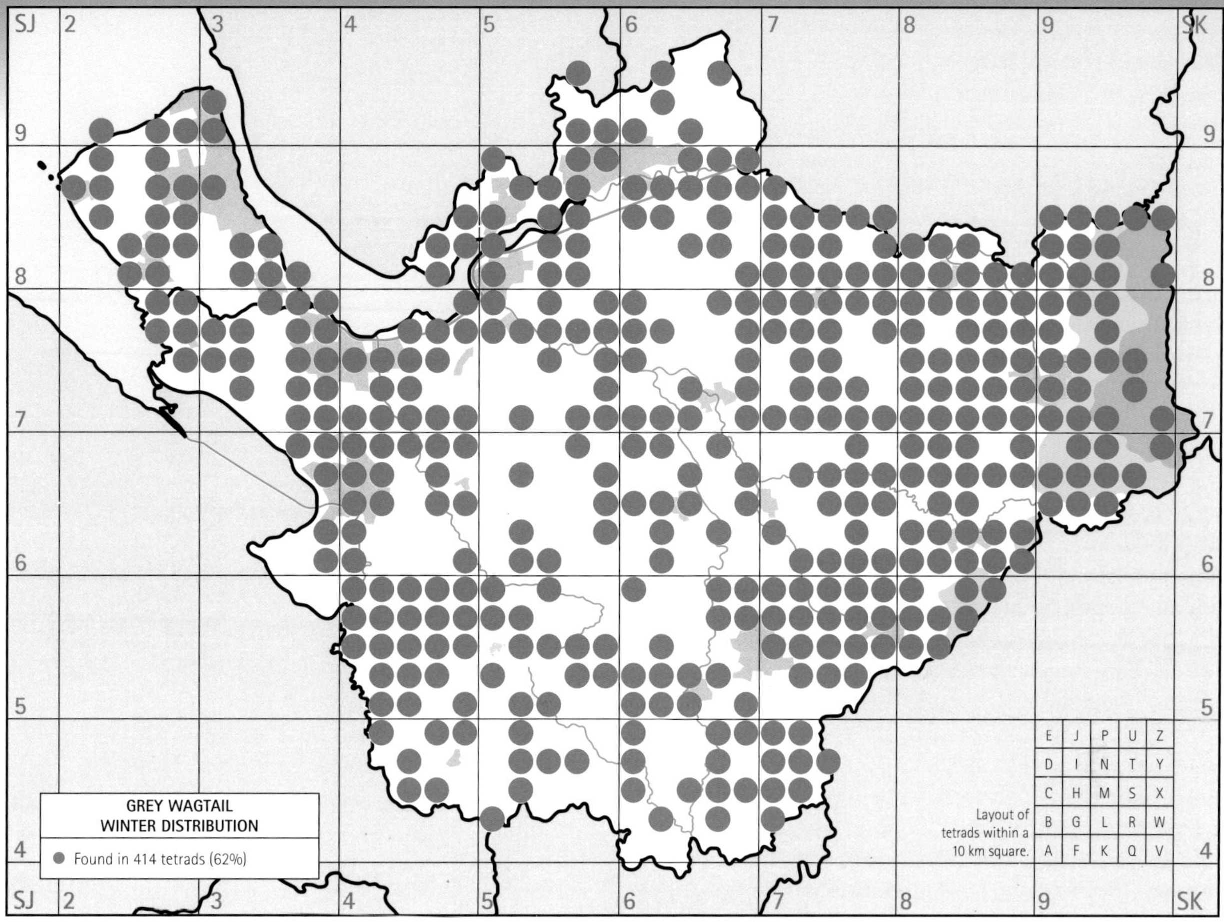
SJ
SK
GREY WAGTAIL
WINTER DISTRIBUTION
Found in 414 tetrads (62%)
Layout of tetrads within a 10 km square.
E J P U Z
D I N T Y
C H M S X
B G L R W
A F K Q V

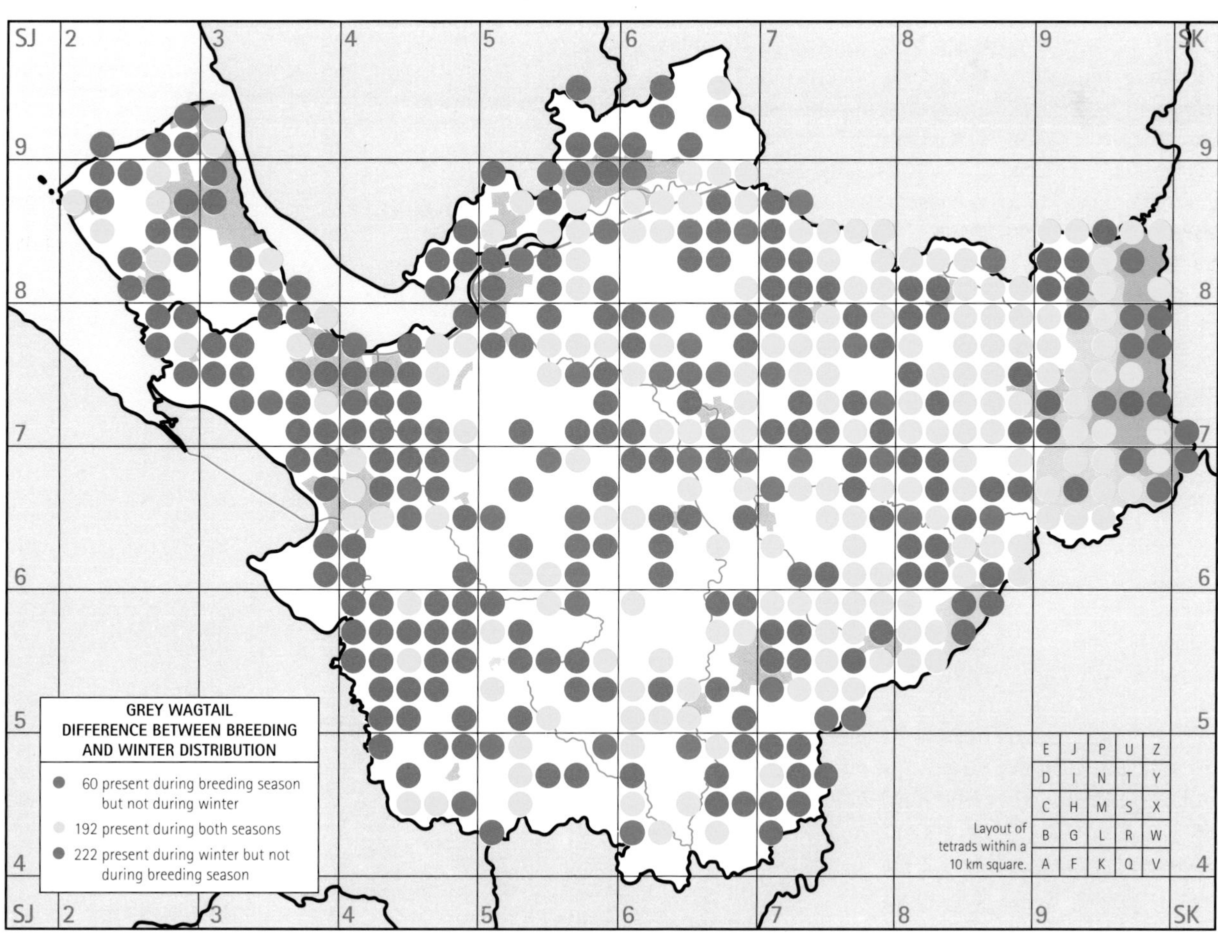
SJ
SK
GREY WAGTAIL
DIFFERENCE BETWEEN BREEDING AND WINTER DISTRIBUTION
60 present during breeding season but not during winter
192 present during both seasons
222 present during winter but not during breeding season
Layout of tetrads within a 10 km square.
E J P U Z
D I N T Y
C H M S X
B G L R W
A F K Q V

Pied Wagtail

Motacilla alba

This is one of our most familiar commensal birds, both by sight and sound, its loud 'chissick' calls being unmistakeable, although the softer 'chewee' indicates a bird on territory. Its close link with man was shown by the submitted habitat codes: more than half of them were human sites, especially rural ones, with most of the remainder being farmland, mainly grassland. Pied Wagtails feed mainly on adult flies, which they catch by a combination of picking off the surface and fly-catching near to the ground if their prey is disturbed into flight (Simms 1992). They noticeably gorge themselves, and feed their chicks, on temporarily abundant species such as mayflies and crane-flies. This prey is most likely to be found on close-cropped grass, grazed farmland being ideal, or mown lawns, bowling greens, playing fields and other sports areas; open areas in man-made sites, such as roads, car parks and farmyards, also attract the species.

Breeding was confirmed in two-thirds of the tetrads with records, most of them by observers seeing recently fledged chicks or adults carrying food. With two broods normal, they can be feeding chicks over an extended period, from early May to late July. The nests themselves, however, can be difficult to find and are usually well hidden on a ledge somewhere. Observers reported nest sites in ivy and other climbing plants and in a variety of human artefacts including a pub windowsill and canal lock gates. In the eastern hills dry-stone walls offer plenty of nooks and crannies, and one pair was seen taking nest material into the roof of the highest pub in Cheshire—the Cat and Fiddle Inn—and later seen carrying food. Most sand quarries have a pair, who can pick plenty of insects off the warm sand, and find a nesting site somewhere amongst the machinery or buildings. They are not deterred by human presence or by the noise and movement of machinery. One pair nested in 1989 and 1990 on a ledge under a sand quarry weighbridge, raising six chicks each year as hundreds of heavily laden lorries passed overhead during the four weeks of the incubation and fledging periods.

The monitoring schemes show that Pied Wagtails exhibit annual fluctuations in breeding population, especially being depressed by hard winter weather, but the national index is now at a similar level to that during our *First Atlas*. Their occupation of Cheshire and Wirral is similar to twenty years ago, despite the figures of 60 tetrads gaining and 63 losing the species. They have increased in a range of tetrads along the centre of the county, where they were thought to have been underrecorded in the *First Atlas*, and have spread more into the Mersey valley and north Wirral, including now breeding on Hilbre. There is no obvious pattern to the tetrads without breeding season records, although there are noticeably fewer tetrads with confirmed breeding in the eastern hills.

SUE & ANDY TRANTER

The BTO BBS analysis shows that the breeding population of Cheshire and Wirral in 2004–05 was 20,120 birds (7,020–33,230), corresponding to an average of about 21 pairs per tetrad with confirmed or probable breeding, or 17 pairs per tetrad in which the species was recorded. This is almost 2% of the national total, showing that Cheshire and Wirral is a favoured county for them.

Sponsored by Norman Scott

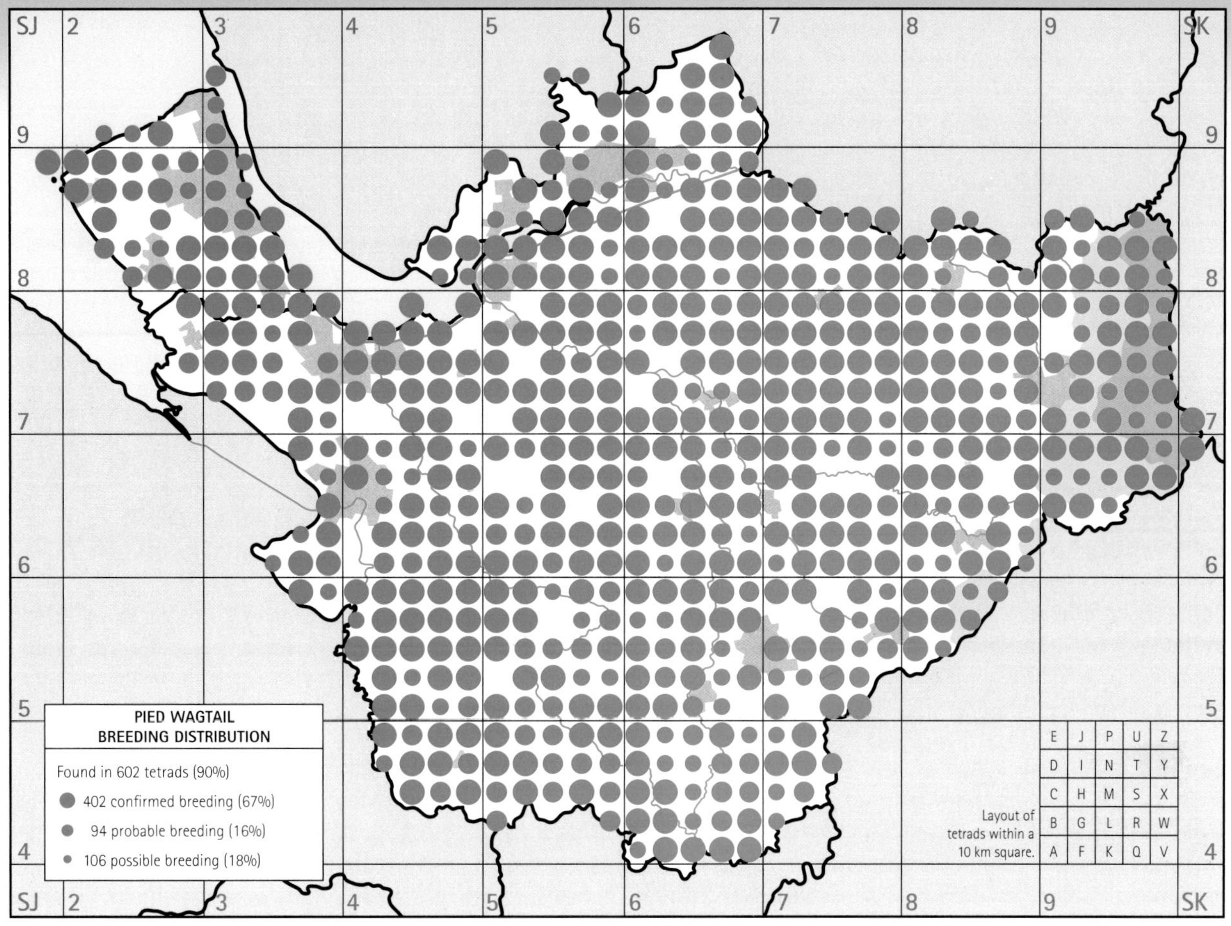

PIED WAGTAIL
BREEDING DISTRIBUTION
Found in 602 tetrads (90%)
402 confirmed breeding (67%)
94 probable breeding (16%)
106 possible breeding (18%)
Layout of tetrads within a 10 km square.

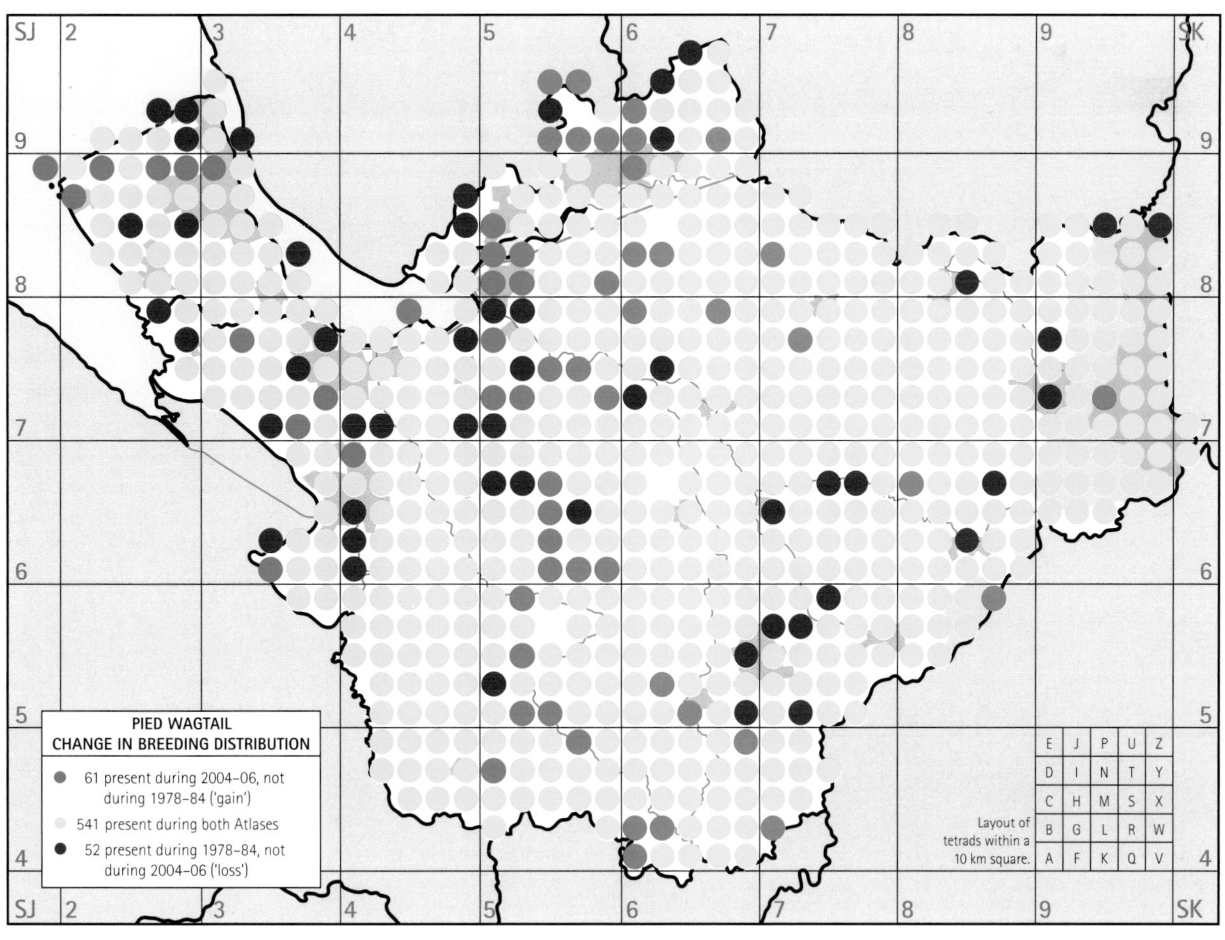

PIED WAGTAIL
CHANGE IN BREEDING DISTRIBUTION
61 present during 2004–06, not during 1978–84 ('gain')
541 present during both Atlases
52 present during 1978–84, not during 2004–06 ('loss')
Layout of tetrads within a 10 km square.

Pied Wagtails feed on insects all year round and have to be adaptable to achieve this. Some of our birds, especially the adults, stay close to their breeding areas while others, and many youngsters, move south, some as far as the Mediterranean. Meanwhile, our wintering population is augmented by arrivals of some Scottish birds (*Migration Atlas*). They also retreat from the highest ground, and this is just evident at the east of our recording area where they quit eight tetrads above 300 m in which a breeding record was obtained. They appear to be missing from some of the most open areas at sea level as well: the Dee and Mersey salt-marshes, and parts of the Mersey valley mosses. Otherwise, the winter distribution is similar to that for the breeding season.

This map would surprise the earlier chroniclers of the county's birds. Coward and Oldham (1900) knew the Pied Wagtail as a partial migrant, 'only a few birds remaining through the winter'. In contrast to the present day, they commented that, especially during a frost, Pied Wagtails were numerous on the Dee marshes; the birds feeding along the high water mark and resorting to the gutters when the tide was out. Boyd (1951) mentioned 'the comparatively few Pied Wagtails that winter here', and Bell (1962) wrote that 'relatively few birds remain through the winter' and that 'the numbers in most areas in winter are very small and widely scattered'. Unfortunately, the annual county bird reports give no indication when Pied Wagtails changed their winter habits to become common and widespread, as now. From 1964 to 1977 there were only three winter records published, two of feeding concentrations at sewage farms and one of a December roost in Wilmslow. A roost at Rolls-Royce, Crewe, drew comment from 1978 to 1980, then fieldwork for the national *BTO Winter Atlas* (1981/82–1983/84) focused the attention of some observers. Pied Wagtails were found in all 40 of the county's 10 km squares, although one-third of them only registered the lowest (one to seven birds) category of abundance. In the cold winter of 1981/82 they were noted as being much more localized in rural areas than during the breeding season. From then on, winter records were published annually in *CWBRs*, mostly of totals at sewage farms and roosts and by 1992, when the annual bird report introduced a summary status line, the species was described as a 'common widespread resident', meaning 1,000–5,000 birds in winter. Pied Wagtails are susceptible to freezing weather, and presumably the milder winters since the late-1980s have allowed them to survive in the county.

RAY SCALLY

As well as continuing to inhabit farmland, especially grassland and farmyards, wagtails move into gardens, and the Pied Wagtail is perhaps the most characteristic bird of sewage treatment plants, where insects are guaranteed. The winter habitat codes showed most birds (49%) in human sites (5% urban, 11% suburban and 33% rural); 41% on farmland, mostly grassland, and 7% spread across all types of fresh water. Flying insects are scarce in winter, so their diet becomes beetles, spiders and invertebrate larvae, supplemented by occasional small seeds and breadcrumbs in human sites. In midwinter, they spend 90% of the daylight hours feeding, taking an average of 18 items per minute. This feeding rate—one small insect every three or four seconds throughout a winter's day—seems incredible but is only just sufficient for a bird to gain enough energy to sustain it through the night (Davies 1982). Most birds were reported during this winter Atlas in ones or twos, but there were eight feeding flocks of over 100 birds, including two each at sewage works and wet stubble fields.

This species is renowned for its urban winter roosts, birds gathering either on the flat roofs of large buildings or in dense evergreen bushes, with laurel especially favoured, although sometimes wagtails roost on the bare branches of trees. Examples were reported during this Atlas of roosts in the town centres of Runcorn, Crewe, Alsager, Wilmslow and Macclesfield. They also have a liking for large building complexes in a mainly rural environment such as motorway service areas, Alderley Park, Daresbury Laboratory and Cheshire Oaks. Several of the larger roosts may number in three figures, with counts submitted of up to 300 in the regular roost around Crewe railway station (SJ75C), up to 200 in Macclesfield town centre (SJ97B) and 120 outside Runcorn Police Station (SJ57K) in January 2005. Their autumn reed-bed roosts are seldom used into the winter period, presumably because they are too exposed for the long cold nights.

Birds of the nominate race, White Wagtails *Motacilla alba alba*, pass through on spring and autumn passage between their breeding grounds in Iceland and their normal wintering quarters in West Africa. In recent years a few have been noted in winter in Britain, including one during this winter Atlas, a bird ringed at Prestbury Sewage Farm SJ87Z in winter 2005/06.

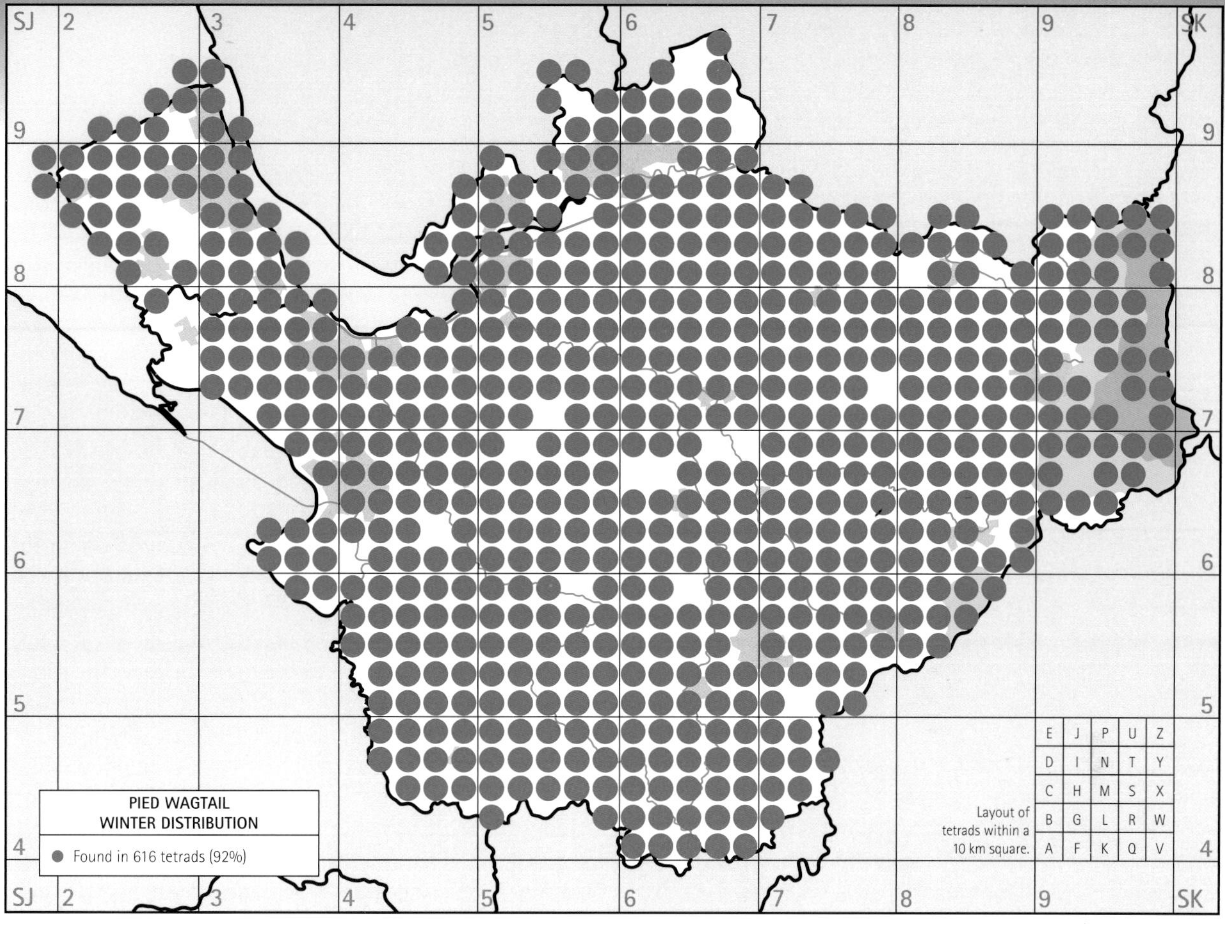
SJ
SK
PIED WAGTAIL
WINTER DISTRIBUTION
Found in 616 tetrads (92%)
E J P U Z
D I N T Y
C H M S X
B G L R W
A F K Q V
Layout of tetrads within a 10 km square.

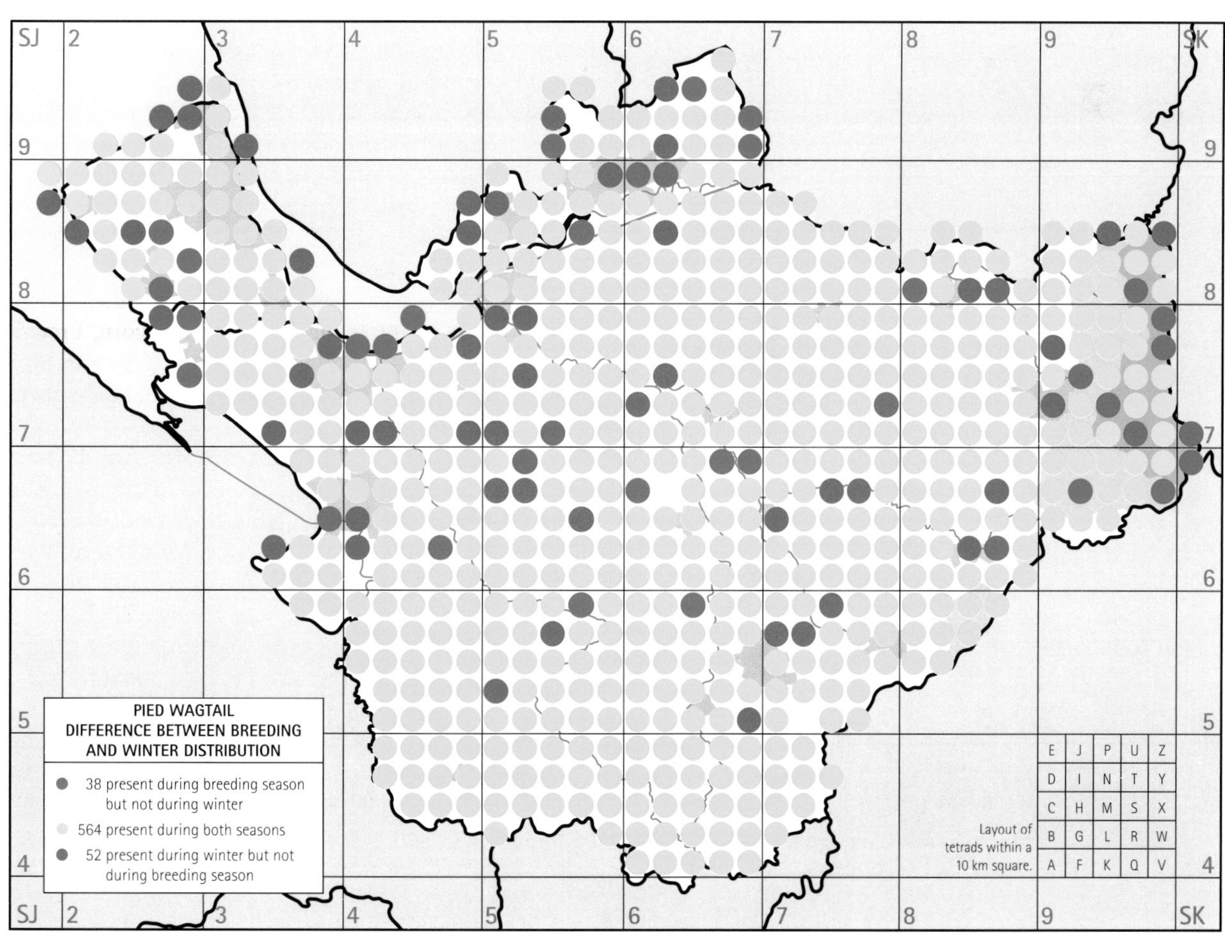
SJ
SK
PIED WAGTAIL
DIFFERENCE BETWEEN BREEDING AND WINTER DISTRIBUTION
38 present during breeding season but not during winter
564 present during both seasons
52 present during winter but not during breeding season
E J P U Z
D I N T Y
C H M S X
B G L R W
A F K Q V
Layout of tetrads within a 10 km square.

Waxwing

Bombycilla garrulus

SIMON BOOTH

The winter of 2004/05 brought an unprecedented influx of (Bohemian) Waxwings to Britain, and their presence in Cheshire was one of the highlights of the first winter of recording for this Atlas. Odd Waxwings have previously been reported in many winters but significant invasions only in 1849/50, 1863/64, 1901/02 (Coward 1900), 1946/47 and 1965/66 (Bell 1967) when a flock of over 80 at Reddish Vale (outside the current recording area), on the early date of 20 November 1965, was noted as 'much the largest flock ever reported in the county'. The maximum counts in *CWBRs* are shown in the graph.

In autumn 2004, the crop of berries, especially of Rowan *Sorbus aucuparia* failed in Fennoscandia owing to very wet weather that caused the fruit to rot on the trees. After the birds turned from their breeding season diet, mainly insects caught by fly-catching, they rapidly found that they had to move south and west to find food.

The Waxwings' origins are shown by ringed birds from Finland, Sweden and Norway caught by ringers during that winter, but the numbers present in Britain, estimated at more than 100,000, suggest that some must have come from farther east in Russia as well. Their course through Britain was well studied in a coordinated effort by many ringers. Birds were colour-ringed in north-east Scotland and subsequently seen farther south, including in Cheshire at Wilmslow and Warrington. In previous years with big Waxwing numbers in Britain, they have tended to move southwards along the eastern half of Britain (as noted by Coward & Oldham 1900), but in 2004/05 most of them moved along a more westerly track, thus favouring Cheshire more than ever before (Oddy 2005). It was not a straightforward movement, however, and individual birds proved to be highly mobile–birds ringed in Warrington were later caught in Sheffield–and careful watching of the main flocks showed a daily turnover in birds.

The first Waxwings were found in the county in late November 2004 and numbers built to a peak during January 2005. Three flocks totalled 690 birds on 19 January, but not all of the flocks were regularly counted and possibly as many as 2,000 birds were in our area at the peak. Numbers dwindled during February and some were still moving around Cheshire and Wirral in March and even into April, after the end of the Atlas winter recording season.

This nomadic species showed its apparent preference for human sites, and almost all records were in habitats of F1 or F2 (urban or suburban areas). Several large flocks formed in the county, notably in the town centres of Macclesfield, Warrington and Runcorn, and at Chester Zoo. These often centred on just a few trees, usually ornamental varieties of rowan, and led to amusing territorial battles with resident Mistle Thrushes, and occasionally with flocks of Redwings and Starlings. After exhausting the fruit there, birds spread out and wandered far and wide in search of more berries. Waxwings will eat almost any berry, of almost any colour or texture, and their agility, deriving in part from their fly-catching days, and helped by their strong claws that allow them to grip well, meant that few berries were beyond their reach. They could be found widely throughout the county, although it needed an element of luck to spot where the birds had moved to, possibly only staying a few hours, and their distribution was probably underrecorded. Also, amazing as

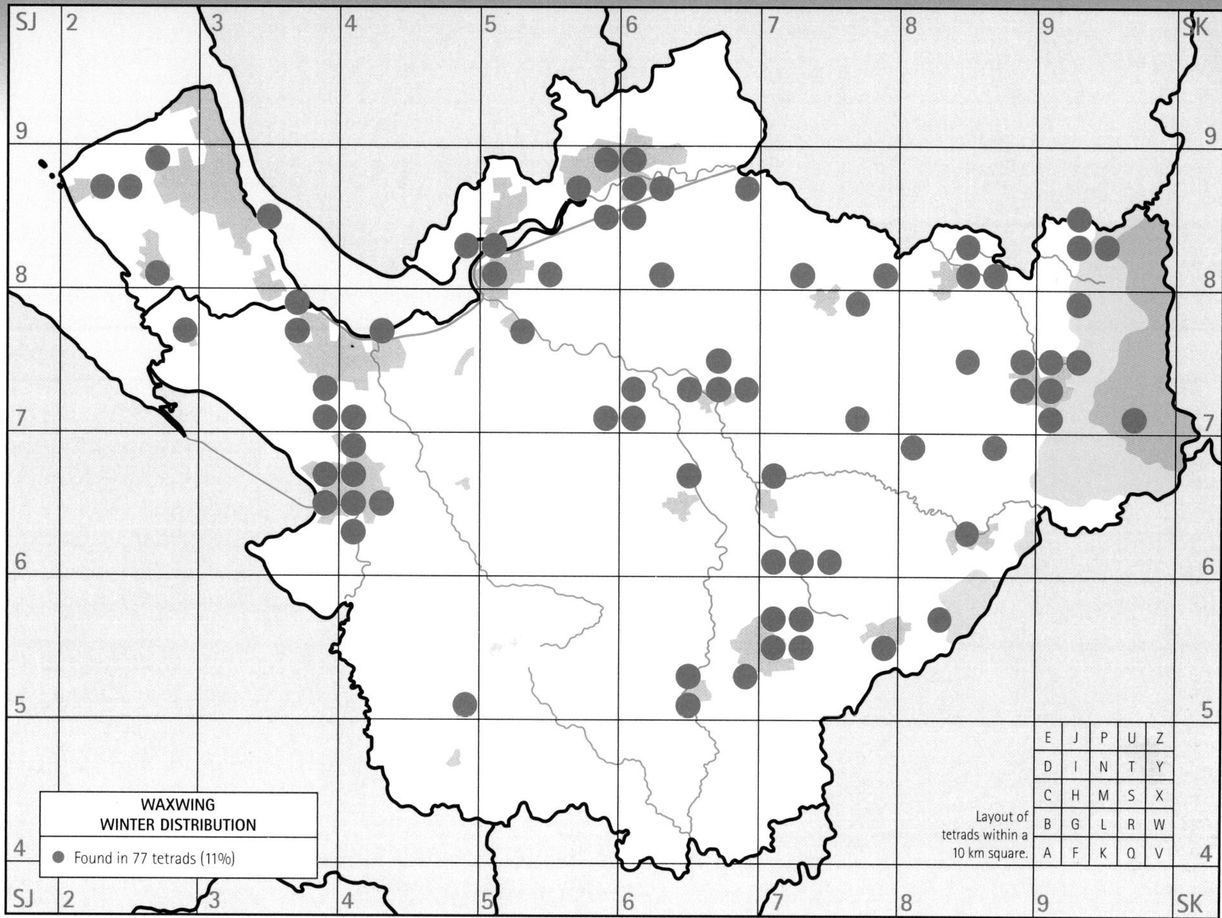

it is to report, some birdwatchers tired of looking for Waxwings in 2004/05!

Most birds were found by seeing the aerial manoeuvres of a flock of birds, perhaps initially confused with Starlings, and some observers detected Waxwings after they had gained familiarity with their call-notes, a pleasing twittering, likened by some to a mechanical sound such as a 'Trimphone', and perhaps sounding closer to a Redpoll than any other bird species. Some birds could be surprisingly invisible in the treetops, but they frequently showed themselves from their habit of feeding in bouts and flying off to rest in nearby trees and rooftops. They used the resting time to digest their meals and deposit the inevitable products—not always welcome in urban settings—although most members of the public were intrigued not only by the antics of the birds but also by those of the people who came to watch them. They were featured on television and radio, in local newspapers and on websites. The extraordinary irruption of 2004/05 may represent a once-in-a-lifetime event for Cheshire and Wirral, and will long be remembered by birdwatchers as providing a marvellous start to our first ever winter Atlas.

This influx was put into context by the next two winters, when there were only three records in 2005/06, all from tetrads that had held birds in 2004/05, and none at all in 2006/07.

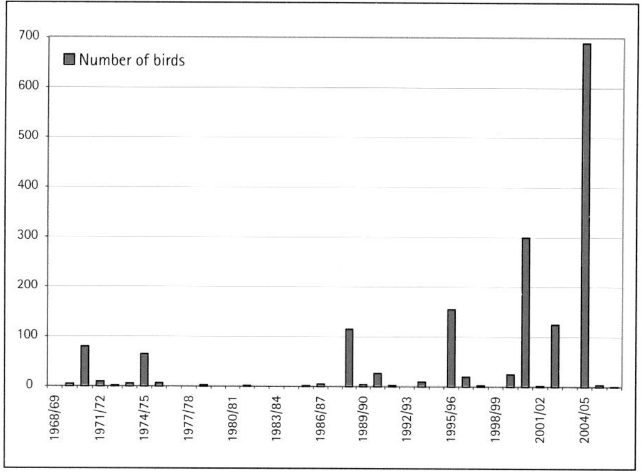

Waxwing wintering numbers.

Dipper

Cinclus cinclus

RICHARD STEEL

This is the characteristic bird of fast-flowing rivers and streams, and is normally found only in Cheshire in the eastern hills. The breeding distribution map shows a reduction from 36 occupied tetrads in the *First Atlas* to 22 now. It is not possible to track their contraction in range because Dippers have been notoriously poorly recorded in the annual county bird reports, as the following quotes illustrate: just four years after our *First Atlas* period, 'there were no confirmed breeding records' in 1988, and by 1992 'there were no breeding records' at all. Richard Blindell single-handedly rectified this in 1994 by locating at least 12 territories along about 10 km of the meandering river Dane from Hug Bridge (SJ96G) to Congleton (SJ86R), but again by 1997 the species was 'underrecorded' and in 2002 'breeding was not confirmed from any site in the county'. This Atlas stimulated more thorough recording of Dippers: fieldworkers confirmed breeding in 13 tetrads, recording nest with young (NY) in four tetrads, recently fledged young (RF) in eight tetrads and one instance of an adult carrying food for its young (FY); pairs were observed in another three tetrads and single birds in six. Not surprisingly, all of the submitted habitat codes were G6 (stream less than 3 m wide) with 12 records or G7 (river more than 3 m wide) with 10 records.

There is no clue from the national picture that might explain a decline in the species since our *First Atlas*. Dipper populations on the BTO's Waterways Bird Survey plots have fluctuated over the last 30 years, but shown little overall trend. The birds are a sensitive indicator of acidity and other water pollution (Tyler & Ormerod 1994). Dippers use their sharp claws to grip onto the riverbed whilst they walk about underwater finding food. Adults eat a lot of shrimps, and feed their young chicks mainly on mayflies or stonefly nymphs, with caddis larvae increasingly important as the chicks grow. According to monitoring by the Environment Agency, the biological quality of east Cheshire's watercourses is deteriorating. Their most recent assessments (2004–06) place the river Dane (SJ96S), Clough Brook (SJ96T), Bosley Brook (SJ96C) and Pott Shrigley Brook (SJ97P) in category C (fairly good), all having been category B (good) a few years earlier.

Most Dippers are monogamous, and often pairs stay together for several years. To reinforce the pair-bond both sexes sing at almost any time of year, although their sweet, rippling notes are often drowned out, to human ears, by the noise of the water, and there were no Atlas records of song. Dippers start their breeding activity in winter and invest a lot of time in their nest, perhaps taking a month to build a large, domed structure over running water, on a ledge (natural or man-made) and sometimes even behind a waterfall or in a culvert. They start laying in March or early April, having advanced this date by about nine days in the last 40 years. Their four or five chicks are flying during May; their early start allows Dippers to refurbish the nest and raise a second brood in July, although perhaps only one-quarter of pairs do so (Tyler & Ormerod 1994).

Although almost all breeding Dippers have been in the eastern hills, especially along the rivers Dane, Dean and Goyt and their tributaries, occasional birds have been found in the lowlands, including a series of records during the 1970s from the Cuddington Brook (SJ57W), with proven breeding in 1975; in 1982 a pair hatched young on the Wych Brook in SJ44M; and in 1994 Dippers bred near Haslington (SJ75H).

The 1994 survey of the river Dane found territory lengths of less than 1 km, and the typical range is 0.5–2.5 km (Tyler & Ormerod 1994), so each tetrad could hold from one to five pairs. With 16 tetrads recorded with confirmed or probable breeding, there might be 25–30 pairs of Dippers in Cheshire.

In 2007 South Manchester Ringing Group started a research project ringing, colour-marking, mapping territories and nest sites and measuring water quality. Within our county boundaries, their members found 12 nests in nine tetrads, with probable breeding in another two tetrads and possible breeding in one; four of these 12 tetrads are blank on the Atlas map. We should know much more about Cheshire's Dippers in the next few years.

Sponsored by N. and K. Parry

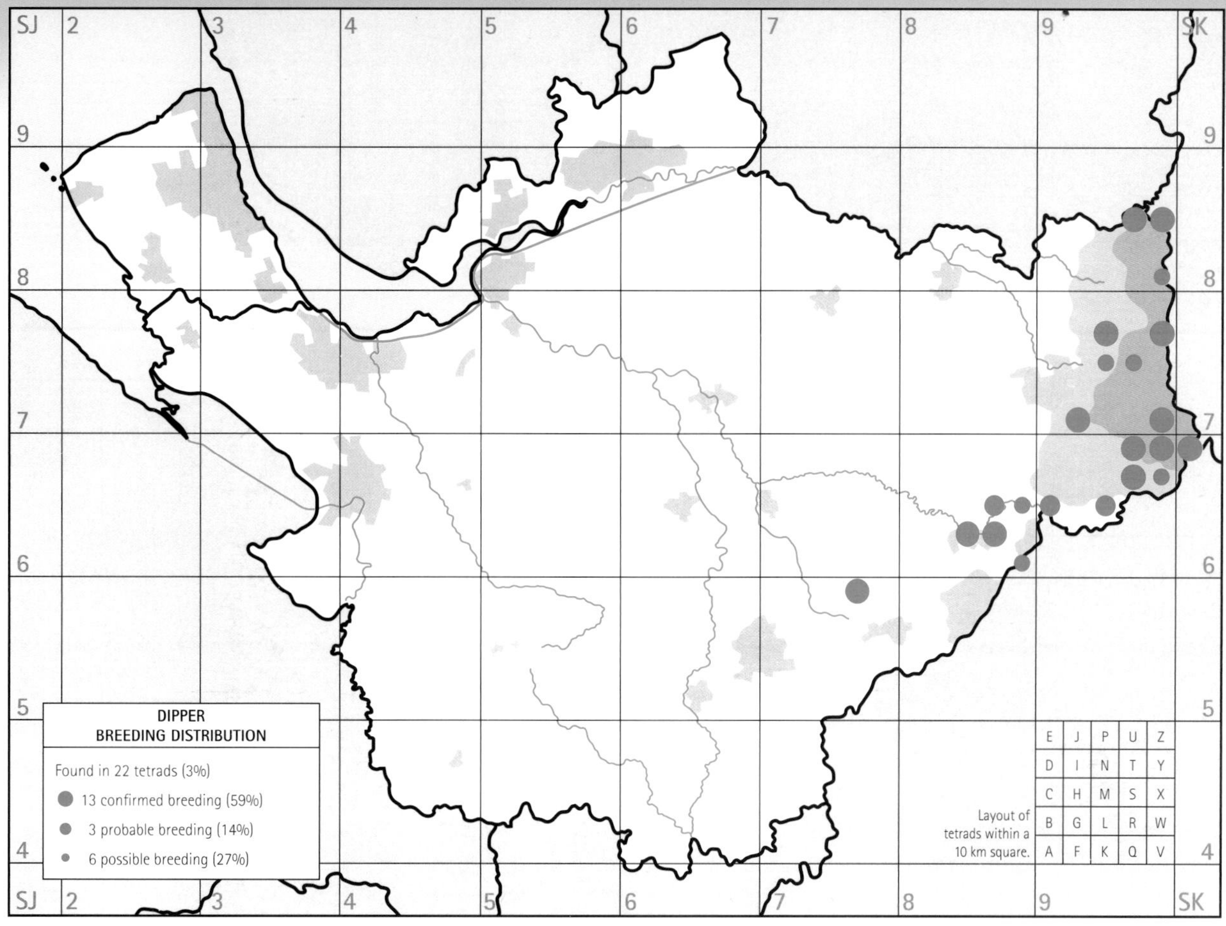
DIPPER
BREEDING DISTRIBUTION
Found in 22 tetrads (3%)
13 confirmed breeding (59%)
3 probable breeding (14%)
6 possible breeding (27%)
Layout of tetrads within a 10 km square.

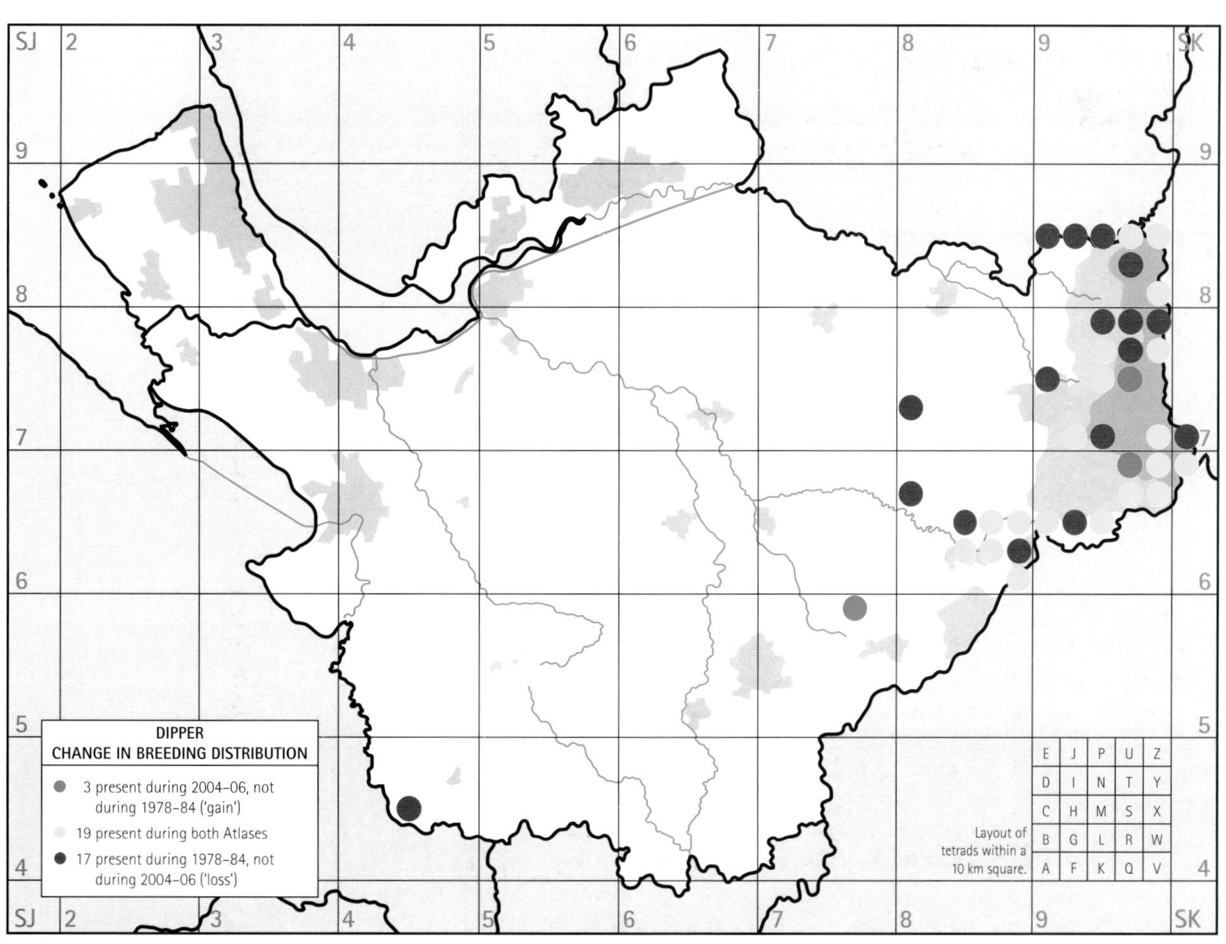
DIPPER
CHANGE IN BREEDING DISTRIBUTION
3 present during 2004–06, not during 1978–84 ('gain')
19 present during both Atlases
17 present during 1978–84, not during 2004–06 ('loss')
Layout of tetrads within a 10 km square.

Most Dippers are sedentary but this Atlas shows clear evidence of altitudinal migration, with some birds descending to lower altitudes in winter. The map illustrating the difference between breeding and wintering distribution shows clearly that most of the nine tetrads occupied in winter but with no breeding season record are to the west, at lower altitude than their breeding range. Omitting the bird holding a territory spanning SJ75T/U, four of the five tetrads occupied in the breeding season only, with no winter record, were above 300 m, while seven of the eight tetrads occupied in winter only, with no breeding season record, were below 200 m, four of them below 100 m. Some of the highest altitude territories, such as in SJ96Y/Z and SJ97V, had birds present in both seasons, however, so some birds are able to survive winters in upland Cheshire. Perhaps some of those at lower altitudes are first-year birds that have been driven out by their parents. Coward, who in his 1910 book described the Dipper as 'an abundant resident on the hill streams in the east', noted that 'many of the birds leave the high ground in the late summer or autumn, and in winter the Dipper is occasionally met with on the lower reaches of the larger streams and on brooks in the plain'.

Midstream stones covered with droppings often indicate Dippers' favoured sites. Many birds maintain winter territories, usually as pairs and often coinciding with their breeding territory, provided that they can provide sufficient of their winter diet, caddis and dipteran flies, shrimps, fish and molluscs. Many of the aquatic invertebrates reach their peak populations during winter, prior to spring emergence, and the upland watercourses seldom freeze so food availability should not be a problem. Dippers often sleep overnight in communal roosts, mostly of two birds but sometimes more, in nooks and crannies under bridges where they can stay warmer on cold, windy nights.

Even in midwinter, residents sing strongly to re-establish their territories and anticipate the breeding season. Apart from the portion of the population that undertakes altitudinal migration, there is remarkably little seasonal difference in the Dippers' lives. This is such an important indicator of the state of our upland watercourses that it deserves monitoring closely.

RICHARD STEEL

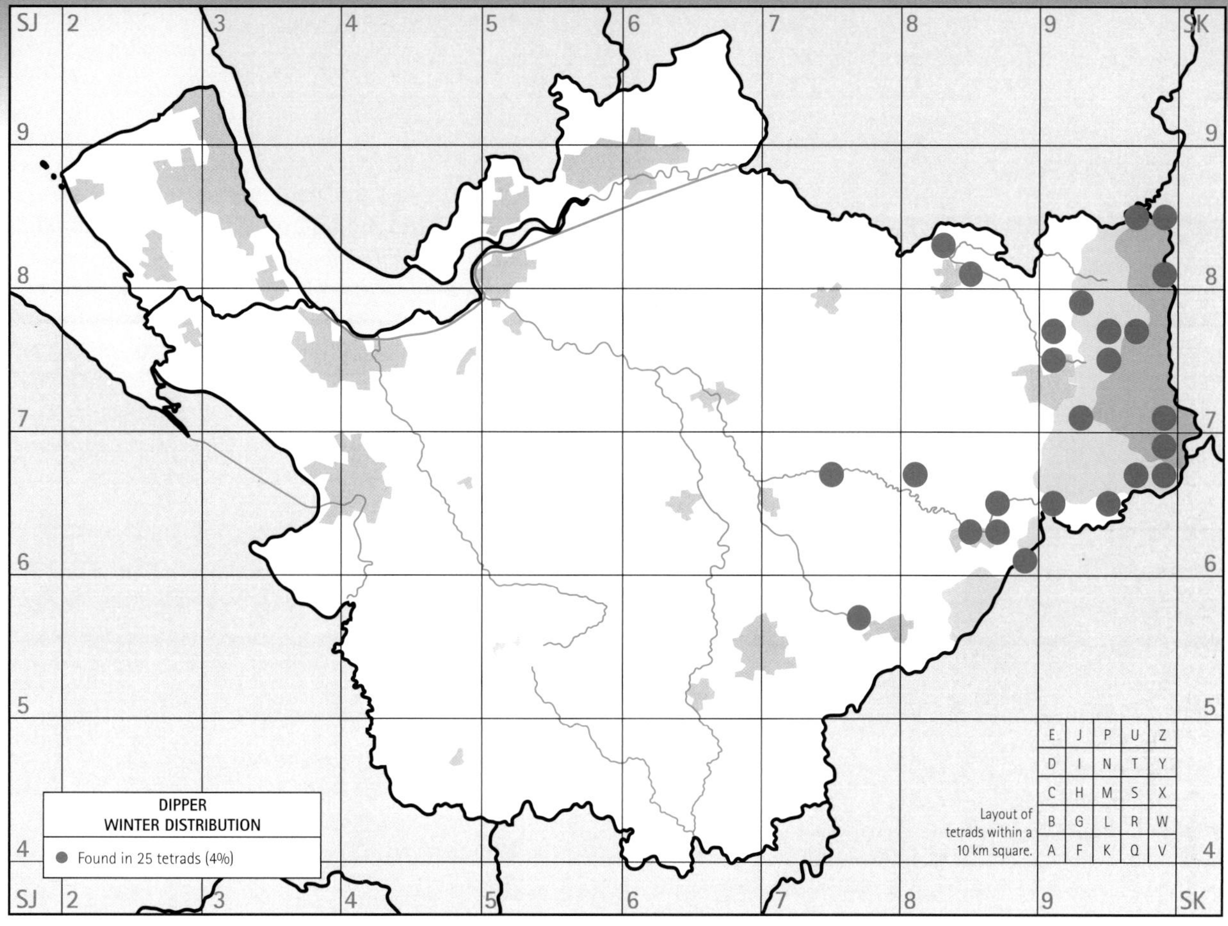
DIPPER
WINTER DISTRIBUTION
Found in 25 tetrads (4%)
Layout of tetrads within a 10 km square.
E J P U Z
D I N T Y
C H M S X
B G L R W
A F K Q V
SJ
SK

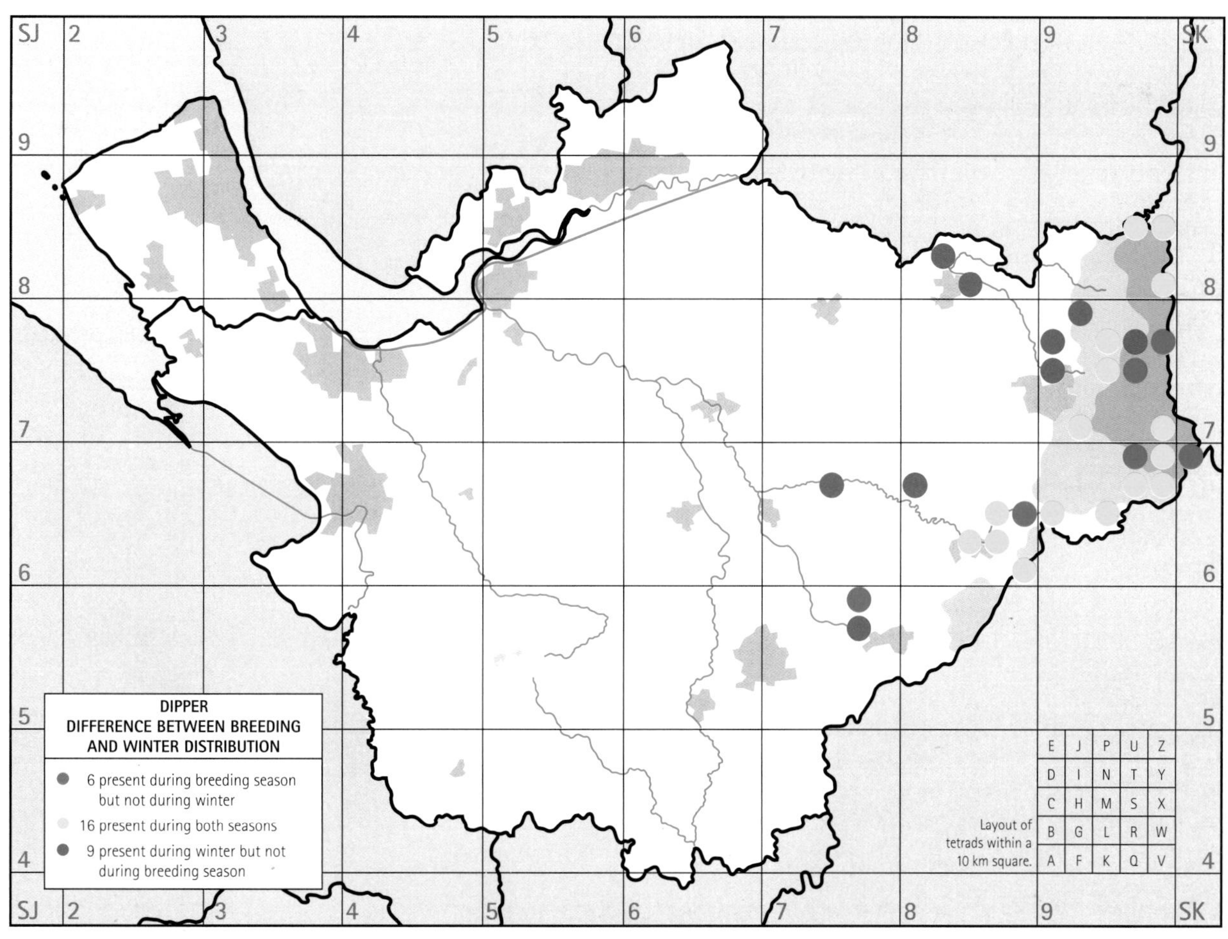
DIPPER
DIFFERENCE BETWEEN BREEDING AND WINTER DISTRIBUTION
6 present during breeding season but not during winter
16 present during both seasons
9 present during winter but not during breeding season
Layout of tetrads within a 10 km square.
E J P U Z
D I N T Y
C H M S X
B G L R W
A F K Q V
SJ
SK

Wren

Troglodytes troglodytes

ANDY HARMER

This Atlas survey showed that Wren is now the county's most widespread breeding species, present in 660 tetrads and only missing from the estuarine salt-marshes. The only change since our *First Atlas* is that Wrens have bred on Hilbre since the mid-1990s, last known in the 1930s (Hardy 1941).

The key to the Wren's success is its ability to thrive in a variety of habitats. Fieldworkers recorded Wrens in farmland (32% of records), woodland (29%), human sites (27%) and scrub (10%). The species' habitat preferences run in the order: first, small woods and clumps of trees with underlying scrub; next, rough vegetation along rivers, streams and ditches; followed by gardens and the edges of farmland ponds, with field hedgerows the least favoured (Williamson 1969). Now, with their population at a high level, it is not surprising that every habitat is occupied.

Wrens were confirmed breeding in 73% of their tetrads, with observers in 163 tetrads recording adults carrying food or a faecal sac, in 206 tetrads seeing recently fledged chicks and finding nests with young or eggs in 111. Male Wrens build several 'cocks' nests', domed balls of moss, leaves and grasses, from which his mate chooses one and lines it with feathers. The same procedure is followed for the almost customary second brood in July. Most nests are in hedges or creeping plants or in holes such as rock crevices, amongst tree roots or, especially in the hills, dry-stone walls and stunted hedges provide numerous nest sites. In farm buildings they often build on an old Swallow's nest, and several observers reported Wrens using nests in artificial sites including under a bridge, in a carport, in honeysuckle against a pole in a garden centre, on the timber frame of a hide at Woolston Eyes, and one found by Tony Coatsworth in Little Bollington (SJ78I), where an adult was feeding chicks in a hanging basket outside a pub.

The BTO analysis of BBS transects shows that this is our seventh most numerous species, with a breeding population of Cheshire and Wirral in 2004–05 of 129,370 birds (108,620–150,110), an average of almost 200 Wrens per tetrad across the county. In the best habitats there are up to 320 birds per tetrad, as the abundance maps shows in scrubby areas along the Mersey valley and south Wirral, and in south-east Cheshire.

There is no long-term trend in the national or local Wren populations but their numbers can fluctuate enormously, dropping to less than one-quarter of their maximum level following the severe winter weather of 1962/63, with other large drops in 1978/79 and 1985/86. In exposed sites almost every Wren might die, with the population restocked from birds surviving in sheltered farmsteads and villages (Peach *et al.* 1995b). In recent years, the limit on their population has been competition from other Wrens as they reach the carrying capacity of the environment.

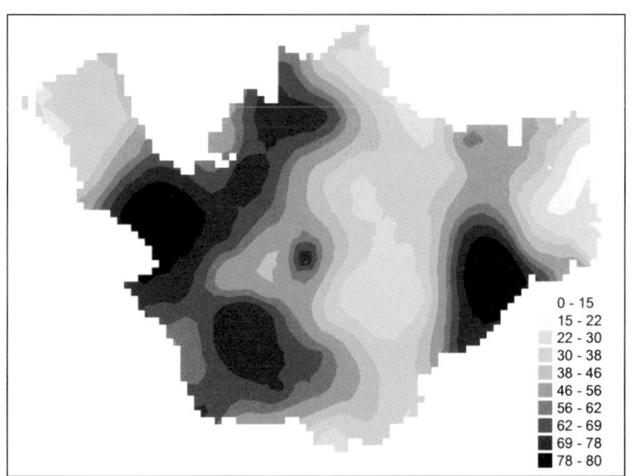

Wren abundance.

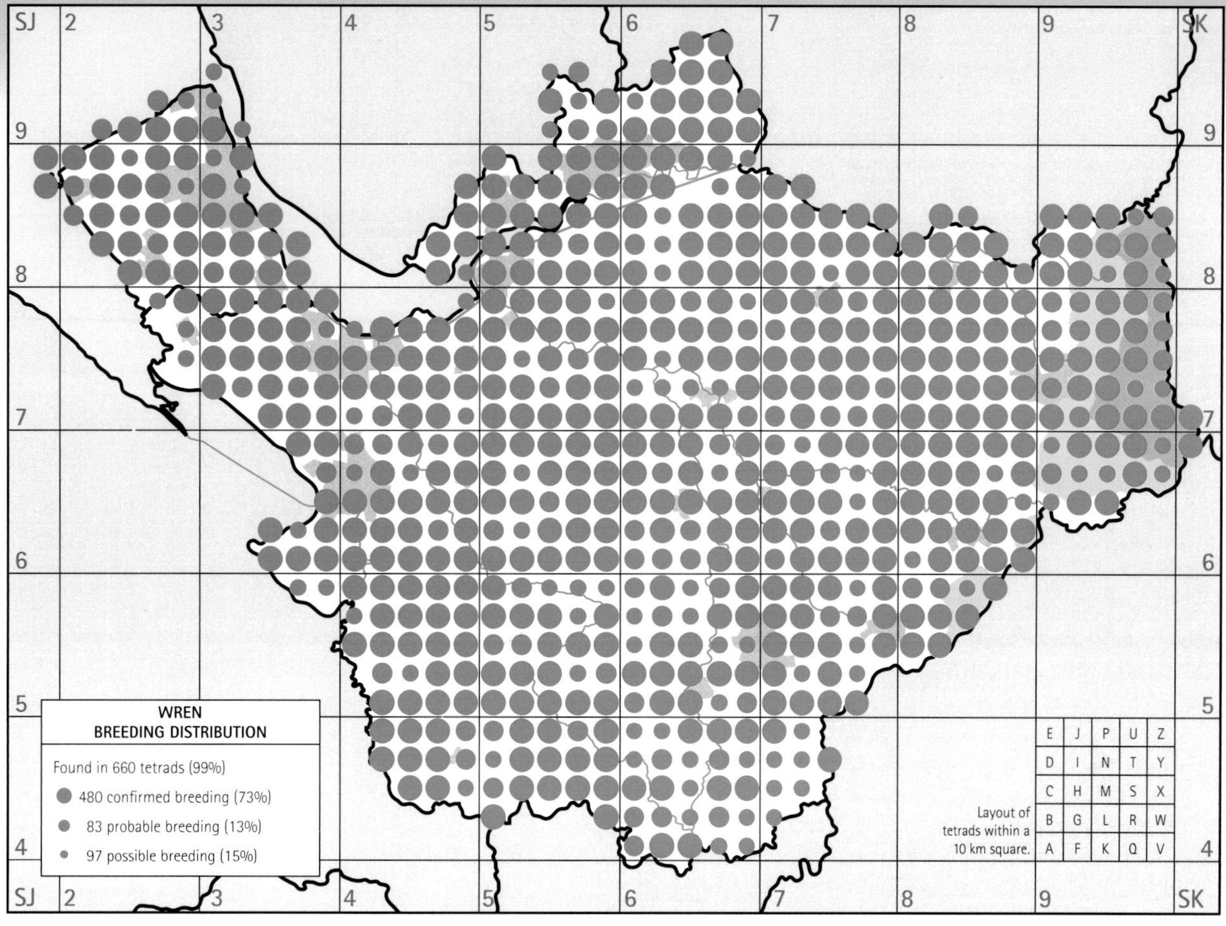
SJ
SK
2
3
4
5
6
7
8
9
WREN
BREEDING DISTRIBUTION
Found in 660 tetrads (99%)
480 confirmed breeding (73%)
83 probable breeding (13%)
97 possible breeding (15%)
E J P U Z
D I N T Y
C H M S X
B G L R W
A F K Q V
Layout of tetrads within a 10 km square.

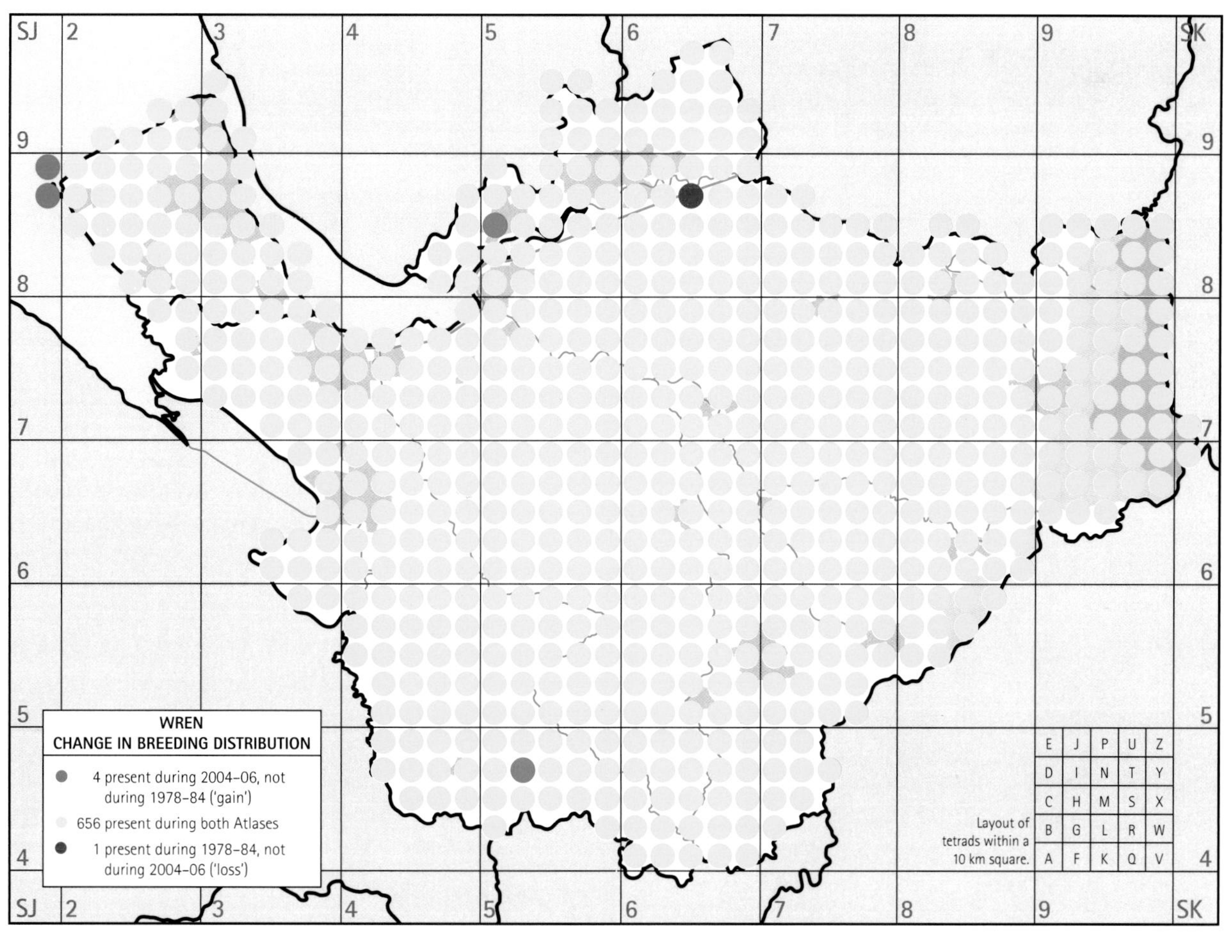
SJ
SK
2
3
4
5
6
7
8
9
WREN
CHANGE IN BREEDING DISTRIBUTION
4 present during 2004–06, not during 1978–84 ('gain')
656 present during both Atlases
1 present during 1978–84, not during 2004–06 ('loss')
E J P U Z
D I N T Y
C H M S X
B G L R W
A F K Q V
Layout of tetrads within a 10 km square.

Some Wrens undertake altitudinal migration (*Migration Atlas*), leaving the highest ground, but surveyors for this Atlas found some birds in virtually every tetrad apart from the highest of all in the county (SK07A), lying above 500 m. Otherwise, many birds stay on or near their breeding areas. Typically of insectivores, many Wrens establish winter territories. Indeed, ensuring overwinter survival is so important to them that competition for territories may start in July (*BTO Winter Atlas*). There is little aggression during winter and many birds are unobtrusive. The odd bursts of winter song seem to be unrelated to declarations of territorial possession. As might be expected from a territorial species, half of the counts submitted by Atlas surveyors were of single birds. Some Wrens do gather into groups, especially in reed-beds and other habitats not used for breeding; these birds contain a majority of females, somewhat smaller than males, that have probably lost out in a contest for a territory.

MIKE ATKINSON

As in the breeding season, Wrens find most of their winter food close to the ground, in ditches, hedges, crevices in walls and the like, which they search assiduously for insects, spiders and some seeds.

Habitat occupation in winter is determined partly by availability of food but especially by shelter from cold and winds. Atlas fieldworkers registered significant drops in almost every category of habitat code except for urban and suburban areas, but with substantial increases in the totals in hedgerows. To some extent birds flitting about in hedges might be more noticeable, with silent birds in woodland or scrub being quite inconspicuous, but there are some real differences in the type of hedges used: in the breeding season, the two categories of hedge (more or less than 2 m in height) were equally occupied, but in winter there were significantly more Wrens recorded in short hedges. The *BTO Winter Atlas* noted that farmland hedgerows were commonly empty in winter, but that certainly is not the experience during this survey. The explanation for the disagreement may be winter temperatures, with the first national winter Atlas collecting data during the relatively cold winters of 1981/82–1983/84, when the first winter had two 10-day spells of subzero temperatures, much colder than during this Cheshire and Wirral Atlas.

As a small resident insectivore the Wren is always vulnerable to hard weather. One way in which they try to keep warm overnight is by sharing roost sites, birds huddling together to minimize loss of heat. One such roost was reported during this Atlas, in house ivy near Mow Cop (SJ85U) where Alan Straw counted 10 birds; the maximum at the same site had been 17 in 2003/04.

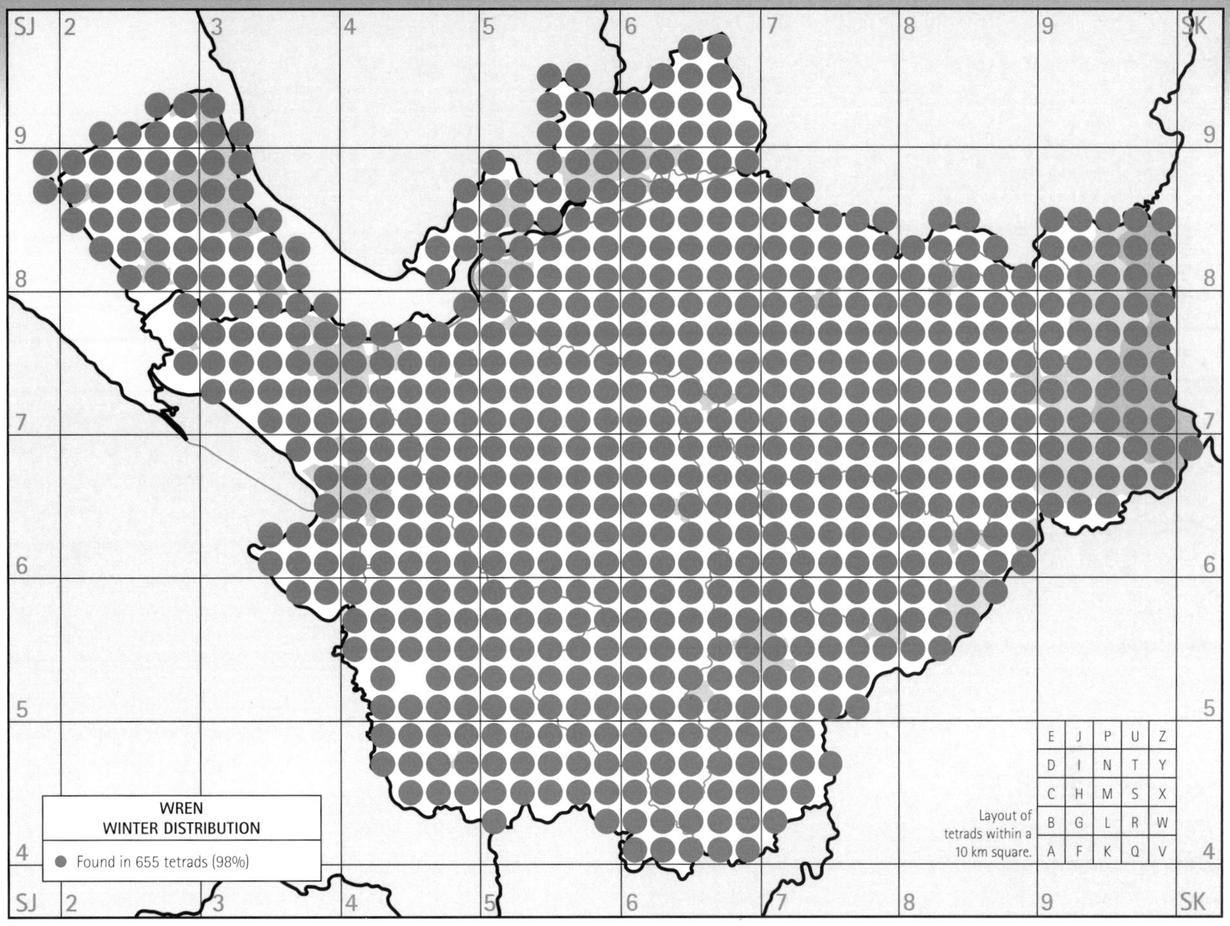
WREN
WINTER DISTRIBUTION
Found in 655 tetrads (98%)
Layout of tetrads within a 10 km square.
E J P U Z
D I N T Y
C H M S X
B G L R W
A F K Q V
SJ
SK

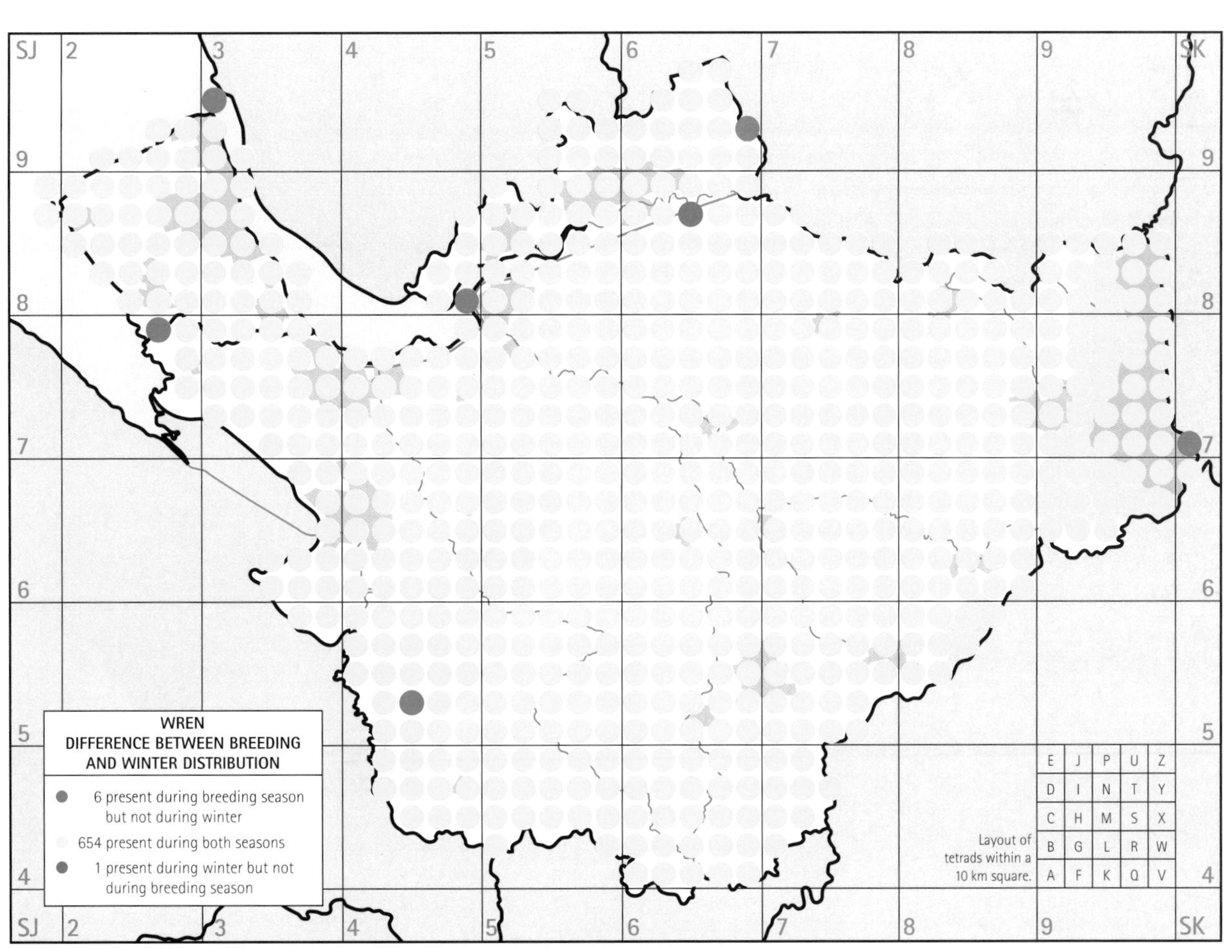
WREN
DIFFERENCE BETWEEN BREEDING AND WINTER DISTRIBUTION
6 present during breeding season but not during winter
654 present during both seasons
1 present during winter but not during breeding season
Layout of tetrads within a 10 km square.
E J P U Z
D I N T Y
C H M S X
B G L R W
A F K Q V
SJ
SK

Dunnock

Prunella modularis

RICHARD STEEL

The Dunnock is one of the most overlooked common birds, but this Atlas shows it to be the ninth most widespread species in Cheshire and Wirral, present in 647 tetrads. Its unusual mating systems and susceptibility to Cuckoo parasitism have made it the subject of much professional study (Davies 1992), and its recent placing on the Amber List of species of conservation concern has concentrated the attention of ringers, nest recorders and some birdwatchers.

Their national population fell by 47% from its peak in 1974 to the zenith in the mid-1990s, much of the drop taking place during the seven years of our *First Atlas*. The reasons for the decline are not well understood but the removal or heavy trimming of farmland hedges cannot have helped. The species has now recovered somewhat from its low point and the national index in 2004 was a little higher than 20 years previously. The BTO BBS analysis shows that the breeding population of Cheshire and Wirral in 2004–05 was 71,680 birds (57,070–86,280). The population corresponds to a mean of almost 110 birds per tetrad in which they were recorded, but the abundance map shows that this average figure covers an enormous range from some suburban areas where there were more than 200 birds per tetrad to some moorland sites where it was quite difficult to find any. Most recorded habitat codes were farmland (38%), mainly hedgerows (20%) and improved grassland (10%), with 32% in human sites, 19% in woodland and 11% in scrub.

In this Atlas survey, relatively few nests were found for such a common bird, and Dunnocks had the lowest proportion of confirmed breeding of any of the top ten most widespread passerines. The four codes referring to nests (NE/NY/ON/UN) were recorded in 75 tetrads, with another 24 'probable breeding' records of birds visiting a likely nest site or carrying nesting material, often moss. Observers found birds carrying a faecal sac or food in 165 tetrads: this can be difficult to see because, when chicks are small, their parents carry tiny food items that are mostly hidden in their bill. Also, Dunnocks are sneaky birds and, if they feel they are being watched too closely, adults often swallow the food they were carrying for their chicks. As usual, many locations furnished proof of breeding through observations of adults with dependent young (188 RF records).

This unobtrusive little bird does not form pairs, but breeds in groups of up to three males and three females, with two males and a female being the most common, making a mockery of the nineteenth-century vicar who thought that the Dunnock was a perfect example of humility and exhorted his parishioners to emulate their behaviour (Davies 1987). Many Atlas fieldworkers noted three or more birds together. This is most likely in prime habitat where population densities are high.

The map shows that Dunnocks were unaccountably missed from a few tetrads, but the only significant gains or losses were at the extremes of the county. They are now probably breeding on Hilbre, a gain since our *First Atlas*. At the highest altitudes, above about 350 m, birds were found in three tetrads at the eastern edge of SJ97 where they were absent twenty years ago, but on the other hand, are now missing from four adjacent tetrads at the south-east of the hill country.

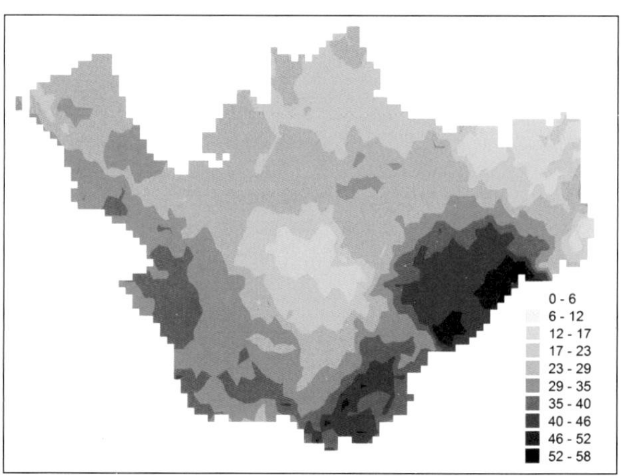

Dunnock abundance.

Sponsored by Peter Walton

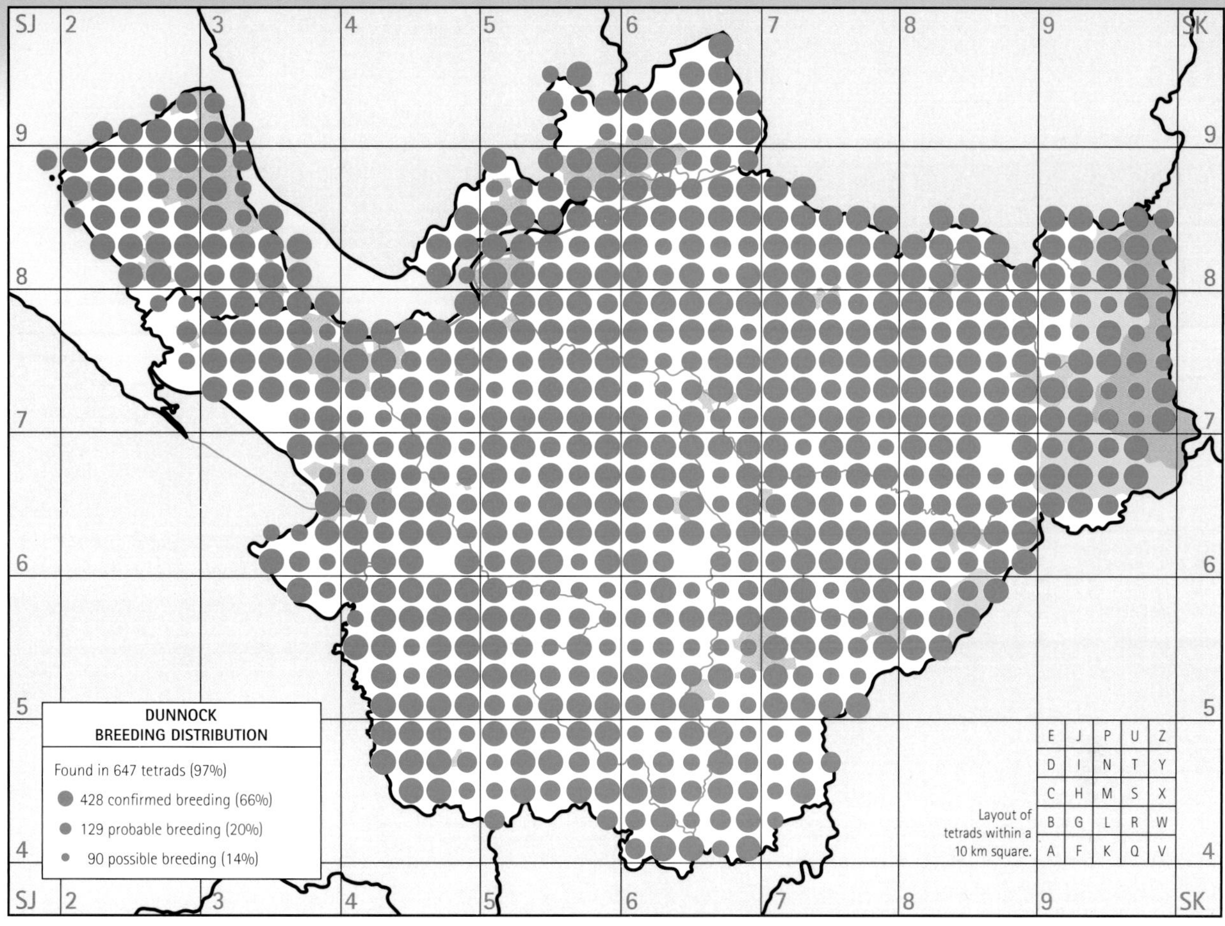
DUNNOCK
BREEDING DISTRIBUTION
Found in 647 tetrads (97%)
428 confirmed breeding (66%)
129 probable breeding (20%)
90 possible breeding (14%)
Layout of tetrads within a 10 km square.
E J P U Z
D I N T Y
C H M S X
B G L R W
A F K Q V
SJ
SK

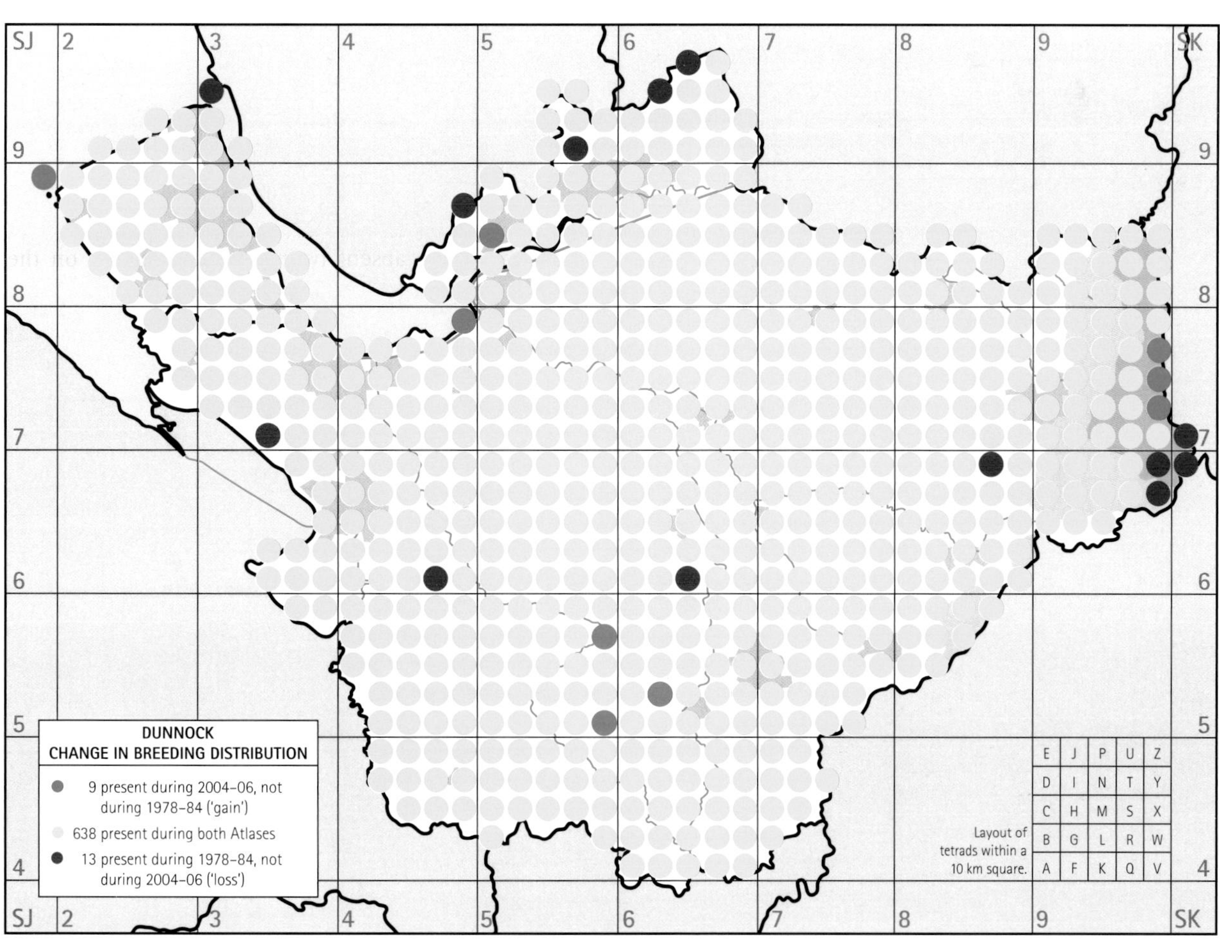
DUNNOCK
CHANGE IN BREEDING DISTRIBUTION
9 present during 2004–06, not during 1978–84 ('gain')
638 present during both Atlases
13 present during 1978–84, not during 2004–06 ('loss')
Layout of tetrads within a 10 km square.
E J P U Z
D I N T Y
C H M S X
B G L R W
A F K Q V
SJ
SK

There is little difference between the Dunnocks' distribution or numbers in the breeding season and winter, and the birds recorded are likely to be the same individuals in both seasons. British Dunnocks are very sedentary, most individuals probably spending their whole lives within an area of radius of 0.1–1 km. Some of the migratory population from Scandinavia appear on passage in eastern Britain, but there is no evidence of any reaching Cheshire and Wirral. The Atlas map shows the species to be missing from three of the highest eastern tetrads, just as it was found to be scarce above 300 m on the moors around Sheffield (Bevington 1991). The main difference in habitat recorded in winter is a drop in the proportion in woodland and scrub, with a substantial rise in birds in hedgerows.

At all seasons, Dunnocks find most of their food on the ground, by gleaning or turning over small leaves. In winter, the diet consists largely of small invertebrates (e.g. beetles, snails, spiders, flies, earthworms and spring-tails) but where food is provided for birds, they take a wide variety of small seeds, fragments of peanuts, breadcrumbs and, less often, berries, small pieces of fat, meat and fruit. The BTO's Garden BirdWatch shows that this is one of the species most likely to be found, Dunnocks ranking as the fourth most widely reported species in the gardens of north-west England.

Wintering Dunnocks tend to be solitary; observers recorded counts for more than 500 tetrads, but half of them were of single birds. I have been surprised to be able to ring up to 20 different birds in a morning at Meadow Bank Farm, Broxton (SJ45W) where they congregate to feed on wildbird seed crops, especially favouring the energy-rich quinoa.

Life can be hard for Dunnocks. In midwinter, individuals feed for over 90% of the daylight hours, dropping to 60–70% in March (Davies 1987) and in hard winters, the slightly smaller, and subordinate, females have to wander in search of food, and suffer higher mortality (*BTO Winter Atlas*).

Despite the rigours of winter, many Atlas fieldworkers noted Dunnocks in song from late January onwards, anticipating an early start to the breeding season.

RICHARD STEEL

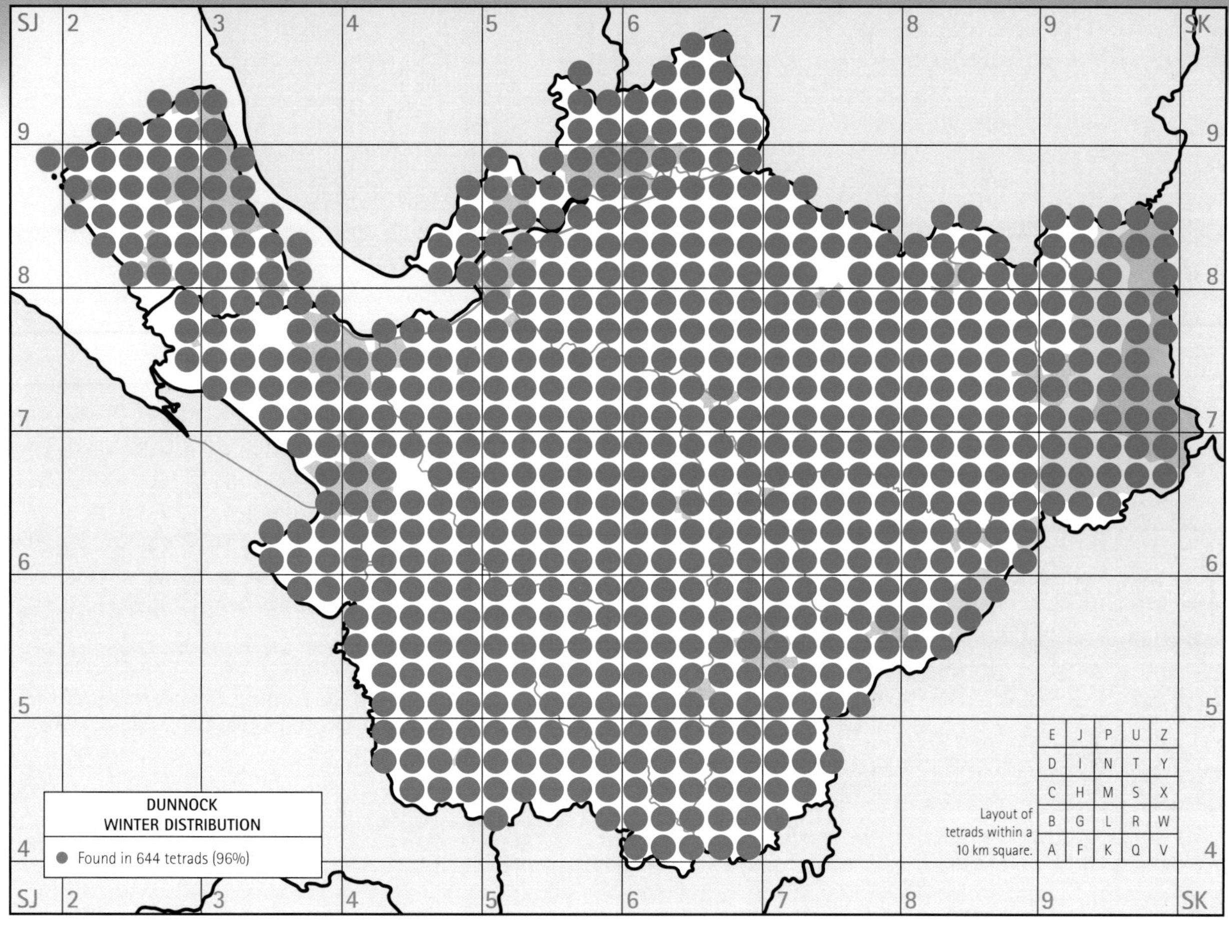
SJ
2
3
4
5
6
7
8
9
SK
9
8
7
6
5
4
DUNNOCK
WINTER DISTRIBUTION
Found in 644 tetrads (96%)
E J P U Z
D I N T Y
C H M S X
B G L R W
A F K Q V
Layout of tetrads within a 10 km square.

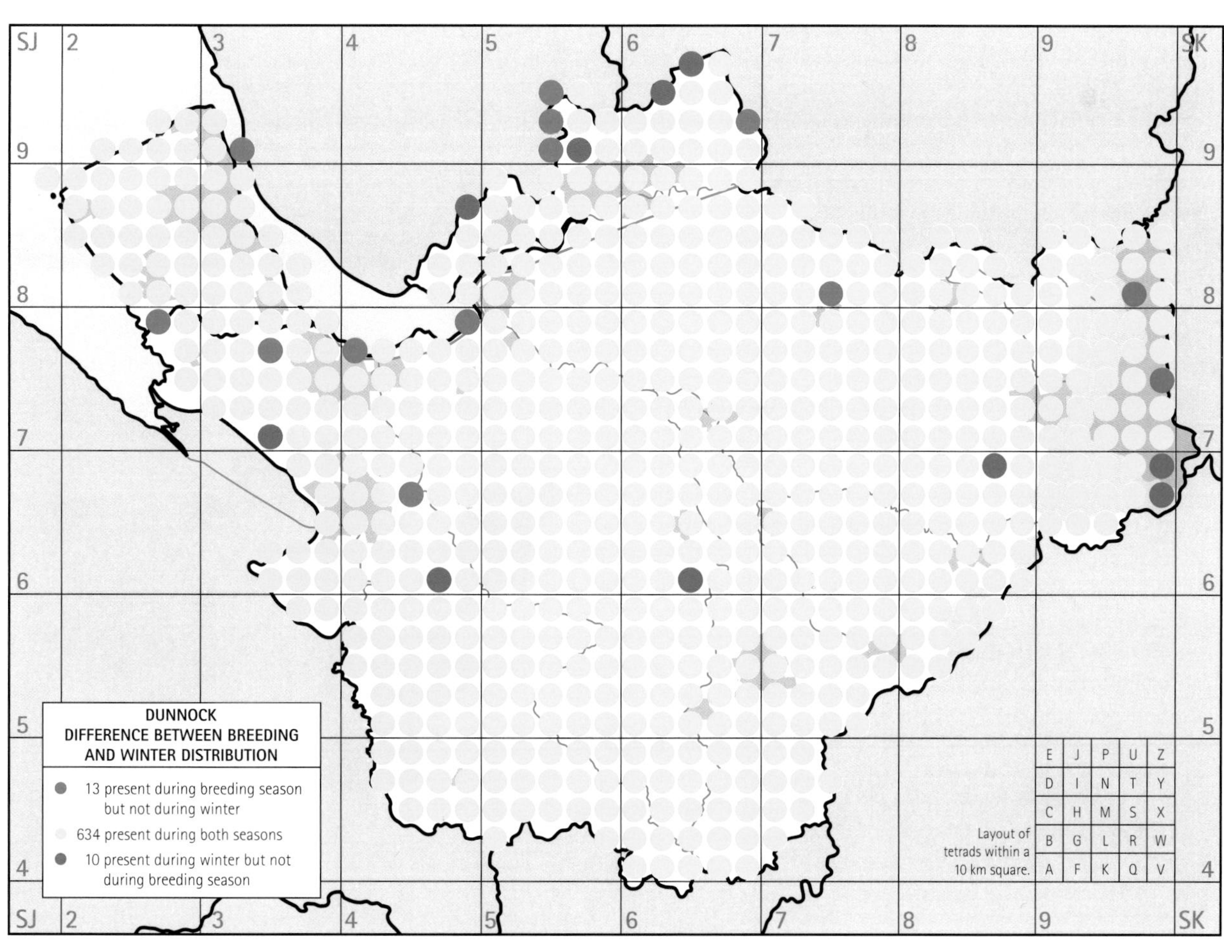
SJ
2
3
4
5
6
7
8
9
SK
9
8
7
6
5
4
DUNNOCK
DIFFERENCE BETWEEN BREEDING AND WINTER DISTRIBUTION
13 present during breeding season but not during winter
634 present during both seasons
10 present during winter but not during breeding season
E J P U Z
D I N T Y
C H M S X
B G L R W
A F K Q V
Layout of tetrads within a 10 km square.

Robin

Erithacus rubecula

STEVE ROUND

This Atlas shows that Britain's national bird tied for second place as the most widespread species in Cheshire and Wirral, being present in the breeding season in 655 tetrads. The only significant difference from our *First Atlas* is that Robins now breed on Hilbre, but they are still missing from two of the highest tetrads.

The national population, and probably that in the county as well, is much higher than twenty years ago. A succession of cold winters had hit their numbers and they reached a low point in the mid-1980s, just after our *First Atlas*, but since then the national population index has risen steadily and in 2004 it was half as high again as 20 years previously. The analysis of BBS transects shows that this is our fifth most numerous species, with a breeding population of Cheshire and Wirral in 2004–05 of 147,520 birds (126,890–168,160), a mean of 220 birds per tetrad. The distribution across the county is relatively even: the abundance map shows that the highest densities exceed 300 birds per tetrad while the lowest are around 100 per tetrad. In the best habitats, broad-leaved woodland with dense understorey, densities can reach 1,000 pairs per tetrad, each pair living in an area averaging just 0.4 ha (one acre) (Mead 1984).

Robins also had one of the highest proportions of confirmed breeding, 87%. The majority of these, in 259 tetrads, came from fieldworkers seeing broods of recently fledged young with their distinctive spotty plumage. Unfortunately some recorders included unaccompanied juveniles, not realizing that they could have travelled some distance from their natal site, perhaps from an adjacent tetrad. In 218 tetrads observers logged parents carrying food or a faecal sac, with nests found in just 90 tetrads. A dedicated nest finder of a former generation (Simson 1966) regarded the Robin as 'just about the most cunning and secretive of our common birds'. Nests are usually in a dark spot, often in a bank, in a hole in a tree or an ivy-covered trunk, but many are in human artefacts. Near Hulme Walfield (SJ86M) Steve and Gill Barber were told by a farmer that he had moved a nest with eggs from a trailer he needed to use, but the nest remained active and young fledged.

Their familiarity with man was shown by the recorded habitat codes, with most in human sites (a total of 35%, 21% being rural), followed by farmland (30%), woodland (27%) and scrub (7%). Robins eat mainly invertebrates in the breeding season, foraging mostly on or near the ground and feeding themselves and their young on any grubs and spiders that they can find.

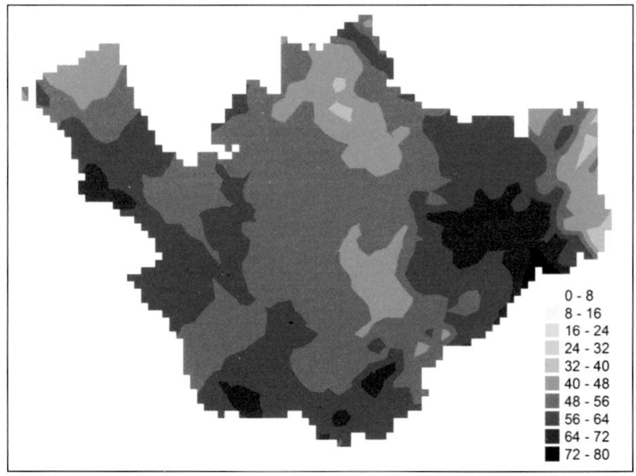

Robin abundance.

Sponsored by Robin Hart

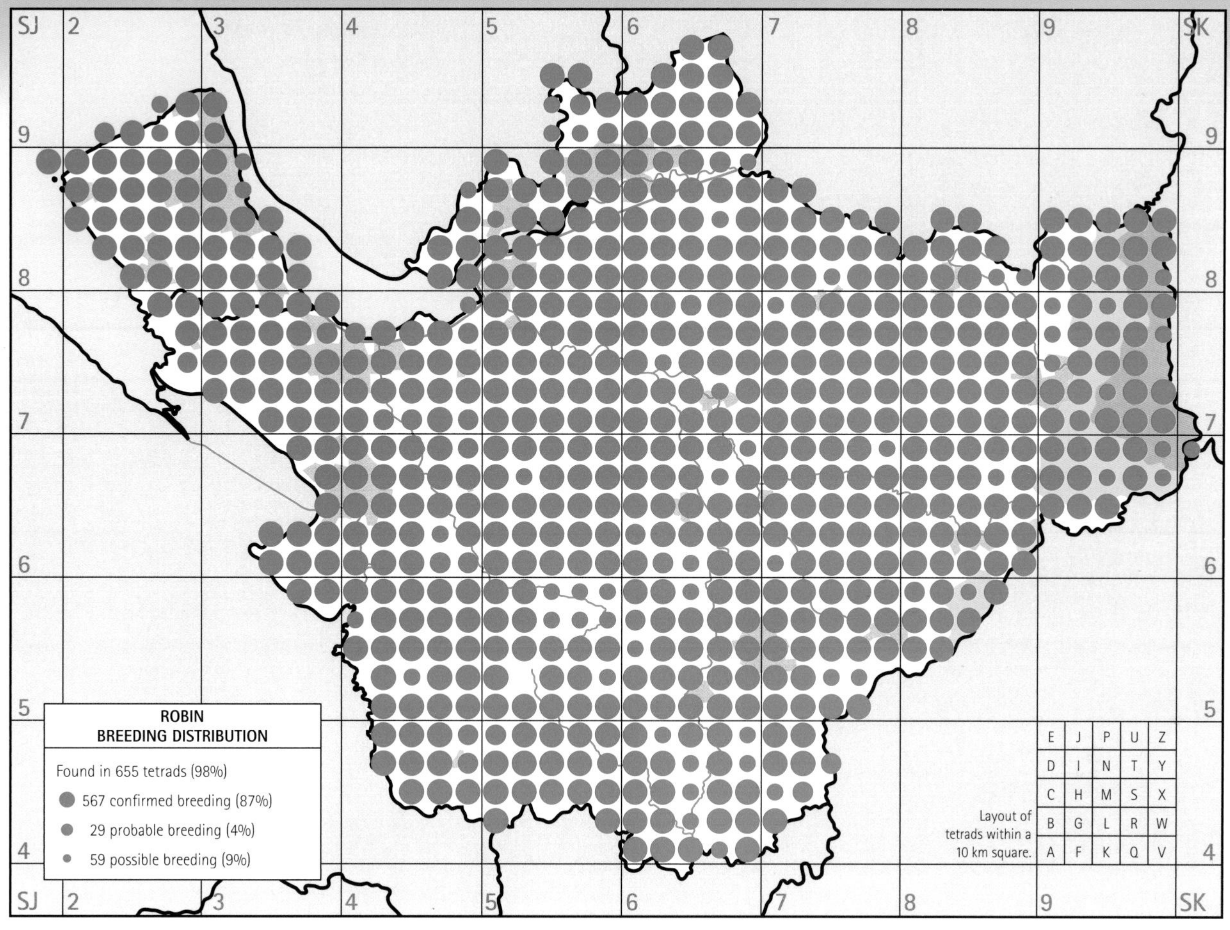

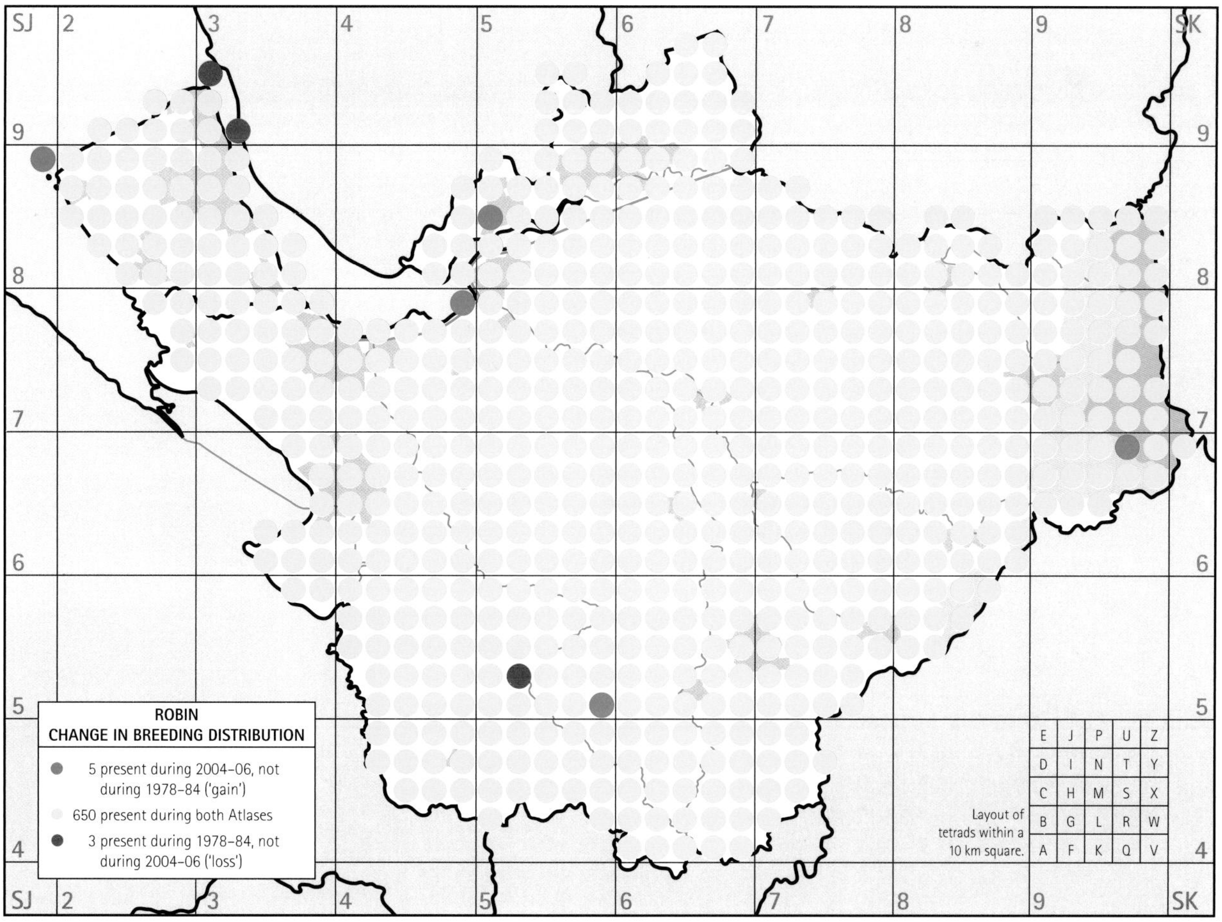

ROBIN
CHANGE IN BREEDING DISTRIBUTION

5 present during 2004–06, not during 1978–84 ('gain')

650 present during both Atlases

3 present during 1978–84, not during 2004–06 ('loss')

Layout of tetrads within a 10 km square.

E	J	P	U	Z
D	I	N	T	Y
C	H	M	S	X
B	G	L	R	W
A	F	K	Q	V

SJ 2 3 4 5 6 7 8 9 SK

STEVE ROUND

There is little difference between the Robin's breeding and wintering distribution, although the winter map shows that they were missing from the two easternmost tetrads. Many birds do move from their breeding areas, however, as shown by one ringed at a feeding station at Linmere, Delamere on 16 January 2003 that was found in Nottinghamshire on 6 April 2003, 99 km away. Male and female Robins set up separate winter territories, often starting in autumn as soon as they finish their moult, with males usually maintaining their breeding territory and females moving away, perhaps up to 5 km (Mead 1984). Unusually, both sexes sing to establish winter territories, using a different song from the breeding season. Birds with territories near street-lights often sing at night.

Robins can be very aggressive in establishment and defence of their winter areas, and the Christmas card picture of many birds together is not often seen. Most of the submitted counts were of one or two, with just 19 records of 10 or more birds. Around well-provisioned feeding areas they seem to call a truce, especially in hard weather.

The presence of abundant cover within 2 m of the ground is an important feature of most occupied sites (*BTO Winter Atlas*) and the Atlas records showed that the main change in winter habitat from the breeding season is a reduction in the proportion of woodland records, with far more reported from hedges. There is a noticeable switch from preferring tall hedges in the breeding season (58% of the breeding season hedgerow records) to short hedges in winter (55% of the winter hedgerow records). They often use a low twig in a hedge as a perch from which to scan the ground and drop onto a spider or beetle. Robins try to find invertebrates on the ground throughout winter, often closely following gardeners to do so, and they also eat soft fruit, seeds, bread and fat. Vegetable food, however, rarely accounts for more than 10% of energy intake, showing the importance of live food and their susceptibility to periods when the ground is hard frozen or covered in snow (*BTO Winter Atlas*).

After the year-end, many males relax their winter territoriality and sing to attract a mate, and, especially in mild weather, some start building nests towards the end of our defined winter period, although they often leave them for several weeks before laying.

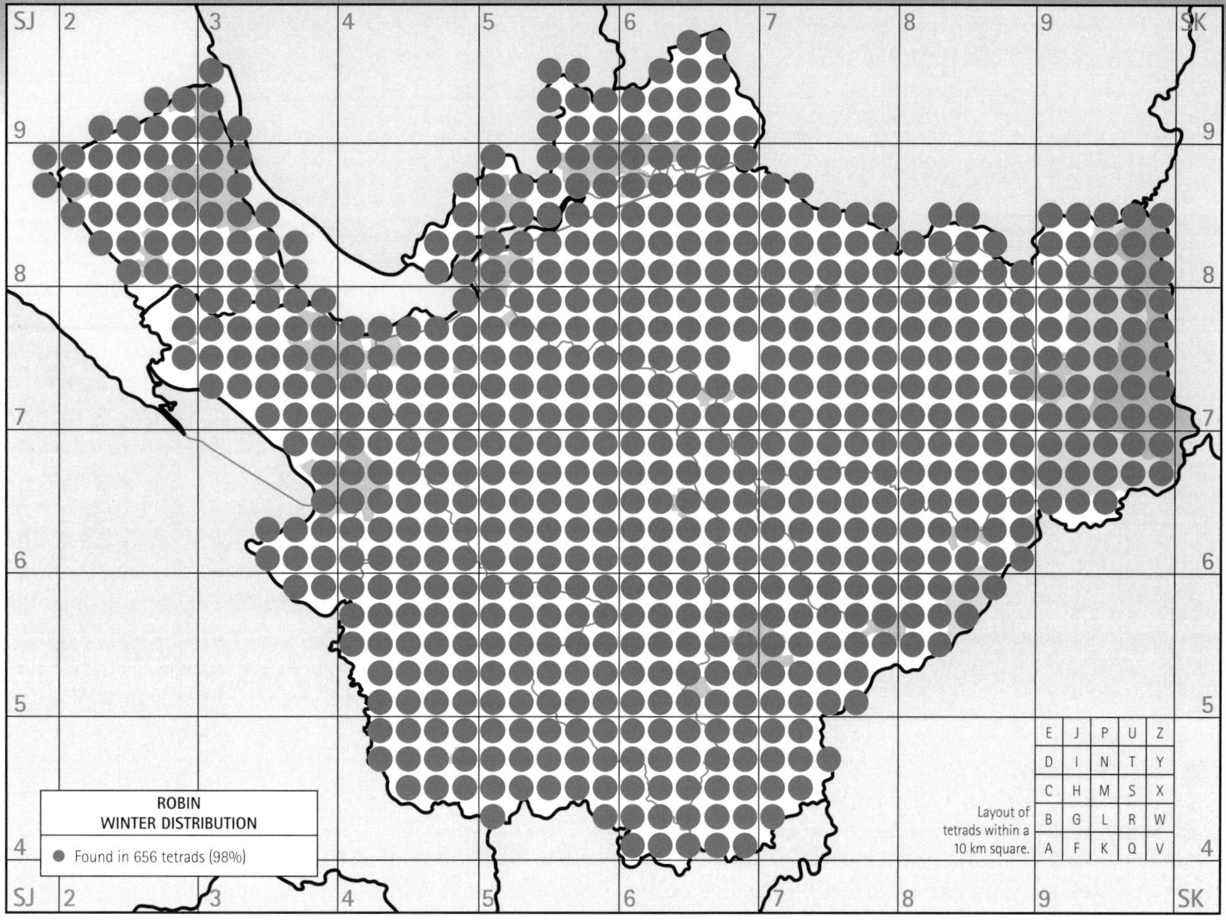
SJ
2
3
4
5
6
7
8
9
SK
ROBIN
WINTER DISTRIBUTION
Found in 656 tetrads (98%)
E J P U Z
D I N T Y
C H M S X
B G L R W
A F K Q V
Layout of tetrads within a 10 km square.

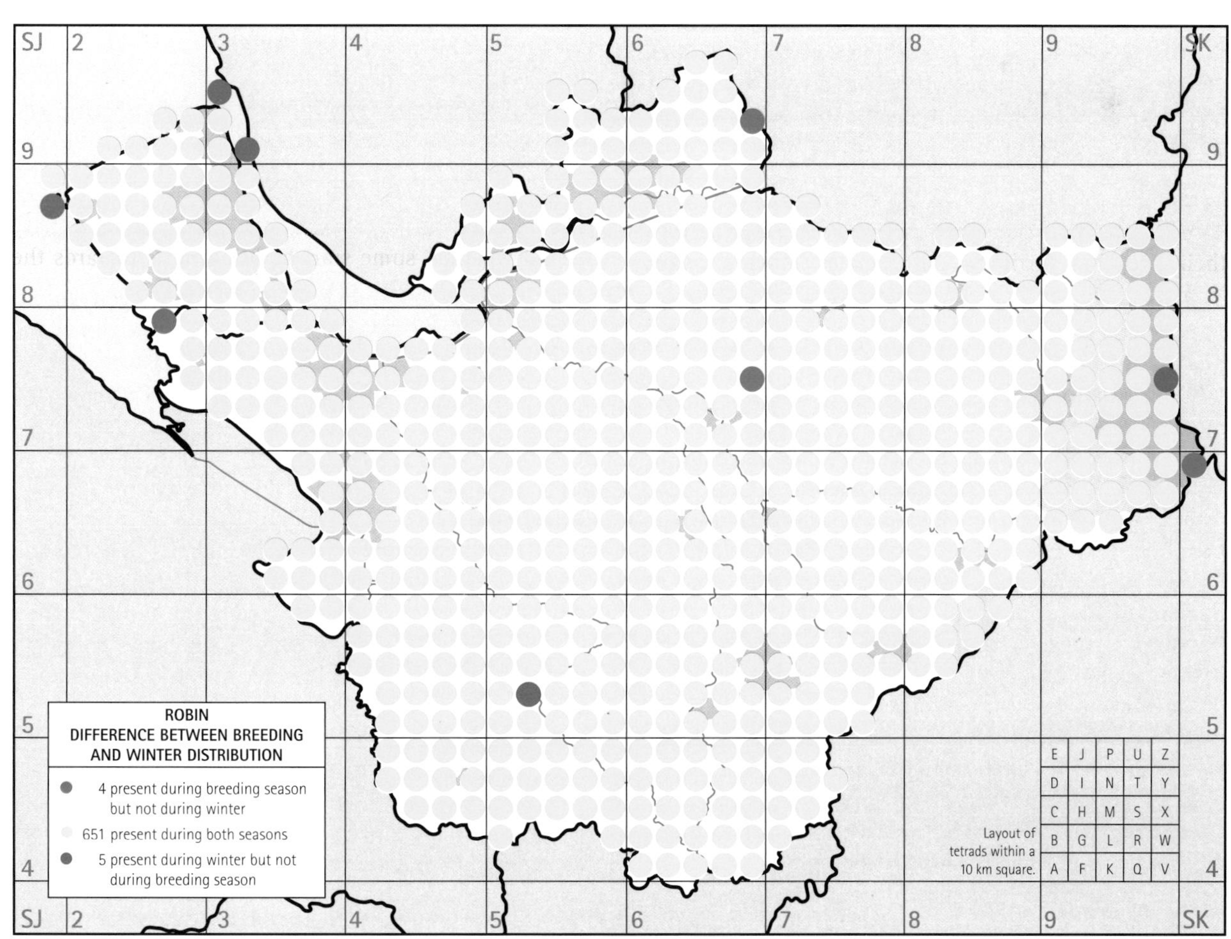
SJ
2
3
4
5
6
7
8
9
SK
ROBIN
DIFFERENCE BETWEEN BREEDING AND WINTER DISTRIBUTION
4 present during breeding season but not during winter
651 present during both seasons
5 present during winter but not during breeding season
E J P U Z
D I N T Y
C H M S X
B G L R W
A F K Q V
Layout of tetrads within a 10 km square.

Redstart

Phoenicurus phoenicurus

RICHARD STEEL

The sound, and sight, of Redstarts enlivening our deciduous woodlands is now almost restricted to the eastern hills of Cheshire. In the *First Atlas* they were sparsely distributed across parts of western and south-western Cheshire, as well as SJ86/87, all areas from which they are now missing. The 'change' map, which omits 'possible' breeding records, shows that their range has contracted so that half of Cheshire's tetrads with Redstarts are now at altitudes above about 250 m. Surprisingly, only 27 out of 45 (60%) of the submitted habitat codes were broad-leaved or mixed woodland, and five of the 13 instances of confirmed breeding were not in woodland, the rest being in scrub, rural human sites and grass moorland. It probably needs an expert ecologist to study the fine differences in habitat requirements between Redstart, Wood Warbler and Pied Flycatcher, to explain why the Redstart is so restricted to our eastern hills, and why Redstarts have contracted in range in Cheshire during a time when the national population is stable or expanding.

Their national population has risen from a low point in the mid-1970s, probably recovering following the worst of the Sahel droughts. Redstarts winter south of the Sahara, in the soudan and guinea savannah belts from central Senegal southwards to Sierra Leone and countries to the east. They have to pass through the Sahel zone and perhaps were hit by the widening of the Sahara and reduced opportunities for pre-migratory fattening in spring. BTO indices show that the recovery in their population continued until the late 1990s, helped by improving breeding performance and progressively earlier laying dates, and their numbers are now roughly stable, and slightly higher than 20 years ago. The reduction in Cheshire Redstarts is not easy to explain.

The males arrive in late April after the leaves break and usually sing from the tree canopy, making them often extraordinarily difficult to see. They are, however, very demonstrative if the nest area is approached, scolding the observer with their loud 'hwee-tuck' alarm, what seems to be a very appropriate mixture of calls typical of the warbler and chat families; some birds repeat just the first or the last part alone. Redstarts are unusually versatile in their choice of nest hole. Cheshire nests have been recorded in tree-holes including old woodpecker holes and nest-boxes, cavities in stone walls, even holes underground. They usually prefer a larger entrance hole than those chosen by other similarly sized birds. The folklore amongst ringers studying the species is that they like to occupy dilapidated nest-boxes, often in the last year before they fall apart. The male selects the nest, singing to attract a female to it. In a seldom-seen display described by Buxton (1950), he signals from inside the hole using his two most prominent plumage features—the red tail and the white frontal patch—which are emphasized in the French name of the species: 'rouge-queue à front blanc'. The male then stops singing for a few days whilst his mate builds the nest, swirls of grass lined with fine grasses and feathers. The drabber female lays an average of six or seven pale blue eggs, and she alone incubates them as the male resumes singing.

The BTO's nest records analysis shows that Redstarts have advanced their first-egg date by a remarkable 11 days in just 20 years from 1984 to 2004. The chicks typically hatch in the last week of May, and it is then very easy to prove breeding when the adults conspicuously carry beakloads of food back to their brood. Redstarts feed in the lower reaches of trees and on the ground, with males especially taking a lot of their prey by aerial fly-catching and hovering at the tips of vegetation. The adults eat fairly large insects, especially adult *Hymenoptera* and beetles, and feed their young a similar diet but with more spiders, especially when the chicks are small (*BWP*, Buxton 1950). Exceptionally, they may have two broods, but none has been reported in Cheshire. The confirmed breeding records for this Atlas came from observations of birds at nests (five), adults with food for their young (three), and recently fledged young (five).

Not much is known about site fidelity and recruitment to the population. One bird in Delamere Forest, ringed as a chick in 2002, returned to the Forest in 2003 to breed in a natural hole about a kilometre from her natal site, and in 2004 again bred in the same territory, with the same male as in 2003, both times using old Great Spotted Woodpecker nests in decaying birch trees just 50 m from each other.

Most sites seem to hold just one or two pairs, and the Cheshire total of breeding Redstarts is unlikely to be much above 50 pairs.

Sponsored by David and Fran Cogger in memory of Jet

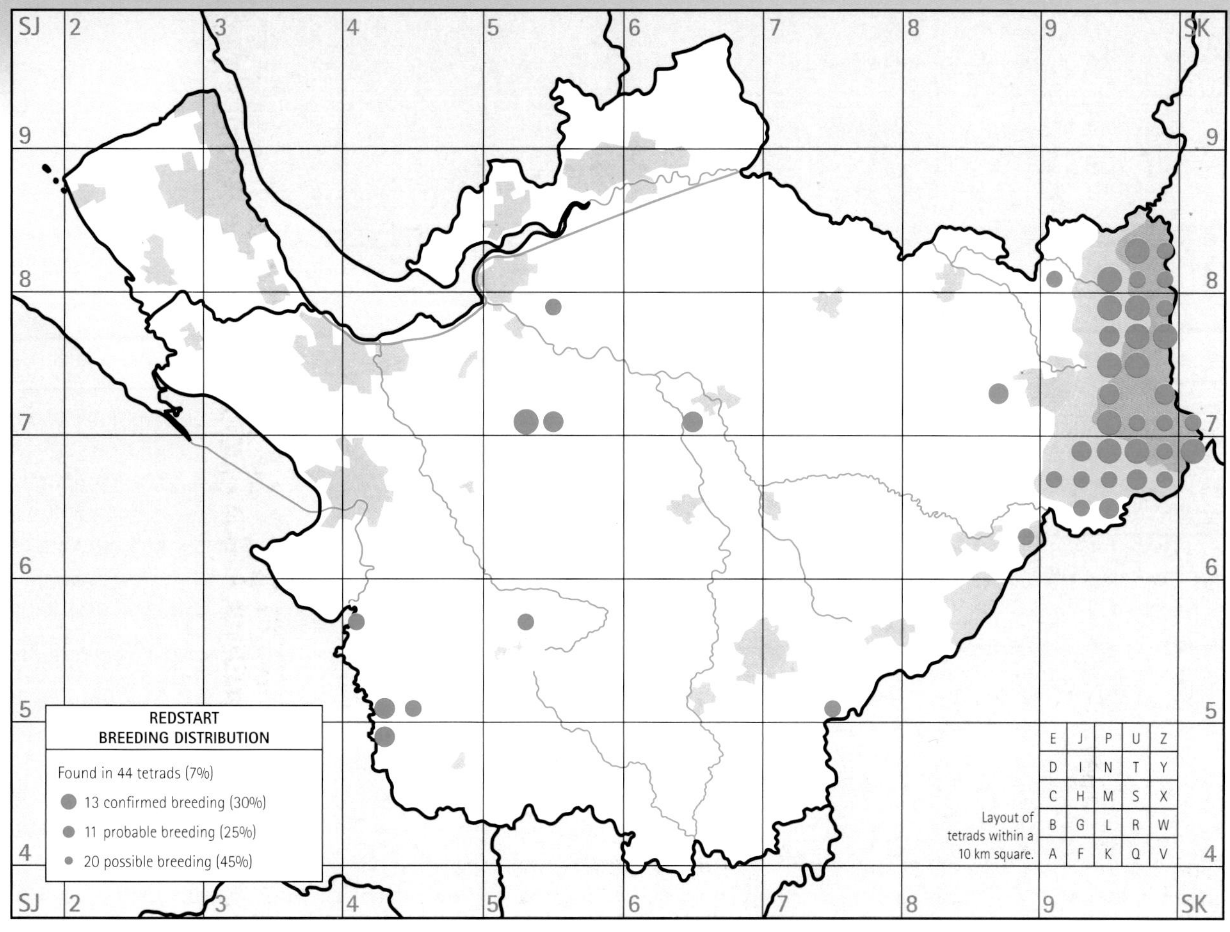
SJ
SK
2
3
4
5
6
7
8
9
REDSTART
BREEDING DISTRIBUTION
Found in 44 tetrads (7%)
13 confirmed breeding (30%)
11 probable breeding (25%)
20 possible breeding (45%)
E J P U Z
D I N T Y
C H M S X
B G L R W
A F K Q V
Layout of tetrads within a 10 km square.

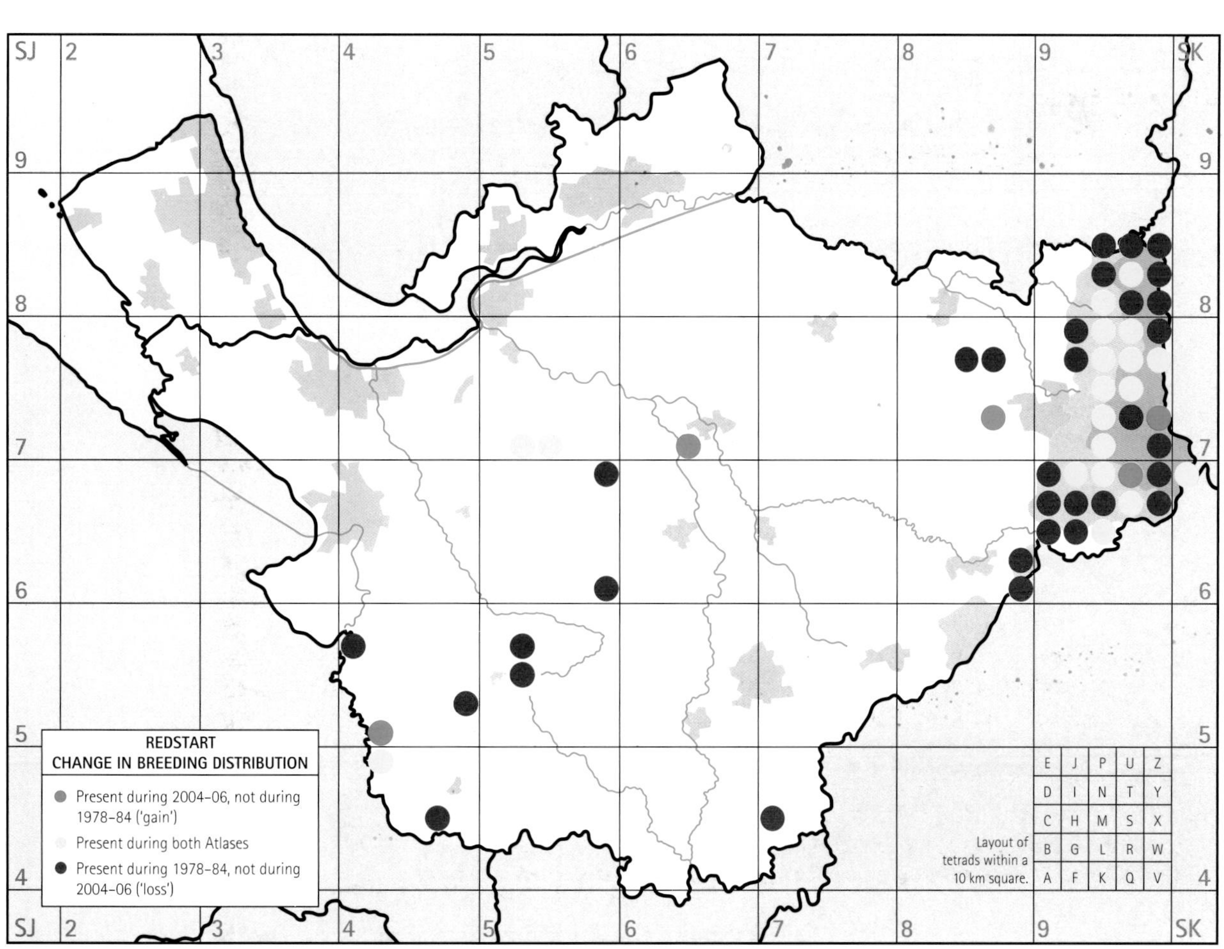
SJ
SK
2
3
4
5
6
7
8
9
REDSTART
CHANGE IN BREEDING DISTRIBUTION
Present during 2004–06, not during 1978–84 ('gain')
Present during both Atlases
Present during 1978–84, not during 2004–06 ('loss')
E J P U Z
D I N T Y
C H M S X
B G L R W
A F K Q V
Layout of tetrads within a 10 km square.

Whinchat

Saxicola rubetra

Every Cheshire ornithologist since Coward has reported the decline of the Whinchat. Hardy (1941) stated that the species was becoming scarcer as a nester. Griffiths and Wilson (1945) commented 'there has evidently been a considerable reduction in the breeding population'. Boyd (1951) wrote that their 'numbers are limited–fewer than twenty years ago'. Our *First Atlas* found them breeding sparsely along the Mersey valley and south of Chester, with a few in the eastern hills and odd scattered records elsewhere, but reported that during the period of the fieldwork (1978–84) they were declining further in their regular areas. Fewer were found after the end of the intensive Atlas fieldwork and, according to the annual bird reports, odd pairs were found at various Cheshire sites until the last confirmed breeding in 1991.

During this survey there were just four records of confirmed or probable breeding: one nest was found in 2005, at Frodsham Marsh (SJ57E)–the first known breeding in the county for 14 years–and pairs were recorded at three other sites. Far more Whinchats pass through the county than ever stay to breed, and the Atlas map is dominated by records of birds on passage: they usually turn up in areas of apparently suitable habitat, and merit an H code, but almost all of them quickly move on. Most birds arrive in May and lone migrants can be found well into June in many years. If they stay to breed, chicks seldom hatch much before mid-June, and often later.

Whinchats perch prominently and feed on insects caught on the ground or in short sallies, with their main targets being beetles, flies, spiders and the larvae and adults of butterflies and moths. This is a chat found in open grassland, meadows and the youngest stages of plantations or open scrubland; it seems to be one of the few species that actively favours areas of bracken. Of the habitat codes submitted for 17 of the records in this survey, nine were in farmland (equally split between improved grassland, unimproved grassland and tilled land), three in semi-natural grassland, two on saltmarsh and three in scrub. Their decline has long been ascribed to mowing of roadside verges and tidying of rough ground (*BTO First Atlas*) and the loss of marginal farmland habitats (Marchant *et al.* 1990). It might be thought that land set-aside from agricultural production would prove suitable, but apparently not.

This species and its close relative the Stonechat neatly illustrate two strategies used by an insectivorous bird to cope with the British winter. Whinchats face the problems of a long migration and the potential hazards of winter in Africa while their cousins, Stonechats, try to stick it out in Britain, suffering in hard winters, or migrating shorter distances. Whinchats breeding in western Europe migrate to winter in the guinea savannah grasslands and the savannah/forest mosaic from the south of Senegal to the Gulf of Guinea coast, eastwards as far as Cameroon (Urban *et al.* 1997). British birds probably inhabit the western part of that range, although no British-ringed bird has been found south of the Sahara (*Migration Atlas*). They have not noticeably suffered from the Sahelian droughts, wintering south of that area and presumably being able to lay down sufficient reserves to cross the widening Sahara desert.

SUE & ANDY TRANTER

● One Whinchat was seen during the winter Atlas period, on 21 November 2004 at the Gowy Marshes (SJ47G). This is the third November record in Cheshire and Wirral, following birds in the Frodsham area on 3 November 1984 and 13 November 1989. Autumn passage is usually complete by mid-October with later October records in just eight years since 1970.

Sponsored by Andy Coxon

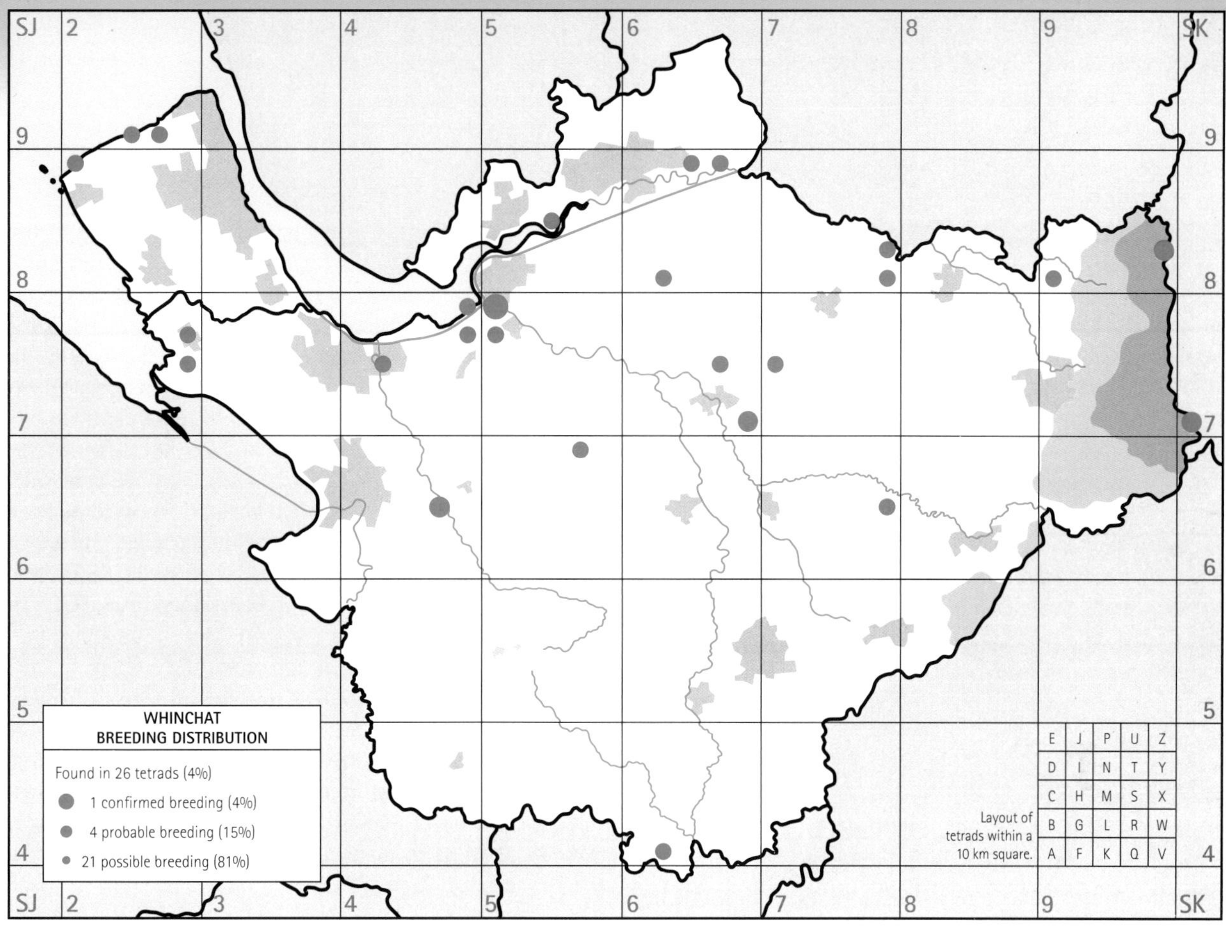
SJ
SK
WHINCHAT
BREEDING DISTRIBUTION
Found in 26 tetrads (4%)
1 confirmed breeding (4%)
4 probable breeding (15%)
21 possible breeding (81%)
Layout of tetrads within a 10 km square.
E J P U Z
D I N T Y
C H M S X
B G L R W
A F K Q V

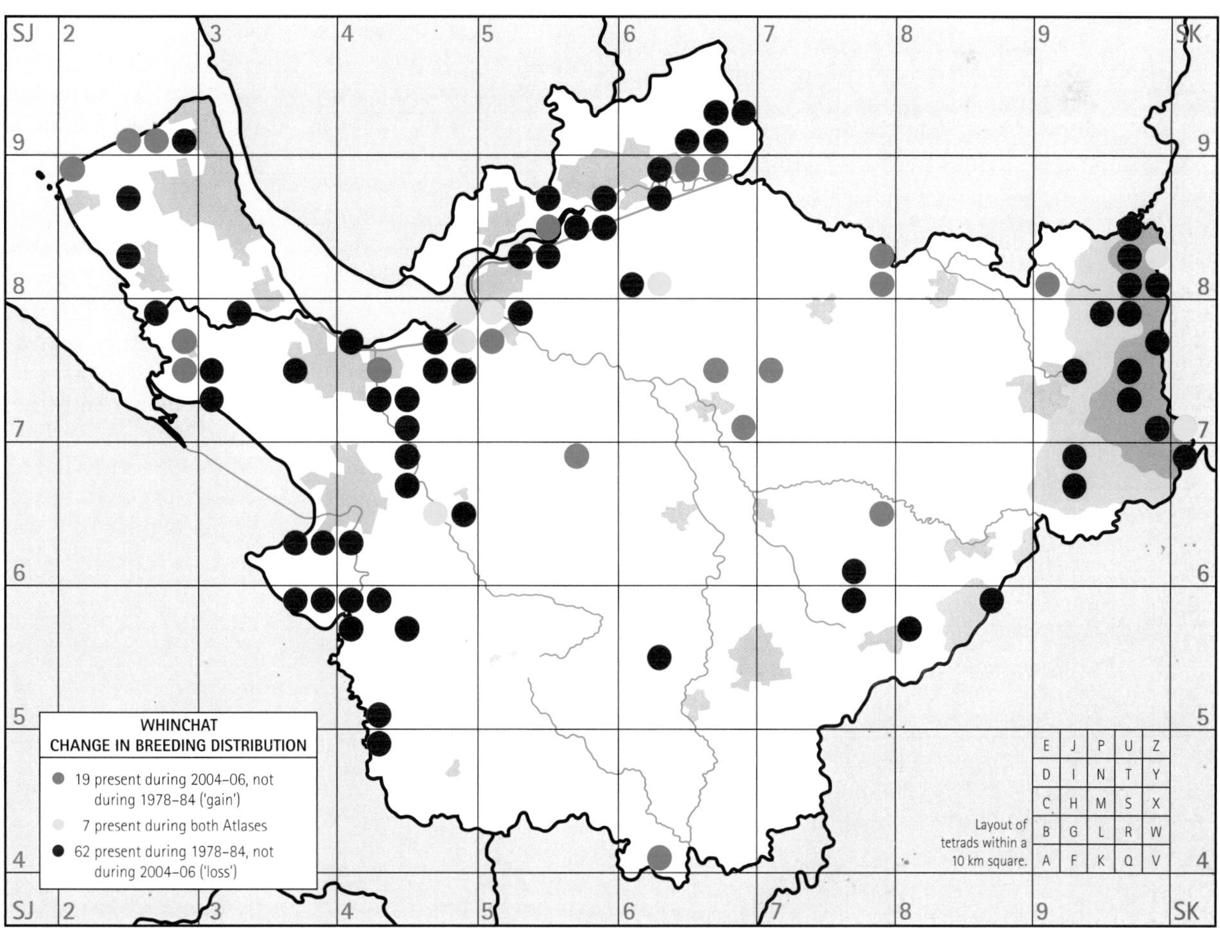
SJ
SK
WHINCHAT
CHANGE IN BREEDING DISTRIBUTION
19 present during 2004–06, not during 1978–84 ('gain')
7 present during both Atlases
62 present during 1978–84, not during 2004–06 ('loss')
Layout of tetrads within a 10 km square.
E J P U Z
D I N T Y
C H M S X
B G L R W
A F K Q V

Stonechat

Saxicola torquatus

STEVE ROUND

Stonechats have undergone a fascinating shift in distribution since our *First Atlas*: twenty years ago, this was a species breeding in the lowest-lying land in the county, mainly in the north Wirral and the Mersey valley. Now, there are far fewer on the coast and others breeding at the highest altitudes in the eastern hills. As an insectivorous resident, this species is susceptible to hard weather and it is tempting to think that warmer winters have allowed them to flourish.

Since the end of fieldwork for our *First Atlas* in 1984, the annual county bird reports have several times lamented the loss of Stonechat as a breeding species, and there are only six records in the 19 years to the start of this Atlas in 2004, one each in 1986, 1990, 1992, 1995, 2002 and 2003. The record near Three Shires Head (SK06E) in 1995 was of special significance, although not noted as such in the *CWBR*, as it appears to be the first recorded breeding in the hills since Coward (1910) said that it 'nests in the hill-country in the east but is not abundant'. Neither Boyd (1946) nor Bell (1962), in their writings on the county's birds, made any comment on its status in the hills. Another pair bred 'in the east of the county' in 2002, then the start of this Atlas in 2004 coincided with a resurgence in records.

It is impossible to know to what extent the increase in fieldwork for this survey yielded more records, but upland breeding was well established in Cumbria and Lancashire long before it was reported in Cheshire. In Lancashire, the tetrad Atlas in 1997–2000 found over 40 pairs in the uplands of Bowland and the west Pennines (Pyefinch & Golborn 2001). In Cumbria, Atlas fieldwork spanning 1997–2001 estimated a total of 1,000 pairs, mostly along the coast but with several hundred in the Lake District hills up to an altitude of 500 m (Stott *et al.* 2002).

Stonechats will breed in a wide variety of habitats, probably the only common characteristic being 'rough' ground, avoiding woodland and most areas in agricultural use. They need scattered bushes, trees, fence posts or wires for use as song-posts and for perching whilst watching for their insect prey. Their catholic taste was borne out in this survey when the 28 occupied tetrads yielded as many as 18 different habitat codes. The most frequent were C5 (dry grassland, six records), B7 (scrub, six records) and E2 (unimproved grassland, five records), with no other code being registered more than twice.

Stonechats start to breed early in the year, with eggs often laid in late March in lowland sites, although later at higher altitude. They nest from ground level up to about a metre, usually at an arm's length deep inside gorse or other dense bush. Most pairs have two broods, and three is not unusual, extending the season into August. With an average of five chicks each time, this high reproductive potential allows them to balance the losses in cold weather, or alternatively allows rapid population growth when overwinter survival is higher.

This is a conspicuous bird, perching prominently and having a loud alarm call, a typically chat-like 'tack tack', albeit with a weak song. Adults with food in their bills, especially when feeding recently fledged broods, are easy to see. The breeding status codes reflect this, with one record of a nest with young, two of adults carrying food for their young and 10 tetrads where observers saw recently fledged young.

As well as the shift in the distribution to the eastern hills, the birds in Delamere represent a return to an area where Oldham found a brood in 1904 (Coward 1910), in 1927 it was said to be nesting regularly (Bell 1962) and Boyd (1951) found them breeding in the 1930s.

There were 13 tetrads with proven breeding at some stage during this Atlas survey. The national population index (dating only from 1994) roughly doubled from 1994 to 2004 and Cheshire and Wirral has shared in this growth. The number of breeding pairs in the county is probably just into double figures, its highest recorded level since 1978.

Sponsored by Irene Blagden

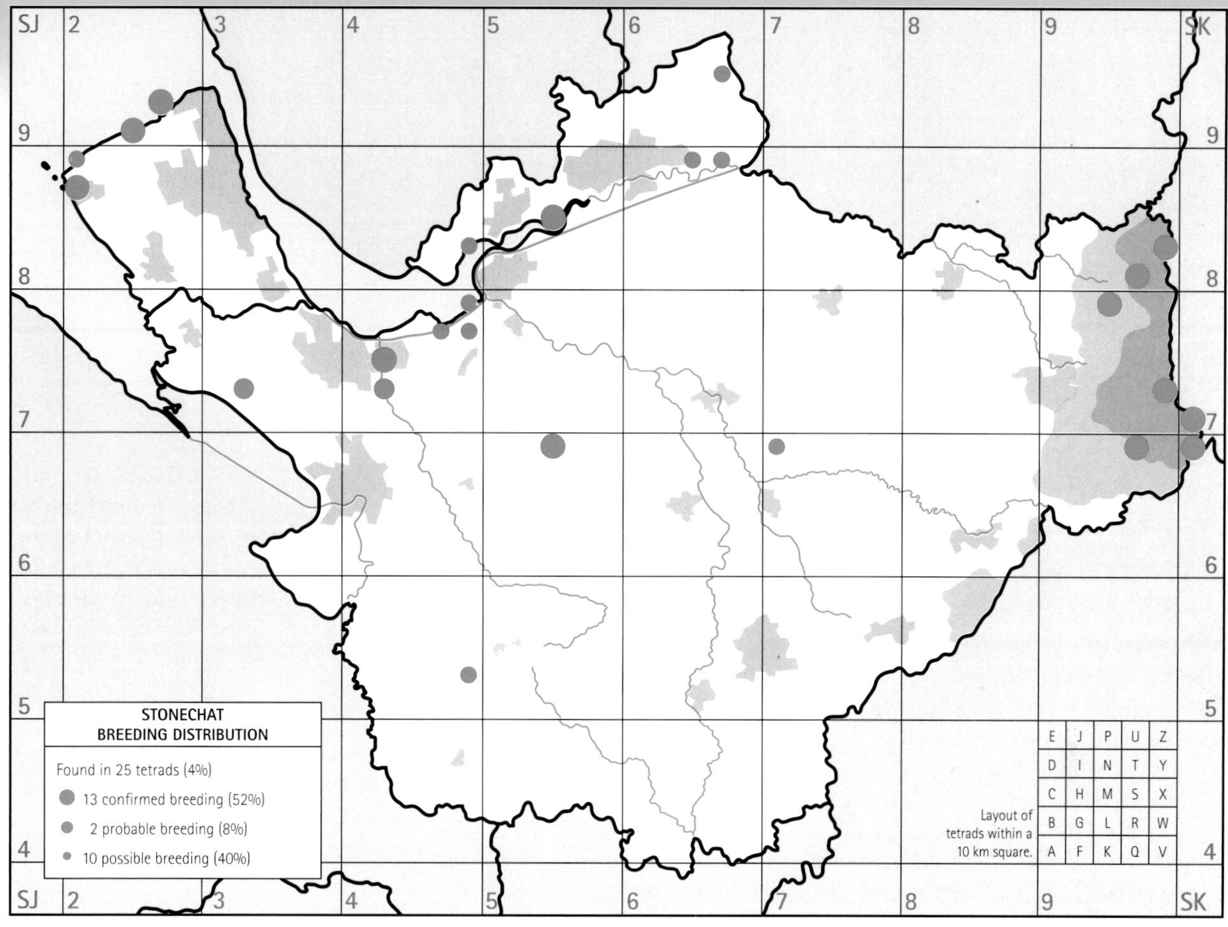
SJ
2
3
4
5
6
7
8
9
SK
STONECHAT
BREEDING DISTRIBUTION
Found in 25 tetrads (4%)
13 confirmed breeding (52%)
2 probable breeding (8%)
10 possible breeding (40%)
Layout of tetrads within a 10 km square.
E J P U Z
D I N T Y
C H M S X
B G L R W
A F K Q V

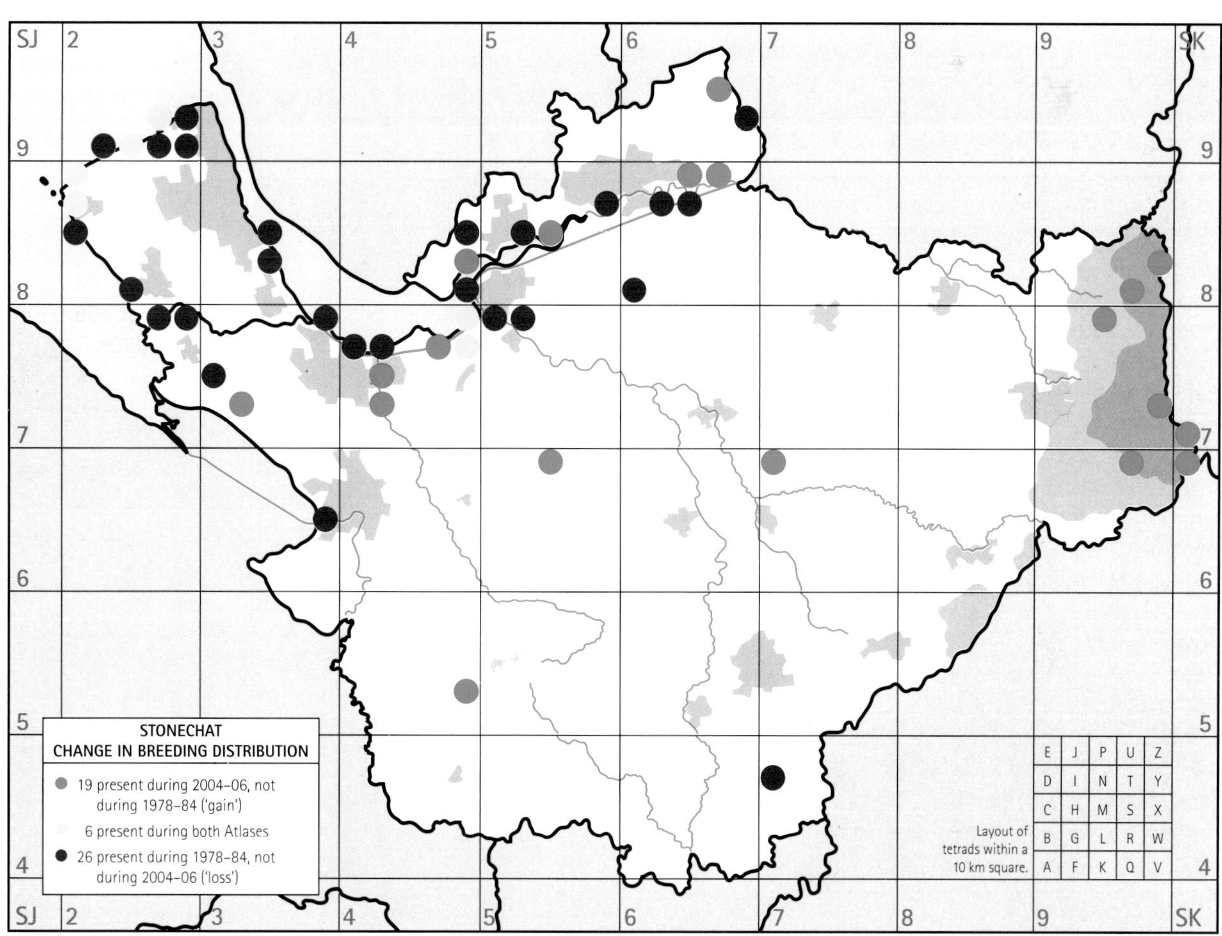
SJ
2
3
4
5
6
7
8
9
SK
STONECHAT
CHANGE IN BREEDING DISTRIBUTION
19 present during 2004–06, not during 1978–84 ('gain')
6 present during both Atlases
26 present during 1978–84, not during 2004–06 ('loss')
Layout of tetrads within a 10 km square.
E J P U Z
D I N T Y
C H M S X
B G L R W
A F K Q V

Many Stonechats are strongly territorial in pairs throughout the winter, either enlarging the breeding territory by a factor of two or three, to ensure the availability of sufficient food, or establishing new winter territories, many of which are coastal and may be totally unsuitable as nesting habitat (*Migration Atlas*). As an early breeding species, many males are singing in January and most birds have staked their territorial claim before the end of February, so some of the mapped 'winter' records will be from breeding birds. In fact, only three of the tetrads with a breeding season record were not also occupied during winter.

The Cheshire and Wirral breeding birds cannot, however, account for all of the Stonechats present in the county during winter. The *BTO Winter Atlas* text, based mostly on experiences in the Channel Islands, misleadingly emphasizes the sedentary nature of the species. The Stonechat has evolved as a partial migrant to guarantee survival of at least a proportion of the population in the event of either migratory or winter catastrophes, and many of the birds found here in winter must have moved in from breeding areas elsewhere. There is no indication of Stonechats wintering here from anywhere outside Britain. The main stronghold of the species within Britain is in north-western Scotland, relatively few of those birds remaining for the winter, with some of them known to have migrated south as far as Spain and Portugal (*Migration Atlas*). Cumbrian-bred birds have been proven to winter in Kent. So, the likely origin of many of the birds wintering in Cheshire and Wirral is northern Britain. A fascinating challenge for the county's ringers would be to test this suggestion.

The Atlas map shows that there are three main components to the Cheshire and Wirral wintering population. Some birds visit the coast; others tough it out in the eastern hills; while a third group follows the lines of rivers, especially the Mersey and the Gowy. All of these areas provide the rough ground that the Stonechat needs, and perhaps the recent habitat improvements in the Gowy corridor—particularly aimed at Barn Owl conservation—have incidentally benefited wintering Stonechats. A wide variety of habitat codes was recorded, with 44% on farmland (mainly grassland and low hedges), 31% semi-natural grassland and marsh (mostly wet areas, grazing marsh, reed-beds and saltmarsh), 8% scrub and 5% bog.

As in the breeding season, their main food is invertebrates, spotted by watching from a perch and taken from the ground. They require a certain warmth for their prey to be active, and the winter distribution of Stonechats nationally is more or less bounded by the 4°C January mean isotherm. All parts of the county comfortably exceeded that criterion, although eastern Cheshire was a little colder than that in January 2006. When their favoured insect prey is scarce, or hard to find, Stonechats occasionally take berries and they can survive for a few days on a vegetable diet.

Coward (1910) quoted Brockholes (1874) that Stonechat was 'a partial migrant, a few remaining all winter', and they knew a few winter records themselves. Boyd (1951), writing about the Great Budworth area, stated that it is 'distinctly uncommon and has been seen only 13 times in 40 years, as a winter visitor'. Bell (1962) added that, as a winter visitor it had been seen 'in most of the last 10 years around West Kirby and Hoylake, and in the Frodsham area'. All of these writers indicate the species' relative scarcity.

PETER TWIST

In this Atlas survey, although fieldworkers were not required to submit records from the same tetrad in more than one winter, in fact for this species some observers did so, giving useful indications of recurrence at wintering sites: records were submitted from 91 tetrads for just one winter, from 27 tetrads for two winters and from two tetrads for all three winters. Most surveyors also gave counts of the Stonechats seen. For the three winters of this survey, 2004/05–2006/07, there were Stonechat records from 57, 48 and 58 tetrads, with totals of 107, 84 and 117 birds. It may not be a coincidence that January 2006 was the coldest of the three years.

These are the largest numbers of Stonechats known to have been wintering in the county since ornithological recording began.

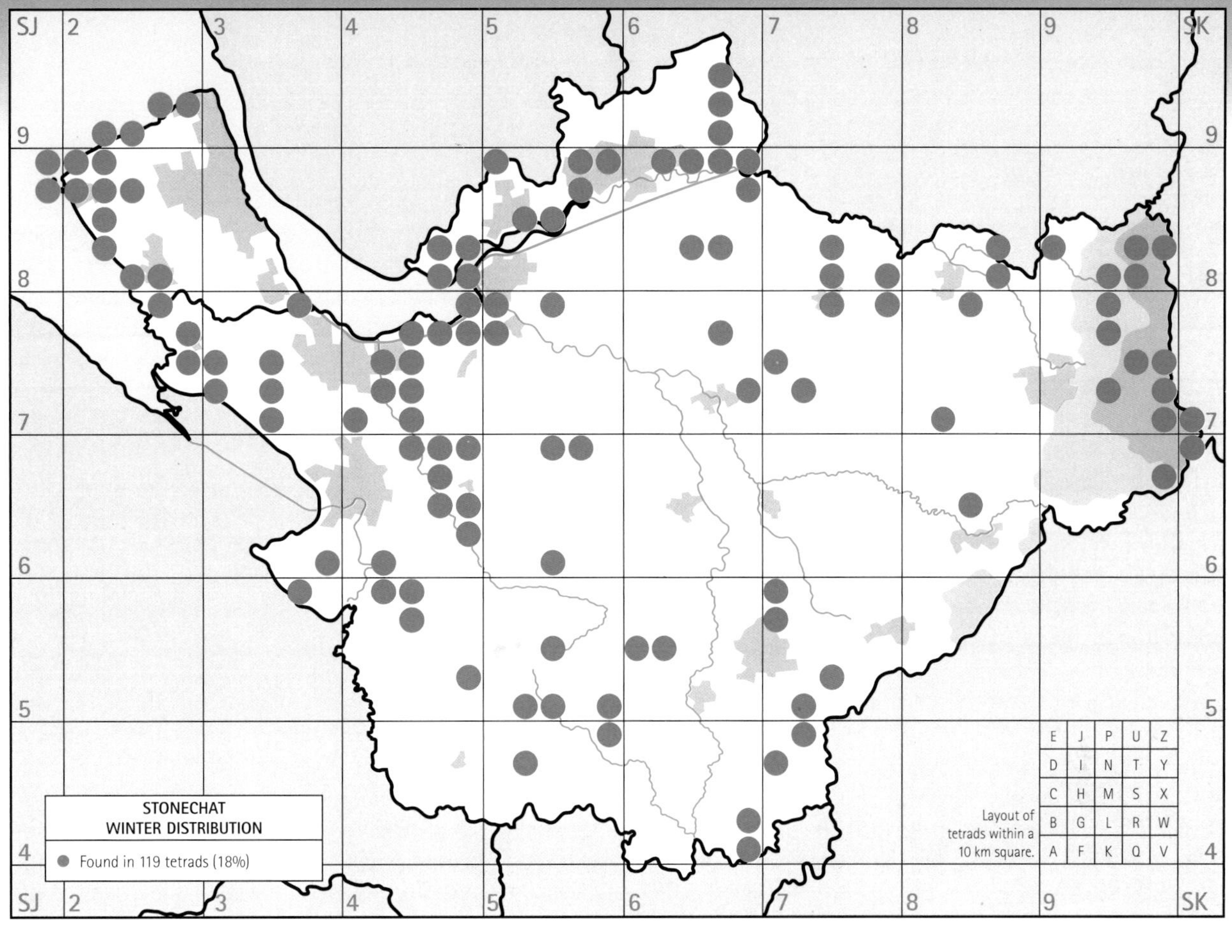
SJ
2
3
4
5
6
7
8
9
SK
STONECHAT
WINTER DISTRIBUTION
Found in 119 tetrads (18%)
Layout of
tetrads within a
10 km square.
E J P U Z
D I N T Y
C H M S X
B G L R W
A F K Q V

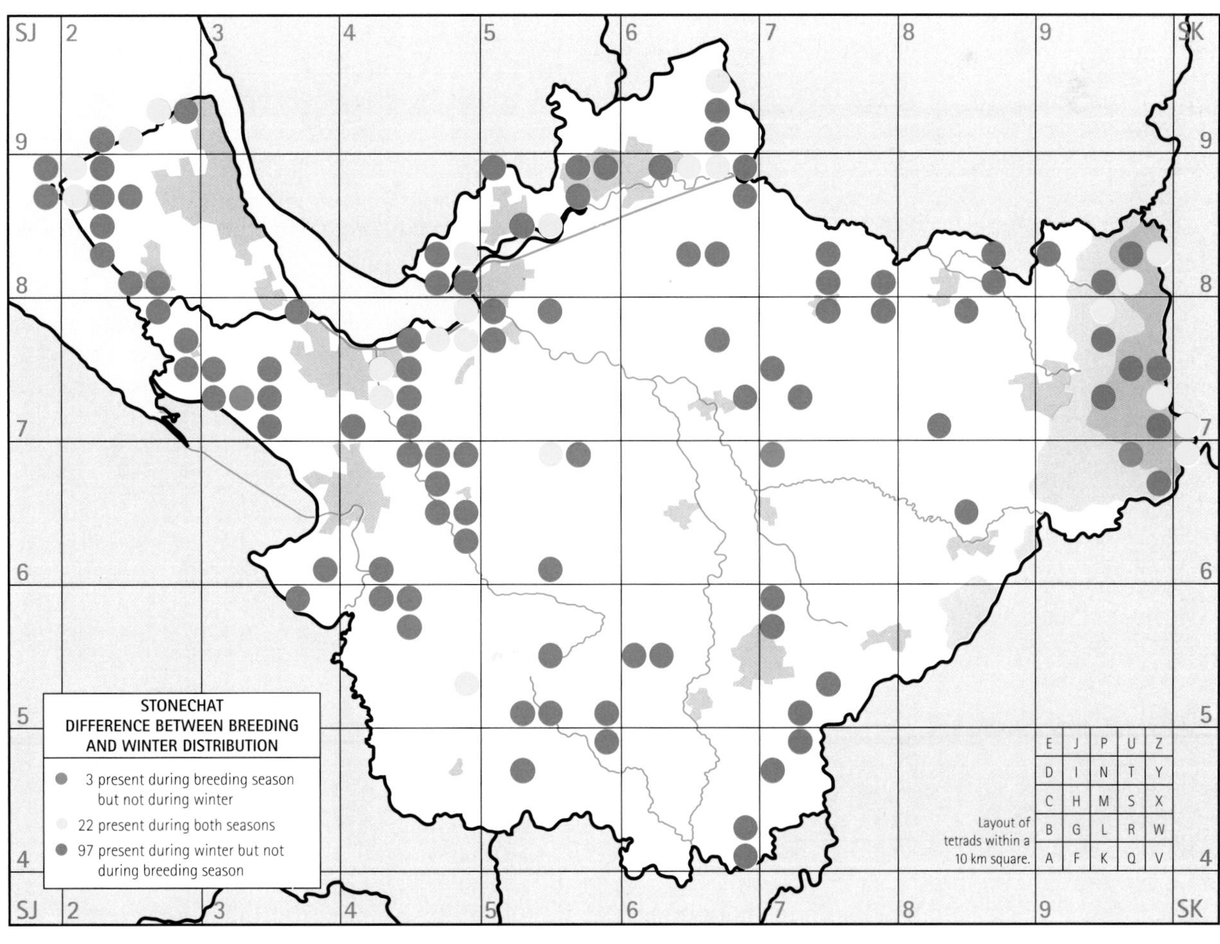
SJ
2
3
4
5
6
7
8
9
SK
STONECHAT
DIFFERENCE BETWEEN BREEDING
AND WINTER DISTRIBUTION
3 present during breeding season but not during winter
22 present during both seasons
97 present during winter but not during breeding season
Layout of
tetrads within a
10 km square.
E J P U Z
D I N T Y
C H M S X
B G L R W
A F K Q V

Wheatear

Oenanthe oenanthe

Wheatears are amongst the first summer migrants to return, eagerly awaited by many birdwatchers. They winter in Africa just south of the Sahel in a broad belt across the continent (Keith *et al.* 1992). No British-ringed bird has been found south of the Sahara, so their exact whereabouts are unknown, but they are probably in Senegal and Mali (*Migration Atlas*). On their return in spring, males arrive before females, and older birds before first-timers. It is not obvious why they migrate so early because they usually take several weeks before nesting. Perhaps Wheatears are driven north by the worsening conditions in Africa, the rising spring temperatures making their ground-based insect prey more difficult to catch (Conder 1989).

Few of the Wheatears seen here stay to breed in the county. In the Atlas map, many records of birds on passage complicate the picture, a lot of these being Greenland Wheatears *Oenanthe oenanthe leucorrhoa*, larger and more brightly coloured than the nominate race which breeds here. This species proved particularly tricky in attribution of O or H codes. Some birds can hang around for long periods, often investigating possible nest holes, but not stay to breed. These records are mapped as 'possible breeding'; some of them were recorded as 'pairs' on passage and these are 'probable breeding' on the distribution map.

RICHARD STEEL

The only confirmed breeding records are in the eastern hills above about 300 m, and here their range has contracted since our *First Atlas*. The 'change' map for this species considers just the tetrads where breeding was proven in one or other Atlas and shows a clear loss from the northern part of the uplands. The reasons for this are not known but changes in the grazing régime are implicated. Surveys of the South Pennine Moors SPA, of which the Cheshire moors are a part, showed a 55% drop between 1990 and 2004–05 in the breeding population of Wheatears (Eaton *et al.* 2007). The loss from the lowlands of Cheshire and Wirral, in which there were three proven breeding records twenty years ago, reflects the national picture. By the time of the BTO's second national Atlas (1988–91) there were range contractions from lowland Britain, tentatively attributed to losses of suitable grassland and declines in rabbit abundance.

Wheatears depend on open areas with close-cropped grassland. They feed mostly on the ground, the usual technique being to hop and peck, birds often hopping several times before they see suitable prey. They eat a wide variety of adult invertebrates, ants, wasps, flies, beetles, spiders and molluscs, ranging from almost inert species to some that are quite fast-moving. They also occasionally fly, taking to the air to pursue insects, especially when they are swarming, and will hover briefly over a prey item.

They nest in a hole, favourite sites being rabbit burrows, holes in walls and underneath a pile of rubble, with the nest entrance normally chosen to be sheltered from the prevailing wind. The male bird stands guard whilst his mate builds a bulky foundation of roots, thin twigs and grasses, lining the nest with feathers. Five or six eggs are normally laid around the first week of May, with about half of Wheatear pairs having a second clutch in mid-June. Despite their slow start to the season, once they start breeding they proceed with haste, and the females having second attempts start building and laying in a new nest almost as soon as the first brood chicks fledge. This is probably because, in common with most species, they time their breeding to coincide with peak availability of food for the chicks. Young birds get most of their energy from grasshoppers, bees, caterpillars and large flies, with smaller prey, including spiders and ants, being fed to them in their first few days of life.

Wheatears had not been well monitored by the annual national surveys until the BBS started in 1994. Since then, there is no clear trend in abundance. The Cheshire population has fallen in the last 20 years and there are now likely to be only around 20–30 pairs of Wheatears breeding in the eastern hills.

Sponsored by John Bannon in memory of a great friend and Cheshire birder, Colin Antrobus

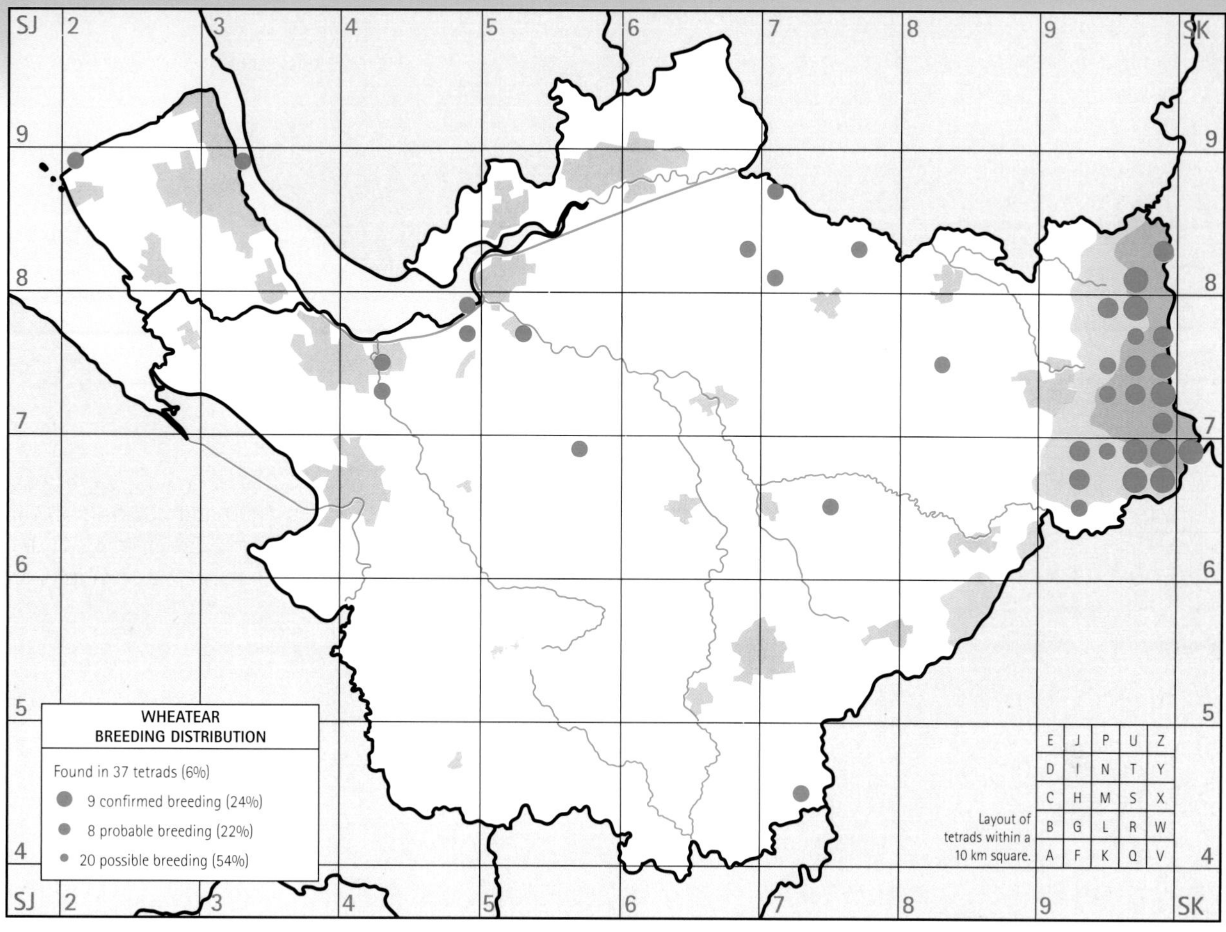
WHEATEAR
BREEDING DISTRIBUTION
Found in 37 tetrads (6%)
9 confirmed breeding (24%)
8 probable breeding (22%)
20 possible breeding (54%)
Layout of tetrads within a 10 km square.
E J P U Z
D I N T Y
C H M S X
B G L R W
A F K Q V
SJ
SK

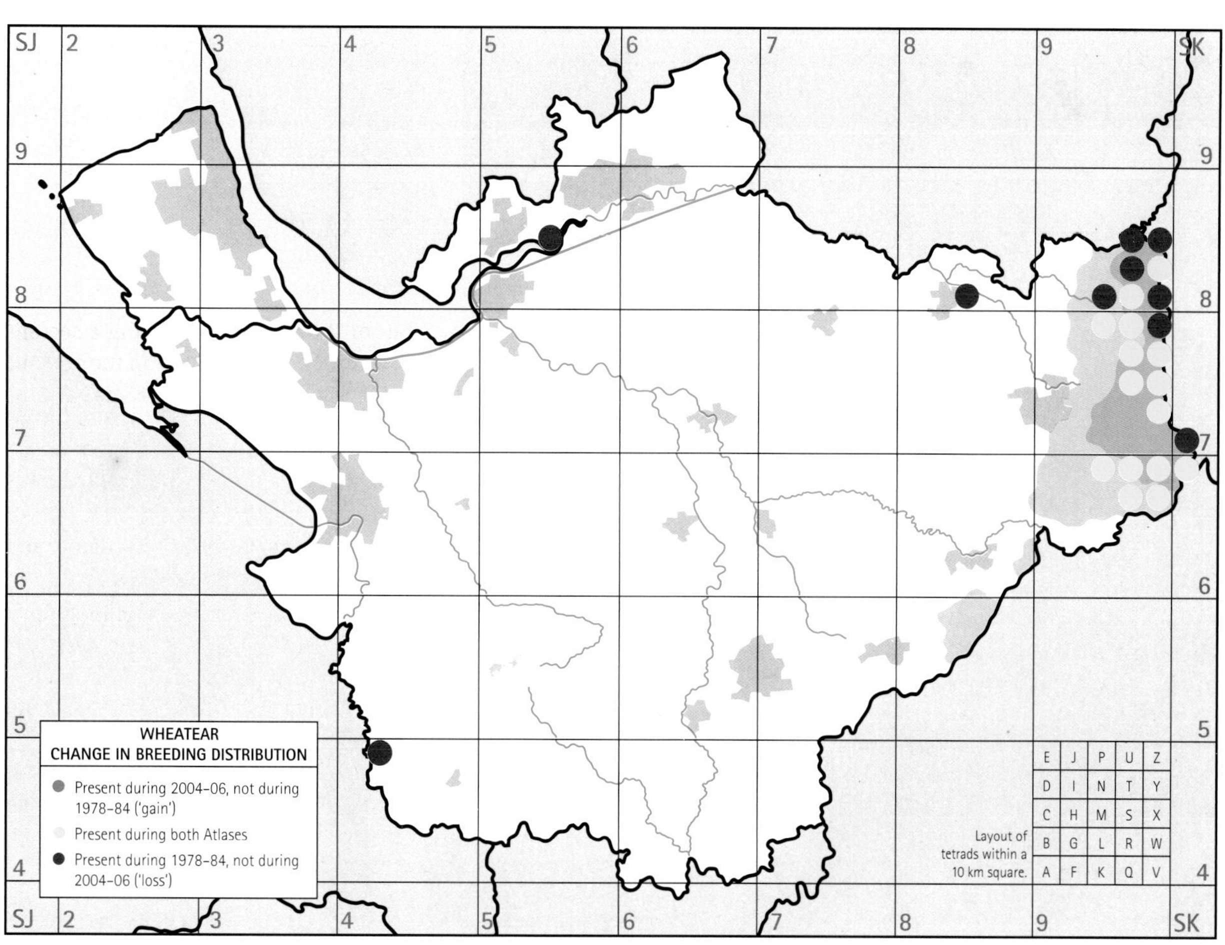
WHEATEAR
CHANGE IN BREEDING DISTRIBUTION
Present during 2004–06, not during 1978–84 ('gain')
Present during both Atlases
Present during 1978–84, not during 2004–06 ('loss')
Layout of tetrads within a 10 km square.
E J P U Z
D I N T Y
C H M S X
B G L R W
A F K Q V
SJ
SK

Ring Ouzel

Turdus torquatus

PHIL JONES

Our only summer migrant thrush, the Ring Ouzel is on the Red List of species of conservation concern because of its rapid population decline. Nationally, the BTO's second breeding Atlas showed a drop of 27% in the number of 10 km squares occupied between 1968–72 and 1988–91, then a further 39–43% range contraction was estimated for the period between 1988–91 and 1999 (Wotton *et al.* 2002). RSPB surveys in the Staffordshire moorlands showed precipitous declines, from 61 pairs in 1985 to 18 in 1992 and five in 1996 (Brindley *et al.* 1992, McKnight *et al.* 1997). No quantitative evidence has been forthcoming of a decline in Cheshire, but in 1991 the *CWBR* stated that there 'appears to be a general feeling' that the species is becoming scarcer on its breeding grounds. Fieldwork for this Atlas shows that they are now breeding only on the very fringes of Cheshire.

Ring Ouzels return early from their winter quarters in the Spanish and Moroccan uplands, birds often arriving during March, and they are usually on territory in the eastern hills in April. They breed at high altitudes in steep areas of gullies, rocky cloughs, rock outcrops and old quarries. They usually nest on or close to the ground in low vegetation, especially heather and bracken, also on rocky ledges and, rarely, in trees. The adults find their food, for themselves and their chicks, mostly on the ground, eating invertebrates, both adult and larvae, including earwigs, bugs, flies, sawflies, moths, beetles, millipedes, snails, slugs and earthworms. Most birds have two broods of chicks and the adults in particular are sustained through their later nesting attempts by the early fruits from plants such as bilberry. Thus, they favour a mosaic of heather moorland for nesting and short grass for foraging, and a loss in quality or availability of either component reduces the attractiveness of an area for Ring Ouzels.

The reasons for the Ring Ouzels' decline are poorly understood. Responsible factors on the breeding grounds include habitat deterioration, increased competition with Blackbirds or the effects of climate change on a high-altitude species. Other suggestions involve afforestation, acid rain, recreational disturbance and increased predation, including by raptors. The use of anthelmintics to control parasites in sheep is likely to reduce substantially the abundance of soil invertebrates (Brown & Grice 2005). Conditions on passage could also have an influence. Numbers of Fennoscandian breeders appear to have held steady and perhaps the earlier timing of spring migration for UK birds, and their more westerly route, gives them greater exposure to hunting pressures, particularly in south-west France (Burfield & Brooke 2005).

The *First Atlas* suggested that the Cheshire population was limited to 9–12 pairs each year; it is probably now down to three or four pairs.

● There were reports of wintering males within the breeding area in 2002/03 and 2003/04, but none during this winter Atlas period.

Sponsored by David Hinkes

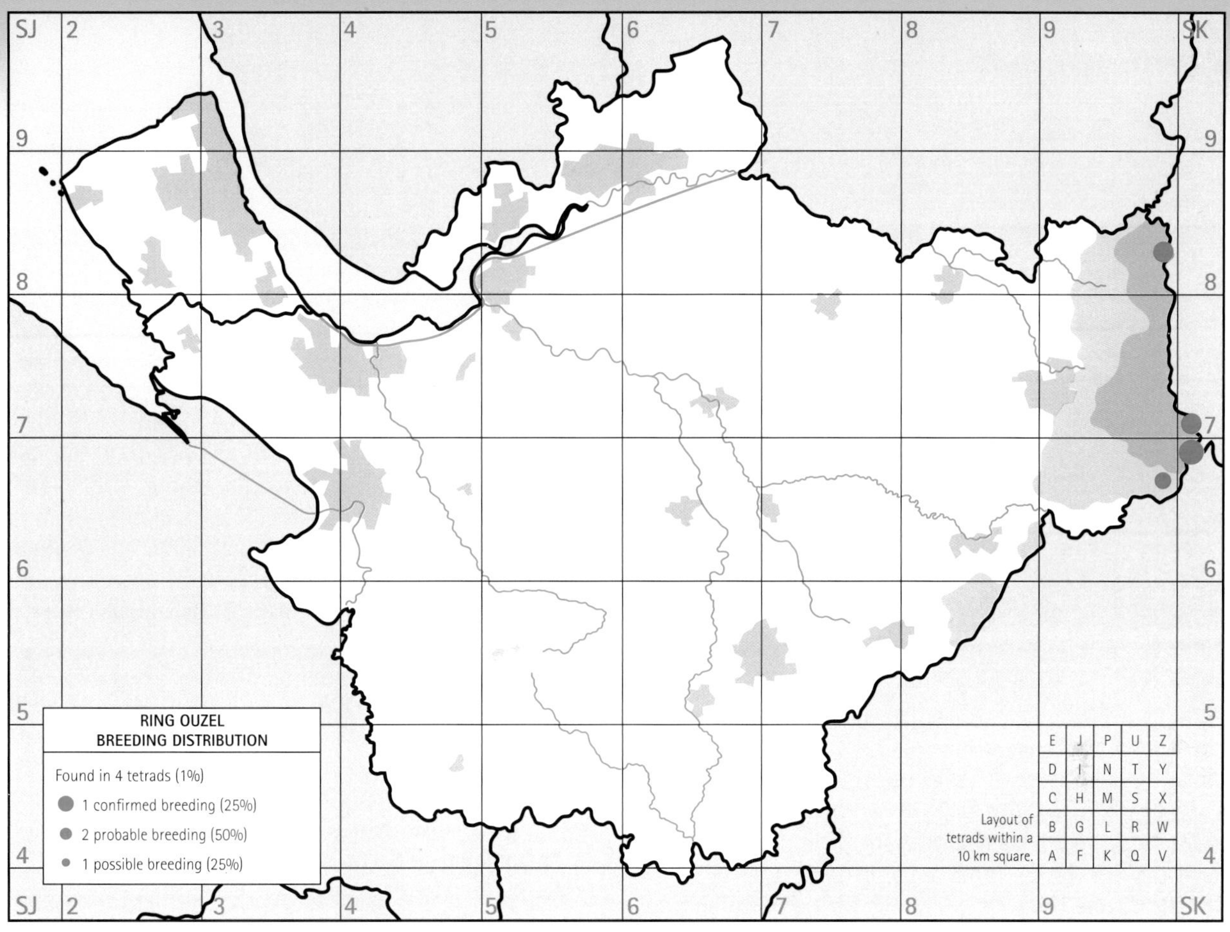
SJ
2
3
4
5
6
7
8
9
SK
9
8
7
6
5
4
RING OUZEL
BREEDING DISTRIBUTION
Found in 4 tetrads (1%)
1 confirmed breeding (25%)
2 probable breeding (50%)
1 possible breeding (25%)
E J P U Z
D I N T Y
C H M S X
B G L R W
A F K Q V
Layout of tetrads within a 10 km square.

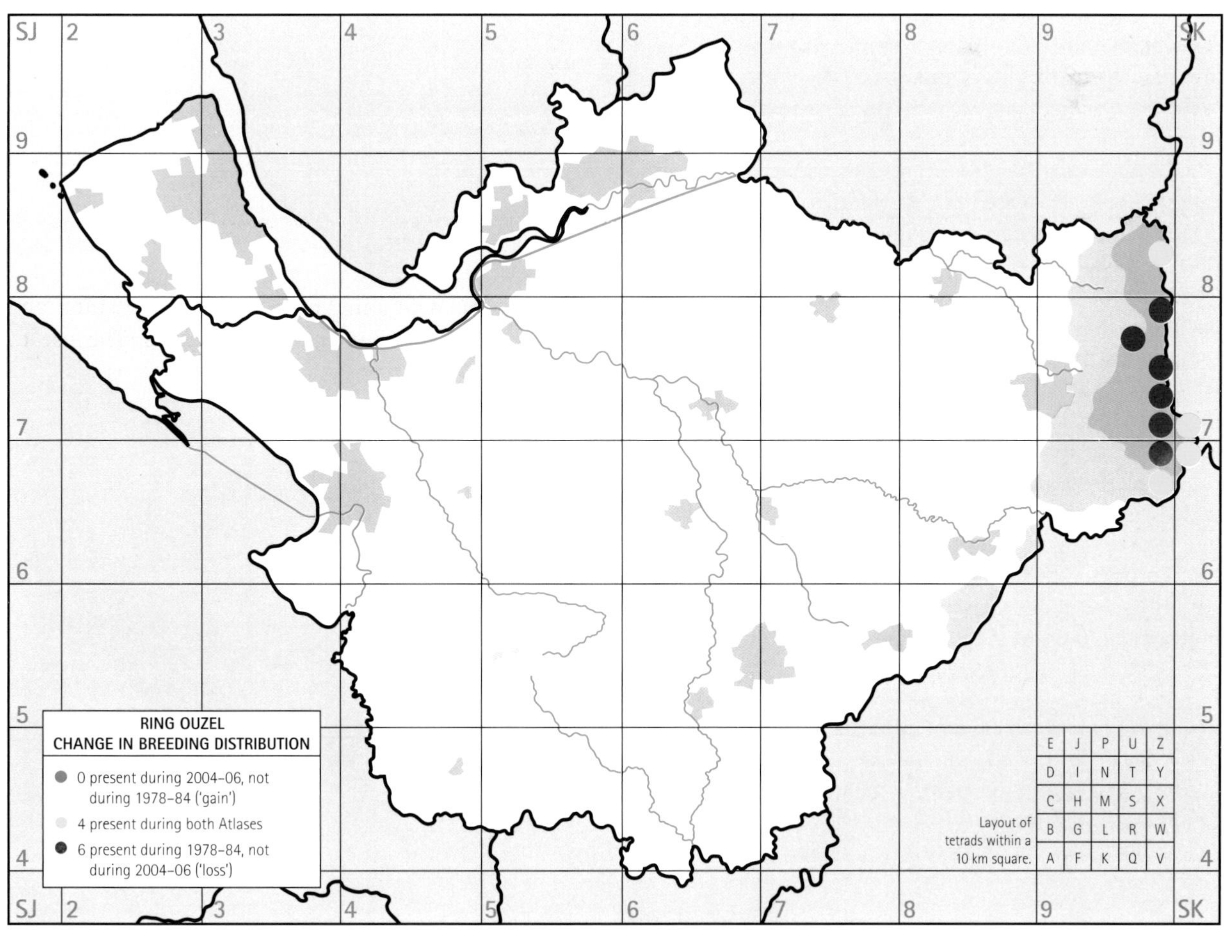
SJ
2
3
4
5
6
7
8
9
SK
9
8
7
6
5
4
RING OUZEL
CHANGE IN BREEDING DISTRIBUTION
0 present during 2004–06, not during 1978–84 ('gain')
4 present during both Atlases
6 present during 1978–84, not during 2004–06 ('loss')
E J P U Z
D I N T Y
C H M S X
B G L R W
A F K Q V
Layout of tetrads within a 10 km square.

Blackbird

Turdus merula

Blackbird was the equal second most widespread breeding species and appears to be almost ubiquitous, with little change from our *First Atlas* across most of the county, apart from odd instances of under-recording. They were, however, more difficult to find, and to prove breeding, in some of the highest eastern tetrads: of the county's 20 tetrads with a mean altitude above 300 m, Blackbirds were confirmed breeding in seven, probably breeding in three, possibly breeding in eight and not found in two, so they have probably declined somewhat in the hill country. They also used to breed regularly on Hilbre at the time of the last Atlas, but then deserted the island, and the female with an incubation patch trapped in 2006 represented the first suspected breeding for some time.

The figure of 89% of Blackbird records being two-letter codes was exceeded amongst the widespread species only by Blue Tit and Starling, showing how easy it is to prove Blackbirds breeding. Such records came from observers seeing adults carrying food (254 tetrads) or with family parties of their spotty-plumaged recently fledged young (182), with nests found (NE/NY/ON) in 146. Observers have multiple opportunities to record them in their long breeding season, from March to August, with birds nesting up to five times following repeated failures, and some successful pairs having multiple broods as well. In 2006 in Chester (SJ46I), Joe O'Hanlon noted one pair that had four broods, although the last one failed.

The main reason for their near-ubiquity in the county is the Blackbirds' ability to exploit almost any type of habitat. Their most-used category was human sites (34% of habitat records), followed closely by farmland (33%, nearly all grassland and hedgerows), and woodland (25%). They were more likely to be found in scrub (7%) than the other breeding thrushes. As recently as the mid-nineteenth century, Blackbirds were almost solely confined to their ancestral woodland habitat, and were never found breeding near houses (Parslow 1973). Surveyors included an F habitat code amongst the returns from 422 tetrads, almost two-thirds of those with the species, with 43 tetrads recording birds in F1 (urban). Provided that they can find sufficient food and a suitable nesting site, they can breed almost anywhere, and this is one of the species most likely to make the popular press with stories of unusual locations.

Blackbirds eat, and feed to their chicks, a wide variety of food. Earthworms are a staple, with invertebrates discovered in leaf litter, bare soil or grass, and caterpillars and adult insects found above the ground. Such animal matter is probably the most nutritious, but at any time of year they also take fruits and most things provided by man.

The BTO BBS analysis shows that the breeding population of Cheshire and Wirral in 2004–05 was 182,810 birds (156,630–209,000), corresponding to an average of almost 140 pairs per tetrad across the entire county. Average figures are not very meaningful, however, as breeding densities can vary enormously, from as high as 1,000 pairs per tetrad in suburbia, through 100 in farmland, to single figures in the difficult upland terrain (*BTO Second Atlas*). In the best habitats a breeding territory may be as small as 0.1 ha, equivalent to a circle 35 m in diameter.

The Cheshire and Wirral total amounts to 1.8% of the birds in the UK, indicating that the county is relatively important for the species (Newson *et al.* 2008). Their conservation status is reasonably secure. The national population index was in gentle decline, by about 10% during the period of our *First Atlas*. This accelerated to reach a low point in the mid-1990s, with numbers on farmland especially reduced and the species Amber listed for a while, but Blackbirds have recovered since, and the present national population is much the same as in 1980.

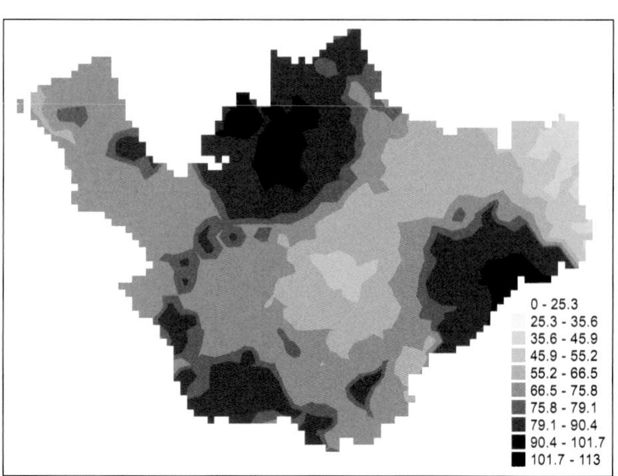

Blackbird abundance.

Sponsored by Mrs Edna Draper

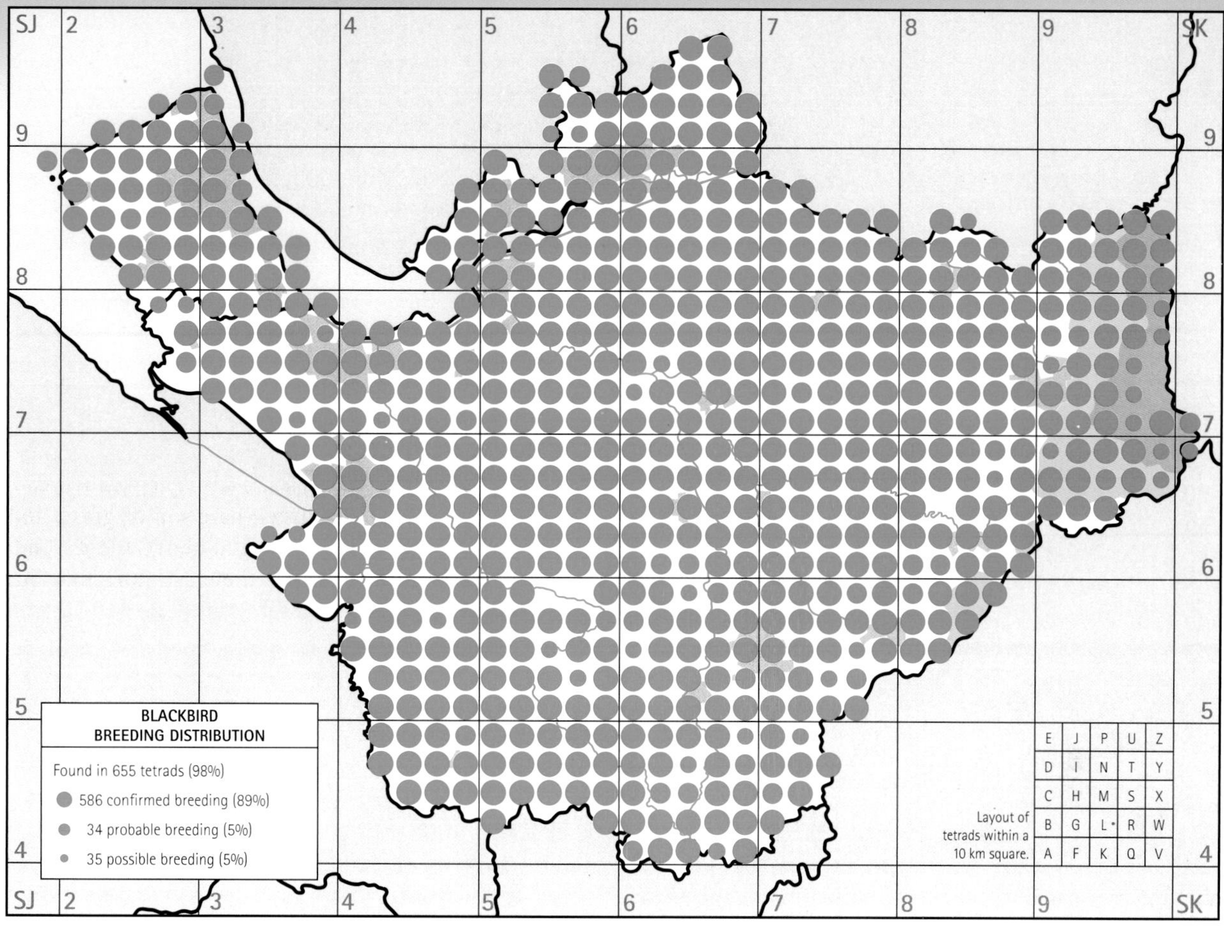
SJ
SK
BLACKBIRD
BREEDING DISTRIBUTION
Found in 655 tetrads (98%)
586 confirmed breeding (89%)
34 probable breeding (5%)
35 possible breeding (5%)
E J P U Z
D I N T Y
C H M S X
B G L R W
A F K Q V
Layout of tetrads within a 10 km square.

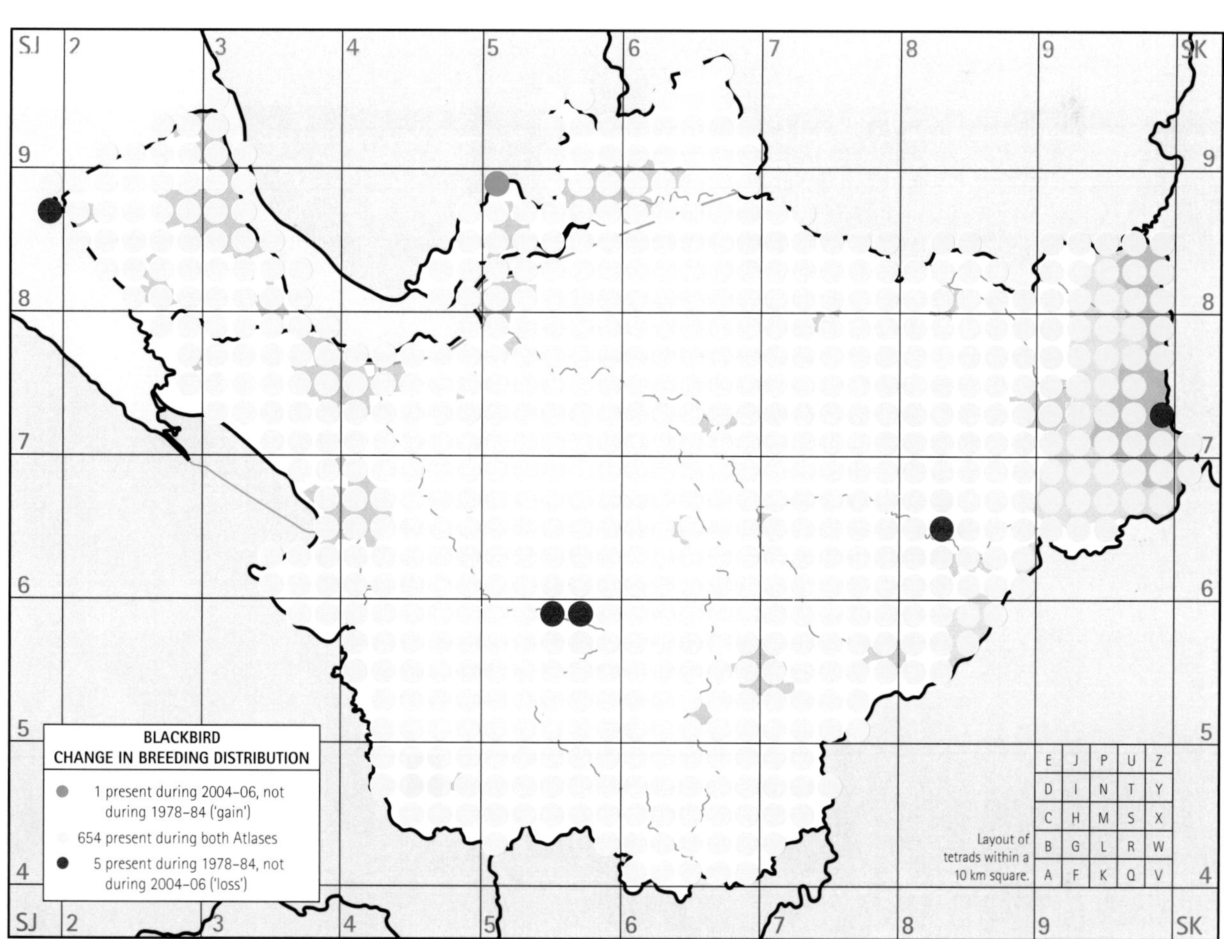
SJ
SK
BLACKBIRD
CHANGE IN BREEDING DISTRIBUTION
1 present during 2004–06, not during 1978–84 ('gain')
654 present during both Atlases
5 present during 1978–84, not during 2004–06 ('loss')
E J P U Z
D I N T Y
C H M S X
B G L R W
A F K Q V
Layout of tetrads within a 10 km square.

Blackbirds were reported from 655 tetrads in winter, everywhere in the county apart from the estuarine salt-marshes. Many of the birds seen will have been the same individuals as in the breeding season, for most British Blackbirds are sedentary, and have become even less likely to move in the last quarter-century (*Migration Atlas*). The tendency of some individuals to leave the country has ceased since Coward (1910) wrote 'in the autumn many of the birds leave us' and Bell (1962, 1967) detailed several examples of ringed birds. Both members of a pair defend a joint territory in winter, although they might split it and argue over the boundary (Brown & Grice 2005).

Winter numbers are augmented by an influx of birds from Fennoscandia, the Baltic States and elsewhere in northern Europe. The northerly birds tend to be larger, and some can be distinguished in the hand; they are more likely to be found in more remote sites, away from people, although some in gardens are foreign birds, as ringers know. Apart from SK07A, birds were found in all of the tetrads in the eastern hill country, in small numbers, with the largest reported flock being 10 birds seen by Steve and Gill Barber, about 450 m above sea level, feeding among a herd of goats at Whitehills (SJ97R).

In winter Blackbirds still like to eat invertebrates whenever they can find them, above all earthworms. On a still, frosty day, Blackbirds in woodland can often be heard from some distance as they noisily scratch through the leaf litter on the woodland floor. But their winter diet contains much more fruit, especially haws, usually taken early in winter, ivy and rowan, with apples as a standby.

The habitats recorded were much the same as in the breeding season—human sites, woodland and farmland, with some in scrub—and the main change is a proportionate reduction in all categories and a huge increase in birds in hedges, with this habitat being recorded in half of all tetrads. More than 40% of the hedge records were in the low (shorter than 2 m) class, and this species may tolerate hedge-trimming better than most, provided that the fruits remain.

Many Blackbirds roost communally, even some of the territorial birds leaving their domain for the night, usually in dense vegetation providing good shelter from winds. Rhododendron scrub under mature trees makes an ideal site, and other suitable roost locations include hedges, conifer plantations, brambles, gorse, and evergreen creepers on buildings (Simms 1978). Surprisingly, as few as eight roosts were reported during this Atlas, with the only substantial count being around 100 at Norton Priory, Runcorn (SJ58L). Other than at roosts, Blackbirds are not often found in large flocks and half of all the submitted counts were of four birds or fewer.

Blackbirds seldom undertake hard-weather movements and are likely to try to tough it out in even the worst of winter conditions (*BTO Winter Atlas*), probably because of the dedication of most resident birds to a territory. By the time our defined winter period finishes at the end of February, many of the immigrants are preparing to depart—birds ringed in winter in the county have been reported near Stockholm, Sweden as early as 11 March, and in Germany on 15 March—and many of the local birds are starting to breed.

SIMON BOOTH

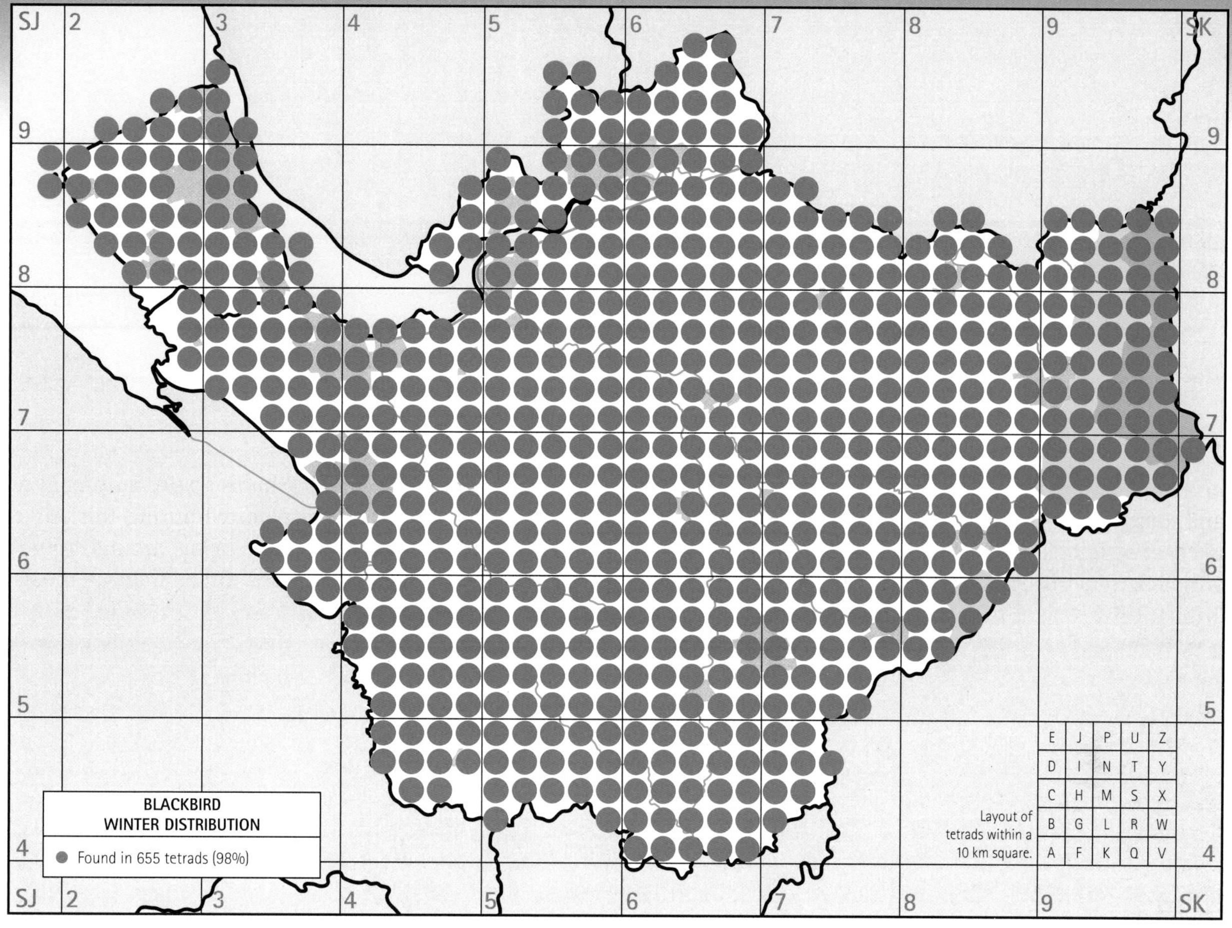
SJ
2
3
4
5
6
7
8
9
SK
9
8
7
6
5
4
BLACKBIRD
WINTER DISTRIBUTION
Found in 655 tetrads (98%)
E J P U Z
D I N T Y
C H M S X
B G L R W
A F K Q V
Layout of tetrads within a 10 km square.

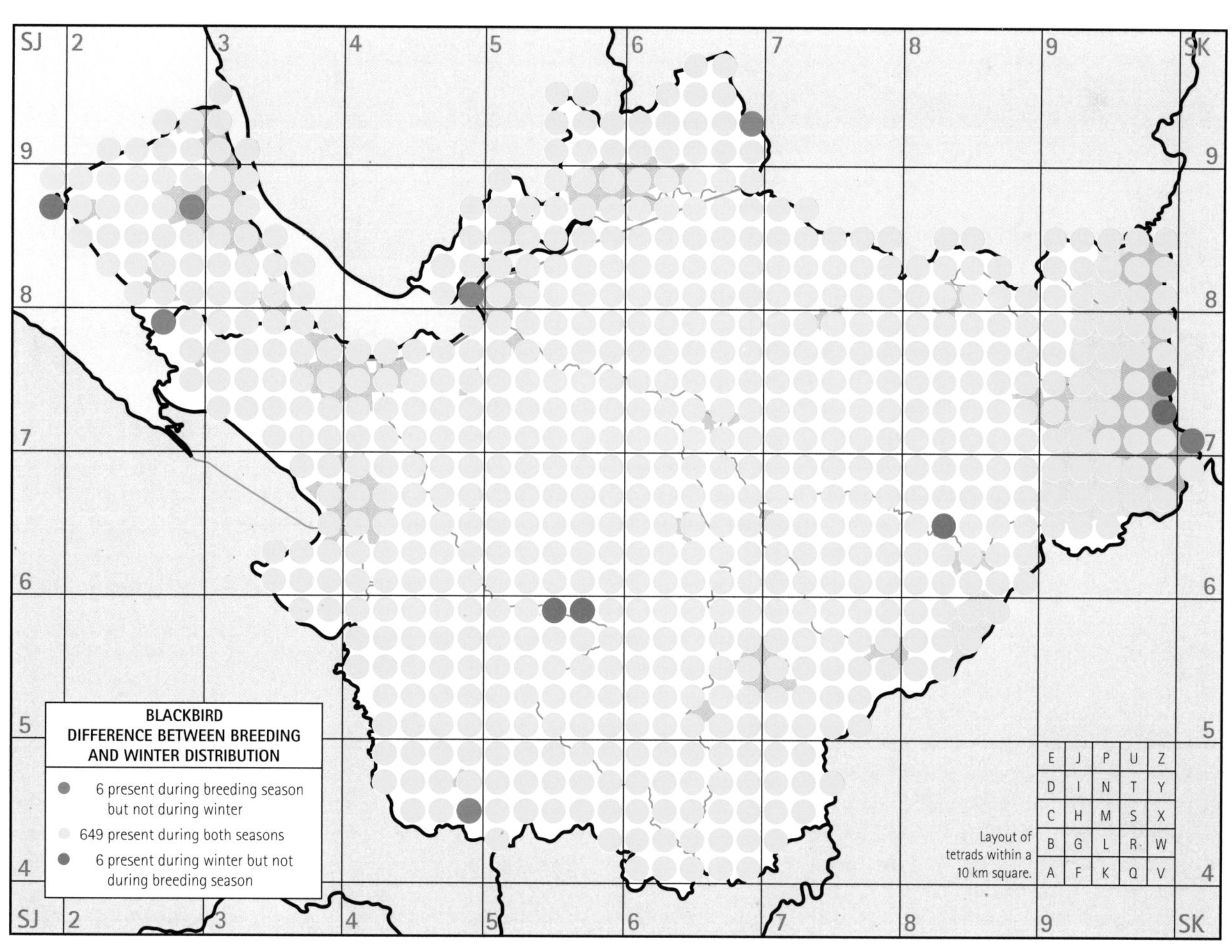
SJ
2
3
4
5
6
7
8
9
SK
9
8
7
6
5
4
BLACKBIRD
DIFFERENCE BETWEEN BREEDING AND WINTER DISTRIBUTION
6 present during breeding season but not during winter
649 present during both seasons
6 present during winter but not during breeding season
E J P U Z
D I N T Y
C H M S X
B G L R W
A F K Q V
Layout of tetrads within a 10 km square.

Fieldfare

Turdus pilaris

STEVE ROUND

About one million Fieldfares migrate to Britain for the winter, quitting their Fennoscandian breeding areas as the rowan crop runs out (*BTO Winter Atlas*). The Atlas map shows that they are widespread in Cheshire and Wirral, and altitude is no bar to them, but urban development obviously is. They were absent from most of Halton and Warrington in SJ58 and SJ68/69, the east Wirral and more local gaps including the Stanlow industrial complex (SJ47D/I) and parts of Chester and Northwich; in only eight tetrads were birds recorded with a habitat code of urban human sites (F1). Fieldfares are also scarce on Hilbre, which appears with a dot on this map because of just one bird in the last year of this survey.

These are gregarious birds, most Fieldfares breeding in colonies and usually being found in winter in flocks, often mixed with Redwings and Starlings, and sometimes amongst Lapwings and Golden Plovers. Even in relative safety amidst their large flocks, Fieldfares are wary, and often fly into the top of a tall tree, all sitting prominently, facing into the wind. Apart from such occasions, however, this is the wintering thrush least likely to be found in woodland (10% of habitat records) or human sites (7%), and the habitat records came overwhelmingly from farmland (78%), mostly improved grassland (34%) and tall hedges (18%). In fields they take about half of their food from the surface, mainly beetles, spiders and flies, digging the rest from the soil including earthworms, centipedes, slugs and larvae of beetles and crane-flies. Atlas fieldworkers reported them on maize stubble (particularly favouring recently slurried areas), flooded meadows, and pastures, often alongside sheep or horses. In the hedges, their staple diet is haws, hips, ivy and holly, and, if they can find them, the protein-rich fruits of mistletoe, juniper, rowan and buckthorn (Snow & Snow 1988). In hard weather they resort to commercial orchards, often in large flocks, to feed on apples, especially favouring the sweeter, softer varieties like Golden Delicious; one or two apples are sufficient to sustain them through a day of hard weather when the ground is frozen, although they will lose condition after a few days without invertebrate food or more nutritious

Sponsored by Heather James

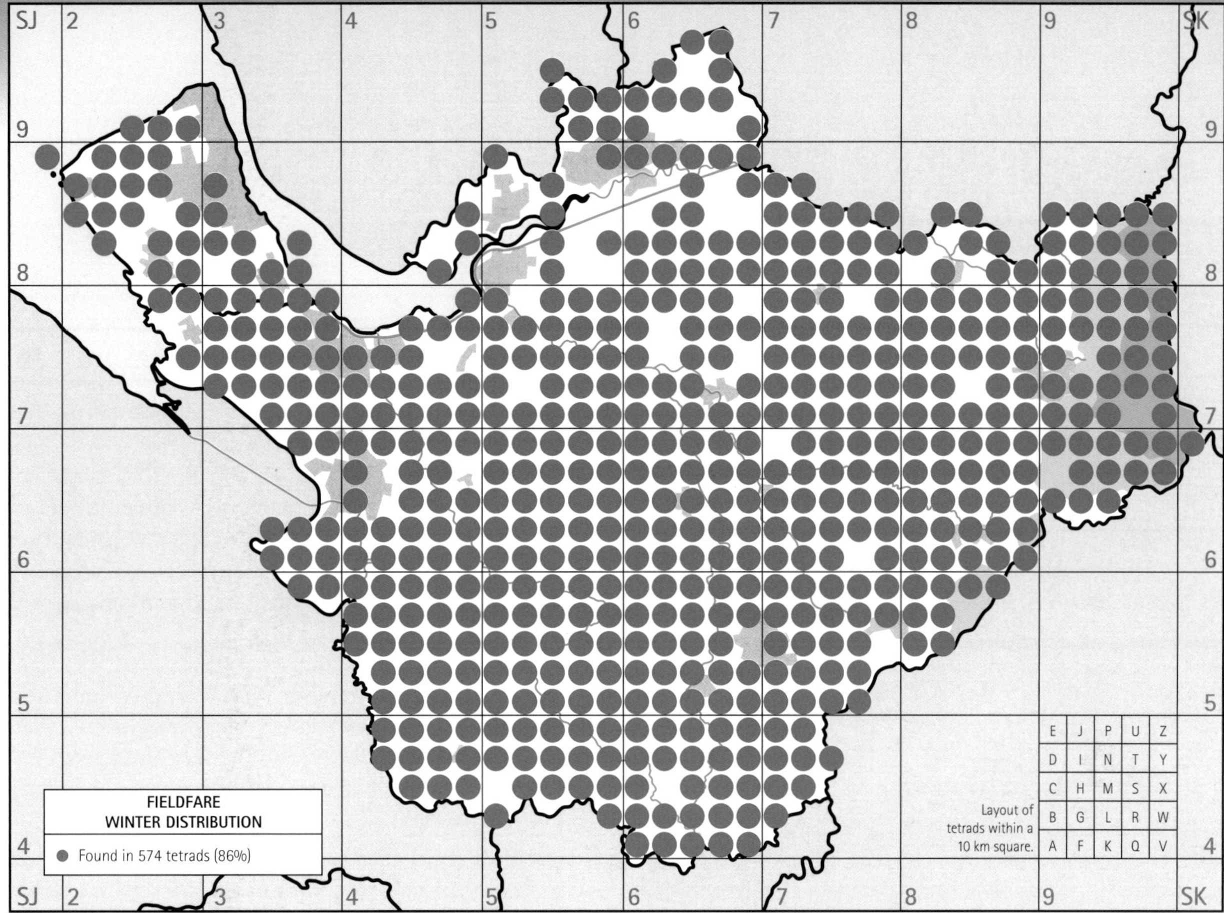

hedgerow fruits (Norman 1995). In prolonged spells of subzero temperatures, many Fieldfares leave the county, but conditions since the 1980s have never been severe enough to provoke their departure.

Most surveyors counted their Fieldfares, providing 771 counts over the three years of the Atlas survey. Although Bell (1962) wrote that they were more numerous in some years than others, there was no evidence for this during the three winters of this Atlas, in contrast to the results for Redwings. Counts of Fieldfares were submitted from almost identical numbers of tetrads in each year, and the median flock size each winter was the same: 50 birds. There were 26 records of large flocks of 500 or more, headed by the 2,000 reported by Charles Hull in SJ65H and the 1,392 laboriously counted by John Bannon just before the end of this Atlas period (26 February 2007) on grazing pasture near No Mans Heath (SJ54E).

Fieldfare roosts are often not as obvious as those of other thrushes, so it was good that they were reported in 20 tetrads, holding from three birds to more than 1,000, in habitats including willows and rhododendron scrub in a large garden. Most Fieldfare roosts are low down, often on the ground (Norman 1994a), but nine of those reported were shared with Redwings.

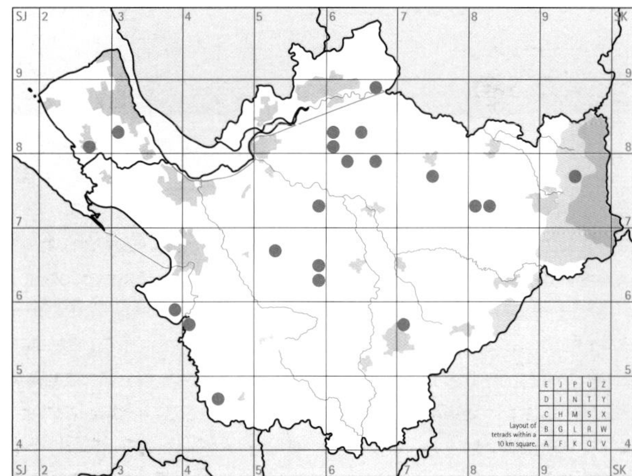

Fieldfare roost map.

Song Thrush

Turdus philomelos

JOHN POWER

Song Thrush numbers have declined greatly in the last 40 years but it is still a relatively common bird and the population decline is not evident in its distribution within the county. The map shows that they were present in 639 tetrads, just eight fewer than in our *First Atlas*. Most of the tetrads without a Song Thrush probably result from underrecording, but their absence from four of the highest in the eastern hills is significant. They have occasionally bred on Hilbre in the past, but not during either of our two Atlas periods (Craggs 1982).

Farmland records contributed 31% (including 11% in hedges) and woodland 29%, with 6% in scrub, but the commonest category of habitat code submitted for this Atlas (33% of records) was F (human sites). Gardens, allotments and farmsteads may well now be the most important sites in the county for Song Thrushes. In a breeding survey in 10 tetrads in a mainly arable farming area of Essex (quoted by Snow 2003), gardens made up just 2% of the area but held 72% of the Song Thrush territories, and in another similar area there was a density of 25 pairs per square kilometre in villages and none in the surrounding farmland. The position in pastoral Cheshire is not as extreme, but it would be fascinating to perform a similar quantitative survey here.

The national population index was in free fall from the early 1970s, dropping by one-quarter during the seven years of our *First Atlas*, but levelled out in the mid-1990s and has now risen again so that the 2004 figure is the same as that of 1984. The substantial decline led to Song Thrush being placed on the Red List of species of conservation concern, and national and local Biodiversity Action Plans written for it: so far, these have led to little action for its conservation but much research into the species' ecology. This shows that the population decline was almost certainly driven by a fall in survival in the juveniles' first winter, and perhaps also the postfledging period, so that there are not enough recruits to replace adult mortality (Thomson *et al.* 1997, Siriwardena *et al.* 1998, Robinson *et al.* 2004). The environmental causes are not known, but changes in farming practices, land drainage, pesticides and predators are all candidates (Fuller *et al.* 1995, Robinson *et al.* 2004).

In Cheshire (without Wirral) the population halved from 1970 to 1986, correlated with, and perhaps caused by, agricultural land drainage; drier soils substantially reduce the number of earthworms near to the surface, removing much of the thrushes' staple diet (Peach *et al.* 2004). They then have to switch to spiders and snails, never as common in Cheshire's sandy, calcium-deficient soils as in many other counties. The current breeding population of Cheshire and Wirral, from the BTO analysis of 2004–05 BBS data, is 17,200 birds (13,410–21,000), corresponding to an average of about 17 pairs per tetrad with confirmed or probable breeding. This is only one-tenth of the county's Blackbird population. Until about 1940, Song Thrushes outnumbered Blackbirds in Britain as a whole, and probably in Cheshire too.

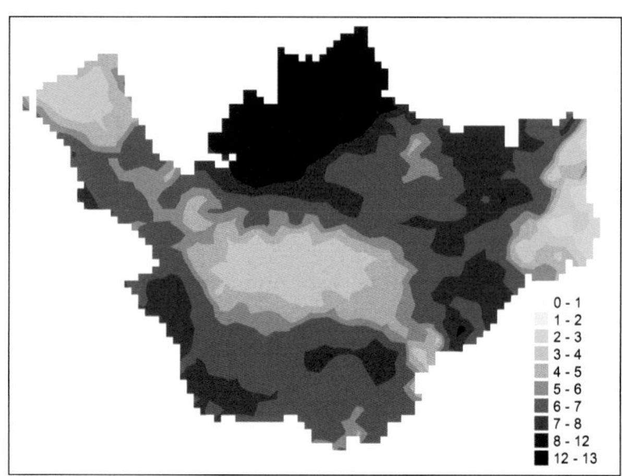

Song Thrush abundance.

Sponsored by Henry Finch

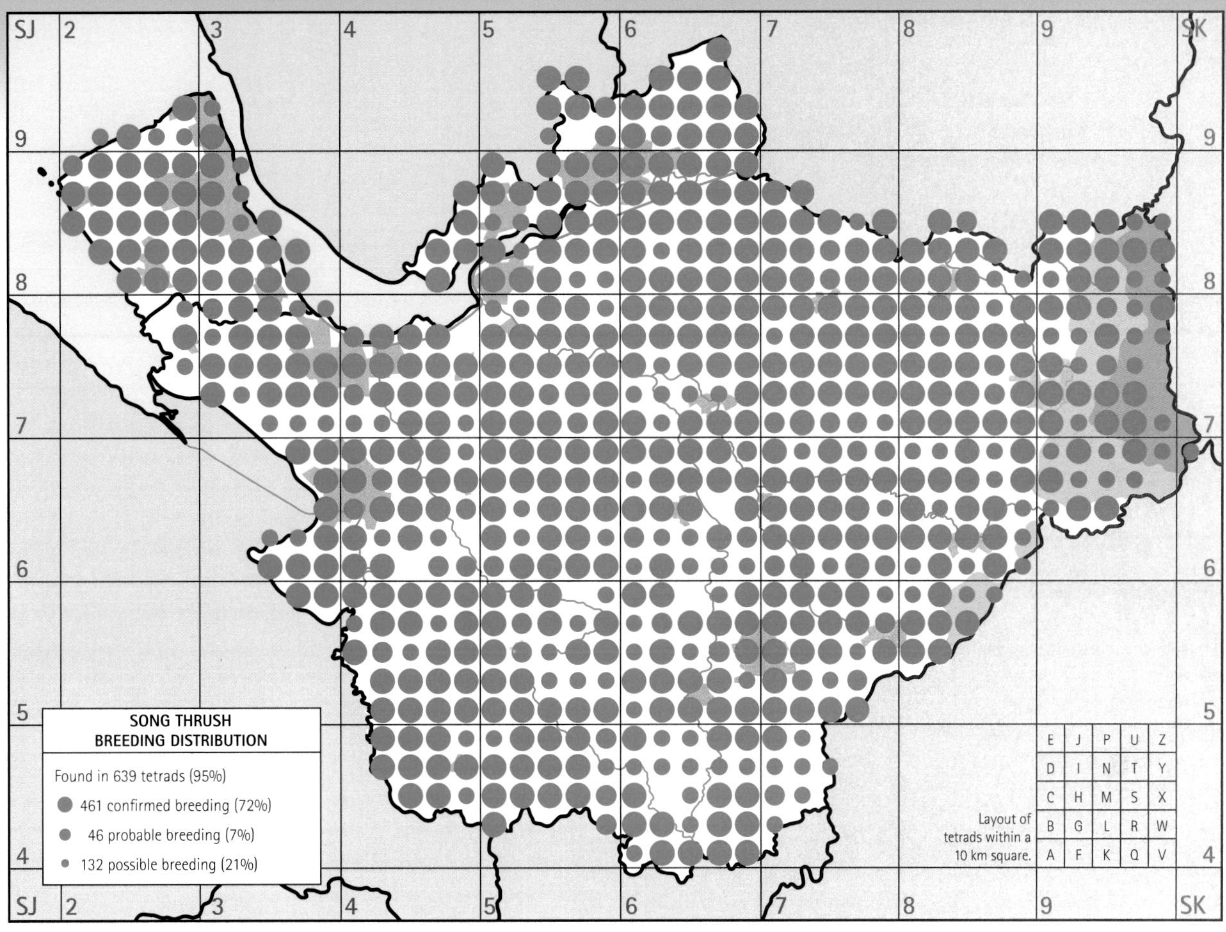
SJ
SK
2
3
4
5
6
7
8
9
SONG THRUSH
BREEDING DISTRIBUTION
Found in 639 tetrads (95%)
461 confirmed breeding (72%)
46 probable breeding (7%)
132 possible breeding (21%)
E J P U Z
D I N T Y
C H M S X
B G L R W
A F K Q V
Layout of tetrads within a 10 km square.

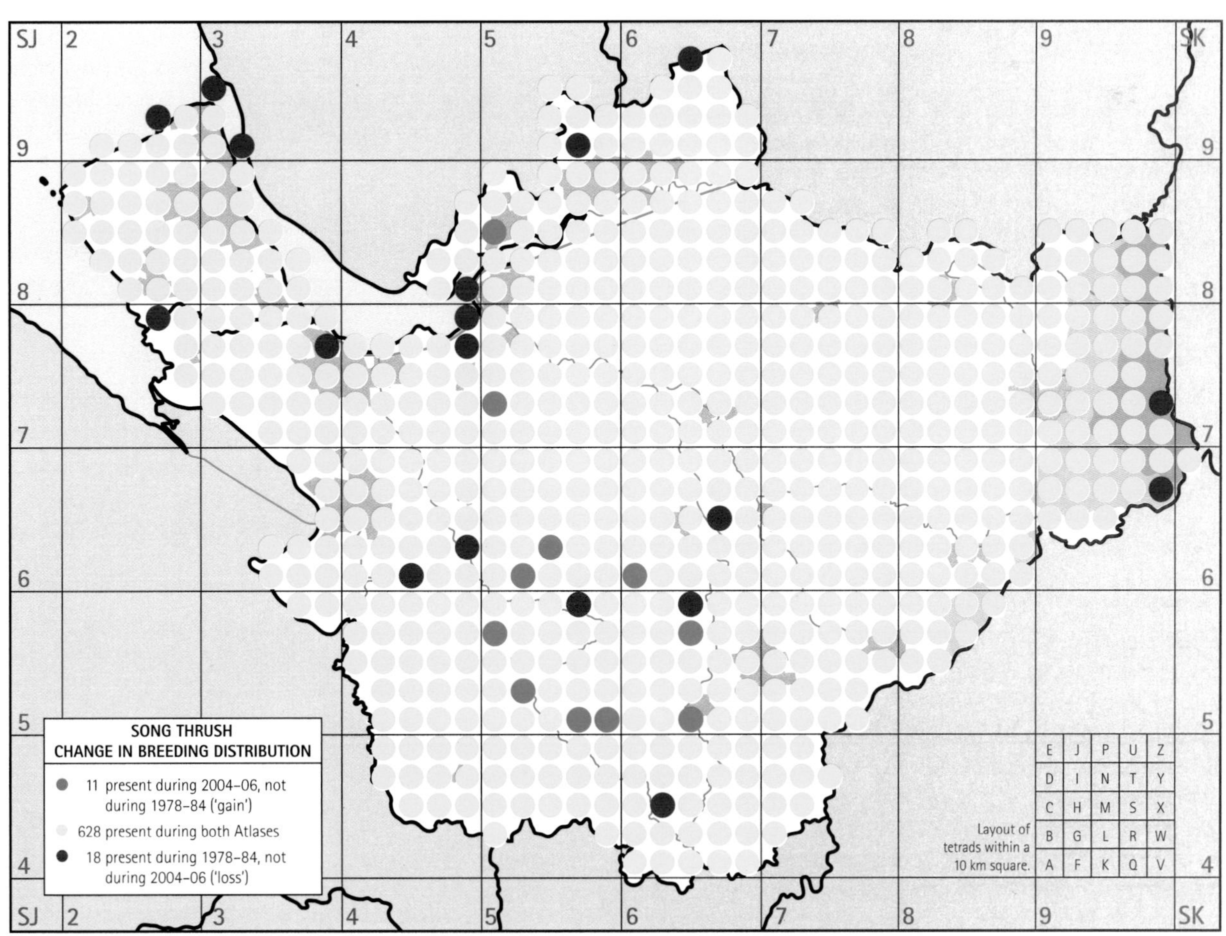
SJ
SK
2
3
4
5
6
7
8
9
SONG THRUSH
CHANGE IN BREEDING DISTRIBUTION
11 present during 2004–06, not during 1978–84 ('gain')
628 present during both Atlases
18 present during 1978–84, not during 2004–06 ('loss')
E J P U Z
D I N T Y
C H M S X
B G L R W
A F K Q V
Layout of tetrads within a 10 km square.

STEVE ROUND

Song Thrushes were recorded in winter in 621 tetrads, 18 fewer than in the breeding season. The map shows that there were a few odd tetrads in which they were not found, but the only places they are truly absent are the estuarine salt-marshes and the eastern hills. This is not a very hardy species, withdrawing from most of the uplands of northern Britain (*BTO Winter Atlas*) and it seems that there is some altitudinal migration even within Cheshire. They were not found in 13 of the highest tetrads, 10 of which were occupied in the breeding season. At the other end of the county, two or three Song Thrushes were counted on Hilbre—where they did not breed—during each winter of this survey.

The movement from the hill country is interesting because it seems that the migratory status of British Song Thrushes is probably changing, as has happened with Blackbirds. Earlier analyses showed that most birds wintered away from their natal area, but nowadays it is suggested that the typical winter behaviour of Song Thrushes should be described as 'residency, interrupted sometimes by cold-weather movements' (*Migration Atlas*). There is more migration from northern Britain than from the south, however, and continued study of the county's birds is warranted, including observations of the dates of return to their eastern breeding sites, and the effect of winter weather on this susceptible species.

In addition to the British-bred Song Thrushes, there is some autumn passage of Fennoscandian birds, mostly moving through on their way to Iberia, but a few stay in Britain for the winter, as do many birds from the Netherlands and Belgium (*Migration Atlas*). These birds are of different races and occasionally 'funny-looking' Song Thrushes—slightly larger and greyer above with whiter underparts—are seen wintering in Cheshire and Wirral. A bird caught at Norton Priory, Runcorn on 12 January 1986 had been ringed on the Norfolk coast on 18 October 1985, and was likely to have been a migrant from Fennoscandia. Not all birds from the east coast are immigrants, however, as another bird caught at the same site on 20 November 1988 was certainly British-bred, having been ringed in North Yorkshire on 18 June that year as a chick in the nest.

In winter, Song Thrushes have a mixed diet of soil invertebrates, especially worms and snails, and fruit from bushes such as rowan, hawthorn, ivy and holly. Several observers noted that they seem to like horse paddocks, where the close-cropped grass allows easy access to earthworms. The only substantial difference in habitat from the breeding season to winter is that the proportion in farmland hedgerows doubled from 11% of records to 22%, mostly at the expense of records from woodland, with little change in other farmland codes and human sites. Even so, out of our five wintering thrushes, this is the one most likely to be found in woodland and least likely to frequent farmland, based on the percentages of submitted habitat codes. Song Thrushes tend not to form large flocks, and more than half of the counts submitted were of single birds. There were only five reported gatherings of 10 or more, including about 12 that David Bowman counted feeding in 200 m of hedgerow near Rixton (SJ68Z) on 19 December 2006, and a large roost found by Steve Binney and Frank Gleeson in winter 2004/05 near Brimstage (SJ38B).

A further indication of the sedentary nature of most of our Song Thrushes is that many birds sing from November onwards, some continuing throughout the winter period, and almost all breeding territories are established by mid-February (Snow 2003), thus merging the two seasons of this Atlas.

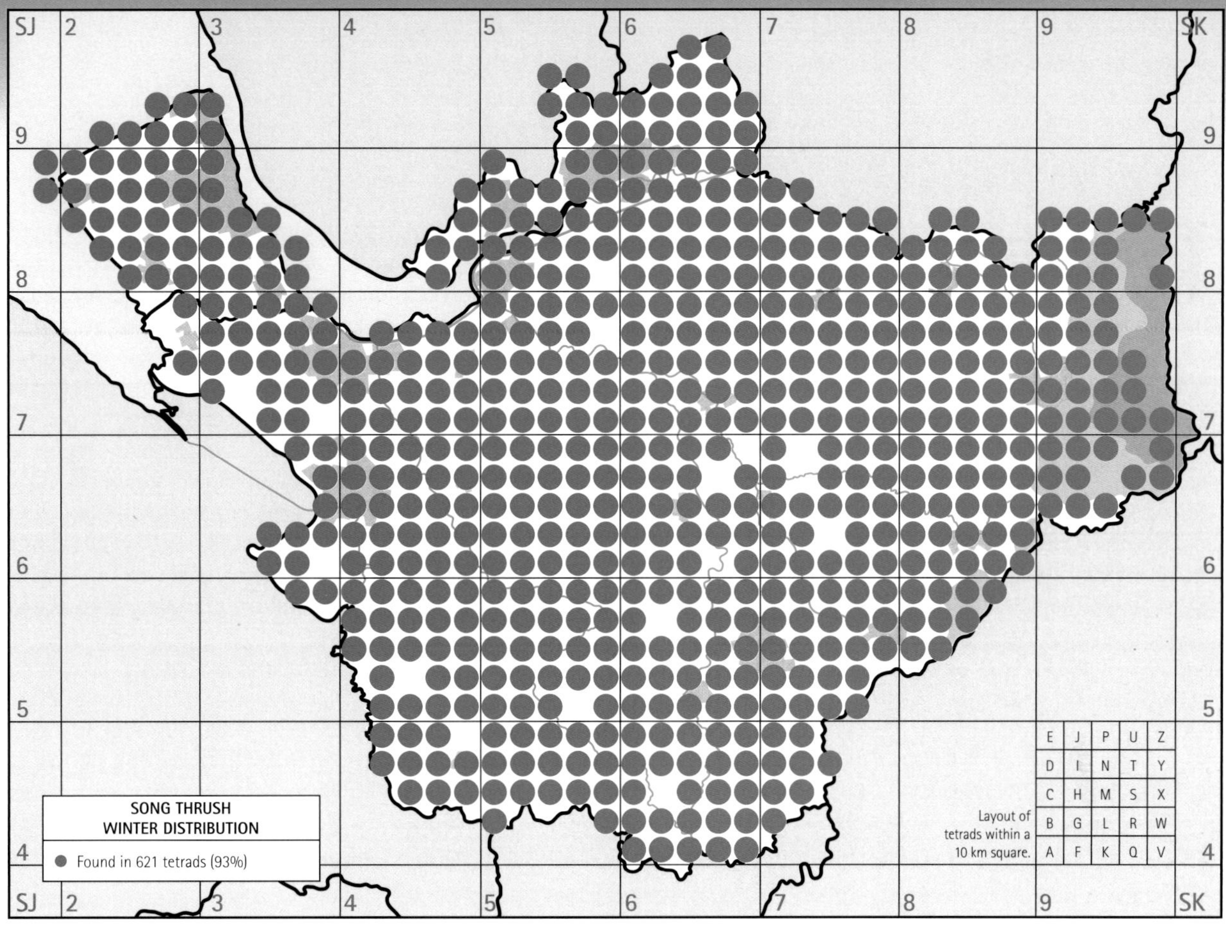
SJ
2
3
4
5
6
7
8
9
SK
9
8
7
6
5
4
SONG THRUSH
WINTER DISTRIBUTION
Found in 621 tetrads (93%)
E J P U Z
D I N T Y
C H M S X
B G L R W
A F K Q V
Layout of tetrads within a 10 km square.

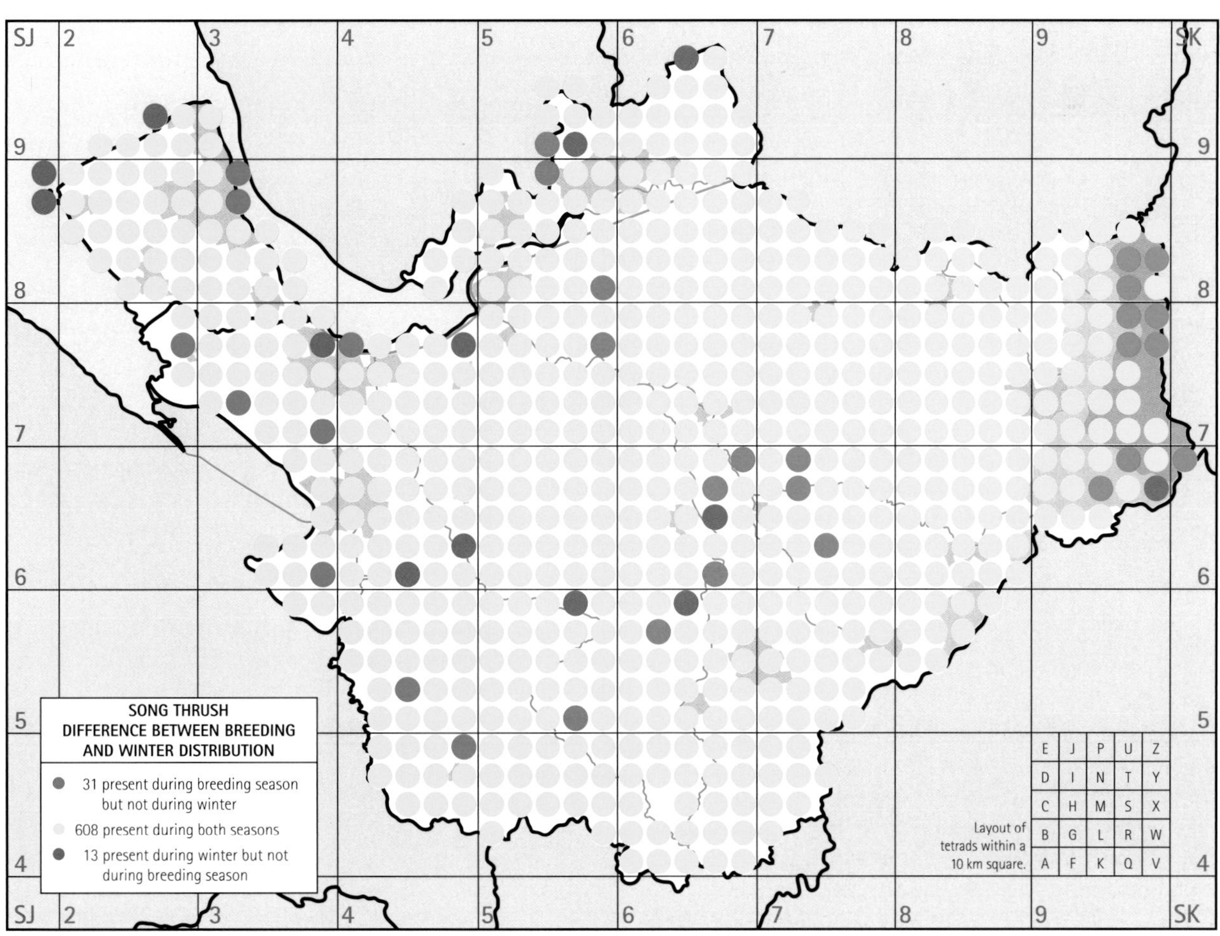
SJ
2
3
4
5
6
7
8
9
SK
9
8
7
6
5
4
SONG THRUSH
DIFFERENCE BETWEEN BREEDING AND WINTER DISTRIBUTION
31 present during breeding season but not during winter
608 present during both seasons
13 present during winter but not during breeding season
E J P U Z
D I N T Y
C H M S X
B G L R W
A F K Q V
Layout of tetrads within a 10 km square.

Redwing

Turdus iliacus

This is our most widespread winter visitor, being found in 603 tetrads. The map suggests that they avoid some urban and industrial areas: the east Wirral conurbation, Stanlow, Runcorn/Widnes, Chester and Northwich, and there were none on Hilbre or the highest hills. Redwings come here for the winter from two different breeding areas, with the birds sufficiently distinct to form two races: *coburni* from Iceland are slightly larger, with more distinct breast markings and legs dark brown rather than the pink of *iliacus* birds from Fennoscandia and Russia. A bird ringed at Norton Priory, Runcorn (SJ58L) in January was caught by a ringer in Arkhangelsk, Russia, near the Arctic Circle 2,750 km away. Most *coburni* winter in Ireland, but ringing has shown that some visit Cheshire and Wirral.

As with all wintering thrushes, their preferred diet is soil invertebrates, especially earthworms, but they eat a wide variety of fruits, and in hard weather will eat nothing else. In many tetrads, Redwings were found on bare ground, including newly ploughed or harrowed fields, or stubble, even maize stubble which often has few other birds; fields recently covered with slurry or manure seemed almost guaranteed to attract Redwings. Several observers commented on their liking for horse paddocks and fields with livestock, sheep or cattle. Fruit-eating birds were noted on holly, ivy, hawthorn and rowan. They were often found in mixed flocks with Fieldfares, and the two species' habitat preferences are very similar. Redwings were mostly reported in farmland (71% of habitat records), mainly mostly improved grassland (29%) and tall hedges (18%), and 8% in human sites. Especially in hard weather, Redwings enter woodland and forage amongst the leaf litter, and broad-leaved or mixed woodland provided 15% of the habitat records.

Most surveyors counted their Redwings, providing 828 counts over the three years of the Atlas survey. There were 11 records of large flocks of 500 or more, headed by the 1,000 reported by Roy and Iona Bowden near Delamere (SJ57L). Numbers can vary greatly from one year to another, figures submitted for this Atlas showing as many birds counted in 2004/05 as in the

STEVE ROUND

Sponsored by Margaret Bain, Barry Taylor and Stephen Taylor

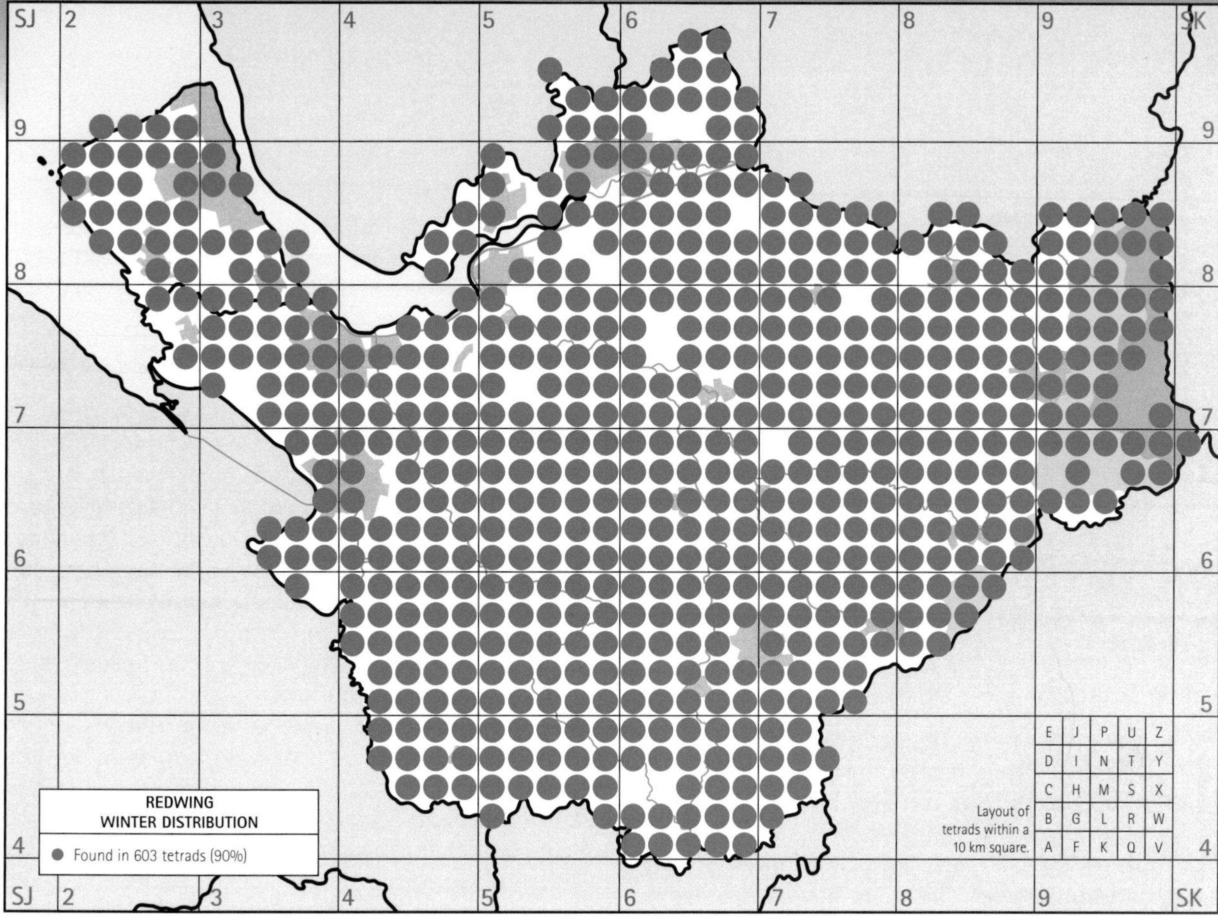

other two winters combined, from similar numbers of tetrads each year; the median flock sizes were 52, 29 and 31 in the three winters. This variation reflects the species' nomadic nature, few birds showing any site fidelity from one winter to another: one ringed at Norton Priory, Runcorn, was in Spain for the next winter, and others have been found in France and Italy. Coward (1910) noted the fluctuation in numbers, and Redwings' susceptibility to hard weather, hard frost or heavy snow driving most birds from the county or into close proximity to man in suburban gardens' berry-bearing bushes. Bell (1962) concentrated on their migration dates, and gave no indication of the species' winter distribution or numbers.

This is one of the few species for which several observers reported roosts, in a variety of sites including rhododendrons under mature trees, *phragmites* and willows, and holding a variety of numbers of birds, from 10 to 300. The excitement of seeing, and hearing, several hundreds of these birds entering a communal roost provides a satisfying end to fieldwork on a winter evening, and it would be good to know more about their night-time haunts: after all, in midwinter Redwings, like all passerines, spend twice as much time in their nocturnal roost as in daytime feeding.

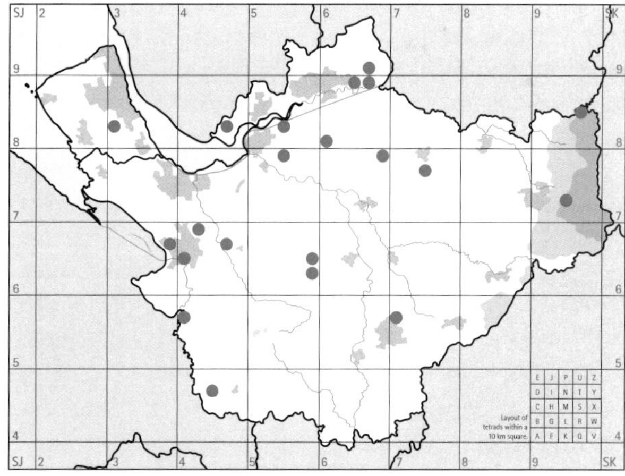
Redwing roost map.

Mistle Thrush

Turdus viscivorus

SUE & ANDY TRANTER

By contrast with our two other common breeding thrushes, Mistle Thrushes are considerably less widespread than in our *First Atlas*, being found in 48 fewer tetrads. The losses have been scattered across the county, but most noticeably in the centre and south of Cheshire where there are now some obvious gaps without the species, as in SJ46/56/64/65/66. This is mostly classic pastoral Cheshire and this is one bird that ought to have benefited from the switch from hay to silage, the earlier grass-cutting exposing a sudden flush of invertebrates that fits well with the Mistle Thrush breeding season (O'Connor & Shrubb 1986) but there must be something else in modern agricultural practice that is inimical to these birds.

Mistle Thrushes are only ever found at relatively low densities: they defend large territories, usually at least 1 ha and some more than 10 ha (Simms 1978), that contain a variety of habitats. Analysis of the submitted habitat codes for this Atlas shows that most birds were in farmland, broad-leaved woodland and human sites. This is the archetypal bird of 'parkland'—open, grassy areas with mature trees. Compared to Blackbirds and Song Thrushes, Mistle Thrushes are more likely to be found in agricultural grassland, including unimproved grassland (especially in the hill country), and much less likely to frequent scrub or farmland hedgerows. They were recorded in 207 human sites, 100 of them urban or suburban habitats, and Mistle Thrushes can breed even in the most built-up settings provided that there are sufficient lawns and flower-beds to provide food. The abundance map suggests that the highest concentrations of Mistle Thrushes are in the most populous north of the county.

Most of the confirmed breeding records came from observers seeing adults carrying food (157 tetrads) or with recently fledged young (155), with nests found (NE/NY/ON), usually in the fork of a tree and often high off the ground, in 68. Some of the probable breeding codes could, with luck, have been converted to proven breeding: in 16 tetrads observers found birds visiting a probable nest site or carrying nesting material, and 22 tetrads provided fieldworkers with a code of A (agitated behaviour or alarm calls), this being one of the more demonstrative species. Some territories are difficult to locate, not least because Mistle Thrushes will fly a long way, up to a kilometre on occasions, if a prime source of food becomes available such as a ploughed field or newly mown pasture or playing field (O'Connor & Shrubb 1986). Others can seem ridiculously easy to find, especially if an adult 'churrs' noisily and flies off with a beak full of worms, or a Magpie goes too near, when ferocious attacks by the thrushes usually deter them from plundering the nest. Despite their being early nesters, often starting in March before there is much vegetation on the trees to conceal them, data from the BTO's nest record scheme show that the success rate of Mistle Thrush nests, with eggs or with chicks, is much higher than that of Blackbirds or Song Thrushes.

Nationally, Mistle Thrush populations have declined significantly since the mid-1970s, especially on farmland, causing them recently to be added to the Amber List of species of conservation concern. The drop has been mostly on farmland rather than woodland areas (Brown & Grice 2005) and the decline is likely to have been driven by reduced annual survival (Siriwardena *et al.* 1998). The national population index fell by 16% during the seven years of our *First Atlas*, and is still dropping, with the 2004 figure 25% lower than that of 1984. In Cheshire and Wirral, the BTO BBS analysis shows that the breeding population in 2004–05 was 6,240 birds (4,190–8,290), corresponding to an average of about 13 birds per tetrad with confirmed or probable breeding, or 11 birds per tetrad in which the species was recorded.

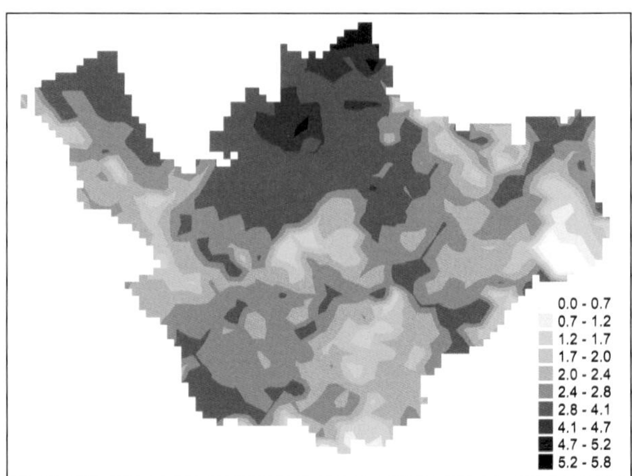

Mistle Thrush abundance.

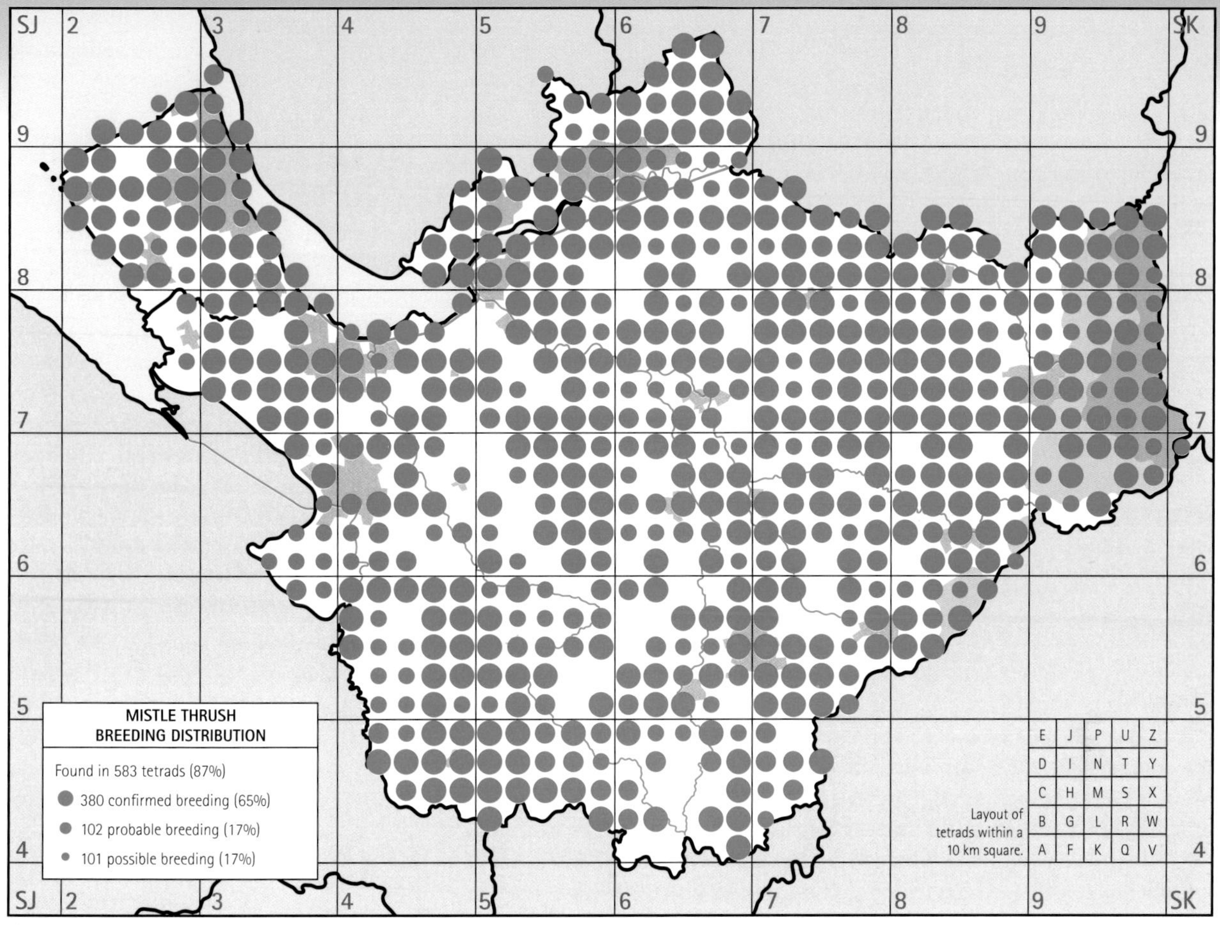
SJ
2
3
4
5
6
7
8
9
SK
9
8
7
6
5
4
MISTLE THRUSH
BREEDING DISTRIBUTION
Found in 583 tetrads (87%)
380 confirmed breeding (65%)
102 probable breeding (17%)
101 possible breeding (17%)
E J P U Z
D I N T Y
C H M S X
B G L R W
A F K Q V
Layout of tetrads within a 10 km square.

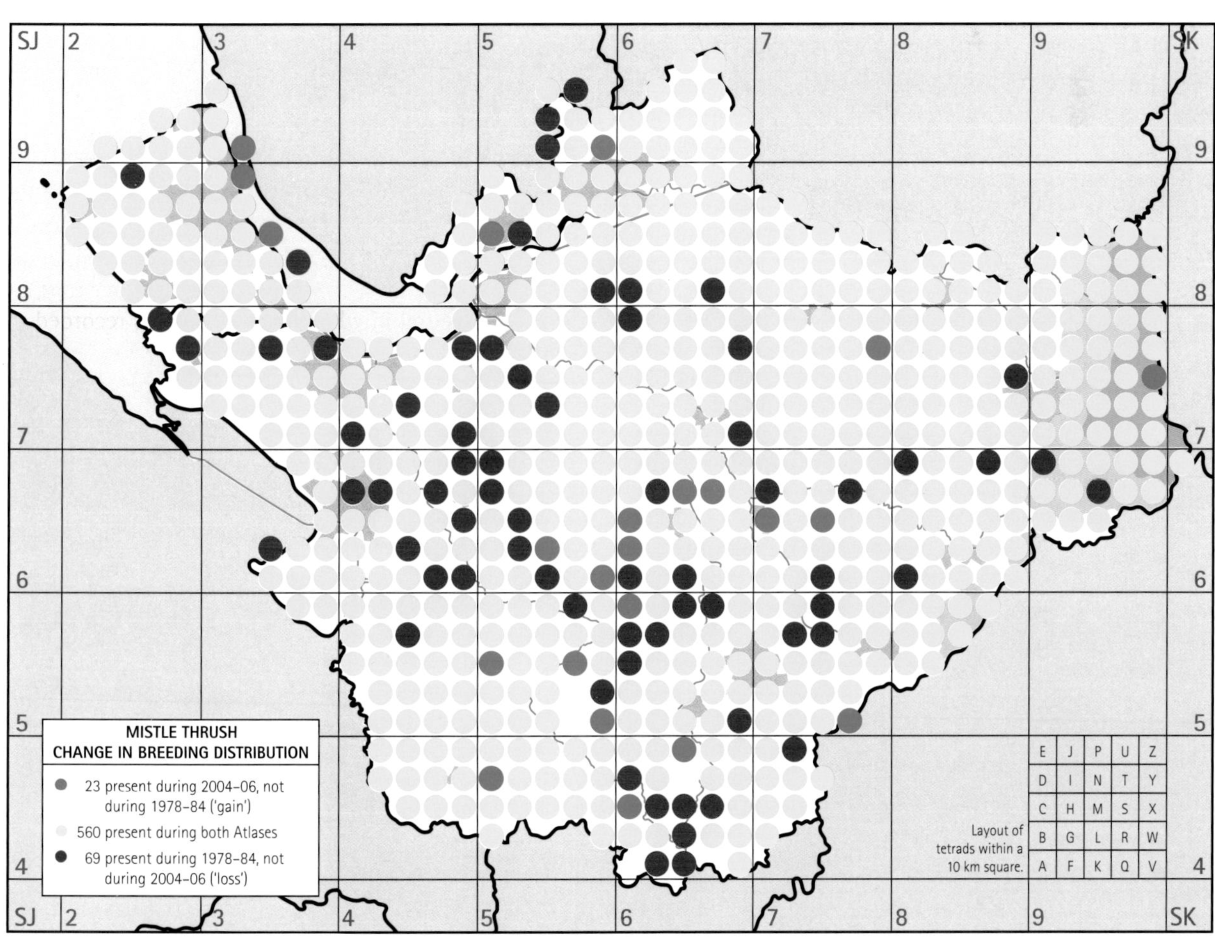
SJ
2
3
4
5
6
7
8
9
SK
9
8
7
6
5
4
MISTLE THRUSH
CHANGE IN BREEDING DISTRIBUTION
23 present during 2004–06, not during 1978–84 ('gain')
560 present during both Atlases
69 present during 1978–84, not during 2004–06 ('loss')
E J P U Z
D I N T Y
C H M S X
B G L R W
A F K Q V
Layout of tetrads within a 10 km square.

Mistle Thrushes are somewhat more widespread in winter than in the breeding season, being found in 606 tetrads, an increase of 23. Adult birds are highly sedentary but first-year birds may disperse short distances (*Migration Atlas*), and it is presumably the young birds who move to fill in many of the gaps in rural Cheshire. None was found on Hilbre during this Atlas. Although it is widely distributed, the density of Mistle Thrushes is low. After the early autumn gatherings break up, this species is seldom found in large flocks. The vast majority of submitted counts were of one or two birds, according with the tendency of adults to maintain territories in winter. There were only 15 counts in double figures, with a maximum of 40 at Toft (SJ77N) counted by Pete Hall.

The habitat records for this Atlas show that, compared to the breeding season, fewer Mistle Thrushes were in woodland (which is primarily used for nesting rather than for feeding) and human sites, and more were located in open farmland. Fieldworkers noted that they often shared their feeding areas with livestock, including sheep on the hillsides, where the thrushes benefit from close-cropped grassland and are able to probe for worms and other soil invertebrates amongst the animals. Studies elsewhere have shown that birds in farmland show a strong preference for feeding on grazed grass fields during winter, especially permanent pastures or long-term leys where soil invertebrate populations have not been affected by cultivation for several years (Wilson *et al.* 1996), and they avoid ungrazed grass and arable crops. In this Atlas, the proportion of Mistle Thrushes using improved grassland was more than double that of Blackbirds or Song Thrushes, but in winter Mistle Thrushes have to compete with the flocks of Fieldfares and Redwings, which are even more likely to favour the grazed pastures. Perhaps it is this rivalry that has led to Mistle Thrushes defending some winter food supplies.

Most adult birds, either as individuals or, more often, as pairs, choose a bush covered with berries, usually holly, mistletoe or haw, occasionally yew or ivy, and keep away all other birds, of every species. They start in October and preserve this supply for their own future needs, seldom eating from their defended bush until late in the winter, and perhaps not even then; some bushes keep their fruit into the breeding season, when the Mistle Thrushes feed them to their chicks. A holly bush that still has its fruit at Christmas, certainly in a hard winter, is almost certainly being defended by Mistle Thrushes (Snow & Snow 1988), and their liking for mistletoe must have been known for centuries, as it led to the species' English name and the scientific name, from *viscum album*. The defence of their chosen bush may break down in the face of concerted attacks by a flock of birds, perhaps in hard weather by Fieldfares. The ornamental rowan trees in Runcorn town centre (SJ58B) visited by Waxwings in January 2005 had been the property of a pair of Mistle Thrushes, but they were no match for the hordes of invading Waxwings, which largely ignored the thrushes' attempts to keep them off. Even Europe's largest thrush had to admit defeat.

RICHARD STEEL

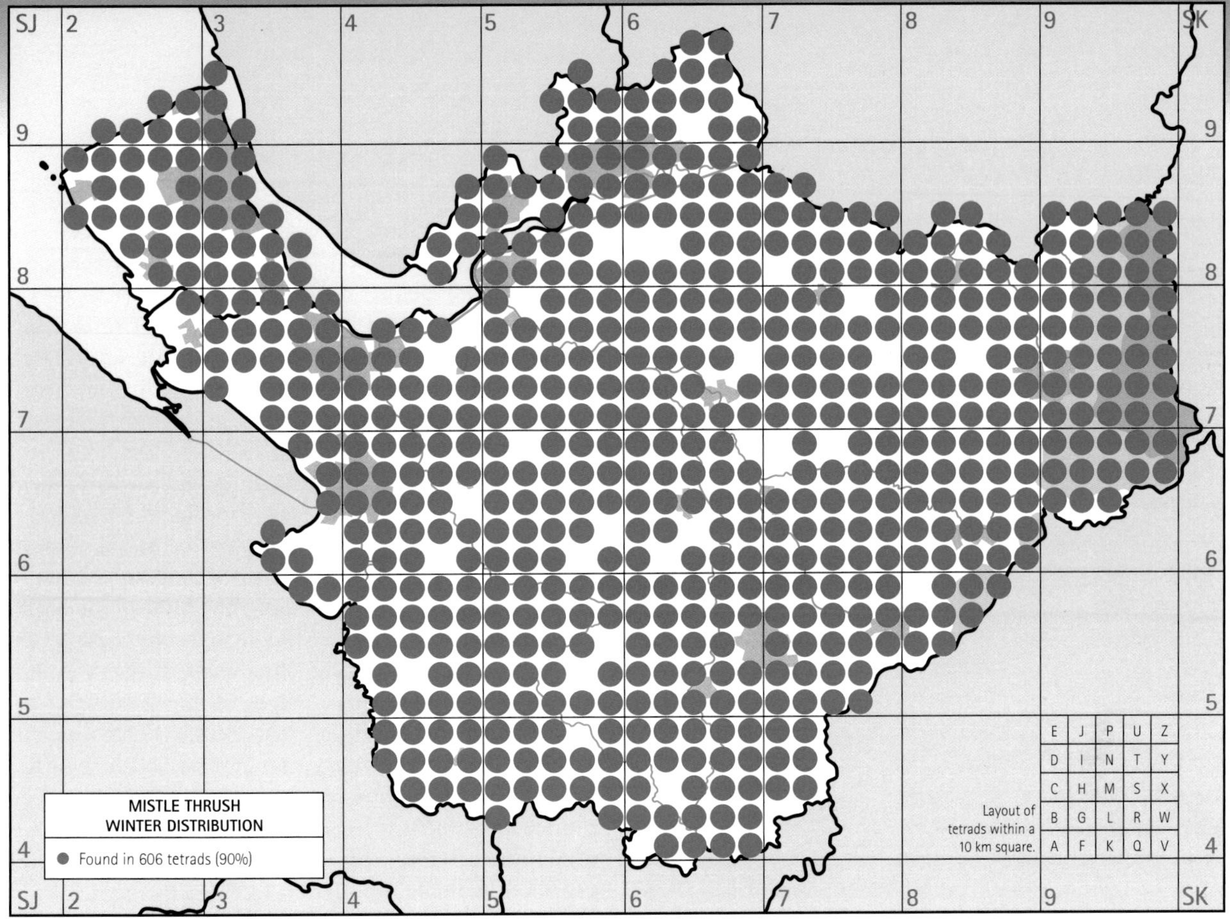
MISTLE THRUSH
WINTER DISTRIBUTION
Found in 606 tetrads (90%)
Layout of tetrads within a 10 km square.
SJ
SK

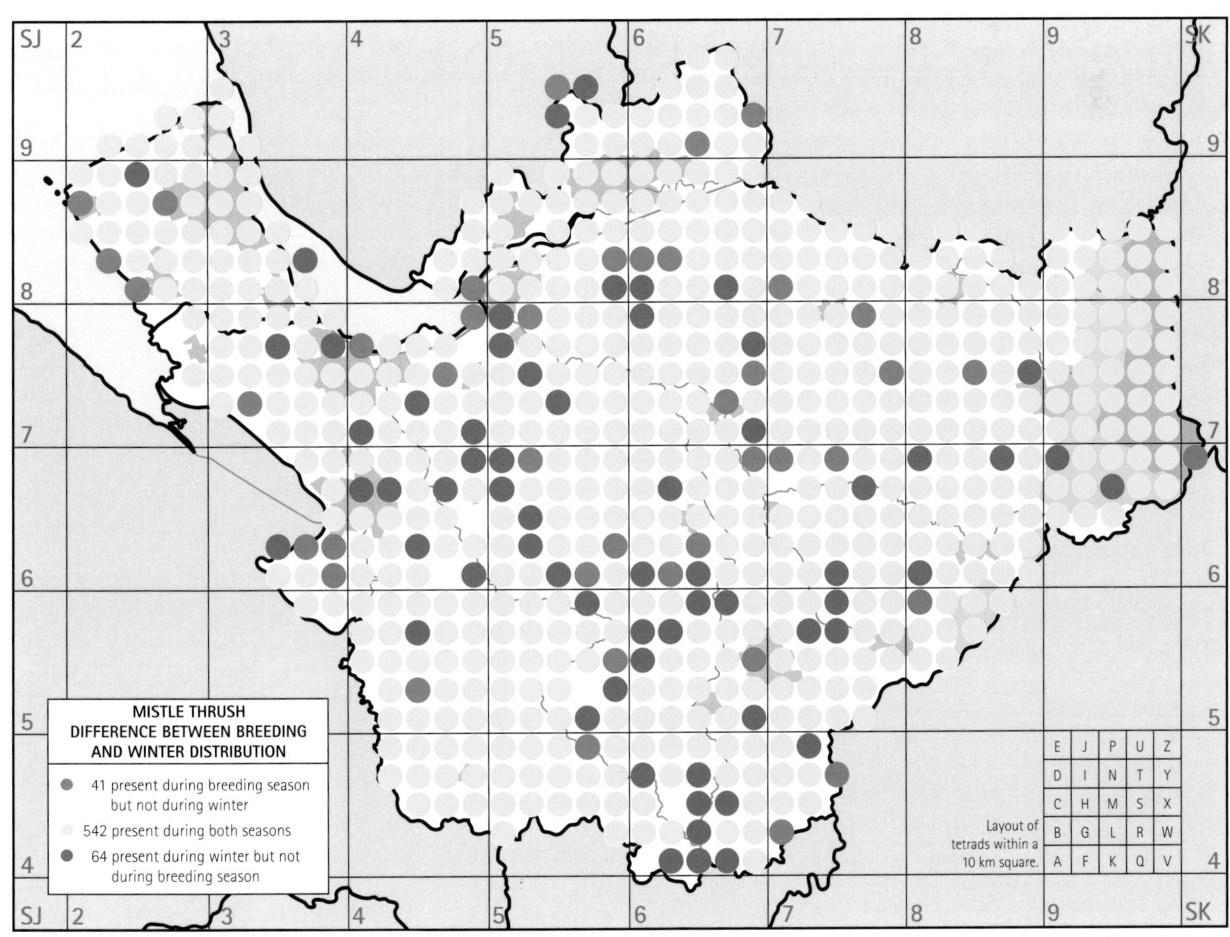
MISTLE THRUSH
DIFFERENCE BETWEEN BREEDING AND WINTER DISTRIBUTION
41 present during breeding season but not during winter
542 present during both seasons
64 present during winter but not during breeding season
Layout of tetrads within a 10 km square.
SJ
SK

Grasshopper Warbler

Locustella naevia

This species is not often seen, spending most of its time skulking in the undergrowth, most records coming from the males' 'reeling' song. Grasshopper Warblers were found in 83 tetrads in this survey, down from 114 in the *First Atlas*. Their strongholds remain as they were twenty years ago: the north and west fringes of Wirral, the Chester area and the Mersey valley. Although they can turn up anywhere, there are now fewer records away from their favoured areas. About half of the 42 new tetrads were adjoining their core areas, whilst most of the 72 'losses' are scattered across the county. Notably, in the *First Atlas* there were 10 tetrads with records around Sandbach/Congleton, where there were none in this survey.

It was not surprising that only 10 tetrads furnished proof of breeding. Nests are difficult to find, built just off the ground in a patch of rough grass or nettles, but they are often surprisingly open when they are located. Grasshopper Warblers seldom use their alarm call—a harsh 'tack'—and often do not perch on their way to and from the nest, the adults carrying small grubs and caterpillars flying fast and low, and often only seen out of the corner of an eye, then creeping the last few metres through the undergrowth to reach the nest. They can, however, be quite obvious when carrying faecal sacs away from their nestlings. I had an unusual experience on 2 and 3 June 2005 at Frodsham when a pair of Grasshopper Warblers was still carrying faecal sacs from chicks that had left the nest. Chicks often scatter from the nest before they can fly and spend several days crawling around in the undergrowth. Grasshopper Warblers in the county start breeding in late April, often having two broods, so evidence of breeding presence can be obtained throughout their extended season, sometimes into early August.

Most of the Atlas records (58 tetrads) were of song. Some of these could have been from birds on passage, and the map might overstate the species' status; but on the other hand, their most sustained singing is usually around dawn and dusk, and sometimes during the night, so some birds might have been missed unless observers were in the right part of the tetrad early in the morning. Although they are often thought of as a bird of damp areas, Grasshopper Warblers will occupy a wide range of habitats, from the lowest to the highest altitudes of the county. The 100 habitat records submitted in this survey comprised as many as 26 different codes. Forty-two of the records were in the category C (semi-natural grassland/marsh), and the top five codes were C7 (reed swamp); C5 (other dry grassland); B1 (regenerating natural or semi-natural woodland); E2 (unimproved grassland); and C6 (water-meadow/grazing marsh).

This species is not well covered by any of the standard BTO surveys, but several pieces of evidence point to a substantial drop in population since the 1960s (Riddiford 1983) and Grasshopper Warbler is now on the Red List of species of conservation concern. They winter in West Africa just south of the Sahara and have also probably suffered from the Sahelian droughts. Habitat changes in Britain—drainage of swampy areas; maturation of scrub; 'tidier' agriculture—will all have reduced their available breeding sites. However, the species has high reproductive potential, as shown by analysis of nest record data (Glue 1990), so, where the habitat is right, they can flourish. Grasshopper Warblers can occur at high densities in areas of suitable habitat, as shown by the regular presence during this survey period of three or four pairs in 2.5 ha at Oxmoor Local Nature Reserve, Runcorn. In 1994 Mike Smith found five pairs in an area of 6 km^2 along the Wirral Way between Heswall and Caldy; two of the pairs had second broods, and young fledged from all seven nests. Their variability, or the variability in their detection, is evinced by the Woolston warbler census figures of 1, 7 and 10 singing males in the three years of this Atlas. Assuming just one pair for each tetrad with possible breeding, and two or three pairs where breeding was probable or confirmed, the current population in Cheshire and Wirral is likely to be in the region of 110–140 pairs, about the same as the estimate twenty years ago. This is around 1% of the English figure.

Sponsored by Jill Thornley

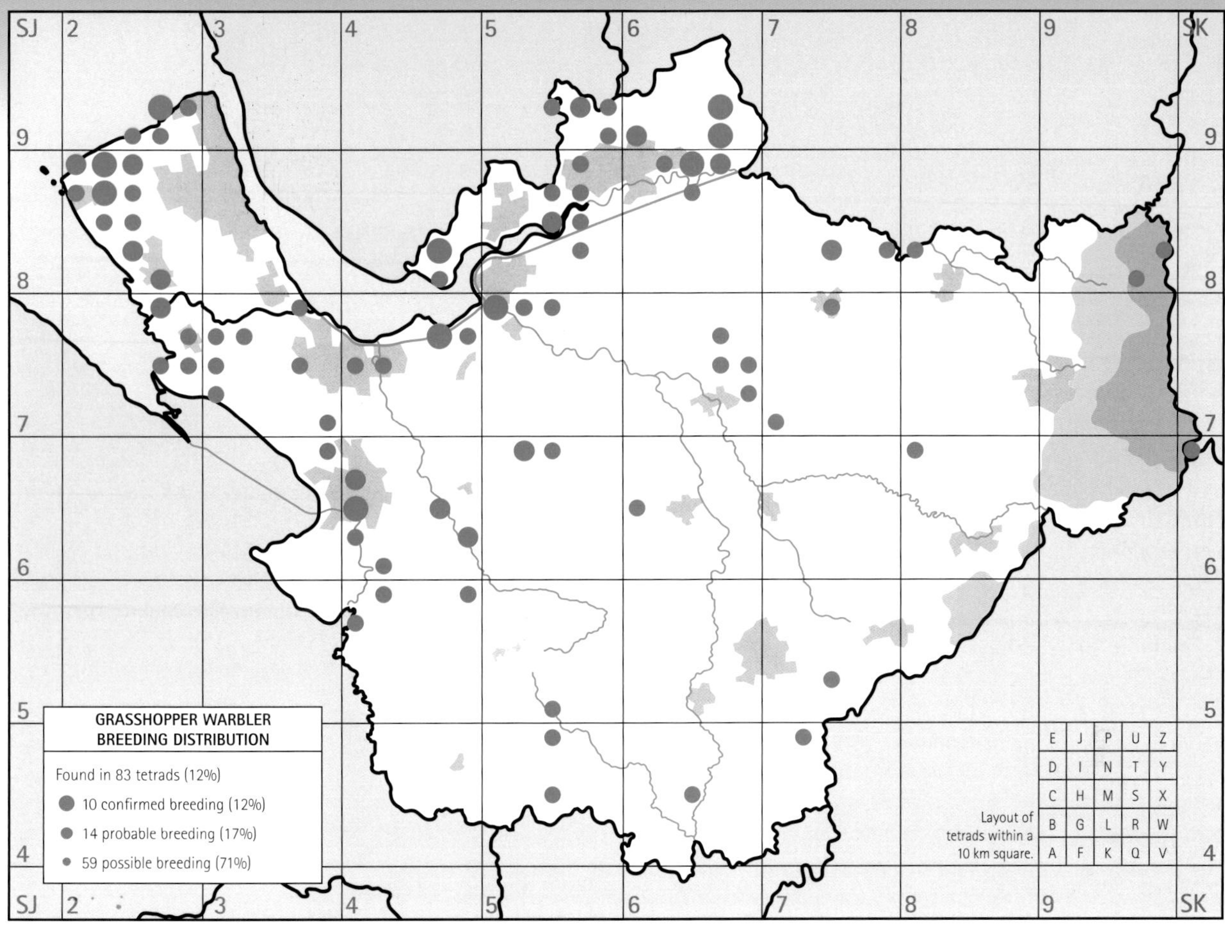
GRASSHOPPER WARBLER
BREEDING DISTRIBUTION
Found in 83 tetrads (12%)
10 confirmed breeding (12%)
14 probable breeding (17%)
59 possible breeding (71%)
Layout of tetrads within a 10 km square.
SJ
SK

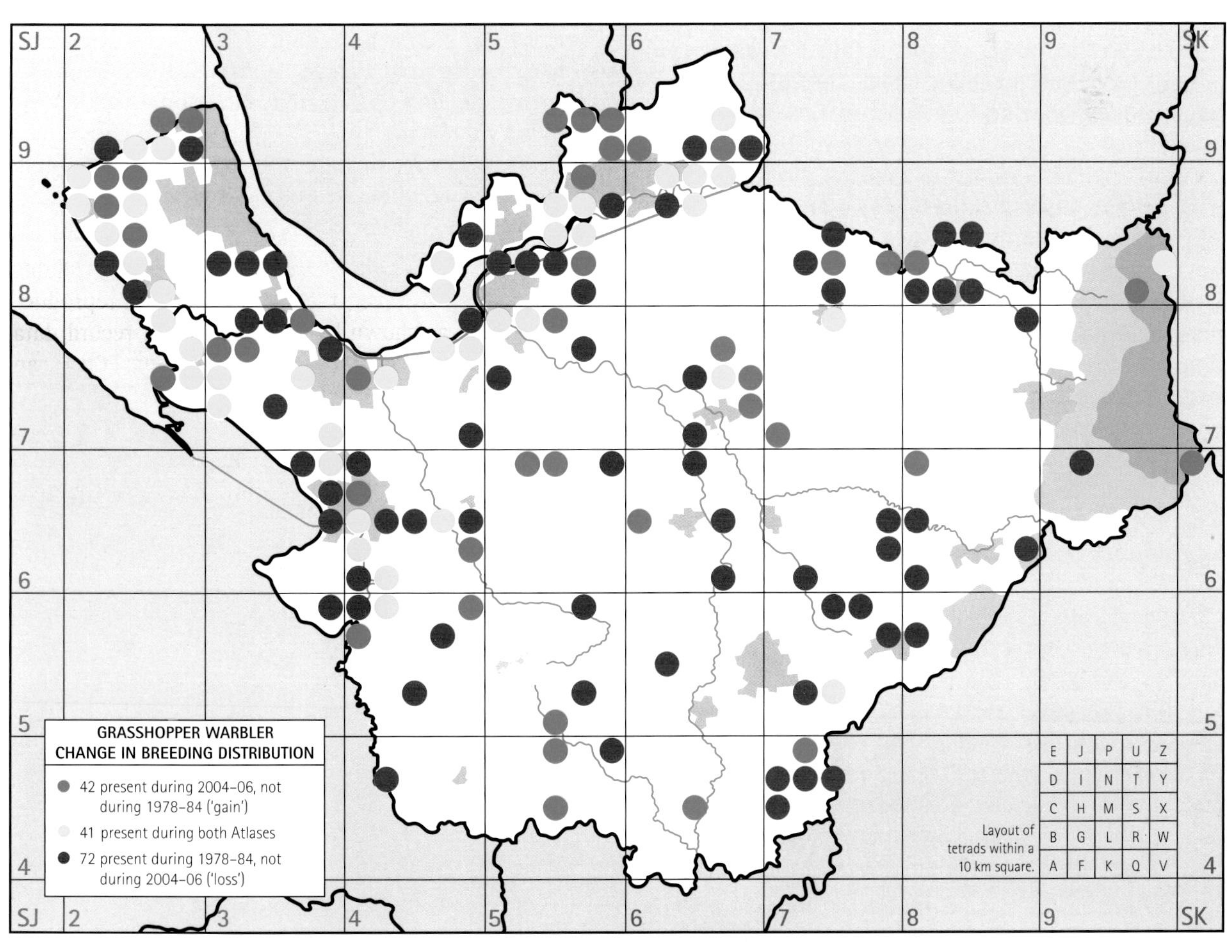
GRASSHOPPER WARBLER
CHANGE IN BREEDING DISTRIBUTION
42 present during 2004–06, not during 1978–84 ('gain')
41 present during both Atlases
72 present during 1978–84, not during 2004–06 ('loss')
Layout of tetrads within a 10 km square.
SJ
SK

Sedge Warbler

Acrocephalus schoenobaenus

Sedge Warblers have slightly increased their range in the county, being found in 210 tetrads, up from 199 in *First Atlas*, but this general picture includes 96 gains and 85 losses. The map shows that they have quite a clustered distribution, with many breeding sites being 5–10 km from the next nearest birds. The newly occupied tetrads are mainly around their existing strongholds: the north Wirral, a few coastal spots around the south Wirral, a crescent across the north of Cheshire from south of Chester to Warrington, a range of sites across the south of the county from Malpas to Sandbach, and locations around Northwich. There was no proven breeding in any tetrad above 100 m in altitude.

This is one of the classic species that migrates to spend the winter in the Sahel. Detailed analysis shows the survival of adult birds closely correlated with the annual West African rainfall, varying from around 50% in the wettest years to as little as 4% in the 1983 drought; this is the main factor driving year-to-year variation in population size (Peach *et al.* 1991). As with several of our trans-Saharan migrants, the national population was at its lowest at the end of our *First Atlas* period, following the failure of the African rains in autumn 1983, but their numbers have risen since, with some fluctuations, and the index in 2004 was 53% higher than in 1984.

The BTO BBS analysis shows that the breeding population of Cheshire and Wirral in 2004–05 was 3,950 birds (with very wide confidence limits from zero to 9,420), corresponding to an average of about 36 birds per tetrad with confirmed or probable breeding, or 19 birds per tetrad in which the species was recorded. Sedge Warblers can breed at high densities at favoured sites. On 15 May 1999, surveyors recorded 256 singing males in the Woolston warbler count, an average of one bird per hectare across the entire site. Changes in vegetation, especially the spread of giant hogweed *Heracleum mantegazzianum* and goose-grass (cleavers) *Galium aparine*, have since made much of the site less attractive to Sedge Warblers, but during this Atlas survey there was an average of 100 males singing there each year. Other sites reported during this period with high totals include Inner Marsh Farm, Frodsham Marsh and Moore/Gatewarth.

Almost half of the Atlas records (99) were of birds singing only, and many observers added comments such as 'moved on', 'did not stay' and 'found on early visit only'. However, most male Sedge Warblers stop, or greatly reduce, their singing soon after pairing, and it is difficult to know whether these S records truly indicate birds that were merely on passage or if they should point to higher levels of breeding status. The females build a nest on or near the ground, with the typical site in rank vegetation often near water, although at the species' stronghold at Woolston most of the nests found have been in nettles and often hundreds of metres away from water. The normal clutch is five eggs, chicks hatching around the beginning of June, with occasional second broods into August. Birds carrying food are very obvious, and one-quarter of the total (52 tetrads) provided FY records.

RICHARD STEEL

Sedge Warblers can use a wide variety of habitats, and records were submitted for this survey with as many as 36 different habitat codes. As many as 45% of the tetrad records were accompanied by a G habitat code (freshwater body) and the top five codes, accounting for more than 60% of the records, were C7 (reed swamp), B1 (regenerating natural or semi-natural woodland), G8 (ditch with water, less than 2 m wide), G3 (lake/unlined reservoir) and C6 (water-meadow/grazing marsh).

Sponsored by Syngenta CTL

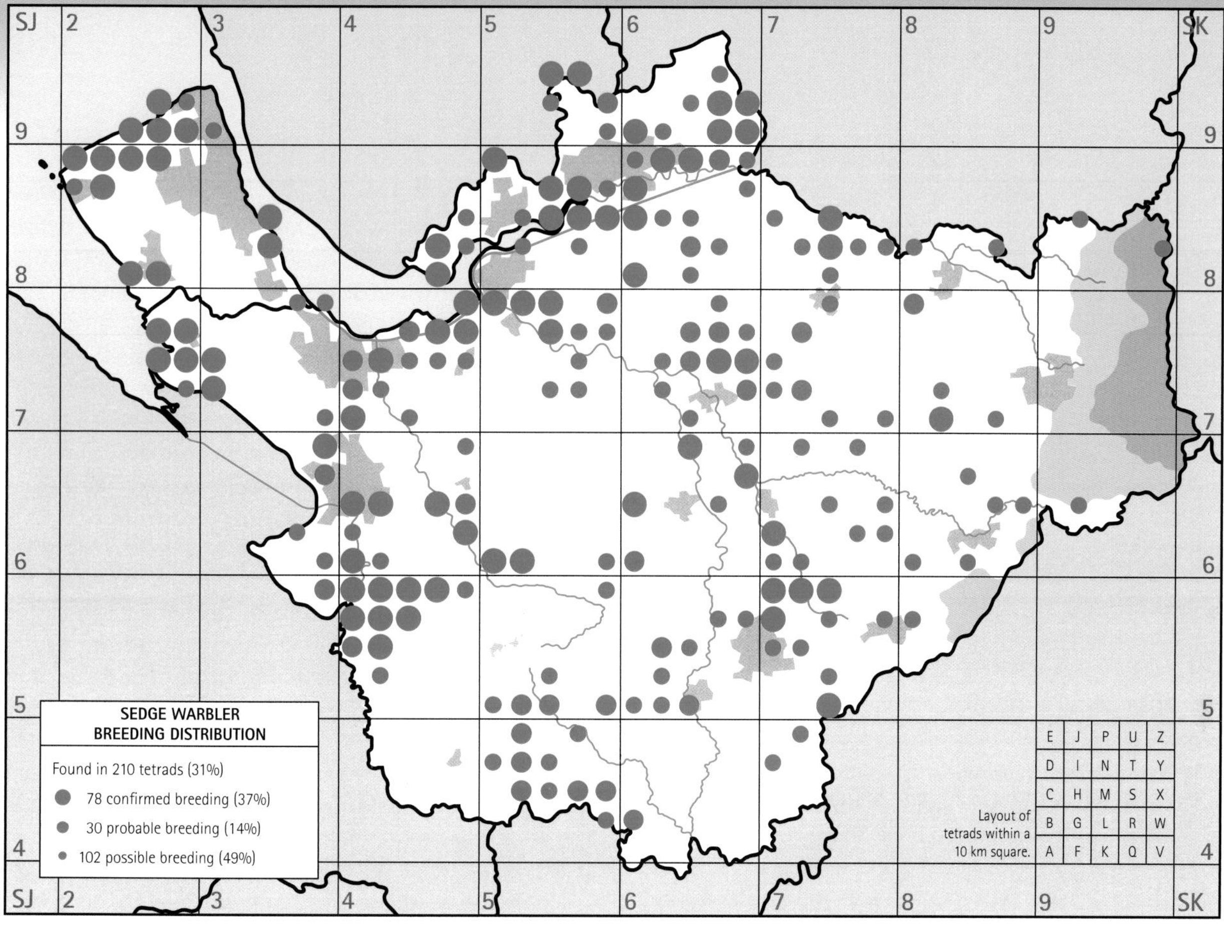
SEDGE WARBLER
BREEDING DISTRIBUTION
Found in 210 tetrads (31%)
78 confirmed breeding (37%)
30 probable breeding (14%)
102 possible breeding (49%)
Layout of tetrads within a 10 km square.
E J P U Z
D I N T Y
C H M S X
B G L R W
A F K Q V
SJ
SK

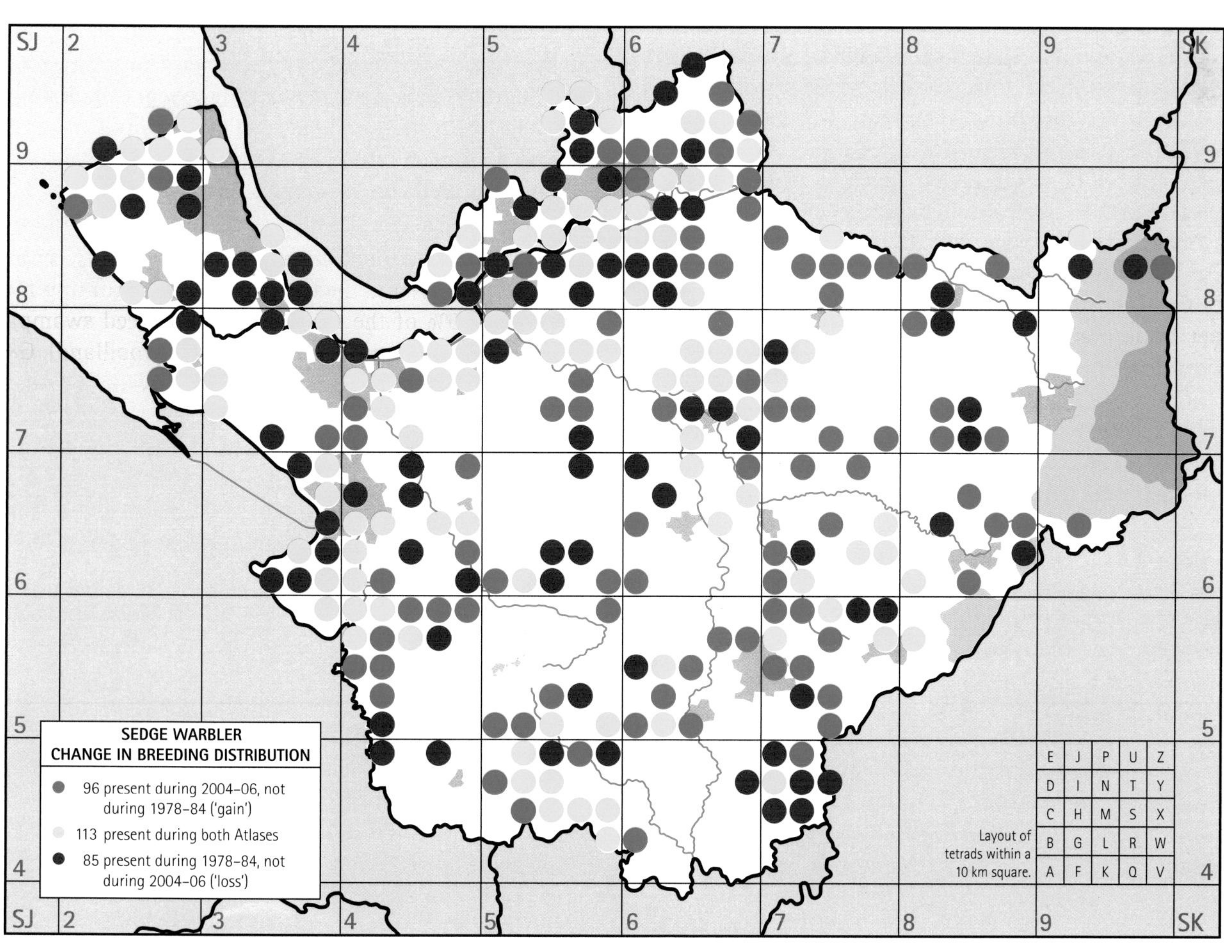
SEDGE WARBLER
CHANGE IN BREEDING DISTRIBUTION
96 present during 2004–06, not during 1978–84 ('gain')
113 present during both Atlases
85 present during 1978–84, not during 2004–06 ('loss')
Layout of tetrads within a 10 km square.
E J P U Z
D I N T Y
C H M S X
B G L R W
A F K Q V
SJ
SK

Reed Warbler

Acrocephalus scirpaceus

STEVE ROUND

This species is appropriately named, for the breeding map and breeding habits of the Reed Warbler are defined by common reed *Phragmites australis*. They seldom breed away from *phragmites* although birds occasionally spill over to use similar plants such as reed canary-grass *Phalaris arundinacea* and reed sweet-grass *Glyceria maxima*. Although they are almost exclusively tied to reed-beds for their nests, they find much of their food in surrounding bushy vegetation. Their conservation should be assured because there are national and local BAPs on the reed-bed habitat; their emphasis, however, is on maintaining or creating reed-beds with a large area: whilst this meets the habitat requirement of other species such as Bittern, Marsh Harrier and Bearded Tit, because Reed Warblers spend so much of their time outside the reed-bed, the perimeter, rather than the area, is the key to conserving high populations of this species. Many reed-filled ditches or the edges of ponds hold one or two pairs, and several observers commented that tiny areas of reeds could be occupied. It was not surprising that 94% of the submitted habitat records were categories C (semi-natural grassland/marsh), almost all of them C7 (reed swamp), or G (fresh water) or H3 (estuarine).

Cheshire used to be at, or near, the north-western limit of Reed Warbler distribution in Britain, but the species is continuing to spread farther north-west (Calvert 2005). It has increased its range in the county, now present in 137 tetrads, up from 101 in the *First Atlas*. Their stronghold is the Mersey valley, from Frodsham Marsh to Woolston, but they can be found anywhere with suitable habitat. They have increased greatly in Wirral, and remain absent from the east of Cheshire.

A Reed Warbler's nest is a work of art, taking a week or more to build from reed leaves and fronds, and lined with reed flowers. Chicks leave the nest before they can fly, then spend about a week crawling through the undergrowth whilst being fed by their parents. This behaviour makes them one of the easiest species in which to prove breeding. Adults are noisy, with obvious alarm calls, and are easy to see perched on the reeds or an adjacent bush with their beaks stuffed with insects. It is a surprise that only just over half of tetrads holding the species furnished proof of breeding. It could be that some males sing for a while, then move on, but it is perhaps somewhat more likely that the late breeding season of this species meant that it did not coincide with the normal period for Atlas fieldwork. This is the latest of the common warblers to arrive and to breed, with adults trickling in during May and into June, and an extended breeding season lasting from early May well into August. Malcolm Calvert has put in more time studying this species than almost anyone in Britain, and finds that about one in five Reed Warblers at Rostherne has a second brood, often dismantling the first nest to reuse the materials in building a second (Calvert 2005).

In more south-easterly parts of Britain, the Reed Warbler is a common host for Cuckoos, but this had only been recorded twice in Cheshire before 1988, when nine nests at Rostherne and three at Woolston were cuckolded that year (Calvert 1988, Smith & Norman 1988). Cuckoos were then recorded from at least four Cheshire Reed Warbler sites over the next few years, including annually at Rostherne 1988–93 and at Woolston until 1995 and again in 1998, but Cuckoo parasitism in the county now seems to have ceased.

As with most species with a clumped distribution, normal census methods do not work, so there are no indices of national or local population. Reed Warblers seem to have been little affected by the expansion of the Sahara and the vagaries of African rainfall, perhaps because they appear to winter farther south beyond the Sahel. There is no doubt that they have increased substantially in Cheshire and Wirral. Although many tetrads hold only one or two pairs, Reed Warblers are present at very high densities at favoured sites. The Rostherne Mere population doubled from around 40 during our *First Atlas* to 80 pairs in 2004. At Woolston the warbler census recorded about 20 singing males in the early 1980s and a total of 150 in 2006; although earlier arrival dates have brought more males in by the mid-May date of this annual survey, *phragmites* has increased enormously at the site. The 2004 *CWBR* reported at least 551 singing males and the breeding population of Cheshire and Wirral must be at least double the *First Atlas* estimate of 300 pairs, and is perhaps as high as 750 or more.

Sponsored by Malcolm Calvert

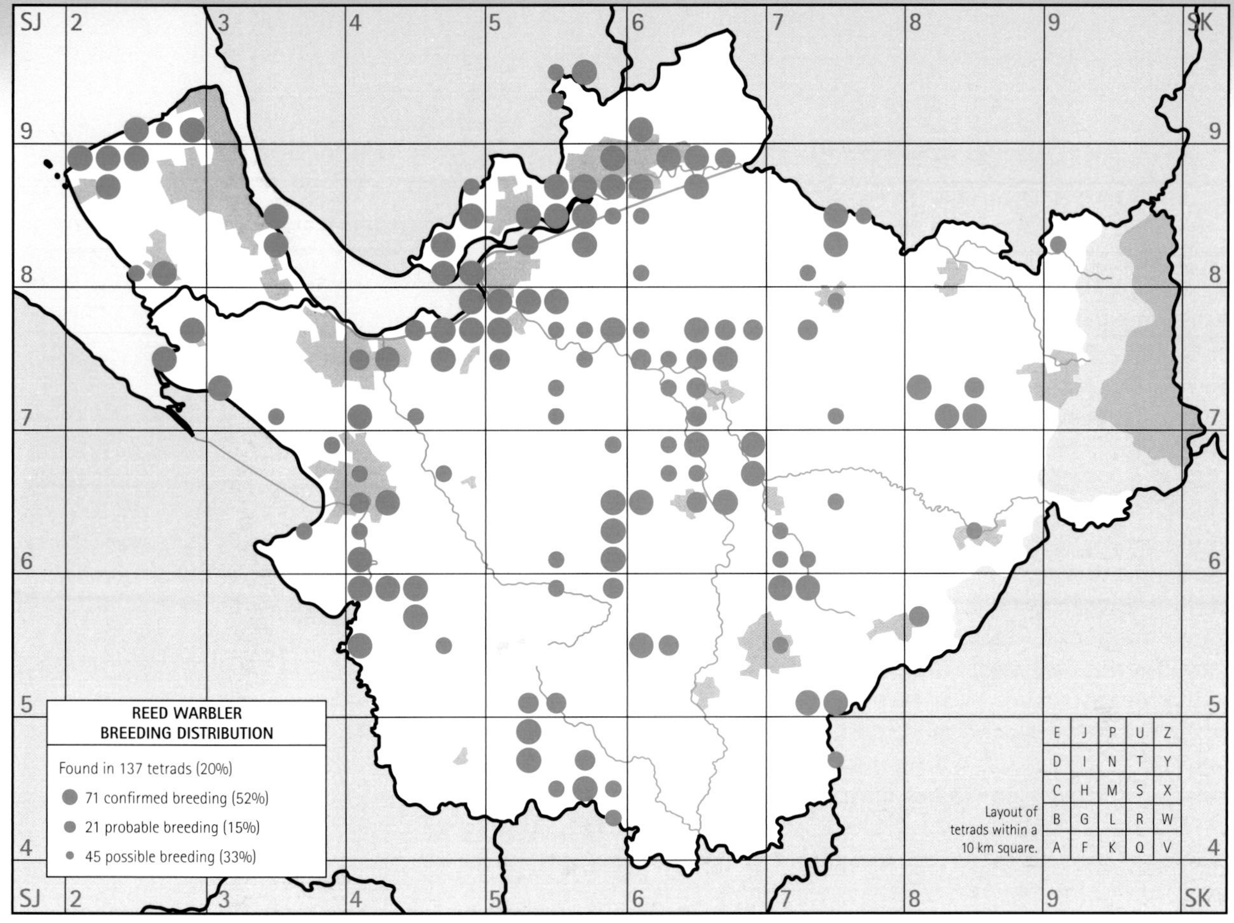
REED WARBLER
BREEDING DISTRIBUTION
Found in 137 tetrads (20%)
71 confirmed breeding (52%)
21 probable breeding (15%)
45 possible breeding (33%)
Layout of tetrads within a 10 km square.
SJ
SK

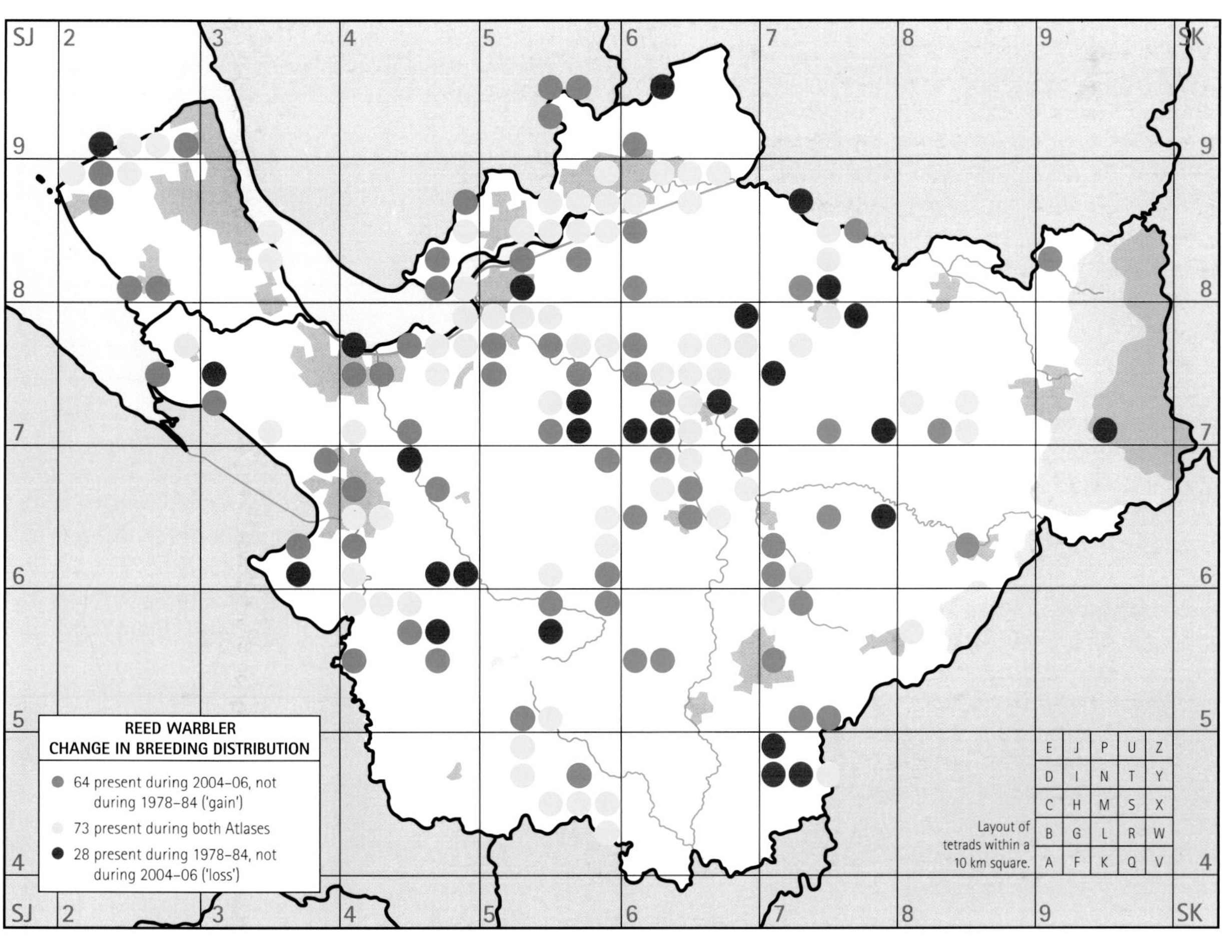
REED WARBLER
CHANGE IN BREEDING DISTRIBUTION
64 present during 2004–06, not during 1978–84 ('gain')
73 present during both Atlases
28 present during 1978–84, not during 2004–06 ('loss')
Layout of tetrads within a 10 km square.
SJ
SK

Blackcap

Sylvia atricapilla

A loud burst of song from a Blackcap deep in the undergrowth is usually the first sign that spring is really here. This is overwhelmingly the woodland *Sylvia*. Habitat codes submitted for this survey showed 48% in woodland, with 22% in scrub, 18% in farmland and 12% in human sites. Blackcaps mainly frequent mature deciduous or mixed woodlands—fewer than 1% of our habitat records are from coniferous woodland (A2)—with a well-developed shrub layer. They are found especially at the woodland edges, perhaps because greater light penetration makes for more luxuriant shrub growth there. When populations are high, as now, some birds spill out into farmland where they occupy overgrown hedgerows, especially if they contain some tall trees. They also appear in urban areas, including areas of human habitation and industrial sites, anywhere where there is enough scrubby undergrowth, especially bramble. Blackcaps were almost twice as likely to be recorded in human sites as any other *Sylvia* warbler.

RICHARD STEEL

The 'change' map shows that in the last twenty years Blackcaps have spread to become almost ubiquitous. They have increased along the Mersey valley and spread into the eastern hills and onto the least well-wooded farmland in the south and south-west of Cheshire. They are now missing only from the very edges of the county—the highest hills, north Wirral coast and the Dee and Mersey salt-marshes.

Although the early songs of Blackcap are unmistakeable, once Garden Warblers arrive, usually at least two weeks later, distinguishing the two species can be difficult. They do respond to each others' songs, with Blackcaps dominating Garden Warblers and trying to keep them out of their territories; but this might just be a reaction against any intruder as they also react against Chiffchaffs entering their area.

As well as singing, the male Blackcap quickly builds a number of flimsy 'cocks' nests', showing them to any arriving female until one decides to stay, choosing one of his nests and lining it. They have a short incubation period of around 13 days, with males taking an almost equal share during daylight hours, and chicks leave the nest after about 11 days, before they can fly properly, and crawl around in the undergrowth. The sharp 'tac' alarm calls of the parents often alert observers to their best chance of proving breeding, FY accounting for 60% and RF a further 27% of the confirmed breeding records. Caterpillars and crane-flies (tipulids) make up much of the chicks' diet, with beetles especially for late broods when the former have declined in abundance.

Blackcaps have changed their breeding schedule remarkably, and were laying 15 days earlier in 2004 than 20 years previously. This could be a response to climate change: with a relatively short migratory journey to return to breed here, they are well placed to react to rising temperatures. British breeding birds spend the winter around the Mediterranean, with variable numbers from year to year crossing the Sahara. They used only to have one brood, with second attempts uncommon, but now some Blackcaps have more time to fit them in, giving them the chance of increased productivity and also allowing fieldworkers more extended opportunities to record breeding behaviour.

In the first county bird report (1964) Blackcap was said to 'breed in small numbers', probably a reflection of the bias in reporting and in birdwatching, but an interesting observation nevertheless. The species has increased consistently in abundance since the late 1970s, although the causes remain unknown. In the 20 years between our Atlas periods (1984–2004) the national population index for Blackcap has risen by 75%. The BTO BBS analysis shows that the breeding population of Cheshire and Wirral in 2004–05 was 12,910 birds (8,570–17,260), corresponding to an average of about 36 birds per tetrad with confirmed or probable breeding, or 21 birds per tetrad in which the species was recorded. Territories can be as small as 0.2 ha, depending on the habitat quality, so there is plenty of room for more Blackcaps in the county.

Sponsored by Bernard Machin

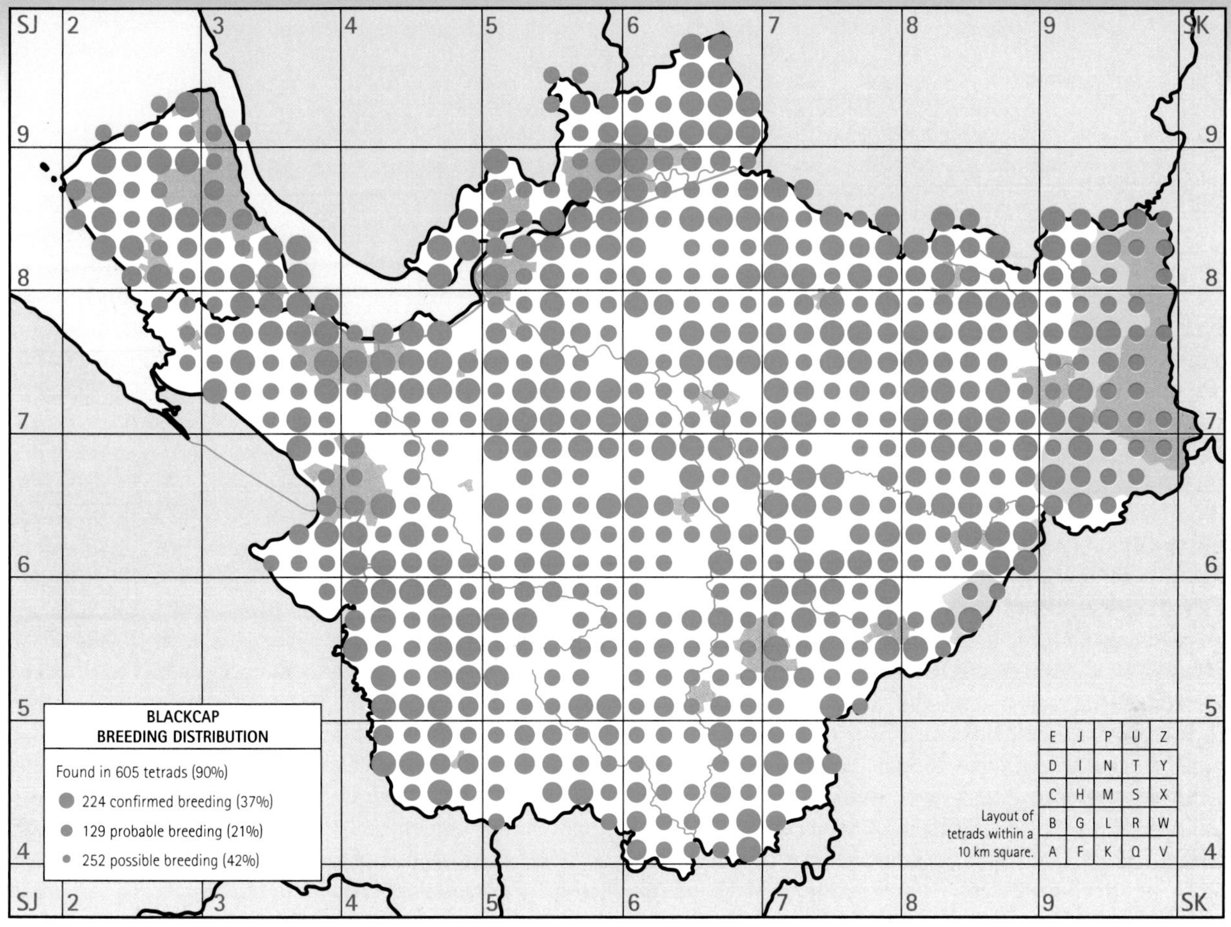
SJ
2
3
4
5
6
7
8
9
SK
BLACKCAP
BREEDING DISTRIBUTION
Found in 605 tetrads (90%)
224 confirmed breeding (37%)
129 probable breeding (21%)
252 possible breeding (42%)
E J P U Z
D I N T Y
C H M S X
B G L R W
A F K Q V
Layout of tetrads within a 10 km square.

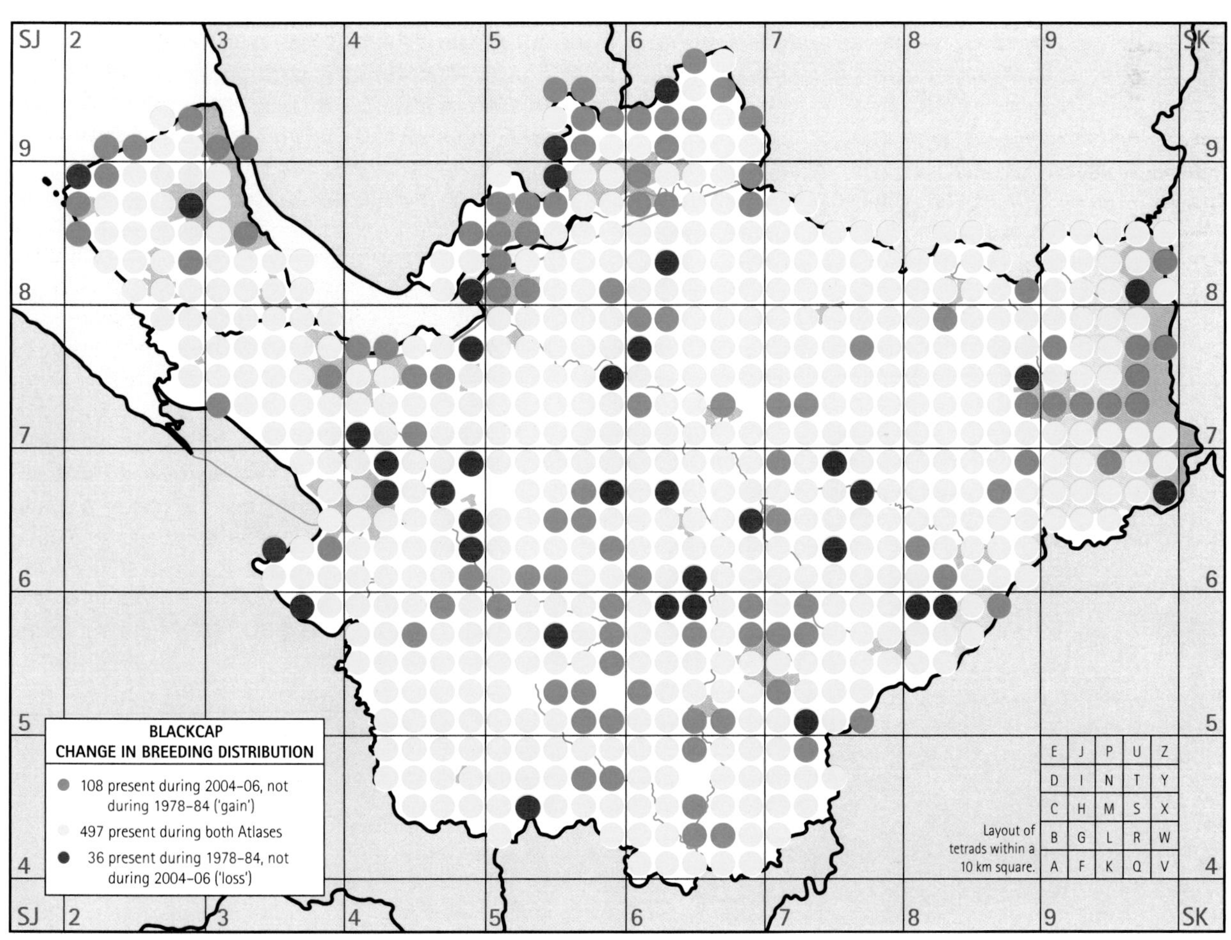
SJ
2
3
4
5
6
7
8
9
SK
BLACKCAP
CHANGE IN BREEDING DISTRIBUTION
108 present during 2004–06, not during 1978–84 ('gain')
497 present during both Atlases
36 present during 1978–84, not during 2004–06 ('loss')
E J P U Z
D I N T Y
C H M S X
B G L R W
A F K Q V
Layout of tetrads within a 10 km square.

The Blackcap's winter presence in 161 tetrads, almost one-quarter of the county, illustrates an amazing story of rapid adaptability. Contrary to the frequent comments, these are not birds that have 'stayed' for the winter. Our wintering Blackcaps are immigrants from breeding areas in southern Germany and Austria which have migrated north-west. When they arrive here, they find a relatively mild climate, and an even warmer urban microclimate; provision of food in gardens also helps them to survive. In spring, they have a shorter return migration than their conspecifics that have wintered in Africa, and so arrive back on their central European breeding grounds earlier and in better condition, thus being able to claim the best territories and breed earlier. It is easy to see how such an advantageous trait can become established and flourish.

The habitat codes show that most birds recorded (69%) were in human (F) habitats, with 15% in broad-leaved or mixed woodland and only 5% in scrub, with 8% in farmland hedgerows. They penetrate even into urban areas, with five records in F1 habitats, 76 in suburban (F2) and 34 in rural areas (F3). Clusters of records around urban areas show up obviously on the map, especially at Macclesfield, Congleton, Wilmslow, Warrington, Northwich, Crewe, Nantwich, Chester and the Wirral towns. Blackcaps do not seem to call in winter, though, and are thus not easy to detect, so a bias towards records from gardens and well-watched places is to be expected.

For a period of seven years in the 1990s, the county bird reports noted the sex of all wintering Blackcaps, totalling significantly more males (255) than females (172). There is, however, no significant difference in the sex ratio of birds ringed in the winter period from 1981 to 2006 by members of Merseyside Ringing Group, so perhaps there are equal numbers present but the males are just more visible to observers. Many of the county's annual bird reports comment that fewer birds are recorded in mild winters. It is not known if this indicates that there are fewer Blackcaps wintering in the county, or if this observation derives from hard weather driving some birds into gardens from where most of the records come.

They take a wide variety of food, including natural foods, especially the most nutritious fruit—berries of *cotoneaster*, holly, honeysuckle and ivy—as well as almost any food provided at a bird table. Many observers comment on their aggression at communal feeders, and they are well able to hold their own with resident British birds. The national survey in 1978/79—a very cold winter—recorded them taking especially bread, fat, apples and peanuts, plus an eclectic range of items of household scraps (Leach 1981).

Coward and Oldham (1900) had 'no evidence that it ever winters in Cheshire', and it seems that Boyd recorded the first, on 23–25 January 1944 near Northwich, closely followed by another on 30 January 1944 at Cotebrook (Boyd 1946). He had never seen one in his Great Budworth parish (Boyd 1951). It is difficult to tell from the literature when the habit of Blackcaps wintering became more common. Bell (1962) states that 'there are no recent Cheshire records' but the first *Cheshire Bird Report* in 1964 gave the species' status as 'winter resident, rare' and recorded three 'winter' birds during that year (two in early November), without any particular comment.

The chart summarizes records each winter, taken from the annual county bird reports. There are some problems in interpretation, not least because some years' reports jumble the early- and late-winter records. It is always difficult to adjudge the status of late-staying or early-arriving summer migrants, and many records are published without dates. From 1964, birds in November and March were counted as 'winter', but from 1975 onwards November birds were declared to be late migrants. In recent years, with an increased population of birds and birdwatchers, and much extended dates for spring and autumn migration, there is no clear division between breeding or passage birds and those wintering

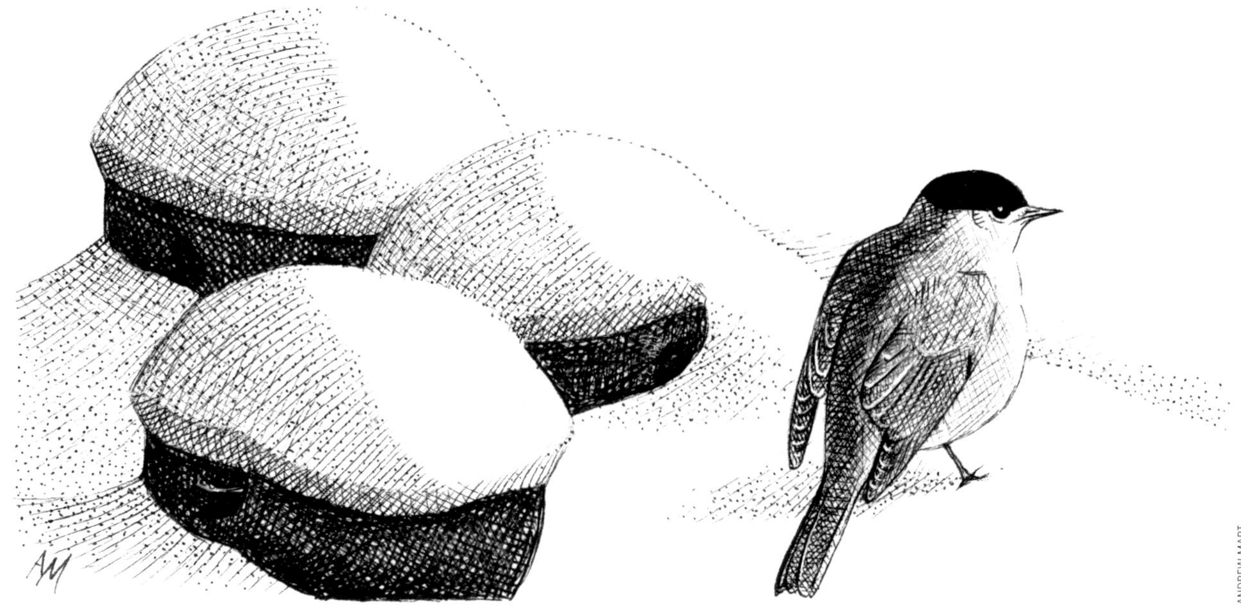

ANDREW MART

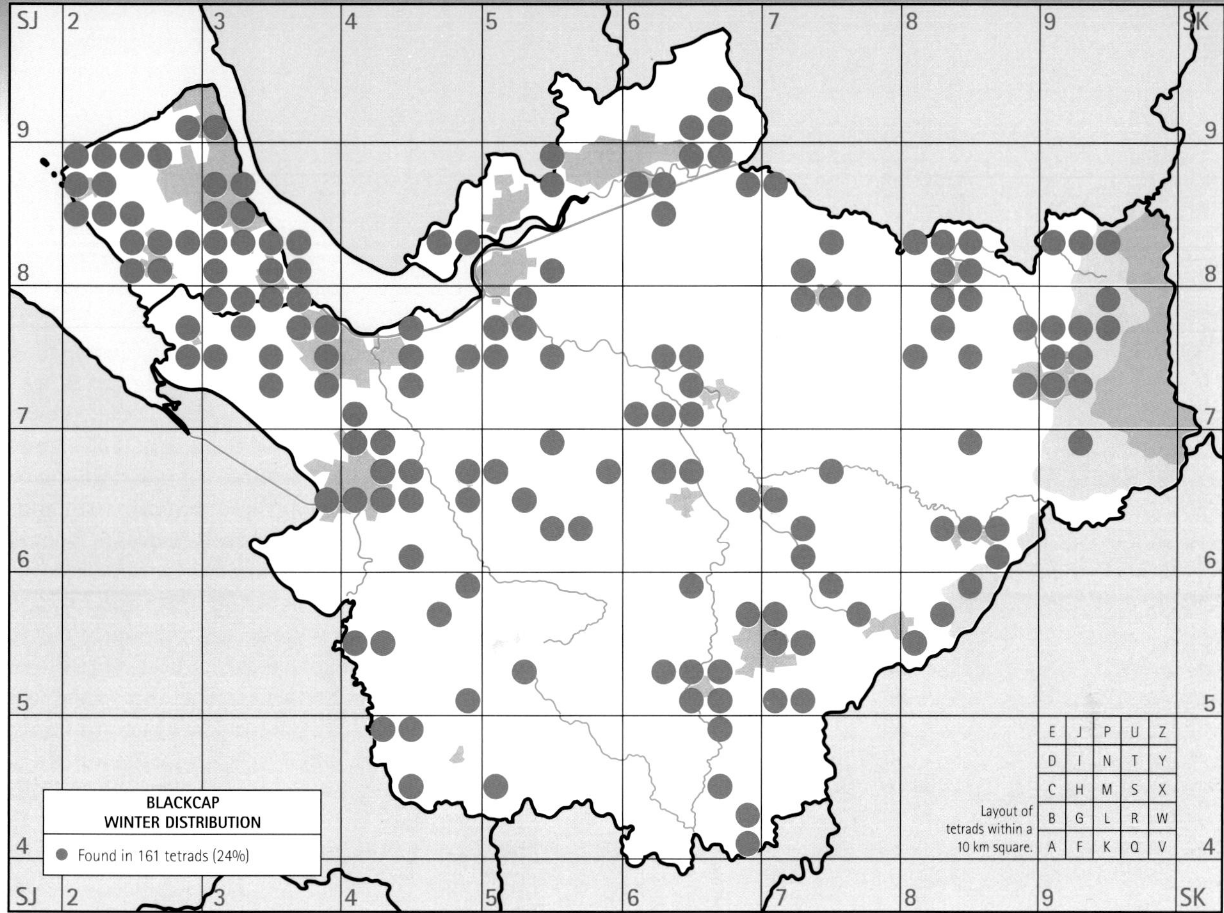

here. With all of those caveats, the chart attempts to count only birds within our defined winter period (16 November to end of February).

Annual records started in 1966/67, but stayed in single figures each winter until 1974/75. The spike in 1978/79, caused by a national survey of the species (Leach 1981), suggested that casual reporting underestimated their numbers by about a factor of two. From then numbers rose gradually through the 1980s, but more or less reached a plateau from 1992/93 onwards, averaging about 60 birds recorded per winter, although with large year-to-year fluctuations. This Atlas has clearly stimulated a higher level of recording, and the likely total of birds each winter in the county is certainly in three figures.

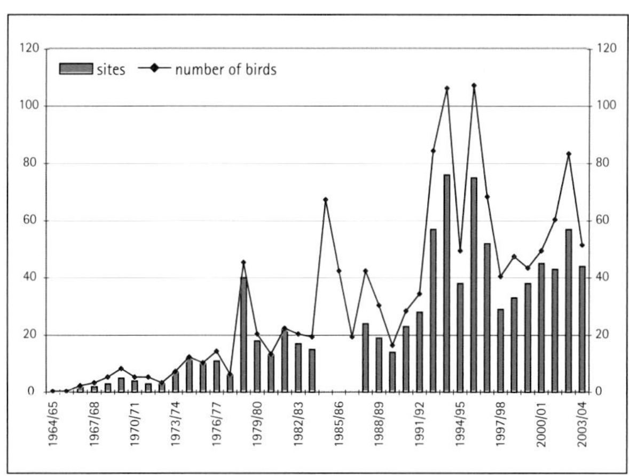

Blackcap wintering numbers.

Garden Warbler

Sylvia borin

RAY SCALLY

The relationship of Garden Warbler to Blackcap is similar to that of Willow Warbler to Chiffchaff; in each pairing, the former is a long-distance migrant, breeding here in scrub habitats and woodland edges while the latter is a shorter-distance migrant, breeding in mature woodlands. Their fortunes are aligned as well, with Blackcap and Chiffchaff increasing greatly in the last twenty years whilst Garden and Willow Warblers are in decline.

However, the substantial fall since our *First Atlas*—a net loss of 46 tetrads occupied by Garden Warbler—came as a surprise, as there had been no suggestion, in Cheshire and Wirral annual bird reports, of any change in status. The 'change' map shows a widespread scatter of gains and losses across the county, with no particular pattern.

The *BTO Second Atlas* (1988–91), surveying on a 10 km^2 grid, found Garden Warblers at their highest densities in Wales and southern England, but missing, or present only at low densities, in much of Wirral, north Cheshire, Merseyside, Lancashire and Greater Manchester. This picture can be amplified at a regional level by examining the figures from the tetrad Atlases of nearby counties. The species was reported from 45% of tetrads in our *First Atlas*, and in 38% of tetrads in this survey. Records came from 74% of tetrads in Shropshire (1985–90) and 32% in Lancashire and North Merseyside (1997–2000). Looking in greater detail, there are clear gradations within those counties. In Shropshire, Garden Warblers were found in 58% of the northernmost one-third of the county, nearest to Cheshire, and 82% of the rest. Within Lancashire and North Merseyside, they were recorded in just 25% of the tetrads south of the Ribble, but 43% north of the Ribble, the same figure as in the whole of Cumbria (1997–2001). A clear picture thus emerges of relative scarcity in Cheshire and Wirral, and parts of adjoining counties.

All of this is, of course, a description of the Garden Warbler's distribution but not an explanation for it; neither does it account for the drop in occupied tetrads in the county since the *First Atlas*. There are several factors probably affecting them: habitat loss on the breeding grounds; competition with other species; and climatic changes, at any point in their life cycle. Scrub is in decline as a British habitat, following reduced woodland planting and management, and there are fewer of their favoured young, open woodlands with internal rides (Rackham 2006). This is an inappropriately named species for modern Britain, and only the largest and most overgrown gardens might hold a pair. On top of unfavourable habitat change, Garden Warblers could be losing out to Blackcaps. Blackcaps dominate inter-specific competition, and arrive here increasingly earlier in spring such that—based on the BTO's national figures—their breeding cycle is now almost two weeks ahead of that of Garden Warblers; 20 years ago, there was only about three days' difference. Climate change could also be adversely shifting the synchronicity between Garden Warblers and availability of their favoured food items, as has been demonstrated for several species (Visser & Both 2005). During the breeding season they feed themselves and their young on caterpillars of the smaller moths and butterflies, as well as small beetles, *Diptera*, *Hymenoptera*, *Hemiptera* (including aphids) and spiders (Simms 1985).

They winter in West Africa, ringed British birds especially being found in Ghana. There is no evidence that their population has fluctuated in line with the Sahelian droughts, and Garden Warblers appear to survive the winter well, having one of the lowest annual mortality rates of any migratory passerine. This balances their low productivity: they have the smallest broods of the common species in the *Sylvia* family, with three or four chicks (Mason 1995).

The present national population is somewhat higher than it was during the seven-year period of fieldwork for our *First Atlas*, making the local contraction in distribution more puzzling. The BTO analysis of 2004–05 BBS data puts the breeding population of Cheshire and Wirral as 3,000 birds (with wide confidence limits from zero to 6,070), corresponding to an average of about 39 birds per tetrad with confirmed or probable breeding, or 12 birds per tetrad in which the species was recorded.

Sponsored by John Headon

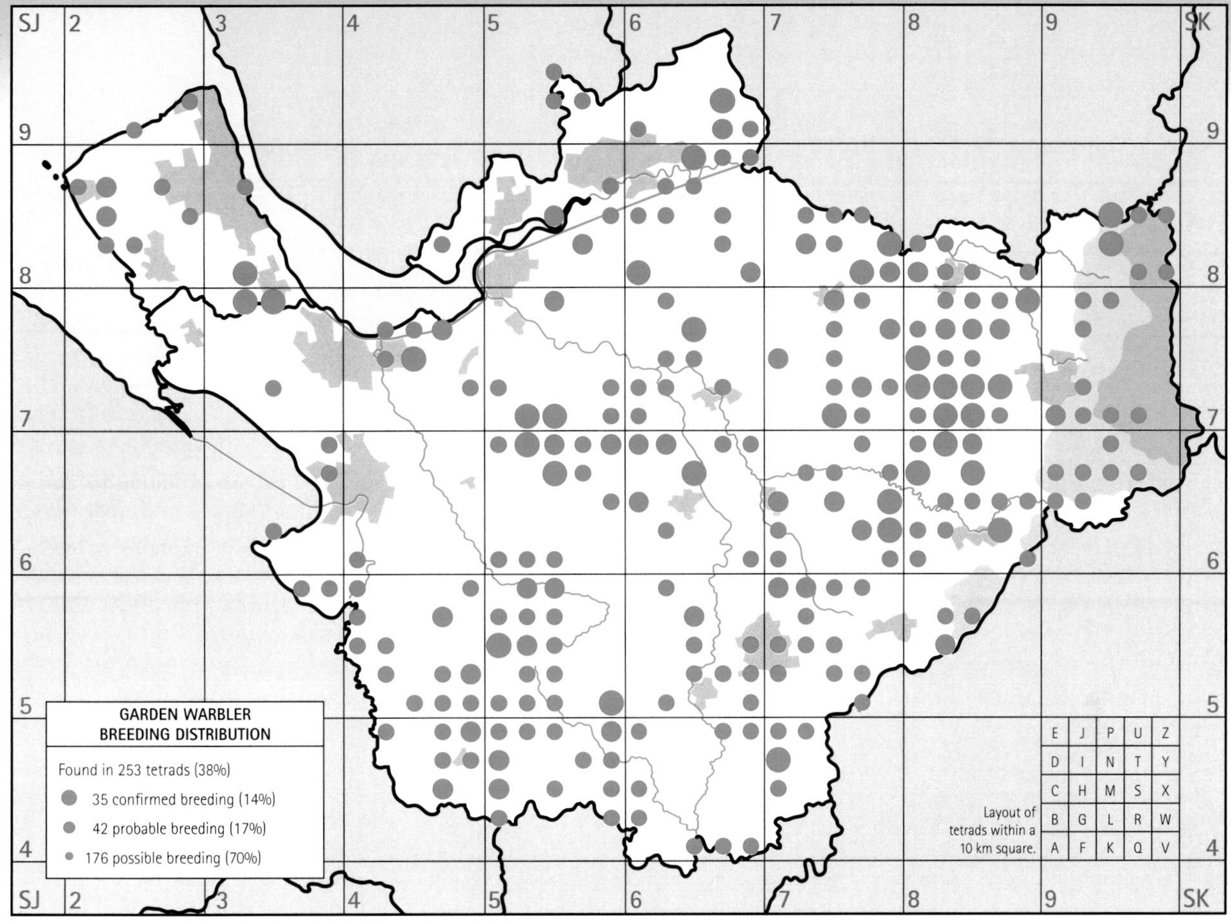
GARDEN WARBLER
BREEDING DISTRIBUTION
Found in 253 tetrads (38%)
35 confirmed breeding (14%)
42 probable breeding (17%)
176 possible breeding (70%)
Layout of tetrads within a 10 km square.
E J P U Z
D I N T Y
C H M S X
B G L R W
A F K Q V
SJ
SK
2
3
4
5
6
7
8
9

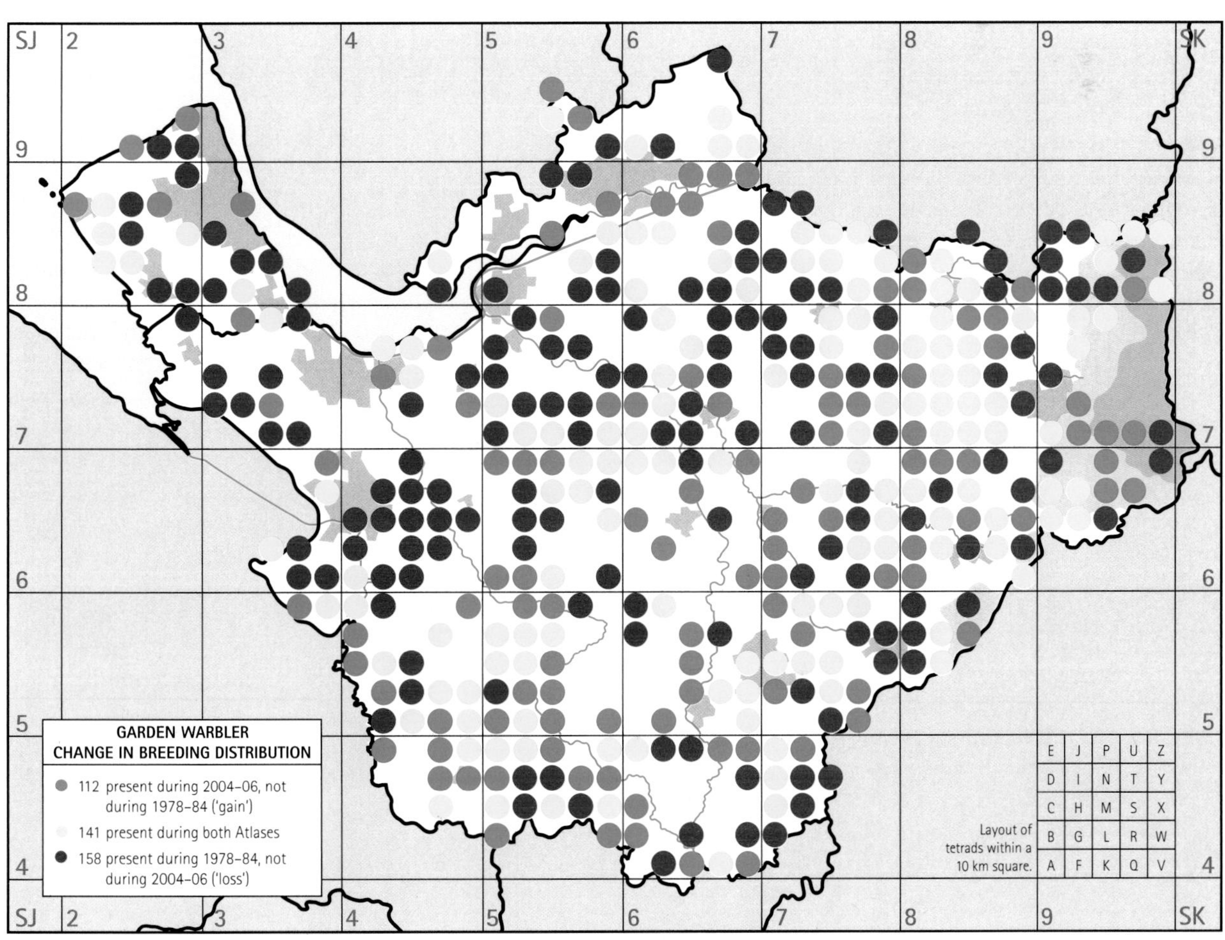
GARDEN WARBLER
CHANGE IN BREEDING DISTRIBUTION
112 present during 2004–06, not during 1978–84 ('gain')
141 present during both Atlases
158 present during 1978–84, not during 2004–06 ('loss')
Layout of tetrads within a 10 km square.
E J P U Z
D I N T Y
C H M S X
B G L R W
A F K Q V
SJ
SK
2
3
4
5
6
7
8
9

Lesser Whitethroat

Sylvia curruca

STEVE ROUND

This is the commonest *Sylvia* warbler across much of agricultural Cheshire, yet is underrecorded as some observers do not recognize its song. The most obvious component of the song is a loud rattle, a bit like the beginning of a Yellowhammer's song or the second half of a Chaffinch's and completely different from any other British warbler; at close distance a weak warble can be heard as well. If some observers find it difficult to detect the species, it can be even more tricky to confirm breeding. More than two-thirds of Atlas records were possible breeding, with just 14% of probable and 18% of records being confirmed breeding (23 FY, 14 RF and 10 others).

Lesser Whitethroat is the hedgerow *Sylvia par excellence.* The recorded habitat codes showed 73% in farmland, with 16% in scrub, 6% in human sites and just 2% in woodland, but hedgerows were mentioned in half of the occupied tetrads, over twice the proportion for any other warbler. These records showed a preference for tall hedges (E8) over short hedges by a factor of more than 5:1. The national nest records (Mason 1976) showed that Lesser Whitethroats nest higher than the other *Sylvias*, most nests at heights of 0.6–1.2 m. They used hawthorn and blackthorn much more than other warblers, also favouring bramble and rose, not just for nesting but also finding their breeding season diet of small soft-bodied insects and their larvae by diligent searching through the shrubs.

The abundance map shows the highest densities in the south-west of Cheshire and along the Wirral peninsula, and the estimate of the county's breeding population in 2004–05 is 3,480 individuals (1,510–5,460), an average of about 13 birds per occupied tetrad. Thus, the county holds about 3.4% of the English population; it is surprising that we have more than our proportionate share for a species with a traditionally south-easterly distribution. An indication of its range is well illustrated by the figures for the Atlases of nearby counties: presence in 37% of tetrads in this Atlas, 16% in Lancashire and North Merseyside (1997–2000) and 5% in Cumbria (1997–2001). This is not just a simple effect of geographical range, however, as Lesser Whitethroats are seldom found anywhere above an altitude of 200 m.

This is one of the few species that migrates south-east in autumn, Lesser Whitethroats wintering south of the Sahara in eastern Africa, mostly at low altitudes in Ethiopia, Sudan and Chad. Thus, they have not been subject to the drought in the Sahel that has impacted many migrants in western Africa, and also appear not to have been affected by the well-publicized periods of drought that have afflicted humans in Ethiopia and Sudan: annual fluctuations in their population are not correlated with African rainfall. A recent paper by BTO and RSPB staff (Fuller *et al.* 2005), however, suggests that pressures during migration and in winter are the most likely causes of the decline in the national population indices, which peaked just after our *First Atlas*, in 1986, and have dropped by 35% in the 18 years from then to 2004.

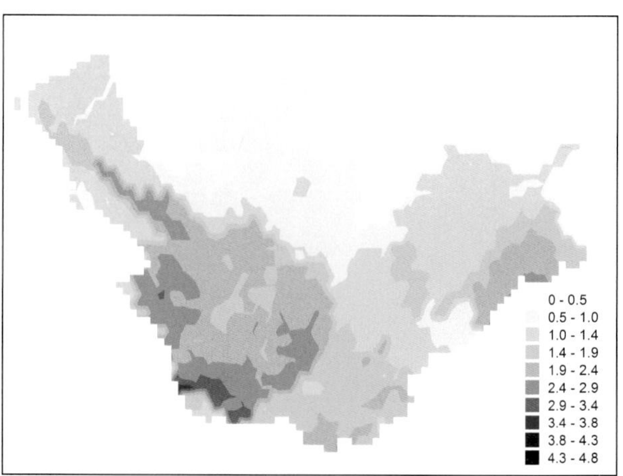

Lesser Whitethroat abundance.

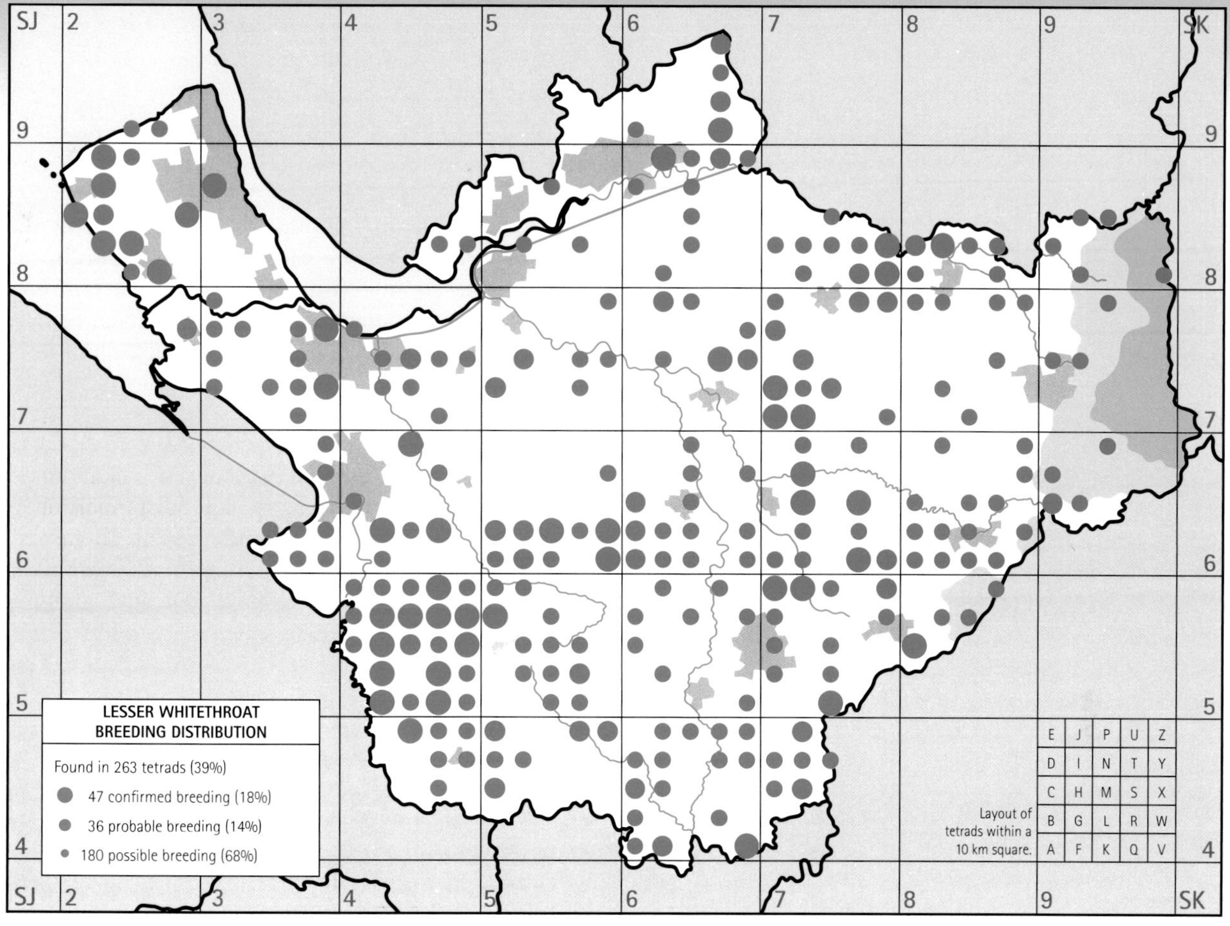
SJ
SK
LESSER WHITETHROAT
BREEDING DISTRIBUTION
Found in 263 tetrads (39%)
47 confirmed breeding (18%)
36 probable breeding (14%)
180 possible breeding (68%)
Layout of tetrads within a 10 km square.
E J P U Z
D I N T Y
C H M S X
B G L R W
A F K Q V

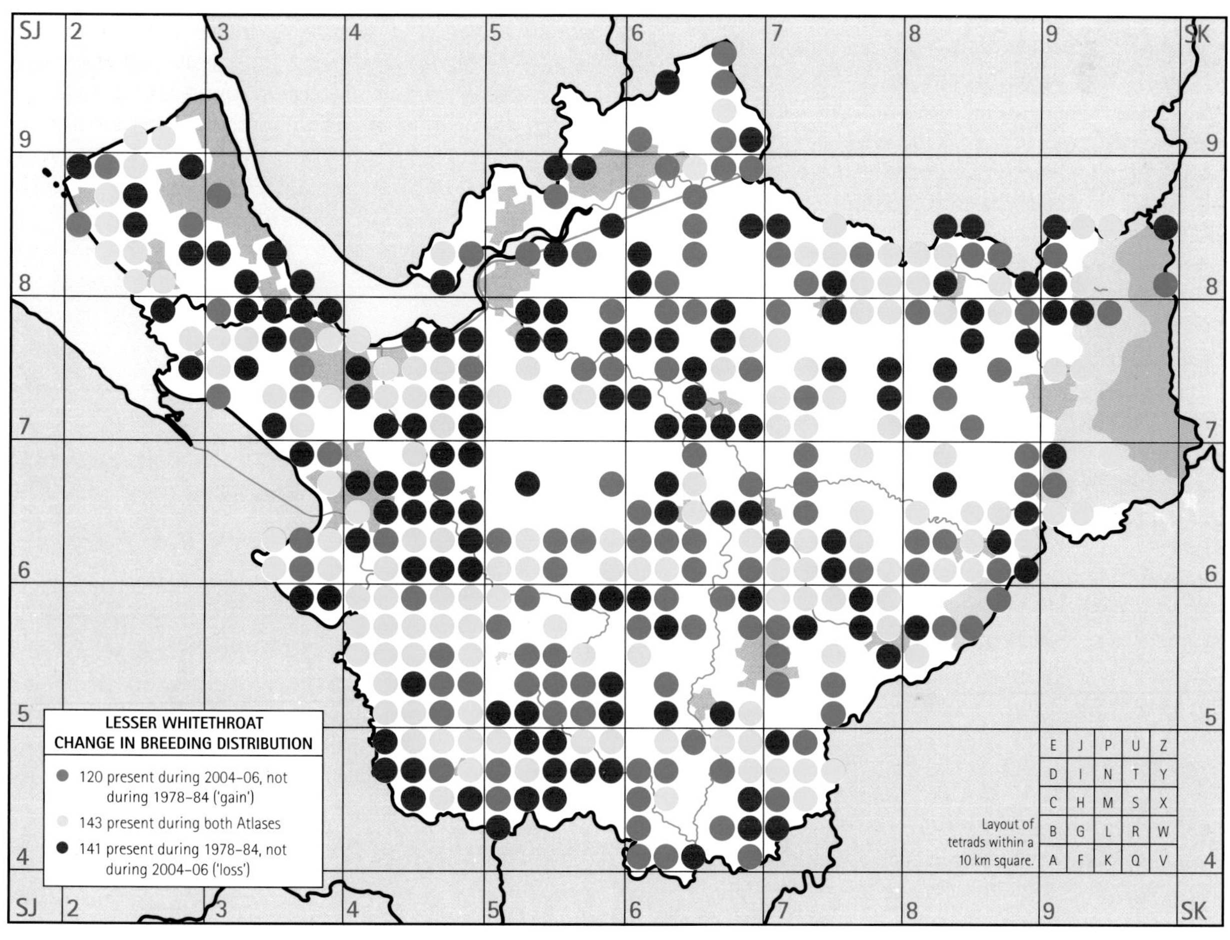
SJ
SK
LESSER WHITETHROAT
CHANGE IN BREEDING DISTRIBUTION
120 present during 2004–06, not during 1978–84 ('gain')
143 present during both Atlases
141 present during 1978–84, not during 2004–06 ('loss')
Layout of tetrads within a 10 km square.
E J P U Z
D I N T Y
C H M S X
B G L R W
A F K Q V

Whitethroat

Sylvia communis

RICHARD STEEL

'Where have all the Whitethroats gone?' was the plaintive cry in 1969, and the title of a famous paper giving the answer (Winstanley *et al.* 1974), following the massive crash in population that first alerted us to the importance of drought in the African Sahel for our wintering birds. But they have bounced back and, although nowhere nearly as common as it was in the 1960s, Whitethroat is again the most abundant warbler in Cheshire and Wirral. The BTO BBS analysis shows that the breeding population of the county in 2004–05 was 16,890 birds (10,410–23,380), corresponding to an average of 44 birds per tetrad with confirmed or probable breeding, or 31 birds per tetrad in which the species was recorded. In prime habitat they can be remarkably numerous, exemplified by the record total of 185 singing males found across 260 ha of SSSI at Woolston in the 2006 census there.

They are obviously still vulnerable to conditions on their wintering grounds, mostly in Senegal and Mali just south of the Sahara, and annual fluctuations in their abundance are closely linked to their overwinter survival and Sahel rainfall (Baillie & Peach 1992). The national population index was at its lowest at the end of our *First Atlas* period, following another failure of the African rains in autumn 1983, but their numbers have risen ever since, and had more than doubled by 2004. This rise in population has been accompanied by a spread in distribution, with presence recorded in a net 42 tetrads more than in the *First Atlas*, but with a patchy picture of 100 gains and 58 losses. The 'change' map shows areas of considerable gains in the southern and eastern parts of Cheshire, as well as towards the north of Wirral: they are still not that common in the south of the county, where they are often outnumbered by Lesser Whitethroats, and the abundance map shows the highest concentrations of Whitethroats in Halton and the Mersey valley. The national Atlases, recording 10 × 10 km squares, show that they avoid the highest land, above about 300 m, but the finer detail of our Atlas suggests that they are scarce above about 100 m, albeit with some scattered records to the east of that contour. Fifty-one per cent of habitat records were from farmland, with 29% scrub, 6% woodland and 7% human sites. They readily move into built-up areas provided that there is a suitable area of overgrown land, typical postindustrial 'brownfield' sites being ideal. This is one of the few species that appears to flourish in low, heavily trimmed hedges provided that there is some ground vegetation present, so they have perhaps not been hit as badly as some others by agricultural intensification, although obviously they would not tolerate complete removal of hedgerows (Lack 1992).

Early in the season, the males are conspicuous, often singing from the top of a bush and performing songflights. Even when hidden from sight, their song is loud and distinctive; descriptions of their song always seem to include the word 'scratchy'. They nest close to the ground in nettles or a suitably impenetrable bush, the female laying four or five eggs from mid-May, with some having second broods in July. When they have young, they draw attention to themselves with their insistent buzzing call, and they are easy to see in a hedge with a beakful of insects (167 FY), this species yielding the highest proportion of confirmed breeding amongst the warblers. Observers in 77 tetrads found broods of recently fledged young, also conspicuous and noisy.

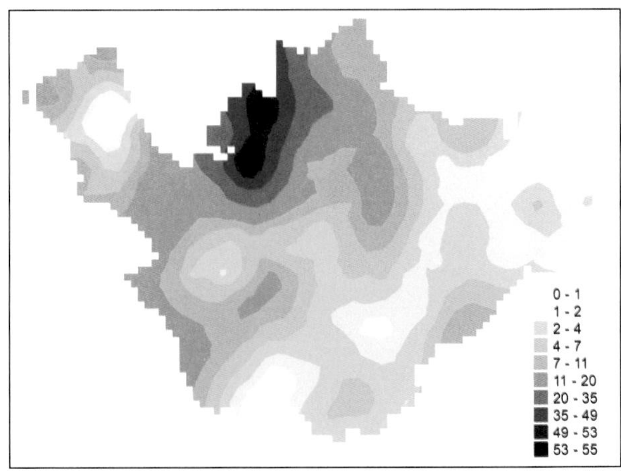

Whitethroat abundance.

Sponsored by Tricia and Mike Thompson

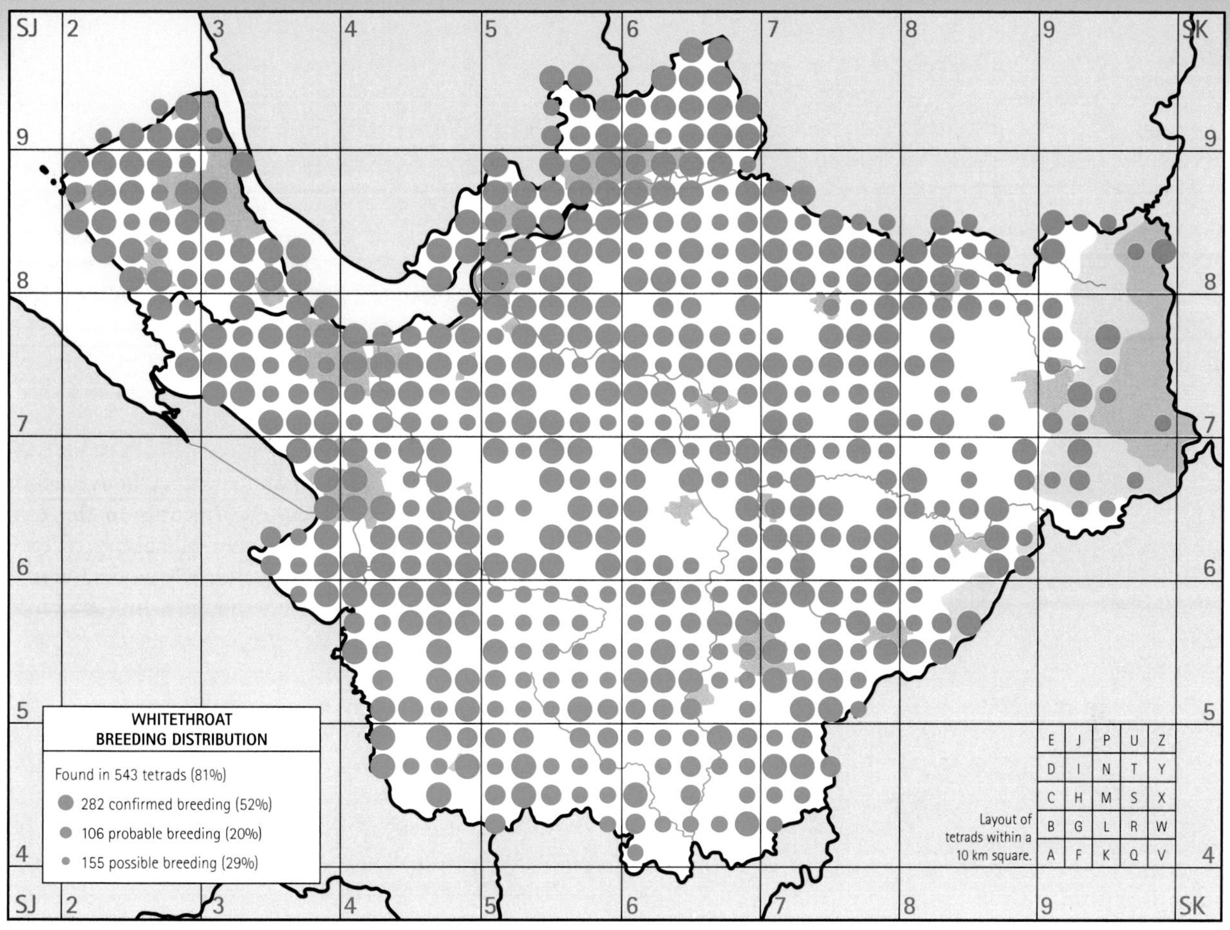

SJ
SK
2
3
4
5
6
7
8
9
WHITETHROAT
BREEDING DISTRIBUTION
Found in 543 tetrads (81%)
282 confirmed breeding (52%)
106 probable breeding (20%)
155 possible breeding (29%)
Layout of tetrads within a 10 km square.
E J P U Z
D I N T Y
C H M S X
B G L R W
A F K Q V

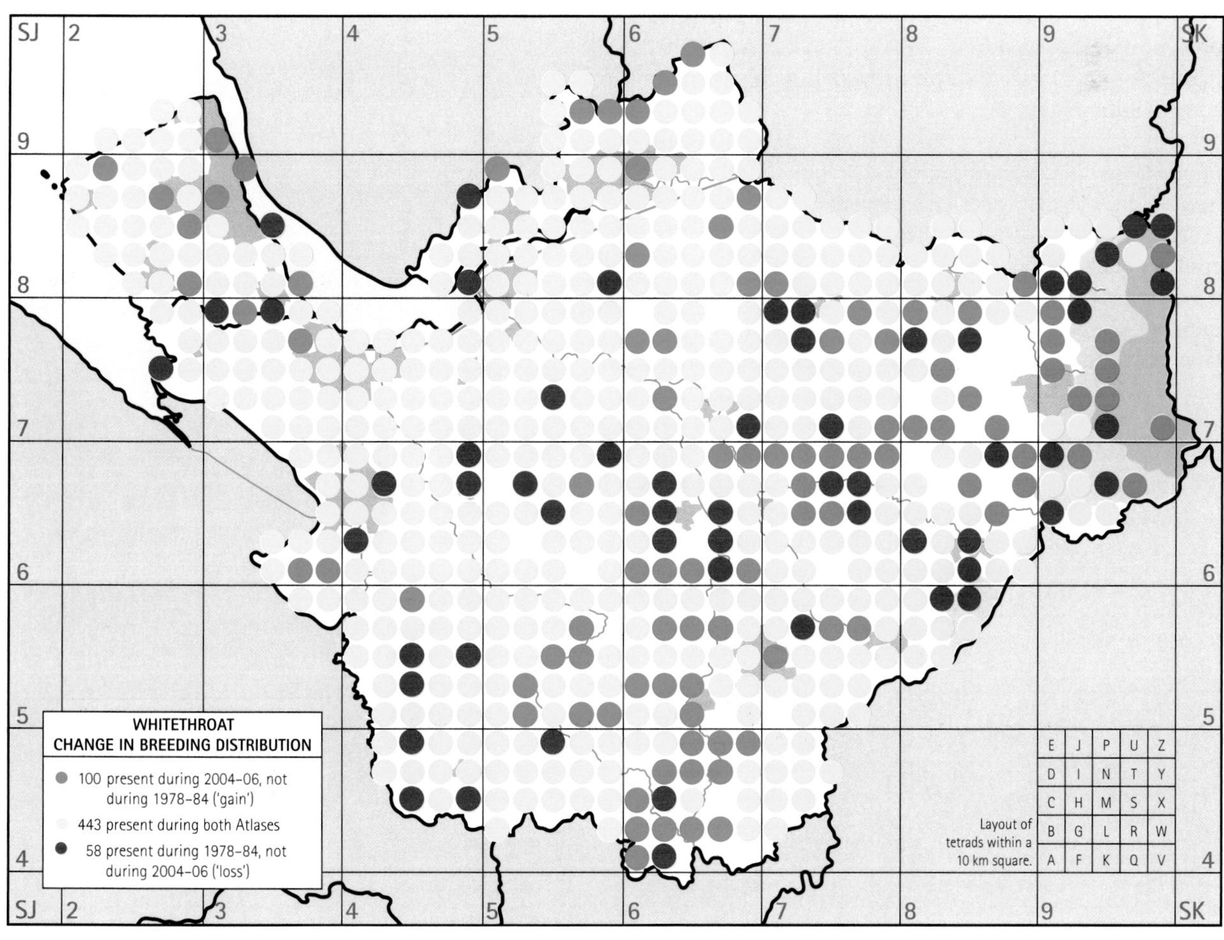

SJ
SK
2
3
4
5
6
7
8
9
WHITETHROAT
CHANGE IN BREEDING DISTRIBUTION
100 present during 2004–06, not during 1978–84 ('gain')
443 present during both Atlases
58 present during 1978–84, not during 2004–06 ('loss')
Layout of tetrads within a 10 km square.
E J P U Z
D I N T Y
C H M S X
B G L R W
A F K Q V

Wood Warbler

Phylloscopus sibilatrix

RICHARD STEEL

The Wood Warbler is a scarce bird in Cheshire and Wirral, having declined greatly in the last decade or so. BTO BBS results show that the UK population dropped by 52% from 1994 to 2004, for unknown reasons, and it is now on the Amber List of species of conservation concern.

This bird lives up to its English name: it is the *Phylloscopus* warbler of mature woodland, and all but one of the habitat codes recorded in this survey were group A (woodland). Its requirements are quite specific: climax woodland, usually deciduous, with at least a 70% closed canopy and little ground cover. Such habitat is mainly located in western Britain, but Wood Warblers have also been found quite widely but thinly distributed across much of lowland England.

Suitable habitat is in short supply in the county and is mainly at the higher altitudes, in east Cheshire including Alderley Edge, the mid-Cheshire Sandstone Ridge and Caldy Hill on Wirral. Favoured sites are visited year after year, often by the same individuals. From 1981 to 1993, eight out of the 29 (28%) Wood Warbler males ringed in Delamere Forest are known to have returned in a subsequent year (Norman 1994b). The suitable area of Delamere Forest supported a small and variable population, from one to eight males each year to 2001. In only half of the years, however, was a female present, and then no more than one in a year. From 2002 to 2005 no birds stayed for more than an odd day, but in 2006 two males set up territory, although neither was successful in attracting a mate. One of them held exactly the same territory used by the last pair of Wood Warblers that successfully nested in the forest, in 2001.

The female builds a domed nest on the ground, often on a slope, with the nest frequently close to a small bush that provides a perch on the way in to feed their chicks. Nests can be easy to find, but the main way of proving breeding is from hearing adults giving alarm calls then seeing them carrying food, usually in mid- or late June. Recently fledged young are all-but impossible to locate, spending their time high in the canopy and rapidly leaving their natal area.

Outside the breeding season, little is known about Wood Warblers in Britain: few are seen or caught on migration. They are one of the few migrants to fly south-east in autumn, apparently moving to Italy to fatten up then seemingly crossing the Mediterranean and the central part of the Sahara desert in one long flight. The wintering grounds probably lie from the Ivory Coast to the Congo basin, around the equator, although it is not known where British birds go within this range, as no British-ringed bird has been reported from its winter quarters (*Migration Atlas*).

This Atlas map greatly overstates the species' distribution. Most tetrads recorded 'possible' breeding only, usually with a male Wood Warbler present and singing, often only for a day or two: for one-quarter of the records, the observer specifically noted that the bird was present for one morning only. Even when they stay for longer, some birds hold territory for several weeks without attracting a mate (Norman 1994b). They sing almost non-stop, mixing two completely different songs, a stuttering, descendent trill and a loud, shrill 'peu peu peu', like a repetition of their alarm call, with much of their song given in flight around the territory. Males often sing close to each other, and are more effective in attracting females to their vicinity than solo males. If they find a mate, many males then set up a second territory whilst the female incubates their eggs, and try to attract another female. The second territory is typically 800 m away and out of earshot of the bird on the nest; they return to their primary territory every 30–40 minutes. All these aspects of their behaviour mean that, without careful study, the population can be exaggerated.

Eighty singing males were recorded in Cheshire (without Wirral) in the 1984 national survey (Bibby 1989), two-thirds of them east of the SJ80 longitude line. During this Atlas survey the county may have been visited by some 10–20 Wood Warblers in a year but the breeding population is only in single figures.

Sponsored by Stephen Atkins

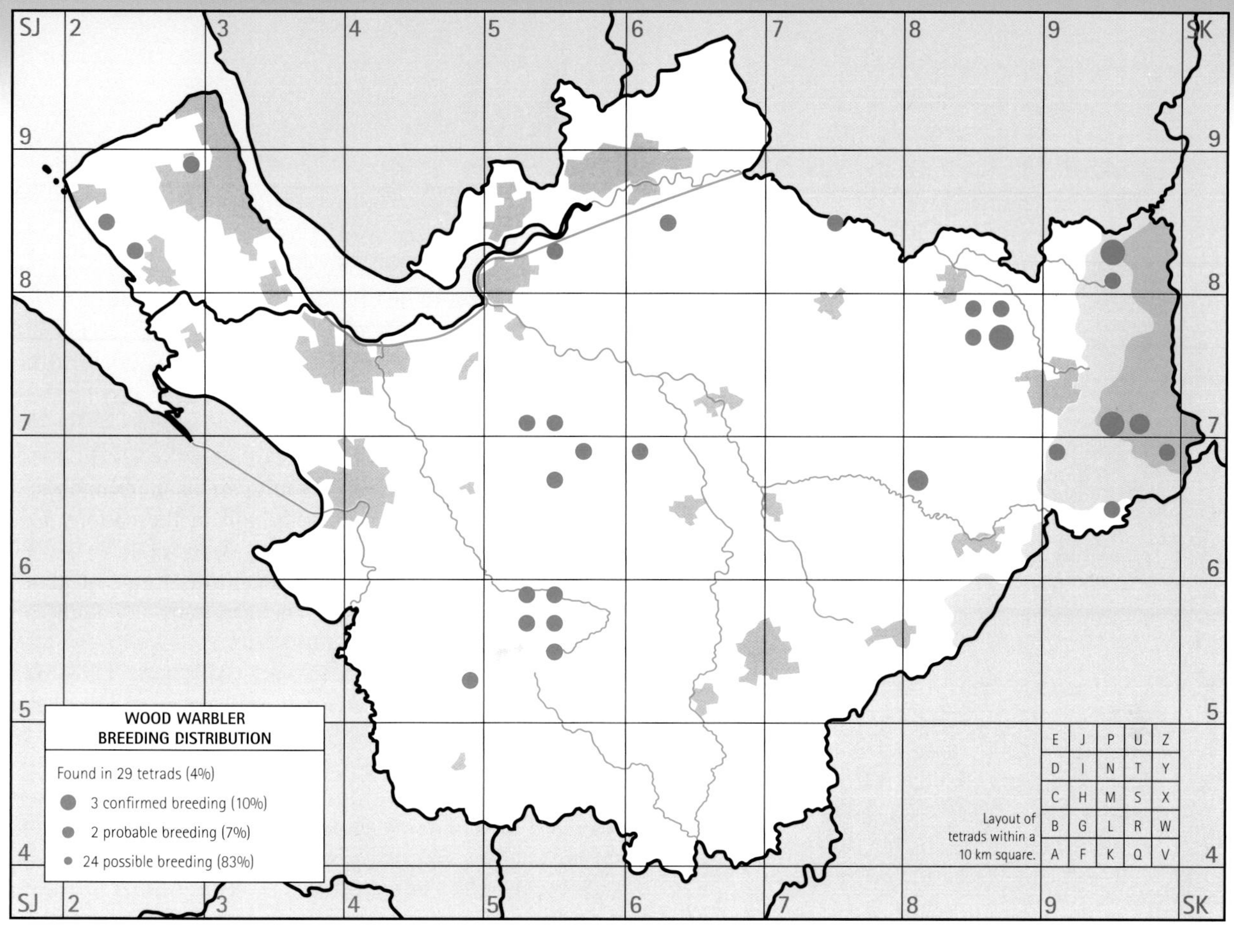
WOOD WARBLER
BREEDING DISTRIBUTION
Found in 29 tetrads (4%)
3 confirmed breeding (10%)
2 probable breeding (7%)
24 possible breeding (83%)
Layout of tetrads within a 10 km square.
E J P U Z
D I N T Y
C H M S X
B G L R W
A F K Q V
SJ 2 3 4 5 6 7 8 9 SK
9 8 7 6 5 4

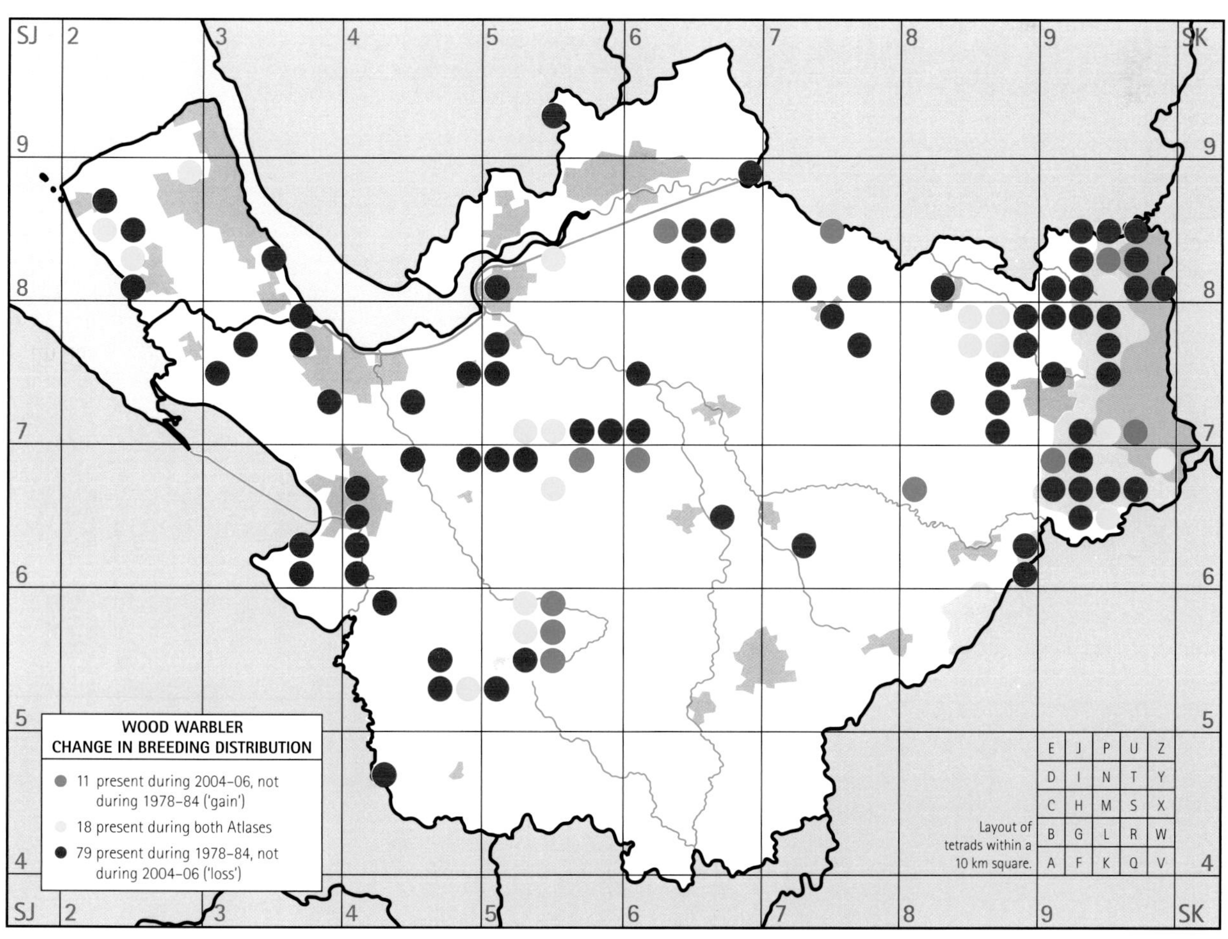
WOOD WARBLER
CHANGE IN BREEDING DISTRIBUTION
11 present during 2004–06, not during 1978–84 ('gain')
18 present during both Atlases
79 present during 1978–84, not during 2004–06 ('loss')
Layout of tetrads within a 10 km square.
E J P U Z
D I N T Y
C H M S X
B G L R W
A F K Q V
SJ 2 3 4 5 6 7 8 9 SK
9 8 7 6 5 4

Chiffchaff

Phylloscopus collybita

PHIL JONES

In the last twenty years, Chiffchaffs have flourished and fieldwork for this Atlas has confirmed that it is now our most ubiquitous warbler and our second most widespread summer migrant: they now occur in 615 tetrads, a net gain of 166 since our *First Atlas*. They are missing only from the treeless areas of the eastern hills and the estuarine fringes, along with the most urban parts of towns such as Birkenhead, Widnes, Northwich and Crewe. The abundance map shows their highest densities in west Cheshire and Wirral. The BTO analysis of Cheshire and Wirral BBS gives a county breeding season population in 2005 of 15,800 (11,630–19,970) Chiffchaffs, an average of 25 birds per tetrad in which they were recorded. The authors of the *First Atlas* suggested a county population, just twenty years previously, of perhaps 1,500 pairs.

Male Chiffchaffs are usually the first summer migrant to reappear in Cheshire and Wirral woods, and they probably spend the longest period in Britain of any migrant species. One ringed individual at Woolston in 1990 was well studied from its arrival on 18 March to its final capture on 26 September, having spent over half of the year at the site. Arrivals by mid-March are usual in most years, with birds instantly recognized by their song, not quite as boring as at first it seems, most birds breaking up their monotonic 'chiff-chaff' with trisyllabic variations and the 'trr' interludes, perhaps increasingly so as the season goes on. When the females arrive, two or three weeks later, they pair rapidly and she quickly builds and occupies a nest. Their typical clutch size is five or six eggs, rather than the Willow Warbler's seven, probably because of the increased load on the female. A male Chiffchaff plays little part in anything to do with the nest; he does not feed the female, and does not feed the chicks. His role appears to be to establish and defend the territory, and he stands guard, singing and giving the alarm when necessary, throughout the breeding period.

The Chiffchaff is mostly a bird of woodland but, as the population has increased, they have spilled out into farmland and other areas. The first birds back each year fill up the preferred deciduous woods, and later-arriving birds—thought to be the one-year-old birds breeding for the first time—occupy poorer quality woods, hedges and elsewhere (Clement 1995). With Cheshire and Wirral being a relatively sparsely wooded county, it is perhaps surprising that such a high proportion of our Chiffchaffs are in woodland: habitat codes reported in this survey were 61% woodland, 19% scrub, 9% farmland and 10% human sites.

In the 20 years between our Atlas periods (1984–2004) the national population index for Chiffchaff has risen by 180%. Lack of management has accelerated the habitat progression from scrub, preferred by Willow Warblers, towards the Chiffchaffs' favoured more-mature woodland; many well-recorded sites have seen a substantial shift in the relative proportions of these two common *Phylloscopus* warblers. Further, the consequent decline of the Willow Warbler has allowed some Chiffchaffs to spread into less-wooded habitats. Finally, their migratory strategy might have benefited this species. In winter, British breeding birds go south to the Mediterranean, with some crossing the Sahara to the region from Mauritania to Guinea-Bissau. Short-distance migrants—such as many Chiffchaffs—tend to have prospered at the expense of those undertaking longer journeys, perhaps because they are better able to adjust their seasons to climate change.

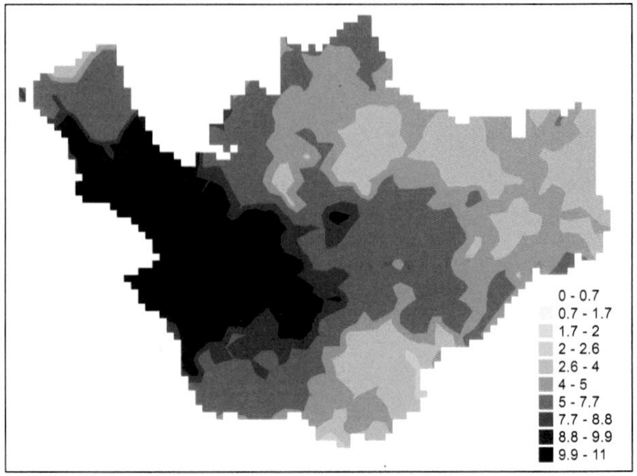

Chiffchaff abundance.

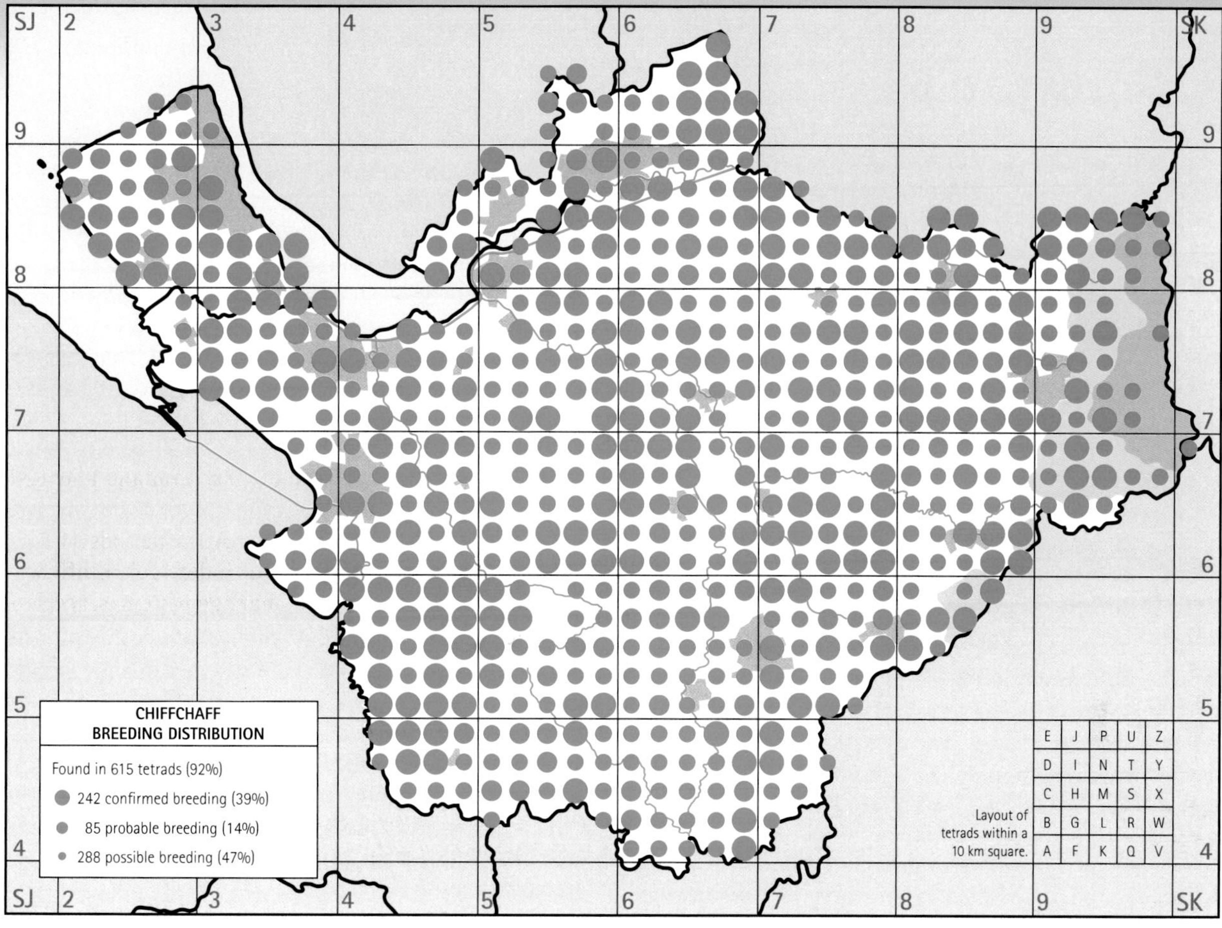
CHIFFCHAFF
BREEDING DISTRIBUTION
Found in 615 tetrads (92%)
242 confirmed breeding (39%)
85 probable breeding (14%)
288 possible breeding (47%)
Layout of tetrads within a 10 km square.
SJ
SK

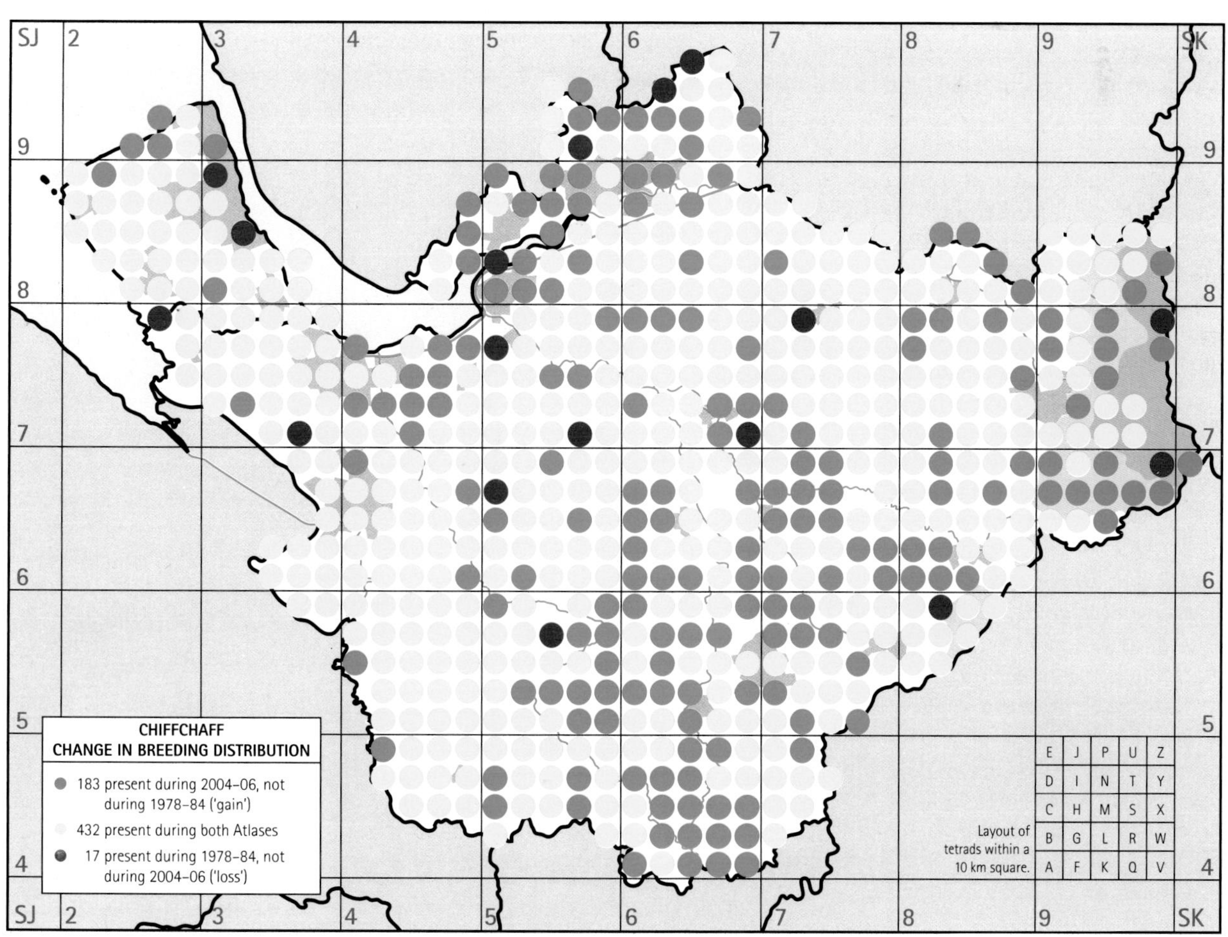
CHIFFCHAFF
CHANGE IN BREEDING DISTRIBUTION
183 present during 2004–06, not during 1978–84 ('gain')
432 present during both Atlases
17 present during 1978–84, not during 2004–06 ('loss')
Layout of tetrads within a 10 km square.
SJ
SK

SUE & ANDY TRANTER

Wintering Chiffchaffs seem to be restless and always on the move, often calling as they go, which helps in detecting their presence. They need to be ever-active to find their insect food, no mean feat in a British winter, adding 10–15% to their body-weight during the day and burning up that fat during the long nights. Four main habitats accounted for nearly all the winter records: suburban and rural human sites (F2 and F3) in 17 tetrads; broad-leaved woodland (A1) in 13; regenerating woodland (B1) in 12; and farmland hedgerows (E8 and E9) in nine. Only 28% of the total was in human sites, compared to 69% of wintering Blackcaps, probably because Blackcaps take a wide range of foods while wintering Chiffchaffs are almost entirely insectivorous. They are by no means our only winter insectivores, sharing that habit with Goldcrest and Wren at least.

The Chiffchaff is a widespread and adaptable species, wintering across a range of more than 40° in latitude. Three races are present in Britain during winter—the nominate *collybita*, which make up the vast majority, and the eastern races *abietinus* and *tristis*, much scarcer but with their presence overemphasized by excessive publicity. Out of nearly 700 wintering Chiffchaffs ringed in Cornwall in 1999–2005, 87% were *collybita*, 6% *abietinus*, 3% intergrades between *collybita* and *abietinus*, 4% intergrades between *abietinus* and *tristis*, and only two birds were *tristis* (Conway 2005). A few of the birds of the nominate race are likely to be British breeders but the majority have probably come here from southern Scandinavia or continental Europe (*Migration Atlas*); as yet, however, there is no definitive evidence from ringed birds in Cheshire and Wirral.

Although there are no records from the highest altitudes, Chiffchaffs have been found in some of the bleakest parts of lowland Cheshire and Wirral, and they appear to be able to stick it out through winter. It is, however, noticeable that well-studied sites record far fewer Chiffchaffs in January and February than in November and December. This could suggest that some move out of the county, or die, during the winter.

Neither Coward (1910) nor Boyd makes any mention of any wintering Chiffchaffs in the county, although Boyd (1946) was told of one in Lancashire from November 1934 to February 1935. The first documented bird was apparently one reported by Eric Hardy in mid-February 1961 at Leasowe, although Bell noted two November records, one of which, at Walton on 23 November 1958, fell within our definition of winter. Another was near Warrington on 11 December 1961 and one on the same date in 1966 near Stockport (not within present-day Cheshire) (Bell 1962). One further bird was ringed on 29 November 1966 at Frankby. The chart summarizes records each winter from the start of the *Cheshire Bird Report* in 1964. There are some problems in interpreting the reports, partly because of changing editorial practice. In the early years, from 1964 to 1976, normal records of this species were ignored and only unusual dates and races were published. In analysing the annual reports from then on, it can be difficult to rule out late-staying or early-arriving summer migrants, or multiple reports of the same bird and duplication of records across the year-end boundary. Nevertheless, a reasonable picture emerges of the extreme scarcity of winter Chiffchaffs until 1976/77, with none or one each winter. Then the number of records from November to February inclusive rose sharply in 1980/81 and averaged about 11 birds at 8 sites each winter during the 1980s and about 17 birds at 12 sites from 1990, until the start of this Atlas stimulated a flurry of extra records. Although mild weather is often quoted as a reason for the increase of wintering records, the yearly fluctuations in Cheshire and Wirral show no correlation with the harshness of the winter weather.

With presence in 65 tetrads, and others probably undetected, work for this Atlas shows that the Cheshire and Wirral wintering population of Chiffchaff is likely to be around 80–100 birds. It will be interesting to put this in the context of the national Wintering Warbler Survey, organized by the BTO in 2006/07, when the results are published.

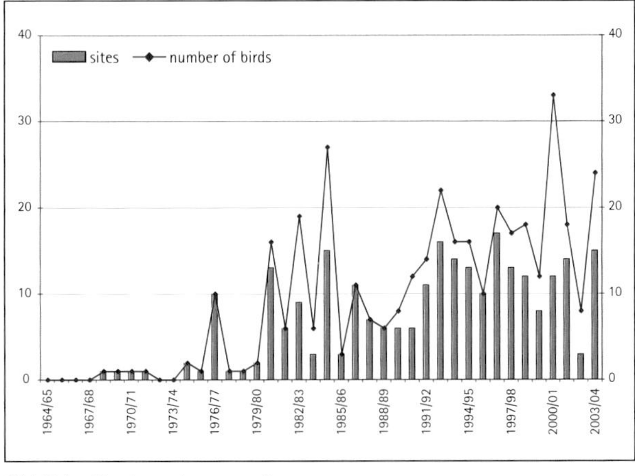

Chiffchaff wintering numbers.

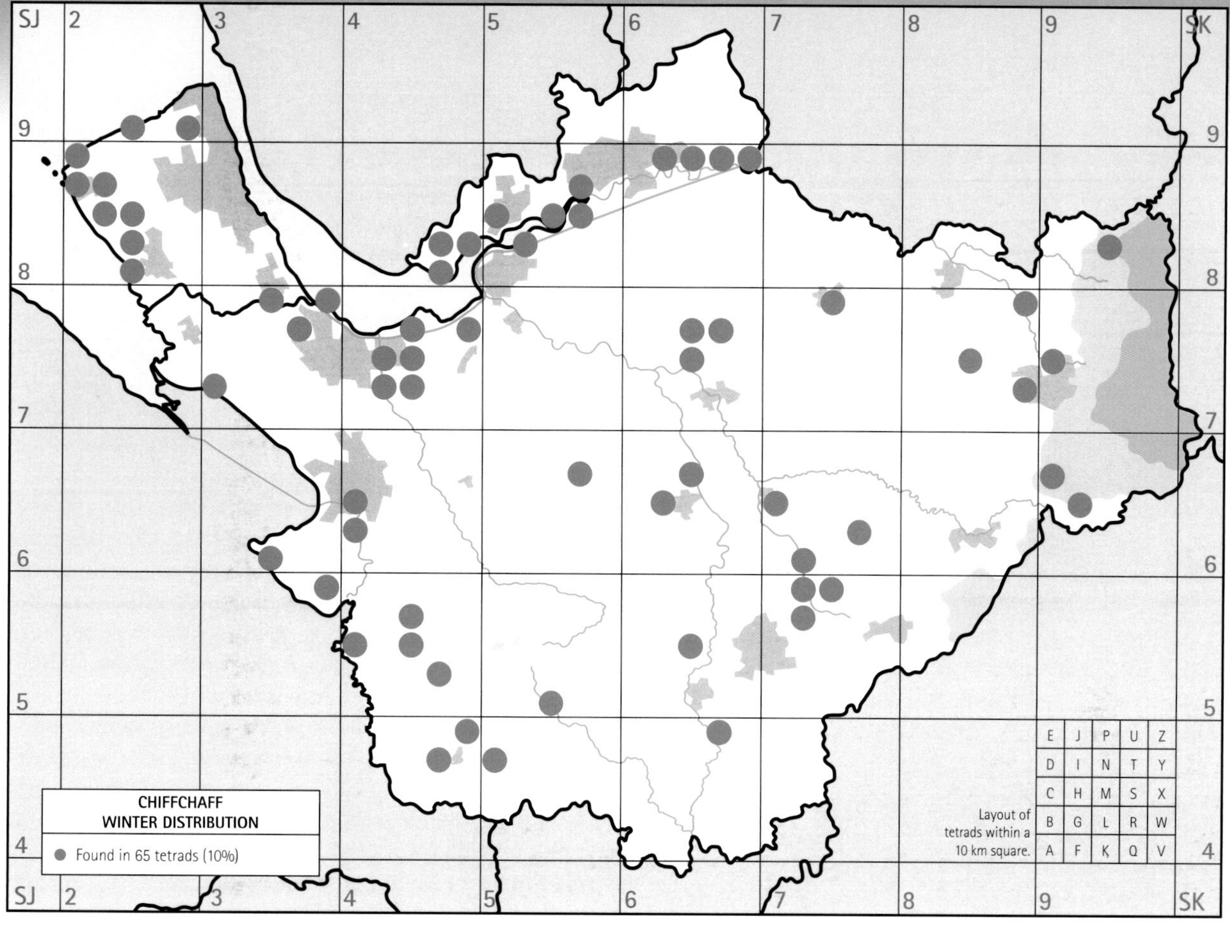
CHIFFCHAFF
WINTER DISTRIBUTION
Found in 65 tetrads (10%)
Layout of tetrads within a 10 km square.
E J P U Z
D I N T Y
C H M S X
B G L R W
A F K Q V
SJ
SK
2
3
4
5
6
7
8
9

Willow Warbler

Phylloscopus trochilus

SIMON BOOTH

The cheering song of the Willow Warbler—sure to raise the spirits of any birdwatcher—is heard much less frequently nowadays, and the 'change' map is depressingly red. The species has dropped from having been the second most widespread summer visitor in the *First Atlas* to rank sixth now. Twenty years ago it was by a long way the most widespread warbler, found in 96% of tetrads, yet has now been overtaken in ubiquity by Chiffchaff, Blackcap and Whitethroat, having been lost from 119 tetrads and gained in just 10. The drop in the county is probably even worse than is suggested by the 'change' map because so many tetrads in this Atlas recorded 'possible' breeding only. At many sites now it seems that a male Willow Warbler will sing for a while, fail to attract a mate and then move on. In our *First Atlas* almost three-quarters of the tetrads in the county recorded confirmed breeding, by far the highest proportion of any warbler, and some people considered this one of the easiest species in which to get a two-letter code. The authors of the *First Atlas* suggested a county population, just twenty years previously, of perhaps 18,000 pairs; the BTO analysis of Cheshire and Wirral BBS gives a breeding season population in 2004–05 of 4,120 (1,960–6,320) individuals.

Willow Warblers have undergone a major decline nationally. They were at their peak in England in 1984, at the end of our *First Atlas*, and the population indices slumped by 62% in the next 20 years, placing them on the Amber List of species of conservation concern. Their decline occurred mainly in the south of Britain, accompanied by a fall in survival rates (Peach *et al.* 1995a), with Scottish populations remaining unaffected. Results from a local study agree with the larger-scale picture, with return rates of birds at Woolston dropping after 1984, perhaps indicating a real decline in the annual survival of the species, coinciding with the national drop in population from 1985 onwards (Norman 2005). With the 'national' decline in Willow Warblers apparently occurring mainly in the south of the UK, in this example of a 'north-south divide', Cheshire is definitely in the south!

This is the *Phylloscopus* warbler of the pioneer scrub, young woodland and sparsely wooded areas dominated by small-leaved deciduous trees like birch, alder and willow. The abundance map shows the highest densities in the scrubby unwooded areas of the eastern hills and north of the Mersey. The habitat codes recorded in this survey show 44% woodland, 32% scrub, 11% farmland and 9% human sites. The fact that there are more woodland than scrub records probably reflects just the availability of these types of habitat rather than the species' preference; Willow Warblers clocked up more B1 (regenerating natural or semi-natural woodland) records than any other species except Whitethroat.

Two factors have worked against the Willow Warblers' favoured habitat, probably reducing their population: the increasing average age of woods, and the long-standing decline in woodland management, both of which mean that there are fewer young, open woodlands with internal rides (Rackham 2006). Willow Warblers avoid the interior of closed-canopy woods, being replaced there by Chiffchaffs or possibly Wood Warblers, but will use their edges and rides within such woods. There is no link between their population changes and the weather in the Sahel region, through which they pass in spring and autumn (Baillie & Peach 1992). The differential survival between northern and southern birds is puzzling but could be explained by an as-yet undetected 'leapfrog' migration with Scottish birds wintering farther south in Africa. All that is known of the wintering grounds of British Willow Warblers is that they appear to lie in the Ivory Coast and Ghana (*Migration Atlas*).

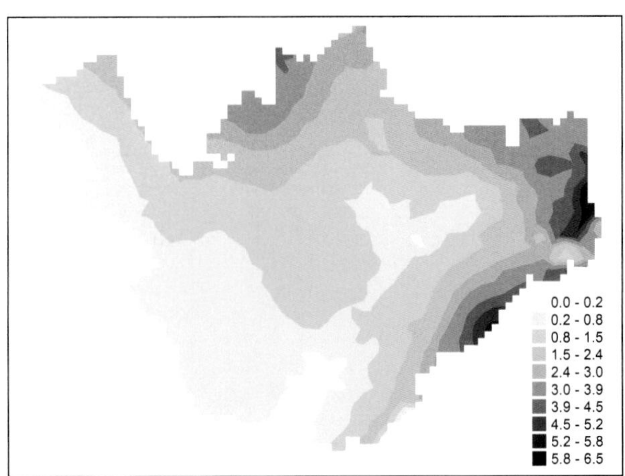

Willow Warbler abundance.

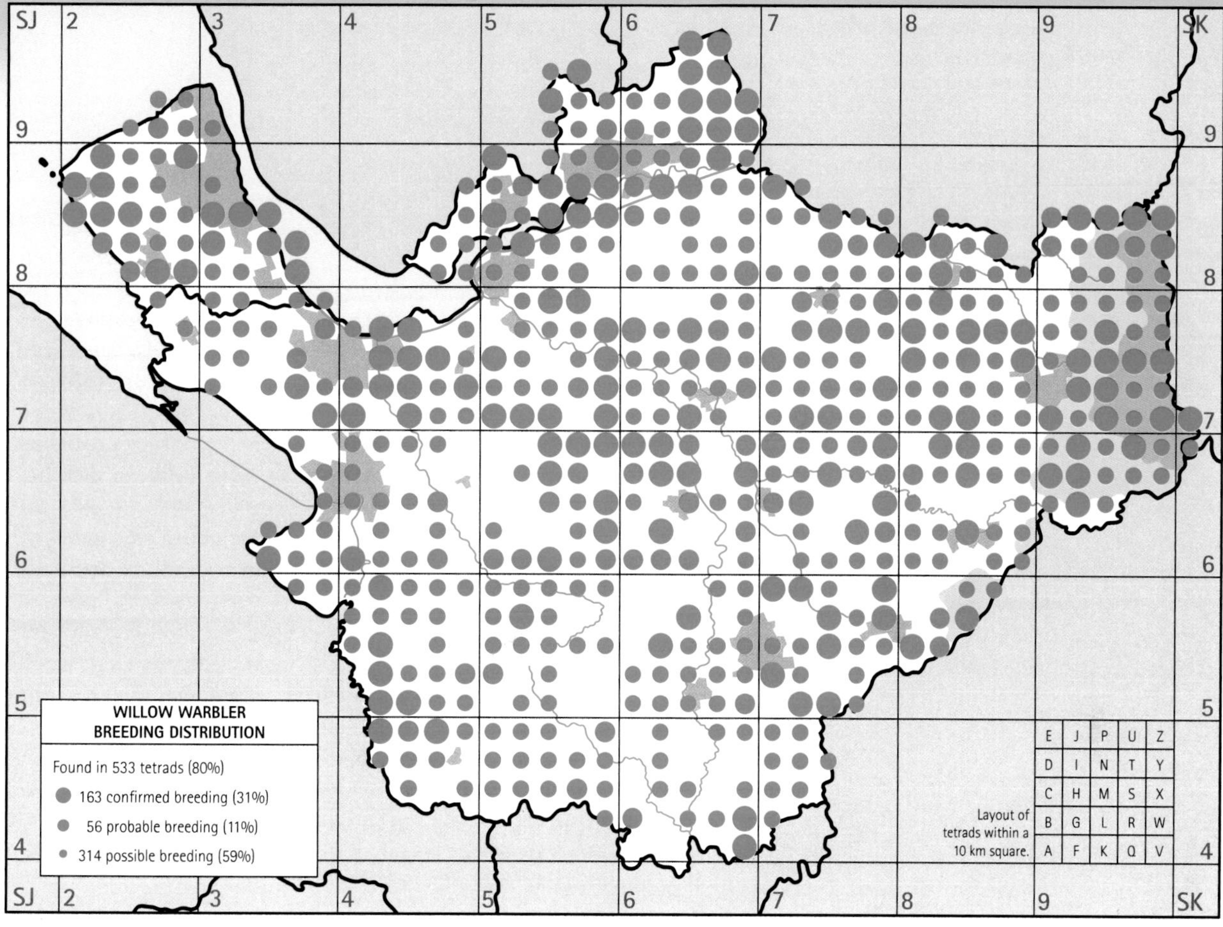
WILLOW WARBLER
BREEDING DISTRIBUTION
Found in 533 tetrads (80%)
163 confirmed breeding (31%)
56 probable breeding (11%)
314 possible breeding (59%)
Layout of tetrads within a 10 km square.
E J P U Z
D I N T Y
C H M S X
B G L R W
A F K Q V
SJ
SK

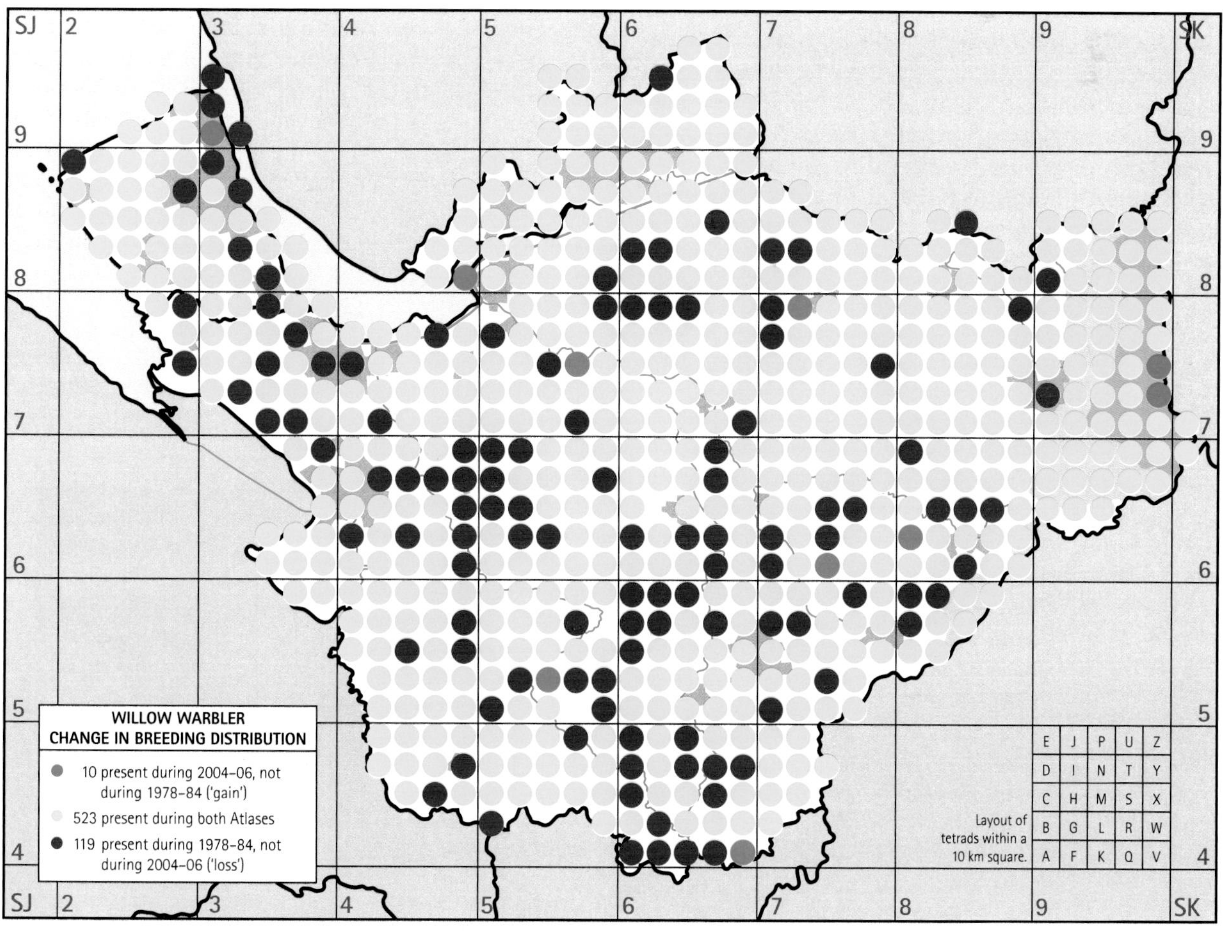
WILLOW WARBLER
CHANGE IN BREEDING DISTRIBUTION
10 present during 2004–06, not during 1978–84 ('gain')
523 present during both Atlases
119 present during 1978–84, not during 2004–06 ('loss')
Layout of tetrads within a 10 km square.
E J P U Z
D I N T Y
C H M S X
B G L R W
A F K Q V
SJ
SK

Goldcrest

Regulus regulus

ANDY HARMER

The maps show that the range of this, our tiniest bird, has increased greatly since our *First Atlas*: it is present in half as many tetrads again (417 compared to 280) and was proven breeding in almost twice as many (133 compared to 70). There is nothing in the national statistics to explain the major increase in Cheshire and Wirral. Although the numbers of this species, as a small resident insectivore, are reduced following hard winters such as those of the late 1970s and early 1980s, the national breeding population was higher throughout our *First Atlas* period than it is now: the English breeding index now is similar to, but somewhat lower than, that during our *First Atlas*. Indeed, the species is currently on the Amber List of species of conservation concern because its population had fallen by more than one-quarter over the period 1975–2000.

Their expansion has taken Goldcrests across most of the county. Their strongholds are the north-east and south-west of Cheshire, with much of Wirral, and around Chester and Congleton. Birds are found at high densities in the Forestry Commission woods around Delamere and Macclesfield Forests although these do not show up on the abundance map as well as the lighter-coloured areas where the species is sparsely distributed or absent.

This is a difficult species to prove breeding, and most records were of possible breeding through observers hearing their high-pitched song (149 tetrads) or finding birds in suitable habitat (45). Probable breeding was scored with records of pairs of birds (59), display or courtship (7), birds visiting a probable nest site (10), carrying nesting material (9), or anxiety calls (5). Most confirmed breeding, in 84 tetrads, derived from observations of recently fledged young: Ann Pym near Swettenham (SJ76Y) noted that a brood 'must have just left the nest when we saw them, like tiny balls of fluff'. Fieldworkers in a further 34 tetrads saw adults carrying a faecal sac or food—Goldcrests feeding themselves and their chicks on insects, especially aphids, springtails and caterpillars, and spiders—and records from just 15 tetrads referred to nests (NY, NE or ON). Their nest is difficult to find, a delicate structure of moss, lichens and spiders' silk, usually suspended beneath a branch of an evergreen tree.

As these comments imply, Goldcrest is indeed the species most likely to be found in coniferous woodland, with the habitat codes from 75 tetrads being given as A2; Coal Tit had 60 such records, but no other passerine was in double figures. Interestingly these are the only two species for which the number of A3 habitat records (mixed woodland, at least 10% of each) exceeds the number of A1 codes (broad-leaved woodland), suggesting that, wherever they can find them, Goldcrests preferentially search out the coniferous parts of a wooded area. In 124 tetrads birds were recorded in human habitats and several observers noted comments of 'conifer in large garden'. They are not solely restricted to conifers, however; indeed, if they were, there would be few Goldcrests in the county because only 1% of the land area of Cheshire and Wirral is coniferous woodland, and only one-fifth of the 1 km squares (585 out of 2687) have *any* coniferous woodland (Haines-Young *et al.* 2002). Not surprisingly from those statistics, the county holds only a low proportion of the UK breeding population of nearly 1,750,000 birds (Newson *et al.* 2008): the BTO's analysis of BBS transects shows that the breeding population of Cheshire and Wirral in 2004–05 was 6,140 birds (2,620–9,670), less than 0.5% of the national total.

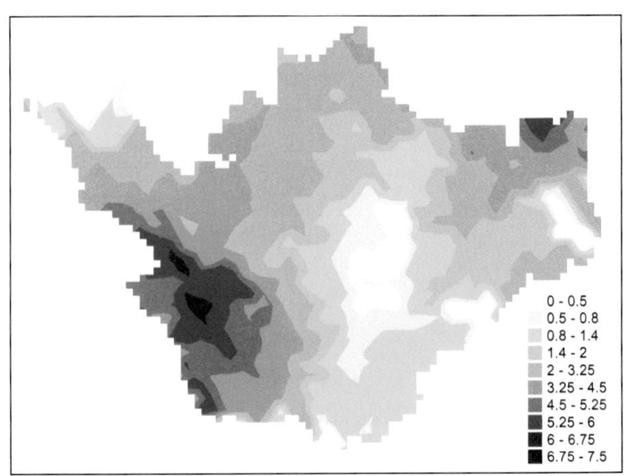

Goldcrest abundance.

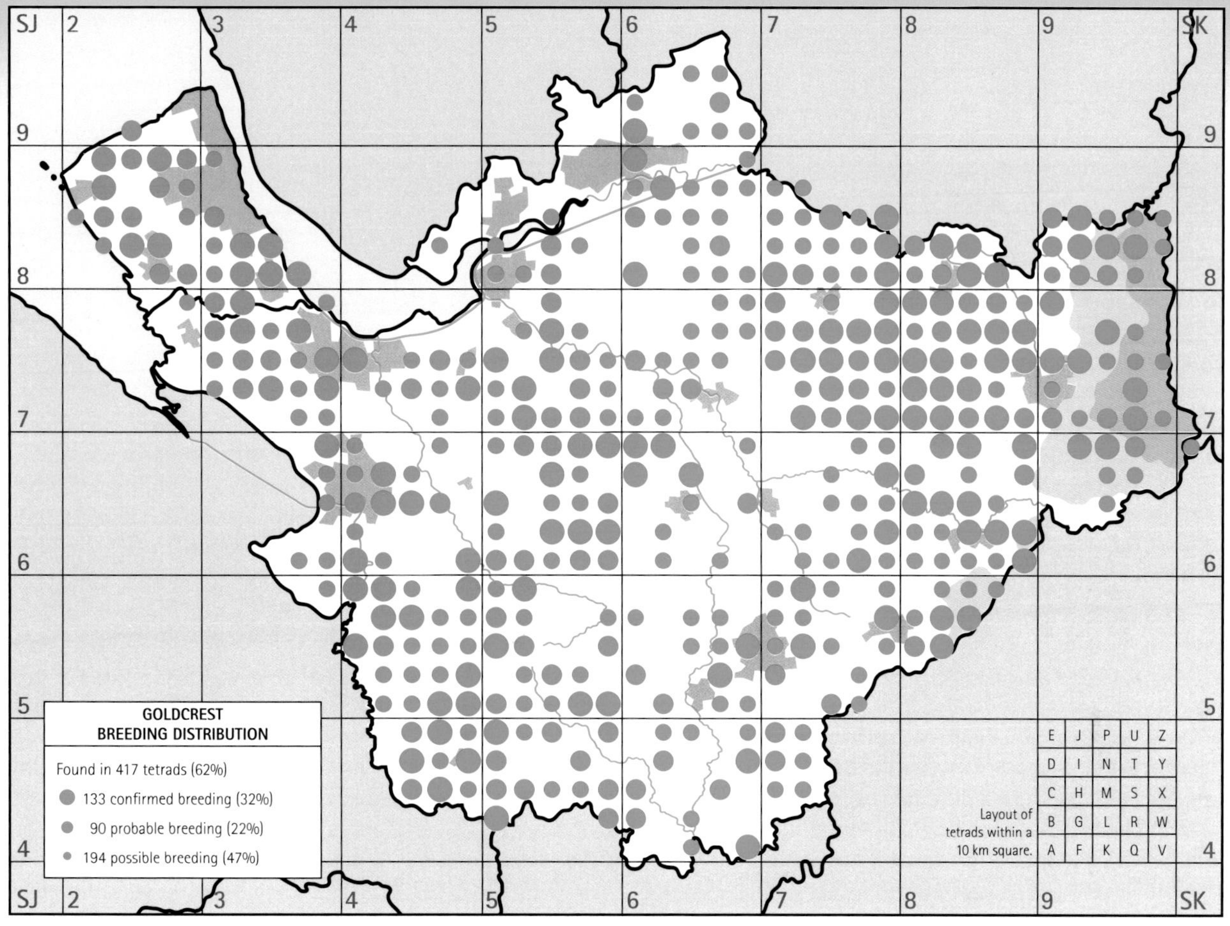
GOLDCREST
BREEDING DISTRIBUTION
Found in 417 tetrads (62%)
133 confirmed breeding (32%)
90 probable breeding (22%)
194 possible breeding (47%)
Layout of tetrads within a 10 km square.
E J P U Z
D I N T Y
C H M S X
B G L R W
A F K Q V
SJ
SK
2
3
4
5
6
7
8
9

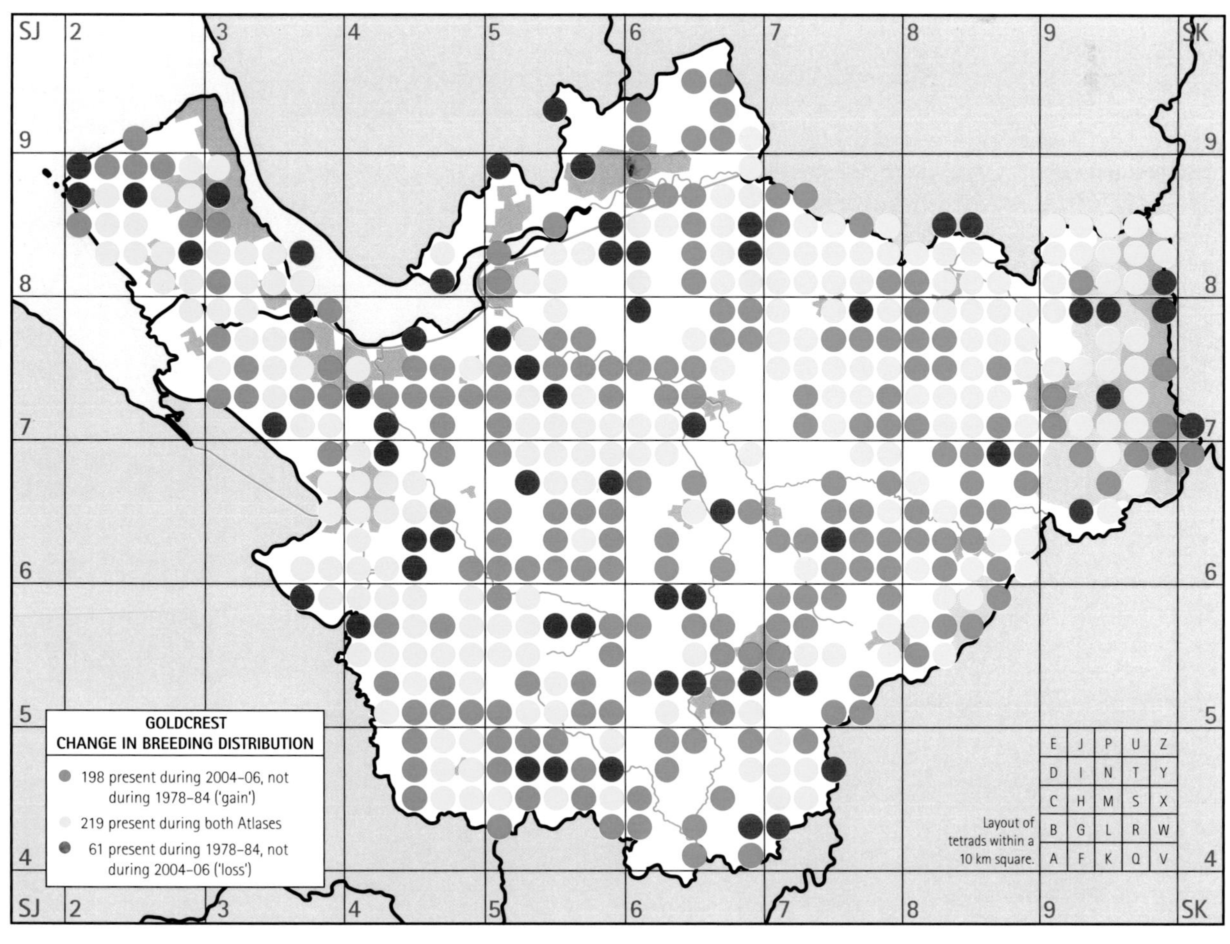
GOLDCREST
CHANGE IN BREEDING DISTRIBUTION
198 present during 2004–06, not during 1978–84 ('gain')
219 present during both Atlases
61 present during 1978–84, not during 2004–06 ('loss')
Layout of tetrads within a 10 km square.
E J P U Z
D I N T Y
C H M S X
B G L R W
A F K Q V
SJ
SK
2
3
4
5
6
7
8
9

Goldcrests become even more widespread in winter, occupying an extra 110 tetrads compared to the breeding season. As noted by Coward (1910) and Bell (1962), they broaden their habitat use and are no longer defined by coniferous woodland, although, as in the breeding season, this is the species most likely to be found in that A2 habitat, recorded in 66 tetrads. They switch to a higher proportion of broad-leaved woodland, with more broad-leaved (157) than mixed (117)—reversing the breeding season order of 103 to 148—perhaps because in winter they have few competitors as insectivorous feeders amongst the twigs in the tree canopy. There are almost the same number of human site records: apart from a slightly warmer microclimate, the environs of habitation have little to offer Goldcrests in winter. The key factor in allowing it to spread out into the relatively treeless areas is the winter occupation of scrub (51 winter records compared to 24 for breeding) and especially of farmland hedges (86 compared to 12). Thus, wintering Goldcrests fill in most of the gaps in their breeding distribution.

Most of the birds recorded in the extra tetrads, however, are likely to be different individuals. Breeding birds probably remain on or near their territory (*BTO Winter Atlas*), and these are presumably those that are occasionally heard singing, even in the depths of winter. Juveniles disperse locally, with the population augmented by some Scottish birds moving south for the winter and some immigrants from northern Europe (*Migration Atlas*). Some birds move around within a winter. One ringed at Norton Priory, Runcorn on 31 December 1994 was found dead in April 1995 near Haverfordwest, Dyfed, 233 km south-west, a classic destination for a hard-weather movement.

They eat almost exclusively small invertebrates and it is remarkable that Britain's smallest bird, weighing about 5 g, can survive through most winter conditions. They spend much of their time searching the undersides of leaves, the needles of conifers and twigs, so they are not much affected by snow, and the only adverse weather that impinges on their feeding is frosting or glazing of trunks and foliage. They forage at all heights from the neck-aching (for the observer) tops of tall trees to ground level if need be, with two reports of birds feeding on the ground in snow. One observer found two small flocks feeding on seed-heads and on dead thistles, where it was most likely that they had found some invertebrate larvae or eggs amongst the plants, and in a garden at Poynton (SJ98B) Goldcrests had learned to feed on fat balls.

Some Goldcrests join mixed-species flocks, especially with Long-tailed Tits and other tits, usually squeaking as they go. Substantial flocks of 'crests are sometimes found: as many as 40 birds were reported in Little Sutton (SJ37T) and similar numbers in a hillside wood near Wildboarclough (SJ97V), with other flocks of around 25 in Abbots Moss (SJ56Z) and Woolston (SJ68U). But three-quarters of records were of just one or two birds, indicating the way that most Goldcrests lead their lives.

STEVE ROUND

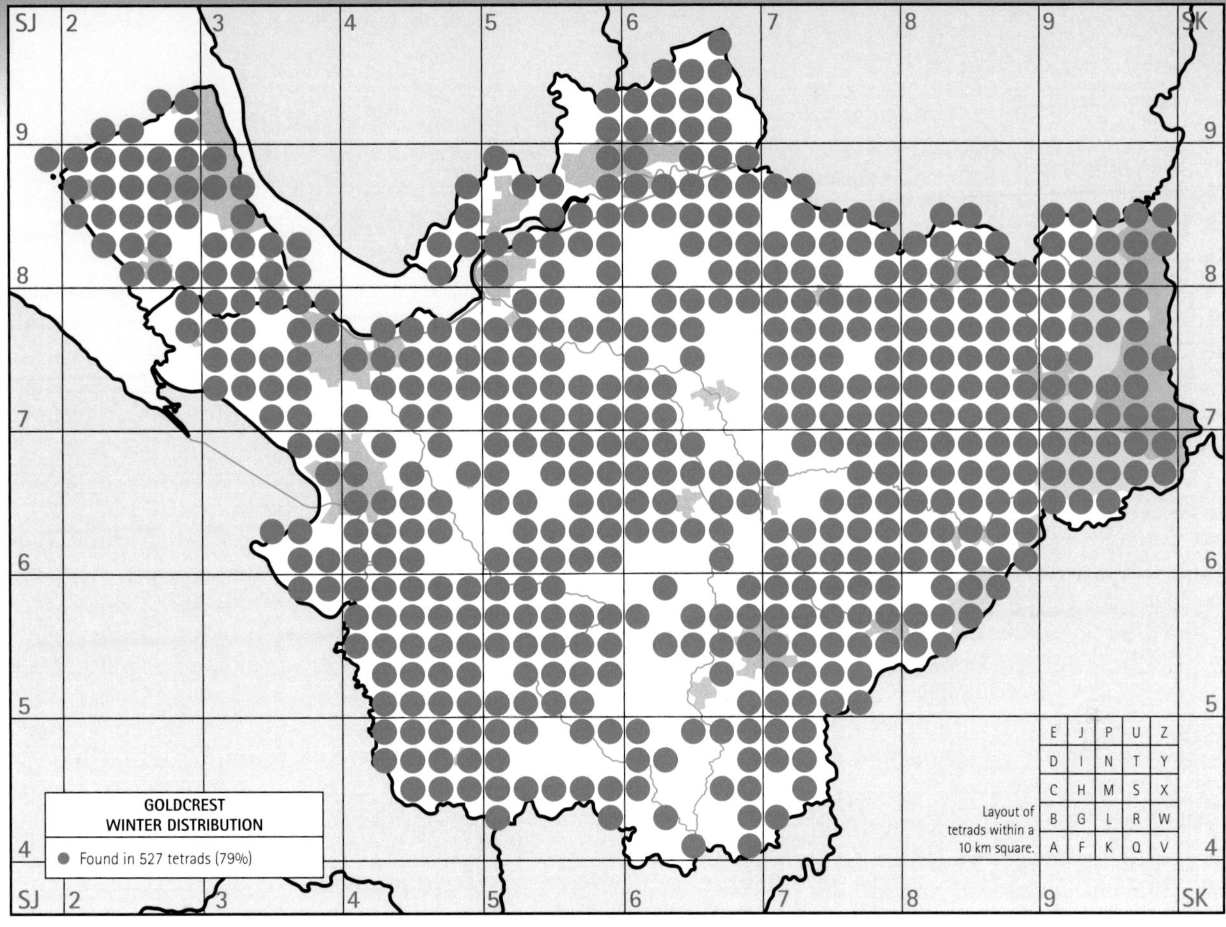
SJ
2
3
4
5
6
7
8
9
SK
GOLDCREST
WINTER DISTRIBUTION
Found in 527 tetrads (79%)
Layout of tetrads within a 10 km square.
E J P U Z
D I N T Y
C H M S X
B G L R W
A F K Q V

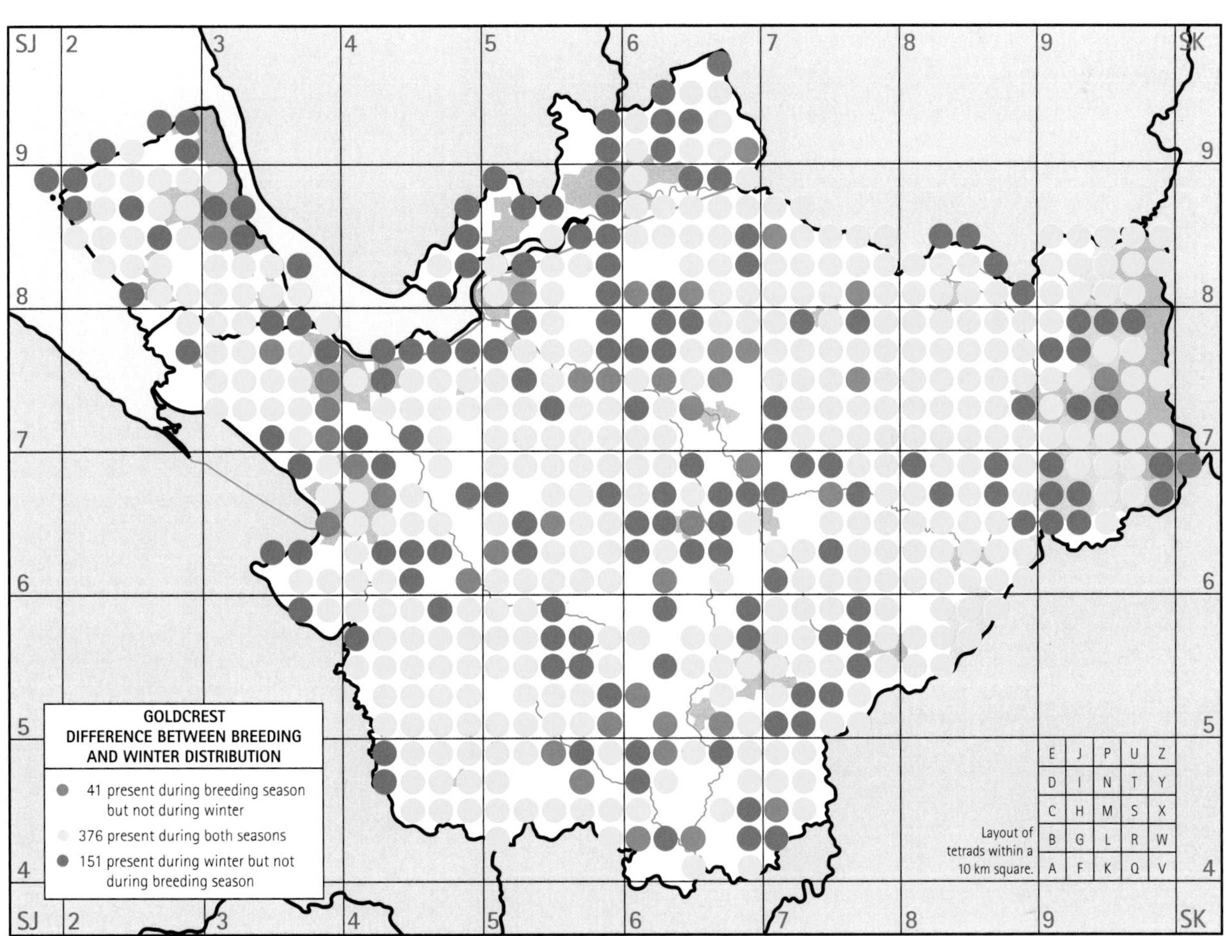
SJ
2
3
4
5
6
7
8
9
SK
GOLDCREST
DIFFERENCE BETWEEN BREEDING AND WINTER DISTRIBUTION
41 present during breeding season but not during winter
376 present during both seasons
151 present during winter but not during breeding season
Layout of tetrads within a 10 km square.
E J P U Z
D I N T Y
C H M S X
B G L R W
A F K Q V

Firecrest

Regulus ignicapilla

Firecrests have been found regularly in Cheshire and Wirral since their mass influx of about 23 birds in 1974/75, still the highest total for the recording area and described by the County Recorder at the time as 'an extraordinary picture of a bird that was hardly known in the county a few years ago'. The species is much sought-after but is elusive and may well be under-recorded because one of their favourite habitats, rhododendron scrub under mature trees, is not often visited by birdwatchers. Thirty-one of the 48 Firecrests ringed in the county by members of Merseyside Ringing Group up to 2003/04 were in this habitat, more than half of them in the last hour of the day, probably preparing to roost in the shrubs (Norman & Ormond 2003).

The first year of this Atlas stimulated widespread recording, and the total of 12 birds in 2004/05 was the county's third highest winter figure of birds seen in the field (20 in 1974/75; 16 in 1993/94; 12 also in 1997/98). On the other hand, just three birds were found in 2005/06 and two in 2006/07. Most of the birds were on their own but up to three were seen in Rivacre Country Park (SJ37Y/Z) and two at Dibbinsdale (SJ38B).

Elsewhere in Britain, Firecrests are said to favour woodland adjacent to rivers or other water (*Migration Atlas*) but there is no evidence for this preference in Cheshire and Wirral. Birds in seven tetrads were recorded as using woodland (five broad-leaved and two mixed), with two in scrub, four in hedgerows and two in suburban gardens. This accords with previous records in the county where almost all Firecrests were in willow-dominated scrub or mature trees (either broad-leaved or coniferous) with rhododendron understorey. The data from ringed birds suggested, although with not enough birds to be statistically robust, that the larger males were more likely to use the scrubby areas, presumably more open and somewhat colder than the sheltered woodland (Norman & Ormond 2003). None of the birds seen during this Atlas was sexed in the field, probably wisely, because females can show some of the golden-orange colour in their crown, although never as much as males, and Firecrests seldom cease their relentless search for insects long enough to allow the observer a perfect view.

According to the records of the Rare Breeding Birds Panel, up to 250 pairs of Firecrests now breed in Britain, almost all in southern England (Holling *et al.* 2007a) but most of the wintering birds are likely to be immigrants from the closer parts of continental Europe (*Migration Atlas*).

● There was one breeding season record during this Atlas period, a bird singing in a small mixed plantation at Derbyshire Bridge (SK07A). Firecrests bred for the first, and only, time in Cheshire and Wirral in 2003, in an area of spruce in Macclesfield Forest (Barber & Barber 2003). Tall Norway spruce, at least 8 m high, is the classic breeding habitat for the species in England (Batten 1973).

SUE & ANDY TRANTER

Sponsored by Mike Crawley

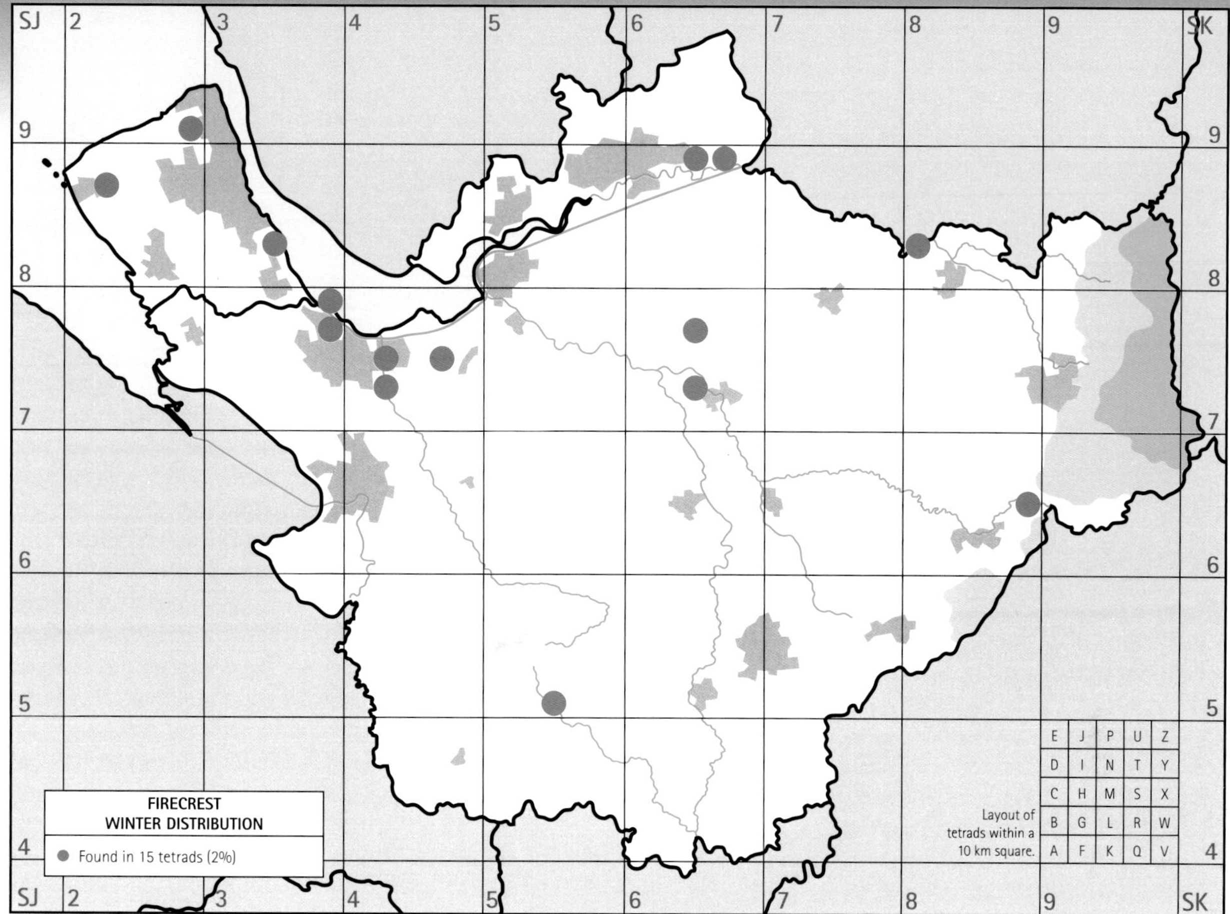
SJ
2
3
4
5
6
7
8
9
SK
9
8
7
6
5
4
FIRECREST
WINTER DISTRIBUTION
Found in 15 tetrads (2%)
Layout of tetrads within a 10 km square.
E J P U Z
D I N T Y
C H M S X
B G L R W
A F K Q V

Spotted Flycatcher

Muscicapa striata

ANDY HARMER

For most people in the county the Spotted Flycatcher is effectively extinct as a local breeding bird, as the map shows an obviously south-easterly distribution, with only a handful of records in the most densely populated four northern boroughs of Wirral, Ellesmere Port and Neston, Halton and Warrington, and birds avoiding the urban areas of Northwich, Macclesfield and Crewe. They were found in only half as many Cheshire and Wirral tetrads as in the *First Atlas*, and confirmed breeding in only 101 compared with 267 tetrads twenty years ago. This is all part of the national decline in the species, whose population index has been in free fall since quantitative national recording started in the mid-1960s, dropping by 75% between our two Atlas periods. The decline is probably driven by low annual survival of first-year birds, in the period immediately after they leave the nest and/or on migration and in their first winter (Freeman & Crick 2003); the widely observed reduction in large flying insects cannot have helped. Spotted Flycatchers undergo one of the longest migrations of all summer visitors to Britain: the species winters from the Gulf of Guinea coast southwards and ringed individuals from northern Europe have been found in South Africa (Urban *et al.* 1997).

Despite being amongst our most confiding birds, Spotted Flycatchers are probably underrecorded. They arrive late—the main influx being in the second half of May—so their breeding activity peaks after that of all other passerines. Their song is weak, infrequent and not well known, a discordant mixture of buzzing and kissing noises—Walter de la Mare's 'grey on grey post, this silent little bird'. So, most Spotted Flycatchers are detected by eye, not by ear. They draw attention to themselves by their characteristic method of feeding, unlike that of any other British species, flying out from a perch to catch a flying insect, usually returning to the same perch. When viewed carefully, however, the bird can be seen to be not 'spotted' and its scientific name, meaning streaked flycatcher, is much more appropriate.

Spotted Flycatchers depend on exposed perches and adequate space to make their aerial sallies, thus avoiding open areas and dense woods, favouring areas with well-spaced mature deciduous trees. Habitat codes submitted in the Atlas showed that most birds were in human sites (42% of records) or broad-leaved or mixed woodland (41%), with 15% in farmland. Eighty-seven of the 107 'human site' records were rural, with villages and cemeteries favoured sites. They place their nests on ledges, and especially favour creeping vine or ivy against a tree or a wall; they take fairly open holes and crevices in trees, including occasionally open-fronted nest-boxes, and especially seem to like half-coconut shells placed in a suitable site, which save them time and effort in nest-building (Clarke 2005). Adult birds seldom feed far away from their nest—usually within 20 m or so—perhaps because they take only one item of food at a time back to their chicks, and a nearby feeding perch minimizes the time taken and their energy expenditure.

As a Red-listed species of conservation concern, the Spotted Flycatcher is now the subject of much study, mostly in its breeding areas. Birds breeding in gardens have much higher success than those elsewhere, with fewer nests predated and more chicks fledging, in better condition (heavier weights) (Stevens *et al.* 2007).

The BTO analysis of Cheshire and Wirral BBS gives a county breeding season population in 2004–05 of 2,060 Spotted Flycatchers (with wide confidence intervals of 520–3,600). Especially with their liking for human habitation, there seems to be plenty of scope for active conservation measures to try to assist this species and attract it back to now-abandoned areas; the efforts of a team of amateurs in Worcestershire shows what can be done (Clarke 2005).

Sponsored by Focalpoint Optics Ltd

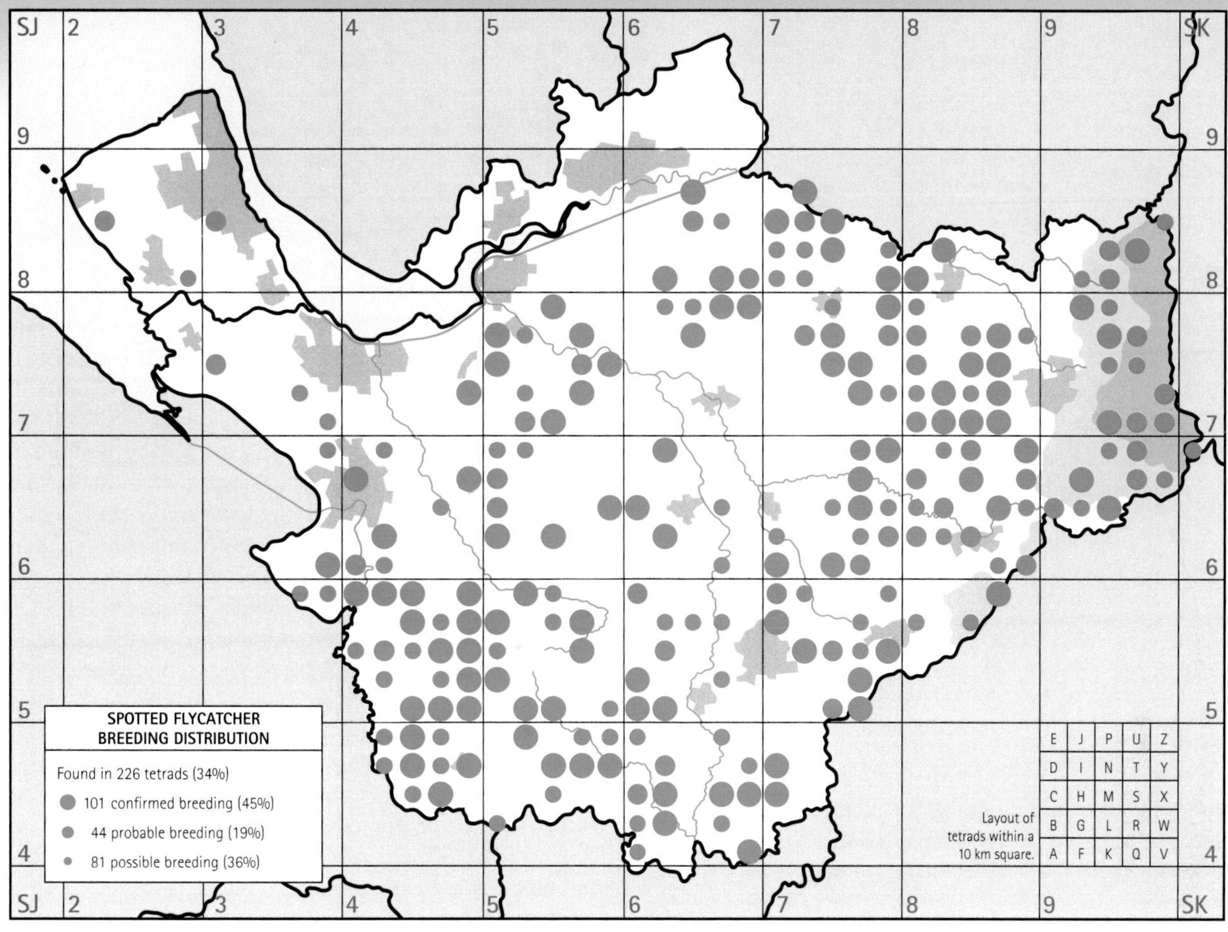
SPOTTED FLYCATCHER
BREEDING DISTRIBUTION
Found in 226 tetrads (34%)
101 confirmed breeding (45%)
44 probable breeding (19%)
81 possible breeding (36%)
Layout of tetrads within a 10 km square.
E J P U Z
D I N T Y
C H M S X
B G L R W
A F K Q V
SJ
SK
2
3
4
5
6
7
8
9

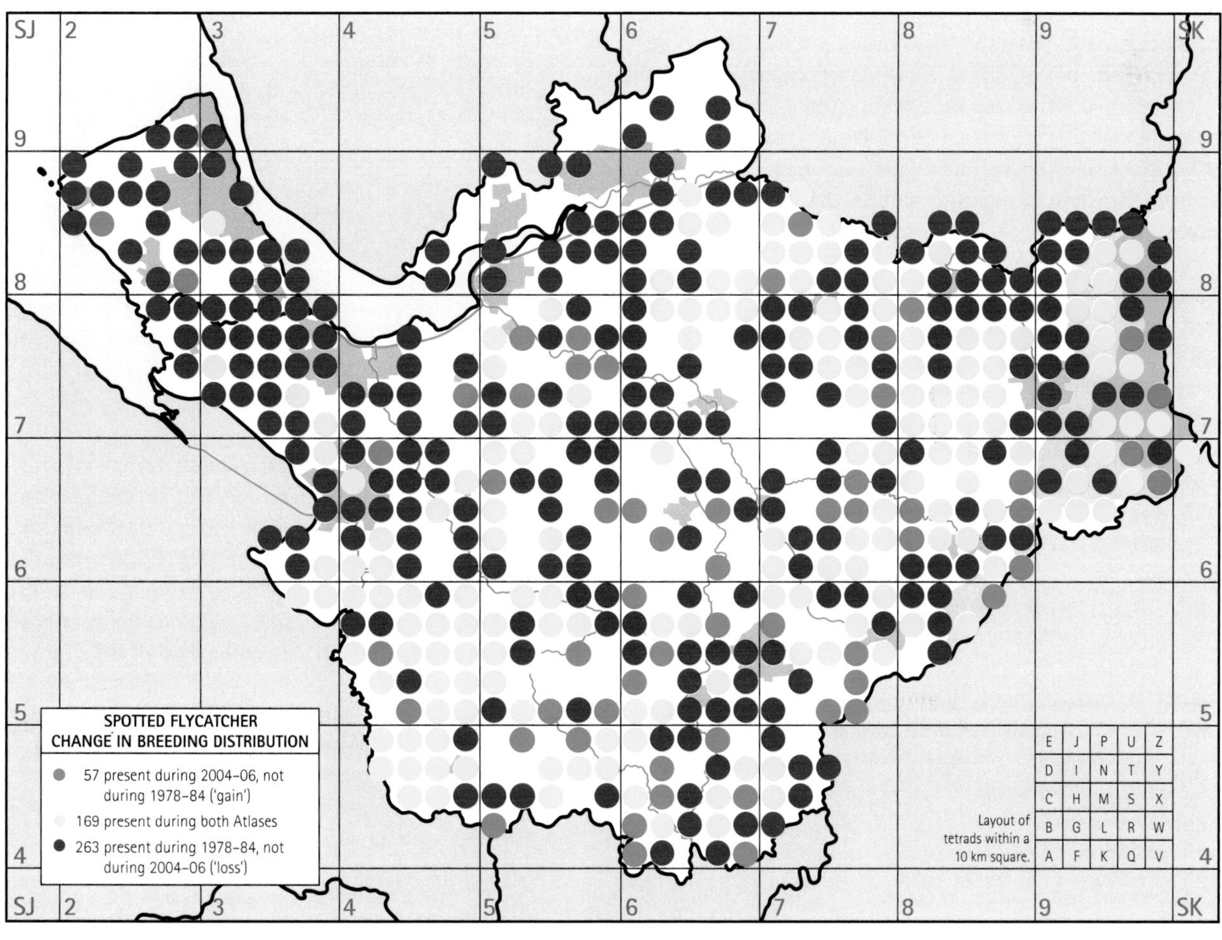
SPOTTED FLYCATCHER
CHANGE IN BREEDING DISTRIBUTION
57 present during 2004–06, not during 1978–84 ('gain')
169 present during both Atlases
263 present during 1978–84, not during 2004–06 ('loss')
Layout of tetrads within a 10 km square.
E J P U Z
D I N T Y
C H M S X
B G L R W
A F K Q V
SJ
SK
2
3
4
5
6
7
8
9

Pied Flycatcher

Ficedula hypoleuca

NORMAN RICHARDSON

Pied Flycatchers are mostly birds of the upland deciduous woods in parts of western and northern Britain, and, as expected, almost all of the habitat codes included broad-leaved woodland. With such preferences, they are never likely to form a major part of the county avifauna, but during the 1990s they seemed to be colonizing Cheshire and Wirral more widely. The number of occupied tetrads with confirmed or probable breeding has doubled in the last twenty years: 23 now and 11 in the *First Atlas*. Their distribution has shifted, however, and only four of the 11 from 1978–84 are still occupied now. Most of the county's Pied Flycatcher nests are in boxes and are regularly studied; natural sites—often holes bored by Great Spotted Woodpeckers in the previous year—are now unusual. This is probably a good choice for the birds because nests in natural holes suffer much higher predation than those in nest-boxes (Lundberg & Alatalo 1992).

Pied Flycatchers winter in West Africa south of the Sahara, in wooded areas on the edge of the savannah and climax forest, with British birds probably from Guinea across to Ghana. Birds usually arrive in the county around the third week of April, the males arriving first and setting up territory around a suitable nest hole. Their weak song is not well known to all observers and possibly some singing males could have been overlooked. The normal clutch is of seven pale blue eggs, which hatch around the end of May in lowland Cheshire. Despite their name, adult Pied Flycatchers eat more ants than anything else, with other *Hymenoptera* (bees, wasps and sawflies) and *Coleoptera* (beetles). On the other hand, most of the food that they bring to their chicks is caterpillars and the larval stages of invertebrates, gleaned from leaves in the tree canopy. In some years they struggle to find sufficient food for all of the chicks. This species may well be suffering from climate change, which is advancing the peak period of food availability for Pied Flycatchers in deciduous forests, whilst in the Netherlands the birds have so far been unable to compensate by breeding earlier (Both *et al.* 2006).

At the end of the *First Atlas* period, the county population was estimated at 10–15 pairs, the highest level since records began, probably occasioned by a surge in numbers in 1984 (Richards 1997). The population has clearly risen since then, although the picture is clouded by the provision of more nest-boxes. According to the annual county bird reports, the total stayed at roughly the 1984 level throughout the 1980s, then 'larger than usual numbers' were reported in 1990 and the county population reached a new plateau during the 1990s, with annual figures of 46–64 males at 16–23 sites, and exceptional totals of 74 males at 25 sites in 1999. This was followed by a crash to 35 males at 14 sites in 2000. There was no apparent drop in the national population index between those two years and the fall must be ascribed to unknown factors, but it affected most localities in the county, widely spaced from each other: Pied Flycatchers bred on Wirral from about 1989 to 1999 but not since. From 2000 to 2003, the Cheshire total was recorded as 30–43 males at 12–18 sites. All of these figures are of 'males', as detailed in *CWBRs*, rather than breeding pairs: some birds hold two territories and others, pioneer prospectors for new sites, do not succeed in attracting a mate. Many of the 'possible' breeding records on the distribution map were likely to have been male birds on passage, and these records are omitted from the 'change' map.

The populations in the South Pennines and in North Wales expanded during the 1980s and 1990s, perhaps fuelling the rise in our county population. Some birds wander quite widely, such as the female that bred in Powys one year then in Delamere Forest the next year. On the other hand, some birds show strong site fidelity: one female ringed in Delamere Forest bred there in 1992, 1993, 1994 and 1996, using the same nest-box in the first two years.

The comprehensive fieldwork for this Atlas uncovered a few more birds than previously, but it is still a scarce species in Cheshire, and has not reoccupied any Wirral site. Most Cheshire birds are along the Sandstone Ridge or in the eastern hills. The 2005 *CWBR* detailed 46 known nesting or territory-holding birds, and during this Atlas period there are likely to have been around 50–60 pairs of Pied Flycatchers breeding in the county.

Sponsored by Clive Richards

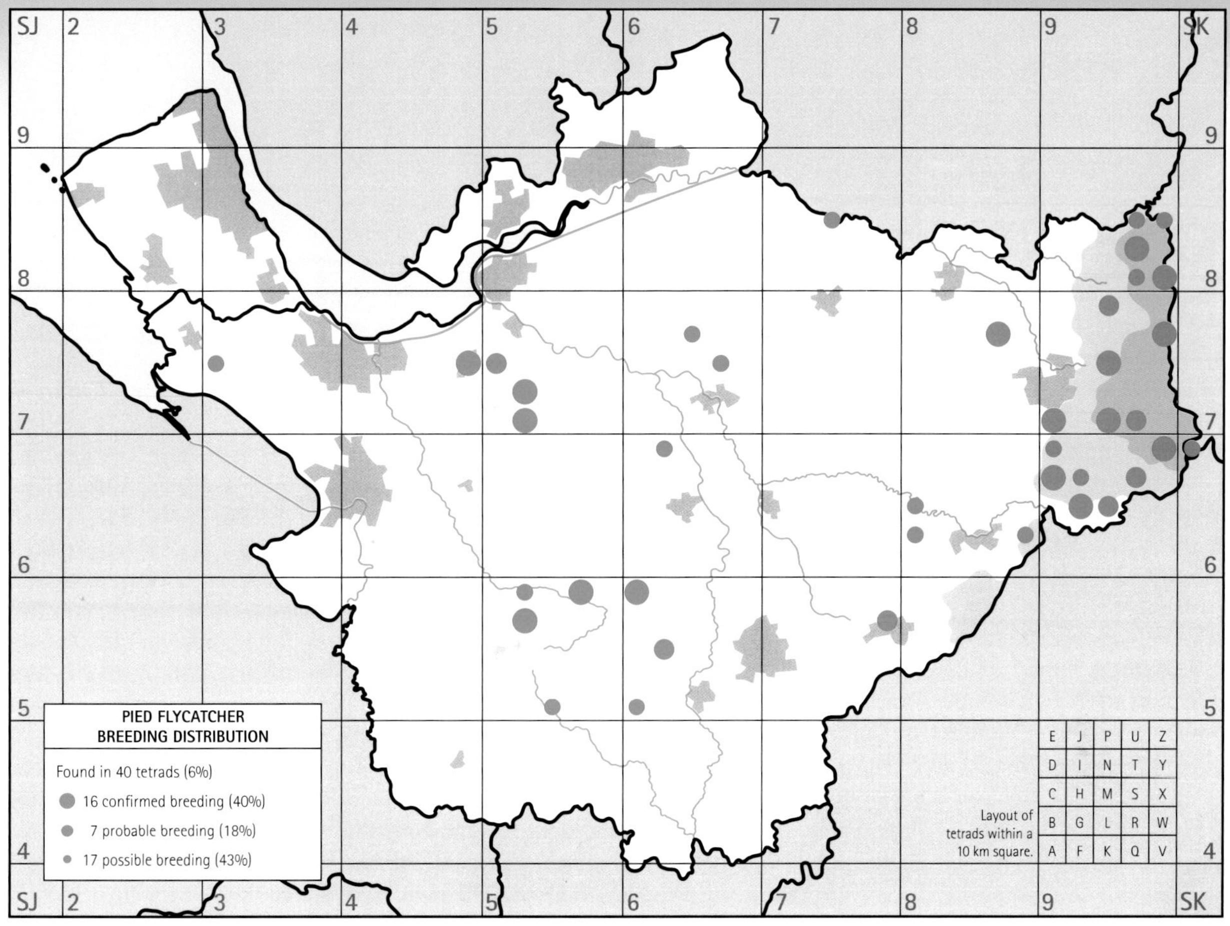
PIED FLYCATCHER
BREEDING DISTRIBUTION
Found in 40 tetrads (6%)
16 confirmed breeding (40%)
7 probable breeding (18%)
17 possible breeding (43%)
Layout of tetrads within a 10 km square.
E J P U Z
D I N T Y
C H M S X
B G L R W
A F K Q V
SJ
SK

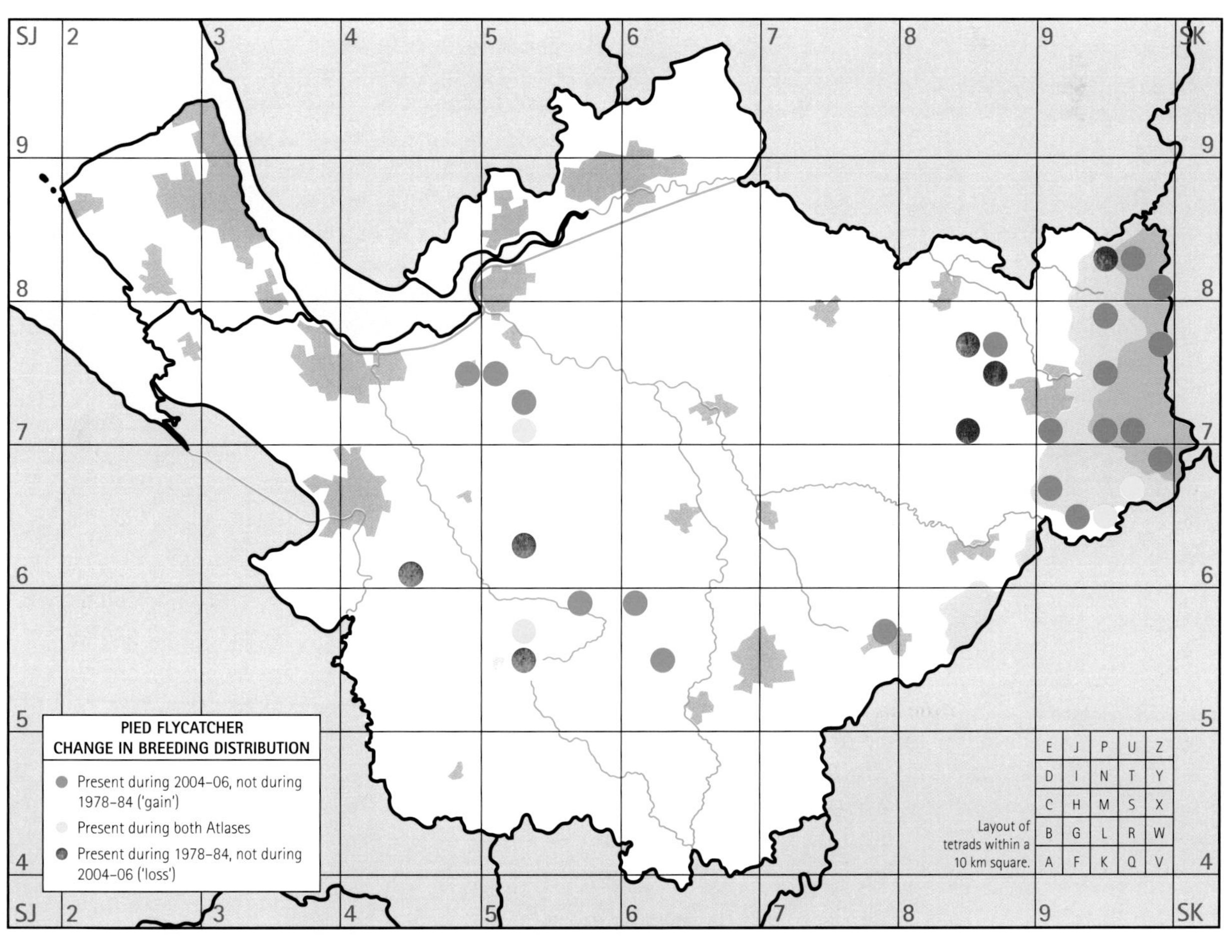
PIED FLYCATCHER
CHANGE IN BREEDING DISTRIBUTION
Present during 2004–06, not during 1978–84 ('gain')
Present during both Atlases
Present during 1978–84, not during 2004–06 ('loss')
Layout of tetrads within a 10 km square.
E J P U Z
D I N T Y
C H M S X
B G L R W
A F K Q V
SJ
SK

Bearded Tit

Panurus biarmicus

Bearded Tits first bred in Cheshire and Wirral in 2003, at Neston Reed-bed (SJ27Y), and again in 2004 to gain their inclusion in this Atlas. This event came out of the blue, there having been no record of the species in the county during the breeding season from 1985 to 2002, and it seems that no-one even knew the birds were at Neston until they were halfway through breeding, indicating just how elusive Bearded Tits can be, even in a well-watched site alongside a much-used footpath (Wells 2003). They are easiest to detect by ear, Bearded Tits making a loud metallic 'ping', unlike the call of any other British species.

The breeding birds are insectivorous, tending to catch relatively slow-moving insects. Good feeding places can shift suddenly from day to day as a change of wind direction or a synchronous emergence of chironomid midges or wainscot moth larvae suddenly produces easy pickings (Bibby 1983). Colin Wells noted that at one stage during the 2003 breeding attempt the birds were leaving the reed-bed to collect insects from the adjacent rushes. Researchers elsewhere have noted that the best feeding sites may be some way from the best nesting areas, entailing frequent flights, perhaps up to several hundred metres, for adults feeding chicks. On one day at Neston, the adults took food to the nest eight times in half an hour (Wells 2003).

PETER SMITH

From the information published in the *CWBRs*, it seems that the Neston birds had just one brood in each year. Elsewhere, they almost always have two broods, often three, and sometimes four in a season lasting as long as September, so that the most successful pairs of Bearded Tits might rear 20 chicks in a year, possibly the highest productive rate achieved by any passerine in Europe. To realize this, some birds overlap nesting attempts, the male building a new nest and his female laying eggs in it whilst they are both still feeding chicks from the first brood; as with most reed-nesting species, the young leave the nest before they can fly, and crawl through the vegetation, and appear to be independent of their parents at 20–25 days old (Bibby 1983). With Bearded Tits at some sites breeding from March onwards, and the birds at Neston not found feeding young until 29 May 2003, could that already have been their second breeding attempt?

They are confined almost exclusively to *phragmites* reed-beds, and ought to benefit from the national and local Biodiversity Action Plans for that habitat. Bearded Tits have bred at Leighton Moss, the RSPB reserve in north Lancashire, from 1973 on, with a peak of 65 pairs in 2000 (White *et al.* 2008). This is the only regular breeding site in north-west England, perhaps because all other reed-beds are too small, and certainly nowhere can match the 79 ha extent of that at Leighton Moss. The best habitats have a range of water levels: nests are likely to be in the drier parts of reed-beds which provide better undercover, and feeding places are most likely to be wet, especially along margins with open water where emerging chironomids may collect or be drifted by the wind. The birds use freshwater or brackish sites. They build their nests in the thick areas of reed litter, and at Leighton Moss have readily taken to using specially designed 'nest-boxes', wigwam-like structures that mimic their natural sites. Bearded Tits in Cheshire and Wirral might be helped by provision and monitoring of such nest structures by workers suitably licensed under Schedule 1 of the Wildlife and Countryside Act 1981.

Bearded Tits are scarce enough to be monitored by the Rare Breeding Birds Panel: the national population in 2004 was 534–556 pairs, at 51 sites in 15 counties (Holling *et al.* 2007a). Numbers have fluctuated over the last 30 years, but there were at least 590 pairs in 11 counties in 1974 and 339–408 pairs at 44 sites in 13 counties in 1992 (Campbell *et al.* 1996). But for now, they are not established members of the Cheshire and

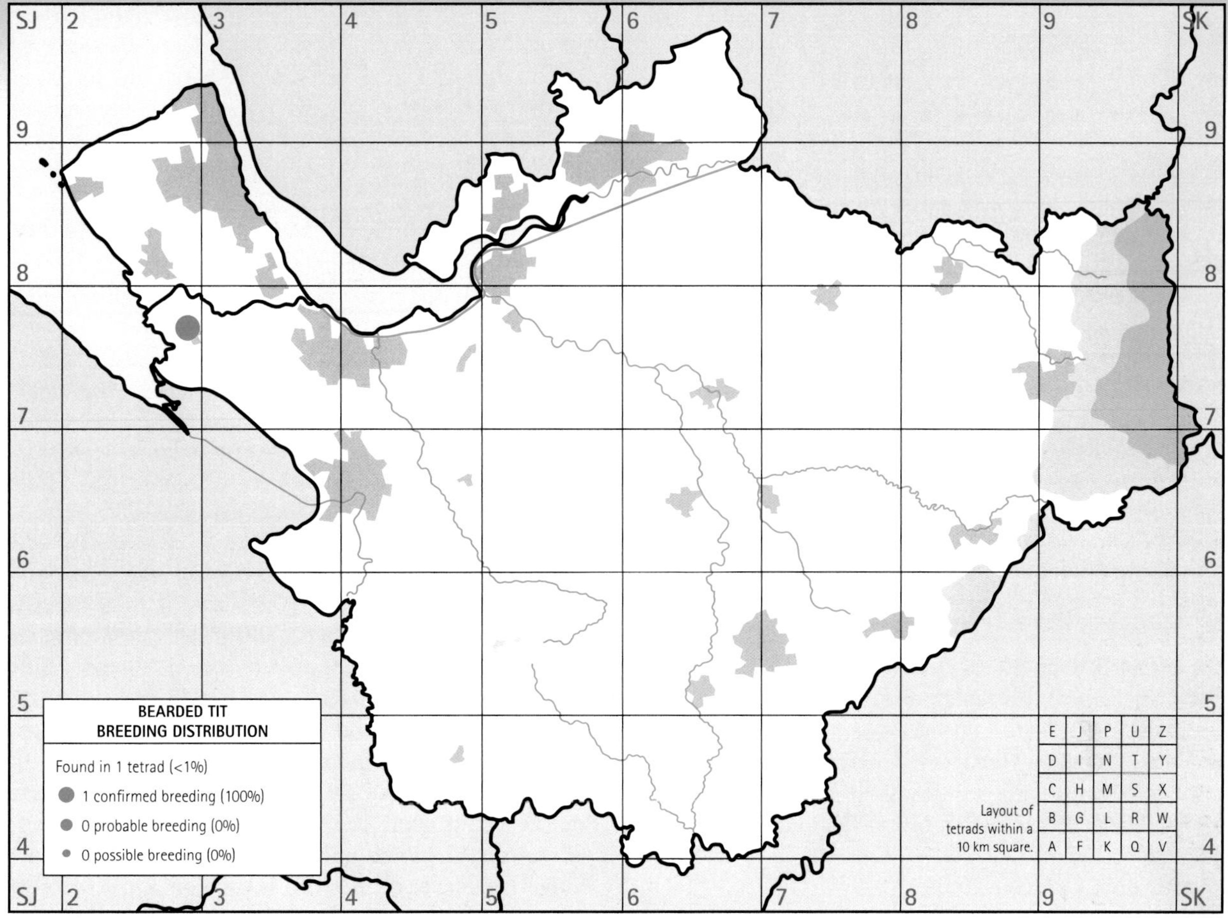

Wirral avifauna. In 2005 there were occasional records from Neston in the first three months of the year, and two were heard calling on 14 April, but there were no further records that year, and in 2006 birds were reported at Neston on 4 and 5 April only.

Bearded Tits continue their association with reed-beds all year round. They switch from their insectivorous summer diet to seed-eating during winter, with changes to their digestive system by elongation of the gut in order to cope (Bibby 1981). Continuing their dependence on *phragmites*, their favourite seed, they also eat other grasses and sedges such as nettles and willow-herbs. During this winter Atlas period, birds were seen, and heard 'pinging', in Neston Reed-bed during winter 2004/05, and in the same habitat at Woolston in 2006/07. At Neston there were four birds on 27 November 2004 and one, two or three birds reported on other dates through the whole winter period; at Woolston four birds arrived in mid-October 2006 and were seen for a few days but there were no further records until two were present on 18 February 2007.

There have been few wintering records of the species in Cheshire and Wirral. In 1965/66 there was substantial immigration to Britain and some reached the county: one caught at Bidston Moss in February 1966 wore a ring from the Netherlands. From 1971 to 1975 birds were also reported in the county, mostly in October, but odd ones during winter. Since then, their scarcity is shown by the few records in *CWBRs*, the only birds in winter being a male at Rostherne on 29 and 30 November 1977, one or two at Neston Reed-bed for 10 weeks over winter 1992/93 and two at Arpley tip (SJ58T) on 4 February 2001.

Bell (1967) described the birds in 1965/66 as the first authenticated records for the county, discounting Coward's (1910) listing of two pairs shot during the nineteenth century; Coward himself questioned the records, but largely because 'the Bearded Titmouse is a species that rarely wanders from its usual haunts', a statement that is now known to be spectacularly wrong.

One of the features of Bearded Tit ecology is their irruptions. In some autumns at some sites, birds gather and rise high above the reeds, perhaps dropping into a new part of the same reed-bed, and on occasion leaving the site and flying long distances. During these movements they tend to travel in pairs: a male and female caught just outside our county boundary at Shotton, Flintshire, by Merseyside Ringing Group in October 1965, bore consecutively numbered Dutch rings. There has been much discussion about what drives these irruptions. The species' extreme output of young can lead to high autumn populations, perhaps putting pressure on food resources and forcing them to move in search of reed seeds. But Bearded Tits showed this behaviour every year since they colonized Leighton Moss, regardless of population or seed availability (Wilson 1993). It is not just one-way traffic: some irrupting birds have returned to the continent, including birds ringed in Flintshire in the 1970s subsequently caught in Germany and the Netherlands.

Numbers may be substantially reduced in severe winters, when reed seeds can become glazed with frost

RAY SCALLY

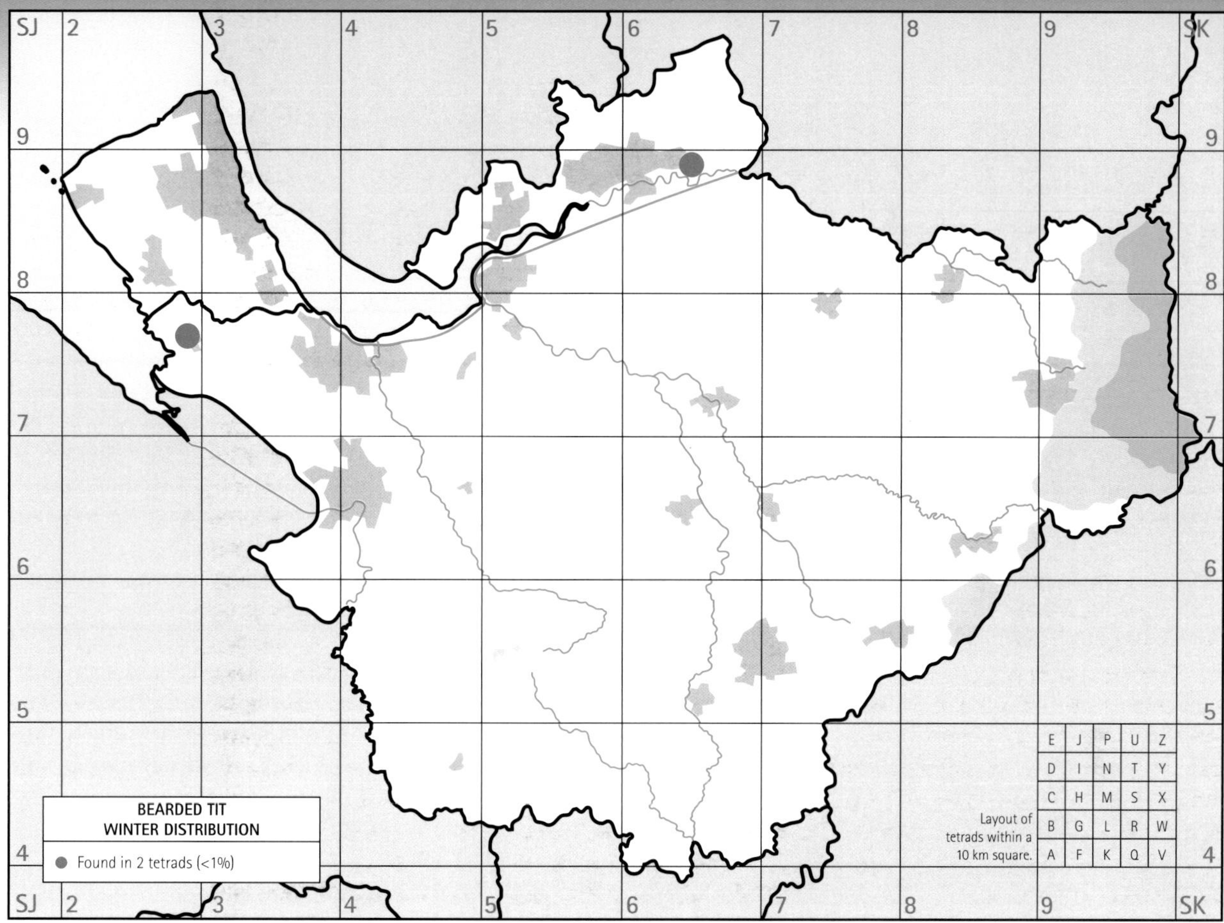

or hidden under snow. The breeding population of Leighton Moss fell following hard winters in 1978/79, 1981/82 and 1985/86–1987/88, and crashed from 65 pairs in 2000 to seven pairs in 2001 after high water levels in late 2000 had submerged the reed litter, their favoured feeding site, followed by midwinter snowfall (White *et al.* 2008).

Long-tailed Tit

Aegithalos caudatus

SUE & ANDY TRANTER

A Long-tailed Tit's nest is a work of art, once seen, never forgotten. It may contain more than 2,000 feathers, and the outside of the nest is bound together, decorated and camouflaged with lichens. Jonathan Guest suggested in our *First Atlas* that the scarcity of Long-tailed Tits breeding in the Mersey valley, Stanlow/Ellesmere Port area and much of east and north Wirral was because of the polluted air and lack of lichens. Since then, reduced levels of atmospheric sulphur dioxide allowed the pioneering epiphytic lichens to move in, as shown on the maps on p. 35 (Fox & Guest 2003), and Long-tailed Tits (and Chaffinches) have also colonized the same areas. The only parts of the county from which they are now absent are some of the highest uplands, the salt-marshes and Hilbre, with other unexpected gaps around Frodsham and odd tetrads elsewhere in which the species was unaccountably missed.

This is the thirteenth most numerous breeding species in the county: the BTO BBS analysis shows that the population in 2004–05 was 37,670 birds (21,140–54,200), corresponding to an average of about 70 birds per tetrad with confirmed or probable breeding, an enormous change from the assumed underestimate in our *First Atlas* of up to 1,500 pairs. Cheshire and Wirral holds a disproportionately high figure of as much as 3.6% of the UK total of just over one million birds. English populations were depressed during most of the period of our *First Atlas*, probably by winter mortality, and the ameliorating climate of the 1990s has allowed their numbers to rise to a level more than 50% higher than 20 years ago. Presumably also in response to warmer weather, Long-tailed Tits are breeding earlier, with average first-egg dates having advanced to about 6 April, nine days earlier in just 20 years.

This is an easy species in which to prove breeding, 71% of records being two-letter codes. Long-tailed Tits are early nesters, usually building most of the nest in February and March, then leaving it for a month or so before lining and using it. The suggestion is that so many nests fall to predation, often to corvids and mustelids—only some 16% of nests yielded fledged young in one detailed study (Glen & Perrins 1988)—that, if a nest has survived intact for a month, usually whilst there are few leaves on the bushes, it is quite likely to serve the birds well for their breeding attempt. Some nests can be quite obvious, and observers in 65 tetrads found an occupied nest with eggs or chicks, with another 79 tetrads providing breeding evidence through adults carrying food or a faecal sac; but the vast majority of records (268) came from fieldworkers seeing parties of recently fledged young. A typical family party comprises the pair of adults and six juveniles, often with an extra one or two adults. If a nest is lost early enough in the season, some pairs build another, but many move to help feed chicks at another Long-tailed Tits' nest nearby. Research has shown that the helpers are almost always related to the male parent, so they are assisting in raising their nephews and nieces, thus having a genetic interest in ensuring the survival of those chicks. This helping is beneficial to all concerned. At nests with helpers, the chicks are more likely to fledge, the parents can reduce their feeding rate and maintain their own condition better, and the chicks are better nourished and weigh more (Glen & Perrins 1988).

Although most habitat records were woodland (298 tetrads), this is by far the most likely of the four common tits (with Coal, Blue and Great Tits) to be found in scrub (139 tetrads). The other main habitat categories were hedgerow (126) and farmland (105); the species is quite tolerant of human presence (139 tetrads in human sites).

Sponsored by Tony and Margaret Hayter

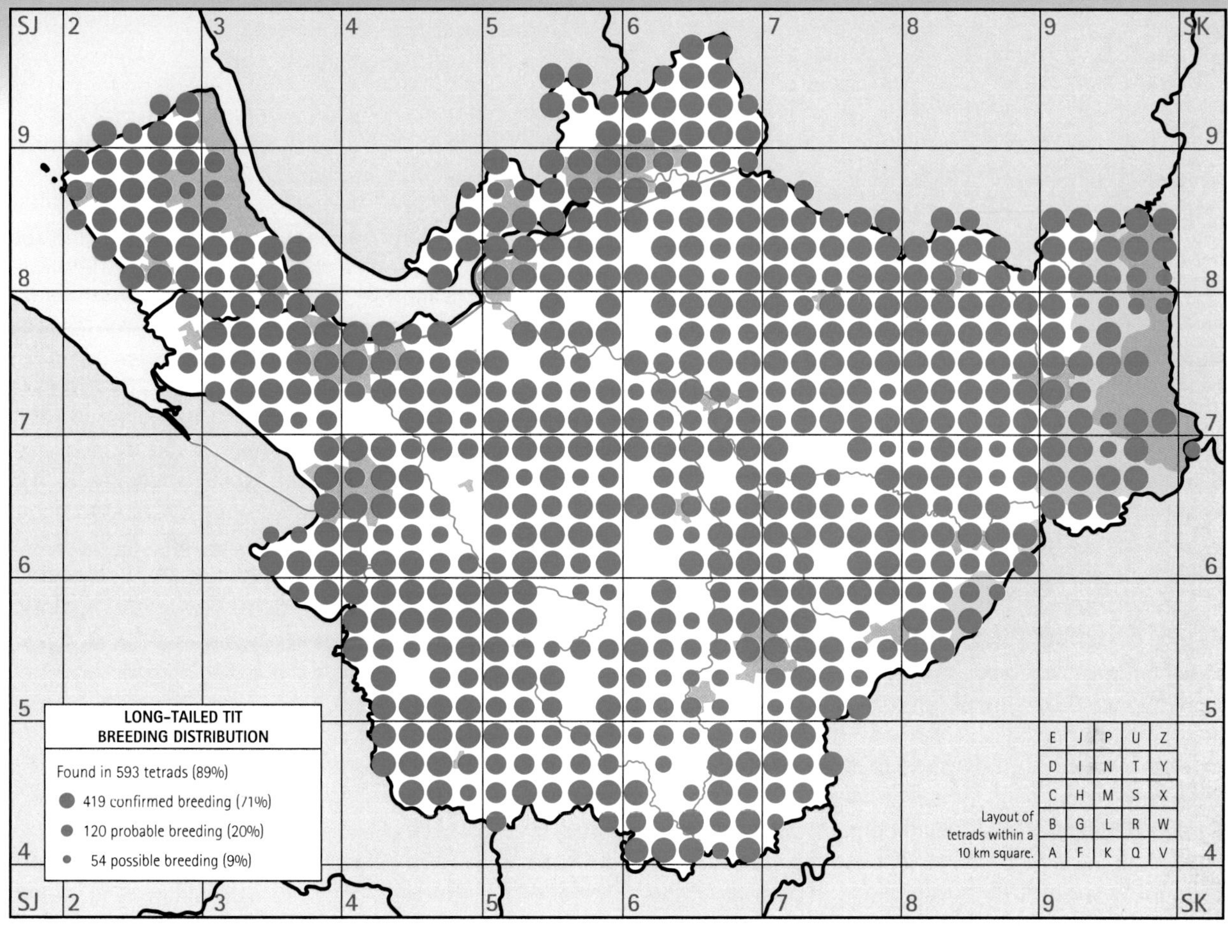
SJ
SK
2
3
4
5
6
7
8
9
LONG-TAILED TIT
BREEDING DISTRIBUTION
Found in 593 tetrads (89%)
419 confirmed breeding (71%)
120 probable breeding (20%)
54 possible breeding (9%)
E J P U Z
D I N T Y
C H M S X
B G L R W
A F K Q V
Layout of tetrads within a 10 km square.

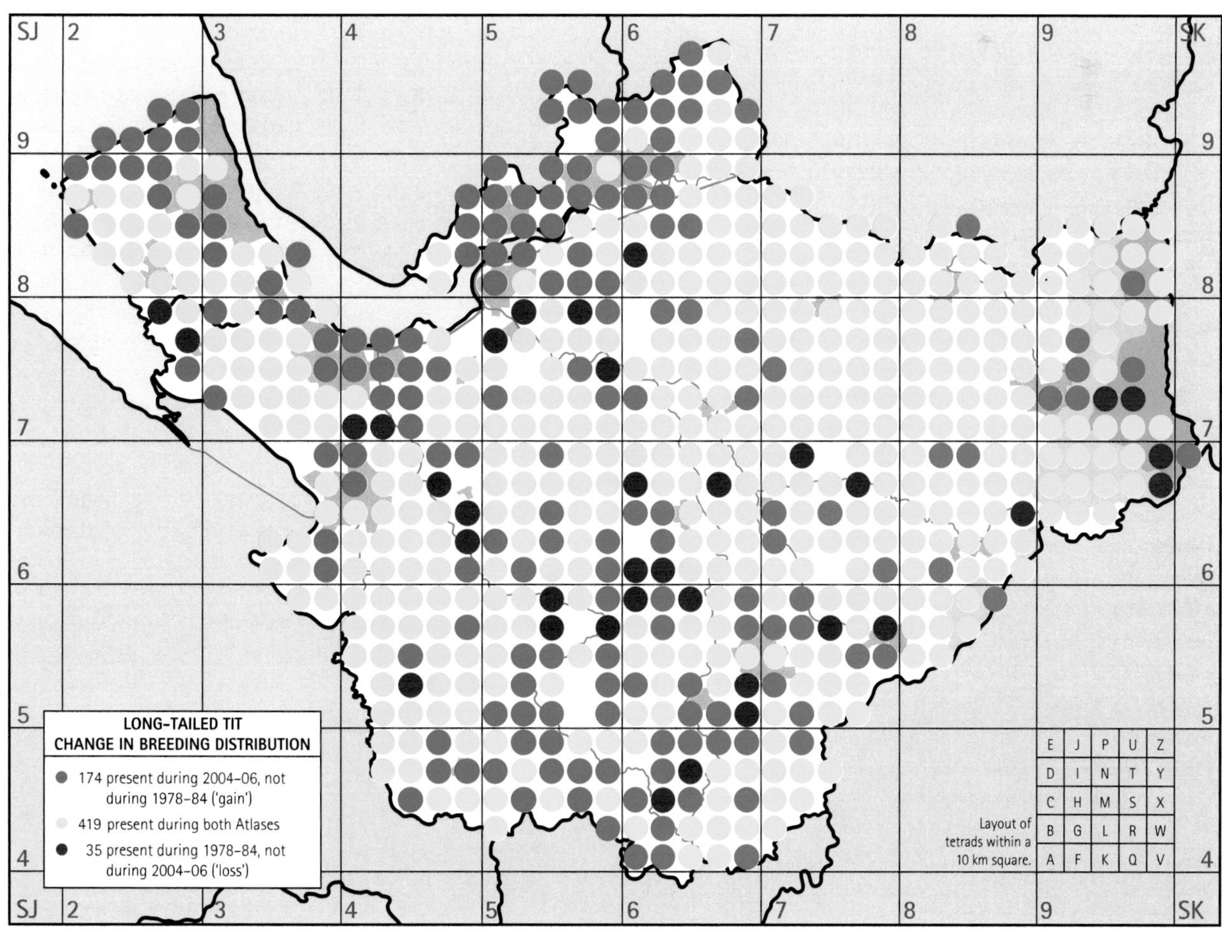
SJ
SK
2
3
4
5
6
7
8
9
LONG-TAILED TIT
CHANGE IN BREEDING DISTRIBUTION
174 present during 2004–06, not during 1978–84 ('gain')
419 present during both Atlases
35 present during 1978–84, not during 2004–06 ('loss')
E J P U Z
D I N T Y
C H M S X
B G L R W
A F K Q V
Layout of tetrads within a 10 km square.

The Atlas maps show that Long-tailed Tits do move somewhat to occupy extra tetrads in winter, and become the eleventh most widespread winter species. There are 573 tetrads with birds in breeding and winter seasons, 49 tetrads having birds in winter only, and 20 with breeding season presence but no winter record. The areas filled in during winter include some of the county's most inhospitable tetrads, five in the highest hills and five in urban east Wirral. Most of our birds appear to be resident or make short distance movements, but some do undertake longer journeys, including a flock of three juveniles, ringed together in June 1981 in Warwickshire and retrapped together on 14 February 1982 at Caldy, 142 km north-west.

As this record suggests, these gregarious birds spend most of their lives together, seldom seeming to be more than one or two bushes apart from each other. The groups are usually family parties, comprising a brood, its parents and any extra adults that helped to raise that brood. Over the three years, 663 Atlas records included counts of flock sizes: 30% of them held more than 10 birds, but only 2% were above 20 in size. The numbers in the larger flocks are difficult to estimate, but on 17 February 2001 I mist-netted two flocks totalling 55 birds going to roost in areas of bramble and rhododendron only 100 m apart from each other.

The winter flocks are generally territorial, holding an average area of around 20 ha, with larger flocks maintaining larger territories (Glen & Perrins 1988). With such large areas, the birds in one flock do not often come into contact with those in another, but when they do, they defend their boundary vigorously. Long-tailed Tits also roost together, low down in a dense thorny bush. This is one of the few British species where the communally roosting birds actually huddle together for warmth on cold winter nights, perhaps the reason that they stay in parties throughout the winter. Nonetheless, winter survival is often difficult for small birds, and prolonged periods of hard weather have hit the species hard in the past as Bell (1962) noted, but the mild winters of the last decade or more have allowed populations to flourish.

Analysis of the habitat codes shows significant shifts between breeding and winter seasons. Woodland is still the most favoured but far fewer birds were reported from scrub (7% of records in winter, 17% during the breeding season) and farmland (7% of records in winter, 13% during the breeding season). Instead, birds are found much more in hedges (25% of records in winter, 16% during the breeding season) and in human sites (22% of records in winter, 17% during the breeding season). These changes indicate that birds are preferentially using the warmer and less windswept areas, where they can keep themselves warmer and are more likely to find insects. Long-tailed Tits are usually insectivorous all year round, although some birds in gardens do learn to feed on peanuts and suet.

RAY SCALLY

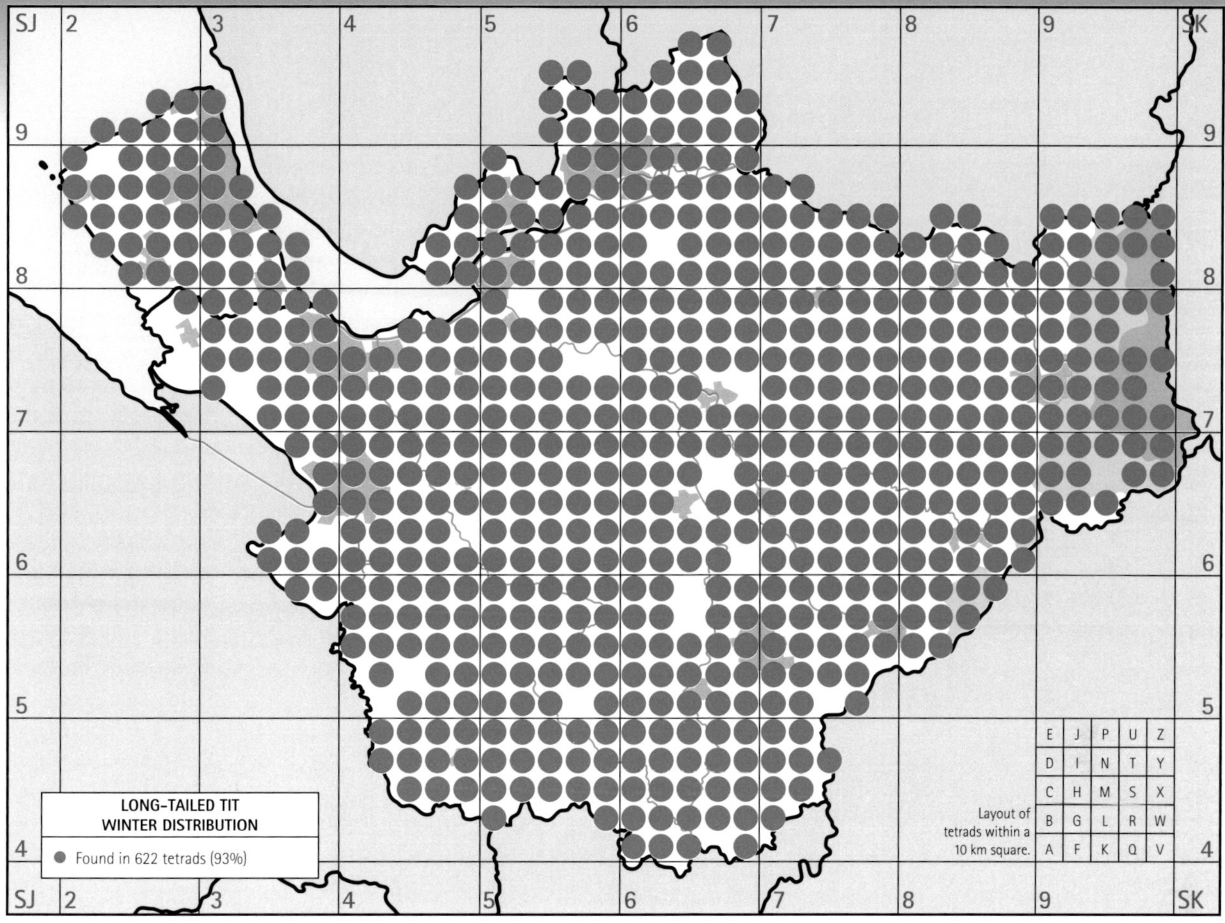
SJ
2
3
4
5
6
7
8
9
SK
9
8
7
6
5
4
LONG-TAILED TIT
WINTER DISTRIBUTION
Found in 622 tetrads (93%)
E J P U Z
D I N T Y
C H M S X
B G L R W
A F K Q V
Layout of tetrads within a 10 km square.

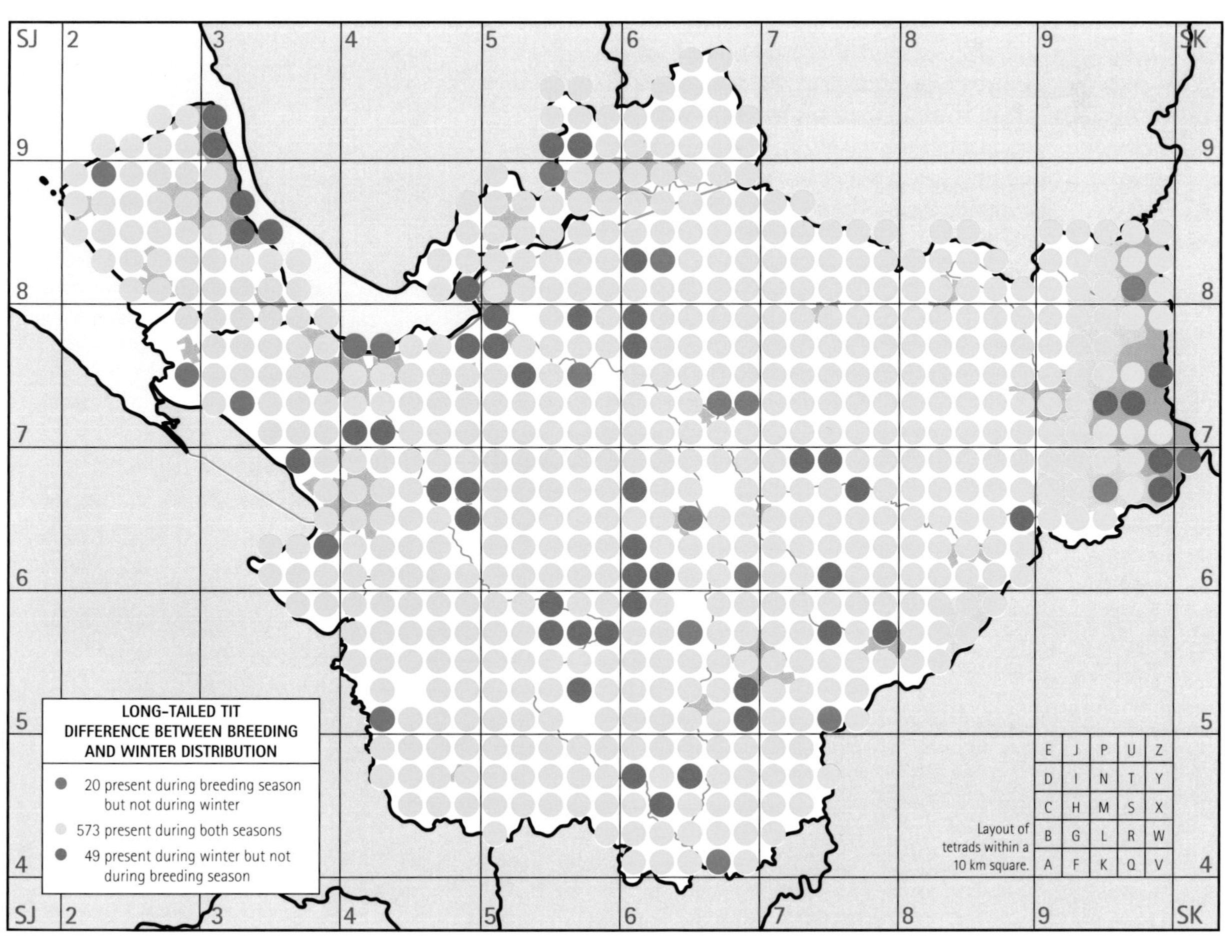
SJ
2
3
4
5
6
7
8
9
SK
9
8
7
6
5
4
LONG-TAILED TIT
DIFFERENCE BETWEEN BREEDING AND WINTER DISTRIBUTION
20 present during breeding season but not during winter
573 present during both seasons
49 present during winter but not during breeding season
E J P U Z
D I N T Y
C H M S X
B G L R W
A F K Q V
Layout of tetrads within a 10 km square.

Blue Tit

Cyanistes caeruleus

SUE & ANDY TRANTER

The analysis of BBS transects shows that this is our second most numerous species, with a breeding population of Cheshire and Wirral in 2004–05 of 195,250 birds (164,480–226,010). This massive total corresponds to an average of more than 150 pairs per tetrad, equivalent to a density of one pair per 2.6 ha across the entire county. This figure is 1.7% of the UK breeding population of 11.3 million birds (Newson *et al.* 2008). National monitoring shows that Blue Tit populations have increased by about 14% in the last 20 years since our *First Atlas*, aided by mild winters, provision of food in gardens and the availability of nest-boxes. The rise in population has been accompanied by decreasing clutch and brood sizes, and a substantial decline in the proportion of young birds in early autumn, in a clear demonstration of density-dependence, suggesting that the British countryside has reached its carrying capacity and is 'full' of Blue Tits.

As in our *First Atlas*, Blue Tits are almost ubiquitous, missing only from a couple of the bleakest upland tetrads, the estuarine salt-marshes and Hilbre, and a handful of tetrads in which it was just bad luck that an observer could not find them. This species provided the highest number of confirmed breeding records, showing how easy it is to prove breeding (92% of records). Surveyors in 140 tetrads saw them carrying food or a faecal sac, and most records (253) came from fieldworkers seeing parties of recently fledged young, but occupied or used nests were recorded in 32 tetrads, and a nest with eggs or chicks in as many as 178. Blue Tits always nest in a hole or crevice of some sort, and observers reported a wide variety: natural holes in oak, ash and alder; and a range of unnatural sites including holes in metal and concrete gateposts, lampposts, telegraph poles and walls. Henry Finch noted them nesting in a weathercock atop Kingsley church spire (SJ57M). In 2001 Blue Tits reared seven young at Woolston in the stem of a dead giant hogweed, and the feat was repeated in a different part of the reserve in 2002; during this survey, in 2006, Steve and Gill Barber saw birds using the same plant near Tiverton (SJ56K), carrying nesting material into a broken (open-topped) stem.

Most Blue Tits were recorded in woodland habitats (375 tetrads), almost all deciduous or mixed, with birds found in scrub in 85 tetrads. The other main habitat categories were hedgerow (125) and farmland (135); in agricultural areas hedgerow trees are crucial for them in providing nest holes and caterpillars. The species is quite tolerant of human presence; the 350 records in the F categories comprised 36 urban, 116 suburban and 198 rural sites.

In their prime habitat of broad-leaved woodland—which can support up to 1,000 pairs per tetrad (Perrins 1979)—they feed their brood on defoliating caterpillars, especially of winter moths, collected from the tree canopy. The adults bring food as often as once a minute throughout daylight hours for the 18–21 days the chicks are in the nest, a total of perhaps 10,000 caterpillars per pair. The timing of Blue Tits' breeding season can vary by up to three weeks from year to year as they try to coincide with the short-lived flush of moth larvae. In recent years (notably 1999, 2003 and 2007) there have been days of torrential rainfall in May, often washing many of the caterpillars from the canopy onto the ground. Although they are readily taken by Blackbirds, Robins and other ground-feeders, it seems that tits do not recognize them as food and continue to search the leaves: many chicks have starved as a result.

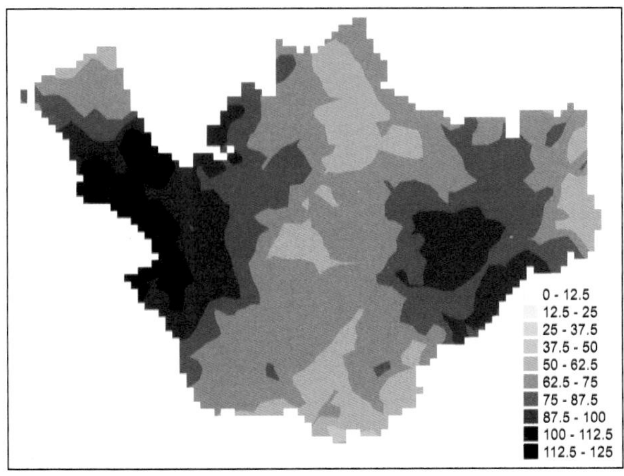

Blue Tit abundance.

Sponsored by Marie Turner

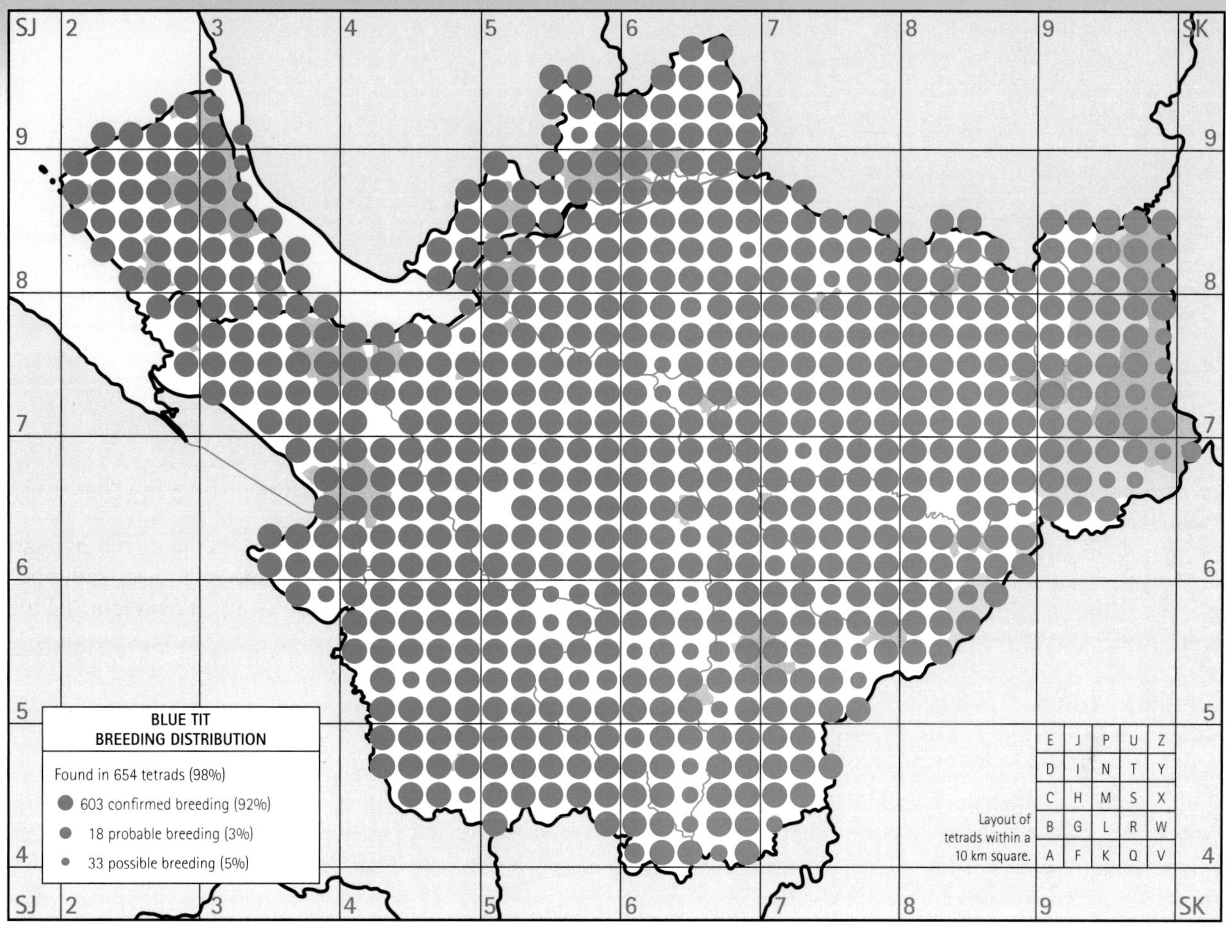
SJ
2
3
4
5
6
7
8
9
SK
9
8
7
6
5
4
BLUE TIT
BREEDING DISTRIBUTION
Found in 654 tetrads (98%)
603 confirmed breeding (92%)
18 probable breeding (3%)
33 possible breeding (5%)
E J P U Z
D I N T Y
C H M S X
B G L R W
A F K Q V
Layout of tetrads within a 10 km square.

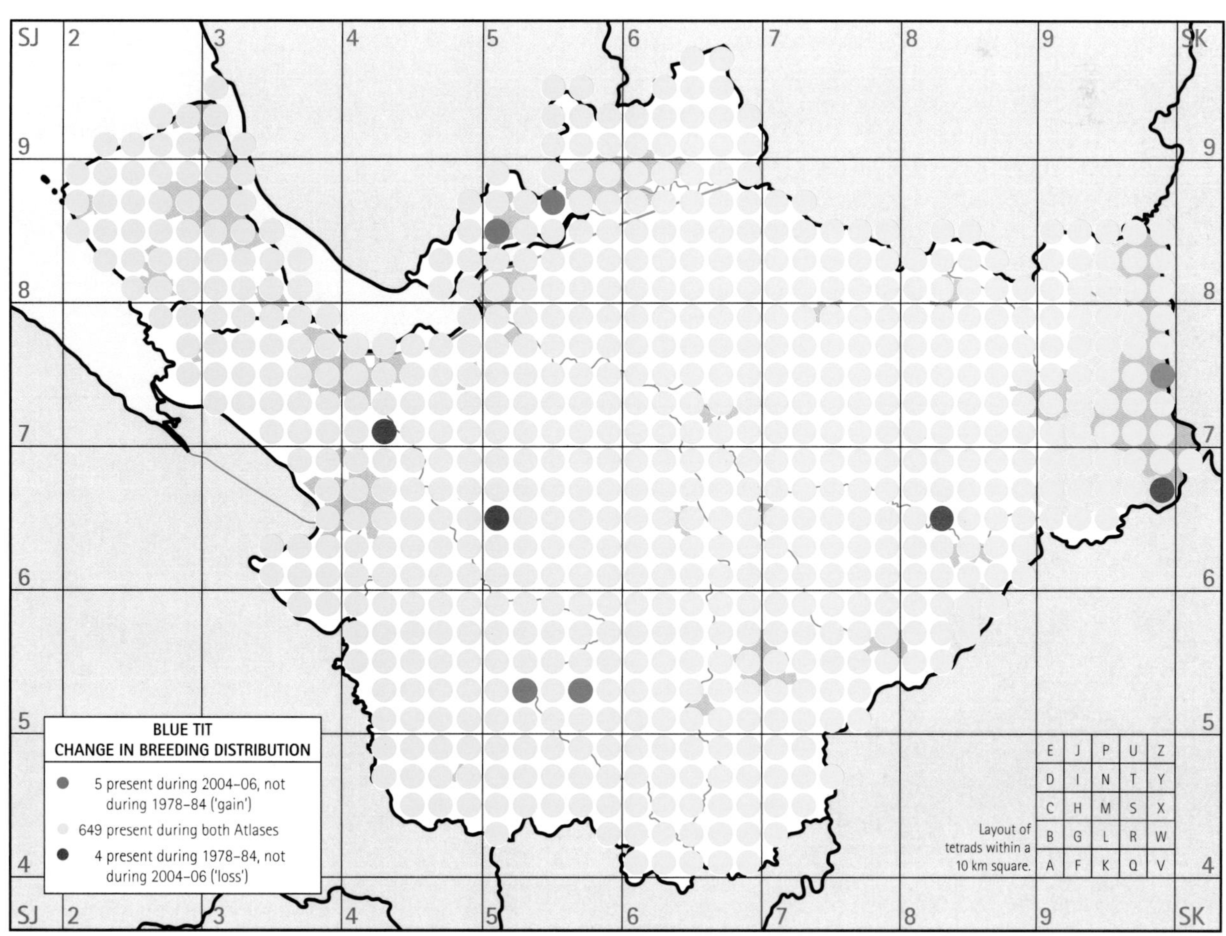
SJ
2
3
4
5
6
7
8
9
SK
9
8
7
6
5
4
BLUE TIT
CHANGE IN BREEDING DISTRIBUTION
5 present during 2004–06, not during 1978–84 ('gain')
649 present during both Atlases
4 present during 1978–84, not during 2004–06 ('loss')
E J P U Z
D I N T Y
C H M S X
B G L R W
A F K Q V
Layout of tetrads within a 10 km square.

There is little difference in the breeding season and winter distribution of Blue Tits in the county. Odd birds occasionally make it to Hilbre and also into the highest eastern hills, but not the estuarine saltmarshes. Blue Tits' habitat use is similar in winter, with most records in woodland and human sites, but there are significant drops in birds reported from scrub (5% of records in winter, 8% during the breeding season) and farmland (8% of records in winter, 13% during the breeding season), with more birds found in farmland hedges (26% of records in winter, 12% during the breeding season).

In natural woodlands, Blue Tits spend most of their time in winter in oaks, searching for insect food amongst the leaves and dead branches, increasingly turning to examining buds when they appear. Beechmast is an important seed, if present, and in gardens they eat peanuts, sunflower and other seeds, bread, suet and other fats. Their former habit—known in Cheshire in the 1930s (Boyd 1946)—of pecking the tops from milk-bottles and drinking the cream is seldom reported these days.

Many writers have had nothing to say about wintering Blue Tits, Coward (1910) and Bell (1962) amongst them, and for many years the annual county bird reports describe only their autumn coastal passage. A detailed study of a relatively small population in suburban Birmingham (Kenrick 1940), which ought to be repeated today, found four components to the population. About 38% of birds were resident, breeding in local nest-boxes and visiting bird tables in winter. A further 12% were summer visitors, seen in successive years but only when breeding. Another one-quarter were winter visitors, seen in successive winters but not during the breeding season, and one-quarter of Blue Tits moved through the area, especially in late winter, and were never seen again.

Blue Tits live in flocks for most of the winter, although the median count submitted for this Atlas was just four birds. After the breeding season, birds move around and invade territories, whose owners no longer defend them. A winter flock consists of a small nucleus of dominant residents and constantly drifting, subservient nomads, its composition frequently changing as some individuals leave and new ones join. Even within the winter flocks, however, some birds will be paired, and these birds often display and roost together, probably in an area that they later use for breeding (Colquhoun 1942).

Most Blue Tits live all their lives within a short distance of their natal site. A bird ringed at Meols as a juvenile in 1992 succumbed to a Sparrowhawk at the same site in 2002 when it was a few months short of the national record for longevity. The median distance of movement of chicks to winter areas is only 3 km, although 5% of birds move more than 68 km and females move farther than males. The distances that a few will travel are shown by the bird caught at Woolston on 24 February 2001 that had been ringed as a chick in 1996 in a nest-box in Grizedale Forest, Cumbria, 111 km away. After midwinter the range contracts as birds move back towards their natal site (or the more distant ones die). For those recruited to the breeding population at one year of age, 95% of them are within 15 km of the natal site and half are within 2 km, showing their essentially sedentary nature (*Migration Atlas*).

By the end of our winter period, many Blue Tits are on territory and choosing nest sites, examining every possibility. I put up a nest-box in my garden on 25 February 2002, and had walked no more than 5 m away before a Blue Tit was looking into the hole, and birds have bred in it every year since.

BEN HALL

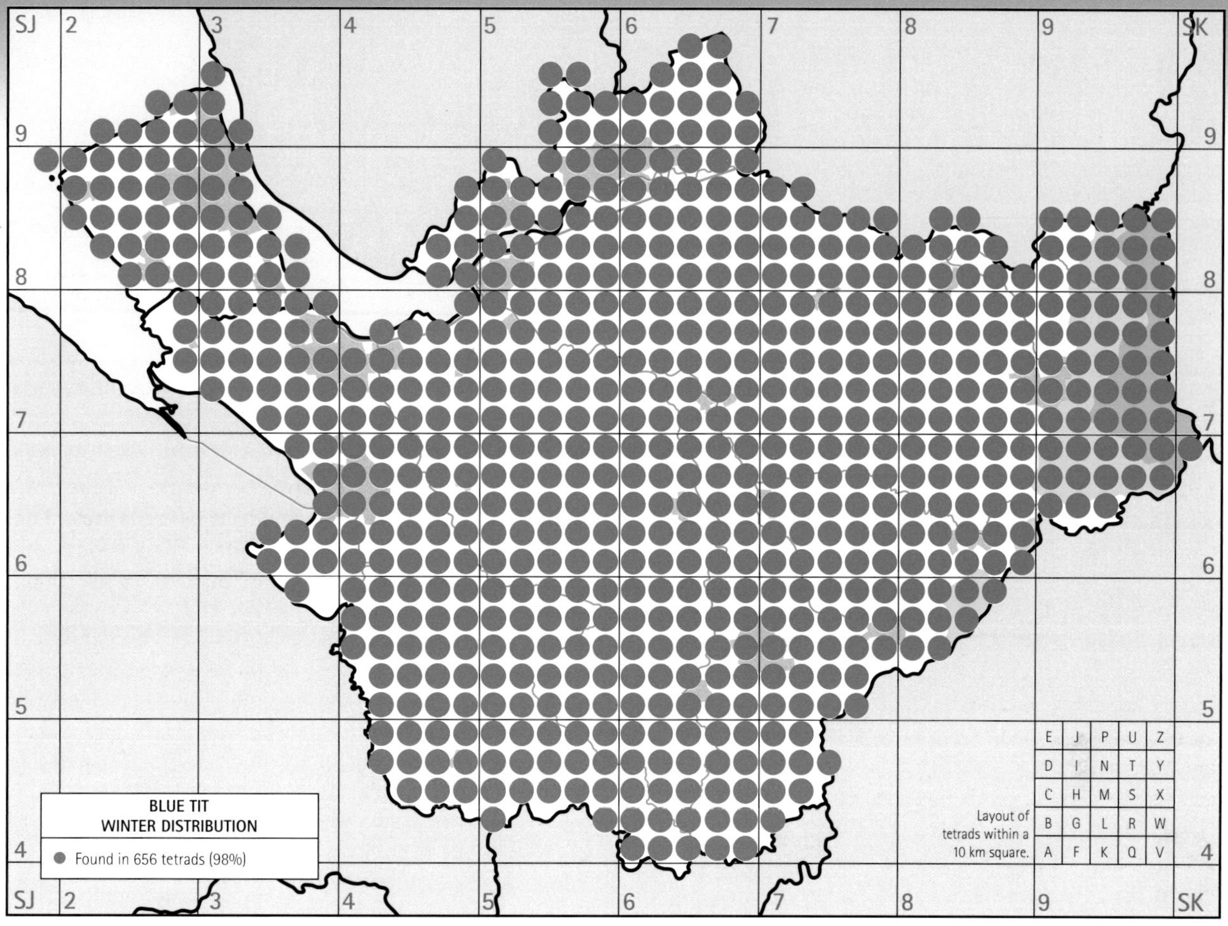
SJ
2
3
4
5
6
7
8
9
SK
BLUE TIT
WINTER DISTRIBUTION
Found in 656 tetrads (98%)
Layout of
tetrads within a
10 km square.
E J P U Z
D I N T Y
C H M S X
B G L R W
A F K Q V

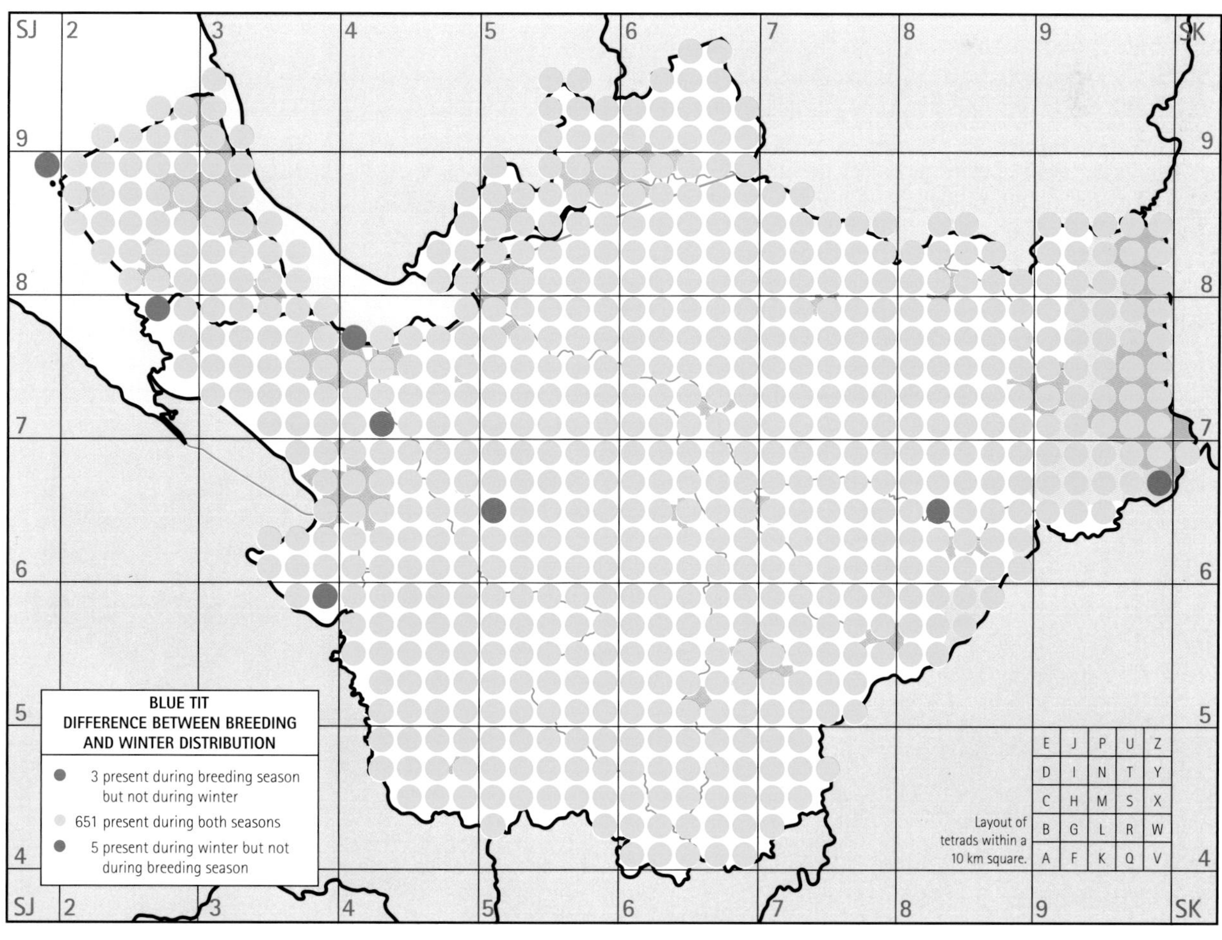
SJ
2
3
4
5
6
7
8
9
SK
BLUE TIT
DIFFERENCE BETWEEN BREEDING
AND WINTER DISTRIBUTION
3 present during breeding season but not during winter
651 present during both seasons
5 present during winter but not during breeding season
Layout of
tetrads within a
10 km square.
E J P U Z
D I N T Y
C H M S X
B G L R W
A F K Q V

Great Tit

Parus major

BEN HALL

Great Tit is the eighth most widespread species across Cheshire and Wirral. This Atlas showed a very similar distribution to our *First Atlas*, with birds almost everywhere except for three of the highest-lying tetrads at the east of the county, Hilbre and the estuaries, and a handful of others where they were not found. This species' division across the habitat classes was almost identical to that of Blue Tits. Most recorded habitats were woodland (374 tetrads) or human sites (333), with fewer in scrub (85 tetrads), hedgerow (129) and farmland (131).

This is an easy species in which to prove breeding (89% of records) and provided the third highest number of confirmed breeding records. Fieldworkers in 281 tetrads saw parties of recently fledged young, usually noisy and conspicuous as they pester their parents for food. Adults carrying food or a faecal sac were reported in 146 tetrads, but occupied or used nests were recorded in 22 tetrads, and a nest with eggs or chicks in 133. Nests were reported from natural sites including holes in oak, alder and birch trees, in numerous nest-boxes and a variety of others including an old Kingfisher hole in a stream bank, holes in walls, gateposts, telegraph poles, a road signpost and a metal lamppost on Runcorn East station (SJ58K). These metal structures must suffer extremes of temperature, but chicks fledged from at least some of them. This is probably the species most likely to interrupt postal services by nesting in a postbox, as Tricia Thompson reported from near Styal (SJ88H).

The BTO BBS analysis shows that the breeding population of Cheshire and Wirral in 2004–05 was 104,160 birds (87,940–120,430), corresponding to an average of about 85 pairs per tetrad with confirmed or probable breeding, and about 1.8% of the UK breeding population of 5.8 million birds (Newson *et al.* 2008). Great Tits nationally have increased by about 22% in the 20 years since our *First Atlas*, probably encouraged by more provision of winter food in gardens and the lack of hard weather to knock them back.

The Great Tit is often said to be the most studied small bird in the world: their breeding has been followed for sixty years in woods near Oxford and for seventy years in the Netherlands (Perrins 1979, Gosler 1993). Their egg-laying dates are proving to be a sensitive and fascinating test of climate change. In Cheshire woodlands, they usually start laying in the second half of April, but can be somewhat earlier or later; Great Tits in gardens breed earlier but raise smaller broods. The laying date of British birds has advanced by about a week in the last forty years, in line with rising temperatures, but the date for emergence of winter moth caterpillars, the chicks' main food, has not shifted as much. In the Netherlands, however, the opposite is true: caterpillar emergence is earlier and Great Tit laying phenology has stayed the same (Visser & Both 2005). In both cases the result is the same: they are increasingly struggling to find enough food for their brood.

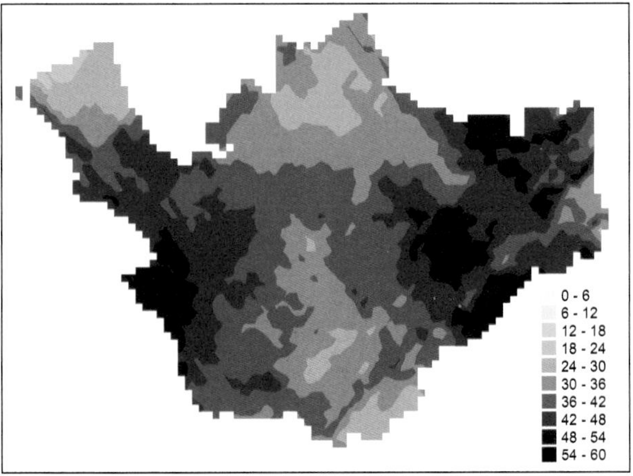

Great Tit abundance.

Sponsored by Paul S. Lewis

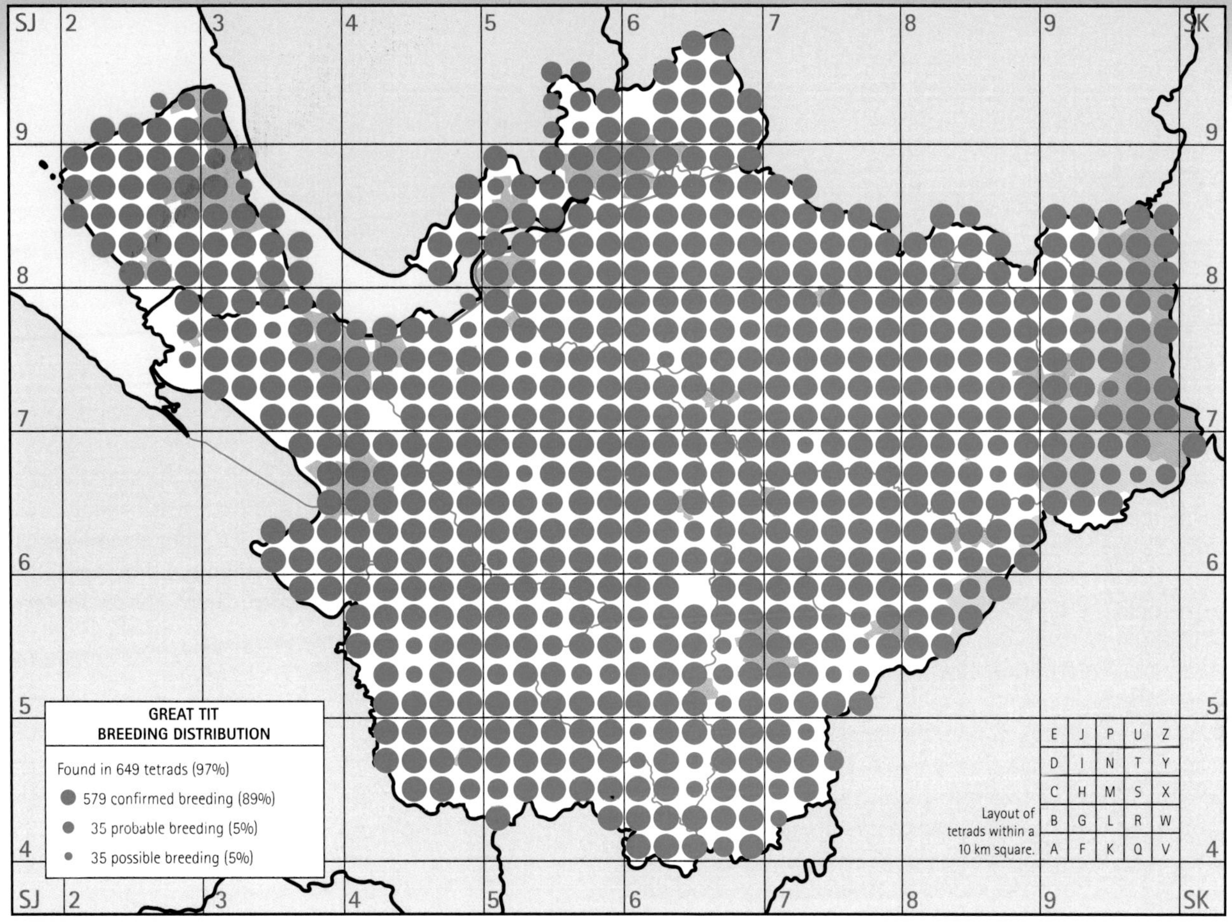
GREAT TIT
BREEDING DISTRIBUTION
Found in 649 tetrads (97%)
579 confirmed breeding (89%)
35 probable breeding (5%)
35 possible breeding (5%)
Layout of tetrads within a 10 km square.
E J P U Z
D I N T Y
C H M S X
B G L R W
A F K Q V
SJ
SK

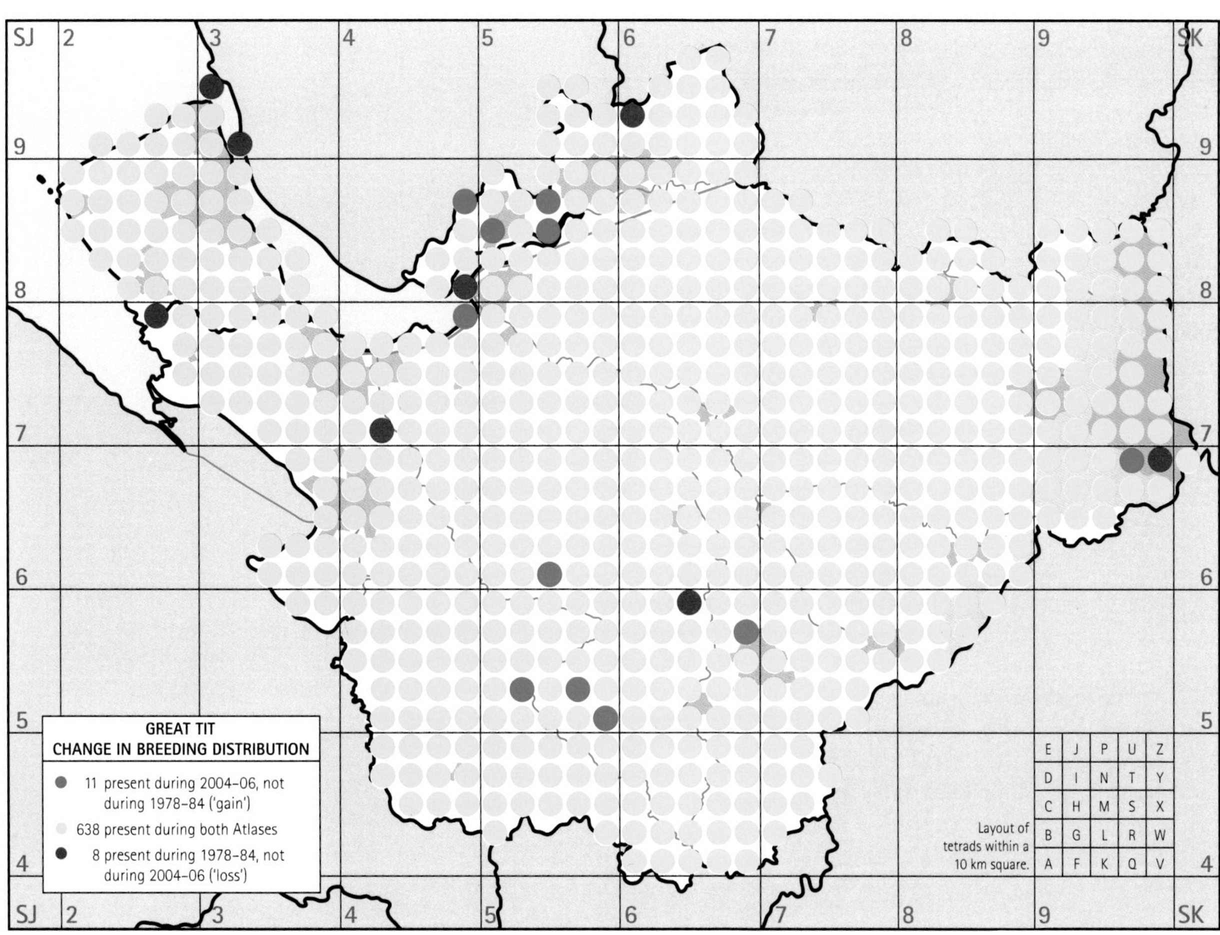
GREAT TIT
CHANGE IN BREEDING DISTRIBUTION
11 present during 2004–06, not during 1978–84 ('gain')
638 present during both Atlases
8 present during 1978–84, not during 2004–06 ('loss')
Layout of tetrads within a 10 km square.
E J P U Z
D I N T Y
C H M S X
B G L R W
A F K Q V
SJ
SK

In autumn, Great Tits gradually shift in diet from invertebrates to seeds and fruit so that, by November, beechmast and hazelnuts provide a major part of their daily intake. Many males remain on their territories year-round provided that they can find enough food, but most birds move into winter flocks that roam around a few hectares of feeding area. These two facts drive the species' winter distribution and habitat use.

The winter map shows that Great Tits explore almost every part of the county, including the tetrads on the fringes–the highest hills and Hilbre–that do not support breeding birds. The habitat codes demonstrate slight reductions in the fraction of records in woodland and human sites, larger decreases in the proportions in scrub (8% in breeding season, 5% in winter) and farmland (12% in breeding season, 7% in winter) while the percentage of records in hedges more than doubled from 12% to 26%. These probably illustrate the species' two main winter feeding areas, woodland and gardens, using hedgerows to move around.

SUE & ANDY TRANTER

Flocks form above all in hard weather, of which there was little during this winter Atlas, so most birds were found in small groups, with a median count of just three. The large numbers are mainly at well-stocked feeding stations close to woodland and, especially, in areas with lots of tree seeds. Great Tits are much more ground-feeders than their close relatives, and can gather into large flocks, especially when feeding on beechmast. I well remember trying to catch Bramblings feeding on the ground under beeches at Petty Pool (SJ66I) on 19 December 1992, but instead finding my mist-nets full with 98 Great Tits. They extract the kernel of beech nuts by making a characteristic neat hole in the side, and the woodland floor can be littered with such evidence. As supplies of nuts become exhausted during the winter, Great Tits move out of the beechwoods in the order of their social dominance: first to go are first-year females, then adult females, followed by first-year males and finally adult males (Gosler 1993).

As well as woodland seeds, the provision of food by humans is thought to be particularly important for Great Tits, which seem to be among the most intelligent of birds and can quickly learn to exploit new opportunities. An extreme effect of garden feeding was found in northern Finland, turning a migratory population into a sedentary one (*Migration Atlas*). Despite the dangers of feeding in British gardens, especially cats, Great Tits' winter survival is higher in suburban areas than in woodland; but the best places to breed are in the woods, and birds have some tricky choices to make in deciding between, or moving between, the two (Gosler 1993).

Great Tits are generally sedentary birds, most males settling to breed within a few hundred metres of their natal site and most females within a kilometre, but half of first-year birds move more than 4 km away during winter, tending to return as spring approaches (*Migration Atlas*). Some birds are already paired within the winter flocks, anticipating the breeding season.

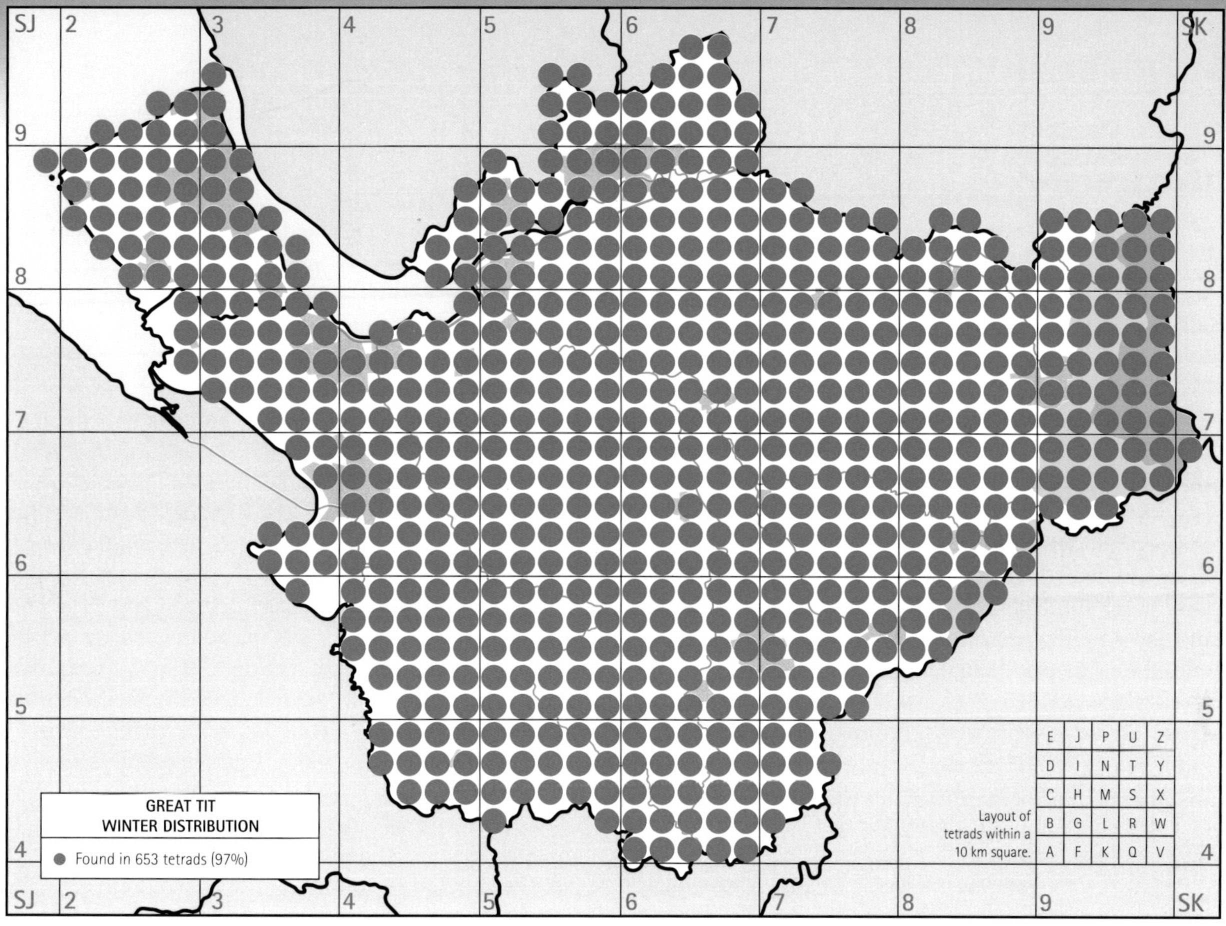
SJ
SK
GREAT TIT
WINTER DISTRIBUTION
Found in 653 tetrads (97%)
Layout of
tetrads within a
10 km square.
E J P U Z
D I N T Y
C H M S X
B G L R W
A F K Q V

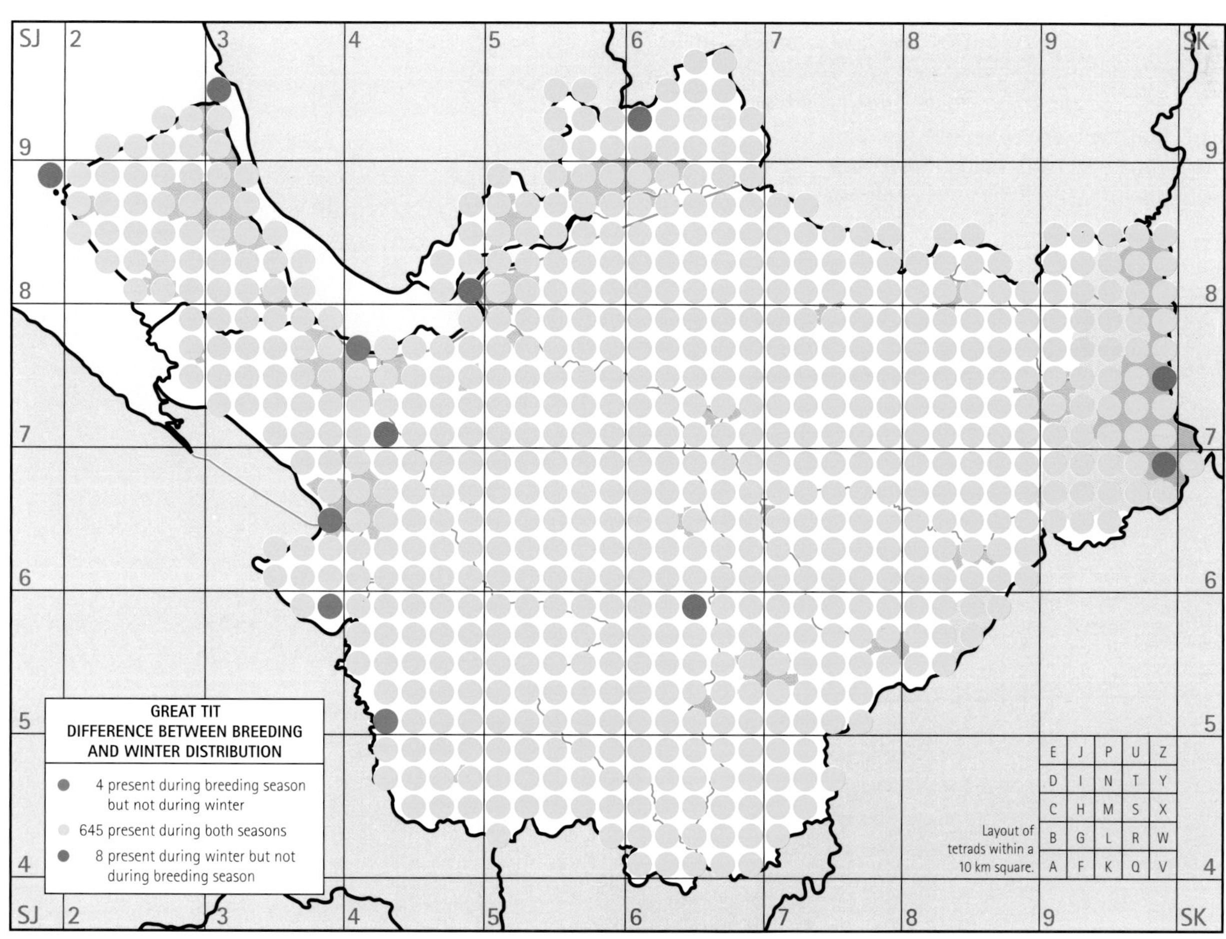
SJ
SK
GREAT TIT
DIFFERENCE BETWEEN BREEDING
AND WINTER DISTRIBUTION
4 present during breeding season but not during winter
645 present during both seasons
8 present during winter but not during breeding season
Layout of
tetrads within a
10 km square.
E J P U Z
D I N T Y
C H M S X
B G L R W
A F K Q V

Coal Tit

Periparus ater

Coal Tits are overwhelmingly birds of woodland, reported in this habitat in 335 tetrads, with only 16 records for scrub, 9 in hedgerow and 16 farmland: the contrast with Blue and Great Tits is stark. Coal Tit is also one of the few species that seems at home in coniferous woodland (A2), with 60 tetrad records. Exceeded only by Goldcrest (75), no other passerine registered in double figures. Gardens, in urban, suburban and rural areas, were used by many birds (154 tetrads in the F categories).

They are widespread across Cheshire and Wirral, present in two-thirds of tetrads, but are absent especially from the sparsely wooded areas of the county, noticeably that in the central southern part of Cheshire, centred on Calveley (SJ65E), and in a band running as far as Tabley (SJ77D). Coal Tits have been lost from this area in the last twenty years, for unknown reasons that would repay further study. They were present in 334 tetrads in both Atlases, with 108 tetrads newly occupied since 1978–84, and 94 losses, giving little net change since our *First Atlas*.

This is by far the most difficult tit species in which to prove breeding (51% of records). Fieldworkers found birds carrying food or a faecal sac in 58 tetrads and parties of recently fledged young in another 132; in only 37 tetrads were nests found. Nest sites reported included natural holes in trees, often low down or even underground amongst the roots, and a variety of man-made artefacts including nest-boxes, pipes and holes in walls, with Martyn Stanyer noting one pair in SJ85H on 15 May 2004 that was taking food into a nest hole in a wall, only a metre from an occupied Great Tit nest. Coal Tits apparently feed on a wider variety of invertebrates than other tits, and are more likely to have a second brood (Perrins 1979).

The BTO BBS analysis shows that the breeding population of the county in 2004–05 was 5,750 birds (2,990–8,520), corresponding to an average of about 10 pairs per tetrad with confirmed or probable breeding, or six pairs per tetrad in which the species was recorded. This is less than 0.5% of the UK breeding population of one million birds, reflecting Cheshire and Wirral's status as one of the least wooded counties in England (Smith & Gilbert 2003).

The national population has fluctuated but shows no clear trend in 20 years; this statement, however, conceals important habitat-specific changes. The numbers on English CBC plots in woodland have dropped slightly, whilst the totals on farmland plots have roughly doubled (Brown & Grice 2005). This behaviour is usually characteristic of a species whose population is high: it 'fills up' its natural habitat, and some individuals spill over into other, suboptimal, habitats. This pattern of Coal Tits moving in to farmland has not been noted in Cheshire and Wirral, however, and perhaps depends on the detailed land-use of the agricultural landscape.

STEVE ROUND

Sponsored by Denise Bebbington

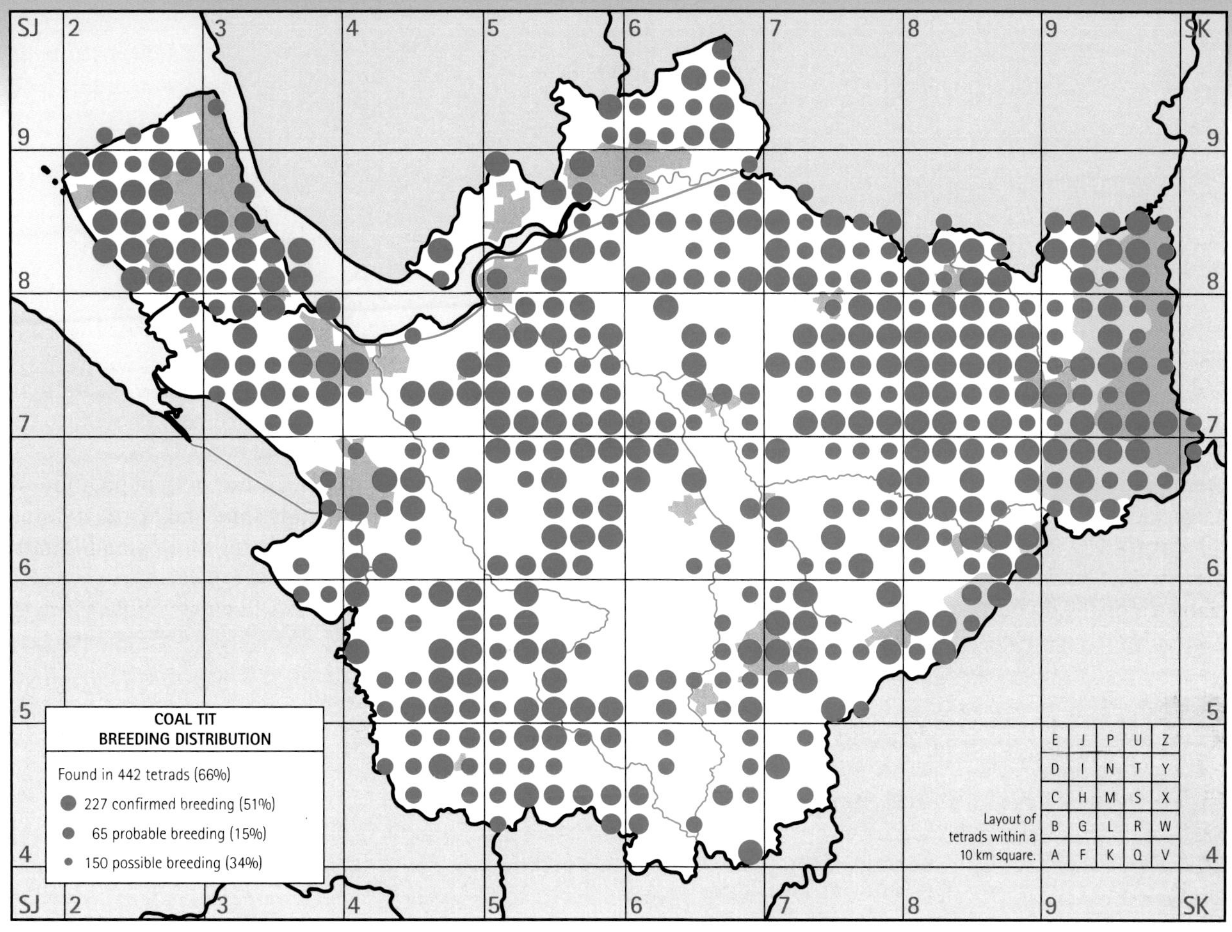
SJ
SK
COAL TIT
BREEDING DISTRIBUTION
Found in 442 tetrads (66%)
227 confirmed breeding (51%)
65 probable breeding (15%)
150 possible breeding (34%)
Layout of tetrads within a 10 km square.
E J P U Z
D I N T Y
C H M S X
B G L R W
A F K Q V

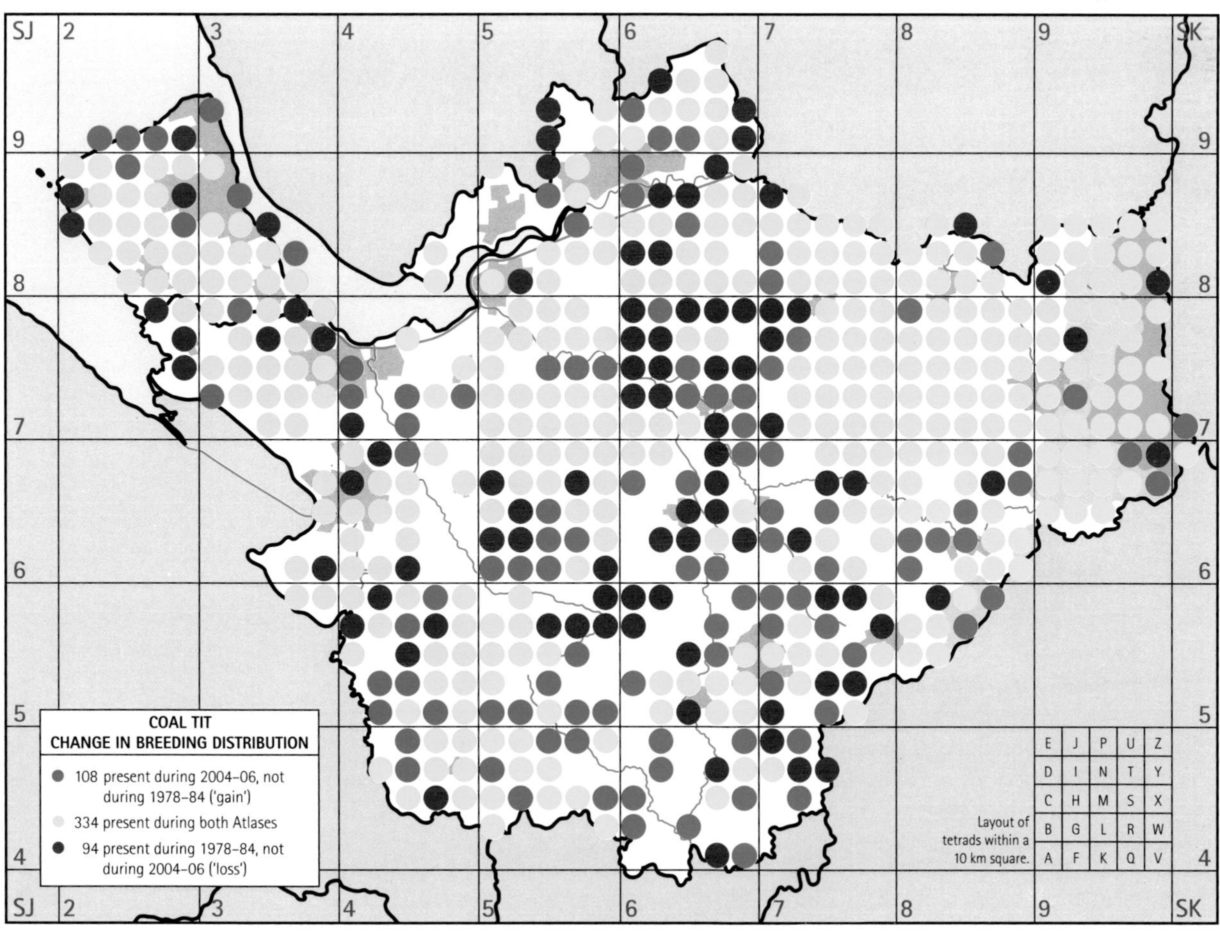
SJ
SK
COAL TIT
CHANGE IN BREEDING DISTRIBUTION
108 present during 2004–06, not during 1978–84 ('gain')
334 present during both Atlases
94 present during 1978–84, not during 2004–06 ('loss')
Layout of tetrads within a 10 km square.
E J P U Z
D I N T Y
C H M S X
B G L R W
A F K Q V

Some Coal Tits spread out and switch habitats in winter, the maps showing them present in an extra 65 tetrads compared to the breeding season, including some of those in the sparsely wooded areas of the county. Woodland is still the most favoured habitat although in significantly fewer tetrads (51% of records in winter, 63% during the breeding season) with their liking for conifers maintained, but far fewer birds were reported from scrub (7% of records in winter, 17% during the breeding season) and farmland (7% of records in winter, 13% during the breeding season). More birds were found in farmland hedges (6% of records in winter, 2% during the breeding season), mostly in mixed flocks with other tits and far more Coal Tits were reported from human sites, mainly suburban and rural (38% of records in winter, 29% during the breeding season).

Over 400 submitted records over the three winters included a count of Coal Tits, but more than half of them were of just a single individual, illustrating that the way that most people encounter the species is by finding an odd one amongst a flock of other birds. Even at their regular haunts, groups of more than a few Coal Tits are seldom seen. At feeding stations in Delamere Forest, I have found that Coal Tit numbers vary substantially from year to year, presumably responding to the biennial cycle in the crop of natural seeds, and the number of gardens visited also changes depending on the yield of beechmast (Glue 1982 and BTO Garden BirdWatch data). Where they share feeding areas, this species is subordinate to all of the other tits and woodland feeders and can suffer if there is a dearth of food. Coal Tits avoid this in two ways: their finer bill makes them more able to exploit small food items amongst clusters of pine needles, and they often hide food in caches during autumn to be retrieved in later times of shortage.

The description of Coal Tit as one of Britain's most sedentary species (*BTO Second Atlas*, *BTO Winter Atlas*) is probably an overstatement. First-year birds disperse up to a median distance of 11 km from their natal site in midwinter (*Migration Atlas*) although, once settled in an area, birds probably do tend to stay put. One regular customer at a Delamere Forest feeding station, hatched in 1996 or earlier and ringed in winter 1997/98, was caught in seven winters and retrapped when at least nine-and-a-half years old in December 2005.

There are occasional influxes of Coal Tits from continental Europe. Although none has been proven to reach Cheshire and Wirral, one wonders about the origins of the first-year bird ringed on 12 October 1985 at Bardsey Island, Gwynedd and retrapped in a ringer's garden 136 km away at Little Sutton (SJ37T) on 15 February 1986. Coward (1910) noted that they were more in evidence in the winter months, which he ascribed to probable immigration.

SHEILA BLAMIRE

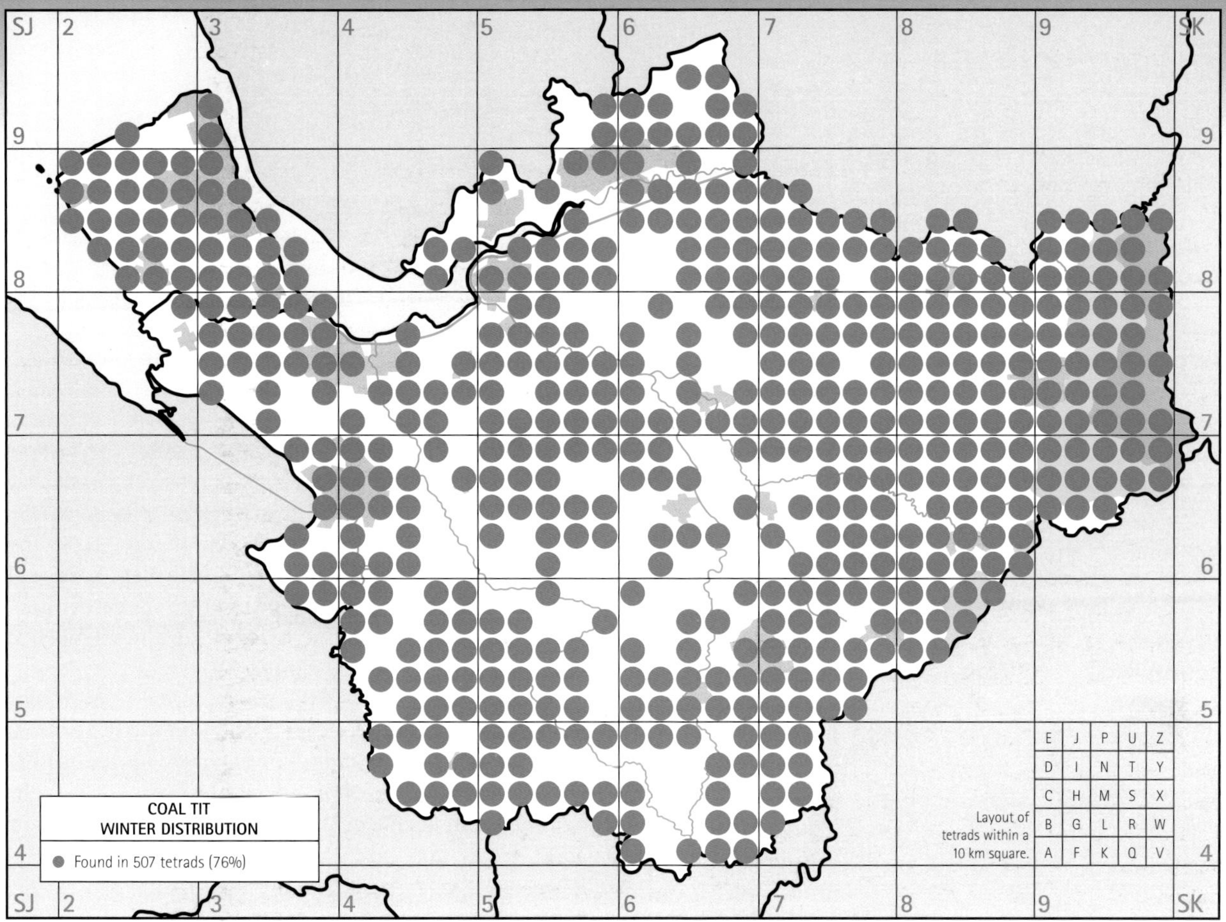
SJ
2
3
4
5
6
7
8
9
SK
9
8
7
6
5
4
E J P U Z
D I N T Y
C H M S X
B G L R W
A F K Q V
Layout of tetrads within a 10 km square.
COAL TIT
WINTER DISTRIBUTION
Found in 507 tetrads (76%)

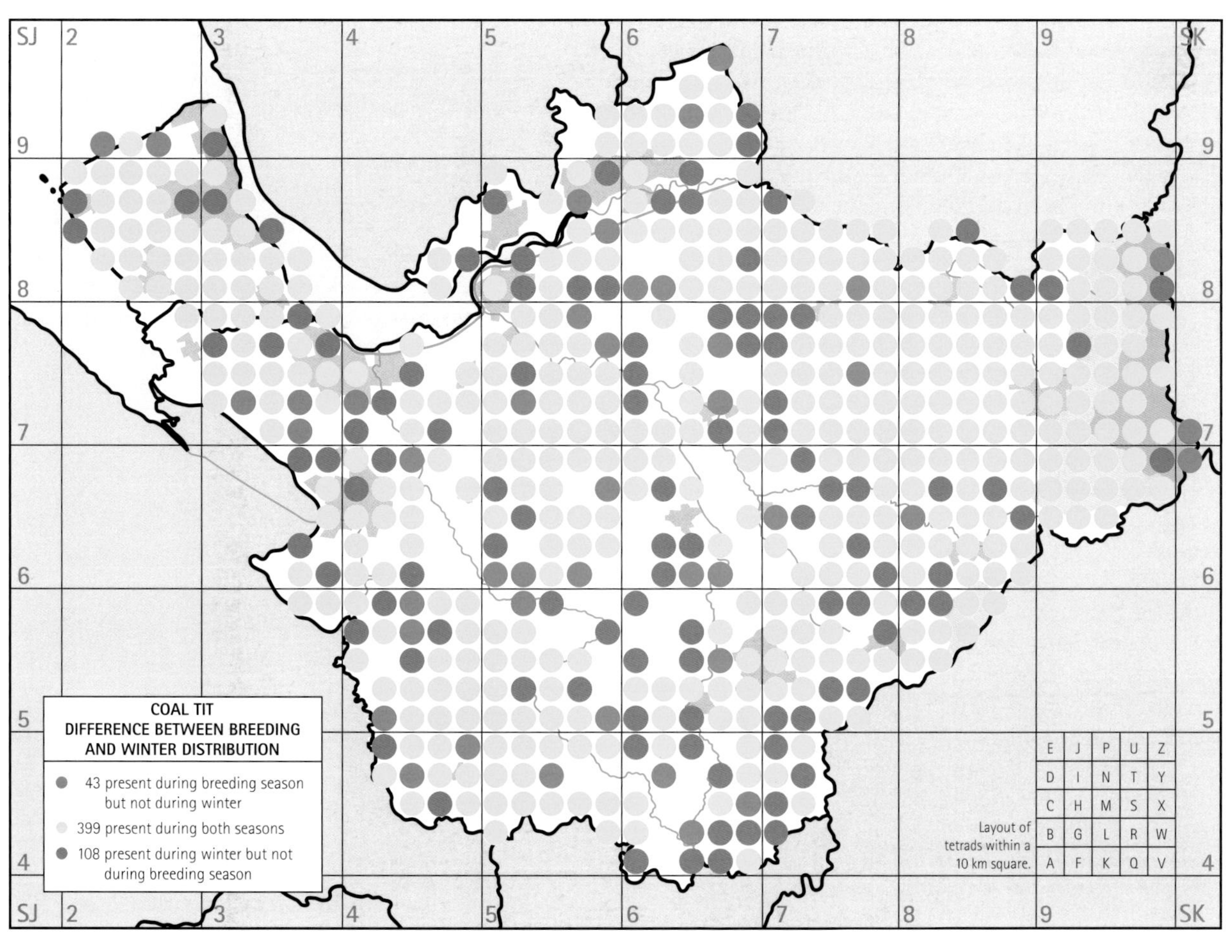
SJ
2
3
4
5
6
7
8
9
SK
9
8
7
6
5
4
E J P U Z
D I N T Y
C H M S X
B G L R W
A F K Q V
Layout of tetrads within a 10 km square.
COAL TIT
DIFFERENCE BETWEEN BREEDING AND WINTER DISTRIBUTION
43 present during breeding season but not during winter
399 present during both seasons
108 present during winter but not during breeding season

Willow Tit

Poecile montana

RAY SCALLY

The Mersey valley is now one of the national strongholds for Willow Tit, such has been the extent of their rapid decline. From being present in 40% of Cheshire and Wirral tetrads twenty years ago, in this survey it was found in just 7%, a drop from 270 tetrads to 49. The 'change' map shows that the decline has taken place across Cheshire, and the species now has only a toe-hold on the Wirral, but they were found in a few new tetrads along the Mersey valley.

The Willow Tit national population dropped during the 1970s but was steady during the period of our *First Atlas*. From 1987, however, it has been in inexorable decline, falling by 77% in 18 years since then and leading to 'Red' status for the species on the list of birds of conservation concern. Detailed analysis shows that the drop has not been uniform and the numbers are stable in their preferred wet habitats (Siriwardena 2004). Farmland is now only rarely occupied, and Willow Tits fare badly in dry woodland. These conclusions are from the nationwide annual censuses, and the recorded habitat codes in this Atlas survey illustrate the species' preference for waterlogged (carr) broad-leaved woodland (10 tetrads) and scrub (14 tetrads), with 11 records from broad-leaved woodland, 5 from mixed woodland and 6 others.

The causes of decline have been suggested to be competition with other tit species or increasing nest predation by Great Spotted Woodpeckers, but neither of these hypotheses stands up to scrutiny in the breeding season for Willow Tits in woodland and their decline is more likely to be caused by winter factors (Siriwardena 2004). At all seasons they differ from the common tits by feeding almost exclusively in the shrub layer, not using the tree canopy or finding food on the ground, and the problem may lie in unknown, but deleterious, changes in their shrubby food sources. Deterioration in the quality of woodland as feeding habitat for Willow Tits, through canopy closure and increased browsing by deer, has been proposed as a cause (Fuller *et al.* 2005). There are relatively few deer in the county (Cheshire Mammal Group 2008), however, and they have not wrought mass destruction here as they have in other counties, so they cannot be blamed for any changes in woodland structure in Cheshire.

Willow Tit is the only species, other than woodpeckers, that excavates its own nest holes, but live trees are too tough for them and they can only nest in rotting wood. Sometimes they do all of the work, only to be evicted by Blue or Great Tits, but other observations show that some Willow Tits can mount a successful defence. Nests are usually low down, typically 1–2 m above ground, on average containing five noisy chicks that often attract an observers' attention—and presumably that of predators as well. However, nests were found in only four tetrads, with adults carrying food for their chicks—almost invariably caterpillars—in five and recently fledged young were observed in a further six. Where the species is common, it is not difficult to prove breeding, but odd pairs can be quite quiet. The song, a sweet warbling, is seldom heard but their nasal call is distinctive and far-carrying. Although their territories can be large—up to 9 ha—Willow Tits do not move far during the year, and the 'possible' breeding records are likely to refer to birds resident in the tetrad.

From being a widespread bird, with a Cheshire and Wirral population estimated at 350–400 pairs during our *First Atlas*, the current county population is unlikely to be much above 50 pairs, with perhaps one-quarter of them at Woolston.

Sponsored by Nantwich Natural History Society

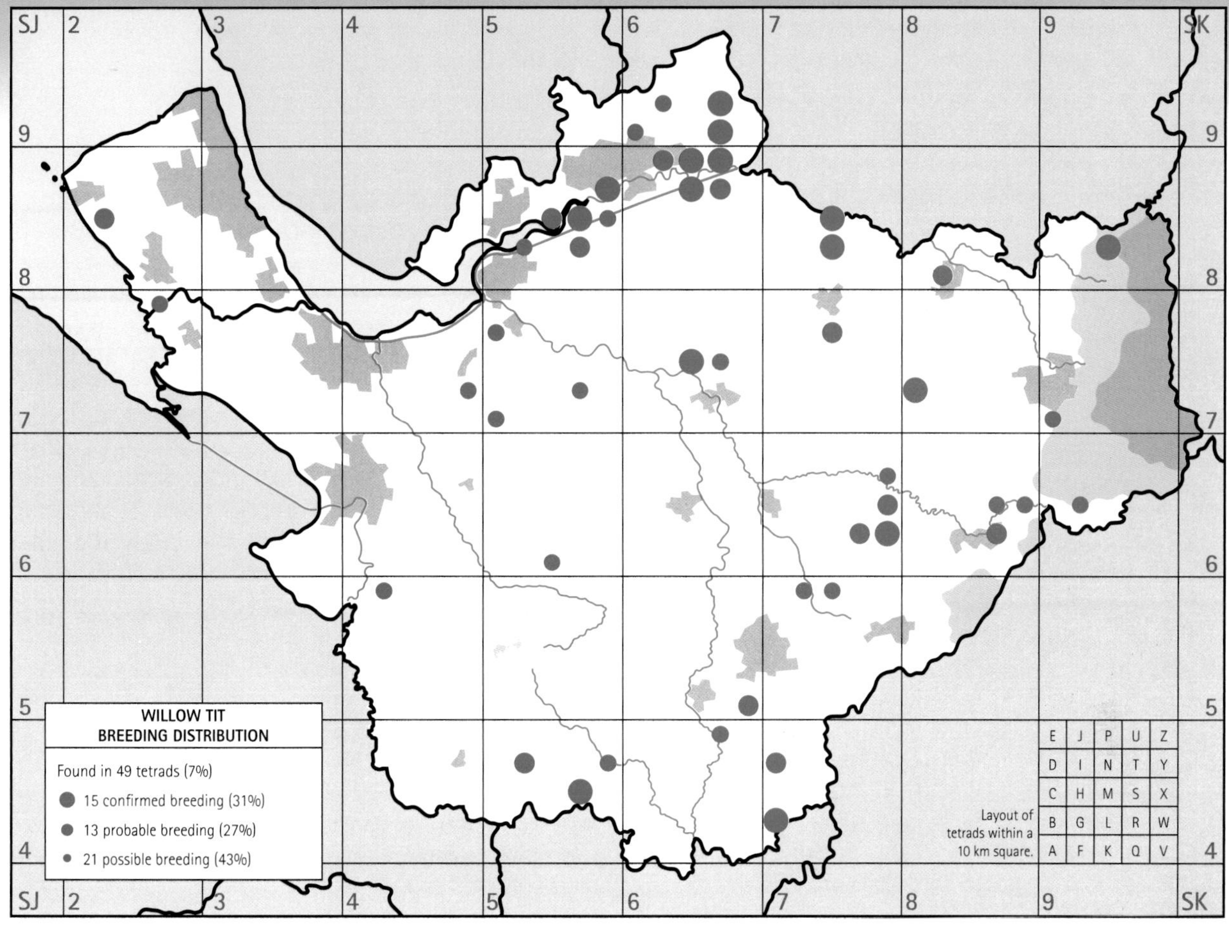
SJ
SK
WILLOW TIT
BREEDING DISTRIBUTION
Found in 49 tetrads (7%)
15 confirmed breeding (31%)
13 probable breeding (27%)
21 possible breeding (43%)
Layout of tetrads within a 10 km square.
E J P U Z
D I N T Y
C H M S X
B G L R W
A F K Q V

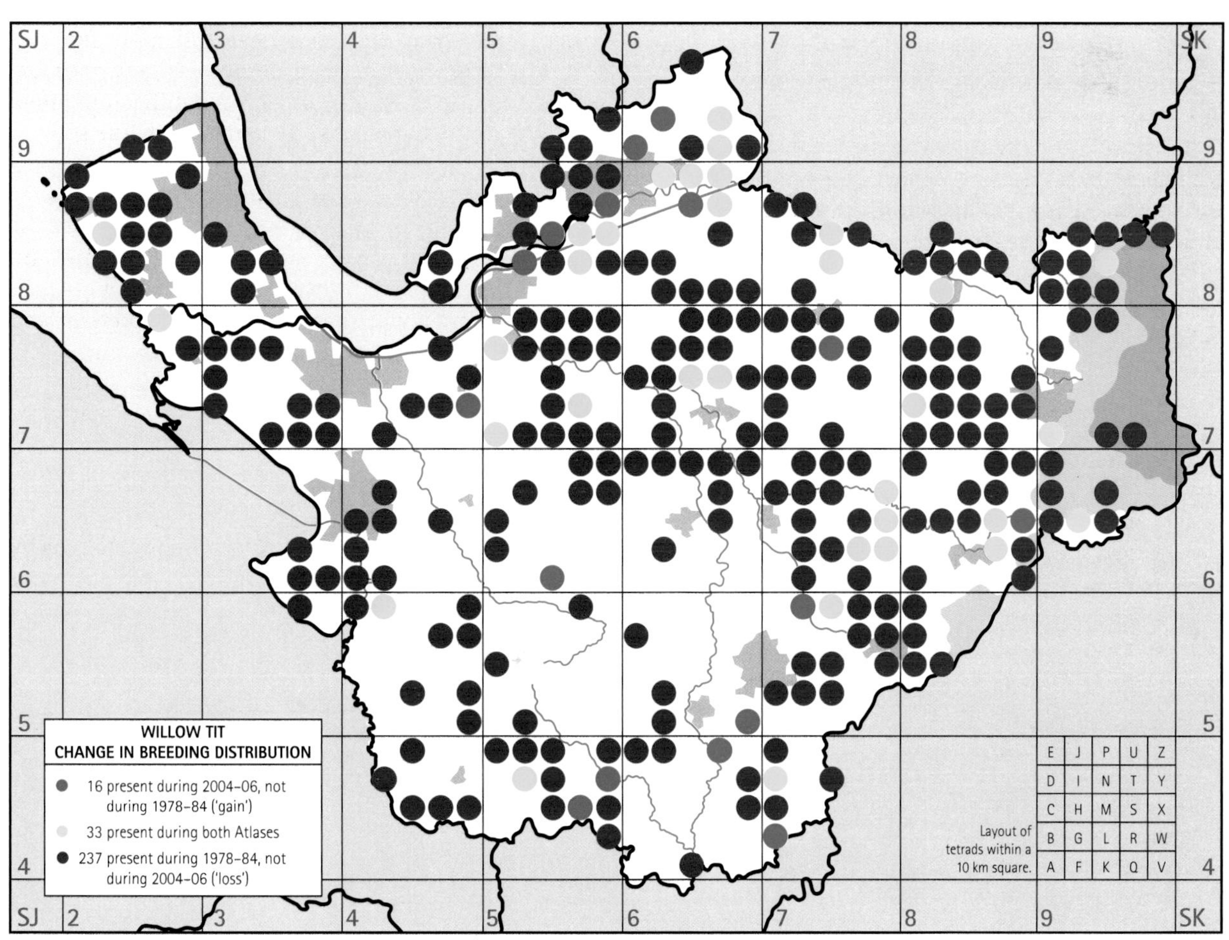
SJ
SK
WILLOW TIT
CHANGE IN BREEDING DISTRIBUTION
16 present during 2004–06, not during 1978–84 ('gain')
33 present during both Atlases
237 present during 1978–84, not during 2004–06 ('loss')
Layout of tetrads within a 10 km square.
E J P U Z
D I N T Y
C H M S X
B G L R W
A F K Q V

STEVE ROUND

As a reportedly highly sedentary species (*Migration Atlas*), there would not be expected to be much difference between the breeding and wintering distributions for Willow Tit. However, this survey shows that they appear to be more widespread in winter. There were 24 tetrads in which Willow Tit was found during the breeding season and not in winter and 30 vice versa. Most of the extra records in winter were within one or two tetrads of one occupied in the breeding season, and could suggest winter dispersal, but others might indicate locations for breeding that had not been found during the breeding season survey. Observers' attention was drawn to this possibility in an Atlas newsletter in December 2005 but few extra records were forthcoming.

It is thought that adult birds probably remain on their territories in winter (*BTO Winter Atlas*) and Willow Tits join mixed-species flocks less readily than other tit species. Unlike other tits, they seldom seem to eat nuts such as beechmast, perhaps because their relatively thin bill is not adapted for cracking them, or it may be just because there are few nut-bearing trees available in their normal habitat. Neither do they take fleshy fruits and they seem to eat invertebrates whenever they can find them, even during winter. Mead (2000) suggested that, as a small sedentary bird, Willow Tit would be susceptible to cold weather but in fact their national population index was stable during the last decade with hard winters—the 1980s—and has crashed since. It does seem likely that lack of winter food, in any weather, is likely to underlie their decline (Siriwardena 2004).

Most of the Willow Tit records were of one or two birds, with three seen together in three tetrads. The winter habitat codes show rather fewer in wet woodland than during the breeding season, just 7 tetrads recording broad-leaved carr, with 10 tetrads holding birds in scrub, 13 records from broad-leaved woodland, and 7 from mixed woodland. Despite their supposedly sedentary nature, there were suggestions that birds had spread out from breeding sites into a wider range of habitats, with 7 records of birds in farmland hedgerows and 11 in human sites, several of them feeding stations. Another indication of their more widespread winter distribution was that there were eight tetrads in which Willow Tits and Marsh Tits were both found during this Atlas; in all cases both species were recorded in the same winter.

The species was not identified in Cheshire until 1912, and neither Boyd (1946) nor Bell (1962) made any significant comment on Willow Tits in winter.

There are probably few British counties in which Willow Tit is more numerous than Marsh Tit. In view of this, and its national decline, a more detailed survey of this species in Cheshire is surely warranted.

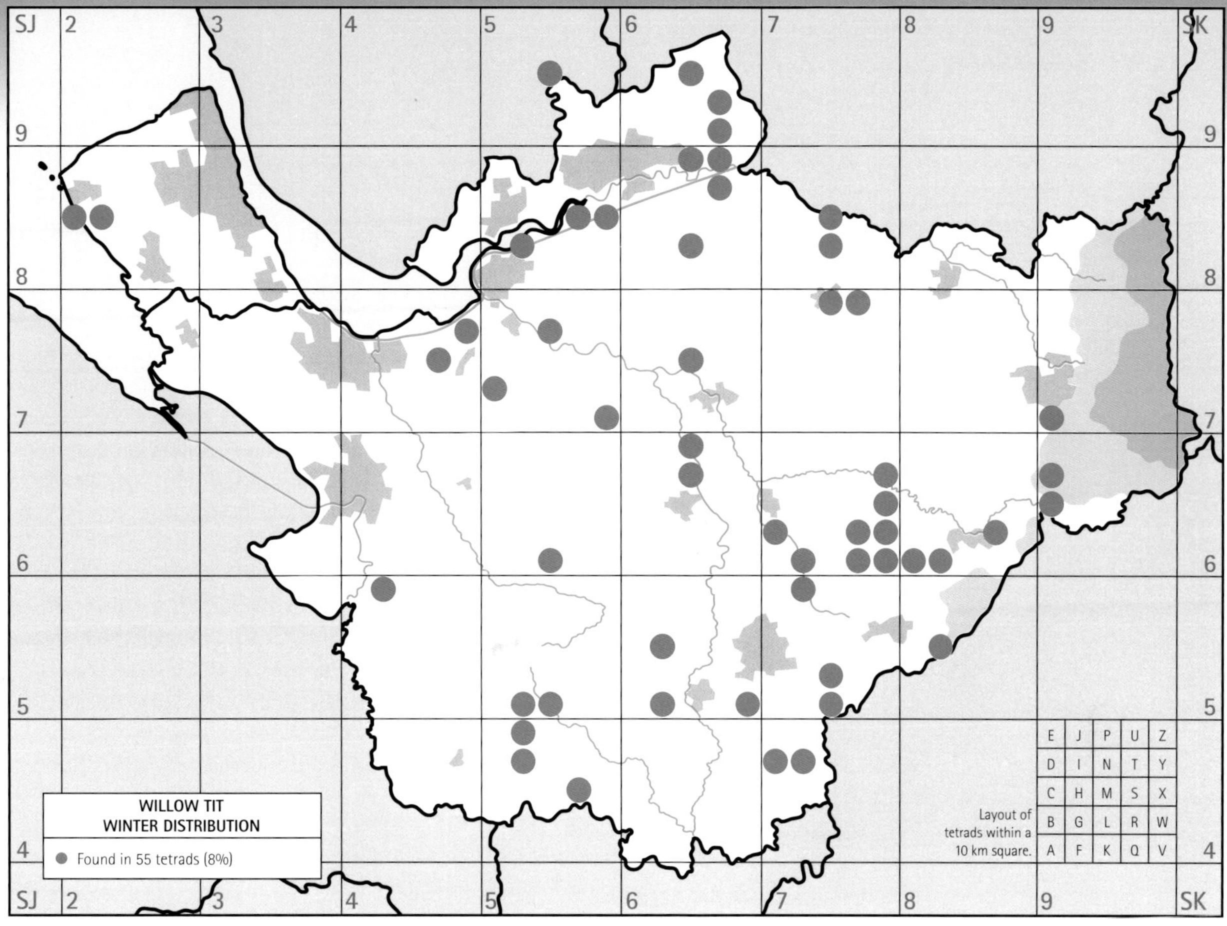
WILLOW TIT
WINTER DISTRIBUTION
Found in 55 tetrads (8%)
Layout of tetrads within a 10 km square.
E J P U Z
D I N T Y
C H M S X
B G L R W
A F K Q V
SJ
SK
2
3
4
5
6
7
8
9

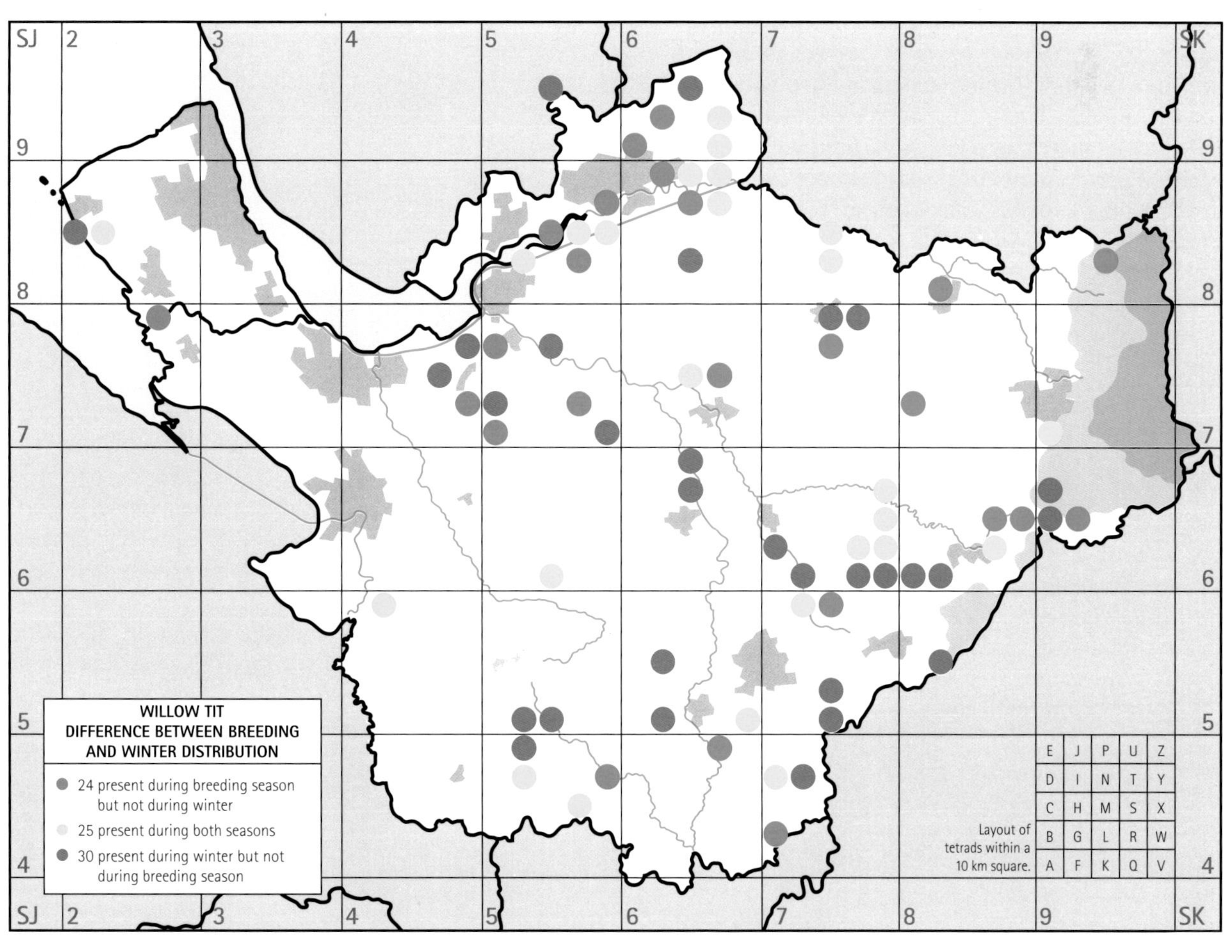
WILLOW TIT
DIFFERENCE BETWEEN BREEDING AND WINTER DISTRIBUTION
24 present during breeding season but not during winter
25 present during both seasons
30 present during winter but not during breeding season
Layout of tetrads within a 10 km square.
E J P U Z
D I N T Y
C H M S X
B G L R W
A F K Q V
SJ
SK
2
3
4
5
6
7
8
9

Marsh Tit

Poecile palustris

RICHARD STEEL

This is the 'brown tit' of mature woodland, especially with oak or beech, and their habitat preference—very different from that of the Willow Tit—is well shown by the codes submitted by observers in this survey. Nearly three-quarters of the records (22 out of 30) were in broad-leaved woodland (A1), with three in mixed woodland (A3), one each in waterlogged broad-leaved and mixed woodland (A4 and A6), and three others. Recent study has shown that the characteristics of the shrubs, especially at heights of 2–4 m, underneath the tall trees are most important for Marsh Tits (Hinsley *et al.* 2007). Damage to the shrub layer, by deer, by shading out due to canopy closure and by managed clearance of shrub cover, may underlie the long-term sustained drop in the abundance of Marsh Tits. They are now on the Red List of species of conservation concern, following a sustained fall in their national population ever since BTO census work started in the 1960s. From a nadir in 1998, there has been a small rise, leaving the national population index with a drop of 20% between our two Atlases, from 1984 to 2004.

Detailed demographic work suggests that the decline may have been driven by low annual survival and that neither increased predation nor interspecific competition is responsible (Siriwardena 2006). Nesting success has improved during the period of decline. They defend territories all year round, 2–8 ha in size, within which they satisfy all of their annual needs, and they are seldom found in woods smaller than 1 ha (Hinsley *et al.* 1995, Broughton *et al.* 2006). Marsh Tits are the lowest in pecking order when competing for nest holes, and they choose small holes in mature trees, close to the ground, that are probably unattractive to other species (Nilsson 1984). They start laying in mid- or late April, becoming earlier with climate change, and the average brood of around seven chicks fledges in early June. Their summer diet is dominated by adult insects, especially moths, bugs, springtails and beetles, and Marsh Tits depend much less on the insect larvae associated with oaks than other tits; they obtain most of their food from the understorey vegetation or from low in the canopy.

The species was found in 160 tetrads in the *First Atlas*, but only 30 tetrads in this survey, just four of them with proven breeding. The 'change' map shows locations that were occupied in the *First Atlas* and still now include much of the county's scarce mature woodland: the lower Weaver valley around Aston, the Wych valley, the Eaton estate and the Peckforton area. It is missing from the north of Cheshire and from Wirral. The loss of Marsh Tits in Cheshire is much more than would have been expected from a 20% drop in their national population, and this is probably a reflection of changes in abundance and distribution being more obvious at the edge of a species' range. In its national distribution, Marsh Tit has an obvious gap in the Mersey valley, and the Lancashire and North Merseyside tetrad breeding Atlas (1997–2000) showed only one record in Lancashire within 25 km of the Cheshire boundary (Pyefinch & Golborn 2001).

Some birdwatchers have difficulty in distinguishing the two species of 'brown tits' although the call of the Willow Tit is completely different, and the map omits records from two tetrads in which the observer was uncertain of the identification. Now that they are both scarce species in Cheshire, they have completely separated in their local distribution: during this Atlas survey there was no tetrad in which Marsh Tit and Willow Tit were both recorded in the breeding season.

Twenty years ago Marsh Tit was a relatively widespread bird, with a Cheshire and Wirral population probably underestimated at 150–200 pairs. In this survey, most of the records were of single birds, or pairs, and the county population is unlikely to exceed 50 pairs. The reasons for this drop are probably worthy of professional study. The oft-quoted cause, loss of understorey from excessive browsing by deer, cannot be the reason in our county where feral deer are still relatively scarce (Cheshire Mammal Group 2008).

Sponsored by Paul Morris

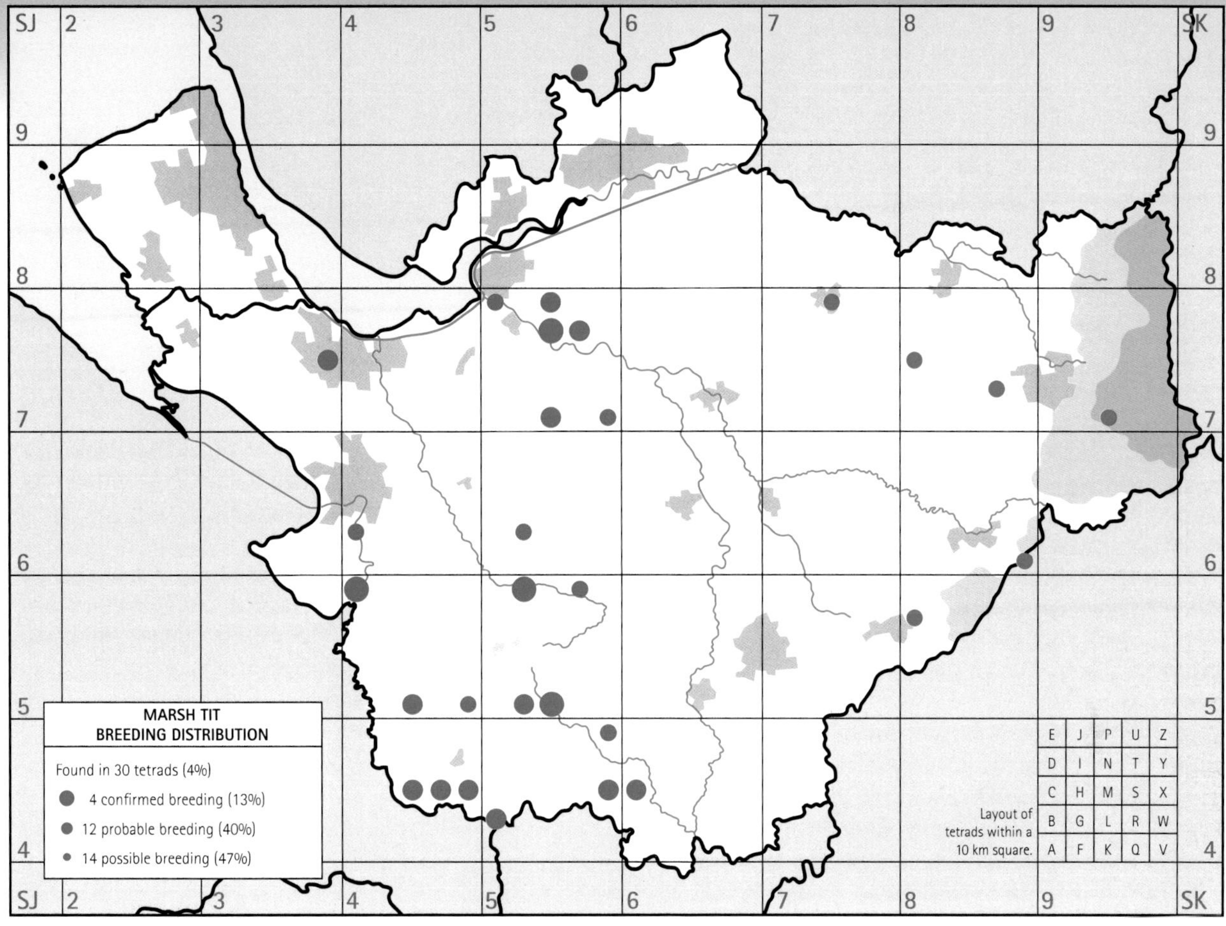
MARSH TIT
BREEDING DISTRIBUTION
Found in 30 tetrads (4%)
4 confirmed breeding (13%)
12 probable breeding (40%)
14 possible breeding (47%)
SJ
SK
Layout of tetrads within a 10 km square.
E J P U Z
D I N T Y
C H M S X
B G L R W
A F K Q V

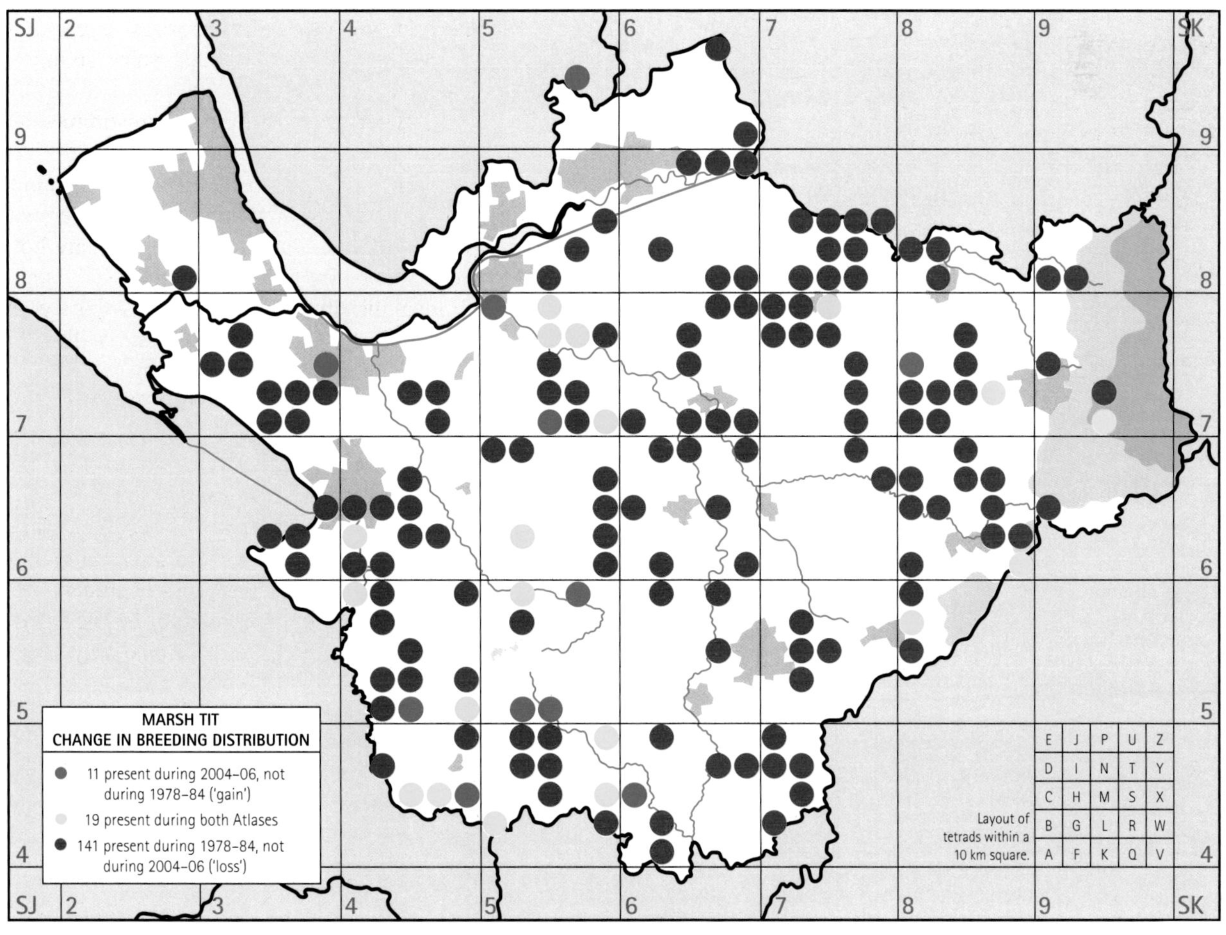
MARSH TIT
CHANGE IN BREEDING DISTRIBUTION
11 present during 2004–06, not during 1978–84 ('gain')
19 present during both Atlases
141 present during 1978–84, not during 2004–06 ('loss')
SJ
SK
Layout of tetrads within a 10 km square.
E J P U Z
D I N T Y
C H M S X
B G L R W
A F K Q V

Marsh Tit adults are amongst the most site faithful of all passerine species. They stay paired throughout the winter and remain on their large territory even in hard weather. They defend it against their neighbours, especially using their loud 'pitchou' calls. Unpaired first-winter birds, on the other hand, join mixed-species tit flocks in winter, which roam at will, and territorial adults do not defend against these birds; indeed, they may well join a roaming flock whilst it moves around their territory (*BTO Winter Atlas*). They can be present but quite elusive at times. In 26 years of ringing in February and March at Aston (SJ56P) I caught Marsh Tits in half of the years, but with a seven-year gap from 1994 to 2000.

Following this description of their habits, it was surprising to find Marsh Tits reported from 50 tetrads in winter, 20 more than in the breeding season. Many of the extra tetrads with winter records were within one or two tetrads of the core breeding sites, and could be interpreted as dispersal of first-year birds, but up to 10 of the records were from isolated tetrads, at least 5 km distant from the nearest known breeding site. Conversely, four tetrads in the east of the county furnished records of single birds in the breeding season, but none was found within those 10 km squares in winter.

Their winter food is more widespread than their apparently restricted breeding requirements. Beechmast is a key part of their diet if present, along with the seeds and fruits of other trees and shrubs, and insects if they can find them. They store food, usually in moss on or near the ground, often for only a few hours during a day, perhaps to avoid it being taken by the other larger and more dominant tit species.

There are no benchmarks for the species' former distribution or abundance. They were not separated from the Willow Tit until 1897, and all Cheshire records of 'brown tits' were lumped in with Marsh Tit; neither Boyd (1946) nor Bell (1962) makes any significant comment on them in winter.

STEVE ROUND

MARSH TIT
WINTER DISTRIBUTION
Found in 50 tetrads (7%)
Layout of tetrads within a 10 km square.
E J P U Z
D I N T Y
C H M S X
B G L R W
A F K Q V
SJ 2 3 4 5 6 7 8 9 SK
9 8 7 6 5 4

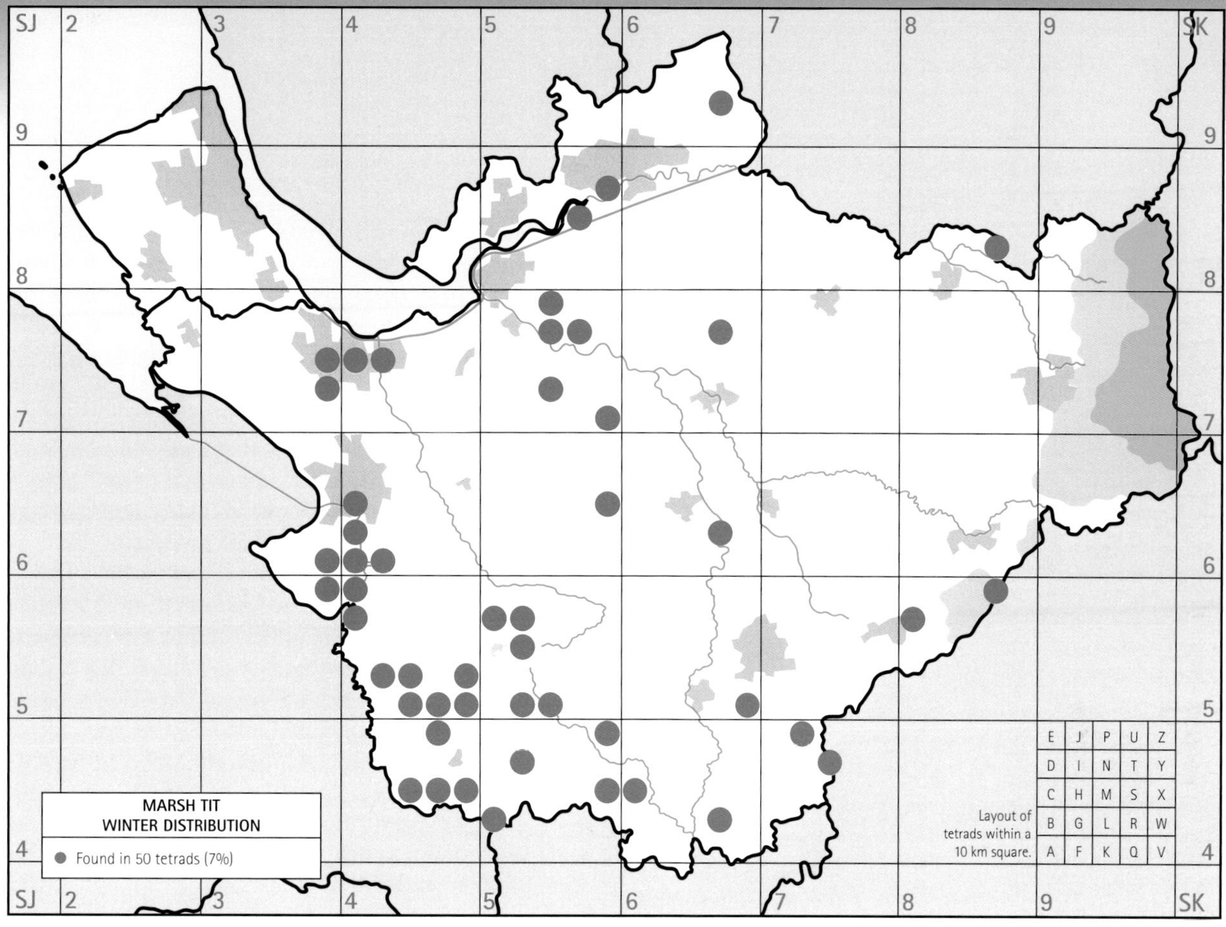

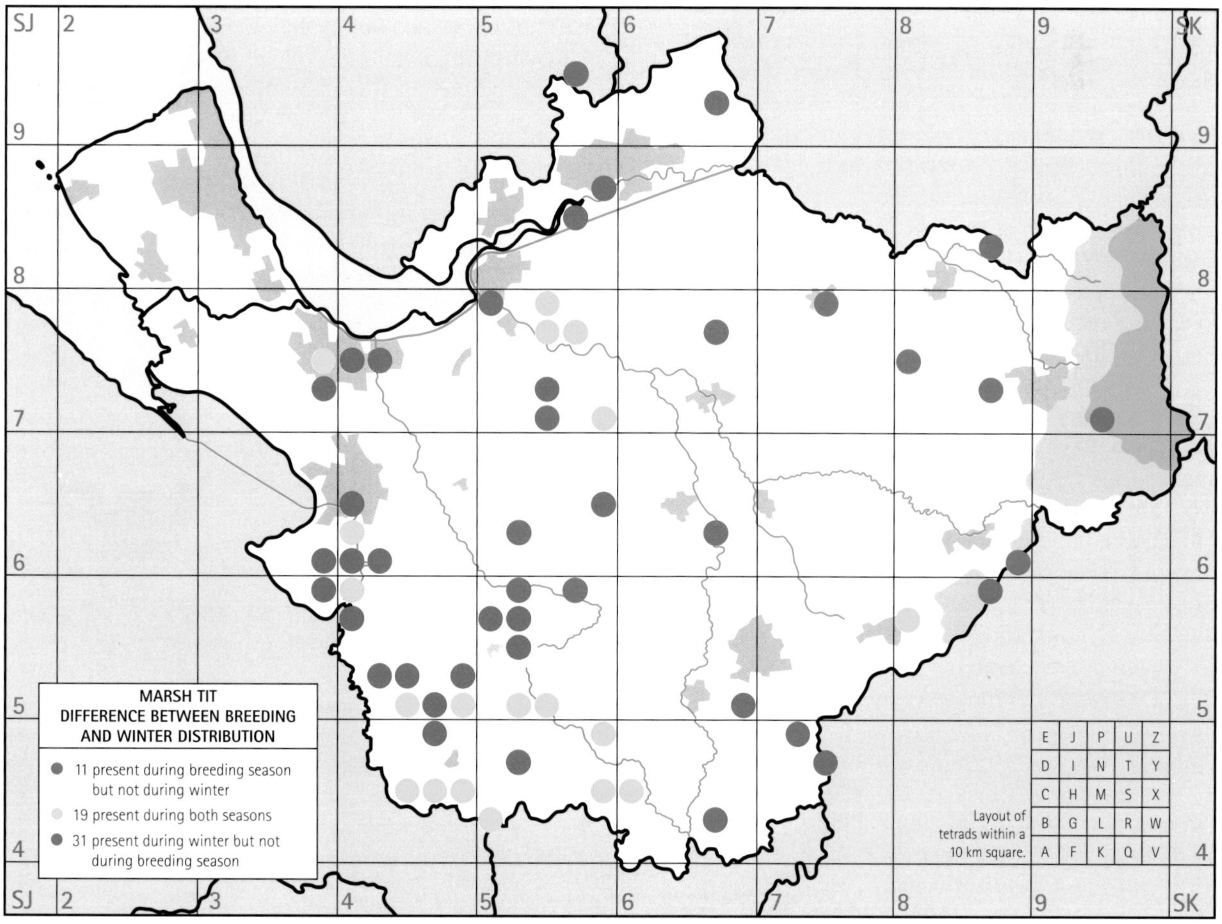

MARSH TIT
DIFFERENCE BETWEEN BREEDING AND WINTER DISTRIBUTION
11 present during breeding season but not during winter
19 present during both seasons
31 present during winter but not during breeding season
Layout of tetrads within a 10 km square.
E J P U Z
D I N T Y
C H M S X
B G L R W
A F K Q V
SJ 2 3 4 5 6 7 8 9 SK
9 8 7 6 5 4

Nuthatch

Sitta europaea

BEN HALL

The expansion of the Nuthatch's range was described in our *First Atlas*, and this Atlas shows them continuing to fill in some of the gaps in their distribution and gradually moving towards the north: they were present in one-third more tetrads than twenty years ago (from 343 to 457), and proven breeding in an extra 50 (from 189 to 239). The abundance map shows their highest density in the wooded areas around Wilmslow, but Nuthatches can now be found almost anywhere in the county with sufficient trees for them to feel at home. The mosslands around the river Mersey used to be a significant barrier for them (*BTO Atlas*, *BTO Second Atlas*) but they have now spread across that, especially in SJ69, and are present in most of south Liverpool (Pyefinch & Golborn 2001). The main areas still without Nuthatches are northern parts of Wirral, Halton and Warrington, the Gowy valley and a band across south central Cheshire from Faddiley (SJ55W) to Cranage (SJ76P).

This is one of our most arboreal species, especially favouring mature deciduous woodland: 'within Europe, the most important tree for Nuthatches is undoubtedly the oak' (Matthysen 1998). The bark of oaks provides plenty of nooks and crannies from which they can glean food for themselves, mostly adult insects, spiders, larvae, pupae and eggs, and for their chicks, who are fed especially beetle larvae and moth caterpillars. The habitat codes submitted for 85% of tetrads were A1 (broad-leaved) or A3 (mixed) woodland. Most of the remainder were suburban or rural human sites and Nuthatches readily use large gardens provided that they contain trees and are adjacent to woodland. A few records came from farmland with tall hedges; hedgerow oaks are probably important in helping the species' spread across the agricultural landscape.

This is generally a noisy and demonstrative species, not easy to overlook, although they go quiet during incubation. Only just over half of tetrads provided evidence of confirmed breeding, however; in our fragmented landscape, some of the birds in isolated woods are likely to have been unmated (*Migration Atlas*). Birds were seen carrying food or a faecal sac in 54 tetrads, and fieldworkers in 108 tetrads saw recently fledged young. Nests were found in 77 tetrads, usually in the trunk of a tree, often high up. Nuthatches cannot excavate their own holes, so rely on taking over an old Great Spotted Woodpecker nest or wherever a rotten branch has fallen and left a suitable cavity. Many nest sites are refurbished and re-used, some of them for five years or more. If the size of the nest hole is not to their liking, most Nuthatches use mud to reduce it to fit themselves and exclude the majority of possible competitors or predators. When the nest has been sufficiently manicured, the pair then line it with bark flakes, Scots pine being especially favoured and often deemed worth flights of hundreds of metres from the nest. During this survey, holes in oaks and nest-boxes were the only sites recorded, apart from Hugh Linn's extraordinary record near Dodleston (SJ36Q) in 2006, when Nuthatches nested in the wreckage of an aeroplane.

Along with their expansion of range, the Nuthatch population has increased considerably, the national index being more than 70% higher than 20 years ago. The reasons for their continued rise are unknown, however. In prime oak habitat, Nuthatches can achieve a density ranging from two to seven pairs per 10 ha (Matthysen 1998). There are few areas in the county as good as that, but it does have an average of more than 12 pairs per tetrad with confirmed or probable breeding according to the BTO's analysis of BBS transects, which found the breeding population of Cheshire and Wirral in 2004–05 to be 7,770 birds (with very wide confidence limits from zero to 16,440).

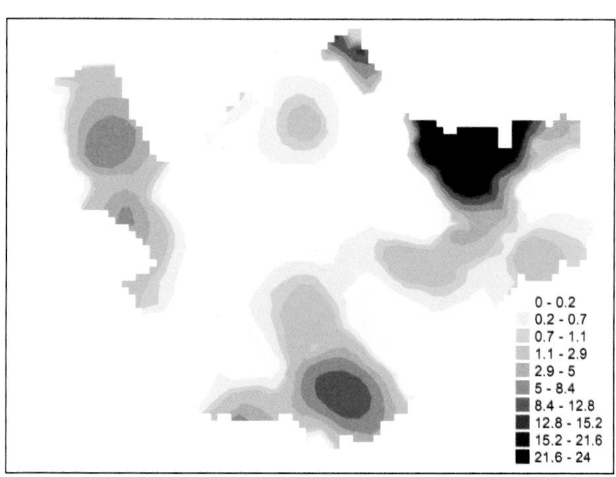

Nuthatch abundance.

Sponsored by AstraZeneca, Club AZ Natural History section

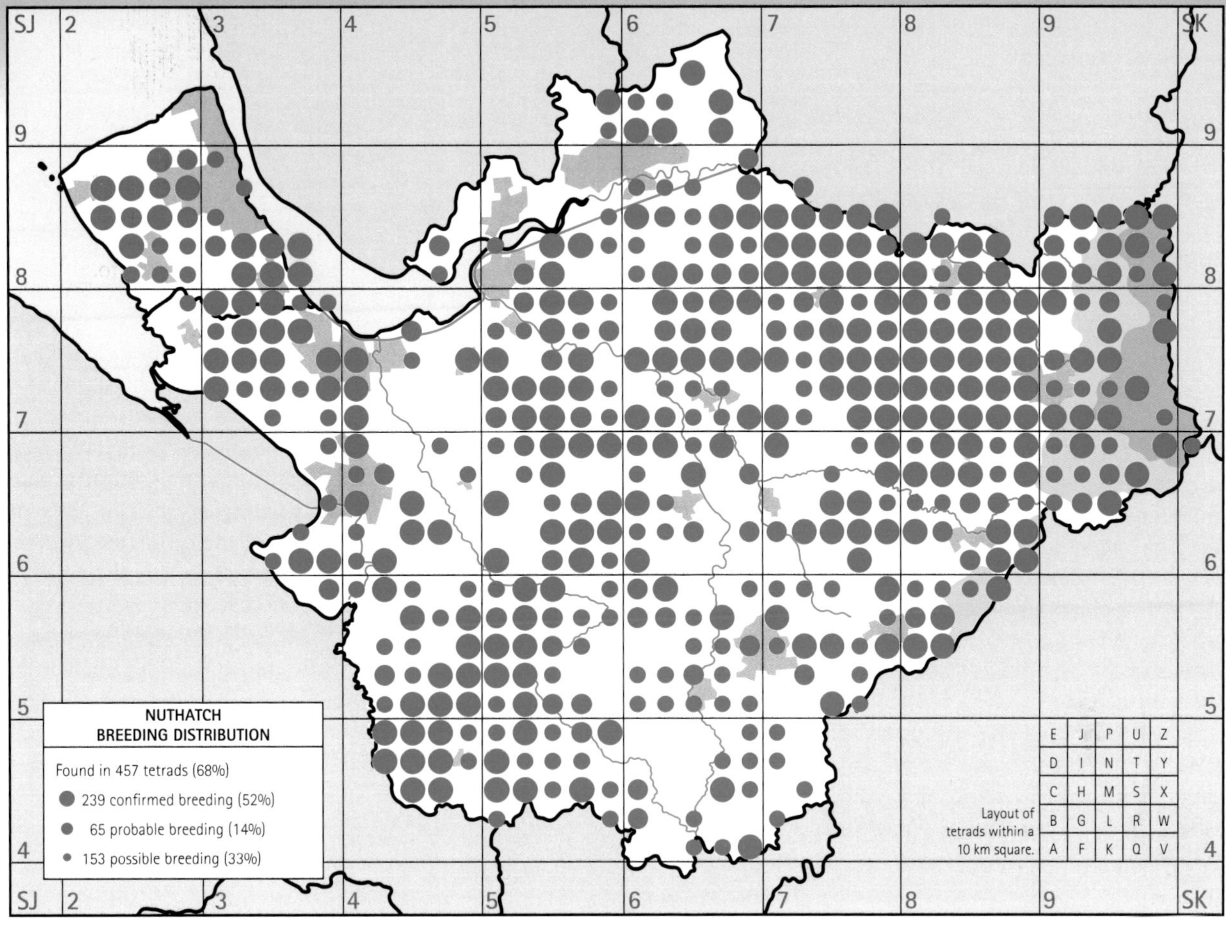
SJ
2
3
4
5
6
7
8
9
SK
NUTHATCH
BREEDING DISTRIBUTION
Found in 457 tetrads (68%)
239 confirmed breeding (52%)
65 probable breeding (14%)
153 possible breeding (33%)
E J P U Z
D I N T Y
C H M S X
B G L R W
A F K Q V
Layout of tetrads within a 10 km square.

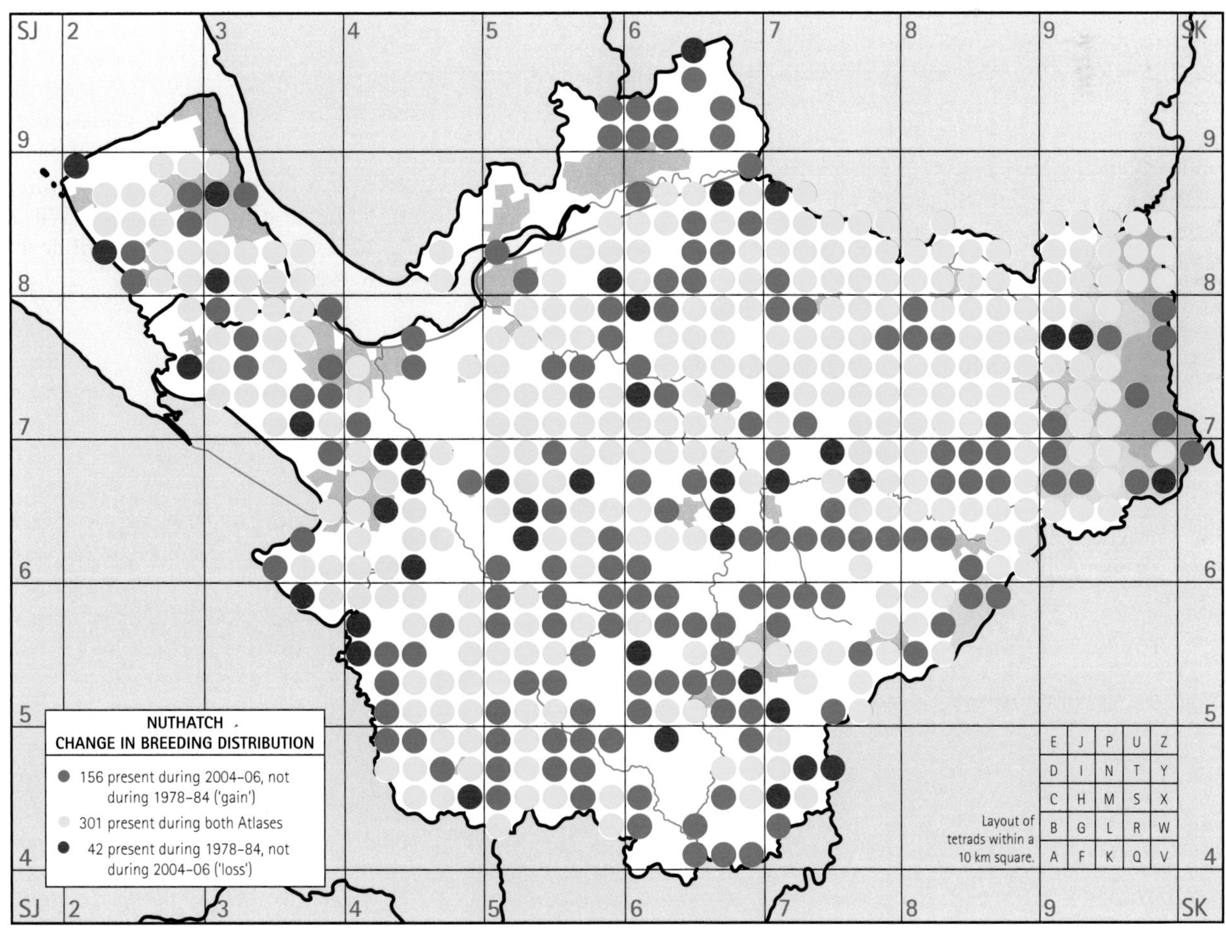
SJ
2
3
4
5
6
7
8
9
SK
NUTHATCH
CHANGE IN BREEDING DISTRIBUTION
156 present during 2004–06, not during 1978–84 ('gain')
301 present during both Atlases
42 present during 1978–84, not during 2004–06 ('loss')
E J P U Z
D I N T Y
C H M S X
B G L R W
A F K Q V
Layout of tetrads within a 10 km square.

Despite their sedentary nature, Nuthatches were found in winter in an extra 37 tetrads without a breeding season record: 407 tetrads had birds in both seasons, 87 with winter presence only, and there were 50 tetrads in which they were found in the breeding season but not in winter. The areas occupied in winter include parts of the Gowy valley and the south central Cheshire band without breeding season presence, and odd tetrads in the northern parts of Wirral, Halton and Warrington, but all these areas remain mostly blank. It is not clear, however, how much these winter records represent birds moving in to these areas and how much is because some Nuthatches become easier to record through visiting gardens: 'human' habitats made up 14% of the submitted habitat codes in the breeding season but 25% of the total in winter, with a corresponding drop in the proportion of woodland records. They can be quite inconspicuous on some winter days, but on others many birds seem to be calling and they are just as easy to detect as they are in spring.

Nuthatches are extremely territorial birds, with some birds starting to establish territories as early as June, as little as two weeks after they fledge (Matthysen 1998)! It is not surprising that the Atlas database shows that 90% of the 376 records where surveyors submitted a count were of one or two birds only, with most of the others, up to a maximum of eight in Delamere Forest (SJ57K), at well-stocked feeding stations. Most territories are established by early autumn, with little exploration by November and December, followed by resurgence in spring, not least because most of the winter deaths occur in late winter and spring as the food remaining from the autumn crop reaches a minimum (*BTO Winter Atlas*). Pairs usually remain together and defend their breeding territory in winter as well as during the breeding season. Juveniles disperse as far as they have to in order to find a suitable territory, although they usually try to fit in to a vacant area near their natal site. In my study of the Delamere Forest population, with more than 500 captures, I have had two instances of birds ringed as chicks moving 1.3 km to a prime territory, both of them males, but that is a long way for a Nuthatch and every other bird has been retrapped at the site where it was ringed. The national database shows that the median distance of movement, for both sexes, is less than 1 km (*Migration Atlas*).

Their winter diet comprises live food when they can find it, especially insects hidden in or under bark, but is mainly vegetarian, especially seeds of trees—hazel, beech, oak (acorns), hornbeam, sycamore, yew and ash—which they often open by wedging them in a tree and hammering on the nut, behaviour that gains them their English name. They readily supplement these natural foods with human-provided fare, mainly peanuts. In times of plenty, Nuthatches store food in caches, mainly tree-crevices, birds usually covering their food with a piece of bark, lichen or moss for retrieval at a later date.

RICHARD STEEL

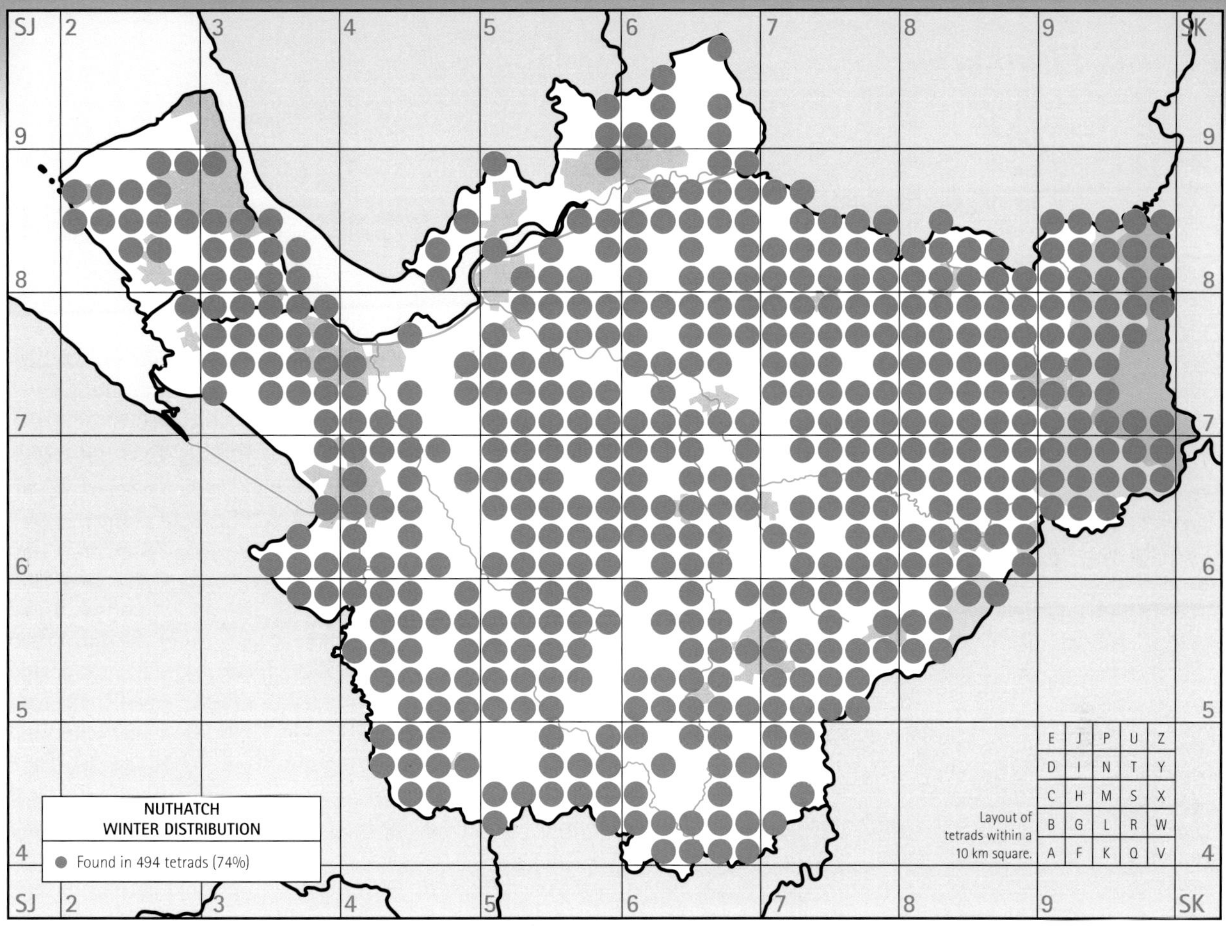
SJ
2
3
4
5
6
7
8
9
SK
NUTHATCH
WINTER DISTRIBUTION
Found in 494 tetrads (74%)
E J P U Z
D I N T Y
C H M S X
B G L R W
A F K Q V
Layout of tetrads within a 10 km square.

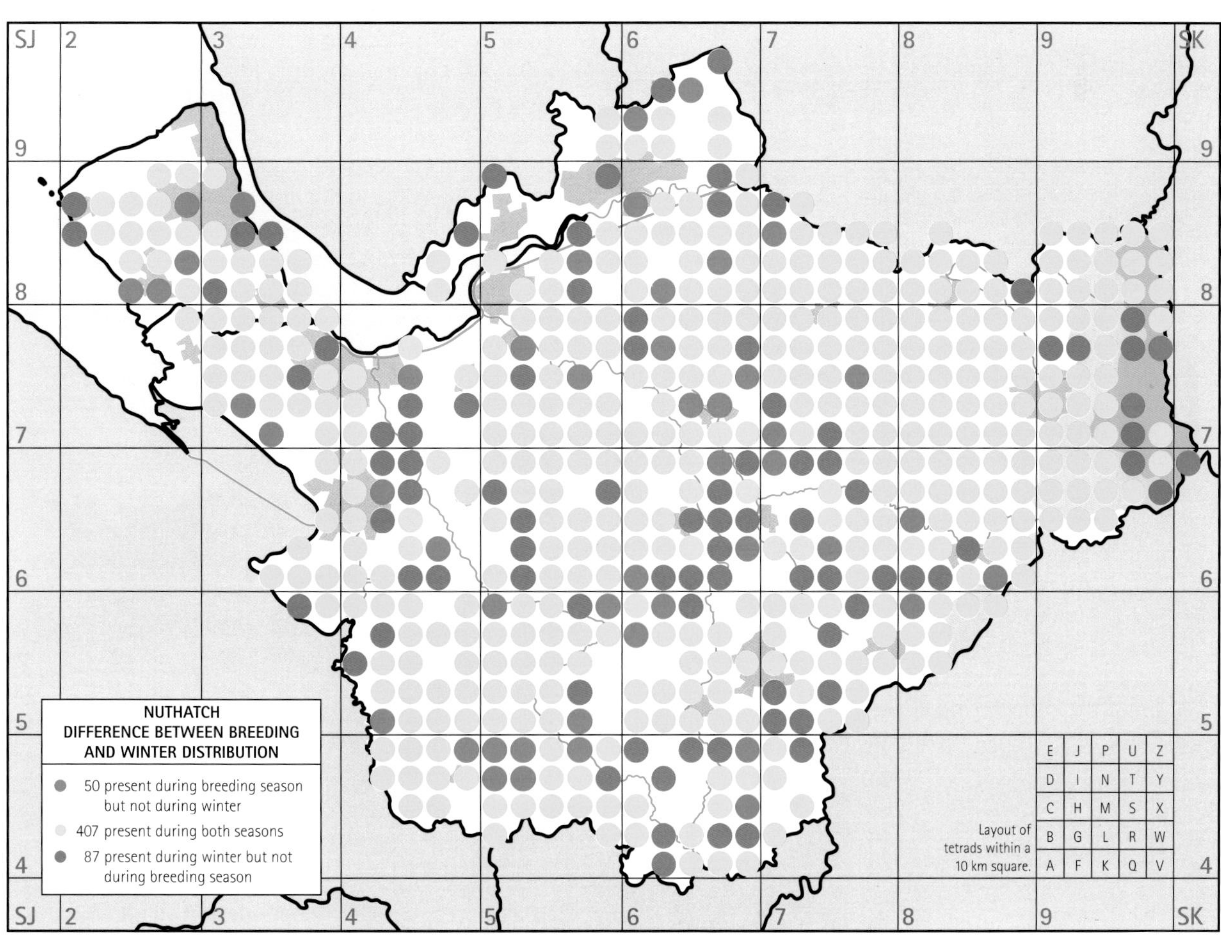
SJ
2
3
4
5
6
7
8
9
SK
NUTHATCH
DIFFERENCE BETWEEN BREEDING AND WINTER DISTRIBUTION
50 present during breeding season but not during winter
407 present during both seasons
87 present during winter but not during breeding season
E J P U Z
D I N T Y
C H M S X
B G L R W
A F K Q V
Layout of tetrads within a 10 km square.

Treecreeper

Certhia familiaris

REN HATHWAY

The substantial reduction in breeding Treecreepers was one of the surprises of this Atlas. From the total in our *First Atlas* of 475 occupied tetrads, this survey showed a drop of 68, with a much larger decline in those with confirmed or probable breeding, falling by 110 from 357 to 247. The 'change' map shows widespread gaps across rural Cheshire, with noticeable losses from several tetrads around Chester and Macclesfield (although they are always scarce in urban areas) and it seems that they have retreated to the core woodland areas, as also suggested by the abundance map. From the submitted habitat codes, 85% of tetrads with Treecreeper records contained woodland, almost all of them broad-leaved or mixed, with 15 records of birds in carr (waterlogged) woods. This might overstate the importance of woodland: trees are essential, but they often use hedgerows with mature oaks.

There seems to be little in the national statistics to explain a drop in occupation of Cheshire and Wirral tetrads. The BTO's population index has fluctuated somewhat, but the UK figure was at the same level in 2004 as in 1980. The BTO's analysis of Breeding Bird Survey transects shows that the breeding population of the county in 2004–05 was 6,270 birds (2,700–9,850). This figure amounts to 2.0% of the UK breeding population of about 319,000 Treecreepers (Newson *et al.* 2008).

This seems to have been one of the more difficult species for many fieldworkers to prove breeding, with 45% of tetrads yielding two-letter codes. In 62 tetrads, recently fledged juveniles were found, often well-camouflaged birds packed side-by-side in a frozen attitude, vertical on a tree trunk as they await the return of their parents. In 71 tetrads, birds were seen carrying food: often a bird carrying food could be watched climbing a tree trunk, then apparently disappear as it slipped behind a broken piece of bark into the nest, and 49 nests were found. Oak and alder were the only species of tree reported, with several birds using nest-boxes, and Treecreepers successfully nested in bird hides at Hattons Hey (SJ57T), as they have done before, and for four years in succession (2002–05) at Doddington Pool (SJ74D). Previously, nests have been reported in bat-boxes, in beech and sweet chestnut trees and in a crack in an outbuilding wall at Inner Marsh Farm (*CWBRs*).

Treecreepers are well known for their feeding habits, starting at the bottom of a tree and working upwards in a spiral, picking insects from crevices in the bark. They especially eat spiders, but will take any insects that they find, and occasionally take wing to catch a small moth or other morsel flying past.

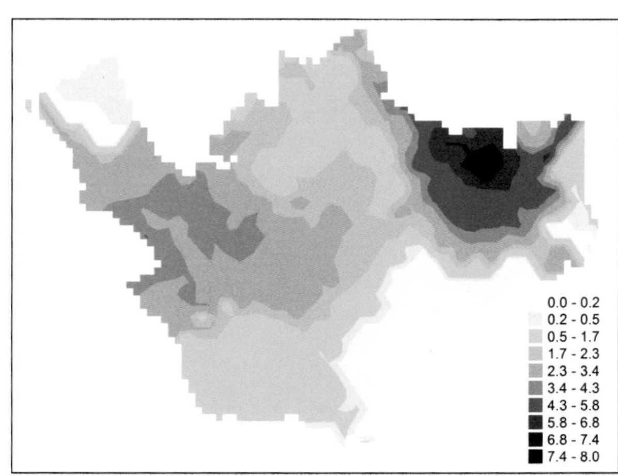

Treecreeper abundance.

Sponsored by Tony Coatsworth and Gina Jones

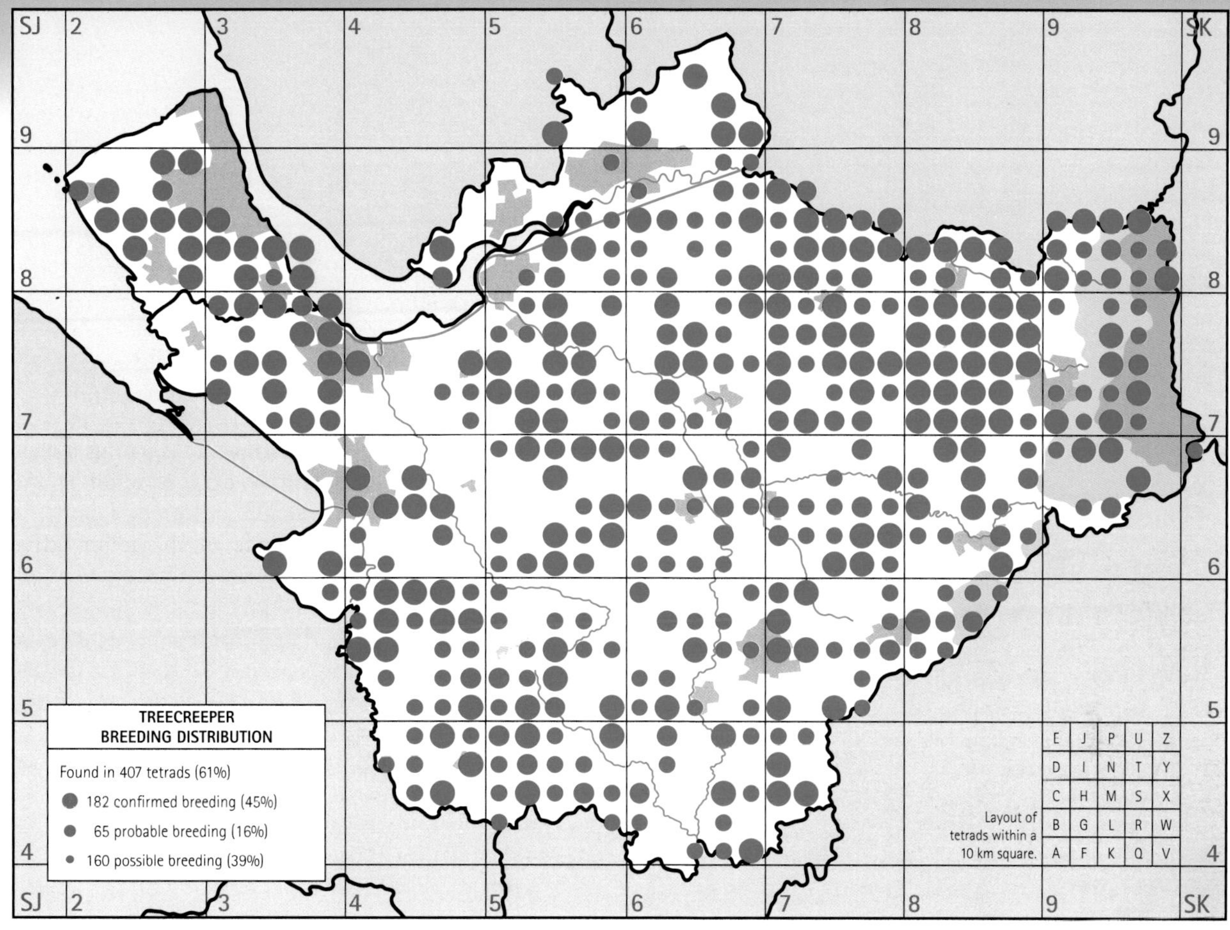

SJ
SK
TREECREEPER
BREEDING DISTRIBUTION
Found in 407 tetrads (61%)
182 confirmed breeding (45%)
65 probable breeding (16%)
160 possible breeding (39%)
Layout of tetrads within a 10 km square.
E J P U Z
D I N T Y
C H M S X
B G L R W
A F K Q V

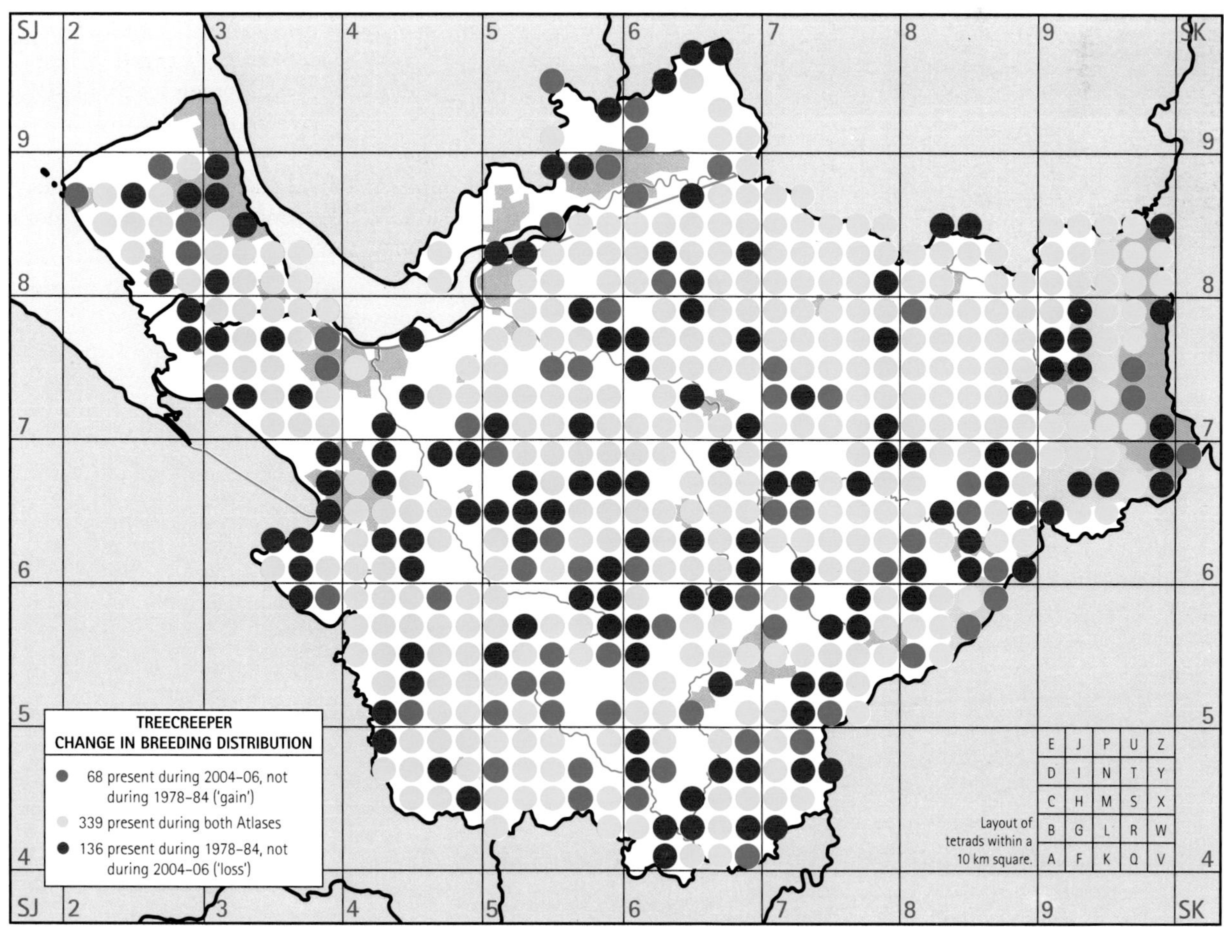

SJ
SK
TREECREEPER
CHANGE IN BREEDING DISTRIBUTION
68 present during 2004–06, not during 1978–84 ('gain')
339 present during both Atlases
136 present during 1978–84, not during 2004–06 ('loss')
Layout of tetrads within a 10 km square.
E J P U Z
D I N T Y
C H M S X
B G L R W
A F K Q V

SHEILA BLAMIRE

Although probably less obvious in winter, when they do not sing and seldom call, and thought to be underrecorded in winter (*BTO Winter Atlas*), Treecreepers were nevertheless found in 54 more tetrads than in the breeding season. The species is scattered widely across the county; areas occupied in winter only include a noticeable cluster in the lower Gowy valley (SJ46/47) and around Macclesfield (SJ97). Adult Treecreepers are thought to maintain their breeding territories all year round, varying in size from 1 to 15 ha. This is a large area for a small passerine but only equivalent to a circle 440 m in diameter, and adults almost never move more than 500 m (*Migration Atlas*). Together with their reluctance to cross open spaces (*BWP*), this vitiates the species' colonization of new areas. The birds found in winter but not in the breeding season are likely to be first-year birds dispersing from their parents' territory. Examination of the winter habitat codes shows almost identical numbers in woodland (369 breeding season, 354 winter), but large increases in the figures for farmland hedgerows (from 23 to 63) and human sites (from 30 to 87), showing those birds spreading out from the core woodland areas into a wider range of habitats.

In winter, Treecreepers continue to search trees for insects and spiders, their long bill allowing them to probe where no other bird can, but they also eat seeds, especially of pines and spruces. Within the last decade Treecreepers have started feeding on peanuts in hanging baskets at a number of sites scattered widely across Britain, in Devon, Buckinghamshire, Carmarthen and several Scottish counties, although this habit seems not yet to have been noted in Cheshire and it would be interesting to document its uptake. They sometimes associate with tit flocks, but usually feed solitarily, not often even with others of their own species. Out of the 724 records of Treecreeper submitted over the three winters, 328 included counts: 240 of them were of a single bird, with 70 records of two together, 12 records of three birds and six counts of four birds.

A fascinating aspect of Treecreeper behaviour is their occasional use of roosting holes which they excavate themselves in soft wood, including dead alder and, famously, redwood (wellingtonia) *Sequoiadendron giganteum* trees. They usually make their roost-holes on the north-east side of the tree, away from the prevailing wind, a wise precaution since winter rainfall has been shown adversely to affect their survival (Peach *et al.* 1995b). Such roosts have not been observed in Cheshire and Wirral—indeed during this survey there were no reports at all of roosting Treecreepers—but it would be an interesting study to visit some of the county's few redwoods to see if Treecreepers here have learned this habit.

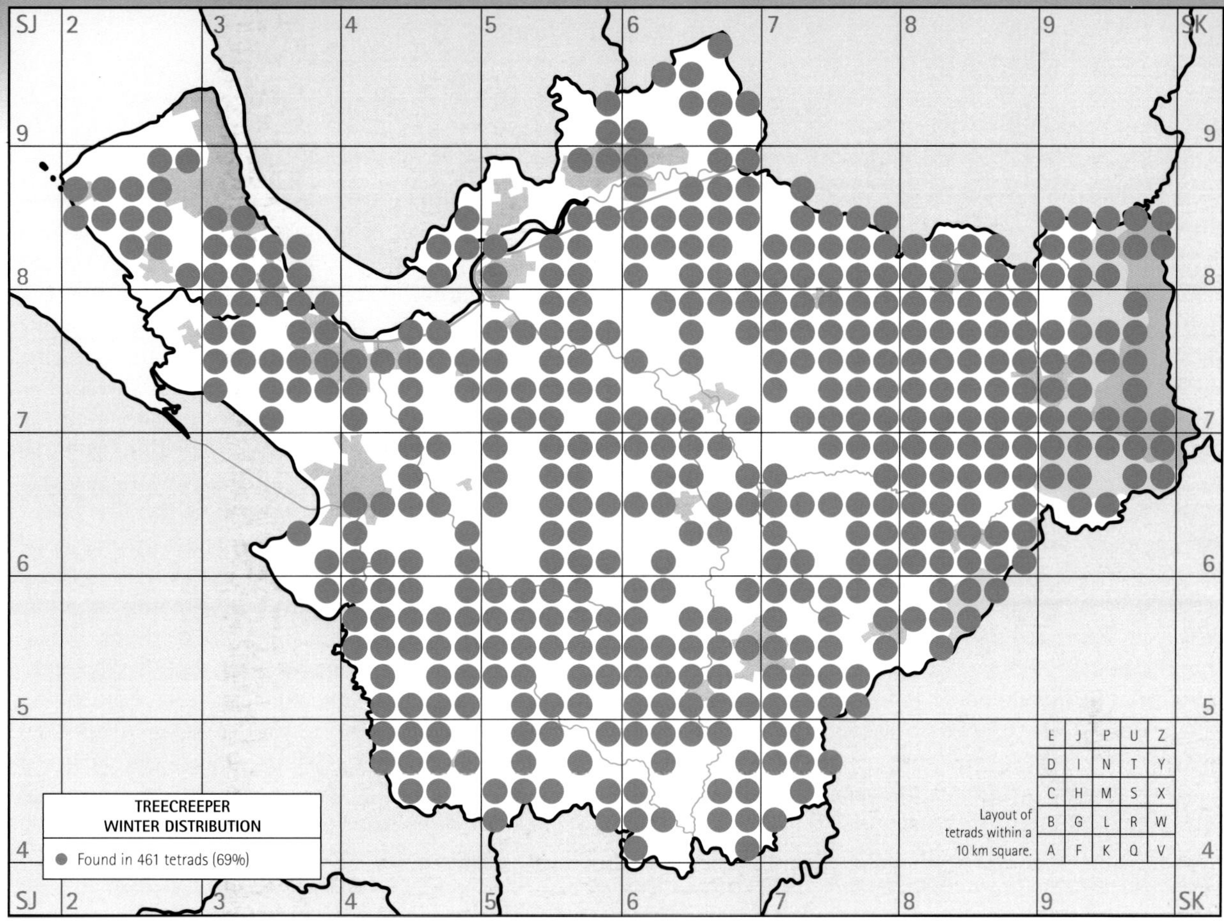
SJ
2
3
4
5
6
7
8
9
SK
TREECREEPER
WINTER DISTRIBUTION
Found in 461 tetrads (69%)
Layout of
tetrads within a
10 km square.
E J P U Z
D I N T Y
C H M S X
B G L R W
A F K Q V

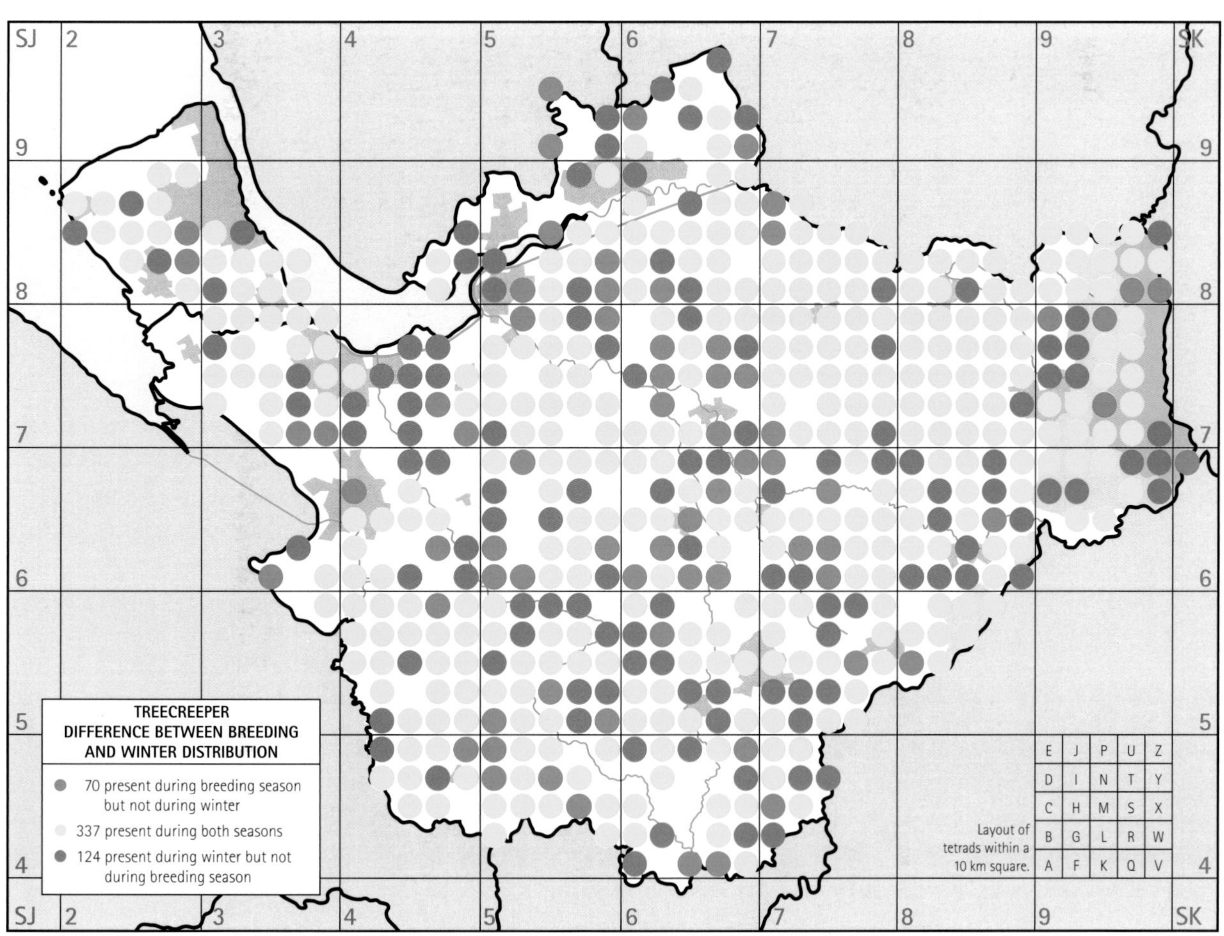
SJ
2
3
4
5
6
7
8
9
SK
TREECREEPER
DIFFERENCE BETWEEN BREEDING
AND WINTER DISTRIBUTION
70 present during breeding season but not during winter
337 present during both seasons
124 present during winter but not during breeding season
Layout of
tetrads within a
10 km square.
E J P U Z
D I N T Y
C H M S X
B G L R W
A F K Q V

Jay

Garrulus glandarius

This is the corvid of woodland: the habitat codes supplied came mostly from woodland (65% of records), mostly broad-leaved or mixed, with 9% in scrub, 17% on farmland and 8% in human sites. Despite their quite restricted needs, Jays have increased their range since our *First Atlas*, with a net gain of presence in 50 tetrads. The 'change' map shows their increase most noticeably along the Mersey valley and in south central Cheshire, and they have particularly moved into urban areas around Widnes, Warrington, Chester and Crewe.

The national breeding population index has fluctuated but with no overall trend, and their numbers are much the same as during our *First Atlas*. According to the analysis of BBS transects in Cheshire and Wirral, their breeding population in the county in 2004–05 was 5,520 birds (2,470–8,570), an average of 10 birds per tetrad in which they were found.

Their display in April can be entertaining to watch, as several birds often chase each other through the trees. This is a good way of locating territories, but the wary birds usually see the human much quicker than the other way round, and often all that can be detected is a raucous squawk and a flash of white rumps as they fly off. Jays' nests are difficult to find. They are secretive birds, usually building in dense scrub or small trees, and their nests are surprisingly small, often little bigger than that of a Blackbird. Only in 25 tetrads did observers record a nest as proof of breeding, and most confirmed breeding came from seeing adults carrying food for their chicks (53 tetrads) or with recently fledged young (91). Amongst the categories of probable breeding, 13 tetrads furnished evidence of birds carrying nesting material, and 11 of Jays visiting a probable nest site.

They forage during the breeding season for invertebrates to feed to their young, especially defoliating caterpillars, beetles and spiders. Jays are well known for predating the eggs and chicks of smaller birds. Parents feed their older chicks some acorns that they have dug up from those stored the previous year, even if they have sprouted and have started to become oak seedlings; Jays seem able to distinguish between the green-stemmed seedlings, newly grown and still palatable, and the brown-stemmed young shoots from previous years, which they ignore (Coombs 1978).

SIMON BOOTH

Sponsored by The Arnold Family (Hebe, Clair and Mark)

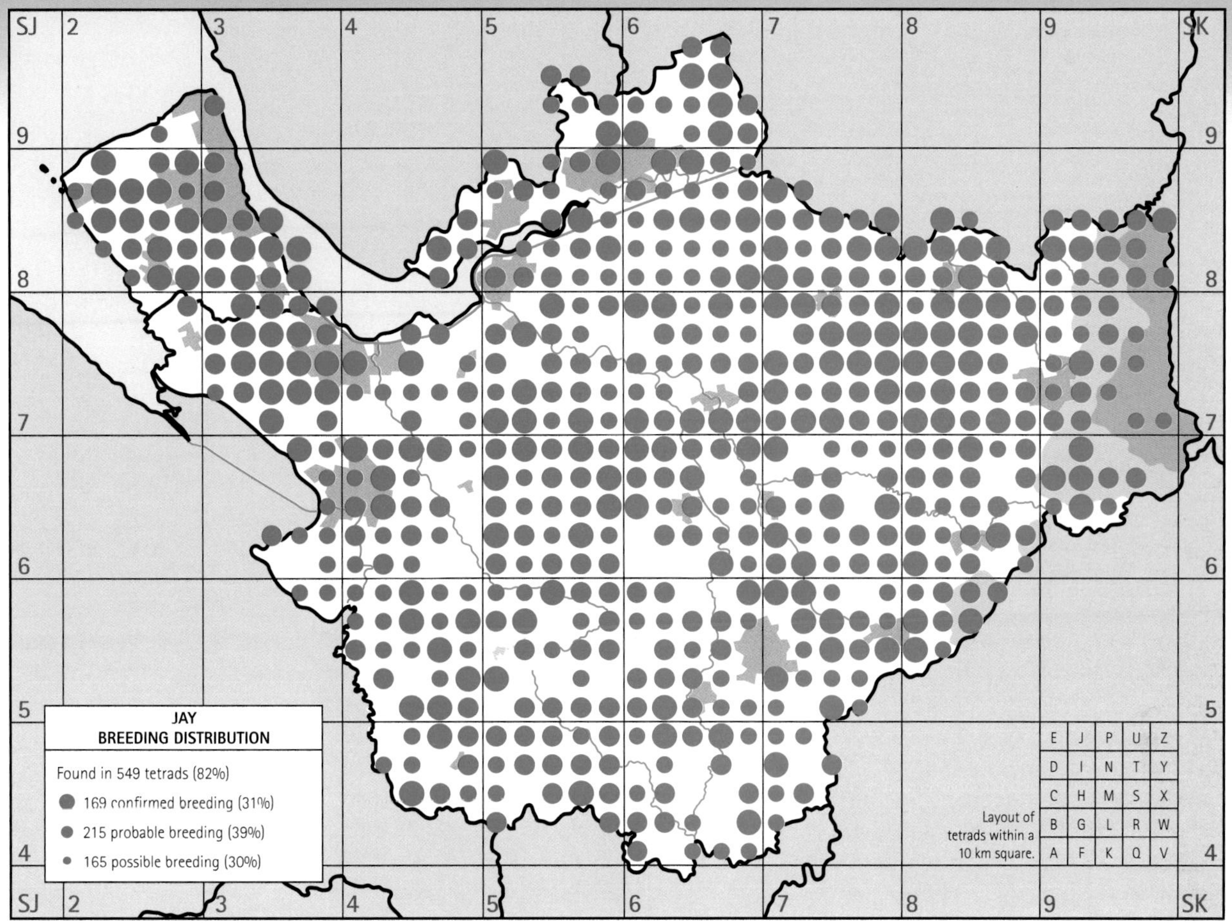
SJ
2
3
4
5
6
7
8
9
SK
9
8
7
6
5
4
JAY
BREEDING DISTRIBUTION
Found in 549 tetrads (82%)
169 confirmed breeding (31%)
215 probable breeding (39%)
165 possible breeding (30%)
E J P U Z
D I N T Y
C H M S X
B G L R W
A F K Q V
Layout of tetrads within a 10 km square.

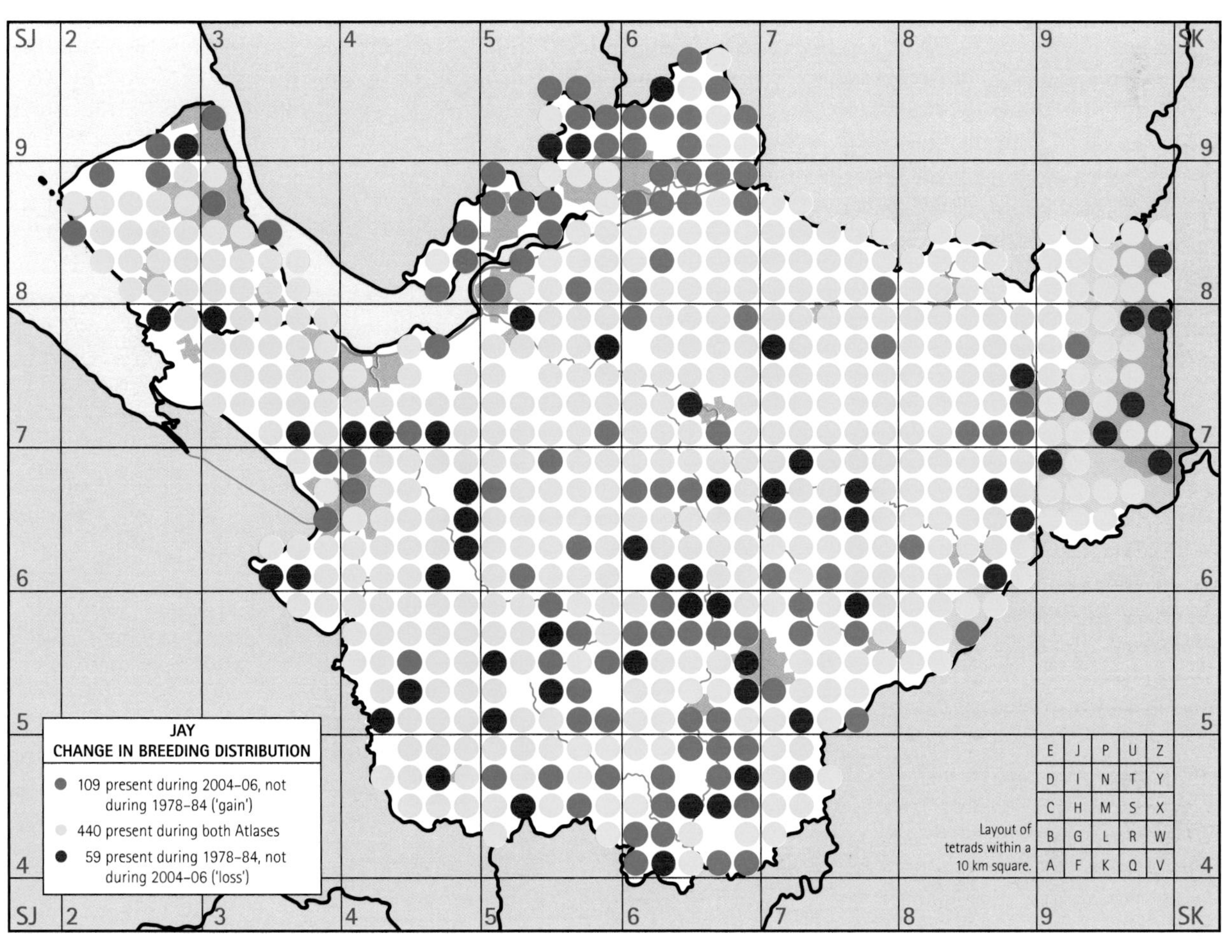
SJ
2
3
4
5
6
7
8
9
SK
9
8
7
6
5
4
JAY
CHANGE IN BREEDING DISTRIBUTION
109 present during 2004–06, not during 1978–84 ('gain')
440 present during both Atlases
59 present during 1978–84, not during 2004–06 ('loss')
E J P U Z
D I N T Y
C H M S X
B G L R W
A F K Q V
Layout of tetrads within a 10 km square.

STEVE ROUND

The position of Jay as the woodland corvid is even more obvious in winter. As many as 59% of the habitat records came from woodland or scrub, more than twice as high a proportion as any other member of the crow family. A further 24% were in farmland, more than half of them hedgerows, and 16% in human sites, over twice the proportion in the breeding season.

The winter Atlas map shows that they moved into some areas where they did not breed, being found in 18 more tetrads, although with gains and losses scattered across the county. A few of the higher altitude squares, vacant in the breeding season, held a bird or two in winter. Most Jays do not move far, British birds being largely sedentary. There is occasional mass immigration from the continent following widespread failure of the acorn crop but Cheshire and Wirral missed out on the last such event, in autumn 1983, with only odd records of more than a few birds, although the publicity given to the invasion perhaps stimulated more recording of the species than normal (*CWBR*).

Jays are at their most conspicuous in October, when they fly to and fro carrying acorns which they store by burying in the ground, although on 26 December 2005, Brian Baird reported a Jay at Great Sankey (SJ58U) eating nuts and berries that it had apparently stored in an old nest. Each bird will cache several thousand acorns, often up to a kilometre or more from the oak tree from which they fell (Coombs 1978). They also hoard beechmast, hazelnuts and sweet chestnuts, and peanuts in gardens, and opportunistically feed on almost anything they can find. They return to the buried items later in the year, starting even a week or two after they finished hiding them, and stored acorns are the Jay's main winter food. Their ability to retrieve the stored items has intrigued various ornithologists and ethologists. It seems to be based entirely on memory, Jays even being able to retrieve items buried under snow when all external clues appear to have been lost (Coombs 1978). They do not return to all that they buried, and some birds die during the winter, so some of the buried acorns turn into oak trees, often a long way from woodland. For this habit of spreading oaks, Jay is a very important species in the British countryside.

Jay is the only corvid that does not form large flocks. Over the three winters, 472 counts were submitted, more than three-quarters of them of one or two birds, with the largest flocks, of eight or nine birds, reported from seven tetrads. Communal roosts of Jays are seldom recorded, and just two were found during this winter Atlas, three birds in SJ56X and eight on 11 February 2007 flying into rhododendrons in large gardens in SJ68L.

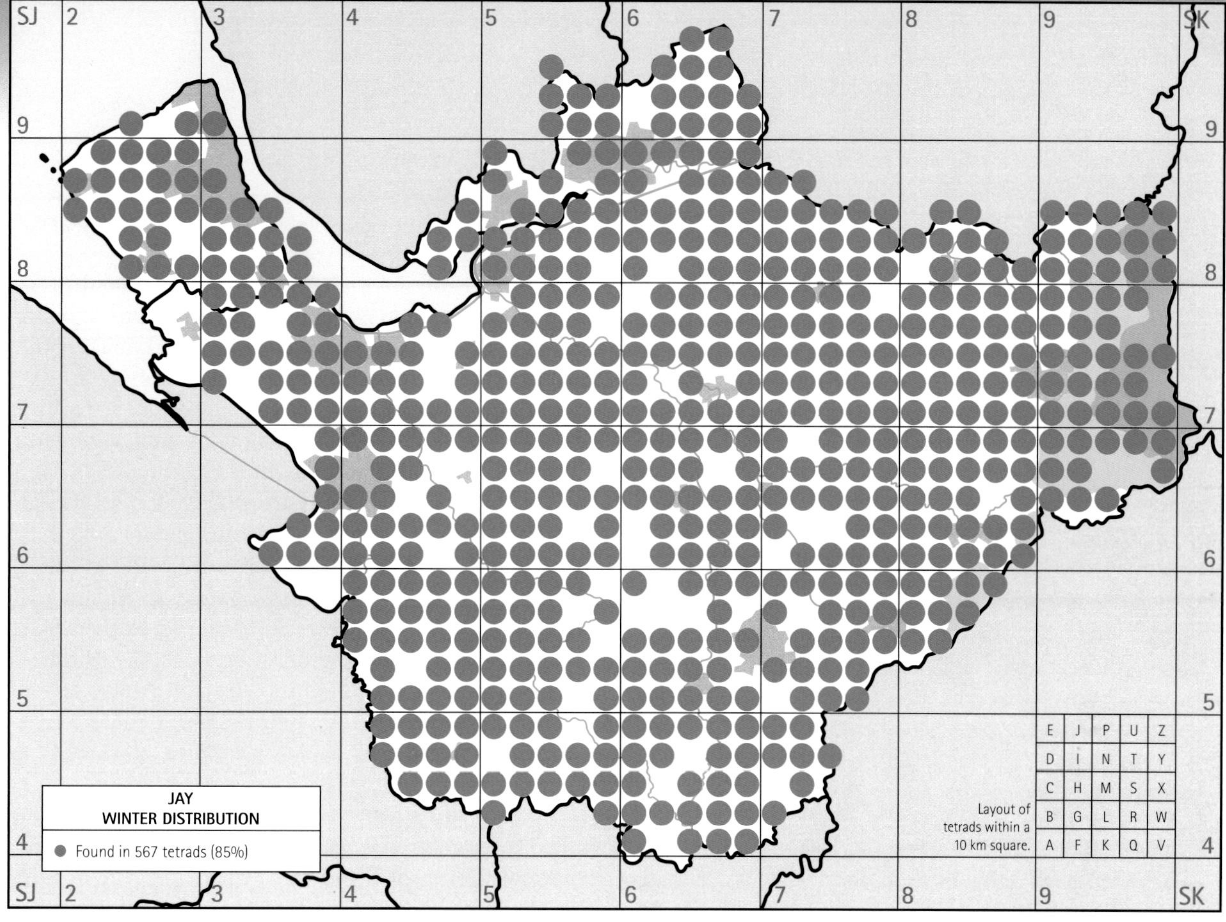
JAY
WINTER DISTRIBUTION
Found in 567 tetrads (85%)
Layout of tetrads within a 10 km square.
E J P U Z
D I N T Y
C H M S X
B G L R W
A F K Q V
SJ
SK

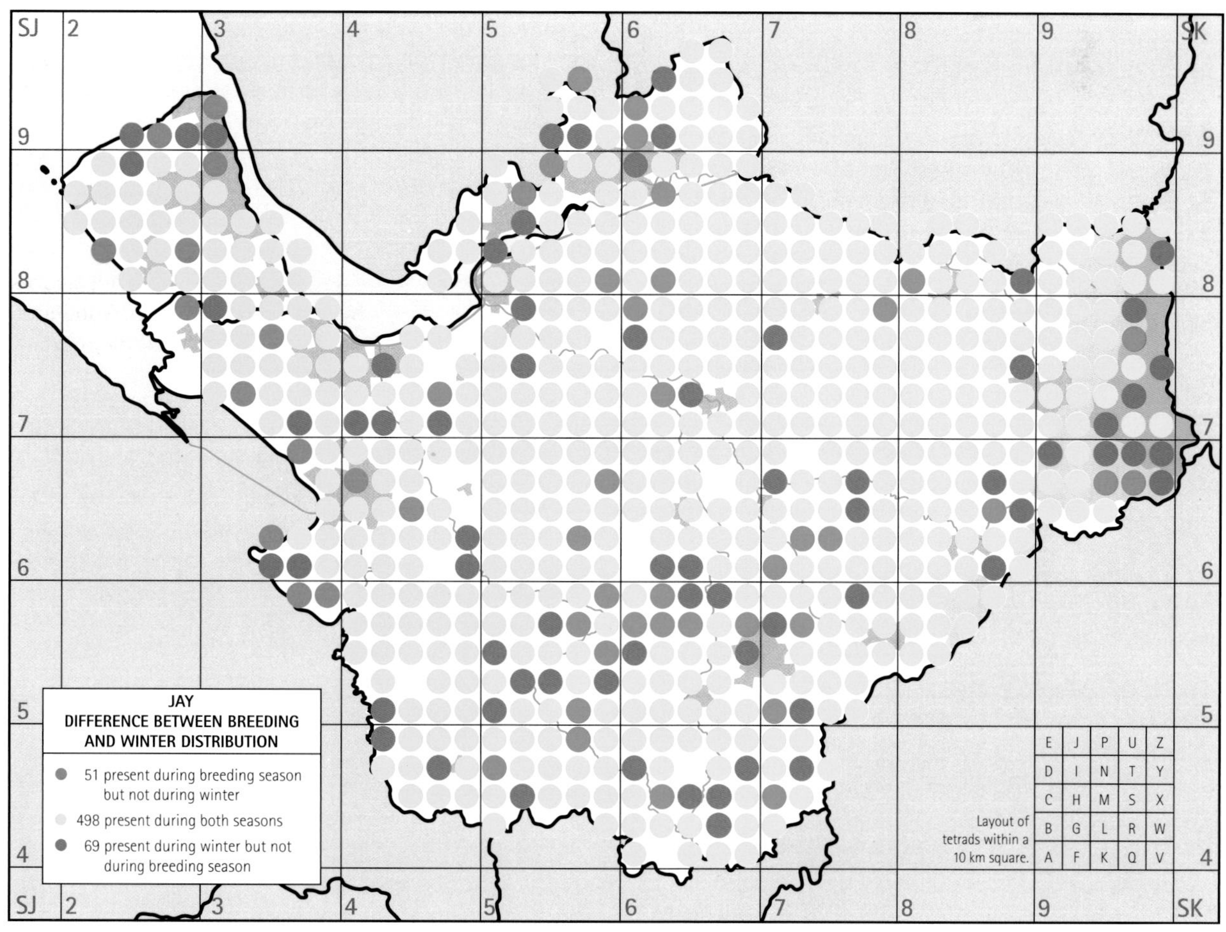
JAY
DIFFERENCE BETWEEN BREEDING AND WINTER DISTRIBUTION
51 present during breeding season but not during winter
498 present during both seasons
69 present during winter but not during breeding season
Layout of tetrads within a 10 km square.
E J P U Z
D I N T Y
C H M S X
B G L R W
A F K Q V
SJ
SK

Magpie

Pica pica

COLIN SMITH

'The Magpie is far too abundant' opined Boyd in 1951. What would he think now, with this as the seventh most widespread breeding bird in Cheshire and Wirral? Their population has probably stabilized now, however, after rising rapidly for many years. During the seven-year fieldwork period of our *First Atlas* the national index climbed by more than one-quarter, but since about 1987 it has levelled off (Gregory & Marchant 1996), leaving the present figure about 10% higher than in 1984. Their distribution in the county shows minor changes since twenty years ago, with a couple of new breeding tetrads in Birkenhead docklands (SJ38J/39F), but still no place for it on Hilbre, and a noticeable loss from six tetrads in the eastern hills. According to the analysis of BBS transects in Cheshire and Wirral, their breeding population in the county in 2004–05 was 14,190 birds (10,650–17,720), an average of 22 birds per tetrad in which they were found. The validity of this survey for producing breeding population figures for Magpie is still being tested, however, because many Magpies live in non-breeding flocks (Birkhead 1991). These flocks make up one-quarter to one-half of the total population and are composed of one-year-old birds, too young to breed, and older birds that have not managed to displace, or replace, a territorial bird.

Probably the main change that Boyd would notice from sixty years ago is the Magpie's move into suburbia (85 tetrads) and urban areas (22). The habitat codes recorded in this Atlas comprised 44% farmland, 25% woodland, 7% scrub and 23% human sites. Some birds are now remarkably tolerant of man, and vice versa, although in some rural areas they are trapped in large numbers. Unless the culling pressure is intense, though, it makes little difference to breeding numbers because most of those taken are non-breeders and a territorial bird that dies is replaced almost immediately by a member of the non-breeding flock, virtually always within 48 hours and sometimes the same day (Birkhead 1991). In rural areas, Magpies actually choose to nest near houses, probably to reduce the likelihood of predation by Carrion Crows, which are much more wary of man!

By far the easiest way to prove Magpies breeding is by seeing their enormous domed stick nests, usually close to the top of a tall tree, which take them three weeks to build, usually during March and often starting in February. They have shown a strong trend to earlier breeding: analysis of the BTO nest record data shows them laying eggs a whole month earlier in 2005 than in 1968, typically starting in late March nowadays. Nests were recorded in 226 tetrads but, once the leaves are out, they can be surprisingly difficult to see and surveyors visiting a tetrad for the first time in late April or May could have missed them. No matter, because recently fledged young are noisy and obvious by their short tails as they harass their parents for food for several weeks and they seldom leave the 5 ha breeding territory: RF was the code for confirmed breeding in 220 tetrads.

Magpies will eat almost anything but adults take mostly invertebrates to feed their young. Around Manchester, beetle larvae, adult beetles, ants and leatherjackets were the main prey (Tatner 1983). They find most of their food in grassland, either agricultural fields or urban greenspace. Many birdwatchers hate Magpies because they occasionally take eggs and nestlings of smaller birds, but they seldom comprise much of a Magpie's diet and several studies have shown such predation to have no effect on the populations of other birds (Gooch *et al.* 1991).

Sponsored by Fran Cogger

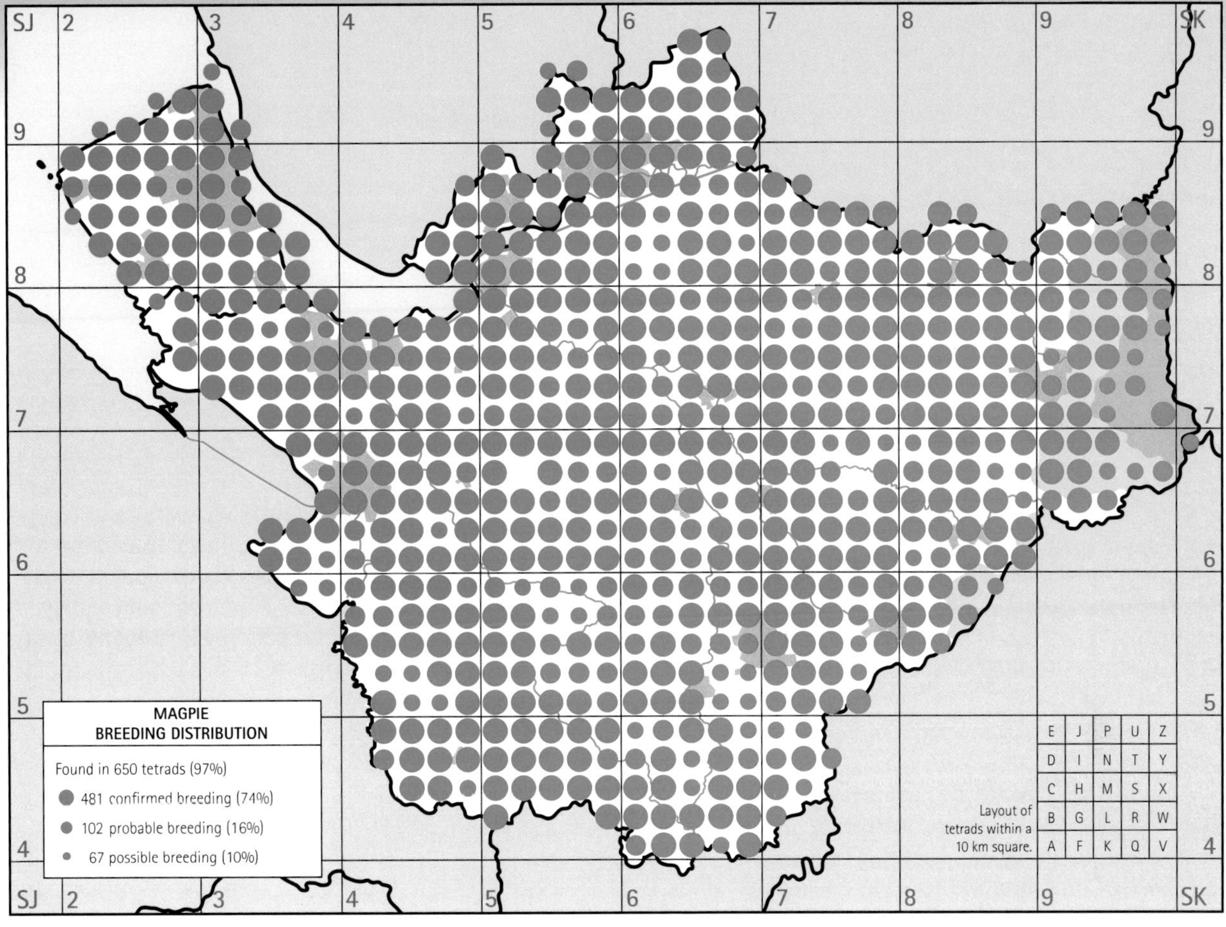
MAGPIE
BREEDING DISTRIBUTION
Found in 650 tetrads (97%)
481 confirmed breeding (74%)
102 probable breeding (16%)
67 possible breeding (10%)
Layout of tetrads within a 10 km square.
E J P U Z
D I N T Y
C H M S X
B G L R W
A F K Q V
SJ 2 3 4 5 6 7 8 9 SK

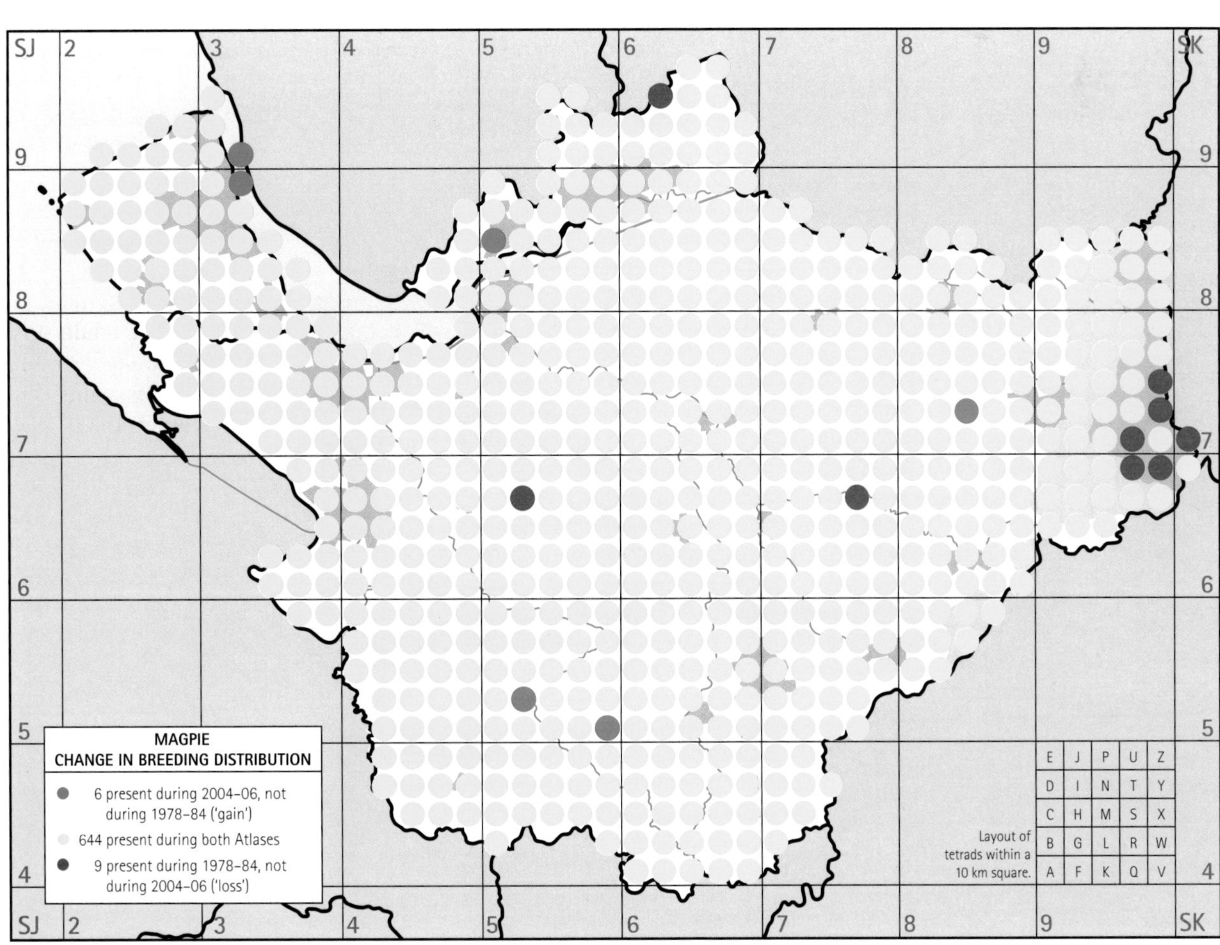
MAGPIE
CHANGE IN BREEDING DISTRIBUTION
6 present during 2004–06, not during 1978–84 ('gain')
644 present during both Atlases
9 present during 1978–84, not during 2004–06 ('loss')
Layout of tetrads within a 10 km square.
E J P U Z
D I N T Y
C H M S X
B G L R W
A F K Q V
SJ 2 3 4 5 6 7 8 9 SK

The distribution map shows that, bar a few odd spots of underrecording, Magpies are ubiquitous in winter. Compared to the breeding season, birds move to fill in the gaps in the Cheshire hills, although not onto Hilbre Island. This is one of the most sedentary of all species, with the median distance of movement of ringed birds less than 1 km, although the daily roamings of non-territorial birds, and the distance they go to roost, are likely to exceed that. There has been no proof of any immigration from the continent to Britain (*Migration Atlas*).

The habitat records show a minor shift onto farmland (53% of winter records, against 44% of breeding records) and commensurate small losses from woodland, scrub and human sites. Within farmland, more birds than in the breeding season were using improved grassland and hedges, and fewer were found on arable land. Magpies were much less likely to be found on stubble than Carrion Crow, Jackdaw or Rook. They eat mostly vegetable material during winter—nuts, seeds and grain—and often store food, although usually for only a day or two (*BTO Winter Atlas*). These intelligent and opportunistic birds will steal from other species, including robbing Jays' cached food, and can be found trying almost anything edible.

Observers submitted 610 counts of Magpies, half of them of four birds or fewer, but there were eight counts of 30 or more, going way beyond the 'one for sorrow, two for joy ...' rhyme, with the largest flock 80 birds at Fiddler's Ferry (SJ58M). Roosts were noted in 13 tetrads, with a typical size of 50 birds, but by far the largest was at Woolston (SJ68P), where Brian Martin counted a minimum of 111 birds on 22 January 2006 entering willows and elders.

By the end of our winter period, many Magpies were showing breeding intent, often starting to build nests in February.

SIMON BOOTH

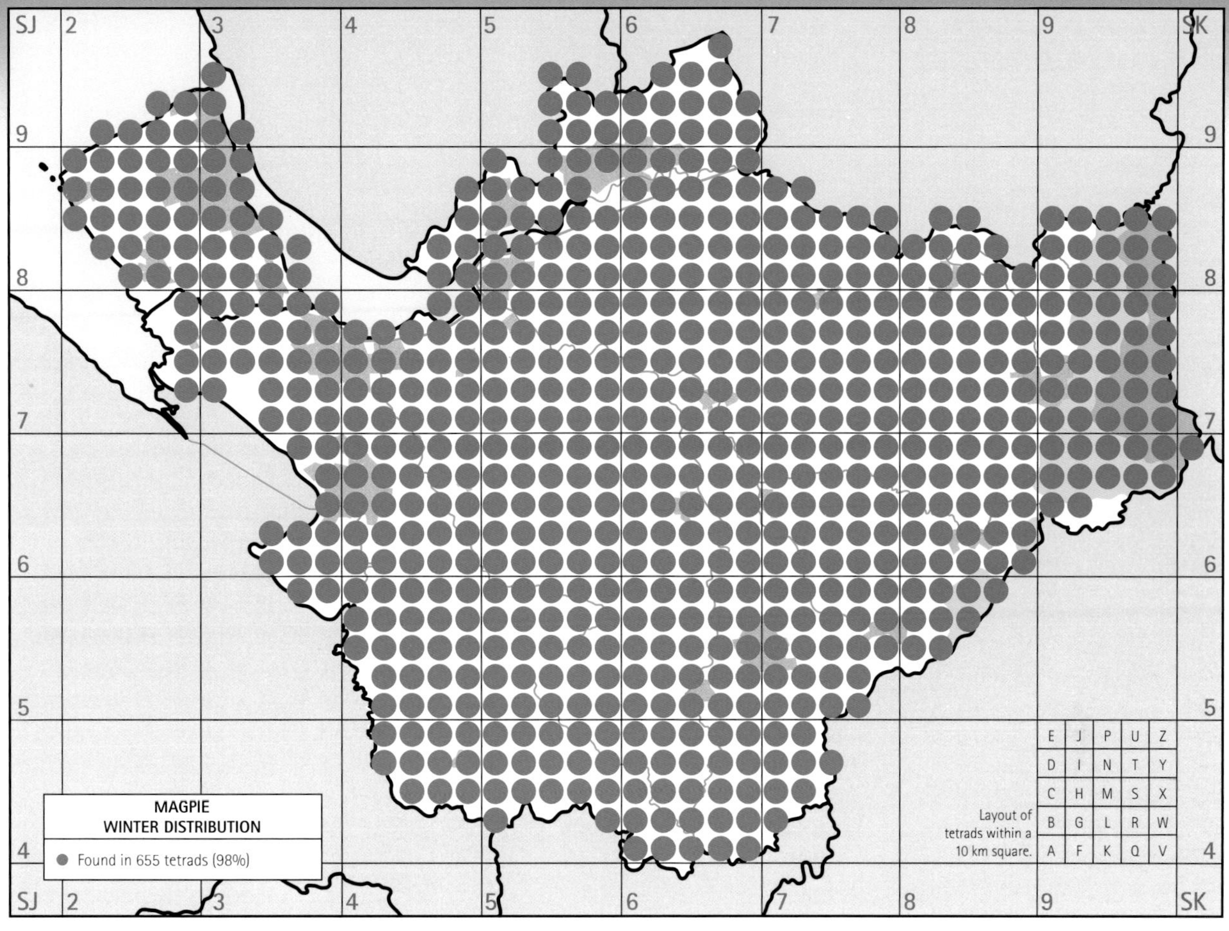
SJ
2
3
4
5
6
7
8
9
SK
MAGPIE
WINTER DISTRIBUTION
Found in 655 tetrads (98%)
E J P U Z
D I N T Y
C H M S X
B G L R W
A F K Q V
Layout of tetrads within a 10 km square.

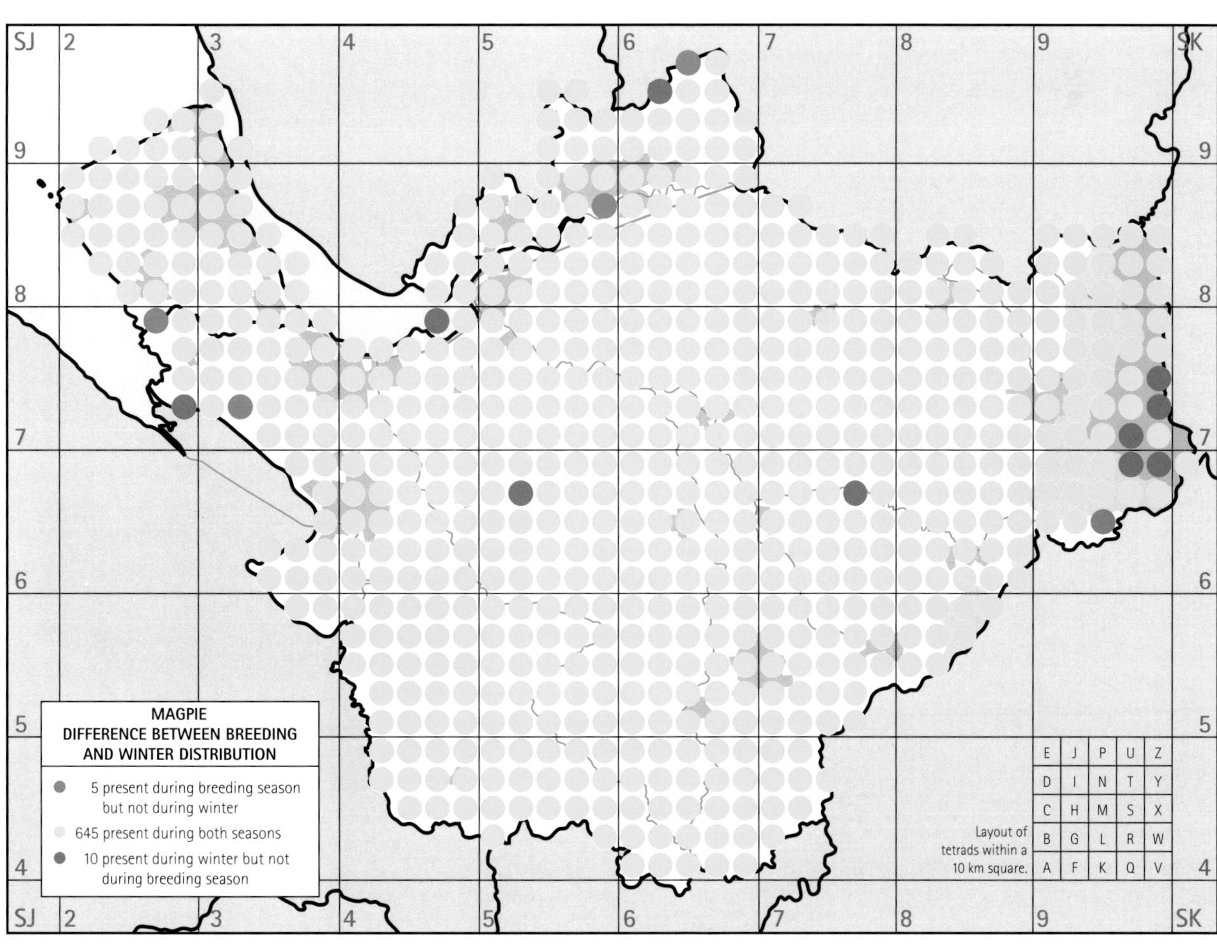
SJ
2
3
4
5
6
7
8
9
SK
MAGPIE
DIFFERENCE BETWEEN BREEDING AND WINTER DISTRIBUTION
5 present during breeding season but not during winter
645 present during both seasons
10 present during winter but not during breeding season
E J P U Z
D I N T Y
C H M S X
B G L R W
A F K Q V
Layout of tetrads within a 10 km square.

Jackdaw

Corvus monedula

STEVE ROUND

This Atlas indicates that Jackdaws have increased substantially across the county. They were found in 61 more tetrads than during the 1978–84 fieldwork period for our *First Atlas*, and the number of tetrads with confirmed breeding went up from 303 to 388. They are still quite sparsely distributed in Wirral, where the 'change' map indicates that they have been lost from a number of tetrads, and along the Mersey valley, a lack that is mirrored in adjacent counties to the north of the Mersey. Jackdaws are missing from a handful of the squares at highest altitude in the east of Cheshire. Throughout the rest of the county they are now almost ubiquitous, having spread to fill in most of the gaps from twenty years ago. The abundance map shows that they are found at highest densities in the agricultural south-west of the county.

Most of the proof of breeding came from observers seeing birds going to or from their nests, for which they use any sort of large hole, filling it with lots of sticks, often leaving some poking out. Observers in 33 tetrads noted Jackdaws nesting in chimneys, and in tree holes in a further 21, with one pair near Crewe (SJ75H) feeding young in a hole in an ash tree about a metre away from an active nest containing noisy Great Spotted Woodpecker chicks. They can make a nuisance of themselves by occupying nest-boxes intended for Barn Owls, and nest widely in church spires. They often form small colonies, with at least eight occupied nests in chimneys of Westwood Grange Country Club, Thornton Hough (SJ27Z) and at least 50 pairs breeding in Dunham Park (SJ78I). The association with buildings shows up in the analysis of habitat codes, with 42% of records in human sites, 34% in farmland and 21% in woodland.

The Jackdaw's diet is very varied, with farmland insects, usually picked from amongst the grass or crops rather than from probing in the ground, often making up the majority. Many birds in woodland feed their chicks on caterpillars, and they are surprisingly agile and adept at clinging on to thin branches in the tree canopy. They eat a lot of vegetable matter, plants and seeds, and will scavenge for almost anything else including carrion (Coombs 1978). These generalist feeding habits allow it to exploit diverse and ephemeral food resources, and must have helped it to ride out changes in agricultural practice. BTO figures show that their breeding total nationally rose by 30% in the 20 years from 1984. According to the analysis of BBS transects in Cheshire and Wirral, their breeding population in the county in 2004–05 was 32,610 birds (21,960–43,250), an average of 58 birds per tetrad in which they were found.

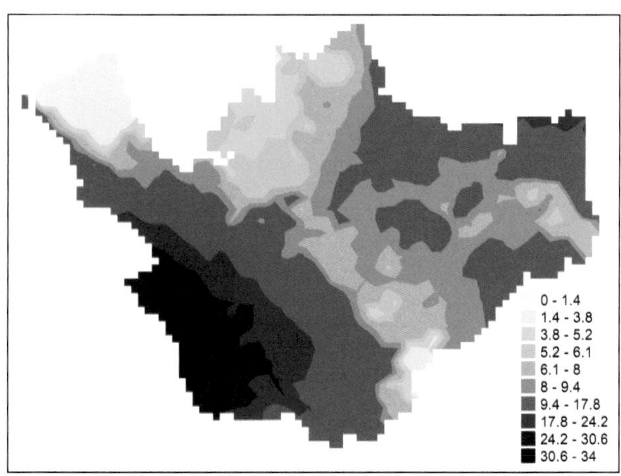

Jackdaw abundance.

Sponsored by John Davies

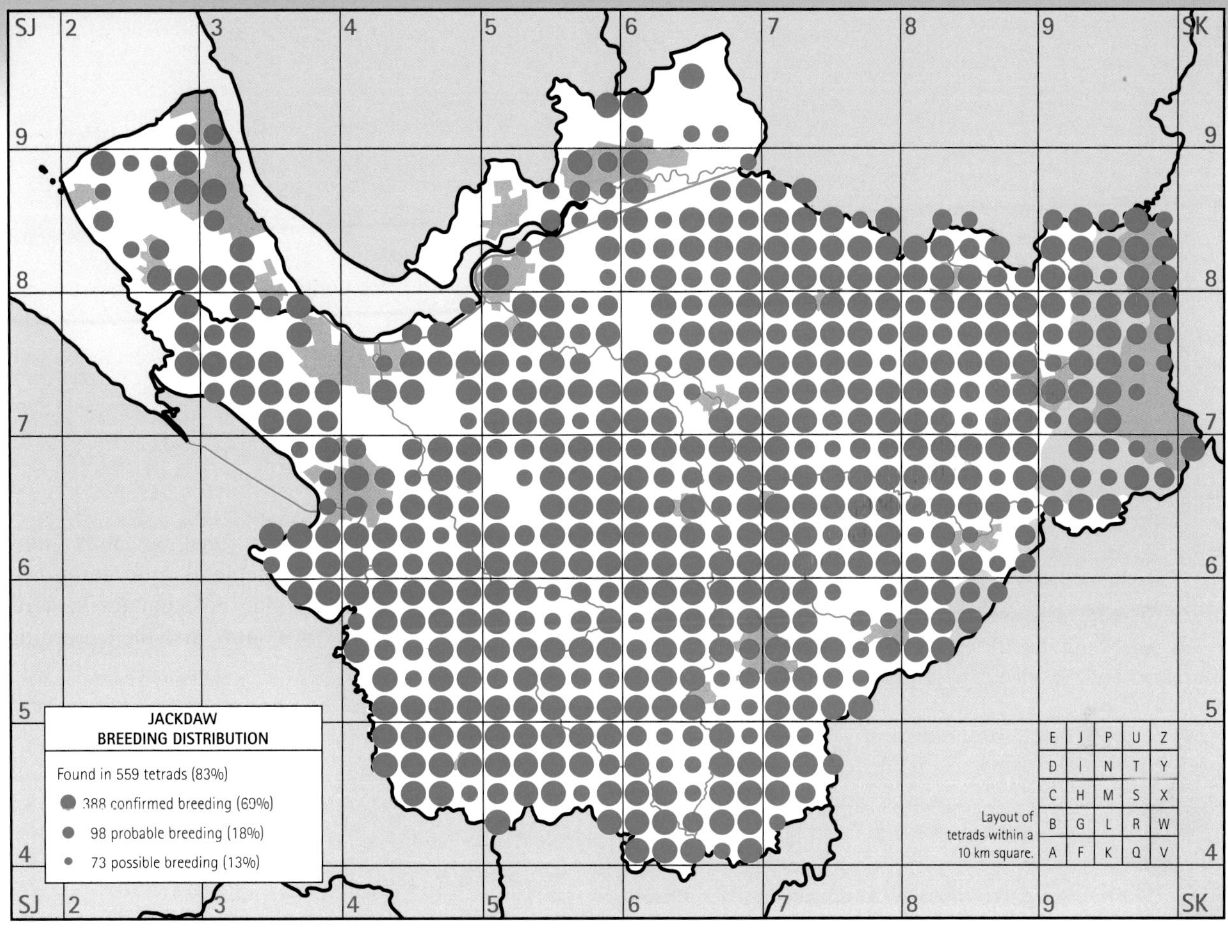
JACKDAW
BREEDING DISTRIBUTION
Found in 559 tetrads (83%)
388 confirmed breeding (69%)
98 probable breeding (18%)
73 possible breeding (13%)
Layout of tetrads within a 10 km square.
E J P U Z
D I N T Y
C H M S X
B G L R W
A F K Q V
SJ
SK

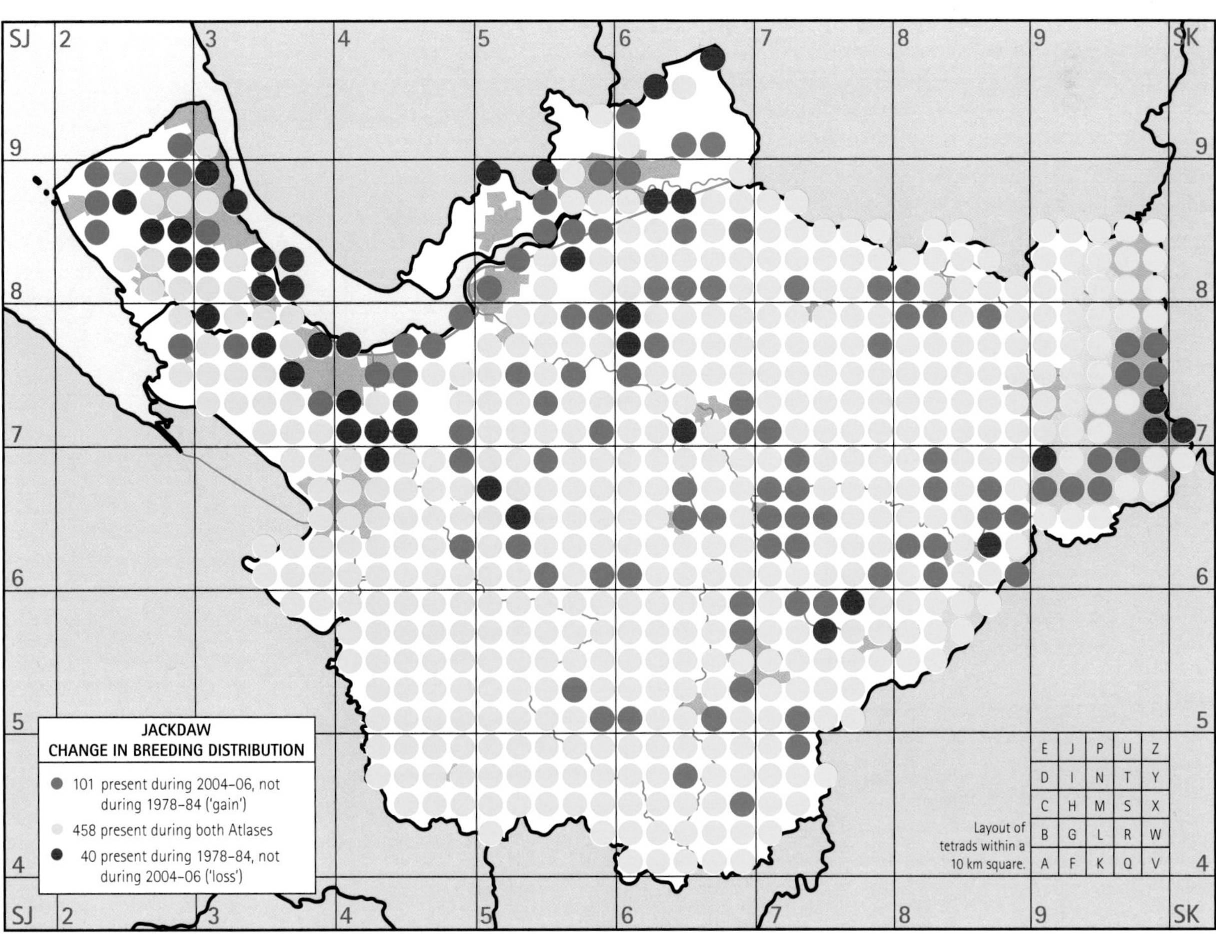
JACKDAW
CHANGE IN BREEDING DISTRIBUTION
101 present during 2004–06, not during 1978–84 ('gain')
458 present during both Atlases
40 present during 1978–84, not during 2004–06 ('loss')
Layout of tetrads within a 10 km square.
E J P U Z
D I N T Y
C H M S X
B G L R W
A F K Q V
SJ
SK

The winter Atlas map for Jackdaws is similar to that for the breeding season, with the main differences in the north of Cheshire and in Wirral. Some breeding tetrads are not occupied, but on the other hand, in winter, Jackdaws are found in a few sites in north Wirral and the Mersey valley where they did not breed, suggesting that their breeding distribution in the north of our area might be limited by a lack of nest sites. English breeding birds are sedentary—and on bright winter days in January some of them show signs of breeding behaviour—but some first-year birds might move south and west for the winter (*BTO Winter Atlas*). Although some immigrants from Scandinavia and the near continent have been found in eastern England, there is no evidence of any having reached Cheshire and Wirral (*Migration Atlas*).

Many of them undertake a shift in habitat for winter, with the proportion recorded in human sites halving to 21% as they slacken the association with potential breeding sites in buildings. Most Jackdaws in winter (58%, up from 34% of breeding season records) are on farmland, especially improved grassland, where they feed on seeds and whatever insects they can find, especially weevils, and small snails. One of the species' specialized foods is ticks, picked from the backs of cattle and especially sheep. In urban areas they use their agility to reach into litter-bins and other sources of food discarded by man.

Jackdaws are gregarious birds and usually found in flocks, often mixed with Rooks, from a few birds strong up to several hundred, and John Headon estimated 2,000 birds near Adlington (SJ98A) in an area of improved grassland left to go to seed. The median count of Atlas records was only 20 birds, however.

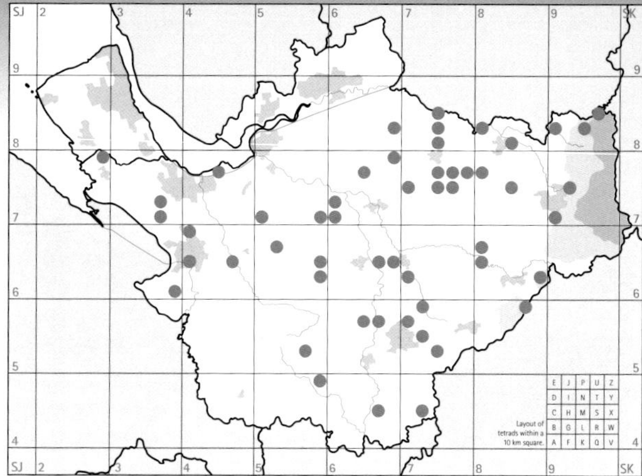

Jackdaw roost map.

One of the features of a late winter afternoon is the loud cackling of flocks of Jackdaws as they make their way to communal roosts. Roosts were recorded in 53 tetrads, as shown on the map. Half of the roost counts were of 50 birds or fewer, but some enormous gatherings were logged, with five of 1,000 or more, all in the east of the county. This is not a complete picture—for instance, a large roost in SJ58 was not reported—but would provide a good base for a thorough study of Jackdaw roosts across the county.

NORMAN RICHARDSON

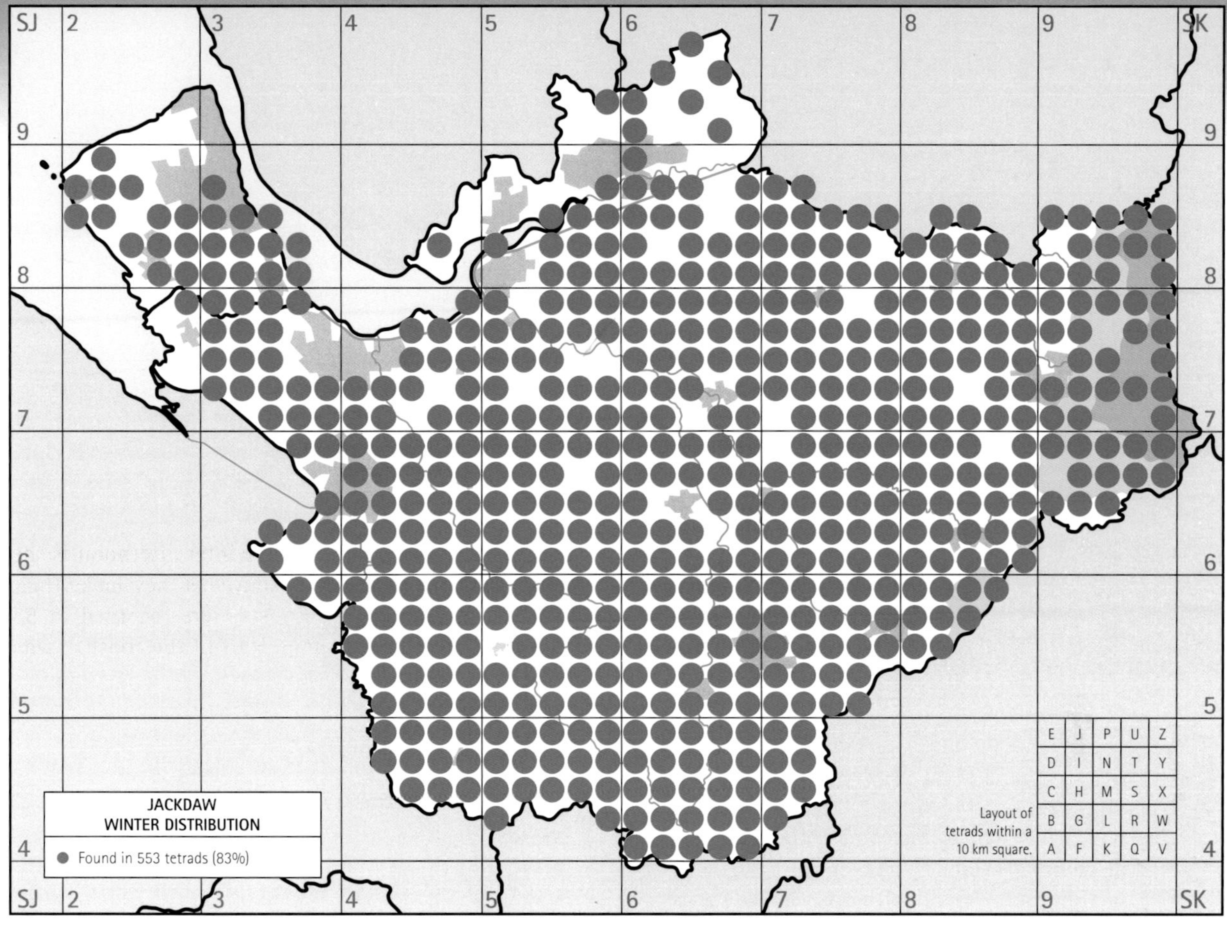
SJ
2
3
4
5
6
7
8
9
SK
9
8
7
6
5
4
JACKDAW
WINTER DISTRIBUTION
Found in 553 tetrads (83%)
E J P U Z
D I N T Y
C H M S X
B G L R W
A F K Q V
Layout of tetrads within a 10 km square.

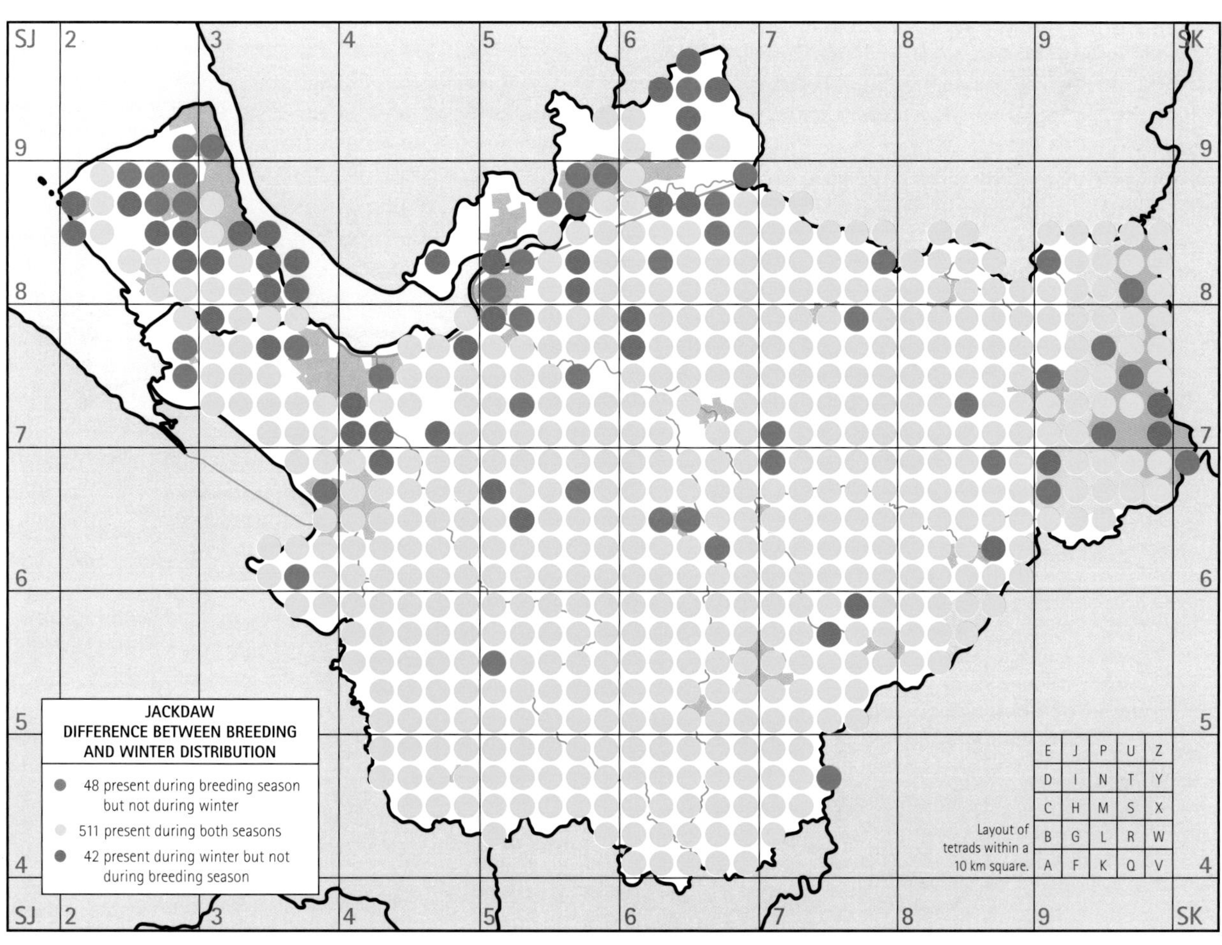
SJ
2
3
4
5
6
7
8
9
SK
9
8
7
6
5
4
JACKDAW
DIFFERENCE BETWEEN BREEDING AND WINTER DISTRIBUTION
48 present during breeding season but not during winter
511 present during both seasons
42 present during winter but not during breeding season
E J P U Z
D I N T Y
C H M S X
B G L R W
A F K Q V
Layout of tetrads within a 10 km square.

Rook

Corvus frugilegus

STEVE ROUND

Rooks are familiar birds and ubiquitous. They are a bird of farmland, mainly feeding on soil invertebrates, especially earthworms, but they will scavenge on urban scraps and flock to landfill sites. Rooks nest colonially in the tops of trees, the largest rookeries holding more than 100 pairs, and are a veritable cacophony of noise during the breeding season. As was said in our *First Atlas*, there is probably no tetrad in the county where Rooks do not appear at some stage during the breeding season, often miles away from a rookery. Some of these are one-year-old birds, too young to breed; family parties similarly can be found far away from breeding sites. We thus follow the same convention as in our *First Atlas* and include, on the distribution and 'change' maps, only the categories of breeding status code referring to nesting sites: confirmed (NY, NE, ON and UN) and probable (B). This Atlas shows a significant reduction in the number of tetrads occupied, from 266 confirmed and 12 probable twenty years ago to 205 confirmed and 4 probable now.

This apparent decline in the county is puzzling. The national picture is of no significant change in breeding distribution between the two BTO Atlases (1968–72 and 1988–91), but a 40% increase in abundance between 1975 and 1996 (Marchant & Gregory 1999). Rooks like areas of mixed agriculture, reaching their greatest density in an optimum combination of 45% tillage and 55% grass, with breeding density declining as farming moves away from that ratio in either direction (Brenchley 1984). With the dominance of grassland through much of Cheshire, the county is not likely to be a stronghold of Rooks. According to the BTO analysis of BBS transects in the county, the breeding population of Cheshire and Wirral in 2004–05 was 9,910 birds (4,620–15,190), an average of 50 birds per tetrad with confirmed or probable breeding. This corresponds only to about half of the average density of Rooks across the UK, perhaps emphasizing the relative unsuitability of pastoral farmland for them.

However, the Breeding Bird Survey is not a good way to census Rooks or any colonial species, and a coordinated count of nests is required. The last census in Cheshire and Wirral, in 1975, found 346 rookeries containing 8,824 nests within the present recording boundaries, a substantial reduction from the previous count in 1944–45 which recorded 439 rookeries with a total of 15,866 nests. If the figure from the BBS were taken at face value, which is not advisable, the present total of around 5,000 pairs would represent a further major decline. Some observers count nests annually, with figures included in the county bird reports, and figures from the largest rookeries appear to be relatively stable for the last decade. Currently the county's largest known colonies, with regular three-figure counts, are at Alderley Park (SJ87M), Inner Marsh Farm (SJ37B), Kelsall (SJ56P), Foden's Flash (SJ75J) and the Crewe/Alsager area.

It is obvious that the present picture is confusing, and a complete census of the occupied nests at the county's rookeries is required. 'The relative conspicuousness of Rook nests makes this one of the simplest breeding bird species to census. However, the extremely clumped, colonial distribution and the turnover in colony location from year to year make it especially important that, to be representative and adequately precise, censuses should cover large geographical areas and be either complete or drawn from a carefully constructed sample' (Marchant & Gregory 1999). Unfortunately, the coverage in Cheshire and Wirral for the last national sample survey in 1996 was so patchy that no useful figures can be obtained.

A rookery survey should also obtain information about the species of tree used—only beech and pine being mentioned in data submitted for this Atlas—and an assessment of the surrounding habitat. The Atlas codes for Rook show 46% of records in farmland and 46% in woodland, with 7% in human sites. These figures are probably of little value because many fieldworkers recorded the nest site rather than the feeding habitat.

Although counts of occupied nests are the best way to assess the breeding population, they do not tell the whole story. Detailed work by Merseyside Ringing Group at some Cheshire and Wirral rookeries shows that they almost always lay four eggs but in most years raise only one or two chicks to fledging. In years with dry spring weather, chicks are often underweight and many die. In wet springs the adults presumably find it easier to obtain worms, and their chicks fare better. The productivity, and recruitment to the population, thus varies considerably from year to year.

Sponsored by Anne and Stephen Young

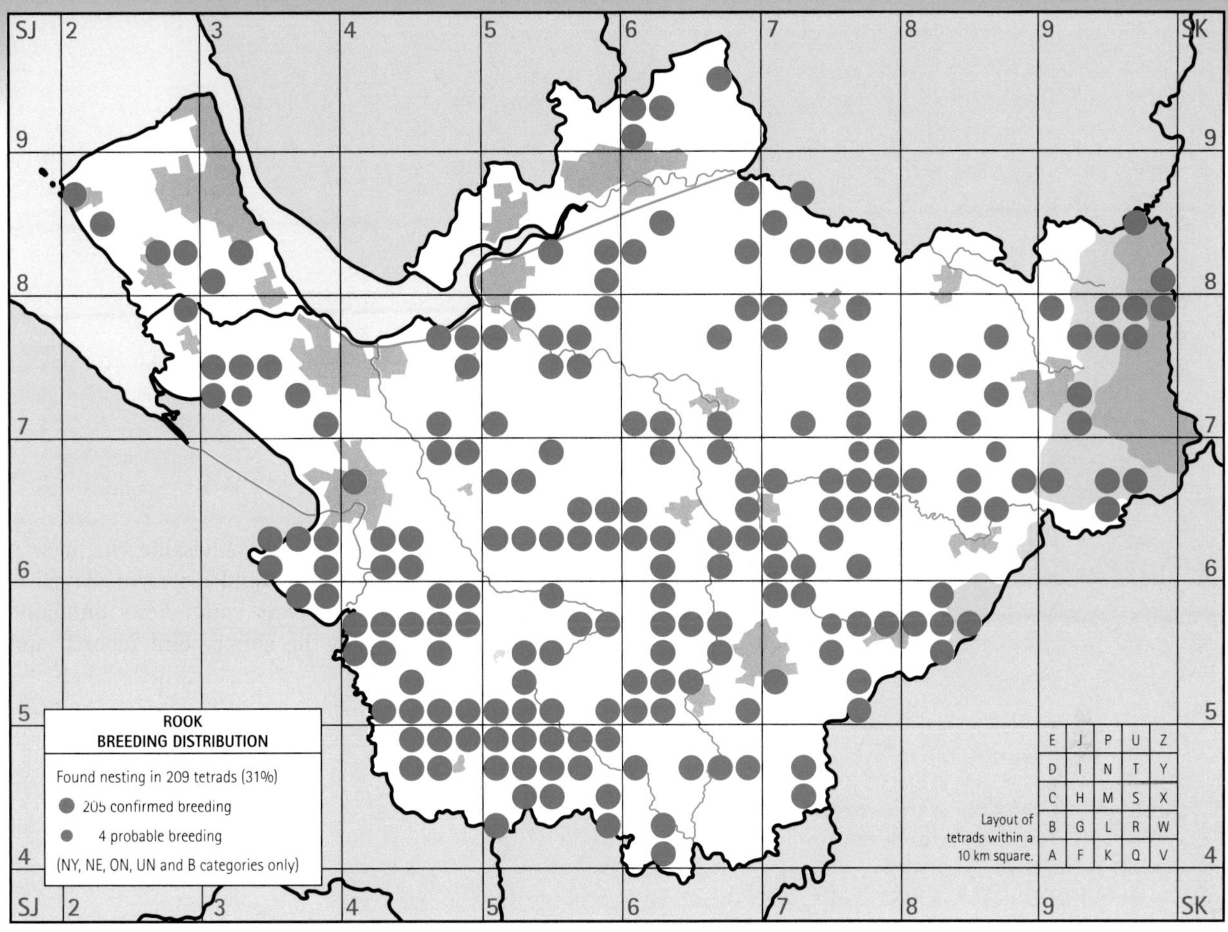
SJ
2
3
4
5
6
7
8
9
SK
9
8
7
6
5
4
ROOK
BREEDING DISTRIBUTION
Found nesting in 209 tetrads (31%)
205 confirmed breeding
4 probable breeding
(NY, NE, ON, UN and B categories only)
E J P U Z
D I N T Y
C H M S X
B G L R W
A F K Q V
Layout of tetrads within a 10 km square.

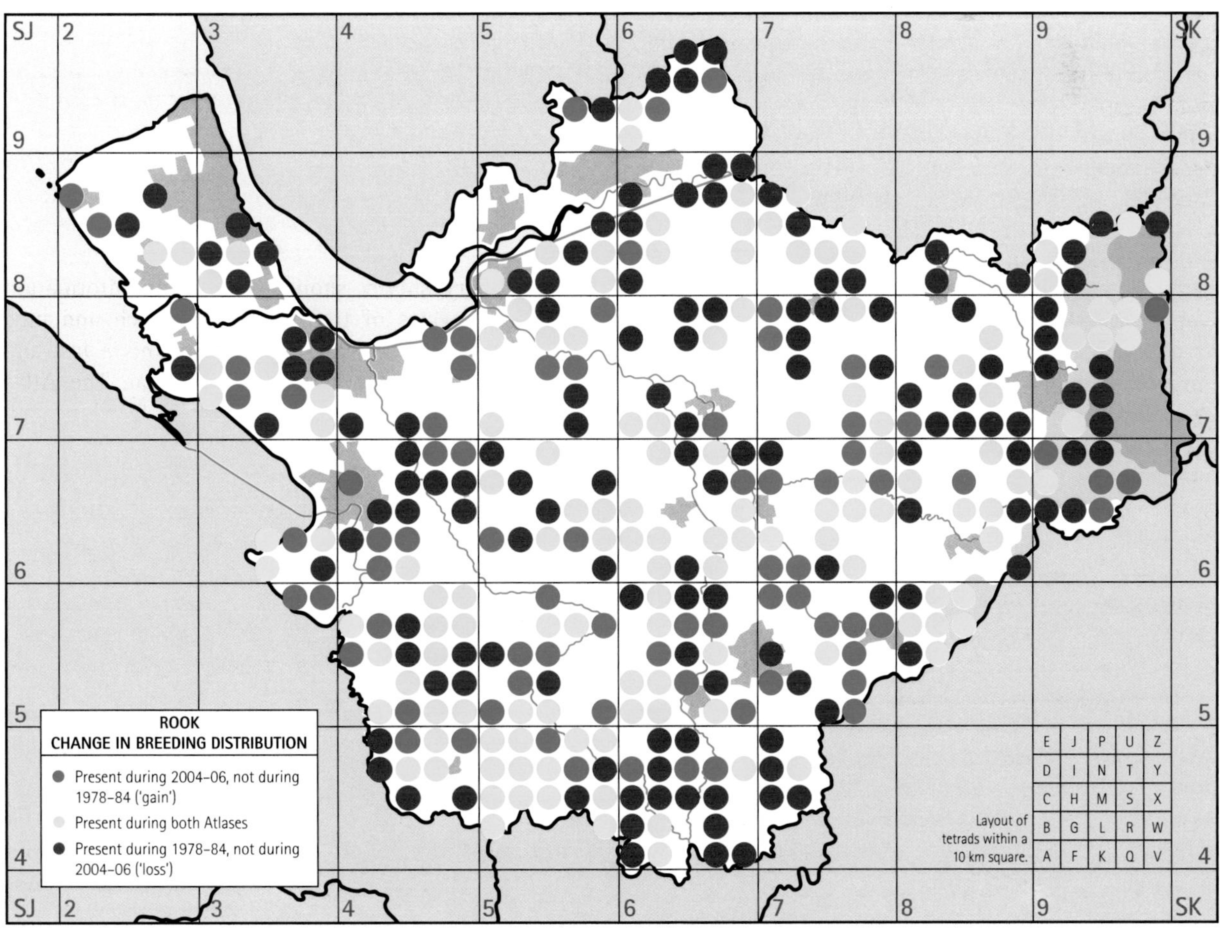
SJ
2
3
4
5
6
7
8
9
SK
9
8
7
6
5
4
ROOK
CHANGE IN BREEDING DISTRIBUTION
Present during 2004–06, not during 1978–84 ('gain')
Present during both Atlases
Present during 1978–84, not during 2004–06 ('loss')
E J P U Z
D I N T Y
C H M S X
B G L R W
A F K Q V
Layout of tetrads within a 10 km square.

STEVE ROUND

This is the most rural member of the crow family and the main determinant of its winter distribution in the county seems to be its avoidance of the most built-up areas. As in the breeding season, only 6% of the species' habitat records were classed as human sites; intriguingly, two-thirds of these were suburban, with few in urban or rural areas. Almost three-quarters (74%) of records of Rooks were on farmland, with the main categories being 42% on improved grassland, 8% unimproved grassland and 6% stubble. Their winter food is mainly seeds, waste root crops and invertebrates, but they scavenge almost anything, and often flock to landfill sites. Many of the 18% of records in woodland can be accounted for by early-returning birds to arboreal rookeries: they refurbish nests from January onwards. Nearly all of the Rooks found in the county in winter will have been local birds: some from farther north in Britain disperse, usually no more than a few kilometres, but this is unusual for most English birds. In some years birds arrive on the east coast from north-easterly and easterly directions, but they seldom penetrate beyond the eastern counties (*Migration Atlas*).

Rooks spend almost all of their lives in flocks. The median size of gatherings reported for this Atlas was 25 birds, with 75 flocks of 100 or more but few flocks (just five reported) of more than 250. The largest were 600 birds at Maw Green tip and adjacent flashes (SJ75E), and 400 on stubble near the Gowy Meadows (SJ47M). Larger flocks gather together noisily at night, with 1,000 in Crewe Hall Woods (SJ75H). Roosts were reported in 43 tetrads; although some are shared with other species, especially Jackdaws, the distribution of reported Rook roosts is quite different, with none in the south Manchester fringe or the south of the county.

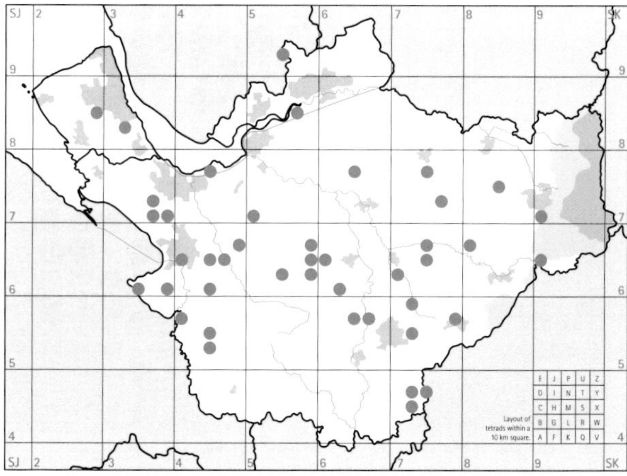

Rook roost map.

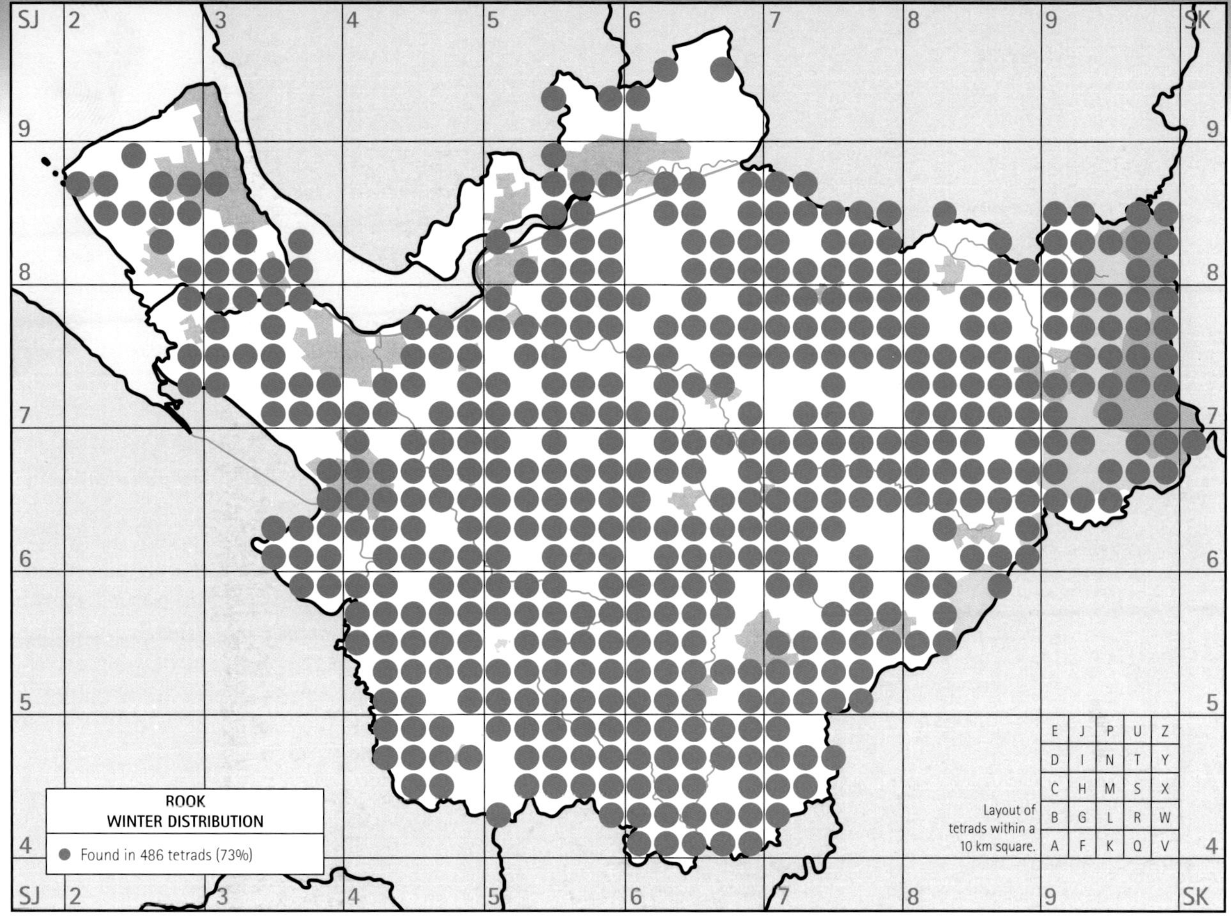
SJ
SK
ROOK
WINTER DISTRIBUTION
Found in 486 tetrads (73%)
Layout of
tetrads within a
10 km square.
E J P U Z
D I N T Y
C H M S X
B G L R W
A F K Q V

Carrion Crow

Corvus corone

ANDREW HART

Apart from odd areas of underrecording, the Carrion Crow is ubiquitous in the county, and ranked tenth in order of the number of tetrads occupied. Since our *First Atlas* they have regularly bred on Hilbre. Although they are wary birds, crows can be found in every town and village as well as all rural areas of Cheshire and Wirral. The habitats recorded were 53% in farmland, 30% in woodland, 4% in scrub and 12% in human sites. The abundance map suggests that the regions of highest density include a band from Runcorn to the south-west of Cheshire and another area in south-east Cheshire, while there are fewer birds around Knutsford and Northwich and much of the Wirral peninsula.

Carrion Crows' nests are normally high in a tree, 10–20 m up, usually firmly supported in the middle of the crown. They are very well constructed, of twigs and fibrous material, filled with earth and mud and lined with wool, feathers and other soft, warm materials. Although these nests often last for two years or more, they are seldom reused by Carrion Crows. They are, however, very important structures for other birds and may often form the base for the nest of a raptor, especially Sparrowhawk, Hobby or Buzzard. Fieldworkers found nests in 295 tetrads; the only species of tree reported, in five tetrads, was oak. Most chicks fledge by early June and then accompany their parents for several weeks. Records of recently fledged young provided proof of breeding in 170 tetrads.

Their omnivorous diet allows them to survive almost anywhere. They eat a lot of grain and weed seeds, but meat is a particularly important food item during the breeding season; they take small mammals, usually caught alive, and—true to their name—carrion, performing an important early-morning job in clearing road-kill (Coombs 1978). On Hilbre, the crows mostly feed by scavenging on the tide line.

The national population has been rising since at least the 1960s (Gregory & Marchant 1996) and the index has shown a 43% rise since 1984. According to the analysis of BBS transects in Cheshire and Wirral, their breeding population in the county in 2004–05 was 30,640 birds (24,080–37,190), an average of 48 birds per tetrad in which they were found. It is not known how that total splits between territory-holding adults and non-breeding flocks, the latter containing one-year-old birds, too young to breed, and subordinate individuals who have not been able to gain a territory. Some of these may be several years old, paired and physiologically ready to breed but, without a territory, are unable to do so (Coombs 1978). The non-breeders are continually testing the territorial birds and pose the biggest threat to Carrion Crows' successful breeding as they will take eggs or young from the nest if it is not sufficiently well guarded.

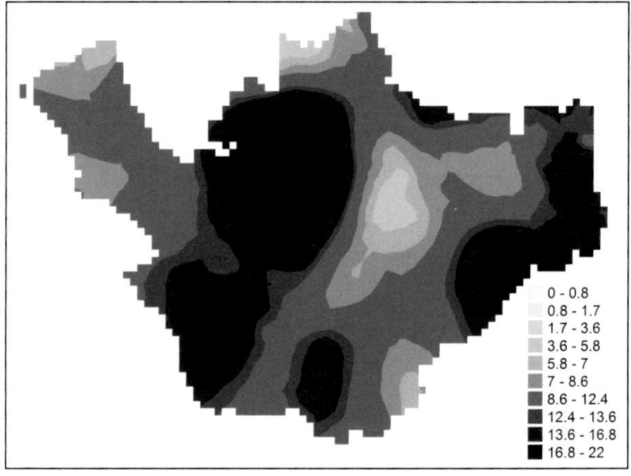

Carrion Crow abundance.

Sponsored by Tom Rowbottom

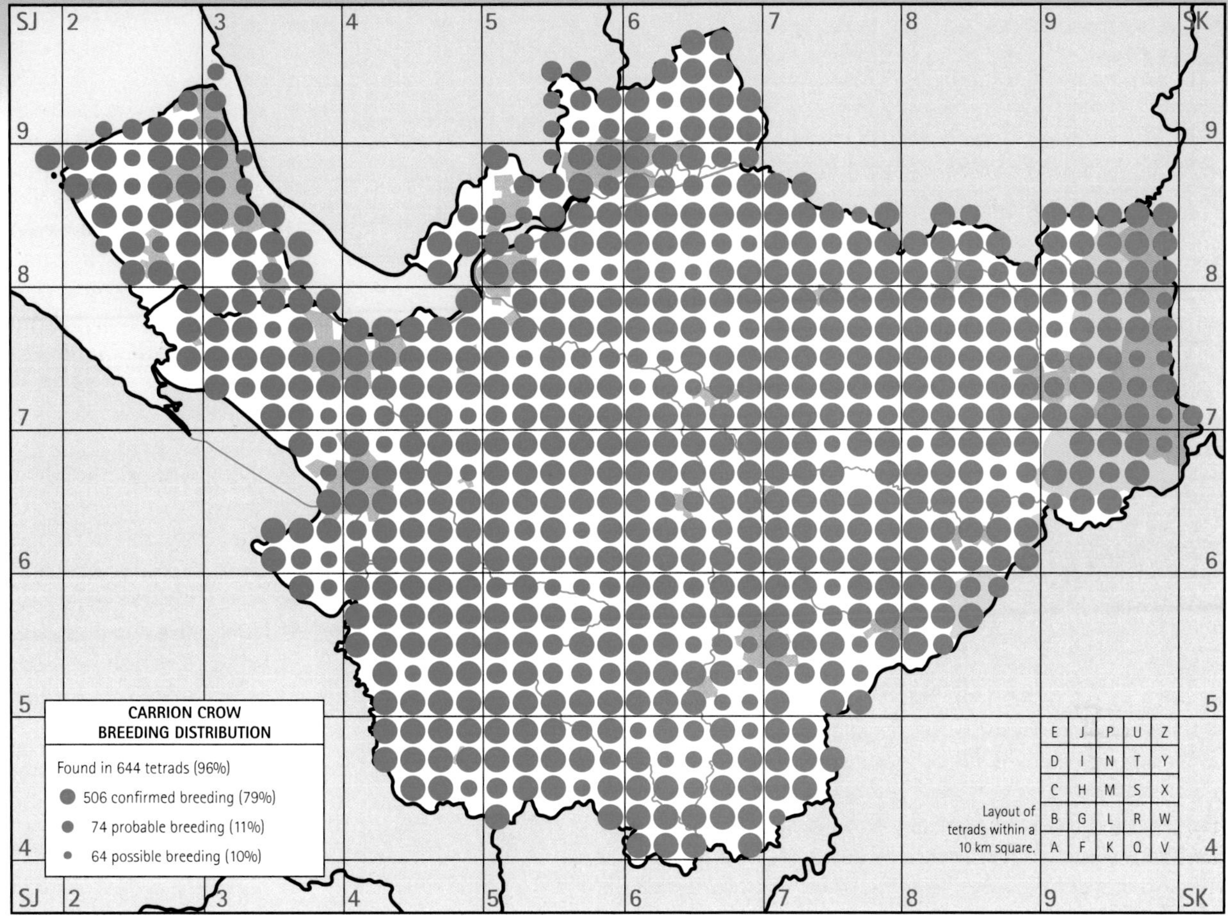
SJ
2
3
4
5
6
7
8
9
SK
CARRION CROW
BREEDING DISTRIBUTION
Found in 644 tetrads (96%)
506 confirmed breeding (79%)
74 probable breeding (11%)
64 possible breeding (10%)
Layout of tetrads within a 10 km square.
E J P U Z
D I N T Y
C H M S X
B G L R W
A F K Q V

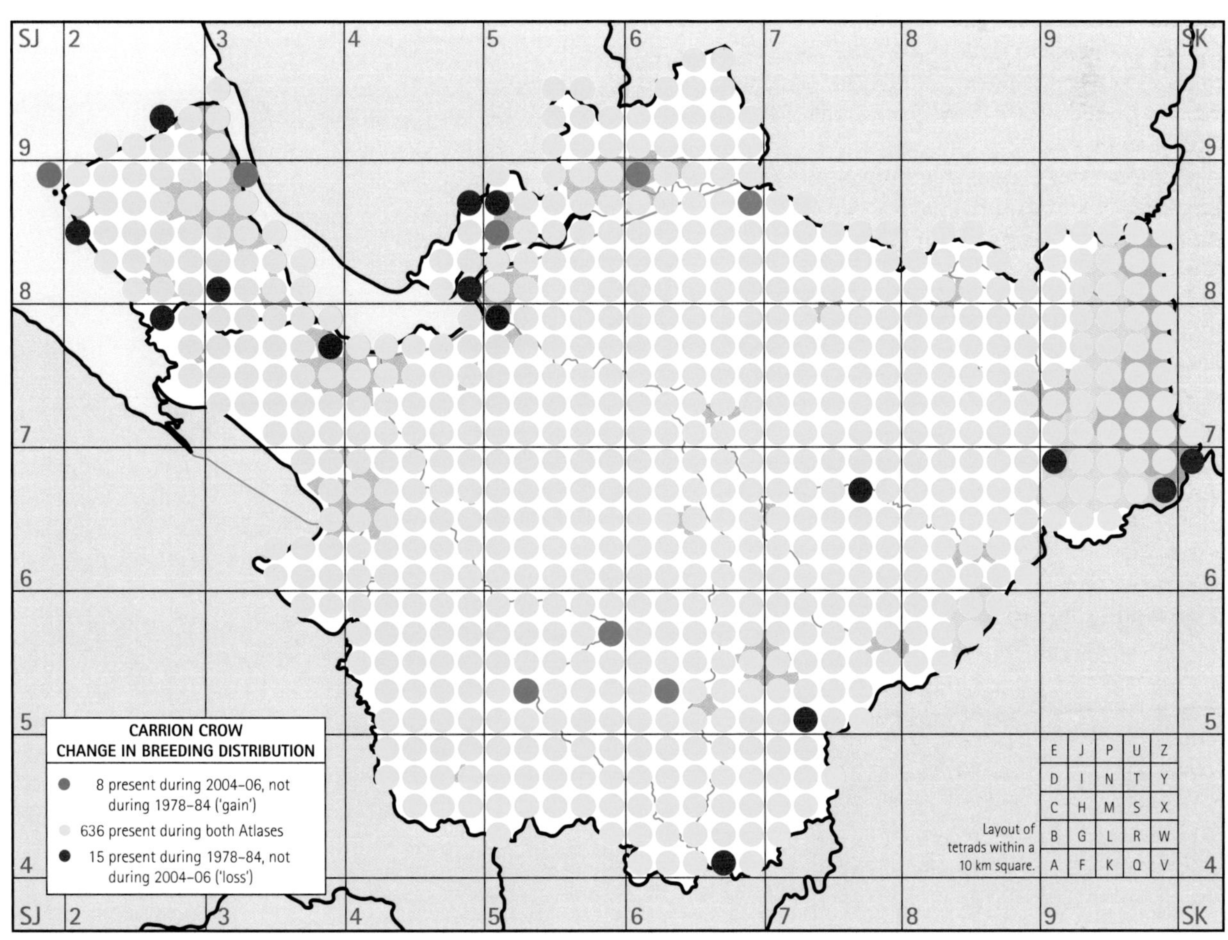
SJ
2
3
4
5
6
7
8
9
SK
CARRION CROW
CHANGE IN BREEDING DISTRIBUTION
8 present during 2004–06, not during 1978–84 ('gain')
636 present during both Atlases
15 present during 1978–84, not during 2004–06 ('loss')
Layout of tetrads within a 10 km square.
E J P U Z
D I N T Y
C H M S X
B G L R W
A F K Q V

With such a territorial bird, breeding adults maintaining their territories all year round, there would not be expected to be much seasonal change in Carrion Crows' distribution. Probably the most notable difference, clearly visible on the map showing difference between breeding and winter, is their occupation of coastal and salt-marsh tetrads on the north Wirral and in both estuaries. The birds visiting these squares are members of the non-breeding flocks, exploiting a wide range of food resources including fish, marine molluscs, salt-marsh seeds and almost anything edible amongst the shoreline detritus.

Their main change in habitat for winter is a shift from woodland (14% of winter records) or scrub (2%) to farmland (67%), mostly improved grassland but including unimproved grassland (7%) and stubble (5%), where there were more records of Carrion Crows than any other corvid. They also seemed to use recently ploughed fields more than other species, along with manured fields and sheep pasture. Many of the records comprising 'human sites' (13% of the total) came from birds foraging at sewage works or landfill sites and scavenging on refuse in retail areas. Such adaptability in their diet underlies the species' success.

Despite the advice to novice birdwatchers that 'if you see one or two, they're Crows; if you see a flock, they're Rooks', the non-territorial Carrion Crows frequently form quite large flocks. Out of 699 counts submitted with Atlas records, only 144 were of one or two birds, with half of them being of 10 birds or more, including 30 flocks of 100 or more. By far the largest were the gatherings of 420 birds on a ploughed field near Kidnal (SJ44U) counted by Neil Friswell on 3 December 2005 and 500 near Thornton-le-Moors (SJ47M) seen by Steve Holmes and Marion Barlow in 2006/07.

Carrion Crows also congregate to roost overnight together, usually in traditional sites in dense woodland; six such gatherings of 100 or more birds were reported during this survey, with up to 300 birds near Higher Whitley (SJ68A). Carrion Crows are usually the last birds to go to roost at night, often well after dusk, and the earliest to leave in the mornings at the first glimmer of daylight. Some local territory-holders join the roosting flocks, and presumably they are especially keen to return to defend their areas against potential intruders (*BTO Winter Atlas*).

PETER SMITH

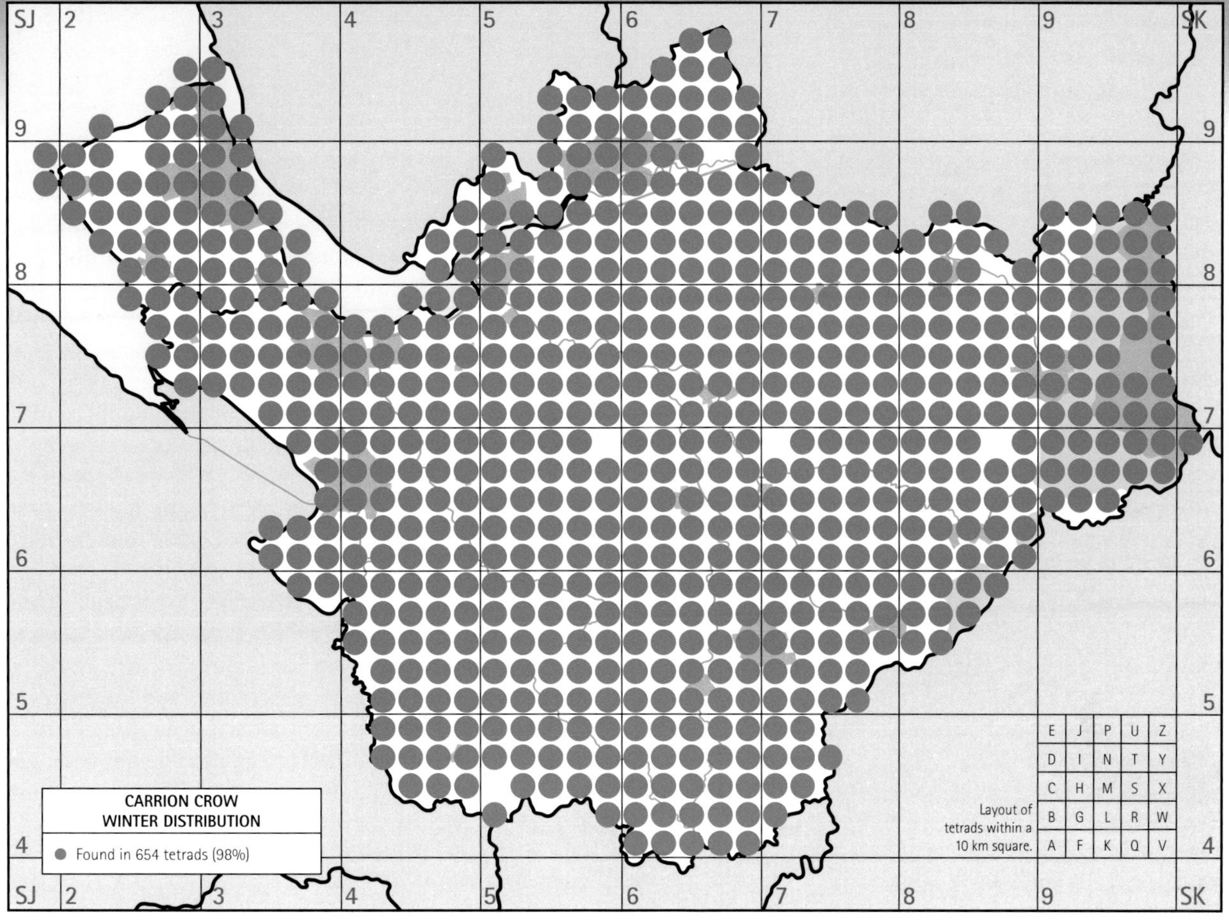
SJ
2
3
4
5
6
7
8
9
SK
9
8
7
6
5
4
CARRION CROW
WINTER DISTRIBUTION
Found in 654 tetrads (98%)
Layout of tetrads within a 10 km square.
E J P U Z
D I N T Y
C H M S X
B G L R W
A F K Q V

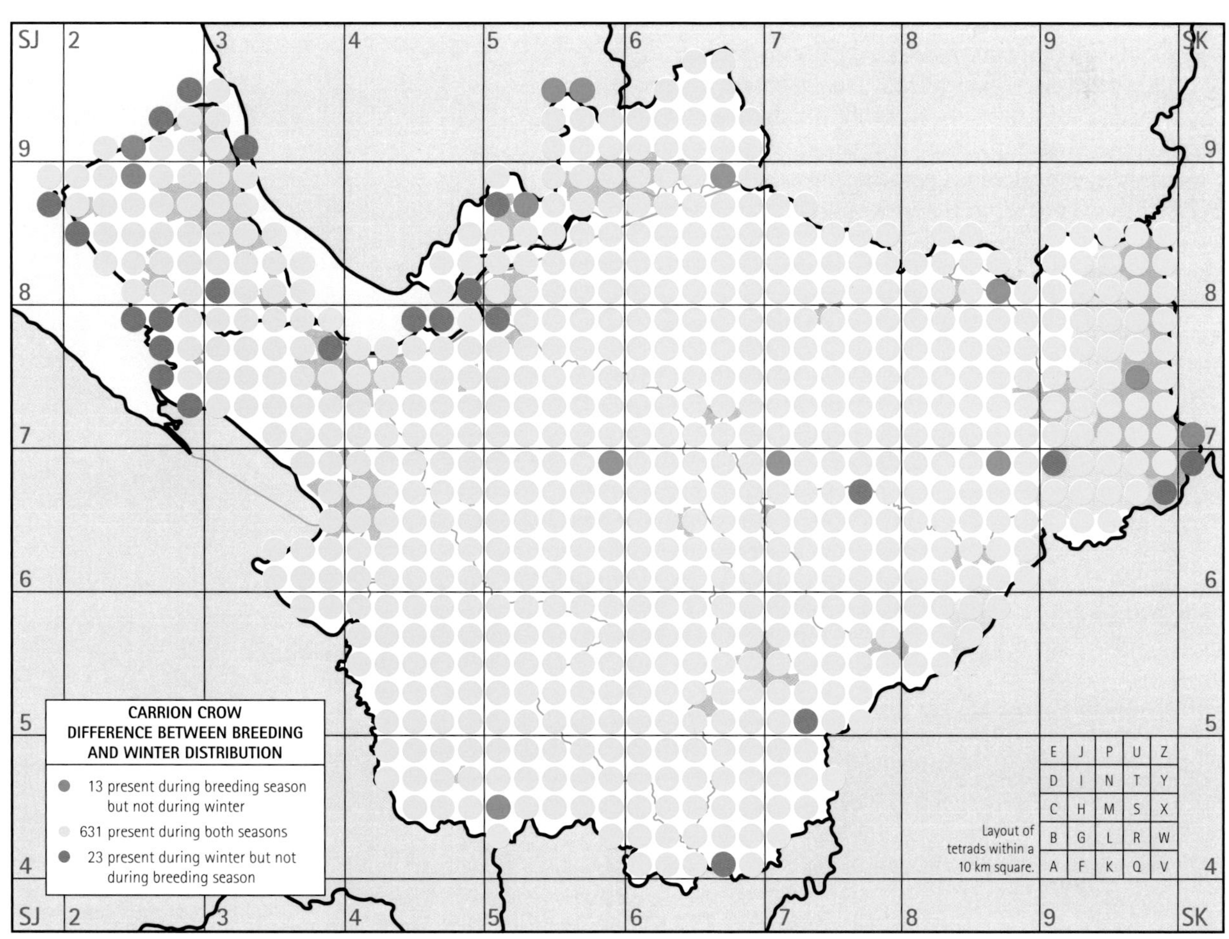
SJ
2
3
4
5
6
7
8
9
SK
9
8
7
6
5
4
CARRION CROW
DIFFERENCE BETWEEN BREEDING AND WINTER DISTRIBUTION
13 present during breeding season but not during winter
631 present during both seasons
23 present during winter but not during breeding season
Layout of tetrads within a 10 km square.
E J P U Z
D I N T Y
C H M S X
B G L R W
A F K Q V

Raven

Corvus corax

STEVE ROUND

The Raven has been another interesting addition to the breeding avifauna of Cheshire (but not quite the Metropolitan Borough of Wirral) since the *First Atlas*, with their nesting in 1991 the first confirmed in the county since 1857 (Wells 1994). They have rapidly taken to nesting on man-made structures and, provided that they can find sufficient food, the adoption of this habit means that there is probably no limit to their distribution. Traditional nest sites are on cliffs, which were soon occupied, and Cheshire Ravens now nest in trees (with a preference for Scots pines), quarries and a range of tall industrial structures—oil storage tanks, power station chimneys, electricity pylons, a hilltop telecommunications mast and Jodrell Bank radio telescope. Probably the best-known local nesting site was in Chester, either on the Town Hall or Cathedral from 1996 to 2003. The spread of the Raven into Cheshire has paralleled that of the Peregrine, and indeed there is now an annual competition on the county's sandstone cliffs between the two species. Ravens usually win, being bigger birds, and earlier nesters, thus in possession before the raptor; once having re-established their nest site, however, they seem to come to an uneasy truce with the Peregrines. Twenty years ago, who would have thought that we could watch aerial battles between these two species in the heart of Cheshire?

The rise in population has been a national phenomenon. With strongholds in south-west England, Wales, Cumbria and Scotland, Ravens were not well monitored by the BTO's Common Birds Census; but, since the instigation of the Breeding Bird Survey, with a wide national coverage, the population index in England has more than quadrupled from 1994 to 2005. During this time, the Welsh population has also doubled and it is likely that the Cheshire birds originated in Wales or the Shropshire hills.

The adults probably mate for life, and maintain their territory year-round. Some traditional nest sites are occupied for decades, the nests themselves becoming enormous structures. Ravens appear to be amongst our hardiest birds, and may start laying eggs as early as the first week of February; most birds in the lowlands are sitting by the first week of March. They endure hard weather in some years, but their wool-lined nests are very warm, and the timing coincides with peak availability of food for chicks, during the lambing season. They lay quite large clutches, four, five or six being normal, and the female incubates the eggs for about 21 days while the male keeps watch, calling her off with an alarm call when intruders, including humans, get too close. An average of three chicks fledge after six or seven weeks in the nest, and then undergo a long period of dependency on their parents, flying as family parties until July, then the young birds disperse and join flocks.

Ravens will eat almost anything, but they are, first and foremost, scavengers and in effect our vulture substitute. In medieval times, they acted as our urban waste disposal system along with Red Kites, but gradually their distribution became confined mainly to the sheep-farming hills, and typical analyses of Raven pellets from upland Britain find half or more of their diet from sheep, with one-quarter rabbits and hares, and the rest comprising small mammals, beetles, vegetable matter and a wide variety of other food. In some areas, though, lagomorphs (rabbits and hares) dominate—often taken as road-kill—and few sheep remains are found. This is likely to apply across most of Cheshire with its low density of sheep, but there are no direct observations of the food taken by Ravens in our area and an analysis of pellets would be useful.

The habitat codes submitted by fieldworkers are not very informative, because some observers have clearly recorded just the nest site, rather than the wide area over which the birds have foraged. In practice, Ravens probably cover any of the Cheshire farmland habitats and tend to avoid areas of dense woodland and built-up places. Territories may be large, up to several square kilometres, although they may share good feeding grounds such as overstocked fields of sheep in the uplands.

The Raven, the world's biggest passerine, can breed at two years old, but most do not start until the age of three or older: 'the average age of first breeding ... is simply not known for the Raven' (Ratcliffe 1997). It is clear that there will be a considerable population of

Sponsored by Christian and Sue Heintzen

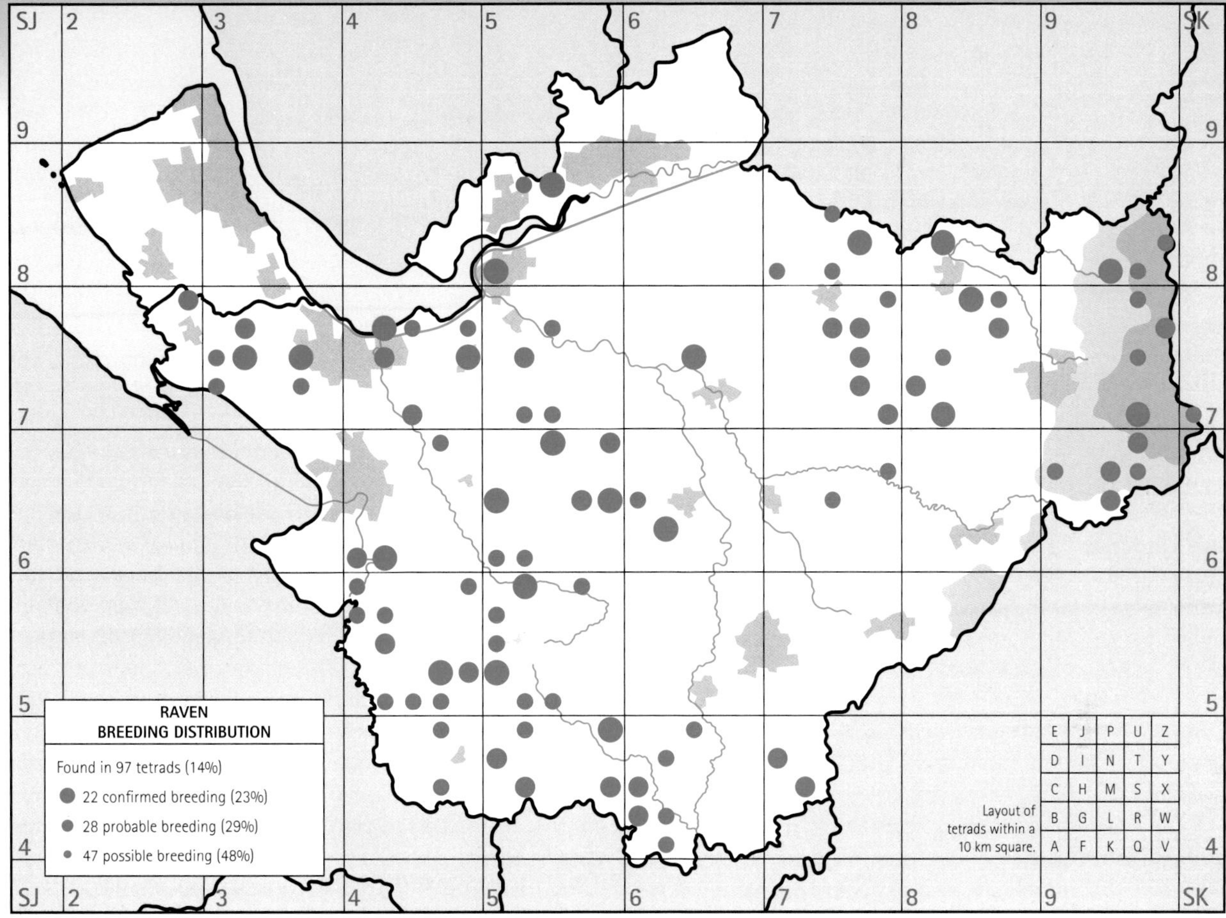

immature birds, probably wandering quite widely, and some adult pairs may hold territory without breeding: estimation of the population is not straightforward.

Only 12 out of the 22 confirmed breeding records refer to nests, with the rest either sightings of recently fledged chicks (RF) or adults with bulging crops returning to the area of a nest (FY); some of these could be from nests in an adjacent tetrad. There were 5 records of display and 22 of 'pairs', some of which were likely to be dispersing adults or two immature birds associating together.

Adopting a conservative approach, during this Atlas period there were probably about 25 pairs of Ravens breeding in Cheshire. In its traditional strongholds, occupying areas of suitable habitat, Ravens nest at a nearest-neighbour mean spacing of 2–4 km, and achieve a density of around one pair per 10 km^2, i.e. one pair per 2.5 tetrads. The county population could thus increase way beyond its present level and a special survey of Ravens in five or ten years' time would be valuable in monitoring its spread.

Breeding Ravens rarely wander far in winter, and indeed many of them start nesting activities within our defined 'winter' period. Non-breeding birds, however, may roam much more widely and the species was reported in winter in almost one-quarter of the county; in addition to the mapped records, there were 77 tetrads for which Ravens were recorded in winter 'in flight' only. There are probably now few parts of the county over which Ravens have not flown, and their distinctive bulky shape with a wedge tail is becoming more familiar to Cheshire and Wirral people. They most often draw observers' attention by their deep 'cronk' call, or their mobbing by other corvids. Roughly speaking, small birds flap and large birds soar, and the wing-loading of Raven is such that it is at the boundary between these two modes of flight, choosing to soar as long as there is sufficient uplift from rising air. They can effortlessly cover a large area, scanning the ground below for suitable food, especially carrion from large mammals. They will, however, eat almost anything including earthworms and beetles, and some seeds, with estuarine birds taking fish and seaweed (Ratcliffe 1997). Some birds are very wary whilst others can become almost tame: two lucky Atlas workers had a bird feeding on their lawn, and Ravens sometimes scavenge on landfill sites.

They obviously used to be extremely scarce in the county. Coward and Oldham (1900) have no records, at any season, after the mid-nineteenth century. Bell (1962, 1967) recorded only one in the first half of the twentieth century, a bird judged to be an 'escape' in 1931, then single winter birds in January 1958 and January 1959, with two over Hilbre in February 1962. Those mentioned in the 1969 and 1971 county bird reports were adjudged to be escaped pets, and the first to be taken seriously were several birds in 1975 and 1976, at various Dee estuary sites and in the east of the county. From 1980 onwards they have been recorded annually in increasing numbers. The 2005 *CWBR* states that 'records from the eastern area predominant as usual' but this Atlas map shows that birds are widespread across the county, with the highest densities of occupied tetrads in the agricultural south-west of Cheshire. Presumably the bird report comment says more about the geographical distribution of regular contributors of records than of the Ravens themselves. Most of the county's birds are using farmland in winter: of the 177 habitat codes submitted, 97 (55%) were of farmland, with 51 woodland, 12 human sites and 9 saltmarsh.

RICHARD STEEL

Most winter Atlas counts were of one or two birds, but there were two flocks of six birds, whilst eight were at Bosley Cloud on 3 January 2005 and Richard Smith also saw eight in 2006/07 near Heswall (SJ28L). These appear to be the largest flocks on record in the county. Some winter gatherings in other counties are large, even reaching hundreds of birds, and similarly large communal roosts have been reported, but not, yet, in Cheshire and Wirral. There must be at least 200 Ravens in winter in the county, made up of 50 breeders, 50 first-winter birds, 100 immature (one- to three-year-olds) and some wandering birds from elsewhere.

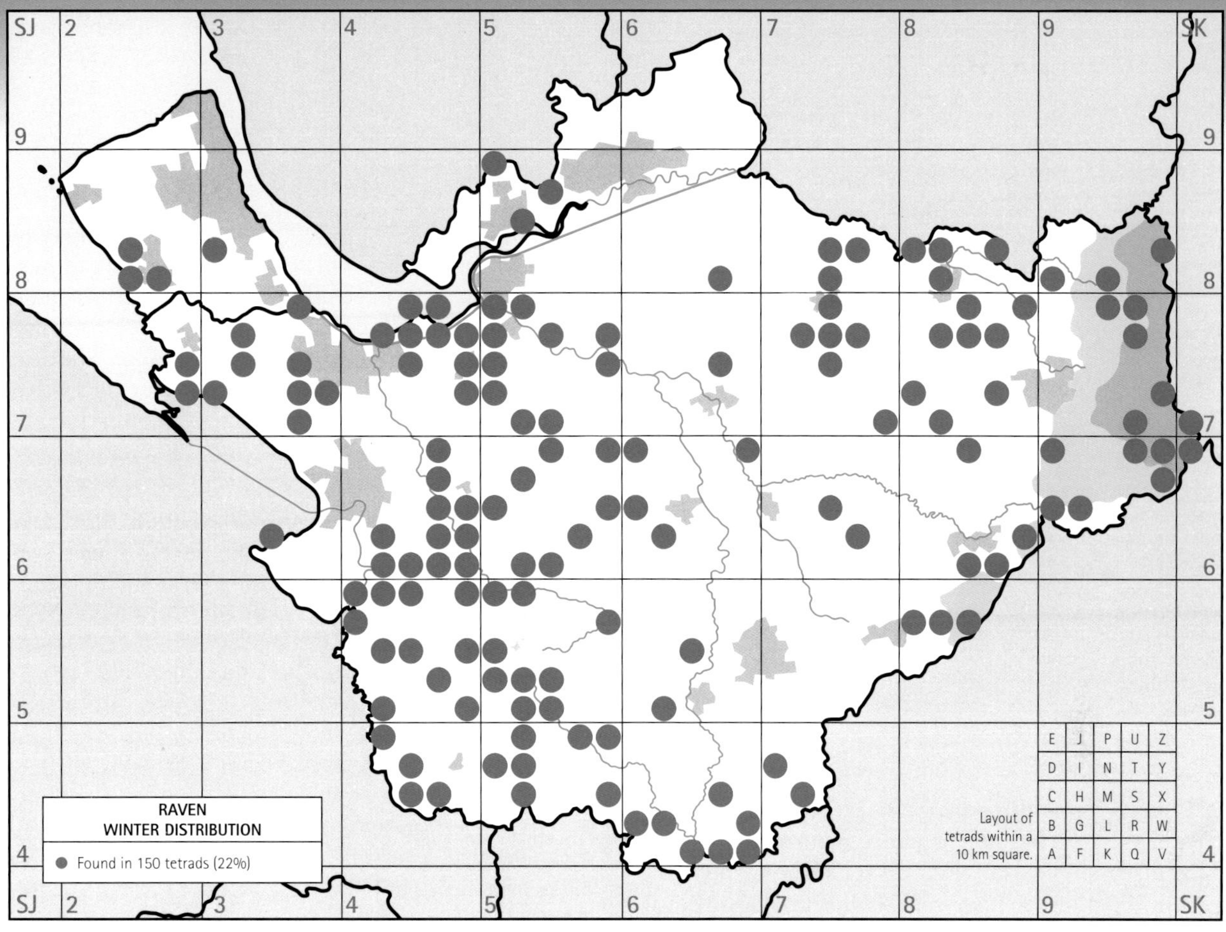
SJ
2
3
4
5
6
7
8
9
SK
9
8
7
6
5
4
RAVEN
WINTER DISTRIBUTION
Found in 150 tetrads (22%)
E J P U Z
D I N T Y
C H M S X
B G L R W
A F K Q V
Layout of
tetrads within a
10 km square.

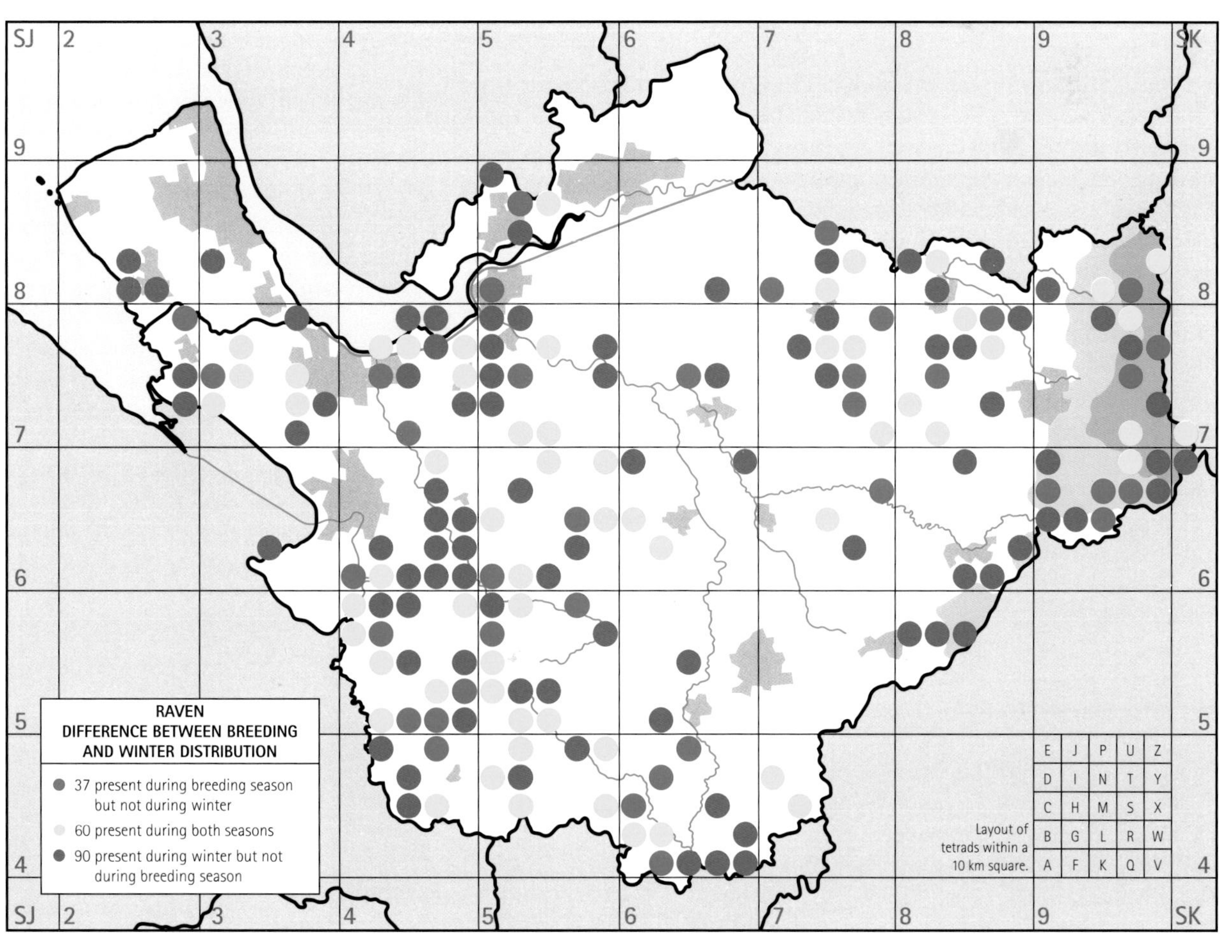
SJ
2
3
4
5
6
7
8
9
SK
9
8
7
6
5
4
RAVEN
DIFFERENCE BETWEEN BREEDING
AND WINTER DISTRIBUTION
37 present during breeding season
but not during winter
60 present during both seasons
90 present during winter but not
during breeding season
E J P U Z
D I N T Y
C H M S X
B G L R W
A F K Q V
Layout of
tetrads within a
10 km square.

Starling

Sturnus vulgaris

ANDY HARMER

Starling was the most widespread breeder in our *First Atlas* but now is not in the top ten in terms of the number of occupied tetrads. As a breeding bird, it has a distribution very similar to that of House Sparrow, both having been lost in the last twenty years from Hilbre and from the eastern hills: of the eleven tetrads above 350 m, they were confirmed breeding in one, possibly breeding in another and missing from nine.

Starling is now on the British Red List of species of conservation concern. The English population peaked in 1978, dropped by about 20% during 1978–84, the fieldwork period for our *First Atlas*, and continued to fall every year since then, such that by 2004 the national index was about 75% lower than just 20 years previously. The slump started earlier, and the decrease was greater, in their secondary habitat of woodland than in their preferred farmland. A detailed analysis of BTO data showed a marked regional effect, with the decline greatest in pastoral areas such as Cheshire. In northwest England, Starlings achieved their greatest concentrations near habitation, especially suburban areas, followed by urban and rural, with fewer on farmland but about five times higher densities on grassland than arable areas (Robinson *et al.* 2005b).

Although Starling is now only the sixteenth most widespread species in the county, judging by the number of tetrads in which birds were found in the breeding season, it is the ninth most abundant species. The analysis of the BBS transects in 2004–05 shows that the breeding population of Cheshire and Wirral is 72,240 (50,190–94,290) Starlings.

The nub of the species' problems has clearly been identified as reduced overwinter survival, especially of first-year birds; despite on average laying more eggs, rearing more chicks, losing fewer nests and laying earlier in some years, which allows more pairs to have second broods, the population is dropping because more birds die in winter (Freeman *et al.* 2007). The reasons for the decline are less easy to define. Although Starlings supplement their winter diet with seeds, and indeed they will eat almost anything they can find, the key food all year round is soil invertebrates, found in areas of short grassland. They like to feed amongst cattle, and perhaps the tendency to keep stock indoors during winter has affected the species. It is not known, however, what has happened in the Cheshire uplands since our *First Atlas* to cause the loss of Starlings. A survey of the upland farmers would be instructive.

Starling chicks need insect food, especially leatherjackets, the larvae of crane-flies (tipulids), which their parents find amongst short-cropped grass, especially mown lawns and salt-marsh; adult birds will fly up to a mile or more to a sure source of food, and are very obvious from late April as they fly back to their nests with a beakful of invertebrates. With chicks squawking in their nests, this must be amongst the easiest of all birds in which to prove breeding, and indeed Starlings had the second-highest percentage of confirmed breeding of all species. In 206 tetrads, birds were seen with food for their young, with a further 13 where adults were noted carrying faecal sacs away from the nest, another obvious feature of this species. Fieldworkers recorded nests in 154 tetrads, which are mostly nowadays in man-made structures, especially under the eaves or in chimneys of buildings; nests in holes in trees are much scarcer than twenty years ago, although six observers noted nests in oak, ash and alder, sometimes in a naturally formed hole and other times using an old woodpecker's nest. In a further 200 tetrads, recently fledged young were seen; this is clearly the least reliable evidence of breeding in a tetrad because youngsters become independent very quickly, within about 10 days (Feare 1984) and some parties of Starlings will fly long distances from their natal site within days of fledging.

The Atlas data show most habitat codes from human sites (60% of records, with 38% rural, 17% suburban and 5% urban), with 28% farmland and 11% woodland or B1 (scrub, regenerating woodland).

Sponsored by Dr P. Griffiths

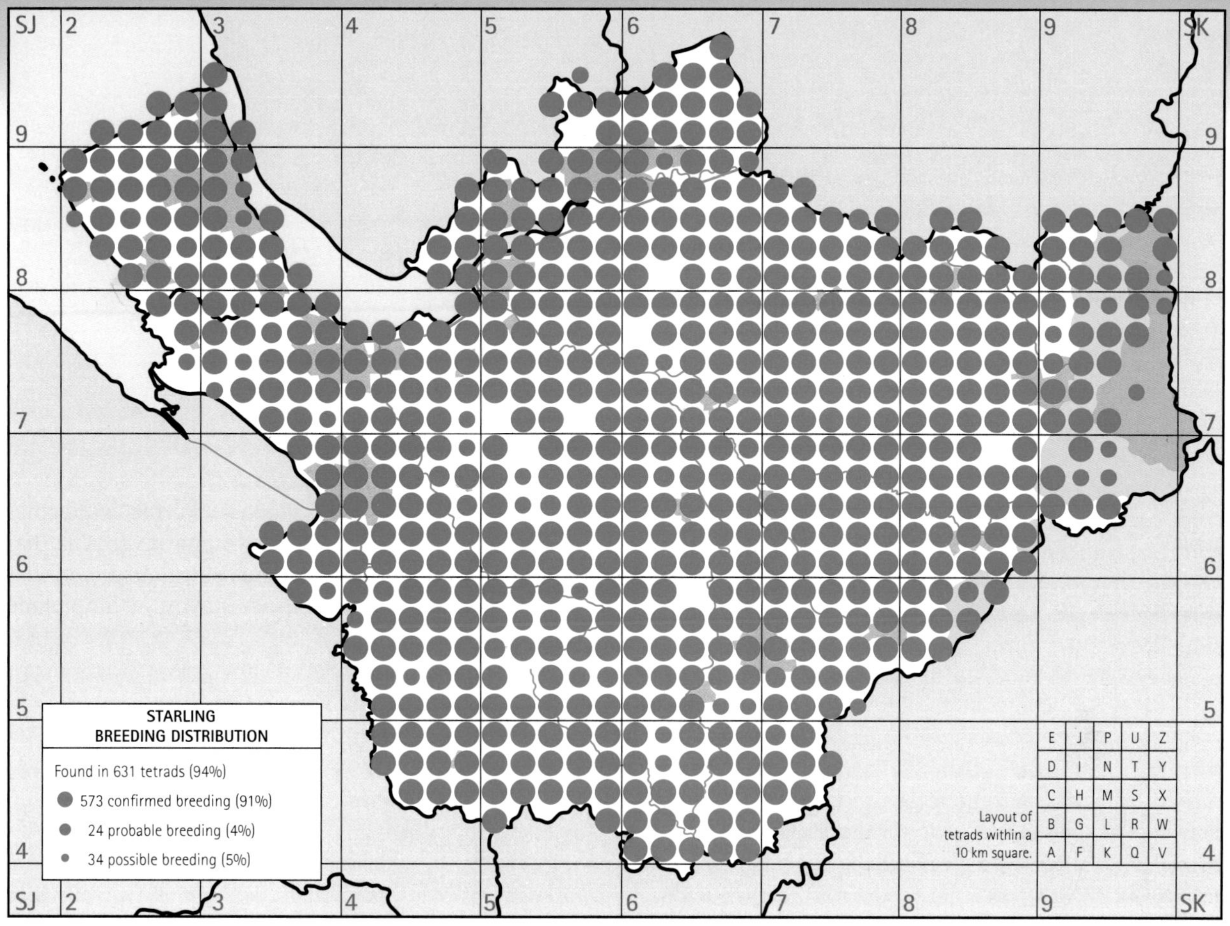
SJ
2
3
4
5
6
7
8
9
SK
9
8
7
6
5
4
STARLING
BREEDING DISTRIBUTION
Found in 631 tetrads (94%)
573 confirmed breeding (91%)
24 probable breeding (4%)
34 possible breeding (5%)
E J P U Z
D I N T Y
C H M S X
B G L R W
A F K Q V
Layout of tetrads within a 10 km square.

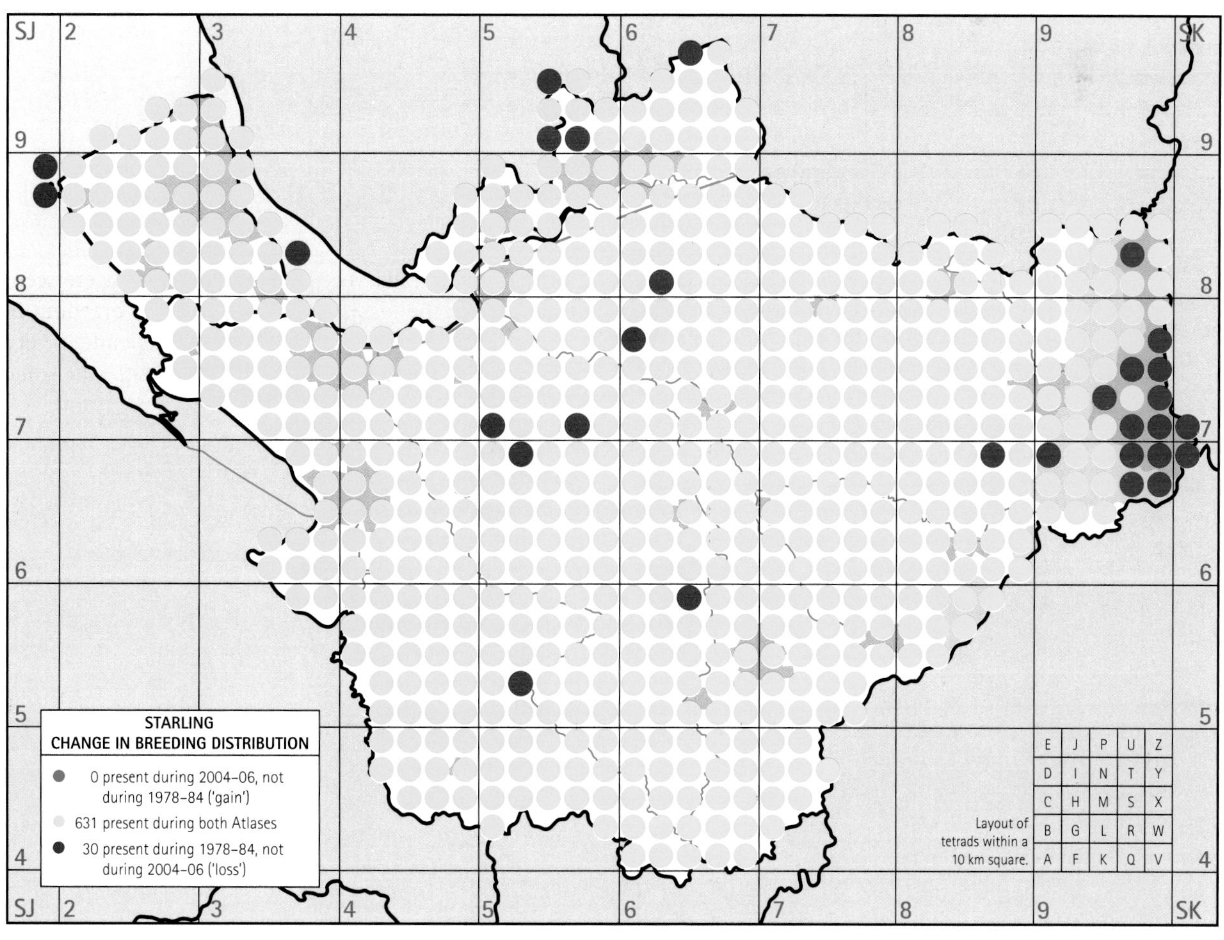
SJ
2
3
4
5
6
7
8
9
SK
9
8
7
6
5
4
STARLING
CHANGE IN BREEDING DISTRIBUTION
0 present during 2004–06, not during 1978–84 ('gain')
631 present during both Atlases
30 present during 1978–84, not during 2004–06 ('loss')
E J P U Z
D I N T Y
C H M S X
B G L R W
A F K Q V
Layout of tetrads within a 10 km square.

Our breeding Starlings are mostly sedentary, or make short movements within Britain, but their numbers are augmented in winter by millions of birds from eastern Europe. Merseyside Ringing Group has 88 records of ringed Starlings overseas, including 12 from as far as Russia, Belarus and the Baltic states. Some of these stay in large flocks in the countryside but others come into gardens and mix with local birds. The Atlas map shows that the winter distribution is similar to that of the breeding season, with the only significant difference being birds present in seven of the tetrads in the eastern hills where they were not found breeding. The habitat codes submitted in winter, however, show a very different distribution from the breeding season, with 60% of the winter records on farmland (including 31% improved grassland), 30% human sites, 7% woodland or scrub, many of these used for roosting, and 3% semi-natural grassland and marsh. The phrase 'human sites' does not only mean habitation, and birds were noted in a number of tetrads feeding on landfill sites or sewage farms.

They spend almost all of their lives in groups from a few birds to many thousands. Large feeding flocks are especially a feature of the south of the county, birds foraging on pasture or stubble, particularly favouring recently slurried fields or those used by cattle or sheep. Starlings are wintering in fewer gardens, according to the BTO's Garden Bird Feeding Survey, having fallen from presence in about 85% of gardens in the mid-1990s to 70% now. Similarly, from its inception in 1979 to 2003, the late-January RSPB Big Garden Birdwatch found Starling to be the most numerous bird in gardens, but it no longer holds the top spot and the numbers of Starlings per garden are down to less than a quarter of those recorded in 1979. These results do not necessarily imply any change in populations, but could indicate changed feeding habits and less need to visit artificial food sources, especially with warmer winters of late.

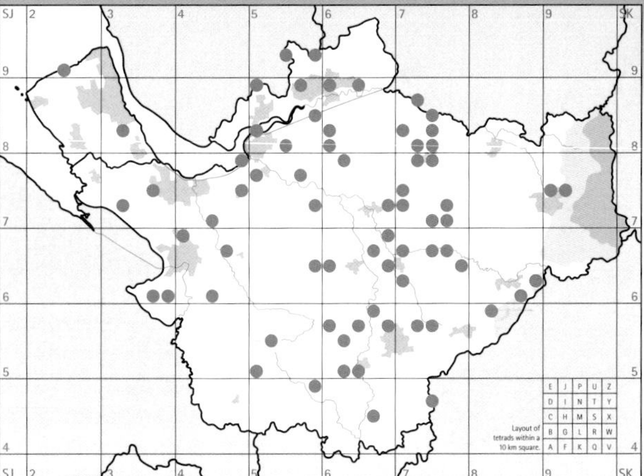

Starling roost map.

Roosting or pre-roosting flocks were reported widely across the county, with some massive counts in the south of the county headed by the half a million birds in Nantwich (SJ65K) in 2004/05, up to 300,000 in conifer windbreak trees near Wardle (SJ65D) in 2005/06 and 250,000 at Bulkeley (SJ55H) in 2004/05. Elsewhere, the Runcorn-Widnes Bridge (SJ58B) has held hundreds of thousands of birds in the past, despite concerted attempts by local authorities at dispersal, and there were estimated to be up to 70,000 there during this Atlas period. Another traditional site is the reed-bed at Rostherne Mere (SJ78L)—mentioned by Coward (1910)—holding a conservatively judged 45,000 in 2006/07. Many smaller roosts were reported, often in *leylandii*, with willows used at Woolston (SJ68P), a plane tree in Warrington town centre (SJ68E), a water tower near Congleton (SJ86Q) and industrial buildings across the county. Large roosts may have a catchment 20 km in radius (*BTO Winter Atlas*), and the map of reported roost sites is difficult to interpret, amalgamating three winters and ignoring changes within a winter. Coordination of counts and mapping flight-lines to roosts would make an admirable project for CAWOS.

RICHARD STEEL

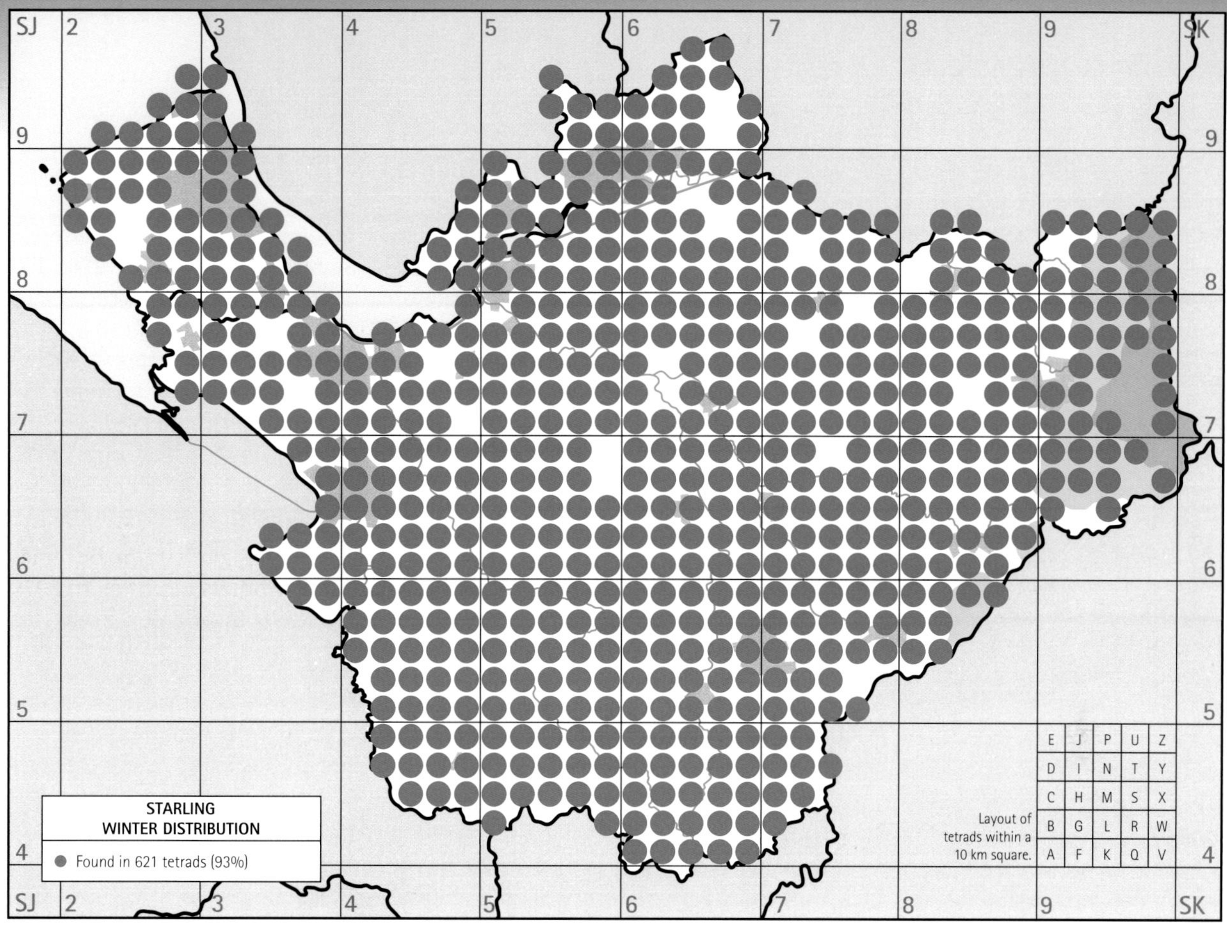
STARLING
WINTER DISTRIBUTION
Found in 621 tetrads (93%)
Layout of tetrads within a 10 km square.
E J P U Z
D I N T Y
C H M S X
B G L R W
A F K Q V
SJ
SK

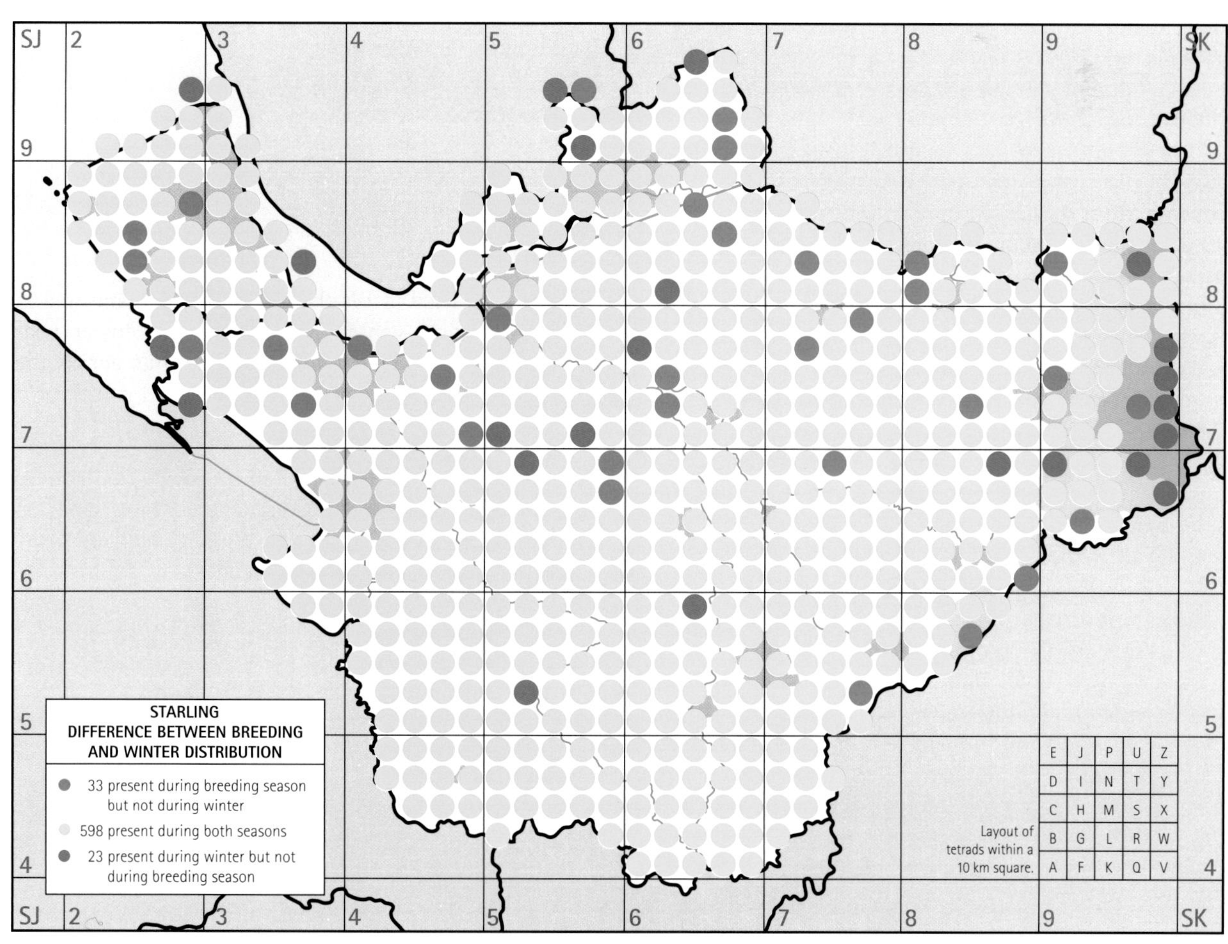
STARLING
DIFFERENCE BETWEEN BREEDING AND WINTER DISTRIBUTION
33 present during breeding season but not during winter
598 present during both seasons
23 present during winter but not during breeding season
Layout of tetrads within a 10 km square.
E J P U Z
D I N T Y
C H M S X
B G L R W
A F K Q V
SJ
SK

House Sparrow

Passer domesticus

The Atlas map reveals that House Sparrow is no longer in the top ten of widely distributed breeding species in the county, but the population figures show that it is our most abundant bird. This apparent paradox is easily explained: as a social/colonial bird, it is not found everywhere but there are often large concentrations where it does occur.

Their population has declined nationally and they have been on the Red List of species of conservation concern from 2005. The population indices showed a 40% drop in breeding numbers in England during the period of our *First Atlas* (1978–84) and there has been a further 45% drop in 20 years since then (1984–2004). However, these data are mainly from rural areas, almost certainly driven by a fall in overwinter survival as has been experienced by many farmland seed-eaters, and their decline has been greatest in eastern and south-eastern England. House Sparrow density in many rural towns (Summers-Smith 2003), and in some urban and suburban areas, appears not to have changed much for many years although there are well-publicized dramatic collapses in populations in the centres of some big cities. There are several research projects, and much speculation, on the reasons for this, including loss of nest sites from tidier building maintenance, increases in cat predation, pollution from unleaded petrol and the overuse of pesticides; but firm results are still awaited.

Apart from odd tetrads of underrecording in the *First Atlas* or this survey, the species has been lost from the far west and far east of our area. House Sparrows do not now breed on Hilbre, where their fortunes have previously been shown to follow the practices of different wardens in keeping chickens, or not (Craggs 1978). The most noticeable area of loss in the last twenty years is the eastern hills. House Sparrows are now missing above approximately the 350 m contour mark; a similar distribution has been observed in the tetrad Atlases of Northumbria, Lancashire and North Merseyside, and Cumbria. It is probably not a simple effect of altitude, however, and is likely to be the change in agricultural practice and habitation, and possibly rainfall, as the weaver family, that includes sparrows, generally inhabits arid lands. There is nothing obvious that has happened in the last twenty years, however, and the decline has occurred unremarked in bird reports, but it does mirror that of Starling.

As well as preferring to be with other sparrows, House Sparrows are seldom found far from people, and 80% of the habitat codes recorded in this survey were category F (human sites) with 17% being farmland. There has been an interesting change in birdwatchers' attitude to the species, it having gone from being ignored, often disliked, to becoming a topic of conversation and often a matter of some pride for those of us who have them living nearby.

The BTO analysis estimated a Cheshire and Wirral breeding population of 211,490 (160,420–262,550) individuals, an average of about 42 pairs per square kilometre across the whole county. Thus, Cheshire and Wirral holds about 2.0% of the UK population; with 1% of the land area of the UK, we have more than our proportionate share of the species. Despite their traditional easterly distribution, perhaps the comparatively benign intensification of our pastoral agriculture has been relatively favourable for sparrows, compared to their fate in the arable counties.

A 2001 survey in urban North Merseyside (White 2002) found amazing variations in the density of breeding House Sparrows, from none to 192 pairs per square kilometre, with an average of 62 pairs per square kilometre. They had almost abandoned central Liverpool and St Helens, but no correlation could be deduced with any geographical or habitat features examined. A similar survey in Cheshire and Wirral would make an admirable project for CAWOS members.

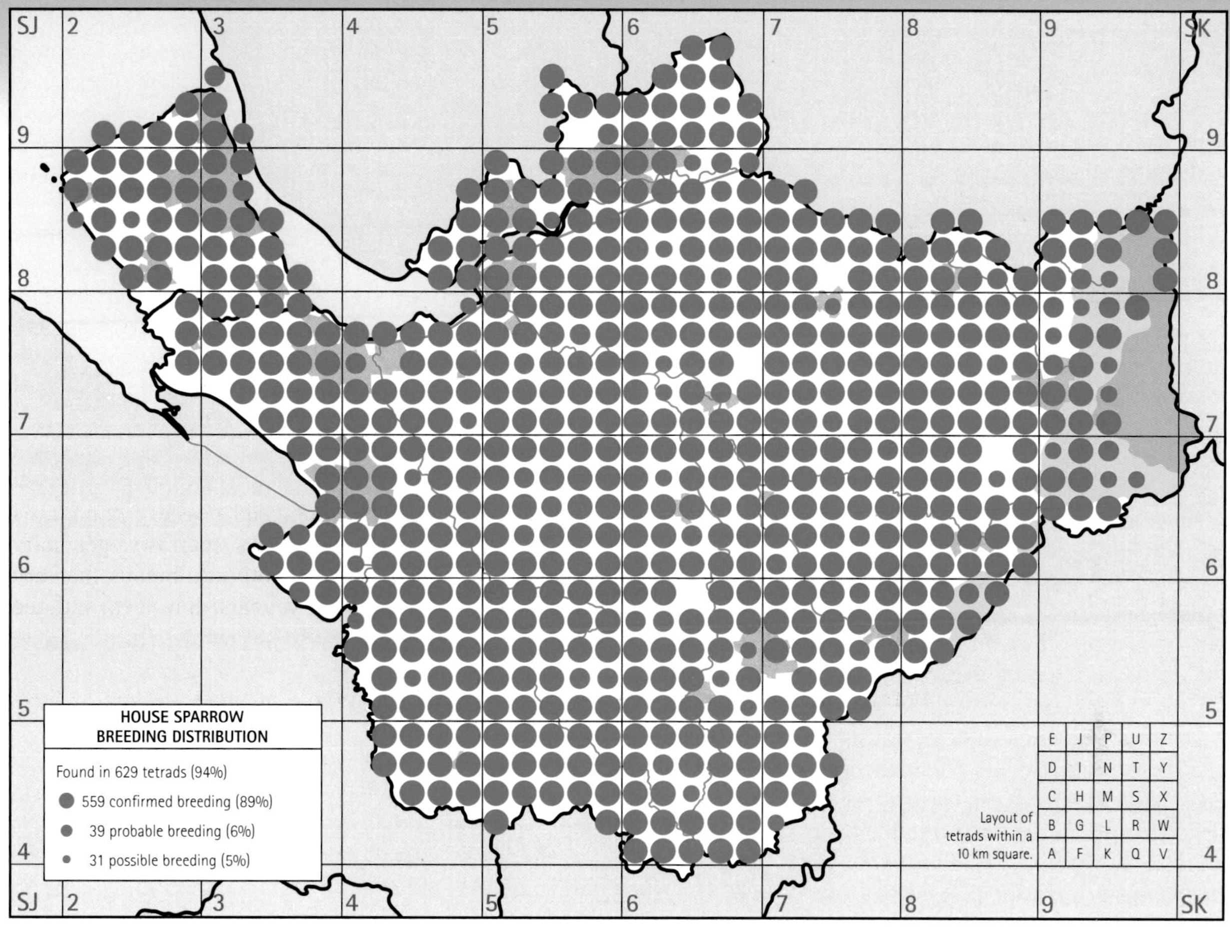

HOUSE SPARROW
BREEDING DISTRIBUTION
Found in 629 tetrads (94%)
559 confirmed breeding (89%)
39 probable breeding (6%)
31 possible breeding (5%)
Layout of tetrads within a 10 km square.
E J P U Z
D I N T Y
C H M S X
B G L R W
A F K Q V
SJ
SK

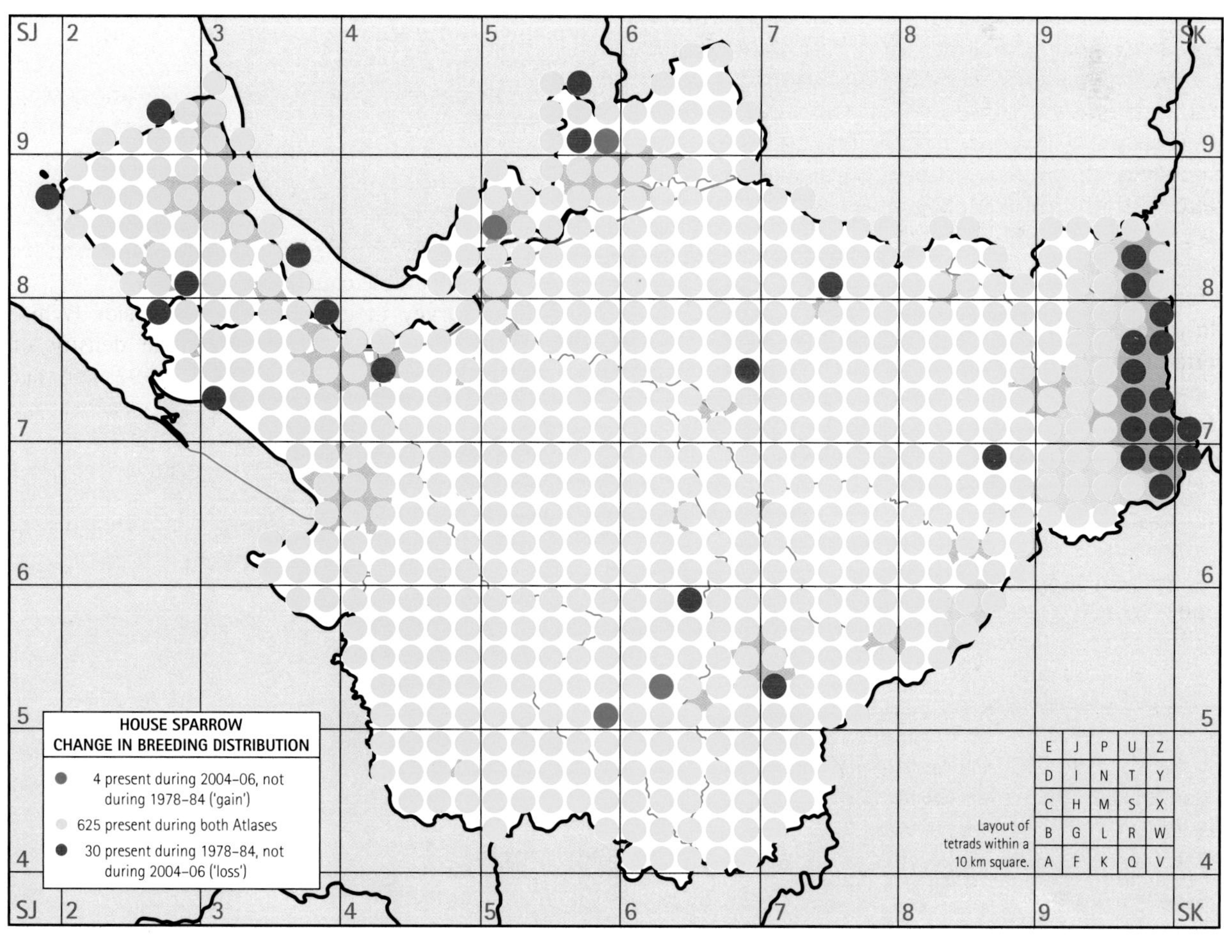

HOUSE SPARROW
CHANGE IN BREEDING DISTRIBUTION
4 present during 2004–06, not during 1978–84 ('gain')
625 present during both Atlases
30 present during 1978–84, not during 2004–06 ('loss')
Layout of tetrads within a 10 km square.
E J P U Z
D I N T Y
C H M S X
B G L R W
A F K Q V
SJ
SK

Most House Sparrows live all their lives within 1–2 km of their natal site, so not much difference would be expected between the breeding and wintering distribution, and this is borne out by the maps. Just nine tetrads had birds in winter where they had not been recorded in the breeding season, and 24 the other way round. These small differences show no significant pattern and are almost certainly due to the vagaries of recording effort. Similarly, there was no meaningful change in the habitat codes recorded.

Adults remain focused on their nest sites all year round, adding material to the nest at any time, and females roost in it on and off throughout the year. They often join flocks along with the males and the first-year birds, however. More than 600 counts of House Sparrows were made by winter fieldworkers, half of them of more than 10 birds, with 35 groups of 40 birds or more including five three-figure flocks. They also roost communally, the pre-roost gatherings often betrayed by the birds' noisy discordant chirruping. Despite this being the time of greatest pressure on their lives, with difficulty in finding sufficient winter food, House Sparrows finish feeding and go to roost extraordinarily early on a midwinter afternoon, usually an hour before sunset. Atlas surveyors recorded roosts in 28 tetrads, especially in evergreen hedges such as privet and *leylandii* or impenetrable bramble or hawthorn, mostly holding 10–40 birds. These were dwarfed, however, by the massive total found by Brian Martin, 200 House Sparrows on 23 November 2006 roosting in laurels in the car park of a Warrington superstore (SJ58Z).

Cheshire's early-twentieth-century ornithologists made no attempt to hide their dislike of House Sparrows, and wrote little about their status. Coward (1910) said that '... with obtrusive familiarity, the bird monopolizes the scraps spread in suburban gardens in winter, frequently to the exclusion of more deserving species, and repays its benefactors by pulling to pieces the crocuses and early spring flowers.' Boyd's view (1951) was that it was '... far too plentiful'. Bell (1962) added nothing, copying the comment on distribution from Coward and Oldham 62 years previously: 'This abundant resident is widespread, except on the bleaker hills in the east, but it frequents isolated farms on the high ground'. Perhaps we can deduce from this that there was little change in its status, although with the disdain for recording House Sparrows, continued in the early county bird reports, it is impossible to be sure.

Nationally, rapid declines amongst House Sparrows wintering in gardens are indicated by the BTO's Garden Bird Feeding Survey (Robinson *et al.* 2005a): it fell from presence in 97% of gardens in the 1970s and 93% in the 1990s to only 83% at the start of this Atlas. The RSPB Big Garden Birdwatch has recorded a drop in average numbers per garden, from 10 in 1979 to 4.4 in January 2007.

RAY SCALLY

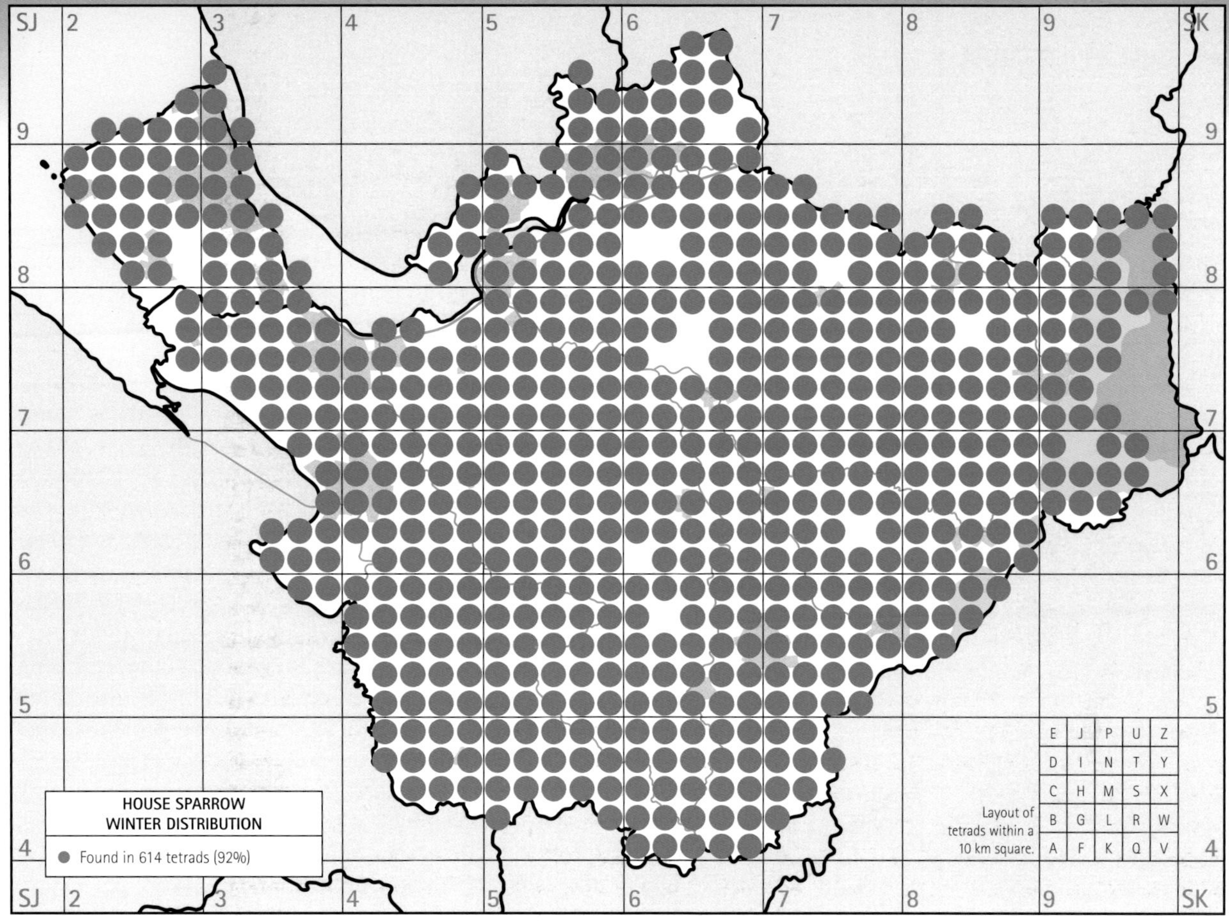

SJ
2
3
4
5
6
7
8
9
SK
HOUSE SPARROW
WINTER DISTRIBUTION
Found in 614 tetrads (92%)
Layout of tetrads within a 10 km square.
E J P U Z
D I N T Y
C H M S X
B G L R W
A F K Q V

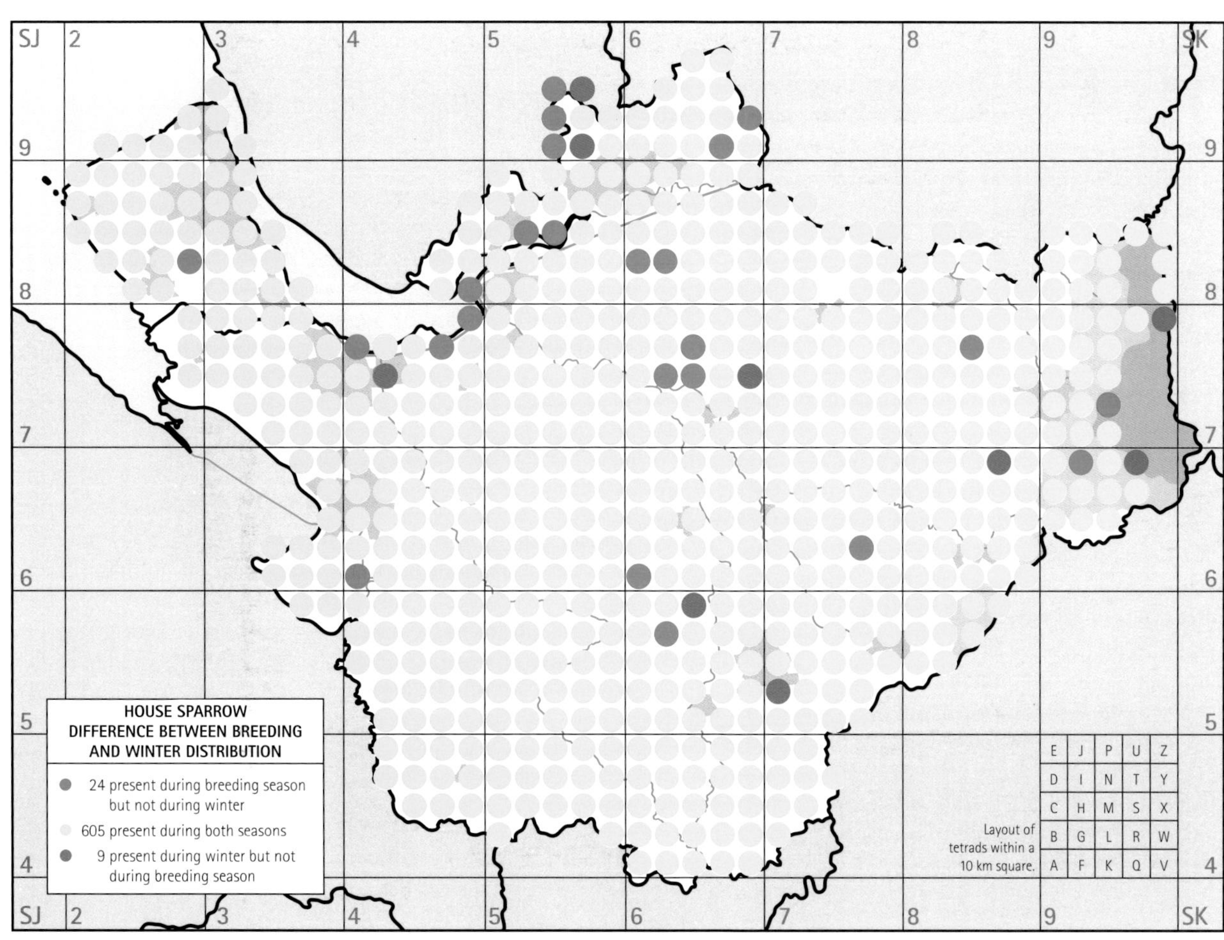

SJ
2
3
4
5
6
7
8
9
SK
HOUSE SPARROW
DIFFERENCE BETWEEN BREEDING AND WINTER DISTRIBUTION
24 present during breeding season but not during winter
605 present during both seasons
9 present during winter but not during breeding season
Layout of tetrads within a 10 km square.
E J P U Z
D I N T Y
C H M S X
B G L R W
A F K Q V

Tree Sparrow

Passer montanus

STEVE ROUND

The Atlas results for this species were awaited with more trepidation than most, as its numbers have declined more steeply in the last 30 years than any other English bird. In the event, many observers commented that they found Tree Sparrows in areas where they had not known them before, their presence often given away by a series of 'chup' calls from deep in a hedge: the species is quite secretive and probably underrecorded in casual birdwatching, as Boyd commented 60 years ago (Boyd 1951).

Tree Sparrow abundance dropped spectacularly in the UK between the late 1970s and the early 1990s. Most of the population crash occurred during the period of our *First Atlas*, so that the national index fell by three-quarters during 1978–84, and continued to decline into the mid-1990s but has risen a little since then. It appears that the low point in their Cheshire and Wirral fortunes probably occurred about halfway between our two Atlases. This species has been hit hard by agricultural intensification, especially the loss of weedy winter stubble, and it seems that the Countryside Stewardship agri-environment scheme is helping to turn round their fortunes. The 'change' map, although showing the species lost from 246 tetrads since our *First Atlas*, does illustrate 44 gains, mainly in the cattle-farming areas of southern Cheshire.

Most Tree Sparrows nest in loose colonies, with some solitary pairs. Cheshire birds appear to be mainly in groups of 5–10 pairs, although 10–50 used to be the normal size (Summers-Smith 1995) and the UK BAP considers a 'large' colony to be one exceeding 20 pairs, possibly worthy of site safeguard measures. Colonies are not dense aggregations, and indeed a casual visitor might not realize that there is more than one or two nests. A typical colony covers an area of 5–20 ha, a diameter of 250–500 m, the size usually limited by the number of available holes for nesting and the amount of suitable food in the vicinity. On a local scale, they show a preference for damp areas, especially for finding copious invertebrates, although breeding adults may fly more than a kilometre to suitable sources of food. Provision of nest-boxes, preferably situated with a few close together, can help in building up numbers, even starting from scratch, but studies elsewhere have shown that it might take six years or more before the birds respond and establish a colony.

Tree Sparrows pair for life, and remain faithful to the same nest site. Their breeding season can extend from April to August, three-quarters of pairs having a second brood and about 40% having a third. They do not hang about: on average, about a week after the first chicks leave the nest, the female has started laying the next clutch of eggs (Summers-Smith 1995).

The breeding population estimate for Cheshire and Wirral in 2004–05 from the BBS analysis is 4,350 (2,100–6,600) individuals. Although probably not as scarce in the county as many observers had feared, it must be remembered that just a quarter of a century ago they were probably amongst the top ten commonest birds in Cheshire. This figure gives an average of around seven pairs per occupied tetrad, but this is a misleading way to express the density of a colonial species with such a clumped distribution. In practice it might mean, on average, one colony per tetrad.

This is predominantly the rural sparrow, and the habitat records show that Tree Sparrows were mainly found in farmland (64% of records), with 26% in human sites, nearly all rural, and 6% woodland and 3% scrub. The map shows that its distribution in the county is now almost defined by avoidance of built-up areas and the highest ground. Our *First Atlas* noted that they were absent from urban areas and scarce (but present in almost all tetrads) in the eastern hills. This Atlas shows that Tree Sparrows have withdrawn from suburban areas as well, with a very local distribution on Wirral, and are now missing from the hill country.

Sponsored by Alan and Judith Straw

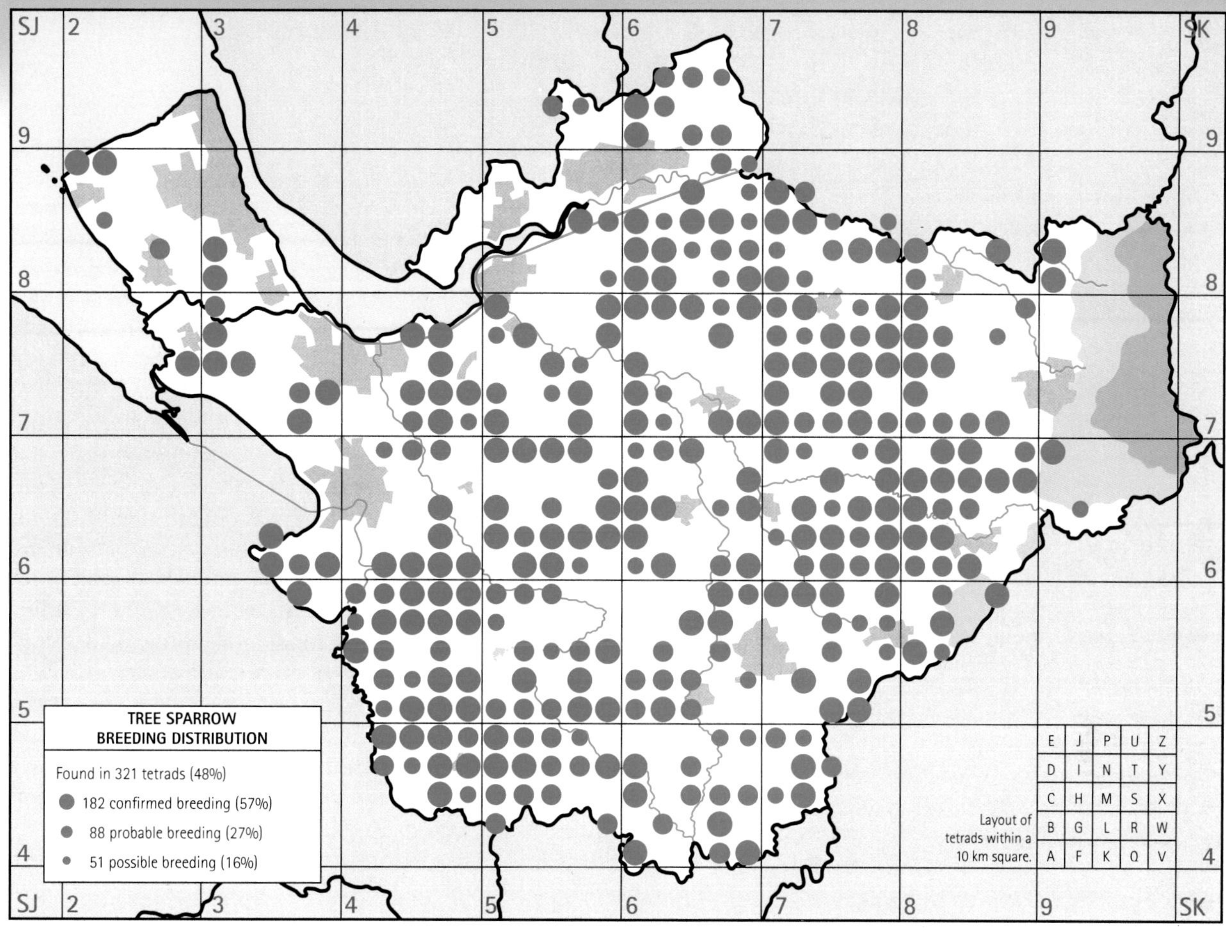
TREE SPARROW
BREEDING DISTRIBUTION
Found in 321 tetrads (48%)
182 confirmed breeding (57%)
88 probable breeding (27%)
51 possible breeding (16%)
Layout of tetrads within a 10 km square.
E J P U Z
D I N T Y
C H M S X
B G L R W
A F K Q V
SJ
SK

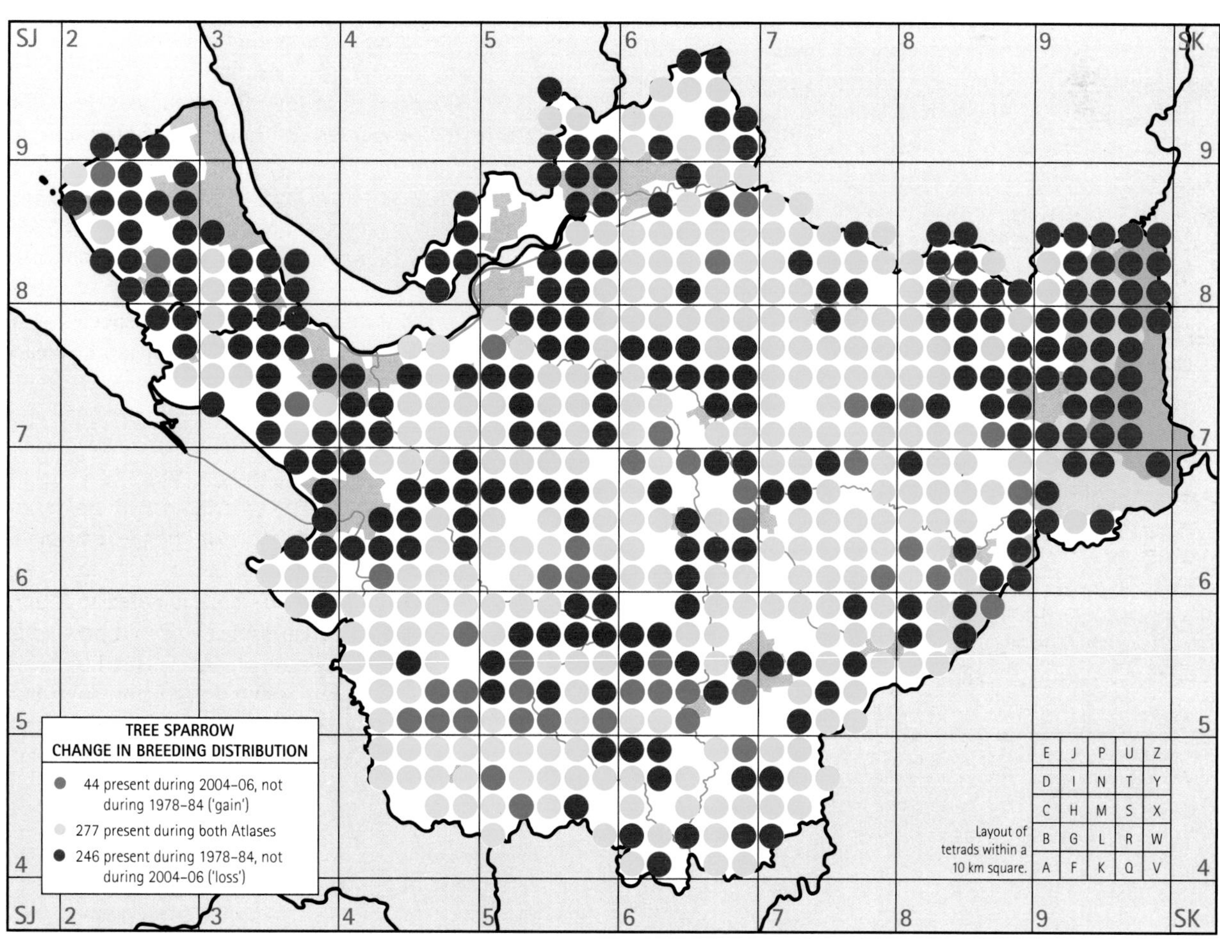
TREE SPARROW
CHANGE IN BREEDING DISTRIBUTION
44 present during 2004–06, not during 1978–84 ('gain')
277 present during both Atlases
246 present during 1978–84, not during 2004–06 ('loss')
Layout of tetrads within a 10 km square.
E J P U Z
D I N T Y
C H M S X
B G L R W
A F K Q V
SJ
SK

DAVID TOLLIDAY

Most adult Tree Sparrows are sedentary, whilst the young birds disperse, avoiding inbreeding by moving a few kilometres. There is a small reduction in the number of tetrads occupied from the breeding season to winter—from 321 to 276—which could be attributed to some birds deserting their breeding areas in the formation of winter flocks. There were 103 tetrads with birds in the breeding season but not in winter, and 58 where they were found in winter only. There is no significant change in habitat codes recorded between breeding and winter seasons, with 66% of winter records from farmland and 30% from human sites (overwhelmingly rural), and a handful from woodland and scrub.

All of them seem to join winter flocks, from a few to several hundred birds in size. Half of the reported groups in this winter Atlas were of five birds or fewer while there were seven three-figure flocks, all in the south of the county. The largest, estimated at 300 birds in 2005/06 and 200 birds in 2006/07, fed on strips of set-aside and stubble in the area north of Comber Mere, covering four adjacent tetrads (SJ54X/Y/SJ64C/D). A flock of 220 birds spent the winter of 2005/06 feeding on stubble and game cover including quinoa at Warmingham (SJ76A). Nationally, a major decline—a drop by a factor of three—has been noted in the sizes of winter flocks recorded in 1980–95 compared to 1965–79 (Shrubb 2003).

It is hard to deduce their former status in Cheshire and Wirral. Previous Cheshire ornithologists wrote little about Tree Sparrows in winter, but Coward and Oldham (1900) commented that they were frequently seen in farmyards or by the roadside in company with House Sparrows, Chaffinches and Yellowhammers. Perhaps the annual county bird reports tell a story: in the 1960s the species was ignored, along with all others that were thought to be common; the reports from 1975 to 1977 list a few large flocks, up to several hundred strong; but by 1982 there were 'few large flocks noted' and in 1983 all flocks larger than 20 birds were listed (*CWBRs*).

Although Tree Sparrows join feeding flocks of other seed-eaters, they tend to stay close to hedges or other suitable cover, and hedgeless fields and the centres of large fields are left to the finches and buntings. Undisturbed flocks frequently move in waves, the birds at the back of the flock flying forward to take up position at the front. They feed in bouts, gorging themselves then retreating to cover where they preen and digest their food.

Tree Sparrows eat some farmland grain, but much less than House Sparrows do: they tend to specialize on smaller seeds such as grasses and annual weeds such as goosefoot and chickweed. They also like oil-rich seeds including sunflowers and rape. In extensive areas of planted wildbird seed crops on farmland near Broxton, I have found that Tree Sparrows ignore the areas dominated by kale and triticale and only frequent plots containing quinoa and millet: birds caught for ringing have had their crops full of these small seeds. However, observations elsewhere (Perkins *et al.* 2007) have found different results, the authors commenting that 'For species with a diverse diet, such as Tree Sparrow, food preference may vary between populations in different locations, due to learned behaviour and adaptation to locally abundant seed types.'

They form communal roosts, especially in thick hedgerows, but in hard weather many birds roost in holes, perhaps those that have been, or will become, their nesting site. Just four roosts were reported from Atlas fieldwork, in adjacent tetrads near Buerton (SJ64V/W) and near Weston (SJ75F/K).

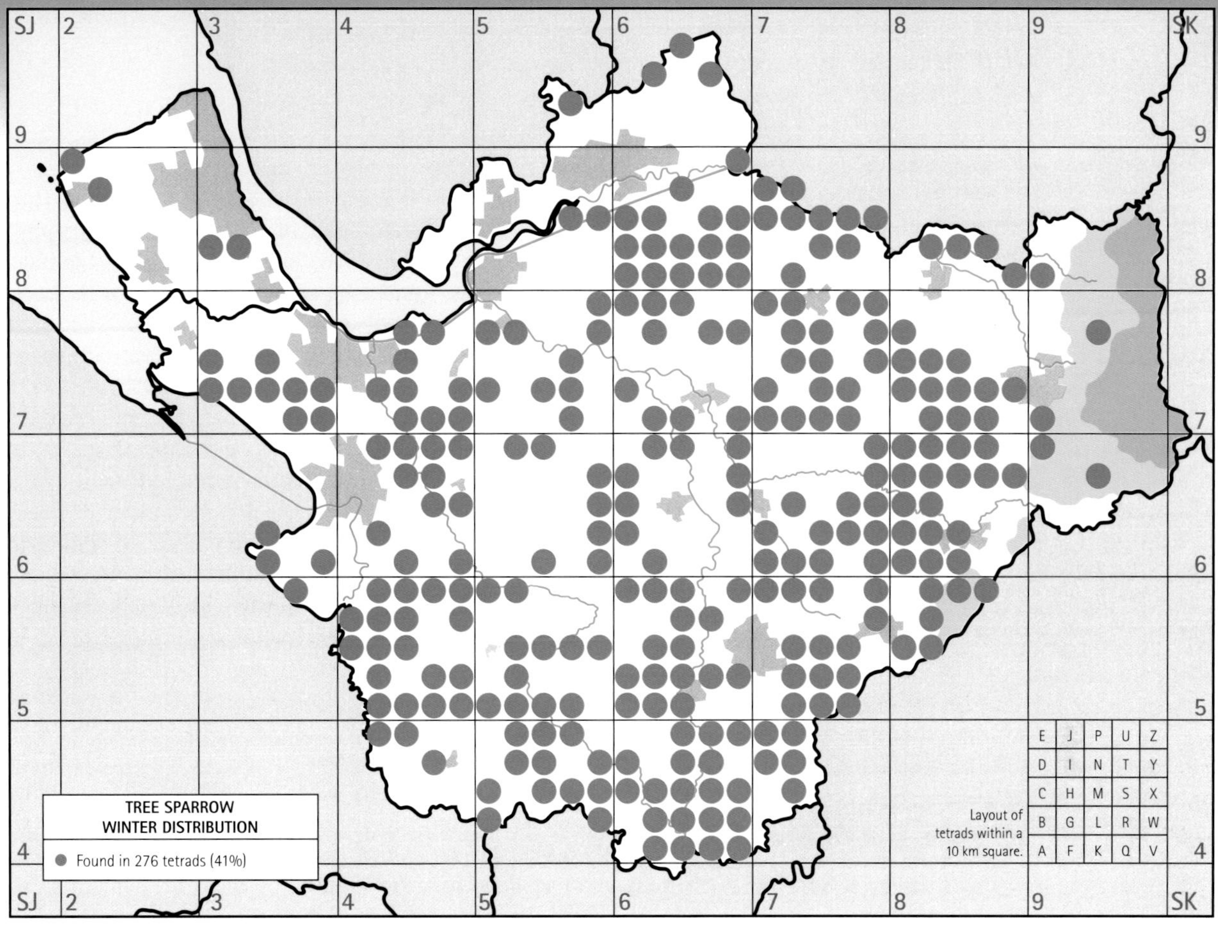
TREE SPARROW
WINTER DISTRIBUTION
Found in 276 tetrads (41%)
Layout of tetrads within a 10 km square.
SJ
SK

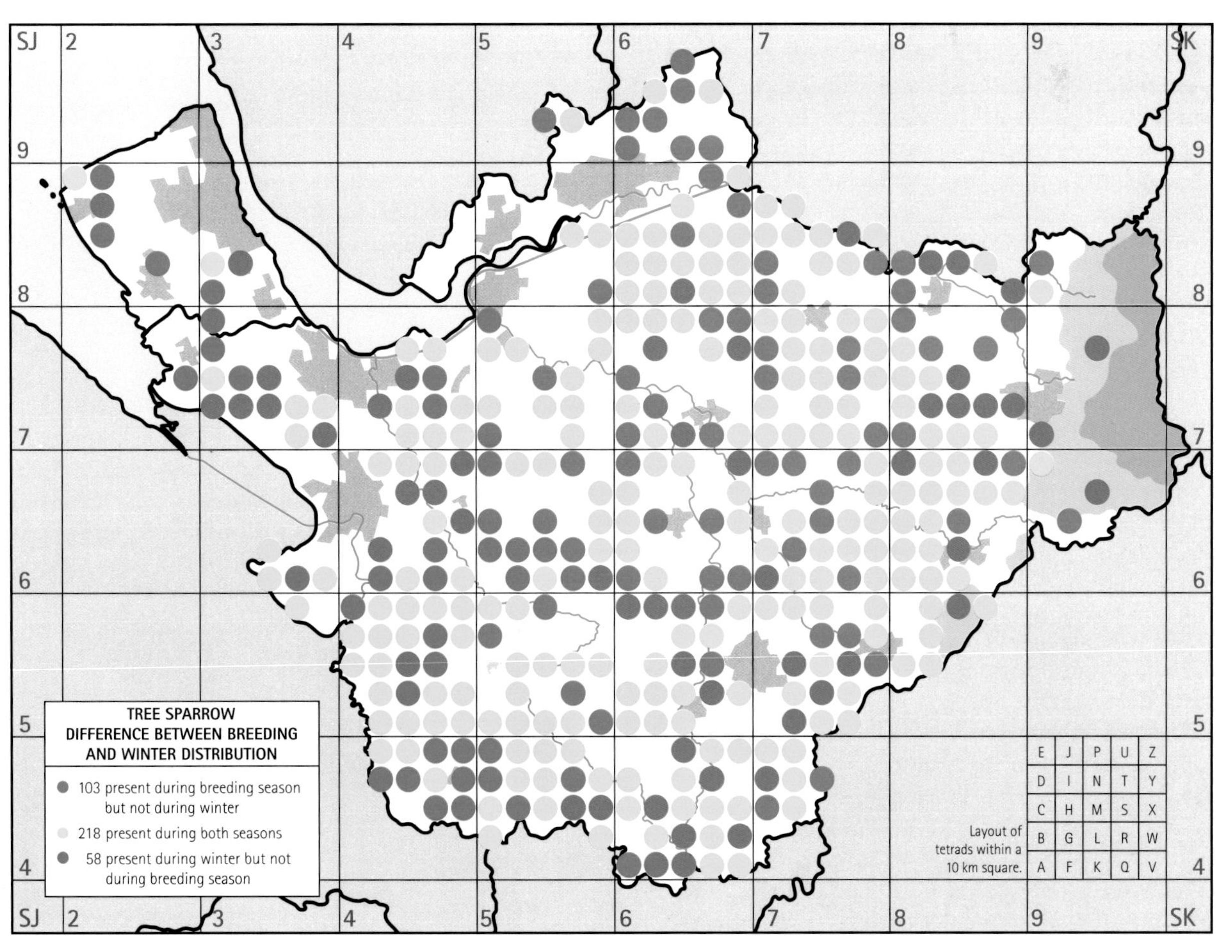
TREE SPARROW
DIFFERENCE BETWEEN BREEDING AND WINTER DISTRIBUTION
103 present during breeding season but not during winter
218 present during both seasons
58 present during winter but not during breeding season
Layout of tetrads within a 10 km square.
SJ
SK

Chaffinch

Fringilla coelebs

RICHARD STEEL

Chaffinch is now one of the most widespread species in the county, being found in the breeding season in 653 tetrads, 97% of the county. The 'change' map dramatically shows how Chaffinches have spread into the two areas from where they were missing in our *First Atlas*, the Mersey valley and north Wirral. In our *First Atlas* it was suggested that the cause of their absence was air pollution, which inhibited the growth of epiphytic lichens that Chaffinches use to bind and camouflage the exterior of their nests. During the 1990s these lichens spread throughout the county, as shown in the maps on p. 35, and it seems that Chaffinches, and Long-tailed Tits, have responded.

As well as being widespread, Chaffinch is the third most abundant species in the county. The BTO BBS analysis shows that the breeding population of the county in 2004–05 was 185,450 birds (159,260–211,640), corresponding to an average of 315 birds per tetrad with confirmed or probable breeding, or 285 birds per tetrad in which the species was recorded. This is an average of about one pair per 2.8 ha across the entire county.

Amongst the characteristics of the fringilline finches (Chaffinch and Brambling) that separate them from the cardueline finches are their defence of breeding territories and their nestling diet, exclusively invertebrates, so in the breeding season Chaffinches behave more like an insectivore than a seed-eater. The adults' habit of carrying food in their bill makes it easier to prove breeding than for other finches, and many birds draw attention to themselves by their territorial alarm call, only heard in the breeding season, a repeated 'hoo-eet' similar to the alarm call of Willow Warblers. Adult Chaffinches are long-lived birds, and they tend to have small broods, four being a typical number, with many pairs producing only one brood each year. The usual nest is in a hedge or low scrub. Breeding was confirmed in 96 tetrads by observers finding nests, with adults carrying food or a faecal sac in 176 and recently fledged young seen in 201. It was not easy to prove breeding in some of the most urban areas where Chaffinches were thinly distributed, however.

Chaffinches are well adapted to suburban and garden habitats, as well as to highly fragmented woodland and hedgerows. Most of the reported habitat codes were farmland (37%), with 28% human sites, 26% woodland and 8% scrub.

Although mostly eating seeds outside the breeding season, Chaffinches have not been hit in the same way as other granivorous species by the agricultural changes of the past fifty years. The national population index has been stable, increasing by about 10% from 1984 to 2004, and their annual survival appears to have reduced somewhat, perhaps suggesting that the population is self-limiting and near to saturation (Siriwardena *et al.* 1999).

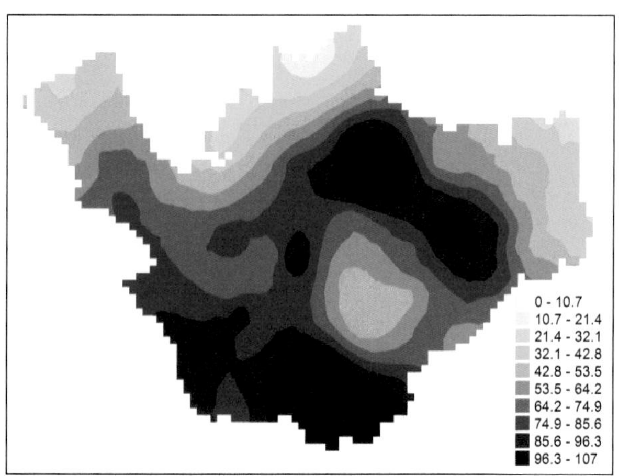

Chaffinch abundance.

Sponsored by Alastair Jenkins

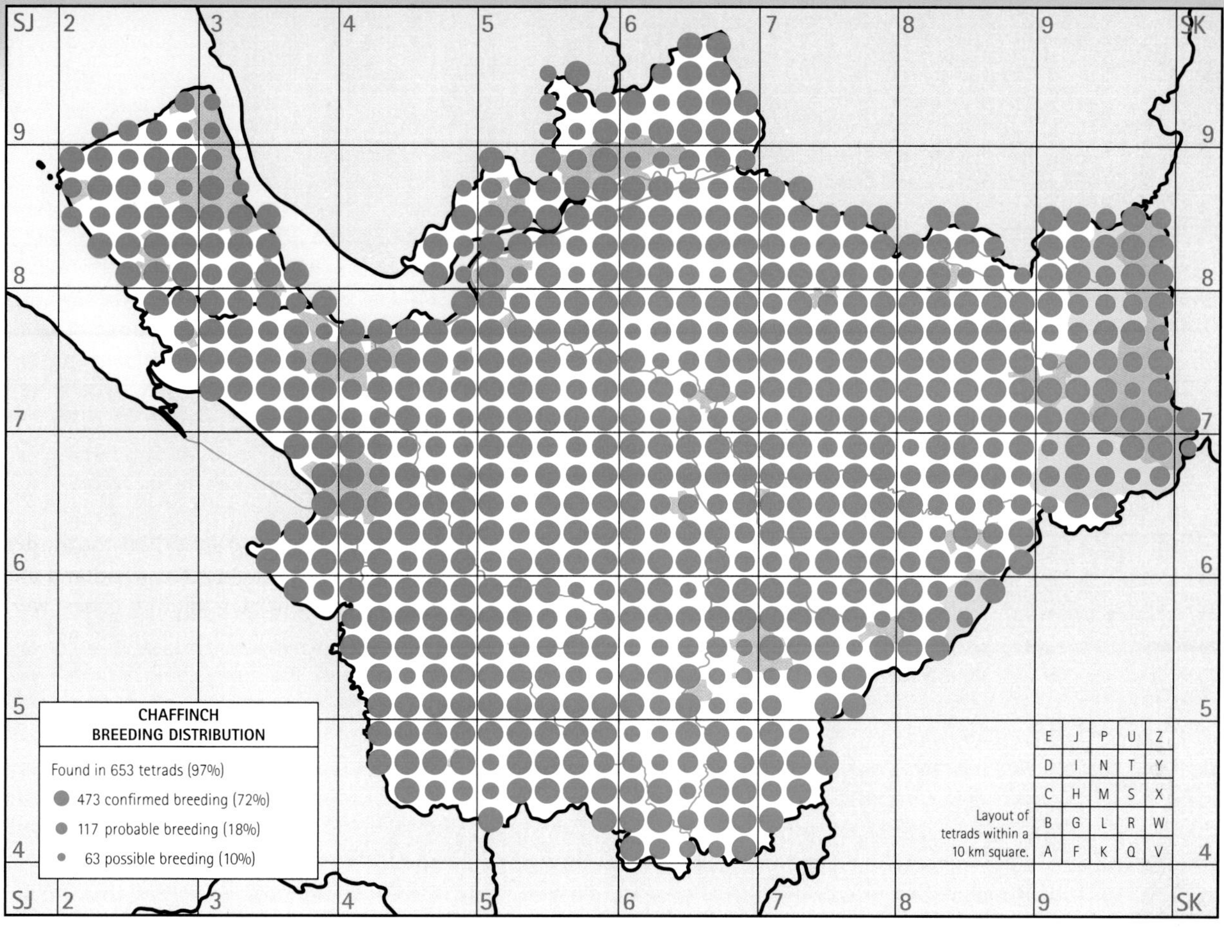
SJ
SK
2
3
4
5
6
7
8
9
CHAFFINCH
BREEDING DISTRIBUTION
Found in 653 tetrads (97%)
473 confirmed breeding (72%)
117 probable breeding (18%)
63 possible breeding (10%)
E J P U Z
D I N T Y
C H M S X
B G L R W
A F K Q V
Layout of tetrads within a 10 km square.

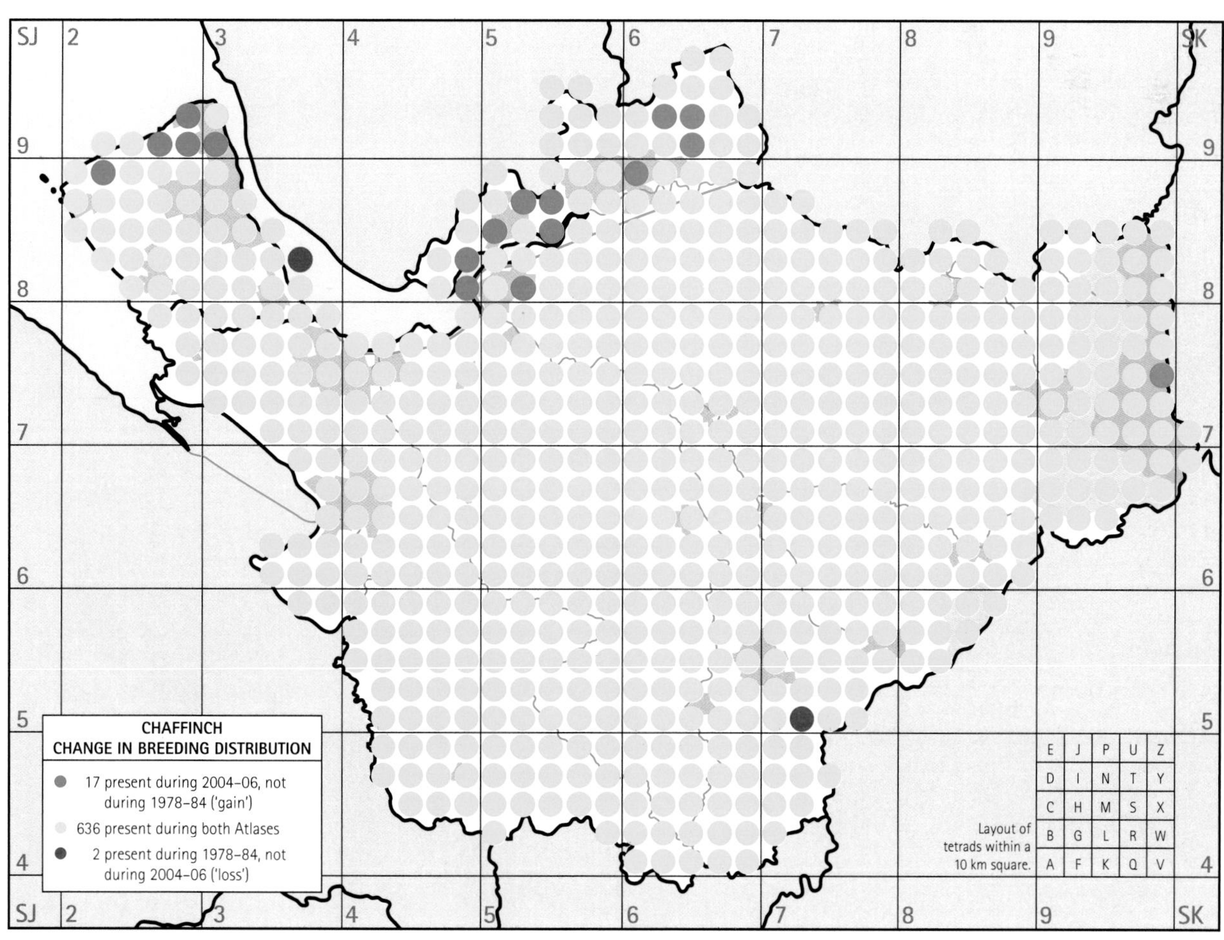
SJ
SK
2
3
4
5
6
7
8
9
CHAFFINCH
CHANGE IN BREEDING DISTRIBUTION
17 present during 2004–06, not during 1978–84 ('gain')
636 present during both Atlases
2 present during 1978–84, not during 2004–06 ('loss')
E J P U Z
D I N T Y
C H M S X
B G L R W
A F K Q V
Layout of tetrads within a 10 km square.

In winter, the population of Chaffinches is roughly doubled by immigration from Fennoscandia (*BTO Winter Atlas*). There are many ringing records in Cheshire and Wirral of birds from Finland, Sweden, Norway and Denmark, and along their migration route here following the coast of Germany, the Netherlands and Belgium. Our breeding birds are resident all year round: their median distance of movement is less than 1 km at all seasons, 90% move no more than 5 km, and the rest, almost entirely first-year birds, less than 50 km (Newton 1972, *Migration Atlas*). Coward (1910) gave no evidence for his statement that the numbers of our breeding birds were reduced by autumn emigration, and that has probably never been true. In prolonged periods of frost some birds leave to fly to Ireland, but hard weather movements have not occurred for some twenty years.

The map shows that they were found everywhere in winter. Their apparent absence from an odd tetrad here and there can only be the result of bad luck for the observers. They are not limited by altitude or vegetation, and were found in a wide variety of habitats. The submitted habitat codes for winter showed a slight shift to farmland (45%, compared to 37% in the breeding season), with commensurate drops in the other three main habitat classes; 25% human sites, 24% woodland and 5% scrub. Half of the farmland codes were hedgerows, with 5% of the total stubble fields.

The sex ratio of wintering Chaffinch flocks is an interesting subject for amateur observation and has aroused much discussion over the years, ever since Linnaeus in 1758 named the species *coelebs* (bachelor) because wintering birds in his native Sweden were almost exclusively male. Gilbert White, in letters dated 1768 and 1770 included in his *Natural History of Selborne*, commented on the vast preponderance of females—at least fifty to one—in wintering Chaffinch flocks around Selborne in Hampshire. By 1949, however, males were reported to predominate in the Netherlands, Belgium and Britain, with females in the majority in Ireland. In Cheshire, my ringing from 1980 to 2007 in a variety of feeding flocks and roosts has found just a slight excess of males, 52% to 48% females (*Migration Atlas*).

In winter the Chaffinch's diet consists almost exclusively of small seeds which they find on the ground. They have catholic tastes, taking a wider range of seeds than any other finch, but cereal and weed seeds are the most important. It is many years since they earned their name as the chaff-finch, and they would not nowadays be noted as the bird that followed the grain harvest. They lack the specialized bill of some other finches, and cannot cope with seeds that are difficult to extract.

The species' status has probably not changed much for a century or more. Coward and Oldham (1900) wrote 'in winter the bird is eminently sociable, and large flocks may be seen in the open fields' and Boyd (1951) said 'big flocks roam the woods and fields, and roost in hollies and other evergreens', comments that could be made today.

Although communal roosts are an obvious feature of this species' behaviour in winter, not many birdwatchers pay them much attention, and roosts were reported in only 12 tetrads in this Atlas, only three of them with flocks estimated larger than 50 birds. The largest was of 200 birds at Norton Priory, Runcorn (SJ58L), taking advantage of the microclimate, especially shelter from winds, provided by rhododendron bushes under mature trees. Chaffinches gather in the tops of the trees from one hour before dusk, indicating that they seldom have difficulty in finding food and have time to spare even on the shortest midwinter days.

PHIL JONES

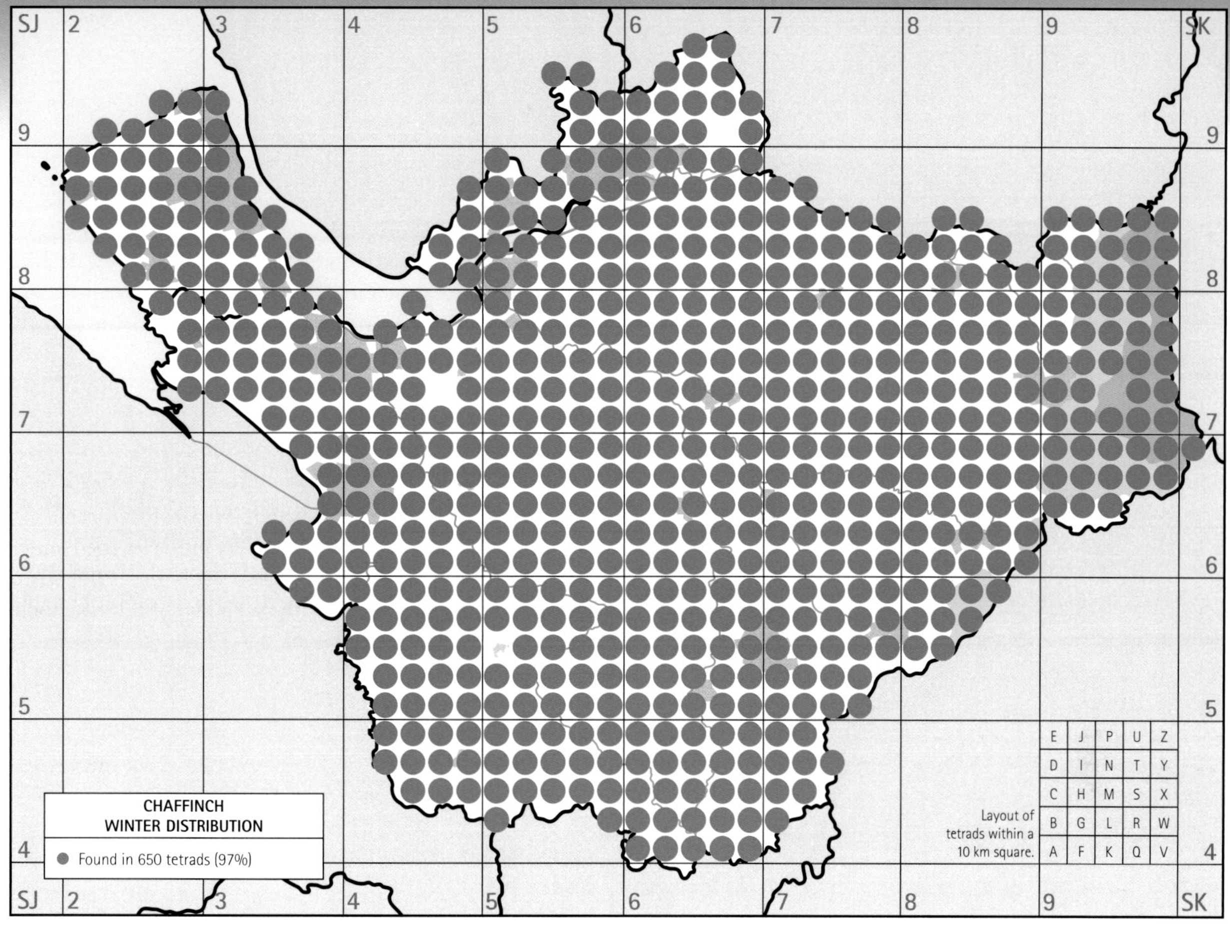
SJ
2
3
4
5
6
7
8
9
SK
9
8
7
6
5
4
CHAFFINCH
WINTER DISTRIBUTION
Found in 650 tetrads (97%)
E J P U Z
D I N T Y
C H M S X
B G L R W
A F K Q V
Layout of tetrads within a 10 km square.

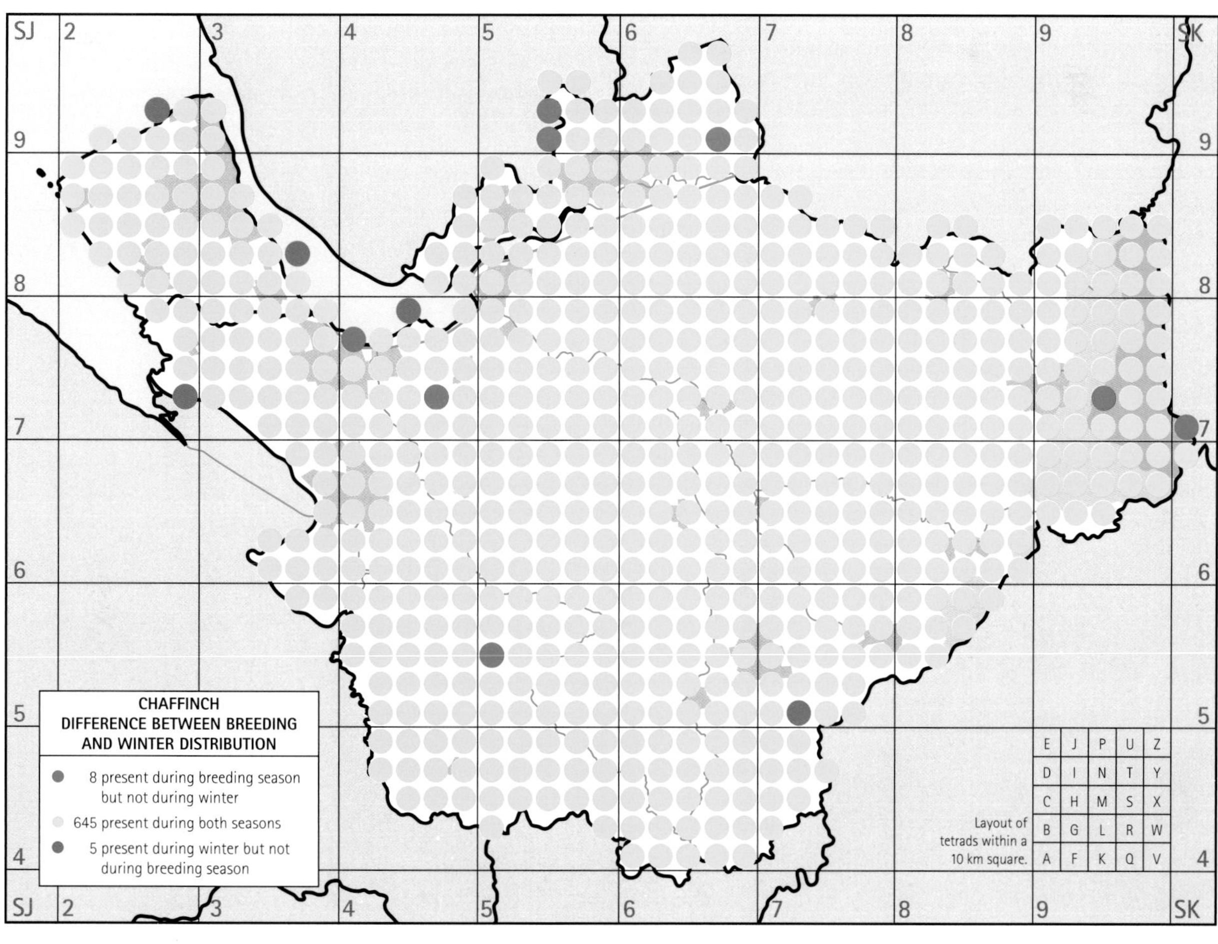
SJ
2
3
4
5
6
7
8
9
SK
9
8
7
6
5
4
CHAFFINCH
DIFFERENCE BETWEEN BREEDING AND WINTER DISTRIBUTION
8 present during breeding season but not during winter
645 present during both seasons
5 present during winter but not during breeding season
E J P U Z
D I N T Y
C H M S X
B G L R W
A F K Q V
Layout of tetrads within a 10 km square.

Brambling

Fringilla montifringilla

RICHARD STEEL

The winter distribution of Bramblings is dictated primarily by the availability of seeds (mast) of beech trees, and flocks leave their breeding grounds in northern Fennoscandia and Russia to roam across Europe in search of an abundant food supply. Their sharp-edged bill, stronger than that of their close relative the Chaffinch, is well adapted for cutting into beechmast (*BTO Winter Atlas*). After exhausting, or failing to find, supplies of beech nuts, some Bramblings move on to occupy a wider range of habitats including open fields and sewage works; observers for this Atlas recorded small numbers, from one to four birds, in gardens in 19 tetrads. Analysis of the Atlas habitat codes shows that most records (37%) were from farmland, of all types, with equal numbers of tetrads (29%) recording human sites and woodland, almost all broad-leaved or mixed, and 4% in scrub. Bramblings were often found with Chaffinches, and several fieldworkers detected them in mixed flocks by their wheezy, buzzing call.

The Atlas map shows that Bramblings were thinly distributed across the county, being reported from 101 tetrads, with a clear concentration towards the north-east of Cheshire. The picture has obviously changed since Bell (1962) observed that 'the records show that flocks are much more likely to be found in the west than the east of the county in most years'. It also seems that the timing of Bramblings' arrival in the county has changed over the years. Coward and Oldham (1900) wrote that they were 'seldom met with in Cheshire before January' and Boyd (1951) said that, in mid-Cheshire, 'they seldom arrive before November and it is often December before the first is seen'. In Bell's experience, it was rare to find any in the east of Cheshire before the New Year (Bell 1962). These comments do not accord with modern findings, with birds in the county typically from October to April.

Their year-to-year fluctuations in distribution and abundance are illustrated by figures for the three winters of this survey. They were reported from 37 tetrads in winter 2004/05; from 55 tetrads in 2005/06; and from 31 tetrads in 2006/07. All the twentieth-century Cheshire ornithologists commented on these variations in Brambling numbers, Coward and Oldham (1900) linking them with the severity of the season, birds being 'fairly plentiful' in hard winters, while Bell (1962) wrote that 'in some years it is very scarce or even absent; in others large flocks are seen'.

According to records submitted to the annual county bird reports, it seems that fewer Bramblings have visited the county over the years. Flocks numbering thousands of birds used to be reported on average every other year, but the last four-figure count was in 1983/84. Flocks at Lyme Park of 250 in 1995/96 and around 300 in 1997/98 were the largest recorded during the 1990s, and from 1999 to 2004 only two flocks in three figures were reported. During this Atlas there were only two flocks of over 50 Bramblings recorded: 250 birds feeding on wildbird seed crops at Broxton (SJ45R/W) in November/December 2005, and 160 in mixed woodland at Cholmondeley (SJ55K) in January 2007.

Although communal roosts are a notable feature of this species' behaviour, only one record of roosting Bramblings was reported during this Atlas, when a small flock of 10 joined Chaffinches at Aston (SJ57P) in winter 2005/06, in rhododendrons beneath mature mixed woodland.

Sponsored by Malcolm Calvert

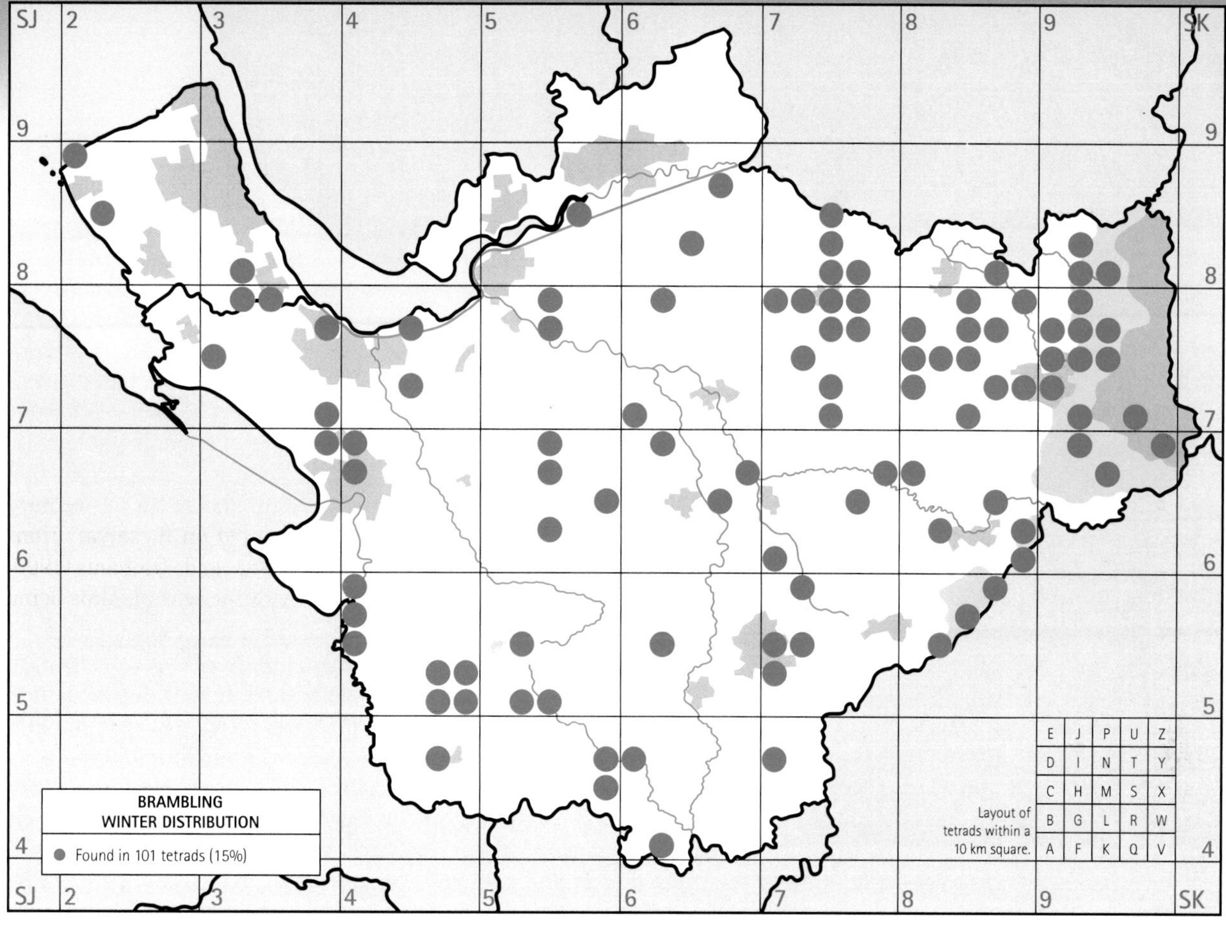
BRAMBLING
WINTER DISTRIBUTION
Found in 101 tetrads (15%)
Layout of tetrads within a 10 km square.
E J P U Z
D I N T Y
C H M S X
B G L R W
A F K Q V
SJ 2 3 4 5 6 7 8 9 SK
9 8 7 6 5 4

Greenfinch

Carduelis chloris

RICHARD STEEL

Greenfinches have expanded their range to fill in most of the gaps in their distribution at the time of our *First Atlas*, across all the agricultural region of southern Cheshire and most of the eastern hills. They were found in an extra 71 tetrads, with 12 losses, a net gain of 59 tetrads to become the eleventh most widespread species, present in 639 tetrads. It was also the eleventh most abundant according to the BTO's analysis of BBS transects, with a breeding population of Cheshire and Wirral in 2004–05 of 49,950 birds (38,170–61,720). This spread in their distribution probably reflects the national rise in population: the index is now 55% up on its low point, around the end of our *First Atlas*. Like most seed-eaters, Greenfinch populations dropped between the mid-1970s and mid-1980s, but their numbers fell much less than those of other species, only by about 20%, probably because they eat a much wider range of foods. The abundance map, as for Goldfinch, shows lower densities of Greenfinches in the more newly colonized areas, with highest numbers in the north and west of the county.

The submitted habitat codes came mainly from human sites (43%) and farmland (34%), with 14% in woodland and 8% in scrub. As many as 27% of the records were from rural human sites (F3) and the surest way to find Greenfinches, on visiting a tetrad, was to go to the edge of a village, next to an overgrown hedgerow. The birds usually give away their presence with their monotonous wheezing calls, and often breed in loose colonies, with several pairs within a small area all sharing the same feeding sites. Adult Greenfinches feed their chicks by regurgitating seeds, with small chicks getting a few invertebrates as well, and in 48 tetrads observers recorded adults taking food to, or faecal sacs from, their nestlings. Nests were recorded in 55 tetrads, a bulky construction usually deep within a hedge or thick shrub such as an evergreen, hawthorn or elder. Family parties with dependent young, accounting for 241 of the tetrads with confirmed breeding, are commonly found around the middle of June. Steve Hind reported birds at Higher Poynton (SJ98L) on 2 July 2006 that were feeding their young on cherries. Mean laying dates are as much as two weeks earlier than 40 years ago, probably driven partly by climate change (Crick & Sparks 1999) and also facilitated by year-round use of gardens for feeding. April is usually the toughest month for Greenfinches, with highest adult mortality as natural food supplies are at their lowest, and provision of extra food for them can make a significant difference to survival and, if the adults are in good condition, allow an early start to the breeding season. Some individuals can be much earlier than the average—I found fledged young in Acton Bridge (SJ67C) on 7 May 2006 whose parents must have started nesting in March—and the products of late broods can still be in juvenile plumage into October or, exceptionally, November, as with a bird ringed in my garden (SJ57K) on 9 November 2005.

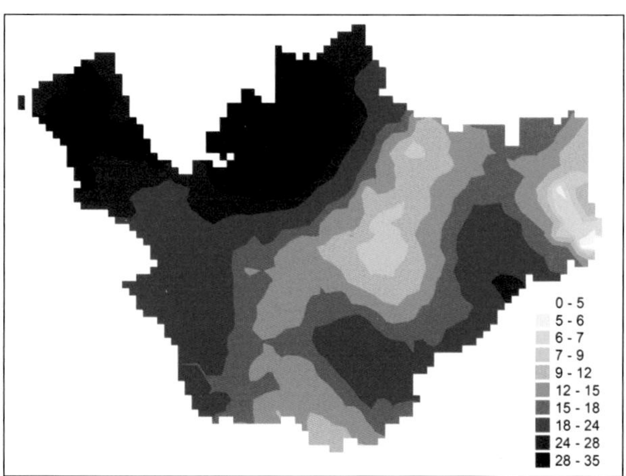

Greenfinch abundance.

Sponsored by Brenda and Michael Arnold

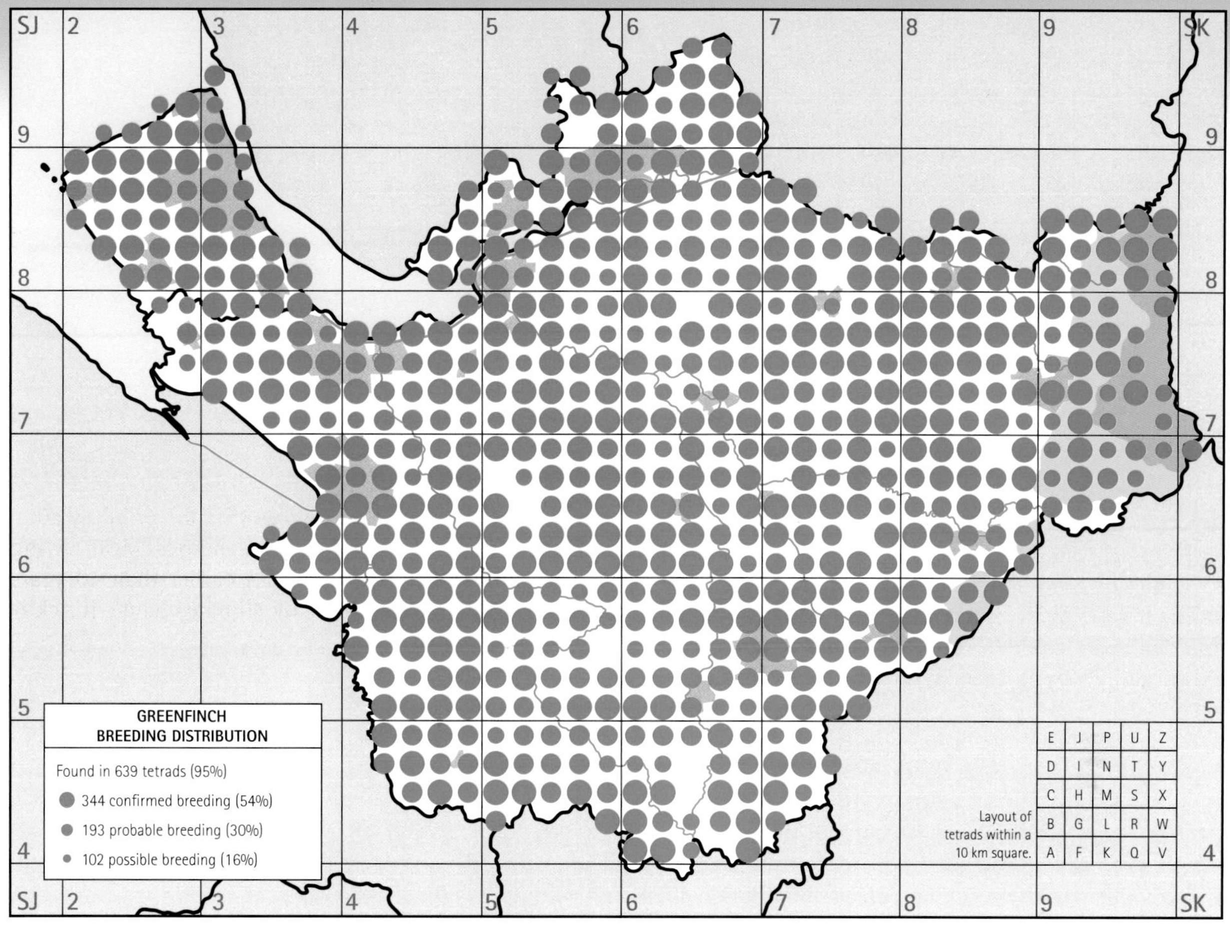
GREENFINCH
BREEDING DISTRIBUTION
Found in 639 tetrads (95%)
344 confirmed breeding (54%)
193 probable breeding (30%)
102 possible breeding (16%)
Layout of tetrads within a 10 km square.
E J P U Z
D I N T Y
C H M S X
B G L R W
A F K Q V
SJ
SK

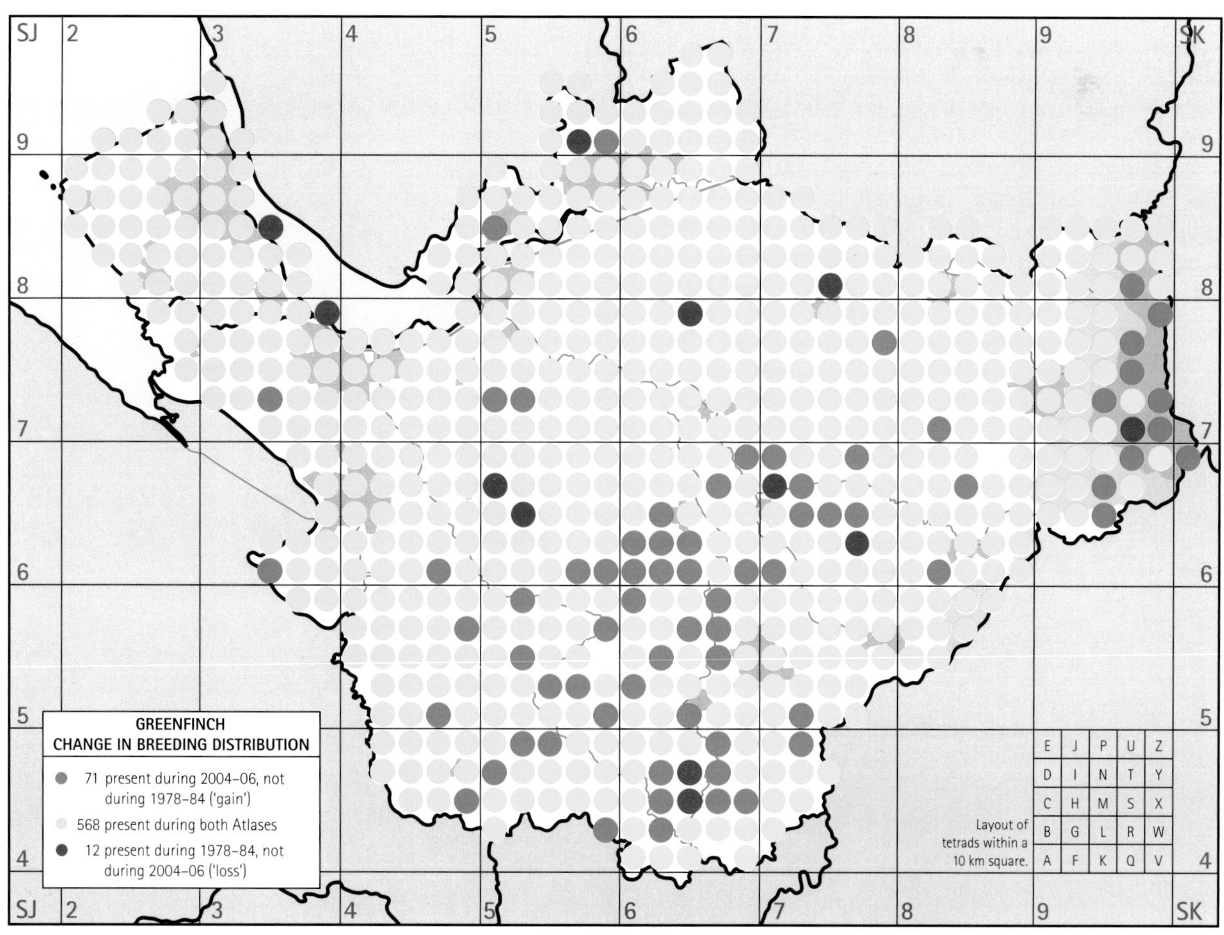
GREENFINCH
CHANGE IN BREEDING DISTRIBUTION
71 present during 2004–06, not during 1978–84 ('gain')
568 present during both Atlases
12 present during 1978–84, not during 2004–06 ('loss')
Layout of tetrads within a 10 km square.
E J P U Z
D I N T Y
C H M S X
B G L R W
A F K Q V
SJ
SK

A century ago, Coward (1910) described the Greenfinch as an abundant resident and partial migrant, and wrote 'in winter, though a few may be met with, it is scarce in most parts of Cheshire'. Migratory parties appeared from the beginning of March, and birds left again in September and October. At some stage they must have substantially shifted from being 'scarce in most parts of Cheshire' to their present status as one of our commonest and most widespread wintering species, but this change was not documented. Bell (1962) agreed that Coward's summary adequately described the Greenfinch's status although Boyd (1951) had called it '... one of the most plentiful birds in the district [around Great Budworth] throughout the year', with flocks of hundreds of Greenfinches noticeable from November to February. Since Coward's time almost two million Greenfinches have been ringed in Britain and Ireland and we now know that most of them are sedentary or make short movements up to 20 km, which might not be much farther than their daily foraging or roosting distances. Fewer than one-in-five birds moves more than 20 km, a clear difference from one hundred years ago. Some Norwegian birds cross to Britain, although few penetrate beyond the east coast, but some British birds move west or south-west for the winter and augment our resident population (*Migration Atlas*).

RICHARD STEEL

This Atlas survey shows Greenfinch to be the fourteenth most widespread species in winter in the county. The map shows them present in 16 tetrads in which they were not recorded during the breeding season, but they were missing from 38, a net loss of 22 tetrads: these were scattered across the county and perhaps attributable to birds joining flocks outside the tetrad. They are scarce in the uplands (*BTO Winter Atlas*) and moved out of seven of the tetrads above 250 m, but on the other hand birds were found in four other high-altitude tetrads where they had not bred. Their recorded distribution across habitats was almost identical to the breeding season: human sites (45%), farmland (34%), woodland (14%) and scrub (8%). Their winter diet is seeds, especially those at the larger end of the size range such as rose-hips, brambles and yew berries. In gardens they can dominate feeders and bird tables providing peanuts and sunflower seeds.

Most Greenfinches in winter join flocks, although many records were just of one or two birds, and the median count was three birds. Fieldworkers logged 24 feeding flocks of 50 or more, including seven flocks of 150 or more, with a maximum of 150–200 birds estimated by Chris Hancock at Whitley Reed (SJ68L). Communal roosts are a regular feature of Greenfinch behaviour in winter, but they were reported from only 16 tetrads. Three of them had flocks estimated larger than 100 birds, all in urban situations, found by Brian Martin in a holly tree in Warrington cemetery and by Colin Lythgoe in laurels in two different sites on either side of Crewe. Others were noted in yew, poplar and rhododendron and they will use any suitable bush or tree that provides sufficient shelter from wind and rain (Newton 1972).

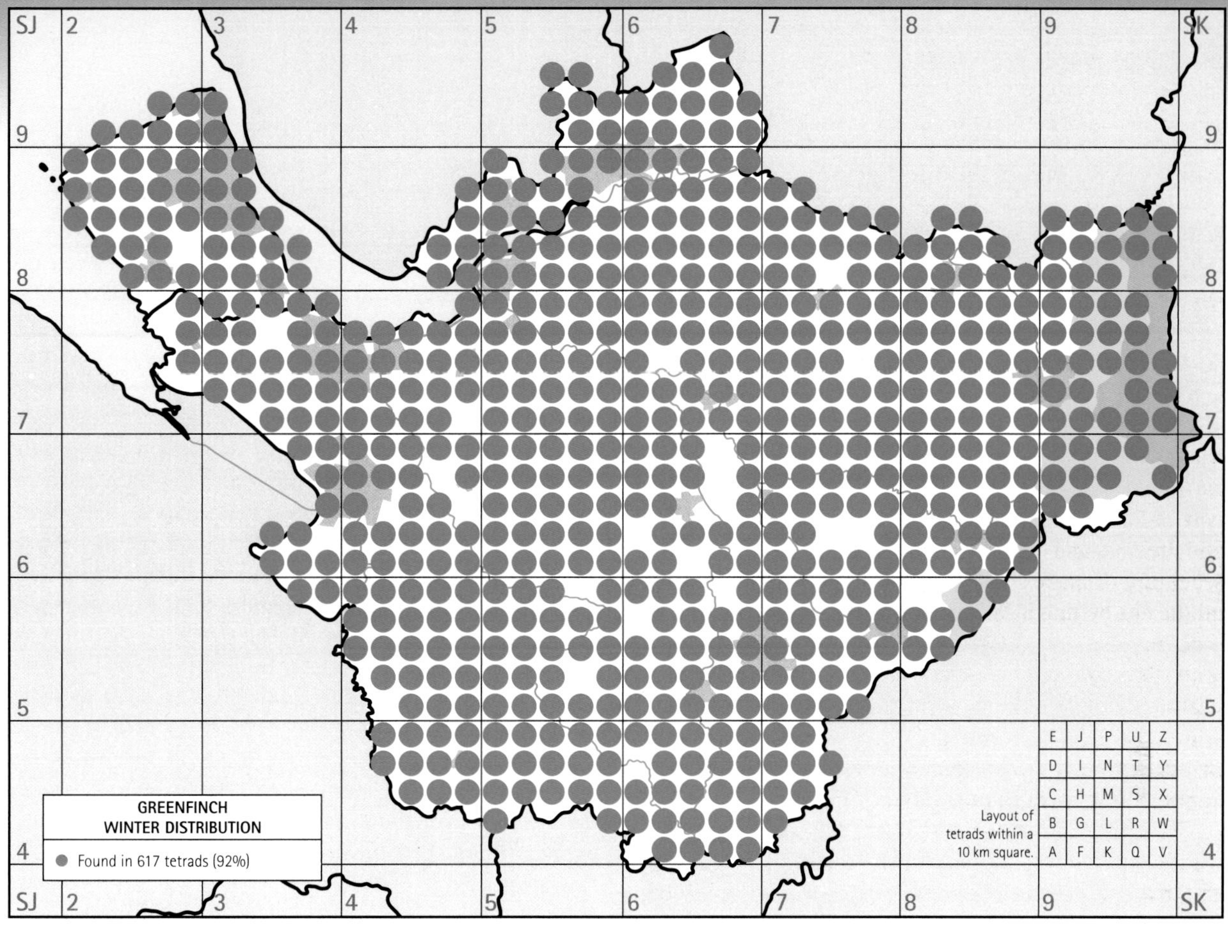
SJ
SK
2
3
4
5
6
7
8
9
GREENFINCH
WINTER DISTRIBUTION
Found in 617 tetrads (92%)
E J P U Z
D I N T Y
C H M S X
B G L R W
A F K Q V
Layout of tetrads within a 10 km square.

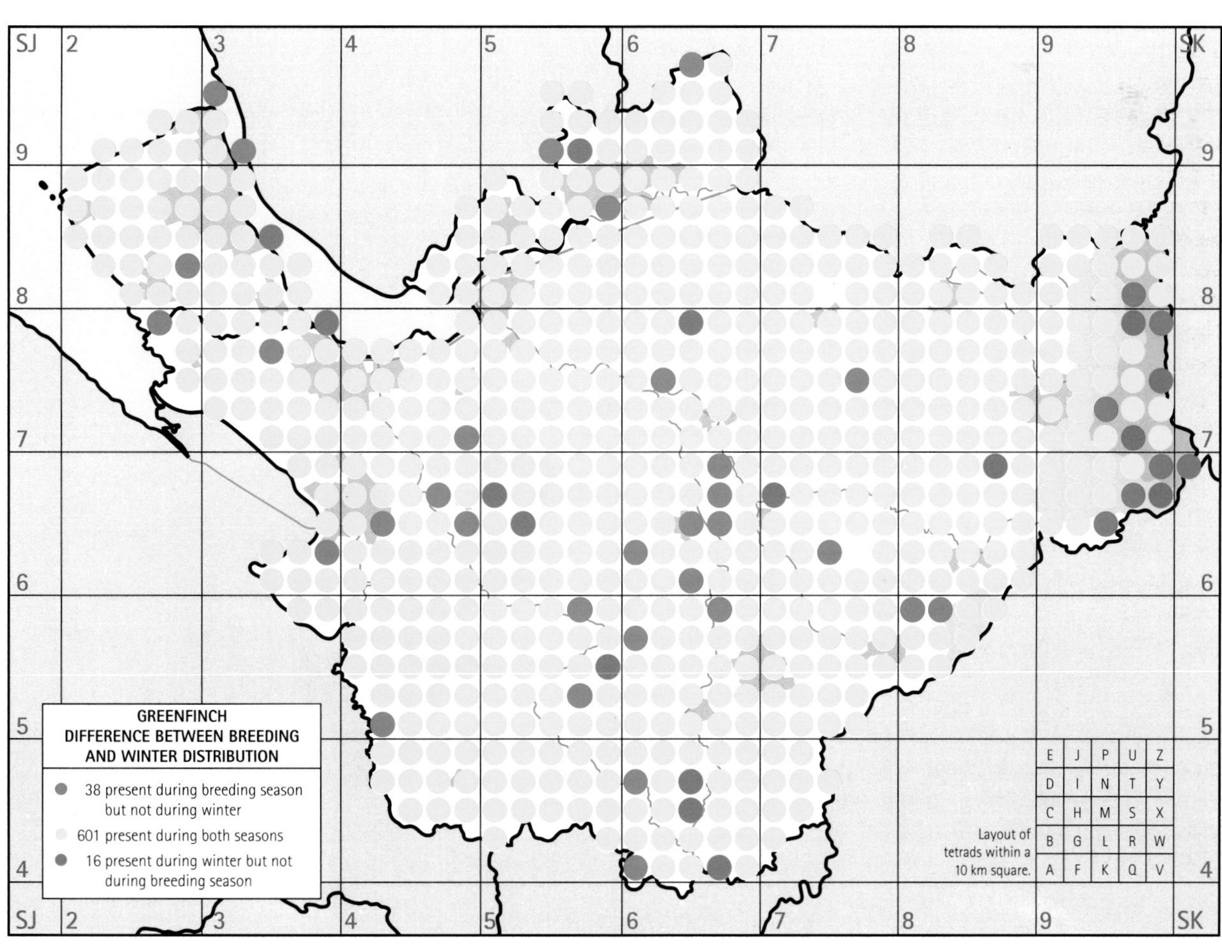
SJ
SK
2
3
4
5
6
7
8
9
GREENFINCH
DIFFERENCE BETWEEN BREEDING AND WINTER DISTRIBUTION
38 present during breeding season but not during winter
601 present during both seasons
16 present during winter but not during breeding season
E J P U Z
D I N T Y
C H M S X
B G L R W
A F K Q V
Layout of tetrads within a 10 km square.

Goldfinch

Carduelis carduelis

The Goldfinch has continued to increase and spread since our *First Atlas* and is now the thirteenth most widespread breeding species in Cheshire and Wirral. Compared to twenty years ago, they are present in 92 new tetrads, with just 14 losses, a net gain of 78 tetrads. They have filled in almost all of the breaks in their distribution in central southern Cheshire and there are now no significant gaps. The abundance map, however, indicates relatively few birds in many of these newly colonized areas. There is a significant cline in their density, with totals of 100 birds per tetrad north-west of a line from Chester to Warrington, decreasing to figures of fewer than 15 birds per tetrad in patches of southern Cheshire and the eastern hills. The average across the whole county is 48 birds per tetrad, and the analysis of BBS transects shows that this is our seventeenth most numerous species, with a breeding population of Cheshire and Wirral in 2004–05 of 30,440 birds (21,640–39,240).

The Goldfinch's fortunes have undergone massive changes over the last 30 years. A rapid decline in population from the mid-1970s to mid-1980s, in parallel with many other seed-eaters, caused them to be placed on the Amber List of species of conservation concern, but numbers have recovered and their status has returned to 'green'; the national index in 2004 was 68% up on 20 years before, although still somewhat lower than at the beginning of our *First Atlas* fieldwork in 1978. These population changes can be explained almost entirely by changes in annual survival rates, probably arising from a reduction in the availability of weed seeds due to agricultural intensification, and subsequent increased use of other food sources such as garden bird tables (Siriwardena *et al.* 1999). The warmer weather of the last two decades has probably also helped this partial migrant to thrive.

Newly fledged chicks can be very obvious when they beg from their parents, and accounted for 214 of the 304 confirmed breeding records. Their nesting season can extend from April to August, allowing plenty of time for two broods, and occasionally three: a very recently fledged chick was being fed by parents in my garden (SJ57K) on 1 September 2006. Some of their nests are very well concealed, often precariously placed near to the end of a long branch, but others can be obvious, especially in their favourite specimen trees such as flowering cherry or laburnum. Goldfinch can be one of the commonest species nowadays in suburbia as long as there are some not-too-tidy areas providing seeds of their preferred food-plants, especially dandelions and groundsels early in their breeding season, with burdocks and thistles for later broods. They feed their chicks with regurgitated seeds and a few small caterpillars. This is mainly a bird of farmland (41% of habitat records) and human sites (36%), with fewer in woodland (11%) or scrub (10%).

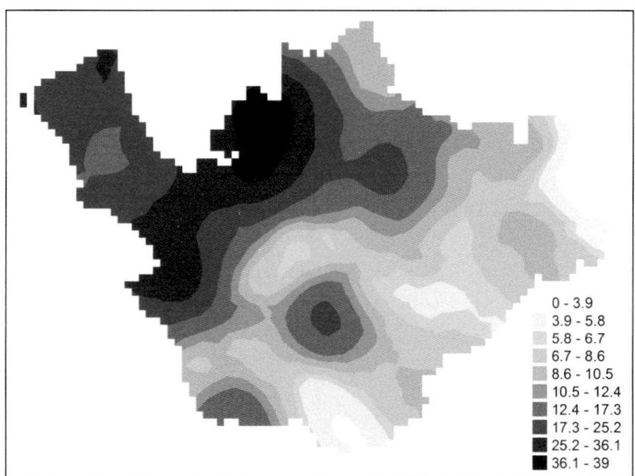

Goldfinch abundance.

Sponsored by Ray and Janet Thorp

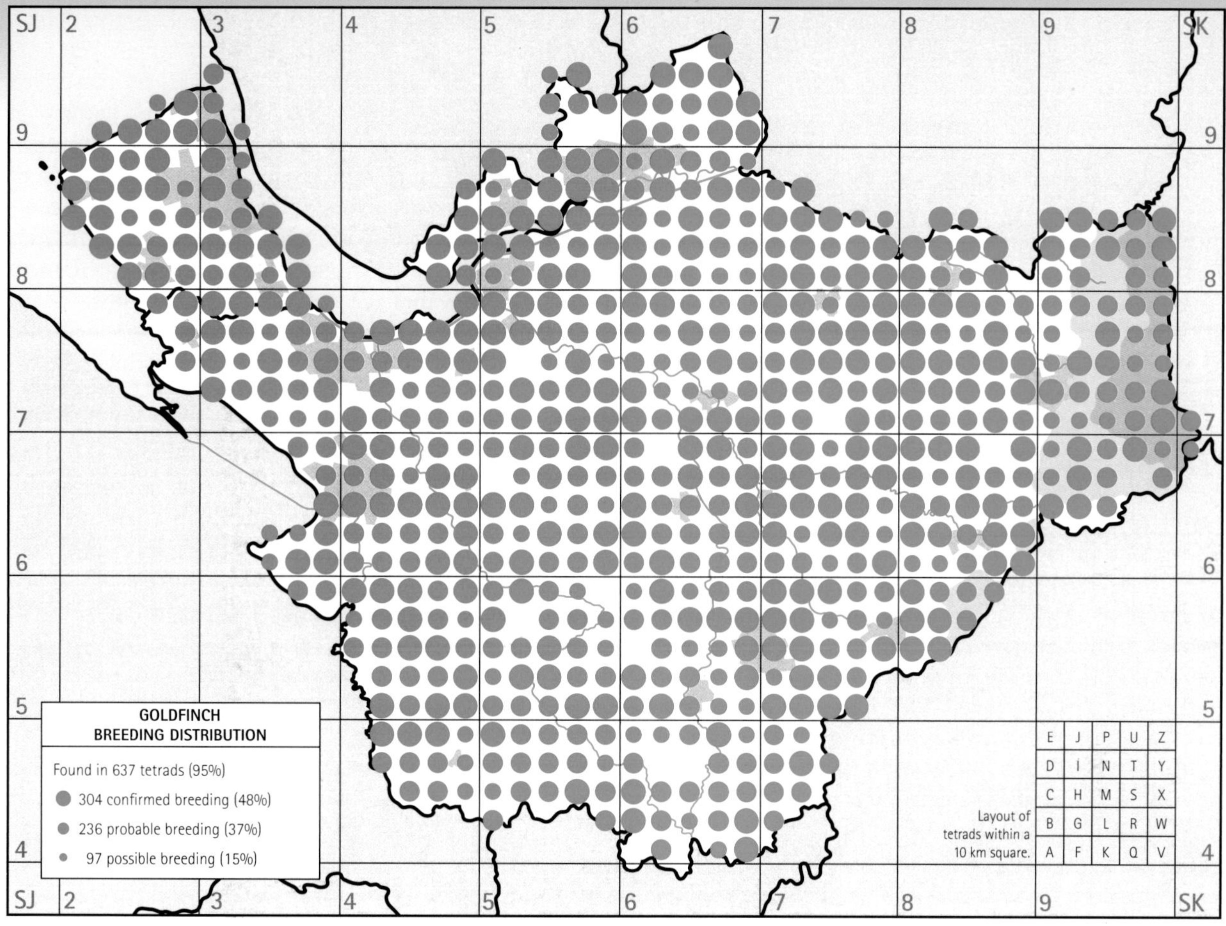
GOLDFINCH
BREEDING DISTRIBUTION
Found in 637 tetrads (95%)
304 confirmed breeding (48%)
236 probable breeding (37%)
97 possible breeding (15%)
Layout of tetrads within a 10 km square.
SJ
SK

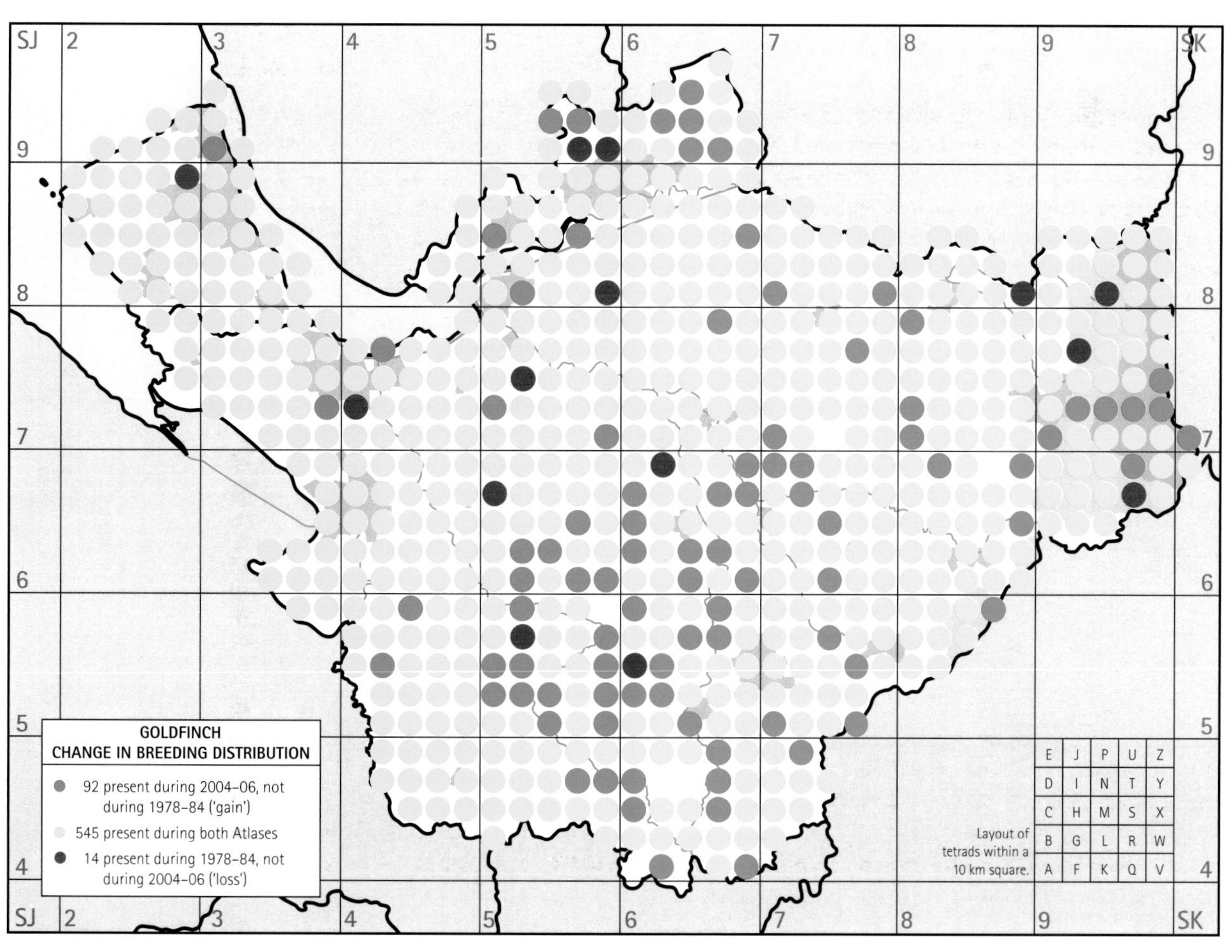
GOLDFINCH
CHANGE IN BREEDING DISTRIBUTION
92 present during 2004–06, not during 1978–84 ('gain')
545 present during both Atlases
14 present during 1978–84, not during 2004–06 ('loss')
Layout of tetrads within a 10 km square.
SJ
SK

Goldfinches were somewhat less widespread in winter than during the breeding season, quitting some of their areas of lowest breeding density, including withdrawing from some of the highest altitudes. There is little difference in habitat occupation between the breeding and winter seasons. Most wintering birds were in farmland (41% of habitat records) and human sites (32%) with an increase in those in woodland (17%) and fewer in scrub (8%). A few birds were reported in seed-rich areas of semi-natural grassland and marsh. A total of 567 tetrads was used in both seasons, with 22 newly occupied in winter and 70 with breeding season presence but birds not found in winter. The empty tetrads are probably because birds have either migrated or joined local flocks. Although many British Goldfinches stay on or near their breeding grounds, most birds leave in the autumn to winter as far south as Iberia and Morocco (*Migration Atlas*). There have been fewer overseas recoveries of ringed birds in recent years, but this could be because hunting has decreased on the continent and this finding has not been tested statistically; the great rise in numbers wintering in the county suggests that the proportion of emigrants has fallen, however, perhaps driven by climate change.

Goldfinches form sizeable flocks, especially early in winter when there are copious supplies of their favoured foods, including thistles, burdocks and teasels. Some birds join Lesser Redpolls and Siskins feeding in alders and birches, but mostly they form single-species flocks to feed on plants where their long, thin bill allows them to exploit seeds not available to other birds; indeed, those able to perform the difficult task of extracting teasel seeds are mostly male Goldfinches that have slightly longer bills than females (*BTO Winter Atlas*). The median flock size reported by Atlas fieldworkers was six birds, but there were 15 flocks of 50 or more including two different groups of 150 birds, but the largest was an estimated 280 birds found by Andy Ankers on Ince Marshes (SJ47T). Goldfinches also roost communally and nocturnal roosts were reported in four tetrads, with the largest of 50 birds in a roadside hazel bush near Bostock Green (SJ66U).

The habit of visiting gardens was almost unknown twenty years ago (*BTO Winter Atlas*) but has become common since then. Thelma Sykes in 1988 described how Goldfinches were attracted to her garden at Saughall, near Chester to drink in warm, dry weather, and elsewhere, birds entered gardens to take seeds of ornamental thistles, teasel, lavender, cornflower, forget-me-not, Mexican aster, pansy and evening-primrose (Glue 1996). Some Goldfinches experimented with hanging on peanut feeders and eating sunflower seeds but the real breakthrough in garden feeding came with the widespread provision of niger seed, which closely approximates their natural food in size but is even more nutritious, containing some 40% of fat and 18% protein. Not only has this changed behaviour enabled many people to enjoy watching Goldfinches, but it may well have helped the species' overwinter survival and assisted an earlier start to the breeding season. Just one (human) lifetime ago, they were scarce birds such that Boyd, on 12 November 1937, wrote 'in much of Cheshire it is still almost an event' to see one, and that they were seldom found in large flocks as in some parts of England (Boyd 1946).

PHIL JONES

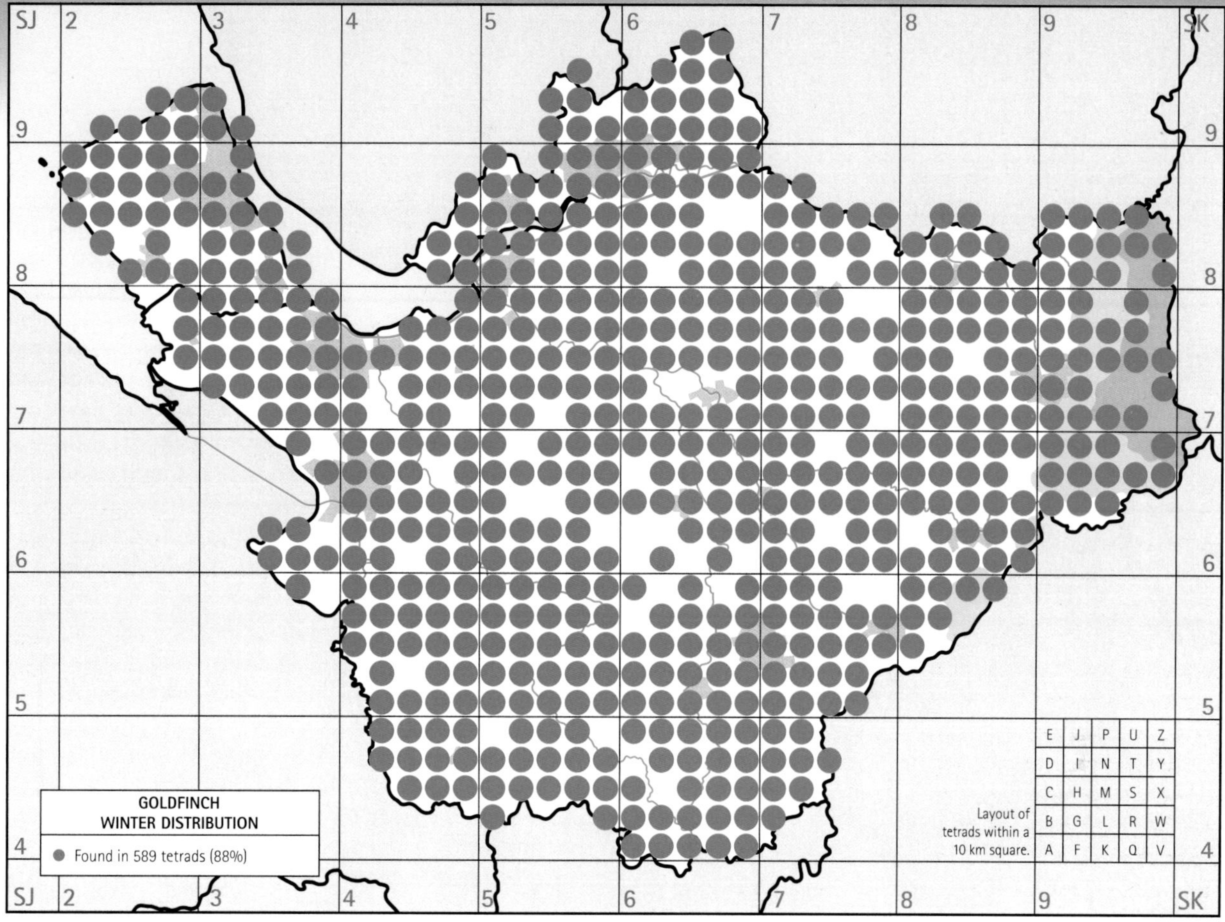
SJ
2
3
4
5
6
7
8
9
SK
GOLDFINCH
WINTER DISTRIBUTION
Found in 589 tetrads (88%)
Layout of
tetrads within a
10 km square.
E J P U Z
D I N T Y
C H M S X
B G L R W
A F K Q V

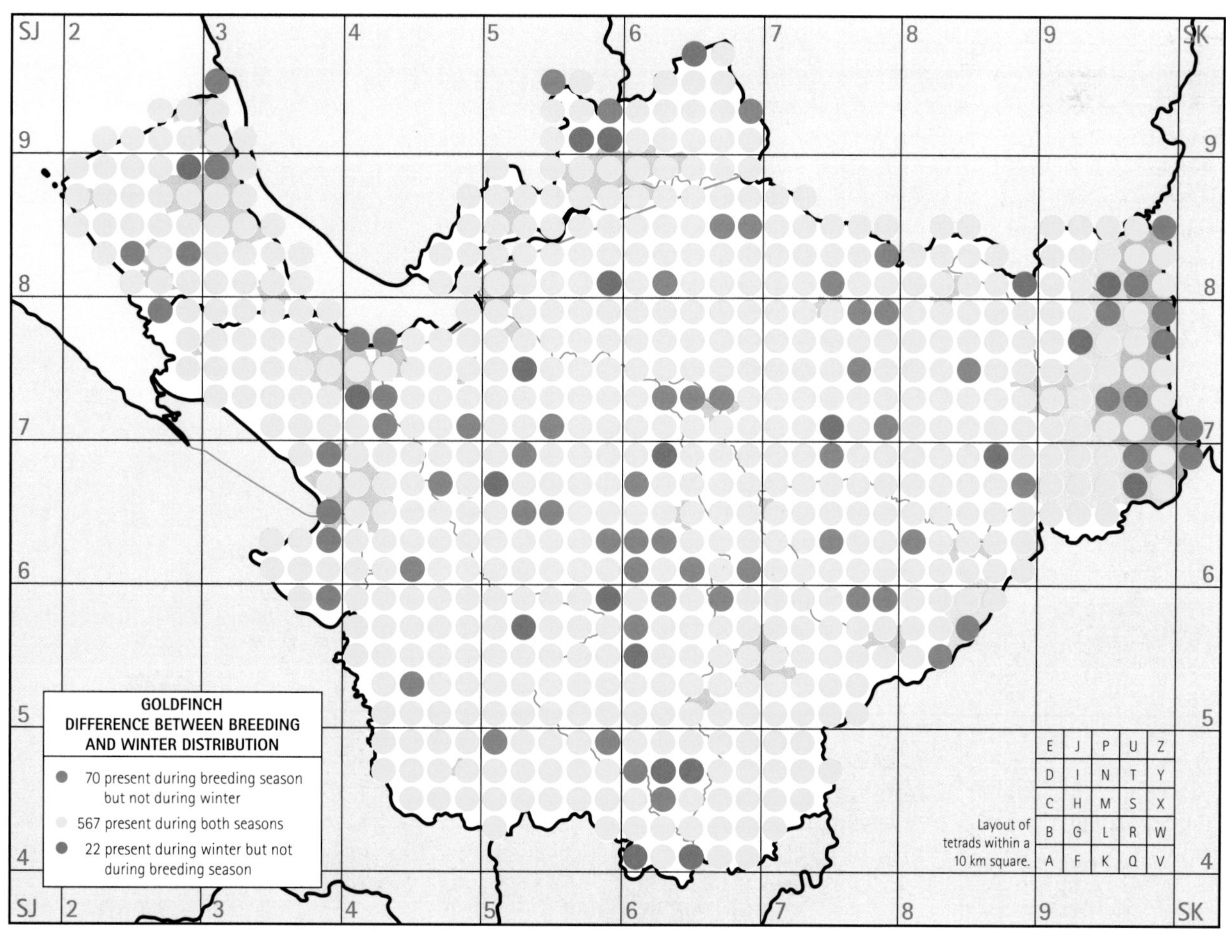
SJ
2
3
4
5
6
7
8
9
SK
GOLDFINCH
DIFFERENCE BETWEEN BREEDING
AND WINTER DISTRIBUTION
70 present during breeding season but not during winter
567 present during both seasons
22 present during winter but not during breeding season
Layout of
tetrads within a
10 km square.
E J P U Z
D I N T Y
C H M S X
B G L R W
A F K Q V

Siskin

Carduelis spinus

REN HATHWAY

The entire life cycle of this woodland finch is dictated by tree seeds. When seeds are abundant, Siskins can breed as early as February; in other years they delay until April or May. Early chicks are fed on the seeds of opening spruce *picea* cones, whereas later broods are reared on seeds from pine cones, with other seeds and insects. Their population may well vary considerably from year to year, as they usually rear two broods when breeding starts early, and only one in other years.

Their breeding range has expanded greatly in Britain (*BTO Second Atlas*), attributed to maturing of conifer forests, and this expansion has included Cheshire. Breeding was first proven in Delamere Forest in 1962 and 1964, with a poorly documented record in Wirral in 1976, but there were no breeding records during our *First Atlas* in 1978–84. The annual county bird reports show that observers mostly concentrate on any large flocks, but they contain sporadic records of birds in 'summer' with breeding proven in 1990, when a pair were feeding young in Lyme Park on 4 June. From then on, records that would merit a breeding status code came from a gradually increasing number of sites, especially Macclesfield Forest, Lyme Park and Alderley Park, with the annual county reports noting birds singing in most years, seen carrying nesting material twice and 'breeding suspected' once. There was no more confirmation of breeding until this Atlas started in 2004, however, but this is a tricky species in which to prove breeding and it is difficult to establish its true status in the county. Many males sing on passage, from late winter onwards, sometimes even performing their 'butterfly' display flight on bright spring mornings, and it can be problematical to separate locally breeding birds from Siskins on their way to breed in Scotland; their wide variability in timing of breeding from year to year further complicates this.

Although most submitted habitat codes were broadleaved or mixed woodland, the Atlas map shows a clear correlation with coniferous woodland, with occupied tetrads in Delamere and Macclesfield Forests, another group of tetrads around Wilmslow and a few scattered records elsewhere. Four tetrads furnished proof of breeding, three of them with observers in gardens seeing recently fledged juveniles being fed by their parents, two of them in May 2004 and the third in 2006. The fourth record comes from 2005 when Sheila Blamire had the good fortune to be able to stand on a slope above Wildboarclough (SJ96U) and look down into a nest in the top of a small pine only 3–4 m tall, where she saw the female Siskin regurgitating food for the chicks whilst the male called nearby.

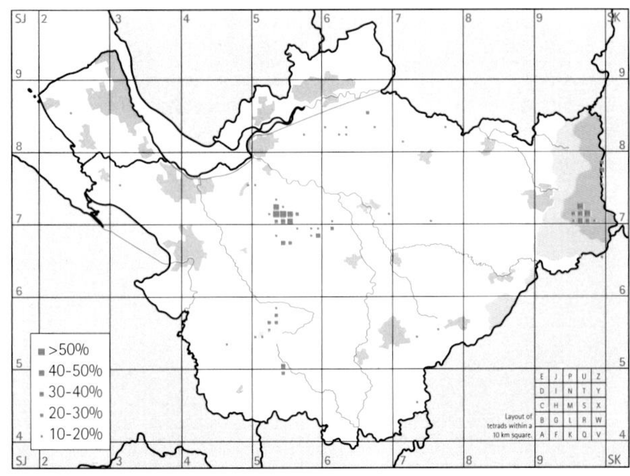

Coniferous woodland land cover.

Sponsored by David Simmons

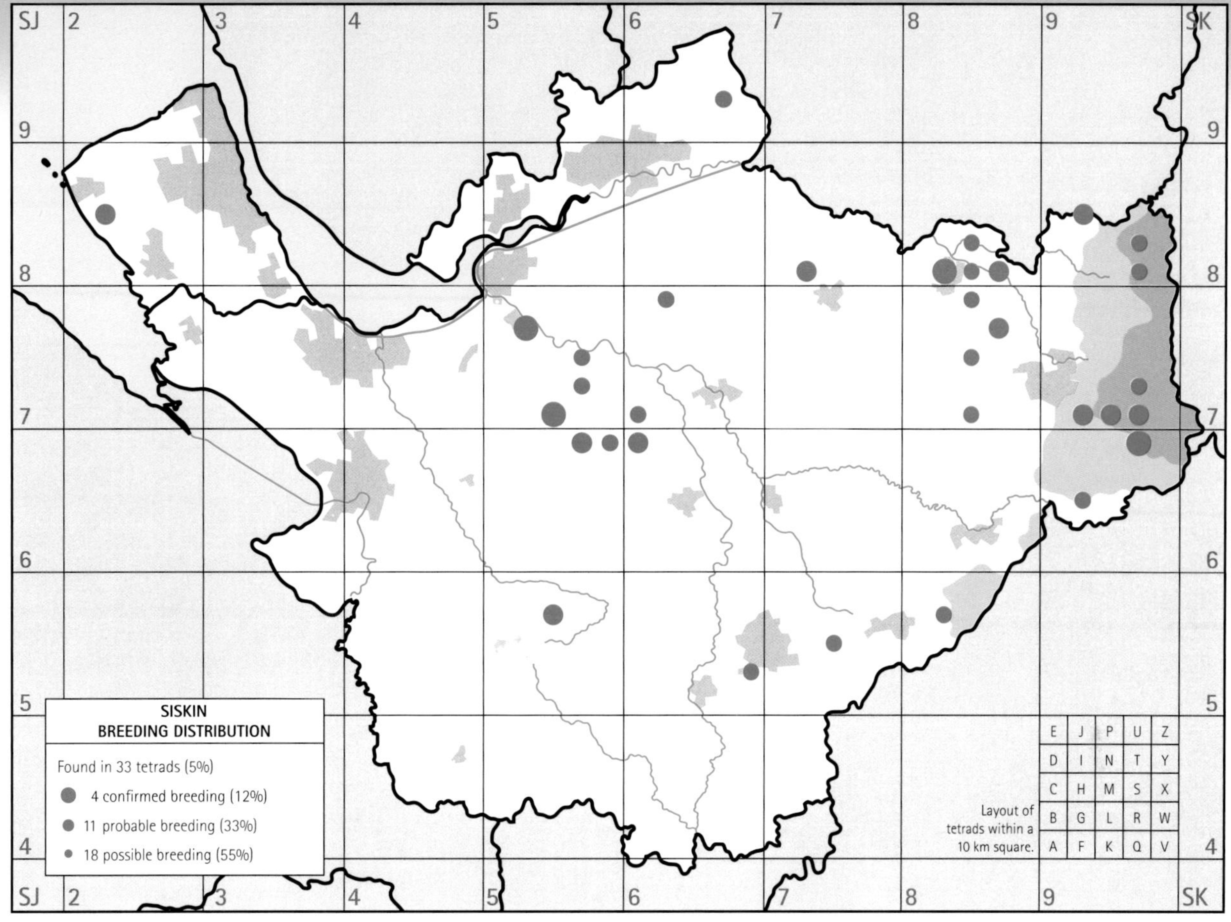
SISKIN
BREEDING DISTRIBUTION
Found in 33 tetrads (5%)
4 confirmed breeding (12%)
11 probable breeding (33%)
18 possible breeding (55%)
Layout of tetrads within a 10 km square.
E J P U Z
D I N T Y
C H M S X
B G L R W
A F K Q V
SJ
SK

RICHARD STEEL

The biennial variation in the natural seed-crop means that in alternate years Siskins tend to stay in woodland, often in quite large flocks and usually in the tops of the trees. In these years many birds move north to their breeding grounds without visiting gardens and feeding stations. Some birders describe this as 'a bad year for Siskins', but it is actually the opposite: natural feeding conditions were so good for the species that they had no need of artificially provided food, and migrated north to breed earlier than normal.

This alternate-year pattern is shown well in the records for this Atlas, and parallels that found for Lesser Redpoll, another finch that feeds on tree seeds; indeed the two species were often found together, especially in waterside alders and birches. In the winters 2004/05 and 2006/07 Siskins were recorded in 82 and 90 tetrads, whereas in the middle winter, 2005/06, they were found in more than twice as many, 189 tetrads. Evidence for the switch between natural food and bird feeders comes from the habitat codes submitted for this Atlas. In 2004/05 and 2006/07, most of the habitat records (51%) were from woodland, with 33% from human sites; in 2005/06, their habitat choice was reversed, with 39% in woodland and 53% of records in human sites.

Siskins are nearly always found in flocks. Of the 266 counts submitted, half of them were of 10 birds or more, and eight tetrads recorded flocks of 100 or more. As well as being far more widespread in 2005/06, far more Siskins were counted in the middle winter, again more in total than the other two winters put together.

Many of the county's ringers have concentrated on this species, the results showing that there are two populations of Siskins wintering here, from breeding areas in continental Europe and in Scotland. These different groups appear to intermingle and are indistinguishable in the field, or in the hand. It is not known where our local breeding birds spend the winter.

Although Siskins are now much more numerous, the species' behaviour has obviously not changed much

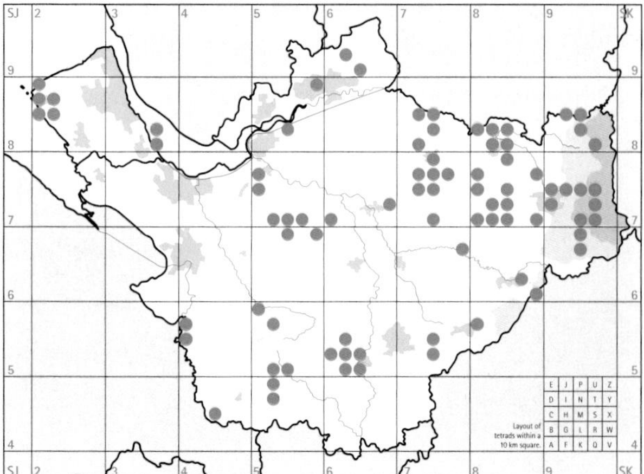

Siskin in winter 2004/05.

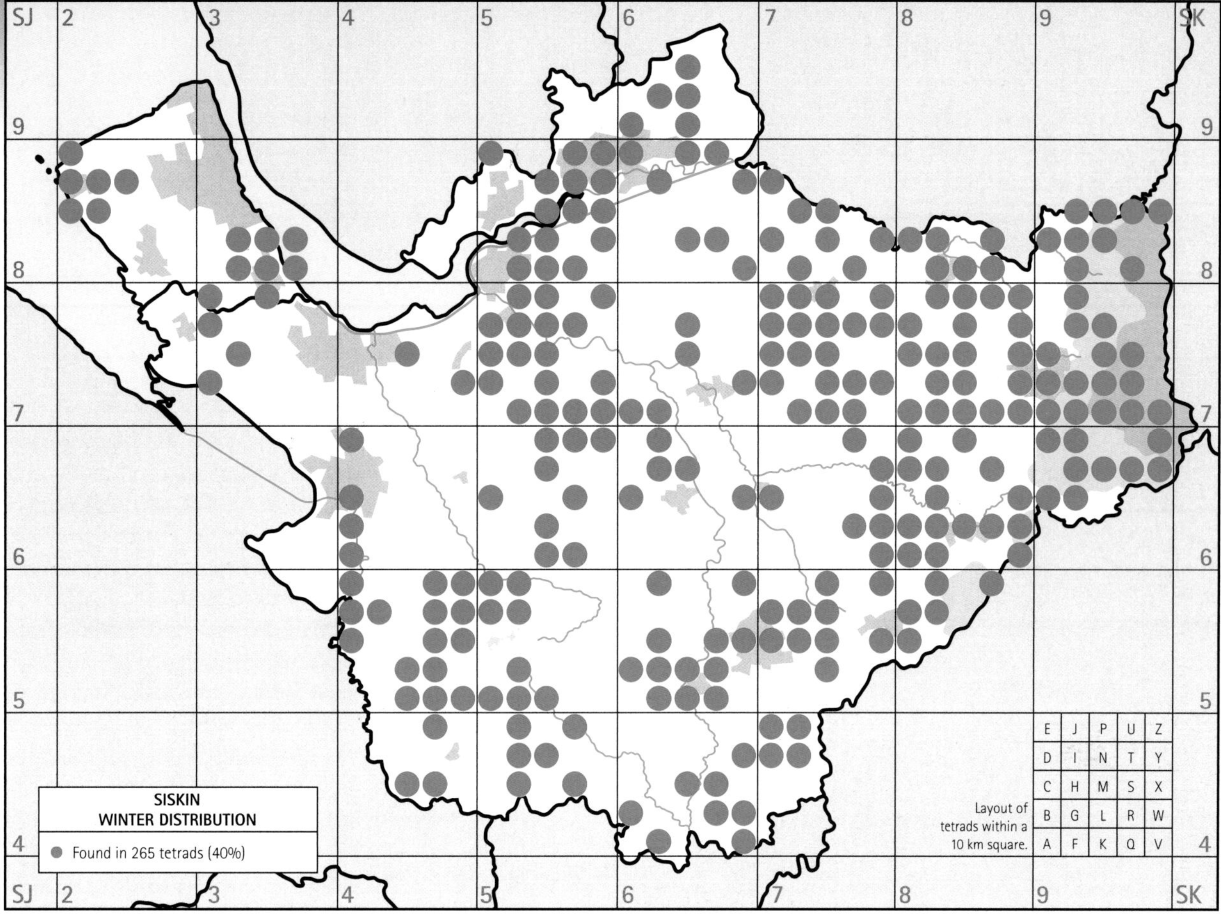

in more than a century. Coward (1910) wrote that the 'Siskin is only known in Cheshire as a winter visitor, sometimes occurring in considerable numbers, but in some seasons being scarce or absent ... almost invariably met with in compact flocks in alders and birches, feeding upon the seeds', and fifty years later, Bell (1962) repeated this statement of their status. The annual county bird reports from 1964 on, however, record no years when Siskins were absent. The number of reports, and of birds, increased considerably from the 1970s as Siskins adopted a new habit of visiting gardens and feeding on peanuts, with most birds now preferring niger seed when it is on offer.

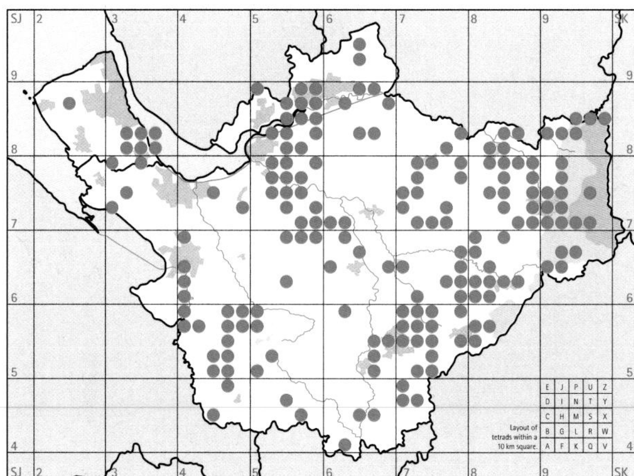

Siskin in winter 2005/06.

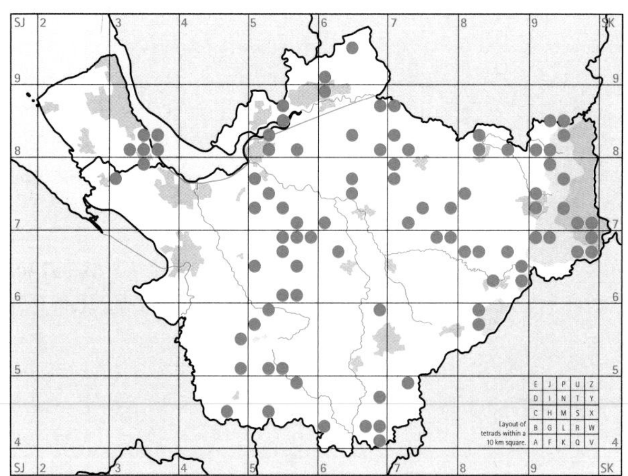

Siskin in winter 2006/07.

Linnet

Carduelis cannabina

This survey shows that breeding season Linnets were recorded in 163 fewer tetrads than during our *First Atlas*. There are some areas where it is still almost ubiquitous, notably the western half of Wirral (and this is one of the few breeding species able to eke out an existence on Hilbre) and a broad swathe from Stanlow to Warrington. The most concentrated losses, evident from the 'change' map, are in the most intensely agricultural areas in the south of the county. Linnets have no problem breeding in urban or industrial sites, provided that there are some suitably weedy areas.

Linnet was one of the first species to suffer from changed agricultural practice from the 1960s onwards, perhaps because their favoured foods, small weed seeds, were among the earliest to be hit by modern herbicides. The national breeding population was already dropping when our *First Atlas* started in 1978, and fell by almost 40% during the seven years of that survey (1978–84) but the population has largely stabilized since then, with the decline arrested as some birds learned to feed on oilseed rape as the seeds ripened during the second half of their breeding season (Moorcroft *et al.* 2006). Their national population index was some 20% lower in 2004 than in 1984. Although the Linnet population has dropped, their distribution has not noticeably contracted at the 10 km square scale, indicating that they remain widespread but at lower density (Fuller *et al.* 1995). Despite their decline, Linnets still make it into the top twenty most abundant passerines in Cheshire and Wirral. The BTO BBS analysis gives an estimate for the breeding population of the county in 2004–05 of 17,830 birds (with wide confidence limits of 9,340–26,330), corresponding to an average of about 52 birds per tetrad with confirmed or probable breeding, or 43 birds per tetrad in which the species was recorded.

Adult birds feed themselves on small weed seeds, and regurgitate the contents of their crops for their chicks. Dandelions are the dominant food for chicks of early broods, with rape assuming key importance from mid-June onwards. Although there is far less rape grown in Cheshire and Wirral than in the arable east of England, Linnets will fly long distances from their nest, foraging flocks moving as far as 3 km to find suitable food. Their long breeding season, from April to the end of August, allows some birds to raise as many as three broods. They nest semi-colonially, especially in gorse, hawthorn or other dense scrub, and each pair defends a small area around the nest, but they do not keep to a feeding territory and breeding birds gather together to feed in flocks. More than two-thirds (68%) of the habitat codes were farmland, mostly grassland, with 3% semi-natural grassland, 17% scrub and 7% human sites.

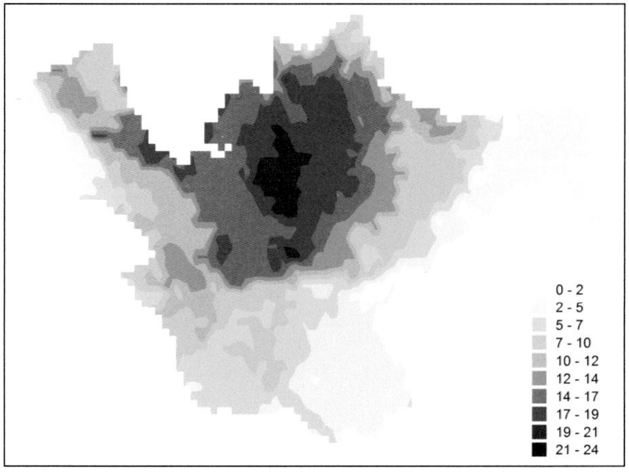

Linnet abundance.

Sponsored by Hilbre Observatory and Ringing Station

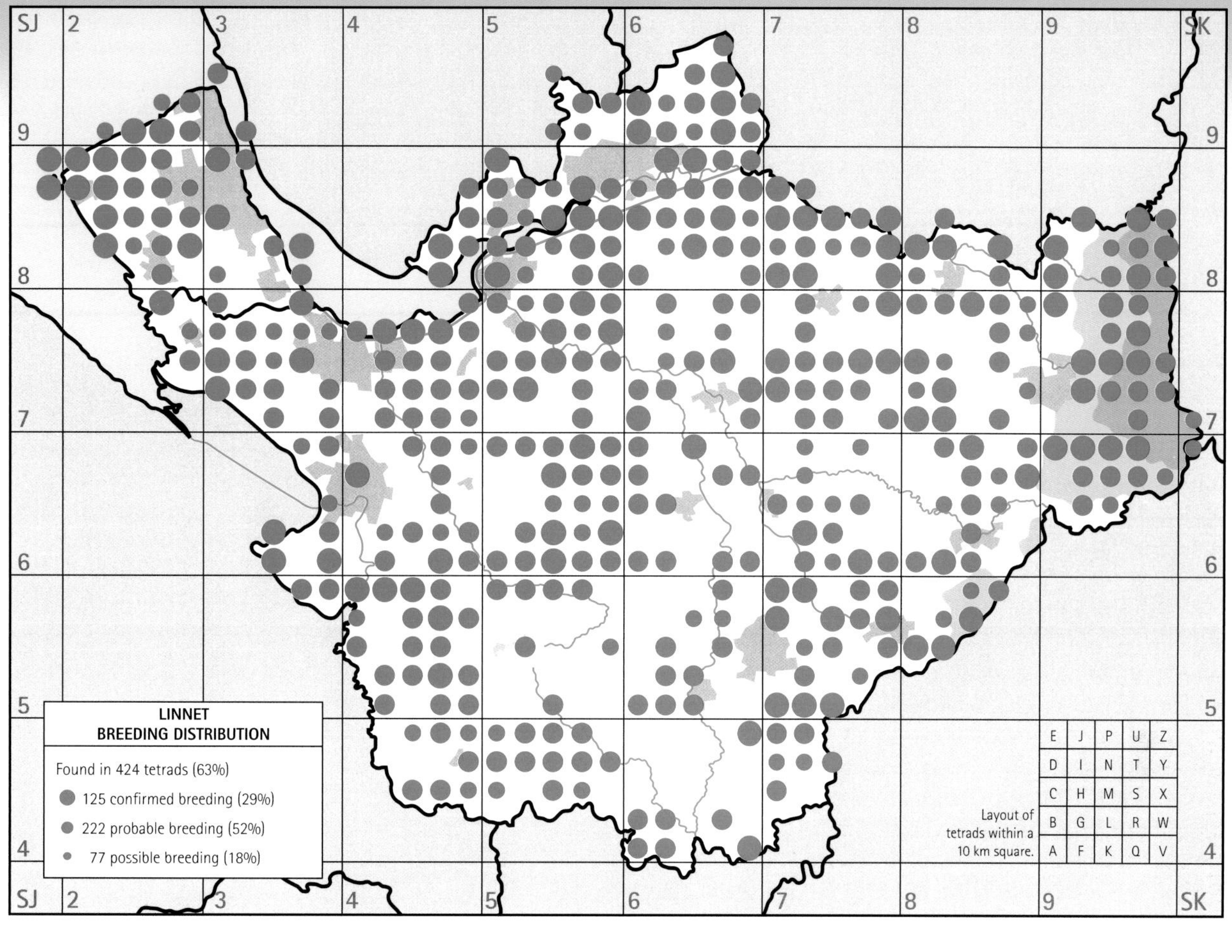

SJ
2
3
4
5
6
7
8
9
SK
LINNET
BREEDING DISTRIBUTION
Found in 424 tetrads (63%)
125 confirmed breeding (29%)
222 probable breeding (52%)
77 possible breeding (18%)
E J P U Z
D I N T Y
C H M S X
B G L R W
A F K Q V
Layout of tetrads within a 10 km square.

SJ
2
3
4
5
6
7
8
9
SK
LINNET
CHANGE IN BREEDING DISTRIBUTION
41 present during 2004–06, not during 1978–84 ('gain')
383 present during both Atlases
202 present during 1978–84, not during 2004–06 ('loss')
E J P U Z
D I N T Y
C H M S X
B G L R W
A F K Q V
Layout of tetrads within a 10 km square.

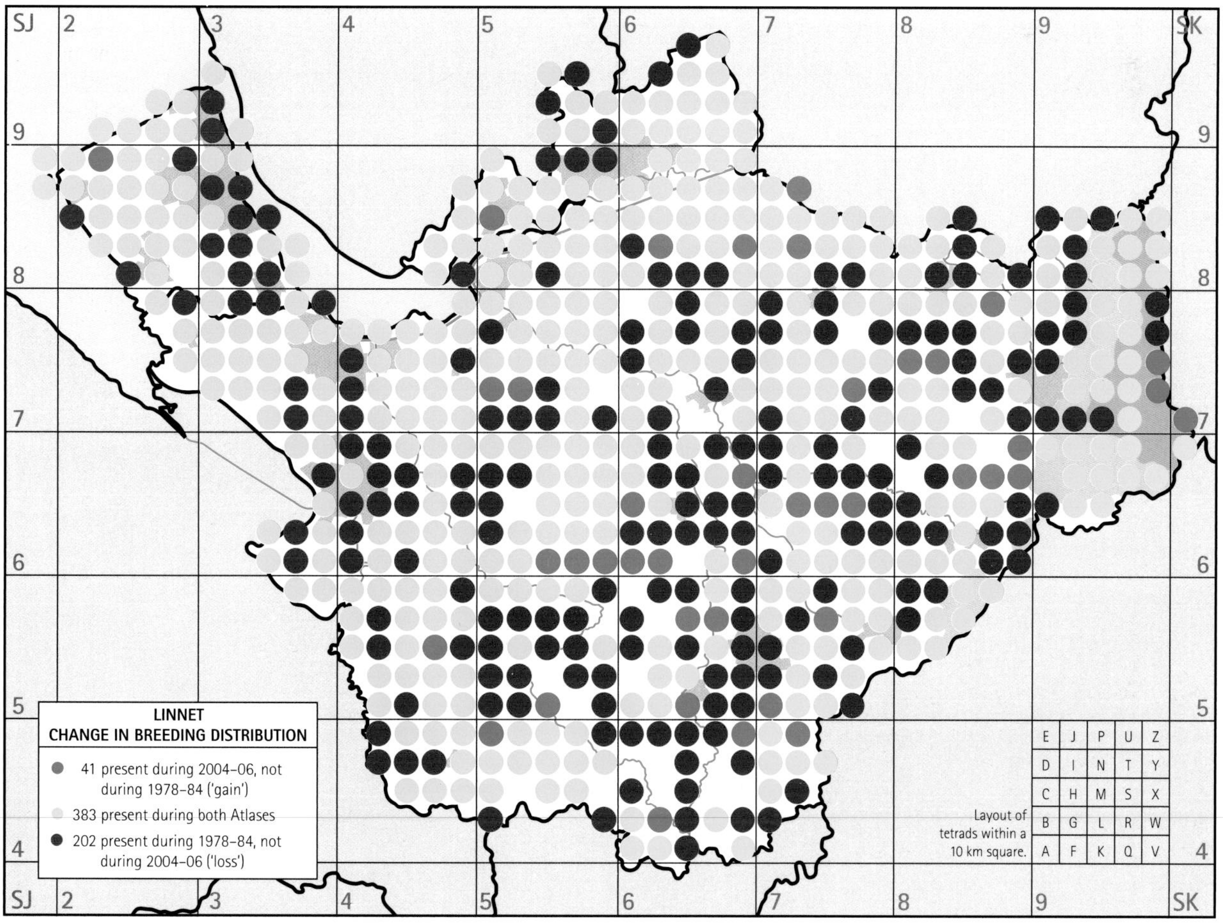

The winter map shows Linnets found in only about half of the number of tetrads compared to their breeding distribution, with a clear contraction in range in the east of the county including only two squares above 150 m in altitude. A marked absence from all areas of higher ground was noted in the *BTO Winter Atlas*, and it is not clear if the birds that breed there undertake altitudinal migration or if it is these birds that preferentially move out of Britain, because Linnets are classic partial migrants. Some British birds remain in winter—apparently an increasing proportion as our winter weather ameliorates—while others move south to winter in a narrow band along the west coast of France, or in Spain (*Migration Atlas*).

Linnets congregate in seed-rich habitats including, during this survey, stubble fields, including weedy maize stubble, game cover, set-aside farmland, derelict industrial land and salt-marshes. The submitted habitat codes show an even greater proportion on farmland (77%) than in the breeding season, with the figure for stubble (14%) higher than most other species. The main other habitats used were scrub (9%), human sites (5%) and semi-natural grassland (4%).

They are gregarious birds at all times of year but especially gather into some large flocks in winter. Eleven tetrads held a flock of 100 or more Linnets, with the largest being 420 birds noted by Colin Lythgoe in SJ74D, feeding in a seeding area of game cover, which conveniently flew onto overhead wires to be counted! They are often found in the same areas as other seed-eaters but seem to keep separate: if disturbed, other species tend to head for the nearest cover whilst the Linnets fly up and circle before descending into the feeding area again. At night, they usually assemble, often in gorse, in communal roosts which also can be large. Just five were reported during this survey, containing up to 150 birds.

None of the previous Cheshire ornithological writers has noted the movement of Linnets away from the hills. Coward (1910) wrote that 'in winter the Linnet is generally distributed, consorting with Chaffinches in the hedgerows and pastures'. Bell (1962) said that 'its present status has altered little since the early part of the century', and added that hard weather movements across the Dee had been seen in January and February. With the warming climate, the annual county bird reports have not recorded a frost-driven movement of Linnets since the early 1980s.

STEVE ROUND

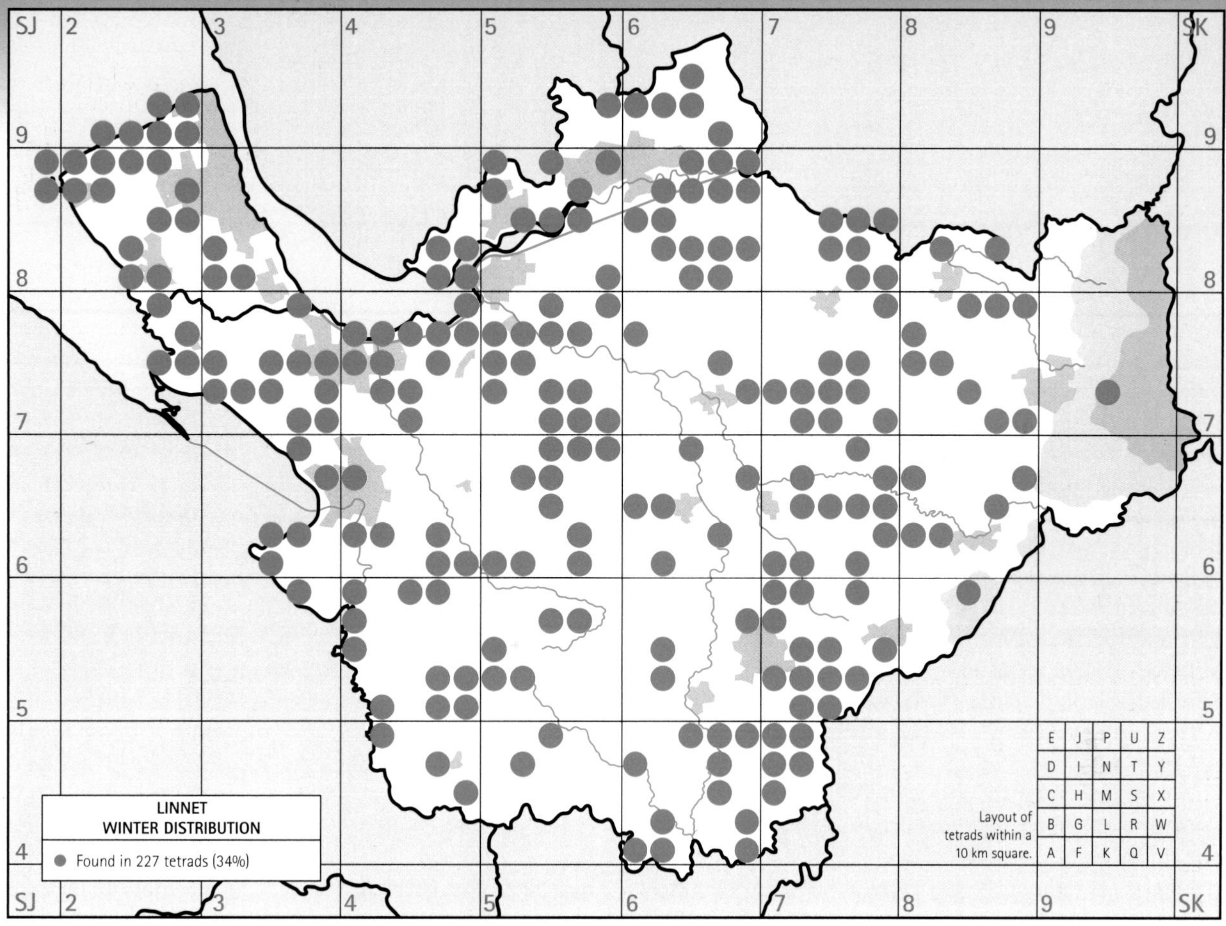
LINNET
WINTER DISTRIBUTION
Found in 227 tetrads (34%)
Layout of tetrads within a 10 km square.
SJ
SK

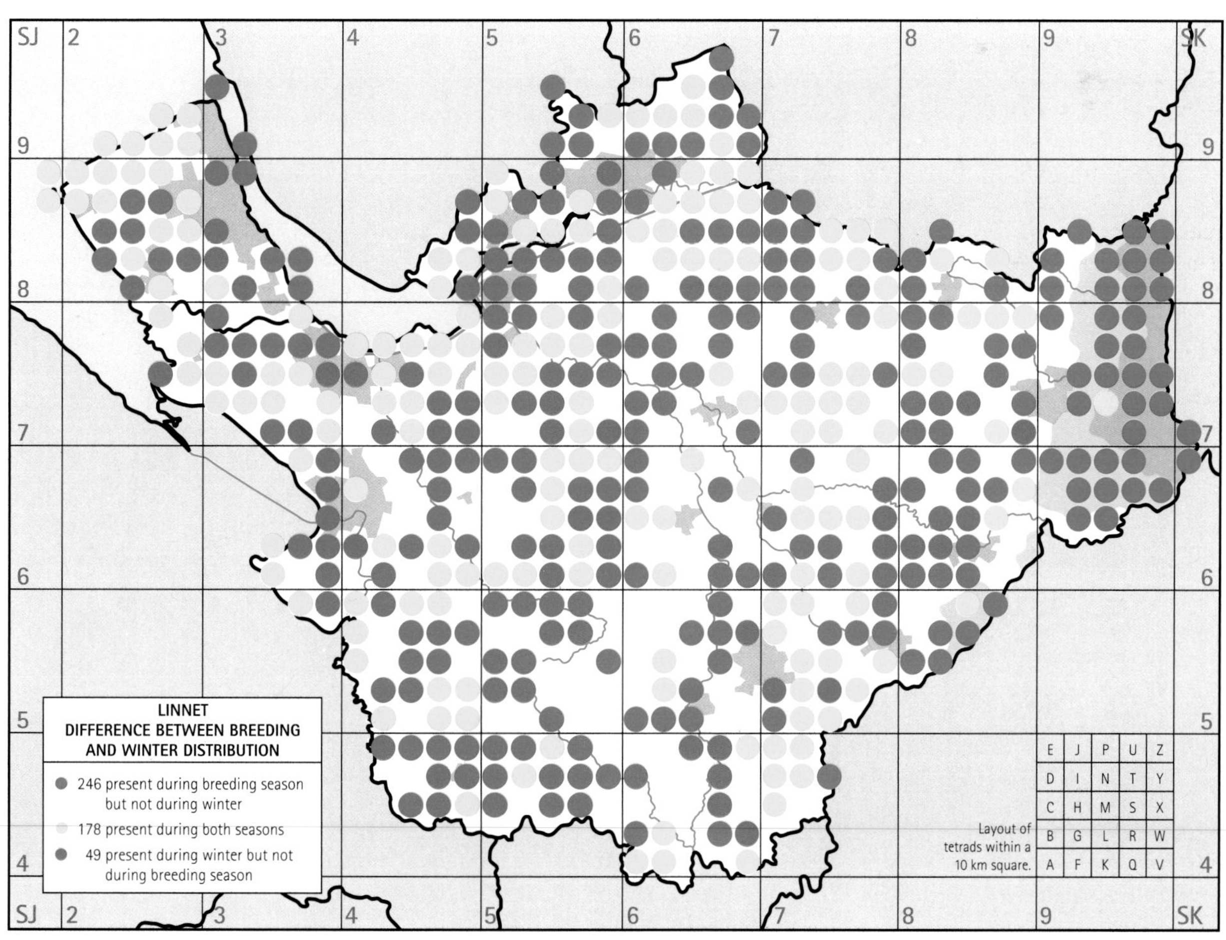
LINNET
DIFFERENCE BETWEEN BREEDING AND WINTER DISTRIBUTION
246 present during breeding season but not during winter
178 present during both seasons
49 present during winter but not during breeding season
Layout of tetrads within a 10 km square.
SJ
SK

Twite

Carduelis flavirostris

There were no records of Twite during the breeding season in this survey, but they bred during our *First Atlas*, in two different habitats at the lowest and highest points of the county. In 1978–84, Twites were recorded in 13 tetrads, one with confirmed breeding, three probable and nine possible. Most of the birds were in the moorland of the eastern hills. Records from this area continued to be submitted to the annual bird reports, the largest count in 1989 with evidence of 'a possible ten pairs on the Cheshire side of the eastern hills'. After that year, however, only sporadic breeding season records were received, with none from 1991 to 1993, odd records in 1994 and 1995, none in 1996, and one singing bird in 1997. Following two years of absence in 1998 and 1999, it was thought that a pair at Shining Tor on 13 July 2000 'may have bred locally'. If they did, they were the last known breeders in the county.

Twite also used to nest alongside the estuaries. In the mid-1970s there were confirmed breeding records at New Ferry and possible breeding at Frodsham, but there has been no summer record from the Mersey for thirty years. On the Dee salt-marsh, a nest was found in 1967, then a pair seen feeding small young in 1979, the origin of the confirmed breeding record during our *First Atlas*. An adult was seen there on 22 June 1980, but there has been no subsequent record.

As a Red-listed species of conservation concern, the Twite's ecology has come in for detailed study in recent years. The breeding season lasts from early May to late July, allowing up to three broods in favourable conditions. They breed at quite low densities, from 2 to 14 pairs per tetrad, nesting in tall heather and bracken in open moorland, but get most of their food from pastures and meadows, possibly as far as 3 km away, flying to and fro on well-defined flight-lines when feeding young. As with other cardueline finches, they eat small seeds such as dandelion and sorrel, storing food in their crops to be regurgitated for the chicks (Brown & Grice 2005).

Their extinction in Cheshire is just part of a wider population decline. Surveys of the South Pennine Moors SPA, including the Cheshire moors, showed an 84% drop between 1990 and 2004–05 in the breeding population of Twites (Eaton *et al.* 2007). The reasons for their demise are not well established, however. Overgrazing by sheep and bracken removal have reduced the area of suitable nesting habitat, and their food supply has greatly diminished as many pastures are overstocked

PETER SMITH

Sponsored by Richard Gabb

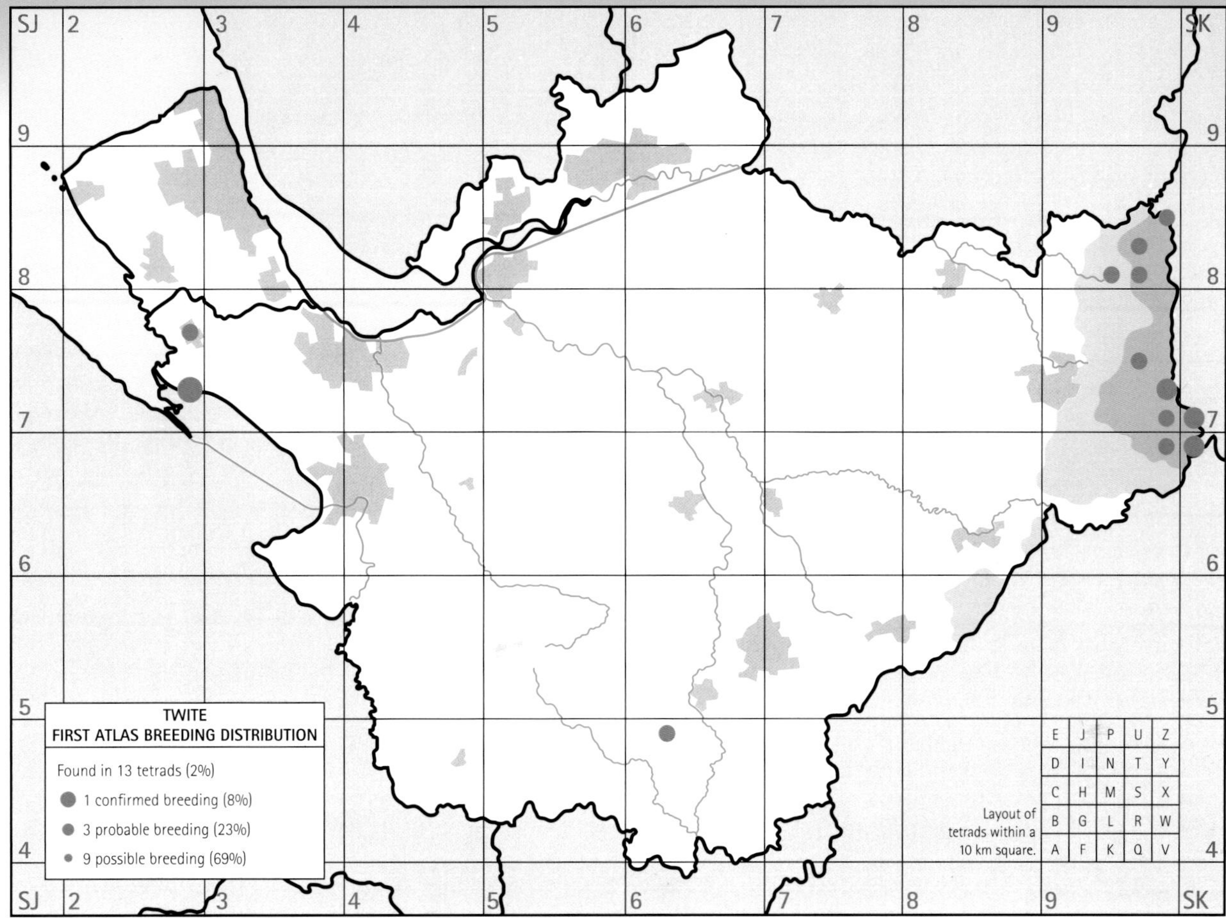

or cut early for silage, so flowers rarely set seed. Even roadside verges, potentially a rich source of seeds, are often cut in the name of 'tidiness' (Brown & Grice 2005). Even without these symptoms of modern countryside management, Twites are northern breeding birds of cool, wet places and climate change will make English moorlands even less hospitable for them: they are likely to be lost from England later this century (Huntley *et al.* 2007).

In winter, Twites flock on seed-rich estuarine salt-marshes and other weedy lowland coastal areas. Those breeding in the Pennines move south-east to winter on the English east coast, and sometimes reach the Netherlands (*Migration Atlas*). Contrary to the statement in the BTO *Migration Atlas*, the Twites wintering on the coasts of Lancashire and Cumbria are now known to have bred in the Hebrides and western Scotland. The source of the birds in Cheshire and Wirral has not been proven, but they are also likely to be of Hebridean stock. Up to half a million pairs breed in Norway, and some of them are thought to winter in Britain. Many Twites have been colour-marked in recent years, so careful observation, or a programme of ringing, could establish the origins of the county's birds.

During the three years of this winter Atlas the Dee salt-marsh tetrads yielded counts of 10, 20 and 45; and, for a few days in January 2005, up to 35 opportunistically fed on football fields in Wallasey after westerly gales. A flock of 13 was counted on stubble in SJ47G and birds were recorded in all three winters in the inner Mersey tetrads, with counts up to a maximum of 30. By far the largest flock was on rough grassland on 10 December 2006 near Frodsham in SJ47T.

This is a fairly typical showing for recent years, and indeed is probably quite similar to their status to any time in the last century. Coward (1910) said that Twites were '... in winter occasionally to be seen in the Dee estuary', and Boyd never mentions the species in his *Country Diary* or *Country Parish* books (Boyd 1946, 1951). Bell (1962) suggested that it was underrecorded as there had been no report at any season for 12 years up to 1949. However, on the Dee estuary since winter 1956–57 flocks up to 200 strong began to appear in each winter, with just odd birds elsewhere in the county. Since then, there have been major fluctuations in their occurrence and numbers, with the Dee being the most likely location but with some periods of several years with none or only a few present.

SUE & ANDY TRANTER

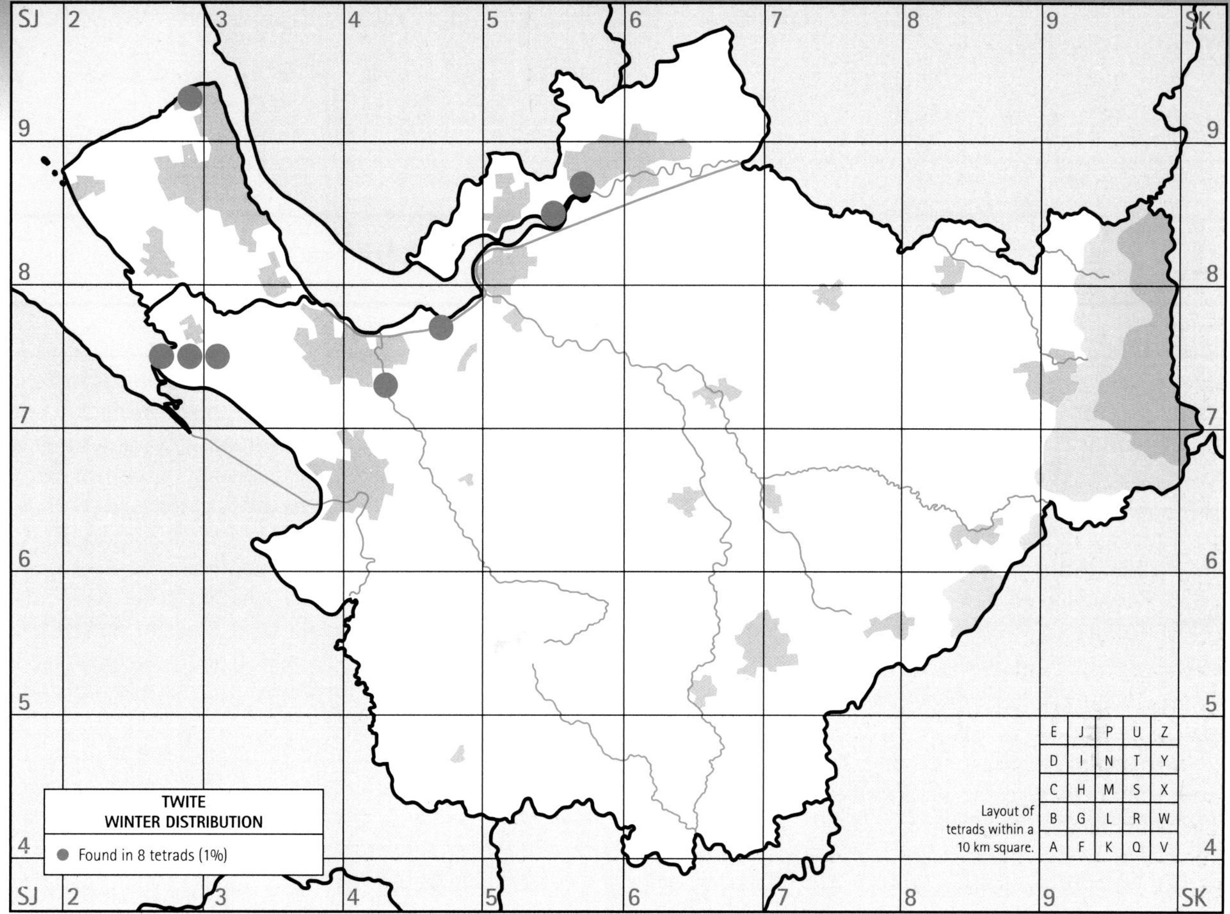

SJ
SK
2
3
4
5
6
7
8
9
TWITE
WINTER DISTRIBUTION
Found in 8 tetrads (1%)
Layout of tetrads within a 10 km square.
E J P U Z
D I N T Y
C H M S X
B G L R W
A F K Q V

Lesser Redpoll

Carduelis cabaret

This species has undergone a massive drop since our *First Atlas*. Redpolls used to breed almost everywhere across the northern half of the county, but now are restricted mainly to the two areas of Forestry Commission coniferous plantations, Delamere and Macclesfield Forests, and the Inner Mersey valley, with scattered records elsewhere in the county.

The fall in Cheshire and Wirral mimics that nationally: the BTO population index peaked in the mid-1970s and has been in free fall since then, to a level where the present national index is about 98% below that at the peak 30 years ago. Despite this precipitous decline, Lesser Redpoll has conservatively been included only on the Amber List of species of conservation concern because the data might not be representative, and only in 2007 has it been added to the UK BAP. Their rapid decrease appears to be driven by drops in productivity and survival rates, possibly linked to smaller areas of suitable young forest growth (Fuller *et al.* 2005). However, the reasons for the decline are not well established and research into its ecology is urgently needed.

Redpolls are birds of pioneer woodland, nesting mainly in birch scrub, alder, sallow and hawthorn, as well as young conifer plantations (Newton 1972). Out of the 75 habitat records submitted during this Atlas, 36 were woodland, 17 scrub and 15 suburban or rural human sites.

As with all the 'woodland finches', this is a difficult species in which to prove breeding, and just three observers were fortunate enough to get a two-letter code (one each of NE, ON and RF). Redpolls are not territorial and several birds may join in display flight, dancing over the treetops: such observations accounted for most of the probable breeding records. Typically, groups of up to six pairs nest close together in loose colonies. They breed from late April to July, with their brief incubation and fledging periods allowing time for up to three broods. In Scandinavia, Common Redpolls may have one brood in one area then move long distances north, perhaps hundreds of kilometres, for a further attempt later in the same season. Early in the breeding season, Redpolls feed themselves and any early broods mainly on the flowers and seeds of willow and associated bud-dwelling insects; they then move on to seeds of grasses and other weeds, but switch to birch seeds as soon as they become available, usually in July.

Although study of the species' habitat needs and life cycle has been lacking, there has been more research on its taxonomy, resulting in the decision in 2000 by the British Ornithologists' Union, the arbiters of the British List, that Lesser Redpoll *Carduelis cabaret* should be treated as a separate species from Common Redpoll *Carduelis flammea*. Lesser Redpolls have an unusual distribution, being restricted largely to the British Isles and nearby continental Europe, and the Alps.

PETER SMITH

Sponsored by Michael Miles

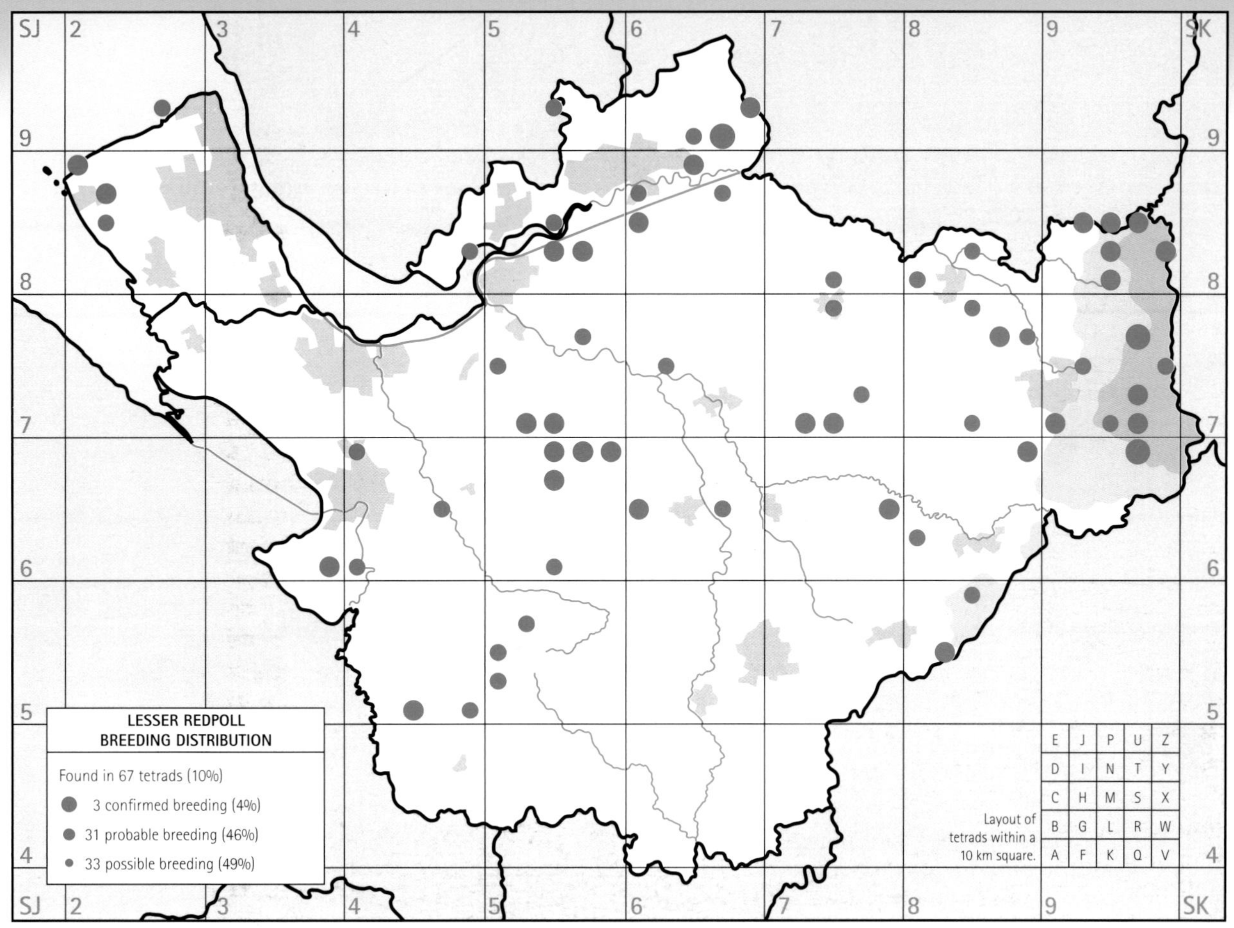
LESSER REDPOLL
BREEDING DISTRIBUTION
Found in 67 tetrads (10%)
3 confirmed breeding (4%)
31 probable breeding (46%)
33 possible breeding (49%)
Layout of tetrads within a 10 km square.
E J P U Z
D I N T Y
C H M S X
B G L R W
A F K Q V
SJ
SK

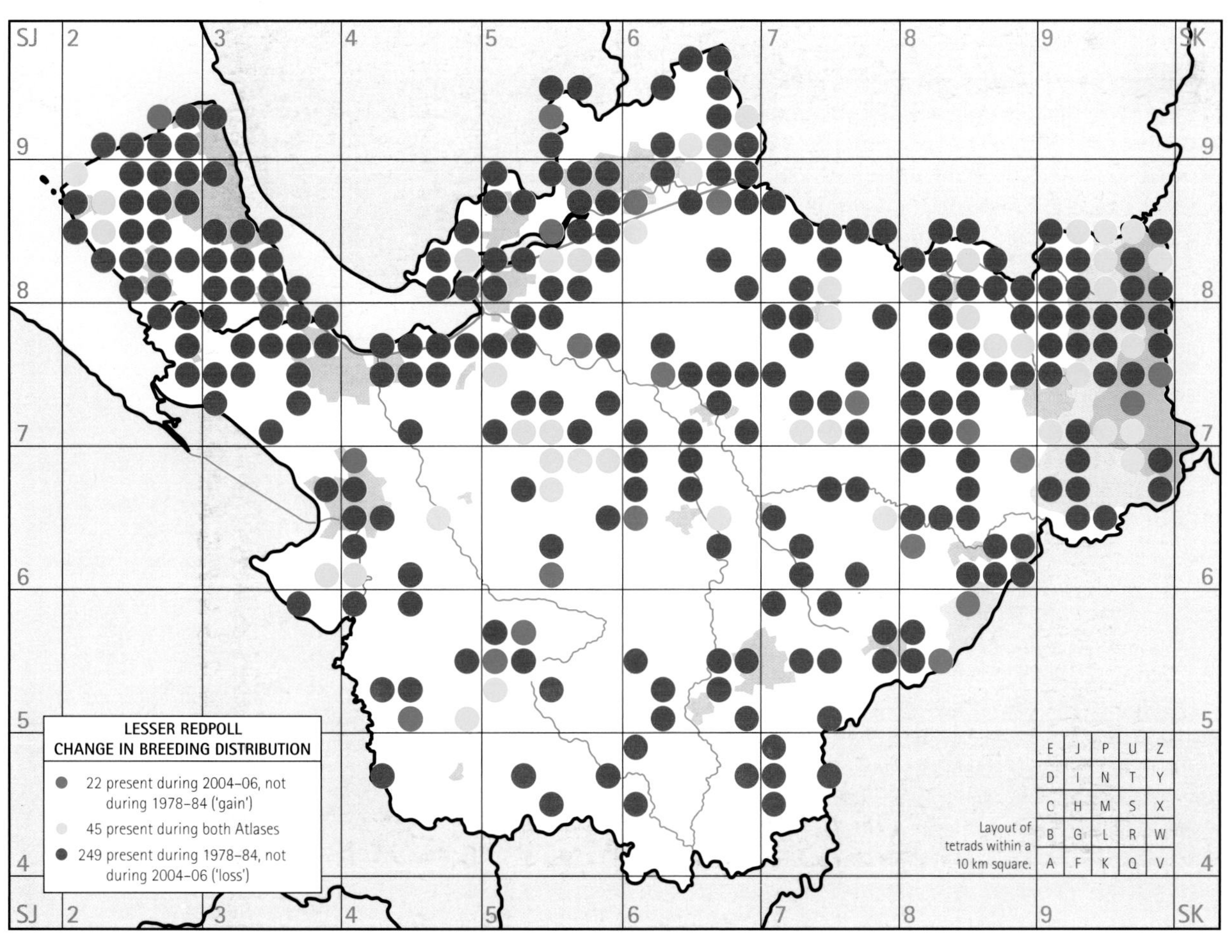
LESSER REDPOLL
CHANGE IN BREEDING DISTRIBUTION
22 present during 2004–06, not during 1978–84 ('gain')
45 present during both Atlases
249 present during 1978–84, not during 2004–06 ('loss')
Layout of tetrads within a 10 km square.
E J P U Z
D I N T Y
C H M S X
B G L R W
A F K Q V
SJ
SK

STEVE ROUND

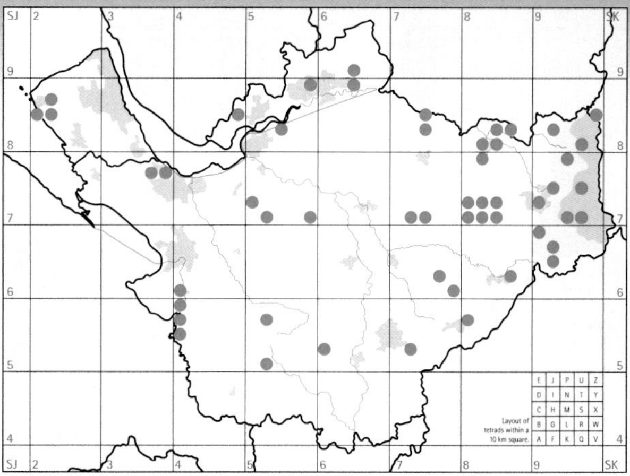

Lesser Redpoll in winter 2004/05.

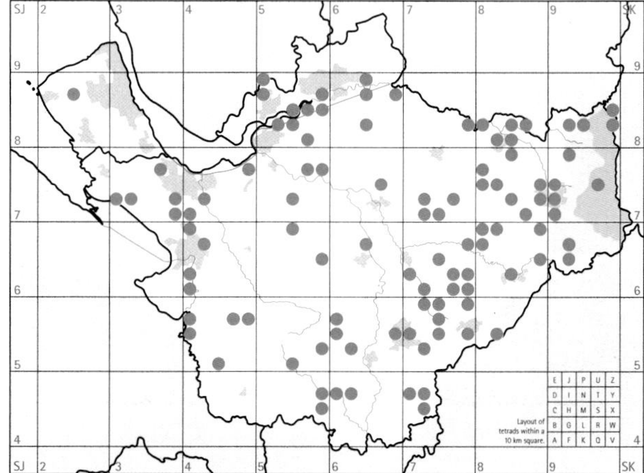

Lesser Redpoll in winter 2005/06.

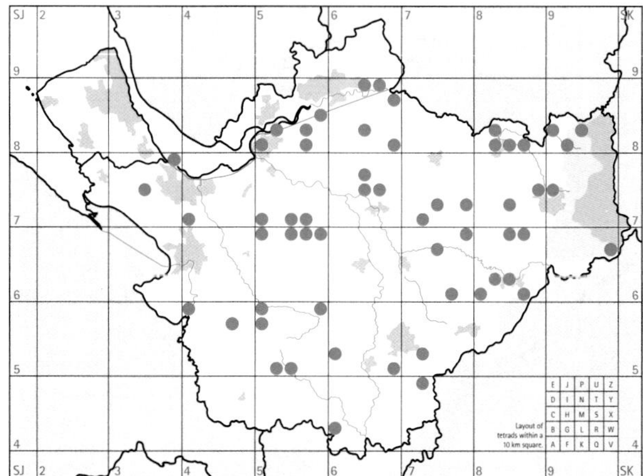

Lesser Redpoll in winter 2006/07.

Lesser Redpolls' winter distribution is dictated largely by the availability of birch seeds, with alder as an acceptable substitute, so they undertake long-distance movements to find them. Southerly migration within Britain is probably annual, and Cheshire and Wirral ringers have many examples of birds from Scottish sites moving through or wintering in the county. A number of birds move on to continental Europe in some years (*Migration Atlas*).

As with other woodland finches, especially the Siskin, their winter occurrence shows a clear biennial pattern. Fieldworkers for this Atlas were not required to submit repeat records for tetrads in which the species had already been found, but many surveyors did do so, and the differences were striking, as seen in the maps for the three separate winters of this survey: in winter 2004/05 Lesser Redpolls were recorded in 52 tetrads; in 2005/06 they were found in 101 tetrads; and in 2006/07 observers reported them from 58 tetrads.

The species is much more widespread than in the breeding season, with larger flocks, the biggest reported being 80 birds. Woodland (42% of habitat records) and human sites (20%) were occupied in much the same proportions as in the breeding season, with fewer (11%) in scrub and 19% of habitat codes from birds frequenting farmland. Lesser Redpolls were often found in waterside locations, usually easier to hear than to see as they kept to the tops of trees, and the lines of some rivers show up in the distribution map, especially the Dee and Mersey. In the east of the county, Lesser Redpolls are widely distributed, but, as in the breeding season, this is now a scarce species on Wirral.

Coward (1910) noted winter flocks sometimes numbering 50–100 birds or more, usually in birches and alders, much the same as nowadays. Bell (1962) described the species as a 'widely distributed resident, and a passage migrant and winter resident in small numbers': depending on the meaning of the terms 'resident' and 'winter resident', which are not defined in the book, this seems the opposite way round to the present status. If true, this suggests that perhaps Redpolls have undergone a long-term variation in abundance or migratory tendency.

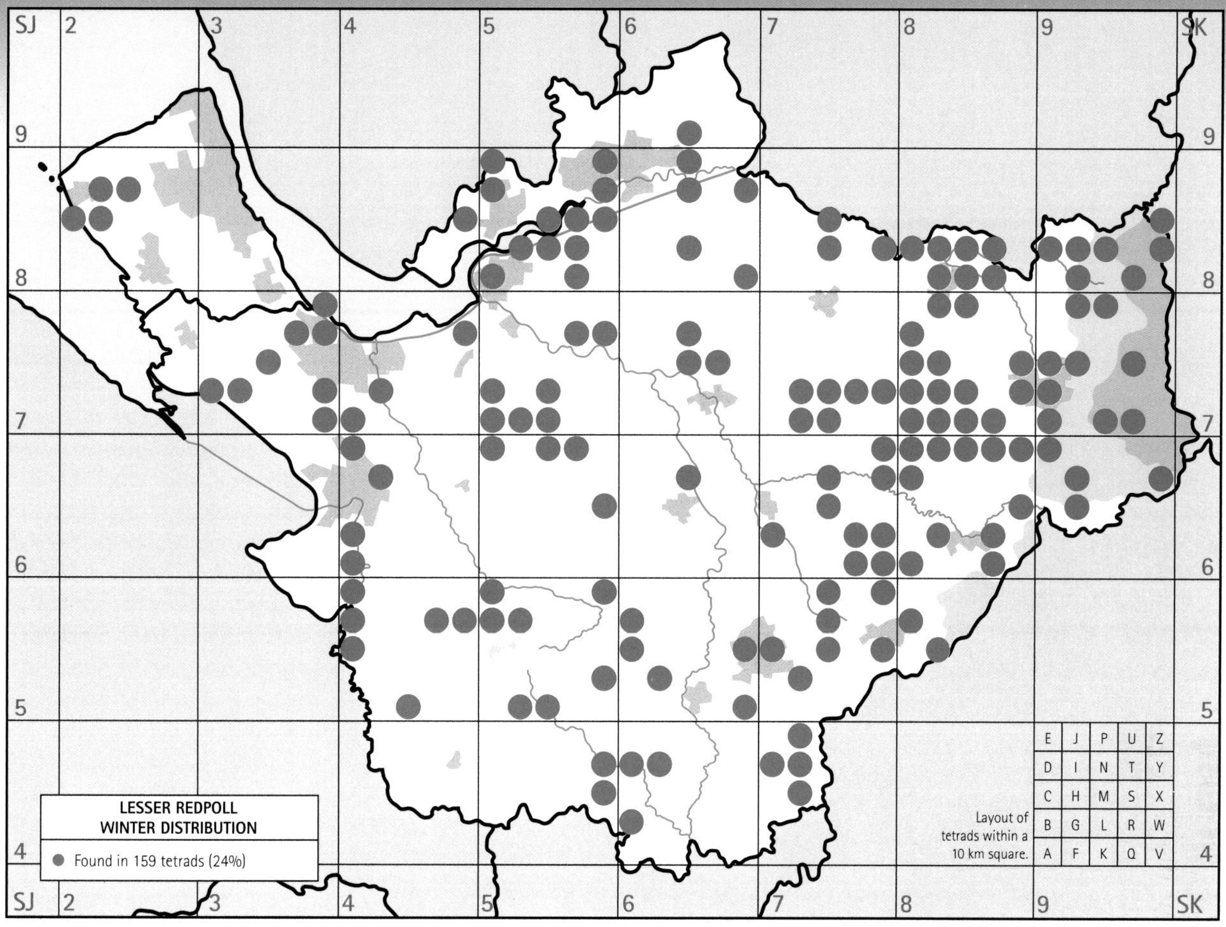
SJ
2
3
4
5
6
7
8
9
SK
LESSER REDPOLL
WINTER DISTRIBUTION
Found in 159 tetrads (24%)
Layout of tetrads within a 10 km square.
E J P U Z
D I N T Y
C H M S X
B G L R W
A F K Q V

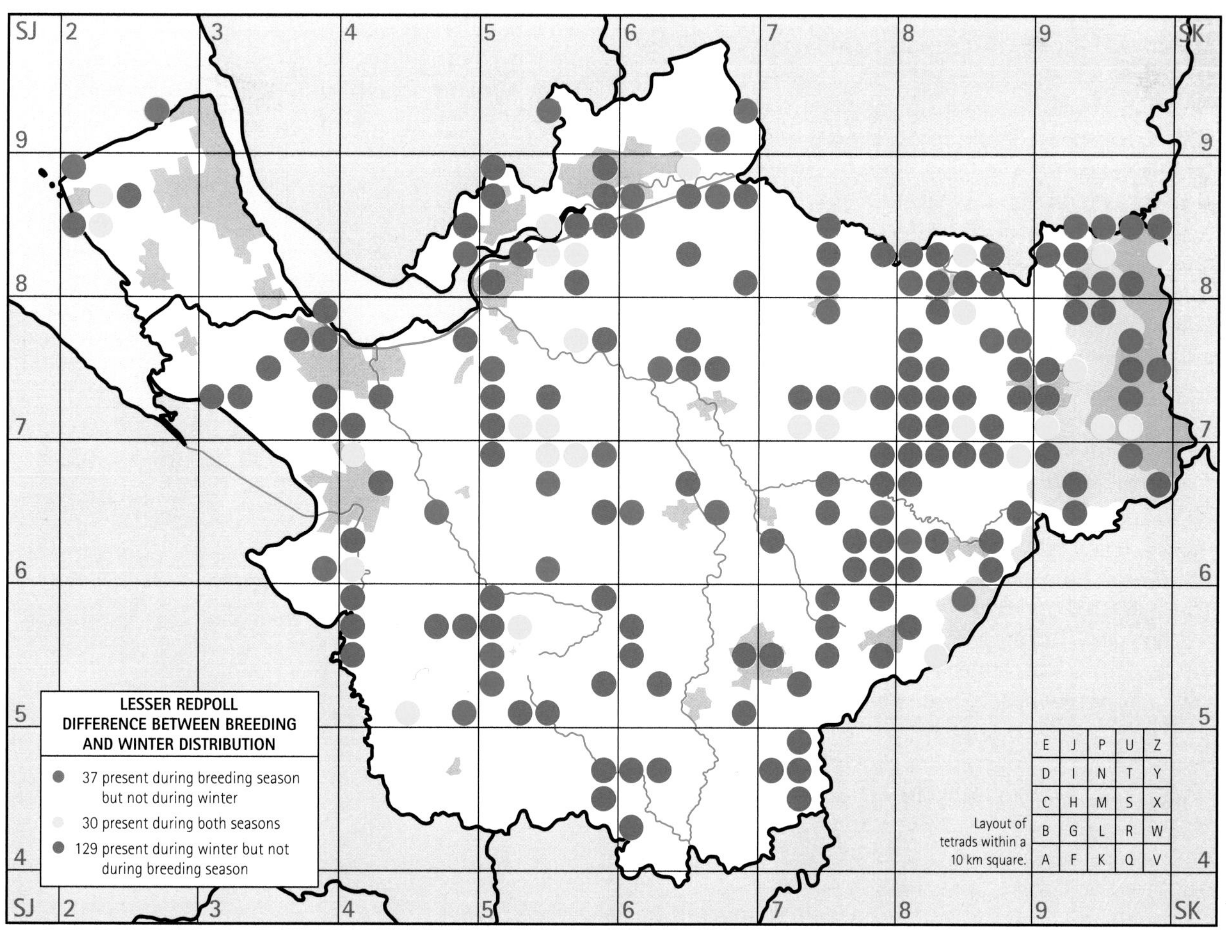
SJ
2
3
4
5
6
7
8
9
SK
LESSER REDPOLL
DIFFERENCE BETWEEN BREEDING AND WINTER DISTRIBUTION
37 present during breeding season but not during winter
30 present during both seasons
129 present during winter but not during breeding season
Layout of tetrads within a 10 km square.
E J P U Z
D I N T Y
C H M S X
B G L R W
A F K Q V

Crossbill

Loxia curvirostra

PETER SMITH

For a species that feeds almost exclusively on the seeds of coniferous trees, it is not surprising that Crossbills were found mostly in the Forestry Commission plantations of Delamere and Macclesfield Forests, or that all of the habitat codes were coniferous or mixed woodland. They almost certainly nest in some of these areas but it is very difficult to confirm breeding and all nine tetrads with birds present are recorded just as possible breeding. Richard Elphick saw two males and one young bird at Alderley Edge (SJ87T) in 2005; the closest to proof of breeding came when Roger Wilkinson reported a family party, including one adult male and at least two birds of the year, just south of Blakemere (SJ57K) on 9 April 2006; and I recorded a flock of 20 birds in the same tetrad on 14 May 2006.

The lives of Crossbills are dictated by the seed crop and they eat little other than conifer seeds: spruce, pine and larch. They are capable of extracting seeds at any stage of ripeness, using their unique bill to prise apart the cones, but it takes extra time and effort on unripe cones and feeding is easiest when the cones are opening naturally, typically during winter and early spring in Scots and Corsican pines. When they are feeding in an area, Crossbills usually stay in the tops of the trees and are best detected by their 'chup' calls and by seeing flakes of cones drifting to the ground. The evidence is completed by finding cones on the ground, open and with the scales forced apart but intact, completely different from those taken by grey squirrels, on which only the inedible centre of the cone remains.

Crossbills are so linked to conifer seeds that they are stimulated to nest by an abundance of food rather than the changes in day length that induce breeding in most other birds. In European spruce forests they can breed from August to May on occasions, but in English pine plantations the season is shorter. Nests with eggs have been recorded in every month from December to June but mostly from February to April (Newton 1972). The timing of Atlas fieldwork does not fit well with the Crossbills' life, and evidence of breeding is perhaps more likely to be obtained during winter surveying.

After the two instances of proven breeding in 1981 described in our *First Atlas* (one of them not mapped, however), the records submitted to the annual county bird reports concentrate on influxes to the county and the only suggestion of breeding in the last quarter-century was in 1998 in Macclesfield Forest when a male was singing, a female seen carrying material into a nearby tree and the male feeding the female. In 1999 Crossbills were 'reported to have bred at Cholmondeley' but with no more information. In other years, flocks including singing males and immatures were in Delamere Forest on 29 April 1989 and from March to May 1990; birds were said to be on territory or singing at Blakemere and The Cloud, Congleton (SJ96B) in 2000; and in 2003, juveniles were noted at Abbots Moss (SJ56Z) and Cholmondeley (SJ55F/K), with family parties seen at Sound Common (SJ64J). Short of dedicated effort and sustained watching, always difficult with flocks of birds at the top of trees in dense woodland, this is as close as it gets to recording breeding in the county.

Sponsored by Michael S. Twist

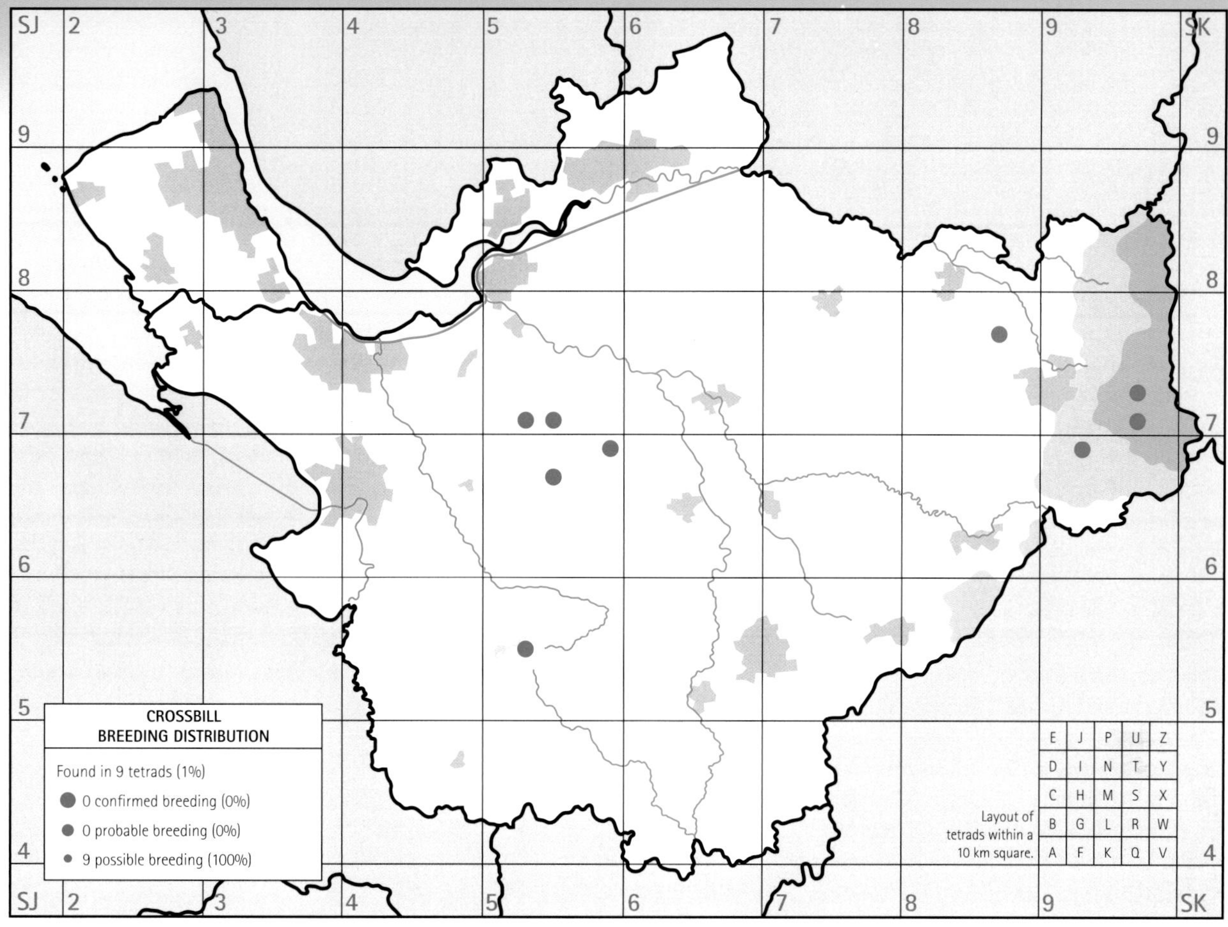
CROSSBILL
BREEDING DISTRIBUTION
Found in 9 tetrads (1%)
0 confirmed breeding (0%)
0 probable breeding (0%)
9 possible breeding (100%)
Layout of tetrads within a 10 km square.
E J P U Z
D I N T Y
C H M S X
B G L R W
A F K Q V

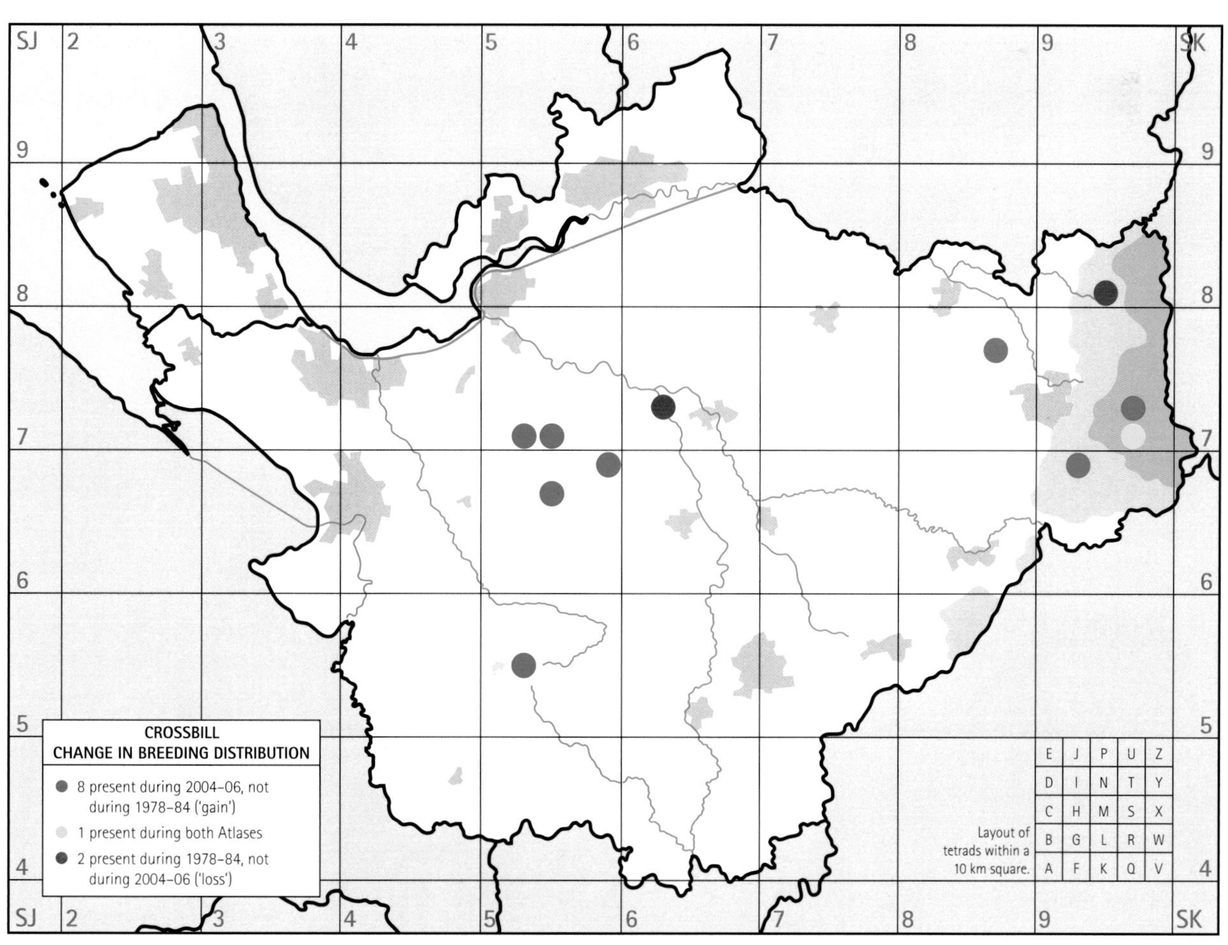
CROSSBILL
CHANGE IN BREEDING DISTRIBUTION
8 present during 2004–06, not during 1978–84 ('gain')
1 present during both Atlases
2 present during 1978–84, not during 2004–06 ('loss')
Layout of tetrads within a 10 km square.
E J P U Z
D I N T Y
C H M S X
B G L R W
A F K Q V

Depending on a single food source with crops that vary sporadically from one year to the next, Crossbills undertake some large postbreeding movements as they try to find another area with enough conifer seeds. These movements occur in summer, usually from late June, as the new year's production of cones is forming. There are occasional massive eruptions from their continental breeding areas, when Crossbills may be seen in large numbers in new places. If the birds find sufficient food to sustain them for a few months, they often then breed in the new area, but are likely to quit for a different site in the following year. The numbers present may vary by a factor of 10 from one year to another, the years of high population coming after an irruption when extra birds have stayed in the area. The largest influxes to the county in recent years were in the summers of 1990 and 1997, the observation of birds showing breeding intent in Macclesfield Forest in 1998 following the latter irruption.

The Atlas map shows birds sparsely distributed in winter, in only 11 tetrads, but broadly in four general areas of coniferous or mixed woodland: Delamere and Macclesfield Forests, Alderley Edge, and the southern end of the Sandstone Ridge. Others were found at Doddington (SJ74D), Daresbury Firs (SJ58R) and Frankby cemetery (SJ28N). Crossbills were reported from just three tetrads during 2004/05, six in 2005/06 and five in 2006/07. Most were in groups of six to eight, with two larger flocks in the Delamere area of 12 and 17 birds.

A century ago, Coward (1910) wrote 'At irregular intervals flocks of Crossbills have occurred, chiefly in the winter, in woodlands in various parts of the county'. Larches were noted as the main attraction, before the mass planting of pines and spruces in the early twentieth century. Boyd (1946) noted an influx into 'the forest country of Cheshire' in July 1935 and noted a flock among the Scots pines in Delamere Forest in March 1943, commenting that 'we have seen little of Crossbills in Cheshire for some years'. Bell (1962) concurred with Coward's general assessment of their status, and since then, *CWBRs* contain few relatively records in the winter period. Large numbers were in Macclesfield Forest in 1993/94, with 59 birds on 15 January 1994, but none at all reported there in the following winter. They were 'very obvious' in Delamere Forest in 1997/98, but the maximum count was only 14, and the only other winter with substantial numbers was 2002/03, with up to 85 in Macclesfield Forest and 16 in Lyme Park (SJ98R).

The three years of this Atlas survey were 'normal' years for Crossbills in Cheshire and Wirral, uncomplicated by irruptions or subsequent extra breeding birds.

ANDREW MART

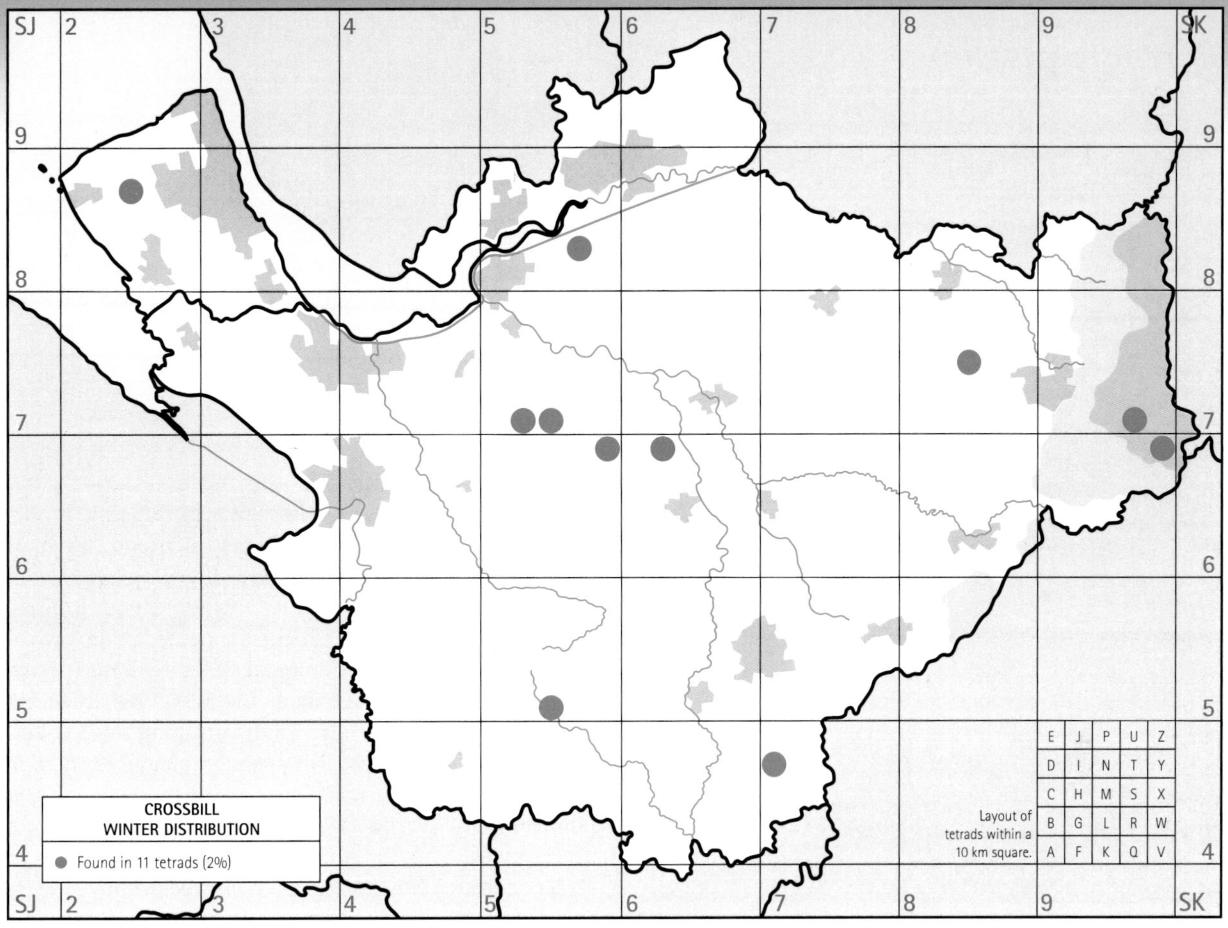
SJ
2
3
4
5
6
7
8
9
SK
9
8
7
6
5
4
CROSSBILL
WINTER DISTRIBUTION
Found in 11 tetrads (2%)
Layout of tetrads within a 10 km square.
E J P U Z
D I N T Y
C H M S X
B G L R W
A F K Q V

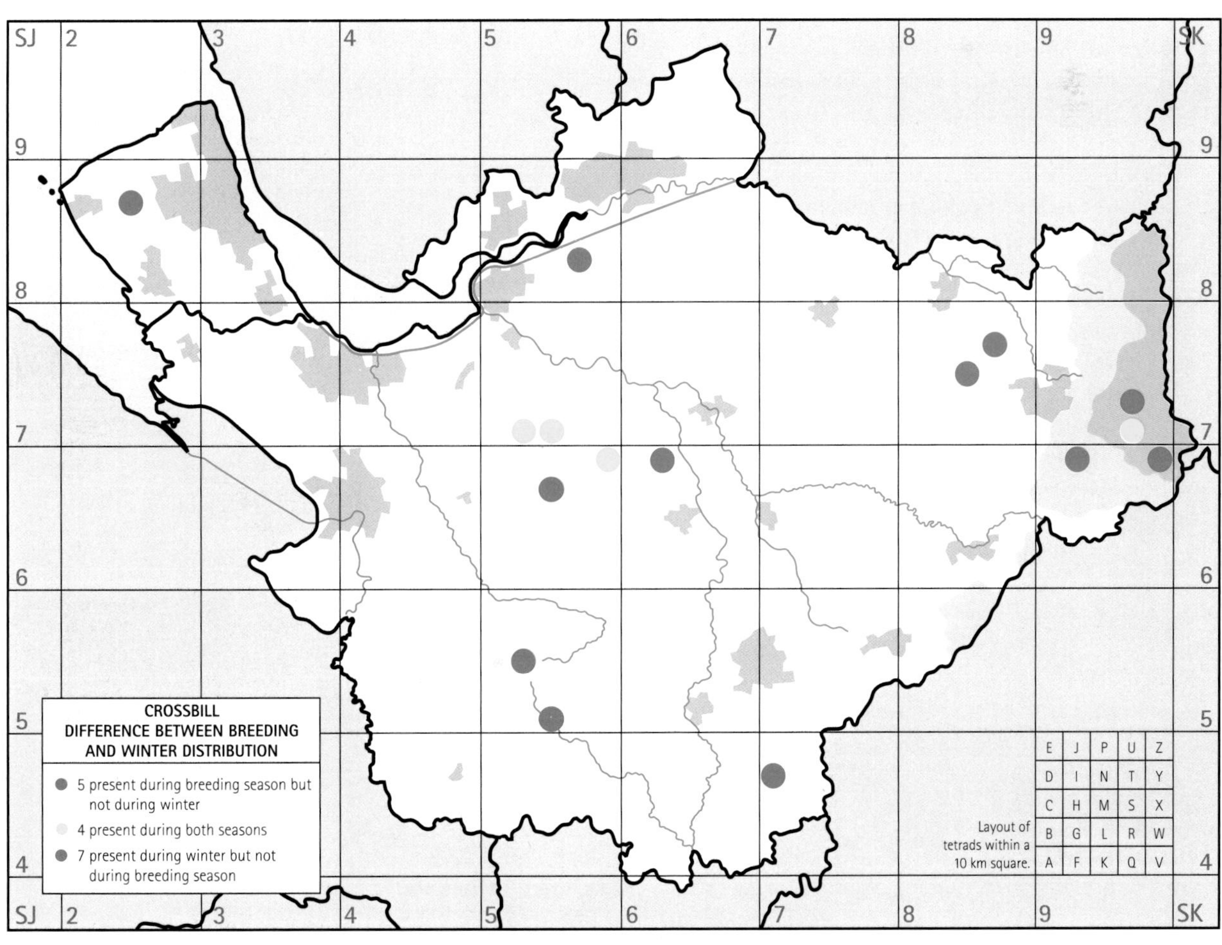
SJ
2
3
4
5
6
7
8
9
SK
9
8
7
6
5
4
CROSSBILL
DIFFERENCE BETWEEN BREEDING AND WINTER DISTRIBUTION
5 present during breeding season but not during winter
4 present during both seasons
7 present during winter but not during breeding season
Layout of tetrads within a 10 km square.
E J P U Z
D I N T Y
C H M S X
B G L R W
A F K Q V

Bullfinch

Pyrrhula pyrrhula

RICHARD STEEL

Because of its big decline in population, the Bullfinch is on the UK's Red List of species of conservation concern, with a Biodiversity Action Plan nationally and locally for its conservation. Bullfinches declined greatly during the period of our *First Atlas*, the national population dropping by 44% in a decade, from the peak in 1974 to 1984. It has continued to decline, with the national index in 2004 about 20% lower than 20 years previously. It was therefore not surprising to find that the breeding distribution map shows a net loss from 65 tetrads compared to the *First Atlas*. There are 83 gains, mostly in the central southern part of Cheshire, but 148 losses spread across the whole of the county. They avoid the highest land in eastern Cheshire, and even the Sandstone Ridge. The habitat records show that most were in broadleaved or mixed woodland (33%), followed by farmland (31%)—where they particularly favour orchards and tall hedges—and scrub (18%). They are the least likely of our finches to use human sites (16% of records), with only three tetrads with an F1 (urban) code.

This is a difficult species in which to confirm breeding, and most records were of pairs seen. Bullfinches are not obviously territorial, and may fly up to a kilometre away from the nest if necessary to reach good feeding areas. Their song is thin and scarcely audible more than a few metres away, but they do indulge in exaggerated mutual displays. Nests are usually well hidden in bramble, hawthorn or similarly inaccessible bushes or hedges, and were found in only 23 tetrads. They rear the chicks on a mixture of soft seeds and small invertebrates, with the proportion of animal material gradually reduced as the chicks grow so that, by the time they leave the nest, they are getting seeds alone. The parents do not carry food in their bills but store it in their special throat-pouches—the only British finch that has this adaptation—so adults seen with bulging cheeks are probably on their way back to a brood. Most of the Atlas records (56) of confirmed breeding came from observers seeing family parties including young birds, distinctively different from their parents, plain brown with no black cap, as the adults feed their young for two or three weeks after they leave the nest. Five observers were lucky enough to have adults bringing their young to garden bird feeders. They nest typically from late May onwards and usually have two broods, making a late end to the season: half-grown chicks were ringed in a nest at Woolston on 4 September 1994.

The reasons for the Bullfinch decline are not understood, but the drop has been much more severe on farmland than woodland and is likely to be linked to removal of hedgerows, and frequent trimming of those remaining, impacting on Bullfinches through loss of nesting habitat and food sources (buds, seeds and fruits).

The BTO analysis of 2004–05 BBS data puts the breeding population of Cheshire and Wirral as 2,580 birds (2,250–2,920), corresponding to an average of eight birds per tetrad with confirmed or probable breeding, or just six birds per tetrad in which the species was recorded. The abundance map shows that the only areas with higher densities were the western edge of Cheshire, south Wirral and the mosslands north of Warrington.

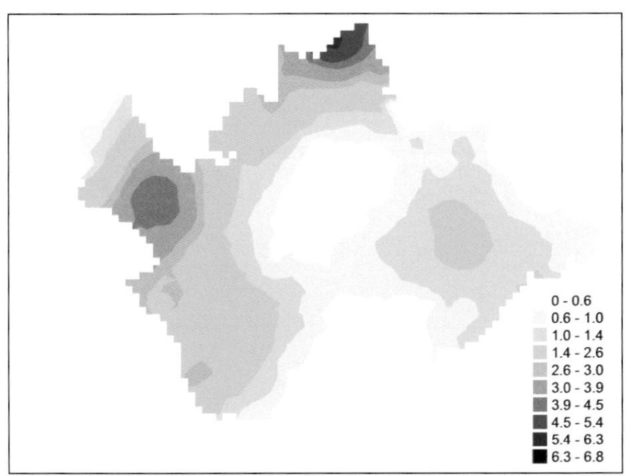

Bullfinch abundance.

Sponsored by Robin Hart

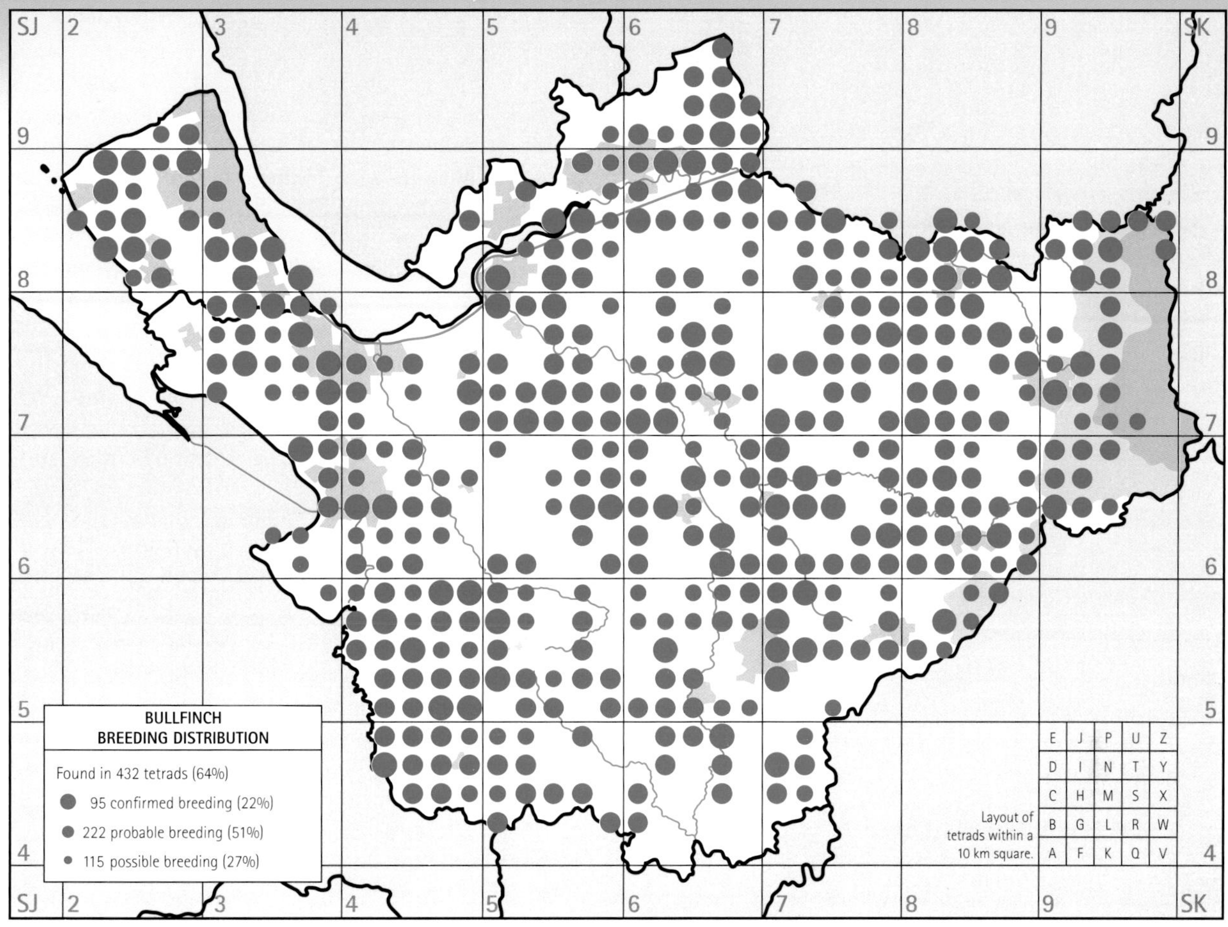
BULLFINCH
BREEDING DISTRIBUTION
Found in 432 tetrads (64%)
95 confirmed breeding (22%)
222 probable breeding (51%)
115 possible breeding (27%)
Layout of tetrads within a 10 km square.
E J P U Z
D I N T Y
C H M S X
B G L R W
A F K Q V
SJ
SK

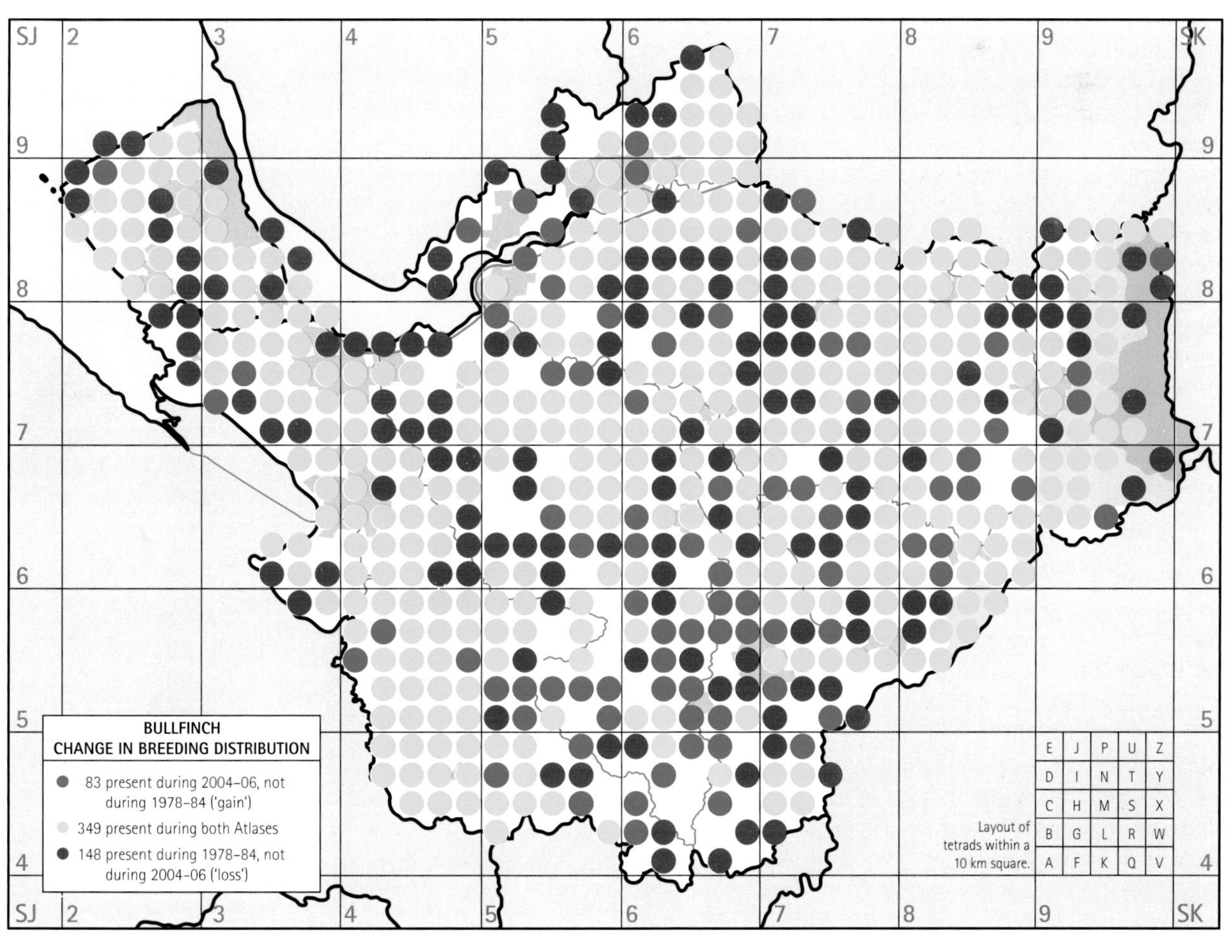
BULLFINCH
CHANGE IN BREEDING DISTRIBUTION
83 present during 2004–06, not during 1978–84 ('gain')
349 present during both Atlases
148 present during 1978–84, not during 2004–06 ('loss')
Layout of tetrads within a 10 km square.
E J P U Z
D I N T Y
C H M S X
B G L R W
A F K Q V
SJ
SK

STEVE ROUND

Bullfinches were reported from 484 tetrads in winter, with 364 tetrads occupied in both seasons, 120 in winter only and 68 in the breeding season only. The winter distribution appears to fill in most of the gaps from the breeding season, and some birds move out of breeding areas into farmland for winter (Brown & Grice 2005). The main changes in recorded habitats from the breeding season are significant drops in birds in woodland and scrub, with large increases on farmland and human sites. The number of tetrads recording birds in hedges doubled between the two seasons, and there were half as many again in human sites: Bullfinches were recorded quite frequently as visitors to bird feeders in gardens or nature reserves. They do not gather into large flocks like some other seed-eating birds, and most counts were of one or two birds, which is how Bullfinches normally spend their lives. Many observers reported seeing male and female together, and Bullfinches appear to pair for life (Newton 1993). Birds may gather together at favoured feeding locations, and fieldworkers reported groups of 8–12 birds in nine tetrads, but they usually arrive and depart from different directions and seldom stay in flocks (*BTO Winter Atlas*). It seems that the presence of Sparrowhawks probably influences Bullfinches' flocking behaviour. When the raptors were scarce or locally extinct in the 1960s and 1970s following poisoning by organochlorine pesticides, Bullfinches were found in some counties in large flocks, sometimes 100 strong, feeding in the centre of fields and orchards, well away from cover; this habit has died out as Sparrowhawks have increased (Newton 1993). There is unfortunately no information on Bullfinch numbers or behaviour in Cheshire and Wirral during this time as it coincided with the dark period in the county's ornithology when bird reports were interested only in migration.

Through the winter, Bullfinches eat whichever seeds they can find, initially those of nettle, birch and rowan, and later those of bramble, dock and ash; in upland areas, they eat heather seeds. Weeds in large fields are not important to them, because the Bullfinch does not forage far from hedgerows and woods, but they do eat seed-bearing weeds in field margins. Where it is available, ash forms a major winter food, but Bullfinches are selective and feed from some trees and not others, choosing those with a lower concentration of the bitter, poisonous phenols and higher fat contents (Newton 1993). As the seed supplies are not replenished during the winter, the size of the initial crops, and the rate at which they are depleted, influence the date when they run out, and Bullfinches have to switch from seeds to buds. Their well-known ability to digest cellulose from buds is a life-saver for the birds, but brings them into conflict with man in gardens and fruit-growing areas. Their favourites include blackthorn, hawthorn and crab apple amongst wild species, as well as buds from cultivated pear and apple trees.

The winter population comprises mostly the same birds as breed here, as Bullfinches seldom move more than a few kilometres. Occasional influxes of birds from Scandinavia—distinguished by their loud 'trumpet' calls rather than the thin piping of the British birds—are usually confined to northern Britain and make no difference to the Cheshire and Wirral numbers. Detailed studies have revealed that individuals may remain for weeks or months within a short distance of a good food source, before suddenly moving to a new site that may be several kilometres away (*Migration Atlas*). This behaviour could account for movements of two local birds. A bird ringed as a nestling at Frankby, Wirral (SJ28M) in June 1986 and retrapped there as a breeding male in June 1988 was found dead in Staffordshire, 74 km away, in January 1989; and another ringed at Woolston (SJ68P) in 1986 as an adult male, and retrapped there in August 1987, was caught in winter 1990 at Aston (SJ57P), 13 km away.

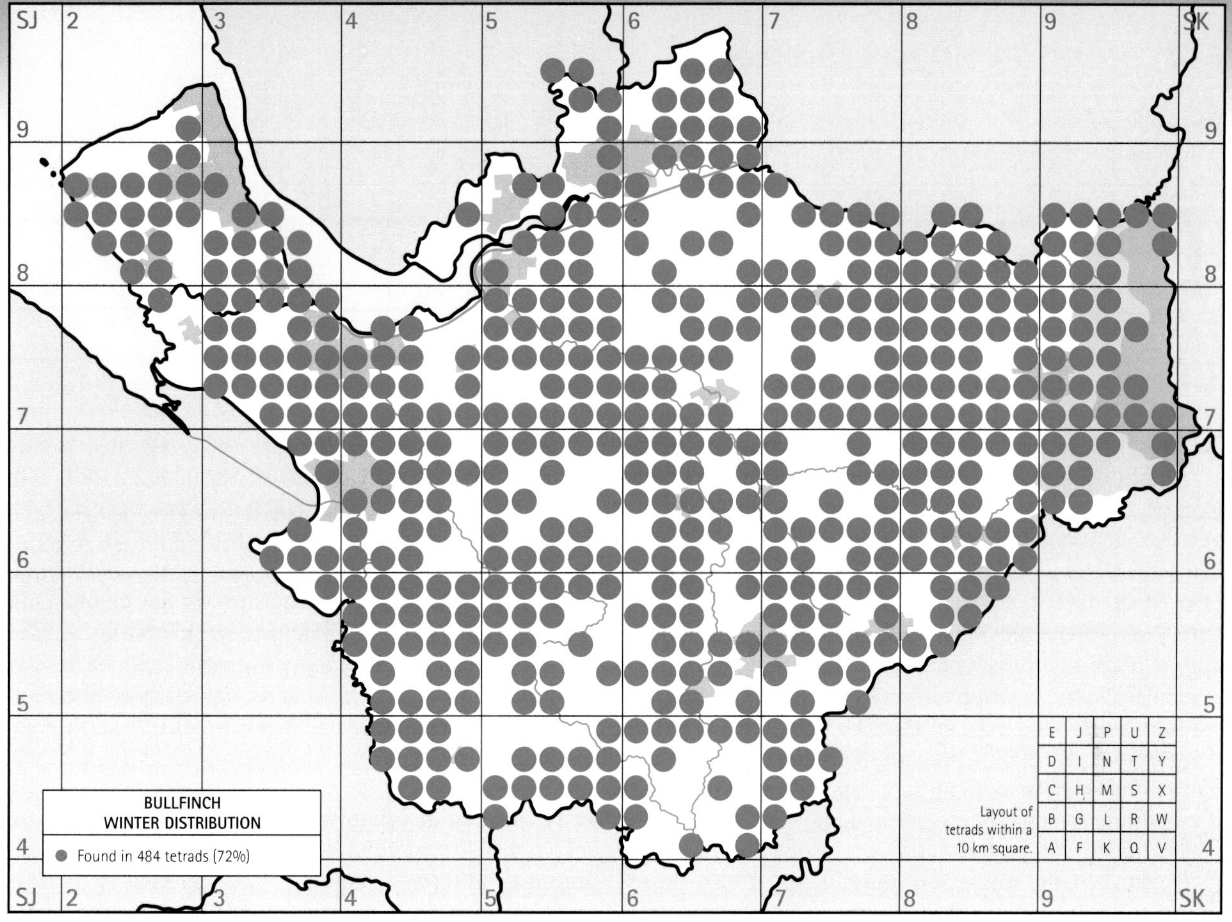
BULLFINCH
WINTER DISTRIBUTION
Found in 484 tetrads (72%)
Layout of tetrads within a 10 km square.
E J P U Z
D I N T Y
C H M S X
B G L R W
A F K Q V
SJ
SK

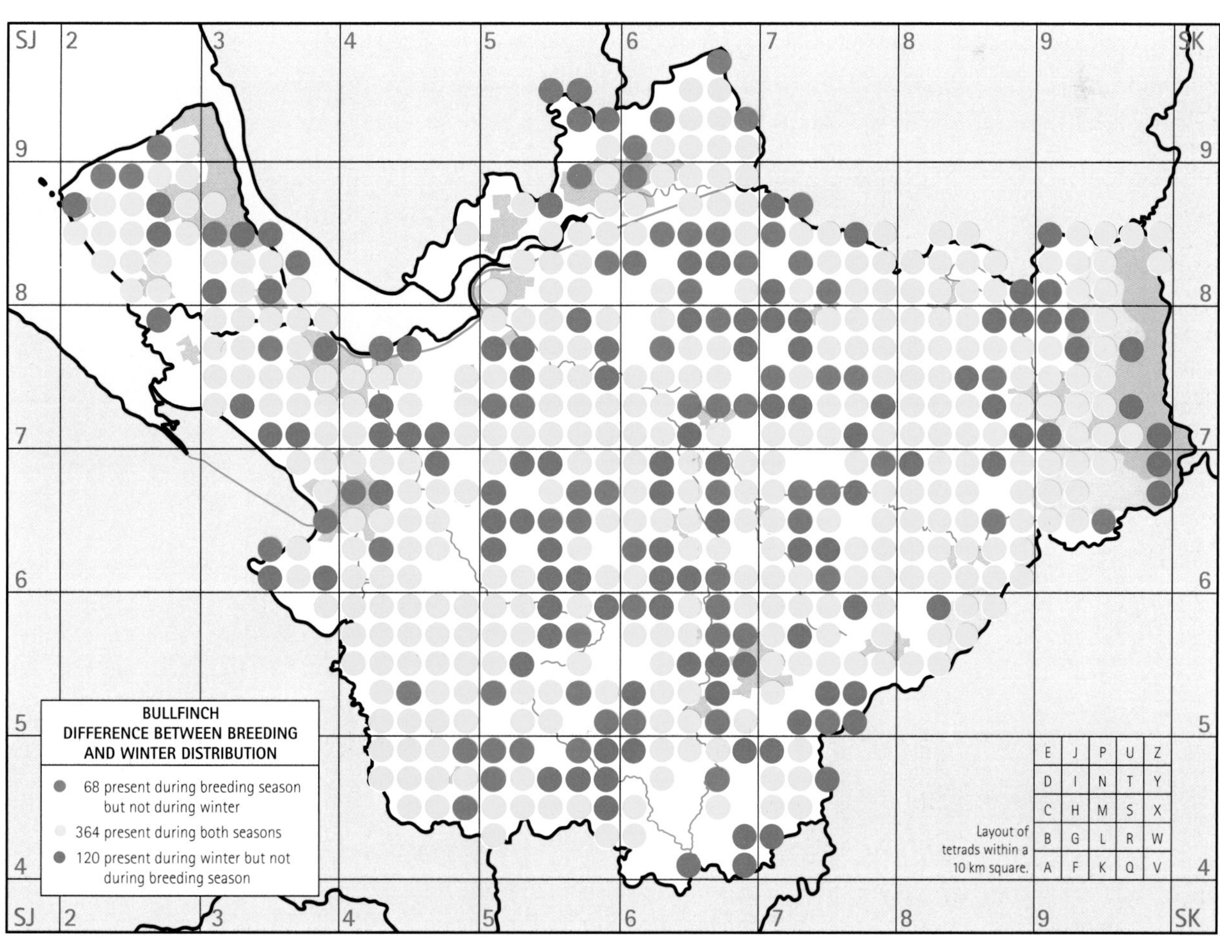
BULLFINCH
DIFFERENCE BETWEEN BREEDING AND WINTER DISTRIBUTION
68 present during breeding season but not during winter
364 present during both seasons
120 present during winter but not during breeding season
Layout of tetrads within a 10 km square.
E J P U Z
D I N T Y
C H M S X
B G L R W
A F K Q V
SJ
SK

Hawfinch

Coccothraustes coccothraustes

This, the UK's largest finch, last bred in the county in 1990, when up to five pairs were found at separate sites in the Eccleston and Eaton Park area (SJ46B), 'with at least three producing young and frequenting the usual cherry trees at the Rectory' (*CWBR*). In 1991, they were 'puzzlingly absent from their Cheshire stronghold', and there have been no records even of possible breeding since then.

Cheshire is not alone in experiencing such a sudden loss of Hawfinches. The authors of the most recent analysis of its status, using county bird reports from across England and Wales, wrote that 'Several counties have documented substantial declines at traditional sites which were previously noted for their wintering and/or breeding concentrations of this species', giving examples from widespread areas including sites in Norfolk, Staffordshire, Derbyshire, Oxfordshire and Kent (Langston *et al.* 2002). Perhaps their loosely colonial nature makes them more prone to such mass desertions if conditions become not to their liking.

Nationally, it appears that their population rose in the late 1970s, was stable through the 1980s then dropped steeply from 1990 onwards, with the total in 1999 perhaps only half of that in 1990 (Langston *et al.* 2002). They are on the Amber List of species of conservation concern because of a moderate contraction of their UK breeding range between the two BTO national Atlases (1968–72 and 1988–91), being found in 31% fewer 10 km squares in the second. Hawfinches have a strangely discontinuous breeding distribution, with strongholds in south-eastern England, and in Gloucestershire, Derbyshire, Nottinghamshire, Yorkshire and Cumbria. An indication of its widespread but scarce status is given by the figures from the Atlases of counties adjoining Cheshire: Hawfinches were recorded in the breeding season in 14 tetrads in Shropshire (1985–90), 7 tetrads in Lancashire and North Merseyside (1997–2000) and 28 tetrads in Cumbria (1997–2001).

Their preferred habitat of deciduous woodland, especially old oaks and hornbeams, is not common in Cheshire and Wirral. Although they are best known for liking cherries, hornbeam seeds provide their staple diet in autumn and winter, with buds, especially of beech, in spring and insects, particularly defoliating caterpillars, in summer (*BTO Second Atlas*).

● It is thought that most British Hawfinches are sedentary (*Migration Atlas*). There are occasional autumn influxes of birds from continental Europe and Scandinavia, where more than one million pairs breed, and odd birds have been reported in the county in winter. One seen briefly at Marbury Country Park (SJ67N) on 31 December 2005 was the first record in any season for five years.

RAY SCALLY

Sponsored by Sheila Blamire

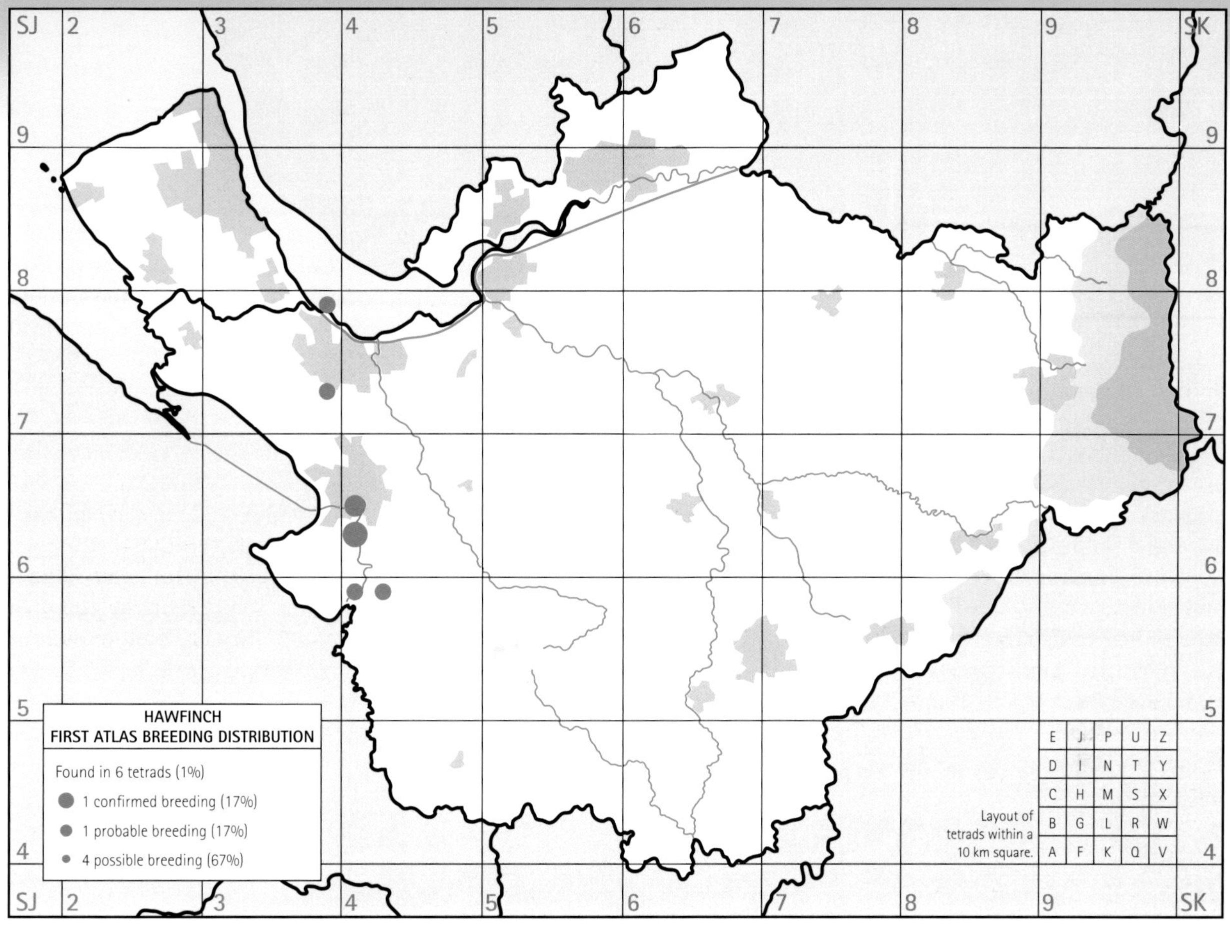
SJ
2
3
4
5
6
7
8
9
SK
HAWFINCH
FIRST ATLAS BREEDING DISTRIBUTION
Found in 6 tetrads (1%)
1 confirmed breeding (17%)
1 probable breeding (17%)
4 possible breeding (67%)
Layout of
tetrads within a
10 km square.
E J P U Z
D I N T Y
C H M S X
B G L R W
A F K Q V

Snow Bunting

Plectrophenax nivalis

Probably 10,000 or more Snow Buntings winter in Britain, mostly along the east coast and the highest hills, but few of them make it to Cheshire and Wirral (*BTO Winter Atlas*). The numbers vary greatly from one year to another. Its rarity and unpredictability, together with the attractiveness of the species make this a bird that is much sought after to brighten a winter's day. They have, however, become distinctly scarcer in recent years, perhaps because of the warming climate.

Snow Buntings have a circumpolar breeding range on the Arctic tundra, with another race (*insulae*), darker and more sedentary, breeding in Iceland and the Scottish mountains: both races winter here, with the birds of the nominate race thought to be from Scandinavia and Greenland. Most of those wintering in England are females and first-year birds (Brown & Grice 2005), males tending to winter farther north, closer to or even on their breeding territories; within Britain, males and adults are likely to winter in montane sites rather than the coast (*Migration Atlas*). As a bird of short, open vegetation, feeding by picking seeds from the ground or low creeping plants, Snow Buntings frequent two habitats, at the lowest and highest altitudes. They particularly favour sandy shores with a carpet of dune-colonizing plants or the lower levels of salt-marshes. In upland areas the main diet is probably seeds of rushes *juncus*, although they will take seeds from moor grasses and heather. They also take invertebrates when they can, especially sandhoppers on the shore.

The records during this winter Atlas were typical of recent years, with birds in five tetrads in 2004/05, in three tetrads during 2005/06 and three tetrads in 2006/07. Hilbre Island (SJ18Z) had one bird in each winter, and birds were in West Kirby (SJ28D) in 2004/05 and 2006/07. All of the Atlas records were of single birds apart from a group of five at Red Rocks (SJ28E). The bird seen by John Oxenham on 3 December 2004

RICHARD STEEL

Sponsored by Syngenta CTL

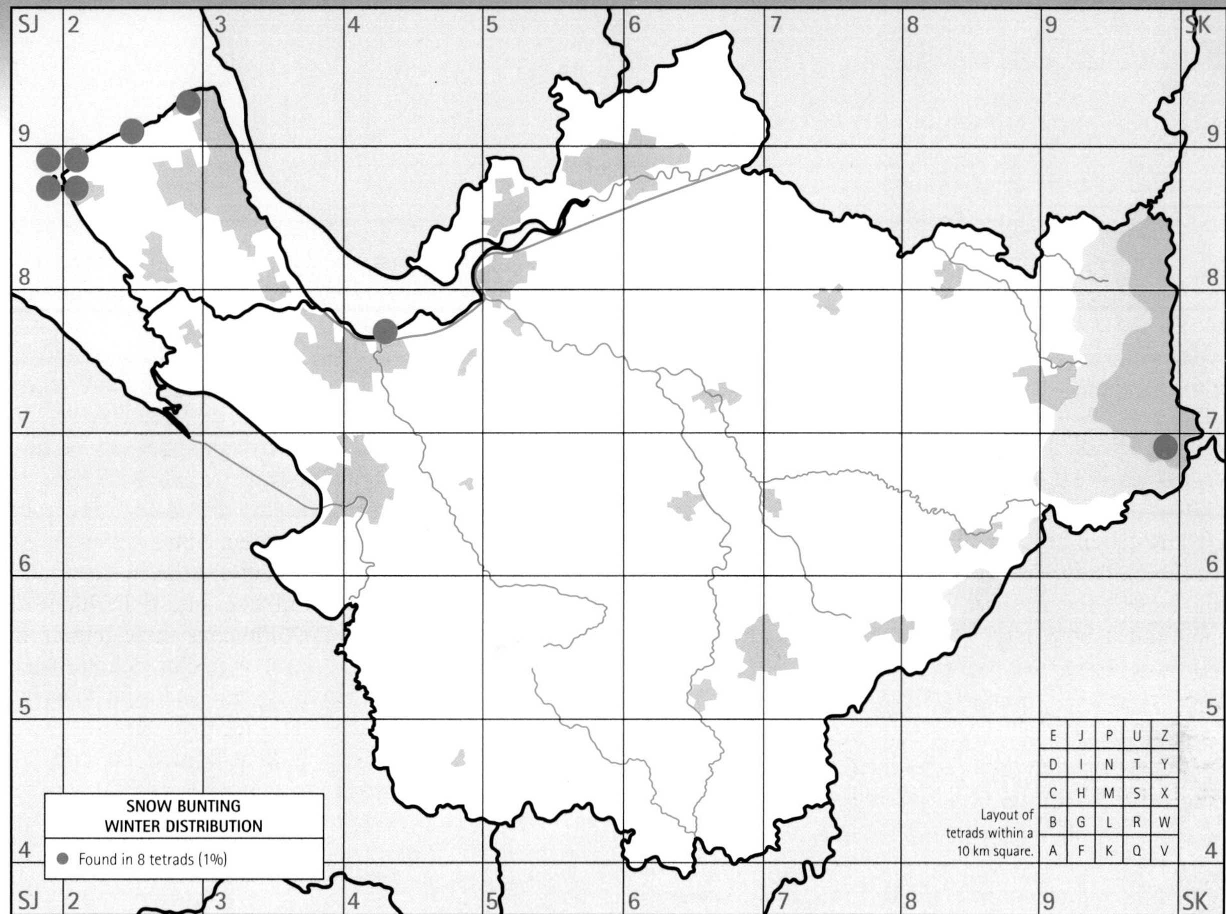

at Birchenough Hill (SJ96Z), 450 m above sea level, was the first in the hills since one in 2001/02.

The coast and the Dee estuary have always attracted the species: Coward (1910) described it as 'a fairly regular winter visitor to the coast'. In more recent times, the county bird reports since 1959 show Snow Buntings in the county in every winter apart from 1994/95, mainly at coastal sites. Leasowe Sandhills (SJ29R) used regularly to hold flocks of 20–40 birds, with a maximum of 70, but was lost to development in the early 1970s and since 1972 there have only been two winters with double-figure flocks along the north Wirral shore. As during this winter Atlas, Hilbre has been the most reliable site for the species, with single birds in many years but flocks of 10 or more in nine winters in the period 1961–2006, most recently in 1998. Along the Mersey small numbers were recorded sporadically in winter until 1982, but there have only been isolated winter records since. In the eastern hills, birds used to be regular, perhaps even annual, until 1934 but records then almost ceased and they are much scarcer now. Since 1961 there have been records in eight years, all on single dates in November and December and mostly of lone birds apart from parties of five on 8 December 1981 and nine on 23 November 1988, both on the slopes of Shutlingsloe (SJ96U). There have been occasional odd birds in the Cheshire Plain, but only six records of single birds in the last fifty years.

Yellowhammer

Emberiza citrinella

Some see this as a typical species of the Cheshire plain, hence the choice of Yellowhammer for the front cover of this Atlas. To others in the county, however, it has become a scarce bird since it was almost ubiquitous in our *First Atlas*. The 'change' map shows the species lost from 222 tetrads, with scattered gains in just 22. There have been two main components to the changes in the last twenty years: Yellowhammers have been lost from the urban fringe, especially around Macclesfield and Congleton, Halton and the Wirral; and very few are now present in the breeding season above an altitude of 100 m. The abundance map shows that the main density of Yellowhammers is around Warrington and the centre of the county.

In many tetrads where they were present, Yellowhammers took a little bit of searching for, as they seldom seemed to be close to habitation or roads. Several fieldworkers commented that they were pleased to discover them quite close to their home, not having realized they were there until they had to survey the area for this Atlas. Their insistent song 'little-bit-of-bread-and-no-cheeeese' is far-carrying, usually audible one or two fields away. 'Song' accounted for most of the possible breeding records, but adults feed their chicks on invertebrates, carried in their bill, and make obvious 'tuck' alarm calls, so FY codes provided most of the confirmed records; only one nest was reported in this survey, however, in Delamere (SJ57Q) by the author. Two or three nesting attempts are possible during the season running from April to August; unusually for a passerine, later nests tend to be more successful.

More than 80% of the submitted habitat records were farmland, and observers in almost half of the tetrads added a code of E8 or E9, indicating the importance of hedgerows to this species. They nest on the ground in field edges or ditches, or low down in hedges. Yellowhammers also use woodland edge, scrub and new plantations but these are suboptimal habitat; they quit the clear-felled areas within Delamere Forest during the 1990s.

Yellowhammer was the last species to succumb to the twentieth-century agricultural revolution: their national population figures held up for longer than for other farmland seed-eaters, uniquely remaining stable throughout our *First Atlas* period, with most of their drop coming from the late 1980s to mid-1990s (Siriwardena *et al.* 2000a), leaving the national index in 2004 at just under half of its value in 1984 and warranting their position on the Red List of species of conservation concern. This difference in timing from other species suggests that Yellowhammers have been affected by different aspects of changes in the countryside, although the reasons are not understood (Brown & Grice 2005). They may well be connected with the increasing specialization of agriculture and the demise of mixed farming. We do not know, but it is likely that Cheshire's Yellowhammers have suffered more than most, because detailed study showed that farms dominated by grass and non-cereal crops were most likely to have lost territories (Kyrkos *et al.* 1998). Even small amounts of arable land, perhaps only one field per farm, in an otherwise grassland landscape, are all that they need to maintain a presence (Robinson *et al.* 2001).

The BTO analysis of 2004–05 BBS data gives the breeding population of Cheshire and Wirral as 7,740 birds (7,110–8,370), corresponding to an average of about 32 birds per tetrad with confirmed or probable breeding, or 21 birds per tetrad in which the species was recorded. This figure is only 0.3% of the UK total, the lowest proportion for any of the farmland passerine species, another intimation that our increasingly specialized pastoral landscape is not, nowadays, prime Yellowhammer country.

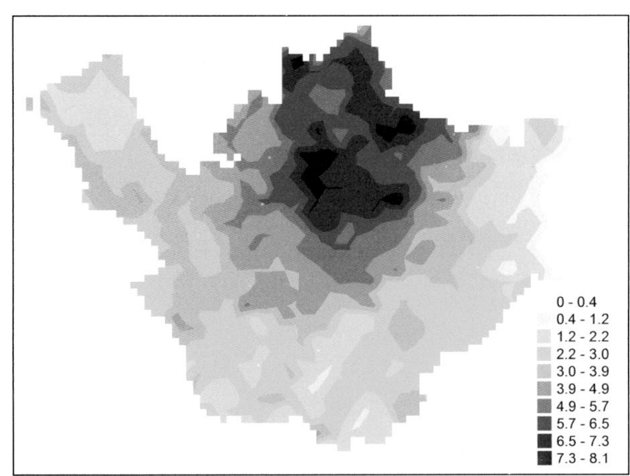

Yellowhammer abundance.

Sponsored by Frank Gleeson

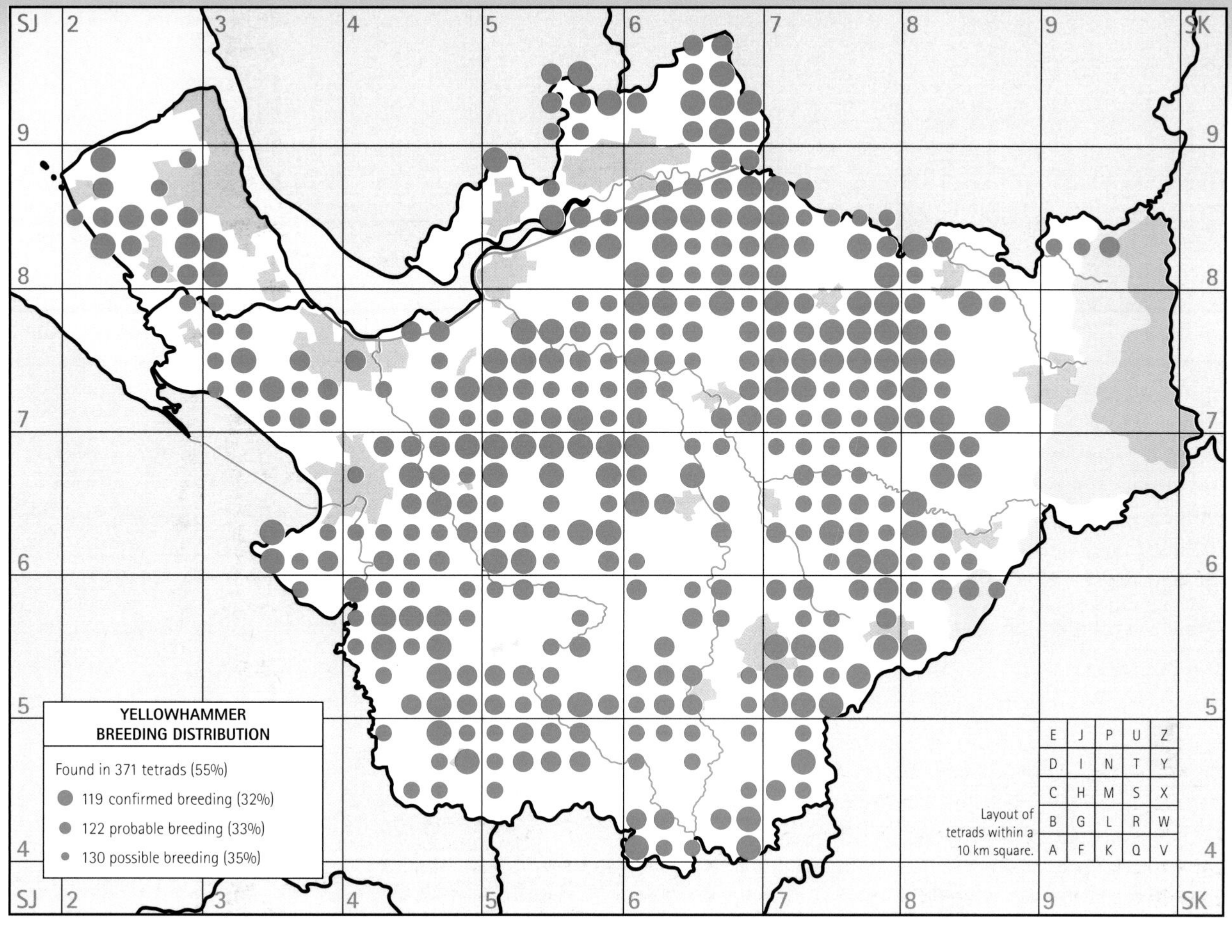
YELLOWHAMMER
BREEDING DISTRIBUTION
Found in 371 tetrads (55%)
119 confirmed breeding (32%)
122 probable breeding (33%)
130 possible breeding (35%)
Layout of tetrads within a 10 km square.
E J P U Z
D I N T Y
C H M S X
B G L R W
A F K Q V
SJ
SK

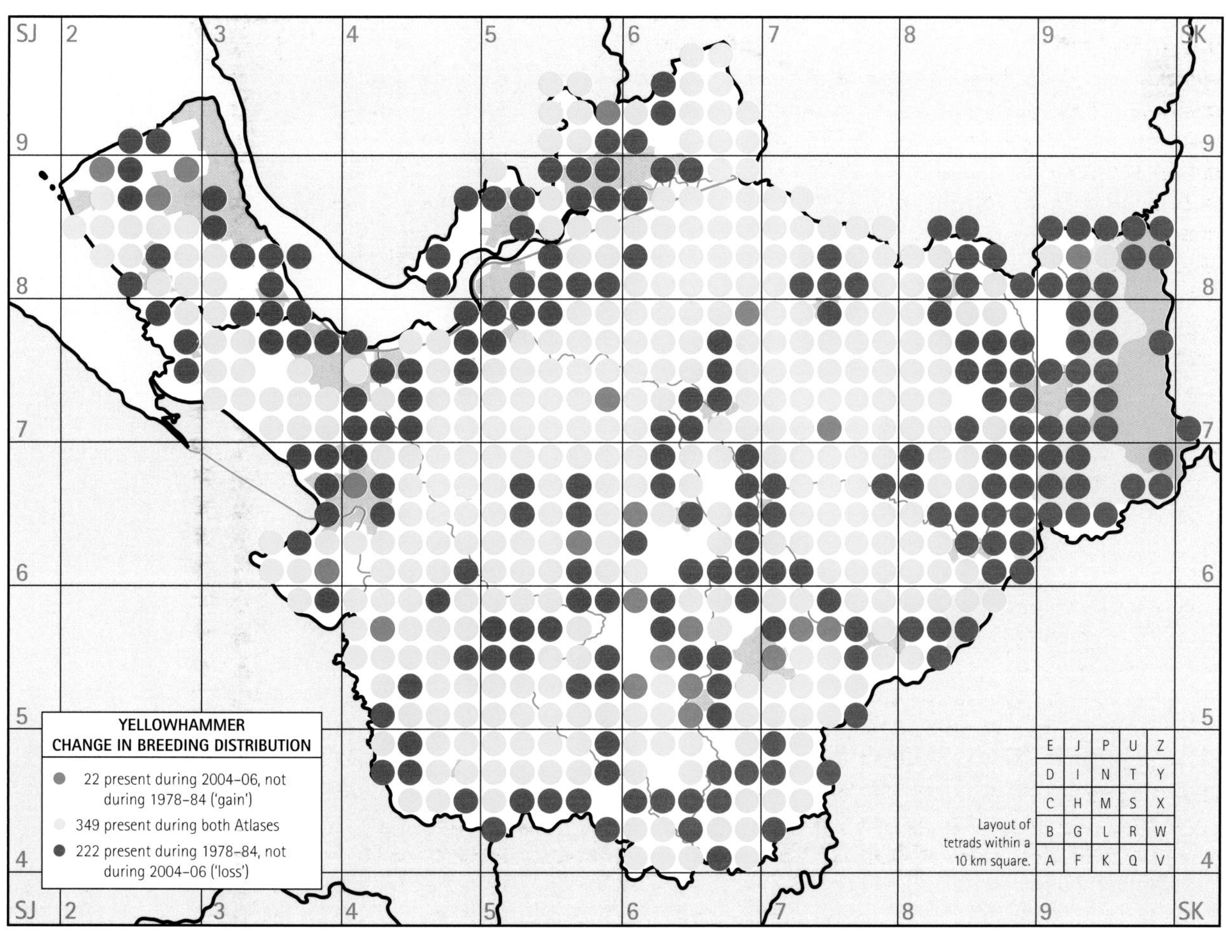
YELLOWHAMMER
CHANGE IN BREEDING DISTRIBUTION
22 present during 2004–06, not during 1978–84 ('gain')
349 present during both Atlases
222 present during 1978–84, not during 2004–06 ('loss')
Layout of tetrads within a 10 km square.
E J P U Z
D I N T Y
C H M S X
B G L R W
A F K Q V
SJ
SK

The winter map for Yellowhammers is much the same as their breeding distribution, as would be expected for this sedentary species. The median distance moved, at any time of year, is less than 1 km, and only 5% of birds move more than 25 km (*Migration Atlas*). There were 222 tetrads with Yellowhammers present in the breeding and winter seasons, 21 occupied in winter only and 149 with breeding season presence only, the latter especially across the agricultural southern half of the county.

The reduction in the number of occupied tetrads in winter is probably because they tend to gather into flocks in winter, often with other farmland seed-eaters. Most groups of Yellowhammers are small, however, numbered in single figures. During this Atlas the largest flock was of more than 100 birds in newly planted woodland at Eddisbury Hill, Delamere (SJ56P), recorded in winter 2005/06 and 2006/07 by Peter and Michael Twist, and fieldworkers noted that several stubble fields held flocks of 70–80 Yellowhammers, at Grappenhall (SJ68I), Buerton (SJ64W) and the Weston area (SJ75F/K). They often roost communally overnight, with gorse a favoured location, although only one roost was reported in this Atlas survey, six birds at Woolston on 14 February 2005.

Analysis of the winter habitat codes shows that this is one of the small passerines most likely to be found in stubble. Some also exploited set-aside fields and seed crops planted for birds under Environmental Stewardship options. Most habitat records included a 'hedge' code, 88 'tall' hedges and 50 'short' hedges. Detailed study has shown that the quality of the winter habitat strongly determines where birds locate territories in summer (Whittingham *et al.* 2005).

Coward and Oldham (1900) called the Yellowhammer 'one of the most familiar of our Cheshire birds'. In their time it was 'plentiful everywhere in the lowlands, and on the Hills up to the edge of the moors. In winter it frequents stubbles and farmyards in company with Chaffinches and sparrows, being as much in evidence at that season as in summer'. Boyd (1951) knew them as 'abundant at all seasons especially on arable farms', and Bell (1962) repeated Coward's assessment, and made no comment on the species in his supplement (1967), so we can deduce that their status remained stable for much of the twentieth century.

RAY SCALLY

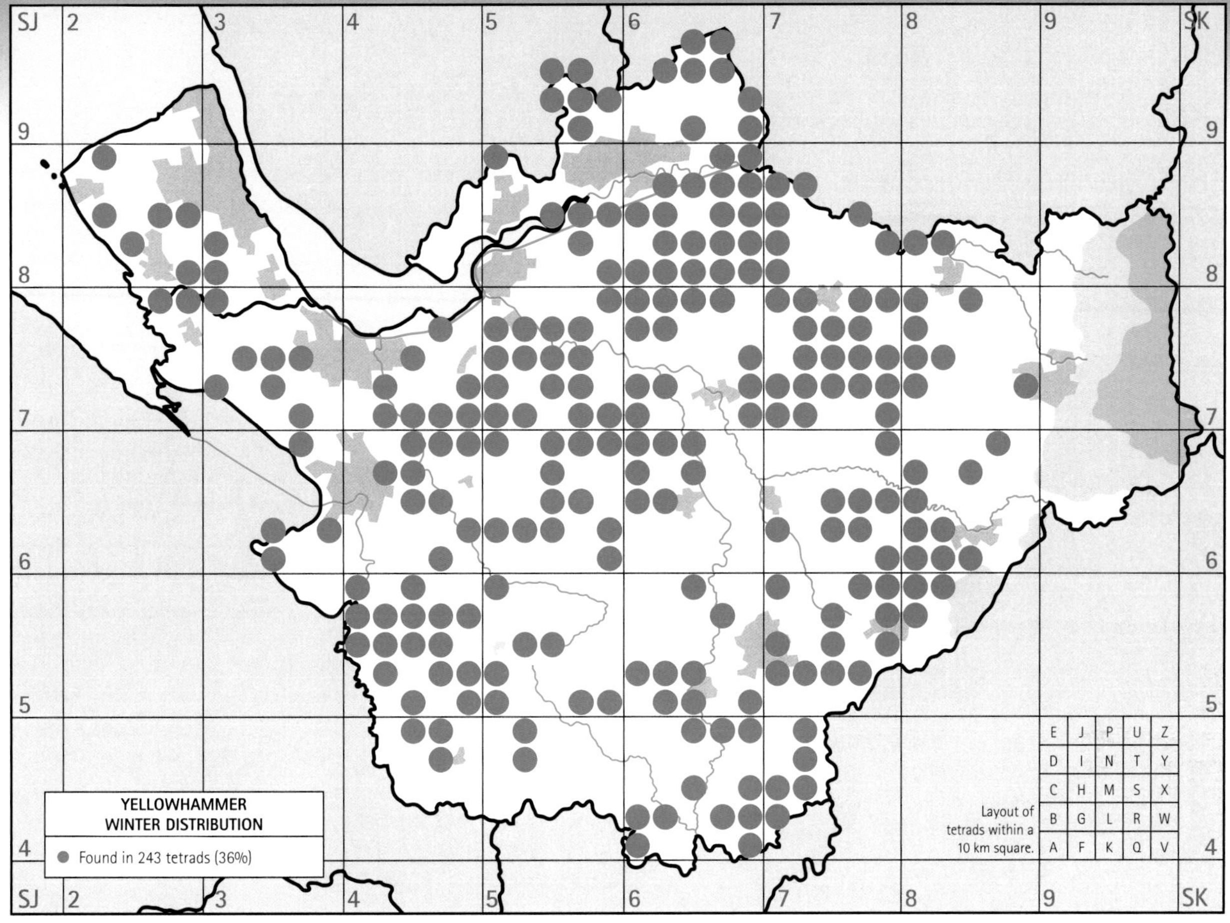
SJ
2
3
4
5
6
7
8
9
SK
9
8
7
6
5
4
YELLOWHAMMER
WINTER DISTRIBUTION
Found in 243 tetrads (36%)
E J P U Z
D I N T Y
C H M S X
B G L R W
A F K Q V
Layout of tetrads within a 10 km square.

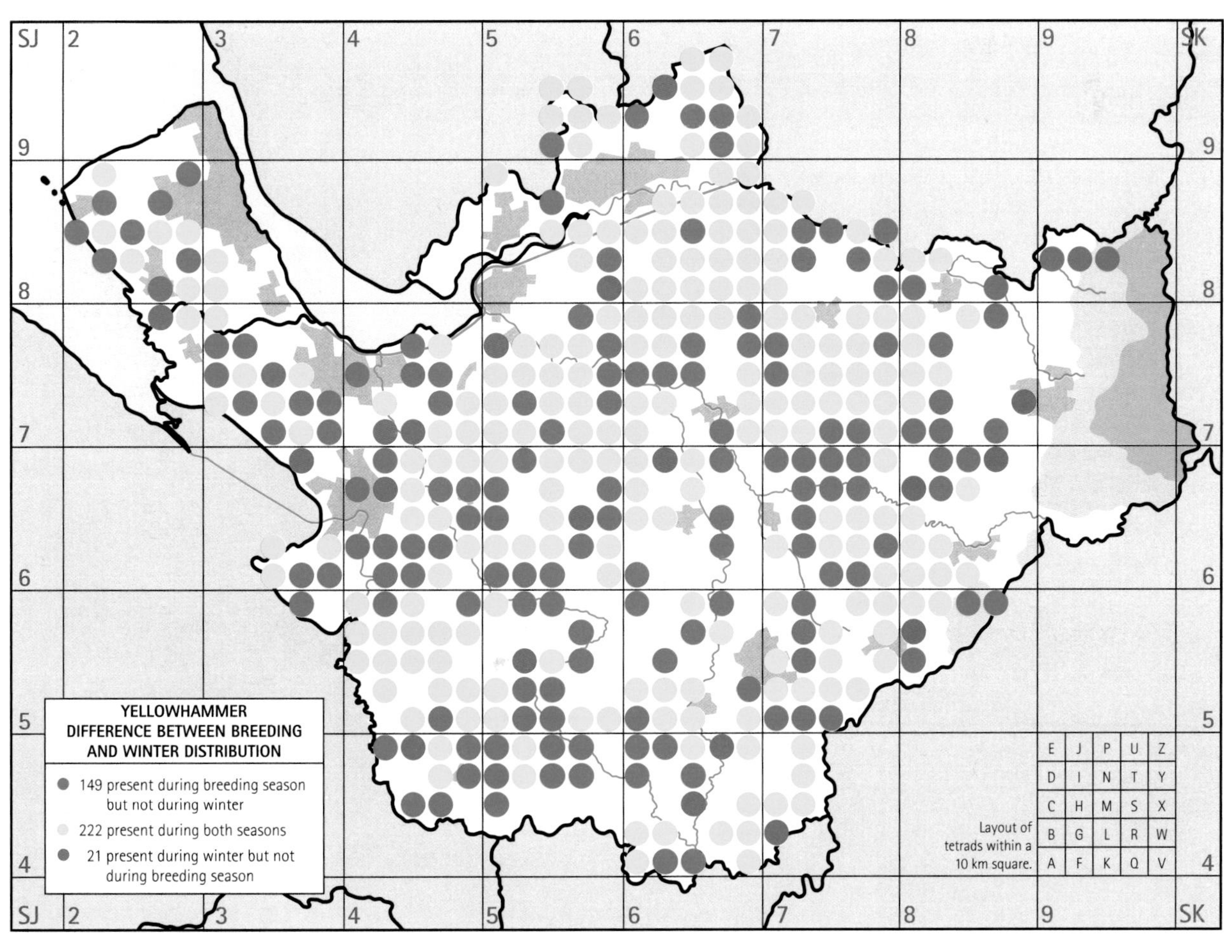
SJ
2
3
4
5
6
7
8
9
SK
9
8
7
6
5
4
YELLOWHAMMER
DIFFERENCE BETWEEN BREEDING AND WINTER DISTRIBUTION
149 present during breeding season but not during winter
222 present during both seasons
21 present during winter but not during breeding season
E J P U Z
D I N T Y
C H M S X
B G L R W
A F K Q V
Layout of tetrads within a 10 km square.

Reed Bunting

Emberiza schoeniclus

RICHARD STEEL

The rapid decline in breeding numbers has put Reed Bunting on the Red List of species of conservation concern, with a national and local BAP to support action for its recovery. The national population index for Reed Bunting crashed to reach a low point in 1984 that was 57% down on their peak just a decade earlier in 1975; the Cheshire and Wirral picture may have been worse, since the fall in northern Britain was greater than in southern areas (Peach *et al.* 1999). Since then, the national index has fluctuated within quite a narrow range and the 2004 figure is little different from that of 20 years before. Thus, the population was falling throughout the period of our *First Atlas*, and the large decrease (169 lost, 54 gained) in occupied tetrads shown in the 'change' map is probably mainly in tetrads surveyed in the early years of our 1978–84 *First Atlas*. This drop is widespread and scattered throughout the county but includes a major loss from most of the Wirral peninsula. It is still, however, a common bird of the damp, scrubby areas in the Mersey valley, and Reed Bunting is perhaps *the* characteristic species of the marl-pit ponds across much of agricultural Cheshire; the only areas showing more than the odd gains since our *First Atlas* are in the south-west of the county.

Demographic analyses suggest that the national decline was driven by decreasing overwinter survival rates, particularly for the inexperienced first-year birds, probably because of reduced availability of small seeds on farmland (Peach *et al.* 1999). The breeding decline was as severe along waterways as on farmland, and deterioration of the Reed Bunting's characteristic wetland habitats may have had a serious effect, through loss of small ponds, unsympathetic river engineering and the encroachment of scrub and carr.

Breeding Reed Buntings occupied a very wide range of habitats. Most contained water or reed-bed, but a significant fraction of birds belie the species' name. During the middle of the twentieth century the species had spread out to occupy some dry habitats, although these are probably suboptimal and much of the population decline seems to have been in these drier areas. Even in apparently favourable habitat, however, there have been waning numbers. This species has been included in most years of the mid-May Woolston warbler census; counts have dropped dramatically from a mean of 103 singing males in the years 1983–89, to 78 males in 1994–97 and a mean of only 36 singing males during the three years of this Atlas. The unmanaged progression from open scrub towards a drier woodland has presumably been inimical to this species. It has also been noticeable across the county that the species has extended its breeding season, with some birds singing into August, probably driven by the poor success of early nests to prolong their season with further attempts. Fieldworkers confirmed breeding in 40% of the tetrads, mostly by seeing adults with a beak full of grubs, the observers' attention probably being drawn by the birds' insistent anxiety calls. Adults feed themselves on small seeds all year round, but have to find the protein-rich invertebrates for their chicks; it may be a reduction in insects that has cut Reed Bunting breeding numbers, especially in drier habitats.

The BTO analysis of 2004–05 BBS data puts the breeding population of Cheshire and Wirral as 4,410 birds (3,930–4,930), corresponding to an average of about 16 birds per tetrad with confirmed or probable breeding, or 10 birds per tetrad in which the species was recorded. The abundance map, although distorted for much of Wirral, shows that the main density of Reed Buntings is along the Mersey valley, where most of their ideal habitat is to be found.

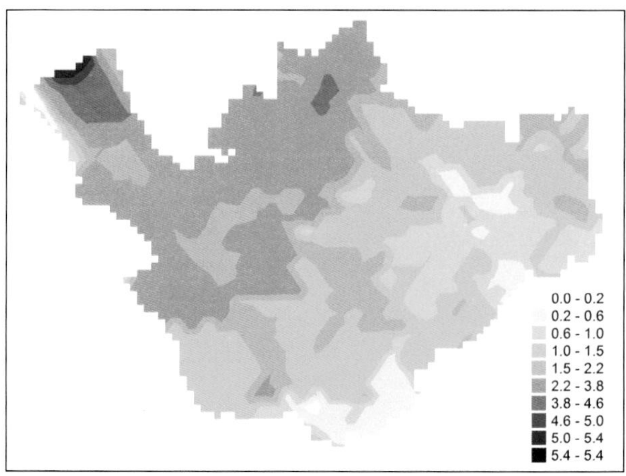

Reed Bunting abundance.

Sponsored by Robin Hart

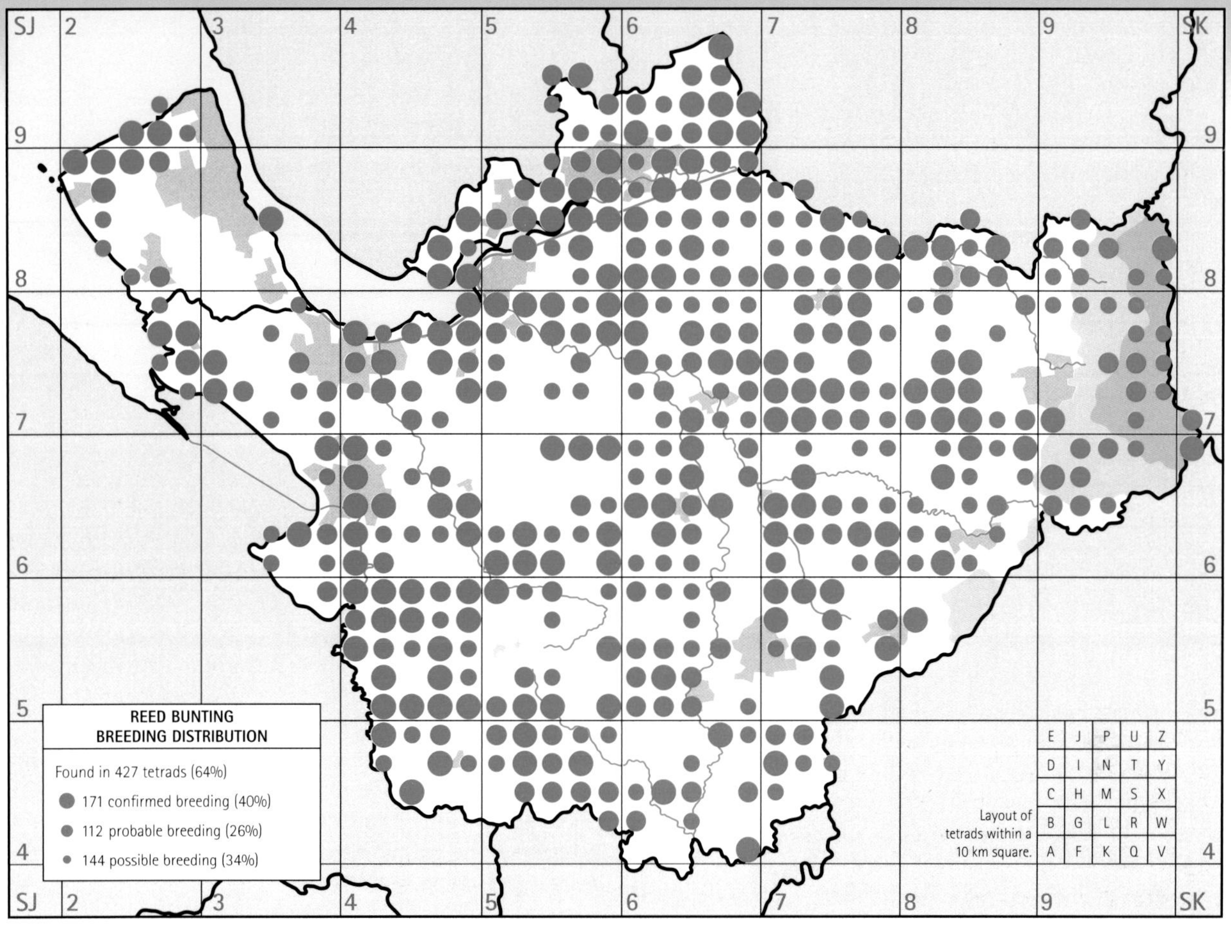
SJ
2
3
4
5
6
7
8
9
SK
REED BUNTING
BREEDING DISTRIBUTION
Found in 427 tetrads (64%)
171 confirmed breeding (40%)
112 probable breeding (26%)
144 possible breeding (34%)
Layout of tetrads within a 10 km square.
E J P U Z
D I N T Y
C H M S X
B G L R W
A F K Q V

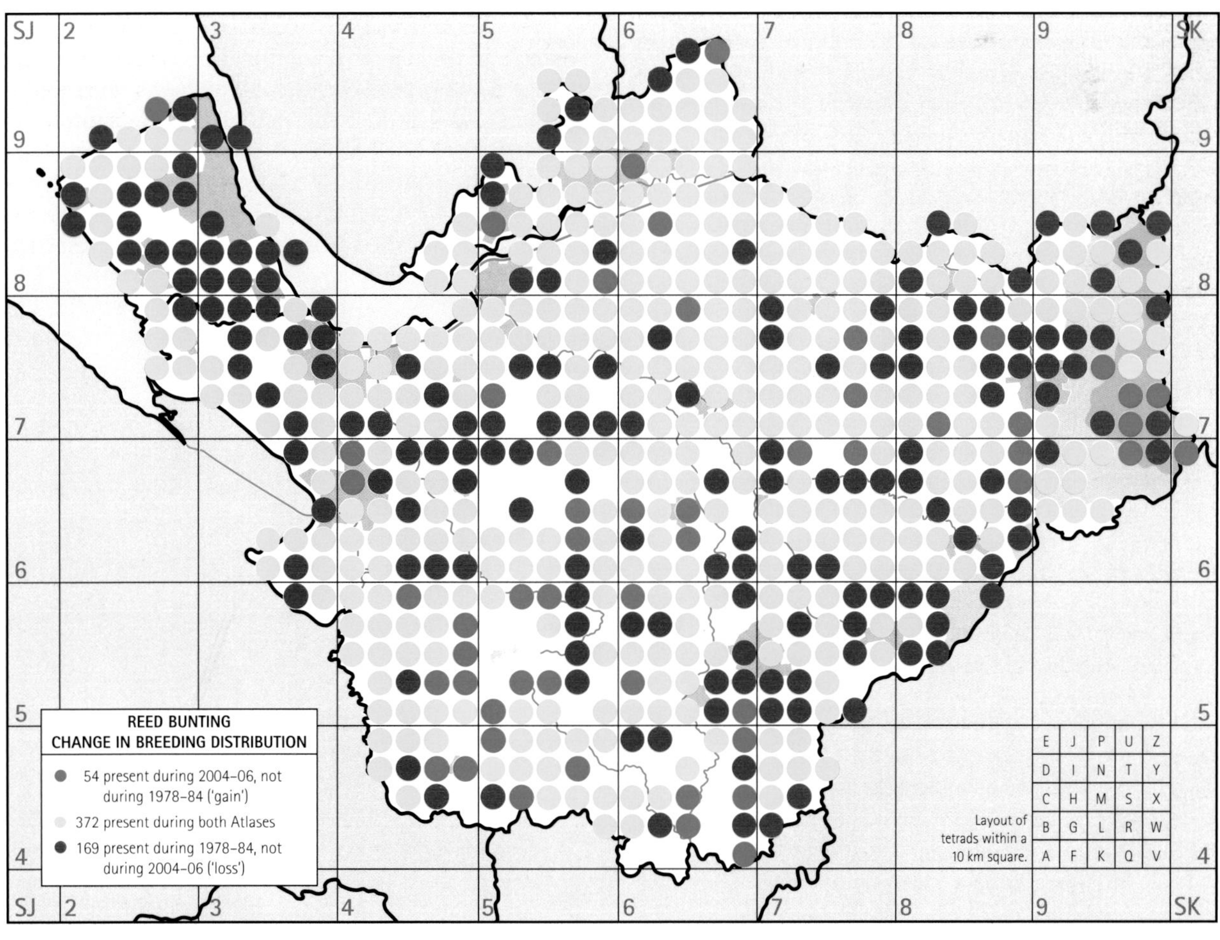
SJ
2
3
4
5
6
7
8
9
SK
REED BUNTING
CHANGE IN BREEDING DISTRIBUTION
54 present during 2004–06, not during 1978–84 ('gain')
372 present during both Atlases
169 present during 1978–84, not during 2004–06 ('loss')
Layout of tetrads within a 10 km square.
E J P U Z
D I N T Y
C H M S X
B G L R W
A F K Q V

This winter Atlas map would come as a surprise to most twentieth-century ornithologists. Coward (1910) noted that 'although a few odd birds, sometimes a male and female evidently a pair, frequently remain throughout the winter, the majority of Reed Buntings leave in the autumn'. They returned in mid-March as one of the earliest spring migrants. Boyd (1951) was used to only small numbers during winter in mid-Cheshire, where he acutely observed that they join the finch-Yellowhammer flocks in the hedgerows. Bell (1962) expanded on the description of their winter status by writing that few remained inland, and that in Wirral, birds from inland localities may have made for the coast. During the mostly cold weather of the national *BTO Winter Atlas* (1981/82–1983/84), Reed Buntings were found in every 10 km square in the county, but only in any numbers along the Mersey valley and west Wirral, a statement that was echoed in the annual county bird report for 1986. From records submitted to the annual bird reports it is not clear when wintering birds became more widespread, but the Woolston report for 1992 noted that the recent run of relatively mild winters had changed their status and the county report for that year introduced one-line status statements for all species in which the Reed Bunting was optimistically declared a 'common widespread resident'. There were noticeably fewer in the county in the colder winters of 1995/96 and 1996/97, when most birds were reported along the frost-free tide-lines and salt-marshes, but since then their wintering numbers have increased greatly.

Life in winter in Cheshire and Wirral is obviously finely balanced for Reed Buntings: the population comprises some residents and some partial migrants, and the equilibrium between them shifts from year to year. The smaller females especially are less able to withstand cold weather and move to the coast or fly south, or die. This is a much-ringed species and there are many records of migration, some as far as the south coasts of England and Wales: in 1990 a Woolston-bred female, for instance, moved to Devon for the winter and then back to Woolston in 1991. There appear to be fewer migratory birds these days, as climate change favours the sedentary individuals. Although the British Reed Bunting population is largely self-contained, there may also be some birds wintering here from continental Europe (*Migration Atlas*); ringed birds moving between Cheshire and Suffolk hint at such an origin.

The map shows that there is some contraction of range, with winter birds found in 323 tetrads, 104 fewer than in the breeding season. There were 252 tetrads with Reed Buntings present in the breeding and winter seasons, 71 occupied in winter only and 175 with breeding season presence only. There is no particular geographical pattern to these shifts, except for a withdrawal from much of the highest land in the east.

Reed Buntings gather into flocks outside the breeding season, but most gatherings are small. Only 14 counts were submitted of more than 25 birds, all in stubble, set-aside or wildbird crops, with the largest, 50 birds, on the Dee salt-marsh. Communal roosts are another feature of their ecology, but only five were reported, with a maximum of 10 birds apart from a substantial roost at Woolston estimated at more than 150 birds on 3 December 2006.

STEVE ROUND

Analysis of the habitat codes submitted shows a wide range spanning all of the habitat groups: 53% farmland; 17% semi-natural grassland and marsh; 16% fresh water; 6% human sites; 4% scrub; and 2% bog. Outside the breeding season, Reed Buntings concentrate on small grass and weed seeds, and weed-rich stubbles are strongly preferred as winter feeding habitat (Wilson *et al.* 1996). Certainly, in this survey Reed Buntings were one of the small passerines most likely to be found in any suitable stubble (E7). The lack of weedy stubble is probably the main factor that reduced the carrying capacity of the winter environment for Reed Buntings compared to that of the early 1970s (Peach *et al.* 1999); this loss has been only partially compensated by Environmental Stewardship options such as set-aside and specially planted seed crops, where Reed Buntings seem especially to favour millet. Observers noted a few birds at 'human' sites, and Reed Bunting is one of the species that occasionally enters gardens, especially in late winter as natural food supplies dwindle, but surveyors for the BTO Garden BirdWatch have reported few since 1998.

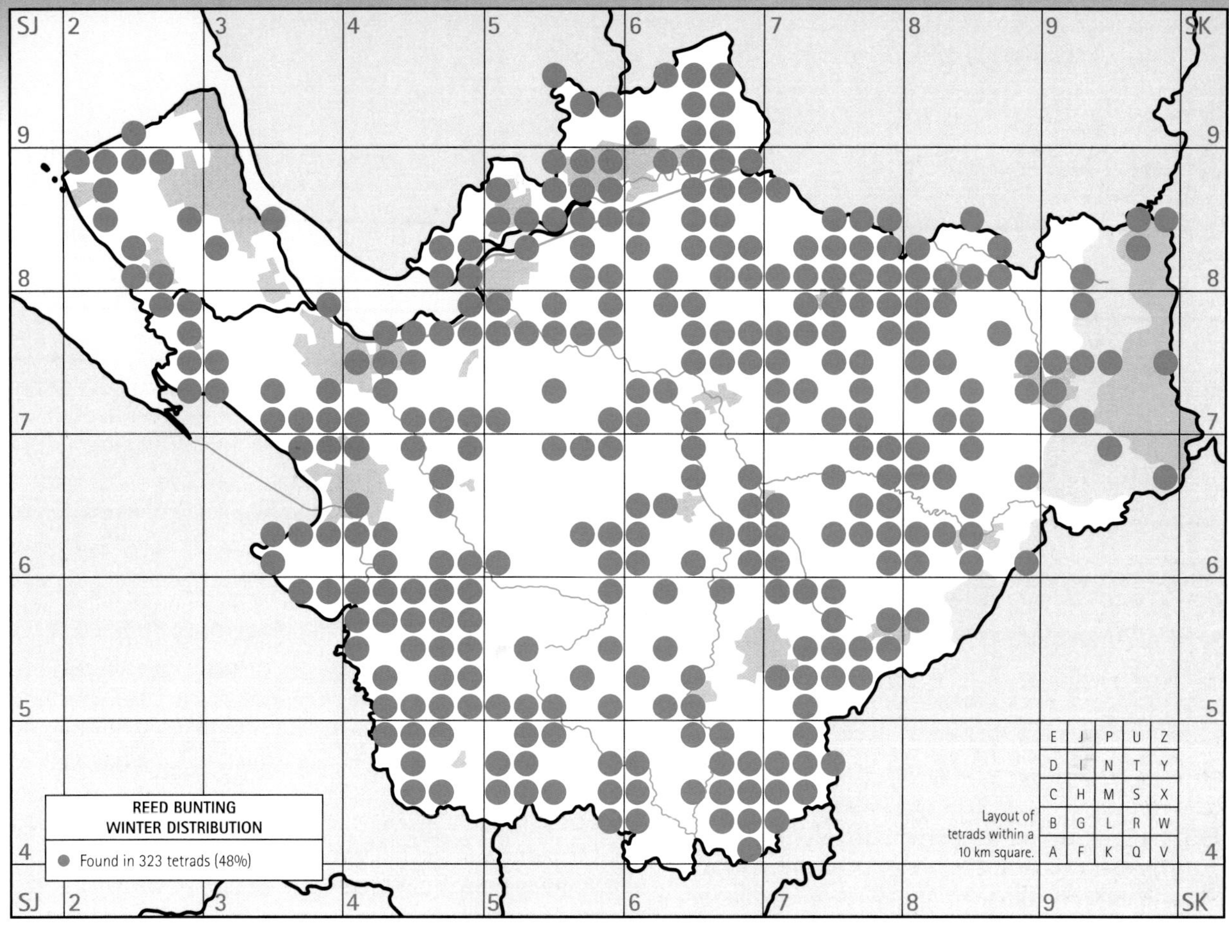
SJ
2
3
4
5
6
7
8
9
SK
REED BUNTING
WINTER DISTRIBUTION
Found in 323 tetrads (48%)
Layout of
tetrads within a
10 km square.
E J P U Z
D I N T Y
C H M S X
B G L R W
A F K Q V

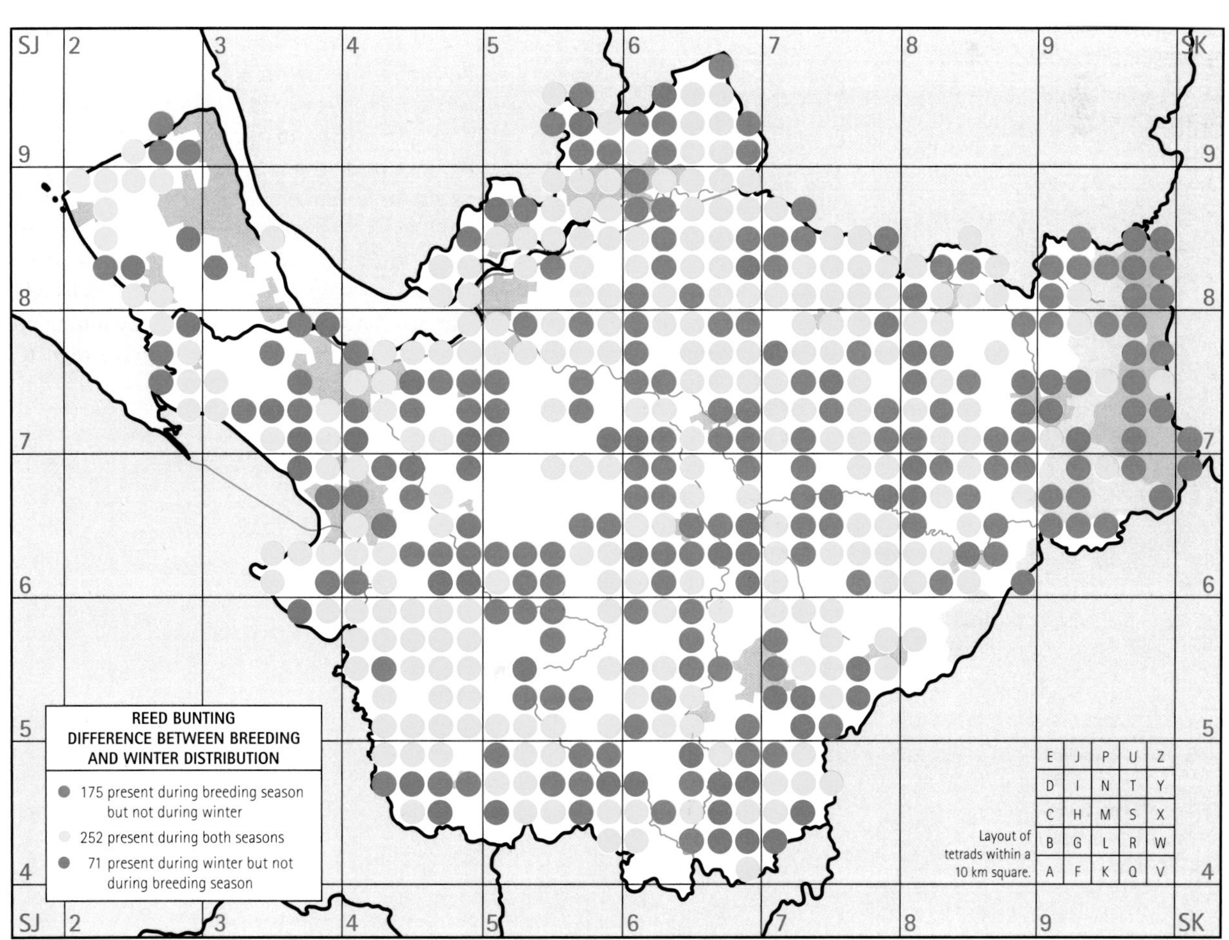
SJ
2
3
4
5
6
7
8
9
SK
REED BUNTING
DIFFERENCE BETWEEN BREEDING
AND WINTER DISTRIBUTION
175 present during breeding season
but not during winter
252 present during both seasons
71 present during winter but not
during breeding season
Layout of
tetrads within a
10 km square.
E J P U Z
D I N T Y
C H M S X
B G L R W
A F K Q V

Corn Bunting

Miliaria calandra

ANDY HARMER

Cheshire can never have been particularly important for the Corn Bunting, as a bird primarily of arable land, but in the last twenty years the species has undergone a major contraction in range within the county, and it is now one of our scarcest breeders.

National surveys show that the population fell precipitously from its peak in 1973, with a 91% drop in the 30 years from then. Much of that drop was during the 1970s and early 1980s, but from the end of our *First Atlas* (1984) to the start of this Atlas (2004), their breeding numbers nationally have seen another 75% fall. Against that background, it is no surprise that it has been lost from Wirral, and the casual reports submitted to *CWBRs* over the last 20 years have shown a steady decline in Cheshire. The species is down from presence in 260 tetrads in our *First Atlas* to just 36 now. It is completely absent from its former strongholds around the Dee, the south Mersey and the lower Weaver valley. A few new sites, including eight tetrads in the southern half of the county that were not occupied twenty years ago, might give some cause for optimism about the Corn Bunting's prospects.

They strongly prefer agricultural areas with mixed arable rotation, and avoid improved grassland. Most of the Cheshire birds are now found in locations where more than half of the land area is devoted to growing cereals. This type of habitat is mainly present in the north of the county, with the species' strongholds around Risley and Hale. Farther north, the Lancashire and North Merseyside breeding bird Atlas (1997–2001) found a healthy (although much reduced) population, with Corn Buntings present in almost all of the lowland non-urban tetrads between the Mersey and the Ribble.

In this survey, nearly all birds were found in agricultural habitats, with the majority of the codes recorded being E3 (mixed grass/tilled land), E4 (tilled land) or E6 (other farming). Six tetrads had records of birds carrying food for their young, and in another six the observer noted pairs of birds, but most Corn Buntings were detected by the observer hearing the jangling song of the male, perhaps followed by a sight of the bulky bird flying across the top of the crop, with his legs characteristically dangling.

This is an unusual passerine species in several ways. They are sexually dimorphic, with males much larger than the females. Some female Corn Buntings pair with an already-mated male, a strategy that clearly works because both females nesting with a polygynous male have similar reproductive success, and both are more successful than a females nesting monogamously (Hartley *et al.* 1995). They are one of the latest breeding passerines in Britain, with a peak of egg-laying in late June, but covering an extended period from late May to late July. Some broods are attended by 'helpers', especially juvenile females that fledged earlier, that assist the parents in feeding the chicks; these are usually half-siblings from a polygynous father.

The nests are almost always on the ground in cereals, field boundaries and rough grass. A clutch of three to five eggs is incubated for about 12–14 days, and chicks leave the nest from about nine days of age, well before they can fly. The chicks are fed almost entirely on invertebrates, especially sawflies, hoverfly larvae and beetles, and loss of these insects is probably instrumental in the decline of the Corn Bunting. After fledging, ripening cereal grain becomes the main food, for adults and juveniles alike.

Few of the Cheshire tetrads now hold more than one or two pairs, and—given its long singing period—it is possible that some of the records refer only to birds moving through. The present county population is unlikely to exceed 70 pairs.

Sponsored by Jean Bulmer

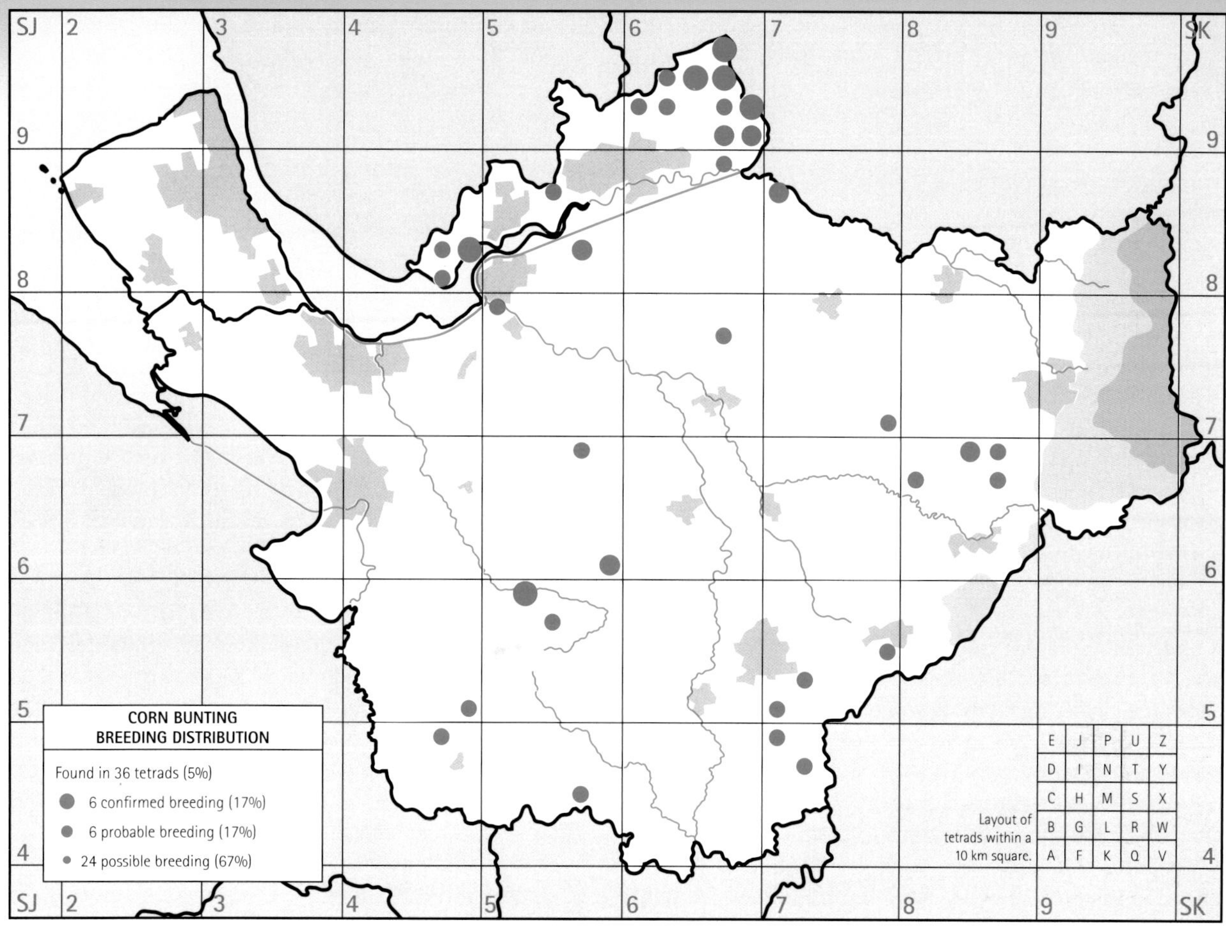
SJ
SK
CORN BUNTING
BREEDING DISTRIBUTION
Found in 36 tetrads (5%)
6 confirmed breeding (17%)
6 probable breeding (17%)
24 possible breeding (67%)
Layout of tetrads within a 10 km square.
E J P U Z
D I N T Y
C H M S X
B G L R W
A F K Q V

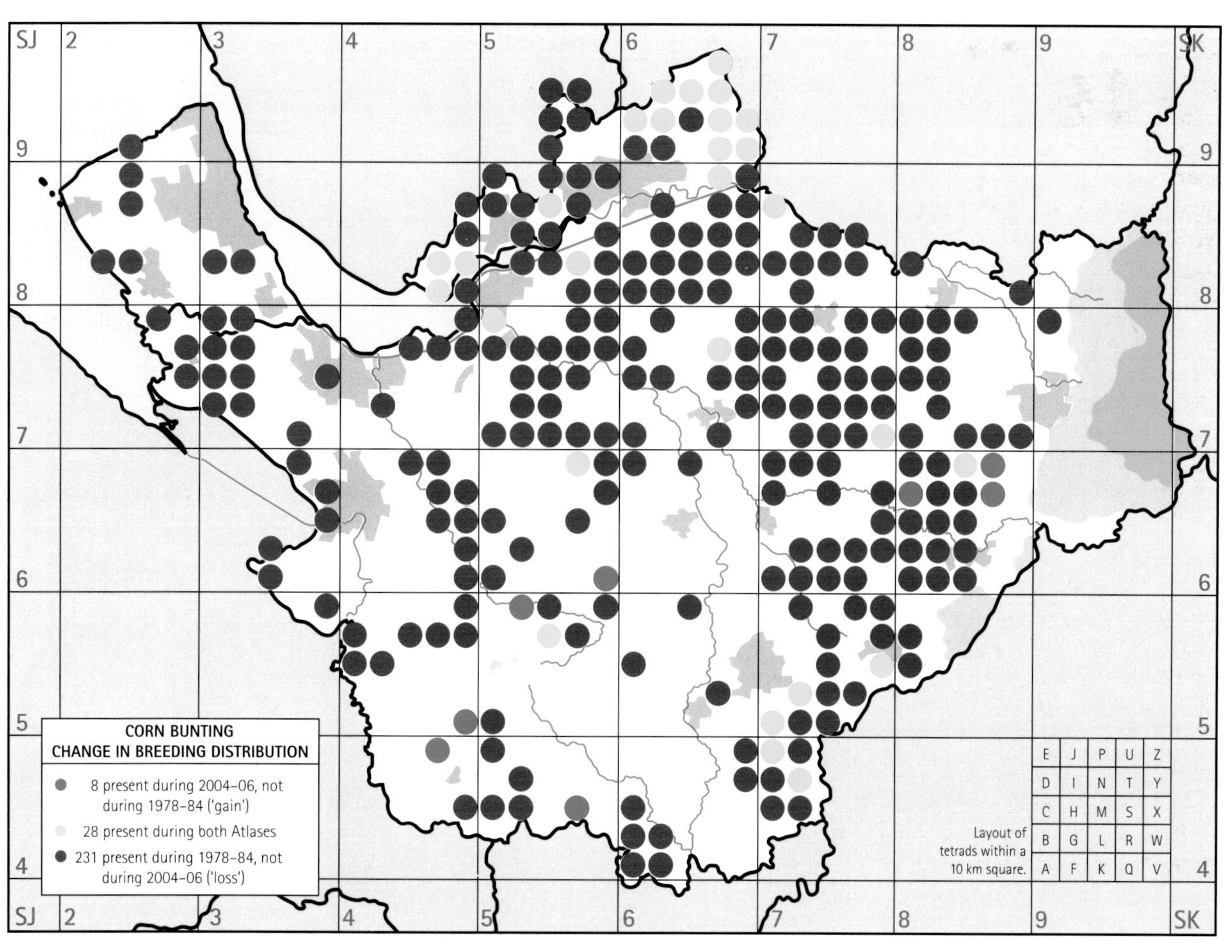
SJ
SK
CORN BUNTING
CHANGE IN BREEDING DISTRIBUTION
8 present during 2004–06, not during 1978–84 ('gain')
28 present during both Atlases
231 present during 1978–84, not during 2004–06 ('loss')
Layout of tetrads within a 10 km square.
E J P U Z
D I N T Y
C H M S X
B G L R W
A F K Q V

Corn Bunting was recorded in winter in only 16 tetrads. They are thought to be largely resident—nationally, the median distance of movement for ringed birds is just 4 km (*Migration Atlas*)—so it is intriguing that seven of the winter tetrads did not have breeding season records, and indeed that 27 of those with breeding evidence did not have birds observed in winter. These observations probably support the notion that there is some short-distance dispersal in winter, with birds returning to the vicinity of their natal areas to breed. They can be an unobtrusive bird in winter, often feeding on the ground in the company of other species, so might have been overlooked in some sites, but some birds reveal themselves by singing occasionally on bright days.

The BTO's winter Corn Bunting survey, in 1992/93, showed that weedy stubble fields were by far the most important feeding habitat during the winter (Donald & Evans 1994), although other habitats, including grassland and salt-marsh, held almost half of the flocks found. They avoid improved grassland and winter cereals. In this survey, observers recorded 20 habitat codes for wintering Corn Buntings: four including tilled land (E3/E4), five on improved grassland, one on the Dee salt-marsh and only three on stubble (E7). The area of winter stubbles has been greatly reduced in recent decades due to the switch from spring-sown to autumn-sown cereals, the decline in mixed farming and the disappearance of undersowing. In addition, increased herbicide and fertilizer use has reduced the abundance of wildflower seeds. Loss of winter food is likely to be a key factor in the species' population decline, probably through reducing survival rates (as with Reed Bunting), but the direct evidence is lacking for Corn Bunting as not enough of them are ringed.

As with all seed-eaters, they join into flocks in winter, although in the 1992/93 BTO survey the most common 'flock' size was just two birds. Most of the flocks recorded were in single figures, and less than 5% exceeded 60. In Cheshire, double-figure flocks are scarce enough to be listed in the annual bird reports: the only such counts during this Atlas period were in the Risley area, about 10 birds in a stubble field on 24 November 2004 in SJ69S and 31 in improved grassland in SJ69Q during 2006/07.

Corn Buntings also form communal winter roosts, travelling up to 4 km from their feeding sites to roost in reed-beds or occasionally in scrub or on the ground. The only roost recorded during this survey was at Hale, Widnes (SJ48R), with 11 roosting in *phragmites* on 21 December 2004.

Not much is on record about the former winter status of Corn Bunting in the county. Coward and Oldham (1900) said that it was 'seldom met with in winter', and Brockholes (1874) considered it absent from Wirral at that season. It may have been overlooked, but there are suggestions that the species used to undertake more winter dispersal. Boyd (1951) noted its 'singularly local distribution' and knew it from nowhere within 12 miles of his home near Great Budworth. He commented on the inappropriateness of its name of 'Common Bunting', still in use in the 1930s, as it is the least common of the three British buntings.

RAY SCALLY

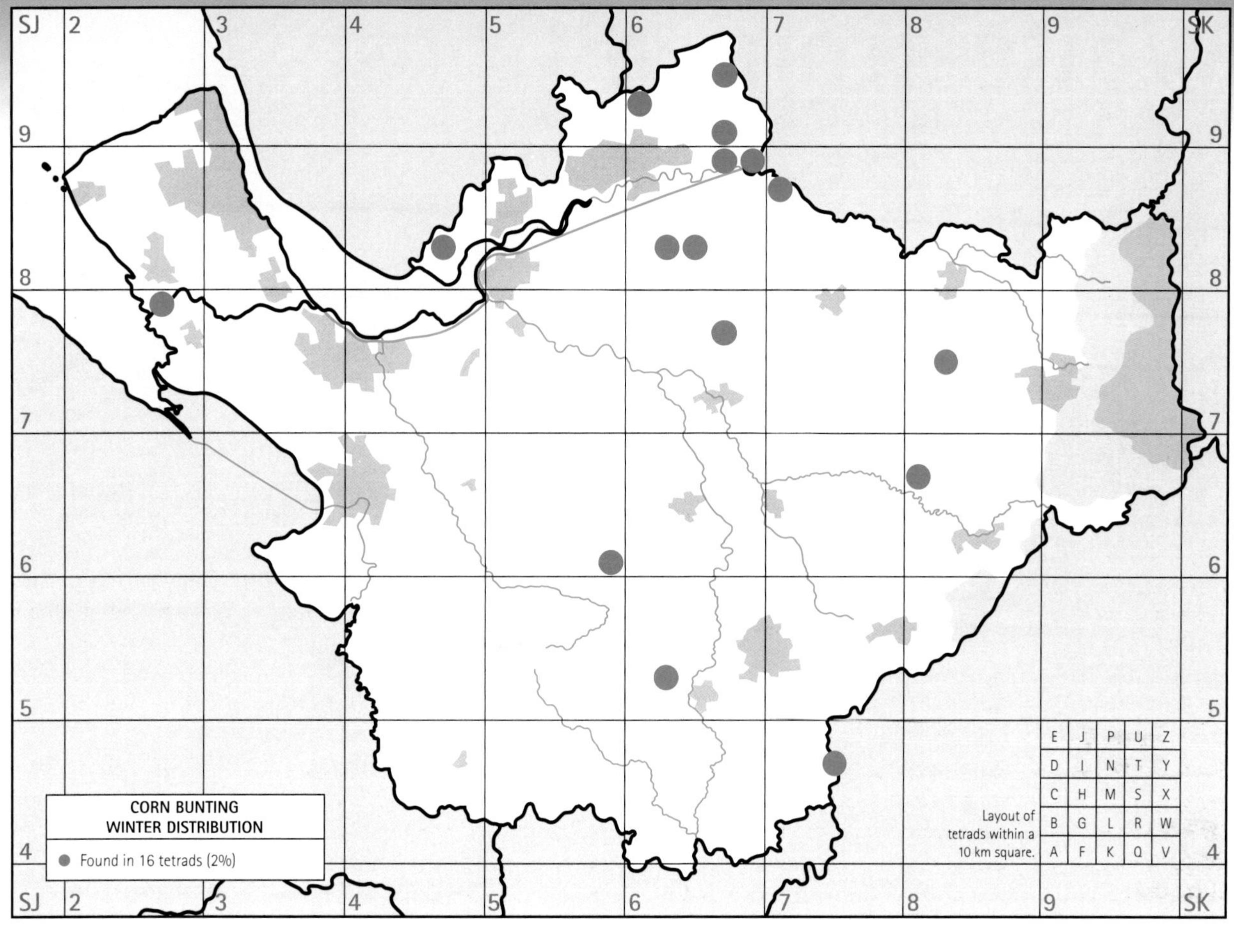
CORN BUNTING
WINTER DISTRIBUTION
Found in 16 tetrads (2%)
Layout of tetrads within a 10 km square.
E J P U Z
D I N T Y
C H M S X
B G L R W
A F K Q V
SJ
SK

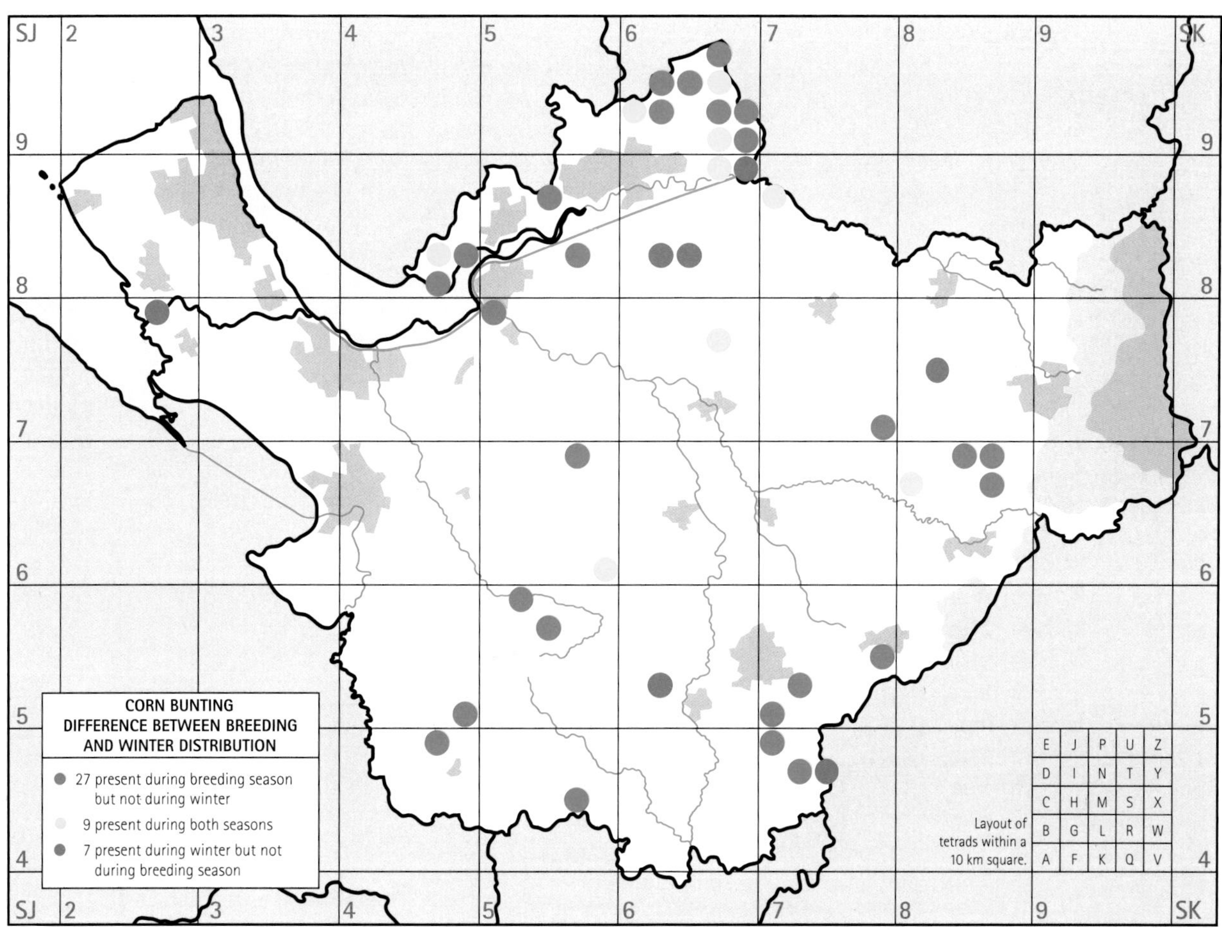
CORN BUNTING
DIFFERENCE BETWEEN BREEDING AND WINTER DISTRIBUTION
27 present during breeding season but not during winter
9 present during both seasons
7 present during winter but not during breeding season
Layout of tetrads within a 10 km square.
E J P U Z
D I N T Y
C H M S X
B G L R W
A F K Q V
SJ
SK

White-fronted Goose

Anser albifrons

There were only three records of White-fronted Geese in the three winters of this survey, all identified as birds of the European (nominate) race *Anser albifrons albifrons* that breeds in arctic Russia and winters mostly in western Europe. Two of the records were on the Dee estuary in 2004/05, with two birds in SJ27X and seven birds in SJ37B; the third record was from SJ75E (Sandbach Flashes), where three adults and four first-winter birds were present for two days from 25 February 2006.

The total of European White-fronted Geese wintering in the UK has declined severely, by more than half in the last 25 years, so the species is listed on the UK BAP priority species list (Eaton *et al.* 2007). The species as a whole is not in trouble—more than one million winter in continental Europe, especially the Netherlands and Germany—but they have shifted their overwintering distribution, probably because of a combination of reduced hunting pressure and the effects of climate change and agricultural intensification (Pollitt *et al.* 2003).

The species' status in Cheshire and Wirral has varied greatly. Coward and Oldham (1900) wrote that it used to be a well-known visitor to the tidal waters of the Mersey estuary in winter, coming down at night from the adjacent mosses. They reported Brockholes (1874) as saying that it occurred occasionally on the Dee Marshes but, by 1900, it was less frequently met with. Coward (1910) added a few records of birds seen or shot on the Dee estuary. Bell (1962) described how it became a regular winter visitor for a period but then reverted to its former status. Typical numbers on the Gowy marshes near Stanlow were 500 in the 1920s, 2,000 during the 1940s and over 4,000 in exceptionally severe frost in January and February 1947. During the 1950s the numbers decreased to maxima of 1,100 in 1953 and 280 in 1957, and from then the area was used very irregularly by flocks up to 150. Birds often fed in the Dee flood-meadows south of Chester and flew to roost on the Mersey, with small groups occasionally visiting the mid-Cheshire meres (Boyd 1951).

The annual bird reports show that numbers have dwindled in the last 25 years, with most records of occasional overflying flocks and a number of odd birds of debatable origin. The largest gatherings of feeding or roosting birds in each decade have been 32 in 1977, 24 in 1984, 20 in 1995 and 16 in 2003, but some years have had only one or two records and this Atlas appears to show the current status accurately.

Sponsored by Mark Greenhough

Egyptian Goose

Alopochen aegyptiaca

This native of trans-Saharan Africa—a shelduck, not a goose—was first introduced to Britain for the royal collection in St James's Park in 1678, and then became a popular bird in collections and large estates. Many were free-flying and wandered somewhat, soon giving rise to feral breeders; the species has never become established like the Canada Goose, however, and perhaps it is not well adapted to Britain's cold winters. It may be relevant that they have flourished here only in the driest parts of the country, a climate more akin to that of its African homelands (Lever 1977). Most of the current population of around 400 pairs is concentrated in Norfolk, but odd pairs have bred in other counties. They are also breeding in Belgium and the Netherlands, where some of the estimated 1,300 pairs have adapted to city parks, although most prefer rural areas, and the geese are now spreading into northern France. When they become established they can breed at high densities: figures of up to 19 pairs per square kilometre have been recorded at preferred breeding sites in the Netherlands, such as small lakes amid marshy woodland and meadows (Hagemeijer & Blair 1997). Egyptian Geese are usually found on large waterbodies or adjacent short grass: they mostly eat grass, with other vegetable matter and some small aquatic creatures. Elsewhere in Britain, most birds appear to be sedentary, or make short flights around their home base.

Egyptian Goose has never been known to breed in the wild in Cheshire and Wirral, although they have in the past been kept on many private waters (Coward & Oldham 1900). In the last twenty years, however, they have bred within a few kilometres of the Cheshire boundary. The *BTO Second Atlas* mapped breeding evidence in SJ69. The Rare Breeding Birds Panel has monitored non-native breeding birds since 1996, and its reports show that Egyptian Geese bred in Greater Manchester at Etherow Country Park, Compstall, Stockport from 1997 to 2002, but not since.

During this Atlas period, up to 10 birds were in the vicinity of Frodsham Marsh/Weaver Bend (SJ47Y/SJ57E) from May to December 2005, with a pair farther up the Weaver (SJ57N) in 2006. Two birds were seen on several occasions at Winsford Bottom Flash (SJ66N) during winter 2005/06, and a single bird appeared to be resident at Poynton Pool (SJ98H). None showed any evidence of breeding activity. The distinction between breeding and winter seasons is not straightforward in this species as Egyptian Geese breed early in the year, nesting from December onwards, sometimes on the ground or in reed-beds but usually in trees, in a hole or an old corvid or raptor nest.

As with most species suspected of being escapes, Egyptian Goose is likely to have been underrecorded in the county. Neither Boyd (1946, 1951) nor Bell (1962, 1967) mentions them, and the first record in the annual bird reports is in 1971, followed by one in 1972 and odd birds in almost every year from 1974 onwards, in very small numbers at a variety of sites including most of the county's well-watched waterbodies. The majority of records are of single birds on single dates although sometimes an individual appears to have stayed for several months. From 1980 to 1985 birds were recorded often at Astbury, Congleton (SJ86L), but the main regular site for many years has been Poynton Pool. Two were there for a week in 1993, with further sightings in 1994 and 1995, an association with the site that was then resumed from 2001 to 2006, mostly single birds being seen on many dates: it is probably significant that this is the nearest waterbody in Cheshire to their breeding site at Etherow Country Park.

Sponsored by Roger and Jayne Nutter

Green-winged Teal

Anas carolinensis

This vagrant from North America owes its place in this Atlas to one drake that lived at Inner Marsh Farm (SJ37B) in winter 2004/05 and then from 27 June 2005 into 2007.

Green-winged Teals were considered to be a race of Teal *Anas crecca*, until 2001 when they were split as a separate species. Their DNA may be different, but the two species appear to be identical in their habitat requirements and food; in the breeding seasons of 2004 and 2006 the bird at Inner Marsh Farm was seen displaying to a female Teal.

Formerly a national rarity, with records assessed by BBRC until 1990, Cheshire's first Green-winged Teal was seen in 1984, followed by another in 1986, the species then being recorded in every year from 1989 except 1995. There are suggestions that only a small number of long-staying or returning individuals are involved: elsewhere, birds have recurred for up to seven successive winters (Brown & Grice 2005). Every bird recorded in the county has been a drake, and they have appeared on most of the county's inland waters and on both estuaries.

RICHARD STEEL

Sponsored by The Wallis family, Greenwich, Connecticut, USA

Red-crested Pochard

Netta rufina

Birds of this species, presumed to have escaped from collections, were recorded in three winter tetrads during this Atlas. A free-flying, unringed drake was seen on Birkenhead Park Lake (SJ38E) on various dates in winter 2004/05, also being found occasionally on the lake in Wallasey Central Park (SJ39A). At Doddington Pool (SJ74D) a female was present from 30 April to 4 June 2004, and another, or the same, female was there on 27 December 2004.

Bell (1962) noted a record of an adult drake at Rostherne, 1 February 1948, with it, or another, there again on 31 December 1948. Extensive enquiries were made about the possibility of the earlier bird being an escape, but the result was negative and it was considered to be genuinely wild. According to Lever (1977), in the 1950s the Red-crested Pochard was a regular autumn migrant to south-eastern England, but since 1962 it reverted to its earlier vagrant status; another influx came in 1986, but none reached Cheshire and Wirral.

The species may well have been overlooked or underreported, the fate of all birds suspected of having escaped from collections, but after 1948 the next one recorded in the county annual bird reports was in 1974. Further birds were noted in 1975 and 1977, then in all but five of the years from 1981 onwards. There are sightings in every month of the year, not least because three or four of the birds have been resident at a site for several months. They have been found on most of the well-watched inland waters, not least because some were reported in the 1980s to have wandered from a collection in Tatton Park, and at the Weaver Bend (SJ57E) and Hilbre Island.

A few Red-crested Pochards have been reported at various sites in the county in the summer over the years, sometimes in pairs, but never with any indication of breeding.

Velvet Scoter

Melanitta fusca

There was just one record of this rare coastal visitor in this Atlas, when at least two, a male and female, were seen off Hoylake Shore (SJ29A) on 16 February 2005.

This is the least abundant of the major wintering sea ducks around Britain. Like most of the other immigrants from Fennoscandia and Russia, the majority is found on the east coast and few reach the Irish Sea (*BTO Winter Atlas*). Coward and Oldham (1900) knew of no records in Cheshire and Wirral, but obviously suspected their presence: '... a little vigilance on the part of local ornithologists would probably result in the addition of Velvet Scoter to the county avifauna'. However, it was not until 1921 that the first was seen by Boyd, off West Kirby on 30 October. Bell (1962) wrote that, since then, it had been reported almost every year in very small numbers, mainly off Hilbre or West Kirby, and occasionally from the Weaver estuary. In the supplement to his avifauna, Bell (1967) said 'records from the coast have been very scarce during the six years' (1961–66) but nevertheless he could list seven occurrences. From then on, birds have been seen in most years, mainly from October to January, although there are perhaps fewer in recent years, with none in 2001, 2004 or 2006.

Almost all records come from the north Wirral and there is only about one per decade from elsewhere in the county, the last in 2000.

Black-throated Diver

Gavia arctica

This is the scarcest of the three wintering divers in the county. Their main winter habitat is normally sandy bays, where they take sand eels, crustaceans and flatfish. Black-throated Divers were recorded in two tetrads during this Atlas: off Hilbre (SJ18Z) in all three winters, counts of one, one and two birds, and off Hoylake (SJ29A) in winter 2004/05, one bird.

As with many seabirds, the number of records has increased markedly over the years, probably reflecting an increase in observers, their use of telescopes, and indeed awareness of what birds might be just off our coasts. Coward (1910) knew only of one shot about 1853 on Puddington Marsh and one shot in the mouth of the Dee in December 1876, with another reportedly shot a week before. Bell (1962) recorded three single birds inland in 1915 and 1916, then the next at West Kirby in 1937. In January 1942 an immature male was shot near Nantwich. From 1950 to 1960 there were 16 reports, mostly from the Dee estuary from September to April, but three inland midwinter records. Bell (1967) added a further eight records, all in the Dee.

The annual county bird reports show that in the 1970s there were about 13 winter records, two of them of two birds together. During the 1980s there were at least 28 winter records—including the record winter count for Hilbre of three birds on 7 December 1984—although the practice in some of the bird reports of aggregating many of the Hilbre records makes it impossible to give precise totals. From about 1990 onwards Black-throated Divers have become somewhat scarcer, with 25 records in 15 years to 2005. The likelihood of finding one inland has decreased as well. From 1970 to 1993 there were 15 records away from the north Wirral, but birds were found inland in only two of the 13 years since then: three in 1997 and one in 2002. This apparent shift in occurrence and distribution deserves study; it coincides with warmer winters, but the causes are unknown.

This species has been little studied but survey work for the *BTO Winter Atlas* showed that the coasts of the Irish Sea are the least likely places in the UK to find the species in winter. Perhaps 1,300 Black-throated Divers winter in Britain, the larger numbers along the east coast probably being immigrants from Scandinavia, while those on the west of Scotland, and presumably the few that visit Cheshire and Wirral, are likely to be from the Scottish breeding population (*BTO Winter Atlas*).

Red-necked Grebe

Podiceps grisegena

Far fewer Red-necked Grebes have been found in Cheshire and Wirral in recent years, probably because they have no need to migrate this far as the warming climate leaves eastern waters ice-free. Their breeding areas, shallow inland waters in Finland and eastern Europe, freeze in winter so they move to the coasts, mostly the Baltic and southern coast of the North Sea, where they can still dive for small fish.

The birds recorded in the course of this Atlas, in 2004/05, were the first in the county in winter since 30 January 1999. One was found on Comber Mere (SJ54X) during WeBS counts on 12 December 2004 and 15 January 2005, with two birds on 16 January 2005, and one was at Woolston (SJ68P) on 9 February 2005.

In the nineteenth century, Coward and Oldham (1900) wrote that '... off the Cheshire shores, as elsewhere on the west coast of England, the Red-necked Grebe is a rather rare winter visitor'. Brockholes (1874) had said it was occasionally obtained in the estuary of the Dee. To Boyd (1951) in central Cheshire, the species was 'a rare and casual winter visitor', only three records: one on Marbury Mere, 29 December 1926 to 22 January 1927; another there, a long-staying bird from 6 February to 12 May 1937; and an immature bird 'on the flashes' 4 and 5 February 1942. Bell (1962) noted an increase in records, ascribed to more observer interest. Nearly all of the records (17 out of 22 known to him) were in January and February.

Since then, the annual county bird reports show that Red-necked Grebes have been recorded in half of the winters from 1964 to 2006, but with more than one bird only in seven of them. The only notable influx was 10 birds in February 1979 when most of the Baltic froze (Chandler 1981).

Slavonian Grebe

Podiceps auritus

There were just two records of Slavonian Grebe, both in the first winter of this Atlas. One was off Hoylake Shore (SJ29A) on 13 February 2005, and then one seen briefly at Inner Marsh Farm (SJ37B) on 19 February 2005, a first record for the site; it could conceivably have been the same bird.

There are two subspecies of Slavonian Grebe that occur in Britain: *arcticus* birds breed in Iceland and northern Norway, with a few in Scotland, and these spend the winter in their breeding range and in Greenland, but not further south. The Slavonian Grebes wintering in England are of the subspecies *auritus*, breeding from Sweden eastwards, these birds mostly wintering around the southern North Sea, with a few flying to the Mediterranean (*Migration Atlas*).

This has always been a scarce bird in Cheshire and Wirral. Only two nineteenth-century records are known: one in a collection labelled 'Burton, January 1839', and an adult in summer plumage shot on Tatton Mere about 1860 (Coward & Oldham 1900). Both of Cheshire's most famous ornithologists logged their only Slavonian Grebe for the county on Marbury Mere (SJ67M): Coward saw one there on 4 November 1916 and, on 6 February 1937, Boyd had the enviable experience, probably unknown to most birdwatchers, of seeing the three larger wintering grebes together when a Slavonian Grebe arrived on Marbury Mere with a Red-necked and 25 Great Crested Grebes (Boyd 1951). Bell (1962) traced a further two records at inland waters: two shot at Cheshire's other Marbury Mere, near Whitchurch (SJ54M) on 10 February 1922, and one at Oakmere on 27 April 1952. Four winter records at Hilbre, 1954–57, are not mentioned in the Liverpool Ornithologists' Club's 1960 checklist for the Wirral, nor by Craggs (1982), and Bell (1962) wondered about their identification. Bell's supplement (1967) added one at Hilbre, October to December 1963 and one on Hurleston Reservoir, 16 January 1966.

Since then, the annual county bird reports show that Slavonian Grebes have been recorded in 25 of the 42 winters from 1964 to 2006; but they are sparsely distributed and only in five winters have more than two birds been found. They have become slightly more common, with seven birds during the 1970s, 17 in the 1980s and 18 in the 1990s. Despite the description in the *BTO Winter Atlas* of their 'essentially coastal' distribution, more than half of the county's birds since 1964 have been inland (28 out of 52 birds).

Fulmar

Fulmarus glacialis

JEFF CLARKE

Most Fulmars pass our coast in the period March to October, and winter records are unusual. Birds were reported in three tetrads for this Atlas, all in winter 2006/07: Hilbre (SJ18Z), Hoylake shore (SJ28E) and off Leasowe (SJ29R).

Coward and Oldham (1900) knew of no winter records, and Bell (1962) could trace only two, both inland: on the river Mersey at Ince on 21 November 1908 and at Witton flashes on 29 January 1929. The next on record is in the county bird report for 1971, on 24 January, followed by singles in 1973, 1974, 1975 and 1977, three in 1979 and five in 1982, then 'throughout the year' in 1982, after which records become jumbled although they were not present in every winter. More recently, in the 10 years from 1996/97 to 2005/06, Fulmars were recorded in six of those winters but not the others. These 10 years yielded a total of only 10 winter records, all in January and February apart from one on 28 December 1997; seven were off Hilbre, two off Hoylake and one over West Kirby town centre.

The origins of the birds seen off the Wirral coast are not known. After fledging in September, young Fulmars spend perhaps four years at sea, dispersing widely (some as far as the fishing grounds off Canada and Greenland) and probably never visiting land. They then spend five or more years visiting colonies until, at about nine or ten years of age, they are ready to breed. Adults occupy their nest sites throughout the year, and all but one of the ringed birds from Scottish colonies found in the Irish Sea outside the breeding season have been immatures (*Migration Atlas*), suggesting that the Wirral birds will be subadults. However, breeding birds will forage for several hundred kilometres from their nest, and this is thought to apply in winter as well (*BTO Winter Atlas*), so adults from the colonies on cliffs along the North Wales coast, in Cumbria and the Isle of Man could well visit this area.

Gannet

Morus bassanus

The normal status of Gannet is a species seen in flight past Hilbre, and some other north Wirral sites, from the second week of March through to the end of October. From 1986 onwards the county bird reports have tabulated the monthly maximum total at Hilbre. In the 20 years to 2005, there were birds in December in four years, in January in five years and in February in eight years. In the midwinter months of December and January, only two of the counts exceeded single figures, 12 birds in January 1994 and 140 in December 1994.

During this Atlas there were winter records from three tetrads: Hilbre (South) (SJ18Y), Hilbre (SJ18Z), where three were seen in 2005/06 and two in 2006/07, and Hoylake Shore (SJ29A), where the 20 birds seen by Jane Turner in winter 2004/05 was one of the largest flocks on record.

First-year Gannets winter off the coasts of West Africa, with older birds increasingly farther north (*Migration Atlas*). Almost all of those seen in winter in British waters are in full adult plumage, thus more than five years old, and are thought to be breeding birds from British colonies (*BTO Winter Atlas*).

This makes even more extraordinary the county's first winter record of the nineteenth century, an immature bird picked up alive at Lymm, 15 January 1865 (Coward & Oldham 1900). An adult bird was 'obtained' between Heswall and West Kirby in early February 1899 (Coward 1910) and Bell (1962 and 1967) traced about 45 records since 1910, in every month except March, but mainly in April and July to October. Gannets are clearly somewhat more often recorded nowadays, although much of this must be attributed to increased observer effort, and they remain scarce in winter.

Sponsored by David Cookson

Spoonbill

Platalea leucorodia

During this Atlas period, two adults briefly visited Inner Marsh Farm (SJ37B) on 2 June 2004.

Spoonbills used to nest in Britain in the sixteenth and seventeenth centuries, but then faded away to become a rare visitor. Only three records exist in the old Cheshire avifaunas, birds shot at Tatton Mere about 1850 or 1860 and at Burton in 1864 (Coward 1910), and one seen at Tabley and Oakmere in April 1920 (Bell 1962).

In recent times this species has been much more commonly found in Britain, and in Cheshire and Wirral. From 1990 onwards it was recorded annually in the county, increasingly showing breeding intent. Then, in 1996, up to five birds were present and a pair displayed and built a nest in a flooded hawthorn hedge at Frodsham Marsh (around the boundary of four tetrads, SJ47Y/47Z/57D/57E), close to several Grey Heron nests. After more than a week of mating rituals, bill clapping, copulation and nest building, the pair abandoned their nest (Schofield 1996). One of the pair had been ringed as a chick in the Netherlands in 1992 and proved to be mobile, being recorded more than 50 times in its life in four European countries (Norman 2000). Birds had also displayed and carried sticks, but no more, in 1996 at Inner Marsh Farm. Spoonbills were again present at Frodsham, with some nest-building seen, in 1997, but that was the end of breeding activities in the county although birds, mostly immatures, were recorded in every year from then to 2003, usually at Inner Marsh Farm (SJ38B). Their occurrences in Cheshire and Wirral have dwindled such that the two birds there for a few minutes in 2004 were the only breeding season records in the three years of this Atlas.

Spoonbills successfully bred in Lancashire in 1999 and built nests in Suffolk in 2002 and elsewhere in northern England in 2004 (Holling *et al.* 2007a).

Five immature Spoonbills overwintered on the Dee estuary in 1997/98, but there were no winter records at all during this Atlas. Most birds migrate to West Africa.

Red Kite

Milvus milvus

For several centuries the fortunes of the Red Kite in Britain have been intimately linked with man's actions. They were common and performed an important role in urban sanitation until Shakespeare's day, being valued and protected in England by Royal Decree—in 1465 killing a kite was a capital offence—although at the same time the King of Scotland was ordering their destruction. The Vermin Act of Queen Elizabeth I (1566) first targeted kites, along with many other species, supposedly to protect grain. The status of the Red Kite in Cheshire can be judged from the numbers killed for which a bounty was paid: 862 birds in the parish of Tarporley in 19 years from 1662 to 1681 and 698 birds in the parish of Bunbury in just eight years from 1715 to 1722, including 256 in the year 1720 alone (Lovegrove 2007). By the late eighteenth century kites were scarce in the county, only found on the large estates, and by the year 1800 they had probably gone, Cheshire bearing the dubious distinction of being one of the first counties to extirpate the Red Kite (Lovegrove 2007). One of the last known to breed in England (in Shropshire) was shot in 1863 and in Scotland they persisted to about 1885.

After that, the only Red Kites breeding in Britain were those in a rump population in mid-Wales, down, at its lowest point in the 1930s, to only one pair that reared young that survived and subsequently went on to become parents themselves, the species thus being almost extinct in the UK. Conservation measures, including 'reward' payments to landowners on whose land they bred, helped the Welsh population to grow, although the productivity was low at only around one chick per pair. The habitat in their mid-Wales remnant area is not particularly good for them and this was just the last area where they were not being persecuted, rather than the best place for them. Some kites had to forage up to 15 km from their nests, whereas in high quality habitat, most food is found within 3 km of the nest (Carter 2001). This has, however, been a great conservation success story and the Welsh Kite Trust estimates that in 2007 there were 670–840 pairs in Wales.

In England and Scotland, Red Kites have been introduced from 1989 onwards to eight separate areas, using nestlings from Sweden, Spain and Wales to maximize the genetic diversity. This has been outstandingly successful in England, populations becoming self-sustaining and new releases being stopped within six years. The project has done less well in Scotland, where the kites' diet makes them susceptible to poisoning. They will eat almost anything, but especially take carrion such as dead rats.

Records in Cheshire and Wirral have increased greatly over the years. The annual bird reports show only 11 records in just nine of the years from 1964 to 1990. The next county record was probably the most instructive to date, a first-year female, known from her wing tags to have come from a nest in mid-Wales, that lived in Tatton Park and adjacent areas from November 1993 until April 1995 when she left, presumably to find a mate elsewhere (Roberts 1995). Since then there have been different birds found in every year in the county, mostly in the period from mid-March to late August, although there are only two records of two birds together, in July 1999 at Cholmondeley and on 31 March 2000 at Barbridge.

Cheshire and Wirral is clearly within the normal dispersal range, at least of immature birds, from several breeding sites, in Wales, the East Midlands and Yorkshire. Young Red Kites, however, show strong natal philopatry, the tendency to return to breed close to the site where they themselves were reared. Kites are social birds, not least with their well-known communal feeding and roosting groups in winter, and the adventurous birds that do breed away from their natal area tend to choose sites near to another existing population rather than in a brand new location. There are examples of recruitment in both directions, for instance, between the reintroduced populations in the Chilterns and East Midlands, 100 km apart, and birds from Germany have moved to breed in Wales (Carter 2001). The proportion of young birds that move long distances also decreases greatly as a population grows in size, thus being largest in the early years of a new group. All of these facts about the species' breeding biology mean that kites can take a long time to spread their breeding range. This was one of the reasons for using several well-separated regions for the reintroduction scheme, and tends to make it less likely that they will naturally colonize new areas, or at least to mean that it will take some time before an odd rogue pair settles well away from their natal site.

The records during this Atlas were typical of recent years. After none in the 2004 breeding season, in 2005 one flew west at Bosley Reservoir (SJ96I) on 23 April, another bird on 28 May was seen first at Sandbach Flashes then during Atlas survey work near Holmes Chapel (SJ76M), and one on 18 June was seen over Henbury (SJ87S) drifting north-west. In 2006, there were reports of probably two birds: what may well have been the same bird on different dates at Overton (SJ44U), Handley (SJ45N) and Tattenhall (SJ45Z), and another on 10 June that flew over Woolston (SJ68N/P).

There were no records during the Atlas winter periods. Apart from a couple of long-staying individuals, winter records in the county have been scarce, with none in November, one in December, none in January and four in February.

Sponsored by Philip French

Osprey

Pandion haliaetus

Ospreys are mainly recorded in Cheshire and Wirral in spring, from late March to May, as they pass through on their return from West African wintering areas to breeding sites in Scotland. Most birds move on within minutes or hours, but some stop for a few days. By far the longest period in the county was logged by a bird that was in the area of Rostherne and Tatton from 3 June to 23 July 1998.

During this Atlas period, there were two instances recorded as possible breeding. One bird frequented the vicinity of Fiddler's Ferry (SJ58M) from 26 June to 25 July 2005, and two birds were reported in the area of Booths Mere (SJ77U) for six days in late May/early June 2005. They obviously were able to find enough fish to sustain themselves.

Ospreys do not start breeding until at least three years of age, and often older (Poole 1989). Immature birds return towards their natal area at two years of age (*Migration Atlas*) and it seems likely that it is the adult birds that migrate quickly to their breeding sites and the subadults that linger in areas such as Cheshire. The Fiddler's Ferry bird was identified from photographs as a two-year-old male.

Ospreys used to be extremely uncommon in the county, the fate of all those known to Coward probably explaining their rarity: three birds, all shot, from 1865, 1890 and 'winter 1893–94' (Coward & Oldham 1900), and another, a female, shot in 1909 (Coward 1910). Bell (1962, 1967) could list only single birds in 1912, 1915, 1940, 1949, 1956, 1957, 1964 and 1965, but sightings have increased in frequency and become annual since 1977. Ospreys have clearly become much more common in Cheshire and Wirral since breeding birds recolonized Scotland in 1954 following their extinction by persecution in 1916. Pairs have nested in England at two sites since 2001, and in Wales since 2003. The British population, at 160–189 pairs in 2004, is now at its highest for well over 100 years (Holling *et al.* 2007a).

Spotted Crake

Porzana porzana

There was just one record of this rare migrant in our Atlas period, when the bird's whiplash call was heard in *juncus* at Inner Marsh Farm (SJ37B) for one night only, 11 May 2005. Spotted Crakes return from their wintering areas in southern Europe and Africa in April or May, and some birds sing through to early July. As detailed in our *First Atlas*, one or two Spotted Crakes nested in the county during the 1930s and single birds were recorded as possibly breeding seven times in the years from then to 1984. The annual county bird reports then list single birds in the breeding season in 1985, 1992, 1995, 2002 and 2003, suggesting more frequent occurrence.

The first Britain-wide survey in 1999 found 73 singing males, including one in Cheshire, not included in the annual bird report (Gilbert *et al.* 2002). In every other year the species is underrecorded, and underreported to the Rare Breeding Birds Panel, who comment 'Around 10–30 pairs of Spotted Crakes probably nest annually in suitable wetlands, although most breeding season records are simply of singing birds, with very few instances of confirmed breeding' (Holling *et al.* 2007a). The RBBP's listing of a bird in Cheshire and Wirral in 2004 is thought to be a mistake for the 2005 bird noted above.

RAY SCALLY

The national survey showed that they favour wet herb habitats, with *phragmites* and wet grass as less-preferred sites; they need tall vegetation and shallow standing water that persists through the breeding season, with a mosaic feeding area of tussocks of wet sedge *carex* or grass species and drier areas. There potentially is habitat meeting this description at several sites in the county.

Corncrake

Crex crex

CLIVE TEMPLE

Just one Corncrake was reported during this Atlas, a bird heard calling on Cuerdley Marsh, Fiddler's Ferry (SJ58M) on 18 June 2005 only.

The last known nesting in Cheshire and Wirral in the early 1970s was followed by an extraordinary record of breeding near Tatton in 1987, when two adults and a juvenile were found dead in late June, all apparently killed by traffic (Broome 1987). There were eight records in the years 1988–2004, all of them on one day only apart from a late September bird present for two days. As with the bird in 2005, they were presumably all on passage between their winter quarters south of the Sahara and breeding grounds in the northern isles. Almost all of the present British population of around 1,000 singing males is on islands in the Inner and Outer Hebrides and Orkney. Since 2003, Corncrakes have also been reintroduced to the Nene Washes in Cambridgeshire in a programme operated by the RSPB, Natural England and the Zoological Society of London (Holling *et al.* 2007a).

Corncrakes breed in tall grass and herbs, particularly hay and silage meadows, and modern agricultural practice, with early cutting of grass, is inimical to them. After a catastrophic decline and the species seemingly headed for extinction in the UK, the population has more than doubled since the start of Corncrake conservation schemes in 1993 (O'Brien *et al.* 2006).

In memory of Jean Martin

Curlew Sandpiper

Calidris ferruginea

Curlew Sandpipers are rare in winter but some birds turn up in the county in autumn on their way from their Siberian breeding grounds to winter in Africa. These, overwhelmingly juveniles, occur in numbers varying from a few birds to three-figure flocks depending on the occurrence of easterly winds to blow them off-course during migration.

The first in winter in the county was shot at New Brighton in January 1891 (Coward & Oldham 1900), followed by only four winter records (December to February) in the next 60 years: 1905, 1942, 1954 and 1956 (Bell 1962). *CWBRs* include single birds on 14 January 1973 at Red Rocks and 17 December 1980 at Meols shore.

In recent years there have been several late records, just extending into our Atlas period: four birds at Inner Marsh Farm to 25 November 1994; one at Fiddler's Ferry on 21 November 1999; two at Frodsham on 17 November 2001; and as many as four at Inner Marsh Farm up to 17 November 2002. It is tempting to think that the warming climate is encouraging a few to stay later.

During this Atlas one juvenile was present all winter 2006/07 at Inner Marsh Farm (SJ37B), paralleling the first known long-staying winter bird, an adult at Frodsham from 6 December 2001 to March 2002.

It is not just in Cheshire and Wirral that wintering Curlew Sandpipers are rare: the mean number, summing the WeBS counts for all of England in the five years from mid-1995 to mid-2000, in the months of December, January and February was one, zero and zero respectively (Brown & Grice 2005).

Arctic Skua

Stercorarius parasiticus

The vast majority of the Arctic Skuas that breed in, or pass through, Britain and Ireland end up crossing the equator to winter in the south Atlantic, mainly off southern Africa but with some birds on the South American coast (*Migration Atlas*). In Cheshire and Wirral, most birds are seen off the Wirral coast in autumn, acrobatically harassing terns to disgorge their latest catch, and winter records are rare. The two birds seen during this Atlas period (both in winter 2006/07) were the first for six years: one was seen off Hilbre (SJ18Z) and another on 4 January 2007 flew in the mouth of the Mersey off Egremont shore, crossing tetrads SJ39B/G.

The first winter bird on record in the county appears to be at Hilbre on 4 December 1960 (Bell 1962). County bird reports from then on confirm its scarcity, with just 12 winter records in 40 years from 1964 to the start of this Atlas. Four of these were in an exceptional period on separate dates from 17 November to 7 December 1982, two in the Mersey mouth and two inland. In total, there have been five records in late November, four in December and two in early January (4 January 1970 and 1 January 1998), and the only February record is an immature bird, seen from a ship in Liverpool Bay on 16 and 20 February 1974. The other sightings came from Hilbre or Red Rocks (six records), the mouth of the Mersey (three) and two inland at Moore and Rostherne. Most sightings were of single birds, but once two were together and on two occasions the observer reported three birds: all of these multiple sightings were from Hilbre or Red Rocks, emphasizing the importance of the mouth of the Dee as the main area frequented by this rare winter visitor.

The unusual nature of winter records was emphasized in the *BTO Winter Atlas* (1981/82–1983/84), when Arctic Skuas were found in only 44 10 km squares, several of them in the exceptional westerly gales of November 1982 that brought Cheshire and Wirral its record numbers. In those three years there were only 11, 8 and 4 records anywhere in the country in the months of December, January and February.

Razorbill

Alca torda

Razorbills are recorded annually, mostly from October to April, with peaks of autumn passage in October and November. Birds have been found at all times of the year, although often with only one or two records per month. The vast majority of records come from Hilbre.

During this Atlas, records were submitted from three tetrads. Hilbre (SJ18Z) reported birds in all three winters, with counts of 3, 2 and 16. A count of 45 birds offshore at Hoylake (SJ29A) by Jane Turner in winter 2004/05 is one of the largest winter flocks on record in the county. A sickly looking individual was at the edge of the tide at West Kirby (SJ28D) in 2006/07.

A century ago Coward (1910) wrote that 'a few birds may often be seen at sea off the Cheshire coast and in the estuaries'. Bell (1962) said that 'although recorded in most months it is most frequently seen in the autumn, chiefly in October and always in very small parties, not exceeding a maximum of four birds'. Both writers overemphasized the occasional storm-driven inland bird, recorded once every twenty years on average. There was no record in the county mapped in the BTO *Winter Atlas* (1981/82–1983/84). Compared to those earlier assessments, Razorbills seem to be more commonly seen these days, but it is perhaps because more observers are scanning the sea with telescopes.

The Razorbills found in winter in our area are almost certainly British-bred birds. Immatures from British colonies move south for the winter, travelling a median distance of almost 1,000 km from their natal site, with some birds reaching West Africa and others entering the Mediterranean. Adults of breeding age also move south, a median distance of nearly 700 km (*Migration Atlas*). Those that are seen in winter in Liverpool Bay are thus most likely to be adults from colonies in northwest Scotland.

Black Guillemot

Cepphus grylle

It is ten years since a Black Guillemot was recorded in Cheshire and Wirral in winter, so it was good that Jane Turner had decided to do some Atlas recording when one flew west past Hoylake Shore (SJ29A) on 12 February 2005.

To Coward and Oldham (1900) this species was 'almost unknown upon the Wirral coast', and it is still a very rare visitor. Bell (1962) could trace no records in the twentieth century until 25 November 1961 when an 'almost full summer plumaged bird' was off Hilbre. According to the annual bird reports there were only about 24 records—at any season—in the 40 years from 1964 to 2003, all single birds except for once two together. Only four of those were within our defined winter period, birds on 7 December 1977, 23 January 1981, 18 November 1982 and 26 November 1995.

Black Guillemots feed inshore in sheltered shallow waters all year round and do not move far from their breeding areas: for ringed birds found dead at any season, the median distance of movement is only 10 km, extraordinarily low for a seabird (*Migration Atlas*). Their winter distribution around the Isle of Man is similar to the breeding map (Sharpe 2007). Nevertheless, with small colonies in Cumbria and Anglesey, and more than 600 adults breeding around the Isle of Man (Mitchell *et al.* 2004), one might have expected more birds to turn up around our coasts.

Little Auk

Alle alle

It can seem hard to believe that this is the most numerous seabird species in the north Atlantic, uncounted millions of Little Auks breeding in huge colonies in the high Arctic, mostly in Svalbard and Greenland. They winter far offshore, usually beyond the continental shelf where they dive in cold waters for crustaceans and seldom come to the attention of man.

The only one found in this Atlas period was recorded by Pete Williams flying past Hilbre (SJ18Z) on 21 November 2006 when he saw it attacked by a Great Black-backed Gull and ditched into the sea. Its fate is not known.

The summary by Coward and Oldham (1900) holds good today: 'The Little Auk has occurred in Cheshire at irregular intervals during the winter months, but even in many years when large numbers have been observed on the eastern coasts none have reached our shores'. Their normal wintering area does include the northern North Sea, beyond the north of Scotland, and some wind-blown birds sometimes reach English coasts but they seldom enter the Irish Sea. Most birds in the county have been seen offshore from Hilbre or the north-west Wirral but a surprising number have been found inland. These could just as likely have been blown across from the east coast as wandered from the west.

The county bird reports list birds in winter on 23 December 1968, 22 November 1975, 18 November 1979, 26 November 1981 and 25 December 1983, with birds off Hilbre on several days in November 1984 and November 1986. The next was on 21 December 1989, with two in winter 1990/91 and three birds together on 24 February 1992. There can be gaps of several years with no records, and it was five years to the next on 29 November 1997, then 26 January 2003 and 6 February 2004.

Ring-necked Parakeet

Psittacula krameri

In its native areas of trans-Saharan Africa and India, this is an abundant and widespread bird. How Ring-necked Parakeets originally became part of the British avifauna seems not to be known and is fast becoming a subject of modern mythology, with one far-fetched story involving their release from Shepperton Studios after filming of *The African Queen* in 1951. They are a commonly kept cagebird, however, and their initial source was likely to have been the pet trade. However they were introduced here, Ring-necked Parakeets were first known to have bred in the wild in Britain in 1969 and are now established feral breeders in south-east England. Their population slowly increased to an estimated 500 birds in 1983 and 1,500 birds by 1996, but now is rising rapidly by an annual average rate of 25% to 30%, with about 6,000 individuals in 2002 (Pithon & Dytham 2002, Butler 2003). They are now common enough to be monitored by the BTO's Breeding Bird Survey.

The breeding area of the birds centred on London is increasing only by 0.4 km a year, and there has been no evidence of any long-distance movement by any of the British birds, so it seems that there are further illegal releases of parakeets fuelling the species' expansion of range. The Rare Breeding Birds Panel has, since 1996, attempted to collect records of non-native breeding birds from county recorders. According to their reports, the first likely breeding records of Ring-necked Parakeet outside southern England during this period came in 2003, when one pair probably bred in Derbyshire in 2003 and 2004, but not 2005, and one pair probably bred and at least six birds were seen regularly in Lancashire in 2004 (Holling *et al.* 2007b).

The species' diet and breeding biology have the potential to cause conflict, with man and with other birds. They eat mainly soft fruits and grain, and in India are considered a serious agricultural pest, although in Britain so far they seem to get much of their food from suburban gardens rather than farmland. They start nesting in February, using medium-sized tree-holes, producing an average of almost two chicks fledging per nest. Recent work based on biometrics has shown that those in this country are of the Indian races (Pithon & Dytham 2001); although of tropical origins, they breed into the foothills of the Himalayas and are quite hardy birds, easily able to withstand what is nowadays a normal British winter. The Ring-necked Parakeets in Britain are now the most northerly breeding parrot populations in the world, although they are not yet known to have bred in Cheshire and Wirral.

The species seems first to have appeared in the county's ornithological literature in 1977 when one was in the Rostherne area from 1 October to 27 November, followed by a female at Hilbre on 11 October 1978. Our *First Atlas* referred to the 'presence of breeding Ring-necked Parakeets in a semi-feral state in adjacent parts of Greater Manchester', and a small population almost certainly bred in Liverpool for a number of years from 1970 to the early 1980s (White *et al.* 2008).

Since the first sighting in 1977, birds have been recorded in Cheshire and Wirral in every year except four, with the information submitted to the annual county bird reports varying from a single record at one site in many years, to eight records from five sites in 2001 and seven records at seven sites in 2004. Most records have been of solo birds, with occasional reports of two birds, often in flight. There are records for every month but with no seasonal pattern, with most from the areas of Hale and Sandbach, and at Poynton Pool where one male lived from October 1990 until it was found dead there on 26 February 1996. No report has ever suggested evidence of breeding, with perhaps the only hint being two birds that 'appeared to be interested in a hole in a tree' at Hale on 16 July 1983.

Within this Atlas period there were several Ring-necked Parakeet records during their potentially long breeding season, scattered across the county. All were single birds and the only records suggesting residence were from Hale (SJ48R) where one was seen several times from April to August 2005. The others were all on single dates, mostly in flight, again with no indication of any breeding behaviour, but in view of the species' rapid expansion they are included here for completeness. In 2004 birds were at Marbury Country Park (SJ67N) and Kenyon (SJ69H), and flying over Woolston (SJ68P), Liscard (SJ39B) and Bath Vale, Congleton (SJ86R). In 2006 records came from near the river Weaver at Warburton's Wood (SJ57N), Oakmere (SJ57Q) and in flight over Mere (SJ78F).

In the winter Atlas period, there were four records of single birds in the eastern half of Cheshire, two of them at least making only brief visits, at Appleton (SJ68H) and Sandbach (SJ76Q) in 2005/06, and at Edleston (SJ65F) and Dunham Massey (SJ78I) in 2006/07. Within their breeding range in Britain, they are well known for communal nocturnal roosts from September to March, usually in tall poplar trees, birds flying from perhaps 20 km to join with their fellows (*Migration Atlas*). This figure implies that any birds, if present, could cover much of the county in their daily range.

Sponsored by Nina and Sarah O'Hanlon

Wryneck

Jynx torquilla

There was one 'possible breeding' record of Wryneck during this Atlas, a bird singing from the railway embankment at Inner Marsh Farm (SJ37B) on 4 May 2005. It was first noticed at 8 am and left at about 12.45 pm, not to be seen or heard again.

Our *First Atlas* quotes a few historical records of nests: in Cheshire about 1884—although the species is mapped as 'not breeding' in Cheshire and 'rare' in Wirral in the last quarter of the nineteenth century (Holloway 1996)—and 1925; and in Wirral in 1934 and 1939. A secondhand report of breeding at Chelford in the 1971 county bird report seems never to have been substantiated. Since then, all of the birds in the county have been on passage, usually in autumn, with a few spring records. The bird recorded in this Atlas was apparently the first noted as singing since 1957 (Bell 1962).

Wrynecks used to be common in central and south-east England, breeding north to Durham and Cumbria, and west to Devon and Wales. The population declined to 150–400 pairs in south-east England by 1954–58, 20–30 pairs in 1966, one pair in 1973 and none in 1974. There were then single breeding records in 1975, 1977, 1978, 1979, 1985, 1986 and 1987, all in south-east England, and probable breeding in Shropshire in 1994. Meanwhile, a few pairs, presumably of Scandinavian origin, colonized northern Scotland and nested annually from 1969, peaking at seven pairs in 1977, then declining with sporadic breeding to 1999, but none since. Only odd birds have lately been found in the breeding season: just three birds were reported to the UK Rare Breeding Birds Panel in each of 2003 and 2004, with merely one each year heard singing (Holling *et al.* 2007a).

The species' habitat was typically orchards or overmature woodland close to unimproved but short-cropped grassland rich in yellow mound ants *Lasius flavus*, their main prey. There has been no real explanation for their precipitous decline but suggested reasons include the grubbing-up of old orchards, loss of grassland and pesticides killing most of the ants (Brown & Grice 2005).

Woodlark

Lullula arborea

A Woodlark singing on Lindow Moss (SJ88F) from 4 to 7 June 2006 was the first authenticated county record in the breeding season for well over one hundred years! The bird, first reported by Bill Gradwell and recorded for the Atlas by Brian Dyke, was in the D6 (drained bog) habitat and obviously found enough to eat and liked the area sufficiently to stay for a while.

A massive contraction in range between the national breeding bird Atlases of 1968–72 and 1988–91 led to Woodlark being placed on the Red List of species of conservation concern, with a Biodiversity Action Plan for its conservation. However, a national survey in 1997 found that the population had increased sixfold since the last survey in 1986, to around 1,500 Woodlark territories, and UK numbers are now at their highest for 50 years. The vast majority of birds breed on sandy soils, either in heathland (in the south) or within forest plantations (in the north and east of their range), particularly in stands of two- and three-year-old trees, although in Devon Woodlarks breed almost exclusively on farmland. Even though they are mainly birds of the south and east of England, by 2003 there were up to 27 pairs in Staffordshire and 21 pairs in Yorkshire (Holling *et al.* 2007a).

The last known breeding in Cheshire and Wirral was in about 1861. There were only around 10 records in the county during the twentieth century, all but two of them from Dee estuary sites on passage in spring or autumn. The exceptions were an undated record in 1934 of a bird singing at Spital, Wirral (Hardy 1941) and an extraordinary winter bird on 3 and 4 January 1997. There were further passage records, one in spring and one in autumn, in 2004 and 2005.

The warming trend is already helping the survival of the proportion of the population that winters in Britain, and climate change is expected to shift Woodlarks' breeding distribution somewhat northwards, although perhaps not as far as Cheshire and Wirral (Huntley *et al.* 2007).

Richard's Pipit

Anthus richardi

Two Richard's Pipits were on the salt-marsh between Red Rocks and West Kirby (SJ28D) from 21 November to 11 December 2005, with one remaining until 12 February 2006. This appears to have been the first record in the county's present boundaries within our defined winter period.

This rarity is normally recorded in the county once every few years, in autumn. During the time when it was treated as a national rarity, from 1958 to 1985, 97% of the total of 1,245 birds found in Britain and Ireland were in autumn, mainly from mid-September to the end of October (Dymond *et al.* 1989). They breed in Siberia, Mongolia and China and winter in southern Asia but some apparently take a westward or north-westward path, mostly arriving in Shetland, or on the east coast or the south-west of England (Brown & Grice 2005). It seems likely that the Wirral birds had arrived earlier in the autumn and gradually made their way here.

Black Redstart

Phoenicurus ochruros

This is one of the few species of bird that actively seems to prefer urban areas, and observers generally need to be active in the F1 habitat to record them. One bird was found during this winter Atlas, on 16 and 17 December 2004 in two adjacent tetrads at Prenton/Woodchurch (SJ28X/Y).

There appear to be two components to the British wintering birds: some breeding birds probably stay all year round, while others arrive from continental breeding areas to the east, finding milder weather here (*Migration Atlas*). This is a rare breeding bird in the UK, covered by the Rare Breeding Birds Panel, with a mean of 67 pairs in the 10 years to 2004. Black Redstarts have bred in Cheshire, in at least 1973, 1974, 1977 and 1995, and recently in adjoining counties: confirmed breeding in Derbyshire in 2003, and possibly in 2004; and pairs probably bred in 2003 in Lancashire and North Merseyside and in 2004 in Greater Manchester (Holling *et al.* 2007a).

Wintering Black Redstarts have obviously become much more common over the years. Coward (1910) had no definite knowledge of any. The first confidently identified in winter was in November 1926, when one frequented a garden at Wistaston, near Crewe, for several days, followed on 20 December 1938 by one at Newbridge near Winsford (Bell 1962). In the years from 1945 to 1961, for which Bell (1962) just gives a monthly summary, there was at least one January record. The annual county bird reports from 1964 onwards list 29 occurrences in winter, with nine first recorded in the second half of November, seven in December, seven in January and six in February. A handful of the birds stayed for weeks, but such occurrences are probably underrecorded. Although averaging fewer than one record per winter, in some years there were up to four, with also some long periods of several years without a winter record: after 1996 there were only three records, for single days each in 2000/01, 2002/03 and 2003/04, until those recorded in this Atlas.

The *BTO Winter Atlas* showed that Black Redstarts were 'largely coastal in distribution', but that is not true of the Cheshire and Wirral records. Ten of the 29 winter records from 1964 to 2003 were at north Wirral migration sites, with the others spread widely across the county and in such odd sites that it seems likely that other birds are being missed.

Cetti's Warbler

Cettia cetti

Our *First Atlas* period ended with Cheshire's first Cetti's Warbler, ringed by the author on 20 April 1984 near Frodsham (SJ57J), and all seemed set for their colonization of the county. Their population was growing, the species was expanding to the north and there is plenty of suitable habitat available for them, especially along the Mersey valley and parts of Wirral. However, it was not to be, and Cetti's Warblers have still not bred in Cheshire and Wirral.

The only records in the period between our Atlases were one at Rostherne Mere (SJ78M) on 8 and 9 May 1989, and a female ringed at Woolston (SJ68U) on 26 September 1998, present until at least 19 December 1998. Two birds ringed in October 2001 and October 2002 in the Wirral were not reported to CAWOS.

This Atlas survey has coincided with a rise in records, including the first in the breeding season since 1989. One or two birds were at Neston (SJ27Y) from 15 February to 31 March 2005, unfortunately not sexed but not reported to sing. Another was reported, seen and heard calling, although not singing, on four dates from 29 March to 10 April 2006, also at Neston. Finally, a male was ringed at Woolston (SJ68U) on 20 July 2006 and sang there to the end of the year.

Although the highly publicized and most intensively watched Cetti's Warblers in the county have been in Neston reed-bed (Williams 2005), they are not really birds of *phragmites*. Detailed study has shown that their best territories are in damp, dense scrub, especially willow carr, with song-posts in small bushes, and reed-beds are rarely visited (Bibby 1982). A particularly favoured habitat is where willow or bramble scrub is invading the edge of extensive reed-beds (Wotton *et al.* 1998). Their diet comprises small flies and other insects, notably caterpillars and beetles, with small snails, spiders and occasional earthworms.

This species is strongly sexually dimorphic, with males significantly larger than females. In established breeding areas, many males are polygamous, holding large territories with up to three females. Males spend most of their time singing and defending the territory but take no part in nest-building or incubation, and only some of them even bother to feed their young. Females paired with polygamous males lay larger clutches and successfully raise more young than those in monogamous pairings, however, suggesting that the polygamous males select the best-quality territories. Because of this habit, breeding surveys of the species count singing males, rather than 'pairs'.

A national survey in 1996 found a total of up to 574 singing males (Wotton *et al.* 1998) and their continued strong increase is shown in the records of the Rare Breeding Birds Panel. By 2004 the population of the UK had more than doubled to at least 1,137 singing males, but no farther north in England than Warwickshire and Leicestershire, with breeding birds also in North Wales, in Anglesey and Caernarfon (Holling *et al.* 2007a). These are the northernmost breeders in Europe, and continued close monitoring of the species will be important for measuring climate change.

In winter, adult Cetti's Warblers stay on or close to their breeding territories, while some first-year birds disperse in all directions (*Migration Atlas*). Two of the Woolston birds detailed above stayed in the same area for several months. Another bird, a first-year female, was ringed at Woolston (SJ68P) just outside our defined Atlas winter dates, on 4 November 2006.

They are vulnerable to hard weather because of their year-round dependence on insect prey, often scarce in winter. Reed-beds are probably more important to them at this time of year when birds can forage amongst the reed litter (Brown & Grice 2005).

It is notable that most of the county's birds have first been found in a ringer's net, without their presence being detected beforehand. The species is skulking and could be overlooked, although their 'chip' calls are quite loud and distinctive, and the males' explosive song is used at any time of year.

As well as those listed earlier, two Cetti's Warblers have been caught at Shotton, just outside the Cheshire and Wirral boundary: one of these had been ringed as a juvenile female in June at Chew Valley Lake, Avon, and wintered at Shotton in two successive years, giving a fascinating insight into the origins and behaviour of one of the region's birds.

Pallas's Warbler

Phylloscopus proregulus

This was a most unexpected species to find in the winter Atlas. The bird, which should have been in China, was discovered by Richard Blindell on 29 January 2005 alongside the Macclesfield Canal near Crossley (SJ86X). It had presumably been somewhere in Britain since arriving in October or November 2004 and stayed at Crossley for almost a month, being heard singing on several dates when the sun shone. The weather was mild during much of its stay but there were three nights of frost, with cold days, in mid-February and then on 20 February there was a biting northerly wind. The Pallas's Warbler was seen on 22 February whilst there was snow on the ground, but not after that date.

Pallas's Warbler is normally insectivorous all year round, like Goldcrests and Wrens, and obviously was able to find enough food in the hedgerows. A good idea of the habitat in the area covered by this bird is given by the different assessments of the four observers who submitted details of this bird as a supplementary Atlas record: two used B1 (regenerating natural or semi-natural woodland), one used B7 (scrub, other) and the fourth chose E9 (farmland with hedge shorter than about 2 m).

According to the note in the annual bird report (Blindell *et al.* 2005) this was only the third winter record in the UK, following ones in Kent (28 January to 24 March 2004) and Cornwall (31 December 2004 to 2 January 2005). Brown and Grice (2005) mention another in Cornwall on 31 December 1999. Cheshire and Wirral's first Pallas's Warbler, at Bidston (SJ29V) on 25 November 1980, was also in the period that we have defined as 'winter'.

Yellow-browed Warbler

Phylloscopus inornatus

A surprising find during this Atlas period was the Yellow-browed Warbler on 27 February 2007, at an unlikely site, a Borough Council work depot on the edge of Crewe (SJ65Y)! It was in a hawthorn hedgerow with some larger trees covered in ivy, the bird first being noticed by its call, then watched for some time as it accompanied two Blue Tits. It is possible that the warbler had been present for most of the month as the observer (Mark Stubbs) had heard a similar call on 3 February.

This is the first ever county record outside the autumn migration period: all previous county records, from the first in 1973 onwards, have been from 21 September, with most in October and three November records. One of these, in a Parkgate garden on 26 and 30 November 1994, falls within our defined winter period. This species does have a history of being found in sites away from the normal rarity hot spots: at least six of the previous Yellow-browed Warblers in the county have been in gardens.

Being insectivorous all year round, Yellow-browed Warblers have to quit their breeding grounds, in Russia east of the Urals, as autumn sets in, and they head for their wintering area in south-east Asia. Some apparently undertake 'reverse migration' and every year hundreds, or thousands, reach northern Europe. Yellow-browed Warblers are unusual in winter, but a few individuals have been recorded in Britain, mostly on the south coast (*Migration Atlas*).

GARY BELLINGHAM

Golden Oriole

Oriolus oriolus

Golden Orioles have never been known to breed in Cheshire and Wirral, but every now and again one turns up in the county, usually a male in the period from mid-May to mid-June. There was one such instance during this Atlas: an immature male was singing at Moore (SJ58X), 21–23 May 2005. This bird was in deciduous woodland (A1), the species' typical habitat.

Golden Orioles are common and widespread breeders across much of Europe, but in Britain are at the north-westward limit of their range. They have been known to breed in England since at least the 1830s, but only ever in small numbers (Brown & Grice 2005). In the last forty years the species has been monitored by the Rare Breeding Birds Panel, in which time the population peaked in the late 1980s at over 40 pairs, but has dropped considerably since then to a level currently (2004) of 3–8 pairs at eight sites. Most birds have been in East Anglia, where they breed especially in plantations of poplar trees in fenland (Holling *et al.* 2007a).

The county avifaunas confirm its rarity in Cheshire and Wirral. There were only two recorded instances during the nineteenth century, a male in May 1830, and a female shot during the 1850s (Coward 1910). Twentieth-century records came in 1907, 1915, 1945 and 1961 (Bell 1962). Authenticated records have been published in the annual county bird reports for 1967, 1974, 1983, 1985, 1986, 1990, 1992, 1993, 1995, 1997 and 1998; Golden Orioles thus seemed to be becoming more frequent, but then there was a run of six years (1999–2004) with no records.

Only one bird was reported in each year apart from 1967, when two males were together, and in 1915 when there were two records, of a pair and a male at different locations (Bell 1962). That record, of 'probable breeding', remains the closest that Golden Orioles have come to gracing the county with a breeding attempt.

Common Redpoll

Carduelis flammea

This bird, split in 2000 as a separate species from Lesser Redpoll, is still known by some birdwatchers by its former name of Mealy Redpoll. During the period of the Atlas there were just three records, all of single birds, in winter 2005/06: Inner Marsh Farm (SJ37B), Frodsham Marsh (SJ47Y) and Fiddler's Ferry (SJ58M), where a bird was reported on three dates in February 2006. They were all in typical habitat of scrub or damp woodland, with birch, alder and willow being especially favoured.

Common Redpolls are almost always in mixed flocks with Lesser Redpolls, presenting an identification challenge as the birds seldom stay still. Coward and Oldham (1900) mentioned the species as quite unknown, then Coward (1910) had two instances of spring records in 1905 and 1907. Bell (1962) traced four winter records from 1911 to 1961, and in his supplement added a record of up to three in the redpoll flocks on Burton marshes in very hard weather from January to March 1963 (Bell 1967).

Since then, there have been two winters with invasions of redpolls, probably triggered by a widespread failure of the birch seed crop in continental Europe. In 1972/73 small numbers were either suspected or definitely identified, especially at Sandbach. The invasion of 1995/96 was much better documented, with up to 50 Mealy Redpolls at Rudheath (SJ67R) and up to 10 in Marbury Country Park (SJ67N) in late December, then reports from 16 sites in early 1996 including 23 birds at Poynton (SJ98G) on 20 January 1996, the same date that one was ringed at Norton Priory, Runcorn (SJ58M), and other reports of up to 15 birds in a flock. Other than these years of mass irruptions, the county bird reports from 1964 onwards contain just 15 records from 10 winters, 10 of them of single birds only and a maximum of four birds, from a range of sites scattered across Cheshire, with only one Wirral record. Thus, the Atlas records are typical of the species.

The identification of this species poses problems for observers, and for the county rarities committee. Nine birds ringed at Thurstaston on 27 February 1987 were somewhat easier to identify, in the hand, and one of them soon proved its provenance by being caught in April 1987 by a ringer in Denmark, the first ever record of a British-ringed Common (Mealy) Redpoll to Denmark. It is known that other Mealy Redpolls have been ringed at Wirral sites but not submitted to the county bird reports.

Lapland Bunting

Calcarius lapponicus

There were two records of this county rarity in this Atlas period, both from the Dee salt-marsh (SJ27X). Colin Wells found one on 15 January 2006, and flushed two during the WeBS count on 19 November 2006.

Although a fairly frequent winter visitor to the east coast of England from their breeding grounds in the Arctic tundra, the species was 'quite unknown' in Cheshire and Wirral in the nineteenth century (Coward & Oldham 1900). Its first identification in the county in October 1956 led to a flurry of records, some in winter including three at Hoylake, November to 3 December 1956, and others at various Dee estuary localities, some outside the county, autumn 1959 to February 1960 (Bell 1962). There were annual records from 1962 to 1966, mostly at Dee sites but also Walton, Warrington, and up to eight birds on Frodsham Marsh (Bell 1967).

Many Lapland Buntings are first located by their distinctive flight call. Most are recorded on autumn passage, often late into November, with fewer in spring. Wintering birds have been recorded roughly annually through the 1980s and the 1990s, usually from the Dee, where they evidently find plenty of seeds to eat. Most records are of one or two birds although a notable exception was the flock of 20 on the Dee on 14 November 1990, reducing to three by 30 December. According to the annual bird reports, in recent years records have been sparse, with one on 13 February 2001 the last before those in this Atlas.

GARY BELLINGHAM

Other species recorded during this Atlas

Other species recorded during the breeding season with possible/probable/confirmed breeding, but not otherwise considered in this book, were:

- Bean Goose
- 'Goose spp'
- Cape Shelduck
- Muscovy Duck
- Guineafowl
- Black Swan
- Wood Duck
- Domestic Duck
- Peacock
- Fan-tailed Pigeon
- Hybrid (Mallard x Pintail) Duck

Other species recorded during the winter season, but not otherwise considered in this book, were:

- 'Goose spp'
- Ruddy Shelduck
- Golden Pheasant
- Bar-headed Goose
- Cape Shelduck
- Muscovy Duck
- Swan Goose
- Guineafowl
- Black Swan
- Harris's Hawk
- Reeves's Pheasant
- Feral Goose
- White-cheeked Pintail
- Domestic Duck
- Peacock
- African Grey Parrot
- Amazon Yellow Headed Parrot
- Aylesbury Duck

Appendix 1

Details of Atlas methodology and results

Genesis of this Atlas

The origins of this Atlas lie in discussions in the mid-1990s amongst various people in Cheshire and Wirral about producing a modern avifauna. Such an enterprise traditionally has two main components: a re-examination of old records of rarities against modern-day recording standards; and comprehensive statements of present status of the birds that regularly use the county. It was clear that the casual records submitted annually for publication in the county bird report—even a top-quality one such as the *Cheshire and Wirral Bird Report* has proven to be, consistently rated amongst the top few in the country—do not provide a basis for a reasonable assessment of most species' status, and that organized survey work is essential.

Early retirement in late 2001 left me (David Norman) with more free time to devote to voluntary activities, and, following informal discussions with a few interested people, in April 2003 I put a proposal to the Council of CAWOS for a project to update our 1978–84 tetrad breeding bird Atlas, with the possibility of adding a winter Atlas as well. This proposal, which included an offer to lead the project and write the book, was enthusiastically accepted, and the work began, with DN known as the Atlas Coordinator.

It was important to recognize from the outset that there is little history of organized bird surveying within the county, apart from that conducted by BTO members. Neither CAWOS nor its predecessor bodies had had any programme of bird surveys to engage their members, and few of the local bird clubs within the county undertake any recording work. During the planning stages of this Atlas a number of concerns were raised about the viability of the project. Three particular issues were thought by some to be potential show-stoppers: (i) there would not be enough volunteers for fieldwork; (ii) surveyors would be reluctant to ask for access to private land; and (iii) observers did not recognize habitat types and would find habitat recording too daunting. These thoughts influenced the design of the Atlas, particularly in trying to make it as simple and undemanding as possible, whilst still delivering state-of-the-art results. In practice, none of these concerns proved to be a problem. The engagement of volunteers, conduct of the fieldwork and standard of coverage achieved have all been extremely successful and substantially raised the level of involvement of Cheshire and Wirral bird recorders, surely laying the basis for future annual survey work as carried out in many other counties.

Objectives of the Atlas

The purpose of the Cheshire and Wirral Bird Atlas was formalized as to:

- Provide a permanent and comprehensive record of the bird species within the county
- Provide baseline data for monitoring future changes in bird populations
- Assess habitat needs of species and document species diversity
- Provide comparisons with historical studies such as the 1978-84 Cheshire and Wirral Breeding Bird Atlas
- Complement existing or ongoing avian monitoring programs at county and national level
- Enable use as a conservation tool and help in land use planning by local authorities
- Assist rECOrd, the local records centre, in providing data for preparing environmental impact assessments
- Promote camaraderie within the birding community
- Recruit and educate birders young and old into recognizing the value of recording for conservation purposes

Recording unit and area

It was clear that the basis for survey had to be the 2×2 km square of the Ordnance Survey grid, a standard recording unit for many local biological Atlases with an area of 4 km^2, called a tetrad. The tetrads forming the recording area for the breeding bird Atlas are defined in three categories as follows:

A those of which the entire land area of 4 km^2 is within Cheshire and Wirral (528 tetrads)

B those of which some area is land, bounded by the sea or the Dee or Mersey estuaries (42 tetrads)

C those of which the land area is shared between Cheshire and another county (101 tetrads)

Categories B and C require some further explanation. In category B, some tetrads have minimal land area, or the land is subject to tidal inundation, offering few possibilities for breeding birds. In category C, there are actually 154 tetrads shared with another county, but the land area in Cheshire varies from a hectare or so up to almost all of the tetrad. We have followed the same definition as for our *First Atlas* and included all those tetrads of which at least 1 km^2 (25% of a tetrad) is in Cheshire, but recorded the birds found in all of the tetrad. One tetrad is common to categories B and C, giving a total of 670 tetrads for the breeding season.

At the planning stage of this project, the convention for choice of category C aroused some discussion, because for some tetrads, up to three-quarters of their area was not in Cheshire and some birds recorded would not be in the county. This system was followed because of several advantages: (i) it was the same as our *First Atlas*; (ii) it was the same as used by other counties; (iii) all Cheshire tetrads have the same land area, allowing comparative analysis; otherwise, all edge tetrads would have had varying expectations of species totals; and (iv) practically, it avoided observers having to decide which side of midriver a Dipper was on!

For winter recording, there is an additional complication because of birds in tetrads offshore, which do not have any permanent land area, thus being unsuitable for breeding birds. There seems to be no standard convention amongst bird Atlases for how to define which offshore tetrads to include. I took advice from Mike Hodgson about the procedure followed in Northumbria, the county with the longest coastline in England (Day & Hodgson 2003) and discussed the subject with a number of local recorders especially in the north Wirral. In principle, birds up to 1 km or more from shore, perhaps even 2 km, could be recorded, and the intention was to add one tetrad going offshore from all the coasts. In practice, it turned out often to be difficult to judge if a bird was in an inshore tetrad or one farther offshore. This is not felt to be a significant drawback, however. Most of the birds were seabirds, often in flight and moving from one tetrad to another; observers wherever possible ensured that individual birds were not double-counted. The number of tetrads for winter recording was 684.

'Cheshire and Wirral' for ornithological purposes is the same as during our *First Atlas*—despite further changes in administrative local authority arrangements—comprising the county of Cheshire and the unitary authorities of Wirral, Halton and Warrington. Although standards have thankfully advanced since the 1970s, when the county boundaries were stretched when a recorder wanted to include a desirable observation at the south end of the Dee or near Manchester, one area of uncertainty still persists, and has to be mentioned because it confuses discussion of the county status of many waterbirds. Even today, *CWBRs* include WeBS counts from the whole of the Dee estuary, bringing in records from some sites which are 15 km or more outside Cheshire and Wirral. Brown and Grice in their *Birds in England* (2005) gave two sets of counts from the border estuaries (Severn, Dee and Solway), those birds counted in England and the count for the whole of each site but, as noted with regret in several of the descriptions of the status of wildfowl and waders, CAWOS has declined to separate records in the county from those in Wales.

An important feature of this Atlas is the ability to make comparisons of bird distribution, for breeding birds between this period and that of our *First Atlas*, and for many species to contrast the breeding and wintering distributions. For comparisons with our *First Atlas*, two tetrads have been omitted, SJ27W and SJ29X because it was felt likely that records had been misattributed to these squares in the *First Atlas*. SJ27W is mainly saltmarsh but had an above-average total of 57 species listed in 1978–84, and SJ29X contains only a tiny area of land, all mown grass and roads, and cannot have held the 19 breeding species included in the *First Atlas*. Comparison maps, especially for the almost ubiquitous species, were distorted by inclusion of these tetrads and it was decided just to exclude them from such maps. The records from SJ27W are on the breeding and winter maps for this Atlas. If they are included on the 'change' maps they give a misleading impression for the almost-ubiquitous species that supposedly have been 'lost' from these two tetrads.

Recording of breeding status

We wanted to measure the distribution and abundance of the county's birds. Probably the most scientifically valid method of doing this is to undertake timed counts. During the planning stages, however, it was felt that this would be too prescriptive and deter potential volunteers, so observers were permitted to visit their tetrads as often as they wished, and to spend as long as they wanted on survey visits. The minimum to achieve reasonable coverage was stated to be two survey visits, at least four weeks apart, once between the beginning of April and middle of May, and once from the middle of May to the end of June, with such visits lasting at least two hours to stand a reasonable chance of finding all species. During each visit observers were urged to visit every type of habitat within the tetrad that was likely to hold any different species. We described the breeding season as being 'from April to the end of June, with adjustments being made for late and early breeders'. It may have been a mistake to mention specific months, because some observers who had been unfamiliar with birds' breeding biology may have taken these dates too literally and thus missed some of the early and late breeding species.

The main advantage of timed counts is that they allow a rigorous determination of abundance. We decided not to use records from all tetrads for this, but to work with a sample from areas within the county covered for the national BBS (see 'Estimating population size of common and widespread birds in Cheshire and Wirral' below).

The first national bird Atlas (1968–72) established the three-category system of confirmed, probable and possible breeding, according to a variety of behaviour indicating different levels of certainty of breeding. This scheme has been widely used, including in our *First Atlas*, and has been adopted as a recommended standard by the European Bird Census Council (EBCC). A number of Atlases, starting with the BTO's second national survey (1988–91), have adopted a two-level method of 'breeding' or 'present', with the former amalgamating the confirmed and probable categories. This system was felt to be preferable in shifting the emphasis onto measuring 'abundance', using a method of relative distribution (how many tetrads were occupied within a 10 km square), rather than obtaining breeding evidence. This two-level system was adopted for very good reasons, but David Gibbons, national organizer of the *BTO Second Atlas*, has said (*personal communication*) that he now wishes that the standard three-category system had been used for that survey.

During the planning stages of our Atlas, we debated long and hard which protocol to use, and eventually decided to require observers to record the highest level of the 16 breeding status codes, which could later be converted to a two- or three-level system. Some of the difference between breeding status codes is a matter of the species' biology and some is a matter of observer competence or experience, or indeed luck, and we waited to see what results were returned before eventually deciding to use the three-level system throughout this Atlas.

We did not, however, adopt one measure of probable breeding from the EBCC list, T: permanent Territory presumed through registration of territorial behaviour (song etc.) on at least two days, a week or more apart, at the same place. This code was also not used in the *BTO Second Atlas*; since, to maximize participation, we specified a minimum of just two visits, at least four weeks apart, it was felt that surveyors would thus be unlikely to record the same individual singing. In any case, there are doubts about the validity of this category as an indicator of 'probable breeding' as persistent song can indicate a pair, but for many species the males go quiet after pairing so a persistently singing male is likely to be unmated. The only difference is that singing birds (S) were counted in the lowest category of breeding.

We also felt that it was important to record the exact breeding status code, rather than just ticking a box in one of two or three columns as has been done in some other Atlases. This had a number of advantages: it allowed a small number of records to be followed up for more information, or mistakes to be corrected; it has been interesting and informative to see the different status codes recorded for different species; it has allowed us to map some species in different ways, especially the colonial nesters that were widely spread in areas where they were not breeding (e.g. Swift, Rook, Grey Heron); and it would allow retrospective analysis or reclassification at a later date if desired.

It is clear from the Atlas results that there is a strong relationship (R^2 = 0.52) between ubiquity and the proportion of confirmed breeding, as shown in Figure 1: the more common a species, as measured by how widespread it is, the more chances that an observer has to record breeding behaviour.

Comparison with other breeding bird Atlases

Although in principle it should be possible to compare results from different county Atlases, in practice some words of caution are needed because the details of the methods have to be taken into account. For instance, a two-level system (breeding/present) requires, as a minimum, a pair of birds to be seen and it could have been much quicker to survey a tetrad just ticking off pairs without seeking any higher level of proof. With limited resources of time or people this could be a better way of organizing an Atlas project. However, some other counties have used this two-level breeding/present system, lumping together the confirmed and probable categories but, confusingly, have described them all as 'confirmed'. Another snag in comparing the system used here with those used elsewhere is that some other Atlases have used the same breeding status codes but have translated them into different levels of breeding category; for instance, attributing 'confirmed breeding' to even a single adult thought to be holding/defending territory, and 'probable breeding' to a singing male in suitable habitat. All of these examples show unfeasibly high apparent levels of 'confirmed' breeding.

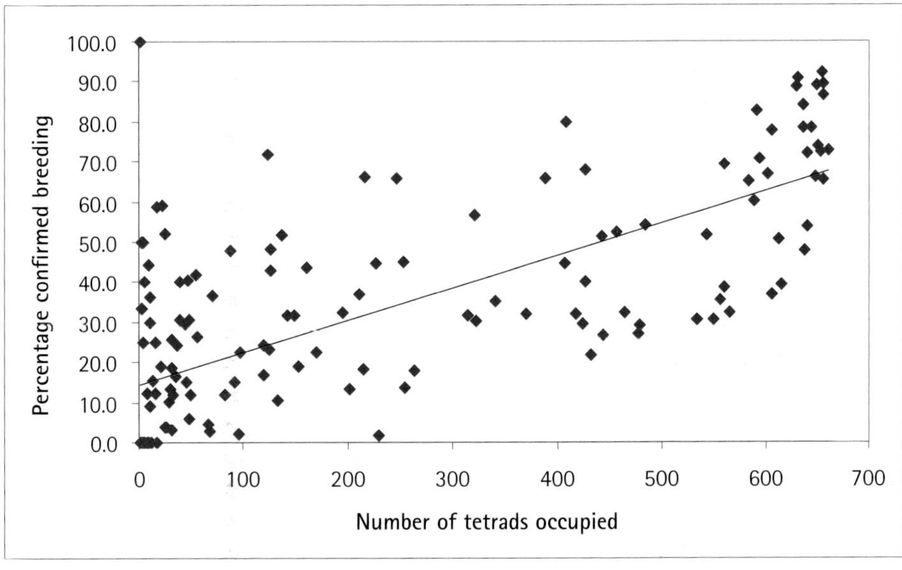

Figure 1: The relationship between the proportion of confirmed breeding and ubiquity of species in this Atlas.

Winter codes

In winter, the main aim was to record every species that was using the tetrad; birds flying over but not using the tetrad were excluded from the Atlas. It was felt that there was not much additional information, apart from habitat details, that would be worth collecting, apart from the size of flocks or roosts. We asked for counts to be included, this request initially being driven by the requirement of the CAWOS database for records to have a number, but in fact the counts, even of a single bird in a tetrad, proved to be especially valuable in allowing a winter population estimate for some species. The winter period was intended to avoid periods of migration and breeding and, to make an Atlas sensible, to cover the time when most birds were settled in one area. Having the same dates for all species, regardless of their biology, inevitably entails a compromise, and 'winter' was defined as 16 November to the end of February. This was the same choice as was made for the *BTO Winter Atlas* in 1981/82–1983/84, although the new national Bird Atlas 2007–11 is taking winter records from the beginning of November.

We briefly considered attempting a year-round Atlas, but decided against it for a variety of reasons, the key one being the questionable value of mapping birds at periods of the year when they are not settled and just moving through the area, making for problems in interpretation and little value from the information. Also, many species are less conspicuous and are difficult to detect, especially during moult periods. Coverage year-round was thought to be more likely to reflect the distribution of recorders than distribution of birds, and observer fatigue may set in, prejudicing the recording of the more important breeding and wintering seasons.

Habitat records

To increase the value of the data for conservation, habitat information was also collected, with observers for every record, breeding or winter, allocating one or more habitat codes according to the standard system devised by the BTO (Crick 1992). This is, we believe, a feature that has not been incorporated into previous Atlases, and aroused much heated discussion at the planning stages. 'Birders don't do habitat' was a phrase frequently used, but in fact all participants in BTO survey work since the mid-1990s have recorded habitat, including for every bird ringed, every nest recorded and every BBS or special survey completed. With some trepidation, and a certain element of autocracy from the Atlas Coordinator, habitat recording was included in the Atlas instructions; it met with little resistance from fieldworkers, proved to be straightforward to do and provided much new information of great interest for many species.

Use of electronic technology for recording and data input

One major change since our *First Atlas* is the increased availability of technology. Twenty years ago, personal computers and mobile phones were not widely available, nor was access to e-mail or the internet. The satellites for the Global Positioning System (GPS) had not been launched. Digital cameras had not even been dreamed of.

In this Atlas, most observers filled in computer spreadsheets with their tetrad data and submitted them by e-mail. We were able to communicate with about two-thirds of fieldworkers by e-mail. We established the website www.cheshireandwirralbirdatlas.org to advertise the project and to provide information and reference material for participants.

In the field, some surveyors took advantage of GPS to obtain accurate locations for observations and tetrad boundaries. In most other types of wildlife recording, their use is now routine, but many birdwatchers apparently think that GPS devices are expensive; in fact, a simple hand-held GPS receiver costs about the same as a bird book, and would probably be the cheapest item in an average birdwatcher's armoury of equipment.

The prompt submission of records meant that preliminary maps could rapidly be produced and regularly shared with observers in the Atlas newsletters. Finally, in contrast to our *First Atlas* where data were collected on paper and the analysis and production of the maps and the book took many years, this Atlas has made it to publication in the calendar year after the end of fieldwork.

Recruitment of fieldworkers

Recruitment was started by placing notices in *Bird News*, the CAWOS newsletter, and by announcements at indoor meetings. The call was taken up by many of the county's local natural history and ornithological societies and RSPB groups, and several members from CAWOS were invited to visit groups to seek out new recruits. Notices were placed in the local press, in local and national birdwatching publications, and in hides and visitor centres throughout the recording area. CAWOS members and birdwatchers covering BTO surveys were often asked to cover tetrads in which they either lived or surveyed.

Recruitment was aided when the Public Rights of Way Unit of Cheshire County Council provided us with laminated maps of the recording area; these were marked with dots to indicate when coverage of a tetrad was complete and, when displayed at many indoor meetings, spurred more volunteers to help to fill the blank areas. In return we helped the Unit by informing them of any footpaths which had been blocked or were otherwise inaccessible. It was emphasized that fieldworkers must obtain permission from landowners for access to private land, and a letter was written by the Atlas Coordinator to facilitate these approaches. In practice, almost all landowners agreed to fieldworkers' requests and in many cases showed considerable interest in the project and provided extra information themselves.

Over 360 birdwatchers sent in records for the Atlas, this being the first experience of systematic bird recording for some of them. Contributors were divided almost equally between CAWOS members and non-members. The former covered two-thirds of the tetrads, but we were keen to stress throughout that all records were valued, from whatever source.

We had hoped to be able to solicit records from a wider community, including farmers, wildfowlers, schools and the general public, with information about nocturnal species hoped for from moth, bat and badger groups, but apart from a few instances of personal contacts, procuring such data proved beyond the resources of our amateur project.

Training

After the initial recruitment phase, over 70 prospective participants attended a one-day meeting on 28 February 2004, just before the start of the project, for training especially in the categories of breeding status and habitat coding. We were able to obtain from the BTO cassette tapes or CDs for those unsure of birdsongs. Notes and discussion of recording techniques and data submission protocols were included in the Atlas newsletters and in a 'Frequently Asked Questions' (FAQ) section on the Atlas website, and the Atlas Coordinator provided advice in person, by telephone or by e-mail to many fieldworkers, especially in the first year or so.

Area coordinators

An important part of the organization was the Area Coordinators, who volunteered to cover, typically, a 10 × 10 km square, containing 25 tetrads, but ranging from two tetrads, in areas at the west and east of the county, to several areas where a coordinator took responsibility for several 10 km squares. Their function was to act as an intermediate level between the Atlas Coordinator and the individual fieldworker, helping with the recruitment of volunteers, keeping in touch with them and giving help where necessary; ensuring full coverage and checking that fieldwork was being done and records submitted; overseeing the data being sent in, including examining for consistency and acting as the first level of quality control. The best of the Area Coordinators added real value to the process, encouraging and supporting fieldworkers in their area, some of them holding discussion meetings with their surveyors, sorting out many small problems and contributing their local knowledge, generally doing more than expected.

Instructions and guidance

Considerable effort was expended to try to make the fieldwork and the recording as straightforward as possible, especially as we recognized that some of those taking part were not used to systematic bird recording. Copies of the 'Instructions and Guidance' notes for the breeding and wintering parts of the survey are included in Appendix 2. These were sent to each registered participant, along with a map of their tetrad.

Effort

We asked observers to record the dates on which they recorded in their tetrad, and the approximate amount of time that they spent on fieldwork. It is recognized that this is not a precise figure, especially for the one-third of fieldworkers who lived or worked in a tetrad that they were surveying.

The mean figures were 30 hours per tetrad for the breeding survey and 18.3 hours per tetrad for winter Atlas work, a total of over 32,500 hours. This does not include supplementary records, nor time spent in fieldwork in other organizations from whom we obtained records, or the other sources of recording (such as WeBS, BBS, heronries counts and so on) whose records and results were incorporated in the Atlas.

We thus estimate that about 50,000 hours of fieldwork were expended on this project.

In addition, countless hours indoors were committed by the Atlas Coordinator, other members of the Steering Group, Area Coordinators, the database manager, artists, photographers and numerous other people involved in this project.

Efficiency of coverage

Given a finite number of observers and finite time available, there is a clear trade-off between continuing to visit a tetrad to find every species and moving on to cover more tetrads. Some dedicated fieldworkers felt that they wanted to persevere in 'their' tetrad and try to find every species present and, in the breeding season, to try to prove breeding for all of them if possible. After investment of a few hours' effort, however, the exact amount depending on the diversity of habitat, the experience of the observer, the stage of the season, and so on, it became increasingly difficult to add extra species and the best option, for the good of the Atlas project as a whole, was to move on to cover a different tetrad. Some observers were reluctant to do that when they knew that there were species probably in the tetrad that they had not yet found, and many surveyors enjoyed getting to know better a tetrad that they had not previously visited. Some other Atlases have given fieldworkers guidance on what would be considered a reasonable level of coverage—the 2nd Pennsylvania Breeding Bird Atlas, for instance, advised surveyors that 75% of the expected number of species was a satisfactory result—but we did not set any targets.

There is clearly an element of uneven coverage from one tetrad to another depending on factors such as the observer's familiarity with the area, their tenacity and temperament. About 120 of our tetrads (18% of the total) were surveyed by people who lived in the square, which makes regular observation easier. In one or two areas the Area Coordinator was more assiduous than most in urging fieldworkers towards 'complete' coverage but, in general, there were not wide variations across the county and we can be reasonably confident that most of the differences seen in the maps are real differences in bird distributions rather than the effects of varying effort or competence.

During this Atlas we had an interesting experiment in efficiency of coverage. Two very experienced observers, who covered more than 10 tetrads each, inadvertently both surveyed two tetrads in the 2006 breeding season, independently of each other, this only being realized months after the end of the season. One tetrad received about six and ten hours of effort from the two surveyors and the other about eight and twelve hours respectively. Out of the total number of species found, both observers recorded 66% (33/50) and 71% (41/58) of them; of the remaining species, each fieldworker found some birds that were missed by the other, roughly in proportion to the time spent surveying.

Our winter instructions called for observers to 'Please feel free to visit your chosen tetrad as often as you like and to spend as long as you want on surveying. The *minimum* to achieve reasonable coverage is to visit twice, once from 16th November to the end of December, and once from 1st January to the end of February. The two dates should be at least four weeks apart. ... We aim to get as complete coverage as possible, so please plan to visit every type of habitat within the tetrad that is likely to hold any different species. To stand a reasonable chance of finding all species, each visit should last *at least* two hours.'

This advice was similar to that for the BBS, and has recently been validated by pilot fieldwork for the BTO Bird Atlas 2007–11 (Gillings 2008). For a wide variety of species, the pilot study showed that, given a finite quantity of field effort, to maximize the number of species found and to minimize error in relative abundance estimates, it is better to distribute survey effort by visiting more tetrads for a shorter period than vice versa.

Weather during the survey

The following comments are generalized and refer to the county as a whole. The two large estuaries have a major influence on the weather of Wirral and much of northern Cheshire, and the eastern hills tend to be colder and wetter than the rest of the area. These brief summaries reflect the influence of the weather during the Atlas period on the birds and on observers' ability to record them.

The three breeding seasons of this Atlas, 2004 to 2006, experienced a variety of weather, as is normal in Britain. All three years were warmer and sunnier than the long-term average. In 2004, changeable April weather allowed most migrants to arrive on or around the normal schedule but the early individuals had to endure some cold and rainy days. May and June were mostly warm and dry, good for most birds and for recording, until gales from late June heralded a wet July and a curtailed breeding season for many species, with relatively few late broods. 2005 was the most equable of the three breeding seasons, with temperatures somewhat above the long-term mean, sunshine about normal and less rain than average. April 2005 was unpredictable, wet and cool at times until the last week of the month, delaying early Atlas recording, but the period from May to July was about as settled as it gets in this country, mostly dry with average temperatures, before August was again changeable and cool. The 2006 breeding season started late, with the coldest March for ten years and a changeable April followed by the wettest May for twenty years. June and July were unusually hot and settled, with the spell broken early in August and another rainy month to end any late breeding attempts for most species.

All three winters of our Atlas were typical of recent times, with rapidly changing weather, often windy and generally mild, with no freezing spells severe enough to force birds to move. During winter 2004/05 there were days of gales, torrential rain and snow, but none of them lasting for long. The hours of sunshine were above normal, as were winter temperatures, and there was not a single day where the temperature stayed below freezing. Drought in southern England dominated the London-based media but rainfall elsewhere, including in north-west England, was average. Winter 2005/06 was the coldest and driest of the three winters, although average temperatures were still above the long-term mean. Our winter Atlas period from mid-November started with overnight frosts before settling to our usual pattern of depressions coming off the Atlantic (warm, windy and wet) alternating with high pressure (cold, calm and dry) for the rest of the winter. Winter 2006/07 was extraordinarily warm (mean temperature for the region 2.3°C above the 1961–90 average) and wet (half as much rainfall again as the long-term average). Unprecedented combinations of winds in the first weeks of our final winter period inhibited some Atlas recording but drove several species of seabird out of the Bay of Biscay and unexpectedly onto the pages of this Atlas.

This summary has been based on the published data from the UK Meteorological Office, especially their seasonal figures for north-west England and North Wales (http://www.metoffice.gov.uk/climate/uk/) and the Central England Temperature record (http://hadobs.metoffice.com/hadcet/), with local information taken from the *CWBRs*, with thanks to Tony Broome and Hugh Pulsford.

Progress of fieldwork

The spread of effort, across the county and across the years, was quite even. Breeding season records from dedicated tetrad visits were received in 2004 from 414 tetrads, in 2005 from 400 and in 2006 from 416 tetrads; including supplementary records those figures go up to 505, 518 and 550 tetrads respectively. There were 188 tetrads recorded as having dedicated visits in all three seasons, with 196 in two seasons and 273 in one season. The running total of tetrads that had received dedicated visits was 414 in 2004, 530 in 2005 and 661 in 2006 (see Figures 2–4).

Although the organizers and Atlas Steering Group had made strenuous efforts to ensure complete coverage during the three breeding seasons, including checking in May 2006 with Area Coordinators that all remaining tetrads were being covered, it became clear during autumn 2006 that not all tetrads had in fact been visited. Nine tetrads, scattered across the county, had received no dedicated recording effort at all in any of the three years. These were surveyed in 2007 by members of the Atlas Steering Group or selected experienced observers; at the same time, the opportunity was taken to make additional visits to a further 14 tetrads where far fewer species had been recorded than expected. It is not felt that this small element of additional effort in 2007 significantly biased the results. Out of the final total of 34,516 unique breeding records, 12,334 (35.7%) were from 2004, 8,572 (24.8%) from 2005, 12,668 (36.7%) from 2006 and 942 (2.7%) from 2007. A total of 30,191 breeding records (87.5%) came from dedicated visits to tetrads and 4,325 as supplementary records. Of the 18,535 confirmed breeding records, 6,618 (35.7%) were from 2004, 4,591 (24.7%) from 2005, 6,909 (37.4%) from 2006 and 417 (2.2%) from 2007.

For all species, the highest levels of the various breeding status codes recorded are shown in Table 1, and the categories of breeding status, compared to those recorded during our *First Atlas*, are shown in Table 2.

The lower proportion of confirmed breeding during this Atlas is almost certainly because of the shorter time span of this survey (three years compared to seven years for our *First Atlas*). To prove breeding in some species requires an element of luck, or increased familiarity with their habits, or improved proficiency at detecting aspects of their behaviour; all of these increase with time. During this Atlas, the proportion of confirmed breeding after the first season was 43.8%, rising to 48.8% after two years' records and 53.7% at the end of the survey.

Winter records from dedicated tetrad visits were received in 2004/05 from 373 tetrads, in 2005/06 from 431 and in 2006/07 from 430 tetrads; including supplementary records those figures go up to 471, 525 and 565 tetrads respectively. There were 163 tetrads recorded as having dedicated visits in all three winters, with 237 in two of them and 284 in just one. The running total of tetrads that had received dedicated visits was 373 in 2004/05, 548 in 2005/06 and 684 in 2006 (see Figures 5–7). Out of the final total of 34,237 unique winter records, 10,747 (31.4%) were from 2004/05, 12,135 (35.4%) from 2005/06 and 11,355 (33.2%) from 2006/07. Being forewarned with the experience from breeding

Table 1: The highest level of breeding status code recorded during this Atlas.

		Breeding Status Code	Total	%
Possible breeding	H	Species present in suitable nesting **H**abitat; no other indication of breeding	5,031	14.6
	S	**S**inging male heard, or breeding calls heard	3,905	11.3
Probable breeding	P	**P**air observed in suitable nesting habitat	4,369	12.7
	D	**D**isplay or courtship	885	2.6
	N	Bird visiting a probable **N**est site	699	2.0
	B	Birds seen **B**uilding a nest, carrying nesting material, or excavating nest cavity	447	1.3
	A	**A**gitated behaviour or anxiety calls from adults suggesting a nest or young nearby	612	1.8
	I	Active brood patch on trapped bird, probably **I**ncubating	33	0.1
Confirmed breeding	DD	**D**istraction **D**isplay or injury-feigning from adults	94	0.3
	UN	Recently **U**sed **N**est (used this season), or eggshells	94	0.3
	ON	**O**ccupied **N**est in use (e.g. high nest or nest hole whose contents cannot be deduced)	2,413	7.0
	FY	Adults carrying **F**ood for **Y**oung	4,320	12.5
	RF	**R**ecently **F**ledged young, still dependent on parents	6,258	18.1
	FS	Adults carrying **F**aecal **S**ac away from nest site	110	0.3
	NE	**N**est with **E**ggs, or adult sitting on nest	869	2.5
	NY	**N**est with **Y**oung, or downy young of nidifugous species	4,377	12.7

	This Atlas (2004–06)		First Atlas (1978–84)	
Confirmed breeding	18,535	53.7%	21,501	61.4%
Probable breeding	7,045	20.4%	7,863	22.5%
Possible breeding	8,936	25.9%	5,630	16.1%
Total	34,516	100.0%	34,994	100.0%

Table 2: Comparison of the results for breeding category in this three-year Atlas and our seven-year *First Atlas*.

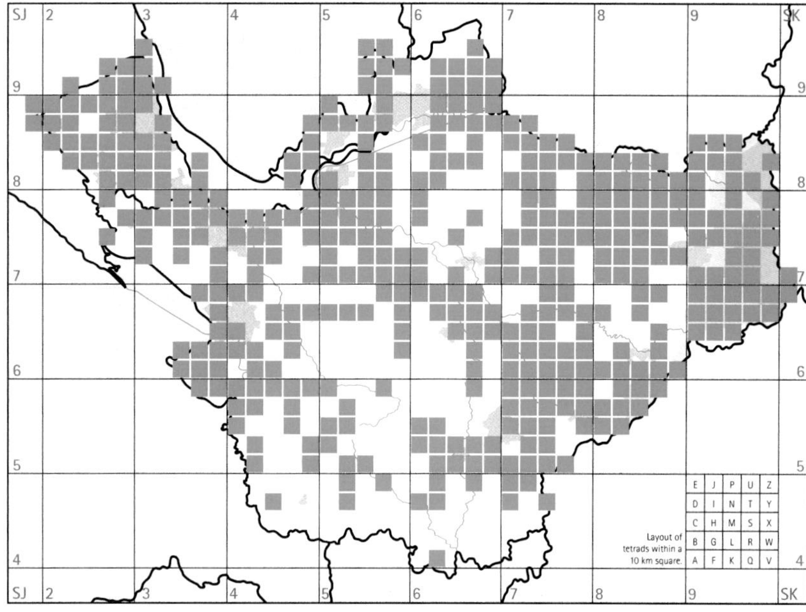

Figure 2: Breeding tetrads with dedicated visits—first year.

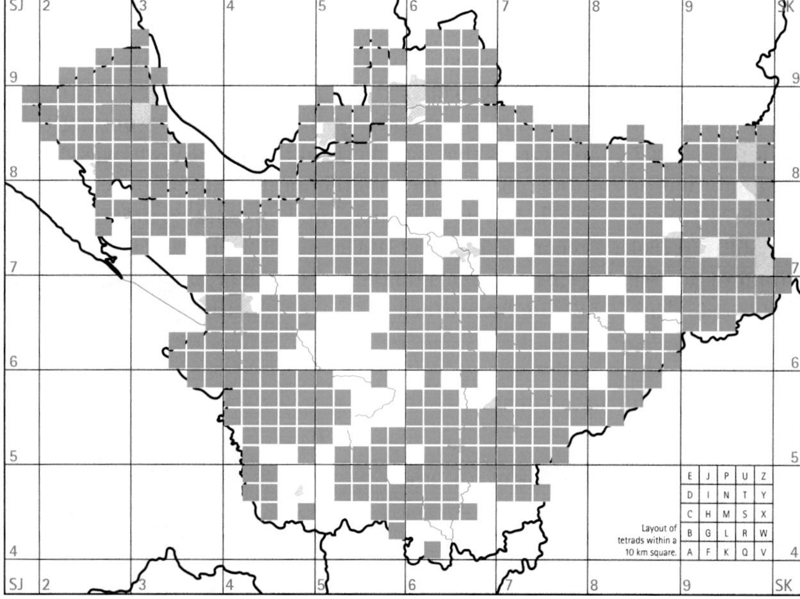

Figure 3: Breeding tetrads with dedicated visits—first two years.

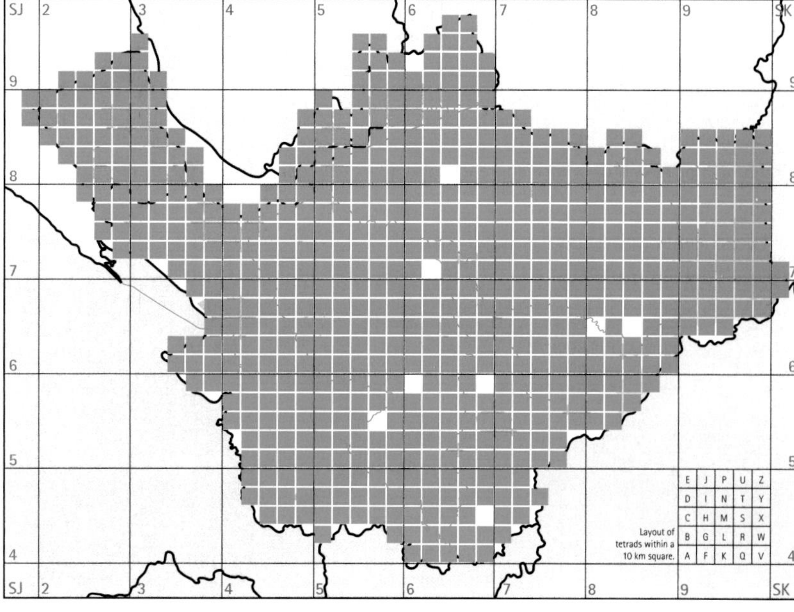

Figure 4: Breeding tetrads with dedicated visits—all three years.

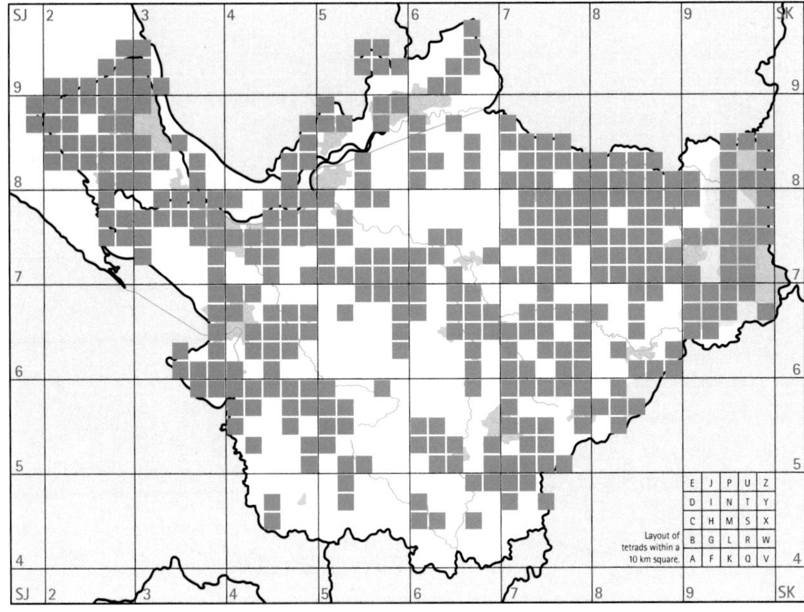

Figure 5: Winter tetrads with dedicated visits—first year.

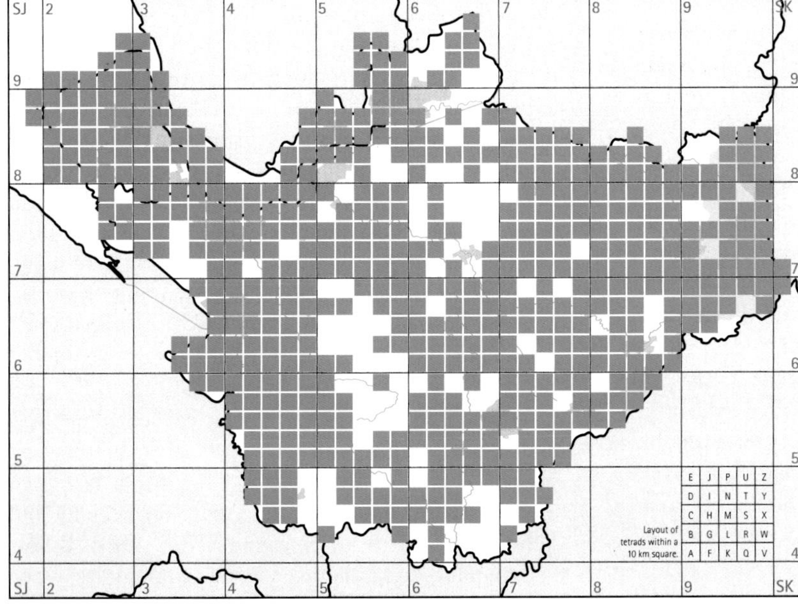

Figure 6: Winter tetrads with dedicated visits—first two years.

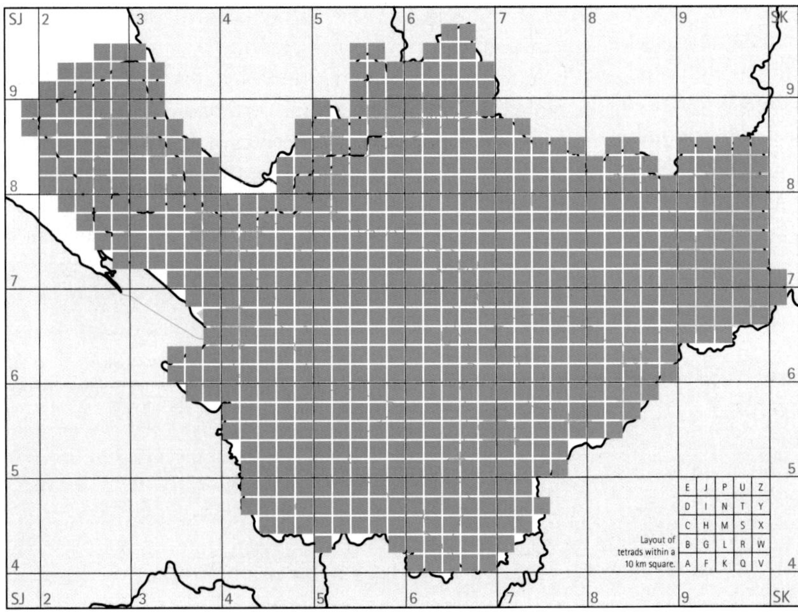

Figure 7: Winter tetrads with dedicated visits—all three years.

season 2006, and knowing that having to delay any winter visits to 2007/08 would have directly impacted on the publication schedule, we applied even tighter control on ensuring full coverage by the third winter season, including flying visits to a few tetrads where the observer or Area Coordinator did not respond to requests for information. Thus, full coverage of all tetrads in the county was achieved in three winters. In total, 29,841 winter records (87.2%) came from dedicated visits to tetrads and 4,396 as supplementary records.

Fieldworkers submitted the results to their Area Coordinators who acted as the first layer of quality control, checking the data for any possible mistakes and querying unexpected records. Most data were submitted electronically using the spreadsheets supplied; an estimated one-quarter of records came in on paper, being transcribed by Area Coordinators, Steering Group members or a volunteer. In the first year, all data were checked by David Norman; after that, Steve Barber took over that role with David Cogger ensuring that all submissions were acknowledged. This provided an extra layer of data validation. All records were added electronically to the Atlas database, which then allowed rapid analysis, production of some preliminary maps and provision of feedback to participants, mainly by occasional newsletters and talks from the Atlas Coordinator.

Although it was felt that the data validation was an important step in ensuring the quality of the records, modifications to submitted records were kept to a minimum and amounted to less than 1% of the total. Reasons for changes included transcription errors, such as incorrectly entered species, tetrads or codes; elimination of double-counting of scarce species nesting in one tetrad but recorded feeding or with fledged young in an adjacent square; downgrading of some probable breeding to possible, especially where observers commented that they had used the D code for song-flights of single birds, and where P had been used for observations of two or more birds, not necessarily paired (although most of these records had no comments and have been left as submitted with a comment in the species text); and some adjustment between H and O, in both directions, based on knowledge/assessment of breeding habitat and likelihood of breeding. Additional reasons for changes to winter records included deletion of records from dates outside our defined winter period; removal of a few records stated to be from wildfowl collections; and correction of F codes to U for some species seen in flight but obviously using the tetrad.

Confidential records

A small number of breeding season records, fewer than 20 in total, were initially submitted in confidence. It is sad to report that the reason for such submissions was usually that the observer feared disturbance to the birds by irresponsible birdwatchers. However, after seeing the maps of all records, all those who had originally submitted confidential data then agreed to publication. All records in this Atlas are mapped accurately.

Estimating population size of common and widespread birds in Cheshire and Wirral

S.E. Newson, British Trust for Ornithology

The analyses of abundance were based on survey work carried out on 109 selected 1 km squares in Cheshire and Wirral. Of these, 69 1 km squares were surveyed through the BTO/JNCC/RSPB Breeding Bird Survey (BBS) in 2004 and/or 2005. An additional 40 1 km pastoral squares were surveyed in 2005, as part of a project to provide a baseline against which change could be monitored following the introduction of the Entry Level Stewardship Scheme (ELS), which encourages farmers to deliver environmental management measures. Full details of the BBS (and fieldwork carried out for ELS survey work which uses the same methodology) are provided by Raven *et al.* (2007). In brief, fieldwork involved two visits to each square, the first between early April and mid-May and the second between mid-May and late June. Birds were recorded in each 200 m section along two 1 km transects. The perpendicular distances of birds from the transect line were recorded in three distance bands (0–25 m, 25–100 m, 100 m or more). Counts began at 0600–0700 hours where possible, to coincide with maximum bird activity, whilst avoiding the concentrated song period at dawn. Flying birds that were actively using resources in a square, such as displaying Skylarks, hovering Kestrels, hirundines and Swifts were assigned to the appropriate distance band; other records of flying birds were not used in our analyses.

Whilst BBS squares were selected according to a random sampling design (Figure 8), ELS squares were selected at random from pastoral squares as classified using landcover data from the Centre for Ecology and Hydrology (CEH) (Haines-Young *et al.* 2002). Unless this sampling design is taken into account, there is the potential to overestimate the population size for species associated with pastoral habitat and underestimate population size for species not occurring in this habitat. For this reason we considered the data as being of two strata, pastoral squares (ELS squares + BBS pastoral squares) and non-pastoral squares. The method for producing population estimates and 95% confidence levels from these data is discussed in brief below.

Observers were asked to exclude juvenile birds from counts where possible because the inclusion of such individuals would inflate estimates of the breeding population. Exploratory analyses of BBS data have shown that such errors are more likely for species that breed early, mainly residents, and that were counted during the late visit. Conversely, most long-distance migrant species are still arriving in the UK during the first visit period, thus counts of these species during this visit may lead to their densities being underestimated. To control for these biases we only used data from early visits for resident species and only from late visits for migrants.

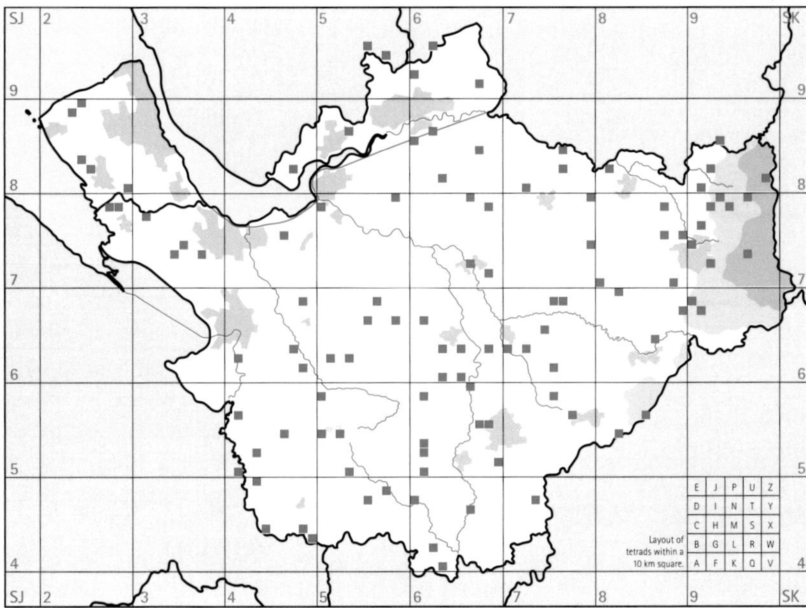

Figure 8: BBS/ELS transects.

Habitat within each 200 m transect section was recorded by volunteers according to a four-level hierarchical coding system that documents the main habitat type in one of nine categories, together with a number of finer level habitat features such as the type of farmland, the nature of field boundaries and the crop (Crick 1992). This is a more detailed version of the same scheme used for habitat recording in this Atlas (p. 5).

Detectability must be taken into account when converting count data into densities, and subsequently population estimates, otherwise these variables will be underestimated. This was achieved using distance sampling software (DISTANCE, version 5.0 Release 2; Buckland *et al.* 2001, Thomas *et al.* 2006) to model the decline in detectability with distance from the transect line. Birds recorded in the final distance band (100 m or more) were excluded from the analyses, because counts within an unbounded category are difficult to interpret. Habitat types differ in the structure of their vegetation and are thus likely to influence detectability to varying extents: this was taken into account in the analysis.

We identified nine main habitat types (broad-leaved woodland, coniferous woodland, mixed woodland, semi-natural grassland/heath and bog, arable, pastoral and mixed farmland, human habitats and waterbodies) based on Crick (1992) and adopted the following stepwise approach. For each species we estimated $f(0)$, i.e. the value of the probability density function of perpendicular distances at zero distance, without including habitat covariates to both half-normal and hazard rate models. We then added habitat as a covariate and established whether the model fit was improved, defined as a reduction in the Akaike's Information Criterion (AIC), and identified the best fitting model. We then fitted a model with both habitat and region as covariates and used AIC to see whether the relative fit of the model improved. If there was no improvement in model fit, the best fitting model with a single covariate or no covariate was regarded as that which best explained heterogeneity in detectability. Once this best fitting model had been chosen for a species, it was applied to the encounters from surveyed squares to produce an estimate of the number of individuals of that species within each square.

In total it was possible to model detectability using the data for Cheshire and Wirral for 61 common and widespread species. For a further 18 species, it was possible to calculate density estimates by assuming the detection probability was the same as calculated by Newson *et al.* (2008) using the entire BBS national data set for 2006. This was done by specifying the probability of detection as a multiplier in the analyses, and fixing the modelled probability of detection by fitting a uniform distribution to the detection function with no adjustments. Although the analyses for these 18 species are statistically valid, for many of them, however, the figures seemed unrealistically too high or low when compared to knowledge of the county's birds, and the data for only four of them are used in this Atlas; these discrepancies deserve further investigation.

To properly account for the sampling design, it was necessary to consider squares as belonging to two strata, pastoral squares (ELS squares + BBS pastoral squares) and non-pastoral squares. For each of the two strata a mean density estimate (and standard error, or SE) was calculated using the GENMOD procedure in SAS (SAS Institute 2001) with which we fitted a log-linear regression model with Poisson error terms and identity link. Density estimates were then multiplied by the area of each stratum in Cheshire and Wirral to obtain a population size estimate for each stratum. The SE for each population estimate was calculated as: area of stratum^2 × SE of the appropriate density estimate. A total population estimate for Cheshire and Wirral was calculated as the sum of stratum population estimates and 95% confidence intervals calculated as the Cheshire and Wirral population estimate ±1.96 (square root of summed SEs).

Comparison with population estimates from our *First Atlas*

Most population estimates presented in our *First Atlas* were of breeding pairs. For comparative purposes, we multiplied these by two to get estimates of the number of individual birds, taking the mean figure when a range was given. However, these figures are not likely to be comparable for species which do not breed in their first years and for which there is a significant non-breeding component to the population. These caveats notwithstanding, the figures from the two Atlases are plotted in Figure 9 for the 65 species for which the BBS/ELS analysis worked. The solid line indicates a total the same in both surveys, with the dotted line showing the present figure twice that for 1978–84. The present estimates are higher for 50 species and lower for 15. It seems implausible that the populations of so many species have risen, and that so few have fallen; the grand total of all the estimates for this Atlas is 2,022,880 and for our *First Atlas* is 1,213,788 individuals. The most parsimonious explanation of these figures is that many of the population figures presented in our *First Atlas*, although thought to have been reasonable at the time, were likely to have been underestimates. One of the reasons for thinking those figures to have been suspect is that several species that are clearly declining in fact appear to have almost identical populations to twenty years ago, including Starling (SG), Skylark (S.), Tree Sparrow (TS), Spotted Flycatcher (SF) and Grey Partridge (P.).

Nevertheless, there are some species whose breeding population has increased or decreased substantially: those that have increased are to the top left of the lines in the figure, and those that have decreased are to the bottom right. Six species have apparently increased by more than one order of magnitude (i.e. at least tenfold). Ranked by the ratio of the estimates from this Atlas to that from the *First Atlas*, these are Buzzard (BZ), Mute Swan (MS), Red-legged Partridge (RL), Long-tailed Tit (LT), Oystercatcher (OC) and Mallard (MA). The first four are certainly known to have increased greatly, and populations of Oystercatcher and Mallard certainly have risen, although a factor of 10 seems improbable. The next in order, in a group indicating rises of between fivefold and tenfold, are Goldfinch (GO), Grey Heron (H.), Tufted Duck (TU), Greenfinch (GR), Jackdaw (JD), Chiffchaff (CC) and Nuthatch (NH); again, all seven have risen in county breeding population in the last twenty years, but there is likely to be a mixture of real increases and underestimates in 1978–84. The next group of 13 species, with calculated increases ranked from a factor of five to a factor of 2.5, comprise Canada Goose (CG), Collared Dove (CD), Lesser Whitethroat (LW), Pied Wagtail (PW), Woodpigeon (WP), Meadow Pipit (MP), Sedge Warbler (SW), Pheasant (PH), Grey Wagtail (GL), Feral Pigeon (FP), Garden Warbler (GW), Whitethroat (WH) and Blackcap (BC). Out of this list it seems likely that Lesser Whitethroat, Meadow Pipit, Sedge Warbler, Feral Pigeon and Garden Warbler may well have been significantly underestimated twenty years ago, but that the others have genuinely increased a lot.

Those at the bottom of the list, whose breeding population appears to have fallen the most, include Willow Warbler (WW), Yellow Wagtail (YW), Song Thrush (ST), Bullfinch (BF) and Reed Bunting (RB), all known to be declining, although the presence of Curlew (CU) and Little Owl (LO) towards the head of that group is more surprising. Magpie (MG) is unexpected below the line, but the presence of Rook (RO) and Moorhen (MH) may well indicate real declines and their county populations should be better studied.

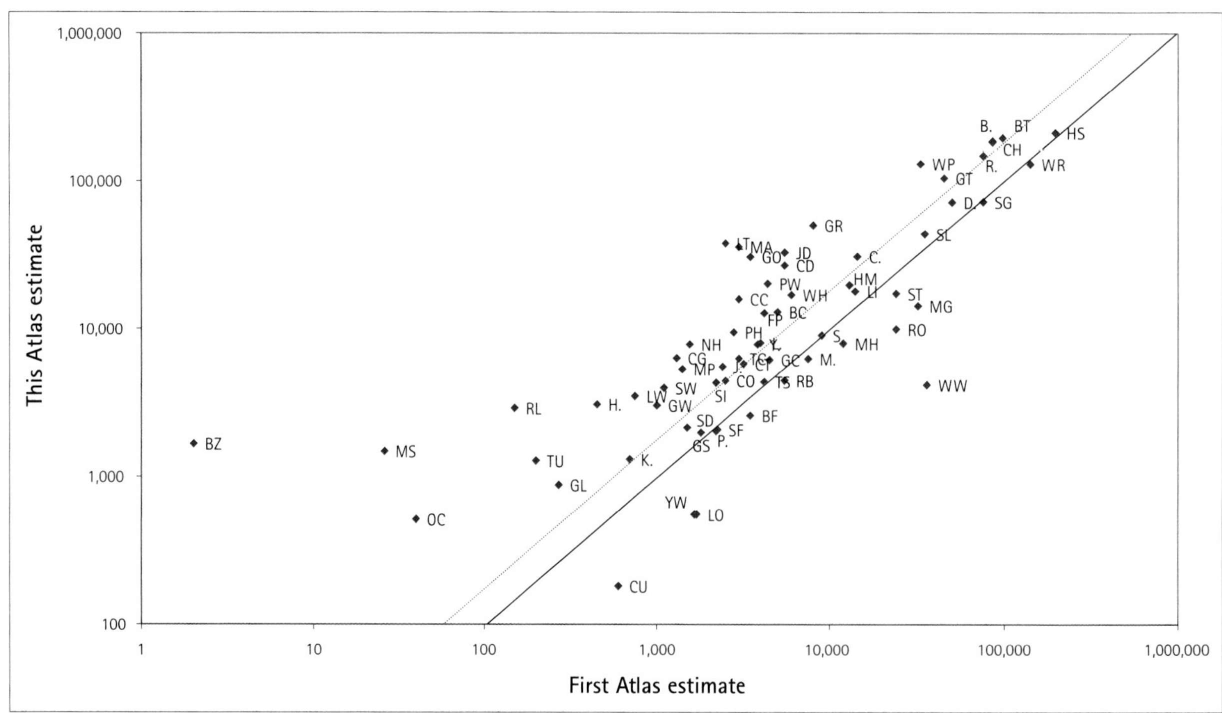

Figure 9: Comparison, for 65 species, between the county population estimates in this Atlas and our *First Atlas*.

Mapping the abundance of birds in Cheshire and Wirral

S.E. Newson, British Trust for Ornithology

Maps of abundance were produced using the densities estimated for surveyed 1 km squares, derived as a by-product of the population estimates work above, and using a statistical approach known as simple co-kriging. Simple co-kriging is one of a number of geostatistical methods that model the statistical relationship between surveyed sites. This approach weights the surrounding counts at surveyed sites to derive a prediction for unsurveyed locations. In these, the weights are based on the distance between measured sites and the prediction location, but also on the overall spatial arrangement in the weights (the spatial autocorrelation). For a full discussion of geostatistics and geostatistical methods see Chilès and Delfiner (1999). These techniques allowed us to produce a prediction surface over the entire area of interest, in this case Cheshire and Wirral.

Because the addition of habitat in the modelling process may improve the resulting predictions of abundance, we first carried out some preliminary analyses to examine which habitat or habitats best predicted abundance of each bird species. For this we used the bird densities and eight aggregate CEH landcover 2000 classes (inland water, moorland/heath and bog, broad-leaved woodland, coniferous woodland, improved grassland, semi-natural grassland, arable and human habitats; Haines-Young *et al.* 2002) to identify the best habitat predictors for each species. These analyses were performed for each species using the GENMOD procedure in SAS (SAS Institute 2001), specifying poisson errors and using a logit link function. The dependent variable used in each model was the density estimates and aggregate CEH landcover data habitat classes as categorical independent variables. This allowed us to identify which habitats were the best predictors of bird densities, and for each species up to three habitats were included in the subsequent co-kriging models. The geostatistical analyses were implemented with the Geostatistical Analyst extension of ArcGIS (Johnston *et al.* 2001) and resulted in contour maps of abundance. Each map was then scaled to best reveal any patterns present in abundance.

This technique has not previously been used to calculate abundance maps at as small a scale as a county.

Some reflections on successes and problems: personal views from the Atlas Coordinator

How well were the Atlas objectives achieved?

The first objective of the Atlas—to provide a permanent and comprehensive record of the bird species within the county—is completely satisfied, along with providing comparisons with historical studies such as the *First Atlas*. The completion in three years, along with rapid analysis and publication, is probably about as fast as could reasonably be achieved for full coverage of the county. The time-scale ought to be as short as possible to avoid the distorting effect of population changes during the survey, as happened disastrously to most farmland birds during the extended period of our *First Atlas*; but one has to balance the desire for a rapid survey with the number of fieldworkers available and obtaining as high as possible evidence of breeding. This has been the first survey to assess the habitat use of species in the county.

The 'social' aspects of the Atlas—to promote camaraderie within the birding community and to recruit and educate birders young and old into recognizing the value of recording for conservation purposes—seem to have been well fulfilled. It was interesting to go to many different gatherings where birdwatchers were present, and to discover how many people were taking part in the Atlas. It seemed odd that about half of those who individually submitted records for the annual *CWBRs* did not take part in the Atlas, despite regular exhortation; on the other hand, about half of the Atlas participants were not members of CAWOS and for many of them it was their first experience of systematic bird recording. Most observers took pleasure in participating, many of them learning a new aspect to their birdwatching; indeed, several wrote of their frustration that they had not previously learned the importance of birds' songs and alarm calls and had not studied birds' behaviour before, so the Atlas brought an enjoyable new side to their hobby. The influx of many new recruits bodes well for the future of bird recording in the county, if the enthusiasm can be marshalled and directed in further projects.

The success of the 'conservation' objectives—to enable use as a conservation tool and help in land use planning by local authorities, and to assist rECOrd, the local records centre, in providing data for preparing environmental impact assessments (EIAs)—will mostly be decided in the future. The Atlas results should be used to inform selection of Local Sites (Sites of Biological Interest). In planning and development control, they should not substitute for thorough site-based surveys and EIAs but provide the county-wide context for importance of bird species.

Similarly, fulfilment of the remaining two objectives—to provide baseline data for monitoring future changes in bird populations; and to complement existing or ongoing avian monitoring programs at county and national level—will depend on the future actions of the county's bird societies, especially CAWOS.

The following are some more detailed comments that may be especially relevant in the conduct of future surveys.

Definition of 'winter'

The breeding season is defined by birds' biology but 'winter' is defined by our calendar. The period from 16 November to the end of February was chosen to cover the period when most birds were expected to be fixed on their winter sites, with least confusion from migration. This defined period is never going to be right for all species. Some birds can be found breeding at any time of year, such as Collared Dove and Feral Pigeon; others normally start breeding during winter, such as Grey Heron, Tawny Owl, Raven and Crossbill. However, with the mild winters of late and the general advance of breeding dates, many species now show breeding behaviour during February, and sometimes January, and it might be better for a future winter survey to exclude the month of February.

Special sites

Perhaps ironically, some of the most troublesome areas for the Atlas included the most regularly watched sites in the county. In some of them, observers recorded within their normal 'site' boundary but not elsewhere within the tetrad, thus missing some habitats and species. In others, surveyors lumped all of the birds from an extensive site into one tetrad, overstating the records from that tetrad at the expense of neighbouring ones, and sometimes using the same habitat code for all species and confusing the habitat analysis.

Supplementary records

It was a surprise and a disappointment that, despite frequent pleas, fewer than one-third of fieldworkers submitted records from outside their 'main' tetrad. In many tetrads the only way to cover all of the square involved moving out of the tetrad and back in again, and surely some valuable extra records have potentially been lost by some observers' not providing supplementary submissions. It is not known how more supplementary records could be collected.

Incorrect use of codes

Although it is not thought that any of these has substantially biased the results, it is clear from examination of the records and from discussion with some fieldworkers that some of the codes were incorrectly applied. Many observers used RF for unfledged young—birds incapable of flight—of nidifugous species. More seriously, some submissions contained unexpectedly high proportions of RF codes and it is suspected that some surveyors used this code for all juvenile birds, whether or not they were recently fledged, thus undoubtedly including some birds that had nested in an adjacent tetrad, or in some cases, much farther afield. DD codes were expected for some waders and a few other species, but odd records were submitted for a wide variety of birds and there was probably some confusion between DD and D. Some observers used D for birds that sing in the air—Skylark, pipits, etc.—or for species whose song-flight is often called 'display'—Snipe, Woodcock, etc.—when only a single bird was involved and S was the correct code. P was occasionally recorded for a flock of birds, rather than strictly for a male and female associating together in suitable breeding habitat, and the colloquial equation of 'pair' for 'two' is unhelpful and should be banished from any birdwatcher's vocabulary. There were many instances of incorrect use of H and O, mostly caused by poor knowledge of the species' breeding habitats, and most of the obvious examples of errors were changed, such as excluding submissions of H for Arctic-breeding waders that have never bred in Britain, or changing O to H for some ubiquitous passerines. Finally, in winter, a few observers had not followed the instructions for recording birds in flight: birds seen flying from one hedge to another, or hovering over a field, were obviously using the tetrad and were recorded as U.

A more comprehensive set of examples of the use of recording codes could have obviated some of these mistakes, but we were wary of providing a long list for fear that the wrong inference could be drawn from omission from such a list, and preferred to rely on the common sense of observers.

Appendix 2

Instructions and guidance to surveyors

Cheshire and Wirral Bird Atlas

INSTRUCTIONS AND GUIDANCE FOR THE BREEDING ATLAS

The aim of this part of the Atlas is to determine the distribution and abundance of all birds breeding in Cheshire and Wirral. Our birdlife is changing rapidly. The Breeding Bird Atlas of Cheshire and Wirral was published over 10 years ago (1992) based on fieldwork now over 20 years old (1978-84), and the only mapping survey of the area in winter was in 1981-84 for The Atlas of Wintering Birds in Britain and Ireland, using 10km squares. This Atlas will allow comparison with the breeding birds of twenty years ago; it will produce data for winter, never before mapped in detail; and it will measure the abundance of birds as well as their distribution. It is essential to have as good information as possible on the birds' present status, and this Atlas will be a key tool to help their conservation.

Fieldwork is planned to cover three breeding seasons (April to the end of June each year) and three winter periods (mid-November to the end of February), from April 2004 to February 2007. Records for other times of year are requested to improve our knowledge, and will be included in the annual Cheshire and Wirral Bird Reports, but they will not be mapped in the Atlas as many birds are moving through our area then. Please e-mail your records for other times of year to submissions@cawos.org; for further advice please e-mail help.submissions@cawos.org.

We hope to achieve as good coverage as possible during the first year of the survey, so **please try to carry out the fieldwork in your chosen tetrads during 2004**. If you cannot do so, please let your Area Coordinator (names on the enclosed list) know as soon as possible.

Fieldwork

The basis for recording is the tetrad, a 2x2km square defined by the even-numbered lines on the National Grid. Use of an Ordnance Survey map is essential; the 1:25000 series is recommended, and a GPS device, if you have one, is very helpful. There is a map provided for each tetrad that you have volunteered to cover. For supplementary records from other areas that you visit, please identify the appropriate tetrad from the enclosed list.

Please feel free to visit your chosen tetrad as often as you like and to spend as long as you like on survey visits. If you cannot visit very often, the *minimum* to achieve reasonable coverage is to survey your tetrad twice, at least four weeks apart, once between the beginning of April and middle of May, and once from the middle of May to the end of June. Such visits should last at least two hours to stand a reasonable chance of finding all species. We aim to get as complete coverage as possible, so please plan to visit every type of habitat within the tetrad that is likely to hold any different species. Try to conduct your surveys during periods when birds are most likely to be detected, by sight and sound – preferably in the early morning, avoiding extremes of weather (heat, cold, wind and rain); if such conditions are unavoidable, please make a note of the weather in the 'general comments' box at the end of the form.

Record every species that you see or hear that is using the tetrad for breeding. Do not include birds that are merely moving through the area (such as gulls, corvids or herons, unless there are breeding birds in the tetrad) or passage migrants. As well as identifying them, watch and listen to find out what the birds are doing, and record the highest level of breeding status (the category closest to the bottom of this list) for each species in the tetrad, using the codes:

O Bird **O**bserved (seen or heard); no more knowledge of the species' status or of habitat suitable for breeding
H Species present in suitable nesting **H**abitat; no other indication of breeding
S **S**inging male heard, or breeding calls heard
P **P**air observed in suitable nesting habitat

D	**D**isplay or courtship
N	Bird visiting a probable **N**est site
B	Birds seen **B**uilding a nest, carrying nesting material, or excavating nest cavity
A	**A**gitated behaviour or anxiety calls from adults suggesting a nest or young nearby
I	Active brood patch on trapped bird, probably **I**ncubating
DD	**D**istraction **D**isplay or injury-feigning from adults
UN	Recently **U**sed **N**est (used this season), or egg-shells
ON	**O**ccupied **N**est in use (e.g. high nest or nest-hole whose contents cannot be deduced)
FY	Adults carrying **F**ood for **Y**oung
RF	**R**ecently **F**ledged young, still dependent on parents
FS	Adults carrying **F**aecal **S**ac away from nest site
NE	**N**est with **E**ggs, or adult sitting on nest
NY	**N**est with **Y**oung, or downy young of nidifugous species

The first two categories ('O' and 'H') are the ones that most often cause problems for some observers. Those recorded as 'O' are of limited value - because they tell us nothing about the possible breeding status - and will not be mapped in the Atlas, although they will be entered into the CAWOS database. So, please try to observe what the bird is doing and use a higher level of coding if appropriate. On the other hand, birds listed as 'H' must be in the normal breeding season for that species, and in suitable nesting habitat. It is not sufficient merely to see a bird during the April-June period.

It is only necessary to record one code of breeding status - the one closest to the bottom of the list - for a species in each tetrad. If, for instance, you find NY on your first visit, you do not need to record any more, although finding the species breeding in different habitats will be useful information. But if you find a species with activity corresponding to one of the single-letter codes, please try to find further evidence to upgrade it to one of the higher levels (a two-letter code) of breeding status on a subsequent visit if you can.

Note that, to record breeding birds, it is not necessary to find nests and please do not approach a suspected nest-site unless you know what you are doing. However, please consider completing a BTO Nest Record Card for any nests found (contact the Atlas Coordinator for advice). For those species on Schedule 1 of the Wildlife & Countryside Act 1981 (marked with shading on the record sheet) it is an offence to disturb them whilst at or near a nest, or with dependent young, unless you have a special licence.

An asterisk * denotes a 'county rarity' for which a reporting form should be completed. If you find a rare breeding species for Cheshire and Wirral, please contact the Atlas Coordinator or County Recorder as soon as possible, so that the record can be followed up.

If you are not sure of a record, do not include it. Record only what you find, not what you expect to be there. If you are told of a bird's presence please do not rely solely on hearsay evidence, but try to see or hear the species yourself.

Please enter on the recording form the dates of your visits and the length of time taken: please spell out the month as April, May or June so that the date is written as, e.g. '5 June 2004' rather than 5/6/04, to avoid confusion with American-style date formats which put the month first.

Extra visits can be made at any time. Visits before April and after June might be helpful in recording the earliest and latest breeding species, and visits at night will be useful for finding the nocturnal species. For extra visits please put the breeding status code and date in the 'comments' column for the species.

If you are covering a tetrad on the boundary, shared with another county, please ensure that you cover all of the habitats within Cheshire. Ideally, if time allows, visit the whole of the square and record birds in all of the tetrad, even though some of it is not in Cheshire, but please indicate under comments which species were only recorded outside the Cheshire boundary.

Records from areas other than your chosen tetrad are very welcome. Please use a 'Supplementary Records Form' for these, unless you have a lot of records for one tetrad, in which case complete a standard Atlas record sheet.

Any additional comments can be very helpful in interpreting records. Please use the 'comments' column alongside each species, or for more general comments, use the box at the end of the form.

Habitat recording

One of the main uses of the Atlas data will be for conservation of birds. To do this, it is important to link the birds to their habitat. Please try to visit every significant habitat type within the tetrad. This may require maps and some local knowledge to identify suitable areas. Local landowners will be able to help if there are, for instance, ponds, woods or reedbeds that are not visible from a road or footpath.

Some species are significantly shifting the types of habitat they use, and work for this Atlas may help us understand some of the changes. Please enter onto the recording form every habitat type in which you found the species breeding, using the habitat codes given on the enclosed list. These codes have been developed by the BTO for use in all sorts of bird recording. They look terribly daunting at first, but don't worry! You will soon get used to them. Just enter a letter and a number for each type of habitat in which you encounter the species; for instance, A1 = broadleaved woodland, C9 = saltmarsh, F2 = suburban human site, G10 = large canal (more than 5m wide). Some of the codes do not apply for Cheshire and Wirral, such as C1 = chalk downland, but are included for completeness.

One of the key things for habitat recording is to look at the habitat from the birds' point of view. For example, you might find a Grey Wagtail nesting amongst the roots of a tree on a river bank, and a Blackbird in the same tree; for the wagtail the crucial habitat is the river (G7) but the Blackbird chose the area because of the cattle-pasture (E1) adjacent to the river. The habitat is mainly determined by where the birds find their food, rather than where they nest. Rooks and Grey Herons, for instance, need fairly tall trees to nest in, but the habitat is defined by the adjacent farmland or ponds and ditches where they feed.

Any extra information on habitat (e.g. species of livestock, dominant crops) is valuable and should be entered in the 'general comments' box at the end of the form.

Please feel free to contact the Atlas Coordinator for advice if you have difficulty with recording habitats.

Access to land

Before entering any land away from public rights of way, please ensure that you have the owner's permission to do so. The 'letter of introduction' provided can be used as an aid to obtaining permission and indeed many landowners, farmers, etc. will be interested in the survey and can often provide valuable local knowledge and data. In case of difficulty, your Area Coordinator or the Atlas Coordinator may be able to help.

We have received valuable assistance from the Cheshire County Council Public Rights of Way Unit. In return they have asked us to inform them of any footpaths that are blocked or otherwise inaccessible. If you find one, please contact David Cogger with the grid reference. Any such footpaths in the local authorities of Halton, Warrington and Wirral should also be reported and will be passed on to them.

Safety

All surveyors should be aware that, even during the breeding season, extremes of hot or cold weather can occur. Such conditions are best avoided for fieldwork, as they are not usually the best for finding birds, and can present a hazard to the unwary. You are advised to check a local weather forecast before undertaking fieldwork; always wear appropriate footwear and clothing, including a hat and sunscreen; and take a supply of food and drink with you. When visiting remote areas always tell someone where you are going and how long you are likely to be away. Stick to your advised route wherever possible. If you have a mobile 'phone, take it with you.

Abundance measurement

An important additional element of the Cheshire and Wirral Atlas will be measuring the abundance of birds. This involves making accurate, timed counts in a number of randomly selected tetrads. If you are interested in volunteering for this aspect of the project, please contact the Atlas Coordinator.

Record Forms

Paper record forms have been included with these instructions, but if you require further copies please contact David Cogger (or simply photocopy them). However, **we urge you to send in your records electronically if at all possible**, either on a floppy disc, or preferably via e-mail or via the Atlas website. To enable this we will be e-mailing you (if we already have your e-mail address) with electronic record forms. If you need further advice regarding electronic submission please e-mail: help.atlassubmissions@cawos.org

Finally …

This survey is a chance not only to get to know the birds of an area much better, and probably to come up with some surprises, but also to contribute to a major project that will see your work published and put to good use for conservation. We hope that you enjoy it. Please let us know how you get on. We shall be producing occasional bulletins on the Atlas, and articles or anecdotes about your tetrad surveying will be very welcome.

Please complete your Atlas Survey Record Cards and return to your Area Coordinator (given on the enclosed list) by 31st July each year (for records on paper), or e-mail your records to atlassubmissions@cawos.org by 31st August.

Cheshire and Wirral Bird Atlas

INSTRUCTIONS AND GUIDANCE FOR THE WINTER ATLAS

The aim of the Winter Atlas is to record the presence or absence of every species in every tetrad of Cheshire and Wirral, and the habitats being used. Approximate counts of any significant concentrations, and notes of any major feeding flocks or roosts, will substantially add to the value of the records. Wintering birds have never been mapped in detail in the county, and this Atlas will be a key tool to help their conservation.

Fieldwork for this survey is planned to cover three winter periods (mid-November to the end of February), from November 2004 to February 2007. We hope to achieve as good coverage as possible during the first year of the survey, so please carry out the fieldwork in your chosen tetrads during winter 2004/ 05. If you cannot do so, please let your Area Coordinator know as soon as possible.

In some ways the winter survey is easier than in the breeding season. An early morning start is not essential; much of the identification will be by sight, although knowledge of calls is very useful to locate some birds; and some species become more conspicuous than when they are breeding.

Most observers are surveying tetrads that they have already covered for the breeding season, and can use the tetrad map provided then. If you are doing a new tetrad, please contact your Area Coordinator or me or David Cogger to be sure that you have it identified correctly.

Fieldwork

The basis for recording is the tetrad, a 2x2km square defined by the even-numbered lines on the National Grid. Use of an Ordnance Survey map is essential; the 1:25000 series is recommended, and a GPS device is very helpful.

Please feel free to visit your chosen tetrad as often as you like and to spend as long as you want on surveying. The *minimum* to achieve reasonable coverage is to visit twice, once from 16th November to the end of December, and once from 1st January to the end of February. The two dates should be at least four weeks apart. Please enter on the recording form the dates of your visits and the approximate length of time taken. Write the date as, e.g. '2 January 2005' rather than 2/1/05, to avoid confusion with American-style date formats which put the month first. We aim to get as complete coverage as possible, so please plan to visit every type of habitat within the tetrad that is likely to hold any different species. To stand a reasonable chance of finding all species, each visit should last *at least* two hours. To do your survey, it is better to avoid the extremes of weather, especially wind and rain – most birds are harder to detect, and survey work is much less enjoyable – but sometimes it is not possible. Fieldwork should be conducted during periods when the birds are most likely to be detected, by sight and sound. For instance, many birds feed most actively in the mornings, but afternoon visits will be needed to find the roosts. In winter, many birds are much more mobile than during the breeding season, and many species flock together, especially for feeding or to roost. A roost can be a daytime gathering, for instance of waders, but usually means a night-time communal concentration. Night-time roosts can often be located by watching a group of birds (thrushes, finches, corvids, Starlings, etc) as they fly off together in late-afternoon.

Extra visits can be made at any time. Please try to make a visit at night to find the nocturnal species: owls' calls, for instance, often can be heard from far away on clear, still nights.

Record every species that you see or hear that is using the tetrad (for feeding, resting, etc.), and put an entry in the 'code' column for each species found. There are only four codes: U = species Using tetrad; C = feeding Concentration; R = Roost; F = Flying over (not using tetrad). Birds in flight require some care in interpretation. For instance, a Kestrel hovering or a Dipper flying along a stream are 'using' the tetrad (U), while a skein of geese flying over or a flock of Starlings on their way to roost are not 'using' the tetrad, and should be entered as 'F'. When you see a significant concentration of birds, please note in the 'Code' column of the recording form C = feeding Concentration or R = Roost, and provide a count if possible of the maximum number: enter this in the 'Count' column. The count should be the maximum seen together, not the sum total throughout the tetrad. What is regarded as a 'significant concentration' varies greatly from one species to another, so please use your own judgment: for most species, any group of more than a few birds visible (or audible) together should be recorded. Some birdwatchers almost automatically count every time they see a flock of birds, whilst others are not used to counting birds. Please do not worry too much about getting *accurate* counts; approximate figures are fine. Flocks of birds not obviously feeding or roosting should be entered as 'U' with an approximate count in the 'Count' column. This might apply, for instance, to a flock of Starlings or thrushes chattering in the tree-tops, or gulls in a field that are not feeding or asleep.

Any additional comments can be very helpful in interpreting records. Please use the 'comments' column alongside each species or the box at the end of the form.

An asterisk * on the recording form indicates a species for which a 'county rarity' reporting form should be completed.

If you are undertaking WeBS counts in an area that spans more than one tetrad, please note the counts separately for the individual tetrads so that they can be incorporated into the Atlas, and fill in the counts on an Atlas record form. Submit the WeBS information in the usual way to your WeBS organiser.

If you are covering a tetrad on the boundary, shared with another county, please visit the whole of the square and record birds in all of the tetrad, even though some of it is not in Cheshire and Wirral.

Supplementary records from other tetrads

Records from areas other than your chosen tetrad are very important. Please use a 'Supplementary Records Form' for these, unless you have a lot of records for one tetrad, in which case you will find it easier to complete a standard Atlas record sheet. A particular example where observers will collect supplementary records is when surveying near to the edges of your tetrads, where birds may often be seen over the 'boundary', and using many footpaths and roads usually entails going out of your chosen tetrad into adjoining ones. Other records can come if you live in a different tetrad from the one you are surveying; or if you regularly watch birds somewhere else. Anyone travelling about the county can also contribute valuable supplementary records: some people carry the recording sheets with them in a car. All of these sorts of records are welcome. Please do not assume that someone else has submitted the record.

'Offshore tetrads' – most tetrad surveyors can skip this section!

There are extra tetrads around the coasts that contain no land, so they were not part of the breeding season survey. But they contain areas exposed at low tides, or areas that remain covered by water, and sometimes hold some bird species that are not found elsewhere in the county, so they will be included in the Winter Atlas.

Recording in these offshore tetrads can be tricky. For safety, observers are advised not to go onto any tidal areas, and recording should be done from the shore. It may be difficult to judge which tetrad birds are in, especially when there are no landmarks in the distance, and it is often difficult to tell how far away birds are. This work requires an element of judgment from observers: please do not spend too much time with a map or GPS trying to decide on the exact location of offshore birds. Regular observers should liaise with the relevant Area Coordinator. Occasional observers should please pass your records to the Area Coordinator with as full details as possible (time, state of tide, any landmarks used, etc).

It can be difficult to observe birds on the water, so seabirds in flight over the sea can be included, provided that they are attributed only to one tetrad. We do not want to omit significant records, but must strive to avoid obvious double-counting. It is recognised that birds such as waders that use one area for feeding and another for roosting will be counted twice, but do not include the areas that they fly over between feeding and roost sites. WeBS counts will be separated into their constituent tetrads and incorporated into the Atlas, so there is no need to duplicate WeBS.

Habitat recording

One of the main uses of the Atlas data will be for conservation of birds. To do this, it is important to link the birds to their habitat. Please try to visit every significant habitat type within the tetrad. This may require maps and some local knowledge to identify suitable areas. Local landowners will be able to help if there are, for instance, ponds, woods or reedbeds that are not visible from a road or footpath.

Most of the habitat codes are the same as used for the breeding bird atlas work, with the additions:
H5 Open Sea
E7 Farmland – stubble (the remains of last season's crop left in the ground, not ploughed)

Access to land

Before entering any land away from public rights of way, please ensure that you have the owner's permission to do so. The 'right to roam' introduced in the Countryside and Rights of Way Act does not give anyone free access to farmland and certain other types of site: permission must be obtained. In the first season of the breeding bird Atlas, many tetrad surveyors found that landowners were very interested in the survey and often provided valuable local knowledge and data. We are keen to build on this 'good PR' for birds by ensuring that landowners are aware of the Atlas. Even when you have had permission for the breeding bird Atlas, it is a good idea to contact the landowners to check that it is still all right for you to visit in winter. The 'letter of introduction' provided can be used as an aid to obtaining permission. In case of difficulty, your Area Coordinator or the Atlas Coordinator may be able to help.

We have received valuable assistance from the Cheshire County Council Public Rights of Way Unit. In return they have asked to us to inform them of any footpaths we find which are blocked or otherwise inaccessible. If you find one, please contact David Cogger and give as accurate a grid reference as you can. Any such footpaths in the Wirral should also be reported and will be passed on to the appropriate body.

Safety

Please bear in mind the safety aspects of surveying in winter. The survey is meant to be enjoyable as well as constructive but it is a winter Atlas Survey and all fieldworkers should be aware at all times that weather conditions can deteriorate quickly and become potentially dangerous to the unwary. You are advised to check a local weather forecast before undertaking fieldwork; always wear appropriate footwear and clothing; and take a supply of food and drink with you. When visiting remote areas always tell someone where you are going (leave a note in your vehicle as well) and how long you are likely to be away. Stick to your advised route wherever possible. If you have a mobile phone, take it with you.

All fieldworkers are volunteering to take part in this survey as part of their hobby, and do so at their own risk. CAWOS are not responsible for and do not maintain any of the land that the volunteers will use and therefore cannot be held responsible for any injuries to their members or others. Surveyors who cause damage to third party property or injury should have cover under their own household insurance for their personal liability.

Finally ...

This survey is a chance not only to get to know the birds of an area much better, and probably to come up with some surprises, but also to contribute to a major project that will see your work published and put to good use for conservation. If you have any questions, please ask your Area Coordinator, look on the Atlas website, or contact the Atlas Coordinator. We hope that you enjoy the Atlas work.

If you are submitting Atlas Survey Record Cards on paper, please return them to your Area Coordinator by 31st March each year. Electronic records are preferred, using the spreadsheet supplied, and should be sent by 30th April, to atlassubmissions@cawos.org, with a copy to your Area Coordinator. Copies of the electronic forms can be downloaded from the Atlas website (www.cheshireandwirralbirdatlas.org).

References

The material cited here is not necessarily the primary source for each piece of work, but is that considered most likely to be accessible, especially to the amateur without access to an academic library. These references include books and journals, particularly *British Birds*, *Ibis*, and the BTO journals *Bird Study* and *Ringing & Migration*, as well as the annual county bird reports, now called *Cheshire and Wirral Bird Report* (*CWBR*) and previously named *Cheshire Bird Report* (*CBR*). Not every book or paper listed here is directly cited in the text, but all have been consulted in its preparation.

Some of the information in the texts has been gleaned from the websites of various organizations, especially the BTO with their two marvellous sources of information, Breeding Birds in the Wider Countryside (www.bto.org/birdtrends) (Baillie *et al.* 2007) and BirdFacts (www.bto.org/birdfacts) (Robinson 2005), and the UK Meteorological Office (www.metoffice.gov.uk/hadobs).

Aebischer, N.J. & Ewald, J.A. (2004) Managing the UK Grey Partridge *Perdix perdix* recovery: population change, reproduction, habitat and shooting. *Ibis* 146 (Suppl. 2): 181–91.

Alström, P. & Mild, K. (2003) Pipits and Wagtails. Helm, London.

Amar, A., Hewson, C.M., Thewlis, R.M., Smith, K.W., Fuller, R.J., Lindsell, J., Conway, G., Butler, S. & MacDonald, M.A. (2006) What's happening to our woodland birds? Long-term changes in the populations of woodland birds. BTO Research Report No. 169, RSPB Research Report No. 19, RSPB, Sandy.

Anderson R. (1993) Wintering Little Grebes. *CWBR* 1993: 84–85.

Anthes, N. (2004) Long-distance migration timing of *Tringa* sandpipers adjusted to recent climate change. *Bird Study* 51: 203–11.

Atkinson-Willes, G.L. (1963) Wildfowl in Great Britain. HMSO, London.

Austin, G.E., Rehfisch, M.M., Allan, J.R. & Holloway, S.J. (2007) Population size and differential population growth of introduced Greater Canada Geese *Branta canadensis* and re-established Greylag Geese *Anser anser* across habitats in Great Britain in the year 2000. *Bird Study* 54: 343–52.

Baillie, S.R., Marchant, J.H., Crick, H.Q.P., Noble, D.G., Balmer, D.E., Barimore, C., Coombes, R.H., Downie, I.S., Freeman, S.N., Joys, A.C., Leech, D.I., Raven, M.J., Robinson, R.A. & Thewlis, R.M. (2007) Breeding Birds in the Wider Countryside: their conservation status 2007. BTO Research Report No. 487. BTO, Thetford (www.bto.org/birdtrends).

Baillie, S.R. & Peach, W.J. (1992) Population limitation in Palaearctic-African migrant passerines. *Ibis* 134 (Suppl. 1): 120–32.

Baker, H., Stroud, D.A., Aebischer, N.J., Cranswick, P.A., Gregory, R.D., McSorley, C.A., Noble, D.G. & Rehfisch, M.M. (2006) Population estimates of birds in Britain and in the United Kingdom. *British Birds* 99: 2–24.

Banks, A.N., Collier, M.P., Austin, G.E., Hearn, R.D. & Musgrove, A.J. (2006) Waterbirds in the UK 2004/05: the Wetland Bird Survey. BTO/WWT/RSPB/JNCC, Thetford.

Banks, A.N., Coombes, R.H. & Crick, H.Q.P. (2003) The Peregrine Falcon breeding population of the UK & Isle of Man in 2002. Research Report No. 330. BTO, Thetford.

Barber, S. & Barber, G. (2003) Firecrests breeding: a first for Cheshire. *CWBR* 2003: 145–47.

Barber, S. & Hargreaves, R. (1999) The Cheshire & Wirral Raptor Study Group's breeding Common Buzzard (*Buteo buteo*) survey in Cheshire & Wirral 1999 & 2000. *CWBR* 1999: 105–11.

Batten, L.A. (1973) The colonisation of England by the Firecrest. *British Birds* 66: 159–66.

Beer, S. (1995) An Exaltation of Skylarks. SMH Books, Pulborough.

Bell, T.H. (1962) The Birds of Cheshire. Sherratt, Altrincham.

Bell, T.H. (1967) A Supplement to The Birds of Cheshire. Sherratt, Altrincham.

Bevington, A. (1991) Habitat selection in the Dunnock *Prunella modularis* in northern England. *Bird Study* 38: 87–91.

Bibby, C.J. (1982) Polygyny and breeding ecology of the Cetti's Warbler *Cettia cetti*. *Ibis* 124: 288–301.

Bibby, C.J. (1983) Studies of West Palearctic birds: 186. Bearded Tit. *British Birds* 76: 549–63.

Bibby, C.J. (1989) A survey of breeding Wood Warblers *Phylloscopus sibilatrix* in Britain, 1984–85. *Bird Study* 36: 56–72.

Bibby, C.J., Hill, D.A., Burgess, N.D. & Mustoe, S. (2000) Bird Census Techniques. 2nd edition. Academic Press, London.

BirdLife International (2004) Birds in Europe: population estimates, trends and conservation status. BirdLife International (Conservation Series No. 12), Cambridge, UK.

Birkhead, M. & Perrins, C.M. (1986) The Mute Swan. Croom Helm, London.

Birkhead, T.R. (1991) The Magpies. T. & A.D. Poyser, London.

Bishton, G. (2001) Social structure, habitat use and breeding biology of hedgerow Dunnocks *Prunella modularis*. *Bird Study* 48: 188–93.

Blindell, R.M., Conlin, A. & Williams, S. (2005) Pallas's Warbler in Cheshire: the first North West wintering record. *CWBR* 2005: 122–24.

Both, C., Bouwhuis, S., Lessells, C.M. & Visser, M.E. (2006) Climate change and population declines in a long-distance migratory bird. *Nature* 441 (4): 81–83.

Boyd, A.W. (1946) The Country Diary of a Cheshire Man. Collins, London.

Boyd, A.W. (1951) A Country Parish. Collins New Naturalist, London.

Brenchley, A. (1984) The use of birds as indicators of change in agriculture. *In* Jenkins, D. (ed.) Agriculture and the Environment, pp. 123–28. ITE Symposium 13. ITE/NERC, Cambridge.

Brickle, N.W. & Harper, D.G. (2002) Agricultural intensification and the timing of breeding of Corn Buntings *Miliaria calandra*. *Bird Study* 49: 219–28.

Briggs, K.B. (1984) The breeding ecology of coastal and inland Oystercatchers in north Lancashire. *Bird Study* 31: 141–47.

Brindley, E., Lucas, F. & Waterhouse, M. (1992) North Staffordshire Moors Survey 1992. RSPB, Sandy.

Brockholes, J.F. (1874) The Birds of Wirral. [Published in Part I of the *Proceedings of the Chester Society of Natural Science and Literature*.]

Bromhall, D. (1980) Devil Birds. Hutchinson, London.

Broome, A.M. (1987). Corncrakes in Cheshire 1987. *CBR* 1987: 84–85.

Broughton, R.K., Hinsley, S.A., Bellamy, P.E., Hill, S.A. & Rothery, P. (2006) Marsh Tit *Poecile palustris* territories in a British broad-leaved wood. *Ibis* 148: 744–52.

Brown, A. & Grice, P. (2005) Birds in England. T. & A.D. Poyser, London.

Brown, A.F. & Stillman, R.A. (1998) The return of the Merlin to the South Pennines. *Bird Study* 45: 293–301.

Brown, L. (1976) British Birds of Prey. Collins New Naturalist, London.

Browne, S., Vickery, J. & Chamberlain, D. (2000) Density & population estimates of breeding Skylarks in Britain. *Bird Study* 47: 52–65.

Browne, S.J. & Aebischer, N.J. (2005) Studies of West Palearctic birds: Turtle Dove *Streptopelia turtur*. *British Birds* 98: 58–72.

Browne, S.J., Aebischer, N.J., Yfantis, G. & Marchant, J.H. (2004) Habitat availability and use by Turtle Doves *Streptopelia turtur* between 1965 and 1995: an analysis of Common Birds Census data. *Bird Study* 51: 1–11.

Buckland, S.T., Anderson, D.R., Burnham, K.P., Laake, J.L., Borchers, D.L. & Thomas, L. (2001) Introduction to Distance Sampling: Estimating Abundance of Biological Populations. Oxford University Press, Oxford.

Buckland, S.T., Anderson, D.R., Burnham, K.P., Laake, J.L., Borchers, D.L. & Thomas, L. (2004) Advanced Distance Sampling. Oxford University Press, Oxford.

Bunn, D.S., Warburton, A.B. & Wilson, R.D.S. (1982) The Barn Owl. T. & A.D. Poyser, Calton.

Burfield, I.J. & Brooke, M. de L. (2005) The decline of the Ring Ouzel *Turdus torquatus* in Britain: evidence from bird observatory data. *Ring. & Migr.* 22: 199–204.

Burton, N.H.K. (2007) Influence of restock age and habitat patchiness on Tree Pipits breeding in Breckland pine plantations. *Ibis* 149 (Suppl. 2): 193–204.

Burton, N.H.K., Musgrove, A.J., Rehfisch, M.M., Sutcliffe, A. & Waters, R. (2003) Numbers of wintering gulls in the United Kingdom, Channel Islands and Isle of Man: a review of the 1993 and previous Winter Gull Roost Surveys. *British Birds* 96: 376–401.

Butler, C.J. (2003) Population biology of the introduced Rose-ringed Parakeet *Psittacula krameri* in the UK. D.Phil. thesis, University of Oxford.

Buxton, J. (1950) The Redstart. Collins, London.

Byerley, I. (1856) Fauna of Liverpool. [Reprinted from the *Proceedings of the Liverpool Literary and Philosophical Society*, 1854.]

Calbrade, N., Entwistle, C.A., Smith, A.J. & Spencer, K.G. (2001) Roof assemblies of Lapwings and plovers in Britain. *British Birds* 94: 35–38.

Calladine, J., Buner, F. & Aebischer, N.J. (1999) Temporal variations in the singing activity and detection efficiency of Turtle Doves *Streptopelia turtur*: implications for surveying. *Bird Study* 46: 74–80.

Calvert, M. (1988) Cheshire Reed Warblers as Cuckoo hosts. *CWBR* 1988: 87.

Calvert, M. (2005) Reed warblers at Rostherne Mere. English Nature, Shrewsbury.

Campbell, L.H., Cayford, J. & Pearson, D. (1996) Bearded Tits in Britain and Ireland. *British Birds* 89: 335–46.

Carter, I. (2001) The Red Kite. Arlequin Press, Chelmsford.

Chandler, R.J. (1981) Influxes into Britain and Ireland of Red-necked Grebes and other waterbirds during winter 1978/79. *British Birds* 74: 55–81.

Chapman, A. (1999) The Hobby. Arlequin Press, Chelmsford.

Cheshire Mammal Group (2008) The Mammals of Cheshire. Liverpool University Press, Liverpool.

Chilès, J.-P. & Delfiner, P. (1999) Geostatistics: Modelling Spatial Uncertainty. Wiley, New York.

Clarke, J. (2005) The Spotted What? Plum Tree Publishing, Worcester.

Clarke, R. (1995) The Marsh Harrier. Hamlyn, London.

Clarke, R. & Watson, D. (1990) The Hen Harrier *Circus cyaneus* Winter Roost Survey in Britain and Ireland. *Bird Study* 37: 84–100.

Clement, P. (1995) The Chiffchaff. Hamlyn, London.

Clements, R. (2002) The Common Buzzard in Britain: a new population estimate. *British Birds* 95: 377–83.

Colquhoun, M.K. (1942) Notes on the social behaviour of Blue Tits. *British Birds* 35: 234–40.

Combridge, P. & Parr, C. (1992) Influx of Little Egrets in Britain and Ireland in 1989. *British Birds* 85: 16–21.

Conder, P. (1989) The Wheatear. Helm, London.

Conrad, K.F., Woiwod, I.P., Parsons, M., Fox, R. & Warren, M.S. (2004) Long-term population trends in widespread British moths. *J. Insect Cons.* 8: 119–36.

Conway, G. (2005) Population composition of wintering Common Chiffchaffs in southern England. *British Birds* 98: 396–410.

Conway, G., Wotton, S., Henderson, I., Langston, R., Drewitt, A. & Currie, F. (2007) Status and distribution of European Nightjars *Caprimulgus europaeus* in the UK in 2004. *Bird Study* 54: 98–111.

Cookson, D. (1993) Cheshire's Mute Swans. *CWBR* 1993: 86–87.

Coombs, C.J.F. (1978) The Crows. Batsford, London.

Coward, T.A. (1910) The Vertebrate Fauna of Cheshire and Liverpool Bay. Witherby, London.

Coward, T.A. & Oldham, C. (1900) The Birds of Cheshire. Sherratt and Hughes, Manchester.

Cowley, E. (2001) June broods are of greatest benefit to Sand Martins *Riparia riparia*. *Ring. & Migr.* 20: 202–08.

Cowley E. & Siriwardena, G.M. (2005) Long-term variation in survival rates of Sand Martins *Riparia riparia*: dependence on breeding and wintering ground weather, age and sex, and their population consequences. *Bird Study* 52: 237–51.

Craggs, J.D. (1982). Hilbre: The Cheshire Island. Liverpool University Press, Liverpool.

Cramp, S., Simmons, K.E.L. & Perrins, C.M. (eds.) (1977–94). Birds of the Western Palearctic, volumes I–IX. Oxford University Press, Oxford.

Crick, H.Q.P. (1992) A bird-habitat coding system for use in Britain and Ireland incorporating aspects of land management and human activity. *Bird Study* 39: 1–12.

Crick, H., Banks, A. & Coombes, R. (2003) Findings of the National Peregrine Survey 2002. *BTO News* 248: 8–9.

Crick, H.Q.P. & Sparks, T.H. (1999) Climate change related to egg-laying trends. *Nature* 399: 423–24.

Cross, A.V. & Davis, P.E. (1998) The Red Kites of Wales. The Welsh Kite Trust, Llandrindod Wells.

Davies, A.K. (1988) The distribution and status of the Mandarin Duck, *Aix galericulata*, in Britain. *Bird Study* 35: 203–08.

Davies, A.K. & Baggott, G.K. (1989a) Clutch size and nesting sites of the Mandarin Duck, *Aix galericulata*. *Bird Study* 36: 32–36.

Davies, A.K. & Baggott, G.K. (1989b) Egg-laying, incubation and intraspecific nest parasitism by the Mandarin Duck *Aix galericulata*. *Bird Study* 36: 115–22.

Davies, N.B. (1982) Territorial behaviour of Pied Wagtails in winter. *British Birds* 75: 261–67.

Davies, N.B. (1987) Studies of West Palearctic birds: 188. Dunnock. *British Birds* 80: 604–24.

Davies, N.B. (1992) Dunnock Behaviour and Social Evolution. Oxford University Press, Oxford.

Davies, N.B. (2000) Cuckoos, Cowbirds and other cheats. T. & A.D. Poyser, London.

Day, J.C. & Hodgson, M.S. (2003) The Atlas of Wintering Birds in Northumbria. Northumberland and Tyneside Bird Club.

Day, J.C., Hodgson, M.S. & Rossiter, B.N. (1995) The Atlas of Breeding Birds in Northumbria. Northumberland and Tyneside Bird Club.

Deans, P., Sankey, J., Smith, L., Tucker, J., Whittles, C. & Wright, C. (1992) An Atlas of the Breeding Birds of Shropshire. Shropshire Ornithological Society.

del Hoyo, J., Elliott, A., Christie, D.A. & Sargatal, J. (eds.) (1992–2007). Handbook of Birds of the World, volumes I–XII. Lynx Edicions, Barcelona.

Donald, P.F. (2004) The Skylark. T. & A.D. Poyser, London.

Donald, P.F. & Aebischer, N.J. (eds.) (1997) The Ecology and Conservation of Corn Buntings *Miliaria calandra*. UK Nature Conservation No. 13. Joint Nature Conservation Committee, Peterborough.

Donald, P.F. & Evans, A.D. (1994) Habitat selection by Corn Buntings *Miliaria calandra* in winter. *Bird Study* 41: 199–210.

Donald, P.F. & Morris, T.J. (2005) Saving the Sky Lark: new solutions for a declining farmland bird. *British Birds* 98: 570–78.

Dougall, T.W., Holland, P.K. & Yalden, D.W. (2004) A revised estimate of the breeding population of Common Sandpipers *Actitis hypoleucos* in Great Britain and Ireland. *Wader Study Group Bulletin* 105: 42–49.

Dymond, J.N., Fraser, P.A. & Gantlett, S.J.M. (1989) Rare birds in Britain and Ireland. T. & A.D. Poyser, Calton.

Eaton, M.A., Austin, G.E., Banks, A.N., Conway, G., Douse, A., Grice, P.V., Hearn, R., Hilton, G., Hoccom, D., Musgrove, A.J., Noble, D.G., Ratcliffe, N., Rehfisch, M.M., Worden, J. & Wotton, S. (2007) *The state of the UK's birds 2006*. RSPB, BTO, WWT, CCW, EHS, NE and SNH, Sandy, Bedfordshire.

Elphick, D. (1979) An inland flock of Curlews *Numenius arquata* in mid-Cheshire, England. *Wader Study Group Bulletin* 26: 31–35.

Elphick, D. (1985) The status of the Mute Swan in Cheshire and Wirral. *CBR* 1985: 83–94.

Etheridge, B. & Summers, R.W. (2006) Movements of British Hen Harriers *Circus cyaneus* outside the breeding season. *Ring. & Migr.* 23: 6–14.

Evans, K.L. & Robinson, R.A. (2004) Barn Swallows and agriculture. *British Birds* 97: 218–30.

Farrer, G.B. (1938) Feathered Folk of an Estuary. Country Life Books, London.

Feare, C. (1984) The Starling. Oxford University Press, Oxford.

Fiuczynski, D. & Nethersole-Thompson, D. (1980) Hobby studies in England and Germany. *British Birds* 73: 275–95.

Forshaw, W.D. (1979) Severe weather movement of Pink-footed Geese in Cheshire and North Wales, 1979. *CBR* 1979: 66–67.

Fox, B.W. & Guest, J.P. (2003) The Lichen Flora of Cheshire & Wirral. Nepa Books, Frodsham, Cheshire.

Freeman, S.N. & Crick, H.Q.P. (2003) The decline of the Spotted Flycatcher *Muscicapa striata* in the UK: an integrated population model. *Ibis* 145: 400–12.

Freeman, S.N., Robinson, R.A., Clark, J.A., Griffin, B.M. & Adams, S.Y. (2007) Changing demography and population decline in the Common Starling *Sturnus vulgaris*: a multisite approach to Integrated Population Monitoring. *Ibis* 149: 587–96.

Fuller, R.J., Gregory, R.D., Gibbons, D.W., Marchant, J.H., Wilson, J.D., Baillie, S.R. & Carter, N. (1995) Population Declines and Range Contractions Among Lowland Farmland Birds in Britain. *Conservation Biology* 9: 1425–41.

Fuller, R.J., Noble, D.G., Smith, K.W. & Vanhinsbergh, D. (2005) Recent declines in populations of woodland birds in Britain: a review of possible causes. *British Birds* 98: 116–43.

Gibbons, D.W., Reid, J.B. & Chapman, R.A. (eds.) (1993) The New Atlas of Breeding Birds in Britain and Ireland: 1988–1991. T. & A.D. Poyser, London.

Gilbert, G. (2002) The status and habitat of Spotted Crakes *Porzana porzana* in Britain in 1999. *Bird Study* 49: 79–86.

Gilbert, G., Tyler, G.A. & Smith, K.W. (2002) Local annual survival of booming male Great Bittern *Botaurus stellaris* in Britain, in the period 1990–1999. *Ibis* 144: 51–61.

Gill, Jr, R.E. (1986) What won't Turnstones eat? *British Birds* 79: 402–03.

Gillings, S. (2008) Designing a winter bird atlas field methodology: issues of time and space in sampling and interactions with habitat. *J. Ornithology* 149: 345–55.

Gillings, S., Austin, G.E., Fuller, R.J. & Sutherland, W.J. (2006) Distribution shifts in wintering Golden Plover *Pluvialis apricaria* and Lapwing *Vanellus vanellus* in Britain. *Bird Study* 53: 274–84.

Gillings, S. & Fuller, R.J. (2001) Habitat selection by Skylarks *Alauda arvensis* wintering in Britain in 1997/98. *Bird Study* 48: 293–307.

Gillings, S., Fuller, R.J. & Sutherland, W.J. (2005). Diurnal studies do not predict nocturnal habitat choice and site selection of Eurasian Golden Plovers *Pluvialis apricaria* and Northern Lapwings *Vanellus vanellus. Auk* 122: 1249–60.

Glen, N.W. & Perrins, C.M. (1988) Co-operative breeding by Long-tailed Tits. *British Birds* 81: 630–41.

Glue, D.E. (1982) The Garden Bird Book. Macmillan, London.

Glue, D.E. (1990) Breeding biology of the Grasshopper Warbler in Britain. *British Birds* 83: 131–45.

Glue, D.E. (1996) Goldfinches feeding in gardens. *British Birds* 89: 459–60.

Glue, D.E. & Boswell, T. (1994) Comparative nesting ecology of three British breeding woodpeckers. *British Birds* 87: 253–69.

Gooch, S., Baillie, S.R. & Birkhead, T.R. (1991) Magpie *Pica pica* and Songbird Populations. Retrospective Investigation of Trends in Population Density and Breeding Success. *J. Appl. Ecol.* 28: 1068–86.

Gosler, A.G. (1993) The Great Tit. Hamlyn, London.

Green, R.E. (1978) Factors affecting the diet of farmland Skylarks *Alauda arvensis. J. Anim. Ecol.* 47: 913–28.

Green, R.E. (1984) The feeding ecology and survival of partridge chicks *Alectoris rufa* and *Perdix perdix* on arable farmland in East Anglia. *J. Appl. Ecol.* 21: 817–30.

Gregory, R.D. & Marchant, J.H. (1996) Population trends of Jays, Magpies, Jackdaws and Carrion Crows in the United Kingdom. *Bird Study* 43: 28–37.

Griffiths, W. & Wilson, W. (1945) The Birds of North Wirral. *North Western Naturalist* 19: 238–51; 20: 37–47; 20: 164–74.

Gruar, D., Barritt, D. & Peach, W.J. (2006) Summer utilization of Oilseed Rape by Reed Buntings *Emberiza schoeniclus* and other farmland birds. *Bird Study* 53: 47–54.

Guest, J.P., Elphick, D., Hunter, J.S.A. & Norman, D. (1992) The Breeding Bird Atlas of Cheshire and Wirral. Cheshire and Wirral Ornithological Society.

Guyomarc'h, J.C., Combreau, O., Puigcerver, M., Fontoura, P., Aebischer, N. & Wallace, D.I.M. (1998) *Coturnix coturnix* Quail. *BWP Update* 2: 27–46.

Hagemeijer, E.J.M. & Blair, M.J. (1997) The EBCC Atlas of European Breeding Birds: Their Distribution and Abundance. T. & A.D. Poyser, London.

Haines-Young, R.H., Barr, C.J., Black, H.I.J., Briggs, D.J., Bunce, R.G.H., Clarke, R.T., Cooper, A., Dawson, F.H., Firbank, L.G., Fuller, R.M., Furse, M.T., Gillespie, M.K., Hill, R., Hornung, M., Howard, D.C., McCann, T., Morecroft, M.D., Petit, S., Sier, A.R.J., Smart, S.M., Smith, G.M., Stott, A.P., Stuart, R.C. & Watkins, J.W. (2002) Accounting for nature: assessing habitats in the UK countryside. DETR, London.

Hamerstrom, F. (1986) Harrier–Hawk of the Marshes. Smithsonian Institution Press, Washington, D.C.

Hancock, M.H., Gibbons, D.W. & Thompson, P.S. (1997) The status of breeding Greenshank *Tringa nebularia* in the United Kingdom in 1995. *Bird Study* 44: 290–302.

Hardy, E. (1941) The Birds of the Liverpool Area. Buncle, Arbroath.

Harper, D. (1995) Studies of West Palearctic birds: Corn Bunting. *British Birds* 88: 401–21.

Hartley, I.R., Shepherd, M. & Thompson, D.B. (1995) Habitat selection and polygyny in breeding Corn Buntings *Miliaria calandra. Ibis* 137: 508–14.

Higginbotham, G.H. (1995) First Confirmed Breeding of Goosander in Cheshire. *CWBR* 1995: 92.

Hinsley, S.A., Bellamy, P.E., Newton, I. & Sparks, T.H. (1995) Habitat and landscape factors influencing the presence of individual breeding bird species in woodland fragments. *J. Avian Biol.* 26: 94–104.

Hinsley, S.A., Carpenter, J.E., Broughton, R.K., Bellamy, P.E., Rothery, P., Amar, A., Hewson, C.M. & Gosler A.G. (2007) Habitat selection by Marsh Tits *Poecile palustris* in the UK. *Ibis* 149 (Suppl. 2): 224–33.

Holland, P.K. & Yalden, D.W. (2002) Population dynamics of Common Sandpipers *Actitis hypoleucos* in the Peak District of Derbyshire–a different decade. *Bird Study* 49: 131–38.

Holling, M. & the Rare Breeding Birds Panel (2007a) Rare breeding birds in the United Kingdom in 2003 and 2004. *British Birds* 100: 321–67.

Holling, M. & the Rare Breeding Birds Panel (2007b) Non-native breeding birds in the United Kingdom in 2003, 2004 and 2005. *British Birds* 100: 638–49.

Holling, M. & the Rare Breeding Birds Panel (2008) Rare breeding birds in the United Kingdom in 2005. *British Birds* 101: 276–316.

Holloway, S. (1996) The Historical Atlas of Breeding Birds in Britain and Ireland: 1875–1900. T. & A.D. Poyser, London.

Hosking, E. (1970) An Eye for a Bird. Hutchinson, London.

Huntley, B., Green, R.E., Collingham, Y.C. & Willis, S.G. (2007) A Climatic Atlas of European Breeding Birds. Lynx, Barcelona.

Hutchinson, C.D, & Neath, B. (1978) Little Gulls in Britain and Ireland. *British Birds* 71: 563–81.

Jenkins, R.K., Buckton, S.T. & Ormerod, S.J. (1995) Local movements and population density of water rails *Rallus aquaticus* in a small inland reedbed. *Bird Study* 42: 82–87.

Jenkins, R.K.B. & Ormerod, S.J. (2002) Habitat preferences of breeding water rail *Rallus aquaticus. Bird Study* 49: 2–10.

Johnston, K., Ver Hoef, J.M., Krivoruchko, K. & Lucas, N. (2001) Using ArcGIS Geostatistical Analyst. ESRI.

Keith, S. Urban, E.K. & Fry, C.H (1992) Birds of Africa Volume IV. Academic Press, London.

Kenrick, H. (1940) A study of Blue Tits by colour-ringing. *British Birds* 33: 307–10.

Kyrkos, A., Wilson, J.D. & Fuller, R.J. (1998) Farmland habitat change and abundance of Yellowhammers *Emberiza citrinella*: An analysis of Common Birds Census data. *Bird Study* 45: 232–46.

Lack, D. (1956) Swifts in a Tower. Methuen, London.
Lack, P.C. (ed.) (1986) The Atlas of Wintering Birds in Britain and Ireland. T. & A.D. Poyser, Calton.
Lack, P. (1992) Birds on Lowland Farms. HMSO, London.
Langston, R.H.W., Gregory, R.D. & Adams, R. (2002) The status of the Hawfinch in the UK 1975–1999. *British Birds* 95: 166–73.
Leach, I.H. (1981) Wintering Blackcaps in Britain and Ireland. *Bird Study* 28: 5–14.
Lees, M. (1994) Habitat and Breeding Population Status of Long-Eared Owls in Cheshire. *CWBR* 1994: 94–96.
Lever, C. (1977) The Naturalized Animals of the British Isles. Hutchinson, London.
Lewis, A., Amar, A., Cordi-Piec, D. & Thewlis, R.M. (2007) Factors influencing Willow Tit *Poecile montanus* site occupancy: a comparison of abandoned and occupied woods. *Ibis* 149 (Suppl. 2): 205–13.
Lovegrove, R. (2007) Silent Fields. Oxford University Press, Oxford.
Lowe, F.A. (1953) The Heron. Collins, London.
Lundberg, A. & Alatalo, R.V. (1992) The Pied Flycatcher. T. & A.D. Poyser, London.
Lythgoe, C. (2001) 2001 SECOS Swift survey. SECOS Report. South East Cheshire Ornithological Society, Sandbach.

Marchant, J.H., Freeman, S.N., Crick, H.Q.P. & Beaven, L.P. (2004) The BTO Heronries Census of England and Wales 1928–2000: new indices and a comparison of analytical methods. *Ibis* 146: 323–34.
Marchant, J.H. & Gregory, R.D. (1999) Numbers of nesting Rooks *Corvus frugilegus* in the United Kingdom in 1996. *Bird Study* 46: 258–73.
Marchant, J.H., Hudson, R., Carter, S.P. & Whittington, P.A. (1990) Population Trends in British Breeding Birds. BTO, Tring.
Marchington, J. (1984) The Natural History of Game. Boydell Press, Woodbridge, Suffolk.
Marques, F.F.C. & Buckland, S.T. (2003) Incorporating covariates into standard line transect analyses. *Biometrics* 59: 924–35.
Marquiss, M. & Newton, I. (1982) The Goshawk in Britain. *British Birds* 75: 243–60.
Martin, B. (1997) A Survey of Summering Swifts *Apus apus* in Cheshire and Wirral and their Conservation Status. *CWBR* 1997: 104–13.
Martin, B. & Smith, J. (2007) A survey of breeding Black-necked Grebes in the UK: 1973–2004. *British Birds* 100: 368–78.
Martin, B.P. (1990) The Glorious Grouse. David & Charles, Newton Abbot.
Mason, C.F. (1976) Breeding biology of the *Sylvia* warblers. *Bird Study* 23: 213–32.
Mason, C.F. (1995) The Blackcap. Hamlyn, London.
Matthysen, E. (1998) The Nuthatches. T. & A.D. Poyser, London.
May, R. (2004) Grouse moors in Cheshire–what future? *CAWOS Bird News* 63: 24–25.
May, R. (2005b) Grouse counts on Piggford and High Moor. *CAWOS Bird News* 67: 14.
May, R. (2005a) Grouse moors in Cheshire–further information. *CAWOS Bird News* 65: 20–22.
McKnight, A., O'Brien, M., Waterhouse, M. & Reed, S. (1997) Breeding Birds of the North Staffordshire Moors 1996. RSPB, Sandy.
Mead, C. (1984) Robins. Whittet Books, London.
Mead, C. (2000) The State of the Nation's Birds. Whittet Books, Stowmarket.
Messenger, A. & Roome, M. (2007) The breeding population of the Hobby in Derbyshire. *British Birds* 100: 594–608.
Mikkola, H. (1983) Owls of Europe. T. & A.D. Poyser, Calton.
Mitchell, J.R., Moser, M.E. & Kirby, J.S. (1988) Declines in midwinter counts of waders roosting on the Dee Estuary. *Bird Study* 35: 191–98.
Mitchell, P.I., Newton, S.F., Ratcliffe, N. & Dunn, T.E. (2004) Seabird populations of Britain and Ireland. T. & A.D. Poyser, London.
Møller, A.P. (1983) Breeding habitat selection in the Swallow *Hirundo rustica*. *Bird Study* 30: 134–42.
Moorcroft, D., Wilson, J.D. & Bradbury, R.B. (2006) The diet of nestling Linnets *Carduelis cannabina* on lowland farmland before and after agricultural intensification. *Bird Study* 53: 156–62.
Morris, A., Burges, D., Fuller, R.J., Evans, A.D. & Smith, K.W. (1994) The status and distribution of Nightjars *Caprimulgus europaeus* in Britain in 1992. *Bird Study* 41: 181–91.
Morton, W.S. (2001) Little Egret: the significance of successful breeding at Frodsham Marsh in the context of their country-wide expansion. *CWBR* 2001: 122–24.
Moss, D. & Moss, G.M. (1993) Breeding biology of the Little Grebe *Tachybaptus ruficollis* in Britain and Ireland. *Bird Study* 40: 107–14.
Murton, R.K. (1965) The Wood Pigeon. Collins, London.
Musgrove, A.J. (2002) The non-breeding status of the Little Egret in Britain. *British Birds* 95: 62–80.
Musgrove, A.J., Collier, M.P., Banks, A.N., Calbrade, N.A., Hearn, R.D. & Austin, G.E. (2007) Waterbirds in the UK 2005/06: the Wetland Bird Survey. BTO/WWT/RSPB/JNCC, Thetford.

Nelson, S.H., Court, I., Vickery, J.A., Watts, P.N. & Bradbury, R.B. (2003) The status and ecology of the Yellow Wagtail in Britain. *British Wildlife* 14: 270–74.
Newson, S.E., Evans, K.L., Noble, D.G., Greenwood, J.J.D. & Gaston, K.J. (2008) Use of distance sampling to improve estimates of national population sizes for common and widespread breeding birds in the UK. *J. Appl. Ecol.* 45: 1330–38.
Newson, S.E., Marchant, J.H., Ekins, G.R. and Sellers R.M. (2007) The status of inland-breeding Great Cormorants in England. *British Birds* 100: 289–99.
Newson, S.E., Woodburn, R., Noble, D.G. & Baillie, S.R. (2005) Evaluating the Breeding Bird Survey for producing national population size and density estimates. *Bird Study* 52: 42–54.
Newton, A. (1893–96) A Dictionary of Birds. Black, London.
Newton, A. (1971) Flora of Cheshire. Cheshire Community Council, Chester.
Newton, I. (1972) Finches. Collins New Naturalist, London.
Newton, I. (1979) Population Ecology of Raptors. T. & A.D. Poyser, Berkhamstead.
Newton, I. (1986) The Sparrowhawk. T. & A.D. Poyser, Calton.
Newton, I. (1993) Studies of West Palearctic birds: 192. Bullfinch. *British Birds* 86: 638–48.
Newton, I., Robson, J.E. & Yalden, D.W. (1981) Decline of the Merlin in the Peak District. *Bird Study* 28: 225–34.

Nilsson, S.G. (1984) The evolution of nest-site selection amongst hole-nesting birds: the importance of nest predation and competition. *Ornis Scand.* 15: 167–75.

Norman, D. (1994a) The Fieldfare. Hamlyn, London.

Norman, D. (1994b) The return rate of adult male Wood Warblers *Phylloscopus sibilatrix* to a peripheral breeding area. *Ring. & Migr.* 15: 79–83.

Norman, D. (1995) Flock composition and biometrics of Fieldfares *Turdus pilaris* wintering in a Cheshire orchard. *Ring. & Migr.* 16: 1–13.

Norman, D. (1999) 'All the birds of the air'—indicators of the environment. Chapter 21 in Ecology and Landscape Development: A History of the Mersey Basin, ed. E.F. Greenwood. Proceedings of a conference held at Merseyside Maritime Museum, Liverpool, 5–6 July 1996. Liverpool University Press & National Museums and Galleries on Merseyside, Liverpool.

Norman, D. (2000) Movements of a colour-ringed Spoonbill. *CWBR* 2000: 119.

Norman, D. (2005) The return rates of territory-holding Willow Warblers. *Woolston Eyes Conservation Group Annual Report* 2005: 65–67

Norman D. & Coffey, P. (1994) The importance of the Mersey estuary for waders in the cold weather of February 1991. *Ring. & Migr.* 15: 91–97.

Norman, D. & Lythgoe, C. (1997) Pesticide analysis of Cheshire Peregrine eggs. *CAWOS Bird News* 34: 26–27.

Norman, D. & Ormond, A. (2003) The Regular Occurrence of Wintering Firecrests in north Cheshire and Wirral. *CWBR* 2003: 141–45.

Oakes, G. (1953) Birds of Lancashire. Oliver & Boyd, London.

O'Brien, M., Green, R.E. & Wilson, J. (2006) Partial recovery of the population of Corncrakes *Crex crex* in Britain, 1993–2004. *Bird Study* 53: 213–24.

O'Connor, R.J. & Shrubb, M. (1986) Farming and Birds. Cambridge University Press, Cambridge, UK.

Oddy, P. (2005) Waxwing influx 2004/05. *CWBR* 2005: 132–37.

Ogilvie, M. (2003) Grebes of the world. Bruce Coleman Books, Uxbridge.

Owen, M., Atkinson-Willes, G.L. & Salmon, D.G. (1986) Wildfowl in Great Britain. Second Edition. Cambridge University Press, Cambridge, UK.

Owen, M. & Mitchell, C. (1988) Movements and migrations of Wigeon *Anas penelope* wintering in Britain and Ireland. *Bird Study* 35: 47–59.

Oxenham, J.V. (2002) An estimate of the number of Red Grouse in Cheshire. *CWBR* 2002: 155–60.

Parker, D.E., Legg, T.P. & Folland, C.K. (1992) A new daily Central England Temperature Series, 1772–1991. *Int. J. Clim.* 12: 317–42.

Parslow, J.L.F. (1973) Breeding Birds of Britain and Ireland. T. & A.D. Poyser, Berkhamsted.

Patterson, I.J. (1982) The Shelduck. Cambridge University Press, Cambridge, UK.

Peach, W.J., Baillie, S.R. & Underhill, L. (1991) Survival of British Sedge Warblers *Acrocephalus schoenobaenus* in relation to west African rainfall. *Ibis* 133: 300–05.

Peach, W.J., Crick, H.Q.P. & Marchant, J.H. (1995a) The demography of the decline in the British Willow Warbler population. *J. Appl. Stat.* 22: 905–22.

Peach, W.J., du Feu, C. & McMeeking, J. (1995b) Site tenacity and survival rates of Wrens *Troglodytes troglodytes* and Treecreepers *Certhia familiaris* in a Nottinghamshire wood. *Ibis* 137: 497–507.

Peach, W.J., Robinson, R.A. & Murray, K.A. (2004) Demographic and environmental causes of the decline of rural Song Thrushes *Turdus philomelos* in lowland Britain. *Ibis* 146 (Suppl. 2): 50–59.

Peach, W.J., Siriwardena, G.M. & Gregory, R.D. (1999) Long-term changes in overwinter survival rates explain the decline of Reed Buntings *Emberiza schoeniclus* in Britain. *J. Appl. Ecol.* 36: 798–811.

Pearce-Higgins, J.W. & Yalden, D.W. (2004) Habitat selection, diet, arthropod availability and growth of a moorland wader: the ecology of European Golden Plover *Pluvialis apricaria* chicks. *Ibis* 146: 335–46.

Perkins, A.J., Anderson, G. & Wilson, J.D. (2007) Seed food preferences of granivorous farmland passerines. *Bird Study* 54: 46–53.

Perrins, C.M. (1979) British Tits. Collins New Naturalist, London.

Perrins, C.M. (2003) The status of Marsh and Willow Tits in the UK. *British Birds* 96: 418–26.

Pithon, J.A. & Dytham, C. (2001) Determination of the origin of British feral Rose-ringed Parakeets. *British Birds* 94: 74–79.

Pithon, J.A. & Dytham, C. (2002) Distribution and population development of introduced Ring-necked Parakeets *Psittacula krameri* in Britain between 1983 and 1998. *Bird Study* 49: 110–17.

Platt, D. (2002) Avocets breeding: a first for Cheshire. *CWBR* 2002: 151–52.

Pollitt, M.S., Hall, C., Holloway, S.J., Hearn, R.D., Marshall, P.E., Musgrove, A.J., Robinson, J.A. & Cranswick, P.A. (2003) The Wetland Bird Survey 2000–01: Wildfowl and Wader Counts. BTO/WWT/RSPB/JNCC, Slimbridge.

Poole, A.F. (1989) Ospreys. Cambridge University Press, Cambridge, UK.

Potts, G.R. (1986) The Partridge. Collins, London.

Prince, P. & Clarke, R. (1993) The Hobby's breeding range in Britain. *British Wildlife* 4: 341–46.

Proffitt, F.M., Newton, I., Wilson, J.D. & Siriwardena, G.M. (2004) Bullfinch *Pyrrhula pyrrhula* breeding ecology in lowland farmland and woodland: comparisons across time and habitat. *Ibis* 146 (Suppl. 2): 78–86.

Pyefinch, R. & Golborn, P. (2001) Atlas of the Breeding Birds of Lancashire and North Merseyside 1997–2000. Hobby Publications, Maghull, Liverpool.

Rackham, O. (2006) Woodlands. Collins New Naturalist, London.

Ratcliffe, D.A. (1993) The Peregrine Falcon. Second (revised) edition. T. & A.D. Poyser, London.

Ratcliffe, D.A. (1997) The Raven. T. & A.D. Poyser, London.

Raven, M.J., Noble, D.G. & Baillie, S.R. (2007) The Breeding Bird Survey 2006. BTO Research Report No. 471. BTO, Thetford.

Rees, E. (2006) Bewick's Swan. T. & A.D. Poyser, London.

Riddiford, N. (1983) Recent declines of Grasshopper Warblers *Locustella naevia* at British observatories. *Bird Study* 30: 143–48.

Richards, C.M. (1997) Pied Flycatchers in Cheshire to 1995. *CWBR* 1997: 114–16.

Roberts, B. (1995) The long-staying Red Kite in Tatton Park. *CWBR* 1995: 93.

Robertson, P. (1997). A Natural History of the Pheasant: Swan Hill Press, Shrewsbury.

Robinson, R.A. (2005) BirdFacts: profiles of birds occurring in Britain & Ireland (v1.2, Jan 2008). BTO Research Report No. 407. BTO, Thetford (www.bto.org/birdfacts).

Robinson, R.A., Crick, H.Q.P. & Peach, W.J. (2003) Population trends of Swallows *Hirundo rustica* breeding in Britain. *Bird Study* 50: 1-7.

Robinson, R.A., Green, R.E., Baillie, S.R., Peach, W.J. & Thomson, D.L. (2004) Demographic mechanisms of the population decline of the song thrush *Turdus philomelos* in Britain. *J. Anim. Ecol.* 73: 670-82.

Robinson, R.A., Siriwardena, G.M. & Crick, H.Q.P. (2005a) Size and trends of the House Sparrow *Passer domesticus* population in Great Britain. *Ibis* 147: 552-62.

Robinson, R.A., Siriwardena, G.M. & Crick, H.Q.P. (2005b) Status and population trends of Starling *Sturnus vulgaris* in Great Britain. *Bird Study* 52: 252-60.

Robinson, R.A., Wilson, J.D. & Crick, H.Q.P. (2001) The importance of arable habitat for farmland birds in grassland landscapes. *J. Appl. Ecol.* 38: 1059-69.

Rock, P. (2005) Urban gulls: problems and solutions. *British Birds* 98: 338-55.

Rose, L.N. (1982) Breeding ecology of British pipits and their Cuckoo parasite. *Bird Study* 29: 27-40.

Sanderson, F.J., Donald, P.F., Pain, D.J., Burfield, I.J. & van Bommel, F.P.J. (2006) Long-term population declines in Afro-Palearctic migrant birds. *Biol. Cons.* 131: 93-105.

SAS Institute. (2001) SAS/STAT user's guide, version 8.02. Cary, North Carolina.

Schofield, C. (1996). Attempted breeding of Spoonbill in Cheshire, 1996. *CWBR* 1996: 13.

Scott, D. (1997) The Long-eared Owl. Hawk & Owl Trust, London.

Sharpe, C.M. (2007) Manx Bird Atlas. Liverpool University Press, Liverpool.

Shawyer, C. (1987) The Barn Owl in the British Isles. Hawk Trust, London.

Shawyer, C. (1994) The Barn Owl. Hamlyn, London.

Shawyer, C. (1998) The Barn Owl. Arlequin Press, Chelmsford.

Sheldon, R.D., Chaney, K. & Tyler, G.A. (2007) Factors affecting nest survival of Northern Lapwings *Vanellus vanellus* in arable farmland: an agri-environment scheme prescription can enhance nest survival. *Bird Study* 54: 168-75.

Shrubb, M. (1993) The Kestrel. Hamlyn, London.

Shrubb, M. (2003) Birds, Scythes and Combines. Cambridge University Press, Cambridge, UK.

Shrubb. M. (2007) The Lapwing. T. & A.D. Poyser, London.

Sim, I.M.W., Gregory, R.D., Hancock, M.H. & Brown, A.F. (2005) Recent changes in the abundance of British upland breeding birds. *Bird Study* 52: 261-75.

Simms, E. (1978) British Thrushes. Collins New Naturalist, London.

Simms, E. (1985) British Warblers. Collins New Naturalist, London.

Simms, E. (1992) British Larks, Pipits and Wagtails. Collins New Naturalist, London.

Simson, C. (1966) A Bird Overhead. Witherby, London.

Siriwardena, G.M. (2004) Possible roles of habitat, competition and avian nest predation in the decline of the Willow Tit *Parus montanus* in Britain. *Bird Study* 51: 193-202.

Siriwardena, G.M. (2006) Avian nest predation, competition and the decline of British Marsh Tits *Parus palustris*. *Ibis* 148: 255-65.

Siriwardena, G.M., Baillie, S.R., Crick, H.Q.P. & Wilson, J.D. (2000a) The importance of variation in the breeding performance of seed-eating birds for their population trends on farmland. *J. Appl. Ecol.* 37: 128-48.

Siriwardena, G.M., Baillie, S.R. & Wilson, J.D. (1998). Variation in the survival rates of British farmland passerines with respect to their population trends. *Bird Study* 45: 276-92.

Siriwardena, G.M., Baillie, S.R. & Wilson, J.D. (1999) Temporal variation in the annual survival rates of six granivorous birds with contrasting population trends. *Ibis* 141: 621-36.

Siriwardena, G.M., Crick, H.Q.P., Baillie, S.R. & Wilson, J.D. (2000b) Agricultural habitat type and the breeding performance of granivorous farmland birds in Britain. *Bird Study* 47: 66-81.

Skutch, A.F. (1987) Helpers at Birds' Nests. University of Iowa Press, Iowa City.

Slater, P. (2001) Breeding ecology of a suburban population of Woodpigeons *Columba palumbus* in north-west England. *Bird Study* 48: 361-66.

Smart, J. & Gill, J.A. (2003). Climate change and the potential impact on breeding waders in the UK. *Wader Study Group Bulletin* 100: 80-85.

Smith, K.W. (2005) Has the reduction in nest-site competition from Starlings *Sturnus vulgaris* been a factor in the recent increase of Great Spotted Woodpecker *Dendrocopos major* numbers in Britain? *Bird Study* 52: 307-13.

Smith, K.W. (2007) The utilization of dead wood resources by woodpeckers in Britain. *Ibis* 149 (Suppl. 2): 183-92.

Smith, K.W., Reed, J.M. & Trevis, B.E. (1999) Nocturnal and diurnal activity patterns and roosting sites of Green Sandpipers *Tringa ochruros* wintering in southern England. *Ring. & Migr.* 19: 315-22.

Smith, M.G. & Norman, D. (1988) Cuckoos at Woolston 1988. *CWBR* 1988: 88.

Smith, R. (2006) The Leach's Petrel wreck. *CWBR* 2006: 124-27.

Smith, R., Ormond, A. & Coffey, P. (2008) Wouldn't it be nice to catch more Black-tailed Godwits? *Merseyside Ringing Group Annual Report* 2006. 28-37.

Smith, S. (1950) The Yellow Wagtail. Collins, London.

Smith, S. & Gilbert, J. (2003) National Inventory of Woodland and Trees. Country Report for Great Britain, Forestry Commission, Edinburgh.

Snow, D. (2003) Song and territories of Song Thrushes in a Buckinghamshire village: a ten-year study. *British Birds* 96: 119-31.

Snow, D.W. & Snow, B.K. (1988) Birds and Berries. T. & A.D. Poyser, London.

Stevens, D.K., Anderson, G.Q.A., Grice, P.V. & Norris, K. (2007) Breeding success of Spotted Flycatchers *Muscicapa striata* in southern England—is woodland a good habitat for this species? *Ibis* 149 (Suppl. 2): 214-23.

Stott, M., Callion, J., Kinley, I., Raven, C. & Roberts, J. (eds.) (2002) The Breeding Birds of Cumbria; A tetrad atlas 1997-2001. Cumbria Bird Club.

Stubbs, M. (2001) The first proved breeding for Hobby in the SECOS area. SECOS Report. South East Cheshire Ornithological Society, Sandbach.

Summers-Smith, J.D. (1963) The House Sparrow. Collins New Naturalist, London.

Summers-Smith, J.D. (1995) The Tree Sparrow. Summers-Smith, J.D. (self-published).

Summers-Smith, J.D. (2003) The decline of the House Sparrow: a review. *British Birds* 96: 439–46.

Tapper, S. (1999) A question of balance: game animals and their role in the British countryside. The Game Conservancy Trust, Hampshire, UK.

Tatner, P. (1983) The diet of urban Magpies. *Ibis* 125: 90–107.

Taylor, I. (1994) Barn Owls. Cambridge University Press, Cambridge, UK.

Thomas, L., Laake, J.L., Strindberg, S., Marques, F.F.C., Buckland, S.T., Borchers, D.L., Anderson, D.R., Burnham, K.P., Hedley, S.L., Pollard, J.H., Bishop, J.R.B. & Marques, T.A. (2006) Distance 5.0. Release 2. Research Unit for Wildlife Population Assessment, University of St Andrews, UK (www.ruwpa.st-and.ac.uk/distance/).

Thomson, D.L., Baillie, S.R. & Peach, W.J. (1997) The demography and age-specific annual survival of British song thrushes *Turdus philomelos* during periods of population stability and decline. *J. Anim. Ecol.* 66: 414–24.

Tubbs, C. (1974) The Buzzard. David & Charles, Newton Abbot.

Tucker, G.M. & Heath, M.F. (1994) Birds in Europe: their conservation status. BirdLife International, Cambridge, UK.

Turner, A.K. (1991) Studies of West Palearctic birds: Swallow. *British Birds* 84: 555–69.

Turner, A. (1994) The Swallow. Hamlyn, London.

Turner, A. (2006) The Barn Swallow. T. & A.D. Poyser, London.

Tyler, S.J. & Ormerod, S.J. (1994) The Dippers. T. & A.D. Poyser, London.

Underhill-Day, J. (1998) Breeding Marsh Harriers in the UK 1983–95. *British Birds* 91: 210–18.

Urban, E.K., Fry, C.H. & Keith, S. (1997) Birds of Africa Volume V. Academic Press, London.

Village, A. (1990) The Kestrel. T. & A.D. Poyser, London.

Vinicombe, K. (1982) Breeding and population fluctuations of the Little Grebe. *British Birds* 75: 204–18.

Visser, M.E. & Both, C. (2005) Shifts in phenology due to global climate change: the need for a yardstick. *Proc. R. Soc. B* 272: 2561–69.

Voisin, C. (1991) The Herons of Europe. T. & A.D. Poyser, London.

Wall, T. (1982) Some preliminary results from cage-trap ringing of waterfowl at Rostherne Mere. *CBR* 1982: 61–65.

Watson, D. (1977) The Hen Harrier. T. & A.D. Poyser, Berkhamstead.

Webb, A., McSorley, C.A., Dean, B.J., Reid, J.B., Cranswick, P.A., Smith, L. & Hall, C. (2004) An assessment of the numbers and distributions of inshore aggregations of waterbirds using Liverpool Bay during the non-breeding season in support of possible SPA identification. JNCC Report No. 373. JNCC, Peterborough.

Wells, C.E. (1994) Review of the Status of breeding Ravens in Cheshire. *CWBR* 1994: 100.

Wells, C.E. (2002) Breeding Water Rail survey of the Dee Estuary 2002. *CWBR* 2002: 153–54.

Wells, C.E. (2003) Bearded Tit breeding: a first for Cheshire. *CWBR* 2003: 148.

Wells, C.E. (2005) Breeding Little Egrets on the Dee Estuary. *CWBR* 2005: 130–32.

Wells, C.E. & Friswell, N. (1998) A major new Shelduck (*Tadorna tadorna*) moult site. *CWBR* 1998: 95–97.

Wernham, C.V., Toms, M.P., Marchant, J.H., Clark, J.A., Siriwardena, G.M. & Baillie, S.R. (eds.) (2002) The Migration Atlas: movements of the birds of Britain and Ireland. T. & A.D. Poyser, London.

White, G. (1789) The Natural History of Selborne. Cassell, London.

White, S. (2002) The distribution and population size of House Sparrows in urban north Merseyside, 2001–2002. *Lancashire Bird Report* 2002: 150–53.

White, S.J., McCarthy, B. & Jones, M. (2008) The Birds of Lancashire and North Merseyside. Hobby Publications, Lancashire & Cheshire Fauna Society, Southport.

Whittingham, M.J., Swetnam, R.D., Wilson, J.D., Chamberlain, D.E. & Freckleton, R.P. (2005) Habitat selection by yellowhammers *Emberiza citrinella* on lowland farmland at two spatial scales: implications for conservation management. *J. Appl. Ecol.* 42: 270–90.

Wiktander, U., Olsson, O. & Nilsson, S.G. (2001a) Annual and seasonal reproductive trends in the Lesser Spotted Woodpecker *Dendrocopos minor*. *Ibis* 143: 72–82.

Wiktander, U., Olsson, O. & Nilsson, S.G. (2001b) Seasonal variation in home-range size, and habitat area requirement of the lesser spotted woodpecker (*Dendrocopos minor*) in southern Sweden. *Biol. Cons.* 100: 387–95.

Williams, S. (2005) Cetti's Warblers at Neston Reed Bed, RSPB Dee Estuary Nature Reserve. *CWBR* 2005: 127–30.

Williamson, K. (1969) Habitat preferences of the Wren on English farmland. *Bird Study* 16: 53–59.

Wilson, A.M., Vickery, J.A. & Browne, S.J. (2001) Numbers and distribution of Northern Lapwings *Vanellus vanellus* breeding in England and Wales in 1998. *Bird Study* 48: 2–17.

Wilson, A.M., Vickery, J.A., Brown, A., Langston, R.H.W., Smallshire, D., Wotton, S. & Vanhinsbergh, D. (2005) Changes in the numbers of breeding waders on lowland wet grasslands in England and Wales between 1982 and 2002. *Bird Study* 52: 55–69.

Wilson, J. (1993) Colonisation by Bearded Tits of Leighton Moss, Lancashire. *British Birds* 86: 352–58.

Wilson, J.D., Taylor, R. & Muirhead, L.B. (1996) Field use by farmland birds in winter: an analysis of field type preferences using resampling methods. *Bird Study* 43: 320–32.

Winstanley, D., Spencer, R. & Williamson, K. (1974) Where have all the Whitethroats gone? *Bird Study* 21: 1–14.

Wotton, S., Gibbons, D.W., Dilger, M. & Grice, P.V. (1998) Cetti's Warblers in the United Kingdom and the Channel Islands in 1996. *British Birds* 91: 77–89.

Wotton, S.R. & Gillings, S. (2000) The status of breeding Woodlarks *Lullula arborea* in Britain in 1997. *Bird Study* 47: 212–24.

Wotton, S.R., Langston, R.H.W. & Gregory, R.D. (2002) The breeding status of the Ring Ouzel *Turdus torquatus* in the UK in 1999. *Bird Study* 49: 26–34.

Wyllie, I. (1981) The Cuckoo. Batsford, London.

Species index

Birds are indexed by the first word of their common name and by the genus of their scientific name. Each species' main account starts on the page given in **bold**, and the scientific names refer only to these accounts. This index excludes Tables 1–10 on pp. 28–32.